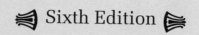

Sixth Edition

Instruction of Students with Severe Disabilities

Martha E. Snell
University of Virginia

Fredda Brown
Queens College,
City University of New York

PEARSON
Merrill
Prentice Hall

Upper Saddle River, New Jersey
Columbus, Ohio

Library of Congress Cataloging in Publication Data

Instruction of students with severe disabilities / [edited by] Martha E. Snell, Fredda
Brown.— [6th ed.]
    p. cm.
  ISBN 0-13-114335-2
  1. Children with disabilities—Education—United States. 2. Special education—United States.
I. Snell, Martha E. II. Brown, Fredda.
  LC4031.I572 2006
  371.91′0973—dc22   2005005089

Vice President and Executive Publisher: Jeffery W. Johnston
Senior Editor: Allyson P. Sharp
Editorial Assistant: Kathleen S. Burk
Production Coordination: GGS Book Services, Atlantic Highlands
Production Editor: Linda Hillis Bayma
Design Coordinator: Diane C. Lorenzo
Cover Designer: Terry Rohrbach
Cover image: Corbis
Production Manager: Laura Messerly
Director of Marketing: Ann Castel Davis
Marketing Manager: Autumn Purdy
Marketing Coordinator: Brian Mounts

This book was set in Garamond by GGS Book Services, Atlantic Highlands. It was printed and bound
by Hamilton Printing Company. The cover was printed by The Lehigh Press, Inc.

Photo Credits: Kimberly and Mike Daswick, pp. 295, 296, 319 (top and bottom), 320, 321, 324–325; Philippa Campbell
and the Children's Hospital Audiovisual Department, pp. 315, 317, 322–323; Karen Schooley, pp. 335–336; Martha Snell, pp. 345,
364, 556; Martha Snell and Karen Schooley, p. 347; Warren C. Rommacher, p. 348; Amy Weatherby, pp. 406, 412, 413, 417;
Douglas Siegel-Causey, pp. 423, 439, 441; Theresa Rebhorn, p. 467; Ginevra Courtade-Little, pp. 504, 506, 509, 516; Courtesy
of Lehigh University Supported Employment, used with permission, pp. 542, 547; Wally Kempe & Associates, p. 613; Philip and
Dianne Ferguson, pp. 617, 618, 627, 632; Robin De Witte, pp. 628, 629.

Pearson Education Ltd.
Pearson Education Singapore Pte. Ltd.
Pearson Education Canada, Ltd.
Pearson Education—Japan

Pearson Education Australia Pty. Limited
Pearson Education North Asia Ltd.
Pearson Educación de Mexico, S.A. de C.V.
Pearson Education Malaysia Pte. Ltd.

10 9 8 7 6 5 4 3 2 1
ISBN: 0-13-114335-2

*For our children, for our partners,
and for our friends and colleagues
who have provided us support
without reservation.*

≋ Preface ≋

In this sixth edition, we have as a foundation many of the same principles about teaching students with severe disabilities that were present in earlier editions because these principles have continued relevance:

- Inclusive schools create new opportunities for *all* students to learn relevant skills and to form supportive social relationships.
- Inclusive schools create new opportunities for teachers to become better teachers of *all* their students.
- Teams of people, not isolated individuals, are responsible for designing, implementing, and evaluating educational programs.
- The skills identified for each student to learn should be functional (matching the student's current and future needs), suited to the student's chronological age, and respectful of the student's and family's preferences.
- To be appropriate, instruction must be planned to suit an individual student.
- To improve education for all students, special education needs to be merged with general education rather than viewed as a separate educational structure to retain the diverse talents of both special and general educators.
- The teaching methods we use need to be research based and effective and appropriate for a variety of students in inclusive settings.

As in the fifth edition, we continue to emphasize that learning is more than increasing specific isolated skills—school efforts must be organized toward the achievement of three outcomes: membership, belonging, and skills. To achieve this, schools must appreciate the relationship between these outcomes and focus on supporting students and their families to develop and work toward a vision of a satisfying, meaningful, and personally determined quality of life. There is great value in building self-determination in our students, as there is for all students; the challenge is to understand the many individualized ways this characteristic can be developed. For example, teachers can match job training opportunities to students' preferences, team

members can teach their students to make choices and initiate preferred activities, and students' problem behaviors are best viewed by their teams as having a legitimate motivation that should drive the development of behavior support planning.

In addition to these principles and foundations, we have incorporated several features into the text to make the text more useful to its readers. One of the most effective ways we learn is through examples. Thus, we begin each chapter with case studies of students and then apply chapter concepts to these individuals. Because heterogeneity is characteristic of those with severe disabilities, our examples are diverse and include individuals ranging in age from preschool to young adult with a variety of abilities and disabilities—cognitive, movement, sensory, behavioral, and emotional.

Over the years, this text has gained a reputation for being both comprehensive and current. The aim of earlier editions was to present issues and strategies documented as effective and not to "jump on treatment bandwagons." The sixth edition maintains this reputation. Because our students with severe disabilities often challenge the available supply of teaching methods, we have described guidelines for designing instruction and procedures for evaluating the effects of instruction on students. We have added a new opening chapter, "Foundational Concepts and Practices for Educating Students with Severe Disabilities," and extensively updated and revised all remaining chapters to reflect the most recent research and practice in the field. There are also activities at the end of each chapter that will help readers apply concepts to individuals and teaching situations. In addition, we have written as we aim to speak—using respectful, people-first language.

Organization of the Text

We begin this edition with five chapters that lay the foundation for the rest of the book. The first two chapters focus on basic concepts central to the education of students with severe disabilities: inclusion and families. The discussion by Michael Giangreco introduces readers to students with severe disabilities by exploring definitions of severe disabilities and how these definitions and societal perceptions affect the lives of these individuals and their families. Giangreco offers us a historic retrospect of where we've been, how far we've come, and where we need to be heading. Finally, Giangreco helps us understand what is meant by appropriate education for students with severe disabilities.

Students grow up as members of families, and families are most often the primary advocates for their children throughout life. In chapter 2, Ann and Rud Turnbull explore the factors that make successful partnerships between home and school. Two such factors are ongoing, reciprocal communication between home and school and interactions that reflect and respect families of diverse cultural backgrounds.

Chapters 3, 4, and 5, written by the editors, with Donna Lehr joining authorship in chapter 3, set forth the basic strategies and tools educators use in concert with other team members to equip students for meaningful participation at home, in school, in the community, and on the job. All other chapters build on this foundation. Three key words sum up the content of this section: assessment, teaching, and evaluation. We have written this section to acquaint the reader with the resources educators rely on; because there are many resources, these chapters are comprehensive and lengthy.

In chapter 6, Rob Horner, Rick Albin, Anne Todd, and Jeff Sprague set forth the principles of positive behavior support. Using comprehensive case examples, these authors describe how the process of functional assessment is conducted and used to design effective behavioral support plans that are based on the values of self-determination, respect, and inclusion.

In chapter 7, Jane Rues and her three coauthors (Carolyn Graff, Marilyn Ault, and Jennifer Holvoet) undertake the task of describing health care procedures required by some students during the school day. This chapter describes how to incorporate special health care procedures into the educational day and how educators can contribute to the prevention of related health problems and conditions.

In chapter 8, Philippa Campbell addresses the related topic of movement disabilities that often are present in our students. Because all team members interact with a student over a range of daily activities, practical knowledge about motor disabilities must be

shared. Students deserve to have consistency and competence in the ways they actively participate daily routines that involve movement.

The skills of caring for oneself, toileting, eating, dressing, and grooming are important goals for all individuals regardless of severity of disability. In chapter 9, Leslie Farlow and Marti Snell provide a comprehensive review of effective methods for teaching self-care skills while also showing how these methods apply to specific students.

One of the most important elements schools can offer students is social relationships with peers. In chapter 10, Ilene Schwartz, along with Debbie Staub, Charles Peck, and Chrysan Gallucci, describe and illustrate techniques that teams can use to promote membership and a sense of belonging and to build a variety of personal relationships among students in classrooms and schools.

Chapters 11 and 12 address communication. First, in chapter 11, Ellin Siegel and Amy Wetherby define nonsymbolic communication and describe the use of movement, gestures, facial expression, and other behaviors to express messages to others. Many of our students reach this level of communication, but their teams may not recognize their skills or use their abilities to express themselves without symbols. These two authors provide a clear framework for understanding nonsymbolic communication and relating effectively to students who communicate in these ways.

In chapter 12, Ann Kaiser and Joan Grim provide us with teaching guidelines for students learning to use words, signs, and picture symbols to express themselves. They describe a set of naturalistic or milieu teaching methods that have been found to be effective in expanding students' beginning communication abilities, whether spoken or augmented, with manual or two-dimensional pictured symbols.

Basic skills in reading, writing, mathematics, science, and social studies can be useful to many students when these skills are taught so that they apply to daily routines. In chapter 13, Diane Browder, Lynn Ahlgrim-Delzell, Ginevra Courtade-Little, and Marti Snell discuss alternate assessment and the link to No Child Left Behind regulations. They elaborate on the importance and process of meaningfully including students with severe disabilities in the general education curriculum. These authors provide guidelines for coordinating alternate assessment with the individualized education program, for accessing the general curriculum, and for applying proven instructional strategies to teach basic academic skills.

Learning skills that increase active participation in home and community life is the topic for chapter 14. Linda Bambara, Diane Browder, and Freya Koger begin with a series of guiding values and principles that characterize the outcomes of skill instruction referenced to students' homes and communities. These themes are coupled with instructional methods found effective with students.

Our special education laws require a clear focus on and preparation for the transition to adulthood. Preparing students for real work in the community is a longitudinal process requiring extensive team effort over the teenage years. In chapter 15, Katty Inge and Sherrill Moon set forth the essential elements of secondary vocational programs that will allow students and their teams to plan the transition from school to adulthood with their teams and then make the transition.

The book closes with chapter 16, in which Phil and Dianne Ferguson discuss, both as parents and as scholars, the promises that adulthood can offer to individuals with severe disabilities. The Fergusons take us on a remarkable journey across the years with their son Ian. This family's story gives us a glimpse of a path that has been "often confusing and frustrating, but also filled with many exciting achievements." The concept of supported adulthood is discussed within the context of current policy, social services, educational practices, and societal expectations.

Acknowledgments

Many people have assisted in the task of developing the sixth edition. We are grateful for the helpful comments of our reviewers at various stages in the revision process: Judy K. C. Bentley, Southwest Texas State University; Sara Pankaskie, Florida Atlantic University; Keith Storey, Chapman University; and Michael L. Wehmeyer, University of Kansas. We would also like to thank many of our students who continually inspire our thinking and writing. We would also like to recognize the contributions of production editor Linda Bayma, editorial assistant Kathy Burk, our editor Allyson Sharp, and GGS Book Services. Their combined efforts have been central to the final quality of this text.

Finally, we are indebted to a small group of students— the children, adolescents, and young adults who add reality to each chapter and whose abilities and disabilities have challenged and shaped our own skills and those of our contributors. Their families and their educators deserve equal votes of gratitude for providing a vast array of teaching ideas, for granting permission to use photographs, and for giving us extensive examples and information.

Marti E. Snell
Fredda Brown

Discover the Merrill Education Resources for Special Education Website

Technology is a constantly growing and changing aspect of our field that is creating a need for new content and resources. To address this emerging need, Merrill Education has developed an online learning environment for students, teachers, and professors alike to complement our products—the *Merrill Education Resources for Special Education* Website. This content-rich website provides additional resources specific to this book's topic and will help you—professors, classroom teachers, and students—augment your teaching, learning, and professional development.

Our goal is to build on and enhance what our products already offer. For this reason, the content for our user-friendly website is organized by topic and provides teachers, professors, and students with a variety of meaningful resources all in one location. With this website, we bring together the best of what Merrill has to offer: text resources, video clips, web links, tutorials, and a wide variety of information on topics of interest to general and special educators alike.

Rich content, applications, and competencies further enhance the learning process.

The *Merrill Education Resources for Special Education* Website includes:

Resources for the Professor

- The **Syllabus Manager**™, an online syllabus creation and management tool, enables instructors to create and revise their syllabus with an easy, step-by-step process. Students can access your syllabus and any changes you make during the course of your class from any computer with Internet access. To access this tailored syllabus, students will just need the URL of the website and the password assigned

to the syllabus. By clicking on the date, the student can see a list of activities, assignments, and readings due for that particular class.
- In addition to the **Syllabus Manager**™ and its benefits listed above, professors also have access to all of the wonderful resources that students have access to on the site.

Resources for the Student

- Video clips specific to each topic, with questions to help you evaluate the content and make crucial theory-to-practice connections.
- Thought-provoking critical analysis questions that students can answer and turn in for evaluation or that can serve as a basis for class discussions and lectures.
- Access to a wide variety of resources related to classroom strategies and methods, including lesson planning and classroom management.
- Information on all the most current relevant topics related to special and general education, including CEC and Praxis standards, IEPs, portfolios, and professional development.
- Extensive web resources and overviews on each topic addressed on the website.
- A message board with discussion starters where students can respond to class discussion topics, post questions and responses, or ask questions about assignments.
- A search feature to help access specific information quickly.

To take advantage of these and other resources, please visit the *Merrill Education Resources for Special Education* Website at

http://www.prenhall.com/snell

Educator Learning Center: An Invaluable Online Resource

Merrill Education and the Association for Supervision and Curriculum Development (ASCD) invite you to take advantage of a new online resource, one that provides access to the top research and proven strategies associated with ASCD and Merrill—the Educator Learning Center. At **www.educatorlearningcenter.com**, you will find resources that will enhance your students' understanding of course topics and of current educational issues, in addition to being invaluable for further research.

How the Educator Learning Center Will Help Your Students Become Better Teachers

With the combined resources of Merrill Education and ASCD, you and your students will find a wealth of tools and materials to better prepare them for the classroom.

Research

- More than 600 articles from the ASCD journal *Educational Leadership* discuss everyday issues faced by practicing teachers.
- A direct link on the site to Research Navigator™ gives students access to many of the leading education journals, as well as extensive content detailing the research process.

- Excerpts from Merrill Education texts give your students insights on important topics of instructional methods, diverse populations, assessment, classroom management, technology, and refining classroom practice.

Classroom Practice

- Hundreds of lesson plans and teaching strategies are categorized by content area and age range.
- Case studies and classroom video footage provide virtual field experience for student reflection.
- Computer simulations and other electronic tools keep your students abreast of today's classrooms and current technologies.

Look into the Value of Educator Learning Center Yourself

A four-month subscription to Educator Learning Center is $25 but is **FREE** when packaged with any Merrill Education text. In order for your students to have access to this site, you must use this special value-pack ISBN number **WHEN** placing your textbook order with the bookstore: 0-13-154901-4. Your students will then receive a copy of the text packaged with a free ASCD pincode. To preview the value of this website to you and your students, please go to **www.educatorlearningcenter.com**. and click on "Demo."

⚞ Brief Contents ⚟

Contents

8

Addressing Motor Disabilities   291

PHILIPPA H. CAMPBELL

9

Teaching Self-Care Skills   328

LESLIE J. FARLOW AND MARTHA E. SNELL

10

Peer Relationships   375

ILENE S. SCHWARTZ, DEBBIE STAUB, CHARLES A.
PECK, AND CHRYSAN GALLUCCI

11

Nonsymbolic Communication   405

ELLIN SIEGEL AND AMY WETHERBY

12

Teaching Functional Communication Skills   447

ANN P. KAISER AND JOAN C. GRIM

13

General Curriculum Access   489

DIANE M. BROWDER, LYNN AHLGRIM-DELZELL,
GINEVRA COURTADE-LITTLE, AND MARTHA
E. SNELL

Note: Every effort has been made to provide accurate and current Internet information in this book. However, the Internet and information on it are constantly changing, so it is inevitable that some of the Internet addresses listed in this textbook will change.

1

Foundational Concepts and Practices for Educating Students with Severe Disabilities[1]

Michael F. Giangreco

University of Vermont, Center on Disability and Community Inclusion

Partial support for the preparation of this chapter was provided by the United States Department of Education, Office of Special Education Programs, CFDA 84.324M (H324M02007), awarded to the Center on Disability and Community Inclusion, University of Vermont. This chapter reflects the ideas and positions of the author and does not necessarily reflect the ideas or positions of the U.S. Department of Education; therefore, no official endorsement should be inferred.

Charles Dickens (1859) wrote the famous words, "It was the best of times, it was the worst of times . . . the spring of hope . . . the winter of despair" to describe the conditions that preceded the French Revolution. This chapter explores how today's educational environment might be considered the best and worst of times for educating students with severe disabilities. The chapter presents a series of foundational concepts and practices organized into three major sections. The first major section addresses the sometimes elusive question, "Who are students with severe disabilities?" by examining definitions, how societal perceptions of people with severe disabilities can affect their lives, as well as reciprocal benefits of interactions between people with and without disability labels. The second major section addresses *the best and the worst of times* by highlighting some of the key areas for optimism and key areas of concern for students with severe disabilities. Finally, the bulk of the chapter addresses *access to appropriate education* by delving into four interrelated aspects of quality education for students with severe disabilities: (a) access to the least restrictive environment, (b) access to appropriate curriculum, (c) access to effective instruction, and (d) access to individually determined supports.

[1] In loving memory of the vibrant life of Erin McKenzie: August 9, 2004 to August 24, 2004.

1

Who Are Students with Severe Disabilities?

Definitions

Although the phrase "severe disabilities" is used extensively in the professional literature, no single authoritative definition exists. The amendments to the Individuals with Disabilities Education Act (IDEA) (1997), a common source of special education terminology, do not define *severe disabilities*. IDEA and its corresponding Code of Federal Regulations (CFR) (1999) do define 13 distinct disability categories (CFR 300.7), several of which reasonably include students considered to have severe disabilities (e.g., autism, deaf-blindness, mental retardation, multiple disabilities, traumatic brain injury), though not all students within these categories have severe disabilities.

Not surprisingly, many definitions describing individuals with severe disabilities focus on deficits such as intellectual, orthopedic, sensory, behavioral and functional impairments; unfortunately, such definitions tell us very little about them as people (McDonnell, Hardman, & McDonnell, 2003). What can be said with some confidence is that individuals with severe disabilities include a widely heterogeneous group in terms of their disability characteristics, capabilities, and educational needs. Their nondisability characteristics (e.g., interests, preferences, personalities, socioeconomic levels, cultural heritage) are as diverse as the general population. What they share in common is the need for extensive and ongoing supports. Sometimes people with severe disabilities are described as having *low-incidence* disabilities because it is estimated that less than 1% of the general population has severe disabilities (see chapter 3 for specific incidence and prevalence information).

The international organization TASH (formerly The Association for Persons with Severe Disabilities) has identified the persons for whom it advocates as those

> *who require ongoing support in one or more major life activities in order to participate in an integrated community and enjoy a quality of life similar to that available to all citizens. Support may be required for life activities such as mobility, communication, self-care, and learning as necessary for community living, employment, and self-sufficiency. (TASH, 2000)*

Snell (2003) reminds us that in addition to their collective diversity and need for lifelong support, individuals with severe disabilities share "the capacity to learn" (p. 2210). Though this may seem too obvious to mention, as recently as the early 1980s there were heated debates in the professional literature about whether individuals with the most severe disabilities were capable of learning and how such judgments affected their rights to be educated. While some questioned the educability of children with the most severe disabilities and the wisdom of educating them (Kaufman & Krouse, 1981), others offered persuasive arguments favoring the pursuit of education for every child, regardless of the perceived severity of their disability (Baer, 1981; Noonan, Brown, Mulligan, & Rettig, 1982). As Baer pointed out, in addition to the potential benefits associated with students learning skills that will be useful to them, approaching *all* students as capable of learning provides us with the opportunity to extend our own understandings of teaching and learning:

> *To the extent that we sometimes finally succeed in teaching a child whom we have consistently failed to teach in many previous efforts, we may learn something about teaching technique.... Too often, in my opinion, we teach children who are not only capable of teaching themselves, but eager to do so; in their wisdom, they cheat us of learning completely how the trick is done because they do some of it for us and do it privately. It is when they cannot do much if any of it for us that we get to find out how to do all of it ourselves, as teachers. (p. 94)*

The stance favoring education for *all* was then— and continues to be—consistent with the federal, *zero reject*, principle embedded in IDEA. The zero-reject provision established that *all* school-aged children, regardless of the severity of their disability, are entitled to a free, appropriate public education (H. R. Turnbull & A. P. Turnbull, 2000). The zero-reject principle was tested in the case of *Timothy W. v. Rochester School District* (1989). A student with severe, multiple disabilities had been denied admission to his local public school because school officials deemed him too severely disabled to benefit from education. Although the federal district court agreed with the school, the U.S. Court of Appeals for the First Circuit overturned the lower court's ruling and strongly affirmed the zero-reject principle as a core component of IDEA.

Societal Perceptions and Expectations

An experience people with severe disabilities often share in common is that frequently the rest of the world seems to define them primarily, sometimes exclusively, by their disability characteristics. This has been referred to as *disability spread*, the tendency to make broad inferences, assumptions, and generalizations about a person based on disability stereotypes within the society (Dembo, Leviton, & Wright, 1975). Some common stereotypes portray persons with disabilities as sick, subhuman, a menace, an object of pity, an object of charity, or a holy innocent (Wolfensberger, 1975). As pointed out by Van der Klift and Kunc (2002), "When disability is seen as the largest component of a person, much of what is unique and human about him or her is obscured" (p. 25). Biklen and Mosley (1988) explained that people with disabilities may not think of themselves in ways that put their disability characteristics at the forefront of their self-perception, instead "preferring to identify with members of particular religious groups, as certain kinds of workers, employees of particular companies, or as fans of particular sports teams (p. 155).

Opportunities for Interaction and Reciprocal Benefit

Since people with severe disabilities require ongoing supports, the ways in which they are perceived and subsequently treated by others can have a major impact on the quality of their lives. While we are quite certain that disability spread adversely affects people with disabilities, we suspect that far too many people without disabilities are missing out on potentially important relationships with people with disabilities because of this artificial, socially constructed barrier to interaction (Bogdan & Taylor, 1989). If you accept the notion that personal relationships are among a small set of the most defining characteristics that influence the quality of a person's life, then disability spread is a problematic issue for those with and without disabilities alike (Taylor & Bogdan, 1989).

So as you continue to read this chapter and the rest of this book about people who have the label of *severe disabilities*, you are encouraged to think about how these individuals are like all other people, like some other people, and uniquely like no other people. Keep in mind that first and foremost they are human beings—they are someone's child, someone's sibling, someone's classmate, or someone's friend. Though they have been born with or acquired disability characteristics that are considered so severe in today's society as to require ongoing and intensive supports, our collective attitudes and responses to a person's disability characteristics can influence how much of a barrier those characteristics are to leading a regular life. As an *Nth Degree* T-shirt worn by a self-advocate says, "Your attitude just might be my biggest barrier" (Wilkins, 2003).

The Best and Worst of Times

In many ways, from an historical perspective, this is the best of times for individuals with severe disabilities, at least thus far. I write this with the full recognition that our current *best* is relative and is a long way from *good* for far too many people labeled as having severe disabilities (more about that when the "worst of times" are discussed in the next section).

The Best of Times: Reasons for Optimism

Table 1–1 highlights areas for optimism about the present and future. Such optimism about our collective potential to make a positive difference in the lives of students with and without disabilities is an essential ingredient of the creative problem solving necessary to tackle such important challenges.

First, nowhere is progress more evident or reason for optimism more warranted than in regard to *inclusive educational opportunities* available to students with severe disabilities (Downing, 2002; Giangreco, Dennis, Cloninger, Edelman, & Schattman, 1993; Jackson,

TABLE 1–1
Areas for Optimism

1. Inclusive education
2. School reform and restructuring
3. Access to the general education curriculum
4. Alternative assessment in statewide accountability systems
5. Transition to adult life (e.g., postsecondary education, supported employment, community living)
6. Positive behavior supports
7. Partnerships between families and professionals
8. Self-determination

TABLE 1–2
Characteristics of Inclusive Education

1. *All* students are welcomed in general education. The general education class in the school the student would attend if not disabled is the first placement option considered. Appropriate supports, regardless of disability type or severity, are available.
2. Students are educated in classes where the number of those with and without disabilities is proportional to the local population (e.g., 10%–12% have identified disabilities).
3. Students are educated with peers in the same age groupings available to those without disability labels.
4. Students with varying characteristics and abilities (e.g., those with and without disability labels) participate in shared educational experiences while pursuing individually appropriate learning outcomes with necessary supports and accommodations.
5. Shared educational experiences take place in settings predominantly frequented by people without disabilities (e.g., general education classes, community work sites, community recreational facilities).
6. Educational experiences are designed to enhance individually determined valued life outcomes for students and therefore seek an individualized balance between the academic-functional and social-personal aspects of schooling.
7. Inclusive education exists when each of the previously listed characteristics occurs on an ongoing, daily basis.

(Giangreco, Cloninger, & Iverson, 1998)

Ryndak, & Billingsley, 2000; McGregor & Vogelsberg, 1998). In schools across the country, students with severe disabilities increasingly are accessing general education schools and classrooms; such options were rare or nonexistent just a decade or two ago. The literature now is replete with examples, strategies, and research focusing on inclusive schooling across the age span (Hunt & Goetz, 1997; Meyer, 2001; Ryndak & Fisher, 2003)—from early childhood education (Wolery & McWilliam, 1998), to elementary school (Janney & Snell, 1997), through middle school (Kennedy & Fisher, 2001) and high school (Fisher, Sax, & Pumpian, 1999; Jorgensen, 1998). Table 1–2 lists seven prominent characteristics of inclusive education.

Inclusion-oriented people seek to establish an ethic that welcomes all children into their local schools and simultaneously pursues a range of individually meaningful learning outcomes through effective educational practices. Though prompted by the needs of students with disabilities, the concept of inclusive education is broader. The outcomes it seeks to promote (e.g., equity, opportunity, social justice) are relevant for any student across a range of diversity characteristics (e.g., race, culture, socioeconomic level) as well as any students (without a specified diversity characteristic) who simply are having difficulty becoming part of the classroom's learning community.

Second, inclusive schooling increasingly is being linked with broader *school reform and restructuring* efforts designed to improve educational opportunities for *all* students (Lipsky & Gartner, 1997; Peterson, Beloin, & Gibson, 1997; Sailor, 2002; Villa & Thousand, 2000). Third, curricular options for students with severe disabilities have extended beyond functional life skills to include greater alignment and *access to the general education curriculum* in this era of standards-based reform (Ford, Davern, & Schnorr, 2001; Gee, 2002; Udvari-Solner, Thousand, & Villa, 2002). Correspondingly, a fourth area for optimism is that students with severe disabilities are now being included in statewide accountability systems using *alternative assessment* approaches (Klienert & Kearns, 2001). This helps ensure the educational progress of students with disabilities is monitored within schoolwide improvement efforts.

Fifth, a significant volume of literature exists on promising practices on *transition to adult life* (Chadsey-Rusch & Rusch, 1996) leading to *supported employment* (Wehman, 2001) and supported *community living* (Horner et al., 1996) (see chapters 15 and 16). An emerging set of examples exist describing *college options* for young adults with moderate and severe disabilities (Doyle, 2000; Grigal, Neubert, & Moon, 2001; Hall, Kleinert, & Kearns, 2000).

Sixth, further cause for optimism comes from the rapidly developing technology of *positive behavior support* (see chapter 6). Increasingly, teams are conducting functional assessments of student behavior in an effort to better understand the functions of those behaviors and their communicative intent (Carr et al., 1999; Dunlap, Newton, Fox, Benito, & Vaughn, 2001; Durand & Merges, 2001; Horner, 2000). Behavior support plans are being developed and implemented by teams to teach students social, communication, and other functional skills as a way to replace problem behaviors. Within the positive behavior support framework, change does not focus exclusively on an individual's

TABLE 1–3

Professional Assumptions About Families That Facilitate Partnership

1. Families know certain aspects of their children better than anyone else.
2. Families have the greatest vested interest in seeing their children learn.
3. Families should be approached in culturally sensitive ways.
4. Family members are likely to be among the only adults involved with a child's educational program throughout his or her entire school career.
5. Families have the ability to positively influence the quality of educational services provided in their community.
6. Families must live with the outcomes of decisions made by educational teams, all day, every day.

(Giangreco, Cloninger, & Iverson, 1998)

problem behaviors but rather more comprehensively on changing environmental conditions that may be contributing to a person's challenging behaviors. Positive behavior support is an evidence-based practice that is designed not only to reduce problem behaviors (e.g., aggression, self-injury, property destruction) but also to "build prosocial behavior, document durable change, generalize across the full range of situations an individual encountered, and produce access to a rich lifestyle" (Carr et al., 1999, p. 4).

Seventh, the continuing development of *partnerships between families and professionals* is an encouraging trend (see chapter 2). Parents are taking an ever-increasing role as full team members rather than passive or perfunctory recipients of professional perspectives (A. P. Turnbull & H. R. Turnbull, 2000). Professionals have increasingly recognized that it is in everyone's best interest for families to be informed and effective consumers of educational and related services. Table 1–3 offers a list of professional assumptions about families that can facilitate constructive partnerships.

Finally, over the past several years, the focus on family involvement has expanded beyond parental involvement to include *self-determination* by individuals with disabilities. Self-determination is pursued by teaching individuals skills to make decisions about their own lives, providing them with opportunities to make decisions, and then honoring their decisions (Bambara, Cole, & Koger, 1998; Wehmeyer, Agran, & Hughes, 2000). As succinctly summarized in self-advocacy circles, "Nothing about me without me!"

The Worst of Times

Though the eight areas of optimism presented in the previous section are encouraging trends, the field of special education is not at a stage of development where the curricular, instructional, and support needs of students with severe disabilities are consistently and sufficiently addressed. Table 1–4 lists six continuing areas of concern.

First, although inclusive educational opportunities have expanded, *uneven and inconsistent access to inclusive classrooms* continues to plague the public school system, especially for students with severe disabilities. The U.S. Department of Education (2002, p. A-138) indicates that placement rates of all students with disabilities in general education classrooms vary substantially from state to state. In only 11 states (Colorado, Idaho, Kansas, Massachusetts, Minnesota, North Dakota, New Hampshire, Ohio, Oregon, South Dakota, and Vermont), between 70% and 88% of all students with disabilities (ages 6 to 21) have their primary placement (at least 80% of the time) in general education classes. In a small number of other states (Hawaii and Texas) and Washington, D.C., the overall placement rates are below 25%. Only half the states report the general education class as the primary placement for more than 60% of their students with any type of disability.

A closer look at categories most likely to include students with severe disabilities (e.g., autism, deaf-blindness, mental retardation, multiple disabilities, traumatic brain injury) depicts a more stark reality. For example, rates of placement in general education

TABLE 1–4

Areas of Continuing Concern

1. Uneven and inconsistent access to inclusive classrooms
2. Questionable quality of curriculum and instruction
3. Too many families are frustrated by the lack of professional responsiveness
4. Continued use of aversive procedures
5. Challenging working conditions for special educators
6. Limited postschool options

classes as the primary placement for students with the label "mental retardation" (p. A-144) are dismal—below 10% in 20 states and a scant 11% to 30% in 23 other states. The general education class placement rates in six states (Colorado, Idaho, Iowa, North Dakota, Ohio, Oregon) range from 31% to 48%. Only two states exceed 50% general education class placement rates for students with the label "mental retardation"—New Hampshire (56%) and Vermont (80%) (U.S. Department of Education, 2002, p. A-144). Unfortunately, the odds that any particular student with a severe disability will be included in a general education class currently depends, in large part, on where that student lives and what disability category has been assigned to him or her. Although placement doesn't equal inclusion, it is a telling indicator of access to general education environments and a first step toward inclusive opportunities.

As we move slowly closer to realizing promises of the IDEA and toward an educational system that supports access to general education curriculum and environments for students with disabilities, serious questions remain about whether progress is simply too slow (Brown & Michaels, 2003):

> *How long should educators accept that in many locations across the country the more "primitive" steps toward inclusion continue to be accepted and reinforced? Can they afford to wait another decade . . . ? In the meantime, what happens to children, especially those with the most severe disabilities . . . ? Is it acceptable for the education field to praise its progress when generations of these students continue to be excluded? (p. 240)*

Second, even in situations where access to inclusive environments is better, *questionable quality of the curriculum and instruction* for students with severe disabilities in general education classrooms continues to be a serious and ongoing issue. Being physically present in settings with same-age peers who don't have disabilities is necessary but not sufficient to be included. Too many students with severe disabilities placed in general education classes are subjected to undesirable conditions, such as being (a) separated within the classroom (e.g., taught primarily by a paraprofessional), (b) taken through the motions of a lesson or activity without having appropriately targeted learning outcomes (i.e., not learning much of value or importance to them), or (c) presented with lesson content that is inconsistent with their level of functioning or learning and communication characteristics. Such practices obviously limit a student's learning opportunities and may contribute to internalized (e.g., withdrawal, lack of responsiveness) or externalized (e.g., self-stimulation, aggression, tantrums) problem behaviors.

In some cases the very concept of inclusive education has become distorted because fragmented, partial, or low-quality implementation efforts have been mislabeled as "inclusive" (Davern et al., 1997). Clashing ideological views and rhetoric among special education scholars has increased confusion about exactly what inclusive education is, and what should be done about it (Brantlinger, 1997). While public debates continue to be waged regarding the *least restrictive environment* provision of IDEA, years pass, and the lives of real children and their families are adversely affected.

Third, *too many families are frustrated by the lack of professional responsiveness* to their children's educational needs (Soodak & Erwin, 2000). While some educators certainly interact with parents and students as consumers and embrace them as partners in the educational process, others still resist, preferring to retain the role of professional as *expert*. Although professionals have expertise within their discipline, those who spend the most time with people who have disabilities often have a different yet equally valuable type of expertise and knowledge about an individual. Family members, close friends, and persons with disabilities themselves have access to expertise and knowledge concerning things such as an individual's likes and dislikes, behavioral tendencies, rest/sleep patterns, idiosyncratic communication behaviors, personal history, and other important information that may contribute to educational and service planning. It is when the respective expertise of professionals and families are combined that teams have the opportunity to experience the synergy that comes from true collaboration.

Fourth, concern exists about the *continued use of aversive procedures* to manage challenging behaviors. Shockingly (pun intended), in an era when electric cattle prods are becoming a thing of the past in American agriculture, some students with severe disabilities continue to be subjected to an arsenal of aversive procedures and punishments in the name of "treatment," resulting in lost learning opportunities, degradation, psychological trauma, physical injury, and, in a small number of cases, even death (Evans, Scotti, & Hawkins, 1999; Weiss, 2003). This problem persists despite the availability of effective, positive alternatives (Horner, 2000; Janney & Snell, 2000).

Fifth, *challenging working conditions for special educators* contribute to the challenges facing students with severe disabilities. Of particular concern is the national shortage of qualified special educators as well as the need to train and retain more of them (Billingsley, 2002). The shortages interfere with students with disabilities receiving an appropriate, quality education (McLeskey, Tyler, & Saunders, 2002). Kozleski, Mainzer, and Deshler (2000) highlighted some of the key factors contributing to special educators leaving the field (e.g., excessive paperwork, large caseloads, lack of administrative support). The field needs a full and capable cadre of special educators to team up with parents, related services providers, and teachers. As so eloquently stated by Brown, Farrington, Ziegler, Knight, and Ross (1999), "because learning is so difficult for students with significant disabilities, they are in dire need of continuous exposure to the most ingenious, creative, powerful, competent, interpersonally effective, and informed professionals" (p. 252).

Finally, *limited postschool options* adversely affect people with severe disabilities. As noted in a report of the National Council on Disability on the implementation of IDEA, "After years of public education, youth with severe disabilities all too often exit school unemployed, without basic skills, lonely, isolated from peers, and disenfranchised from the larger society" (Giangreco & Snell, 1996, p. 100). Unfortunately, this statement is as true today as it was in 1996.

If you are interested in improving the lives of people with severe disabilities through education, there is plenty to motivate you to act, regardless of whether you see this point in time as the best or worst of times. For those of you motivated by positive news, there is a continually growing set of examples and body of literature documenting steady progress to encourage your continuing contributions to these efforts. If it is the slow pace of progress or ongoing injustices facing people with severe disabilities that fuels your fire, there is plenty of motivation to act and work to do!

Access to Appropriate Education

The remainder of this chapter offers foundational information and ideas about access to appropriate education of students with severe disabilities in four main areas: (a) access to the least restrictive environment,

(b) access to appropriate curriculum (c) access to effective instruction, and (d) access to individually determined supports.

Access to the Least Restrictive Environment

IDEAS's least restrictive environment (LRE) provision clearly establishes that "to the maximum extent appropriate, children with disabilities... are educated with children who are nondisabled" (CFR 300.550 [b][1]). The LRE provision states that "special classes, separate schooling, or other removal of children with disabilities from the regular educational environment occurs only if the nature or severity of the disability is such that education in regular classes with the use of supplemental aids and services cannot be achieved satisfactorily" (CFR 300.550 [b][2]).

Ironically, it has been this second part of the LRE provision that, at times, has been used to justify the continued segregation of students with the most severe disabilities. Across the country, far too many students who are designated as having severe disabilities are almost automatically placed in self-contained special education classes or schools, sometimes requiring them to travel far greater distances than their siblings and neighbors each day to attend school as they are bussed to regional programs. IDEA provides clear and compelling clarification about placement and LRE issues in Appendix A (Notice of Interpretation) of the Code of Federal Regulations (CFR) (1999):

> *Even though IDEA does not mandate regular class placement for every disabled student, IDEA presumes that the first placement option considered for each disabled student by the student's placement team, which must include the parent, is the school the child would attend if not disabled, with appropriate supplementary aids and services to facilitate such placement. Thus, before a disabled child can be placed outside the regular education environment, the full range of supplementary aids and services that if provided would facilitate the student's placement in the regular classroom setting must be considered. (p. 12472)*

IDEA is clear that the default placement—in other words, the starting point—for *all* students with disabilities is the general classroom with appropriate supports. Many school districts never seriously consider general class placement of students with severe disabilities because they rely on the part of the LRE provision that allows for removal of students with disabilities if "the nature or severity of the disability is such that education in regular classes with the use of supplemental aids and services cannot be achieved satisfactorily." Appendix A of IDEA offers some powerful language that provides additional clarification on this point:

> *In all cases, placement decisions must be individually determined on the basis of each child's abilities and needs, and not solely on factors such as category of disability, significance of disability, availability of special education and related services, configuration of the service delivery system, availability of space, or administrative convenience. Rather, each student's IEP forms the basis for the placement decision. (CFR, 1999, p. 12472)*

Teams that are responsible for making placement decisions must make those decisions in ways that are consistent with the law. This means discarding many of the common reasons students with severe disabilities are denied access to general education classes. IDEA does *not* say students with disabilities should be denied access to general education classes

- if they have a particular label (e.g., autism, mental retardation) or are at a certain level (e.g., severe),
- if they function at different levels than their classmates,
- if they are pursuing different learning outcomes than their classmates,
- just because it hasn't been done that way before in the school,
- if it is administratively inconvenient or if needed services are not currently in place,
- if they require supports or accommodations, or
- if the adults in the school are unaccustomed to the characteristics presented by the students.

Therefore, placement teams should shift away from asking, "Who is appropriate to exclude?" It would be more constructive and consistent with IDEA to ask, "How can we change our practices so that more students with disabilities can be successfully included and educated?" By approaching this challenge proactively, people with varying philosophical orientations can, it is hoped, come together around a simple purpose to ensure that students' lives should be better because they went to our schools.

Access to Appropriate Curriculum

IDEA provides a potent framework to enhance the lives of students with disabilities through *special education* and the development of an *Individualized Education Plan (IEP)*. Special education is defined as "specially designed instruction, at no cost to parents, to meet the unique needs of a child with a disability" (20 U.S.C. secs. 1400 [sec. 602][25]). Specially designed instruction means "adapting . . . content, methodology, or delivery of instruction to meet the unique needs of the child that result from the child's disability; and to ensure access of the child to the general education curriculum" (34 CFR 300.26 [b][30]).

As described in IDEA, special education is a service, not a place (Taylor, 1988). At its heart, special education refers to the *individualized* ways we provide instruction to students in an effort to respond to their unique learning characteristics resulting from their disability. This can take a variety of forms or combinations. Sometimes individualization means (a) *changes in curriculum* to account for a student's present level of functioning or special learning needs, (b) *adaptations to the delivery of instruction* (e.g., sensory, physical, behavioral, environmental) that allow a student to have access to learning opportunities, or (c) use of *different instructional methods* applied to the general education curriculum or to individually determined learning outcomes that extend beyond the general education curriculum.

Individualized Participation Options Within General Education

One of the most basic barriers for students with severe disabilities accessing special education within general education settings is the difficulty some people have conceptualizing how to retain curricular and instructional integrity. People ask logical questions such as, "I don't understand. How does it makes sense for a student with a severe cognitive disability to be in a fifth-grade class when he can't do fifth-grade work?" Such legitimate questions deserve answers. But placing a student in an age-appropriate general education classroom does make sense when we shed the notion that the student must participate at the same level or necessarily should have the same learning outcomes as his or her classmates without disabilities. The question isn't whether the student performs at grade level but whether his or her individual needs can be met within the general class context with special education plus supplemental supports and aids.

Within general education classes and activities, the participation of students with severe disabilities can be broadly characterized along two dimensions: (a) their *program* (e.g., individualized curriculum, IEP annual goals, learning outcomes from the general education curriculum) and (b) their *supports*, namely, what is provided to assist the student in accessing and pursuing achievement of his or her educational goals (e.g., materials, adaptations, learning strategies, personnel). As shown in Figure 1–1, this can be conceptualized as four basic options for including students with severe disabilities (or any student for that matter) within typical class activities; each is described in the following sections. During the course of a school day, even sometimes within a single activity, an individual student will move within these different options depending on the nature of the activity and their individual needs. This approach requires deliberate collaboration between teachers, special educators, and related services providers (Janney & Snell, 1997; Snell & Janney, 2004).

Option A: No Accommodations Required

Option A exists when a student is pursuing the general education program available to students without disabilities and can pursue that program with typically

FIGURE 1–1
Inclusion Options Within General Education Environments and Activities

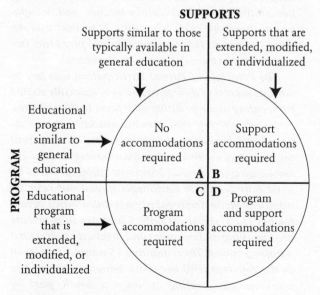

(Adapted from Giangreco & Meyer, 1988)

available supports (e.g., teacher, classmates, classroom equipment). It should be noted, however, that supports that are typically available can vary widely from class to class or school to school.

The participation of students with severe disabilities can be characterized as option A during certain parts of the day (if it were all of the time, they would not be in need of special education). For example, in a primary classroom, when the teacher is reading the class a story, the student with severe disabilities may not require a specialized program or supports. The teacher may position the child close to her so that she can show each page and respond if the student's attention wanders. The teacher may have a peer sit close in case the student starts to lose her balance while seated on the floor with the rest of the class; but these types of simple actions are not specialized.

It is important to recognize times when the participation of a student with a severe disability can be within option A because (a) it provides opportunities for teachers to interact with students who have disabilities in typical (nonspecialized) ways, (b) it allows classmates to see that the student doesn't always need extra help, and (c) it allows the student to avoid unnecessary supports that may inadvertently interfere with peer interaction or teacher engagement. Many students with severe disabilities have paraprofessional support while they are in general education class activities. There can be a tendency to provide such support, even at times when it is not needed. Using the previous example, having the student with a severe disability sit beside or on the lap of the paraprofessional not only may be unnecessary but also may have unintended negative consequences (e.g., stigma, create unnecessary dependency, interfere with peer interactions, interfere with teacher engagement). Teams should continually look for option A opportunities by considering how naturally available supports can be utilized (Nisbet, 1992).

Option B: Support Accommodations Required

Option B exists when a student with disability requires extended, modified, or otherwise individualized supports while pursuing the general education program. For example, in order for a student with deaf-blindness to access the general education program, he may require tactile signing from an interpreter as a necessary support. Similarly, a student with severe orthopedic or multiple disabilities might require a tape recorder and adapted switch to "take notes" during a high school class.

Option C: Program Accommodations Required

Option C exists when a student requires extension, modification, or individualization to the content of the general education program but does *not* require specialized supports. For example, the teacher might adjust the (a) amount (e.g., 4 new vocabulary words instead of 10), (b) the level (e.g., posing less complex questions), or (c) the type of content (e.g., 1:1 correspondence instead of fractions). Across each of these possibilities, once the content adjustment is made, the student does not require other specialized supports—though like option A, natural supports might be provided.

Option D: Program and Support Accommodations Required

Option D exists at times when a student needs extension, modification, or individualization of both the general educational program and the supports to participate.

> Following a small-group geometry lesson on calculating the angles of various types of triangles, the teacher has planned a variety of activities for students to practice what they learned during the lesson. For Jamie, a student with severe disabilities, the content of the lesson and follow-up activities have been focused on discriminating triangles from other shapes; this represents individualization in the content of the general education math program. Making such discriminations also supports his communication; he is learning to extend his ability to discriminate beyond actual objects to symbolic representations. Additionally, rather than being asked to complete a paper-and-pencil task, he requires tactile materials that he can hold and feel, visual cues to highlight the three sides of the triangles, as well as individualized prompting and feedback on his performance; these represent support accommodations. So, for this math activity, Jaime receives both program and support accommodations (option D).

Within both options C and D, teams may employ the *principle of partial participation* (Baumgart et al., 1982). This principle asserts that it is important for individuals with severe disabilities to participate in whatever parts of activities they can, even if they cannot participate in every aspect and that they "can acquire many skills that will allow them to function, at least in part, in a wide variety of least restrictive school and

nonschool environments and activities" (Baumgart et al., 1982, p. 19). Ferguson and Baumgart (1991) remind us that, like any principle, partial participation can be misused. They identified passive participation, myopic participation, piecemeal participation, and missed participation as common error patterns that have occurred when people have attempted to apply the principle of partial participation. Partial participation is designed to foster socially valued roles for people with disabilities that have a positive influence on their image and personal competencies (Wolfensberger, 2000).

> Consider Kendra, a middle school student with multiple disabilities who has severe oral-motor problems (e.g., difficulty chewing and swallowing). Many foods that Kendra is helped to eat fall out of her mouth. When in the noisy, bustling cafeteria, she seems particularly distracted. Her parents identified eating in busy environments as a priority because the family often finds themselves eating in these types of public places.
>
> School personnel, however, were concerned that eating in the cafeteria was socially problematic for Kendra and would detract from how she was perceived by others. So since she moved into this school district a year ago, she has been eating lunch in a private area while working on goals to improve her eating and drinking skills with a paraprofessional. Unfortunately, this practice, while intended to be respectful of her, took an all-or-nothing approach. A subgroup of Kendra's educational team, including her mother, special education teacher, and occupational therapist, came up with a plan that was designed to respect her dignity while also providing her with access to the cafeteria with classmates.
>
> The Principle of Partial Participation was key to various aspects of their plan that systematically shifted from eating alone to eating with peers in the cafeteria. First, recognizing that Kendra quickly became fatigued and her eating skills deteriorated as time went on, they decided that rather than having Kendra eat her entire lunch in one 20-minute sitting, she was offered four 5-minute minimeals spread out over 90 minutes. During the regularly scheduled lunch period for her class, she spent only 5 minutes in a private area working on her eating and drinking goals with a paraprofessional. The remaining 15 minutes was spent in the cafeteria with her peers, hanging out just like everyone else—eating is only a small part of lunchtime in a middle school cafeteria. After she had

been going to the cafeteria for a couple of weeks and seemed more comfortable, 5 of the 15 minutes were spent working on eating and drinking goals, though slightly differently than in the private setting. Kendra's parents and occupational therapist identified a specific set of foods that she was able to chew and swallow most effectively without spilling. She would still lose food occasionally; this would also allow her peers to learn that some people eat differently and for the adults to model that it's not a big deal. Kendra continued to work on eating more challenging, messy foods in private. The team met regularly to discuss Kendra's progress. As time passed, they gradually shifted her eating to the cafeteria completely, though she still didn't eat her entire meal during the scheduled lunchtime. The team used partial participation by offering her only certain foods in the cafeteria and using only part of the time for eating; these modifications in the usual lunch routine allowed Kendra to be more fully part of the life of the school.

While option D (program and support accommodations required) will be necessary, at least part of the time, for students with severe disabilities, teams should make every effort to consider when options A, B, or C are possibilities and be conscious of not over using option D. Even when a student has a severe disability, it is rare that their participation would need to be characterized as option D all the time.

Understanding how the participation of a student with severe disabilities can be characterized using these options can help some team members conceptualize the inclusion and meaningful participation of these students. Equally as important, some general education teachers experience great uncertainty when they are unclear about the nature of a student's participation in their class and their role with the student. These teachers want to know what is expected of the student in their classroom and what is expected of them as teachers. Clarifying the options for participation in a variety of class activities can help alleviate teachers' anxieties and establish a firm foundation on which to establish inclusion that retains curricular and instructional integrity.

Multilevel Instruction and Curriculum Overlapping

Inclusion options C and D often lead teams to ask an important question "How can individualized curricular content be addressed appropriately in the classroom when students without disabilities are pursuing different curricular content?" Lack of clarity about this issue can lead to one of the most common and anxiety-producing questions asked by classroom teachers: "How do you expect me to incorporate an individualized curriculum for a student with disabilities while teaching the rest of my class?" Unfortunately, all too often the solution to this challenge is for a paraprofessional to operate a parallel educational program in the back or side of the classroom. Such an approach minimizes the potential benefits of participation in a general education class. Delegating primary instructional responsibilities to a paraprofessional also may relegate students with disabilities, presumably the students with most significant learning challenges, to receiving their instruction from the least qualified personnel who tend to be undertrained and undersupervised (Giangreco & Doyle, 2002). Two alternatives include *multilevel curriculum/instruction* and *curriculum overlapping* (Giangreco & Meyer, 1988).

Multilevel curriculum/instruction occurs when a student with disabilities and peers without disabilities participate together in a shared activity such as a science lab experiment. Each student has individually appropriate learning outcomes that may be at any of multiple levels (i.e., below, at, or above grade level), all within the same curriculum area (Campbell, Campbell, Collicott, Perner, & Stone, 1988). This approach builds on classic concepts presented in the *Taxonomy of Objectives* (Bloom, 1956). While one student may be learning at a basic knowledge or comprehension level, another student simultaneously may be working on a more advanced application or synthesis levels.

Imagine fourth-grade students playing a small-group social studies board game designed by their teacher and special educator to learn about their neighborhood, town, and state. The teachers have prepared a set of 10 game cards for each student that target individual learning outcomes. For one student, the game cards require applying knowledge about the roles of community helpers (police, firefighters, store clerks, postal workers) by moving game pieces to respond to scenarios on cards (e.g., "Move your player to the place where you might go if you wanted to send a card to your grandmother for her birthday."). For another, game cards have the student answer questions about where she lives (e.g., street address, phone number, recognizing photos of neighbors). A third student is using map skills such as north, south, east, and west to respond to questions (e.g., "If you started at the Bookstore, went two blocks north and one block east, where would you be?"). In this example, all the students have individualized social studies learning outcomes.

Multilevel curriculum/instruction can include variations across subject content, level of learning outcomes pursued, or both.

In one seventh-grade social studies class focusing on American history from the Revolution through the Civil War, the topic is the same for Joseph, a student with disabilities, and his classmates without disabilities. But his level of learning outcomes is adapted to suit him (e.g., historical people, places, events). In Joseph's algebra class, however, the subject content for Joseph is different than for many of his classmates, focusing on counting and basic computation (e.g., adding). In this case, the level and quantity of the learning outcomes would be adapted as well. In both classes, Joseph is working on individualized learning outcomes within the same curriculum content area as his classmates, just at a different level.

Curriculum overlapping starts in the same way as multilevel curriculum/instruction; a student with disabilities and peers without disabilities participate together in a shared activity where each student has individually appropriate learning outcomes. Curriculum overlapping differs in that the learning outcomes being pursued within a shared activity come from two or more different curriculum areas; this is unlike the multilevel curriculum/instruction examples, where they were all within the same curriculum area.

In a middle school biology class, students are grouped in teams of three for lab. They are assembling a model of a human heart. Two of the students have goals related to the identification, anatomy, and physiology of the human heart. The third student, who has severe disabilities, participates in helping to assemble the model heart but is working on communication and social skills (e.g., taking turns, following instructions, responding to yes/no questions, maintaining socially acceptable behavior for longer periods of time).

Curriculum overlapping tends to be used more frequently when the differences between the level of learning outcomes being pursued by most of the students in class and the student with a severe disability

are the greatest. So as you consider the following example, remember that before employing curriculum overlapping, the team should first consider whether the student could pursue the same learning outcomes as the rest of the class or whether multilevel curriculum/instruction is a viable option. If neither of those options is appropriate, it is time to consider curriculum overlapping.

In a middle school math class, six students are arranged in a circle for a game that involves throwing and catching a beach ball covered with numbers to practice multiplication. The game starts by having one student call a classmate by name and then toss the ball: "Terry, I'm throwing the ball to you." After catching the ball, the student is asked to multiply the two numbers touching his or her thumbs. All the students have math learning outcomes except for Jesse, a student with profound intellectual disabilities. Jesse participates in the same activity but with a series of nonmath goals. He is learning to orient toward a person who calls his name, react to the tossed ball by moving his arms to attempt a catch, and match to a sample by pointing to a photograph of a classmate who is in the group, then orienting toward that classmate before being assisted to toss the ball.

At times, both multilevel approaches and curriculum overlapping can be used within the same activity. By pursuing more than one learning outcome within class activities, students with severe disabilities are provided with numerous opportunities to learn and practices skills throughout the school day. Recent research has demonstrated the effectiveness of embedding individually determined learning outcomes within general class activities (McDonnell, Johnson, Polychronis, & Risen, 2002). In rare instances, it may be necessary to plan an alternate activity if a student needs to work on a high-priority goal that doesn't lend itself to being incorporated into multilevel or curriculum overlapping options.

Curricular Balancing Act

Ensuring access to a relevant, individualized curriculum for a student with severe disabilities also requires a balancing act in at least two ways. First, a sound curriculum establishes a *balance between focus and breadth.* Providing access to a breadth of learning outcomes that includes but is not limited to general education curriculum ensures that students with disabilities will have opportunities that may have been denied them in the past. A sound curriculum establishes a clear focus, based on a reasonably small set (e.g., five to eight goals and related objectives) of the highest educational priorities agreed to by the team; these are documented as IEP goals (Giangreco, Cloninger, & Iverson, 1998).

Historically, curriculum for students with severe disabilities has emphasized the identification of chronologically age-appropriate and functional skills needed to function in current and future environments (Brown, Nietupski, & Hamre-Nietupski, 1976; Brown et al., 1979). While these foundational concepts remain contemporary 30 years after they were first articulated in the professional literature, variations on the themes have been expanded.

Today, the basis for selecting IEP goals and objectives for students with severe disabilities has shifted to place a greater emphasis on determining which goals and objectives are most likely to result in positive lifestyle improvements (Carr et al., 1999; Horner 2000). Research is beginning to tackle elusive concepts such as identifying, validating, and increasing the indices of "happiness" in individuals with profound, multiple disabilities (Green & Reid, 1996; 1999; Logan et al., 1998). By asking parents who have children with disabilities and people with disabilities themselves what does or would contribute to living a "good life," we can better identify and select goals and objectives that will contribute to the development of *valued life outcomes* (Giangreco et al., 1998) such as the following:

- Being safe and healthy
- Having a home now and in the future
- Having meaningful relationships
- Having choice and control that matches one's age and culture
- Participating in meaningful activities in various places

The Perez family has three children. Their youngest, Juanita, has severe disabilities and is in first grade. Juanita's special education teacher, Ms. Brown, shared information with the team, including Mr. and Mrs. Perez, about an educational planning process called "COACH" (Choosing Outcomes and Accommodations for Children) (Giangreco et al., 1998). After becoming familiar with the process, Mr. and Mrs. Perez agreed to try this approach to planning Juanita's IEP. The first step was a structured family interview during which the parents were

asked questions about valued life outcomes for Juanita and then guided through a series of questions about potential learning outcomes. The questions then assisted the family in identifying the five highest priorities for Juanita that would be translated into IEP goals and objectives to be focused on during the school year. These priorities included (a) expressing "more," (b) making choices when given options, (c) responding to yes/no questions using eye gaze, (d) calling others to her using a switch and recorded message, and (e) using a switch to activate leisure devices (e.g., CD player, battery-operated toys). Each of these priorities was cross-referenced to one or more valued life outcomes. For example, being able to activate toys was designed to give Juanita more choice and control and was hoped to be a point of connection that might serve to extend her relationships with other children her age. In step 2 of COACH, the team considered a set of additional learning outcomes to establish the breadth of Juanita's educational program. They did this by systematically looking at the general education curriculum in each subject area as well as nine functional skill categories included in COACH to decide what learning outcomes would make the most sense for Juanita. From these listings, they selected a series of skills, such as imitating skills used in daily life, eating finger foods, drinking through a straw, and increasing the amount of time she could sustain attention to a task, among others. From the general education curriculum, they started with skills such as recognizing symbols, distinguishing between shapes, writing her name using an adapted stamp, and using a variety of art media, among others.

Second, a sound curriculum *balances the assessed level of appropriateness with a measure of challenge*. An age-old tenet of instruction is that a student's learning outcomes should be selected at an *appropriate level of difficulty* based on assessment data—neither too easy nor too difficult. Rather, targeted learning outcomes should be reasonably attainable yet challenging, though not so challenging as to be unattainable or frustrating. Although it is logical to select instructional targets based on the student's current level of functioning and known learning characteristics, quality instruction should *provide ample opportunities for students to surprise us with their capabilities*.

Therefore, we should never presume to know the upper limits on a student's abilities, especially if the student has not been sufficiently exposed to a concept or skill or has not received ongoing, competent instruction. This is consistent with Donnellan's (1984) *criterion of the least dangerous assumption*, which asserts that "in the absence of conclusive educational data, educational decisions should be based on assumptions which, if incorrect, will have the least dangerous effect on the student" (p. 142). For example, if an individual with a severe disability is nonverbal and does not have a fluent augmentative method of language or communication, it would be most dangerous to assume that he or she does not understand much, if any, of what is said to or near him or her. It would be less dangerous to assume that he or she understands everything being said to or near him or her. Similarly, it would be most dangerous to prevent the student's exposure to general education curriculum and least dangerous to provide not only exposure but also instruction.

Juanita's team did not select any science learning outcomes for her because they felt, based on existing assessment data, that the concepts were too advanced for her. Recognizing that this could be a dangerous assumption given her limited communication skills, they decided to include her in science class and start with curriculum overlapping so that the learning outcomes she focused on during science were primarily communication and social skills. By including her in the science activities and exposing her to instruction in this area along with her classmates, they are providing her with opportunities that would not deny the possibility that she understands more than they were currently able to discern. At least at the outset, accountability for learning during science class will focus on the non-science communication and social skills. Over time, based on the teacher's observations during science activities, Juanita's additional learning outcomes may be expanded in the future to include science outcomes.

Access to literacy instruction is a prime example of how curricular balance and applying the criterion of the least dangerous assumption have changed the educational opportunities available to students with severe disabilities and corresponding professional practices (Erickson & Koppenhaver, 1995). Historically, literacy instruction has been extremely limited for individuals with moderate or severe disabilities

(e.g., teaching functional sight words). Conventional wisdom suggested that our limited teaching time should be spent almost exclusively on teaching functional life skills rather than selected academics. To date, professionals have not been successful in teaching literacy skills to the majority of students with severe disabilities, but increasingly this option is being explored. Additionally, there is a recognition that every child, regardless of the severity of their disability, can begin to work on some early literacy skills. Some students, many of whom people previously would have not considered teaching literacy skills, are developing skills in reading and writing (Erickson, Koppenhaver, Yoder, & Nance, 1997). This has occurred because of a change in attitude, followed by opportunity, and effective instruction.

In Juanita's case, the team agreed that as a first grader she was much too young to forgo literacy instruction. Instead, they made a conscious effort to expose her to books in English and Spanish since her family is bilingual. Daily she was shown books, read to, assisted to turn the pages, and otherwise shown the wonders of stories and reading. At the same time, she worked on skills such as (a) directing and sustaining attention to objects, books, activities, or interactions; (b) establishing consistent response modes (e.g., pointing, eye gaze, activating a switch); (c) differentiating or discriminating between various objects, photos, or symbols; or (d) matching to a sample. While everyone was hopeful that these efforts would provide important foundations for literacy, they agreed that working on these skills was worthwhile regardless of whether Juanita's literacy proficiency ever reached the heights of functional reading. Her pursuit of important early literacy skills would likely have generalized implications for the development of related skills in domains such as communication, social skills, and recreation.

Although access to the general education curriculum is designed to give students opportunities to learn a wide variety of new skills, exposure to new curriculum content can initiate curiosity about a topic that can become a lifelong interest and a point of connection to others regardless of an individual's skill level. We all know people who are not great musicians but who love music. You may know someone who is not particularly versed in science but through exposure to astronomy has become fascinated with the moon and

Box 1–1

March 24, 2003

Dear Mrs. B. & Mr. G.

Erin attended the State Thespian Conference with the Drama Club this past weekend. When she saw that *The Tempest* was the Friday night play and it was by Shakespeare she was all excited; she definitely knows his name from your classes. On Sunday morning, there was a comedy entitled, *The Works of Shakespeare*. Erin insisted on attending after she heard that it was about Shakespeare and she loved it!

Saturday night, we saw one of the best musical presentations I have ever seen, of *Les Miserable*. Now Erin says she has to get the CD. She was mesmerized, but then we all were-just a phenomenal performance. At intermission she said the play was about what she had learned in history class. She made that connection!

This reinforces for me the need for all students to access the general education curriculum, even if they can't describe all the nuances of what they are learning about. I doubt very much that Erin would have been exposed to Shakespeare or any other great literature in the special education classroom for students with cognitive and developmental disabilities. That would have been unfortunate. Theatre has helped Erin to continue to make connections between literature and what she has learned in class. She watches the video from last year's school performance of "The Crucible" all the time.

Please keep Erin's experiences in mind when you and your colleagues are planning. *All* students, with any disability label, should have the opportunity to be part of the mix. You never know what any particular student might get out of a lesson or experience.

Thank you for giving Erin the opportunity to access great literature in your classes.

Barb McKenzie

stars. Such interests can hold great meaning to people. Consider the above letter (see Box 1-1) written by a parent to two high school English teachers about her daughter, Erin, who has a passion for theater (Erin has Down syndrome).

Access to Effective Instruction

Over the past several decades, the field of educating students with severe disabilities has relied extensively on the use of systematic instructional methods to pursue meaningful curricular outcomes because of their strong theoretical foundation and documented effectiveness (Alberto & Troutman, 1995; Snell & Brown, 2000). This set of instructional methods, such as chaining, shaping, prompting, and error correction, offered a bright spot in a special education system that was all too often characterized by unnecessarily low expectations, too much instructional downtime, limited access to peers without disabilities, and questionable curriculum. Use of these and other systematic

instructional methods played a major role in documenting the wide range of skills and functional routines people with severe disabilities could learn if offered consistent, quality instruction (Brown, Evans, Weed, & Owen, 1987). In fact, the use of these methods was instrumental in helping to establish, once and for all, the educability of people perceived as having the most profound disabilities.

Ironically, as students with severe disabilities have gained more access to general education classes with higher expectations, peers without disabilities, and a broader curriculum, new questions have been raised about the integrity of their instruction. The field is wrestling with the challenge of how to utilize the time-tested, evidence-based, systematic instructional approaches in new and contextually viable ways (Logan & Malone, 1998; McDonnell, 1998). In part, this has included a shift from individual instruction and small homogeneous groups to mixed-ability groupings where there is only one student with a disability with classmates who do not have disabilities.

Consider the case of Lisa, a high school student with severe disabilities. In the past, although she was included in general education classes, typically she was separated from the rest of the class for individualized instruction with a paraprofessional who implemented a systematic instructional plan that had been developed by the special educator. Although this plan had certain positive features (e.g., use of systematic instructional procedures, attention to functional skills), the lessons had no contextual relevance to the classrooms where they were being delivered. This resulted in Lisa's not being a true member of the classroom community since she had no substantive involvement with the classroom teachers or peers. When the team began planning ways to embed important learning outcomes for Lisa into class activities and creating opportunities for classmates to help each other learn, Lisa actually had more real opportunities for learning than ever before. The team met on a regular basis in an effort to evaluate how their plans were working and continually explore ways to use the best of validated instructional approaches in ways that were more natural and contextually grounded.

As teams pursue instructional integrity, it is important to remember that the principles of teaching and learning do not change because a child gets a disability label or because those who were once in a special class are now supported in a general class (see Box 1-2). Many doors have been opened for people with severe disabilities using foundational principles of instruction, and these remain critical for learning in inclusive settings. As with all strategies, however, the specific and changing learning environments and individual learning needs of each student will shape how strategies are used and adjusted to fit the evolving context.

Know Each Student's Characteristics

Quality instruction always starts by making sure you know your students. This means more than being familiar with their disability diagnosis, though that is important to understand. It means understanding their cognitive, physical, and sensory characteristics that affect instruction. It also means being cognizant of their social/emotional traits (e.g., temperament, behaviors), motivations, preferences and dislikes, interaction patterns, and creative attributes. Understanding such aspects of your students supports *individualization*, a hallmark of special education, and encourages the development of instructional approaches that build on each student's strengths and preferences.

Select Meaningful Learning Outcomes

Quality instruction really matters only if it is applied to meaningful learning outcomes. Highly effective instruction applied to irrelevant, nonfunctional, or chronologically age-inappropriate learning outcomes is a waste of the student's time as well as your own. Effective teams establish and maintain a positive sense of urgency about their work without simultaneously creating undue stress on the student or team. They know that, relatively, they have precious little time to teach, so their curricular selections and instructional intensity matter. Though much of the curricular aspects related to instruction were mentioned earlier in this chapter (e.g., functionality, age appropriateness, balance of breadth and focus), there are a few additional considerations when selecting meaningful learning outcomes.

Consider the frequency with which a learned skill will be used both now and in the future. Clearly, skills that are used frequently and have current and future utility generally are more important than those that are used infrequently or won't be useful in the future. Selecting meaningful learning outcomes is always a

 Box 1–2 Generic Principles of Quality Instruction

1. Know each student's characteristics
2. Select meaningful learning outcomes
3. Establish shared expectations among team members
4. Create a motivating learning environment
5. Select effective teaching methods
6. Provide sufficient and consistent learning opportunities
7. Use data to make instructional decisions

judgment. Sometimes, skills with a lower frequency of use can be extremely important to being safe (e.g., street crossing, evacuating a building in response to an alarm) or to personal preferences (e.g., the leisure skills one enjoys, predictable environments, unstructured time). For individuals with the most severe and multiple disabilities, a major consideration is the extent to which a learned skill will allow a person to control his or her environment (Brown & Lehr, 1993). For example, learning to use an adapted microswitch may allow a person with severe, multiple disabilities to activate a wide variety of electrical or electronic devices across a range of places and activities (e.g., communication, cooking, leisure, work).

Establish Shared Expectations Among Team Members

As curricular and instructional planning continues, team members need to establish shared expectations. From a logistical standpoint, ensuring that team members strive toward being on the same wavelength regarding philosophy, curriculum, and instruction can be a challenge simply because students with severe disabilities typically have teams with numerous members. Such teams often include parents, teachers, special educators, paraprofessionals, and related services providers such as speech-language pathologists, physical therapists, occupational therapists, orientation and mobility specialists, and psychologists. When teams are too large, it poses challenges in selecting meeting times and communicating. Team membership often changes substantially each school year with parents and students being the members most likely to remain on the team for extended periods of time.

Having multiple perspectives from numerous members can be a valuable asset to an educational planning team. Managing the group's size and diversity of input is important to enhance the productivity of the group and to avoid the stereotypical problems of team meetings, such as (a) being unclear about the purpose of the meeting, (b) getting off on tangents, (c) having the meeting dominated by one person or more members, or (d) leaving the meeting feeling like it was waste of time. Effective interactions among members can be facilitated through a variety of collaborative teamwork practices (Rainforth & York-Barr, 1997; Thousand & Villa, 2000). Establishing shared expectations means that all members should (a) know the student's learning-related characteristics, (b) be aware of the student's priority learning outcomes (e.g., IEP goals), (c)

be aware of the breadth of learning outcomes that are targeted for instruction (e.g., general education curriculum), (d) know when learning outcomes will be addressed throughout the school day, (e) know what general supports or accommodations need to be made for the student, (e) know the student-specific instructional procedures and adaptations, and (f) know what information to collect about the student's progress.

It is critical that all team members clearly understand the distinction between a *learning outcome* and a *general support*. A learning outcome is a goal or objective the team has targeted for the student to learn, such as "pointing to a desired food item on a communication board" or "finding one's own locker." This requires student responding and is designed to result in a change in student behavior (e.g., the acquisition of a new skill). A general support, on the other hand, refers to what will be provided for a student so that he or she may have access to education, participate in school, and pursue identified learning outcomes. On IEP documents, the terms used to describe general supports vary from place to place (e.g., accommodations, modifications, supports, management needs). General supports tend to cluster in one of six main categories (Giangreco et al., 1998):

1. Personal needs (e.g., support to eat, catheterization, provide medication)
2. Physical needs (e.g., repositioned at least hourly)
3. Teaching others about the student (e.g., teach staff and classmates about the student's augmentative communication, teach staff seizure management procedures)
4. Sensory needs (e.g., auditory amplification system, tactile materials, large-print materials)
5. Providing access and opportunities (e.g., environmental modifications, access to cocurricular activities, access to materials in the student's native language, computer access)
6. Other general supports (those not clearly addressed in any other category) (e.g., class notes recorded, extended time to complete tasks, communication with the family)

Drawing a distinction between general supports and learning outcomes is important because too often goals and objectives listed on IEPs for students with severe disabilities are written as passive general supports (e.g., repositioned at least hourly) rather than active learning outcomes (Downing, 1988; Giangreco, Dennis, Edelman, & Cloninger, 1994).

The volume, range, and complexity of information that teams exchange in the process of establishing shared expectations require practical documentation in addition to the IEP. There are a variety of ways that a team's shared expectations for a student can be clarified. First, a one- or two-page *program-at-a-glance* is a simple and concise way to summarize a student's learning outcomes and general supports for daily use (Giangreco et al., 1998, p. 132).

A second way to clarify the team's shared expectations are in lesson or program plans that explicitly describe how a student with a severe disability will pursue his or her learning outcomes within typical class activities. Such plans can also be effective reminders of basic information such as (a) operational definitions of target skills, (b) how to arrange the environment to facilitate learning (e.g., seating arrangement, materials), (c) methods for introducing tasks, and (d) what to do if the student doesn't respond in a reasonable length of time, responds incorrectly, or responds correctly. Having all team members clear about how to respond under these varying circumstances is critical to ensuring instructional consistency.

Third, general supports can be effectively documented through photographs or video clips, such as (a) how to safely transfer a student between their wheelchair and other places (e.g., stander, toilet, floor), (b) how a student should be appropriately positioned in his or her wheelchair, or (c) specialized feeding techniques. Finally, a *transition book*, which presents photos and short descriptive information, can be a friendly and effective way to introduce the personal and learning characteristics of a student with a severe disability to new team members and peers (Doyle, 2000).

Create a Motivating Learning Environment

Although it may seem obvious, the importance of *creating a motivating learning environment* where all students feel welcomed cannot be underestimated. Establishing a sense of belonging is considered a key building block for effective learning (Kunc, 2000). Studies of students with severe disabilities in elementary and middle schools highlight the limitations of part-time participation in general classes and the importance of participating in shared experiences (Schnorr, 1990, 1997). In order for students with disabilities to develop meaningful relationships with peers who do not have disabilities and access to a broad range of meaningful learning outcomes, they must share learning experiences with peers on an ongoing basis.

Select Effective Teaching Methods

Part of instructional access involves selecting effective teaching methods as a starting point for intervention. Students with disabilities often respond favorably to many of the same teaching methods that are common and effective for students who do not have disabilities. Some of these common methods include modeling and demonstration, repeated practice, guided discovery, participatory activities, using educational games or play, using positive and negative examples, giving corrective feedback, or cooperative group learning approaches. Challenges arise when students do not progress adequately when you have relied on typical instructional methods. In such cases, it is often necessary to be more precise in the application of methods, break the skills down into smaller components, or use different instructional methods, such as task analysis, chaining, shaping, and time delay (see chapters 4, 9, and 13). Consider the case of Tom and how he learned a new skill because of the use of a systematic instructional procedure and how it had an impact on his life.

Tom had a traumatic brain injury resulting in severe physical, cognitive, and sensory disabilities including blindness, loss of language, the inability to walk, sit up independently, or use his arms and hands. Tom was fed through a stomach tube, though his parents had worked with him so that he could eat soft foods and drink by mouth. His only consistent, voluntary skill was some head movement side to side when supported from behind, the ability to open and close his mouth, and some chewing. Tom communicated primarily through vocalizations. For example, he made a groaning sound that everyone easily recognized as discomfort. This usually meant it was time to get him out of his wheelchair for a while. At a meeting when Tom was 14 years old, his parents were asked for their input into Tom's IEP goals for the year. Tom's father said, "I don't care what he learns; I just want to know that he can learn." Building on Tom's strengths, the team decided to teach Tom to respond to the verbal instruction, "Open up" to open his mouth to receive, food, drink, medicine, and have his teeth brushed. The team knew that Tom currently didn't respond to "Open up" or any other instruction, but he did open his mouth wide when his lower lip was touched lightly (e.g., by a spoon with food). Some team members wondered if he was actually responding to the lip touch or something else, such as the air movement of something coming toward him, smell, or cues from some residual vision. Their assessment convinced them that it was the touch cue only that caused him to open his mouth. They decided to use an instructional procedure called "time delay." This started by simultaneously pairing the cue that they knew Tom responded to (i.e., touching the lip with a spoon) with the cue they wanted him to respond to (i.e., the verbal instruction "Open up"), followed by giving him a spoon of fruit yogurt. This simultaneous pairing is known as a zero delay because there is no time between the presentations of both cues. This was done numerous times throughout the day when Tom would normally be expected to open his mouth in an effort to help Tom to make the connection between the two cues. After this had been done for a few days, a 1-second time delay was put between the cues. The teacher would say "Open up," then wait 1 second before touching his lip. Over the next couple of weeks, the time delay between asking Tom to "Open up" and touching his lip was gradually increased in 1-second intervals, always followed by a small bite to eat or sip to drink. When the time delay got to 5 seconds, Tom opened his mouth to accept the food before his lip was ever touched—he had responded to the instruction! Time delay had been successfully used to transfer control from the one cue to another. Some people might think that this didn't matter much, but it did! For the first time in years, people who worked with Tom were excited and encouraged that he had learned a new skill. People interacted with him differently, more positively, as someone capable of learning. They were anxious to find out what else Tom could learn. Tom will always need substantial support from others, but this small change had a big impact.

Provide Sufficient and Consistent Learning Opportunities

Once instructional methods have been selected, with the individual student's learning characteristics in mind, the team needs to ensure that sufficient and consistent learning opportunities are provided for the student. A scheduling matrix (Giangreco et al. 1998, p. 161) provides a way for a team to ensure that a student's IEP goals and additional learning outcomes are incorporated into the daily or weekly schedule. A

scheduling matrix is set up as a simple grid. Listed across the top are regularly occurring class activities (e.g., arrival, language arts, math, science, physical education, lunch, recess). It can be helpful to note the amount of time devoted to each activity. For example, arrival time may be only 10 or 15 minutes at the beginning of the day, whereas a full hour might be devoted to language arts. The time frame is important to know because the number of learning outcomes that can reasonably be addressed will vary accordingly. Since daily schedules often change (e.g., one day math is at 9:00 a.m., a different day it is at 10:30 a.m.), when using a schedule matrix it is not crucial to arrange the general class activities in a specific order according to the schedule. Once a team determines which learning outcomes will be addressed in each class, that match will be the same regardless of what time the class occurs or on which day of the week. In this way, the scheduling matrix can then be used to clarify which of a student's learning outcomes can be embedded within all classes (e.g., express greetings and farewells, respond to yes/no questions, follow instructions, make choices when presented with options) and which will be targeted to specific classes or activities that make the most sense.

During computer class, Joshua will engage in individual active leisure by activating single-response software on a computer using an adapted microswitch. During language arts, he will identify photos and symbols, summon others, and do classroom jobs.

Providing sufficient and consistent learning opportunities requires persistence and creativity on the part of team members to embed opportunities for learning within class activities. Although the team wants to provide a reasonable level of planned consistency, since students with severe disabilities often present a very unique constellation of learning characteristics, team members need a certain level of instructional flexibility. They need room to explore new approaches, combinations of approaches, and capitalize on unscheduled, teachable moments.

Use Data to Make Instructional Decisions

Along with this flexibility comes accountability in the form of data collection. Just as we collect data and examples of work completed by students who do not have disabilities to monitor and document progress and to be accountable for our teaching, teams have a responsibility to do the same for students with severe disabilities (see chapter 5). Individualized data provide the essential information for making reasoned instructional decisions (Farlow & Snell, 1994).

As we think about collecting data on student learning, it is important to remember that performance related to specific IEP goals and objectives is only part of what is necessary. Regardless of the extent of student progress, it is important for each priority goal to be evaluated on the basis of its real impact on a person's life. Wolf's (1978) classic article introduced the field of applied behavior analysis to the assessment of *social validity*. Wolf argued that we must augment objective observable measures of behavior with subjective perspectives of consumers if we are to achieve outcomes of social importance. He suggested that we evaluate (a) the social significance of the goals being sought, (b) the social appropriateness of the procedures being used, and (c) the social importance of the effects. The concept of social validity acknowledges that a student's attainment of an established goal is not necessarily synonymous with its importance or meaningful changes in the student's life.

> *Maria is learning a set of social skills (e.g., responds to the presence of others, greeting, taking turns) with the intention that the attainment of these skills will contribute to establishing or extending friendships with peers. Merely knowing that she has acquired those skills is a good first step, but it is incomplete until we determine whether her relationships with peers have changed for the positive and whether her improved skills contributed to those socially important changes.*

Sometimes, socially important outcomes can occur even when target skills are not achieved. There may be circumstances where a student does not progress much in development of the targeted skill but where the nature of the instructional arrangement (e.g., peer involvement in typical class activities) leads to improvement in valued life outcomes because something in the environment has changed (e.g., access to typical settings, attitudes of classmates). Improvements in valued life outcomes for individuals with severe disabilities can be enhanced by a combination of skill acquisition on their part as well as changes in the environment, especially the attitudes and actions of the people in those environments.

Access to Individually Determined Supports

As described earlier, one of the defining characteristics of people with severe disabilities is that they require ongoing supports. A primary mechanism within IDEA to provide support is through the provision of *related services*:

> *The term "related services" means transportation, and such developmental, corrective, and other supportive services (including speech-language pathology and audiology services, psychological services, physical and occupational therapy, recreation, including therapeutic recreation, social work services, counseling services, including rehabilitation counseling, orientation and mobility services, and medical services, except that such medical services shall be for diagnostic and evaluation purposes only) as may be required to assist a child with a disability to benefit from special education, and includes the early identification and assessment of disabling conditions in children. (20 U.S.C. sec. 1400 [sec. 602][22])*

For many students with severe disabilities, special education services alone are not sufficient for them to receive an appropriate education; in such cases, the provision of related services are essential. The availability and array of related services recognizes the reality that no single discipline embodies the varied knowledge and skills necessary to effectively support the education of the full range of students with disabilities. One of the primary challenges of providing related services is ensuring that a student receive appropriate supports yet at the same time being careful that those services do not inadvertently interfere with the student's access to the least restrictive environment, appropriate curriculum, or effective instruction.

Team Decisions About Related Services

All too often, related services for students with severe disabilities are based on separate, discipline-specific goals and perspectives. Such scenarios highlight that merely assigning a group of individuals to the same student does not make them a team. It is the way these individuals interact together that ultimately distinguishes whether they are accurately referred to as a *group of individuals* or a *team*.

At the very outset of making team decisions about related services, it is helpful to understand and acknowledge that all decision making is based on underlying assumptions and values. Sometimes these are clearly understood and agreed to by team members. It is when they are unclear or conflicting that it becomes problematic because it increases the probability that team members will be working at cross-purposes, sometimes without even realizing why this is happening. Though honest disagreements about values will certainly exist among some team members, it is preferable that disagreements are in the open and that members strive toward identifying shared values that can guide their decisions. Having shared values can assist members in evaluating proposed actions as consistent or inconsistent with the team's approach. Listed in the following sections are three common value systems teams might encounter. The first two are inconsistent with sound educational practices; the third is suggested as a desirable alternative.

More Is Better Some team members are continually advocating for *more* related services. If one session of a particular therapy is recommended, they think two would be better and three better yet. The *more-is-better* approach is misguided because it confuses quantity with value. Often, although it is rooted in benevolent intentions, the more-is-better approach can have unintended, negative consequences for students by interfering with participation in other school activities. What is the student missing when he or she is spending time receiving a service someone has advocated for but that is not necessary? Providing more services than necessary may do the following:

- Decrease time for participation in activities with peers who do not have disabilities
- Disrupt class participation and membership by removal from class activities
- Cause disruption in acquiring, practicing, or generalizing other important skills
- Cause inequities in the distribution of resources when some students requiring services remain unserved or underserved
- Overwhelm families with an unnecessarily large number of professionals
- Result in stigmatization by the provision of special services
- Create unnecessary or unhealthy dependencies
- Unnecessarily complicate communication and coordination among team members

Return on Investment Another misguided value system, called *return on investment*, places a high value on serving students who have a favorable history and prognosis for being "fixed"—those likely to contribute the most, economically, to society. The return-on-investment approach fails to recognize the many noneconomic contributions made by people, including those with the most severe disabilities.

The return-on-investment value orientation is based on a curative mentality that sends negative messages to children with disabilities and their families. Imagine what it might be like to continually get the message, "You are not OK the way you are. In order to be OK, your disability has to be fixed and you need to be more like us (people without disabilities)." Increasingly, self-advocates are asking that their disabilities be viewed as a form of natural human diversity and that others' efforts be less about "fixing" a person's disabilities and more about accepting individuals for who they are and providing necessary and self-determined supports.

In addition, the return-on-investment approach tends to discriminate against individuals with the most severe disabilities. It seeks to justify the differential valuing of people and the services they receive on the basis of the severity of their disability characteristics. Anytime schools sanction practices that imply that some students are more worthy of staff time and resources than other students, there is a serious problem. All children are worthy, although they have differing needs.

Only as Specialized as Necessary An alternative value system is referred to as *only as specialized as necessary*—providing enough but not too much. This value orientation is based on the notion that, like other things people *need* (e.g., food, water, sleep, sunshine, time with others), our aim should be to get what we need in balance with all the other things we need rather than in the most amount possible. This involves both trade-offs and individualization when determining the appropriate type and amount of service for each student. This determination will be a collective best judgment of team members. Although this value system is contemporary, its conceptual basis within special education pre-dates federally protected educational rights for students with a full range of disabilities (Reynolds, 1962) and has a strong legal foundation in a U.S. Supreme Court precedent (*Board of Education of the Hendrick Hudson School District v. Rowley*, 1982).

The only-as-specialized-as-necessary approach seeks to identify and draw on natural supports, including those currently existing and available to students without disabilities (e.g., guidance counselor, teachers, school nurse, peers, educational support teams). In cases where more specialized services are deemed necessary, ongoing data should be collected in an effort to document the impact of the services while the team continues to explore alternatives that would allow students with disabilities to receive needed supports in the most natural and sustainable ways possible. This approach supports the provision of needed services and acknowledges the contributions made by various disciplines but takes precautions to avoid the inherent drawbacks of providing well-intentioned but unnecessary services.

It is important to recognize that the only-as-specialized-as-necessary approach does not necessarily mean that "less is always best" or "only a little is plenty." Some advocates have voiced concerns that this approach might be misused to justify denial of needed services; this certainly is not its intended use. When used as intended, the only-as-specialized-as-necessary approach results in students receiving needed services. Further, it is meant to be a value orientation agreed to by the team, which includes the family. In summary, it is most important that teams understand the value orientations held by their members and that they work toward a shared value system that will contribute to making educationally sound support service decisions.

Educational Relevance and Necessity

When considering a value orientation such as the only-as-specialized-as-necessary approach within the context of the IDEA definition of related services and putting it into practical use requires that teams ask themselves challenging questions about the educational relevance and necessity of a proposed service. *Educational relevance* exists when a proposed service can be explicitly linked with a component of a student's educational program (e.g., IEP goals, general education curriculum).

Lisa, an occupational therapist, has made various recommendations to support the handwriting skills of Adam, a student with autism, based on her evaluation of him. If handwriting is included as a goal or objective on Adam's IEP or is part of the general education for which the student needs special education,

then the recommended occupational therapy supports are educationally relevant.

Educational relevance alone is not sufficient to warrant service provision; services must also be *educationally necessary*. A service is educationally necessary if, after establishing its educational relevance, the team determines that the service is essential. In many cases, IEP teams are asking the wrong questions, such as "Could the proposed related service help?" When this question is posed, the answer is almost always "Yes." But this is not the question that the IDEA poses in the definition of a related service. The question may be more appropriately posed like this: "If the student does not receive a proposed related service, is there reason to believe that he or she will not (a) have access to an appropriate education or (b) experience educational benefit?" This question requires a higher standard of accountability to answer "Yes" than the one asking whether it could help. If a team does answer "Yes," it clearly suggests educational necessity.

Consider the following two scenarios: (a) A parent takes her child with a disability to a private clinic for an evaluation and a consultant recommends music therapy once a week as a related service. (b) A therapist recommends therapeutic horseback riding twice a week. First, consider the following question to assist your team in determining whether a proposed related service is educationally necessary. Will the absence of the service interfere with the student's access to or participation in his or her educational program this year? If the team answers "Yes," the service under consideration probably *is* educationally necessary. If the team answers "Yes" to any of the following questions, the service under consideration probably *is not* educationally necessary (Giangreco, 2001).

- Could the proposed service be addressed appropriately by the special educator or classroom teacher?
- Could the proposed service be addressed appropriately through core school faculty or staff (e.g., school nurse, guidance counselor, librarian, bus drivers, cafeteria staff, custodians)?
- Has the student been benefiting from his or her educational program without the service?
- Could the student continue to benefit from his or her educational program without the service?
- Could the service appropriately be provided during nonschool hours (as established in the 1984 U.S.

Supreme Court decision, *Irving Independent School District v. Tatro*, 1984)?

- Does the proposed service present any undesirable or unnecessary gaps, overlaps, or contradictions with other proposed services?

If the team asked the question "Could these services help?" it could be quite easy to answer "Yes." It would be more difficult to answer "Yes" if the question was asked a different way: "If the student does not receive music therapy or therapeutic horseback riding as a related service, is there reason to believe that he or she will not be able to receive an appropriate education?" This aspect of educational relevance is rooted in the *Rowley* decision *Board of Education of the Hendrick Hudson School District v. Rowley* (1982). In that case, the Court established that if a student was receiving educational benefit without the service, it was evidence that the service was not needed, even though providing the service might help. In such cases, schools are not required to provide the proposed service.

This type of scrutiny of service provision presents many gray areas and points of potential conflict among team members, which is why it is so important to continually build a shared understanding as a team. Ultimately, unnecessary services take away from rather than improve a student's educational program. Conversely, well-conceived and well-carried-out related services can make a substantial contribution to a student's educational program.

Jamal is a student with multiple disabilities, including deaf-blindness. The related services providers on his team have worked closely with the special educator, his classroom teacher, and his parents to ensure that his related services are both educationally relevant and necessary. The physical and occupational therapists have selected and modified equipment (e.g., specialized seating, arm/hand supports, adapted computer interface) that allows Jamal access to many learning opportunities. The speech-language pathologist has developed an augmentative communication system and corresponding instructional approaches that create opportunities for Jamal to communicate more effectively with teachers and peers. The vision and hearing specialists have adapted materials and learning environments (e.g., tactile labels, individualized amplification) to allow Jamal access to the general education curriculum.

These are only a few of the many ways that educationally relevant and necessary related services can be imperative for some students with disabilities. Making effective team decisions is not always easy but definitely is important.

Summary

Regardless of your role on the team, how you approach the task of educating students with severe disabilities depends quite substantially on the attitudes and dispositions you bring to this important task. One of the best places to look for encouraging and affirming perspectives is to families who have accepted their child with a severe disability unconditionally. That leads me to my colleague and friend, Susan Yuan, who has three children, all of whom are now young adults. Her youngest, Andreas, has severe disabilities. In a recent essay, she wrote about "seeing with new eyes" by using metaphors to help people think about individuals with severe disabilities differently (Yuan, 2003). Susan's metaphor regarding Andreas was that of a bicycle. She likened her earlier parenting experiences with her two older daughters to riding a basic bike with fat tires, no gears, and a coaster brake. She knew basically what to expect and was able to figure it out. When Andreas was born, one of her first reactions was, "No way I could be a good mother to him!" He wasn't like the bike she was accustomed to riding.

Sticking with the bicycle metaphor, to many people in our society the constellation of characteristics presented by Andreas would lead them to thinking of him as a bike that was broken or missing some parts. Such a perspective leads to many of the traditional ways our society limits opportunities and provides services for people with disabilities. You don't take a broken bike out for a ride on the recreation path; first you try to fix it. If it can't be fixed, some consider discarding it. Others become sentimental or hopeful and put the bike in the garage and tinker with it now and then; but their expectation is that it will never be a bike they can really ride or fully enjoy.

Rather than thinking of Andreas as a broken bike, Susan extended the metaphor by coming to think of him as a fancy Italian racing bike, with many gears, hand brakes, and racing handlebars. This bike wasn't broken; she just hadn't learned to ride it yet. She came to see this new bike as more complex, more sensitive, more responsive than a typical bike. On top of it all, it was a tandem bike that both parents would need to learn to ride together, move together, and get in sync. She closed her essay this way:

> *Though I may not be ready for the Tour de France, I have become quite comfortable and capable with my own fancy, complex bicycle, known in the metaphorical world as my son, Andreas. Yes, he has his own unique characteristics, idiosyncrasies, peculiarities—don't we all! As I enter the 30th year of an incredible journey, I am still tinkering with the gears, appreciating that this bike has a mind of its own, and enjoying the ride. (p. 210)*

As you proceed with your learning and your practice, part of the work is the struggle to find a balance between attending to the undoubtedly special needs of individuals with severe disabilities and their right to live regular lives. As a community of educators, we know quite a lot about what we think makes for effective education, but there is so much we don't know or simply don't do regularly enough. A key aspect of this work is creativity and unwavering persistence. By combining these elements, we have a reasonable chance for making the kinds of individual, collective, and incremental breakthroughs that can make a difference in people's lives.

References

Alberto, P. A., & Troutman, A. C. (1995). *Applied behavior analysis for teachers* (4th ed.). Upper Saddle River, NJ: Merill/Prentice Hall.

Baer, D. (1981). A hung jury and a Scottish verdict: "Not proven." *Analysis and Intervention in Developmental Disabilities, 1*(1), 91-98.

Bambara, L. M., Cole, C., & Koger, F. (1998). Translating self-determination concepts in support for adults with severe disabilities. *Journal of the Association for Persons with Severe Handicaps, 23,* 27-37.

Baumgart, D., Brown, L., Pumpian, I., Nisbet, J., Ford, A., Sweet, M., Messina, R., & Schroeder, J. (1982). Principle of partial participation and individualized adaptations in educational programs for severely handicapped students. *Journal of the Association for the Severely Handicapped, 7*(2), 17-27.

Biklen, S. K., & Mosley, C. R. (1988). "Are you retarded?" "No, I'm Catholic": Qualitative methods in the study of people with severe handicaps. *Journal of the Association for Persons with Severe Handicaps, 13,* 155-162.

Billingsley, B. (2002). Improving special education teacher retention: Implications from a decade of research. *Journal of Special Education Leadership, 15*(2), 20-26.

Bloom, B. S. (Ed.). (1956). *Taxonomy of educational objectives: Handbook I: Cognitive domain.* New York: McCay.

Board of Education of the Hendrick Hudson Central School District v. Rowley, 102 S. Ct. 3034 (1982).

Bogdan, R., & Taylor, S. J. (1989). Relationships with severely disabled people: The social construction of humanness. *Social Problems, 36,* 135-147.

Brantlinger, E. (1997). Using ideology: Cases of nonrecognition of the politics of research and practice in special education. *Review of Educational Research, 67*(4), 425-459.

Brown, F., Evans, I., Weed, K., & Owen, V. (1987). Delineating functional competencies: A component model. *Journal of the Association for Persons with Severe Handicaps, 12,* 117-124.

Brown, F., & Lehr, D. H. (1993). Making activities meaningful for students with severe multiple disabilities. *Teaching Exceptional Children, 25*(4), 12-16.

Brown, F., & Michaels, C. A. (2003). The shaping of inclusion: Efforts in Detroit and other urban settings. In D. Fisher & N. Frey (Eds.), *Inclusive urban schools* (pp. 231-243). Baltimore: Paul H. Brookes.

Brown, L., Branston, M. B., Hamre-Nietupski, S., Pumpian, I., Certo, N., & Gruenewald, L. (1979). A strategy for developing chronologically age-appropriate and functional curricular content for severely handicapped adolescents and young adults. *Journal of Special Education, 13,* 81-90.

Brown, L., Farrington, K., Ziegler, M., Knight, T., & Ross, C. (1999). Fewer paraprofessionals and more teachers and therapists in educational programs for students with significant disabilities. *Journal of the Association for Persons with Severe Handicaps, 24,* 249-252.

Brown, L., Nietupski, J., & Hamre-Nietupski, S. (1976). The criterion of ultimate functioning and public school services for severely handicapped students. In M. A. Thomas (Ed.), *Hey, don't forget about me! Education's investment in the severely, profoundly, and multiply handicapped* (pp. 2-15). Reston, VA: Council on Exceptional Children.

Campbell, C., Campbell, S., Collicott, J., Perner, D., & Stone, J. (1988). Individualized instruction. *Education New Brunswick—Journal Education, 3,* 17-20.

Carr, E. G., Horner, R. H., Turnbull, A., Marquis, J. G., McLaughlin, D. M., McAtee, M. L., Smith, C. E., Ryan, K. A., & Doolabh, A. (1999). *Positive behavior support for people with developmental disabilities: A research synthesis.* Washington, DC: American Association on Mental Retardation.

Chadsey-Rusch, J., & Rusch, F. R. (1996). Promising transition practices for youths with disabilities. *Contemporary Education, 68,* 9-12.

Code of Federal Regulations (CFR). (1999). *Assistance to states for the education of children with disabilities and the early intervention program for infants and toddlers with disabilities: Final regulations, 34,* Parts 300 and 303.

Davern, L., Sapon-Shevin, M., D'Aquanni, M., Fisher, M., Larson, M., Black, J., & Minondo, S. (1997). Drawing the distinction between coherent and fragmented efforts at building inclusive schools. *Equity and Excellence in Education, 30*(3), 31-39.

Dembo, T., Leviton, G. L., & Wright, B. A. (1975). Adjustment to misfortune: A problem of social-psychological rehabilitation. *Rehabilitation Psychology, 22,* 1-100.

Dickens, C. (1859). *Tale of two cities.* London: Chapman and Hall.

Donnellan, A. (1984). The criterion of the least dangerous assumption. *Behavior Disorders, 9,* 141-150.

Downing, J. (1988). Active versus passive programming: A critique of IEP objectives for students with the most severe disabilities. *Journal of the Association for Persons with Severe Handicaps, 13,* 197-210.

Downing, J. (2002). *Including students with severe and multiple disabilities in typical classrooms: Practical strategies for teachers* (2nd ed.). Baltimore: Paul H. Brookes.

Doyle, M.B. (2003). "We want to go to college too": Supporting students with significant disabilities in higher education. In D.L. Ryndak & S. Alper. (Ed.). *Curriculum development for students with disabilities in inclusive settings* (pp. 307-322). Boston: Allyn & Bacon.

Dunlap, G., Newton, J. S., Fox, L., Benito, N., Vaughn, B. (2001). Family involvement in functional assessment and positive behavior support. *Focus on Autism and Other Developmental Disabilities, 16,* 215-221.

Durand, V. M., & Merges, E. (2001). Functional communication training: A contemporary behavior analytic intervention for problem behaviors. *Focus on Autism and Other Developmental Disabilities, 16,* 110-119, 136.

Erickson, K., & Koppenhaver, D. (1995). Developing a literacy program for children with severe disabilities. *Reading Teacher, 48*(8), 676-684.

Erickson, K.A., Koppenhaver, D.A., Yoder, D. E., & Nance, J. (1997). Integrated communication and literacy instruction for a child with multiple disabilities. *Focus on Autism and Other Developmental Disabilities, 12,* 142-150.

Evans, I. M., Scotti, J. R., & Hawkins, R. P. (1999). Understanding where we are going by looking at where we have been. In J.R. Scotti & L.H. Meyer (Eds.), *Behavioral intervention: Principles, models, and practices* (pp. 3-23). Baltimore: Paul H. Brookes.

Farlow, L. J., & Snell, M. E. (1994). *Making the most of student performance data: Innovations, Research to Practice Series.* Washington, DC: American Association on Mental Retardation.

Ferguson, D. L., & Baumgart, D. (1991). Partial participation revisited. *Journal of the Association for Persons with Severe Handicaps, 16,* 218-227.

Fisher, D., Sax, C., & Pumpian, I. (1999). *Inclusive high schools.* Baltimore: Paul H. Brookes.

Ford, A., Davern, L., & Schnorr, R. (2001). Learners with significant disabilities: Curricular relevance in an era of standards-based reform. *Remedial and Special Education, 22,* 214-222.

Gee, K. (2002). Looking closely at instructional approaches: Honoring and challenging all children and youth in inclusive schools. In W. Sailor (Ed.), *Whole-school success and inclusive education: Building partnerships for learning achievement and accountability* (pp. 123-141). New York: Teachers College Press.

Giangreco, M. F. (2001). *Guidelines for making decisions about IEP services.* Montpelier: Vermont Department of Education.

Giangreco, M. F., Cloninger, C. J., & Iverson, V. S. (1998). *Choosing outcomes and accommodations for children: A guide to educational planning for students with disabilities* (2nd ed.). Baltimore: Paul H. Brookes.

Giangreco, M. F., Dennis, R., Cloninger, C., Edelman, S., & Schattman, R. (1993). "I've counted Jon": Transformational experiences of teachers educating students with disabilities. *Exceptional Children, 59,* 359-372.

Giangreco, M. F., Dennis, R. E., Edelman, S. W., & Cloninger, C. J. (1994). Dressing your IEPs for the general education climate: Analysis of IEP goals and objectives for students with multiple disabilities, *Remedial and Special Education, 15*(5), 288-296.

Giangreco, M. F., & Doyle, M. B. (2002). Students with disabilities and paraprofessional supports: Benefits, balance, and band-aids. *Focus on Exceptional Children, 34*(7), 1-12.

Giangreco, M. F., & Meyer, L. H. (1988). Expanding service delivery options in regular education schools and classrooms for students with severe disabilities. In J. L. Graden, J. E. Zins, & M. J. Curtis (Eds.)., *Alternative educational service delivery systems: Enhancing instructional options for all students* (pp. 241-267). Washington, DC: National Association of School Psychologists.

Giangreco, M. F., & Snell, M. E. (1996). Severe and multiple disabilities. In R. Turnbull & A. Turnbull (Eds.), *Improving the implementation of the individuals with disabilities education act: Making schools work for all of America's children* (pp. 97-132). Washington, DC: National Council on Disability.

Green, C. W., & Reid, D. H. (1996). Defining, validating, and increasing indices of happiness among people with profound multiple disabilities. *Journal of Applied Behavior Analysis, 29,* 67-78.

Green, C. W., & Reid, D. H. (1999). A behavioral approach to identifying sources of happiness and unhappiness among individuals with profound multiple disabilities. *Behavior Modification, 23,* 280-293.

Grigal, M., Neubert, D., & Moon, M. S. (2001). Public school programs for students with significant disabilities in post-secondary settings. *Education and Training in Mental Retardation and Developmental Disabilities, 36,* 244-254.

Hall, M., Kleinert, H. L., & Kearns, J. F. (2000). Going to college! Postsecondary programs for students with moderate and severe disabilities. *Teaching Exceptional Children, 32*(3), 58-65.

Horner, R. H. (2000) Positive behavior supports. *Focus on Autism and Other Developmental Disabilities, 15,* 97-105.

Horner, R., Close, D., Fredericks, H. D. B., O'Neill, R., Albin, R., Sprague, J., Kennedy, C., Flannery, B., & Heathfield, L. (1996). Supported living for people with profound disabilities and severe behavior problems. In D. H. Lehr & F. Brown (Eds.), *People with disabilities who challenge the system* (pp. 209-240). Baltimore: Paul H. Brookes.

Hunt, P., & Goetz, L. (1997). Research on inclusive educational programs, practices, and outcomes for students with severe disabilities. *Journal of Special Education, 31,* 3-29.

Irving Independent School District v. Tatro, 104 S. Ct. 3371 (1984).

Jackson, L., Ryndak, D., & Billingsley, F. (2000). Useful practices in inclusive education: A preliminary view of what experts in moderate and severe disabilities are saying. *Journal of the Association for Persons with Severe Disabilities, 25,* 129-141.

Janney, R., & Snell, M.E. (1997). How teachers include students with moderate and severe disabilities in elementary classes: The means and meaning of inclusion. *Journal of the Association for Persons with Severe Disabilities, 22,* 159-169.

Janney, R., & Snell, M. E. (2000). *Teacher's guides to inclusive practices: Behavioral support.* Baltimore: Paul H. Brookes.

Janney, R., & Snell, M. E. (2004). *Teacher's guides to inclusive practices: Modifying schoolwork (2^(nd) edition)*. Baltimore: Paul H. Brookes.

Jorgensen, C. M. (1998). *Restructuring high schools for all students: Taking inclusion to the next level.* Baltimore: Paul H. Brookes.

Kauffman, J. M., & Krouse, J. (1981). The cult of educability: Searching for the substance of things hoped for; the evidence of things not seen. *Analysis and Intervention in Developmental Disabilities, 1*(1), 53–60.

Kennedy, C. H., & Fisher, D. (2001). *Inclusive middle schools.* Baltimore: Paul H. Brookes.

Kleinert, H. L., & Kearns, J. F. (2001). *Alternative assessment: Measuring outcomes and supports for students with disabilities.* Baltimore: Paul H. Brookes.

Kozleski, E., Mainzer, R., & Deshler, D. (2000). Bright futures for exceptional learners: An action agenda to achieve quality conditions for teaching and learning. *Teaching Exceptional Children, 32*(6), 56–69.

Kunc, N. (2000). Rediscovering the right to belong. In R.A. Villa & J. S. Thousand (Eds.), *Restructuring for caring and effective education: Piecing the puzzle together* (2nd ed., pp. 77–92). Baltimore: Paul H. Brookes.

Lipsky, D. K., & Gartner, A. (1997). *Inclusion and school reform: Transforming America's schools.* Baltimore: Paul H. Brookes.

Logan, K. R., Jacobs, H.A., Gast, D. L., Murray, A. S., Daino, K., & Skala, C. (1998). The impact of typical peers on the perceived happiness of students with profound multiple disabilities. *Journal of the Association for Persons with Severe Handicaps, 23,* 309–318.

Logan, K., & Malone, D. M. (1998). Instructional contexts for students with moderate, severe, and profound intellectual disabilities in general education classrooms. *Education and Training in Mental Retardation and Developmental Disabilities, 33,* 62–75.

McDonnell, J. (1998). Instruction for students with severe disabilities in general education settings. *Education and Training in Mental Retardation and Developmental Disabilities, 33,* 199–215.

McDonnell, J., Hardman, M., & McDonnell, A. (2003). *An introduction to persons with moderate and severe disabilities: Educational and social issues* (2nd ed.). Boston: Allyn & Bacon.

McDonnell, J., Johnson, J. W., Polychronis, S., & Risen, T. (2002) Effects of embedded instruction on students with moderate disabilities enrolled in general education classes. *Education and Training in Mental Retardation and Developmental Disabilities, 37,* 363–377.

McGregor, G., & Volgelsberg, R. T. (1998). *Inclusive schooling practices: Pedagogical and research foundations: A synthesis of the literature that informs best practices about inclusive schooling.* Baltimore: Paul H. Brookes.

McLeskey, J., Tyler, N., & Saunders, S. (2002). *The supply and demand of special education teachers: The nature of the chronic shortage of special education teachers.* Gainesville: University of Florida, Center on Personnel Studies in Special Education.

Meyer, L. H. (2001). The impact of inclusive education on children's lives: Multiple outcomes, and friendship in particular. *International Journal of Disability, Development and Education, 48*(1), 9–31.

Nisbet, J. (Ed.). (1992). *Natural supports in school, at work, and in the community for people with severe disabilities.* Baltimore: Paul H. Brookes.

Noonan, M. J., Brown, F., Mulligan, M., & Rettig, M. (1982). Educability of severely handicapped persons: Both sides of the issue. *Journal of the Association for Persons with Severe Handicaps, 7*(1), 3–14.

Peterson, J. M., Beloin, K., & Gibson, R. (1997). *Whole schooling: Education for a democratic society.* Detroit: Whole Schooling Consortium.

Rainforth, B., & York-Barr, J. (1997). *Collaborative teams for students with severe disabilities: Integrating therapy and educational services* (2nd ed.). Baltimore: Paul H. Brookes.

Reynolds, M. C. (1962). A framework for considering some issues in special education. *Exceptional Children, 28,* 367–370.

Ryndak, D. L., & Fisher, D. (Eds.). (2003). *The foundations of inclusive education: A compendium of articles on effective strategies to achieve inclusive education* (2nd ed.). Baltimore: TASH.

Sailor, W. (Ed.). (2002). *Whole-school success and inclusive education: Building partnerships for learning achievement and accountability.* New York: Teachers College Press.

Schnorr, R. (1990). "Peter? He come and he goes . . .": First graders' perspectives on a part-time mainstream student. *Journal of the Association for Persons with Severe Handicaps, 15,* 231–240.

Schnorr, R. (1997). From enrollment to membership: "Belonging" in middle and high school classes. *Journal of the Association for Persons with Severe Handicaps, 22,* 1–15.

Snell, M. E. (2003). Education of individuals with severe and multiple disabilities. In J. W. Guthrie (Ed.), *Encyclopedia of education* (2nd ed., pp. 2210–2213). New York: Macmillan.

Snell, M. E., & Janney, R. (2004). *Teacher's guides to inclusive practices: Collaborative teamwork* (2nd edition). Baltimore: Paul H. Brookes.

Soodak, L. C., Erwin, E. J. (2000). Valued member or tolerated participant: Parents' experiences in inclusive early childhood settings. *Journal of the Association for Persons with Severe Handicaps, 25,* 29–41.

TASH. (2000, March). TASH resolution on the people for whom TASH advocates. Retrieved July 18, 2003, from http://www.tash.org/resolutions/res02advocate.htm

Taylor, S. J. (1988). Caught in the continuum: A critical analysis of the principle of the least restrictive environment. *Journal of the Association for Persons with Handicaps, 13,* 41–53.

Taylor, S. J., & Bogdan, R. (1989). On accepting relationships between people with mental retardation and non-disabled people: Towards an understanding of acceptance. *Disability, Handicap and Society, 4,* 21–36.

Thousand, J., & Villa, R. (2000). Collaborative teaming: A powerful tool for school restructuring. In R. A. Villa & J. S. Thousand (Eds.), *Restructuring for caring and effective education: Piecing the puzzle together* (2nd ed., pp. 254–291). Baltimore: Paul H. Brookes.

Timothy W. v. Rochester School District, 559 EHLR 480 (D.N.H. 1988), 875 F.2d 954 (1st Cir. 1989), cert. denied, 493 U.S. 983 (1989).

Turnbull, A. P., & Turnbull, H. R. (2000). *Families, professionals and exceptionality: Collaborating for empowerment* (4th ed.). Upper Saddle River, NJ: Merrill/Prentice Hall.

Turnbull, H. R., & Turnbull, A. P. (2000). *Free appropriate public education: The law and children with disabilities* (6th ed.). Denver: Love Publishing.

Udvari-Solner, A., Thousand, J. S., & Villa, R. A. (2002). Access to the general education curriculum for all. In J. S. Thousand, R. A. Villa, & A. I. Nevin (Eds.), *Creativity and collaborative learning: The practical guide to empowering students, teachers, and families* (2nd ed., pp. 85–103). Baltimore: Paul H. Brookes.

U.S. Department of Education. (2002). *To assure the free and appropriate public education of all children with disabilities: Twenty-third annual report to congress on the implementation of the Individuals with Disabilities Education Act.* Washington, DC: Author.

Van der Klift, E., & Kunc, N. (2002). Beyond benevolence: Supporting genuine friendship in inclusive schools. In J. S. Thousand, R. A. Villa, & A. I. Nevin (Eds.), *Creativity and collaborative learning: The practical guide to empowering students, teachers, and families* (2nd ed., pp. 21–28). Baltimore: Paul H. Brookes.

Villa, R. A., & Thousand, J. S. (2000). *Restructuring for caring and effective education: Piecing the puzzle together* (2nd ed.). Baltimore: Paul H. Brookes.

Wehman, P. (2001). *Life beyond the classroom: Transition strategies for young people with disabilities* (3rd ed.). Baltimore: Paul H. Brookes.

Wehmeyer, M. L., Agran, M., & Hughes, C. (2000). *Teaching self-determination: Basic skills for successful transition.* Baltimore: Paul H. Brookes.

Weiss, N. (2003, January/February). Excerpts from the testimony of Nancy Weiss, executive director, TASH, at the New Jersey Restraint Bill Hearings, January 16, 2003. *TASH Connections, 29*(1/2), 6.

Wilkins, D. (2003). Your attitude. Retrieved August 2, 2003, from http://www.thenthdegree.com/advocacy.asp#YOUR%20ATTITUDE

Wolery, M., & McWilliam, R. A. (1998). Classroom-based practices for preschoolers with disabilities. *Intervention in School and Clinic, 34*(2), 95–102.

Wolf, M. M. (1978). Social validity: The case for subjective measurement, or how applied behavior analysis is finding its heart. *Journal of Applied Behavior Analysis, 11,* 203–214.

Wolfensberger, W. (1975). *The origin and nature of our institutional models.* Syracuse, NY: Human Policy Press.

Wolfensberger, W. (2000). A brief overview of social role valorization. *Mental Retardation, 38*(2), 105–123.

Yuan, S. (2003). Seeing with new eyes: Metaphors of family experience. *Mental Retardation, 41,* 207–211.

Fostering Family–Professional Partnerships

Ann Turnbull
Rud Turnbull

Mr. and Mrs. Bridge regard themselves as very lucky. It's not just that their daughter Libby has been "in the right place at the right time" all of her life. It's more that Libby has always been in an inclusive setting of one kind or another and that the Bridges have had positive relationships with Libby's teachers and other educators.

Libby is 11 years old and is in a fifth-grade general education classroom. Her cerebral palsy, mental retardation, epilepsy, and visual impairment do not inhibit her from enjoying friendships with her peers and teachers, liking school, and delighting in taking the school bus from her Kansas City, Kansas, home to her school. How did Libby's situation come to be? What paths did she take?

Libby's first school experience was in an early intervention program affiliated with a local university; the program did not practice any form of inclusion because it was exclusively for students with disabilities. From there, however, Libby went to a school that employed the practice of "reverse integration"—she was in a special setting, but students from general education programs spent some time in her class throughout each school day.

While Libby was still in that program, school district administrators asked Mr. and Mrs. Bridge whether they wanted her to participate in the district's inclusion program. The Bridges were plagued by doubt, fearing that their daughter would not receive the attention she needs to benefit from school. After considering their options and discussing it at length together, with Libby's present teachers, and with the district's special education staff, however, they opted for inclusion.

Libby has since exceeded their expectations for her; so too has the full-inclusion program. When Libby started the new school, she could not walk without assistance. Naturally, her parents were worried about the stairs in the building of her new school. How would Libby ever get around? Several options were discussed. Given that Libby has a significant mobility impairment and that the school building is old, it is unlikely that the school district would install an elevator for her or any other students or faculty. Instead, if necessary, it would either schedule all her classes on the ground floor or install a chair lift if such a device could be retrofitted to the existing stairwells without impeding access by the students and faculty, especially during an emergency. This would only be done if the lift safely gives Libby access to second-floor classrooms. A few months later, however, they were thrilled as they watched Libby make her way down the hall and successfully negotiate the steps—without need of any of the environmental adaptations. Libby's teachers, paraprofessionals, and related services providers had great expectations for her, which paid off.

Libby benefits from the support of her large family—both her immediate and her extended family. She lives with her parents and her two sisters, Hilary and Hayley, ages 9 and 4. Her grandparents live nearby and enjoy spending time with her, giving her parents time for themselves and for Libby's sisters and helping to balance the Bridges' life so it does not center on only Libby. The grandparents also help the Bridges with problem solving and brainstorming to meet Libby's special needs. In all that they do, they provide much-needed emotional support: support that began from Libby's very first days and early diagnosis. In Libby's life, the norm is acceptance within the home and, now, within the school.

That is not to say, however, that there are no concerns. Indeed, a major concern for the family is Libby's upcoming move to middle school. Libby will go from an inclusive program in an elementary school to a middle school that does not support inclusion. Instead of taking a short bus ride to her nearby home school, she will ride a bus across the city for nearly an hour.

In addition to these two school concerns (the lack of inclusion and the bus ride), Mrs. Bridge is worried about Libby's developmental changes and their implications for the family. Libby is unable to provide any self-care; all her needs are taken care of by family members when at home and by educators while at school. Her inevitable development from being a child to a teenage girl to a grown woman will pose challenges related to hygiene and perhaps even sexuality.

Mr. and Mrs. Bridge have never liked being asked what they see for Libby in the future. Yet it is a question that follows them constantly. Libby's teachers began asking it when she was a baby and have continued to ask it at every stage of Libby's transition, from early intervention to elementary school and now from elementary school to middle school.

Mrs. Bridge explained the family's quandary in the simplest and most poignant terms: "It's hard enough to figure out what she's going to be doing next year, much less where she'll be after high school. I don't think we like to think that far into the future—especially now because everything is so good. We'd rather she just stay in elementary school the rest of her life and never grow up, and we'll live forever."

When the Bridges do venture beyond the safety of today and look into their and Libby's future, they say that they can only hope that Libby will work in a supported employment setting but that she will continue to live with them in the family home. "Nobody will love her like her mom, father and sisters, so if you ask me that question now, that's what I'll say—that she'll stay with us forever."

 Introducing the Hanaoka Family

Having immigrated from Japan to the United States only 4 years ago, Ms. Hanaoka and her daughter, Emily, age 12, face culture shock in more ways than one. It is not merely that they now need to acclimate to their new country and in particular its midwestern mores; it is also that Emily has two concurrent disabilities—mental retardation and autism. Ms. Hanaoka has been a single parent since the accidental death of her husband 8 years ago. Emily is a bright-eyed and energetic child and shares her mother's love for music. This love for music cements their bond and makes the mother–daughter relationship all the more vital—it breathes life into each of them and necessitates careful cultivation by Emily's special and general educators.

The family's history, together with the tight mother–daughter bond, is relevant to educators. Needing to reenter the work force on her husband's death, Ms. Hanaoka, a musician, began to investigate further training to advance her career. When she learned of a well-regarded and long-established music therapy graduate program at the

University of Kansas, she decided to come to Kansas with her daughter.

Ms. Hanaoka's decision rested on something else equally important. She had become discouraged at the educational opportunities available in Japan for Emily and other children with severe disabilities. In particular, she was eager for Emily to be in a school where she could interact with peers who did not have disabilities. Although some general education programs and schools for children without disabilities in Japan are beginning to accommodate children with disabilities, Emily was rejected for admission to a regular school; its faculty regarded her disability as too significant for them to address. More discouraging was the realization that the special schools to which Emily was referred did not provide individualized teaching. That approach occurred only if a teacher was trained and motivated to individualize for the students' benefit.

So began a sequence of events. She would investigate the possibilities for herself and her daughter. She would apply to graduate school at the University of Kansas, receive an acceptance letter, arrange for a student visa, plan a move, locate housing, and, along the way and not at all incidentally to everything else facing the family, plan and undertake the daunting task of helping Emily, who tends to rely on structure and predictability, adjust to moving far from home.

Once in Kansas, Ms. Hanaoka found the hoped-for educational opportunities for Emily. But finding them was only one accomplishment. Making sure that they benefited Emily was another one altogether—an endeavor that has turned Ms. Hanaoka into an enthusiastic and tireless advocate for her daughter, hardly an easy task given her own workload as a full-time graduate student, her status as a single parent, and cultural dissonance between some of the mores of Japan and those of Kansas.

Having been placed initially in one school and its special education program where there were students with various disabilities, Emily is now in a program in a different school designed especially for elementary-age students with autism. Ms. Hanaoka had not been wholly satisfied with Emily's first placement, nor is she entirely satisfied with Emily's present program.

Yes, she has some concerns about the program's exclusivity and restriction to students with autism, but she admits being pleased with the progress Emily has made. She also is delighted with the teachers' enthusiasm and professionalism. She has found her own interactions with school personnel to be fruitful, although she characterizes the processes and terms of the Individuals with Disabilities Education Act as confusing and says she must constantly advocate for clear and effective communication from Libby's teachers. Happily, Libby's teachers' abilities and attitudes contrast sharply with the preparation and effectiveness of many teachers in Japan, where there is a severe shortage of specially trained teachers of students with special needs.

Ms. Hanaoka hopes Japanese law will be amended to ensure that services are as appropriate and individualized as those she experienced in the United States. In the meantime, she is trying to learn as much as possible about the types of services available in the United States to persons with disabilities and their families, intending to provide information to her Japanese friends back home who have children with disabilities.

These two families—the Bridges and the Hanaokas—offer us two windows through which we can gain a clearer understanding of family life. You will continue to learn about these families as we address two major trends that have significantly affected the nature of family–professional partnerships. The first is the Individuals with Disability Education Act, which governs how educators interact with families. The second is the family systems perspective, which provides a framework through which professionals can understand families' preferences, strengths, and needs.

Individuals with Disabilities Education Act: Parental Rights and Responsibilities

The immediate purpose of the Individuals with Disabilities Education Act (IDEA) has always been to provide a free, appropriate public education to all students with disabilities. To accomplish that outcome, IDEA has always recognized that families play an important role in the child's education. Accordingly, IDEA provides a basis on which families and professionals may enter into partnerships with each other.

When Congress reauthorized IDEA in 1997 (P.L. 105-17), it strengthened parents' roles in their children's education and sought to ensure that families will have more meaningful opportunities to participate in their children's education at school and at home. How does IDEA express this intent?

First, IDEA enhances parents' and families' roles by providing the framework of opportunities within which parents, families, and students on the one hand and educators on the other can participate in shared decision making. Second, IDEA increases procedural safeguards that parents, families, and students may invoke to ensure that they have those opportunities. To clarify how IDEA carries out congressional intent, it is helpful to examine IDEA's six principles (H. R. Turnbull & Turnbull, 2000). For the sake of brevity, we use the word "parent" to refer to parents and other family members IDEA covers, unless we indicate otherwise. We also use the acronym "LEA" to refer to local educational agencies and "SEA" to refer to state educational agencies.

IDEA's Six Principles

Figure 2-1 highlights the educational process for implementing IDEA's six principles—zero reject, nondiscriminatory evaluation, appropriate education,

FIGURE 2–1
Process for Implementing IDEA's Six Principles in Educational Decision Making

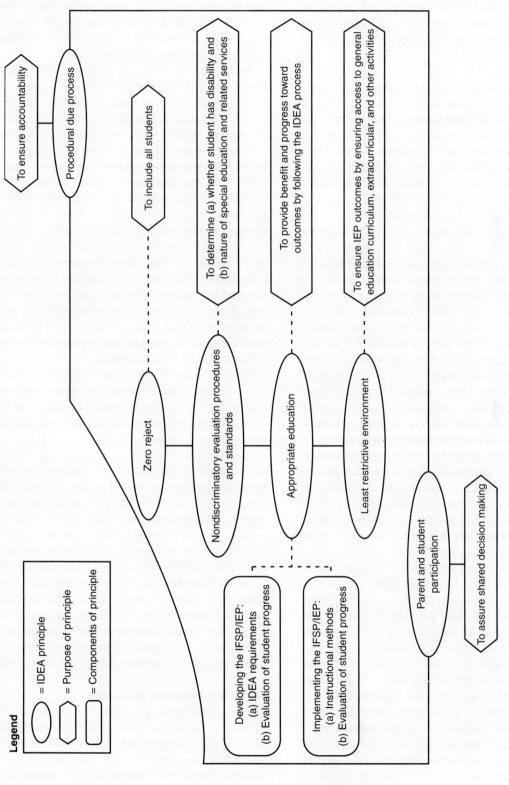

Legend

⬭ = IDEA principle

⬡ = Purpose of principle

▢ = Components of principle

To ensure accountability

Procedural due process

To include all students

Zero reject

Nondiscriminatory evaluation procedures and standards

To determine (a) whether student has disability and (b) nature of special education and related services

To provide benefit and progress toward outcomes by following the IDEA process

Appropriate education

Developing the IFSP/IEP:
(a) IDEA requirements
(b) Evaluation of student progress

Implementing the IFSP/IEP:
(a) Instructional methods
(b) Evaluation of student progress

To ensure IEP outcomes by ensuring access to general education curriculum, extracurricular, and other activities

Least restrictive environment

Parent and student participation

To assure shared decision making

least restrictive environment, parent and student participation in shared decision making, and procedural due process. In this section, we will briefly highlight key requirements associated with each of these principles.

Zero Reject

IDEA's first principle is that of zero reject. This is a rule against the exclusion from school of any age-eligible student who has a disability. The type or severity of the student's disability is irrelevant; zero reject means precisely what it says: all students will be included in a free, appropriate public education. All means all. "All" includes Libby and Emily; their many different disabilities do not result in exclusion but instead make it all the more important for them to be educated.

IDEA connects the zero-reject principle to parental rights and responsibilities in myriad ways. Under IDEA's early intervention provisions, families and their infant or toddler children may receive a large number of services (set out in an individualized family support plan [IFSP]) designed to develop the children's capacities, minimize their potential for developmental delays, and enhance families' capacities to work with their children. If families consent to early intervention, they can benefit from and influence the nature and extent of early intervention services they are offered. Libby benefited from early intervention services, including physical therapy and speech therapy at infant-development centers. Emily, of course, did not; those services were unavailable in Japan.

In light of IDEA's cardinal rule that public education should be "free" to parents, IDEA provides that parents such as the Bridges not be required to use private insurance benefits to pay for their children's education, but families may offer to pay for services or to ask an insurer to pay for services that an LEA must otherwise provide without cost (such as physical or occupational therapy). If a family's insurance policy obligates the insurer to pay, the insurer must. Only rarely, however, do parents ask their insurance carrier to pay for something that the schools must provide; they try to preserve their insurance for risks that are not covered by IDEA and to stay inside the "cap" that insurance contracts place (a cap is the maximum amount of funds that the carrier must pay for the insured). Although Ms. Hanaoka was brought up in her Japanese culture to not question authority, it was now important to her and Emily that she questioned the professionals about why music therapy was not provided and advocated for it to be a related service for Emily. She may succeed if she can demonstrate that music therapy is "neces-

sary" for Emily to benefit from such components of special education in the same way as speech-language interventions. IDEA provides that a student is entitled to a related service only if the service is necessary to yield a benefit from special education.

Finally, ever since the U.S. Supreme Court decided in *Honig v. Doe* (1988) that IDEA limits the power of LEAs to discipline students with disabilities, the issue of school discipline has been a controversial topic. Concerns about "school safety" and "law and order" brought the matter of school violence and discipline to a head when IDEA's reauthorization was before Congress in 1995–1997. The ultimate resolution of the conflict between those who wanted "no cessation" of IDEA rights and those who wanted safer schools (some people thought schools would be safer if students with disabilities could be expelled or suspended) resulted in a rule of "no cessation" of services. Whenever a student with a disability is disciplined (under IDEA, discipline is a sanction for violating a school code and consists of in-school or out-of-school suspension or change of placement for more than 10 days in any school year), the LEA must continue to provide free, appropriate public education to the student, regardless of whether the behavior for which the discipline is imposed is a "manifestation" of the student's disability. Thus, parents may assume (as a general rule) that once their children are classified into special education, they will continue to receive special education benefits.

An example of this situation involves Eddie, who has a long-standing pattern of challenging behavior, especially aggression toward others, property destruction, and self-injury. In the past, students like Eddie were frequently suspended from school or allowed to come to school for only a small portion of the school day. When they engaged in challenging behavior, the common response was to call their parents to pick them up from school. Given the new zero-reject requirements, parents have stronger rights for their children to remain in special education and to benefit from a functional assessment and implementation of a comprehensive positive behavioral support plan (Carr et al., 2002; Lucyshyn, Dunlap, & Albin, 2002).

Nondiscriminatory Evaluation

IDEA's second principle is one of nondiscriminatory evaluation, namely, an evaluation that is not biased as a result of the student's language, culture, or other characteristics. The evaluation has two purposes: (a) to determine whether the student has a disability and (b) if so, to specify what kind of special education and related services the student should receive.

IDEA grants parents rather expansive rights to have their perspectives taken into account when professionals evaluate their children. Under IDEA, parents (a) are members of the evaluation team (indeed, the evaluation team also is the team that develops the student's individualized program), (b) must be given a copy of the evaluation report and documentation concerning their child's eligibility (or lack of eligibility) for special education, (c) may submit to the team and require it to consider evaluations and information that they (the parents) initiate or provide, (d) have a right to be notified that the team has determined that it does not need any additional data for the purposes of deciding whether their child remains eligible for special education (i.e., still has a disability), and (e) have a right to request an assessment to determine whether their child continues to be eligible for special education (i.e., the team does not have to conduct the assessment unless the parents request one).

Because parents are presumed to act in the best interests of their children, they also may give or withhold consent to the initial evaluation, all reevaluations, and any exit evaluation. If they do give their consent, it is good for that evaluation only and not for any other evaluations or for the student's placement into or out of special education.

If the school has taken reasonable measures to secure the parents' consent (e.g., certified mail, registered mail, telephone, or fax or home visits) and if the parents have failed to respond to the school's request for consent, the school may evaluate the student (initial evaluation or reevaluation). If the parents refuse to give consent, the LEA may go to mediation or a due process hearing to try to get permission to evaluate the student. (We discuss mediation and due process hearings later in this chapter.)

Parents may also secure (at their own expense) an independent evaluation and require the school's evaluation team to consider it. Parents also may charge the cost of an independent evaluation to the LEA if the LEA's evaluation is not appropriate or if the reevaluation was ordered by a due process hearing officer or court. This means that team evaluations may not be completely influenced only by LEA members. Thus, the Bridges and Ms. Hanaoka may secure an independent evaluation of their children and require professionals on the evaluation team to take it into account during their evaluation. An independent evaluation of Emily's

cognitive and other needs may be warranted if the school-based evaluation team fails to assess her needs and strengths in her native language, as is required.

Appropriate Education

IDEA's third principle is one of appropriate education, namely, one that complies substantially with all IDEA processes and that benefits the student (*Board v. Rowley*, 1982). The linchpin for an appropriate education is the student's IFSP (for infants and toddlers, birth through age 2) or Individualized Educational Plan (IEP) (for students ages 3 through 21). Figure 2–2 highlights the IEP content requirements and shows that the IEP must provide related services for students. In addition to services for the student, IDEA also provides that parents may benefit from related services for their child. Among these services are (a) family training, counseling, and home visits; (b) parent counseling and training; (c) psychological services; (d) coordination of services for infants and toddlers and their families; (e) social work services; (f) speech-language pathology services; and (g) assistive technology and services. It is clear that the more the parents can take advantage of related services by getting them written into the IEP, the more parents, students, and educators are likely to benefit.

IDEA's IFSP and IEP requirements enable families and professionals to work together as partners in planning and implementing the student's appropriate education. In developing an IEP, the team must consider both the parents' concerns and the student's strengths. This requirement rebalances the "power" within the IEP team by requiring the team to address parental concerns.

An LEA must take certain steps to ensure that one or both of the student's parents are members of any group (including the IEP team) that makes decisions on the child's educational placement. These steps include advance notice of the meeting, mutually convenient scheduling of the meeting, and arranging for interpreters for parents who are deaf or non-English speaking, which is not the case with Ms. Hanaoka, whose English is quite good. If the parent(s) cannot attend the meeting, they may participate through individual or conference telephone calls.

The LEA may have an IEP meeting without parent participation only when it can document that it attempted unsuccessfully to have a student's parents participate. The documentation should include detailed records of telephone calls, copies of letters to and from the parents, and the results of any visits to the parents' homes or places of work.

FIGURE 2–2

Required Contents of Individualized Educational Plan (IEP)

The IEP is a Written Statement for each student, ages 3 to 21. Whenever it is developed or revised, it must contain the following:
- The Student's present levels of educational performance, including
  - How the disability of a student (age 6 through 21) affects his or her involvement and progress in the general curriculum, or
  - How the disability of a preschooler (age 3 through 5) affects his or her participation in appropriate activities
- Measurable annual goals, including "benchmarks" or short-term objectives, related to
  - Meeting needs resulting from the disability to enable the student to be involved in and progress in the general curriculum
  - Meeting each of the student's other disability-related needs
- The special education and related services and supplementary aids and services that will be provided to the student or on the student's behalf, and the program modifications or supports for school personnel that will be provided so that the student
  - Can advance appropriately toward attaining the annual goals
  - Be involved and progress in the general curriculum and participate in extracurricular and other nonacademic activities
  - Be educated and participate with other students with disabilities and with students who do not have disabilities in general education
- The extent, if any, to which the student will not participate with students who do not have disabilities in general education classes and in extracurricular and other nonacademic activities of the general curriculum
- Any individual modifications in the administration of statewide or districtwide assessments of student achievement, so that the student can participate in those assessments; moreover, if the IEP determines that the student will not participate in a particular statewide or districtwide assessment or any part of an assessment, why that assessment is not appropriate for the student and how the student will be assessed
- The projected date for beginning the services and program modifications and the anticipated frequency, location, and duration of each
- Transition plans, including
  - Beginning at age 14, and each year thereafter, a statement of the student's needs that are related to transition services, including those that focus on the student's courses of study (e.g., the student's participation in advanced-placement courses or in a vocational education program)
  - Beginning at age 16 (or sooner, if the IEP team decides it is appropriate), a statement of needed transition services, including, when appropriate, a statement of the interagency responsibilities or any other needed linkages
  - Beginning at least 1 year before the student reaches the age of majority under state law (usually, at age 18), a statement that the student has been informed of those rights under IDEA that will transfer to the student from the parents when the student becomes of age
- How the student's progress toward annual goals will be measured and how the students parents will be informed, at least as often as parents of students who do not have disabilities are informed, of the student's progress toward annual goals and the extent to which the progress is sufficient to enable the student to achieve the goals by the end of the school year

---

Note: From *Exceptional Lives: Special Education in Today's Schools* (p. 64), (2nd ed,) by Ann P. Turnbull, H. Rutherford Turnbull, Marilyn Shank, and Dorothy Leal, copyright 1998. Reprinted by permission of Prentice-Hall, Inc., Upper Saddle River, NJ.

Parents are not exactly "voting" members of IFSP and IEP teams because IDEA does not provide how a team makes decisions (e.g., whether members vote or reach decisions through other means). Clearly, however, professional members of the team must take the parents' perspectives into account in all decision making and must give the parents a copy of the IFSP/IEP. Not surprisingly, the Bridges and Ms. Hanaoka have attended every IEP meeting related to their respective children. Not all parents are so diligent; some want to attend but cannot, others attend some but not all meetings, and some simply do not attend (for various reasons).

Parents may invite other family members or other individuals knowledgeable about their child to attend the IFSP and IEP team meetings. This provides parents with supportive allies and the entire team with additional information. For example, Mrs. Bridge's mother has attended in the past, as has Libby's 9-year-old sister, Hilary. Mrs. Bridge said that having other children at a meeting can "be very enlightening. Plus, I think it's helpful just to have their opinions, because I think they, a lot of times, come up with better ideas on how to solve a problem with Libby than the adults do." Similarly, Ms. Hanaoka has been accompanied by one of her music therapy professors and by several graduate-student members of the university's Asian Students' Association. The professor provides support on technical terms and some aspects of special education programming and placement, and the fellow students provide emotional support and interpreter services.

Each IEP must contain a statement of (a) how the student's progress toward the IEP annual goals will be measured and (b) how the child's parents will be informed regularly (at least as often as parents are informed of progress of their nondisabled children) of their child's progress toward the annual goals and the extent to which that progress is sufficient to enable the student to achieve the goals by the end of the year.

Nearly all infants and toddlers (birth through age 2, sometimes referred to as birth to 3) leave early intervention programs and enter early childhood education programs. That is why their IFSPs must describe the steps that will be taken to ensure a smooth transition and to involve the parents in transition planning. Moreover, infants and toddlers who do transition to early childhood programs may now "carry" their IFSPs with them; they do not have to get a new "I-plan" (at age 3, the IEP) because their IFSP is "portable" until they are 9 years old. (Portability exists only if the state chooses to have such a policy and the parents and the early childhood "receiving" program agree to the IFSP being carried forward.)

The portability provision is important to both the infant and the parents. The infant is assured that there will be no disruption in services and thus no loss of beneficial programming, and the parents continue to have an I-plan that includes services for them. Basically, the portability provisions recognize that the IFSP approach is solid and that benefits of early intervention should be sustained over time.

Beginning at age 14 and annually thereafter, the student's IEP must contain a statement of the student's transition service needs and focus on the student's course of study (such as participation in a vocational education program). At age 16, the IEP must contain a statement of transition services for the student (see chapter 15 for a discussion of transition). And when a student attains the age of majority (usually age 18), the student is entitled to exercise his or her IDEA rights independently of his or her parents.

Indeed, a year before becoming of age, a student is entitled to a notice concerning what rights will transfer to him or her on attaining the age of majority. This provision means that parents need to begin to consider, at least a year before the student's age of majority, how to ensure that the student knows about IDEA rights and is capable of exercising them. A curriculum in self-determination or self-advocacy (including

knowledge of rights, responsibilities, and decision-making processes) is especially important. Libby and Emily will benefit from curricula that focus goals and objectives on skills related to self-determination (Field & Hoffman, 2002; Mithaug, Agran, Martin, & Wehmeyer, 2003; Wehmeyer, Agran, Palmer, & Mithaug, 1999).

If an of-age student has been adjudicated by a court to be legally incompetent as an adult, the court-appointed guardian (who may be a parent) is entitled to exercise the student's rights. If, however, a student has not been adjudicated incompetent but is regarded (by whom, it is not clear, but probably by the evaluation or IEP team) to be incapable of providing informed consent regarding his or her educational program, the SEA may appoint the student's parents or another appropriate individual to represent the student's educational interests (the "education surrogate"). These provisions help parents avoid legal guardianships and require the evaluation or IEP team to make a different kind of judgment (about capacity to consent) than they have been making in the past and, in turn, to use different kinds of evaluations and to know the legal standards for competency and incompetency.

Since IDEA's initial implementation in the mid-1970s, research has consistently reported that parents have limited participation and influence in IEP conferences (H. R. Turnbull & Turnbull, 2000). There is little evidence in the professional literature that a genuine collaborative partnership among families and professionals has characterized many IEP conferences. Research on participation of families from culturally and linguistically diverse backgrounds especially highlights the "uneven table" (Kritek, 1994) at which many families are expected to negotiate (Harry, Kalyanpur, & Day, 1999; Kalyanpur & Harry, 1999). A Puerto Rican mother in one of Harry's studies commented,

It is only their opinions that matter. If I do not want the child in a special class or if I want her in a different school, they will still do what they want. Because that is what I try to do, and Vera [the social worker] talked with them, too, and tried to help me, but—no! Our opinions are not valued. Many parents do not want their child in a special class or in a school so far away, but they keep quiet. It is very hard to struggle with these Americans. In America, the schools are for Americans. (Harry, 1992, p. 486)

We believe that educators have an affirmative duty to ensure that all parents, especially ones such as

Ms. Hanaoka who are from culturally and linguistically diverse backgrounds, have opportunities for genuine and trusting partnerships with educators throughout the IFSP and IEP process (Harry, Allen, & McLaughlin, 1995).

Least Restrictive Environment

IDEA provides that students with disabilities, ages 3 through 21, are to be educated, to the maximum extent appropriate for each, with students who do not have disabilities; the student may be removed from the regular educational environment only when the nature or extent of the student's disability is so great that the student cannot be educated satisfactorily in regular classes even with the use of supplementary aids and services. These provisions create a rebuttable presumption in favor of placement in regular educational environments. They enable Libby and Emily to have access to education in that environment (20 U.S.C. sec. 1412[a][5]).

A "presumption" is a rule of law that drives individuals into a predetermined result. For example, there is a presumption of innocence when an individual is charged by the state with a crime. The presumption (of innocence) drives the judge or jury to favor the accused. The presumption, however, is rebuttable. It may be set aside if the facts so warrant it. Thus, the state may have sufficient evidence to convict the accused; the presumption of innocence is then rebutted by the facts.

Under IDEA, the presumption is that the student will be educated with students who do not have disabilities. That presumption, however, may be set aside when the student's needs are so great that, even with related services and with supplementary aids and services, the child cannot be educated satisfactorily in the regular education environment.

IDEA does not define "the regular education environment." Instead, it uses such terms as "general curriculum" and "regular class" (20 U.S.C. secs. 1414[b][2][A]; 1414[c][1][B][iii]; 1414[d][1][A][iii]; 1414[d][1][A][iv]; 1414[d][1][B][ii] and [iv]; 1414[d][4][ii][II]). The problem, then, is whether "LRE" has the same meaning as "general curriculum" or "regular class" or both. The courts have interpreted IDEA to mean that LRE includes the academic, extracurricular, and other school activities (20 U.S.C. sec. 1414[d][1][A][iii][II]; *Board of Education v. Holland*, 1994; *Daniel R.R. v. State Board of Education*, 1989). So for all interests and purposes, the LRE includes but is not limited to the general (academic) curriculum; it is not limited to that curriculum because IDEA allows students to be placed in more separate and segregated programs along a continuum of restrictiveness (20 U.S.C. sec. 1412 [a][5]). Libby and Emily benefit from the presumption. Each receives some academic instruction in the same rooms with peers who do not have disabilities, albeit through an adapted curriculum and with the benefit of a paraprofessional. Each participates in all other school activities, such as field trips, social occasions, recess, and lunchtime, often with the support of peers who volunteer to be in their respective circles of friends.

IDEA also provides that infants and toddlers in early intervention programs will receive services in "natural environments," namely, those in which peers without disabilities participate, to the extent appropriate for the child with a disability.

Four settings comply with the "natural environments" rule. These are the child's home, full- or part-time participation in preschool programs operated by public agencies (e.g., Head Start), segregated private schools (in which there are only children with disabilities) or integrated private schools (in which there are children with and without disabilities), and classes in general education elementary schools (with children who do not have disabilities).

These options are justified on the basis that the child's needs are valued more greatly than the child's placement; there is no federal mandate for early intervention programs, and thus compliance with the natural-environments rule is shaped by the laws, policies, and practices of state and local agencies; and the natural-environments rule is a rebuttable presumption similar to the LRE rule for children ages 3 through 21 and is interpreted and applied in the same manner as that rule (*P.J. v. State of Conn. Bd. of Ed.*, 1992).

The rebuttable nature of the natural-environments rule is made explicit by the language of the statute itself, providing that separate settings such as hospitals are permissible only when the child requires extensive medical treatment (20 U.S.C. sec. 1436[d][5]; Early Intervention Program for Infants and Toddlers with Disabilities, Part 3, Rule, 57 *Fed. Reg.* 18986, 19002 [1991]; 58 *Fed. Reg.* 40958, 40982, 40983, 40986, 40973 [1993]; 64 *Fed. Reg.* 18290 [1998]; 64 *Fed. Reg.* 12406, 12536 [1999]). Were these settings (such as hospitals) impermissible, the natural-environments rule would be an irrebuttable presumption, and no placement would be allowed except in an integrated setting (Stowe & Turnbull, 2001).

The placement decision may not be made until after the child has been given a nondiscriminatory evaluation; it is made on the basis of that evaluation and by the members of the child's IFSP team when they prepare the IEP or IFSP. They may not decide, without an evaluation and without conforming to the IFSP process, that the child will have a certain placement. Parents are members of that team and thus have a role in deciding how the LRE rule applies to their child.

Parent and Student Participation in Shared Decision Making

Parents may participate in general ways in making decisions about their child's education. They have the right to have access to their children's school records and to limit the distribution of those records to people who do not "need to know" what they contain. They also have the right of access to the school district's general records about special education, such as the records showing how many students receive special education services and the amount of money the district receives and spends for special education. Obviously, they do not have the right to see the other students' records. In addition, parents generally have the right to see the state's special education plan, to receive public notice of hearings on the plan, and to comment on the plan. They are entitled to serve on the state advisory council on special education, and they must constitute the majority of the council's membership. Finally, parents of infants and toddlers are entitled to serve on the state's interagency coordinating council on early intervention and must constitute a majority of the membership of the council.

Most of all, however, parents have a right to participate in the evaluation and IEP team meetings, and their children, whatever their age and however challenging their disabilities may be, also have a right to be members of the IEP team "whenever appropriate." When is it appropriate? Basically, whenever parents and educators decide it is. Student participation can be especially effective if a student has been instructed in a curriculum that emphasizes self-determination. Parents and teachers can encourage students to take on roles that are consistent with their preferences, strengths, and needs. For example, students can work with their parents and teachers in advance to prepare for an IEP meeting, learn how to share with others the work in which they take the most pride, describe their goals, and express preferences about their educational program. Because IEP meetings can intimidate even

adults, it is especially important to work with students in advance of the meeting to plan the way that they would most like to share information. One possibility might be to develop a portfolio of their work and of information about their goals that they could bring to the meeting and review with the adult participants. It is essential for other IEP team members to listen with respect to the student's contributions, ask questions, and incorporate their contributions as collaborative decisions are made. A student's mere presence at a meeting can cause educators and parents to be more strength oriented and give more consideration to students' perspectives. This is especially important to consider for students who have limited communication (such as Libby and Emily).

It may be that some parents from culturally and linguistically diverse backgrounds, as well as from European American backgrounds, might not agree that it is important for their child's voice to be heard. Cultural values strongly influence whom families consider to be appropriate decision makers and the extent of autonomy that might be extended to someone who is not yet an adult. That may be the case with Ms. Hanaoka when she first comes to Kansas, but it also may be that she will adopt the more American custom of having Emily participate and express her own desires about her education. We encourage educators to ask families about their thoughts on student input and to reach agreement on what is appropriate for a particular student's participation.

Procedural Due Process

Procedural due process is a technique for accountability and refers to IDEA's safeguards for assuming that the student receives free, appropriate public education. Parents have the right to be informed in writing about an LEA's proposed evaluation of their child for placement into special education, to receive information in their native language or other mode of communication, and to consent in writing or to withhold consent.

Parents have the right to receive written notice before an LEA proposes to change or refuses to change a student's identification, evaluation, or placement or to change the provisions of a free, appropriate public education to their child. They have the right to receive a written notice (similarly written or translated) of their due process rights on three occasions: at the initial referral of the student for evaluation, on each notification to them of an evaluation or IEP meeting, and on their filing of a complaint about the LEA's violation of their child's IDEA rights. These notices must be in the parents' native language or other mode of communication or must be translated orally to the parents if they are unable to read.

Parents are entitled to use mediation to resolve their disputes with an LEA or, if they do not want to use mediation, to have a due process hearing before an impartial person. The hearing is like a civil trial, with both the parents and the LEA having the right to be represented by lawyers and to produce evidence; the losing party may appeal to a state-level hearing officer and then to the courts, and if the parents prevail (win), they may recover the fees they paid to their lawyers.

Parents must give the LEA notice that they are planning to file a complaint against the LEA and set out in the notice the student's name, a description of the problem related to the student, and a proposed resolution of the problem. If they are represented by a lawyer, the lawyer must give this notice or face the possibility that his or her fees will be reduced (if he or she is entitled to recover the fees from the LEA).

In a national, random sample survey of parents of students with disabilities, 31% of the parents of students with severe disabilities reported that they had considered suing the school or had threatened to sue because of their disappointment in the quality of services provided (Johnson & Duffett, 2002). More than twice as many parents of students with severe disabilities indicated their consideration of suing than did parents of students with mild disabilities. These data should be of concern to every teacher of students with severe disabilities. If one third of the parents are dissatisfied to the point of considering suing, it is essential that we learn more from parents about their preferences concerning educational partnerships. As you complete this chapter, you will learn about the family systems approach, which is a way that you can begin to understand the individual strengths and needs of families as the basis for forming the most effective partnership possible. Certainly it is a far better investment of time and energy to focus on building effective partnerships as contrasted to spending time involved in a lawsuit.

Summary of Six Principles
Through each of its six principles, IDEA strengthens parents' rights. Five principles (zero reject, nondiscriminatory evaluation, appropriate education, least restrictive

environment, and parent and student participation in shared decision making) establish a framework within which parents acquire rights to affect their children's education; the due process principle establishes a mechanism for parents to hold the LEA accountable for complying with IDEA.

Supporting Families to Be Educational Advocates

Learning the broad IDEA principles and the specific requirements can be overwhelming for many families. That is why an extensive national resource network exists for parents—Parent Training and Information Centers (PTIs). Currently, there are 70 PTIs funded by the U.S. Department of Special Education, Office of Special Education and Rehabilitative Services. Each state has at least one PTI, and some states have two or more. Each PTI must have a private, nonprofit status. Typically, PTIs are directed by parents of children with disabilities, and under IDEA the majority of staff members must be parents. Teachers should refer families of students in their classrooms to their respective state PTIs.

PTIs vary in their specific activities, although they all share the same primary purpose of preparing parents to be effective advocates in educational decision making. They provide a broad range of workshops, conferences, other training opportunities, and even one-to-one assistance to families. Many PTIs have IDEA information in languages other than English and have staff who are from diverse cultural and linguistic groups.

In addition to PTIs, Community Parent Resource Centers (CPRCs) are useful resources to traditionally un/underserved families. Whereas PTIs typically have statewide mandates, CPRCs are located in communities characterized by cultural and linguistic diversity. CPRCs give special emphasis to parents with low incomes, parents of children who are English-language learners, parents who live in empowerment zones, and parents who have disabilities. CPRCs offer intensive, culturally relevant support to families. Both PTIs and CPRCs can be valuable resources to educators and to the families they serve. If there were one where Ms. Hanaoka lives, she most certainly would benefit from it; without one, however, she has secured support from one of her professors and from members of the university's Asian Students Association.

There is a national technical assistance program for the PTIs and CPRCs that is a part of the Minnesota

PTI—the PACER Center. This national network—Technical Assistance Alliance for Parent Centers—provides information and ongoing staff development, technology access, and a range of other informational resources for the national PTI and CPRC networks (http://www.fape.org). On the Website of the Technical Assistance Alliance for Parents (http://www.taalliance.org), you can find a resource list that contains the names, addresses, and contact information for all the PTIs and CPRCs. Parents should be encouraged to contact their state PTI as well as the Alliance to obtain training opportunities and printed information developed specifically for families.

In addition to the FAPE project, the National Association of State Directors of Education sponsors Web-based training on IDEA for educators and administrators (http://www.ideainfo.org). They provide extensive information that can enable you to continue to expand your knowledge of IDEA's requirements and the effective implementation of those requirements.

Many parents participate in educational partnerships to implement all six IDEA principles. Even with resources and training available, however, some parents may opt for a less active role. Parents of students with disabilities are a heterogeneous group with different preferences, strengths, and needs, just as are the parents of children not identified with disabilities.

Indeed, legislative assumptions regarding parents' participation were not based on research data (H. R. Turnbull & Turnbull, 1982); these assumptions were based more on ways that advocates, policymakers, and legislators think parents should participate. True, the assumption that many parents want to be involved has led some professionals to assume that all parents want to be involved. But parent participation in the decision making process may be detrimental to some parents and extremely helpful to others (A. P. Turnbull & Turnbull, in press). Similar to parents of children without disabilities, some parents of children with disabilities have many other critical day-to-day concerns that may prevent participation, other parents do not value or feel confident about schools, and still other parents believe that all educational decision making is the teacher's job. Research over the past 30 years highlights a consistent pattern that many parents participate passively in educational decision making (A. P. Turnbull & Turnbull, in press). The evidence reveals an interesting perspective about families and educators:

The term "parent involvement" sums up the current perspective. It means we want parents involved with us. It means the service delivery system we helped create is at the center of the universe, and families are revolving around it. It brings to mind an analogy about the old Ptolemaic view of the universe with the Earth at the center. . . .

Copernicus came along and made a startling reversal—he put the sun in the center of the universe rather than the Earth. His declaration caused profound shock. The Earth was not the epitome of creation; it was a planet like all other planets. The successful challenge to the entire system of ancient authority required a complete change in philosophical conception of the universe. This is rightly termed the "Copernican revolution."

Let's pause to consider what would happen if we would have a Copernican revolution in the field of disability. Visualize the concept: The family is the center of the universe and the service delivery system is one of the many planets revolving around it. Now visualize the service delivery system at the center and the family in orbit around it. Do you see the difference? Do you recognize the revolutionary change in perspective? We would move from an emphasis on parent involvement (i.e., parents participating in the program) to family support (i.e., programs providing a range of support services to families). This is not a semantic exercise—such a revolution leads us to a new set of assumptions and a new vista of options for service. (A. P. Turnbull & Summers, 1987, pp. 295-296)

The revolution in parent involvement has led researchers and practitioners to recognize families' preferences, strengths, and needs. The next section reviews the progress that has been made in working within this family systems perspective.

A Family Systems Perspective

A system is defined as a "set(s) of elements standing in inter-relation among themselves and with the environment" (Bertalanffy, 1975, p. 159). Systems theory assumes that a system can be understood only as a whole. A familiar saying is that "the whole is greater than the sum of the parts." Professionals can enhance their understanding of the Bridge and Hanaoka families by understanding and applying a family systems perspective.

Systems theory has been applied to family sociology and family therapy in terms of how families interact as a whole system. Before the family systems approach within the field of special education, educators were concerned primarily about how much progress the child with a severe disability was making in acquiring developmental skills. Sometimes their intense concern for development resulted in parents being highly involved in carrying out instructional programs at home (A. P. Turnbull, Pereira, & Blue-Banning, 1999; A. P. Turnbull, Turbiville, & Turnbull, 2000). An unintentional consequence of this emphasis sometimes was that the mother spent her time with the child who had the disability at the expense of her other children, her spouse, and herself. Another unintentional consequence was to shift the role of parents from being nurturers to teachers and to shift their home from having family activities to having school activities. A mother of a child with Down syndrome who is highly involved in being a teacher of her son now reflects back on the early intervention years and provides this perspective:

> *I readily became James' teacher. His playtime at home became "learning time"—actually all his time was learning time. Any free time we had was to be spent on his therapy or to be spent feeling guilty that we weren't doing his therapy. (A. P. Turnbull et al., 1999, p. 165)*

This mother went on to describe how this emphasis on her son's development caused her to believe that the key to his acceptance in life would be achievement.

The family systems view is interested in the well-being of all family members across all domains of family quality of life. It does not single out education or developmental milestones as the priority for children and youth who have disabilities. Furthermore, it recognizes the support needs of parents, siblings (such as Libby's two sisters), and other family members (such as Libby's grandparents).

The application of family systems theory to special education requires fundamental changes in answer to the following question: Who is the consumer of services delivered by special education professionals and other related professionals? In the past, the student has been viewed as the sole consumer. The family systems approach identifies the whole family as the consumer of services. It also seeks to have a much broader view than education or skill development only. Figure 2–3 depicts the family systems framework we will discuss

FIGURE 2–3
Family Systems Framework

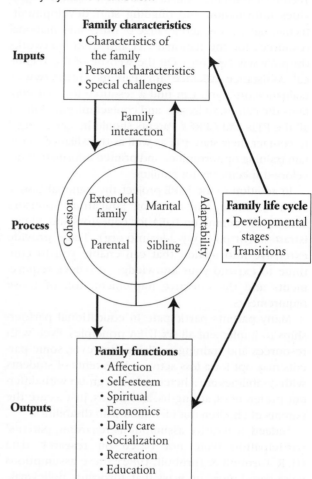

Source: Turnbull, A. P., Summers, J. A., & Brotherson, M. J. (1984). *Working with families with disabled members: A family systems approach* (p. 60). Lawrence: University of Kansas, Kansas Affiliated Facility. Adapted by permission.

in the remainder of this chapter. The components of the framework and their interrelationships within the family system follow:

1. *Family characteristics* describe the whole family as a unit (e.g., size and form, cultural background, socioeconomic status, geographic location), the family's personal characteristics (e.g., health, coping styles), and the family's special challenges (e.g., poverty, abuse). These characteristics are the underlying input to the system that shapes the way in which the family interacts.

2. *Family interaction* is the hub of the system, the process of interaction among individual family members and subsystems. Subsystem interactions are influenced by, and in turn influence, what family members do to respond to individual and collective family needs.

3. *Family functions* are the output of the interactional system. Based on its characteristics (input), the family interacts (a process) to produce responses that fulfill family affection, self-esteem, economic, daily care, socialization, recreation, and education needs.

4. *Family life cycle* introduces the element of change into the family system. As the family moves through time, developmental and nondevelopmental changes alter the family's characteristics and needs; these, in turn, produce change in the way the family interacts.

The family systems model enables educators to recognize each family's complexity and uniqueness. Each family is composed of so many attributes that it can interact in an almost endless variety of ways. A family is not a static entity; it is constantly changing and also resists change. The unique characteristics of each family must be considered. To have only one way of interacting with families, one type of policy or program, or one idea of how families "should" be would be a disservice to every family encountered. What may be suitable for the Bridges would not be for the Hanaoka family. For example, Mrs. Bridge may want Libby to live at home with her and her husband throughout her adult life, whereas Mrs. Hanaoka may have the vision that Emily will live in her own apartment supported by a caregiver who is also her roommate.

Each of these four components—characteristics, interaction, functions, and life cycle— provides a different perspective from which families view their family member's exceptionality, the services that are offered, the professionals they encounter, and their everyday life experiences. The following sections briefly discuss each of the four components outlined in Figure 2–3 and highlight issues relevant to special educators. For a more comprehensive description of these elements, see A. P. Turnbull and Turnbull (in press).

Family Characteristics

When you think of the range of families within your community alone, you will recognize that family characteristics are infinitely diverse. This diversity greatly influences the impact of a child with a severe disability on the family and family responses to meeting the child's needs. Three considerations in understanding family characteristics are (a) characteristics of the family as a whole, (b) personal characteristics of each family member, and (c) characteristics of special challenges.

Characteristics of the Family

Families vary in areas such as size, form (e.g., dual vs. single parents, original vs. reconstituted family), culture, socioeconomic status, and geographic location. Obviously, although the Bridge and Hanaoka families have much in common, they also differ from each other in many ways. For example, there are many more Bridge family members than Hanaoka family members. In this section, we focus on culture as illustrative of variations in family characteristics.

Culture provides the "lens" within which individuals and families form a sense of group identity (Gollnick & Chinn, 2002). It involves many considerations, including race, ethnicity, geographical location, religion, income status, sexual orientation, gender, disability status, and occupation. People often equate culture with race or ethnicity, but culture is a broader concept than that. For example, the Bridge family is European American and are part of the majority culture of their community. By contrast, Ms. Hanaoka is of a different race and has a different cultural heritage: hers is Asian, specifically, Japanese. These differences can be substantial, but they are by no means bound to be so, especially because Ms. Hanaoka is herself a professional and now is being inculcated with American (Western) influences. Aside from the inculcation, Ms. Hanaoka describes a difference of opinion she had with Emily's teacher concerning the IEP goal that the teacher recommended for teaching Emily proper table place setting, including placement of knives. Ms. Hanaoka explained that in her culture knives were rarely used at the table. Chopsticks might be used, and food is prepared in a way so that cutting is not necessary. She felt that this goal, therefore, would be a waste of time for Emily and would not be a functional skill.

Culture influences marriage ceremonies, religious beliefs and practices, rites of passage (e.g., bar or bat mitzvah), holiday celebrations, holy day observations, rituals surrounding deaths and burials, a person's perception of his or her relationship to the world, political beliefs, attitudes toward independence and work, and, in general, parenting practices (e.g., the extent to which it is appropriate for children and youth to be self-determining). For example, self-determination is a value that suggests people should be the primary causal agents in their life decisions and that acting autonomously is not only appropriate but also preferred (Wehmeyer, 2001). A study of cultural diversity reveals that some families emphasize values such as family unity and permanence, interdependence, and protectiveness much more than self-determination (A. P. Turnbull & Turnbull, 1996). Quotes from Latin American parents suggest those values:

- "It is against the family for the children to live alone as adults."
- "The family is a service vocation on behalf of the member with the disability."
- "Family interdependence is the soundest possible way of support for each member."
- "Children are always children. They do not go their own way, as a rule." (A. P. Turnbull & Turnbull, 1996, pp. 200-201)

This should not be interpreted to mean that all Latin American parents hold these values; on the contrary, there is tremendous variability within cultures as well as among cultures. Consider the child of parents who hold the previous values regarding self-determination and the implications of these values for what is appropriate to teach in a self-determination curriculum and for the development of transition programs when students move from high school to adulthood. From a European American perspective, it can be easy to assume that appropriate goals are employment, independent living, and community contribution (Hanson, 1992). The Bridges, for example, see work in Libby's future but not living on her own in her own apartment or home.

While you need to be aware of cultural differences, you also need to be careful not to stereotype families based on this awareness. To say that all people of color, in comparison to the dominant European American culture in the United States, value family unity and permanence, interdependence, and protectiveness is contrary to the real-life experiences of many individuals in these groups. You should always strive to enhance cultural self-awareness and cultural competence so that you can, in turn, create partnerships with families that are respectful of their cultural values (Gollnick & Chinn, 2002; Kalyanpur & Harry, 1999; Lynch & Hanson, 2004) as well as respectful of their individual family characteristics.

Personal Characteristics

Personal characteristics include the aspects of a member's disability, each family member's mental and physical health status, and individual life management skills. The characteristics of a child's disability contribute to shaping the impact of the child's needs and strengths on the family system and the ability of the family system to be responsive. In contrast to Emily, Libby has multiple disabilities (a combination of cerebral palsy, mental retardation, epilepsy, and visual impairment), but that does not mean that their families' needs, related to disability, differ. Both need knowledge about the nature and extent of disability and the likely trajectory of their child's development and future (assuming FAPE is available to them).

The characteristics of a child's disability include many factors, such as the nature of the disability, the extent or degree of the disability, the time of onset, and future prognosis. A child with medically complex needs often requires families to make adaptations in daily routines in providing ongoing assistance, purchase special equipment, and interact frequently with medical personnel (Jones, Clatterbuck, Marquis, Turnbull, & Moberly 1996). Children with problem behavior can place inordinate demands on family members and create stress in activities both within and outside the home (Lucyshyn et al., 2002; A. P. Turnbull & Ruef, 1997). A child with later onset of disability (disability caused from an accident during school years) can cause major family readjustments in dealing with the immediacy of the crisis and in recurring long-term rehabilitation (Michaud, Semel-Concepion, Duhaine, & Lazer, 2002).

Regardless of the particular nature of the disability, children and youth also provide a broad array of positive contributions to their families, including happiness and fulfillment, strength, personal growth, an expanded social network, career or job growth, and pride in accomplishments (Scorgie & Sobsey, 2000; Summers, Behr, & Turnbull, 1989). Thus, for professionals to understand the impact of the child with a severe disability, they will need to understand both the child's demands on and the child's contributions to the family. Some people assume that a severe disability always produces greater stress on the family than a mild disability. As one parent of a young adolescent commented,

Don has been labeled profoundly retarded. He is not able to do anything to take care of himself, cannot walk, and has no language. But I remind myself that

I never have to chase him around the house, he never talks back or sasses, he doesn't have to enter the rat race of teenage years like my other sons, and he does not try to hurt himself.

According to Mr. and Mrs. Bridge, Libby has contributed to the family by "teaching her sisters how to be helpful and compassionate." Mr. Bridge particularly likes Libby's smile, her eyes, and her laughter; Mrs. Bridge enjoys the times that Libby shows affection and the connection between them is obvious. Thus, while the family experiences challenges related to caring for Libby, they also experience joy from their relationships with her. And just as Libby has affected her family positively, so too does Emily's love of music reinforce her mother's career. More than that, Emily provides companionship to her mother; that is especially important given that Ms. Hanaoka is a single parent. Professionals should be encouraged to understand the impact of disability within the context of each family's situation and in light of their values and perceptions.

Special Challenges

The final aspect of family characteristics relates to the special challenges that families face. Families face many challenges over and above a child's exceptionality, from less extreme ones (such as moving to a new community, changing jobs, or having a new baby) to more extreme challenges (such as death of a family member, which happened in the Hanaoka family). Additional extreme challenges include substance abuse, exposure to violence, having a family member who is incarcerated, having teenage parents, having parents with mental retardation, and living in poverty.

Poverty challenges many families, especially those whose children have disabilities. Approximately twice as many youth with disabilities live in households with an annual income less than $25,000, as contrasted to approximately one third of youth without disabilities (U.S. Department of Education, 2002). Furthermore, youth without disabilities are about five times more likely to live in a family with a household income of more than $50,000 as contrasted to youth with disabilities. An analysis of national data related to family incomes has shown that (a) the number of American children living in poverty has increased significantly over the past decade, (b) these children are most likely to live in single-parent households, and (c) both poverty and living in a single-parent household are more likely to occur for children with a disability as contrasted to children without a disability (Fujiura & Yamaki, 2000).

The National Research Council (NRC) investigated issues associated with the disproportionate number of students from diverse racial and ethnic backgrounds who receive special education services. A particular concern was the disproportionate number of African American students identified as having mental retardation or emotional disturbances. The NRC (2002) concluded that a major issue in disproportionate identification is the greater likelihood of students from diverse backgrounds experiencing poverty. For example, African Americans have been found to be two and a half times more likely than European Americans to experience poverty (Fujiura & Yamaki, 2000). Because of the high association of poverty with other risk factors including dangerous toxins, lower birth weight, poor health care, and poor nutrition, it is clear that poverty creates many special challenges for students and families.

Poverty can also have an impact on a family's sense of shaping its own destiny. In Kozol's (1995) disturbing and compelling analysis of a South Bronx neighborhood, he states,

So long as there are ghetto neighborhoods and ghetto hospitals and ghetto schools, I am convinced there will be ghetto desperation, ghetto violence, and ghetto fear, because the ghetto is itself an evil and unnatural construction.....Perhaps this is one reason why so much of the debate about the "breakdown of the family" has a note of the unreal or incomplete. "Of course the family structure breaks down at a place like the South Bronx!" says a white minister who works in one of New York City's poorest neighborhoods. "Everything breaks down in a place like this. The pipes break down. The phone breaks down. The electricity and heat breaks down. The spirit breaks down. The body breaks down. The immune agents of the heart break down. Why wouldn't a family break down also?" (p. 162)

Educational Implications of Understanding Family Characteristics

Families vary widely in their characteristics. These characteristics, in turn, shape the way that families interact, carry out their functions, and change or stay the same over the life cycle. Rather than adhering to an idealized image of what a family "should be," the most successful way to form partnerships with families is to recognize and respect their diversity across these three elements—characteristics of the family as a whole, personal characteristics of individual members, and special challenges. By understanding elements within each component, you can identify a family's preferences for partnerships, for ongoing communication with you, and for planning their child's services and supports.

Family Interaction

Family–professional partnerships typically are mother–professional relationships. But do not assume, as many do, that mother and family are synonymous. The members of some families are related by blood or marriage, whereas others are related by preference (a close family friend who is regarded as a family member). The family is a unit of interaction. Each family member is affected by the disability of the child, and the child is affected by each family member. The goal of educators should be to form a partnership with multiple family members who have an interest in supporting the child's education, including mothers, fathers, siblings, and extended family members.

You should keep in mind that any interaction with the child or other member ripples throughout the whole family. A home visit can be a totally positive experience, or it can create family stress because of a perception of having one's privacy violated or because of the need to alter the schedule of activities or responsibilities (Klass, 1996). Scheduling a parent conference to discuss the child's progress can create an argument between two working parents about which one will take time off from employment. Working on a child's social skills can enhance a sibling relationship that was threatened by embarrassment over inappropriate public behavior. Requesting parents to follow through on instructional programs at home can strengthen their relationship with their child but may also create major tensions. Just how much time do Mr. and Mrs. Bridge have for being "follow-through" educators for Libby, given that they also are raising her two sisters? How much time does Ms. Hanaoka have for raising Emily, given that Ms. Hanaoka is newly arrived in the United States and enrolled in a demanding doctoral program? What support does either family have for that role, assuming the family wants to perform it? The tensions between parent and child can then spill over into a marriage, sibling interactions, and interactions with

extended family, neighbors, bosses, and coworkers. Interaction with any member of the system has implications for all members.

From the perspective of family interaction, two major concepts are critical: (a) family subsystems and (b) ways that families establish balance through their cohesion and adaptability.

Family Subsystems
The family systems framework highlights four major subsystems within traditional nuclear families:

1. Marital subsystem—marital partner interactions
2. Parental subsystem—parent and child interactions
3. Sibling subsystem—child and child interactions
4. Extended family subsystem—whole family or individual member interactions with relatives, friends, neighbors, and professionals

Variations in subsystems exist in many families, such as single parents, stepparents, families with one child (Ms. Hanaoka) or many children (the Bridges), families with extensive extrafamilial subsystems (such as the Bridges), and families that consist of people who are not related by blood or marriage to each other but perform the same roles as people who are related by blood and marriage. We will highlight information on marital and sibling subsystems.

Marital Subsystem
There is a common assumption that children with disabilities—particularly severe disabilities—place their parents at greater risk for serious marital problems. Some research suggests there is a higher incidence of marital disharmony and divorce in families who have a child with a disability (Hodapp & Krasner, 1995; Murphy, 1982); however, other studies have reported no differences between couples with and without children with disabilities in relation to marital satisfaction (Benson & Gross, 1989; Kazak & Marvin, 1984). Some studies have found that children with disabilities do not affect the marriage in either a positive or a negative way (Abbott & Meredith, 1986; Young & Roopnarine, 1994). This research, however, has not specifically addressed the severity of the disability as a factor. Effect on the marriage, like so many other aspects of the family system, is an individual consideration in light of multiple other characteristics operating simultaneously within the family.

A highly consistent research finding is that families who have higher levels of marital satisfaction also adjust better to their child with a disability (Scorgie, Wilgosh, & McDonald, 1998; Simmerman, Blacher, & Baker, 2001; Willoughby & Glidden, 1995). A strong marriage makes a big difference in overall family quality of life. It is important, however, to remember that many single parents also experience strong family well-being (A. P. Turnbull & Turnbull, 2001); Ms. Hanaoka is one of those families—a confident albeit challenged "new American" whose culture, determination, and informal supports sustain her.

Professionals can support families' marital well-being by listening and responding to parents' preferences for the support that they themselves need in caring for their son or daughter. For example, Mr. and Mrs. Bridge make decisions about Libby's education together. The educators working with Libby support this process by scheduling meetings at times when both parents can attend. Variations in the marital subsystem exist in many families.

> Ms. Hanaoka recalls that her husband tried to hide Emily's disability from his family and to deny that the possibility even existed. When it was no longer possible to deny or hide his daughter's disability, he avoided sharing the responsibility for daily care of Emily and often complained about the effects of her behavior on their family life. It was only after his death that Ms. Hanaoka was able to openly and easily solicit assistance and support from sources outside the family.

Parents of children with severe disabilities, similar to those of children without disabilities, may be in same-sex marriages. Same-sex marriages may occur in families in which parents have been in heterosexual relationships, had children, and then have taken those children into same-sex partnerships, legal unions, and/or marriages. Some children in same-sex marriage are adopted or are born through in vitro fertilization (Lamme & Lamme, 2002). Although we have not been able to find research that specifically addresses children and youth with severe disabilities in these relationships, reviews of literature of the well-being of children who grow up with same-sex parents consistently show that children develop positively in terms of psychological, intellectual, behavioral, and emotional development (Fitzgerald, 1999; Tasker, 1999). There are many steps that you can take to welcome children from these families into schools and to welcome their

parents as well. Some suggestions include (Lamme & Lamme, 2002) the following:

- Provide electronic and library resources on diverse families including same-sex parents.
- Promote a respectful school environment and ensure that harassment related to homophobic terms is not acceptable within the school culture.
- Just as you might sponsor African American, Hispanic, or women's history month, also consider celebrating Gay Pride Week.

Sibling Subsystem

Some studies about siblings have found that brothers and sisters of siblings with disabilities have higher incidence of emotional problems, lower self-esteem, and greater responsibilities for household chores (Fisman, Wolf, Ellison, & Freeman, 2000). Other studies have found the opposite is true (Cuskelly & Gunn, 2003; Hannah & Midlarsky, 1999). Values that Mrs. Bridge wanted to pass on to her children include acceptance of differences and compassion for others. She is happy that Hilary and Hayley are learning these values through interactions with Libby. Mrs. Bridge speaks of the unconditional acceptance that the girls show Libby, saying,

> It's just normal to them. This is who she is. I have always appreciated that in them. . . . They like to go in her room and watch movies—but they watch them with her, they don't ignore her. They all eat popcorn together. During the movie, they'll reach over and stroke her hair or tickle her or something. I think that's what I like the most.

For Emily and her mother, however, there is only the two of them: no father and no siblings. Their family routines are quite different from those of the Bridges.

A national resource for siblings is a program called "Sibshops," which has the goal of providing information and emotional support for brothers and sisters (Meyer & Vadasy, 1994). An evaluation of the Sibshops program with school-age siblings found that siblings became more aware of special needs and improved their relationship with their sisters or brothers (Dyson, 1998). If your community does not sponsor Sibshops, you might consider collaborating with families, educators, adults with disabilities, and other community citizens to start a Sibshop program. (A helpful Website is http://www.thearc.org/siblingsupport.)

An especially helpful way to become sensitive to sibling issues is to listen to sibling perspectives. Siblings can be invited to IEP conferences or to have discussions with teachers or related service providers outside the IEP conference. Another possibility for gaining information is to read the perspectives of siblings that are often provided in newsletters of family organizations and in a new book featuring perspectives of 45 siblings ranging in age from 4 to 18 (Meyer, 1997). For example, Jessica, 9 years old, has an older brother with autism. She comments,

> *In some ways my life is different from kids who have a normal brother, because most of my schedule revolves around Danny. Sometimes I can't go to special activities because my mother has no one to watch Danny and can't take me. I think parents, teachers, and doctors should have more understanding for siblings, because they go through difficult experiences with their brothers or sisters. (Meyer, 1997, p. 27)*

Establishing Balance: Cohesion and Adaptability

Family therapists have identified two dimensions in establishing balance in family relationships: cohesion and adaptability. Cohesion is the bridge between close emotional bonding and individual independence. Carnes (1981) uses an example of "the touching of hands" to describe cohesion:

> *The dilemma is how to be close yet separate. When the fingers are intertwined, it at first feels secure and warm. Yet when one partner (or family member) tries to move, it is difficult at best. The squeezing pressure may even be painful. . . . The paradox of every relationship is how to touch and yet not hold on. (pp. 70–71)*

We urge you to help families learn to touch and yet not hold on by encouraging them to have a balanced view rather than a singular focus on the child with the disability, helping them obtain respite care when needed, referring them to their community's resources, and helping the child build a social support network.

Again, cultural values come into play. As in the previous example about self-determination, some families stress interdependence and may not encourage individual independence as much as a teacher might think appropriate for his or her own family. While an educator may think it right to encourage independence of all

students with severe disabilities, that same educator will have to consider what "independence" means to each student's parents. There may be parents who reject the idea of supported employment and want their son or daughter to stay at home as an adult to ensure security and safety.

What might be your response to such a situation? Some alternatives you might consider in widening the scope of possibilities for a student is to truly listen to the parents' concerns. Consider how more safety and security might be added to supportive employment options. Connect the parents with other parents who have chosen a variety of options for their older sons or daughters with a disability. Finally, consider if there might be a business venture that the student could do with other family members, such as owning and stocking vending machines.

Adaptability is a family's ability to change and create new responses to emerging situations (Olson, Russell, & Sprenkle, 1980). Many families establish interaction patterns. For example, the mother may assume responsibility for bathing, dressing, feeding, and toileting a child with severe physical disabilities. This pattern may become so ingrained that the mother is unable to leave town for a vacation or a visit with extended family or even to have a break from these duties. If the mother is ill or an emergency arises, a family crisis related to parents' roles is likely to occur. One way to help families achieve successful interactions is to encourage them to develop an array of alternatives and options consistent with their cultural values. For families who believe that it is too much trouble to train others for caregiving, you might be able to persuade people who are willing to provide caregiving to come to your classroom for tips from you on how they might best provide support. This would prevent parents from having to provide this orientation for those who might be able to help them.

Educational Implications of Understanding Family Interaction

Supporting families requires developing educational programs that are as responsive to the family system as possible. IEP goals can foster successful family inclusion. For example, students can be taught leisure skills consistent with the recreation interests of the parents and siblings, or priority can be given to self-help, communication, and social skills that lead to increasing contact with grandparents (Seligman, Goodwin, Paschal, Applegate, & Lehman, 1997) and neighbors.

Professionals can provide information to extended family or friends and help them gain confidence in handling matters related to the child's seizures, feeding, positioning, and responding to unique language modes.

Families must meet the needs of all members, not just for the child or youth with a disability. Professionals may perceive a parent's absence from a conference or failure to follow through on home teaching as denying the child adequate attention. An alternative explanation is that the parent is attending to the needs of the marriage, other family members, or himself or herself. Successful families balance needs of all members rather than placing one member in a focal position and meeting that person's needs at the expense of others. (It is also critically important for individuals with disabilities to learn to respect needs and preferences of other family members and know that they sometimes take priority over their own.) A critical self-determination skill that you might teach students is recognizing that happy family relationships sometimes require that priority be given to preferences of other family members. Successful families find the level of cohesion and adaptability that works for them. As professionals assist families in planning for experiences with those outside the family system and for future transitions, respecting the families' definitions of cohesion and adaptability is especially important.

Family Functions

Families exist to serve individual and collective needs of their members. Attending to family functions is one way to characterize how families serve their needs. Family functions can be characterized in many ways. Figure 2-4 highlights these functions and some tasks performed by family members to meet them.

Family functions are not independent of each other. One function may facilitate another function, as when the socialization function of developing an individual friendship leads to an intimate personal relationship that meets a teenager's need for affection. On the other hand, one function may impede progress in another functional area. For example, economic hardship often affects a family's other daily care needs (e.g., nutrition, health care), in turn impinging on a parent's or child's self-esteem.

A son or daughter with a disability can affect a family in negative, neutral, and positive ways. In the next sections, we highlight effects on the economic and

FIGURE 2–4
Family Functions and Tasks

1. *Affection:* Developing intimate personal relationships, expressing sexuality, giving and receiving nurturance and love, and expressing emotions
2. *Self-esteem:* Establishing self-identity and self-image, identifying personal strengths and weaknesses, and enhancing belonging and acceptance
3. *Economic support:* Generating income and handling family finances, paying bills, earning allowances, and handling insurance matters
4. *Daily care:* Purchasing food, preparing meals, providing health care, maintaining the home, providing transportation, and taking general safety measures
5. *Socialization:* Fostering individual and collective friendships, developing social skills, and engaging in social activities
6. *Recreation:* Developing and participating in hobbies or clubs, setting aside everyday demands, and going on vacations
7. *Education:* Participating in school-related activities, continuing education for adults, doing homework, providing for career development, and developing a work ethic

socialization functions of families. For a thorough discussion of all family functions, see H. R. Turnbull and Turnbull (1997).

Economic Needs

All families must have income and a way to spend the money earned to meet food, clothing, shelter, and other needs. The presence of a son or daughter with a severe disability can create excess expense (Birenbaum & Cohen, 1993; Fujiura, Roccoforte, & Braddock, 1994). Some of the devices and services for a child with a severe disability may include adaptive feeding utensils; special clothing; lift-equipped vans; bathroom adaptations, such as support and safety bars; ongoing medications required for seizures and other physiologic needs; body braces; voice synthesizers; hearing aids; adaptive seating equipment; ongoing evaluations by specialists; specially adapted furniture; hospital beds; respirators; suctioning equipment; adaptive exercise equipment; remote control devices for televisions, radios, and lights; positioning equipment, such as prone standers; adaptive toys; and adaptive mobility devices, such as walkers and crutches. Many devices require ongoing servicing and periodic replacement. Even families fortunate enough to have the best health insurance coverage find that costs of buying and maintaining many adaptive devices and medical services are not fully covered. Mrs. Bridge comments,

When we got her first wheelchair we had to pay the majority of that one. I made the comment to one of our friends that we're spending the money that we could have saved over the years for a car ...probably in the end it all evens out. We probably will end up helping purchase cars for the other girls where she won't need one. Libby is receiving SSI and Medicaid that has been very helpful because that is the reason that I have been able to not work and to take her all the places that she needs to go and attend all the meetings that we need to go to ... I wouldn't have been able to put the time in if I had to work so I think because of that help, Libby has benefited.

The economic impact on families varies in light of the nature and extent of the child's disability and, of course, on the family's own resources (predictably, Ms. Hanaoka's resources are slight, her husband having died and she being a graduate student).

Costs associated with providing for the needs of one family member can limit the funds available for the other family members. Parents and other family members may forgo attending to their own needs to afford services for the child with a severe disability. Parents may know that a child could benefit from the purchase of some special piece of equipment and not be able to afford it.

The presence of a family member with a disability may prevent parents from obtaining employment because of the level of care and supervision required. One study found that 32% of the parents of children or adults with a developmental disability reported that they had given up a paying job to provide care, not taken a paying job, or refused a job transfer or a promotion to provide care to the family member with a disability (Agosta, Bass, & Spence, 1986).

This was the case for Mrs. Bridge. She found that she was unable to work outside of the home after Libby was born. She explained, "I have found it literally impossible to work. You can't say to [an employer] 'I'd like to work, but I need Tuesday afternoons and Thursday and every other Friday off,' so Libby and I

spent all the time going to doctors and therapy and I just have never gone back to work ...We still haven't found it possible for me to do that."

Many families, however, report that the child with a disability requires less money. Some less active children require less frequent clothing and footwear replacements. The child may not feel compelled to have expensive items associated with growing up, such as a complex stereo system, personal telephone, a car, undergraduate and graduate education, and extensive travel.

The largest source of support for families is currently Title XIX of the Social Security Act, Home and Community Based Services (HCBS) (Braddock, 2002; Parish, Pomeranz-Essley, & Braddock, 2003). First authorized in 1981, the HCBS waiver was increasingly available to families who have children with disabilities under the age of 18 and also available to adults with disabilities living in community settings (Braddock, Hemp, Rizzolo, Parish, & Pomeranz, 2002). In a study conducted in 2000, Parish et al. (2003) reported that 19 states provided a cash subsidy for family support totaling $69 million to 26,000 families. The families exercised control over how the HCBS funds were spent. Studies that have been conducted on the impact of family support consistently report high levels of satisfaction on the part of families and an increase in quality of life (Heller, Factor, Hsieh, & Hahn, 1998; Melda, Agosta, & Smith, 1995).

Braddock et al. (2002) have provided an ongoing national profile of family support funding (see also Parish, Pomeranz, Hemp, Rizzolo, & Braddock, 2001). Although there has been a continuous expansion of family support initiatives since the 1980s, only 3.6% of the national budget for developmental disability services is devoted to family programs. Medicaid funding currently accounts for approximately one half of all family support funding (Braddock, 2003).

One of the most exciting economic developments for families is the current effort by the federal government's Centers for Medicare and Medicaid services to provide "individualized" or "self-determined" funding (Braddock et al., 2002; Parish et al., 2003; Weiner, Tilly, & Alecxih, 2002). Now being implemented in approximately half the states for adults, this approach puts far more control into the hands of individuals with disabilities and their trusted allies in using funds to pursue community inclusion, productivity, and independence.

There are still many issues to be resolved about the flow, accountability, and outcomes of individualized funding, but from our own personal and professional perspectives, we see individualized funding as the most hopeful and promising economic resource available to families whose children have significant disabilities.

Because states differ in how family support and individualized funding programs are administered, we encourage families and professionals to contact state PTIs to find out about the state family support resources available, as well as any other programs that provide financial resources to families. The local Social Security Office can provide information about eligibility criteria to receive Supplemental Security Income (SSI) and Social Security Disability Insurance. In many states, people who qualify for SSI are also eligible for Medicaid funds to meet medical expenses. In addition, professionals can provide economic-related information to families in other ways (A. P. Turnbull & Turnbull, in press):

- Identify appropriate community contacts and provide parents with names and telephone numbers of persons to contact regarding estate planning, disability benefits, or family subsidies.
- Provide information on financial planning and government entitlement funds, such as SSI, as part of a family resource library.
- Encourage parents who have been successful in obtaining financial resources or who have completed financial planning to provide assistance to other parents who have financial questions.
- Provide information to help families investigate scholarships and financial aid.

Socialization Needs

Parents often are disappointed that their sons and daughters with severe disabilities have limited friendships. In a study of friendships, over two thirds of 17 families of children, teens, and adults with challenging behavior describe the absence of even one friendship for their children with challenging behavior. Parents' comments included the following:

Danny has no relationships outside his family. Jessie has no friends at school. . . . She has only been there 1 1/2 years. (A. P. Turnbull & Ruef, 1997, p. 216)

Interestingly, one of the parents of a young adult in this study warned, "The older you are and the longer you wait, the more difficult it becomes" (A. P. Turnbull & Ruef, 1997, p. 218). Of the 17 families, only one of the parents mentioned even having a vision for future friendship: "My dream is that the phone will ring, and someone will invite her to play" (A. P. Turnbull & Ruef, 1997, p. 218).

Ms. Hanaoka has made it a point to have many respite workers spend time with Emily and to develop a friendship with her. She encourages the respite workers to learn some basic Japanese words and to "connect" with Emily from her own cultural perspective. Ms. Hanaoka has also stocked their home with a variety of typical children's games. She believes that it will be helpful for Emily to learn to play these games so that she might play more easily with other children when opportunities arise.

Parents of students with moderate and severe to profound disabilities indicated in a research study that approximately one fourth of the school week should be related to friendship and social relationship development (Hamre-Nietupski, 1993). Although parents appear to be very interested in a strong friendship curriculum emphasis (Westling, 1996), the primary focus of school curriculum has been on academics, functional skills, employment, and independent living; friendship has not gotten adequate attention (Sowers, Glang, Voss, & Cooley, 1996).

We encourage educators to be mindful that sometimes what can seem like friendships for children with severe disabilities are really helping relationships (e.g., peer tutoring and behavioral monitoring). Evans, Salisbury, Palombaro, Berryman, and Hollowood (1992) reported that girls more frequently than boys tended to interact with peers with severe disabilities by serving as caretakers in tasks such as moving the student around the room, getting materials for them, and making sure that their special needs are met. One of the key aspects in friendships is reciprocity—what students with and without disabilities derive from their relationships with each other (Grenot-Scheyer, Staub, Peck, & Schwartz, 1998; Salisbury & Palombaro, 1998). Friendships often revolve around companionship (going places together, participating in school activities, engaging in sports and activities), emotional support (tending to feelings, expressing affection and caring, enhancing self-esteem), and instrumental support (providing information, providing practical help, providing advocacy) (A. P. Turnbull, Blue-Banning, & Pereira, 2000a).

Schaffner and Buswell (1992) describe three approaches to friendship facilitation:

1. Finding opportunities—arranging activities and opportunities to bring children and youth with and without disabilities together.
2. Making interpretations—highlighting to others a person's strengths and commonalities.
3. Making accommodations—changing or adapting the environment to increase an individual's participation.

You as a teacher can use these very same strategies to facilitate friendships of students in your class (A. P. Turnbull, Pereira, & Blue-Banning, 2000).

A broad range of people can be friendship facilitators, including general and special education teachers, related service providers, paraprofessionals, family members, community citizens, and classmates (Calloway, 1999; Meyer, Park, Grenot-Scheyer, Schwartz, & Harry, 1998; A. P. Turnbull, Pereira, & Blue-Banning, 2000). Many teachers have used the "Circle of Friends" approach with success in students with disabilities (Thousand, Villa, & Nevin, 2000). Chapter 10 provides more information on friendship facilitation.

In addition to what professionals can do to directly facilitate friendship, they also can encourage parents to consider being facilitators. Box 2-1 summarizes methods used by parents whose children had at least one successful friendship with a child or teen without a disability (A. P. Turnbull et al., 1999). Although all the parents in the study that focused on parent facilitation reported enjoying their role as a friendship facilitator, other parents may have problems in addressing this family function. As a parent of a middle school student with mental retardation commented,

> I have found this area [parent facilitation] to be very frustrating … it is a very difficult area … how do parents overcome or balance a provider's services and activities and the tendency for a group of kids to take advantage of the parent of the child with a disability. My experience is that we drive to the movies, go to the pool, we are being taken advantage of by kids sometimes. You kiss a lot of frogs before you find the prince. (A. P. Turnbull et al., 1999, p. 96)

You might find yourself in a situation in which you see great possibilities for a student with a severe disability developing friends, but his or her parents are not interested in being a friendship facilitator. What options exist? You might consider how you and other educators might first facilitate friendships in order to enable parents to "see success" and then feel more hopeful about their own contributions in this regard. Additionally, sometimes brothers and sisters, peers, and other community citizens can make valuable contributions in terms of promoting friendships. From a family systems perspective, it is important to recognize that even though you may perceive friendships to be very important, families may have other priorities. In some situations, families may believe that friendships are just as important or even more important than you think they are, but the family may have no unclaimed minutes to take on one more responsibility.

Educational Implications of Family Functions

Educators must recognize all family functions. It can be easy to focus only on the education function and to encourage parents to spend as much time as they possibly can on this one function. The best way to support students with disabilities and their families is to recognize that families are stretched across all of these functions and that for most families there are not enough hours in each day to do each function justice. The feeling of not having enough time to attend to one's family needs is strongly linked to parental stress and even depression (Herman & Marcenko, 1997). Thus, it is important that you "do no harm" by putting even more time demands on the family.

IFSPs and IEPs can be developed from the perspective of what the child might learn that would contribute to meeting family functions. For example, children can develop friendships that enable them to have invitations so that they spend time away from home. This can result in the parents not having to pay for child care, to have time for themselves—a help for the economic family function as well as for the socialization family function. Additionally, children and youth can learn to attend to their own personal care needs and complete family chores such as washing dishes, emptying the trash, and making their beds. All these tasks can relieve another family member from having to do them, which contributes to the daily care family function that might enhance time for family recreation.

Educators need to find the balance with families and their own interests in being friendship facilitators and in encouraging others to take on this role so that

Box 2–1 Parental Facilitation Strategies

Building a Foundation

- Accepting children unconditionally (e.g., loving the "disabled portion" of the child and perceiving the child as "whole" rather than "broken")

Creating Opportunities

- Supporting participation in community activities (e.g., enrolling the child for a class at the community arts center and supporting the teacher to interact comfortably with the child)
- Advocating for inclusion in the neighborhood school (e.g., working to have the child attend the neighborhood school rather than be bused to a school across town)
- Initiating and facilitating a "Circle of Friends" (e.g., starting a Circle of Friends or encouraging someone else to do so to encourage friendships within the school and community settings)
- Setting sibling-consistent expectations (e.g., similar to siblings inviting friends over to spend the night, encouraging the child to do the same)

Making Interpretations

- Encouraging others to accept the child (e.g., discussing their child's strengths and needs with others and supporting others to know how to communicate comfortably)
- Ensuring an attractive appearance (e.g., ensuring that the child is dressed and groomed in a way that is likely to draw positive and appropriate attention)

Making Accommodations

- Advocating for partial participation in community activities (e.g., encouraging a scout leader to know how to adapt projects to enable partial participation in completing them)

too much responsibility does not fall to the parents alone.

Family Life Cycle

Families differ in characteristics, and those differences influence interaction patterns that affect the family's ability to meet its functional needs. Each family is a unique unit and changes as it goes through stages and transitions of the family life cycle. Two dimensions of the family life cycle important for educators to understand include: (a) life cycle stages and (b) life cycle transitions.

Life Cycle Stages

Family life cycle has been described as a series of developmental stages that are periods of time in which family functions are relatively stable (Carter & McGoldrick, 1999). Many tasks facing families of adolescents are different from those facing families of preschoolers. Researchers and theorists disagree concerning the number of life cycle stages that exist. Some

have identified as many as 24 stages although others have identified as few as six (A. P. Turnbull & Turnbull, 2001). The number is not as important as the tasks that families are responsible for accomplishing at each stage. Six stages are identified here: (a) birth and early childhood, (b) elementary school years, (c) adolescence, (d) early adulthood, (e) middle adulthood, and (f) aging.

> Now that Libby Bridge is about to leave elementary school and enter middle school, she also is about to change physically and perhaps emotionally. The impending changes raise discomfiting issues. Who, for example, will teach or assist her as her menstrual cycles begin? Given that Libby is unable to provide any self-care and that all of her needs have been taken care of by family or teachers, what roles will they have with respect to her adult physical changes?

Table 2-1 identifies possible parental issues encountered at the first four life cycle stages, which are the stages in which families and educators have the most contact.

TABLE 2–1

Possible Parental Issues Encountered at Four Life Cycle Stages

Life cycle stage	Parents
Early childhood (ages 0–5)	Obtaining an accurate diagnosis
	Informing siblings and relatives
	Locating support services
	Clarifying a personal ideology to guide decisions
	Addressing issues of stigma
	Identifying positive contributions of exceptionality
	Participating in IFSP/IEP conferences
	Learning about IDEA rights and responsibilities
Elementary school (ages 6–12)	Establishing routines to carry out family functions
	Adjusting emotionally to implications of disability
	Clarifying issues of inclusive practices
	Participating in IEP conferences
	Locating community resources
	Arranging for extracurricular activities
	Establishing positive working relationships with professionals
	Gathering information about educational services available to the family and the child
	Setting great expectations about the future for their child
	Understanding different instructional strategies
Adolescence (ages 13–21)	Adjusting emotionally to possible chronicity of disability
	Identifying issues of emerging sexuality
	Addressing possible peer isolation and rejection
	Planning for career and vocational development
	Arranging for leisure-time activities
	Dealing with physical and emotional change of puberty
	Planning for postsecondary education
	Planning for the transition from school to adult life
	Addressing issues of preferred postschool outcomes
Adulthood (from age 21)	Addressing the need for preferred living situations
	Adjusting emotionally to adult implications for intensive support
	Addressing the need for socialization opportunities outside the family
	Initiating career choice or vocational program
	Adjusting to the changes that adult life will have on family decision making

Although some families' tasks and issues tend to be stage specific, others permeate all stages. An example of the latter is advocating for inclusive experiences. Many families strongly favor inclusion (Erwin & Soodak, 1995; Erwin, Soodak, Winton, & Turnbull, 1997; Ryndak, Downing, Jacqueline, & Morrison, 1995; Soodak et al., 2002) and are the major advocates for their children in obtaining inclusive experiences starting during the early childhood stage and continuing throughout the entire life span. As inclusion advocates, families often invest tremendous energy at each stage to access experiences that enable their children to be in typical settings:

1. Birth and early childhood: Participating in the nursery within their religious organization, attending neighborhood and community playgroups and child care, and participating in community recreation programs designed for young children

2. Elementary school years: Attending neighborhood schools and being placed in general education programs, taking advantage of typical extracurricular activities such as Scouts and community recreation, and developing friendships with classmates with and without disability

3. Adolescence: Attending inclusive secondary schools, participating in extracurricular activities consistent with preferences, and enjoying friendships and dating

4. Early adulthood: Participating in supported employment, developing a home of one's own, and participating in community activities consistent with preferences

Families who commit themselves early to inclusion and advocate for inclusive experiences across the life span often spend a great amount of time and energy educating others, making logistic and support arrangements, and troubleshooting when special issues arise. But many families are unfamiliar with the American school system and laws that govern it (especially IDEA). Some parents come from a cultural tradition of deference to professionals, relatively nondirect advocacy, and close family interdependence. Professionals who tell parents they "must advocate" for inclusion may be cutting across the grain of family life, even though their efforts are well intentioned and may be culturally appropriate for the majority of students in American schools. Professionals can become reliable allies for families in (a) fostering inclusive experiences both within and outside the school and (b) anticipating future barriers to inclusion and helping eliminate them. Many families would be relieved to feel that the bulk of advocacy is not on their shoulders (Wang, Mannan, Poston, Turnbull, & Summers, 2004).

A second pervasive issue across the life span is development of self-determination skills. Researchers in the self-determination field describe self-determination as being composed of the following four essential characteristics: (a) self-realization, (b) self-regulation, (c) psychological empowerment, and (d) autonomous actions (Wehmeyer, Kelchner, & Richards, 1996). These skills help children and youth with severe disabilities to live their lives according to their own personal values and preferences. Although the major emphasis within the special education field has been on development of self-determination skills at the adolescent level (Wehmeyer, 2001), it is critically important for families and educators to recognize that the foundation of self-determination starts during the birth and early childhood stage and evolves throughout the entire life span (Brown & Cohen, 1996; Erwin & Brown, 2003). Early on, families determine, explicitly or implicitly, the extent to which they value and emphasize opportunities for their son or daughter to express preferences and make choices. Consistent with their cultural values, families carry out tasks at each stage that contribute to either enhancing or impeding development of self-determination skills.

Many barriers challenge both families and professionals in the life cycle enhancement of self-determination, including (a) being unclear about the extent of self-determination that is appropriate to expect, (b) being unfamiliar with instructional strategies to teach self-determination skills, (c) giving priority to attending to other needs of the child and placing self-determination at a lower level of priority, and (d) having cultural clashes with the expression of self-determination (Powers, Singer, & Sowers, 1996). On the last point of cultural clashes, it is important to note that there are many different cultural interpretations of self-determination. For example, autonomy is one of the essential characteristics identified as integral to self-determination; however, Navajo traditions have expectations that all individuals, including children and youth, will act in an interdependent way and consider broad needs of the larger group as contrasted to making decisions about acting in an individually autonomous manner (Frankland, Turnbull, Wehmeyer, & Blackmountain, 2004). From the earliest years, families and professionals must clarify their values and priorities related to self-determination and recognize that its development is a long-term life cycle issue (Palmer & Wehmeyer, 2002). Clarification is important now for the Bridge family and Libby's teachers; her entry into middle school is a good time to discuss these matters, especially since IDEA now requires transition planning to begin when Libby is 14 years old. Emily's teachers may want to discuss Ms. Hanaoka's culturally based expectations for Emily's independence.

Life Cycle Transitions

Transitions represent the periods of change as families move from one developmental stage to another. One way to think about life cycle stages and transitions is that stages are similar to plateaus and that transitions resemble peaks and valleys that divide those plateaus. Because transitional times represent changes in expectations and often in service systems, they typically are the times families identify as the most challenging (Westling, 1996). These transitions may involve movement from the intensive care nursery to the home and community, from early intervention to preschool, from preschool to kindergarten, from elementary to middle school (as for Libby Bridge), from middle school to high school, and from high school into adulthood (Blacher, 2000; Clark & Davis, 2000; Pianta & Cox, 2000; Sax & Thoma, 2002).

Cultural values strongly influence life cycle issues. For example, Navajo youth typically are regarded as adults just after puberty in contrast to most European American youth, who are generally seen as adults around ages 18 to 21 (Deyhle & LeCompte, 1994). Sexual maturity for females is celebrated in a Navajo puberty ceremony referred to as Kinaalva. After this ceremony, pregnancy, even at an early age, has a meaning very different from its significance in European American culture (Deyhle & LeCompte, 1994). Thus, it is critically important to understand transitions from a cultural point of view.

Different cultures have various kinds of rituals they consider appropriate, such as baptism, first communion, bar or bat mitzvah, graduation, and voting. Because these rituals serve as symbols of ongoing development for the family, they help reorient family perspectives toward changes that are occurring throughout transition. A special challenge for families who have a child with severe disabilities is that the child often does not have access to many of these rituals and therefore does not have the experience of transition. Educators can support families by encouraging and supporting them to include their child in these rituals. (See chapter 16 for further discussion of symbols of adulthood.)

Some families may believe that their children should not participate in rituals because of their disability. For example, a mother may think that her child cannot benefit from having religious confirmation experiences. Perhaps you might convene parents whose children have been confirmed and parents who fear that the experience might not be "realistic" for their child. Leaders in a religious community might not encourage parents because they may never have had the experience of including a person with a severe disability. It may be valuable to invite the religious leaders to the IEP meeting (of course, with parental consent) so they can learn about classroom adaptations and how these same adaptations might be done in confirmation classes. A key point is that many parents are led to believe that normal events are unrealistic for their children. The more you can foster a partnership of reliable allies working together toward inclusive experiences related to family rituals, the more likely it will be that the child will truly belong as part of that celebration. In addition to participation in celebrations and rituals, there are many other ways that professionals can collaborate with families in enhancing successful transitions. Table 2–2 includes tips for doing this.

TABLE 2–2

Tips for Enhancing Successful Transitions

Early Childhood
- Begin preparing for the separation of preschool children from parents by periodically leaving the child with others
- Gather information and visit preschools in the community
- Encourage participation in "Parent to Parent" programs, in which veteran parents are matched in one-to-one relationships with parents who are just beginning the transition process
- Familiarize parents with possible school (elementary and secondary) programs, career options, or adult programs so that they have an idea of future opportunities

Childhood
- Provide parents with an overview of curricular options
- Ensure that IEP meetings provide an empowering context for family collaboration
- Encourage participation in "Parent to Parent" matches, workshops, or family support groups to discuss transitions with others

Adolescence
- Assist families and adolescents in identifying community leisure-time activities
- Incorporate into the IEP skills that will be needed in future career and vocational programs
- Visit or become familiar with a variety of career and living options
- Develop a mentor relationship with an adult with a similar disability and with an individual who has a career that matches the student's strengths and preferences

Adulthood
- Provide preferred information to families about guardianship, estate planning, wills, and trusts
- Assist family members in transferring responsibilities to the individual with an exceptionality, other family members, or service providers, as appropriate
- Assist the young adult or family members with career or vocational choices
- Address the issues and responsibilities of marriage and family for the young adult

Educational Implications of Family Life Cycle

Support must be provided consistent with life cycle stages and transitions according to each families' preferences, strengths, and needs. There has been a strong emphasis in the special education literature on the transition of youth with disabilities from school to adulthood; this transitional planning is now mandated to begin at age 14. A key role of educators is to support families throughout the transitional process (Blue-Banning, Turnbull, & Pereira, 2000; Hughes & Carter, 2000). Features of person-centered planning (see also chapters 3 and 15) can be used (a) to bring together family, professionals, friends, and community citizens; (b) to envision the preferred life from the perspective of the individual and family; and (c) to work together to translate that vision into daily and weekly supports and services (Bui & Turnbull, 2003; Holburn & Vietze, 2002; A. P. Turnbull et al., 1996).

  Box 2–2 Planning for Angela

Background

Angela Sloan, who has a moderate-to-severe disability, has just turned age 16 and is in her first year in your high school career education class. You are considering a variety of community jobs for her but are faced with a difficult family situation. Angela's parents have gone through an adversarial divorce, and they are not on speaking terms. Ms. Sloan, Angela's mother, regularly attends parent–teacher conferences and IEP meetings and communicates often using a notebook that goes between home and school. Mr. Sloan also has expressed an interest in being kept informed.

Ms. Sloan is concerned with Angela's functional academic and socialization skills. She has strongly expressed her preference that Angela stay in school and spend her days attending inclusive classes, such as home economics, child development, and computer literacy.

However, Mr. Sloan has discussed with you his preference that Angela spend as much time working as possible. He has a friend who owns a clothing store. The friend has told Mr. Sloan that Angela will have a job there when she graduates. Mr. Sloan believes that if Angela begins developing job skills for the clothing store now, she can graduate at 18 and go to work.

Angela spent part of last year working in an office through the career education program. She was very proud of her job and was sad when school ended and a summer job placement could not be arranged. Angela has expressed her desire to work in an office again. Lately, she has been moody and uncooperative when others in her class leave to go to work and she attends the computer literacy class. You appreciate all points of view but tend to believe that Angela's preferences should be honored.

Issue: Whose Preferences Are Acted On?

Discussing this issue with both parents is going to be difficult. They are at opposite ends of the spectrum, yet both have valid reasons for their positions. Whatever your decision, it will appear that you are siding with one parent over the other or with Angela. Therefore, compromise is needed. In addition, respecting the preference of Angela, who appears to be acting in a self-determining way, is crucial.

You think that a person-centered planning process will prove valuable (see chapters 3 and 15). You want to get together with Angela, her parents, friends, advocates, and other professionals to formulate a vision of what Angela's life could look like and to develop an action plan. However, bringing together the parents in a large-group situation is challenging. Before jumping into a group situation, you consider the following options:

1. Pay close attention to Angela's mood as she participates in different types of activities. Support her in learning to communicate her preferences to her parents. Give priority to teaching self-determination skills.
2. Help Ms. Sloan understand the importance of vocational preparation and emphasize that such preparation can include more than job skills. Angela can work on social skills and begin to establish a circle of work friends who will still be there when her school friends graduate.
3. Talk with Mr. Sloan about the need to allow maximum growth and opportunities for Angela. Graduation at age 18 may be premature for her. If his friend has promised a job, it may be there in 2 years or in 5 years.
4. Compromise on community vocational experiences for the time being. Set up appropriate in-school job experiences, such as working in the school office, which would be consistent with Angela's preferences for office work.

5. Start small. Get each stakeholder to compromise on at least one thing. The job in school may appease everyone for the time being, until you can work on the rest.

6. Begin to talk with Mr. and Ms. Sloan about their perceptions of Angela. Look at her desire to establish some independence and to state her preferences. Encourage Angela to make her own decisions at school. Keep in mind that it may be difficult for Mr. and Mrs. Sloan to support Angela's self-determination. Provide examples of how Angela is expressing her preferences and making decisions at school.

7. Have the parents come to see Angela working in school. Point out her pride and self-esteem when she works.

8. Gradually increase Angela's time in community settings, including vocational sites. It may be for 1 hour this year, 2 hours the next, and so on. As you build trust with Mr. and Ms. Sloan, they will begin to understand your position, and you will begin to understand theirs.

What other options can you suggest? What do you see as the pros and cons of each option? To what extent do you believe that Angela can be her own advocate, and what advocacy support does she need from others? How might you create a win-win-win situation for Angela, Ms. Sloan, and Mr. Sloan, or is that possible?

Summary

Historically, parent and professional partnerships have not been as positive and productive as they might be. IDEA has established ground rules for both educational professionals and parents in their interactions with each other. Associated with each of the six major principles of the law—zero reject, nondiscriminatory evaluation, appropriate education programs, least restrictive alternative, parent and student participation in shared decision making, and due process—are requirements for family–professional partnerships.

IDEA alone does not ensure collaboration among parents and professionals. All parties must work within the guidelines to develop partnerships to meet families' individual needs and preferences. Preferred educational roles of parents and other family members vary across families. Likewise, the level of involvement sought by different family members fluctuates.

Professionals must be encouraged to view students within the broader context of family life. A family systems perspective recognizes the true complexity of families and offers a framework to understand the characteristics, interactions, functions, and life cycle issues of families.

The challenge is exciting. Preparing individuals who have severe disabilities with the academic, social, emotional, and vocational skills necessary to meaningfully participate in society is a complex task. It requires innovative efforts by families and professionals working toward shared goals. The possibilities are boundless, and the benefits for persons with disabilities are unlimited if all parties apply their energies and imaginations in a partnership of progress.

Suggested Activity: A Tale of Two Families

The Angelino Family

The Angelino family has five children, and a sixth is on the way. The children are ages 14 (girl), 12 (boy), 10 (girl), 7 (boy), and 6 (girl). They all attend a nearby parochial school. Mr. Angelino owns a butcher shop that had been his father's and that was begun by his grandfather, who immigrated from Italy in 1904. The butcher shop at one time had upstairs living quarters for the family, but about 10 years ago the family moved into a large, Victorian-style house about a block away.

Mr. Angelino's youngest brother once came back from college with ideas about expanding the business and marketing the family's secret recipe for Italian sausage, but Mr. Angelino (the oldest son) decided against it because it would take too much time away from the family. He is fond of saying, "We ain't rich, but we got a roof over our heads, food in our bellies, and each other. What more could we want?" This youngest brother is the only one in the family with a college education, and he is also the only one who scandalized the family by marrying a non-Catholic. Mr. Angelino uses his little brother as an example of the detrimental effects of "too much education."

Both Mr. and Mrs. Angelino come from large families; most of their brothers and sisters still live in the "Little Italy" section of this large eastern city. All grandparents are dead, with the exception of Mrs. Angelino's mother (Mama). Mama lives in the home with them and is very frail. One of Mrs. Angelino's brothers or sisters is sure to stop by nearly every day, bringing children, flowers, or food, for a visit with Mama. They often take Mama for drives or to their homes for short visits, depending on her health, and help with her basic care.

Life with the Angelinos can be described as a kind of happy chaos. Kids are always running in and out of the butcher shop, where the older brothers and male cousins are often assigned small tasks in return for a piece of salami or some other treat. The old house is always full of children—siblings and cousins—from teenagers to toddlers. Children are pretty much indulged until they reach age 9 or 10, at which time they are expected to begin taking responsibility, which is divided strictly along traditional gender-role lines. Child care, cooking, and cleaning are accomplished by the women: older sisters or cousins, aunts or mothers. Evening meals are a social event. There is virtually always at least one extended family member or friend at the table, and everyone talks about the events of the day, sometimes all at once, except when Mr. Angelino has something to say, at which point everyone stops to listen. Mr. Angelino is obviously a very affectionate father, but he expects his word to be obeyed. Bed times, rules about talking at the table, curfews, and other rules are strictly enforced. This situation is beginning to cause conflict with the oldest daughter, who wants to date and spend more time with her friends from school. Mrs. Angelino is often sympathetic to her children's requests, but her husband has the final say.

All in all, life in the Angelino home is warm, close, and harmonious. Mrs. Angelino, as she approaches her eighth month of pregnancy with this last "surprise" child, shares her contentment with her priest: "I don't know what I have done to deserve so many blessings from the Good Lord."

The McNeil Family

Mr. and Mrs. McNeil have been married for 2 years, and she is expecting their first child. Mr. McNeil is the youngest partner in a prestigious law firm in this midwestern city. Everybody considers him upwardly mobile and thinks it phenomenal that he should achieve a partnership only 3 years out of law school. Mrs. McNeil has a degree in interior design. She worked full time for a while for a decorating firm in another city. After her marriage, Mrs. McNeil moved to this city, where she has a part-time, on-call job with an exclusive architectural firm. She has ambitions of starting her own business.

Mr. McNeil is an only child. His parents live on the East Coast. They are both successful in business—his father is a banker, his mother a real estate broker. They

have always demanded perfection from their son, and he seems to have lived up to their expectations. Mrs. McNeil has one younger sister. Her parents live on the West Coast. They are both professional persons: her father is a college professor, and her mother is a social worker. Mrs. McNeil's family has always been very close. She calls her parents about once a week, and the family occasionally has conference calls with the parents and the two siblings to decide some important issue or to relay some big news. Mrs. McNeil's parents place no demands on her except that she be true to herself. They often tell her how proud they are of her accomplishments.

Both sets of parents are experiencing grandparenthood for the first time with Mrs. McNeil's pregnancy. They are thrilled. It sometimes seems to the McNeils that their parents vie with each other in the gifts they give them. The McNeils refuse the more extravagant gifts to make the point that they are indeed making it on their own, and they have discussed some strategies for disentangling themselves from so much contact with their parents.

The McNeils' avant-garde apartment is the scene of much entertaining with his law firm associates and her artistic friends and decorating clients. Although their social spheres overlap somewhat, each has separate groups of friends and pursues individual interests. They call this "giving each other space," and they consider it an important strength in their marriage. The McNeils believe strongly in supporting each other's careers and in sharing family responsibilities; they divide cooking and cleaning in a flexible way, according to whoever has the time. They are also attending Lamaze classes together and are looking forward to sharing childbirth.

Exercise

The babies Mrs. Angelino and Mrs. McNeil are expecting will have a severe cognitive and physical disability.

1. Use the family systems framework to predict the preferences, strengths, and needs of both families in terms of characteristics, interaction, function, and life cycle.
2. The Angelinos and McNeils have different cultural values. How would you characterize the cultural values of each family? How do you think these cultural values influence what they consider to be appropriate self-determination for each of the parents (mother and father) as well as for their children with

and without a disability (assume that the McNeils have more children who do not have a disability).

3. Given their views on appropriate levels of self-determination, identify two ways that you might work with each family in addressing self-determination within a culturally responsive framework.

References

Abbott, D. A., & Meredith, W. H. (1986). Strengths of parents with retarded children. *Family Relations, 35*, 371-375.

Agosta, J. M., Bass, A., & Spence, R. (1986). *The needs of the family: Results of a statewide survey in Massachusetts*. Cambridge, MA: Human Services Institute.

Benson, B. A., & Gross, A. M. (1989). The effect of a congenitally handicapped child upon the marital dyad: A review of the literature. *Clinical Psychology Review, 9*, 747-758.

Bertalanffy, L. von. (1975). General system theory. In B. D. Ruben & J. Y. Kim (Eds.), *General systems theory and human communication* (pp. 6-20). Rochelle Park, NJ: Hayden.

Birenbaum, A., & Cohen, H. J. (1993). On the importance of helping families: Policy implications from a national study. *Mental Retardation, 31*, 67-74.

Blacher, J. (2000). Transition to adulthood: Mental retardation, families, and culture. *American Journal on Mental Retardation, 106*(2), 173-188.

Blue-Banning, M. J., Turnbull, A. P., & Pereira, L. (2000). Group action planning as a support strategy for Hispanic families: Parent and professional perspectives. *Mental Retardation, 38*(3), 262-275.

Board of Education v. Holland, 4 F. 3d 1398 (9th Cir., 1994).

Braddock, D. (2002). *The state of the states: Public policy toward disability at the dawn of the 21st century*. Washington, DC: American Association on Mental Retardation.

Braddock, D. (2003). *The State of the States in Developmental Disabilities Project*. Boulder: University of Colorado, Department of Psychiatry.

Braddock, D., Hemp, R., Rizzolo, M. C., Parish, S., & Pomeranz, A. (2002). *The state of the states in developmental disabilities: 2002 study summary*. Boulder: University of Colorado, Coleman Institute for Cognitive Disabilities and Department of Psychiatry.

Brown, F., & Cohen, S. (1996). Self-determination and young children. *Journal of the Association for Persons with Severe Handicaps, 21*, 22-30.

Bui, Y. N., & Turnbull, A. (2003). East meets west: Analysis of person-centered planning in the context of Asian American values. *Education and Training in Developmental Disabilities, 38*(1), 18-31.

Calloway, C. (1999). 20 ways to promote friendship in the inclusive classroom. *Intervention in School and Clinic, 34*(3), 176-177.

Carnes, P. J. (1981). *Family development 1: Understanding us*. Minneapolis: Interpersonal Communications Programs.

Carr, E. G., Dunlap, G., Horner, R. H., Koegel, R. L., Turnbull, A. P., Sailor, W., Anderson, J. L., Albin, R. W., Koegel, L. K., & Fox, L.

(2002). Positive behavior support: Evolution of an applied science. *Journal of Positive Behavior Interventions, 4*(1), 4-16, 20.

Carter, B., & McGoldrick, M. (Eds.). (1999). *The expanded family life cycle: Individual, family, and social perspectives*. Boston: Allyn & Bacon.

Clark, H. B., & Davis, M. (2000). *Transition to adulthood*. Baltimore: Paul H. Brookes.

Cuskelly, M., & Gunn, P. (2003). Sibling relationships of children with Down syndrome: Perspectives of mothers, fathers, and siblings. *American Journal on Mental Retardation, 108*(4), 234-244.

Daniel R.R. v. State Board of Education, 874 F. 2d 1036 (5th Cir., 1989).

Deyhle, D., & LeCompte, M. (1994). Cultural differences in child development: Navajo adolescents in middle schools. *Theory into Practice, 33*(3), 156-165.

Dyson, L. L. (1998). A support program for siblings of children with disabilities: What siblings learn and what they like. *Psychology in the Schools, 35*(1), 57-63.

Erwin, E. J., & Brown, F. (2003). From theory to practice: A contextual framework for understanding self-determination in early childhood environments. *Infants & Young Children, 16*(1), 77-87.

Erwin, E. J., & Soodak, L. C. (1995). I never knew I could stand up to the system: Families' perspectives on pursuing inclusive education. *Journal of the Association for Persons with Severe Handicaps, 20*, 136-146.

Erwin, E. J., Soodak, L. C., Winton, P. J., & Turnbull, A. (1997). I wish it wouldn't all depend on me: Research on families and early childhood inclusion. In M. J. Guralnick (Ed.), *Early childhood inclusion: Focus on change* (pp. 127-158). Baltimore: Paul H. Brookes.

Evans, I. M., Salisbury, C. L., Palombaro, M. M., Berryman, J., & Hollowood, T. M. (1992). Peer interactions and social acceptance of elementary-age children with severe disabilities in an inclusive school. *Journal of the Association for Persons with Severe Handicaps, 17*, 205-212.

Field, S., & Hoffman, A. (2002). Lessons learned from implementing the steps to self-determination curriculum. *Remedial and Special Education, 23*(2), 90-98.

Fisman, S., Wolf, L., Ellison, D., & Freeman, T. (2000). A longitudinal study of siblings of children with chronic disabilities. *Canadian Journal of Psychiatry, 45*, 369-375.

Fitzgerald, B. (1999). Children of lesbian and gay parents: A review of the literature. *Marriage & Family Review, 29*(1), 57-75.

Frankland, H. C., Turnbull, A. P., Wehmeyer, M. L., & Blackmountain, L. (2004). An exploration of the self-determination construct and disability as it relates to the Diné (Navaho) culture. *Education and Training in Developmental Disabilities, 39*, 191-205

Fujiura, G. T., Roccoforte, J. A., & Braddock, D. (1994). Costs of family care for adults with mental retardation and related developmental disabilities. *American Journal on Mental Retardation, 99*, 250-261.

Fujiura, G. T., & Yamaki, K. (2000). Analysis of ethnic variations in developmental disability prevalence and household economic status. *Mental Retardation, 35*, 286-294.

Gollnick, D. M., & Chinn, P. C. (2002). *Multicultural education in a pluralistic society* (6th ed.). Upper Saddle River, NJ, and Upper Saddle River, NJ: Merrill/Prentice Hall.

Grenot-Scheyer, M., Staub, D., Peck, C.A., & Schwartz, I. S. (1998). Reciprocity and friendships: Listening to the voices of children and youth with and without disabilities. In L. H. Meyer, H. S. Park, M. Grenot-Scheyer, I. S. Schwartz, & B. Harry (Eds.), *Making friends: The influences of culture and development* (pp. 149–167). Baltimore: Paul H. Brookes.

Hamre-Nietupski, S. (1993). How much time should be spent on skill instruction and friendship development? Preferences of parents of students with moderate and severe/profound disabilities. *Education and Training in Mental Retardation, 28*, 220–231.

Hannah, M. E., & Midlarsky, E. (1999). Competence and adjustment of siblings of children with mental retardation. *American Journal on Mental Retardation, 104*(1), 22–37.

Hanson, M. J. (1992). Families with Anglo-European roots. In E. W. Lynch & M. J. Hanson (Eds.), *Developing cross-cultural competence: A guide for working with young children and their families* (pp. 63–88). Baltimore: Paul H. Brookes.

Harry, B. (1992). An ethnographic study of cross-cultural communication with Puerto Rican-American families in the special education system. *American Educational Research Journal, 29*, 471–494.

Harry, B., Allen, N., & McLaughlin, M. (1995). *Communication versus reciprocity with families: Case studies in special education.* Baltimore: Paul H. Brookes.

Harry, B., Kalyanpur, M., & Day, M. (1999). *Building cultural reciprocity with families.* Baltimore: Paul H. Brookes.

Heller, T., Factor, A., Hsieh, K., & Hahn, J. E. (1998). The impact of age and transitions out of nursing homes and for adults with developmental disabilities. *American Journal on Mental Retardation, 103*, 236–248.

Herman, S. E., & Marcenko, M. O. (1997). Perceptions of services and resources as mediators of depression among parents of children with developmental disabilities. *Mental Retardation, 35*, 458–467.

Hodapp, R. M., & Krasner, D. V. (1995). Families of children with disabilities: Findings from a national sample of eighth-grade students. *Exceptionality, 5*(2), 71–81.

Holburn, S., & Vietze, P. M. (2002). *Person-centered planning: Research, practice, and future directions.* Baltimore: Paul H. Brookes.

Honig v. Doe, 484 U.S. 305, 108 S. Ct. 592, 98 L. Ed. 2d 686 (1988).

Hughes, C., & Carter, E. W. (2000). *The transition handbook.* Baltimore: Paul H. Brookes.

Johnson, J., & Duffett, A. with Farkas, S., and Wilson, L. (2002). *When it's your own child: A report on special education from the families who use it.* New York: Publisher of Public Agenda.

Jones, D. E., Clatterbuck, C. C., Marquis, J. G., Turnbull, H. R., & Moberly, R. L. (1996). Educational placements for children who are ventilator assisted. *Exceptional Children, 63*, 47–58.

Kalyanpur, M., & Harry, B. (1999). *Culture in special education.* Baltimore: Paul H. Brookes.

Kazak, A. E., & Marvin, R. S. (1984). Differences, difficulties, and adaptation: Stress and social networks in families with a handicapped child. *Family Relations, 33*, 67–77.

Klass, C. S. (1996). *Home visiting: Promoting healthy parent and child development.* Baltimore: Paul H. Brookes.

Kozol, J. (1995). *Amazing grace: The lives of children and the conscience of a nation.* New York: Crown.

Kritek, P. B. (1994). *Negotiating at an uneven table: Developing moral courage in resolving our conflicts.* San Francisco: Jossey-Bass.

Lamme, L. L., & Lamme, L. A. (2002). Welcoming children from gay families into our schools. *Educational Leadership, 59*, 65–69.

Lucyshyn, M. J., Dunlap, G., & Albin, R. W. (Eds.). (2002). *Families & positive behavior support: Addressing problem behavior in family contexts.* Baltimore: Paul H. Brookes.

Lynch, E. W., & Hanson, M. J. (Eds.). (2004). *Developing cross-cultural competence: A guide for working with young children and their families.* Baltimore: Paul H. Brookes.

Melda, K., Agosta, J., & Smith, F. (1995). *Family support services in Utah: Striving to make a difference.* Salem, OR: Human Services Research Institute.

Meyer, D. J. (Ed.). (1997). *Views from our shoes: Growing up with a brother or sister with special needs.* Bethesda, MD: Woodbine House.

Meyer, D. J., & Vadasy, P. F. (1994). *Sibshops: Workshops for siblings of children with special needs.* Baltimore: Paul H. Brookes.

Meyer, H., Park, H. S., Grenot-Scheyer, M., Schwartz, I. S., & Harry, B. (1998). *Making friends: The influences of culture and development.* Baltimore: Paul H. Brookes.

Michaud, L. J., Semel-Concepion, J., Duhaine, A. C., & Lazer, M. F. (2002). Traumatic brain injury. In M. L. Batshaw (Ed.), *Children with disabilities* (pp. 525–545). Baltimore: Paul H. Brookes.

Mithaug, Agran, Martin, & Wehmeyer. (2003).

Murphy, A. T. (1982). The family with a handicapped child: A review of the literature. *Developmental and Behavioral Pediatrics, 3*(2), 73–82.

National Research Council. (2002). *Minority students in special and gifted education.* Washington, DC: National Academy Press.

Olson, D. H., Russell, C. S., & Sprenkle, D. H. (1980). Marital and family therapy: A decade review. *Journal of Marriage and the Family, 42*, 973–993.

Palmer, S. B., & Wehmeyer, M. L. (2002). *Self-determined learning model for early elementary students: A parent's guide.* Lawrence: University of Kansas, Beach Center on Disability.

Parish, S. L., Pomeranz, A., Hemp, R., Rizzolo, M. C., and Braddock, D. (2001) Family support for persons with developmental disabilities in the US: Status and trends. Policy Research Brief. Minneapolis: University of Minnesota, Institute on Community Integration.

Parish, S. L., Pomeranz-Essley, A., & Braddock, D. (2003). Family support in the United States: Financing trends and emerging initiatives. *Mental Retardation, 41*(3), 174–187.

Pianta, R. C., & Cox, M. J. (2000). *The transition to kindergarten.* Baltimore: Paul H. Brookes.

P.J. v. State of Conn. Bd. of Ed., 788 F. Supp. 673 (D. Ct. 1992).

Powers, L. E., Singer, G. H. S., & Sowers, J.A. (Eds.). (1996). *On the road to autonomy: Promoting self-competence in children and youth with disabilities.* Baltimore: Paul H. Brookes.

Ryndak, D. L., Downing, J. E., Jacqueline, L. R., & Morrison, A. P. (1995). Parents' perceptions after inclusion of their children with mild or severe disabilities. *Journal of the Association for Persons with Severe Handicaps, 20*, 147–157.

Salisbury, C. L., & Palombaro, M. M. (1998). Friends and acquaintances: Evolving relationships in an inclusive elementary school. In L. H. Meyer, H. S. Park, M. Grenot-Scheyer, I. S. Schwartz, & B. Harry (Eds.), *Making friends: The influences of culture and development* (pp. 60–80). Baltimore: Paul H. Brookes.

Sax, C. L., & Thoma, C. A. (2002). *Transition assessment: Wise practices of quality lives.* Baltimore: Paul H. Brookes.

Schaffner, C. B., & Buswell, B. E. (1992). *Connecting students: A guide to thoughtful friendship facilitation for educators and families.* Colorado Springs: PEAK Parent Center.

Scorgie, K., & Sobsey, D. (2000). Transformational outcomes associated with parenting children who have disabilities. *Mental Retardation, 38*(3), 195–206.

Scorgie, K., Wilgosh, L., & McDonald, L. (1998). Stress and coping in families of children with disabilities: An examination of recent literature. *Developmental Disabilities Bulletin, 26*(1), 22–42.

Seligman, M., Goodwin, G., Paschal, K., Applegate, A., & Lehman, L. (1997, December). Grandparents of children with disabilities: Perceived levels of support. *Education and Training in Mental Retardation and Developmental Disabilities, 32*, 293–303.

Simmerman, S., Blacher, J., & Baker, B. L. (2001). Fathers' and mothers' perceptions of father involvement in families with young children with a disability. *Journal of Intellectual and Developmental Disability, 26*(4), 325–338.

Soodak, L. C., Erwin, E. J., Winton, P., Brotherson, M. J., Turnbull, A. P., Hanson, M. J., & Brault, L. M. J. (2002). Implementing inclusive early childhood education: A call for professional empowerment. *TECSE, 22*(2), 99–102.

Sowers, J. A., Glang, A. E., Voss, J., & Cooley, E. (1996). Enhancing friendships and leisure involvements of students with traumatic brain injuries and other disabilities. In L. E. Powers, G. H. S. Singer, & J. A. Sowers (Eds.), *On the road to autonomy: Promoting self-competence in children and youth with disabilities* (pp. 347–372). Baltimore: Paul H. Brookes.

Stowe, M. J., & Turnbull, H. R. (2001). Legal considerations of inclusion for infants and toddlers and for preschool-age children. In M. J. Guralnick (Ed.), *Early childhood inclusion* (pp. 69–100). Baltimore: Paul H. Brookes.

Summers, J. A., Behr, S. K., & Turnbull, A. P. (1989). Positive adaptation and coping strengths of families who have children with disabilities. In G. H. S. Singer & L. K. Irvin (Eds.), *Support for caregiving families: Enabling positive adaptation to disability* (pp. 27–40). Baltimore: Brookes.

Tasker, F. (1999). Children in lesbian-led families: A review. *Clinical Child Psychology and Psychiatry, 4*(2), 153–166.

Thousand, J. S., Villa, R. A., & Nevin, A. I. (2000). *Creativity & collaborative learning: The practical guide to empowering students, teachers, and families.* Baltimore: Paul H. Brookes.

Turnbull, A. P., Blue-Banning, M. J., Anderson, E. L., Turnbull, H. R., Seaton, K. A., & Dinas, P. A. (1996). Enhancing self-determination through Group Action Planning: A holistic emphasis. In D. J. Sands & M. L. Wehmeyer (Eds.), *Self-determination across the life span: Independence and choice for people with disabilities* (pp. 237–256). Baltimore: Paul H. Brookes. Turnbull, A. P., Blue-Banning, M. J., & Pereira, L. (2000). Successful friendships of Hispanic children and youth with disabilities: An exploratory study. *Mental Retardation, 38*(2), 138–153.

Turnbull, A. P., Pereira, L., & Blue-Banning, M. J. (1999). Parents' facilitation of friendships between their children with a disability and friends without a disability. *Journal of the Association for Persons with Severe Handicaps, 24*, 85–99.

Turnbull, A. P., Pereira, L., & Blue-Banning, M. J. (2000). Teachers as friendship facilitators: Respeto and personalismo. *Council for Exceptional Children, 32*(5), 66–70.

Turnbull, A. P., & Ruef, M. (1997). Family perspectives on inclusive lifestyle issues for people with problem behavior. *Exceptional Children, 63*(2), 211–227.

Turnbull, A. P., & Summers, J. A. (1987). From parent involvement to family support: Evolution to revolution. In S. M. Pueschel, C. Tingey, J. W. Rynders, A. C. Crocher, & D. M. Crutcher (Eds.), *New perspectives on Down syndrome: Proceedings on the state-of-the-art conference* (pp. 289–306). Baltimore: Paul H. Brookes.

Turnbull, A. P., Turbiville, V., & Turnbull, H. R. (2000). Evolution of family-professional partnership models: Collective empowerment as the model for the early 21st century. In J. P. Shonkoff & S. L. Meisels (Eds.), *The handbook of early childhood intervention* (2nd ed., pp. 630–650). New York: Cambridge University Press.

Turnbull, A., & Turnbull, R. (1999). Comprehensive lifestyle support for adults with challenging behavior: From rhetoric to reality. *Education and Training in Mental Retardation and Developmental Disabilities, 34*(4), 373–394.

Turnbull, A. P., & Turnbull, H. R. (1996). Self-determination within a culturally responsive family systems perspective: Balancing the family mobile. In L. E. Powers, G. H. S. Singer, & J. A. Sowers (Eds.), *On the road to autonomy: Promoting self-competence in children and youth with disabilities* (pp. 195–220). Baltimore: Paul H. Brookes.

Turnbull, A. P., & Turnbull, H. R. (2001). *Families, professionals, and exceptionality: Collaborating for empowerment* (4th ed.). Upper Saddle River, NJ: Merrill/Prentice Hall.

Turnbull, A. P., & Turnbull, H. R., E. J. Erwin, & L. C. Soodak (2005). *Families, professionals, and exceptionality: A special partnership.* (3rd ed.). Upper Saddle River, NJ: Merrill/Prentice Hall.

Turnbull, H. R., & Turnbull, A. P. (1982). Parent involvement in the education of handicapped children: A critique. *Mental Retardation, 20*, 115–122.

Turnbull, H. R., & Turnbull, A. P. (1997). The constitutional and programmatic grounding of IDEA. *Journal of the Association for Persons with Severe Handicaps, 22*(2), 83–85.

Turnbull, H. R., & Turnbull, A. P. (2000). *Free appropriate public education: The law and children with disabilities* (6th ed.). Denver: Love.

U.S. Department of Education. (2002). *To assure the free appropriate public education of all children with disabilities: Nineteenth annual report to Congress on the implementation of the Individuals with Disabilities Education Act.* Washington, DC: Author.

Wang, M., Mannan, H., Poston, D., Turnbull, A. P., & Summers, J. A. (2004). Parents' perceptions of advocacy activities and their impact on family quality of life. *Research and Practice for Persons with Severe Disabilities, 29*, 144–155.

Wehmeyer, M. L. (2001). Self-determination and mental retardation. *International Review of Research in Mental Retardation, 24*, 1–48.

Wehmeyer, M. L., Agran, M., Palmer, S. B., & Mithaug, D. (1999). *A teacher's guide to implementing the self-determined learning model of instruction (adolescent version)*. Lawrence, KS: Beach Center on Disability.

Wehmeyer, M. L., Kelchner, K., & Richards, S. (1996). Essential characteristics of self-determined behavior of individuals with mental retardation. *American Journal on Mental Retardation, 100*, 632–642.

Weiner, J. M., Tilly, J., & Alecxih, L. M. B. (2002). Home and community-based services in seven states. *Health Care Financing Review, 23*(2), 89–114.

Westling, D. L. (1996, June). What do parents of children with moderate and severe disabilities want? *Education and Training in Mental Retardation and Developmental Disabilities, 31*, 86–114.

Willoughby, J., & Glidden, L. (1995). Fathers helping out: Shared child care and marital satisfaction of parents of children with disabilities. *American Journal on Mental Retardation, 99*, 399–406.

Young, D. M., & Roopnarine, J. L. (1994). Fathers' child care involvement with children with and without disabilities. *Topics in Early Childhood Special Education, 14*, 488–502.

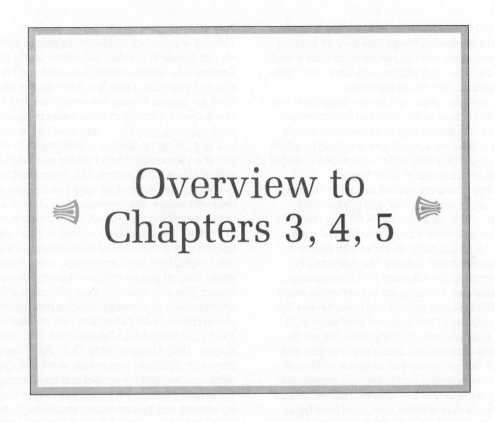

Overview to Chapters 3, 4, 5

Chapters 3, 4, and 5 describe the important process of developing instructional programs for students with severe disabilities. Many phases are involved, from assessing the student through developing an individualized education program (IEP), putting it into place, and evaluating the progress on IEP goals and objectives. Each student is unique, and you must individualize the process for each student. To help you understand the material more readily, we apply many of the concepts in the chapter to three students: Timothy, Jenny, and Christine. These students differ in their ages, instructional settings, abilities and disabilities, and behavioral characteristics.

 Timothy, Jenny, and Christine

Like their peers, students with extensive support needs benefit from learning useful skills, from having social connections with others their age, and from belonging to and actively participating in groups (Billingsley, Gallucci, Peck, Schwartz, & Staub, 1996; Staub, Schwartz, Gallucci, & Peck, 1994). These three basic needs—skills, relationships, and membership—should not be a surprise: They are the same for all people. The presence of severe disabilities does not negate such needs, though the challenges for meeting them may be greater.

Timmy does not initiate greetings or play with others, but he knows how to wave when prompted and will play alone with blocks for long periods of time. He has just joined a preschool of children his age who do not have autism. His parents and teachers are hoping that this context will enable him to learn how to interact with and engage in parallel and cooperative play with others his age. Timothy also participates in one-to-one instruction at home.

Jenny is a member of Ms. Alpern's fifth-grade class and just joined Girl Scouts this year. Her classmates and the other girls in her Girl Scout troop know that Jenny has more difficulty remembering things than they do but also that memory strategies, such as her personal daily schedule and calendar, which use picture reminders, a number line, and a calculator, help her to remember.

Christine, like many others with severe disabilities, has spent most of her school years attending self-contained classrooms with little opportunity to interact with nondisabled peers at school. As a result, she is lacking in school friends, in taking part in social activities with peers, and in the social skills characteristic of older teens.

In the next three chapters, we will use three student outcomes (i.e., skills, membership, and relationships; Billingsley et al., 1996) as a framework for describing the principles that teams follow as they develop and implement educational programs for students with severe disabilities in inclusive school settings. The outcomes for which team members aim influence the curriculum and the methods they use. Attending school alongside peers without disabilities creates options and opportunities that do not exist in separate, "handicapped only" settings. It also changes teachers' roles in many ways. We will describe how these changes can create opportunities and reduce barriers. We recognize that while the number of schools practicing meaningful inclusion has increased in recent years, the majority of students with severe disabilities still experience very isolated lives apart from typical classmates (F. Brown & Michaels, 2003), detached from peers in community activities and at work, and accompanied primarily by their family members or by paid companions. It is true that these patterns of segregated association and education are currently balanced in our country with laws to prevent discrimination against people with disabilities and to create the less restrictive educational environments (Bateman & Linden, 1998). Still, the widespread prevalence of their isolation seems to be maintained both by beliefs that separation is better and by rigid traditions, such as special buildings, programs designed for labeled groups of people, and the methods educators use to place students with disabilities. Another strong force, one that blocks movement toward inclusion, is the confusion that comes with inexperience and the anticipation of change. As Norm Kunc (1991) has expressed it, "Don't confuse 'I don't know how to do it' with 'it's not a good idea.'" These next three chapters—and much of the entire book—are written to address this confusion and to teach readers how to educate students with severe disabilities in inclusive school settings.

In addition to this framework of desirable student outcomes (i.e., relationships, membership, and skills) in the organization of the next three chapters, three students, 4-year-old Timothy, 10-year-old Jenny, and 20-year-old Christine, help us illustrate and explain the concepts we introduce.

Timothy

Timothy, 4 years old, has been diagnosed with autism. He has severe intellectual disabilities and is nonverbal. Timothy lives at home with his parents and his older sister, who is 7 years old. Timothy is a handsome little boy who does not appear to have any disabilities until he engages in any one of a variety of stereotyped behaviors (e.g., hand flapping, jumping up and down) or ritualistic behaviors (e.g., lining up objects, repeatedly watching one section of a videotape). When Timothy was diagnosed with autism at age 2, his mother, Ms. Simms, explored a variety of educational models that were available for young children with autism. Ms. Simms's exploration of autism involved searching the Internet for information on autism. To her delight, there was easy access to chat rooms and list Listservs on autism as well as an abundance of information ranging from basic knowledge about autism to finding family support groups and even how to sue your school district. She also went to a local bookstore and found a whole section of recently published books addressing young children with autism and their families (e.g., Cohen, 1998; L. K. Koegel & LaZebnik, 2004; R. L. Koegel & Koegel, 1995; Maurice, 1996; Quill, 2000; Sandall & Schwartz, 2002). As she started to sift through all the material, she realized the conflict and controversy that existed in the field. Perhaps the only area in which there was agreement was that education should begin as early as possible and should be intensive (Cohen, 1998). However, how intensive and what it looked like varied greatly.

Ms. Simms's decision about the best program for Timothy was a difficult one. Each model that she read about seemed to have advantages, focusing on different but important aspects of development. Each boasted successes. What was especially difficult was that most of the special education professionals she approached seemed to promote their own model to the exclusion of the others. Professionals were not offering Ms. Simms an integrated, individually determined model for Timothy. Rather, each professional described how Timothy could fit into their model.

After much stress and anxiety about what the best course would be, Timothy's family finally decided to put several pieces together, regardless of the individual messages they received from professionals. The new program that they designed consisted of 10 hours each week of one-to-one intensive discrete trial instruction at home, delivered by a specially trained graduate student; 3 hours each day in an inclusive preschool program; and two 1-hour sessions each week with a speech and language therapist at a clinic.

Jenny

Jenny is an expressive and energetic fifth grader who experienced trauma during birth, resulting in some degree of neurological impairment. Her seizure disorder causes significant short-term memory difficulties that affect her learning. Her basic academic skills—reading, spelling, and math—are at a mid-first-grade level. Jenny's accommodations include use of a calculator, a math facts chart, a written/pictorial schedule, and oral and typed responses in place of written responses. A full-time teaching assistant works with Jenny and others in the classroom. Jenny participates with the fifth grade except for three periods: a daily one-to-one reading tutorial with her special education teacher, alternate activities in place of social studies twice weekly with a small group and the assistant, and speech and phonemic awareness with a speech teacher twice weekly.

Jenny enjoys social interactions and works well with peers during cooperative activities (with little adult involvement). Jenny is very involved in school activities and frequently invites friends to her home to play. Her classmates have been given some very basic information to help explain how Jenny learns and why she engages in certain behaviors.

Sometimes when Jenny feels "overloaded" she engages in a rapid display of hand and arm movements— these interfere with peer social interactions. Her teacher is working with her to recognize these situations and request a "break" to change her environment and activity instead of engaging in these hand and arm movements. Across time, Jenny's ability to attend to group directions, take turns as part of a group activity, and participate in a multiple step task has greatly improved.[1]

Christine

Christine, who turned 20 last spring, is actively involved in the transition from school to adulthood. She has a winning personality and often jokes around with others, but she also has clear viewpoints and preferences about her daily and weekly activities, her friends, and her life. Her school day is divided between the community and post–high school program, which is based at a nearby university. Because she has cerebral palsy, she uses a wheelchair for much of the day and uses a variety of means to communicate: sounds, facial expressions, gestures, words, yes or no responses, and a computerized, portable communication device. Christine has limited vision, which, along with her cerebral palsy, means she must often depend on others for help. It is her communication skills that enable her to have ongoing active involvement in "running her life" by making choices, indicating her preferences, expressing her feelings, and sharing her perspective with her family, friends, and team. Her communication device, a Dynavox, has a low-volume auditory scanning system that allows Christine to listen and then select her response with a hand-operated switch; she is learning to efficiently select the relevant category of responses from

a menu of communication categories, organized with options that fit her daily life. She scans the choices and selects, activating a spoken response. It has taken Christine and her team a long time to identify, refine, and use this complex system, and the system continues to grow to reflect changes and growth in Christine's life.

Christine's IEP is geared to her transition needs: finding a job she likes and can be actively involved in, learning the job and its related skills (e.g., interacting with others, understanding job responsibility, taking care of her personal needs at the work site), using community services and leisure options, and getting ready to exit school services and enter the adult service system. She also participates in the university drama club and the pep group and eats often at several campus spots. Christine is involved with Best Buddies (**http://www.bestbuddies.org/home. asp**), a national organization that helps universities and other groups organize to "match" typical people with people who have mental retardation for the purpose of friendship. The Best Buddies group at the university has been in place for several years; students engage in activities (athletic and music events, pizza and movie parties, and just hanging out) as in buddy pairs and in small groups during the academic year.[2]

References

Bateman, B. D., & Linden, M. A. (1998). *Better IEPs* (3rd ed.). Longmont, CO: Sopris West.

Billingsley, F. F., Gallucci, C., Peck, C. A., Schwartz, I. S., & Staub, D. (1996). "But those kids can't even do math": An alternative conceptualization of outcomes for inclusive education. *The Special Education Leadership Review, 3*, 43–56.

Brown, F., & Michaels, C. A. (2003). The shaping of inclusion: Efforts in Detroit and other urban settings. In D. Fisher & N. Frey (Eds.), *Inclusive urban schools* (pp. 231-243). Baltimore: Paul H. Brookes.

Cohen, S. (1998). *Targeting autism: What we know, don't know, and can do to help young children with autism and related disorders.* Berkeley: University of California Press.

Koegel, L. K., & LaZebnik, C. (2004). *Overcoming autism*. New York: Viking.

Koegel, R. L., & Koegel, L. K. (1995). *Teaching children with autism: Strategies for initiating positive interactions and improving learning opportunities.* Baltimore: Paul H. Brookes.

Kunc, N. (1991, April). *Integration: Being realistic isn't realistic.* Speech presented at the On Common Ground Conference, Virginia Statewide Systems Change Project, Charlottesville, VA.

---

[1]Jenny's case was contributed by Maria Beck.

[2]Christine and her parents provided her case information with additional input from others who know her well.

Maurice, C. (Ed.). (1996). *Behavioral intervention for young children with autism*. Austin, TX: PRO-ED.

Quill, K. A. (2000). *Do-watch-listen-say: Social and communication intervention for children with autism*. Baltimore: Paul H. Brookes.

Sandall, S. R., & Schwartz, I. S. (2002). *Building blocks for teaching preschoolers with special needs*. Baltimore: Paul H. Brookes.

Staub, D., Schwartz, I. S., Gallucci, C., & Peck, C. A. (1994). *Four portraits of friendship at an inclusive school. Journal of the Association for Persons with Severe Handicaps, 19*, 314-325.

3

Meaningful Assessment

Fredda Brown
Martha E. Snell
Donna Lehr

The Importance of Assessment

Because assessment outcomes influence so many aspects of a student's educational experience, the development of an assessment process that produces meaningful and usable results is critical. There are many reasons that assessments are conducted and still more ways in which the results are used in the development of educational programs. Some assessment strategies contribute to the development of sound educational programs, while others may yield information that is less helpful or that is perhaps even an obstacle to the development of high-quality educational programs.

Traditionally, classification and placement decisions in special education have relied on assessments of intellectual functioning (H. R. Turnbull & Turnbull, 2000), academic achievement, and perceptual-motor skills (Gresham, 1983). However, these types of assessments for students with severe disabilities fail to provide useful information to educators (Downing & Perino, 1992; Silberman & Brown, 1998). Understanding how an assessment can be used inappropriately is as important as

understanding its appropriate use. Usually, it is not the instruments themselves that are inappropriate but rather the applications of the assessment information derived from them. The importance of appropriate assessment has been stressed by the Council for Exceptional Children (CEC) (2004) in their recently issued "Policy on Assessment and Accountability." The rationale for such a statement recognizes the "important role that standardized and other student assessments play in documenting educational accountability, and in ensuring sound educational decisions are made toward achieving the highest possible academic standards" (p. 70).

Unfortunately, it is not possible to recommend only one or two comprehensive assessment instruments. Students with severe disabilities are likely to have many areas of skill development where assessment is of value (e.g., mobility, daily living skills, language, social interactions, quality of life, relationships, and community skills), but no single instrument can measure this wide range of skills. Thus, assessing students with severe disabilities requires an interdisciplinary team effort at all phases of the assessment process, including selecting

TABLE 3–1

Sample of Nondiscriminatory Evaluation Procedures

Standard	Description	Reference in IDEA
Cultural bias	• Tests and materials are not to be discriminatory on a racial or cultural basis	20 U.S.C. § 1414(b)(3)(A)(1)
	• Tests and materials are provided and administered in the student's native language or other mode of communication unless it is not feasible to do so.	20 U.S.C. § 1414(b)(3)(A)(ii)
Test validity and administration	• Tests must be validated for the specific purpose for which they are used.	20 U.S.C. § 1414(b)(3)(B)
	• Tests must be administered by trained and knowledgeable personnel.	
	• Tests must be administered in accordance with any instructions from the producers.	
Evaluation process	• Use a variety of tools and strategies to gather relevant functional and developmental information to determine whether the student has a disability, and the content of the IEP, including information that enables the student to participate in the general curriculum.	20 U.S.C. § 1414(b)(2)(A)
	• Must not use any single procedure as the sole criterion to determine presence of disability, or, if so, student's appropriate education.	20 U.S.C. § 1414(b)(2)(B)
	• Use technically sound instruments to assess across four domains: cognitive, behavioral, physical, and developmental factors.	20 U.S.C. § 1414(b)(2)(C)
	• Use tools and strategies that assist the team directly in determining that the student's educational needs are satisfied.	20 U.S.C. § 1414(b)(3)(D)
	• Review existing evaluation data, classroom-based assessments and observations, and teacher and related services observations.	20 U.S.C. § 1414(C)(1)(A)
Parent participation	• Parents must be members of the evaluation team.	20 U.S.C. § 1414(d)(1)(B)
	• Parents must be given a copy of the evaluation report and documentation concerning eligibility (or lack of).	
	• Parents may submit to the team and require it to consider evaluations and information that they initiate or provide.	
Parent consent	• Parents may give or withhold consent to initial evaluation, all reevaluations, and any exit evaluation.	20 U.S.C. § 1414(c)(3)
	• If the school has taken reasonable measures to secure parent consent and if parents have failed to respond to the school's request for consent, the school then may evaluate the student.	20 U.S.C. § 1414(a)(1)(C), and (C)(3)
	• If the parents refuse to give consent, the school may go to mediation or a "due process hearing" to evaluate the student.	20 U.S.C. § 1414(a)(1)(C)
Reevaluation	• Must occur at least every 3 years.	20 U.S.C. § 1414(a)(2)(A)
	• Must occur, if "conditions warrant" it, more often than every 3 years (e.g., a dramatic improvement or deterioration in the student).	
	• Must occur if the student's parents or teacher requests it, because they may have or need new information about the student to make the student's special education more effective.	

Note: Adapted, with permission, from Turnbull, H. R.,(III) & Turnbull, A.P. (1998). *Free appropriate public education: The law and children with disabilities* (5th ed.). Denver: Love.

the assessments, conducting the assessments, interpreting the results, and determining program priorities. Nor is it possible to rely on commercially available assessments. Assessments should reflect each student's strengths and needs and his or her unique social, emotional, and physical environment. No single commer-

cially available assessment is capable of capturing this information for the wide range of learners with severe disabilities. Thus, teachers must also design assessments that can be individualized for each learner.

The types of assessments that professionals perceive as appropriate and meaningful are strongly influenced

Box 3–1 Assessment and Evaluation Practices Required by IDEA

- Team must include parents and student, special educators, specialists, and regular educators who are responsible for evaluation, program delivery, monitoring, and placement decisions.
- Parent participation in assessment must be increased.
- Evaluation must be linked to the IEP and program.
- Evaluation must take into account the student's participation in general curriculum.
- Classroom-based data must be generated and considered.
- Assessment must focus equality on four domains, cognitive, behavioral, physical, and developmental.
- Teams must use "tools and strategies" that indicate whether the school is meeting the student 's educational needs.
- Teams must use bias-free assessment instruments and procedures.
- Parent and teacher observation must be reflected in the assessment data that teams gather and use.

Note: Adapted with permission from Turnbull, H.R., & Turnbull, A.P. (1998) *Free appropriate public education: The law and children with disabilities* (5th ed.). Denver: Love, p. 115.

by three variables. First, the purpose of the inquiry and the ways in which the assessment data are to be used determine which instruments are appropriate. Second, the team's educational philosophy determines the educational goals seen as appropriate. A third variable that influences the content and use of assessment is the legal requirements for assessment. The Individuals with Disabilities Education Act (IDEA) requires a multidisciplinary, multifaceted, nonbiased evaluation before classifying a student as eligible for special education services and providing special education (H. R. Turnbull & Turnbull, 2000). Additionally, IDEA requires the assessment of progress of students on individually determined goals and objectives. Table 3–1 reflects the assessment and evaluation standards and procedures that are set forth by IDEA. The No Child Left Behind Act (NCLB) also specifies legal requirements for assessment, stating that all students, including those with severe disabilities, must be assessed relative to statewide academic standards.

This chapter reviews assessment issues and practices as they relate to individuals with severe disabilities. Specifically, it discusses the purposes of assessment and the types of assessment used for these purposes, the relationship between assessment and program planning, and, most important, meaningful assessment of learning and life quality (see Box 3–1).

Definitions of Disability

The issues of testing and assessment are integrally related to the definition of disability. While definitions of disability provide the basis from which identification practices evolve, Ysseldyke and Algozzine (2000)

caution us about the use and effects of labels, as labels are a simple way to confirm that individuals in our society differ from each other. It follows then that definitions of disability and evaluation strategies evolve to reflect changing societal values, attitudes, and expectations (Thompson et al., 2004; White, 1985; Ysseldyke & Algozzine, 2000). This evolution is illustrated by changes in the definition of mental retardation over the past two decades. In 1983, mental retardation was defined as "significantly subaverage general intellectual functioning existing concurrently with deficits in adaptive behavior and manifested during the developmental period" (Grossman, 1983, p. 1). This definition revised earlier ones that did not include the criteria of adaptive behavior (Heber, 1959, 1961).

The addition of the concept of adaptive behavior resulted in a significant change in assessment practices. No longer was mental retardation evaluated exclusively on the basis of measurement of "intelligence." Additional information was necessary regarding adaptive behaviors and required the gathering of more meaningful and relevant information. This change expanded the types of instruments used to measure the behavior of individuals with disabilities and added a new dimension to assessment, that is, the measure of an individual's adaptation to environmental demands.

More recently, an ecological viewpoint has become the basis for defining individuals with disabilities. For example, The Association for Persons with Severe Handicaps (TASH) (2000) defines individuals with severe disabilities as follows:

These persons include individuals with disabilities of all ages, races, creeds, national origins, genders and sexual orientation who require ongoing support in one or more major life activities in order to participate in an integrated community and enjoy a quality of life similar to that available to all citizens. Support may be required for life activities such as mobility, communication, self-care, and learning as necessary for community living, employment and self-sufficiency.

TASH (2000), in response to the negative impact of using a label such as *severe disabilities,* chose to move away from defining people by specific personal characteristics and instead characterized these individuals with disabilities in relation to societal attitudes and treatment. Individuals with severe disabilities are further described by TASH as being those who are characterized as follows:

* Are most at risk for being excluded from the mainstream of society
* Are perceived by traditional service systems as being most challenging
* Are most likely to have their rights abridged
* Are most likely to be at risk for living, working, playing, and/or learning in segregated environments
* Are least likely to have the tools and opportunities necessary to advocate on their own behalf
* Historically have been labeled as having severe disabilities
* Are most likely to need ongoing, individualized supports in order to participate in inclusive communities and enjoy a quality of life similar to that available to all citizens

In 2002, the American Association on Mental Retardation (AAMR) revised its definition to reflect changing views about individuals with cognitive disabilities:

Mental retardation is a disability characterized by significant limitations both in intellectual functioning and in adaptive behavior as expressed in conceptual, social, and practical adaptive skills. The disability originates before age 18. (Luckasson et al., 2002, p. 1)

In this definition, an individual's disability is both related to their intellectual and adaptive behavior and influenced by the context within which an individual lives: the immediate social setting, the neighborhood, the community, and the culture and supports provided in these contexts. AAMR continues to place an emphasis on assessing the level and type of individualized *supports* needed by the person to function in the

home, school, and community. Luckasson et al. (2002) refer to five assumptions essential to the application of this definition:

1. Limitations in present functioning must be considered within the context of community environments typical of the individual's age peers and culture.
2. Valid assessment considers cultural and linguistic diversity, as well as differences in communication, sensory, motor, and behavioral factors.
3. Within an individual, limitations often coexist with strengths.
4. An important purpose of describing limitations is to develop a profile of needed supports.
5. With appropriate personalized supports over a sustained period, the life functioning of the person with mental retardation generally will improve. (p. 1)

In the new AAMR Supports Intensity Scale (Thompson et al., 2004), supports refer to those resources and strategies (e.g., individuals, money or other tangible assets, assistive devices, or environments) that enable individuals with developmental disabilities to live meaningful lives in integrated community settings. According to Thompson et al. (2004), implications of the supports paradigm are the need to:

(a) identify, describe, and understand people in regard to their pattern and intensity of supports needs, and
(b) focus on planning and service delivery on providing supports that reduce the gap between an individual's level of personal competence and the demands of the settings in which the person participates. (p. 6)

This new assessment approach is not based on a philosophy of deficits but rather on the philosophy of personalized support: people with intellectual disabilities have *support needs* that should be identified and used to guide planning and service delivery. This support philosophy increases the likelihood that each individual will participate more fully in a self-determined and independent life (Thompson et al., 2002).

Purposes of Assessment

Different types of assessments provide different types of information. Just as teachers should select an educational intervention to match the particular targeted

TABLE 3–2

Varying Purposes and Characteristics of Assessment in the Education of Student with Severe Disabilities

Assessment Purpose	Types of assessment	Primary assessors	Time of assessment
Screening	• Newborn and infant measures • Motor and sensory functioning measures • Specific domains	• Medical staff • Occupational, physical, and speech therapists • Psychologists	• Early in child's life • After head injury
Diagnosis and placement	• IQ tests • Adaptive behavior tests • Motor and sensory functioning tests	• Psychologist or educational specialist • Occupational, physical, or speech therapists	• Early in the child's life • After head injury
Curriculum and program development	• Ecological analysis • Adaptive behavior tests • Task analysis assessment • Alternate statewide assessment	• Educational team • Psychologists	• Throughout school years at regular intervals
Evaluation • Student progress	• Direct observation of IEP behaviors and skills under criterion conditions • Training and probe data	• Teacher • Educational team	• Daily, weekly, or biweekly
• Quality of life • Program	• Program evaluations • Quality of life evaluations	• Educational team	• Biannually, annually, or as determined by team

skills, so teachers should select an assessment to match the purpose. Assessments are used to gain information for the purposes of screening, placement, curriculum development, and student evaluation (cf. Browder, 2000; Salvia & Ysseldyke, 2004). The professionals involved in each of these areas, the instruments or strategies used, and the timings of the measurements vary according to the purpose of the assessment. Table 3–2 describes these variations.

Screening

A screening test is a broad and quickly administered measure used to determine whether students are significantly different from their peers and require further evaluation, not to obtain information to make instructional decisions or to determine why a problem exists. Medical personnel and psychologists use screening instruments with young children who are delayed in their development to determine if in-depth assessment is needed and whether referral for evaluation to determine eligibility for special programs or related services (e.g., speech, physical, or occupational therapy) is warranted (Browder, 2000). Students with

severe or multiple disabilities, however, typically do not go through formal educational screening evaluations, as often their disabilities are obvious (Gaylord-Ross & Holvoet, 1985). For such students, assessment begins with diagnostic testing.

Screening tests cover a variety of areas, including vision, hearing, gross motor, fine motor, and communication skills. Early childhood screening instruments, however, have little value as a child grows older since such instruments focus on the early milestones of normal development. Since many students with severe disabilities do not necessarily follow typical sequences of development or do so at such a delayed pace, assessment of students relative to those milestones does not result in the identification of age-appropriate functional skills appropriate for inclusion in curriculum.

Screening may begin as early as the prenatal period, with the use of chorionic villus sampling, amniocentesis, and alphafetal protein screening to determine the presence of certain chromosomal and genetic disorders and ultrasound to determine the presence of structural anomalies. Immediately following birth, medical staff use screening devices to check for obvious handicapping conditions or genetic and metabolic disorders (White, 1985) and the physiological and behavioral status of the newborn. The Apgar scoring system (Apgar, 1953; Apgar & Beck, 1973) is used to quickly evaluate a newborn's heart rate, respiration, reflexes, muscle tone, and general appearance at 1 minute, 5 minutes, and 10 minutes after birth. The Brazelton Neonatal Behavioral Assessment Scale (BNBAS) (Brazelton & Nugent, 1995) is used to assess the newborn relative to 27 behavioral measures. These general measures assess alertness, activity level, self-quieting activity, smiles, sleep patterns, and specific behaviors (e.g., the newborn's response to environmental stimuli, such as a light, sounds, and a pinprick on the bottom of the foot). The Apgar test and the BNBAS alert hospital staff to newborns who are in distress and signal medical personnel to follow up with more refined evaluations of the health status of the infants. They do not, however, predict long-term outcomes.

Screening instruments for infants and older children vary in terms of the range of skills included. The Denver Developmental Screening Test II (Frankenburg et al., 1990) and the Developmental Profile II (Alpern, Boll, & Shearer, 1986) cover a variety of domains of development, such as personal and social, fine and gross motor, language, and self-help. Other frequently used screening instruments for young children include the Bayley II Developmental Assessment (Bayley, 1993) and the Battelle Developmental Inventory—2nd Edition (Newborg, 2004). (See **http://www.fpnotebook. com/PED48.htm** for a comprehensive listing of screening assessments appropriate for young children.) It is important to remember that the purpose of these screening tests is to determine if further, more precise assessment is needed, not to determine instructional objectives.

Other screening instruments may focus on only one domain of interest, such as vision or hearing. Unfortunately, some screening instruments, such as traditional visual acuity tests, cannot be adequately administered to students with severe disabilities because of the complex verbal instructions or the cognitive discriminations required (Cress et al., 1981). (For an extensive review of assessments of sensory impairments, see Lewis and Russo, 1998.)

Diagnosis and Placement

The next step in the assessment process is further testing of the child to identify the disorder and possible cause of the delay or disorder and to make eligibility, classification, and placement decisions (Salvia & Yesseldyke, 2004). Determination of classification and eligibility is made by the assessment team or the IEP team, which makes its decision on the basis of evidence from several sources, as required by IDEA. IDEA specifies that multifaceted assessment be used for the purpose of determining eligibility for special education services. Once a delay or a disability is suspected, either through screening or observation, diagnostic testing is conducted to learn more specific information about the delays or disabilities. The primary measures used to diagnose individuals with severe disabilities are intelligence tests and tests of adaptive behavior (Snell, 2003). Typically, these tests are administered by psychologists, education specialists, or therapists. Accurate psychological testing is difficult because of potential movement, vision, hearing, and communication challenges as well as possible problems with cooperation during the assessment sessions (Snell, 2003).

Many tools have been developed to identify students on the autism spectrum. The Gilliam Autism Rating Scale (GARS) (Gilliam, 1995), for example, was designed for use by parents, teachers, and other professionals to help identify and diagnose autism in individuals ages 3 through 22 and to estimate the severity of the problem. Other tools that are easily used to determine if a child falls on the autism spectrum include the Checklist for Autism in Toddlers (CHAT) (Baron-Cohen, Allen, & Gillberg,1992) and the Childhood Autism Rating Scale (CARS) (Schopler, Reichler, & Rochen-Renner, 1998). The Autism Diagnostic Observation Checklist (ADOS) (Lord, Rutter, DiLavore, & Risi, 1999) and the Autistic Diagnostic Interview—Revised (ADI-R) (Lord, Rutter, & Le Couteur, 1994) require more specialized training and experience working with students with autism and related disorders.

Curriculum and Program Development

A major purpose of assessment is to gather information useful for the development of an appropriate educational program. This phase of the assessment process is usually coordinated by the teacher, who directly observes and assesses the student and also collects pertinent information from parents, psychologists, and therapists.

Some assessment instruments, such as criterion-referenced tests and certain adaptive behavior scales, are more suited than others for the purpose of determining curriculum content. These assessments provide meaningful information about what should be taught to students. Other instruments, such as intelligence tests, are inappropriate for this purpose—they are designed to measure general intelligence and should not be translated into instructional goals and objectives. In contrast, ecological inventories of functional environments (discussed later in this chapter) are informal instruments that lead to the identification of critical age-appropriate and functional skills for students with severe disabilities and translate readily into curricular content. Assessment instruments should be carefully inspected to determine their intended purposes.

Alternate statewide assessments are specialized types of assessment designed to evaluate students with severe disabilities relative to statewide academic curriculum standards. IDEA requires that all students, including those with severe disabilities, "have access to, participate in, and make progress in the general curriculum" (U.S. Department of Education, 2003), and states are required to include students with severe disabilities in statewide accountability systems designed to measure yearly progress in meeting the state's standards. Since many students with severe disabilities are not able to participate in general statewide assessments, even with accommodations, states have been required to develop alternate methods of assessments for those students and have been permitted to develop alternate standards based on the general education curriculum (U.S. Department of Education, 2003). Results of these assessments provide program planners with information about levels of proficiency of individual students relative to the state's general curriculum standards.

Evaluation

Evaluation is another component of the assessment process. It is not enough to develop an educational program for a student; teams must be accountable for the programs they develop and the impact of the educational program on the student and his or her family. Three important areas of evaluation include the progress the student is making, the impact of the educational program on the student's quality of life, and evaluation of the total educational program.

Student Progress
Evaluation of student progress is a critical form of educational measurement. Teachers are required to include in each student's IEP a statement of how the

student's progress toward each of the specified objectives will be measured and the extent to which that progress is sufficient to enable the student to achieve the annual goals. (See chapter 5 for a review of measurement strategies.) Recently, however, it has been recognized that simple measurements of each student's progress on specific IEP objectives is insufficient. Measurement of broader outcomes (e.g., quality of life) is considered an important part of comprehensive evaluation of educational outcomes.

Quality of Life
Documentation of success on student outcomes has extended beyond the use of quantitative measures of performance and should include qualitative measures as well (Evans & Scotti, 1989; Haring & Breen, 1989; Meyer & Evans, 1993; Meyer & Janney, 1989; Voeltz & Evans, 1983; Wolf, 1978). Many efforts are being made to evaluate each individual's quality of life, but because of the subjective nature of this concept, there are wide variations in opinion on exactly what should be measured. There is, however, growing consensus about what the core quality-of-life dimensions are. These include emotional well-being, interpersonal relations, material well-being, personal development, physical well-being, self-determination, social inclusion, and human rights (Hatton, 1998; Schalock, 1996). Because an individual's quality of life is influenced by the settings and environments in which they participate and the opportunities available to them (Wehmeyer, 1996), assessment strategies must include this range of personal variables.

Program Evaluation
Program evaluation examines the quality of the program (e.g., educational, residential, vocational) offered to an individual and its impact on the individual and, at times, the individual's family. Many times, an individual's lack of progress can be attributed to inadequacy of services provided. It becomes ludicrous to agonize over instructional modifications when the problem is that the educational program itself does not support the target outcomes (e.g., literacy, numeracy, community integration, interdependence). For example, statewide alternate assessments provide data about how well a school district or state is doing in ensuring that students have access to instruction on the statewide curriculum standards or alternate standards based on the general curriculum standards. Some

evaluations may focus on specific aspects of a program. Another example is the Communication Supports Checklist (McCarthy et al., 1998), which assesses a program's settings and practices in terms of its support and respect for meaningful communication for all individuals in the environment. Bailey et al. (1998) suggest that focusing solely on the extent to which a program is implementing its practices is not sufficient. They suggest that focus should shift to the actual results, benefits, and impact on the people whom the practices are supposed to serve.

Factors Related to Meaningful Assessment

To understand assessment, familiarity with certain terms and testing issues is necessary. The following sections introduce specific assessment concepts needed to evaluate the potential utility of various assessment instruments in educational programs.

Test Reliability

Reliability refers to the extent to which a (standardized) instrument is *consistent* in measuring whatever it purports to measure. If an assessment is repeated within a short interval of time, a student should receive the same score or rating. Reliability is usually measured by some form of reliability coefficient, ranging from 0 to 1, or by the standard error of measurement derived from it. Salvia and Ysseldyke (2004) state that tests should have reliability coefficients in excess of .60 if the scores are for administrative purposes or are reported for group scores; however, when tests are used to make decisions regarding individual students, the reliability coefficient should be over .90.

Reliability does not address the content of what is being assessed, only its consistency. A teacher may reliably measure a student's ability to "place pegs in a pegboard within 1 minute" as part of an assessment of vocational readiness. The measure may be very reliable (consistent) across time, and two evaluators may agree on the student's test performance (interrater reliability). Yet, although reliability is established, the skill has no relationship to preparing for a vocation. The concept of reliability does not address the purpose or the content (validity) of what is being measured.

Test Validity

Test validity refers to the extent to which a test measures what it is supposed to measure; in other words, validity concerns the *content* of the test. If a test measures irrelevant information, it lacks validity, and the test results cannot be meaningfully interpreted. For example,

> *Christine's team would like to assess her receptive language skills. But the measure the speech and language pathologist typically uses requires pointing to objects and pictures. The team knows the test results would not be a valid measure of communication since Christine has great difficulty using her hands as a result of cerebral palsy and has limited vision.*

Instead of measuring Christine's receptive language, this test would measure her motor skill of pointing to visual stimuli. Thus, this test lacks *content validity* for this student.

Content validity is also lacking if a test does not sample a broad enough range of skills to determine whether competency is sufficient. If the self-help domain of a particular test includes only toileting, dressing, and brushing hair, the test may be deemed an insufficient measure of a student's general self-help skills. Thus, the test would be judged invalid.

Criterion-related validity refers to the extent to which scores on a test agree with (concurrent validity) or predict (predictive validity) some given criterion measure. For example, if you are questioning the criterion-related validity of a hypothetical "Smith's Test of Adaptive Behavior," you must determine whether the student's score on this test relates to his or her scores on another test that is presumed to be a valid measure of adaptive behavior or whether the score can accurately predict the student's performance in community settings.

Data Gathering

There are three basic methods of gathering assessment information: direct testing, observation in the natural environment, and interviewing. Each of the methods provides different information and has its own advantages and disadvantages.

Direct Testing

Direct testing is a method of data collection that requires the teacher to provide the student with an arranged opportunity to respond to specific stimuli.

The teacher presents the student with certain materials or instructions to determine if the student can perform the target behavior. Direct testing may occur in either isolated settings or in more natural settings.

Timothy's teacher takes him into the bathroom; provides a toothbrush, toothpaste, cup, and towel; and then asks him to brush his teeth. His teacher then observes what components of the task he performs.

Although this approach enables his teacher to observe whether Timothy brushes his teeth in an appropriate setting and with the same materials used at home, Timothy is being assessed on his ability to perform toothbrushing when he is told to do so, not whether he brushes his teeth at appropriate times.

To the greatest extent possible, direct testing should occur in the criterion environment (where the skill is naturally used), at the appropriate times, and using the criterion materials. If his teacher were to assess Timothy by bringing him into the classroom and providing him with an electric toothbrush instead of the regular toothbrush he typically uses at home, the information gathered likely would not be representative of how he brushes his teeth at home.

When using the direct testing approach, a contrived opportunity is arranged for the student to demonstrate a specific skill or behavior. At times, this is a difficult approach to use because some behaviors do not naturally occur or do not occur frequently enough in a classroom, but they are still important to assess.

Jenny's teacher wants to assess her skill in handling money. Although the criterion environment is the school cafeteria, her teacher first uses direct testing to gather information in the classroom to get a general idea of Jenny's skill. The teacher keeps in mind, however, that Jenny's performance in the classroom may be different from what it would be in the school cafeteria. If Jenny demonstrates the desired skill in the classroom, her teacher will then conduct a second, more contextually valid assessment of the skill in the school cafeteria.

A disadvantage of this approach is that often the test cues, conditions, and materials are only similar to, not the same as, those found in the natural environments. The differences may affect a student's test performance negatively, making it unclear whether further instruction is needed. In the money handling example, the teacher can arrange to use some of the same materials that are used in the cafeteria when she tests Jenny in the classroom (e.g., one-dollar and five-dollar bills, Jenny's wallet); however, there may not be much that her teacher can do to replicate the great numbers of students on the cafeteria food line or the impatient cashier that awaits her at the end of the line.

Observation in the Natural Environment

Observation in the natural environment is a method of data collection in which the teacher observes the student in the setting where a behavior naturally occurs and with people whom the child is familiar. This is especially important for children with severe disabilities whose performance may be very different in unfamiliar settings, with unfamiliar examiners, and using unfamiliar materials (Nelson, van Dijk, McDonnell, & Thompson, 2002). The major advantage of assessing a student in the natural environment is that the teacher may observe more typical performance of the target skill and a wider range of related behaviors than in the more contrived testing situation previously described. In other words, the teacher can see if the student demonstrates associated skills, such as movement to the location of the activity, initiation of the skill, ability to find solutions to problems that arise in the natural environment, and social behaviors.

Christine and a peer from her drama club, along with her teaching assistant, went to the mall to find a certain type of makeup that they needed for an upcoming production. Her special education teacher and her teaching assistant planned to assess several of Christine's skills and routines while at the mall (e.g., purchasing from a store, ordering and eating in the food court). Her teacher knew Christine's skills ordering and eating lunch in the school cafeteria; however, she was interested in determining her skill at the food court, where there were many unknown variables. For example, at the food court, Christine would not know the food server, the waiting line would be made up of people whom she did not know, different food choices would be available, and she would have to solve the problem when the food options on her communication device did not match the pictures of the food choices available.

To increase the value of data gathering in the natural environment, observations should sample a range of all the relevant settings (e.g., classroom, home, playground, bathroom) at appropriate times of the day (e.g., before or after lunch, morning, afternoon), using criterion arrangements (e.g., group, one-to-one, free play). Because each of these variables may influence the student's performance, observations over several days are the preferred method to obtain data that accurately represent the student's ability.

One disadvantage of observing in the natural environment is that the relevant behavior may not occur at the time of the observation. For example, a teacher may decide to take a student into the community to assess the appropriateness of his response to strangers. The ideal way of assessing this would obviously be to take the student to a mall and observe his behavior if a stranger were to approach him; however, there is a good chance that no stranger will approach on that particular day at that particular time. Furthermore, purposely allowing a student to be in a vulnerable situation where a stranger may approach may be dangerous and unethical.

Interviewing

Some assessments require that information be obtained by interviewing others who know the student well. The Adaptive Behavior Scales (Lambert, Nihira, & Leland, 1993; Nihira, Leland, & Lambert, 1993) and the Vineland Adaptive Behavioral Scales (Sparrow, Balla, & Cicchetti, 1984) are two assessments of adaptive behavior that obtain information by interview. O'Neill et al. (1997) use an interview format for one component of their comprehensive assessment of problem behaviors.

Interviews may be with family members, staff from a supported living arrangement (if the student does not live at home), current and past teachers, the student, or any other person who knows the student well. The major advantage with interviews is that the information provided by the informants is likely to reflect the student's typical performance in natural settings with naturally occurring cues and consequences. The major disadvantage is that the interview data may be less accurate and more subjective than direct observation.

Interviewing family members is an informative strategy for finding out about the activities in which a family engages, parents' preferences for particular activities, and student likes and dislikes. Used in conjunction with the other types of information gathering, educators can become more knowledgeable about the student's home environment. This method is also a constructive way of involving parents in the program and letting them know that their input is critical for the development of a sound educational program. It is important, however, that the interview process and the information gathering be done in a culturally sensitive manner and be respectful of families from diverse cultural backgrounds (Chen & Dote-Kwan, 1998). Researchers in the area of positive behavior supports are increasingly focusing on the need for including families in the functional behavioral assessment process and the collaborative development of behavior intervention plans. These researchers stress the importance of family values and beliefs in the development of behavior intervention plans that are contextually compatible with family routines and practices (Albin, Lucyshyn, Horner, & Flannery, 1996; Moes & Frea, 2000).

If family members, for whatever reason, are not available for an interview, other strategies should be implemented to try to facilitate meaningful participation. Some families may be more available for a phone interview, and others may prefer to complete and return a written questionnaire. If a written questionnaire is used, it should be simple to complete, not lengthy, presented in the family's native language, and culturally sensitive. This brief questionnaire should be designed to assess the family's ideas and priorities concerning their child's present and future needs at home, at school, and in the community. Variables such as student preferences and dislikes and the family routines and the child's participation in these routines are important to assess and will be critical for the development of a meaningful educational program. Completing such questionnaires before an IEP meeting prepares family members to reflect on functional educational outcomes that are relevant in current and potential future environments.

Scoring

Assessment scoring systems vary widely. Some tests require a simple dichotomous response (e.g., "yes" the student has the skill or "no" the student does not have the skill), while other instruments require more complex or multiple-level responses on dimensions such as degrees of independence (e.g., can do skill given no assistance, minimal assistance, maximum assistance) or frequency (e.g., can do the skill never, some of the time, frequently, or always).

Each approach serves different purposes. The dichotomous scoring method (e.g., yes or no) represents broad student outcomes or skill mastery. This is important in some contexts. For example, when assessing a skill in the community, we may wish to learn whether a student either has or has not mastered the entire skill sufficiently for independent use. If the student can cross a street only "some of the time," certainly the teacher would conclude that this does not represent a sufficient level of mastery! In this case, a dichotomous scoring method is appropriate.

Further, if teachers are interested in what students can do independently in natural settings, then scoring must be related to meaningful units of behavior (F. Brown, Evans, Weed, & Owen, 1987; F. Brown & Lehr, 1993), such as making a choice, communicating, or demonstrating a social interaction skill, and represent meaningful partial participation (Baumgart et al., 1982). A teacher then knows that an increase in a total score indicates an increase in the functional competence of the person being assessed.

In contrast to the dichotomous scoring method, the multiple-level scoring method is most appropriate for monitoring student progress in an instructional program. In terms of instruction, progressing from performing a skill with maximum assistance to performing the same skill with minimum assistance may be significant for a student just learning that skill. Thus, a scoring system sensitive to small student changes in independence or to consistency of performance is most appropriate and provides information that a teacher needs to determine the adequacy of the instructional interventions.

Norm-Referenced Assessments

Norm-referenced tests determine the extent of deviation from the norm and are standardized around the average score of the normative group so that half the sample scores above the average score and half scores below it (Lewis & Russo, 1998). These measures usually compare the performance of students with disabilities to nondisabled students of the same age. Norm-referenced measures allow the evaluator to determine whether a given student is developing the same skills as the majority of students in the normative sample.

As these assessments use the normal sequence of development to determine which skills an individual should be achieving, they are considered to follow a *developmental approach*. Using this approach, prevalent in the early 1970s (Browder, 2000), the mental age

(MA) of a student was determined by comparing his or her skills to the age at which a normally developing child acquired those skills. The educational needs of persons with severe disabilities was then thought to be best met by focusing on the mental age as derived from the developmental assessment (Browder et al., 2004). Justification for this approach rests on at least three assumptions: (a) normal development constitutes the most logical ordering of behaviors, (b) many behaviors within normal development are prerequisite behaviors, and (c) behaviors acquired by a nondisabled child are appropriate measures for an individual with a disability who is at the same developmental level (Guess & Noonan, 1982).

IQ Tests

The IQ test is the most popular norm-referenced test, and along with adaptive behavior scales, it typically makes up the diagnostic component of assessment. IQ tests are designed to measure learning ability, or "intellectual capacity." "Intelligence," however, is a construct that one infers from a person's performance (Salvia & Ysseldyke, 2004), so the practice of assigning numeric values to a construct (e.g., IQ score) and using these numbers to make important decisions is questionable to many professionals. Intelligence tests sample behaviors such as discrimination, generalization, motor behavior, vocabulary, inductive reasoning, comprehension, sequencing, detail recognition, understanding of analogies, abstract reasoning, memory, and pattern completion (Salvia & Ysseldyke, 2004).

Some frequently used IQ tests are the Bayley Scales of Infant Developmental II (Bayley, 2003), McCarthy Scales of Children's Ability (McCarthy, 1972), Stanford-Binet Intelligence Scales (5th edition) (Roid, 2003), Wechsler Intelligence Scale for Children, Fourth Edition (Wechsler, 2003), and Wechsler Preschool and Primary Scale of Intelligence Revised (Wechsler, 2002).

There are many problems in administering IQ tests to students with disabilities and in applying the test results. Certainly, the more severe an individual's disability, the less appropriate is the application of an IQ test. Few, if any, standardized intelligence tests include students with severe disabilities in their normative samples (Sigafoos, Cole, & McQuarter, 1987). Often, and for various reasons, students with severe or profound disabilities are unable to score on these tests; consequently, infant intelligence tests are sometimes used for students with severe disabilities who are not in infancy (Evans, 1991; Gaylord-Ross & Holvoet, 1985). The inappropriateness of intelligence tests is then further exacerbated by the lack of age appropriateness. Evans (1991) reflects:

> *Extrapolation of scores or the derivation of IQ scores from scales designed for use with infants or for other special purposes is an especially hazardous practice that provides some continued professional expectation that scores can be meaningfully assigned to people falling within the lower ranges. (p. 40)*

Another major disadvantage is the misuse of the information that intelligence tests provide. They are used to make decisions about students and services on the basis of very limited data, and they are inappropriately used to measure student progress.

Much legal controversy exists over the use of intelligence tests in special education. In litigation, such as *Mills v. Board of Education* (1972), *Hobson v. Hansen* (1967), and *Larry P. v. Riles* (1984), courts ruled that exclusion or grouping of students on the basis of standardized tests is unconstitutional.

Developmental Scales

There are several advantages to using developmental scales in the assessment process. Developmental test items are written in observable terms, so presence or absence of a skill can usually be determined reliably. For students with sensory or movement disabilities, however, developmental items must be adapted so that the disability does not prevent assessment of the actual ability being tested. Student progress on the measures can then be noted by periodic administration of the instrument.

Developmental scales give information on functioning in various skill areas, and because skills are listed chronologically, they may provide direction for the next skills to be taught, especially for young children. When used for educational assessment, the items that a student can and cannot do are determined. The first items that a student cannot do are then targeted for intervention. Finally, the familiarity of many disciplines with normal developmental theory may increase communication among disciplines.

There are, however, many problems with applying the developmental approach to students with severe and profound disabilities. First, this approach assumes that the sequences of behavior typical of nondisabled

students are relevant for students with severe or profound disabilities. However, a person with disabilities may develop in a different sequence or may skip skills typically demonstrated by normally developing students. Prostheses or environmental adaptations may render demonstration of typical developmental sequences unnecessary. For example, White (1985) points out that although head control is a prerequisite for normal walking, it is not a prerequisite for use of a motorized wheelchair. Therefore, although the student may have failed the head control item included in an assessment, the evaluator should not stop probing higher-level gross motor skills. Given individualized adaptations, this student may score on many other more advanced skills while failing more basic skills.

Second, because the developmental approach assumes that certain behaviors must be present before other behaviors can be acquired, the results may influence some teachers to instruct students on skills that are neither age appropriate nor functional for adapting to their daily environments (Guess & Noonan, 1982) and that lead to lower expectations. For example, a 15-year-old student who has severe disabilities may fail the item "points to parts of doll" on the Bayley Scales of Infant Development (Bayley, 1993), an item that is usually passed by babies by the time they are 26 months. Instruction on this skill would require materials that are not appropriate for a 15-year-old student, and it is a skill that would have little relevance for that student. Focus on these types of assessment items would naturally have an impact on our expectations of students. Linehan, Brady, and Hwang (1991) found that assessment reports based on developmental measures led respondents to have lower expectations for individuals with severe disabilities than did reports based on functional, ecological approaches.

A third potential danger is that skills are sometimes not assessed within the context of functional routines. Take, for example, the skill of grasping—generally considered an important skill. However, unless grasping is related to other skills or functional contexts, it has little meaning. Grasping of a brush during grooming, a spoon while eating, or a toy during play provides more contextually relevant assessment information than does grasping of a 2-inch wooden dowel. Likewise, "scans objects" is important when it is related to materials used in daily routines (e.g., scan the workbooks to find the one with your name on it, scan the DVDs to find one you like).

Fourth, the purpose for assessing a skill may not be apparent and therefore lead to inappropriate assessment, administration, and interpretation of results.

Some developmental test items, for example, appear simply because of their high reliability at certain ages, such as the classic item of "imitating a bridge built of three 1-inch cubes." However, what ability this item actually is meant to test is not clear (White, 1985). If it is used to assess the fine motor ability of a student, then a child who has little fine motor control or is unable to manipulate a prosthetic device would obviously fail the item. However, if the intent is to assess imitation, then some alternative strategy must be developed to allow the child to demonstrate this cognitive ability given his or her physical capabilities.

Fifth, some teachers assume that because an item is on an assessment, it must be meaningful for instructional purposes. For example, the skill "builds tower of three blocks" is an item that is commonly found on developmental scales. Before considering instruction on such an item, the teacher must question the purpose for assessing this particular skill. Is it to determine the motor ability of the student, whether the student can play with blocks, or simply because tower building (like bridge building) is another reliable milestone of development often found in early childhood measures? If a specific rationale for the assessment of that particular item (e.g., motor ability) is determined, then the teacher must decide whether this basic function is a relevant instructional objective for the student. If the teacher concludes that the play function of the item is relevant, the teacher should translate the item into a form that is meaningful for the student's age and specific environment (e.g., age-appropriate materials and functional context). Caution must be taken however, not to contrive situations that would not otherwise be considered for instruction.

Some developmental instruments relate more directly to the program development component of the assessment process. These instruments are accompanied by curriculum guides. Some of these assessments include the Assessment, Evaluation, and Programming System (AEPS-R) for infants and children (Bricker, 2002); the Carolina Curriculum for Preschoolers with Special Needs (Johnson-Martin, Attermeier, & Hacker, 1990); Learning Accomplishment Profile (LAP) (Nehring, Nehring, Bruni, & Randolph, 1992). Although these instruments were developed with instructional implications in mind, a teacher must still carefully evaluate the relevance of particular test items for each student. The student's age, interests, motor or sensory disabilities, and home and community environments must be considered in the decision-making process.

Siegel-Causey and Allinder (1998) suggest that assessment practices based on norm-referenced tests are often "limited in their ability to document and provide instructionally relevant information on those aspects of children's lives most valued by parents and practitioners, specifically children's membership in inclusive settings, their social relationships with nondisabled children, and development of competence in relevant functional skills" (p. 173). Regardless of the well-known problems with using IQ and other norm-referenced tests with individuals having disabilities, the practice continues. Sigafoos et al. (1987) examined the cumulative school files of 143 students with severe disabilities, ranging from 6 to 20 years of age. The researchers found that criterion-referenced tests were used infrequently in comparison to norm-referenced tests, including IQ tests. It is our position that IQ tests have no value in planning educational programs for students with disabilities, while norm-referenced developmental measures have general *programming value only for younger children* with disabilities and when used in combination with consideration of the student's age, interests, motor and sensory abilities, and home and community environments.

Criterion-Referenced Assessments

Unlike norm-referenced tests, which compare a student's performance to the performance of other students, *criterion-referenced tests* compare a student's performance to a predetermined level of mastery (criterion), regardless of the performance of other students. The specific adaptive or functional behavior identified in a test provides the measure for the assessment. Criterion-referenced tests are used to measure general adaptive behavior (e.g., riding a city bus, buying lunch in the school cafeteria, hand washing), specific domains of adaptive behavior, and academic performance.

Tests of Adaptive Behavior

IQ tests and other norm-referenced assessments focus on conceptual intelligence, while adaptive behavior scales focus on the skills a person displays as he or she engages in typical tasks in the daily environment (Thompson et al., 2004). *Adaptive behavior* is defined as "the collection of conceptual, social, and practical skills that have been learned by people in order to function in their everyday lives" (Luckasson, 2002, p. 73). It is important to consider the individualized nature of adaptive behavior and the connection between an individual's adaptive behavior and his or her chronological age and sociocultural context, both of which influence opportunities, motivation, and performance of adaptive skills (Luckasson, 2002).

> *The social, academic, and behavioral expectations for Christine, who is 20 years old, are very different than the expectations for Timothy, who is 4 years old. In addition, that Timothy lives in an urban area, where there are many stores, public transportation, streetlights, and so on, will shape the types of skills that should be assessed as he becomes older. Christine, who lives in a more suburban setting, will need to learn different ways to travel and get along in her environment.*

The concept of adaptive behavior has encouraged educators to assess behaviors that have relevance to a student's functioning in society. Measures of adaptive behavior are usually checklists of skills required to function in the daily environment. For example, the Adaptive Behavior Scale—School (second edition) (Lambert et al., 1993) includes the domains of independent functioning, physical development, economic activity, language development, numbers and time, prevocational or vocational activity, self-direction, responsibility, and socialization. These scales can provide information that can contribute, at least in part, to the identification of needed functional skills and areas in which to concentrate instruction (Siegel-Causey & Allinder, 1998).

However, adaptive behavior measures have been criticized on several counts. First, adaptive behavior is difficult to measure because the concept remains vague and inadequately defined, making interpretation subjective (Greenspan, 1999). Even though over 200 adaptive behavior measures have been developed in the past two decades, most disagree on the construct of adaptive behavior (Thompson, McGrew, & Bruininks, 1999). In a recent survey of state definitions of mental retardation, Denning, Chamberlain and Polloway (2000) found that 44 states used traditional definitions of mental retardation (i.e., significant limitations in both adaptive behavior and IQ) rather than the 2002 definition, which focuses on assessing support needs and providing support. Second, although these

measures focus on skills required in daily living, they often do not assess an individual's ability to adapt to changing circumstances. An item such as "able to catch a bus to work" may assess a skill necessary for functioning in the work world, but it does not address the individual's ability to solve the problem that would arise if the correct bus failed to come on time (Evans & Brown, 1986). Third, the high correlation between adaptive behavior and IQ leads many educators to conclude that adaptive behavior measures and IQ tests may be measuring the same abilities (Adams, 1973; Baumeister & Muma, 1975). Fourth, the information obtained from most current tests of adaptive behavior do not indicate much more about the severity of the problem or its cause than do more simplified screening instruments (Gaylord-Ross & Holvoet, 1985). Fifth, for some students with severe multiple or profound disabilities, the gap between current and expected performance may be so great that the focus may inappropriately shift to deficits rather than strengths (Nelson et al., 2002).

Table 3–3 describes the domains, or content areas, covered by four frequently used scales that measure adaptive behavior. In this table, Luckasson et al. (2002) analyze the domains according to the three-dimensional framework of conceptual, social, and practical skills. Some adaptive behavior scales, such as the Inventory for Client and Agency Planning (ICAP) (Bruininks, Hill, Weatherman, & Woodcock, 1986); Scales of Independent Behavior, Revised (SIB-R) (Bruininks, Woodcock, Weatherman, & Hill, 1996); and Vineland Adaptive Behavior Scales (Sparrow et al., 1984), include computer components that provide options such as direct scoring, visual profiles of the student's performance across domains, identification of priority areas, items missed, and items successfully passed.

The tests listed in Table 3–3 assess adaptive behavior across multiple domains (e.g., community living skills, socialization, self-help skills). Other instruments assess a single domain. One excellent example is the Assessment of Social Competence (ASC) (Meyer et al., 1985), which was designed as a comprehensive measure of social functions necessary for everyday participation in integrated community environments. In this scale, 11 categories, or functions, are identified to represent the skills involved in social interactions. The concept of function is used to emphasize the idea that the *purpose* of a skill (e.g., greeting people) is more important than the *form* of the skill (verbalizes "hello").

TABLE 3–3
Correspondence Between Three Dimensions of Adaptive Behavior and Empirically Derived Factors on Existing Measures

Instrument	Conceptual skills	Social skills	Practical skills
AAMR Adaptive Behavior Scale–School and Community (Lambert, Nihira, & Leland, 1993)	Community Self-sufficiency	Personal-social responsibility	Personal self-sufficiency
Vineland Adaptive Behavior Scales (Sparrow, Balla, & Cicchetti, 1984)	Communication	Socialization	Daily living skills
Scales of Independent Behavior–Revised (Bruininks, Woodcock, Weatherman, & Hill, 1996)	Community living skills	Social interaction and communication skills	Personal living skills
Comprehensive Test of Adaptive Behavior–Revised (Adams, 1999)	Language concepts and academic skills Independent living	Social skills	Self-help skills Home living

Source: Luckasson, R., Borthwick-Duffy, S., Buntinx, W. H. E., Coulter, D.L., Craig, E. M., Reeve, A., et al. (2002). *Mental retardation: Definition, classification, and systems of supports* (10th ed.). Washington, DC: American Association on Mental Retardation.

Many forms can achieve the same purpose for the individual, and the forms of social skills change according to age, setting, and a variety of other factors. Each social function of the ASC is divided into seven or eight levels that represent increasing forms of social sophistication. The lower levels do not represent younger age equivalents but instead less complex strategies for accomplishing the same function. For example, function 1 of the ASC is "initiate," which focuses on the individual's joining an ongoing interaction or starting a new one. The following are eight increasingly sophisticated levels of this "initiation" function, with an example of each level:

1. Initiates behavior inconsistently in the presence of others (e.g., sometimes vocalizes in the presence of other persons)
2. Consistently initiates behavior with other persons (e.g., moves or reaches out to obtain attention)
3. Uses common greetings and initiations (e.g., hovers around a peer activity but joins only when invited)
4. Initiates interactions based on the situation (e.g., shares an object with another person who wants it)
5. Initiates goal-directed social interaction (e.g., after greeting a peer, gets out a favorite game to play)
6. Attends to contextual details when initiating a social interaction (e.g., waits until another person is not busy to initiate interaction)

7. Bases initiations on direct experience with similar activities previously done with a particular person (e.g., initiates activity only with peers who have been friendly in the past)
8. Bases initiations on indirect knowledge and inference (e.g., invites one friend rather than another, based on the judgment that the selected person likes the chosen activity)

Assessment of Academic Performance

Comprehensive assessment of students with severe disabilities includes assessment in all areas of development, including academic skills. The following sections provide a brief discussion of the types of assessments that are used to assess academic skills, including the alternate assessment of students on statewide academic standards.

Since there are no formal assessments of academic skills specifically designed for students with severe disabilities, teachers often use instruments designed for typical students. For example, the Brigance Diagnostic Inventory of Early Development (Brigance, 1991) and the Brigance Comprehensive Inventory of Basic Skills Revised (Brigance & Clascoe, 1999) are frequently used assessments of the academic skill performance of typically developing children between the ages of birth to age 7 and ages 5 to 13, respectively. These tests are designed to assess students' skills in a number of areas, including reading and math. The assessments are criterion and norm referenced and can be administered directly with a student by a teacher or paraprofessional who carefully follows the directions regarding administration specified in the manual. When these assessments are used with students with severe disabilities, as they sometimes are, the information gained is often invalid and unreliable and can lead to identification of skills to teach that are not critical to development of functional academic skills. The artificiality of the "testing" situation, the one-time assessment opportunity, the extent to which the assessment relies on the typical sequences of development of academic skills, and the lack of consideration of the functionality of the skills assessed can affect the meaningfulness of the information derived from these assessments. (See also the previous section "Developmental Scales.")

Teachers wanting to assess academic skill development of students with severe disabilities via direct observations are often aided by commercially available guides or checklists. For example, the Syracuse Community Referenced Curriculum Guide (Ford et al., 1989), designed specifically for students with severe disabilities, includes scope and sequence charts of functional academic skills. Teachers use these charts to gain an understanding of what skills are considered to be important to target for instruction and as a curriculum-referenced checklist to identify what skills students presently have based on teacher observation of prior demonstration of those skills. Teacher-made skills checklists are an additional method of assessment of academic skills frequently used. Teachers, either individually or as a part of curriculum development committees, identify functional academic skills considered to be critical, develop checklists of those skills, and then consider students' skills relative to those checklists.

Academic skills of students with severe disabilities are also being assessed in today's schools through systems of assessment that are specifically designed to evaluate the progress of students (and their programs) in meeting each state's high academic content standards. States are required to assess *all* their students, including students with severe disabilities, relative to state-adopted standards (Elementary and Secondary Education Act, 1994; IDEA, 1997). Lawmakers recognized, however, that students with severe disabilities would be unable to demonstrate their acquisition of academic skills through use of the general statewide tests, typically paper-and-pencil tests, even with accommodations. Consequently, states were required to develop alternate methods of assessment for their students with severe disabilities. Considerable variation exists, however, in the academic areas assessed, the ways the skills are described, and the methods of assessment utilized (Thompson & Thurlow, 2001).

Initially, many states based their alternate assessments on measurement of students' skills in functional domains, such as self-care, domestic, and community living skills (Thompson & Thurlow, 2001). This gradually has shifted to the content of the assessment being linked to each state's academic standards and assessment being conducted on those same academic areas that are assessed for students without disabilities. For example, while many states have delineated *standards* in the areas of reading, writing, mathematics, history, science, technology, the arts, health, and other areas, statewide *assessments* may be limited to the areas of reading, writing, and mathematics. Consequently, alternate assessments are limited to those areas as well. States have are now engaged in the process of translating the standards to enable meaningful access for these students (Browder & Spooner, 2003).

At this point, there are a variety of approaches to alternate assessment developed by different states. For example, the Pennsylvania Alternate System of Assessment identified the critical essence of each of the standards in reading and mathematics and translated them into relevant, functional applications of the skills (Pennsylvania Alternate System of Assessment Leadership Team, 2004). A sampling of the skills are then embedded within performance tasks on which students are assessed. Massachusetts identified a range of "entry points" to that state's standards for students who qualify for alternate assessment based on levels of complexity. For example, a sixth- to eighth-grade learning standard in the Massachusetts Science and Technology Content Standards is "recognizes that heat is a form of energy and that temperature change results from adding or taking away heat for a system" (Massachusetts Department of Education, 2001, p. 300). Three suggested entry points delineated for this standard are "classify and sort items as hot or cold," "read a temperature gauge," and "recognize that hot items will cool down over time" (p. 301) Furthermore, the state noted that "access skills," including motor, communication, and social skills, may be necessary to teach within the context of standards-based instruction before more specific academic skills can be prioritized and assessed.

Teachers then assemble a portfolio of evidence of student performance on a sampling of academic skills.

Roeber (2002) identified different types of evidence that may be used to determine achievement relative to academic standards. The first, portfolio assessment, is the most frequently used method of alternate assessment (Quenemoen, Thompson, & Thurlow, 2003). Portfolio assessment is a collection of samples of student work that are referenced to a state's standards. Teachers are responsible for collecting these pieces of evidence that include permanent products of student work, observational data collected over a period of time, or video and/or audio recordings of student performance. Portfolios are scored by teams of evaluators using specific rubrics designed to identify the quality and quantify a student's performance and their level of independence in demonstrating the academic skills linked to the state's standards.

A performance assessment is accomplished by directly assessing a student on tasks specifically designed to assess academic skills (Roeber, 2002). The tasks may be paper and pencil in nature or may be functional tasks into which academic skills such as literacy or numeracy tasks are embedded (Pennsylvania Alternate System of Assessment Leadership Team, 2004). For example, a student may be asked to demonstrate their literacy skills by using a store directory to identify the location of specific items in the store. Roeber (2002) also noted that some states are using checklists to assess students on achievement of academic standards. Quenemoen et al. (2003) found that nine states reported using this method in 2001. Checklists are used to guide teachers in observing or recalling student performance on specific academic skills that are linked to the state standards. Roeber (2002) pointed out that while use of checklists have the advantage of being easy to use, they may not yield reliable data. Some states use checklists as one part of a multicomponent assessment of students' academic skills.

Multidimensional Framework for Conceptualizing Functional Assessment

The assessment process is only as meaningful as the behavior or skill outcomes that are identified and measured. These outcomes should reflect what current best practice has identified as important. According to Siegel-Causey and Allinder (1998), the best educational practice standards include those characterized as follows:

- Grounded both in research and values
- Focused on school and community-based instruction
- Referenced to neighborhood schools
- Facilitative of social and instructional integration of students with and without disabilities
- Coordinated between related services and educational personnel

Meaningful and functional assessment of students with severe disabilities must reflect this range of outcomes. For many years, acquisition of functional skills was considered to be the sole outcome of educational programs. This focus then expanded to include social inclusion and self-determination. Finally, with new requirements of NCLB, access to the general curriculum was added to the range of meaningful outcomes that must be assessed (Browder et al., 2004). It is clear that assessment of functional skill acquisition or just academic development, while important, is not sufficient to demonstrate a meaningful or comprehensive educational experience. Billingsley, Gallucci, Peck, Schwartz, and Staub (1996) state that this narrow focus "fails to acknowledge the breadth of outcomes that may contribute to the ability of students to lead fulfilling lives" (p. 44). These authors developed a three-part framework to represent the important outcomes for students with severe disabilities (Table 3-4).

One domain of the conceptual framework is *membership* (belonging) in formal and informal groups of the classroom and school community. Membership can take at least five forms: role in small group, class membership, friendship cliques, school membership, and activities outside of school. A second domain of the conceptual framework refers to the variety of personal *relationships* formed with other children. Billingsley et al. identified five major patterns of interaction: play or companionship, helpee, helper, peer partner, and adversarial. The third domain of the framework is *skills*. This part of the model focuses on such traditional skill areas as the use of appropriate social or communication skills; the degree of change in using academic skills, such as reading, writing, and math; and progress in using functional skills that increase the student's degree of independence and control of the environment.

Taken together, the three components can be used to plan assessment, organize assessment information,

TABLE 3–4

Definitions of Outcome Categories

Membership	Relationships	Skills
Belonging to a group (treated as a member, accommodations made to include, shared rituals and symbols)	Patterns of interaction that typically develop between peers	Behavioral competencies that develop over time and are the traditional focus of special education
Role in small group Student plays an essential role in multiple groups across the school day.	**Play/companionship** Student engages in reciprocal social interactions with peers.	**Social/communication skills** Student learns ways to interact with peers appropriately, to engage cooperatively, to be understood through a system of communication, and to attend to and understand others, even if only in part.
Class membership Student involved in class activities, takes turns with class responsibilities, participates in class privileges, and active in class routines.	**Helper** Student offers or provides appropriate levels of help to peers.	
	Peer/reciprocal Student engages in reciprocal task-related interactions with peers.	**Academic skills** Student learns basic skills or facts in reading, writing, math, science, and social studies.
Friendship cliques Student is a stable member of consistent group of friends.	**Adversarial** Student is involved in negative interactions with one or more peers.	**Functional skills** Student learns practical routines such as dressing, eating, mobility, putting things away, grooming, making purchases, safe street crossing, etc.
School membership Student is involved in schoolwide activities, attends assemblies, and other school functions.		
Outside of school activities Student is a regular participant in extracurricular activities of clubs. Necessary accommodations are present.		

Note: Adapted, with permission, from Billingsley, Gallucci, Peck, Schwartz, and Staub, (1996), p.47.

and determine if the appropriate range of assessments were conducted. For example, if assessments were conducted for a student that covered the areas of skill acquisition and relationships but did not include any information about membership, additional strategies would need to be initiated to assess needs in this area. Likewise, if assessments were conducted for a student in the areas of relationships and belonging, then the educational team would need to explore ways to assess skills, including alternate assessment, as described previously.

The following sections demonstrate how a wide variety of informal assessment strategies can contribute to the collection of assessment information that focuses on a broad framework of meaningful outcomes.

Informal Environmental Assessment Strategies

We have reviewed many issues related to the use of standardized measures for students with developmental disabilities. The most critical point is that these measures provide little useful data for educational programs, while nonstandardized, or alternative, assessment procedures provide more relevant and useful data regarding educational programs and student's achievement of desired outcomes (Browder, 2000; Knowlton, 1998; Siegel-Causey & Allinder, 1998).

This section reviews a variety of assessment strategies that focus on the relationship between an individual and specific environmental demands. As is true with all criterion-referenced tests, environmental assessment strategies examine the environment to determine the skills and supports needed by the individual. In this case, however, rather than using commercially prepared instruments, strategies are applied to assess environments relevant to a particular student. Consequently, the procedure is individualized. The purposes of environmental assessments are to identify functional routines and activities required across relevant settings, such as home, school, work, and community, and to measure or estimate a student's performance on specific routines and activities found within those settings.

Before describing specific environmental assessment strategies, it is useful to consider a number of guidelines that increase the validity of the environmentally based assessment process: the who, when, and where of assessment (Silberman & Brown, 1998).

Who Assesses

IDEA formally identifies individuals who must participate on an evaluation team: the student's parents; at least one general education teacher of the student (if the student is or may be participating in the general education setting); at least one special education teacher; a representative of the school district who is qualified to provide or supervise instruction; an individual who can interpret the instructional implications of evaluation results and, at the parents' or school's discretion, other individuals who have knowledge or special expertise; and the student (when appropriate) (H. R. Turnbull & Turnbull, 2000).

Participants in an environmental assessment may include these evaluation team members but at times may be more inclusive and collaborative. Professionals and others who know the student well are expected to offer information about the student's behavior and performance in a variety of the student's natural environments. Who these people are will vary according to the abilities and disabilities, age, characteristics, and needs of the student (Orelove, Sobsey, & Silberman, 2004; Silberman & Brown, 1998). For example, a bus driver is not likely to be an "informant" on a developmental assessment but may be important in the assessment of the students' traveling routines.

Special education law has long encouraged student participation, when appropriate, but student participation in educational planning has been the exception more than the practice (Wehmeyer & Sands, 1998). With increased focus on self-determination, student participation in educational planning is increasing. In fact, IDEA (1990) mandated that students age 16 and older be provided with transition plans based on their needs, interests, and preferences; IDEA amendments of 1997 then mandated that students be invited to participate in the transition planning process (Wehmeyer & Sands, 1998).

Trends in educating students with disabilities emphasize the involvement of each student in critical elements of the education process. Students with severe disabilities represent a challenge to achieving this goal. Participation in programmatic efforts to increase student involvement and self-determination in the education process often requires communication skills that

are difficult for individuals with severe, multiple disabilities (Gothelf & Brown, 1998). Increasing participation in the educational process, however, must be seen not as an obstacle but as a challenge. A variety of strategies are available for determining preferences of individuals who have difficulty communicating. For example, effective observational assessments of student preferences may involve (a) noting the nonverbal forms of communication (e.g., looking toward item, engagement), (b) interviewing people who know the student well, and (c) observing the person's behavior in a variety of environments and contexts (F. Brown, Gothelf, Guess, & Lehr, 1998; Gothelf & Brown, 1998; Silberman & Brown, 1998).

Timothy's one-on-one home instructor, Juliet, reported that he would intermittently cry and throw his materials on the floor. Mrs. Simms and Juliet decided to more closely observe Timothy's behaviors to try to determine what he might be communicating with his behavior. For 1 week, they kept track of variables such as when the behaviors occurred, in which activities they occurred, and how long he would participate before the onset of the behaviors. They discovered that the disruptive behaviors typically occurred during the same two sessions and would occur after about five trials into the session. The two sessions in which the behavior occurred were the matching colors (using large plastic pegs) and matching shapes (using foam shapes) programs. Mrs. Simms and Juliet made several hypotheses about what Timothy might be expressing about his curriculum. They decided to try several program changes in these two activities to test their hypotheses and note Timothy's response to them: shorten the sessions, take a brief break after three trials, and change the materials to more functional ones. By noting Timothy's response to these changes, they would be testing their hypotheses. Consequent changes in his programs would thus reflect Timothy's contribution to his educational program.

When and Where to Assess

Standardized assessments are conducted in settings that are, to the greatest degree possible, free from distractions (McLoughlin & Lewis, 1994), including, for example, special testing areas or therapy rooms. These practices are used to get as "pure" a reading as possible on the individual's responses to test items. However, environmental assessments have a different mission: to explore the individual's performance in settings in which he or she routinely participates. Thus, assessment will be conducted, to the greatest degree possible, in those routine settings—including all the distractions that are typically found in those settings (Silberman & Brown, 1998)—and interviews will focus on gaining information concerning the individual's behavior and performance in those settings.

Problems in response generalization and stimulus overselectivity further necessitate assessing performance in everyday settings using materials natural to the context. Some children like Timothy may be able to perform a skill in natural contexts but not in a contrived setting.

Timothy was tested for "verbal imitation" in the speech therapy room. Sitting directly across from Timothy, Ms. Rivera, his therapist, presents a verbal cue (e.g., "say ball"), hoping to elicit an imitation of her verbal stimulus. Timothy makes only a few correct responses to the list of words and frequently leaves his seat during testing. Observations during music group in his preschool, however, indicate that during songs such as "Old MacDonald's Farm," Timothy imitates the teacher or peer's choice of animal sounds. His mother also has reported that, at home, Timothy will imitate his older sister's verbalizations of excitement (e.g., "wow," "cool," "go") when they watch videos together.

Other times, the student may be able to perform a skill in contrived settings but not in the natural settings. This is particularly likely when skills have been taught only in the isolated setting.

In the speech therapy room, Timothy was successfully taught to "sort" objects of like color and shape (e.g., reds go in the red pile and blues in the blue pile; triangles go in the triangle bin and squares in the square bin). However, when his teacher observed him putting away toys after free play, Timothy did so randomly rather than putting the foam blocks with the other foam blocks and the wood blocks in the wood block bin.

Because we are interested in assessing the student's performance in typical routines, assessment is most valid in those settings, using those materials that are natural to those settings and with all the distractors associated with those settings. Not only is it informative to know what the student can or cannot do, but it is

critical to consider the reason for failure. Downing and Demchak (1996) suggested that when a student cannot perform an item on an assessment, we must determine whether the student is actually unable to perform the skill, lacks motivation in that context, or has no reason to perform the skill when requested. This information is critical in designing and modifying education programs.

Ecological Inventories

Ecological inventories are informal assessments that require teachers to consider areas of instruction arranged in "domains of adult functioning," or skill categories (L. Brown et al., 1979). These domains may include domestic, leisure, community, school, and vocational areas. The domestic domain includes skills performed in and around the home—self-care, clothing care, housekeeping, cooking, and yard work. In the leisure domain are spectator or participant skills that may take place in the community, at school, or at home. The community domain includes skills such as street crossing, using public transportation, shopping, eating in restaurants, and using other public facilities. The vocational domain includes skills involved in attaining meaningful employment, some of which occur in the middle school and high school settings but most of which take place in community locations. Historically, the activities and skills identified under each of the four domains (i.e., domestic, leisure, community, and vocational) were used to develop the school program for a student with severe disabilities. With neighborhood-inclusive schools being the standard for best practice, the school domain is also examined to determine the school-specific routines (e.g., eating in a cafeteria, using a locker, attending assembly) that should be assessed for a particular student.

L. Brown et al. (1979) refer to their assessment strategy as a "top-down" approach to skill building. That is, they begin with the requirements of independent adult participation within each domain. This practice ensures identification of skills that are functional. The ecological approach differs from the developmental approach, in which instructional objectives are chosen from the bottom up, starting with skills normally performed by infants and proceeding to those considered more advanced.

When IEP goals and objectives address skills that are functional for a person, the chances that those skills, once learned, will be used and thus naturally maintained are increased. Since learning is often slow and skill loss through disuse is predictable for students with severe disabilities, target skills that meet the criterion of functionality can facilitate good conditions for skill retention.

Ecological inventories are tailored to encourage skill generalization in several ways. First, functionality is defined for each student by a variety of individuals familiar with this student and the student's current and potential home, school, community, leisure, and work environments. Second, typically we will see some redundancy in skills and activities that are required across environments (e.g., using the bathroom occurs in many different settings). Skills that are more often required will be deemed "higher priority" and more naturally supported by teachers, peers, and coworkers in those environments.

Another advantage of using ecological inventories over commercially prepared tests is their flexible content (L. Brown et al., 1979). The content is not predetermined; rather, it depends on each student's life circumstances. Considering the variability in students and their environments and their subsequent demands, individually determined assessment content is an asset. For example, the demands and activities in urban settings are quite different than those in rural settings. Certainly, recreational options in various communities differ greatly, as do the leisure preferences of students and their families. The age and family culture of the student also will be determining factors in the types of environments and activities in which they engage. If one's goal is to assess a student's ability to adapt within a particular environment, the content of the assessment should reflect the unique requirements of the community and family context.

According to L. Brown et al. (1979), there are five phases of the ecological inventory process:

1. Identify the curriculum domains
2. Identify and survey current and future natural environments
3. Divide the relevant environments into subenvironments
4. Inventory these subenvironments for the relevant activities performed there
5. Determine the skills required for performance of the activities

The teacher, working with school and family members, proceeds through each phase in order.

Curriculum Domains

For many students, all five domains (i.e., domestic, leisure, school, community, and vocation) are relevant. However, teachers and parents need not concern themselves with the vocational domain until the later elementary years. Rather than the traditional academic or developmental categories, curriculum domains are used because they (a) represent the major life areas, (b) lead to the selection of practical skills, and (c) emphasize the functional goals of self-sufficiency. However, use of curriculum domains does not mean that communication, motor, social, or academic skills are forgotten. Rather, the domains are used as contexts in which to embed and teach those skills.

Most often, the ecological inventory focuses on elementary, middle school, high school, and older students. However, when considering very young children, many professionals do not feel comfortable with trying to predict possible adult environments (Lehr, 1989). Several educators describe application of the *criterion of the next environment* for preschool children. For young children, the skills that are identified should focus on social behavior and skills needed for the next environment, such as an inclusive kindergarten. Figure 3-1 shows the different domains identified for Timothy and Christine, reflecting the differences in their ages; Timothy's assessment will reflect four domains, and Christine, who is older, is expected to participate in all five domains.

Current and Future Natural Environments

The next step requires the teacher to identify and examine the environments in which the student currently lives, learns or studies, works, and plays. Although it is difficult to predict future environments, it is necessary to identify them as early as possible. For Timothy, who is only 4 years old, several environments are relevant—his own home (an apartment), the babysitter's home, various shops in his neighborhood, the school yard, and his preschool. A future environment will be the elementary school in his neighborhood. By contrast, Christine's relevant environments at age 20 include her home, the university campus, various job sites that she is sampling (e.g., the library), and different facilities in the community in which she and her family participate (e.g., recycling center). Figure 3-1 reflects variations in the types of environments

FIGURE 3–1

Examples of Domains, Environments, and Subenvironments Individualized for Timothy and Christine

Timothy:

Domain	Domestic	School	Community	Leisure
Environments	Apartment	Preschool	Grocery store	School yard
Subenvironments	Elevator	Classroom	Shopping cart area	Benches
	Kitchen	Bathroom	Food aisles	Playground
	Bathroom	Hallway	Deli counter	Baseball field
	Bedroom	Playground	Cashier	Water fountain
	Fire escape	Main office	Parking lot	Basketball court

Christine:

Domain	Domestic	School	Community	Leisure	Vocational
Environments	Private house	High school	Recycle center	Movie theatre	Library
Subenvironments	Kitchen	Homeroom	Parking lot	Ticket booth	Check out desk
	Bathroom	Cafeteria	Cans area	Concession stand	Hallways
	Bedroom	Classrooms	Newspaper area	Theater	Restroom
	Den	Bus stop	Bottles area	Bathroom	Break area
	Yard	Bathroom	Office	Video games	Stacks

Note: Adapted, with permission, from Silberman, R. K., & Brown, F. (1998). Alternative approaches to assessing students who have visual impairments with other disabilities in classroom and community environments. In S. Z. Sacks & R. K. Silberman (Eds.), *Educating students who have visual impairments with other disabilities* (p. 81). Baltimore: Paul H. Brookes.

identified for assessment for Timothy, who lives in an urban setting, and Christine, who lives in a suburban environment.

Subenvironments

Further division is necessary to identify the activities most likely to be required in each environment for the student. Because Timothy and Christine live in different environments (i.e., apartment and private house), it follows that the subenvironments will also be different (Figure 3–1). For example, Timothy uses an elevator, while Christine has access to a backyard. The diversity in these two students' ages, living environments, and a

variety of other variables underscore the need for assessments that will be sensitive to individual lifestyles.

Relevant Activities

What are the essential activities that occur in these subenvironments? Because there are potentially an endless number of possible activities that could occur, teachers must consider a variety of factors as they determine which activities are most relevant: (a) activities that are considered to be mandatory for successful participation in the various environments, (b) the number of times an activity is needed in other subenvironments

FIGURE 3–2
Examples of Activities in One Subenvironment in the School Domain for Timothy and Christine

	Timothy	Christine
Environment	**Preschool**	**High School**
Subenvironment	Classroom	Homeroom
Activities	Morning group	Pledge to flag
	Snack	Attendance
	1:1 discrete trial instruction	Hand in notices
	Centers	Pack new notices
	Toileting and handwashing	Review day's schedule
	Recess	
	Music group	

Note: Adapted, with permission, from Silberman, R.K., & Brown, F. (1988). Alternative approaches to assessing students who have visual impairments with other disabilities in classroom and community environments. In S. Z. Sacks & R. K. Silberman (Eds.), *Educating students who have visual impairments with other disabilities* (p. 82). Baltimore: Paul H. Brookes.

in which the student participates, (c) the student's current skills, (d) the student's preferences and interests, (e) the priorities of the family, (f) the specific physical characteristics of the setting in which the activity will occur, (g) the potential for the student's meaningful partial participation in the activity, and (h) the contribution of this activity to the student's relationships and belonging. Figure 3-2 provides examples of activities found in one subenvironment of the school domain for Timothy and Christine.

Skills Required

This step requires that activities be broken down into teachable units, or task analyzed. A task analysis (described in more detail in chapter 4) is a detailed description of each behavior needed to accomplish a complex behavior (Alberto & Troutman, 1999). As task analysis relates to assessment, the student is asked to perform a selected task or activity, and the student's performance on each component is recorded (see

chapter 5 for examples of evaluating performance on task-analyzed activities). The teacher then knows which components of the chain need to be addressed (e.g., taught, environmental modifications made). Although each skill is separated for measurement and teaching, the teacher must not lose sight of the activity or clusters of related skills that must be performed together in the natural environment. For Christine, the "call Best Buddy to confirm lunch" includes many related skills: initiating the call following an examination of her day's schedule, preparing her message on the Dynavox, using her switch to identify the number and make the call, and playing her message once her Buddy answers or the message comes on.

The Component Model of Functional Life Routines: Ensuring Meaningful Task Analysis
F. Brown et al. (1987) identify areas of concern in the standard application of task analysis for assessment. First, most task analyses are designed with a very limited scope of skills. Traditionally, tasks are broken down

within the context of observable motor skills (e.g., pick up the hairbrush, bring to head, brush down left side of hair) and do not identify related or critical skills associated with meaningful performance of an activity in the natural environment. For example, they may exclude skills such as initiation, social, communication, problem solving, choice, and monitoring the quality of an activity. These excluded skills are skills that could enable students (especially those with severe physical disabilities) to have more control over the routine, or self-determination.

Second, the beginning and ending points of behavioral chains are often arbitrary or inconsistent. Often, a task analysis begins with a teacher's verbal cue (e.g., "it's time to go to lunch") rather than an expectation that the student will respond to a natural environmental cue (e.g., the lunch bell sounds). In many task-analyzed activities, students are often not expected to end a task in the way that their nondisabled peers do. For example, ending a task may mean putting away the materials that were used (e.g., put the game back in the box and on the shelf); for other students, especially those who do not have the physical ability to put away materials, ending a task may mean indicating when they would like the activity to end.

Third, because the usual division of an activity into smaller steps focuses on the motor aspects of the activity, teachers often focus on participating in just those components of the activity. For a student with multiple disabilities, such as Christine, this means that partial participation in activities centers around physical expectations and outcomes. This may present an obstacle to Christine participating in a way that she finds meaningful or satisfying. Partial participation should allow the student greater control, or self-determination, over personal routines and activities (F. Brown & Lehr, 1993).

For a student like Timothy who can physically participate extensively in the routine, teachers should identify an appropriate range of skills to more closely represent mastery. For example, the Adaptive Behavior Scales—Public School Version (Lambert et al., 1993) breaks down "washing hands and face" into the following components: (a) washes hands and face with soap and water without prompting, (b) washes hands with soap, (c) washes face with soap, (d) washes hands and face with water, and (e) dries hands and face. Would successful performance of these four parts imply that the student has mastered this skill? These core skills do not sample the range of behaviors necessary for functional use of the routine. To use this skill in the natural environment, Timothy would also be expected to know, for example, when his hands needed washing, to check to make sure they are clean, and to know where to find more soap when the soap runs out.

The Component Model of Functional Life Routines (F. Brown et al., 1987; F. Brown & Lehr, 1993) outlines several ways in which an individual can meaningfully participate in activities. Performing motor (or core) skills is only one of three ways that participation can occur in any given routine. *Extension skills* extend the core skills and create a more comprehensive routine and thus provide a more meaningful evaluation of student competence. Extension skills include (a) initiation, (b) preparation, (c) monitoring the quality, (d) monitoring the tempo, (e) problem solving, and (f) terminating.

Extension skills provide options for meaningful participation in the activity without extensive physical requirements. For example, a student may not be able to eat independently but may initiate independently by pointing on her communication board that she wants to eat or terminate mealtime by indicating that she is finished eating. The student can also monitor the quality of the routine by indicating that her blouse is dirty from lunch and needs to be changed, even though she may not be able to independently change her own blouse.

Enrichment skills are not critical to the independent performance of a routine. They do, however, add to the quality of the routine and, as such, may be considered to be equally as important as the skills already mentioned. If educators are concerned with the quality of students' lives, then their assessment procedures should reflect this concern. Enrichment skills include expressive communication, social behaviors, and choice. If one were doing class recycling, commenting on the activity may not be crucial to accomplishing the task, but it may make this task a more pleasant experience and also offers functional practice of the communication skill. Choosing between two or more feasible alternatives (e.g., a book to have read, a CD to play, a hairstyle) is also not crucial to the performance of a routine but adds to the quality of a student's experience as well as providing more control over daily life.

Each resulting skill in a component analysis represents a meaningful unit of behavior: all items are relevant to the demands of the natural environment and are particularly important for students with severe physical disabilities. Students like Christine often

FIGURE 3–3

Task Analysis of "Plays Game with Peer and Adult" Using The Component Model of Functional Life Routines

Student: _Timothy_

Age: _4_   Date: _____

Domain: _Leisure_

Routine: _Plays game with peer and adult_

Plays Game with Adult	Yes	No	NA	With Adaptations	Comments
1. Lets you or peers know in some way it is time to play game (*initiate*)					
2. Selects game of choice					
3. Selects peer(s) to play with (*choice*)					
4. Arranges play area, gets materials, or arranges with others for things to be done (*prepare*)					
5. Performs basic steps of the game (*core*)					
6. Attempts to improve skills or increase enjoyment for self or others (*monitor quality*)					
7. Spends appropriate amount of time engaged in game (*monitor tempo*)					
8. If a problem arises (e.g., can't find game piece) will take action to remove problem (*problem-solve*)					
9. Puts away materials, arranges for others to put away, or lets other know he is done playing (*terminate*)					
10. Expresses or communicates about any aspect of the activity (e.g., enjoyment, request) (*communication*)					
11. Responds appropriately with peers during game, such as sharing and taking turns (*social*)					

Note: Adapted with permission from Brown, F., Evans, I. M., Weed, K. A., & Owen, V. (1987). Delineating functional competencies: A component model. *Journal of the Associations for Persons with Severe Disabilities, 12*(2), 122.

"bottom out" on many assessments because core motor skills are the usual focus. In interpreting a core skill assessment, a teacher would likely conclude that the student should begin to learn the specific motor movements of the skill as determined by a detailed task analysis. Using the component model, however, the student may be able to engage in other, more meaningful and more satisfying aspects of the routine. With the component model, team members not only assess relevant items and score meaningful dimensions of behavior but also include these items as relevant goals in the student's educational program. The items identified using this approach are closely aligned with the mission of Billingsley et al.'s (1996) outcome framework: to identify those skills that would facilitate the individual's membership and belonging in settings that are valued by the individual, family members, and other members of his or her community.

Figure 3-3 is an example of the component model applied to the activity of "plays a game with peer and adult," which was identified as an objective for Timothy. In addition to delineating meaningful units of behavior, the format depicted in Figure 3-3 can be used to record baseline and to assess progress during instruction. Note that in this analysis of the activity, "performs basic steps of the game" is only one of a total of 11 steps. This implies that playing the game itself is only one part of the activity and that there are many other ways that we are expecting Timothy to participate. If the game playing (e.g., following the rules of the game) was the goal, this step should be further task-analyzed.

Examples of Ecological Inventories

We are not recommending a single format for completing an ecological inventory because ecological inventories should be individualized to assess the variables deemed critical by the educational team. Figure 3-4 is an example of an environmental inventory format. This inventory does not specify the type of scoring used to measure the core skills (e.g., performance level of the activity or routine), nor does it specify the type of component skills that will be measured. The inventory should be individualized according to variables such as the context; the student's age, strengths, and needs; and component skills identified by the team as important. For some students, a dichotomous performance score of "yes" or "no" may be appropriate; for others,

the team may be interested in the level of prompt needed for the student to complete the activity (e.g., verbal, model, physical assistance). Assessment of component skills will also vary according to the needs of the individual student. Problem solving and initiation may be critical skills for one student; assessing another student's social and communication skills across the school day may be of interest.

Figure 3-5 shows a section of the ecological inventory that Mr. Grayson and Ms. Johnston (Timothy's special education and preschool teachers) completed to examine the subenvironments and activities involved from the time of Timothy's arrival at school through "centers" time. The activities typically expected of other children in his class in each of the subenvironments (e.g., hallways, bathroom, morning group) were listed down the left side of the form. The team was interested in assessing Timothy's performance in the activities using a three-part scoring system (i.e., assistance needed on most steps, some steps, or independent performance), so these are indicated across the top of the form.

It was also decided by his team that, in addition to assessing his basic performance of the activities, assessment of several component skills would be revealing. Discussion focused on Timothy's inconsistent initiation and termination of activities. Termination was of particular interest to his teacher, who reported that sometimes Timothy would get upset and cry when he was asked to leave one activity and begin another. On the other hand, Timothy would terminate too quickly when he did not care for the activity or the interaction. Mr. and Mrs. Simms were especially interested in their son exhibiting social and interaction skills with others, so this too was assessed within activities. Finally, everyone agreed that assessing Timothy's choice making and communication skills would address his IEP goals and foster self-determination and cognitive development. The team felt that it would be especially critical to assess these skills within the context of his daily activities because much instruction in these areas occurred in one-to-one and therapeutic settings.

In addition to the school domain, Mr. Grayson assessed three other domains: leisure, community, and domestic. Peers, family members, and various other teachers and therapists were involved in interviews on one or more of these domain areas.

FIGURE 3–4

Blank Form for an Environmental Inventory

Student: Environment: Date: Informants: Methods:									
Domain:		**Performance Level**		**Component Skills**					**Comments**
		(Check one)		**(Check skills that are displayed)**					
Subenvironments/Activity									

FIGURE 3–5

Sample from Environmental Inventory for Timothy

Student: Timothy
Environment: Preschool
Date: October 1999
Informants: Parents, preschool teacher, teaching assistant, speech therapist, 1:1 instructor
Methods: Interview and observation

Domain: School	Performance Level (Check one)			Component Skills (Check skills that are displayed)					Comments
Subenvironments/Activity	Assist on most steps	Assist on some steps	Independent	Initiates	Has related social skills	Makes choices	Terminates	Communicates	
Parking lot and building entrance									
• Enters			X	X					
• Greets children	X								
• Greets adults	X								
Hallways									
• Greets others	X								
• Hangs up coat		X		X		X	X		
Bathroom									
• Toilets		X		X			X		Terminates too quickly
• Washes hands		X				X	X		Terminates too quickly
• Checks appearance		X					X		Terminates too quickly
Morning group									
• Sits in place		X				X			
• Interacts with others	X				X		X		Terminates too quickly; only interacts with Melinda

FIGURE 3–5 (*Continued*)

Domain: School	Performance Level (Check one)			Component Skills (Check skills that are displayed)					Comments
Subenvironments/Activity	Assist on most steps	Assist on some steps	Independent	Initiates	Has related social skills	Makes choices	Terminates	Communicates	
Morning group continued									
• Follows instructions	X								
• Uses materials	X								Doesn't want to terminate
• Imitates actions		X							
• Raises hand for attendance		X							
Centers									
• Follows schedule		X				X			Seems to enjoy looking at schedule and choosing
• Shares with others	X					X		X	Shares only with certain peers; terminates quickly
• Uses materials		X							Doesn't want to terminate
• Switches centers following bell cue		X							Hard to switch activities once he is involved in one
• Interacts with others	X				X		X	X	Terminates too quickly; interacts easily with Melinda

Even though important to curriculum development for students with severe disabilities, the ecological inventory strategy can be very time consuming. What strategies might the team use to make the process more efficient and still identify functional outcomes that can be considered as IEP goals? Often there is more than one student in a given school setting whose IEP process will benefit from this assessment. Thus, teams might first develop a general environmental inventory in a computer file for a particular school setting that includes common subenvironments and activities. When applied to a specific student, the inventory will naturally be individualized. As the student changes grades, computer files can simply be reviewed with the team and revised; entirely new inventories need not be designed until there is a change in the school setting.

When designing ecological inventories, it is important to remember that the general process does not take into consideration the subjectivity of the assessors. Although the process very much ensures identification of skills that are functional for the individual, the skill sequences identified by two raters may be substantially different. For example, a teacher who has had extensive training in communication may identify numerous communication opportunities within her ecological inventory. A second teacher who has had extensive experience teaching students with multiple disabilities may focus on the physical demands of an environment.

Teachers need to be sure that ecological inventories identify not only the observable activities and skills that are associated with competent performance in natural environments but also related skills (i.e., extension and enrichment skills) that may not be quite so apparent. In addition to communication and motor skills, subtle social skills, such as smiling at a waitress and giving eye contact to the cashier at a restaurant, may not be consistently identified. Although not always critical to the performance of the routine, these behaviors may nonetheless be crucial to socially appropriate performance of an activity. Similarly, some language competencies may not be observable because they do not occur at that specific place or time of the activity. That is, "attending a school assembly" or "going to a movie" may be identified as an activity within the school domain and divided into its component parts, but "communicating about the assembly" or the "movie" later in the day or "sitting by a friend in the assembly" or "inviting a friend to the movies" probably would not be identified in an inventory.

Applications of Ecological Inventory

Several authors have applied the ecological inventory strategy to the assessment of critical, or related, skills, using the life domains as contexts in which critical skills can be identified and functionally assessed. Others have formalized the ecological inventory approach by providing more structure or systematizing the approach. For example, Sigafoos and York (1991) use an ecological inventory approach to determine priority communication targets for instruction. In their assessment, the final step of the inventory, or the task analysis, is expanded to include communicative behavior. According to Sigafoos and York, at least six communication variables should be included and explored in an ecological analysis: (a) the communicative demands of relevant activities (e.g., ordering food, requesting a movie ticket); (b) the naturally occurring opportunities for teaching communication skills (e.g., "more" when you run out of work supplies); (c) the communicative intents, or functions, that are required to meet environmental demands and opportunities (e.g., initiate, maintain, reject, comment); (d) the specific vocabulary needs of activities, that is, the words frequently used in the activities in which the student will participate; (e) the most effective communication modes for specific environments and activities (e.g., a cashier in the fast-food restaurant may understand a picture but not a sign); and (f) the natural cues and consequences that should be used to establish participation in activities (e.g., responding to the school bell to change classes rather than a teacher prompt).

The Syracuse Community-Referenced Curriculum Guide for Students with Moderate and Severe Disabilities (Ford et al., 1989) is a curriculum guide that uses the ecological approach. This guide focuses on the four domains of (a) self-management and home living, (b) vocational, (c) recreation and leisure, and (d) general community functioning. Also included in this guide are sections on functional academic skills (e.g., reading, writing, money handling, time management) and embedded skills (i.e., social, communication, motor). Each scope and sequence chart lists the major goal areas of the domain and examples of the sequence of possible activities relevant to students as they progress through the school years. Thus, the goal (or function) remains the same across time, but the form of the activity in which students participate may differ (e.g., a child in kindergarten may learn to prepare a simple snack, a high school student may learn to plan a menu).

Choosing Options and Accommodations for Children (COACH) (Giangreco, Cloninger, & Iverson, 1998) is another assessment and planning tool. It is a comprehensive curriculum guide that helps the team develop annual goals and objectives and determine general supports and accommodations that the student needs to participate in the educational program. There are a wealth of forms to facilitate assessment, implementation, and evaluation of priority goals and objectives. The COACH offers a comprehensive system for helping the educational team move from assessment and identification of objectives to implementation and evaluation of the educational plan within the context of the general education program.

Functional Assessment of Problem Behaviors

A comprehensive assessment of problem behaviors is the cornerstone for developing effective and positive behavioral strategies. Recent efforts to reduce severe problem behaviors, such as self-injury, aggression, and property damage, have focused on assessment of the variables that functionally control behavior. In other words, the relationship between the inappropriate behavior and the environment becomes the focus of assessment. The term "functional behavioral assessment" refers to the process used to identify the antecedent and consequent events that occasion and maintain problem behavior (Lennox & Miltenberger, 1989). (See chapter 6 for an in-depth review of functional assessment and the development of positive behavior support programs.)

Many problem behaviors are attributed to specific pragmatic intents; that is, the behavior serves a specific function for the individual and is a form of communication for the individual. Durand (1990) classifies controlling variables into four categories, or functions, for the individual: (a) social attention (the behavior elicits attention for the individual), (b) escape (the behavior results in the individual's being removed from an unpleasant situation), (c) access to tangible consequences (the behavior results in access to reinforcing events or materials), and (d) sensory feedback (the behavior provides auditory, visual, or tactile stimulation).

Once the function of the behavior is determined (e.g., escape from difficult tasks), the student should be provided with and instructed on a more appropriate way of communicating the same message (e.g., raise hand to obtain for assistance rather than hitting oneself to escape the difficult task). That is, the behavior taught to the individual should be functionally equivalent to the problem behavior (Durand & Carr, 1991; Durand & Merger, 2001; Haring & Kennedy, 1990; Koegel, Koegel, & Dunlap, 1996; O'Neill et al., 1997). This strategy has been termed "functional communication training."

Functional assessment indicated that some of Timothy's crying, which was typically accompanied by throwing materials and falling to the ground, resulted in his "escape" from nonpreferred activities. His teachers, the speech and language therapist, and his parents scheduled a meeting to design a program to teach him how to indicate "break" to escape from nonpreferred activities, both at school and at home. The goal would be for Timothy to refuse participation or terminate an activity in a socially acceptable way rather than "tantruming" to escape from or avoid the activity. An important part of the meeting would be to discuss and decide on what communication mode would be used to indicate "break." Timothy's language objectives included both speech and using a communication board (with speech as the goal); however, it would be important to give Timothy a way to indicate "break" that would be quick, easy to execute, and easily understood by others (e.g., a card with the word "break" or a picture of a stop light on it, the sign for "break" or "finished").

When a student engages in problem behaviors, it is critical to examine a variety of educational and curricular variables that might be associated with the behaviors (Dunlap & Kern, 1993: Dunlap, Kern-Dunlap, Clarke, & Robbins, 1991; Knoster, 2000). This process is often a challenge for the team as they proceed with functional behavior assessment, but it is a critical component of the development of an educational program for students who engage in behaviors that interfere with learning.

A comprehensive functional assessment should provide information concerning the function of the behavior as well as other environmental variables that maintain the behavior. The range of possible variables that may contribute to the presence of problem behavior is as wide, varied, and unique as are individuals. There are a variety of comprehensive assessments and program development guides to help teams through this process (e.g., Carr et al., 1994; Durand, 1990; Janney & Snell, 2000; O'Neill et al., 1997; Willis, LaVigna, &

Donnellan, 1993). In a summary of variables that are included in a variety of published functional behavior assessments, F. Brown (1996) identified four major areas that teams should include in their assessment: *environmental variables* (e.g., when and where is it most and least likely to happen, in what activities is it most and least likely to occur), *communication variables* (e.g., whether the student has the skills to communicate in a more appropriate way, whether others understand the student's communicative attempts), *choice/control variables* (e.g., whether the student is thwarted from doing preferred activities, whether the student values the activities in which he or she is involved), and *teaching/instructional variables* (e.g., whether tasks are too difficult or not sufficiently challenging, whether team members are adequately prepared to implement the behavior support plan, whether prompting strategies are too intrusive).

Four strategies frequently used to conduct functional analysis include (a) informant assessment or interview, (b) rating scales, (c) direct observation, and (d) systematic manipulation of controlling variables (or analog assessments). Analog assessments "involve the manipulation of various antecedents and consequences that are presumed to be important and observing their effect on an individual's problem behavior" (Durand, 1990, p. 66). (See chapter 6 for a comprehensive description of each strategy.) As an example, we can apply one component of the process, manipulation of controlling variables, to Timothy, who exhibits tantrum behaviors (e.g., cries, throws materials, falls to the ground).

Through the functional assessment process, Timothy's tantrum behaviors were hypothesized to be motivated by a desire to escape from the activities during which they occur. To test this hypothesis, Mr. Grayson, his special education teacher, planned to set up a period of time (e.g., Monday during music group) in which Timothy would be allowed to "escape" each time that he begins a tantrum (i.e., Mr. Grayson reinforces the tantruming). This would be repeated on Wednesday and Thursday. Data from these days would be compared with the data from Tuesday and Friday, in which escaping by tantruming is not reinforced (i.e., his teachers attempted to redirect him back to his activities). If the data reveal higher levels of tantrums on Monday, Wednesday, and Thursday, then Mr. Grayson can conclude that the tantruming is a function of the escape that it produces; that is, the tantruming increases when it is reinforced by

escape from the activity. Mr. Grayson could use this information to design or revise current instructional strategies. As described previously, he and others from the team might design a functional communication training program to teach Timothy to escape in a more appropriate way (e.g., sign "break," show break card).

Further, Mr. Grayson might examine Timothy's scheduled activities that are associated with tantruming to see if they are (a) needed, (b) preferred or disliked, and (c) on an appropriate difficulty level. Some activities associated with Timothy's tantrums might not be necessary and could be eliminated from his schedule (e.g., matching colored blocks). However, other activities associated with his problem behavior might not be dispensable, so Mr. Grayson would need to investigate further. Are certain activities too difficult and should they be simplified, or should Timothy be taught to request help? Are the activities simply disliked? If so, Mr. Grayson could make one or several program improvements: (a) teaching Timothy to request periodic breaks, (b) preceding the problematic activities with simpler activities (Horner, Day, Sprague, O'Brien, & Heathfield, 1991), (c) allowing Timothy to schedule when he will complete nonpreferred activities (F. Brown, 1991), or (d) following participation in nonpreferred activities with a choice of preferred activities (positive reinforcement for participation in nonpreferred activities).

Functional assessment of behavior problems is an important element of assessment that teachers should use when developing support plans for students who exhibit serious behavior problems. The assessment process should involve the entire educational team because functional assessment requires a study of a student throughout his or her daily activities.

Assessment of Student Preferences and Choices

The opportunity to express one's preferences and to make and enjoy choices is important to everyone. Consistent with this basic life quality tenet, recent law requires that educational and rehabilitation programs for persons with disabilities reflect the use of an individual's preferences and allow choice making (Hughes, Pitkin, & Lorden, 1998). While related, choice and preference do not mean the same thing. *Choice can be observed when an individual acts to get or engage in something* as an opportunity occurs, but a *preference is something consistently chosen over time* and is observed only by its effect on the individual over time. "While choice is an observable behavior, preference, on the other hand, is inferred from the act of choice" (Hughes et al., 1998, p. 299). We usually assume that choices reflect an individual's preferences, although they may not always do so.

Assessment Procedures

There is an abundance of research on the identification of reinforcers and preferences and the effects of offering opportunities for choice making to individuals with severe disabilities (e.g., Bambara, Ager, & Koger, 1994; Hughes et al., 1998; Ivanic & Bailey, 1995; Kern et al., 1998). An extensive review of research over the past 20 years indicates that increasing choice-making opportunities is associated with increases in appropriate behavior and the decline of undesirable responding (Kern et al., 1998). Knowing what an individual prefers is important for several reasons. First, preferred stimuli may be used to reinforce target behaviors or skills. This traditional approach involves making preferred stimuli available singly or offered as a choice to students contingent on specific target behaviors; the outcome is that the strength or quality of the behavior is likely to improve.

Second and, perhaps more important, offering opportunities to choose between preferred activities or events seems to increase students' active involvement and promote their motivation during instruction (Hughes et al., 1998). A student's control in an activity is increased when asked to select the task, the materials (e.g., markers or colored pencils), the location, the classmates to participate with, or the order of the tasks. Increased involvement and motivation are good reasons to individually assess the activities, events, and objects each student prefers and to offer many opportunities for choices within the context of daily routines across the day (Bambara, Koger, Katzer, & Davenport, 1995; F. Brown, Belz, Corsi, & Wenig, 1993). Typically, students' preferences vary during the day and from day to day. Since most students with severe disabilities cannot verbally inform us of these changes, initially, more comprehensive assessments should be followed by intermittent (or even daily) "mini-assessments" to determine what activities or items are currently preferred (Mason, McGee, Farmer-Dougan, & Risley, 1989; Roane, Vollmer, Ringdahl, & Marcus, 1998). As a simpler alternative to mini-assessment, others suggest that offering

a choice of items and letting the student select, rather than having a teacher select, the preferred item is a more efficient way to be sure activities are reinforcing (Horner & Carr, 1997). In the following section, we review several comprehensive and mini-assessment methods that have been successful in identifying preferences with students who have severe disabilities (Lohrmann-O'Rourke & Browder, 1998).

Interview Interviewing those who know the student well to identify a pool of potentially preferred activities and objects has not been found to be an effective method by itself. The opinions of others assessed through interviews do not usually identify reliable preferences when not used in combination with direct observation methods (Green et al., 1988); however, interviews can provide some idea of activities to assess further through direct observation.

Comprehensive Assessment A comprehensive assessment of a person's preferences involves multiple opportunities to interact with or choose from a pool of potentially interesting activities, foods, or objects. The outcome is a rank ordered set of potential reinforcers from highly preferred (e.g., approached 80% of the time) to less preferred, not preferred, or avoided. Researchers using these assessment methods have found that when those items that were consistently approached or chosen were then used as consequences for certain behaviors, the preferred items produced consistently higher rates of responding than did nonpreferred items. Usually, one of two methods are used for systematic, comprehensive assessment of preferences: approach-avoidance (e.g., Pace, Ivancic, Edwards, Iwata, & Page, 1985) or forced choice (e.g., Fisher, Piazza, Bowman, & Amari, 1996).

Approach-avoidance involves presenting single items to a student and waiting for a short, standard period of time (e.g., about 5 seconds). Approach and avoidance responses must be defined individually for each student. Examples of approach responses are making eye contact with the item, moving toward the item, and making a positive vocal expression. Avoidance responses may include behavior such as pushing the item away, making a movement away from the item, and making a negative vocalization. If the student approaches the item, that item is made available for another short interval (e.g., 5 seconds). If the student does not approach the item, it is removed, and shortly after the student is given an opportunity to sample the activity with prompts (e.g., help Timmy turn on a tape recorder to play music). Following any opportunities to sample an activity, the student is given another approach opportunity with the same activity; if the student approaches it, an additional 5 seconds is given to engage with that item.

Another variation of this approach involves free access to a group of 10 or more potentially reinforcing items that involve various types of stimuli and social attention (e.g., tactile: Koosh ball; play: ball; drink: water, cola; social: praise, hugs) (Dyer, 1987). Any items that are consumed are replenished, and social attention is provided intermittently. An observer watches and rates the individual's approach and avoidance responses to each item or event.

In a forced choice method, items are presented in pairs, and each item in the pool of potential reinforcers is presented randomly with every other item. The same general procedures used in the approach-avoidance method are used, except that items are presented in sets of two. The findings from this method may be more consistent than when items are presented alone.

Brief Assessment Brief assessment methods can be used to update comprehensive assessments for students who have severe disabilities (Mason et al., 1989; Roane et al. 1998). Roane et al. (1998) used a method that provided a student with 5 minutes of free access to a group of items (previously determined to be preferred). Before free access was given, the student was led around a table and given contact with each item in the preferred group; if the student did not initiate contact with the item, the teacher assisted (by modeling or physically prompting the item's use). Then the teacher began the brief preference assessment by (a) gathering the items, (b) arranging them in a circle on a table, and (c) letting the student manipulate any of them, several at a time, or none at all. No items are removed from the array. The teacher used a 10-second partial interval recording procedure to record the student's contact with any particular item (this recording procedure is explained in chapter 5). This method was reported as taking less time and resulting in less student misbehavior but still identifying items students found to be reinforcing. When teachers do not control the presentation of various stimuli as in forced choice assessment format but provide free access, students appear more likely to participate willingly.

Considerations for Assessing Preferences

While the assessment methods we describe were used with students who have severe disabilities, these students demonstrated intentional behavior (see chapter 11) and typically did not have motor or sensory limitations such as Christine's. Because our current methods for assessing preferences with students who have severe disabilities are less inclusive of students with extensive motor and sensory limitations, team members must make adjustments to these approaches when they are used with any particular student (Green & Reid, 1996; Ivancic & Bailey, 1995):

- The student's approach and avoidance response should be identified in observable terms.

  Christine does not visually seek out items associated with preferred activities but smiles and sometimes laughs when engaged in activities she enjoys. Timothy does not show emotions in this way but instead persists in the activities he likes and cries when they are removed.

- Potential preferred items and activities need to be presented so the student is aware of them.

  Depending on the activity option, Christine's team members tell her the name of the activity, let her experience any movement involved, hear noise associated with the activity, and feel objects involved in the activity.

- Items or activities should be sampled in ways that are meaningful to the student.

  Simply telling Timothy about a new activity (e.g., "Timothy, you can play with the water table today") will not provide a meaningful sample. Timothy needs to watch others use the water table and be encouraged to try it himself before his preference is assessed.

When designing and conducting preference assessments, there are also many considerations that concern the social validity of the assessment process. The following guidelines can increase the social validity of the assessment and its application to inclusive settings (Lohrmann-O'Rourke, Browder, & Brown, 2000):

- Assessments should be conducted in settings and within contexts that are as natural as possible.

- Assessments should be conducted by individuals who know the student well.

  A behavioral consultant recently hired by Timothy's preschool was interested in determining Timothy's preferences. Using a forced choice format, he systematically presented a variety of stimulus items to Timothy. Timothy avoided contact not only with the behavioral consultant but with all items presented by the consultant. It was concluded that the results measured not his preference for the stimuli that were being assessed but his level of comfort with the consultant. Plans were made to have his teacher learn how to conduct the assessment.

- Stimuli presented to the individual should be valued by the individual and represent a range of stimuli that reflect events or activities preferred by individuals who do not have disabilities.

  When his teacher presented the stimulus pairs to Timothy, he was able to judge Timothy's approach-avoidance to each item. Mr. Grayson was concerned, however, that although these items were chosen and thus were assumed to be preferred, they did not represent the events and activities that Timothy seemed most to enjoy (e.g., cartoons, building blocks, "hi fives").

- In addition to identifying potential reinforcers, results of preference assessments should lead to information that will contribute to the improvement of daily life (i.e., noncontingent access to preferred events).

  When it was concluded that music was a potential reinforcer for Timothy, some team members suggested that listening to music be contingent on Timothy's performance during group activities. Other team members thought that, because we now know how much Timothy likes music, he should have more access to music and that music should be a context in which he learns other skills. After much discussion, the team decided that there should be more music in his life!

Program Quality and Quality of Life

When professionals view each student with disabilities as having all the feelings, hopes, and needs of their more typical peers, focus on the assessment and evaluation of small skill changes seems inadequate. Although

teachers must still remain accountable for the assessment, instruction, and evaluation of skill learning (process measures), other critical areas in students' lives require evaluation. Outcome measures (see chapter 5 for a more detailed description) refer to the general effect of a program on a person's quality of life. Assessment should reflect a range of meaningful outcomes for the individual, school, family, and community (Billingsley et al., 1996; Meyer & Janney, 1989). Among the variables assessed are social life (the activities performed with other people), the social network, and the social supports a person has (Kennedy, Horner, & Newton, 1990); control and choices in daily life (F. Brown, 1991; Meyer & Evans, 1989); and the extent of social and physical integration, family participation, and physical accessibility. The following sections review some strategies to assess the quality of an individual's program and factors associated with a good quality of life.

Program Quality Indicators (PQI)

The PQI (Meyer & Eichinger, 1994), in its third revision, was developed for use by school districts and consumer groups to evaluate the quality of inclusive schooling and to guide program development and improvement. The PQI checklist contains 38 items organized into four sections. Within each of these areas are items that represent the most promising practices in educational and related services for students with disabilities:

1. Local Education Agency District Indicators include 10 items, among which are policies on placement in home school and inclusive classes, philosophy of mission statement, staff development and unification, and policy for medical and behavioral emergencies.
2. Building Indicators include nine items examining practices related to areas such as family–school relations, transportation, site-based management, extracurricular opportunities, team planning meetings, services in general education, instructional arrangements, and use of paraprofessionals and volunteers.
3. Educational Placement and Related Services Indicators lists nine items focusing on the design of the instructional setting, including areas such as regular education membership and social relationships, daily schedules, regular education instruction,

differentiated instruction, curricular and instructional adaptations, student expectations, support services, and transition planning.

4. Individual Student and Program Indicators has nine items that examine the school's response to educational, linguistic, cultural, age-related, and ability-related diversity as well as opportunities for self-actualization and enrichment.

The PQI was organized into these sections to enable various school personnel to use the specific section for which they have specific responsibility and in which they are most interested. For example, district office personnel may be the most appropriate to evaluate the first component, while district- and building-level administrators may be most appropriate to evaluate the third component since they are responsible for decisions regarding educational placement and assignment of services (Meyer & Eichinger, 1994).

Person-Centered Approaches to Assessment

Person-centered planning is an approach that emerged in the mid-1980s to allow us to better understand the experiences of people with developmental disabilities and more respectfully and effectively support them to expand those experiences to achieve a desired quality of life (Cohen, 1998; Holburn, 2002; Holburn & Vietze, 2002; O'Brien, O'Brien, & Mount, 1997). This approach is qualitatively different from traditional educational, diagnostic, and standardized assessment approaches because it shifts focus of control from the interdisciplinary team to the person with disabilities and his or her family, and it is their hopes and dreams that determine and direct the education program and supports (Knowlton, 1998; Sands, Bassett, Lehmann, & Spencer, 1998; A. P. Turnbull et al., 1996). Kincaid (1996) suggests that person-centered planning activities share a commitment to seeking five essential goals, outcomes, or valued accomplishments in the individual's life: (a) being present and participating in community life, (b) gaining and maintaining satisfying relationships, (c) expressing preferences and making choices in everyday life, (d) having opportunities to fulfill respected roles and to live with dignity, and (e) continuing to develop personal competencies.

Two widely used person-centered planning tools, McGill Action Planning System or Making Action Plans (MAPS) and Personal Futures Planning, will be

discussed here. MAPS (Forest & Lusthaus, 1989; Pearpoint, Forest, & O'Brien, 1996; Vandercook, York, & Forest, 1989) involves having typical students who know the individual well participate in several planning sessions. In MAPS, the individual and members of the individual's inner circle discuss several questions: (a) What is the individual's history? (b) What are your dreams for her or him? (c) What is your nightmare about him or her (e.g., fears about the future)? (d) Who is she or he? (e) What does he or she like? (f) What are his or her strengths, gifts, and talents? (g) What are his or her needs? (h) What would an ideal day for her or him look like? (i) What do we need to make this ideal real?

MAPS serves as a guide for the individual's circle of friends to identify critical areas of focus. The group meets regularly with the facilitating teacher or school staff and the focus individual, informally evaluating their actions, discussing improvements and new ideas, and continuing to support the focus individual. Sometimes when elementary-age students are involved the nightmare question is omitted (Snell & Janney, 2000).

In Personal Futures Planning (Mount & Zwernik, 1988), a facilitator trained in the planning process leads a group of key people through planning steps. The key people may be related to the focus individual as close friends, family members, staff, or others with whom the person spends a lot of time. Whenever possible, the focus individual is included in the planning process; advocates or spokespersons may be present to help the focus person communicate. The first task of the group is to write a personal profile for the focus individual. Personal profiles consist of three kinds of information about the individual: (a) history, (b) accomplishments, and (c) preferences and desires. A second meeting addresses the individual's future plan. Third, the same participants proceed through seven steps: review the personal profile, review the trends in the environment that may affect the individual, find desirable images of the future, identify obstacles and opportunities, identify strategies to implement the plan, identify actions to get started, and identify any needs for system changes.

At age 18 before Christine made the transition to the post-high school program at the nearby university, her parents and the rest of her educational team were joined by a few of her friends from the university and two high school students who knew her well to complete a person-centered plan. They hoped the plan would help them further center all their efforts around Christine's interests and life. The first activities took most of an afternoon and involved describing (a) who was at the meeting; (b) the people in Christine's life; (c) the places she frequents at home, work, school, and in the community; (d) her history; (e) her health issues; (f) her preferences; (g) things that promote respect and detract from the respect of others; (h) strategies that work and don't work; (i) hopes and fears; (j) barrier and opportunities; and (k) the themes of her life (Kincaid, 1996). The group was pleased with their efforts to gather all this information and planned during their second meeting to design a future plan for Christine.

Prioritizing Skills from Assessment Information

Literally hundreds of skills and activities identified in the assessment process are relevant for a student. Teaching all of these is, of course, not possible or desirable. Following the assessment process, the team must select which skills and activities will become the core of the individualized education program. Prioritizing skills and activities is an important step because it defines the activities in which the student will participate for the year. A team approach is critical in this step of the educational process. Rainforth, York, and Macdonald (1997) reflect that "it is natural for service providers to see priorities from the vantage [point] of their own discipline. A collaborative and consensual approach to determining priorities may be the most difficult aspect of designing the IEP, since it frequently requires one or more team members to let go of what they view as important from their discipline's perspective" (p. 160).

Many criteria for selecting priorities have been discussed in the literature. Figure 3–6, based on the format used by Dardig and Heward (1981) and Helmstetter (1989), identifies many criteria that should be considered when prioritizing objectives from assessment information. No single objective can meet all the guidelines, and certainly some objectives may meet only a few but are still critical (e.g., health-related objectives). The relative importance of each criterion varies from student to student, especially given variations in family values, lifestyles, and perspectives (Rainforth et al., 1997). The following are additional questions that

should be considered when selecting IEP objectives that reflect current best practices.

Does the objective reflect the student's chronological age, culture, preferences, and profile of strengths and needs? The student must be recognized as an individual with a chronological age and level of physical maturity, a culture, a family history and context, preferences (including likes and dislikes), and personal strengths and needs. Many students have clear strengths in their adaptive skills and in other personal abilities.

Because Christine's vision and spoken communication are very limited, her family, team members, and friends have learned that several strategies are important. For example, it is best when peers, parents, and teachers tell her what will happen next in simple terms, follow familiar routines while avoiding surprises when possible, dodge strategies that rely only on vision, and read her "body language." She is very social and enjoys being around others when these simple guidelines for interaction are respected. This profile of strengths and needs for Christine has guided the team in selecting work sites for her to sample, and the profile also suggested some preparation steps for each site. As an example, the team guessed that Christine would enjoy (a) assisting in checking out books at a nearby elementary school library and (b) being a greeter at Wal-Mart. They hypothesized this because both jobs allowed active engagement and offered many social opportunities.

Does the objective focus on functional skills and lead to meaningful routines and activities? Another guideline for selecting IEP objectives is functionality, or skill usefulness, a measure of how necessary and important a skill is to a particular person, given his or her current and future environments. Applying the functionality guideline to learning objectives means that no generic bank of IEP objectives can be universally taught. What is functional for one person may not be for another.

Applying the functionality guideline also means looking to the future and planning outcomes for the upcoming stages in the student's life cycle: entering preschool, moving into elementary school, starting middle school and becoming an adolescent, going to high school, taking a job, moving away from home, retiring, and facing death. If parents and preschool teachers plan for Timothy, now 4 years old, to be included at

FIGURE 3–6

Examples of Criteria Used for Setting Priorities

Student: _____

Person(s) completing form: _____

Date: _____

List each activity or objective that is being considered for instruction.

Rate each activity or objective using: 3 = strongly agree with statement; 2 = agree somewhat with statement; 1 = disagree somewhat with statement; 0 = disagree strongly with statement

Criteria	Activity/Objective								
1. Can be used in current environments									
2. Can be used in future environments									
3. Can be used across environments and activities									
4. Facilitates interactions with nondisabled peers									
5. Increases student independence									
6. Is chronologically age-appropriate									
7. Student can meaningfully participate									
8. Student rates as high priority or highly preferred									
9. Family rates as high priority									
10. Improves health or fitness									
11. Meets a medical need									
12. Promotes a positive view of the individual									
13. Student shows positive response to activity									
14. Supported by related service staff									
15. Student can achieve, accomplish, or control a meaningful part of the activity									
Total									

Note: Adapted with permission from Dardig, J. D., & Heward, L. (1981). A systematic procedure for prioritizing IEP goals. *The Directive Teacher, 3,* 6–7, and Helmstetter, E. (1989). Curriculum for school-age students: The ecological model. In F. Brown & D. H. Lehr (Eds.), *Persons with profound disabilities: Issues and practices* (p. 254). Baltimore: Paul H. Brookes.

age 5 in his neighborhood school kindergarten and identify the necessary supports to achieve this, planning will influence the supports and skills delineated in Timothy's current IEP. By using assessment strategies that involve families, friends, present and upcoming teachers, or program staff, a team will be able to understand their students' present lives and formulate ideas about future expectations, possibilities, and hopes.

Can the student participate in the activity in a meaningful way? A student may be able to learn an activity so that it can be performed in its entirety in the natural environment. For these students, the appropriate range of participation necessary for competent performance of the skill in relevant contexts should be ensured (e.g., by initiation, problem solving, quality monitoring). Many students, however, are not able to attain independence in important, needed, or enjoyed skills or activities. Some of the cognitive and motor requirements of tasks may appear to present insurmountable obstacles for an individual student. However, partial participation (Baumgart et al., 1982) can open the door to many possibilities for including that student instead of excluding him or her because "she (or he) will never be able to do that!" Adaptive or prosthetic aids, adapted materials, rule or schedule adaptations, and personal assistance strategies are ways in which a student can meaningfully participate in an activity (Baumgart et al., 1982).

Meaningful participation can also be facilitated by focusing on extension and enrichment skills. For example, initiating, monitoring quality, terminating, choosing, social interacting, and communicating are ways to participate in a routine that do not require extensive motor participation (F. Brown et al., 1987; F. Brown & Lehr, 1993).

Does the objective reflect the student's personal and social needs? Planning an IEP by "functional" guidelines alone may mean that personal and social domains are slighted and that supports are viewed narrowly to include only teachers, therapists, and educational materials. This guideline stresses the importance of the relationships and membership domains. Regardless of the presence or degree of a disability, children, adolescents, and adults need friends to participate in activities in a way that increases self-esteem. In fact, the presence of a disability may increase the need for supportive friends. Objectives that facilitate friendships, supports, and membership in the school and community should be given high priority.

Summary

Assessment is a complex but critical component of program development. If used wisely, information gathered from assessments becomes the cornerstone of program development. Although there are no easy formulas for the selection of an appropriate assessment process for any one student, this chapter reviews the advantages and disadvantages of a variety of assessment strategies and describes how they can best be applied. The assessment process determines whether the outcomes that are identified and measured are meaningful. Focusing solely on academic development or skill development, as was done historically, is not sufficient. Assessment outcomes should also be referenced to the domains of relationships and membership (Billingsley et al., 1996). Involvement in person-centered planning strategies is an excellent way to guide teams and ensure that they focus on those elements that will contribute to the quality of an individual's life.

The chapter discusses developmental approaches to assessment, assessments of adaptive behavior, environmental assessment approaches, assessments of program quality and quality of life, and variables to consider when prioritizing skills for instruction. Teachers must know the appropriate uses—and be aware of the inappropriate uses—of the wide range of assessments and assessment strategies.

Suggested Activities

1. Select one student in your class and carefully examine the assessments that are in his or her file.
   a. How many norm-referenced tests and criterion-referenced tests do you see?
   b. Are there any environmental assessments?
   c. Are there any questionnaires eliciting input from this student's family?
   d. If the student has problem behaviors, are there any functional behavioral assessments?
2. Select a different student and carefully examine the instructional objectives targeted on his or her IEP. How do the objectives compare to the 15 criteria listed in Figure 3-6? How do the objectives compare with the following four criteria:
   a. Does the objective reflect the student's chronological age, culture, preferences, and profile of strengths and needs?

b. Does the objective focus on functional skills and lead to meaningful routines and activities?
c. Does the objective reflect the student's personal and social needs?
d. Can the student participate in the activity in a meaningful way?

References

Adams, J. (1973). Adaptive behavior and measured intelligence in the classification of mental retardation. *American Journal of Mental Deficiency, 78*, 77–81.

Alberto, P. A., & Troutman, A. C. (1999). *Applied behavior analysis for teachers* (5th ed.). Upper Saddle River, NJ: Merrill/Prentice Hall.

Albin, R. W., Lucyshyn, J. M., Horner, R. H., & Flannery, K. B. (1996). Contextual fit for behavioral support plans: A model for "goodness of fit." In R. L. Koegel, L. K. Koegel, & G. Dunlap (Eds.), *Positive behavioral support: Including people with difficult behavior in the community* (pp. 81–98). Baltimore: Paul H. Brookes.

Alpern, G., Boll, T., & Shearer, M. S. (1986). *Developmental Profile II*. Los Angeles: Western Psychological Services.

Apgar, V. (1953). A proposal for a new method of evaluation of the newborn infant. *Current Researches in Anesthesia and Analgesia, 32*, 260–267.

Apgar, V., & Beck, J. (1973). Is my baby all right? New York: Trident Press.

Bailey, D. B., McWilliam, R. A., Darkes, L. A., Hebbeler, K., Simeonsson, R. J., Spiker, D., & Wagner, M. (1998). Family outcomes in early intervention: A framework for program evaluation and efficacy research. *Exceptional Children, 64*, 313–328.

Bambara, L. M., Agar, C., & Koger, F. (1994). The effects of choice and task preference on the work performance of adults with severe disabilities. *Journal of Applied Behavior Analysis, 27*, 555–556.

Bambara, L. M., Koger, F., Katzer, T., & Davenport, T. (1995). Embedding choice in daily routines: An experimental case study. *Journal of the Association for Persons with Severe Handicaps, 20*, 185–195.

Baron-Cohen, S., Allen, J., & Gillberg, C. (1992). Can autism be detected at 18 months? The needle, the haystack, and the CHAT. *British Journal of Psychiatry, 161*, 839–843.

Bateman, B. D., & Linden, M. A. (1998). *Better IEPs* (3rd ed.). Longmont, CO: Sopris West.

Baumeister, A. A., & Muma, J. R. (1975). On defining mental retardation. *Journal of Special Education, 9*, 293–306.

Baumgart, D., Brown, L., Pumpian, I., Nisbet, J., Ford, A., Sweet, M., Messina, R., & Schroeder, J. (1982). Principle of partial participation and individualized adaptations in educational programs for severely handicapped students. *Journal of the Association for the Severely Handicapped, 7*, 17–27.

Bayley, N. (1993). *Bayley Scales of Infant Development II*. San Antonio, TX: Psychological Corporation.

Billingsley, F. F., Gallucci, C., Peck, C. A., Schwartz, I. S., & Staub, D. (1996). "But those kids can't even do math": An alternative conceptualization of outcomes for inclusive education. *Special Education Leadership Review, 3*, 43–55.

Brazelton, T. B., & Nugent, J. K. (1995). *Neonatal behavioral assessment scale* (3rd ed.). London: MacKeith.

Bricker, D. (2002). *Assessment, evaluation and programming system (AEPS-R) for infants and children*. Baltimore: Paul H. Brookes.

Brigance, A. (1991). *Brigance diagnostic inventory of early development*. North Billerica, MA: Curriculum Associates.

Brigance, A., & Glascoe, F. P. (1999). *Brigance Comprehensive Inventory of Basic Skills Revised*. North Billerica, MA: Curriculum Associates.

Browder, D. M. (2001). *Curriculum and assessment for students with moderate and severe disabilities*. New York: Guilford.

Browder, D., & Spooner, F. (2003). Understanding the purpose and process of alternate assessment. In D. L. Ryndak & S. Alper (Eds.), *Curriculum and instruction for students with significant disabilities in inclusive settings* (pp. 51–72). Boston: Allyn & Bacon.

Browder, D., Spooner, F., Ahlgrim-Delzell, L., Flowers, C., Algozzine, B., & Karvonen, M. (2004). A content analysis of the curricular philosophies reflected in states' alternate assessment performance indicators. *Research and Practice for Persons with Severe Disabilities, 28*, 165–181.

Brown, F. (1991). Creative daily scheduling: A nonintrusive approach to challenging behaviors in community residences. *Journal of the Association for Persons with Severe Handicaps, 16*, 75–84.

Brown, F. (1996). Variables to consider in the assessment of problem behaviors. *TASH Newsletter, 22*, 19–20.

Brown, F., Belz, B., Corsi, L., & Wenig, B. (1993). Choice diversity for people with severe disabilities. *Education and Training in Mental Retardation, 28*, 318–326.

Brown, F., Evans, I. M., Weed, K. A., & Owen, V. (1987). Delineating functional competencies: A component model. *Journal of the Association for Persons with Severe Handicaps, 12*, 117–124.

Brown, F., Gothelf, C. R., Guess, D., & Lehr, D. H. (1998). Self-determination for individuals with the most severe disabilities: Moving beyond chimera. *Journal of the Association for Persons with Severe Handicaps, 23*, 17–26.

Brown, F., & Lehr, D. (1993). Meaningful outcomes for students with severe disabilities. *Teaching Exceptional Children, 4*, 12–16.

Brown, F., & Michaels, C. A. (2003). The shaping of inclusion: Efforts in Detroit and other urban settings. In D. Fisher & N. Frey (Eds.), *Inclusive urban schools* (pp. 231–243). Baltimore: Paul H. Brookes.

Brown, L., Branston, M. B., Hamre-Nietupski, S., Pumpian, I., Certo, N., & Gruenewald, L. (1979). A strategy for developing chronological-age-appropriate and functional curricular content for severely handicapped adolescents and young adults. *Journal of Special Education, 13*, 81–90.

Bruininks, R. H., Hill, B. K., Weatherman, R. F., & Woodcock, R. W. (1986). *Inventory for client and agency planning (ICAP)*. Riverside, CA: DLM Teaching Resources.

Bruininks, R. H., Woodcock, R. W., Weatherman, R. F., & Hill, B. K. (1996). *Scales of independent behavior—revised (SIB-R)*. Riverside, CA: DLM Teaching Resources.

Carr, E. G., Levin, L., McConnachie, G., Carlson, J. I., Kemp, D. C., & Smith, C. E. (1994). *Communication-based intervention for problem behavior*. Baltimore: Paul H. Brookes.

Chen, D., & Dote-Kwan, J. (1998). Early intervention services for young children who have visual impairments with other disabilities and their families. In S. Z. Sacks & R. I. Silberman (Eds.), *Educating students who have visual impairments with other disabilities* (pp. 303-334). Baltimore: Paul H. Brookes.

Cohen, S. (1998). *Targeting autism: What we know, don't know, and can do to help young children with autism and related disorders.* Berkeley: University of California Press.

Council for Exceptional Children. (2004). Policy on assessment and accountability. *Teaching Exceptional Children, 36,* 70-71.

Cress, P. J., Spellman, C. R., DeBriere, T. J., Sizemore, A. C., Northam, J. K., & Johnson, J. L. (1981). Vision screening for persons with severe handicaps. *Journal of the Association for the Severely Handicapped, 6*(3), 41-50.

Dardig, J. D., & Heward, W. L. (1981). A systematic procedure for prioritizing IEP goals. *The Directive Teacher, 3,* 6-7.

Denning, C. B., Chamberlain, J. A., & Polloway, E. A. (2000). An evaluation of state guidelines for mental retardation: Focus on definition and classification practices. *Education and Training in Mental Retardation and Developmental Disabilities, 35,* 226-232.

Downing, J. E., & Demchak, M. A. (1996). First steps: Determining individual abilities and how best to support students. In J. E. Downing (Ed.), *Including students with severe and multiple disabilities in typical classrooms* (pp. 35-61). Baltimore: Paul H. Brookes.

Downing, J., & Perino, D. (1992). Functional vs. standardized assessment procedures: Implications for educational programming. *Mental Retardation, 30,* 289-295.

Dunlap, G., & Kern, L. (1993). Assessment and intervention for children within the instructional curriculum. In J. Reichle & D. Wacker (Eds.), *Communicative approaches to the management of challenging behavior* (pp. 177-203). Baltimore: Paul H. Brookes.

Dunlap, G., Kern-Dunlap, L., Clarke, S., & Robbins, F. R. (1991). Functional assessment, curricular revision, and severe problem behaviors. *Journal of Applied Behavior Analysis, 22,* 387-397.

Durand, V. M. (1990). *Severe behavior problems: A functional communication training approach.* New York: Guilford.

Durand, V. M., & Carr, E. G. (1991). Functional communication training to reduce challenging behavior: Maintenance and application in new settings. *Journal of Applied Behavior Analysis, 24,* 251-264.

Durand, V. M., & Merger, E. (2001). Functional communication training: A contemporary behavior analytic intervention for problem behaviors. *Focus on Autism and Other Developmental Disabilities, 16,* 110-119.

Dyer, K. (1987). The competition of autistic stereotyped behavior with usual and specially assessed reinforcers. *Research in Developmental Disabilities, 8,* 607-626.

Evans, I. M. (1991). Testing and diagnosis: A review and evaluation. In L. H. Meyer, C. A. Peck, & L. Brown (Eds.), *Critical issues in the lives of people with severe disabilities* (pp. 25-44). Baltimore: Paul H. Brookes.

Evans, I. M., & Brown, F. (1986). Outcome assessment of student competence: Issues and implications. *Special Services in the Schools, 2*(4), 41-62.

Evans, I. M., & Scotti, J. R. (1989). Defining meaningful outcomes for persons with profound disabilities. In F. Brown & D. Lehr (Eds.), *Persons and profound disabilities: Issues and practices* (pp. 83-108). Baltimore: Paul H. Brookes.

Fisher, W. W., Piazza, C. C., Bowman, L. G., & Amari, A. (1996). Integrating caregiver report with a systematic choice assessment to enhance reinforcer identification. *American Journal on Mental Retardation, 101,* 15-25.

Ford, A., Schnorr, R., Meyer, L., Davern, L., Black, J., & Dempsey, P. (1989). *The Syracuse community-referenced curriculum guide for students with moderate and severe disabilities.* Baltimore: Paul H. Brookes.

Forest, M., & Lusthaus, E. (1989). Promoting education equality for all students: circles and maps. In S. Stainback, W. Stainback, & M. Forest (Eds.), *Educating all students in the mainstream of regular education* (pp. 43-57). Baltimore: Paul H. Brookes.

Frankenburg, W. K., Dodds, J., Archer, P., Bresnick, B., Maschka, P., Edelman, N., & Shapiro, H. (1990). *The DENVER II.* Denver: Denver Developmental Materials, Inc.

Gaylord-Ross, R. J., & Holvoet, J. (1985). *Strategies for educating students with severe handicaps.* Boston: Little, Brown.

Giangreco, M. F., Cloninger, C. J., & Iverson, V. S. (1998). *C.O.A.C.H.: Choosing outcomes and accommodations for children* (2nd ed.). Baltimore: Paul H. Brookes.

Gilliam, J. E. (1995). *Gilliam autism rating scale (GARS).* Austin, TX: PRO-ED.

Gothelf, C. R., & Brown, F. (1998). Participation in the education process: Students with severe disabilities. In M. L. Wehmeyer & D. J. Sands (Eds.), *Making it happen: Student involvement in education planning, decision making, and instruction* (pp. 99-121). Baltimore: Paul H. Brookes.

Green, C. W., & Reid, D. H. (1996). Defining, validating, and increasing indices of happiness among people with profound multiple disabilities. *Journal of Applied Behavior Analysis, 29,* 67-78.

Green, C. W., Reid, D. H., White, L. K., Halford, R. C., Brittain, D. P., & Gardner, S. M. (1988). Identifying reinforcers for persons with profound handicaps: Staff opinion versus systematic assessment of preferences. *Journal of Applied Behavior Analysis, 21,* 31-43.

Greenspan, S. (1999). What is meant by mental retardation? *International Review of Psychiatry, 11,* 6-18.

Gresham, F. M. (1983). Social skills assessment as a component of mainstreaming placement decisions. *Exceptional Children, 49,* 331-336.

Grossman, H. J. (Ed.). (1983). *Classification in mental retardation.* Washington, DC: American Association on Mental Deficiency.

Guess, D., & Noonan, M. J. (1982). Curricula and instructional procedures for severely handicapped students. *Focus on Exceptional Children, 4,* 1-12.

Haring, T. G., & Breen, C. (1989). Units of analysis of social interaction outcomes in supported education. *Journal of the Association of Persons with Severe Handicaps, 14,* 255-262.

Haring, T. G., & Kennedy, C. H. (1990). Contextual control of problem behaviors in students with severe disabilities. *Journal of Applied Behavior Analysis, 23,* 235-243.

Hatton, C. (1998). Whose quality of life is it anyway? Some problems with the emerging quality of life consensus. *Mental Retardation, 36,* 104-115.

Heber, R. (1959). *A manual on terminology and classification in mental retardation.* Willimantic, CT: American Association on Mental Deficiency.

Heber, R. (1961). Modifications in the manual on terminology and classification in mental retardation. *American Journal of Mental Deficiency, 65,* 499-500.

Helmstetter, E. (1989). Curriculum for school-age students: The ecological model. In F. Brown & D. Lehr (Eds.), *Persons with profound disabilities: Issues and practices* (pp. 239-264). Baltimore: Paul H. Brookes.

Hobson v. Hansen, 269 F. Supp. 401 (D.D.C. 1967).

Holburn, S. (2002). How science can evaluate and enhance person-centered planning. *Research and Practice for Persons with Severe Disabilities, 27,* 250-260.

Holburn, S., & Vietze, P. M. (2002). *Person-centered planning: Research, practice, and future directions.* Baltimore: Paul H. Brookes.

Horner, R. H., & Carr, E. G. (1997). Behavioral support for students with severe disabilities: Functional assessment and comprehensive intervention. *Journal of Special Education, 31,* 84-104.

Horner, R. H., Day, M. H., Sprague, J. R., O'Brien, M., & Heathfield, L. T. (1991). Interspersed requests: A nonaversive procedure for reducing aggression and self-injury during instruction. *Journal of Applied Behavior Analysis, 24,* 265-278.

Hughes, C., Pitkin, S. E., & Lorden S. W. (1998). Assessing preferences and choices of persons with severe and profound mental retardation. *Education and Training in Mental Retardation and Developmental Disabilities, 33,* 299-316.

Ivancic, M. T., & Bailey, J. S. (1995). Current limits to reinforcer identification for some persons with profound disabilities. *Research in Developmental Disabilities, 17,* 77-92.

Janney, R. E., & Snell, M. E. (2000). *Practices for inclusive schools: Behavior support.* Baltimore: Paul H. Brookes.

Johnson-Martin, N. M., Attermeier, S. M., & Hacker, B. (1990). *The Carolina Curriculum for preschoolers with special needs.* Baltimore: Paul H. Brookes.

Kennedy, C. H., Horner, R. H., & Newton, J. S. (1990). The social networks and activity patterns of adults with severe disabilities: A correlational analysis. *Journal of the Association for Persons with Severe Handicaps, 15,* 86-90.

Kern, L., Vorndran, C. M., Hilt, A., Ringdahl, J. E., Adelman, B. E., & Dunlap, G. (1998). Choice as an intervention to improve behavior: A review of the literature. *Journal of Behavioral Education, 8,* 151-169.

Kincaid, D. 1996. Person-centered planning. In L. K. Koegel, R. L. Koegel, & G. Dunlap (Eds.), *Positive behavioral support: Including people with difficult behavior in the community* (pp. 439-465). Baltimore: Paul H. Brookes.

Knoster, T. P. (2000). Practical application of functional behavioral assessment in schools. *Journal of the Association for Persons with Severe Handicaps, 25,* 201-211.

Knowlton, E. (1998). Considerations in the design of personalized curricular supports for students with developmental disabilities. *Education and Training in Mental Retardation and Developmental Disabilities, 33,* 95-107.

Koegel, R. L., & Koegel, L. K. (Eds.). (1995). *Teaching children with autism: Strategies for initiating positive interactions and improving learning opportunities.* Baltimore: Paul H. Brookes.

Koegel, R. L., Koegel, L. K., & Dunlap, G. (1996). *Positive behavioral support: Including people with difficult behavior in the community.* Baltimore: Paul H. Brookes.

Kunc, N. (1991, April). *Integration: Being realistic isn't realistic.* Speech presented at the On Common Ground Conference, Virginia Statewide Systems Change Project, Charlottesville, VA.

Lambert, N., Nihira, K., & Leland, H. (1993). *Adaptive Behavior Scale—School.* Austin, TX: PRO-ED.

Larry P. v. Riles, 793 F. 2d. 969 (9th Cir. 1984).

Lehr, D. (1989). Educational programming for young children with the most severe disabilities. In F. Brown & D. Lehr (Eds.), *People with profound disabilities: Issues and practices* (pp. 213-238). Baltimore: Paul H. Brookes.

Lennox, D. B., & Miltenberger, R. G. (1989). Conducting a functional assessment of problem behavior in applied settings. *Journal of the Association for Persons with Severe Handicaps, 14,* 304-311.

Lewis, S., & Russo, R. (1998). Educational assessment for students who have visual impairments with other disabilities. In S. Z. Sacks & R. I. Silberman (Eds.), *Educating students who have visual impairments with other disabilities* (pp. 39-71). Baltimore: Paul H. Brookes.

Linehan, S. A., Brady, M. P., & Hwang, C. (1991). Ecological versus developmental assessment: Influences on instructional expectations. *Journal of the Association for Persons with Severe Handicaps, 16,* 146-153.

Lohrmann-O'Rourke, S., & Browder, D. M. (1998). Empirically based methods to assess the preferences of individuals with severe disabilities. *American Journal on Mental Retardation, 103,* 146-161.

Lohrmann-O'Rourke, S., Browder, D. M., & Brown, F. (2000). Guidelines for conducting socially valid systematic preference assessments. *Journal of the Association for Persons with Severe Handicaps, 25,* 42-53.

Lord, C., Rutter, M., DiLavore, P. C., & Risi, S. (1999). *Autism Diagnostic Observation Schedule-WPS Edition* (ADOS-WPS) Los Angeles: Western Psychological Services.

Lord, C ., Rutter, M., & LeCouteur, A. (1994). Autism Diagnostic Interview- Revised: A revised version of a diagnostic interview for caregivers of individuals with possible developmental disorders. *Journal of Autism and Developmental Disorders, 24,* 649-685.

Luckasson, R., Borthwick-Duffy, S., Buntinx, W. H. E., Coulter, D. L., Craig, E. M., Reeve, A., et al. (2002). *Mental retardation: Definition, classification, and systems of supports* (10th ed.). Washington, DC: American Association on Mental Retardation.

Mason, S. A., McGee, G. G., Farmer-Dougan, V., & Risley, T. R. (1989). A practical strategy for ongoing reinforcer assessment. *Journal of Applied Behavior Analysis, 22,* 171-179.

Massachusetts Department of Education. (2001). *Resource guide to the Massachusetts curriculum frameworks for students with significant disabilities.* Malden, MA: Author.

Maurice, C. (1996). *Behavioral intervention for young children with autism: A manual for parents and professionals.* Austin, TX: PRO-ED.

McCarthy, C. F., McLean, L. K., Miller, J. F., Paul-Brown, Romski, M. A., Rourk, J. D., & Yoder, D. E. (1998). *Communication supports checklist for programs serving individuals with severe disabilities.* Baltimore: Paul H. Brookes.

McCarthy, D. (1972). *Manual for the McCarthy scales of children's abilities.* New York: Psychological Corporation.

McLoughlin, J. A., & Lewis, R. B. (1994). *Assessing special students* (4th ed.). Upper Saddle River, NJ: Merrill/Prentice Hall.

Meyer, L. H., & Eichinger, J. (1994). *Program quality indicators (PQI): A checklist of most promising practices in educational programs for students with severe disabilities* (3rd ed.). Seattle: Association for Persons with Severe Handicaps.

Meyer, L. H., & Evans, I. H. (1989). *Nonaversive intervention for behavior problems: A manual for home and community.* Baltimore: Paul H. Brookes.

Meyer, L. H., & Evans, I. H. (1993). Meaningful outcomes in behavioral intervention: Evaluating positive approaches to the remediation of challenging behaviors. In J. Reichle & D. P. Wacker (Eds.), *Communication and language intervention series: Vol. 3. Communicative alternatives to challenging behavior: Integrating functional assessment and intervention strategies* (pp. 407–428). Baltimore: Paul H. Brookes.

Meyer, L. H., & Janney, R. E. (1989). User-friendly measures of meaningful outcomes: Evaluating behavioral interventions. *Journal of the Association for Persons with Severe handicaps, 14,* 263–270.

Meyer, L. H., Reichle, J., McQuarter, R. J., Cole, D., Vandercook, T., Evans, I. M., Neel, R., & Kishi, G. (1985). *The assessment of social competence (ASC): A scale of social competence functions.* Minneapolis: University of Minnesota Consortium Institute.

Mills v. Board of Education of the District of Columbia, 348 F. Supp. 866 (D.D.C. 1972).

Moes, D. R., & Frea, W. D. (2000). Using family context to inform intervention planning for the treatment of a child with autism. *Journal of Positive Behavior Interventions, 2,* 40–46.

Mount, B., & Zwernik, K. (1988). *It's never too early, it's never too late: A booklet about personal futures planning.* St. Paul, MN: St. Paul Metropolitan Council.

Nehring, A. D., Nehring, E. F., Bruni, J. P., & Randolph, P. L. (1992). *Learning accomplishment profile diagnostic standardized assessment.* Lewisville, NC: Kaplan School Supply.

Nelson, C., van Dijk, J., McDonnell, A. P., & Thompson, K. (2002). A framework for understanding young children with severe multiple disabilities: The van Dijk approach to assessment. *Research and Practice for Persons with Severe Disabilities, 27,* 97–111.

Newborg, J. (2004). *Batelle development inventory—2nd edition.* Chicago: Riverside.

Nihira, K., Leland, H., & Lambert, N. (1993). *Adaptive Behavior Scales—Residential & Community* (2nd ed.). Austin, TX: PRO-ED.

O'Brien, J., O'Brien, C. L., & Mount, B. (1997). Person-centered planning has arrived . . . or has it? *Mental Retardation, 35,* 480–488.

O'Neill, R. E., Horner, R. H., Albin, R. W., Sprague, J. R., Story, K., & Newton, J. S. (1997). *Functional assessment and program development for problem behavior: A practical handbook* (2nd ed.). Pacific Grove, CA: Brooks/Cole.

Orelove, F. P., Sobsey, D., & Silberman, R. K. (2004). *Educating children with multiple disabilities* (4th ed.). Baltimore: Paul H. Brookes.

Pace, G. M., Ivancic, M. R., Edwards, G. L., Iwata, B. A., & Page, T. J. (1985). Assessment of stimulus preference and reinforcer value with profoundly retarded individuals. *Journal of Applied Behavior Analysis, 18,* 249–255.

Pearpoint, J., Forest, M., & O'Brien, J. (1996). MAPS, circles of friends, and PATH: Powerful tools to help build caring communities. In S. Stainback & W. Stainback (Eds.), *Inclusion: A guide for educators* (pp. 67–86). Baltimore: Paul H. Brookes.

Pennsylvania Alternate System of Assessment Leadership Team. (2004).

Quenemoen, R., Thompson, S. & Thurlow, M. (2003). *Measuring academic achievement of students with significant cognitive disabilities: Building understanding of alternate assessment scoring criteria* (Synthesis Report 50). Minneapolis: University of Minnesota, National Center on Educational Outcomes. Retrieved April 16, 2004, from **http://education.umn.edu/NCEO/OnlinePubs/Synthesis50.html**

Rainforth, B., York, J., & Macdonald, C. (1997). *Collaborative teams for students with severe disabilities: Integrating therapy and educational services* (2nd ed.). Baltimore: Paul H. Brookes.

Roane, H. S., Vollmer, T. R., Ringdahl, J. E., & Marcus, B. A. (1998). Evaluation of a brief stimulus preference assessment. *Journal of Applied Behavior Analysis, 31,* 605–620.

Roeber, E. (2002). *Setting standards on alternate assessments* (Synthesis Report 42). Minneapolis: University of Minnesota, National Center on Educational Outcomes. Retrieved April 16, 2004, http://education.umn.edu/NCEO/OnlinePubs/Synthesis42.html

Roid, G. H. (2003). *Stanford-Binet intelligence scales* (5th ed.). Chicago: Riverside.

Salvia, J., & Ysseldyke, J. E. (2004). *Assessment in special and inclusive education* (9th ed.). Boston: Houghton Mifflin.

Sandall, S. R., & Schwartz, I. S. (2002). *Building blocks for teaching preschoolers with special needs.* Baltimore: Paul H. Brookes.

Sands, D. J., Bassett, D. S., Lehmann, J., & Spencer, K. C. (1998). Factors contributing to and implications for student involvement in transition-related planning, decision making, and instruction. In M. L. Wehmeyer & D. J. Sands (Eds.), *Making it happen: Student involvement in education planning, decision making, and instruction* (pp. 25–44). Baltimore: Paul H. Brookes.

Schalock, R. L. (1996). Reconsidering the conceptualization and measurement of quality of life. In R. L. Schalock (Ed.), *Quality of life: Vol. 1. Conceptualization and measurement* (pp. 123–139). Washington, DC: American Association on Mental Retardation.

Schopler, E., Reichler, R., & Rochen-Renner, B. (1998). *The Childhood autism Rating Scale (CARS).* Los Angeles, CA: Western Psychological Services.

Siegel-Causey, E., & Allinder, R. M. (1998). Using alternative assessment for students with severe disabilities: Alignment with best practices. *Education and Training in Mental Retardation and Developmental Disabilities, 33,* 168–178.

Sigafoos, J., Cole, D. A., & McQuarter, R. J. (1987). Current practices in the assessment of students with severe handicaps. *Journal of the Association for Persons with Severe Handicaps, 12,* 264–273.

Sigafoos, J., & York, J. (1991). Using ecological inventories to promote functional communication. In J. Reichle, J. York, & J. Sigafoos (Eds.), *Implementing augmentative and alternative communication: Strategies for learners with severe disabilities* (pp. 61-70). Baltimore: Paul H. Brookes.

Silberman, R. K., & Brown, F. (1998). Alternative approaches to assessing students who have visual impairments with other disabilities in classroom and community environments. In S. Z. Sacks & R. K. Silberman (Eds.), *Educating students who have visual impairments with other disabilities* (pp. 73-98). Baltimore: Paul H. Brookes.

Snell, M. E. (2003). Education of individuals with severe and multiple disabilities. *Encyclopedia of education* (2nd ed., pp. 2210-2213). New York: Macmillan Reference USA.

Snell, M. E., & Janney, R. E. (2000). *Practices for inclusive schools: Social relationships and peer support.* Baltimore: Paul H. Brookes.

Sparrow, S. S., Balla, D. A., & Cicchetti, D. V. (1984). *Vineland adaptive behavior scales.* Circle Pines, MN: American Guidance Service Inc.

Staub, D., Schwartz, I. S., Gallucci, C., & Peck, C. A. (1994). Four portraits of friendship at an inclusive school. *Journal of the Association for Persons with Severe Handicaps, 19,* 314-325.

The Association for Persons with Severe Handicaps. (1989, May). *TASH resolutions and policy statements.* Seattle: Author.

The Association for Persons with Severe Handicaps. (2000). *TASH.org.*

Thompson, J. R., Bryant, B. R., Campbell, E. M., Craig, E. M., Hughes, C. M., Rotholz, D. A., et al. (2004). *Supports intensity scale: Users manual.* Washington, DC: American Association on Mental Retardation.

Thompson, J. R., Hughes, C., Schalock, R. L., Silverman, W., Tasse, M.J., Bryant, B., et al. (2002). Integrating supports in assessment and planning. *Mental Retardation, 40,* 390-405.

Thompson, J. R., McGrew, K. S., & Bruininks, R. H. (1999). Adaptive and maladaptive behavior: Function and structural characteristics. In R. L. Schalock (Ed.), *Adaptive behavior and its measurement: Implications for the field of mental retardation* (pp. 15-42). Washington, DC: American Association on Mental Retardation.

Thompson, S., & Thurlow, M. (2001). *2001 State special education outcomes: A report on state activities at the beginning of a new decade.* Minneapolis: University of Minnesota, National Center on Educational Outcomes. Retrieved September 10, 2004, from http://education.umn.edu/NCEO/OnlinePubs/2001StateReport.html

Turnbull, A. P., Blue-Banning, M. J., Anderson, E. L., Turnbull, H. R., Seaton, K. A., & Dinas, P. A. (1996). Enhancing self-determination through group action planning. In D. J. Sands & M. L. Wehmeyer (Eds.), *Self-determination across the life span* (pp. 237-256). Baltimore: Paul H. Brookes.

Turnbull, A. P., & Turnbull, H. R. (1990). *Families, professionals, and exceptionality.* Upper Saddle River, NJ: Merrill/Prentice Hall.

Turnbull, H. R., & Turnbull, A. P. (2000). *Free appropriate public education: The law and children with disabilities* (6th ed.). Denver: Love.

U.S. Department of Education. (2003, December 9). *Federal Register, 68*(236), 68698.

Vandercook, T., York, J., & Forest, M. (1989). The McGill action planning system (MAPS): A strategy for building the vision. *Journal of the Association for Persons with Severe Handicaps, 14,* 205-215.

Voeltz, L. M., & Evans, I. M. (1983). Educational validity: Procedures to evaluate outcomes in programs for severely handicapped learners. *Journal of the Association for the Severely Handicapped, 8,* 3-15.

Wechsler, D. (2002). *Wechsler preschool and primary scale of intelligence—Revised.* San Antonio, TX: Psychological Corporation.

Wechsler, D. (2003). *Wechsler intelligence scale for children (WISC-IV).* San Antonio, TX: Psychological Corporation.

Wehmeyer, M. L. (1996). Self-determination as an educational outcome: Why is it important to children, youth, and adults with disabilities? In D. J. Sands, & M. L. Wehmeyer (Eds.), *Self-determination across the life span: Independence and choice for people with disabilities* (pp. 17-36). Baltimore: Paul H. Brookes.

Wehmeyer, M. L., & Sands, D. (Eds.). (1998). *Making it happen: Student involvement in education planning, decision making, and instruction.* Baltimore: Paul H. Brookes.

White, O. R. (1985). The evaluation of severely mentally retarded individuals. In B. Bricker & J. Filler (Eds.), *Severe mental retardation: From theory to practice* (pp. 161-184). Reston, VA: Council for Exceptional Children.

Willis, T. J., LaVigna, G. W., & Donnellan, A. M. (1993). *Behavior assessment guide.* Los Angeles: Institute for Applied Behavior Analysis.

Wolf, M. M. (1978). Social validity: The case for subjective measurement, or how applied behavior analysis is finding its heart. *Journal of Applied Behavior Analysis, 11,* 203-214.

Ysseldyke, J. E., & Algozzine, B. (2000). *Critical issues in special and remedial education* (3rd ed.). Boston: Houghton Mifflin.

Ysseldyke, J., & Olsen, K. (1999). Putting alternate assessments into practice: What to measure and possible sources of data. *Exceptional Children, 65,* 175-185.

4

Designing and Implementing
Instructional Programs

Martha E. Snell
Fredda Brown

To design educational programs, teams select and combine ideas that are not only practical and efficient but also substantiated, logical, consistent with current knowledge, and likely to realize change in the desired directions. The principle of parsimony (Etzel & LeBlanc, 1979) provides an uncomplicated standard for teams making decisions about how to teach their students: *Select the simplest but still effective approach.* First the principle cautions educators against selecting questionable methods not based on evidence. Second, when team members are faced with several teaching approaches that all work, the principle advises them to choose the least complicated. This chapter provides guidelines for making these important decisions.

Designing educational programs to teach needed skills requires that team members consider many factors and make numerous decisions. Decisions are made after team members share their different perspectives on the student, engage in relevant discussion and problem solving, and then reach consensus as a team. When decisions are made by majority vote or by experts or authority figures without reaching consensus, the team will not be equally invested in the decision or the outcome. Nonconsensus decisions are based on a narrower range of thinking and risk being of poorer quality. To design and implement individualized programs, teams should reach agreement on each of the following ten steps; the first six address writing individualized educational programs (IEP), while the last four concern designing and implementing instruction:

1. Using an ecological inventory to define the student's unique needs and characteristics in everyday terms
2. Prioritizing the student's needs and recognizing his or her strengths
3. For each need, defining the students' present level of performance in measurable terms
4. For each need, writing measurable annual goals that can be achieved in a year
5. Identifying the educational supports and services that address the student's needs

111

6. Writing the IEP after identifying the intermediate short-term objectives or benchmarks leading from present level of performance to goal level
7. Designing plans to teach what's on the IEP
8. Implementing the instructional plans
9. Gathering data to assess and report on the student's progress
10. Improving instruction based on student data

Developing and Writing IEPs

There are many variations in the IEP forms and procedures used by school systems and by teachers and ultimately in the specificity and utility of their contents. Still, all IEPs should be accurate road maps created collaboratively for a particular student by an educational team; IEPs must actively guide team members throughout a school year, not sit passively in file cabinets. IEP goals set the general direction for instruction and give a basis for developing detailed instructional plans, but they need not be detailed enough to be considered the equivalent of the instructional plan (Bateman & Herr, 2003). IEPs are agreements between team members on the focus and decisive elements that will become a particular student's educational program for a year's time unless changed by team consensus. This means that goals and objectives should be both measurable and specific enough to translate into classroom instruction. As specified in the Individuals with Disabilities Education Act (2004) in Sec. 614(d) (1) (A) (i), the IEP must include "a statement of the child's present levels of academic achievement and functional performance, including how the child's disability affects the child's involvement and progress in the general education curriculum . . . " Furthermore for "children with disabilities who take alternate assessments aligned to alternate achievement standards, a description of benchmarks or short-term objectives . . . " continues to be required in IEPs.

What Is a High-Quality IEP?

"The IEP is a firm, legally binding commitment of resources" by a school system and thus must be written with great care (Bateman & Linden, 1998, p. 60). Resources range widely from basic to specialized services and supports. Basic resources include buildings, transportation, professional and paraprofessional staff,

instructional materials, and staff development; more specialized services and supports include related services personnel, educational programs designed to teach specific objectives, curriculum modifications, training on and support for collaborative teams and positive behavior support, augmentative and alternative communication devices, transportation to job settings in the community, and job coaches. The IEP is a document in which a student's many unique needs are addressed in a highly individualized way.

To develop an IEP, teams work together to assess and reach consensus on the following:

• *Unique needs and characteristics*: Based on assessment information, what are a student's unique educational needs or characteristics that the IEP should address?
• *Present level of performance (PLOP)*: For each unique need, how is the student currently performing?
• *Educational services*: What will the educational team and district do, and what services will be furnished in response to each unique need or characteristic? When will these services begin? What will be their frequency, location, and duration?
• *Annual goals, objectives/benchmarks (G/O/B)*: What student accomplishments (written as measurable G/O/Bs) address these needs and link to that student's present level of performance? What student accomplishments will verify that the services provided are effective (Bateman & Linden, 1998, p. 100)?

The IEP constitutes the educational team's and district's design for providing special education, related services, supplementary aides and services, assistive technology, program modifications, and personnel support. IEP G/O/Bs are written to be indicators of learning and program evaluation. Measuring G/O/Bs enables a school to judge if the services and educational program are successful.

Another essential element of the IEP concerns transition. At age 14 (or younger, if appropriate), IEPs must include a statement of each student's transition service needs, while by age 16 (or younger, if appropriate), transition services must be addressed in the IEP as an individualized transition plan (ITP). ITPs may well include interagency linkages between the school and adult services. Transition services are "a coordinated set of activities," not a haphazard plan, aimed at fostering movement from school to postschool life. These services include instruction, related services, community experiences, development of employment and adult living skills, and, as is often needed with most students who have severe disabilities, the acquisition of daily living skills and functional vocational assessment. Thus, the focus of the IEP changes during the teen years to include the transition to the postschool years: higher education (for some students), adult life, and work.

Listed among the "worst sins" of an IEP are five failures: failure to individualize; failure to address all a student's educational needs; failure to specify needed services; failure to write clear, meaningful, and measurable goals and objectives; and failure to clearly describe a student's present levels of functioning (Bateman & Linden, 1998, p. 88). When teams write IEP objectives based on inquiry in the four areas listed earlier, many of these failures can be prevented. The next section will trace the steps IEP teams take to design and implement instructional programs.

Writing IEPs

Define Student's Unique Characteristics and Needs in Everyday Terms

To write the IEP for a student, a team needs first to identify the student's characteristics and needs. The results from the ecological inventory will reflect the student's skill characteristics and serve as the team's primary guide for defining a student's needs. As described in chapter 3, the team meets and agrees on activities and skills that are important to a particular student in the environments he or she frequents: school and home and, if older, in the community and at work as well. Next, the special education teacher usually takes the lead in interviewing other team members about the student's participation and ability in activities and skills performed in these environments. Interview results are recorded on an ecological inventory form such as described in chapter 3 (Figures 3–5 and 3–6) with ratings of performance level and component skills (e.g., initiation, has related social skills, communicates) and comments about performance or priority. The ecological inventory usually yields many student needs. Several other environmental assessments discussed in chapter 3 also will contribute to the process of defining a student's unique needs (e.g., functional behavioral assessment, preference assessment).

Timmy has distinctive ways of communicating that often are difficult to understand. His tantrums and

self-stimulatory behavior seem to say he is not happy with what's happening, but adults and peers don't always know what he needs or wants. The team agrees that understandable communication with familiar people is a primary need at home and school. This is also clearly reflected in his assessment.

Prioritize Student's Needs and Recognize Strengths

Next, the team meets again to discuss the ecological inventory assessment results with the goal of determining the student's priority needs for the upcoming year. This can be done more efficiently as a group prior to the IEP meeting but also can be coordinated by the special education teacher through separate interactions with team members. chapter 3 listed some criteria teams will consider when deciding what needs are most important (Figure 3–6). Most educators agree on several criteria that should be met when selecting priority skill needs for students with severe disabilities. Priority skill needs should (a) reflect the student's chronological age and preferences, (b) mirror the family's culture, (c) focus on functional skills that lead to meaningful participation, (d) be useful across activities and settings now and in the future, and (e) facilitate interactions with nondisabled peers.

As teams focus on a student's needs, the student's strengths and preferences should not be forgotten. Teaching with preferred activities or materials will promote students' motivation to participate and learn. Expecting students to use their skill strengths means that skills are not forgotten and that teachers can build on these strengths to teach more complex behaviors.

Christine's team identified paid jobs and volunteer work as priority needs. They also know that she enjoys participating in the care of cats and dogs. This preference is one her team will use as they identify potential work and volunteer settings for her to sample early in her final 2 years of school.

Define the Student's Present Level of Performance

In one section of the IEP, the team describes the student's *present level of performance* (PLOP) for each unique area of need. Because the PLOP defines the starting point or baseline for measuring the year's progress, it must be stated in measurable terms.

To know whether Timmy has improved on his IEP goals by June, his team clearly states what his skill

TABLE 4–1
A Working Draft of Timothy's IEP

Unique Needs	Present Level of performance	Specialized Educational Service	Annual Goals
Knowing the preschool schedule of activities	Doesn't go to next activity unless physically prompted	Speech and language pathologist	Will use a picture schedule and go to daily school activities on his own 4 of 5 days
Making requests	Protests when needs aren't met; doesn't use words or pictures to request or choose; about half the time, he leads an adult to a location to indicate need	Speech and language pathologist	Will use a vocabulary of several signs (help, more, break) and 15 picture cards to indicate his wants by handing the card to staff or peers without help; will point to item or hand picture to indicate choice all the time
Listening to and looking at books	Looks at book pictures half the time but mainly when asked to touch a specific picture; does not select book from a choice	Special education teacher	Will look at book pictures and match picture symbols to book pictures when read to him; will select a book from a choice, open it, and turn pages
Dressing/undressing at toileting, arrival, recess, departure	Allows others to dress/undress him; initiates only on last step of removing his jacket	Special education teacher	Without prompting, will pull his pants up and down at toileting and will put on and take off his coat at arrival, recess, and departure (except for fasteners)

level is at the beginning of the school year. His team first reaches consensus on his unique needs, defines his PLOP for each need, and sets an annual goal. Later they will identify any needed specialized services as well as the short-term objectives or benchmarks to get Timothy from his PLOP to his annual goal (Table 4-1).

Identify the Educational Supports and Services That Address Student's Needs
The team also determines any specialized educational services or other "developmental, corrective, or supportive services" that "are required to assist a child with a disability to benefit from special education" (Section 300.16). While some potential services are listed in the law, it is not an inclusive list, and teams will use this guideline to make their decision (Bateman & Linden, 1998). Teams must define clearly in the IEP how much time will be committed to each service (frequency, location, and duration) and when services

will begin. Specialized services are broad and include special education, related services, supplementary aids and services, and more. Special education includes direct instruction (one on one, small or large group), instructional support (e.g., providing assistance in a routine, monitoring transitions), and consultation between staff (planning, problem solving, collecting data, coaching staff). Related services include occupational, physical, and communication therapy and consultation as well as vision and mobility services and adaptive physical education. Special education and related services may be provided in the context of a general education classroom (services pulled "into" the classroom) or provided apart from the general education classroom (services given when the student is "pulled out" from the general education classroom, given in a resource room, in the community, or in a self-contained classroom). Other specialized educational services that may be determined by the IEP committee include supplementary aids, modifications, personnel support, accommodations, and staff training and teamwork. All services must be provided by the school (or contracted out) at no cost to the parent and are chosen based on the student's needs, not on the availability of those services in the school district.

Write Measurable Annual Goals and Identify the Intermediate Short-Term Objectives or Benchmarks

The steps that come before writing goals and objectives ensure that IEPs will focus on needed skills that are viewed by all team members as meaningful for and suitable to the student. When teams write goals and objectives, the focus changes to "measurability," a requirement of IDEA. All goals, objectives, and benchmarks must be measurable; however, the amount of time required to achieve them differs (Bateman & Herr, 2003). Goals are written to be reached within the school year, while objectives and benchmarks are written to be reached in 6 to 9 weeks. The PLOP, based on student need, is the starting point in identifying G/O/Bs; the PLOP is linked to an annual goal by short-term objectives or benchmarks (O/B) as shown in the following formula. The fourth element in this formula is any specialized educational services (e.g., special education, related service) provided through the IEP that helps move a student's performance from its present level to the goal level:

PLOP → O/B → O/B → O/B → O/B → Goal → Special Education and Related Services →

For Jenny, these four elements work together to achieve priority skills.

Jenny's team has identified telling time to the hour as an annual goal on her IEP. She will be given daily special education services during math instruction in the general education setting and individual instruction twice weekly. They identify the PLOP-to-goal sequence in this way:

- *PLOP: Jenny does not tell time but recognizes numbers from 1 to 12.*
- *Short-term objectives:*
  - *She will identify the numbers on an analog clock correctly.*
  - *She will identify the little and big hands of the clock correctly.*
  - *She will read the numbers the little hand points to correctly.*

- *She will use the rule for telling time by the hour without errors on 9 of 10 opportunities: the little hand points to the hour (says "five"), and the big hand points straight up to the 12 (says "o'clock")*
- *Goal: She will tell time to the hour without prompts on 9 out of 10 opportunities.*

Goals and objectives are written so they (a) specify the target behavior in observable terms and (b) identify a simple criterion that tells how well the student must perform to meet the goal or objective (e.g., four out of five opportunities; for a distance of 50 yards; all the time; with no errors; without prompting or assistance). Sometimes the conditions for performance will need to be stated explicitly (e.g., given a numberline, Jenny will "count on" for addition up to 15), but other times this is unnecessary (e.g., Timmy will use a picture schedule . . . the picture schedule is assumed). While it can be challenging for teams to make all goals and objectives measurable, it is essential.

The IEP and Inclusion

We know that inclusion can lead to social benefits and skill improvements for students with severe disabilities (e.g., Dugan et al., 1995; Fisher & Meyer, 2002; Haring and Breen, 1992; Hunt & Goetz, 1997; Hunt, Soto, Maier, & Doring, 2003; Kennedy, Shukla, & Fryxell, 1997; Shukla, Kennedy, & Cushing, 1998). The outcomes of inclusion for students without disabilities also have been studied and found beneficial (e.g., Cushing & Kennedy, 1997; Dugan et al., 1995; Kishi & Meyer, 1994; Shukla et al., 1998). IDEA (1997) and its earlier versions require that the least restrictive environment for each student be used "to the maximum extent appropriate" and that "supplementary aids and services" be added to the general education classroom and activities when needed to make that setting work satisfactorily for students with disabilities. While the inclusion of students with disabilities has been quietly working in many schools for years, some school administrators and professional organizations still draw battle lines and debate the meaning and values of inclusion. Educators and parents of students with disabilities who have practiced inclusion typically are more vocal in their support of inclusion. Administrators may waver, depending on state practices and cost. Court decisions on inclusion have shifted back and forth between being nonsupportive and supportive in recent years. The move from separate programs to inclusive programs is complex and appears to be advanced more by modeling than mandating. The position a state department of education takes on inclusion influences the direction school systems in that state take. Similarly, the view of a school system's administrators have on inclusion appears to influence the practices individual schools in that district follow (Snell & Janney, in press). This means that inclusion is practiced very unevenly; for example, where a student with severe disabilities lives may be the single strongest factor determining whether a student attends an inclusive school or receives special education primarily in a self-contained classroom.

Placement decisions are supposed to be made only *after* the IEP is written. It is the IEP team that plays a controlling role in deciding a student's placement. Unfortunately, many schools continue to use a continuum of options based on level of disability to determine placement; thus, placements are made on variables other than the IEP and are not individualized. This practice does not meet the spirit of the law. Although the law does not mandate inclusion in general education with nondisabled peers, it "continues to express a preference . . . for placement in the regular classroom" (Bateman & Linden, 1998, p. 13). Consistent with this preference, the team will list in the IEP the modifications/accommodations needed to make progress in the general curriculum. In addition, the IEP team must include at least one general education teacher (if the child is or may be participating in a general education environment) who takes part in discussions about how to modify general curriculum in the classroom to ensure involvement and progress.

Influences on Goals and Objectives

Beside student needs, the goals and objectives a team selects for a student are influenced both by the characteristics of the skill itself and by the student's stage of learning. These influences and their impact on teaching will be discussed next.

Characteristics of the Skill
Relationship Between Instructional Objectives
The relationship between the short-term objectives and the goal is important, as it predicts the order for instruction. For example, if the short-term objectives vary

from simple to complex, they will need to be taught in this order, an objective arrangement that Bateman and Herr (2003) refer to as a *ladder relationship.*

> *For Timmy to meet the goal of using 20 picture cards to indicate his wants to staff or peers without help, his team specified four quarterly benchmarks of increasing difficulty: (a) he will use five pictures, (b) 10 pictures, 15 pictures, and (d) all 20 pictures (goal).*

Sometimes short-term objectives address an array of skills that are needed to meet the goal but that can be taught in any order or all at once (e.g., putting on shirt, pants, and socks all contribute to a goal of getting dressed independently). Bateman and Herr call this a *pie relationship* between objectives, wherein all the short-term objectives contribute to the goal, but none are prerequisite to each other. Sometimes there is a mixed relationship—the order of teaching some objectives leading to a goal is flexible (pie), but other objectives are interdependent, and teaching order is set (ladder). For example, Jenny's previously mentioned time-telling objectives have primarily a ladder arrangement, but the first two objectives have a pie relationship—that is, one could be taught either first or second, or they could be taught together (identify clock numbers, identify big and little hands). Knowing whether to teach students' short-term objectives in a particular order will help teams plan their teaching schedules and coordinate instruction across students.

Discrete and Multiple-Stepped Skills Target skills that consist of many behaviors chained together in sequence (cleaning tasks, assembly jobs, dressing) are approached differently by teachers than discrete skills that are disconnected from other behaviors, such as naming familiar people, making numeral/quantity matches, and reading words correctly. Target skills that involve a single, isolated response are called *discrete responses;* these responses are individually distinctive and can stand alone (e.g., matching prices to coins, identifying pictures of class activities by going to the location or materials, reading words). By contrast, most other target behaviors are viewed as being *multiple-stepped responses* and involve the performance of a sequence of multiple behaviors or steps to complete a task. These skills require a task analysis of the responses that are performed in order to complete the task or activity. For example, the following tasks involve multiple steps: sweeping the floor, playing Uno, eating at a fast-food restaurant, brushing one's teeth, operating a CD player, and counting out combinations of coins to pay for a product.

Examine Timmy's goals and decide if they are discrete or multiple stepped:

- When given the verbal direction, "Timmy, wash your hands," he will wash his hands by completing 8 of the 12 task steps independently.
- During breakfast time at preschool, Timmy will choose his own cereal and eat cereal and milk using a regular bowl and spoon and without spilling on four of five trials.
- When asked to point to a particular color from a choice of at least three colors, Timmy will correctly point to red, blue, green, yellow, black, and white on three of four probes.
- Timmy will always use a correct tripincer grasp when holding a crayon, markers, chalk, or paintbrush.

If you identified the first two goals as multiple-stepped tasks and the last two as discrete tasks, you are correct. His team members will write task analyses for the first two skills that will guide both assessment and teaching. His teachers might teach all the task steps in order (total task chaining) or "chunk" the steps and teach them as clusters of steps. Alternately, they could teach just one step in the sequence at a time in a forward or backward order (backward or forward chaining). (These strategies are discussed later in this chapter.) Typically, the last response is followed by reinforcement, either natural (e.g., completing a task and taking a break, getting the help that was requested) or artificial (e.g., teacher praise, participation in a preferred activity) or both.

Discrete behaviors may be taught separately (e.g., reading prices) or taught as a step within a larger chain of functionally related behaviors (e.g., reading prices during the task of getting a snack from a vending machine). The distinction between discrete and multiple-stepped behaviors is not always clear. Many discrete behaviors can be divided into steps. For example, reading words involves a sequence of behaviors: look at the word, make the initial letter sound, and blend with the medial and final sounds to say the word. How teams decide to view a target behavior depends on the behavior and the student and also influences instruction and measurement.

While the discrete skills do not require a task analysis, the team needs to agree on the skill and any prerequisites skills (often called a skill sequence). Before teaching Timothy color naming, it might help to teach color matching. Discrete skills are likely to be taught in a ladder fashion, gradually making the task expectations harder.

Timothy's teachers decide to teach red and blue matching first and then will add two more colors while still giving him opportunities with red and blue. With grasping, the occupational therapist suggests that they start with learning to grasp magic markers (Timothy gets to choose which fruit smell and color) and then teach him the same grasp with crayons, paintbrushes, and finally chalk. As each new material is introduced, Timothy will still be expected to use the same grasp with materials already learned.

Academic discrete skills (e.g., counting, labeling) often are taught through skill sequences—a listing of related skills arranged from simple to more difficult that are taught separately in sequence over a period of time.

Timothy first learned to match pictures, then to locate named pictures, and finally to name pictures by signing. The money management skills that Jenny is learning are part of a generalized math skill sequence for using coins and bills (Table 4-2).

Many of the skills are discrete, while some may be more logically taught as a chain of responses.

After several years of money instruction, Jenny has mastered steps 1 through 12; she is now working on counting quarters and soon will learn to count combinations of all coins. Her teachers schedule regular application of these skills in school to make small purchases. For example, skills 7 and 12 require Jenny to count out a given amount of money, which is required when paying library fines (5 cents a day), buying her school lunch (80 cents) or milk (20 cents), and buying pencils (25 to 35 cents) and paper (2 to 5 cents) in the school store.

Task Analysis   Analyzing a task is not trivial. Consider how Timothy's teachers planned for his active participation in the arrival routine.

TABLE 4–2

Jenny's Skill Sequence for Using Coins to Make Purchases

1. Identification of pennies and stating their value (discrete responses)
2. Counting pennies by ones (chained response) and identifying the total amount (discrete)
3. Identification of nickels and stating their value (discrete responses)
4. Identification and stating the values of nickels and pennies in a mixed order (discrete responses)
5. Counting nickels by fives (chained response) and identifying the total amount (discrete)
6. Counting combinations of pennies and nickels (counting by fives, then counting on by ones) (chained response) and stating the total amount (discrete response)
7. Counting combinations of pennies and nickels to yield a written or stated price (chained response)[1]
8. Identification of dimes and stating their value (discrete responses)
9. Identification and stating the values of dimes, nickels, and pennies in a mixed order (discrete responses)
10. Counting dimes by 10s (chained response) and identifying the total amount (discrete response)
11. Counting combinations of pennies, nickels, and dimes (counting by 10s, then counting on by fives and then ones) (chained response) and stating the total amount (discrete response)
12. Counting combinations of pennies, nickels, and dimes to match a written or stated price (chained response)[1]
13. Identification of quarters and stating their value (discrete responses)
14. Identification and stating the values of nickels and pennies in a mixed order (discrete responses)
15. Counting quarters by 25s (chained response) and identifying the total amount (discrete response)
16. Counting combinations of pennies, nickels, dimes, and quarters (counting by 25s, then counting by 10s, fives, and ones) (chained response) and stating the total amount (discrete response)
17. Counting combinations of pennies, nickels, dimes, and quarters to match a written or stated price (chained response)[1]

[1]Making purchases.

Task analysis

Before teaching Timothy the morning routine, the special education teacher, Ted Grayson, watched others perform the task and analyzed the steps. They identified both the responses they wanted Timothy to learn and the relevant stimulus that Timothy would learn to attend to (Table 4-3). Ted also asked Timothy's preschool teacher, Carlene Johnson, to use the preliminary task analysis and observe students at arrival to double-check the steps. Carlene piloted the task analysis for Timothy to be sure that the steps made sense for him. When she found that some steps were too hard for Timothy (the car door and the building door were too difficult for him to open alone), she added adult help to those steps. In other cases, she made one step into two steps: (a) getting his photo card and (b) selecting an activity by placing his photo beneath the activity picture. Next, Timothy's mother looked at the task analysis and added her ideas. Because Timothy could perform very little of the task during the initial pilot, Ted and Carlene anticipated that Timothy would be in the acquisition stage of learning and thus left the main focus of the task analysis on the core steps of the task. However, the preschool staff suggested adding the enrichment skill of communicating a greeting.

Task analysis typically proceeds through a process:

1. Use ecological inventory results to identify an individually functional and age-appropriate skill that is an important target for a particular student
2. Define the target skill simply, including a description of the settings and materials most suited to the natural performance of the task
3. Perform the task and observe peers performing the task, using the chosen materials in the natural settings while noting the steps involved
4. Adapt the steps to suit the student's disabilities and skill strengths, employing the principle of partial participation and component analysis as needed to enable participation that is both age appropriate and functional
5. Validate the task analysis by having the student perform the task but provide assistance on steps that are unknown so that performance of all steps can be viewed
6. Explore adding simple, nonstigmatizing adaptations to steps that appear to be unreasonable targets in an unadapted form; revise the task analysis
7. Write the task analysis on a data collection form so that steps (a) are stated in terms of observable behavior, (b) result in a visible change in the product

TABLE 4–3
A Sequence of Stimuli and Responses Involved in Timothy's Arrival Routine

Stimulus	Response
• Car stops	Get out of car
• See school, hear mom say and gesture, "Let's go"	Walk into school
• See school door	Open and walk through door
• See hallway	Walk down hall
• See blue classroom door	Open door and go in
• See cubbies and others removing jackets	Remove jacket
• See hook with his photo and others hanging jackets	Hang jacket
• Smiles and praise from teacher	Move away from cubby
• Teacher shows activity board, "What do you want to do, Timothy?"	Get his photo card; look at the activity board, pick activity, attach photo by activity
• Teacher: "You want the sand box! Good choice."	Go to the sand box

or process, (c) are ordered in a logical sequence, and (d) are written in second-person singular so that they could serve as verbal prompts (if used), using language that is not confusing to the student and enclosing in parentheses details essential to assessing performance

Figure 4-1 shows the final task analysis of Timothy's arrival routine. Note how the steps in Table 4-3 were modified when the team followed this validation process. The form in Figure 4-2 allows team members to easily record teaching and testing data and anecdotal comments to explain a student's performance.

Stages of Learning

The ways we teach students who are just beginning to learn a skill will differ somewhat from the ways we teach students who are more experienced. A student's stage of learning for a given skill will reflect the extent of experience and the current performance and should be evident from reading the PLOP. Learning stage has a powerful influence on how a student is taught.

Think of two skills you have: one that is known and easily performed (e.g., crocheting or driving an automatic car) and one you are just learning (e.g., knitting or driving a stick shift). Now describe how you feel when you perform both skills. Have you used phrases like the following?

- *For the skill you know well*: "I'm confident and at ease. It seems mechanical to do this skill." "I'm pretty fast." "I don't make mistakes, unless something unusual comes up."
- *For the skill you are learning to perform*: "I'm careful; I check each step before I do it." "I'm very slow." "I make a lot of mistakes, but if I get some help or just keep trying, I get better."

For *all* individuals, learning appears to move through different stages related to one's grasp of the target skill (Browder, 2001; Liberty, 1985). These stages are illustrated in Figure 4-2. When students with severe disabilities are compared to their typical peers, we know that their learning progresses more slowly, forgetting happens more often, and generalization of skills from one set of conditions to another is rarely automatic. With quality instruction, students with severe disabilities can certainly learn the skills they need to know, but these learning characteristics mean that their teachers must take more care in planning instruction.

As shown in Table 4-4, some teaching strategies are more influential at certain points in learning than at other points. Initial teaching strategies used should match the student's current stage of learning (his or her PLOP) for each priority skill. A student's stage of learning has an impact on the conditions identified in a goal or objective for performing a skill, the complexity of the skill chosen to teach, the focus of instruction, and the criterion set for achieving a goal or objective. For many priority skills, the student's PLOP will be in the acquisition stage; thus, initial short-term objectives will aim to move the student from acquisition to one or more of the advanced stages of learning. Goals are meant to be achieved within the school year and thus are likely to focus on an advanced stage of learning the target skill.

In chapter 3, we discussed the Component Model of Functional Life Routines (Brown, Evans, Weed, & Owen, 1987) and its effect on task analysis. This model emphasizes the range of complexity that is possible in the skills we target to teach. For example, a task's core steps are only part of the task and can be supplemented with extension skills (such as initiating, preparing, monitoring tempo and quality of performance, problem solving, and terminating) and enrichment skills (making choices, commenting, or being

FIGURE 4–1
A Task Analysis of Timothy's Arrival Routine at Preschool

Teachers: Carlene Johnson, Ted Grayson, Jo Milano
Student: Timothy
Day(s): Daily at arrival
Probe Schedule: First Tuesday each month
Settings: Bus/car arrival area, sidewalk, hallway, classroom
Stage of Learning: Acquisition
Baseline/Probe Method: Multiple opportunity task analytic assessment (4-second latency)
Instructional Cue: Arrival at preschool in family car; parent/sitter: "Let's go to school"
Target: Morning arrival routine
Teaching Method: Constant time delay (0, 4 seconds)

Task Steps \ Dates	9/21	9/22	9/23	9/24	9/27	9/28	9/30	10/1	10/4	10/5
Delayed prompt →	–	–	0	0	4	4	4	4	4	–
1. Unbuckle your seat belt (assist buckle and straps)	–	–	✓	✓	✓	✓	✓	+	+	–
2. Open your door (assist from outside car)	–	–	✓	✓	✓	✓	✓	✓	✓	–
3. Get out of car and close the door (assist one hand)	+	–	✓	✓	✓	✓	✓	✓	✓	–
4. Walk to preschool (on sidewalk)	–	–	✓	✓	✓	✓	✓	✓	✓	–
5. Open the door (assist pulling)	–	–	✓	✓	✓	✓	✓	+	+	+
6. Walk to your room	+	–	✓	+	+	+	+	+	+	+
7. Open the door and go in	–	–	✓	✓	✓	✓	✓	✓	+	+
8. Look at teacher, or peer, wave hello	–	–	✓	✓	✓	✓	✓	✓	✓	–
9. Find your cubby	+	+	✓	✓	✓	+	+	+	+	+
10. Take off your coat	–	–	✓	✓	✓	✓	✓	✓	✓	–
11. Grab it (by the collar)	–	–	✓	✓	✓	✓	✓	✓	✓	–
12. Hang it up (on hook)	–	+	✓	✓	✓	✓	+	+	+	+
13. Get your picture (from table)	–	–	✓	✓	✓	✓	✓	✓	✓	+
14. Put your picture (on board) where you want to play	–	–	✓	✓	✓	✓	✓	✓	✓	–
15. Go play (goes to selected activity)	–	–	✓	✓	✓	✓	✓	✓	+	+
Total independent	3	2	0	0	1	2	3	5	6	8
Baseline/Teach/Probe	B	B	T	T	T	T	T	T	T	P

Anecdotal Comments

Task analysis: Arrival routine
Student: Timothy

Date	Teacher	Anecdotal Comments
9/23	Carlene	Waited for help on most steps
9/25	Ted	Seemed sleepy, ear infection meds
10/4	Ted	He's more sure
10/5	Jo	Great probe!

[Located on back of task analysis]

Materials: Activity picture chart, garment or backpack

Recording Key: Test: + correct, – incorrect; Teach: + unprompted correct, ✓ prompted correct, – unprompted/prompted error (gestural/partial physical prompt); NR no response

Latency Period: 0 seconds, 4 seconds for 3 of 5 teaching days

Criterion: 10 of 15 steps correct (67%)

FIGURE 4–2
Stages of Learning

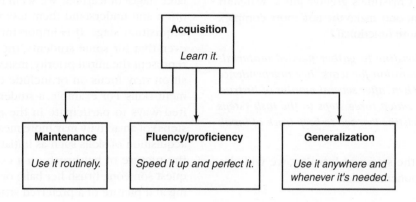

TABLE 4–4
Teaching Focus and Characteristics of the Learning Stages

Acquisition Stage	Maintenance Stage	Fluency/Proficiency Stage	Generalization Stage
Focus	**Focus**	**Focus**	**Focus**
Teach the core steps while keeping errors low	Prevent forgetting and promote perfection through regular use	• Speed performance up to its typical rate or • Perfect the skill so it suits the student's age	• Teach student to perform well when there are changes in stimuli (setting, materials, people) • Teach student to adapt performance as needed
Characteristics	**Characteristics**	**Characteristics**	**Characteristics**
• Student may perform none of the task or up to about half of the task (0% and 60% correct or 0 to 6 steps on a 10-step task) • May need to cue or prompt initiation • Need to use an errorless or low-error prompt system • May need to break skill into smaller components (objectives) • Need to give more continuous positive feedback	• Student performs more than half the task • "Schedule it" and expect student to perform • Add to the skill to make it more functional (e.g., initiates, prepares, terminates/cleanup) • Enrich skill with communication, choice, or social behaviors • Drop all intrusive requests • Fade intrusive prompts • Shift attention to natural cues and prompts • Thin out reinforcement • Shift to natural reinforcement	• Student performs more than half the task • Add realistic speed and quality criteria • Add to skill to make skill more functional (e.g., monitors speed and quality) • Enrich skill with communication, choice, or social behaviors • Drop all intrusive requests • Fade intrusive prompts • Shift attention to natural cues and prompts • Thin out reinforcement • Shift to natural reinforcement	• Student performs more than half the task • Vary settings • Vary instructors, supervisors, others • Vary materials • Vary conditions expected for skill and teach problem solving • Enrich skill with communication, choice, or social behaviors • Drop all intrusive requests • Fade intrusive prompts • Shift attention to natural cues and prompts • Thin out reinforcement

social). Adding extension and enrichment skills to the core steps of Christine's greeter job at Wal-Mart (Table 4–5) will not only make the task more complex but also make it more functional.

By teaching Christine to gather needed materials (step 1) in preparation for work, her independence was expanded. Then, after several months of instruction, the team added three steps to the task (steps 10 to 12) so Christine learned to keep track of break time.

As we discuss the stages of learning, we will also draw on the Component Model.

Acquisition Stage "Learn it" is the slogan for this stage. Typically, skills in this stage are new skills, performed with accuracy varying from 0% to about 60% of the steps correct or no steps to 6 steps of a 10-step task (Farlow & Snell, 1995). The focus of early learning is usually on the accurate performance of the core steps of a skill. But, as was explained in chapter 3, when the student is successful in this stage, teaching may be expanded to include some extension and enrichment skills, such as initiating the task, preparing for the task, terminating the task, and making choices in the task (Brown et al., 1987). Teaching simpler versions of skills makes sense during acquisition, when the tendency to make errors is high. Probably most research on skill instruction has addressed learning during the

acquisition stage. Despite the importance of the three later stages of learning, we seem to focus on them less often and understand them less well than we do the acquisition stage. It is important to remember, however, that for some students, the core skills may not represent the initial priority; instead, their initial acquisition may focus on or include extension or enrichment skills. For example, a student who has very limited ways to participate in the motor aspects (core steps) of an activity may more meaningfully begin with acquisition of skills such as initiating (e.g., pointing to the picture of hairbrush on a communication to request someone brush her hair) or choosing (e.g., looking at a picture of a preferred snack to indicate to her teacher what she would like to eat).

Advanced Stages For learners in advanced stages of learning, teachers generally will want to do the following:

1. Fade all artificial prompts except those built into the task or setting (adapted materials, partial participation, others who model naturally).
2. Thin the frequency of reinforcement and fade artificial reinforcement; shift to natural frequencies and sources.
3. Check to see if the student is *initiating* the skill or waiting for a teacher cue.

TABLE 4–5
Task Steps in Christine's Job at Wal-Mart

1. Prepare materials for work (communication device and switch, money for drink, sales bill box that fits on tray) (Assistance placing in backpack)
2. Take school bus to Wal-Mart (Assistance with wheelchair)
3. Report to work supervisor; sign in using name stamp (Assistance with wheelchair)
4. Find out which greeting station to fill
5. Pick up any sales pages to give to customers; place in box on tray (Assistance putting sales pages in box)
6. Report to greeting station (Assistance with wheelchair)
7. Position chair so that it maximizes her view of customers who have entered the store and allows them to pass close to her chair (Assistance with wheelchair)
8. Use Dynovox® to greet each customer, using one of several greetings (e.g., "Welcome to Wal-Mart. Help yourself to a sales sheet.")
9. Refer customer's questions to assistant or respond directly as appropriate.
10. Leave job when watch signals a break; take 20-minute break in cafeteria (Assistance with wheelchair and getting money from backpack)
11. Return to job when watch signals the end of break (Assistance with wheelchair)
12. Work until watch signals the time to go (Assistance with wheelchair)
13. Report to the supervisor; sign out (Assistance with wheelchair)
14. Take bus back to school (Assistance with wheelchair)

4. Introduce periodic but realistic barriers to task performance so that students can learn to *problem solve*.
5. Be sure the task includes *preparation* and *termination* steps.
6. Add self-monitoring of speed or quality if the student needs to learn these components.
7. Examine the possibilities for enriching the task through communication, social skills, and choice making. Make these added skills ones that do not stigmatize but that match expected behavior for student's gender and age and personal preference.

Maintenance Stage This stage uses the motto "use it routinely." Skills in this stage while still imperfect are good enough to use with some level of independence. The adage "practice makes perfect" applies to this stage and reminds us of two things: (a) forgetting is best remedied through regular use, and (b) functional skills, because they are needed, offer extensive opportunities for practice. Researchers have addressed various aspects of promoting skill maintenance in situations with little or no supervision. Teachers addressing maintenance learning will expect the student to use the skill during all the routines in the day when the skill is needed.

> *Rather than simply teach Jenny to tell time during math time using an unplugged clock and flashcards, her teachers will have her use this skill at the end of every class activity.*

Fluency or Proficiency Stage This stage uses the catchphrase "speed it up and perfect it." Skills in this stage of learning are performed with an accuracy above 60%, but the quality of performance at this level still needs improvement (Farlow & Snell, 1995). For example, some students learn to monitor the tempo (rate and duration) of the task performance (e.g., Can I count out the money fast enough not to hold up the line of customers? Am I emptying the dishwasher quickly enough?). Other students focus on improving the quality of task performance (e.g., Is the floor clean enough? Did I staple the top left corner of the pages?). Still other students work on both tempo and quality of skills while also improving accuracy.

> *Jenny will work on looking at the clock, reporting the time quickly and accurately, and identifying the next activity in her schedule.*

Generalization Stage The goal of this stage is to learn to "use it anywhere and whenever it is needed." In this stage, students are exposed to more variations of task materials and environments. They particularly need to learn problem solving, as natural stimuli change and adaptations in responses are required.

> *Jenny will be taught to tell time using the variety of analog clocks that exist at home and school. This means clocks with an incomplete array of numbers or numbers that are not roman numerals.*

Translating IEPs into Action

Articulating the Teaching Structure

The structure teachers provide students refers to how they manage, direct, support, and encourage students during instruction. Structure consists of what the teacher does before a student responds (antecedent methods) and what the teacher does in reaction to the student's response (consequence methods). For the best outcomes, teachers will match teaching structure to the student's stage of learning and preferences and adjust it to suit how the student responds (attention, accuracy, quality, speed, self-correction, social behavior). Antecedent and consequent structure encompasses many elements:

- *Antecedent to a student's responding*: Teacher and peer proximity, requests and prompts, opportunities for choice, student arrangement, and task materials
- *Consequent to the student's responding*: Teacher and peer reactions such as reinforcement, corrections, task choice, and task change

The context and logistics of the teaching activity also contribute to structure (time schedule, grouping, location, frequency and duration of instruction). Teams will define how much and what type of structure is appropriate for teaching particular skills to particular students. In the sections that follow, we describe some of the options teams have when designing teaching plans. But first, let us integrate stages of learning with teaching structure

Structure and Stage of Learning
Early Stages The teaching structure used should relate to students' stages of learning or their present ability to perform each IEP objective. As a general rule,

somewhat greater structure is used when teaching a new skill (acquisition stage) in order to shape performance and to prevent and minimize errors. For example, students require more direction and assistance to avoid errors on new skills, but that assistance should be gradually faded out; they also benefit from having ongoing feedback on their accuracy (e.g., praise for correct responses as well as for attempts or prompted correct responses and more assistance after errors). Typically, to teach skills in the acquisition stage, teachers are physically closer than usual to the student, so they can assist as needed and provide feedback. In addition, students need to have some repetition in the task steps and stimuli so that they can master a chain of responses; only later in learning should they be expected to adjust their performance to suit wide variations in the task materials, method, or setting. This does not mean that teaching in real locations or natural situations should be avoided or that initial instruction should be limited to one setting. However, teachers should provide enough structure initially to avoid confusing learning conditions.

Timothy's greeting skill is still in the acquisition stage of learning. His teachers talk with his parents to define the target behavior. How Timothy will be taught to greet others depends on what he already can do and what his peers do. Given his beginning social and language ability, Timothy should not yet be taught a different greeting for everyone; instead, he'll learn to use the same raised hand movement for saying "hello" and "good-bye" to peers and adults. Next, the team plans how to prompt his response, emphasizing the natural cues that ultimately signal greeting.

Later Stages

During later stages of learning, teachers should gradually "pull away" from the learner, give less direct supervision, emphasize natural forms of reinforcement and error correction, and teach the student to self-monitor their performance while reducing external reinforcement, supervision, and assistance. For example, during the maintenance stage of learning (a) students should have regular opportunities to use the same skill under familiar conditions, (b) structure should be gradually reduced, and (c) teachers should lessen their assistance and fade their presence and approval so that the skill comes more under the control of natural cues and stimuli.

Jenny has learned to get her daily schedule from her desk each morning when she arrives at class. Then she checks with her teacher for any schedule symbols to move or new symbols to add. With minimal reminders, she uses it regularly throughout the day, moving completed symbols to the back of the card and checking what's next.

Maintenance is a stage that many teachers forget or at least find difficult to implement because it requires shifting from an active teaching role (e.g., prompting, praising) to distancing themselves and giving intermittent attention. Researchers have found that when students cannot predict teachers' supervision of their work on a task they know fairly well, they attend better and complete more of the task (Dunlap & Johnson, 1985). Maintenance is an important stage of learning.

Multiple-Stepped Tasks and Stage of Learning

When the priority skill involves a chain or sequence of steps or several routines together, as do many functional tasks, students' present level of performance may be uneven. Students may perform with varying competence on composite skills (at several different stages of learning) within one routine. The teaching structure (antecedents and consequences) and logistics (how often and where to teach) must be adjusted to mesh with a student's varying performance, as Ms. Washington did when working with Christine in her greeter job at Wal-Mart.

One of Christine's work experiences was being a greeter at Wal-Mart. Some of the skills involved in this job were new (having people take advertising flyers from a box on her tray, greeting customers she did not know), but other parts of the job involved skills used before in other settings (greeting using her speaking communication device, ordering a drink, taking a work break). She participated in this job for 3 weeks and came to know the entire routine for which she was responsible. Many of the 14 task steps (Table 4-5) were partially performed with assistance from her teacher.

During acquisition, Christine's special education teacher, Ms. Washington, focused on the core steps of Christine's greeting customers. Christine was good at greeting others with her Dynovox® at school but not as a greeter at Wal-Mart. Two other task steps—using her signaling watch to start or stop work or break and ordering and purchasing a drink during break—were not new skills, but using them at Wal-Mart was new (skill generalization stage). Slowly, Christine's performance improved in accuracy even as Ms. Washington started to fade out her prompts and reduce her praise. When Christine met the initial acquisition criterion of independence on 9 of 14 steps, Ms. Washington modified her teaching methods to promote skill maintenance and improved accuracy. First, Ms. Washington spent less time directly instructing Christine and expected her to continue greeting while she stood quietly alongside. Ms. Washington also modified the reinforcement used during acquisition. Instead of giving continuous praise for each task step completed, Ms. Washington gave praise only for completing the entire task.

As we will discuss in chapter 5, by far the best way to make decisions about changing the structure of a teaching program is for team members to observe the student performing the skill and collect and examine performance data as a team; by pooling relevant information and solving problems together, a team can reach agreement on any needed changes, implement the changes, and then observe the outcome.

Teacher, Location, and Grouping

Once goals and objectives are written, team members shift their focus to designing specific teaching programs. As teams move through steps to design and implement teaching plans, they will answer a series of questions:

- Who will teach, when, and where?
- What arrangement (e.g., individual, small group, tutoring, large group) will be used?
- What supports and adaptations will be given, if any?
- What teaching methods will be employed?

Teaching plans are ultimately the responsibility of the special education teacher with input from other team members. When the student is taught in the general education classroom or during integrated activities (such as library, lunch, or art), teaching programs must mesh with classroom schedules, planned activities, available staff, and feasible grouping arrangements to take advantage of the opportunities for learning with and around peers. In this section, we describe the options available to address the first two questions,

which involve logistics (who will teach and when) and context (where and in what arrangement).

Who Will Teach? Teams have many options for who will teach: the general or special education teacher, a paraprofessional, related services staff, and students. The more cohesive the team, the more likely that teaching plans will fit into ongoing school activities and suit multiple instructors. If cooperative learning groups are used in classrooms, peers will help teach each other. In addition, older students (typical or with disabilities) in a cross-age tutoring program may be taught to serve as the tutor of younger students (typical or with disabilities). All adults who teach also need to be involved in team conversations about the student's progress so that any problems can be solved together. When instructors communicate as a team, having multiple instructors can be beneficial because it (a) encourages students to generalize their learning across people, (b) provides the team with broader experience in teaching the student, and (c) prevents overinvolvement or isolation of instructors with students.

Several researchers have studied students in inclusive elementary classrooms and found that who taught (general or special educator, paraprofessional, another student) made little difference in the student's level of academic responding (Hunt, Soto, Maier, Muller, & Goetz, 2002; Logan, Brakeman, & Keefe, 1997; McDonnell, Thorson, & McQuivey, 1998). What seems to influence a student's academic responding in these classrooms is a combination of factors: (a) whether there is team collaboration on students' objectives and educational supports; (b) the arrangement used: the rate of engagement is slightly higher when the number of students are fewer (cooperative group or small-group or one-to-one instruction versus whole-class instruction); (c) whether instruction is directed toward the student, which seems to improve a student's rate of responding (i.e., being given opportunities to respond, having materials provided, and being given feedback); and (d) having individualized instruction: academic responding increases when teaching is tailored to the student.

A practice often used by schools and IEP teams is to pair students having more extensive support needs with paraprofessionals for much of the day. Sometimes, however, when a single teaching assistant spends much of the school day with a single student, problems can result. Giangreco, Edelman, Luiselli, and MacFarland (1997, p. 11) studied this staffing practice and identified eight undesirable patterns that may develop when teaching assistants are in the exclusive role of assisting a single student. Teaching assistants may do the following:

1. Obstruct the general educator's role by having complete control in implementing the student's program
2. Isolate the student from classmates by removing or distancing the student from other students and activities
3. Promote dependency on adults
4. Affect peer interactions negatively by their constant proximity and their sometimes protective approach
5. Use less-than-competent teaching
6. Encourage a loss of personal control by failing to promote choice making or peer interaction
7. Be insensitive to the student's gender, for example, by taking male students into female bathrooms
8. Distract classmates, for example, by involving the student in activities that differed from classmates

Schools and educational teams are advised to rethink their practices and policies concerning the use of paraprofessionals so that these problems are eliminated. Individuals who have written about pairing paraprofessionals with students who need support have made some suggestions about addressing these potential difficulties (Doyle, 2002; Giangreco et al., 1997; Hall, McClannahan, & Krantz, 1995; Snell & Janney, 2005). First, it is important to broaden the responsibilities of general education classroom teachers so that they are involved with the special education teacher in the supervision of special education teaching assistants. Second, classroom teachers and paraprofessionals should have basic training in systematic instruction, including ways to promote peer interaction. Third, the classroom teacher should feel ownership of the students with disabilities in their classrooms. Fourth, paraprofessionals need job descriptions that set forth their responsibilities and the line of supervision. When their responsibilities include participation on the student's planning team, paraprofessionals have input and can benefit from team thinking. Fifth, students' schedules should be designed so they are truly integrated into class activities and peer interactions, using adaptations as needed to promote meaningful involvement; simply being present with an assistant does not constitute meaningful inclusion. Finally, for students who need more personal assistance and the

support of a paraprofessional, several practices may reduce the possibility of isolation: (a) assign two assistants to a single student, each for part of the day, and let assistants rotate among other students; (b) assign assistants to classrooms rather than to students; (c) vary a student's support so it rotates among team members; and (d) design teaching arrangements so team members reduce one-to-one instruction and increase instruction in pairs or small groups of students with mixed abilities.

When and Where Will Teaching Occur? Like other students, students with severe disabilities learn both inside and outside the classroom: in hallways, other classrooms, and the cafeteria; outside the school on playgrounds; at the bus loading areas; and in the community. As these students grow older and their IEP objectives include skills or activities not targeted for typical students, their instruction will expand into alternative settings beyond the general education classroom. As a general rule, some alternate teaching settings away from the general education classroom but in the school (with or apart from peers) are necessary during the later elementary and middle school years.

In place of participating in language arts, Jenny instead receives one-to-one instruction in following school routines more independently.

During the middle school, high school, and post–high school years, as the instructional focus for students with severe disabilities shifts to include more functional academic, community, and job-related skills, the alternative teaching settings expand to include stores, offices, libraries and other pubic buildings, streets and sidewalks, restaurants, and work settings in the nearby community. Teams still must plan for general education classes or school activities that maximize students' continued contact with peers.

Christine spends the bulk of her school week learning vocational skills in community settings, but she participates in the Best Buddies Chapter on the university campus, where her post–high school class is located and she is active in the drama club.

In inclusive schools, special education instruction may be provided in a variety of ways, each of which must involve team planning:

• *The general education classroom and "consultation" from special education*: The student with disabilities along with classmates is taught by the classroom teacher, using the same or adapted methods but with no extra staff support.

- *Collaborative teaching (also called team teaching or coteaching)*: Two or more team members (typically the special and general education teachers) plan and teach all the students in the class (students

with and without disabilities) cooperatively, usually for part of the day.

- *Pull-in with collaborative teaming*: The special education teacher or another team member (e.g., related services staff, paraprofessional) teaches or provides support to the student(s) with disabilities in the context of a general education classroom or

FIGURE 4–3

Team Support Approaches for Timothy, Jenny, and Christine

	Team Support Approaches			
Student	**Pullout with Collaborative Teaming**	**Pull-in with Collaborative Teaming**	**Collaborative Teaching**	**General Educator with Team**
Timothy (age 4), preschool	Timothy leaves daily with the SLP for intensive communication training. Special educator and paraprofessional teach Timothy self-toileting.	All special staff provide Timothy with support in classroom activities. Special educator facilitates peer support twice a week; the SLP alternates.	Special and general educators regularly "run" a craft group, oversee centers during structured play, and participate in teaching special unit activities. Timothy is part of these activities.	During recess and two free play sessions a week, Ms. Johnson and her assistant carry out Timothy's communication and social objectives using methods designed by the team.
Jenny (age 10), fifth grade	SLP, assistant, and tutor work for 30-minute sessions three times a week, in the library, in the cafeteria, on the playground, and around the school on self-management and errands.	M–F: Teaching assistant and special educator are scheduled to provide support to Jenny in the classroom (math, reading, writing). On Fridays, special educator runs "lunch bunch" peer support group for fourth and fifth graders.	M–W–F: Special educator and classroom teacher conduct science classes and related cooperative group activities.	Ms. Alpern follows the team plans for Jenny's arrival and departure, monitors Jenny's work during shared reading, and oversees the "lunch bunch" group twice a week.
Christine (age 20), post-high school at nearby university and community	Christine participates in campus and community-based instruction for part of each day accompanied by one of several team members, depending on the teaching plans and schedule. Every 6 weeks, the PT checks her equipment. M–F: Christine is pulled out for bathroom breaks.	Paraprofessional, SLP, or her Best Buddy companion alternate in accompanying Christine to drama club and to lunch at the campus grill or student union; services are focused on making and communicating choices and social interactions with others.	Periodically used; Special education teacher spent time initially in drama club and with Best Buddies teaching peers how to communicate with Christine.	Someone is always present with Christine at drama club, but the club president, faculty adviser, and other members now interact confidently with her.

Note: SLP=speech and language pathologist; M–F=Monday through Friday; M-W-F=Monday, Wednesday, Friday; PT=Physical therapist; TA=teaching assistant.

school activity. Classmates typically are involved in the same or similar activities as the students with disabilities and may participate together in small or large groups or alongside.

- *Pullout with collaborative teaming (also called alternative activities)*: Support is provided to the student with disabilities by special education staff or another team member (e.g., related services staff, vocational teacher) in a setting away from the general education classroom for a particular reason identified by the team (e.g., to give privacy, more space, access to materials not in the classroom). The student who is removed from the general education setting may be accompanied by other classmates. Any use of pullout depends on team collaboration to be effective and needs to be regularly reevaluated.

Often students with severe disabilities receive their special education services in more than one of these ways. Teams determine what approaches to use, depending on the student's needs and characteristics, the services offered, and the skills targeted (Hunt et al., 2002). For example, despite their differences in age and needs, Timothy's, Jenny's, and Christine's schedules reflect all four approaches (Figure 4-3).

What Teaching Arrangement? Most students with severe disabilities, much like their typical peers, can acquire the ability to learn in groups and can also benefit from observing others learn. The skill objective, the setting, and the instructor influence whatever teaching arrangement is chosen (one to one, student pair, small group, or large group). When students present difficulties attending or staying with a small group, the team must build these skills.

One-to-One Instruction On a practical level, one-to-one instruction has *not* proven to be as beneficial to students with severe disabilities as many educators have thought. The rationale for this approach is to minimize distractions and thus enable stimulus control (Rotholz, 1987). Some confuse the notion of individualized instruction for students with individual instruction, but they are not synonymous. Individualized instruction is teaching designed to suit a specific student and can be delivered in a variety of teaching arrangements.

One disadvantage of one-to-one instruction is the failure of generalization. Skills mastered by students with autism and other severe disabilities in one-to-one arrangements do not automatically generalize to larger groups of students (Koegel & Rincover, 1974) or to people other than the original teacher (Rincover & Koegel, 1975). Another disadvantage is the exclusion from other pupils, which means that opportunities are lost for peer-to-peer teaching, peer reinforcement, social interaction, and students' incidental learning of other students' material through observation (Farmer, Gast, Wolery, & Winterling, 1991; Stinson, Gast, Wolery, & Collins, 1991). In contrast, group instruction allows opportunities to acquire taking turns, waiting, and imitation of others—skills that have practical value in everyday life. Finally, one-to-one instruction is not cost effective in terms of teacher time. It results in increased "downtime" (noninstructional time) for students. Thus, one-to-one instruction should be reserved for teaching tasks in which (a) privacy is required, (b) other students cannot easily be included (e.g., job training), (c) an older student teaches a younger student in a supervised tutoring program, and (d) short-term intensive instruction is needed during part of the day for a specific skill.

If a student cannot work in a group, there should be IEP objectives directed toward that goal. Teams will want to consider several strategies that build these skills by varying the arrangement: tandem instruction, sequential instruction, concurrent instruction, and combination instruction are explained in Table 4-6.

Enhanced Group Instruction Enhanced group instruction (EGI) (Kamps, Dugan, Leonard, & Daoust, 1994; Kamps, Leonard, Dugan, Boland, & Greenwood, 1991) has been found to promote effective responding and learning in small groups of students with intellectual disabilities and autism. Teachers working with groups of three to five students made tasks interesting and promoted learning by (a) requesting frequent student-to-student responding, (b) using fast-paced and random trials, (c) rotating materials and concepts taught, (d) using multiple examples of each concept taught (a minimum of three sets per concept), and (e) using individualized sets of materials for each student. These strategies meant that students were handling learning materials and actively and repeatedly responding to the teacher and classmates on task concepts. As a result,

TABLE 4–6
Methods to Build Group Participation Skills

Tandem Instruction

Start with one-to-one instruction and fade in other students one at a time until there is a group. With students who appear to have difficulties, use simple requests to "sit quietly," "put your hands down," or "look at this" or fade continuous reinforcement for staying with the group and participating. Koegel and Rincover (1974) found that while gradually increasing the group size from one to eight students, attending skills were shaped along with students' ability to tolerate less reinforcement. However, the same attending skills can be shaped in the context of the group itself. Thus, tandem instruction can be used part of the day while the same student participates in some groups for short periods at other times of the day, a strategy that reduces the disadvantages of gradually fading out one-to-one teaching (Rincover & Koegel, 1975).

Sequential Instruction

Teach students in a sequential manner (each student gets one turn, while others wait their turn) (Brown, Holvoet, Guess, & Mulligan, 1980). Reinforcing group members who attend to others as they take a turn increases the possibility for observational learning. Alternately, waiting time can be replaced with another activity for students who are not good at waiting, but these students will have less opportunity to learn by observing others. When sequential instruction is used, it is better to give turns contingent on being ready or contingent on being prompted to be ready than to give turns to students who are inattentive or misbehaving. Thus, turns should not be given in strict sequential order.

Concurrent Instruction

Direct instruction toward an entire group, with individuals responding or with group responding in unison (Reid & Favell, 1984). When the diversity of a group is increased, teachers must adjust their presentation of content so that all students can understand (e.g., use words, signs, and concrete objects to describe the task or concept being taught) and allow a variety of response levels and modes so that all students can participate.

Combination Groups

In many classrooms, it is not unusual to address a concept with a large group or class, give instructions for an activity applying that concept (concurrent), and then divide into smaller groups, often of mixed ability levels. Groups may have both independent or cooperative activities geared to individual abilities and goals. The teacher may provide directions to one group at a time or teach each group using turn taking (sequential). Students who have difficulty working in a group may be faded gradually into a group (tandem model) from a one-to-one teaching arrangement in the same classroom, as Koegel and Rincover (1974) did with students having autism. Likewise, students first may be taught to work independently for brief periods (e.g., cutting out 10 words and matching them to 10 pictures), after which they join a small group, where individualized instruction is continued during turn taking (Rincover & Koegel, 1975). The latter example is a combination of tandem and sequential models.

---

they were focused on the target stimuli, participating in the target response, and reported as being interested in the group activity. While all the students in these studies had disabilities, many of these group strategies for making instruction interesting and focused are often used in heterogeneous groups in general education classrooms and appear to have the same effects with a diverse array of students (Hunt, Staub, Alwell, & Goetz, 1994; Snell & Janney, 2000b; Tomlinson, 2001). To the extent that enhanced group instruction makes teaching more effective for *all* learners, it has the features of a *universal design* in that it benefits most if not all students.

Observation Learning It is not surprising that students with severe disabilities can learn by watching others. Researchers have shown positive learning effects from having one student observe another

student acquire academic skills (e.g., spelling one's name, adding, using a calculator, identifying community signs) and nonacademic skills (e.g., sharpening a pencil) (Doyle, Gast, Wolery, Ault, & Farmer, 1990; Singleton, Schuster, & Ault, 1995; Stinson et al., 1991; Whalen, Schuster, & Hemmeter, 1996). In these studies, which involved only pairs or small groups of students with disabilities, students not only learned the skills they were taught directly but also acquired some of their classmates' skills that they observed or that had been presented to them incidentally. Learning through observation in small groups works well when:

- Group members have the same type of task (identifying over-the-counter medications) but are taught with different materials (each student learns two different medications) rather than when all have the same materials.

- Typical classmates model functional tasks for students with severe disabilities while simply verbalizing each step they perform (e.g., spelling their name with letter tiles, using a calculator) (Brown & Holvoet, 1982; Werts, Caldwell, & Wolery, 1996).

During preschool, Timothy's teacher often pairs Timothy with two peers to help teach him routines such as putting things in his cubby and getting ready for snack. Josh and Meredith are good models; they make sure Timothy is watching and then perform one small step at a time while telling him with words and gestures what they are doing.

Students as Tutors Students without disabilities have been found to be effective instructors of students with severe disabilities in one-to-one arrangements. First, when tutors learned to use enhanced group instruction (Kamps, Walker, Locke, Delquadri, & Hall, 1990) and to teach word reading, their tutees made as much progress as they did when taught one on one or in small groups by teachers or paraprofessionals. Shukla et al. (1998) demonstrated that adolescents who were underachievers could learn to be as effective as special educators in getting their tutees to engage in class tasks while also improving their own engagement.

In order to be effective instructors, students must (a) indicate an interest and volunteer, (b) be provided with teaching methods and supervision, and (c) be involved in one-to-one arrangements, not small groups. Good student tutoring programs are often combined with friendship clubs, peer support groups, and classroom problem solving (Snell & Janney, 2000a). We think that the best version of student tutoring programs is cross-age tutoring, a common practice in many schools that involves older students teaching younger students rather than students of their age. Whenever one student teaches another, the relationship is a helping one, not a reciprocal or balanced relationship. Thus, when students are of different ages and older students fill the teaching role, their helping relationship does not compete with peer friendship. Other versions of using students as teachers that avoid this problem of one-way teaching among peers include classwide or reciprocal peer tutoring and peer assistance with cooperative groups, in which students take turns teaching each other (one student may have a disability) (Delquadri, Greenwood, Whorton, Carta, & Hall, 1986; Dugan et al., 1995). Still, many effective tutoring programs have been

reported from preschool to high school in which peers have been taught to tutor classmates with disabilities on communication, social skills, and academic tasks (e.g., Gilberts, Agran, Hughes, & Wehmeyer, 2001; Hughes et al., 2000; Staub, Schwartz, Gallucci, & Peck, 1994; Staub, Spaulding, Peck, Gallucci, & Schwartz, 1996). Peer tutoring programs become more acceptable when they are balanced with efforts to promote friendships and nonhelping reciprocal relationships between classmates and peers with disabilities (Hughes & Carter, in press; Snell & Janney, 2000a).

Twice a week, Jenny looks forward to sessions with her seventh-grade tutor, Rita. After checking in at the tutoring office and getting the lesson plan and Jenny's record book, Rita takes Jenny to a tutoring station in the library. There they review what Jenny has done over the past few days in her classes: getting around the school, carrying out tasks without being distracted, and using picture or word guides to remember task steps. Then Jenny reads the task for that day from her schedule (return old class books and pick up new class books from library), reviews the steps, gets the materials, and completes the task with reminders as needed from Rita. Afterward, Jenny self-evaluates with Rita's input. Before returning to the middle school next door, Rita shows the tutoring supervisor Jenny's record; once a month, Rita is observed by the tutoring supervisor. Rita takes pride in her work and knows that it will help Jenny next year in middle school.

Cooperative Learning Groups Strategies to promote cooperation among students working toward a group goal have had widespread application in regular education programs (Johnson & Johnson, 1997). Many of the strategies for successful group instruction are evident in cooperative learning groups, with the added advantage that students learn to cooperate with others while shifting competition with others to competition with oneself (Snell & Janney, 2000a). Slavin (1991) defines cooperative learning methods as "instructional techniques in which students work in heterogeneous learning teams to help one another learn academic material" (p. 177). In contrast to the group arrangements just described, cooperative learning groups work more independently from the teacher (although cooperative learning groups receive instructions on the purpose of the activity, have ongoing supervision, interact with the teacher, and require a great deal of teacher planning).

In preschool, Timothy's teachers make frequent use of cooperative groupings. The 4- and 5-year-olds form groups of five children for cooperative activities. These activities change daily and involve art (making a mural together), music and dance, building with blocks or other materials, science, cooking, or games. The small groups are balanced so that children who need extra assistance and those who are more independent are spread across the groups. Group membership changes several times over the school year. Following simple directions given by Ms. Johnson, the groups move to the activity, get settled, receive instructions, participate together, finish the activity, and clean up. After instructions or a demonstration of the activity, Ms. Johnson and Mr. Grayson help group members decide who will do what to contribute to the activity. For example, Timothy, who likes to put things in their places, is often given the responsibility of putting materials away in his group. Marion and Charles, each in different groups, enjoy passing out items to group members and need practice naming group members, so they are often given such tasks.

Several examples of cooperative learning groups have involved students with severe disabilities in general education classrooms. Dugan et al. (1995) demonstrated that fourth graders with autism could learn skills such as word recognition, peer interaction, and academic engagement alongside their peers in social studies cooperative groups. Hunt et al. (1994) taught second graders to use positive feedback and prompts to assist classmates with severe movement, cognitive, and communication disabilities to respond in cooperative groups. The students with disabilities rotated to new cooperative groups in the classroom every 8 to 10 weeks. Not only did peers achieve their academic objectives even when serving as mediators, but target students also learned motor and communication objectives that were embedded within the cooperative activity and generalized these skills to new groups, peers, and activities. While the typical students focused on learning geometry from shapes and money skills, their classmates with disabilities worked on communication and motor IEP objectives since the group activity allowed many opportunities to request turns and to move task materials. Both studies lend support for the use of cooperative learning groups as a means for promoting meaningful inclusion of students with severe disabilities in general education classrooms.

Group Instruction Guidelines Teachers can both facilitate observational learning and maximize motivation, thereby adding to the benefits that group instruction has over one-to-one instruction. For example, when teaching small groups of students the same general content, teachers can do the following:

1. Involve all members by using individualized instruction, teaching the same concept at multiple levels of complexity, and allowing for different response modes and modified materials
2. Keep the group instruction interesting by (a) keeping turns short, (b) giving everyone turns, (c) making turns dependent on attending, (d) giving demonstrations, and (e) using a variety of task materials that can be handled
3. Encourage students to listen and watch other group members as they take their turns and praise them when they do
4. Actively involve students in the process of praising and prompting others
5. Allow students to participate in demonstrations and handle materials related to the skill or concept being taught
6. Keep waiting time to a minimum by controlling group size, teacher talk, and the length of each student's turn.
7. Prompt cooperation and discourage competition among group members

In a later section of this chapter, we will review a model for designing schoolwork and individualized supports for students who are members of inclusive classrooms (Janney & Snell, 2004). This model depends on collaborative teamwork among special and general educators, paraprofessionals, related services professionals, and family members. The goal of teams is to meaningfully include students as members of general education classrooms who are active participants both socially and instructionally. Next we will review the effective teaching options team can draw on to plan instruction.

Current Student Performance and Updated Goals and Objectives

Sometimes, IEP objectives must be adjusted following observation to match changes in the teaching conditions or a student's performance. This is especially true when objectives are written in the spring and taught the following fall. While the general skill priority is not likely to change, some aspects of the conditions, behaviors, or criteria may change, especially if the student has changed schools or classrooms. Often the student's current level of performance has only been estimated, not assessed. Assessing skills just prior to teaching is also a good idea, as it gives a *baseline level of performance* against which to compare performance when teaching begins. Periodic assessment of skills once instruction begins (also called *probe performance*) helps the team understand how a student's training progress compares with performance under criterion or test conditions.

Informal Assessment The method of informal assessment chosen must suit the target skill. Most often, informal assessment involves direct observation of a student as he or she attempts to perform the task or discrete behavior under criterion conditions. Sometimes informal assessment involves examining the "permanent product" that results from a student's performance of a skill (e.g., examining, then determining the number of correct place settings, the fraction of a lunch packed, or whether a coat and backpack are hung up in the correct place). (Evaluation methods are described in more detail in chapter 5.) When planning the informal assessment of target behaviors, teachers should remember that the assessment conditions must represent the conditions stated in the behavioral objective. The conditions should be as natural as possible and match the times and places for performance as well as the materials, adaptations, and individuals present (if any).

On two mornings when Timothy arrives, he is assessed on the morning arrival routine (Figure 4-1) using the same conditions under which he will be taught. Since the routine is similar to the one he follows when he leaves before lunch (steps 1 through 12 are reversed in order, and the last three are omitted), his team decides to target the departure routine for instruction as well. Teaching will occur naturally on arrival and departure, but tests of his progress (probes) will take place about once a month during arrival. When Timothy's baseline performance of the morning routine was assessed, he could carry out 3 (20%) of 15 task steps the first day and 2 (13%) of 15 on each of the next day. He consistently was able to find his cubby (step 9). If the baseline data are ac-

curate, Timothy's performance places him in the acquisition stage of learning, which means that a lot of teaching will be needed.

Refine Goals and Objectives Baseline data and observations should be used to refine IEP goals and objectives, specify realistic performance criteria, and identify aim dates (the date a student is predicted to meet the criteria for an objective). After some informal observation in the fall, Timothy's original instructional objectives were adjusted to reflect his baseline performance and the modified target skills (Table 4-7).

When teachers set *aim dates*, it is easier to judge how a student's current level of skill performance compares with the goal or criterion level (Farlow & Snell, 1995; Liberty & Haring, 1990; Wolery, Alt, & Doyle, 1992). An aim date is the date the team expects a particular student to reach the criterion for an instructional objective. Once instruction begins, teachers combine this date with the student's performance during the first 3 training days to create an *aim line* by which to judge progress. The aim line is drawn onto the student's graph of performance data. The aim line is a visible reminder of the team's expectation of student progress. When progress dips below the aim line, teams determine whether to modify the program. (The procedure of setting and using an aim date is discussed in more detail in chapter 5.)

For the first self-management and social objectives, Timothy's team sets their aim dates 8 weeks after the initiation of teaching, as all preschoolers receive performance evaluations just before the holiday break. Because Timothy performed accurately on only a few steps, the teachers judged his learning to be in the acquisition stage. Thus, they planned to use structured antecedent and consequence methods, and they established criteria far less than 100%. The teachers reasoned that once the acquisition criteria were met, they would modify the teaching methods (e.g., provide less structure for partially learned steps), increase the performance criteria, and make the task analysis more complex to suit him in the later stages of learning. The teachers were pleased, though, that even during baseline, Timothy performed several steps, although not consistently, and attempted three other steps.

TABLE 4–7
A Sample of Timothy's Goals and Objectives for Self-Management and Social Interaction

Area: Self-Management in School Routines
(two objectives, one goal: ladder relationship)

Objective 1: On arrival at and departure from preschool, Timothy will exit the car, walk to and enter class, greet familiar people, remove and hang his outer garments in his cubby, and select and go to a play activity at a criterion level of 10 of 15 steps (67%) for arrival and of 8 of 12 steps (67%) for departure during two training sessions (using partial participation on some steps as indicated in the task analysis). **Aim Date:** December 17, 2004

Objective 2: When given an opportunity in preschool to select a play activity using a picture activity chart, Timothy will get his photo card and place it under an activity picture and then go to that activity on three out of four opportunities (embedded across morning). **Aim Date:** March 4, 2005

Goal: Timothy will follow all preschool routines on his own Monday through Friday by the end of the school year. **Aim Date:** June 10, 2005

Area: Social Interaction with Adults and Peers
(one objective, one goal: ladder relationship)

Objective 1: Timothy will greet and indicate farewell to the familiar adults and peers at preschool at the time of their and his arrival and departure by looking at them and using a wave on three out of four natural opportunities during the day. **Aim Date:** December 17, 2004

Goal: Timothy will interact socially with his teachers and peers at preschool by looking at them, greeting (waving), making requests and choices (using pictures, gestures, or words), and playing with or by peers on three out of four natural opportunities during the day. **Aim Date:** June 10, 2005

Selecting Teaching Methods

Antecedent Methods

The initial steps Timothy's team took to plan his morning routine instruction involved: (a) defining the skills or behavior chains and identifying teaching conditions, (b) assessing his or baseline level of performance for the routine, and (c) refining his instructional objectives. Next, the team planned how he would be given assistance (prompts) on the steps that he could not or did not complete in a manner that drew his attention to the relevant stimuli to be learned. They also decided how that assistance would be faded. This phase of writing an instructional plan focused on the antecedent methods.

Instructional antecedents are the planned and incidental stimuli in the learning situation: a teacher's instructional cues or task directions, setting, classmates' activities, teaching and task materials, opportunities for making choices, and teaching prompts. Closely related are the instructional consequences, which address the ways instructors and others in the environment respond to student behavior. While the teaching setting (e.g., general education classroom, resource room,

playground, work setting) has a major bearing on the antecedents and consequences, so do the target skills, a student's stage of learning for each skill, and other student characteristics, such as age, preferences, and communication abilities.

Discriminative Stimuli Learning is a process of understanding how to respond to specific and changing signals or stimuli in the environment.

> *Timothy has learned that in the presence of food at the kitchen table when he is hungry, if he makes the "eat" or "drink" sign or if he says "Mmm" for "more," he will get food. Timothy has also learned to indicate through his own personalized gestures and facial expressions some of the things he wants and does not want at meals.*

Timothy's use of certain signs in the presence of food and drinks have been reinforced for so long that he has learned which responses lead to food. Discriminative stimuli (also referred to as S^Ds) are those relevant aspects of a task or situation in the presence of which a particular behavior is frequently reinforced.

Discriminative stimuli can include aspects of a task setting, teacher requests, materials, the time of day, the student's physical state (e.g., empty stomach, full bladder), and other contextual stimuli. Initially, a teacher's reminders and assistance or prompts are the stimuli that control a student's response. But once the task-discriminated stimuli are learned, they control the student's response, and therefore prompts from others are not needed.

Last month, Christine started sampling a job at an elementary school library close to campus. Her job was checking out books. Initially, she did not understand what to do when someone asked her to scan or check out a book. She did not know what to do when someone placed a book into the book holder on her lap tray. Now she is alert to critical stimuli that "tell" her it is time to press the book scanning switch. For example, a child asking her to check out a book, followed by the thud of the book against the metal end of the slanted book holder on her tray, signals to her that the book is ready to be checked out. She clicks the scanner switch and knows that if there is no beep from the scanner, the book was not put in the holder correctly (with the bar code positioned up and under the scanner). The absence of a beep is a different stimulus, which she responds to by pushing her communication device to say, "Oops! Can you put the book in the right way?"

Teaching involves shifting the control from prompting stimuli to natural task stimuli. For most students, the goal is to respond in the presence of natural cues rather than teacher-applied stimuli, such as requests and prompts. For example, students should respond to the discriminated stimulus of a dirty mirror or the fact that cleaning it is part of their job before a teacher requests its cleaning. Similarly, when materials run out, students should initiate a search for more materials rather than wait for the teacher to remind them. If the goal is for natural task stimuli to control behavior, teachers must incorporate them into the instructional plan. Teaching in natural settings and at natural times lets teachers use environmental cues. Initially, for most tasks in the acquisition stage of learning, an instructional cue or request is necessary to evoke the behavior. Instructional requests need to be carefully planned:

1. State requests so the student easily understands them

2. Phrase them as requests ("Read this," "Tie your shoes,"), not questions ("Can you read this?" Do you want to tie your shoes?")
3. Provide requests only when the student is attending
4. Give them only once at the beginning of the task rather than repeating requests over and over
5. Pair the request with relevant, natural task stimuli: times, of day, materials, and settings

Opportunities for Student Choice The use of choice making as an antecedent strategy is relatively new in the literature. For example, a student might be offered one of a number of choices at the beginning, during, or after completing a task: (a) "Which of several activities or chores do you want to work on?" (b) "Where do you want to do this activity?" (c) "Who would you like as a work partner?" (d) "When do you want to take a break?" and (e) "What do you want to do on break or after you are done?" (Brown, 1991). Reviews of choice-making research over the past several decades lend strong support to the practice of increasing choice-making opportunities as part of teaching; giving students choices is associated with both the improvement of appropriate behavior and the decline of problem behavior (Horner & Carr, 1997; Kern et al., 1998).

At the same time, there are some things we do not know about the best ways to suit choice-making strategies to students or how choice works. For example, is it the opportunity to make a choice and have some control that results in the generally favorable effects on a student's behavior? Or do the effects of choice-making strategies result primarily from experiencing reinforcing or preferred events (Kern et al., 1998)? Horner and Carr (1997) suggested two reasons why choice may reduce problem behavior. First, when given a choice, a student will choose the most preferred option at that time (while the teacher may not know what is preferred at that moment, which may be different than what was preferred the day before). Second, when an activity is chosen by a student (rather than the same activity chosen by a teacher and offered to the student—even when the activity is one that is known to be "preferred"), it seems less likely to result in problem behavior because "choosing may reduce the aversive properties of tasks and activities" (p. 97). Others have espoused the motivating power of sharing control with learners (Koegel, Koegel, & Carter, 1999). For example, following a student's lead during recess or centers and teaching that student in the context of his or her chosen activity is a commonly used teaching strategy with young children and with children who have autism (Koegel, Camarata, Koegel, Ben-Tall, & Smith, 1998; Schepis, Reid, Ownbey, & Parsons, 2001). We know that having opportunities to make choices is a recommended element of both teaching programs and behavioral support interventions and a valued part of life. Thus, it is important to include IEP objectives related to making choices and to include choice making in students' daily schedules.

Student Skills Involved in Choice Making Independent choice making requires several student skills: (a) having some preferred activities or events, (b) being aware of the options (visually, tactilely, or auditorally scanning the choices), (c) expressing intent or choice by making an observable response (gazing at, pointing to, or picking up an item), (d) making a choice when offered options, and (e) engaging in the choice. One of these crucial skills is intent (described in more detail in chapter 11), which can be inferred from a person's behavior but not measured directly. Intentional behaviors are the communicative behaviors by which we judge that a person prefers one thing over another (Snell, 2002). A student shows intent when one or several behaviors occur, such as the following:

- Persistent responding until a goal is accomplished
- Changing one's signal or response until a goal is accomplished (e.g., pointing, whining, then taking a parent by the hand and leading him or her to the location of the goal activity)
- Alternating one's gaze between a goal and a communication partner in the vicinity (looking up at a toy on the shelf, then looking at parent, and back to the toy)
- Waiting for a response from a communication partner
- Stopping communication signals when the goal is met
- Showing satisfaction when the goal is met or dissatisfaction if the goal is not met

Perhaps the best way to teach intent and the skill of choice making is to identify reinforcing or preferred activities and to offer them on a predictable and frequent basis while varying the choice options and using communication a student can understand. (See chapter 3 for assessment of preferences and 11 for ideas on teaching intent.)

Teacher Skills Choice making involves not only several student skills but also certain teacher or adult behaviors. To use choice making as an antecedent strategy, teachers must (a) be aware of an individual's preferences, (b) know how to offer choice options so the student is aware of them, (c) offer a choice that is compatible with the ongoing activity and student, (d) pause for the student to respond, (e) know what student response indicates a favorable choice and a rejection, and (f) provide the choice and time to engage in that choice activity.

Stimulus and Response Prompting Prompting is another major category of antecedent strategies. Behavior must occur before it can be shaped and various types of assistance given before the response increases the likelihood that the learner will perform the desired behavior or a better approximation. Prompts may be associated primarily with the task stimuli (materials) or the response. Stimulus prompts or stimulus modification procedures involve manipulating the relevant and irrelevant task stimuli and gradually changing the teaching stimuli from simpler to more challenging levels. Stimulus modification procedures are used by teachers to improve the chance of a correct response. A classic example of this approach are the stimulus-fading procedures used by Gold (1972) involving color coding of several key parts of bicycle brake pieces to make the assembly task easier for workers with disabilities. Given color-coded parts, the workers simply matched the colors of the parts to be joined. Eventually, the color coding was eliminated or faded.

While stimulus prompts are more time consuming to prepare and use than response prompts, they may be used by students independent of a staff member being present. Prompting students to be successful during instruction by modifying curriculum, class materials, and work directions are important strategies for teaching in the general education classroom. The modifications in class materials might be slowly faded or might be permanent. If gradually faded, they resemble stimulus prompts. For example, name-writing worksheets might have dotted letters that are gradually eliminated, and reading flash cards might be made in four sets—cards with a picture superimposed on the word, two sets of cards with the pictures faded in different degrees, and card with only words.

Response prompts are actions taken by the teacher before a student responds (or after an error) to increase the probability of a correct response. Response prompts are "portable" (the teacher performs them for the student), and they often do not involve materials. Most response prompts used during early stages of learning require a teacher to perform them close to or on the student, but there are many options for "teacher-free" response prompts when students learn to use as task reminders pictures guides, audio- or videotaped instructions, or computer-generated response prompts. Teacher-free response prompts such as these are more successful in later stages of learning. Typical response prompts that teachers provide include verbal instructions, gestures or pointing movements, models, and physical assists. Regardless of the type of prompt, all response prompts given by teachers should be faded as students learn to respond to natural task, environmental, and internal stimuli (Wolery et al., 1992; Wolery & Gast, 1984). To do this, teachers should draw students' attention to natural stimuli by doing the following:

- Matching verbal prompts with the actual words used in the setting where the skill ultimately will be performed

  On her library job, Christine's teachers use the words "scanner" and "beep" because that's what library staff and the students say.

- Emphasizing the type of prompt most prevalent in the natural setting

  When Jenny missed the teacher's directions, her assistant tells her to watch what her friends seated nearby are getting from their desks and do the same.

- When a student skips an important task step, calling attention (with gestures, words, and positioning) to the step (materials, location) that occurred just before the omitted step so the student attends to the relevant natural stimuli

  Timothy pulled up his pants, flushed the toilet, then started to leave the bathroom when the teacher called him back, positioned him facing the sink, and said, "What's next?"

- Using natural prompts and correction procedures whenever possible during fluency, maintenance, and generalization

  Christine has learned to listen for the scanner beep after she activates the switch in order to judge if the library book was placed in the book holder correctly.

- Teaching students performing in the later learning stages to ask for assistance when prompts are faded

  While learning to return the classroom's books to the library, Jenny performs well enough that, if she needs help, she must ask for it; otherwise her instructors only assist if danger is a possibility.

Types of Instructional Prompts Prompts come in many forms (e.g., words, visual demonstrations, physical movement) and are often combined. Prompts differ in the amount of assistance they provide, the student skills required, and their intrusiveness. Teams should choose single prompts or combinations of prompts that suit the skill and setting and the student's preferences, abilities, and stage of learning. Arranged roughly in an order from requiring more student skill to be effective to requiring less student skill, Table 4–8 provides some information on prompts and considerations in using each type (Wolery et al., 1992).

Response Latency In terms of giving instructional prompts, response latency can be defined as the period of time allowed for a student to respond without assistance or to respond following a prompt. Without the opportunity to initiate, students may become prompt dependent and fail to learn the target response. The length of the response latency period depends primarily on the student and, in part, on the response, or task step. For many students without significant movement difficulties and for many tasks, a latency of 3 to 5 seconds often suits them during the acquisition stage of learning. The full latency is provided both before any assistance is given (allowing the student time to initiate the response without help) and after assistance is given (allowing the student time to respond to the prompt). If a student makes an error before the latency is over, it is important to gently interrupt the error with a second prompt or with a prompt that provides more assistance.

When Timothy is standing by his cubby, Carlene waits about 4 seconds to see if he will take off his jacket. If he does not or starts to but stops, she uses a combined gestural and physical prompt (points, then tugs gently at his jacket) and then waits about 4 more seconds for him to initiate.

TABLE 4–8

Definitions, Examples, and Pros and Cons of Common Prompts

Definition and Examples	Pros and Cons
Spoken or Signed Prompts	
• Words or manual signs that tell the student how to respond ("Spray the mirror"); not the same as instructional cues (e.g., "Clean the bathroom") or directions • Match to fit student's comprehension of words/signs and the amount of prompt needed (e.g., nonspecific prompts like "What's next?" may be good later in learning but provide little information)	Pros: • Can be given to a group and used from a distance • Do not require visual attention; involve no physical contact Cons: • Must be heard and understood by student and followed • Level of complexity varies highly • May be hard to fade
Pictorial or Written prompts	
• Pictures or line drawings that tell the student how to perform a behavior; pictures may show the completed task or one or more steps in the task; words may accompany pictures if student can read • May be used as permanent prompts that are not faded • Level of abstraction needs to fit student (e.g., photos, drawings, line drawings, letters, numbers, words)	Pros: • Can be used unobtrusively; do not require reading • Can promote independence even when used as permanent prompts • Standard symbols may help maintain consistency Cons: • Pictures may be poorly drawn or taken; if lost, pictures may not be replaceable • Some actions are difficult to illustrate • Must be seen and understood by student and followed • Level of abstraction varies
Gestural Prompts	
• Movements made to direct a person's attention to something relevant to a response • Pointing toward the desired direction; tapping next to the material needed	Pros: • Unobtrusive, more natural cues • Can be given to a group and used from a distance; requires no physical contact Cons: • Must be seen and understood by student and followed
Model Prompts	
• Demonstrations of the target behavior that students are expected to imitate • Models often involve movement (showing a step in shoe tying) but may involve no movement, as in showing a finished task (show one place set at a table and match to sample) or be verbal ("sign 'want ball'") • Models may be complete (show entire step) or partial (show part of the step); if the model is done on a second set of materials, it need not be undone • Model prompts usually match task steps	Pros: • No physical contact with person is needed; can be used with a group and given from a distance • Versatile: models suit many target behaviors • Complexity of model can be adjusted to suit student's level of performance • Others can be effective models on a planned or incidental basis; modeling can be unobtrusive Cons: • Require students to attend (see, feel, or hear the model) and to imitate • If model is too long or complex, imitation will be difficult
Partial Physical Prompts	
• Brief touching, tapping, nudging, or lightly pulling or pushing a student's hand, arm, leg, trunk, jaw, etc.	Pros: • Give some control over student responding with little physical contact

TABLE 4–8 (Continued)
Definitions, Examples, and Pros and Cons of Common Prompts

Partial Physical Prompts	
• Used to help a student initiate a response or a sequence of responses. • Follow the rule: "as little as necessary."	• Useful when vision is limited Cons: • Can be intrusive; some students do not like to be touched; can't be used at a distance • Care must be taken not to injure or throw student off balance

Full Physical Prompts	
• Full guidance through a behavior, often involving hand-over-hand assistance (as in using a spoon or smoothing a bed spread) or movement of the trunk and legs (as in assisting crawling or walking forward) • Physical prompts should match task steps • Follow the rule "as little as necessary" while being sensitive to any student movement and easing physical control; does not involve force	Pros: • Allows total control over response, thereby reducing errors • Useful when vision is limited Cons: • Highly intrusive, unnatural, and stigmatizing in public; some students do not like to be touched; can't be used at a distance • Care must be taken not to injure through tight holding, to force compliance with a movement, or to throw student off balance

Adapted from *Teaching students with moderate to severe disabilities* (pp. 38–41) by M. Wolery, M. J. Ault, and P. M. Doyle (1992), New York: Longman. Adapted with permission.

If a student seems to require more time to initiate responding, the teacher must determine the student's natural response latency by timing the student as he or she performs a known task involving similar movements. The time that it takes for the student to "get the response going" should be the latency used.

Because of her cerebral palsy, Christine is aware of the need to move before she can actually make a required move. Her teachers use response latencies longer than 5 seconds for responses that involve her hands and arms.

Prompt Fading Fading is the gradual changing of prompts controlling a student's performance to less intrusive and more natural prompts without noticeably increasing student errors or reducing student performance. Fading of prompts is not an exact science (Riley, 1995). Often teams must observe a student's performance and adjust their methods so that fading is not too fast (thus keeping errors low) and not too slow (thus keeping motivation for the task high).

Prompts are faded in many ways, for example, reducing the number of prompts provided (model and verbal instructions faded to just verbal instructions), decreasing the amount of information provided by a prompt, or reducing the amount of physical control. Although it is important to transfer behavior control from training prompts to natural cues quickly, removal of prompts too quickly is certain to hamper successful transition. Fading is most successful when it is planned and completed systematically. Making observations of students performing without any prompts is the best way to judge if they can carry out the task without assistance. Once all prompts have been faded and the student still makes the correct response, learning or independent performance is demonstrated.

Prompting Systems Prompts may be used singularly, in combination, or as part of a prompting system. Some systems employ a hierarchy; that is, prompts are arranged either in a most-to-least order of intrusiveness, called "most-to-least prompting" (e.g., physical-model-verbal), or in a least-to-most order of intrusiveness, often called a "system of least prompts" or "least-to-most prompting" (e.g., verbal-model-physical). Several other prompt systems (time delay, graduated guidance, and simultaneous prompts) have been used to teach a variety of self-care, play, and academic skills during the acquisition stage of learning to students who have severe disabilities (e.g, Denny et al., 2000; Parrott, Schuster, Collins, & Gassaway, 2000; Reese &

Snell, 1990; Sewell, Collins, Hemmeter, & Schuster, 1998). These prompt systems work differently, and Table 4–9 sets forth a description of prompt systems ordered roughly from the easiest to use and potentially least intrusive to the most complex and most intrusive.

Still, none are easy to use, and each requires practice for teachers to become fluent users. One of the main advantages of these systems, if used correctly, is that students generally learn with few errors. The reader is referred to several other sources for more

TABLE 4–9
Commonly Used Response Prompt Systems and Considerations for Use

Description of Prompt System	Supportive Research and Considerations for Use
Constant Time Delay	
• Select prompt that controls the response and determine how many trials will be given at 0-second delay. • During initial requests to respond, the prompt is given at the same time as the request (0-second delay), making early trials look like simultaneous prompting. • After a trial, several trials, or session(s), the delay between the task request and the prompt is lengthened to 4 seconds (or longer). If the student does not respond correctly in 4 seconds, the prompt is given. • Initially reinforce prompted correct responses, later differentially reinforce. • Always reinforce unprompted correct responses. • Continue giving delayed prompts until learning occurs (responds correctly without the prompt over several trials). • If errors occur, interrupt with the prompt; after several consecutive errors, reintroduce 0-second delay for one trial or more. • Response fading is part of the procedure as students learn that anticipating the delayed prompt enables faster reinforcement and/or completion of the task.	Supportive Research: Evidence of success for both discrete and chained responses within a range of tasks and students with disabilities. Considerations: Initially, student does not have to wait for assistance. Easier to use than progressive delay or prompt hierarchy. Only one prompt or two combined prompts (verbal 1 model) are used; prompt(s) must work for student. Requires practice in using; need to count off the delay silently. Responses made before 4 seconds (correct anticipations) should receive more reinforcement than prompted responses. If an error is repeated, use progressive delay, change program, or simplify task. Can be used with forward or backward chaining or when a total task format is used. Recommended Use: During early to late acquisition as well as other phases, but change to a less intrusive prompt. Good with chained or discrete tasks; equally effective but easier to use than progressive delay and more efficient than increasing assistance system.
Simultaneous Prompting	
• Request student to perform the target behavior while prompting at the same time. Model prompts are often used. • Reinforce both prompted correct and independent correct responses. • Before every training session, give an opportunity to perform without prompting (probes) (or following a set number of trials) to determine when to fade prompts. • Fading of prompts occurs when probes alert teacher to stop prompting, prompting is stopped, and student continues to respond correctly.	Supportive Research: Increasing number of applications; successful with discrete behaviors (naming photos and reading) and the chained tasks of hand washing and dressing for young students with mild to severe disabilities. Considerations: Student does not have to wait for a prompt. Procedure is relatively easy to use. Must use probes to determine when to fade. Recommended Use: During early to late acquisition phase. Seems to work well when student cannot use less intrusive prompts. Perhaps less useful in later stages of learning.
System of Least Prompts (Increasing Assistance)	
• Select a response latency and two to four different prompts that suit student and task; arrange prompts in an order from least assistance to most assistance (e.g., verbal, verbal 1 model, verbal 1 physical). • Student is asked to perform the task and allowed the latency to respond.	Supportive Research: Extensive with both discrete and chained tasks; less support with students who have multiple, severe disabilities and with basic self-care tasks. In comparisons with delay, outcomes are the same or less efficient (errors, time to criterion, etc.). More efficient to use a prescriptive (individually suited) set of prompts than the traditional three (verbal, model, physical) but

TABLE 4–9 (*Continued*)

Commonly Used Response Prompt Systems and Considerations for Use

Description of Prompt System	Supportive Research and Considerations for Use
System of Least Prompts (Increasing Assistance) (*Continued*)	
• Whenever a correct response (or a prompted correct) is made, reinforcement is given and the next training step/trial provided. • If student makes an error or no response, the first prompt in the hierarchy is given and the latency waited. If the student again makes an error or no response, the next prompt is given and the latency provided, and so on through the last level of prompt. • Errors are interrupted with the next prompt. • The last prompt should be adequate to produce the response. • Prompt fading generally occurs as students learn to respond to less intrusive prompts and then become independent.	may be more difficult for staff. Considerations: While hierarchies of verbal, model, and physical prompts are most prevalent, many options for simpler hierarchies exist (gestural, gestural + partial physical, gestural + full physical). Requires a lot of practice to use consistently but versatile across tasks. May be intrusive and stigmatizing. Some question the amount of time between task stimuli and responding and the change of response modalities across different prompts. Can be used with forward or backward chaining or when a total task format is used. Recommended Use: If learning is in acquisition, avoid more than two levels of prompt. If learning is in fluency stage, this is more efficient than decreasing assistance. Reduce intrusiveness of prompts for use in later learning phases.
Progressive Time Delay	
• Similar to constant delay, except delay interval is gradually increased from 0 to 8 or more seconds. • Determine delay levels and how many trials will be given at each level; plan error approach. • During initial requests to respond, the prompt is given at the same time as the request (0-second delay), making early trials look like simultaneous prompting. • After a trial, several trials, or session(s), the delay between the task request and the prompt is lengthened by 1- to 2-second increments up to 8 (or more) seconds, where delay remains until student learns. • Errors and corrects are handled as in constant delay, except delay may be reduced partially or completely when errors occur and then increased gradually or quickly when prompted correct responding returns. • Response fading is part of the procedure as students learn that anticipating the delayed prompt enables faster reinforcement and/or completion of the task.	Supportive Research: Extensive support for discrete tasks; good for chained tasks across a range of students with disabilities and tasks. Considerations: Same as for constant delay. Progressive is more difficult to use, particularly with chained tasks. Reducing and then increasing delay for repeated errors is also complex. Produces fast learning with few errors. Better than constant delay for students who have difficulty waiting because the delay is gradually increased and the ability to wait is shaped. Can be used with forward or backward chaining or when a total task format is used. Recommended Use: During early to late acquisition; good with chained or discrete tasks; equally effective with constant delay but less easy to use; more efficient than increasing assistance system.
Most-to-least Prompt Hierarchy (Decreasing Assistance)	
• Select a response latency and two to four different prompts that suit student and task; arrange prompts in an order from most assistance to least (e.g., verbal 1 physical, verbal 1 model, verbal). • The first prompt should be adequate to produce the response. • Determine the criterion for progressing to a less intrusive prompt (e.g., so many minutes of training at each level, a certain number of corrects in a row). • Student is asked to perform the task and allowed the latency to respond. Whenever a correct response (or a prompted correct) is made, reinforcement is given, and the next training step/trial is provided.	Supportive Research: Convincing support for use with students having severe disabilities and a range of skills (self-care, mobility, following directions). Considerations: Teachers must plan how to fade prompts and implement these plans, or students may become prompt dependent. Can be used with forward or backward chaining or when a total task format is used. Recommended Use: Better for teaching basic skills in acquisition than a least-to-most system. Works well when student cannot use less intrusive prompts (e.g., cannot follow verbal direction, imitate, or does not wait for prompts) and makes many errors.

TABLE 4–9 (*Continued*)
Commonly Used Response Prompt Systems and Considerations for Use

Description of Prompt System	Supportive Research and Considerations for Use
Most-to-least Prompt Hierarchy (Decreasing Assistance) (*Continued*)	
• Prompt fading generally occurs when teachers substitute less intrusive prompts for more intrusive ones and students learn to respond to less intrusive prompts and then become independent.	Good when target task is chained and requires fluent movement. Less useful in later stages of learning.
Graduated Guidance	
• Select a general procedure to use: (a) Gradually lighten physical assistance from full hand over hand, to partial, to light touch, to shadowing. Shadowing means that the teacher's hands are close to the student's involved body part (hand, mouth, arm) but not in contact, ready to assist if needed. (b) Hand-to-shoulder fading, which uses a full physical prompt applied at the hand and then faded to the wrist, the forearm, the elbow, the upper arm, the shoulder, and then to shadowing; hand-to-shoulder fading has been accompanied by ongoing verbal praise and tactile reinforcement, with concrete reinforcers given at the end of a task chain. (c) Reducing the amount of pressure from initial full hand-over-hand assistance, to two-finger assistance, to one-finger guiding, and then shadowing. • Prompts are delivered simultaneously with task request, and the student's movements through the task are continuous. • Develop a plan to fade prompts. Begin fading when there is evidence that student can perform with less assistance: (a) sensing the student's assistance with the response through tactile cues, (b) improved performance (less help or no help) during probe or test trials, (c) student initiates the task, or (d) what seems like an adequate amount of training. • Prompts are arranged roughly in an order from requiring more student skill to be effective to requiring less student skill.	Supportive Research: Supported by mostly older, research in institutional groups and self-care tasks with intensive training methods. Several more recent school applications (Denny, Marchand-Martella, Martella, & Reilly, 2000; Reese & Snell, 1990). Considerations: Typically used with chained tasks, a total task format, no latency, and intensive training but can be used without intensive training. A latency may be used to help judge when fading is appropriate (Reese & Snell, 1990). While procedure is not complex (physical prompt only and then fading), it requires many teacher judgments about when to fade prompts; may not be systematic. Prompts may be faded too quickly causing errors. Can be highly intrusive because only physical prompts are used. Recommended Use: Use during early to later acquisition only and after other, less intrusive systems have not worked.

extensive detail on these methods and their use with students (Billingsley, 1998; Demchak, 1990; Schuster et al., 1998; Snell, 1997; Wolery, Ault, Doyle, Gast, & Griffen, 1992).

The prompts, prompt system, and the response latency a team selects for teaching a student should be chosen to suit that student's skills (e.g., how long she can wait, how well she follows spoken or signed requests, whether she imitates models or responds to pointing, if she tolerates physical touch) and also the student's preferences (Demchak, 1990). Perhaps the most efficient approaches for learners in the acquisi-

tion stage are constant time delay and prescriptive increasing of assistance or system of least prompts. Both these approaches also can be used in later learning stages if prompt intensity is lessened. Thus, a teacher might use indirect verbal prompts (such as "What's next?" or the confirmation "That's right" or just say "Keep going" if a student pauses too long) or replace more extensive prompts with individualized cues or gestures that the student understands (teacher looks in direction of correct choice or the next step, nods toward materials needed in the forgotten step, or gives hand motions to go faster).

Researchers have found that constant time delay is one of the most effective and efficient prompting methods and also is versatile across a range of academic, communication, and practical skills that involve either discrete responses or a chain of responses (Wolery et al., 1992). For example, time delay yielded fewer errors and less disruptive behavior than did the system of least prompts when young children with autism were taught academic tasks (matching pictures to objects, receptive identification of objects, numeral identification, word reading) (Heckman, Alber, Hooper, & Heward, 1998). Clearly, teams must select prompt procedures to suit individual students and then monitor each student's progress as instruction progresses.

Applications of Prompt Systems Constant Time Delay Jenny's teachers use constant time delay to teach the skill sequence for using coins to make purchases (Table 4–2). When teaching step 1, Jenny first learned to name pennies and to state their value; in step 3, nickels were taught while alternating opportunities with pennies. Each coin was added in while alternating turns with those previously learned. In the first session(s) on any new coin, her teachers started with 0-second delay trials, using a model (verbal or visual) prompt. What follows illustrates how Jenny was taught to name and know the value of pennies (step 1):

TEACHER: [Shows penny] "Name this coin . . . penny." [Verbal model prompt, 0-second delay]
JENNY: "Penny."
TEACHER: "Right, penny. What's a penny worth?" [Immediately holds up a card with the 1 cent price on it: a visual model prompt at zero delay]
JENNY: "One cent."
TEACHER: "Right! A penny's worth 1 cent."

After several successful zero delay trials on coin and price naming for the penny, the teacher paused 4 seconds before giving the model, hoping that Jenny would try to answer if she knew or wait if she was uncertain:

TEACHER: [Shows a penny] "Name this coin." [Counts off 4 seconds to herself and then gives a verbal model prompt] "Penny."
JENNY: [Waits for the prompt] "It's a penny."
TEACHER: "Right, penny. What's a penny worth?" [Counts off 4 seconds to herself and then holds up a card with the 1 cent price on it: a visual model prompt]

JENNY: [*Before* the card is shown, Jenny responds] "One cent."
TEACHER: "That's exactly right! A penny's worth 1 cent."

The teacher continued trials at 4-second delays until Jenny was able to name the coin and the value without the delayed prompt, which happened during the first 15-minute session. Then the teacher added the nickel, starting again at zero delay but alternating 4-second delay trials with the known penny, saying, "Here's one you know!" If Jenny missed the penny, she would repeat the trial at zero delay and then follow with a 4-second delay trial before giving a trial on the nickel again. The next day they reviewed the two coins by starting them both at 0 seconds. If correct, the penny was presented every so often at 4 seconds, while the nickel was continued for several more trials at 0 seconds before being faded to 4 seconds. Eventually, Jenny was working on naming all four coins and their values (step 14) in a random order without any prompting.

Wolery et al. (1992) give helpful general rules about using zero-delay trials:

- When all students in a group are learning the same skill, fewer zero-delay trials are needed because they can learn from each other.
- When multiple behaviors are being taught (as in chained tasks or with Jenny's coin and value naming response), more trials at zero delay are needed.
- Those with past success learning by time delay may need fewer zero-delay trials.
- Younger students with less familiarity with direct instruction may need more zero-delay trials.

The goal is that teachers use as few zero-delay trials as they can but that the prompt not be delayed until the student consistently responds correctly on zero-delay trials (Wolery et al., 1992, p. 57).

System of Least Prompts Timothy's teachers are using a system of least prompts to teach him to use the bathroom. They teach across all steps in the task, or a total task approach (this is discussed later in the chapter). They start by giving him a 3-second latency to respond. If he does not respond or makes an error, they use a gestural prompt (point to the item associated with the step) and wait 3 more seconds. If this does not work, they give a gestural and physical prompt (point and touch him lightly or nudge him toward the materials). These two levels of prompts suit him better than verbal prompts or full physical prompts. The most effective and preferred prompts and prompt system need to be determined for each student. Timothy's instruction on the first three teaching steps looked like this:

TEACHER: "It's time to use the bathroom." [Instructional cue, waits a 3-second latency]

Timothy continues sitting as others head to the bathroom. [No response]

Teacher goes close to him, gets in his view, and points toward the bathroom. [Gestural prompt]

Timothy looks in that direction but does not move. [Approximation but incomplete response]

Teacher tugs gently on his sleeve and points toward the bathroom. [Gestural and physical prompt]

Timothy gets up and moves to the bathroom door. [Prompted correct on first task step]

TEACHER: "Good job Timothy!"

Timothy continues into bathroom and stops by toilet. [Unprompted correct on second task step]

TEACHER: "Great!"

Timothy stands without taking further action for the entire latency. [No response on third step]

Teacher points to his loose elastic waistband pants. [Gestural prompt]

Timothy grabs his pants, pulls them down, and sits on the toilet. [Prompted correct on third step]

TEACHER: "Good pulling your pants down, Timothy!" [Pats him on the shoulder]

Instruction continues through each remaining step of the chained task.

Prompt systems are effective, systematic ways to teach, but these two examples emphasize the importance of designing the specific method to suit the student and then practicing the methods until team members are consistent in their use.

Alternatives to Response Prompt Systems

There are a number of alternatives to the structured response prompting systems described in Table 4–9.

Universal Design When materials and curricula reflect a collective or common design, they are usable by more people. Curb cuts accommodate wheelchairs but also bikes, strollers, and shopping carts. Telephones with larger and lighted numbers are easier for all to use. Reading class material that is available digitally (rather than only in a textbook form) can be converted easily to other languages, made larger for viewing, printed in Braille, and read aloud by a screen reader (Center for Applied Special Technology, 2004). The logic behind universal design is that materials and curricula should be created from the start to have alternative ways of being accessed so more individuals can participate successfully with fewer teacher modifications and prompts. This approach requires us to think differently—not just teachers but also publishers, urban designers, car manufacturers, computer programmers, and others. Because universal design increases accessibility, it also can reduce the necessity for prompts.

Once Mr. Evans, the middle school science teacher, met Jenny on her visit to the school with her fifth-grade classmates, he decided to go ahead with a universal design approach for the science lab. He had been inspired by his colleague Ms. Rayfield, who had had a student with limited vision in her geography class this year. She'd read about universal design and decided to rearrange her classroom so that every student had a direct line of vision to the chalkboard and the classroom maps. Using the same logic, Mr. Evans learned from Jenny's teacher that she could use simple word/picture directions, and he knew that all his other students would benefit from having clear directions too. Using the Boardmaker for Windows® software program (Mayer-Johnson, Inc., 1998) to produce standard pictures and input from Jenny's teacher and the middle school reading consultant, Mr. Evans labeled the science equipment and work stations and added simplified directions for assembly, cleanup, and safety. He introduced picture labels first to students, followed by teaching the picture directions.

Naturalistic Teaching Procedures Naturalistic teaching or prompting procedures include such approaches as following the student's lead or interest, embedding or teaching within the activity, giving the student an opportunity to respond, using simple prompts if there is no response or an error, and providing natural reinforcers such as a turn to participate in the activity, with assistance if needed, or access to the item requested (Kaiser, Hancock, & Nietfeld, 2000; Keogel, Koegel, Harrower, & Carter, 1999; Koegel et al., 1999). Naturalistic methods use a flexible response latency, planned prompts, a means to handle errors, and reinforcing consequences, but they are always used in the context of ongoing routines. The student's interest becomes the guide for where and when to teach and the source for motivating them to respond. Naturalistic teaching procedures have been very successful with communication and social skills and with young students (e.g., Kaiser et al., 1998); some of these approaches are described further in chapter 12. Naturalistic approaches can be combined with planned structured teaching (also called discrete trials) so that students are both motivated and perform with few errors.

Timothy's team was most successful in teaching him to sign "help" when he needed it. For example, they approached and taught him when he was seen struggling with his jacket, trying to reach a toy, fussing because he could not get on the swing, or looking for a paintbrush or crayon. His team used a model approach for signals that were in acquisition and a delay approach for signals he knew fairly well but failed to use. The "help" sign was not readily used by Timothy, so staff began by getting close to him and establishing "joint attention" on the item of interest (kneeled down and looked with him at his jacket zipper). If Timmy signed help, immediate help was given to him; but if he didn't or if he used his other signals (whining, moving the teacher's hands to his jacket), the teacher silently modeled the help sign. If Timothy signed correctly, the teacher said, "You need help with your zipper!" and gave help. If his signing was unclear, the teacher repeated the model closer to him and gave help when his sign was clear.

Stimulus Modification Procedures Stimulus modification procedures also can be useful in some teaching situations, particularly when teaching academic skills. Stimulus modification procedures involve a gradual change in the teaching stimuli over successive teaching trials, from an easy discrimination to a more difficult discrimination. The change in the stimulus is so gradual that difficulty on any given trial is about the same if the student has learned each previous

discrimination. Most examples of these methods act to reduce errors to a minimum and have excellent research support. But they also require that the student have accurate vision to be effective and often demand extensive preparation of teaching materials (Wolery et al., 1992). Computer-assisted versions of stimulus modification procedures may be an efficient option to teacher-made materials and have been applied to reading instruction for students with severe disabilities.

Two commonly used stimulus modification procedures include stimulus fading and stimulus superimposition. Stimulus fading involves the pairing of an irrelevant stimulus (color or size) with a relevant stimulus (the word on the red card matches the picture shown, the big object matches the picture shown) and gradual fading of the irrelevant stimulus (background color or object size). Stimulus superimposition involves the placement of a known stimulus (a picture) over another that is not known (the word for the picture) and slowly modifying the intensity, clarity, or salience of the known stimulus until it is not visible. Both methods are used to teach an association between the two stimuli.

A simple application of stimulus modification procedures can be used to teach with a variety of task materials, allowing the student to become used to changes in the irrelevant stimulus dimensions. Researchers like Kamps and her colleagues (Kamps et al., 1991, 1994) not only rotated materials often during small group instruction but also used multiple exemplars—a minimum of three sets of materials per concept taught—to promote learning.

Jenny counts many different sets of materials (e.g., movable objects, coins, art materials; immovable dots, pictures, words) during a given day as she does practical math problems, but the counting response does not change.

General Guidelines for Using Naturalistic and Structured Prompts and Cues Effective use of natural prompts or prompt systems involves the following:

1. Select the least intrusive prompt that is effective for the student and task.
2. Select a prompt(s) that suits the student; combine prompts if necessary.
3. Choose natural prompts that are related to the target behavior (e.g., responses that involve movement

may be best prompted with a gesture or partial physical prompt, verbal responses may be prompted with verbal prompts).

4. Highlight natural prompts (e.g., call attention to peers clearing their own dishes).

5. Always wait a latency period (e.g., 3 seconds) before and after the prompt so that learners have a chance to respond without assistance. (Or, with systems like time delay and simultaneous prompting, shift to a delayed prompt or a prompt-free probe so that the student has an opportunity to respond without assistance.)

6. Avoid repeating a prompt for the same response. Instead, if a prompt does not work, try more assistance.

7. Prompt only when the student is attending.

8. Devise a plan to fade prompts as soon as possible.

9. Do not introduce prompts unnecessarily.

10. Reinforce a student for responding correctly to a prompt during early acquisition; later, encourage learning through differential reinforcement.

Selecting Consequence Teaching Methods

Recall Timothy's objectives and teaching program for arrival at school. After selecting the prompts and response latency and deciding how to offer choices, the team talked to resolve the following questions regarding the consequences they provide to him: (a) How will we reinforce him for completing each step and the whole task? (b) Will we teach one steps at a time through chaining or teach the whole task at once? (c) How will we handle errors (no responses and incorrect responses)? Before they began instruction, they also planned how and when to evaluate his learning progress.

General consequence strategies involve the presentation of positive reinforcement or planned ignoring or extinction. Technically, punishment includes anything that reduces the probability of a behavior occurring (e.g., the presentation of aversives or the contingent removal of positive reinforcers following a response), but a broader nontechnical definition of punishment extends to take in a variety of harm categories that cause pain, temporary loss of ability, and prolonged loss of freedom or pleasure (Singer, Gert, & Koegel, 1999, p. 89). Such aversive methods are not regarded as acceptable teaching or disciplining strategies on both moral and educational grounds (Singer et al., 1999). While IDEA does not prohibit punishment or aversive interventions, it does favor positive

approaches to addressing problem behavior or positive behavior support (PBS), which is the only specifically identified approach in the 1997 amendments to IDEA that must be considered by the educational team. (See chapter 6 for a full discussion.) This statute language is viewed by many as a "presumption in favor of PBS" which "is also a presumption against the use of aversive interventions" (Turnbull, Wilcox, Stowe, & Turnbull, 2001, p. 14). Unfortunately, case law (recent court decisions on punishment and students with disabilities) provides few safeguards for students at risk for aversive interventions from schools (Lohrmann-O'Rourke & Zirkel, 1998). Thus, because the courts continue to lend support to aversive methods, schools and educational teams must be vigilant in advocating for and enforcing the supportive school practice of positive behavior support. Our discussion is limited to nonpunitive consequences and ways to effectively manage behavior.

Positive Reinforcement Positive reinforcement occurs when preferred consequences (called positive reinforcers) are given contingent on a behavior and it leads to an increase in the performance of that behavior. Thus, to reinforce means to strengthen behavior by increasing its frequency, duration, or intensity. Positive reinforcement is involved not only in all the prompting methods discussed in the previous section but also in other consequence procedures: shaping, chaining, and error correction. This interdependent or contingent arrangement between behaviors and consequences lets teachers build behaviors purposefully. What is reinforcing for one person will not necessarily be reinforcing for another, particularly with students who have more extensive disabilities; therefore, the activities and objects an individual student finds reinforcing must be determined through informal assessment involving observation (see chapter 3).

"Preference" is a newer term than "reinforcer" but often is used as its synonym. The distinction between the two terms seems to relate more to who is in control: the adult (teacher, therapist, parent) who reinforces or the student who has a preference for something. Traditionally, reinforcement is manipulated by adults for the purpose of increasing the frequency or intensity of a target behavior. Preferences can also be determined in the same manner as reinforcers. By contrast, the opportunity to experience a preferred event may be more under the control of the individual student and may be made available in the context of everyday routines through choice making offered by another or self-initiated by the student (self-reinforcement). Preference, as a concept, is more consistent with fostering self-control or self-determination than is reinforcement. We use the terms as loose synonyms but recognize that opportunities to choose and indicate preferences encourage self-determined behavior, while the tight control of reinforcers by others may not.

Types of Reinforcement Although reinforcers (preferred activities and objects) have unlimited range and vary from tangible items and activities to abstract thoughts of self-approval, all reinforcers are either primary (unlearned or unconditioned) or secondary (learned or conditioned). The first category includes the universal, or automatic, reinforcers to which everyone responds (although not continuously) without instruction. Primary reinforcers for someone who is feeling hungry, thirsty, or cold include food, drink, and warmth, respectively; primary reinforcers serve to return a person who is physically uncomfortable to a comfortable state. Secondary reinforcers develop reinforcing value through their association with primary reinforcers. Secondary reinforcers begin as neutral stimuli, but with repeated pairings with already existing reinforcers, they take on their own reinforcing value.

> *Timothy has learned to enjoy playing with blocks with his classmates because it involves putting things in order and creating large structures, things that he already enjoyed. Christine began listening to rock music for pleasure because listening to music was something her peers liked. Christine smiles when she gets her paycheck for work; she knows that money buys CDs and other things she enjoys.*

Secondary reinforcers commonly used in educational settings include task completion, attention, approval, favorite activities, check marks, stickers, and tokens. It is important to couple simple but specific praise with known reinforcers so that praise acquires reinforcing value for students. The goal is for students to not only enlarge their options for reinforcement but also replace artificial, primary, or age-inappropriate reinforcers for those that are naturally occurring and suited to their chronological age.

Reinforcement Schedules Schedules of reinforcement indicate the frequency and pattern of student responses that are reinforced. Reinforcement may be given according to the number of responses performed (ratio schedules) or the passage of time in relation to the performance (interval schedules). Reinforcement schedules may be based on an absolute, predetermined number of responses (which are then called fixed ratio schedules) or an absolute, predetermined amount of time (which are then called fixed interval schedules). Presentation of one reinforcer for every occurrence of the target response is a fixed ratio schedule of one, or FR:1. This is commonly called continuous reinforcement. All other schedules may be generally called intermittent reinforcement. An FR:5 schedule is a fixed pattern of reinforcement for every fifth correct response. It is also an intermittent schedule because reinforcement is not given for every response.

In contrast to fixed schedules, variable schedules produce a changing, nonfixed number of reinforcements but offer reinforcement on a schedule that is an average of the reinforcement pattern selected. If a teacher specified a variable ratio schedule of reinforcement of VR:5, reinforcement will be delivered on an *average* of every fifth correct response. This VR:5 pattern may consist of three, seven, two, or eight occurrences of a target behavior followed by reinforcement. These numbers average out to reinforcement every fifth correct response. Variable schedules of reinforcement in classrooms are less predictable to students than are fixed schedules and produce more stable rates of behavior.

In interval schedules, the first target response occurring after a regular time period of so many seconds or minutes (fixed interval, or FI) or an average period (variable interval, or VI) is reinforced. In many classrooms, reinforcement schedules are time based (at the end of a class period) and teacher dispensed; feedback and social praise may be as meager as once every 10 minutes. In a classroom of 25 students, this converts to an even thinner reinforcement schedule. Classroom reinforcement schedules are more often variable than fixed. Teachers may provide opportunities for students to choose a preferred activity when they judge the quality or quantity of work done is good enough or sufficient time has passed. Because "enough" and "sufficient" tend to change over time, a variable schedule results.

Because of the powerful influence of reinforcement schedules on behavior, teachers should apply several rules for scheduling reinforcement when planning instruction:

- During the acquisition stage of learning, more instances of behavior should be encouraged by the continuous provision of small amounts of contingent reinforcement (e.g., a smile and task-specific praise, fulfilling a request, sorting words read correctly into the "Awsome" pile, a "high five" or a "Yes!") rather than larger amounts of reinforcement given less often.

When Jenny was first successful counting out combinations of pennies and nickels without help, Ms. Dailey made a "big deal" by cheering whenever she was right. After these sessions, Ms. Dailey reinforcement more by telling Ms. Alpern and having Jenny show off her new skill.

- After a higher rate of more accurate behavior has been established (later in the acquisition stage), reinforcers should be faded slowly from a continuous to an intermittent schedule, which requires more behavior for each reinforcement. This strengthens the behavior as the student learns to tolerate periods of nonreinforcement rather than to abruptly give up and stop responding when reinforcement is not forthcoming.

Jenny is working on counting out combinations of dimes, nickels, and pennies and still requires prompts to start with the dimes and count by tens. Ms. Dailey praises every prompted correct response. When Jenny performs without any prompts, Ms. Dailey is extra enthusiastic and lets Jenny write those amounts on her "I Did It By Myself" chart. Periodically, for review, Ms. Dailey also gives easy trials counting out nickels or pennies or the combination. Instead of praising her for every correct response, Ms. Dailey simply confirms Jenny's accuracy ("OK, 15 cents").

- Fixed schedules of reinforcement produce uneven patterns of behavior because the individual can roughly predict how far away the next reinforcement is based on the last instance. Behaviors on fixed schedules can extinguish quickly following reinforcement because the students recognize the absence of reinforcement.

To increase her students' responsibility for keeping their classroom neat, Ms. Alpern and the class decided to use "Clean Teams" who would have assigned responsibilities for various parts of the class. Initially, Ms. Alpern gave Friday "Clean Team" inspections and awards, which meant that the room was clean on Friday but not the rest of the week.

- Variable schedules generally produce more even patterns of behavior than do fixed schedules because the individual cannot predict the occasions for reinforcement. Behaviors that have been reinforced by variable reinforcement schedules are also more resistant to extinction, so they are more durable if reinforcement stops for a given period of time.

Now, Ms. Alpern gives random spot checks and awards, and the room is usually pretty neat.

- Reinforcers must be reassessed periodically (Lohrmann-O'Rourke, Browder, & Brown, 2000; Mason, McGee, Farmer-Dougan, & Risley, 1989; Roane, Vollmer, Ringdahl, & Marcus, 1998) so that they continue to be reinforcing to the student.
- Reinforcers must be suited to the student's chronological age, the activity, and the learning situation. Aim for replacing less appropriate reinforcers with ones that have more availability in natural environments used by the student.

None of the team members wanted to use food to reinforce Timothy, even though his mom reported they had been successful in his tutoring sessions at home. They talked about what activities he liked, what the other 4-year-old boys liked, and what he could easily do in the preschool. They took this list and tried each activity out, giving him a "sample" first and then letting him choose. He showed clear preferences for block building, the water table, putting blocks away, CD-ROM stories, and riding a tricycle.

- The more immediately a reinforcer is presented following performance of the behavior, the greater its effect.

Timothy's teachers and his peers respond quickly when he uses his picture symbols to initiate a request or interaction. As a result, he is using his picture board more and more to communicate requests.

- Satiation results from the overuse of a reinforcer, and its reinforcing effect may be reduced. To avoid satiation, teams should (a) explore new reinforcers with students, (b) preserve the special quality of objects or activities selected as reinforcers, (c) use intermittent reinforcement because it requires fewer reinforcers for more behavior and reflects more natural schedules, and (d) give students opportunities to choose preferred activities rather than selecting and presenting reinforcers to students.

Other Consequence Strategies for Building Skills

Two frequently used strategies to build or expand new behaviors include shaping and chaining. Addressing errors is also a consequence strategy.

Shaping Shaping involves the reinforcement of successive approximations of a goal response. Instructors provide praise and other reinforcers for better and better performance over time. Shaping is a strategy inherent in most teaching methods that use positive reinforcement—for example, systematic prompting procedures all involve shaping or a gradual increase of the teacher's expectations or criteria for reinforcement over repeated teaching opportunities. This practice acts to improve the student's responding.

Chaining Chaining refers to teaching students to perform a sequence of functionally related responses in an approximate or exact order to complete a routine or task (e.g., clearing a table of dirty dishes, making a sandwich, brushing teeth, printing one's name, or completing an addition problem). Most skills we perform and teach students to perform consist of a chain of small component responses. Learning the sequence of responses involves performing each discrete step of the chain in the correct order and in close temporal succession. Reinforcement is provided by others or by oneself as longer sequences in the chain are performed and as the chained behavior is completed.

When she first started teaching Timothy to zip his jacket, Timothy's occupational therapist would connect the zipper plackets, put Timothy's fingers on the zipper pull, start the movement, and then encourage Timothy to pull the zipper up an inch. When he did, he was enthusiastically praised. Over several weeks, a few more steps earlier in the chain were added so that he now grasps the zipper pull by himself right after the therapist connects the zipper. Backward chaining worked well for this task.

Each component of the chain becomes a conditioned reinforcer for the previous response and a discriminative stimulus for the next response in the chain.

By December, when Jenny would count out a mixed pile of pennies and nickels, she sometimes stopped, started over or just paused and self-corrected, but usually finished with the total amount, "That's 14 cents!"

Chaining often is used in combination with shaping. Shaping and the three basic chaining strategies (i.e., forward, backward, and total task) that teams choose from when planning teaching programs are described in Table 4–10 (and later in chapter 9).

TABLE 4–10
Skill-Building Consequence Strategies and Considerations for Use

Description	Examples	Considerations for Use
Shaping		
Building skills by reinforcing successive approximations or improved attempts at a target behavior. Precision in skill performance is improved over time. Requires instructor to focus carefully on student's response and make quick judgments about each response in comparison to earlier occurrences and the goal criterion. Rather than wait for the final form, reinforcement is given when the student shows any improvement. Involves differential reinforcement, or changing the ongoing rules for what is "good enough."	Useful with many skills, discrete or chained responses (e.g., making transfers from wheelchair to toilet, walking, dressing, social skills, speaking, signing, work tasks, academics, etc.).	A time-consuming process that requires careful observation of the student's small changes in performing the target behavior. Depends on good teaming when multiple instructors are involved. Team must define each level of expected improvement. Shaping can be made more efficient by using a discriminative stimulus (instructional cue) and combining sometimes with prompts.

TABLE 4–10 (*Continued*)

Skill-Building Consequence Strategies and Considerations for Use

Description	Examples	Considerations for Use
Response Chaining: Forward Chaining		
Task analyze steps and measure baseline performance. Begin instruction by starting with the student performing any learned steps in order up to the first unmastered response, at which point instruction occurs. Reinforcement is given quickly after the training step, while more extensive reinforcement may be given after the last step in the chain is completed. The remainder of the chain may be either completed by the teacher or by the student with assistance, but the routine should be finished before another training opportunity. Once this segment of the chain is mastered, through additional trials, instruction shifts to the next unmastered step, while prior learned steps are performed in sequence but without assistance.	Useful with many self-care routines (grooming tasks, dressing, using the toilet). May suit many home management and vocational tasks. Appropriate for some chained academics tasks (e.g., use of number line, telephone dialing, calculator use). (Not as useful in school or community setting when assistance through the unlearned part of the task is more obvious and may be stigmatizing.)	Usually combined with prompting to teach the target step as well as shaping across the entire chain. May work better than total task for some learners who have multiple disabilities or for longer tasks. Initial mastery of single responses in the chain may be faster but slower overall. Replace with backward chaining when task has an especially reinforcing end. Replace with total task if chain is performed less often; may want to switch to total task after half the steps are learned. May need to create more training opportunities or learning will be slow. Involves a lot of teacher effort to complete unlearned portion of task.
Response Chaining: Backward Chaining		
Task analyze steps and measure baseline performance. Instruction begins by either completing or helping the student perform the entire chain of behavior up until the last step of the chain, at which point instruction occurs. After additional opportunities and when the student has mastered the last step, teaching shifts to the next-to-last step of the chain, but the student is expected to perform the last step(s) unassisted. Reinforcement is given quickly after the training step, while more extensive reinforcement occurs only after the last step in the chain is completed. As the remaining steps are taught, learned, and added in a backward order, the entire chain is performed, and the learner is reinforced.	Useful with many self-care routines (grooming tasks, dressing, using the toilet). May suit many home management and vocational tasks. Appropriate for some chained academics tasks (e.g., use of number line, telephone dialing, calculator use). (Not as useful in school or community setting when assistance through the unlearned part of the task is more obvious and may be stigmatizing.)	Similar to forward chaining. The main advantage over forward chaining and total task is being assisted through and completing the task quickly and getting reinforcement early in learning. Usually combined with prompting to teach the target step as well as shaping across the entire chain. May work better than total task for some learners who have multiple disabilities or for longer tasks. Initial mastery of single responses in chain may be faster but slower overall. Replace with total task if chain is performed less often; may want to switch to total task after half the steps are learned. May need to create more training opportunities or learning will be slow. Involves a lot of teacher effort to complete unlearned portion of task.
Response Chaining: Total Task		
Task analyze steps and measure baseline performance. Instruction begins by starting with the first step in the chain and teaching each successive step in order until the chain of responses are completed.	Has been used successfully with all sorts of chained tasks: self-care; mobility; daily living; community, vocational, and social interactions; and some multiple-step academic routines.	Works best if the chain is not too long (chained tasks can be subdivided) or a single training trial can be too lengthy.

TABLE 4–10 (*Continued*)
Skill-Building Consequence Strategies and Considerations for Use

Description	Examples	Considerations for Use
Response Chaining: Total Task		
All steps needing instruction are taught in order and concurrently during each performance of the chained routine. Reinforcement is given quickly (e.g., praise) after each response for corrects and improved performances and again at the end of the chain (e.g., a short leisure break).		Main advantages are that all teaching opportunities are used (each step is taught each time) and that the task is completed. May produce faster learning than other chaining methods. May be combined with repeated training just on difficult step(s) of a routine, although this is usually rather unnatural. This seems to be a more natural approach than the other options.

To teach behavior chains, the cluster of responses is first divided into an ordered list, or task analysis, of separate teachable behaviors. The number of steps into which a chain is divided varies with different students and skills. Since chaining may proceed forward or backward across the sequence of behaviors or may involve instruction across all steps concurrently, a team must select the order in which to teach the task components. The chaining approach selected and the teaching procedures used depend on the student, how fast the student learns under various teaching conditions, the length and complexity of the chain, the opportunity to perform the chain, and the component responses already known. (Refer to chapter 5 for more examples of task analytic assessment.)

Handling Errors The final consequence strategy frequently used in teaching involves handling errors in a way that promotes learning. While teachers plan instruction so that errors are minimized, when they do occur, the teacher may ignore them, provide specific feedback so students aware of the errors, or gently interrupt and correct them in several ways. Errors include both incorrect responses and nonresponses. Incorrect responses can be missed steps in a chain or discrimination errors (skipping several key steps when washing dishes, signing "eat" instead of "help," or reading "men" instead of "women") or mistakes that are not related to the target response and may involve disruptive behavior (e.g., splashing the dishwater excessively, leaving the teaching group, throwing flash

cards). By contrast, nonresponses may simply consist of waiting too long, not trying the task at all, or looking away from the task because of distraction or boredom. The procedures chosen depend on both the type of error (incorrect response, problem behavior, nonresponse) and the student's skills (e.g., performance on the task, skills at understanding teacher feedback, and preferred ways of having mistakes dealt with). To maintain a reinforcing environment for learning, it is important to minimize the potential for student errors. If there are many errors, instruction needs to be improved, and if there is repeated error correction, instruction may become aversive to students, but it certainly becomes inefficient.

When errors that involve incorrect discriminations occur, however, teachers can use several strategies: (a) ignore errors and not give any reinforcement, (b) provide clear and immediate feedback to students, (c) follow errors with assistance, or (d) have students participate in correcting their errors. The last two approaches are examples of error correction. Technically, error correction procedures are response prompting procedures—teachers prompt students to make the correct response (Wolery et al., 1992). However, the timing differs in that error correction is conducted *after* the student responds and has made an error, while response prompting is provided *before* the student's response.

Errors that involve problem behavior often are motivated by the student's interest in escaping from the task for some reason or needing assistance because the task is too difficult. Teams need to study the situation, determine the cause (e.g., session too long, involves lots of correction and little success, provides no student choice), and improve the teaching plan.

The cause of errors that involve nonresponding, like problem behavior errors, also need to be analyzed. When some students are motivated to escape from a task that is too long, involves too much waiting, or is somehow boring to the student, they do so by withdrawing, not attending, not responding, or being easily distracted. Other students are challenged by a tendency to be highly distracted even when teaching is carefully planned to be motivating. Usually, preventing errors by improving the motivation to participate is the best means for addressing nonresponding errors.

Most prompt systems we discussed earlier in this chapter come with "built-in" methods for preventing and for handling errors, but teams still need to decide what approach works best with a given student and task.

When adults use words to correct Timothy's errors, he does not attend or react. He is often resistant when physical corrections are attempted. But gesture cues (pointing to materials involved or moving materials

from the missed step into his view) are often effective. Jenny becomes resistant if teachers verbally point out her errors. The "No" word seems to be a stimulus for anger. Her teachers have found better ways to prevent and to address her mistakes in early learning tasks. First, they start by getting her attention or pausing for her to get ready. Second, they use a systematic prompt strategy such as time delay for academic tasks and least prompts for chained tasks because these methods make prompts available before errors typically occur. So if she fails to respond or makes an error, they say nothing, provide assistance instead, and then praise her efforts. Finally, her teachers have learned that interspersal of known responses is a great way to motivate her, so when working on new words, problems, or routines, they add in items, questions, or steps that review responses she already knows well.

Table 4–11 gives descriptions of ways to handle errors and lists considerations for their use. When a student has learned more than half a skill and moves into the fluency, maintenance, or generalization stage, less structured and informative error correction procedures should be used. Because the student is now

TABLE 4–11
Strategies for Handing Incorrect Response Errors and Considerations for their Use

Strategy	Considerations for Use
• In early learning, it may be best to gently interrupt errors with a prompt (as in most prompt systems). • After an error, provide feedback (pause, hold up index finger, "not quite") and give another immediate opportunity to perform while increasing the assistance (as in a system of least prompts) • Gently stop an error and wait and see if the student will self-correct. Direct student's attention to relevant task stimuli, add prompts as needed. Reinforce any self-corrections. • Later in learning, it may be good to follow some errors by waiting for the student to self-correct; if this does not occur, give assistance to correct the error. • Simplify those responses that are frequently missed or performed wrong. • Gently interrupt errors and provide several immediate opportunities to practice the missed response (or steps in a chained task) that are frequently missed.	• Incorrect responses can be missed steps in a chain or discrimination errors. Repeated error correction is aversive for most students and inefficient. Analyze performance data to decide how to improve instruction. Consider the student's stage of learning and motivation for the task as well. • Sometimes improving the antecedents may be necessary to reduce errors: (a) improve the task analysis of the steps frequently missed (b) use backward chaining to teach these steps (c) use simpler prompts (gestural model instead of verbal) (d) replace a prompt hierarchy with a single prompt system (time delay) (e) provide a permanent prompt like a picture sequence (f) use stimulus prompts like color coding temporarily • During later learning, allowing or prompting students to self-correct lets them experience the natural stimuli resulting from the error and learn ways to improve the situation. Self-correction needs to be used carefully so as not to endanger or embarrass the student.

more proficient at the skill, errors are less frequent and may be caused by distraction or carelessness rather than by not knowing what to do.

> *In several math, punctuation, reading, and spelling tasks, Jenny and her classmates are working on improving their accuracy and speed. Teachers have students (a) correct their own worksheets and give them time to redo those they missed and (b) count up the number they got correct in flash card drills or timed math fact tests and enter the number on their personalized bar graph.*

When students have moved beyond acquisition into advanced stages of learning, one of the following procedures may be chosen:

1. The student who makes an error or hesitates may be given a few seconds to self-correct. Some errors, if uninterrupted, will provide natural learning opportunities for students. If a correction is not forthcoming, then one of the other procedures can be tried.
2. The error may be acknowledged (holding up an index finger, saying "Oops" or "Not quite") without providing negative or harsh feedback. Efforts to soften acknowledgment of an error, however, should not result in confusing or ambiguous feedback. The teacher then requests another try on the same step ("Try it again"). If a second error results, some assistance is given.
3. A minimal prompt ("What's next?") or verbal rehearsal of the last step correctly performed ("You just finished getting the plates, now what's next?") may be provided as soon as the error is stopped. If the student stops before a step is complete, the teacher may confirm and urge the student to continue ("That's right, keep going").

There are many other methods for correcting errors; however, to be effective, error correction procedures must reflect the following characteristics:

- Be suited to the learner's age, level of understanding, and preferences
- Be suited in the amount of assistance and reinforcement (if any) to the student's stage of learning for that task
- Be applied immediately and consistently but unemotionally
- Be nonstigmatizing, humane, and socially valid and not endanger the student

- Provide enough help to correct the error quickly but not so much as to create dependency on the teacher
- Be followed by additional opportunities to respond to the task or step
- Encourage and reinforce independence

Planning and Designing Instruction for the General Education Class

Adapting General Education Class Work and Activities

Often students with severe disabilities require planned adaptations to participate meaningfully in classroom activities and schoolwork with their peers in general education. When teams decide adaptations are needed for meaningful classroom participation, they should be "only as special as necessary." Adaptations need not be intrusive, annoying, distracting, or pushy to students or to their peers or to staff. The best adaptations should "facilitate both social involvement and instructional participation in class activities" (Janney & Snell, 2004). Teachers often report that adaptations for students with severe disabilities do not meet these requirements (Coots, Bishop, & Grenot-Scheyer, 1998; Werts, Wolery, Snyder, & Caldwell, 1996).

Ways to Conceptualize Adaptations

General and special education teachers in inclusive elementary classrooms make modifications in three areas in order to include students with severe disabilities (Janney & Snell, 1997): (a) their roles and responsibilities (changing who does what so that the student with disabilities can learn alongside peers); (b) class routines and physical environment, in order to keep students together; and (c) instructional activities. To include students with disabilities, teachers tend to modify instructional activities by using academic adaptations, such as simplified tasks (e.g., fewer and/or easier spelling words); social participation strategies that allow social, though not academic, responding (e.g., holding a book that others are reading); and parallel activities that differ from classmates' and are carried out separately but in the classroom (e.g., doing money problems at a table while classmates add and subtract in the front of the classroom).

There are other ways to conceptualize modifications that team members make to include students with severe disabilities among nondisabled peers. First, the principle of partial participation suggests that teams work together to plan for each student's active and meaningful involvement even if full participation is not a realistic goal for that student (Baumgart et al., 1982). Second, Giangreco and Putnam's (1991) system for making adaptations views all school and classroom activities as being one of three types:

- *Same activity*: A student with disabilities participates in the same class activity or schoolwork, with no adaptations required.

    Jenny uses the restroom just like other fifth-grade girls; Like his peers, Timothy usually hangs up his coat and backpack; Jenny answers roll call as do classmates; when Christine arrives, she signs the attendance record like other members attending weekly drama club meetings.

- *Multilevel activity*: One or more students with disabilities (or without) participate in the same activity as the rest of the class but learn at different levels of difficulty.

    Timothy uses a picture schedule rather than using words to remember; Jenny has fewer spelling words and uses a calculator in place of adding in her head; in the library and classroom, Christine and Jenny listen to books on tape instead of reading.

- *Curriculum overlapping activity*: One or more students with disabilities participate in the same class activity but work on different target skills from classmates.

    Jenny passes out corrected papers to become fluent with classmates' names, while others complete division and fraction problems. Christine moves through the halls and across campus when her peers change classes in order to practice greeting those she knows and responding to peers by vocalizing and using her communication device.

Although general, these approaches are helpful ways to organize adaptations. Many authors have contributed to schoolwork adaptation methods for students with severe disabilities (e.g., Giangreco, Cloninger, & Iverson, 1993; Janney & Snell, 2004; Kennedy & Horn, 2004; Ryndak & Alper, 2003).

A Model for Making Adaptations

We now briefly summarize a comprehensive model that builds on other adaptation approaches and suits students with many types of special education or other learning needs who are members of general education classes (Janney & Snell, 2004). Our discussion is limited to adaptations for students with severe disabilities. We encourage readers to seek more in-depth analysis (Janney & Snell, 2004). There are several prerequisites for using the model: students are enrolled in neighborhood schools and based in general classrooms while being educated by teams of collaborating general and special educators. In addition, students' IEP objectives are linked to the general education curriculum, and their IEPs include teaching and testing accommodations that facilitate them to make progress in learning. Figure 4-4 portrays the three types of adaptations in this model (curricular, instructional, and alternative adaptations) and their categories:

- *Curricular goals*: Alter what is taught (supplementary, simplified, and alternative goals)

FIGURE 4–4
A Model for Making Adaptations

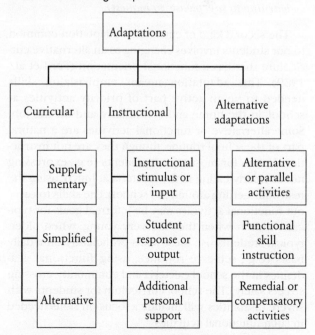

Source: Adapted from *Teachers' Guides to inclusive practices: Modifying schoolwork* (2nd ed.), by R. E. Janney and M. E. Snell, 2004, Baltimore: Paul H. Brookes. Reprinted with permission.

- *Instructional methods and materials*: Alter how students are taught, how students respond, or the amount of personal support provided
- *Alternative adaptation*: Change to a more functional version of learning routines or activities and coordinate them with classroom teaching

Curricular Adaptations   For students like Timothy, Jenny, and Christine, one type of curricular adaptation will consist of simplifying the content to be taught. Simplified adaptations make the *same* content less difficult than that taught to others in the class or group and are similar to multilevel adaptations. For example, rather than learning to "Find the length of the missing side of the triangle" on an eighth-grade math worksheet like most students will do, a student with a simplified curriculum might be expected to "Circle all the right triangles" (Ryndak, 2003). For Jenny and Timothy, a simplified curriculum means other changes.

> *Jenny has shorter weekly spelling word lists and reading passages for social studies at a first-, not a fifth-, grade level and is learning to use a calculator to add and subtract to 25. Timothy is learning to associate pictures with new classroom vocabulary words (his peers learn to say the words) and to select and show pictures to request things (his peers are learning to say "please" to request).*

The second kind of curriculum adaptation common to our students involves changing to an alternative curriculum that has a functional orientation (Ford et al., 1989). This adaptation means emphasizing skills needed to be an active part of priority activities at school, in the home and community, and on the job. Some alternative or functional activities are a natural part of the school routine, though they are not instructional goals for most typical students (e.g., expressing needs clearly, eating in the cafeteria at lunch, using the restroom, getting around the school). The skills to carry out functional activities may be informal goals for typical children when they are very young; when older, typical students use these skills proficiently on a daily basis (e.g., self-care routines, using functional academics in the school cafeteria and community, crossing streets safely). The school curriculum for students with severe disabilities will include a focus on skills needed in such functional activities.

> *Jenny is learning to identify coins and match coins to values, to tell time to the hour, and to run routine*

errands around the school without getting lost or distracted. Most of her simplified and alternative curriculum objectives are taught within fifth-grade class activities.

Christine's curriculum involves primarily functional skills: fluent communication with others, ability to work at a real job with meaningful involvement, partial participation in all self-care routines, and interaction during social activities with typical peers on and around campus and at home. Christine's team members teach this alternative curriculum within the community and on campus (e.g., during Best Buddy activities, at lunch, at drama club, at the campus exercise gym, and during tutoring sessions in the campus resource room).

Instructional Adaptations   There are two *primary* categories of instructional adaptations (Figure 4–4) and a third option. The primary categories involve either how an instructor teaches (instructional stimulus, or input) or how the student behaves or performs during instruction (student's response, or output). Both input and output can be adapted in several ways: (a) level of difficulty or amount, (b) modality, and (c) format or materials (Table 4–12). The general rule is that teams should use adaptations only when necessary, keep them simple, and avoid adaptations that stigmatize students. Usually, input adaptations fit these three requirements more easily than do output adaptations, which require changing what the student does so that it differs from peers.

> *Jenny's classroom teacher gives short, simple instructions for tasks accompanied by demonstrations (input adaptations). Jenny, along with some classmates, understands the instructions more naturally and with less teacher effort than if the teacher had developed special task worksheets or teaching materials for her (output adaptations).*

The third option for instructional adaptations involves adding support in the form of another person: a classmate, paraprofessional, older student tutor, teacher, or related services staff. In an earlier section of this chapter, we discussed these options and their advantages and disadvantages. When students have acquired the basics of a skill or routine, teaching support by an adult or peer should be faded, and the students should be encouraged to perform more on their own and to look to peers for guidance if needed. Classmates as models are the best choice because they are a

TABLE 4–12
Instructional Adaptations of Input and Output

Adapting the instructional stimulus (input)		
Level of difficulty/amount	**Modality**	**Format/materials**
• Uses simpler vocabulary with gestures for explanations • Records a passage (that others read) at simpler level and adds pictures • Reduces the number of problems or spelling words • Uses more cues, prompts, and feedback during practice activities	• Reads text out loud to students • Uses slides, overhead pictures, and manipulative objectives to accompany oral presentations • Gives demonstrations with simple explanations • Provides audiotapes or CD-ROM with textbook • Gives lecture material in brief 5-minute units	• Uses large-print books and materials, increases font size, or makes photo-copy enlargements • Enlarges worksheet to allow more space for larger handwriting style • Adds pictures or symbols to text • Gives demonstrations, simulations, and role plays
Adapting the student's response (output)		
Level of difficulty/amount	**Modality**	**Format/ materials**
• On timed problem worksheet, circles numbers named by teacher rather than completes math problems • Completes selected steps in an art or science project • Reads content in same area but at simpler level and with pictures • Solves only the even-numbered math problems on a homework worksheet	• Listens and gives yes or no answers to questions rather than written responses to written questions • Demonstrates how to do something rather than tells how • Draws pictures in journal rather than writes • Follows steps of pictures for completing multiple step science or writing task	• Carries out functional task rather than solves nonapplied problems (e.g., count out needed pencils for group, hand them out to check) • Completes a drawing, molds clay, or makes music to describe a book character's feelings rather than writes an essay

Source: Adapted from *Teachers' guides to inclusive practices: Modifying schoolwork* (2nd ed.), by R. E. Janney and M. E. Snell, 2004, Baltimore: Paul H. Brookes. Reprinted with permission.

natural part of most classrooms, particularly when teachers encourage peer-to-peer support. Thus, the option for adding personal support should be carefully chosen and regularly assessed for its need.

Alternative Adaptations Sometimes teams plan alternative adaptations that are coordinated with classroom instruction. These changes from scheduled classroom routines include activities that supplement ongoing classroom activities but are designed specifically for an individual student with an IEP. The purpose of alternative adaptations is to provide meaningful activities when the team has not yet figured out how to adapt the ongoing classroom activity so that a student can be successful. Sometimes classroom activities are just too long, and students can participate only part of the time but need an alternative task for the rest of the

time. Other times the student needs small-group or one-to-one instruction from a specialist in such areas as communication. The challenge is to coordinate any alternative instruction with the general education class to avoid activities that are "too special" and separate.

Figure 4–4 shows three types of alternative adaptations: (a) alternative or parallel activities, (b) remedial or compensatory instruction, and (c) functional skill instruction. Parallel activities are conducted in the classroom with team planning to promote activities that are done in normative ways, include peers if possible, and tie in with classroom themes. Sometimes parallel activities are part of a behavior support plan.

Jenny is encouraged to request a limited number of short breaks when she is unable to sit and work. At these times, she goes to one of several locations and jumps rope, runs in place, or uses the exercise bike, then records her time and reports back to class. She shares her exercise times each week with her physical education and classroom teachers. Jenny now manages her activity level well.

Remedial instruction may be used to address basic skills in reading, writing, and math when the student benefits from additional instruction that is more intense than can happen in the classroom. But motor, speech, and communication goals also may be the reason for intensive one-to-one teaching sessions.

Jenny spends time daily receiving direct instruction on reading with one or two other students. Timothy spends two sessions a week at school receiving intensive communication instruction on a one-on-one basis outside the classroom with the speech and language pathologist, but the rest of his communication instruction is done in the classroom among classmates and in the context of ongoing activities.

Finally, students with severe disabilities often have functional skills on their IEP that classmates are not working on. These can be worked on within the classroom alongside peers who are working on other objectives, or they can be taught in parallel activities or in settings outside the classroom, such as the school or community.

Several times a week, Jenny is taught to get around the school independently. Christine spends much of each school day away from the scheduled campus activities (e.g., drama club, exercise period at the gym, Best Buddies activities) in order to prepare for a job.

It is important with all alternative activities (especially those that take place outside the classroom: remedial and functional instruction) that scheduling be synchronized with the class timetable for activities to minimize disruptions and deemphasize differences between students. Teams who choose alternative adaptations to support students must regularly review these adaptations to see if other adaptations can be devised that do not require instruction apart from classmates.

General and Specific Adaptations Of all the adaptations just described, any that are used within predictable school routines like arrival, circle, reading groups, social studies, journal time, library, and lunch and can be used over and over are called *general adaptations*. Once put in place during the first month of school, general adaptations require little adjustment or planning. By contrast, *specific adaptations* relate to the changes teachers make regularly as the semester moves on and their instructional content shifts, as new themes are addressed, and as more advanced skills are taught. Specific adaptations are planned by teachers on a regular basis as classroom content changes. Specific adaptations require that the general educator and the special educator be in close touch to share this information and problem-solve any needed adjustments or materials; special educators typically are responsible for preparing new materials that reflect changes in class content.

The predictable morning routines in Jenny's fifth grade include arrival, journal, reading, language skills, break, spelling, math, shared reading, and lunch. A set of general adaptations was planned by the team for each routine and used daily. During arrival and journal, Jenny followed the same routine as others, but general adaptations were added to journal and reading to enable her participation. During journal, Jenny narrates her entry to a teaching assistant who helps her write down the content in simple sentences. Then Jenny locates the needed word cards from her word bank of known words; she reads her journal entry, independently rewrites it on the computer, and reads it again. During reading, Jenny and several classmates receive direct instruction in a small group taught by either the teacher or the special educator. Both examples involve a simplified curriculum adaptation with input and output instructional adaptations.

Jenny leaves the classroom during language skills to participate with either the speech and language pathologist or the teaching assistant in various activities to build her independence and communication (e.g., using the library, running errands without distractions or getting lost) (alternative adaptation involving functional skills). Her seventh-grade peer tutor visits twice weekly at this time with others on a tutoring team from the middle school next door; the tutor continues work on independence (alternative adaptation involving functional skills). After a social break with classmates, Jenny participates in spelling by learning her own shortened list of useful words (simplified curriculum adaptation). In math, Jenny works on her math objectives with the teacher or assistant in a small group; her individualized problems involve instruction followed by independent problem solving with coins, calculator, number line, counting out amounts, and solving story problems (functional curriculum, output adaptations). During shared reading, Jenny tutors a first grader on word drill games and reads a story with extra monitoring from teachers (simplified curriculum adaptation), while her classmates also work with other first graders.

Because preschools and elementary schools have identifiable morning and afternoon routines, they will have two sets of general adaptations that are used daily. Since secondary classes have individual routine patterns and repeated activities, a set of general adaptations is needed for each class. After general adaptations are in place, teams shift their focus to specific adaptations that define the changes teachers make on a daily, weekly, or monthly basis as their instruction shifts to new topics, skills, or activities. Specific adaptations link the student to the topics and themes being studied by classmates; these adaptations depend on regular short-term planning between the general and special education teachers.

The specific content for each reading group in Jenny's classroom changes every 1 to 2 weeks and requires new words (e.g., American Revolution period: frontier, names of tribes and explorers). The special and general educators discuss the content during their weekly planning sessions and find or create simpler reading materials that are related (simplified curriculum adaptation); they also plan the math activities, relating them to Jenny's IEP objectives and defining practical classroom applications that can be used for practice. For example, Jenny might count out necessary science materials for each cooperative group (functional curriculum adaptations). To promote her ability to follow directions independently, Jenny is in charge of getting and returning library books for various unit topics in science and social studies, so the speech and language pathologist checks weekly on the books needed (functional curriculum).

Using the Model Applying this model to plan for the inclusion of students in general education, team members follow six steps (Janney & Snell, 2004):

1. *Gather and share information about the student, classroom, and routines (before school starts or*

in first month): The team collects information about the student and the classroom during preparation before an IEP meeting, before school starts, or in the first few weeks of school. A "Program at a Glance" form is completed for each student with an IEP (Figure 4-5). This form summarizes IEP objectives, accommodations, academic and management needs, and any special needs.

Knowing when and what kind of adaptations will be necessary depends a lot on the classroom routines and structure, types of activities and teaching approaches, curriculum, climate, behavior rules and expectations, and testing and homework practices. Information about the classroom is gathered by the special education teacher through class observations and teacher interviews early in the school year. Information is used to identify when and what adaptations will be necessary so that they fit with ongoing routines. In secondary schools, information must be gathered for each class, as classes often differ, while elementary classrooms are divided into predictable routines. Elementary "specials" like music, physical education, and art often have fairly individualized routines and thus should be observed separately as well.

When a student's main focus in general education is the embedded social, motor, and communication skills (as for Christine), the special educator will provide more detailed ecological assessment of the student's performance in order to explore ways to improve participation. Table 4-13 shows such an assessment of Christine during the second meeting of the drama club when typical club routines were already in place (e.g., sign in near the stage; socialize during refreshments and before call to order; when faculty advisor or club leader starts talking, get quiet and attend; review club business; decide on acting activities; participate in activities; socialize and leave at end). The observation provided useful ideas to the team on ways to improve Christine's participation through additional skills or adaptations.

2. *Determine when adaptations are needed:* A program matrix is especially valuable for students who have an altered (functional) curriculum. The matrix is a form for plotting a student's IEP objectives against class activities and times. Matrices help teams determine when and where all objectives, but especially altered curriculum objectives, will be taught. Figure 4-6 illustrates when and where Jenny's simplified academic objectives and her alternative objectives will be taught and when and where her self-management and social skills will be embedded during

FIGURE 4–5

Jenny's Program at a Glance

Student: Jenny		
Grade: 5	Teacher: Ms. Alpern	Date: 9/6/04

Brief IEP Objectives

Math:
—"Count on" for addition to 15
—"Count on" for subtraction from 15
—Use calculator to add and subtract from 25
—Identify coins, match to values, and count combinations of pennies, nickels, and dimes
—Count out named amounts of coins (pennies, nickels, dimes)
—Count quarters by 25s; count combinations of all coins and state value
—Compare two-digit numbers: state bigger or smaller
—Tell time to hour and match time to events
—Identify month, day, year

Reading and Writing:
—Decode consonant-vowel-consonant words
—Decode short vowel words with blends & digraphs
—Write two related sentences in journal
—Use of correct beginning, ending, and medial vowels in writings
—Answers comprehension questions about reading

Social:
—Approach peers to initiate task
—Complete cooperative task with peers, without adult prompting
—Socialize in age-appropriate ways during class breaks and at lunch ("Lunch Bunch" group)

Accommodations and Adaptations

Accommodations:
—Calculator
—Number line
—Manipulatives to aid adding/substraacting
—"Money" chart (modification of 100s chart)
—Personal schedule
—Personal calendar
—Full-time teaching assistant in her classroom

Adaptations:
—Curriculum: Use both simplified and functional curriculum adaptations
—Instructional: Use input and output (see Classroom Participation Plan)
—Instructional/additional student support:
Special education teaches the 1:1 or 1:2 reading tutorial for 40 minutes every day in classroom. Desk near front of class and next to model peers.
—Alternative Activities (functional skill instruction):
During language arts with speech and language pathologist, teaching assistant, and peer tutor

Self-Management Needs

—Self-monitor activity level; ask for breaks to use extra energy or use relaxation exercises
—School independence: complete routine errands around the school without getting lost
—Make snacks, pack lunch independently

Comments/Special Needs

—Use "beat the clock" system to speed task completion
—Peers provide model and help with organizational issues

Source: Adapted from *Teachers' guides to inclusive practices: Collaborative teaming*, by R. E. Janney and M. E. Snell, 2000, Baltimore: Paul H. Brookes. Reprinted with permission.

the day. With one exception, Jenny's morning schedule is spent with her class; during language activities, she works with her assistant or the speech and language pathologist on self-management and communication and twice a week with her middle school tutor on the same activities. Matrix blocks can be coded to indicate if additional support is required or if the adaptation is general or specific (and thus requires new materials).

3. *Decide how team members will plan:* We have found that planning goes more smoothly when the special educator and the classroom teacher(s) determine their planning strategies early in the year. Planning strategies include when and where to meet, how long and how often, how materials that need adapting will be exchanged between general and special education teachers, and what to do if problems arise. Therefore, in late August or early September, the special educator

TABLE 4–13

Detailed Ecological Assessment of Classroom Procedures to Plan Adaptations

Class: Drama Club (alternate Thursdays 4–6) Club President: Paul Faculty adviser: Mr. Fullen	Student: Christine Teaching Assistant: Ms. Washington Date: 9/16/04 (second meeting) Time: 4–6

Typical Sequence of Steps/Procedures	Target Student Participation
1. Students file in several at a time, most socializing from prior acquaintance 2. Students sign in on the club attendance notebook located on the stage 3. Students get a drink and chips from the meeting refreshment area and then mingle and socialize 4. Club president call the group to attention and reviews club business, seeking discussion and a member vote on several fund-raising issues 5. Mr. Fullen takes ideas for drama activities and group decides to focus first on some warm-up exercises (voice and movement) and then on improvisation exercises 6. Group divides into five stations for different improvisations; groups rotate after about 10 minutes 7. Paul gives club announcements and ends meeting 8. Students talk and socialize, leaving in small groups or singles	1. Christine is wheeled in to a location away from other students. 2. Ms. Washington goes to the attendance book and signs Christine in. 3. Ms. Washington wheels Christine to the refreshment area and pours a drink for Christine into her sport cup on her tray. Several students talk to Christine, but do not understand how to pause for her to respond. 4. Christine is quiet and looks at Paul but does not participate in voting. 5. Christine is quiet and looks in Mr. Fullen's direction. She laughs with others when he shows some improvisations. 6. Ms. Washington wheels Christine to one group, close enough so she can hear and see larger movements of students. Christine is attentive to students who act, laughs at the right times, but does not participate. 7. Christine is attentive to Paul. 8. Several students go to Christine after the meeting and make conversation. Christine listens but is not successful communicating with her AAC device.

Skills Needed to Increase Participation	Adaptations Needed to Increase Participation
1. Teach peers how to interact with Christine 2. Raise hand to signal teacher for response or turn and to vote 3. Ability to access and use Dynovox categories programmed 4. Practice and adapt improvisations to suit Christine; teacher involve class in obtaining suggestions	1. Position Christine by peers before meeting starts. 2. Adapt sign-in procedure; maybe have peer sign in for her. 3. Assistant provides some translation of Christine's remarks or intent as needed; direct others to talk to Christine or prompt Christine to respond. 4. Program Dynovox with vocabulary suited to club activities. 5. Position Christine close to demonstrations and use extra lighting to improve her perception.

Source: Adapted from *Teachers' guides to inclusive practices: Modifying schoolwork* (2nd ed.), by R. E. Janney and M. E. Snell, 2004, Baltimore: Paul H. Brookes. Reprinted with permission.

completes a planning form that addresses these questions with each teacher who has students with disabilities. These regular meetings may be sometimes attended by related services staff, usually are of short duration (15 to 20 minutes), and are scheduled for the whole year on a weekly or alternate weekly basis.

Ms. Dailey (Jenny's special educator) meets weekly for 20 minutes during prep time with Ms. Alpern (fifth-grade teacher) to review Jenny's progress, solve

any problems that have arisen, and exchange the materials that need adaptations (e.g., journal topics, reading focus, spelling words, classroom applications for functional math, science unit).

4. *Plan and implement adaptations, first general, then specific*: Once designed, general adaptations do not require weekly planning and can be put into place early on, often during the first few weeks of school. Both general and specific adaptations still need to be

FIGURE 4-6
Program Planning Matrix for Jenny's Morning Schedule

Student: _Jenny_   Class: _Ahern/5th_   Date: _9/06_

IEP Objectives	Arrival	Journal	Reading	Language Arts	Break	Spelling	Math	Shared Reading	Lunch
Alternate Activity with Collaborative Planning	No	No	No	Yes	No	No	No	No	No
Math:									
Count on for add/subtract							X		
Calculator for add/subtract							X		
ID coins, match to value							X		X
Tell time to hour, associate	X	X	X	X	X	X	X	X	X
ID month, day, year		X	X			X	X		
Reading & Writing:									
Decode CVC, short vowel		X	X					X	
Write 2 related sentences		X	X					X	
Write using B,E,M vowels		X	X					X	
Answers comp. questions		X	X	X				X	
Functional Skills:									
Self-monitor activity level	X	X	X	X	X	X	X	X	X
Use personal schedule	X	X	X	X	X	X	X	X	X
Use personal calendar	X						X		
Run routine errands				X					
Social Skills:									
Approach peer, initiate task	X			X	X		X	X	X
Complete task with peer	X			X	X		X	X	X

ID, Identify ___; CVC, Consonant-vowel-consonant ___; B,E,M, Beginning, ending, medial placement .

Source: Adapted from *Teachers' guides to inclusive practices: Modifying schoolwork* (2nd ed.), by R. E. Janney and M. E. Snell, 2004, Baltimore: Paul H. Brookes. Reprinted with permission.

160

practical, team generated, socially valid, and individualized while also being "only as special as necessary." Since students with severe disabilities have simplified and alternative curriculum objectives, the adaptation plan uses three columns to detail (a) the class schedule of activities, (b) the student's objectives for each activity, and (c) the general adaptations made in procedures and materials to teach or support the student in that activity. For preschool and elementary students, these plans reflect the morning and afternoon "chunks" of the day (see Table 4–14 for part of Jenny's morning plan), while secondary students have a plan for every general education class they are enrolled in.

Once general adaptations are planned and in place, teams meet to determine the specific adaptations for changing class content (e.g., unit topics, topics from classroom curriculum, science focus, spelling words, field trip content and procedure). Teams will find it helpful to record their decisions on weekly forms that address morning and afternoon periods (elementary classrooms) or specific classes in secondary school. Table 4–15 shows a partially completed afternoon form illustrating a weekly plan for Jenny's science class.

5. *Plan and implement alternative activities, if needed*: Teams may identify a need to supplement classroom activities with alternative or functional instruction. Alternative instruction may involve pullout (intensive specialized instruction, community-based learning) or may take place in the classroom using parallel instruction.

TABLE 4–14

A Sample of Jenny's Classroom Participation Plan with General Adaptations

Time and Activity	IEP Objectives	General Adaptations in Procedures and Materials
8:40–9:00: Arrival	• Use personal calendar and schedule • Put things away, no prompt • Socialize with peers • Approach peer to initiate task • Complete task, no prompt	• With teaching assistant, locates and names month and day, adds special events, and identifies activities for arrival and completes them • Monitor checking off "things away" on schedule • Keep her with class during social opportunities • Monitor asking peer to help class task • Monitor task completion with peer; check off "task done"
9:00–9:30: Journal writing	• Write two related short sentences; type on computer • Decode CVC and short vowel words with blends and digraphs • Use correct vowels (B,E,M) in writings	• Narrates journal entry in topical area to teaching assistant • Writes known words from memory or copies from word bank card • Writes letters for other words • Reads aloud • Copies independently on computer file, prints, adds to journal, and rereads to peer at table
9:30–10:15: Reading groups	• Prior three objectives • Comprehension questions about reading	• Select two or three reading vocabulary words from content being read; J. points to and reads, then adds to word bank if correct three times • Teacher reads selection to group (alternate with students reading first) • Ask J. simplified questions about content of reading similar to other students in group; restate if wrong and prompt as needed • Students read aloud sentences from their version of story adjusted to reading level • Students complete worksheet or activity-matched reading content and vocabulary

Source: Adapted from *Teachers' guides to inclusive practices: Modifying schoolwork* (2nd ed.), by R. E. Janney and M. E. Snell, 2004, Baltimore: Paul H. Brookes. Reprinted with permission.

TABLE 4–15
Partially Completed Weekly Plan for Specific Adaptations for Science

Subject	Class Objectives	Activities	Specific Adaptations
Science: Pollution and ecology	• Define pollution, give examples from nearby community and distant community • Key concepts: clean water, litter, land fill, sewage, sewage treatment, fertilizers, and animal waste	• Slide show from forestry agent on farm pollution • Videos and readings on pollution and solutions • Cooperative groups research and present one method to curb pollution	• Picture-word vocabulary cards; personal set for Jenny • Homework worksheets on content covered; simplified for Jenny • Group work: Locate, cut, and mount pictures to illustrate presentation; type captions written by or with others

While his classmates are involved in free play, Timothy has daily 20-minute intensive training in another room with the speech and language pathologist on using picture and signing communication.

As an alternative to fifth-grade language skills period, Jenny is taught to carry out errands around the school without prompts or getting lost. This activity will help her next year in middle school, when she will be moving between classes in a bigger school.

Christine receives daily community-based instruction apart from her university peers.

There are several reasons for teams adding alternative or functional activities to a student's schedule: (a) to provide intensive instruction in basic academic or communication skills; (b) to create additional opportunities to learn self-care, motor, or social skills; (c) to obtain community-based instruction on functional skills; and (d) to create another in-class option if the team is unsure about adapting a classroom activity for meaningful participation. When used, alternative activities should be designed to give intensive instruction on important IEP objectives that a student would not otherwise receive. Because these activities often separate the student from classmates, their importance should be reviewed regularly. To reduce the disruptive or separate nature of alternative activities, they should be designed, when possible, to meet several guidelines (Janney & Snell, 2004):

• Schedule the student to come and go from the activity at natural class breaks when others also are in transit
• Match alternative activity times to the same times peers participate in activities not suited to the student but don't schedule them during important class routines
• Add peers into the activity as appropriate
• Coordinate classroom themes with the alternative activity to prevent isolation from classmates

6. *Monitor and evaluate*: Teams need to oversee and appraise the effects that individual adaptations have on the following:

• A student and his or her learning of IEP goals (e.g., has the student mastered target objectives, is the student using skill, what is the student's attitude toward adaptations?)
• School staff using them (e.g., are they easy to use, cost effective, unobtrusive?)
• Teaching setting (e.g., what are peers' attitudes toward adaptations, do they disrupt or facilitate class routines, are they nonstigmatizing?).

Regular team sessions are the primary forum for this monitoring process. Teams will use both objective and anecdotal records of the student's performance to assess the effects on student progress and team and peer opinion to assess the effects of the adaptations on both the staff and the teaching setting.

Teachers' Instructional Record Keeping

Responsible teaching is not possible without some written documentation, but if paperwork takes too much time, teaching suffers. At the very minimum, teachers need *simple and team-generated data collection forms* and readily available *guidelines for teaching students and monitoring their progress*. Written programs (i.e., lesson plans, program formats, or teaching guides) should specify the essential elements: the student, objective(s), start and aim date, teaching time and setting, instructor(s), arrangement, materials, evaluation procedure and schedule, and teaching procedures (e.g., instructional cue, prompt and fading methods, error correction procedure, reinforcers, and rough schedule). Written programs also give general instructions for changing procedures during later stages of learning. When teaching programs

TABLE 4–16
Brief Teaching Guide for Timothy's Arrival Program

Brief Teaching Guide		
Student: Timothy Simms	**School:** St. Stephen Preschool	**Start Date:** 9/27/99
Teachers: Carlene Johnson, Ted Grayson, & Jo Milano (SLP)		**Aim Date:** 12/17/99

Objective: On arrival at and departure from preschool, Timothy will independently exit the car, walk to enter the preschool class, greet familiar people, remove and hang his outer garments in his cubby, and select and go to a play activity at a criterion of 10 of 15 steps (67%) during two training sessions (using partial participation on some steps as indicated in the task analysis).

Stage of Learning: Acquisition	**Arrangement:** One to one, naturalistic	
Teaching Times: At arrival and departure	**Teaching Days:** M–F	**Test Day:** Alternate F

Setting: car, bus/car area, sidewalk, halls, classroom, cubby

Instructional Cue: Arrival or departure cues, "Let's go to preschool" "Let's go home"

Teaching Procedure: Constant time delay (0, 4 seconds) across total task

Prompt(s): Gestural (point, tap) *with* partial physical (gentle pressure or nudge). Use his name if he is not attending. Do not use verbal prompts.

Materials: Natural materials involved in task; activity board, student photo cards; task analysis

Reinforcers: Praise, smile, deep pressure rub on shoulder, play activities during free time in and outside

Description of Teaching Procedures: For first 2 days, use zero delay; then delay prompt 4 seconds. Use zero delay for one day after long absences, vacations, or on all steps following four or more error steps in one session. The goal is to increase his unprompted correct responses.

Teacher Antecedents[1]	Student Responses[2]	Teacher Consequences[3]
Follow task steps. Stand close and attend carefully; no verbal prompts, only instructional cue. Count seconds to self; use procedure with each task step. Start by giving cue, wait delay, then give prompt on time if no response. Give full prompt even if he responds after you start it. Withhold prompt when he initiates response before 4 seconds have ended. As he successful on a step, include gesture prompts that draw his attention to peers nearby who are performing the same task.	1) Prompted correct 2) No response 3) Error (includes starting response but not completing it correctly) 4) Unprompted correct response (he initiates the response before you prompt) 5) Correct responses (prompted or unprompted) made when peers are nearby	1) Follow prompted corrects with immediate praise 2) Follow a no response with a prompt 3) Interrupt errors with a prompt as soon as error is obvious; stand close, give prompt so he can see 4) Follow unprompted corrects with enthusiastic praise/back rub 5) Encourage peers to praise him when his things are in cubby and when he makes an activity choice

TABLE 4–16 (*Continued*)
Brief Teaching Guide for Timothy's Arrival Program

Brief Teaching Guide (*Continued*)

Maintenance: Thin and fade reinforcer to end of task; give activity board choices. Require use of arrival procedure to participate in play activity.

Fluency: If performance is slower than peers, time it and set goals for reducing the duration.

Generalization: With parents, task analyze his home routine; adjust the school and home procedures so they are similar.

Evaluation: Use the task analysis of steps to record training and assessment (baseline/probe) data. Take 2 days of baseline using a multiple opportunity task-analytic procedure to identify what his level of skills are for each step of the task; once teaching begins, probe using single opportunity task-analytic assessment. Record all responses as independent (correct +) or errors (incorrectly performed or no response). Graph both baseline data and probes as single opportunity assessments (give credit only for correct responses made before the first error). Graph training data as independent (+) and prompted: GP (gestural physical prompt). Record all data on a dated task-analytic data collection form; attach a graph. Draw an aim line on the graph that reflects aim date and criterion performance.

[1] How the teacher uses antecedent methods (instructor directions, how to present materials, what cue(s) to give, what prompts to give, how long to wait, etc.).
[2] How the student may respond or perform (correct, approximation, no response, error, inappropriate behavior).
[3] How the teacher responds to each type of student response.

are briefly described with this level of detail, there are several advantages:

- Successful program methods can be used again with the same student (and modified for others), while those that yield little or no learning can be modified more precisely.
- Programs are more likely to be implemented consistently regardless of who teaches.

Timothy's team has completed a task analysis data collection form for his arrival program (Figure 4-1) that lists the target behaviors in order, along with the instructional cue, teaching method (constant time delay), the prompt (gestural or partial physical), the response latency, and the recording key. His team can use information recorded on this form to detect day-to-day progress and to identify particular steps that may appear either to be mastered or to be consistently difficult; anecodatal notes help the team hypothesize whether changes in performance result from learning or from problems in the classroom or at home. Use of this information encourages teams to be data based in their decisions and consistent in their teaching, making it easier for Timothy to learn when multiple instructors participate. Staff also refer to the brief teaching guide (Table 4-16), which describes the constant time delay method they use with Timothy.

Teams should devise or adopt *easy-to-use* program forms to guide teaching and data collection. Team members may want to combine written program materials with demonstrations, practice and feedback, and in-class coaching, as these training methods have been shown to be effective in teaching staff to use new procedures correctly and consistently (Schepis et al., 2001). The special educator often assumes the responsibility for completing, organizing and updating instructional records and data collection forms, and making them available to other team members. In the next chapter, we will discuss in depth how student performance data are used to modify and improve instruction.

Summary

Teaching students effectively involves many steps and decisions. Students with significantly differing abilities need instructional experiences that not only focus on appropriate educational goals and objectives and but also reflect effective and efficient teaching techniques. To keep errors to a minimum during early learning and also to facilitate skill generalization, teams must plan instruction so that structure, support, and stage of learning are properly balanced regardless of the location where teaching occurs. But to promote skill maintenance, fluent and proficient performance, and generalization of skills, teams must adjust their teaching procedures to reduce structure, fade prompts, and shift the student's attention to the natural cues and stimuli that must come to control their behavior.

Special education teachers cannot accomplish the best practices described in this chapter if they work alone. Collaboration and problem solving among educators, administrators, and parents are the primary means for successfully including students who have disabilities. While teaching in inclusive schools makes planning more complicated, the outcomes are richer. Only inclusive settings allow the benefits of normalized social contexts and linkage with the general education curriculum.

Suggested Activities

1. Use Table 4–17 to evaluate the school program you work in or are familiar with. If possible, gather a group of educators and an administrator and involve them in this evaluation process. Rate the school on the following school practices using a scale from 0 (not present) to 4 (schoolwide evidence of its practice):

- Students' IEP objectives address priority skills and are linked to the general education curriculum. Students' IEPs include teaching and testing accommodations that facilitate them to make progress in learning.
- Collaborative teaming is predicable and supported by school staff and administrator. Teams plan for individualized adaptations, use problem solving, and reach consensus among team members. Relevant team members are involved.
- All students are members of general education classrooms alongside age peers; their membership is valued.
- Instruction is planned, individualized, and systematic.

With the focus group, rank order those needing improvement and brainstorm the actions needed to tackle each using an issue-action problem-solving form, as shown after the following rating grid.

2. Examine the IEP of a student with more extensive support needs. If the student is being included with his or her peers in general education activities, observe over one of several days and check on how adequately his or her IEP objectives are being

TABLE 4–17
Needs Assessment of Best Practices and Issue Action Problem-Solving Form

Supportive Practice	Not Present	Spoken About but not Practiced	Some Evidence of its Application	Good Evidence of its Application	Schoolwide Evidence of its Application
List below:	0	1	2	3	4

Issue	Action	Taken by whom	Taken by when

addressed. Complete a matrix for this student by listing IEP objectives down the left side and the class schedule across the top. Indicate with checks the activities during which it would be logical to teach each objective. Note when (or if) "pullout" is being used. Explore how inappropriate instances of pullout might be replaced with adaptation of classroom activities. If the student is not included in general education activities, observe a class (or classes) that might be suitable for the student to be included. Complete a matrix as you did previously, then explore the steps needed to implement change.

3. For this same student, apply the model in Figure 4-6 for making adaptations (Janney & Snell, 2004). If the student is assigned to your caseload, then implement the six steps for using the process. If the student is one you work with during a practicum experience, then evaluate the adequacy of adaptations currently used in the student's program. Start with the student's matrix; determine what kinds of curricular, instructional, and alternate adaptations are being used; and decide if they are appropriate. Explore how improvements can be made.

References

Bateman, B. D., & Herr, C.M. (2003). *Writing measurable IEP goals and objectives*. Verona, WI: IEP Resources, Attainment Co.

Bateman, B. D., & Linden, M. A. (1998). *Better IEPs* (3rd ed.). Longmont, CO: Sopris West.

Baumgart, D., Brown, L., Pumpian, I., Nisbet, J., Ford, A., Sweet, M., Messina, R., & Schroeder, J. (1982). The principle of partial participation and individualized adaptations in educational programs for severely handicapped students. *Journal of the Association for Persons with Severe Handicaps, 7*(2), 17-27.

Billingsley, F. F. (1998). Behaving independently: considerations in fading instructor assistance. In A. Hilton & R. Ringlaben (Eds.), *Best and promising practices in developmental disabilities* (pp. 157-168). Austin, TX: PRO-ED.

Browder, D. M. (2001). *Curriculum and assessment for students with moderate and severe disabilities*. New York: Guilford.

Brown, F. (1991). Creative daily scheduling: A non-intrusive approach to challenging behaviors in community residences. *Journal of the Association for Persons with Severe Handicaps, 16*, 75-84.

Brown, F., Evans, I. M., Weed, K. A., & Owen, V. (1987). Delineating functional competencies: A component model. *Journal of the Association for Persons with Severe Handicaps, 12*, 117-124.

Brown, F., & Holvoet, J. (1982). The effect of systematic interaction on incidental learning of two severely handicapped students.

Journal of the Association of the Severely Handicapped, 7(4), 19-28.

Center for Applied Special Technology. 2004. *Universal design for learning*. Retrieved February 28, 2004, from http://www.cast.org/udl

Coots, J. J., Bishop, K. D., & Grenot-Scheyer, M. (1998). Supporting elementary age students with significant disabilities in general education classrooms: Personal perspectives on inclusion. *Education and Training in Mental Retardation and Developmental Disabilities, 33*, 317-330.

Cushing, L. S., & Kennedy, C. H. (1997). Academic effects of providing peer support in general education classrooms on students without disabilities. *Journal of Applied Behavior Analysis, 30*, 139-152.

Delquadri, J., Greenwood, C. R., Whorton, D., Carta, J. J., & Hall, R. V. (1986). Classwide peer tutoring. *Exceptional Children, 52*, 535-542.

Demchak, M. (1990). Response prompting and fading methods: A review. *American Journal on Mental Retardation, 94*, 603-615.

Denny, M., Marchand-Martella, N., Martella, R. C., Reilly, J. C., Reilly, J. F., & Cleanthous, C. C. (2000). Using parent-delivered graduated guidance to teach functional living skills to a child with Cri du Chat Syndrome. *Education and Treatment of Children, 23*, 441-454.

Doyle, M. B. (2002). *The paraprofessional's guide to the inclusive classroom: Working as a team* (2nd ed.). Baltimore: Paul H. Brookes.

Doyle, P. M., Gast, D. L., Wolery, M., Ault, M. J., & Farmer, J. A. (1990). Use of constant time delay in small group instruction: A study of observational and incidental learning. *Journal of Special Education, 23*, 369-385.

Dugan, E., Kamps, D., Leonard, B., Watkins, N., Rheinberger, A., & Stackhaus, J. (1995). Effects of cooperative learning groups during social studies for students with autism and fourth-grade peers. *Journal of Applied Behavior Analysis, 28*, 175-188.

Dunlap, G., & Johnson, J. (1985). Increasing the independent responding of autistic children with unpredictable supervision. *Journal of Applied Behavior Analysis, 18*, 227-236.

Etzel, B. C., & LeBlanc, J. M. (1979). The simplest treatment alternative: The law of parsimony applied to choosing appropriate instructional control and errorless-learning procedures for the difficult-to-teach child. *Journal of Autism and Development Disorders, 9*, 361-382.

Farlow, L., & Snell, M. E. (1995). *Making the most of student performance data* (AAMR Research to Practice Series). Washington, DC: American Association on Mental Retardation.

Farmer, J. A., Gast, D. L., Wolery, M., & Winterling, V. (1991). Small group interaction for students with severe handicaps: A study of observational learning. *Education and Training in Mental Retardation, 26*, 190-201.

Fisher, M., & Meyer, L. H. (2002). Development and social competence after two years for students enrolled in inclusive and self-contained educational programs. *Research and Practice for Persons with Severe Disabilities, 27*, 165-174.

Ford, A., Schnorr, R., Meyer, L., Davern, L., Black, J., & Dempsey, P. (1989). *The Syracuse community-referenced curriculum guide*. Baltimore: Paul H. Brookes.

Giangreco, M. F., Cloninger, C. J., & Iverson, V. S. (1993). *Choosing options and accommodations for children (COACH): A guide to planning inclusive education*. Baltimore: Paul H. Brookes.

Giangreco, M. F., Edelman, S. W., Luiselli, T. E., & MacFarland, S. Z. C. (1997). Helping or hovering? Effects of instructional assistant proximity on students with disabilities. *Exceptional Children, 64*, 7–18.

Giangreco, M. F., & Putnam, J. W. (1991). Supporting the education of students with severe disabilities in regular education. In L. H. Meyer, C. A. Peck, & L. Brown (Eds.), *Critical issues in the lives of people with severe disabilities* (pp. 245–270). Baltimore: Paul H. Brookes.

Gilberts, G. H., Agran, M., Hughes, C., & Wehmeyer, M. (2001). The effects of peer delivered self-monitoring strategies on the participation of students with severe disabilities in general education classrooms. *Journal of the Association for Persons with Severe Handicaps, 26*, 25–36.

Gold, M. W. (1972). Stimulus factors in skill training of the retarded on a complex assembly task: Acquisition, transfer, and retention. *American Journal of Mental Deficiency, 76*, 517–526.

Hall, L. J., McClannahan, L. E., & Krantz, P. J. (1995). Promoting independence in integrated classrooms by teaching aides to use activity schedules and decreased prompts. *Education and Training in Mental Retardation and Developmental Disabilities, 30*, 208–217.

Haring, T. G., & Breen, C. G. (1992). A peer-mediated social network intervention to enhance the social integration of persons with moderate and severe disabilities. *Journal of Applied Behavior Analysis, 25*, 319–334.

Heckman, K. A., Alber, S., Hooper, S., & Heward, W. L. (1998). A comparison of least-to-most prompts and progressive time delay on the disruptive behavior of students with autism. *Journal of Behavioral Education, 8*, 171–201.

Horner, R. H., & Carr, E. G. (1997). Behavior support for students with severe disabilities: Functional assessment and comprehensive intervention. *Journal of Special Education, 31*, 84–104.

Hughes, C., & Carter, E. (2006). *Success for all students: Promoting inclusion in secondary schools through peer buddy programs*. Boston: Allyn and Bacon.

Hughes, C., Rung, L. L., Wehmeyer, M. L., Agran, M., Copeland, S. R., & Hwang, B. (2000). Self-prompted communication book use to increase social interaction among high school students. *Journal of the Association for People with Severe Handicaps, 25*, 153–166.

Hunt, P., & Goetz, L. (1997). Research on inclusive educational programs, practices, and outcomes for students with severe disabilities. *Journal of Special Education, 31*, 3–29.

Hunt, P., Soto, G., Maier, J., & Doering, K. (2003). Collaborative teaming to support students at risk and students with severe disabilities in general education classrooms. *Exceptional Children, 69*, 315–332.

Hunt, P., Soto, G., Maier, J., Muller, E., & Goetz, L. (2002). Collaborative teaming to support students with augmentative and alternative communication needs in general education classrooms. *Augmentative and Alternative Communication, 18*, 20–35.

Hunt, P., Staub, D., Alwell, M., & Goetz, L. (1994). Achievement by all students within the context of cooperative learning groups. *Journal of the Association for Persons with Severe Handicaps, 19*, 290–301.

Janney, R. E., & Snell, M. E. (1997). How teachers include students with moderate and severe disabilities in elementary classes: The means and meaning of inclusion. *Journal of the Association for Persons with Severe Handicaps, 22*, 159–169.

Janney, R. E., & Snell, M. E. (2004). *Practices for inclusive schools: Modifying schoolwork* (2nd ed.). Baltimore: Paul H. Brookes.

Johnson, D. W., & Johnson, F. W. (1997). *Joining together: Group theory and skills* (6th ed.). Upper Saddle River, NJ: Prentice Hall.

Kaiser, A. P., Hancock, T. B., & Nietfeld, J. P. (2000). The effects of parent-implemented enhanced milieu teaching on the social communication of children who have autism. *Journal of Early Education and Development [Special issue], 4*, 423–446.

Kamps, D. M., Dugan, E. P., Leonard, B. R., & Daoust, P. M. (1994). Enhanced small group instruction using choral responding and student interaction for children with autism and developmental disabilities. *American Journal of Mental Retardation, 99*, 60–73.

Kamps, D. M., Leonard, B. R., Dugan, E. P., Boland, B., & Greenwood, C. R. (1991). The use of ecobehavioral assessment to identify naturally occurring effective procedures in classrooms serving students with autism and other developmental disabilities. *Journal of Behavioral Education, 1*, 367–397.

Kamps, D. M., Walker, D., Locke, P., Delquadri, J., & Hall, R. V. (1990). A comparison of instructional arrangements for children with autism served in a public school setting. *Education and Treatment of Children, 13*, 197–215.

Kennedy, C. H., & Horn, E. M. (2004). *Including students with severe disabilities*. Boston: Allyn & Bacon.

Kennedy, C. H., Shukla, S., & Fryxell, D. (1997). Comparing the effects of educational placement on the social relationships of intermediate school students with severe disabilities. *Exceptional Children, 64*, 31–47.

Kern, L., Vorndran, C. M., Hilt, A., Ringdahl, J. E., Adelman, B. E., & Dunlap, G. (1998). Choice as an intervention to improve behavior: A review of the literature. *Journal of Behavioral Education, 8*, 151–169.

Kishi, G. S., & Meyer, L. H. (1994). What children report and remember: A six-year follow-up of the effects of social contact between peers with and without severe disabilities. *Journal of the Association for Persons with Severe Handicaps, 19*, 277–289.

Koegel, L. K., Koegel, R. L., Harrower, J. K., & Carter, C. M. (1999). Pivotal response intervention. I: Overview of approach. *Journal of the Association for Persons with Severe Handicaps, 24*(3), 174–185.

Koegel, R. L., Camarata, S., Koegel, L. K., Ben-Tall, A., & Smith, A. E. (1998). Increasing speech intelligibility in children with autism. *Journal of Autism and Developmental Disorders, 28*, 241–251.

Koegel, R. L., Koegel, L. K., & Carter, C. M. (1999). Pivotal teaching interactions for children with autism. *School Psychology Review, 28*, 576–594.

Koegel, R. L., & Rincover, A. (1974). Treatment of psychotic children in a classroom environment: I. Learning in a large group. *Journal of Applied Behavior Analysis, 7*, 45-59.

Liberty, K. A. (1985). Enhancing instruction for maintenance, generalization, and adaptation. In C. Lakin & R. H. Bruininks (Eds.), *Strategies for achieving community integration of developmentally disabled citizens* (pp. 29-71). Baltimore: Paul H. Brookes.

Liberty, K. A., & Haring, N. G. (1990). Introduction to decision rule systems. *Remedial and Special Education, 11*, 32-41.

Logan, K. R., Brakeman, R., & Keefe, E. B., (1997). Effects of instructional variables on engaged behavior of students with disabilities in general education classrooms. *Exceptional Children, 63*, 481-497.

Lohrmann-O'Rourke, S., Browder, D. M., & Brown, F. (2000). Guidelines for conducting socially valid systematic preference assessments. *Journal of the Association for Persons with Severe Handicaps, 25*, 42-53.

Lohrmann-O'Rourke, S., & Zirkel, P. A. (1998). The case law on aversive interventions for students with disabilities. *Exceptional Children, 65*, 101-123.

Mason, S. A., McGee, G. G., Farmer-Dougan, V., & Risley, T. R. (1989). A practical strategy for ongoing reinforcer assessment. *Journal of Applied Behavior Analysis, 22*, 171-179.

Mayer-Johnson, Inc. (1998). *BoardMaker for Windows®*. Salona Beach, CA: Author.

McDonnell, J., Thorson, N., & McQuivey, C. (1998). The instructional characteristics of inclusive classes for elementary students with severe disabilities. *Journal of Behavioral Education, 8*, 415-437.

Parrott, K. A., Schuster, J. W., Collins, B. C., & Gassaway, L. J. (2000). Simultaneous prompting and instructive feedback when teaching chained tasks. *Journal of Behavioral Education, 10*, 3-19.

Reese, G., & Snell, M. E. (1990). Putting on and removing coats and jackets: The acquisition and maintenance of skills by children with severe multiple disabilities. *Education and Training in Mental Retardation, 26*, 398-410.

Riley, G. A. (1995). Guidelines for devising a hierarchy when fading response prompts. *Education and Training in Mental Retardation and Developmental Disabilities, 30*, 231-242.

Rincover, A., & Koegel, R. L. (1975). Setting generality and stimulus control in autistic children. *Journal of Applied Behavior Analysis, 8*, 235-246.

Roane, H. S., Vollmer, T. R., Ringdahl, & Marcus, B. A. (1998). Evaluation of a brief stimulus preference assessment. *Journal of Applied Behavior Analysis, 31*, 605-620.

Rotholz, D. A. (1987). Current considerations on the use of one-to-one instruction with autistic students: Review and recommendations. *Education and Treatment of Children, 10*, 271-278.

Ryndak, D. L. (2003). Portrait of Maureen before and after inclusion. In D. L. Ryndak, & S. Alper (Eds.), *Curriculum and instruction for students with significant disabilities inclusive settings* (pp. 459-479). Boston: Allyn & Bacon.

Ryndak, D. L., & Alper, S. (2003). *Curriculum and instruction for students with significant disabilities in inclusive settings* (2nd ed.). Boston: Allyn & Bacon.

Schepis, M. M., Reid, D. H., Ownbey, J., & Parsons, M. H. (2001). Training support staff to embed teaching within natural routines of young children with disabilities in an inclusive preschool. *Journal of Applied Behavior Analysis, 34*, 313-327.

Schuster, J. W., Morse, T. E., Ault, M. J., Doyle, P. M., Crawford, M. R., & Wolery, M. (1998). Constant time delay with chained tasks: A review of the literature. *Education and Treatment of Children, 21*, 74-106.

Sewell, T. J., Collins, B. C., Hemmeter, M. L., & Schuster, J. W. (1998). Using simultaneous prompting within an activity-base format to teach dressing skills to preschoolers with developmental delays. *Journal of Early Intervention, 21*, 132-145.

Shukla, S., Kennedy, C. H., & Cushing, L. S. (1998). Adult influence on the participation of peers without disabilities in peer support programs. *Journal of Behavioral Education, 8*, 397-413.

Singer, G. H. S., Gert, B., & Koegel, R. L. (1999). A moral framework for analyzing the controversy over aversive behavioral interventions for people with severe mental retardation. *Journal of Positive Behavior Interventions, 1*, 88-100.

Singleton, K. C., Schuster, J. W., & Ault, M. J. (1995). Simultaneous prompting in a small group instructional arrangement. *Education and Training in Mental Retardation and Developmental Disabilities, 30*, 218-230.

Slavin, R. E. (1991). Cooperative learning and group contingencies. *Journal of Behavioral Education, 1*, 105-115.

Snell, M. E. (1997). Teaching children and young adults with mental retardation in school programs: Current research. *Behaviour Change, 14*, 73-105.

Snell, M. E. (2002). Using dynamic assessment with learners who communicate nonsymbolically. *Alternative and Augmentative Communication, 18*, 163-176.

Snell, M. E., & Janney, R. E. (2000a). *Practices for inclusive schools: Social relationships and peer support*. Baltimore: Paul H. Brookes.

Snell, M. E., & Janney, R. J. (2000b). Teachers' problem solving about young children with moderate and severe disabilities in elementary classrooms. *Exceptional Children, 66*, 472-490.

Snell, M. E., & Janney, R. E. (2005). *Practices for inclusive schools: Collaborative teaming* (2nd ed.). Baltimore: Paul H. Brookes.

Staub, D., Schwartz, I. S., Gallucci, C., & Peck, C. A. (1994). Four portraits of friendship at an inclusive school. *Journal of the Association for Persons with Severe Handicaps, 19*, 314-325.

Staub, D., Spaulding, M., Peck, C. A., Gallucci, C., & Schwartz, I. S. (1996). Using nondisabled peers to support the inclusion of students with disabilities. *Journal of the Association for Persons with Severe Handicaps, 21*, 194-205.

Stinson, D. M., Gast, D. L., Wolery, M., & Collins, B. C. (1991). Acquisition of nontargeted information during small-group instruction. *Exceptionality, 2*, 65-80.

Tomlinson, C. A. (2001). *How to differentiate instruction in mixed-ability classrooms* (2nd ed.). Alexandria, VA: Association for Supervision and Curriculum Development.

Turnbull, H. R., Wilcox, B. L., Stowe, M., & Turnbull, A. P. (2001). IDEA requirements for use of PBS: Guidelines for responsible agencies. *Journal of Positive Behavior Interventions, 3*, 11-18.

Werts, M. G., Caldwell, N. K., & Wolery, M. (1996). Peer modeling of response chains: Observational learning by students with disabilities. *Journal of Applied Behavior Analysis, 29*, 53–66.

Werts, M. G., Wolery, M., Snyder, E. D., & Caldwell, N. K. (1996). Teachers' perceptions of the supports critical to the success of inclusion programs. *Journal of the Association for Persons with Severe Handicaps, 21*, 9–21.

Whalen, C., Schuster, J. W., & Hemmeter, M. L. (1996). The use of unrelated instructive feedback when teaching in a small group instructional arrangement. *Education and Training in Mental Retardation and Developmental Disabilities, 31*, 188–202.

Wolery, M., Ault, M. J., & Doyle, P. M. (1992). *Teaching students with moderate to severe disabilities*. New York: Longman.

Wolery, M., Ault, M. J., Doyle, P. M., Gast, D. L., & Griffen, A. K. (1992). Choral and individual responding during small group instruction: Identification of interactional effects. *Education and Treatment of Children, 15*, 289–309.

Wolery, M., & Gast, D. L. (1984). Effective and efficient procedures for the transfer of stimulus control. *Topics in Early Childhood Special Education, 4*, 57–77.

Measurement, Analysis, and Evaluation

Fredda Brown
Martha E. Snell

To evaluate the impact of a school program on a student, educators must formulate specific strategies for measurement. Three basic reasons for developing measurement strategies are (a) to document what has occurred, (b) to identify the variables responsible for the occurrence (Wacker, 1989; Zirpoli & Melloy, 2001), and (c) to understand when and why learning is occurring or not occurring. Measurement strategies enable teachers to better predict future performance, and prediction helps teachers decide if program modifications are necessary.

Ongoing evaluation of student progress is an integral part of the teaching-learning process, and teachers must develop expertise in collecting data on their student's learning and making changes in instruction based on analysis of these data (Ryndak, Clark, Conroy & Stuart, 2001). With the increasing focus on educating students with severe disabilities alongside their typically developing peers in general education settings, data collection strategies become more of a challenge. Each teacher must balance the need for data to make instructional decisions and to evaluate program effec-

tiveness with the needs of the regular classroom. Although many teachers question the value of data and find data difficult to manage (Farlow & Snell, 1994; Fisher & Lindsey-Walters, 1987; Zirpoli & Melloy, 2001), it is widely accepted that teachers make better instructional decisions when they base them on student performance data (Farlow & Snell, 1989; Meyer & Janney, 1989; Utley, Zigmond, & Strain, 1987). Professionals need to choose data collection strategies that are unobtrusive but that still provide sufficient information to determine program effectiveness (Test & Spooner, 1996). There is an obvious need for data collection strategies that are user friendly (Meyer & Janney, 1989) and that do not require significant sacrifices of teacher time (Zirpoli & Melloy, 2001). According to Meyer and Janney (1989), user-friendly methods are those that can be managed in real classrooms and that are reflective of meaningful outcomes (not just isolated behaviors). Walther-Thomas, Korinek, McLaughlin, and Williams (2000) suggest the KISS principle for inclusive classrooms—*k*eep *i*t *s*imple yet *s*ensitive.

Teachers must be concerned with two levels of measurement. These are process measures and outcome measures (Haring & Breen, 1989). *Process measures* focus on fine-grain, small units of behavior, such as the individual responses within a complex chain or performance of the entire chain (e.g., a task analysis for using a vending machine, frequency of positive interactions with peers) (Haring & Breen, 1989). *Outcome measures* do not provide this level of detailed information on behaviors that occur within a situation. Rather, these measures offer information regarding the general effect of a program on a person's quality of life. Outcome measures include, for example, a student's performance on individualized education plan (IEP) objectives at the end of a school year, test scores, or development of friendships. Process measures, which focus on a specific, discrete target behavior, lack the breadth necessary to assess the broader impact of interventions (Storey, 1997) and typically represent only a temporary change in a controlled setting. Outcome measures offer a more meaningful measurement, reflecting a range of significant outcomes for the individual, school, family, and community (Meyer & Janney, 1989). As described in chapter 3, a broad outcome framework, such as the one described by Billingsley, Gallucci, Peck, Schwartz, and Staub (1996) that includes the domains of skills, membership, and relationships, is necessary to represent a meaningful educational experience for students with severe disabilities.

It is critical that administrative, teaching, and related service practitioners evaluate student progress with outcome data (Snell, 2003). According to Haring and Breen (1989), outcome measures that reflect the success of an inclusive education program include acceptance, friendships, and social participation. Social participation includes such things as the role of the student in the social network, the number of after-school outings with nondisabled friends, and the time spent in social interactions with nondisabled peers.

Meyer and Evans (1993) included in their criteria for successful outcomes of behavioral interventions those related to self-determination and quality of life, such as less restrictive placements, greater participation in integrated school experiences, subjective quality-of-life improvements (e.g., happiness, satisfaction, choices, and control), improvements perceived by significant others, and expanded social relationships and informal support networks. Gothelf and Brown (1998) describe the case of a young man who lived in a facility where he received contingent electric shock for the self-injurious behavior of scratching. He wore a shock device 24 hours per day at his school program and in his group home. After many thousands of shocks, his self-injury was significantly reduced although not entirely. Using the process measure of "rate of scratching" as the only measure of success, it could be concluded that the contingent electric shock was effective. However, Gothelf and Brown point out that the program was far from effective not only because it was an unacceptable strategy but also because there was little impact on the quality of his life. Consider the following outcomes that accompanied the behavior reduction: wearing a shock device 24 hours each day, inability to manage his own behavior without the shock device, going to school and living in a group home with individuals who all had severe behavior problems, having no control over daily activities (e.g., what to eat, when to go to bed or wake up), limited social interaction with individuals without disabilities, limited social interaction with unpaid individuals, self-reports of being unhappy, no control over his own future, and living in a different state than his family. Outcome data revealed how limited this intervention was for him.

Measurement not only must accurately describe current performance on priority skills but also must reach beyond this traditional assessment of isolated skill increases or behavior reduction to assess the outcomes that make a significant difference in the individual's life. Meyer and Janney (1989) state, "In contrast to a limited outcome such as a temporary change in one target behavior in a controlled clinical setting, an expanded definition of effectiveness would require evidence of a range of more meaningful outcomes for child, school, family, and community" (p. 263). In the previous example of the young man receiving an aversive program, significant outcomes would include, for example, self-management of his behavior, living in his own home, designing his own daily routines, pursuing and acquiring a job of his preference, and selecting his own personal care assistants. However, process data are still needed to guide the instruction and are necessary for measurement of skill domains.

This chapter reviews a variety of outcome and process measures as well as some basic concepts, such as defining and measuring behavior, determining reliability, designing data sheets, and graphing data. Furthermore, we discuss measurement and its meaningful implementation within the context of current best practices and philosophy.

Measurement

Data, if wisely used, can provide information critical to the development, evaluation, and revision of instructional efforts (Farlow & Snell, 1994; Zirpoli & Melloy, 2001). However, measurements of behavior change are of little importance if they do not provide meaningful information. Two characteristics of the data must be considered to determine if a measurement system is meaningful: (a) data must reflect important behavior, and (b) data must be sufficiently accurate, or reliable.

Measurement of Important Behaviors

Data should reflect important and significant behaviors. Simply being accurate and reliable is not sufficient. For example, a teacher can accurately measure the number of times Jenny was able to complete a preschool puzzle; however, because a preschool puzzle is not age appropriate for Jenny, who is in fifth grade, it would not be a meaningful measure. Teams should consider a series of questions to determine if their measurement strategies are meaningful:

- Do these data measure behaviors or skills that are valued by the student, his or her parents, and the community or society?
- Do these data reflect the qualitative changes that we hope to see in this student?
- Are the level or types of changes in the student significant?

Many efforts have been made to describe the criteria for evaluating the validity and importance of behavior changes. Researchers and clinicians have used the following five criteria to evaluate the success of behavioral change efforts: (a) statistical significance, (b) clinical significance, (c) social validity, (d) educational validity, and (e) quality of life.

Statistical Significance

Experimental or *statistical significance* involves comparing behavior during or following an intervention with what it was prior to the intervention and asking if that difference is beyond what might be expected by chance (Kazdin, 1976). Often, statistical analysis is used to evaluate the success of an intervention in a research study, but it is not sufficient as a sole criterion for evaluating change, nor is it practical for teams to apply in school.

Clinical Significance

Therapeutic or *clinical significance* is the importance of the change achieved in the behavior (Kazdin, 1976), or the comparison between the change in behavior that has occurred and the level of change required for the individual to more adequately function in society (Risley, 1970). In other words, if the result of an intervention makes no improvement in the student's life (e.g., eat independently), even though there is statistical significance, the change does not meet the criterion of clinical significance.

Social Validity

Social validity also refers to the significance of a change in an individual's life. In an analysis of the development of applied behavior analysis, Baer, Wolf, and Risley (1987) state, "We may have taught many social skills without examining whether they actually furthered the subject's social life; many courtesy skills without examining whether anyone actually noticed or cared; many safety skills without examining whether the subject was actually safer thereafter; many language skills without measuring whether the subject actually used them to interact differently than before; many on-task skills without measuring the actual value of those tasks; and, in general, many survival skills without examining the subject's actual subsequent survival" (p. 322).

Social validity is a concept that addresses qualitative aspects of the educational program. It focuses on the acceptability of the educational goals, the instructional methods used, and the importance and social acceptability of the behavior change (Kazdin, 1977; Wolf, 1978). Social validation procedures can be used to determine whether the learned behavior is functional or meaningful (Kazdin, 1980). There are two methods for determining social validity. *Social comparison* contrasts the student's performance with the performance of the student's nondisabled peers. This standard checks against imposing unnecessarily rigorous performance criteria or stopping instruction before the student reaches a socially acceptable level of performance.

At Timothy's team meeting, it was suggested that a behavioral objective be developed to teach him to sit in his seat and keep his hands in his lap and his feet on the floor for 15 minutes. Mrs. Johnson, his general education teacher, questioned the objective, "I'm not sure any of the children in the class can sit like that for 15 minutes!" Mr. Grayson, Timothy's special education teacher, suggested that he observe Mrs. Johnson's class during a variety of activities and record data on a few typically developing children to determine the range of the duration and the "styles of sitting" displayed by the other students. Mr. Grayson agrees that observing peers will help set a more appropriate goal for Timothy's paying attention in class.

The second method used to determine social validity is *subjective evaluation*. In this method, the opinions of significant people, because of their expertise or familiarity with the student, are used to judge the significance of the behavior change. For example, McGrath, Bosch, Sullivan, and Fuqua (2003) provided social skills training to a preschooler with autism and his nondisabled peers in his class. Using individual and peer training strategies, the researchers were effective in increasing both the preschooler's rate of social initiations and responses to the other children in his class and the type of play in which the child participated with his nondisabled peers (e.g., cooperative versus solitary play). To test social validity and clinical significance, the researchers enlisted the participation of a clinical psychologist and a preschool teacher who were not involved in the study to rate pre- and postintervention videotapes showing the child playing with his peers. Using a 10-point scale, the two professionals viewed randomly ordered videotape clips (so they would not know which were preintervention and which were postintervention sessions) to judge a variety of play related variables (e.g., Does he appear to have fun? Do the peers appear to have fun? Is he invited to play by other children?). Results of these social validity measures indicated that the two professionals agreed that during the preintervention phase, the preschooler with autism had negligible interactions with his peers, that only rarely did he appear to have fun, and that his peers did not invite him to play. However, judgment on the postintervention videotapes revealed that the preschooler had more frequent play interactions with his peers and that his peers always seemed to have fun. Although both professionals agreed that there was an increase in being invited to play following intervention, there was inconsistent judgment about the extent of this improvement (i.e., "often" versus "rarely").

Taber, Alberto, Seltzer, and Hughes (2003) extended social validity measures to the students who participated in their study. These researchers taught the safety skill of "what to do when lost in the community" to six students with moderate cognitive disabilities. In this study, the researchers focused on how to use cell phones when in the community. The students were taught either to answer their cell phone and give the caller (e.g., teacher) detailed information about where they were or to identify when they were lost and use the speed dial on their phone to gain assistance. In addition to interviewing teachers and paraprofessionals about the utility of the safety skill taught and if it was easy to teach, the researchers also interviewed the students both before and after the study. Prior to the study, students were asked if they would like to learn how to use a cell phone and if and why they considered this an important skill. Following the completion of the study, the students were queried if they liked learning the skill and if they still thought it was an important skill. Interestingly, before the intervention, many students' responses about why this skill was important had to do with social reasons (e.g., "I can look cool"); following intervention, all students responded that using a cell phone was important "in case you got lost."

Educational Validity

Voeltz and Evans (1983), in response to the narrow ways in which special education outcomes have been evaluated, offered the term *educational validity* to describe a more inclusive set of criteria for program evaluation for individuals with severe disabilities. To demonstrate educational validity, three criteria must be met. First, *internal validity* criteria must be met. That is, teachers should feel confident that the behavior change occurred as a function of the educational intervention.

Timothy's team reached consensus that, although they did not want to set an objective that Timothy sit in his seat for 15 minutes, having him sit in his seat long enough to complete a short activity would be a valuable goal. Mr. Grayson, familiar with the literature on the positive impact of choice on activity participation, suggested that their intervention be based on providing Timothy with more choices of activities and see if this strategy would increase the length of time he sat in his seat. Following intervention,

Mr. Grayson was happy to report to the team that the use of more choices seemed to be effective—Timothy was sitting for longer periods of time. His mother, however, questioned this finding when she shared with the team that she does not think he feels very well because of spring allergies and that in general he seems to be lethargic and sitting more. Mr. Grayson then wondered if the change in Timothy's in-seat behavior was a function of his new choice program or spring allergies.

Second, the criterion of *educational integrity* should be demonstrated. Educational integrity refers to the implementation of the procedures. It answers the question, "Did the educational intervention occur as specified in the treatment plan?" This is an important question to ask. Consider trying to analyze why a new intervention is not working. If we are not sure whether the various team members are implementing the strategy in the same way, we cannot determine if it is the program that is not effective or if it is just the inconsistent teaching. The final criterion is the *qualitative significance* (social validity) of the behavior change. Teams must question whether the behavior change benefited the student and was considered to be valuable by significant others in the student's natural environment (Voeltz & Evans, 1983).

Quality of Life
In addition to the qualitative aspects of social and educational validity, other criteria are increasingly being suggested as critical in the evaluation of program success. Meyer and Evans (1989) delineate eight possible outcomes to evaluate the effectiveness of a teaching program:

- Improvement in target behavior
- Acquisition of alternative skills and positive behaviors
- Positive collateral effects and absence of side effects
- Reduced need for and use of medical and crisis management services for the individual or others
- Less restrictive placements and greater participation in integrated community experiences
- Subjective quality-of-life improvement—happiness, satisfaction, and choices for the individual
- Perceptions of improvement by the family and significant others
- Expanded social relationships and informal support networks

Certain measurement procedures in community settings promote less-than-normalized lifestyles and interactions, thus detracting from the individual's quality of life. For example, teaching staff may be so interested in recording prompting levels necessary to complete a leisure activity that they forget to notice whether anyone is having fun (Brown, 1991; Brown & Lehr, 1993)! Professionals are recognizing that critical components of program evaluation are choice and control over one's life (e.g., Bambara, & Koger, 1996; Bannerman, Sheldon, Sherman, & Harchik, 1990; Brown, 1991; Brown & Lehr, 1993).

It is critical that each individual, to the greatest degree possible considering the child's age, have control over the activities in which he or she participates, the option to refuse participation, the sequence in which the activities take place, and the times at which activities occur (see also chapter 3). Opportunities for self-determination are also associated with better postschool outcomes (McGlashing-Johnson, Agran, Sitlington, Cavin, & Wehmeyer, 2003; Wehmeyer & Schwartz, 1997). Interestingly, Agran, Snow, and Swaner (1999) found that although most of the special education professionals he surveyed supported the notion that self-determination was an important outcome, they did not necessarily include IEP goals related to self-determination. Inclusion of these goals on the IEP would better ensure the team's commitment to self-determination.

Evaluating educational impact on quality-of-life factors is important if we are to take seriously our commitment to effecting and expecting meaningful change in the student's life. However, measurement of qualitative components of life is often challenging. For example, limited cognitive and communication skills make it difficult for educators and even families to understand a student's definitions or visions of quality of life (Brown, Gothelf, Guess, & Lehr, 1998). Holburn (2002) points out that often the strategies that are used to improve students' quality of life (e.g., person-centered planning) and the collateral outcomes of these strategies (e.g., community inclusion, improved relationships) are difficult to measure but nonetheless necessary.

Thus, recent trends look beyond simple quantitative reports and see each individual within the context of a meaningful life. Measurement strategies must support the evaluation of these important outcomes. The next sections discuss specific strategies relevant to process measures.

Accurate and Reliable Measurement

When a team has decided that a change in a student's behavior is a goal (e.g., increase social interactions, decrease inappropriate verbalizations, extend use of sign language to peers), one of the first steps in the process is to define the behavior. A precise description of the behavior is necessary to ensure that everyone is observing the same thing. For example, if "improve manners" is a goal, it is unlikely that the student, parents, teachers, teaching assistants, and therapists automatically agree on what "appropriate manners" are. To some, appropriate table manners mean sitting up straight, arms off the table, napkin in lap, and chewing with one's mouth closed. Others, however, may feel that some of these components are unnecessarily formal. Indeed, for some students, eating with their mouths closed is physically unrealistic.

To prevent ambiguity, an *operational definition* of the target behavior is created; that is, the behavior must be described in a way that is observable and measurable. Agreement on what constitutes a behavior is critical to the development of reliable and valid measurement and evaluation systems. The description of a behavior must be specific enough to allow two or more observers to read the definition and make the same judgment about the occurrence or nonoccurrence of the behavior (Baer, Wolf, & Risley, 1968). Table 5-1 compares terms that are vague and descriptions that are observable and measurable. These terms represent a sample of the goals determined for Timothy and Christine. The concepts of "functional" and "meaningful" behaviors should not be confused with the standard of describing behaviors in observable and measurable ways. Designing an operational definition to objectively describe a behavior does not ensure that the definition is functional or meaningful to an individual. For example, the statement "When shown either a red or blue block, Jenny will point to the red or blue block placed in front of her" is observable and measurable. It is not, however, a meaningful activity for Jenny.

Quantitative Measures

Teams must know whether each student's instructional program is effective in helping the student accomplish the objectives delineated in his or her IEP. Thus, process measures (or formative evaluation) are crucial to the ongoing assessment of instructional programs and student performance. Many teachers resist data collection because they feel they cannot afford

TABLE 5–1
Vague Versus Observable Descriptions of Behavior

Student	Vague	Observable
Timothy	Interacts appropriately with peers	Takes turns during board games
		Waves "hi" to peers when enters classroom in the morning
		Passes and receives materials to and from peers during group activities
	Improves grooming	Wipes face after meals
		Asks for assistance to tie shoes
	Increases academic skills	Signs or verbally identifies colors
		Signs or verbally identifies shapes
		Signs or verbally identifies pictures in a book
Christine	Increases community participation	Goes to grocery store with peer once each week to purchase snacks for drama class after school rehearsals
		Uses communication device to greet the cashier in the grocery store
	Understands job responsibilities	Completes sequence of job tasks recorded on communication device
		Requests help when needed during job tasks

the time. However, such teachers may find 4 months into the school year that their intervention is not working. A student with severe disabilities, or any other student, cannot afford to participate in an ineffective intervention for 4 months! Frequent and ongoing data collection provides us with ongoing feedback about the student's progress and provides important information to guide program modification.

Rationale

Research has shown that instructional decisions are enhanced with the use of data and that such decisions positively influence student performance (Farlow & Snell, 1994; Fuchs & Fuchs, 1986; Holvoet, O'Neil, Chazdon, Carr, & Warner, 1983; Utley et al., 1987; White, 1986). Fuchs and Fuchs (1986) found that teachers are more effective when they use student performance data rather than subjective teacher judgment for making instructional decisions. These researchers also found greater improvements in student performance when the teachers used graphed data rather than ungraphed data to make decisions. Utley et al., (1987) found that teachers and teachers in training make more accurate judgments about student performance when they use data (graphed, ungraphed, or both) than when they base their judgments on observation.

When teachers begin to measure individual student performance, some other advantages become obvious. Precise measurement of behavior allows teams to see even small changes in the behavior, giving everyone the message "Keep up the good work!" This encourages the continued use of promising instructional programs. Continuing an instructional strategy is frustrating when one does not feel that any progress is being made. Student performance data also allow the team to see when a program is not as effective as planned so that they can design modifications and not let precious instructional time be wasted.

Student performance data can enhance communication with others in the same ways that precise definitions of behavior do. Saying, based on intuition, that someone is "doing better in cooking" or "seems to be initiating interactions more frequently" is vague, subjective, and possibly inaccurate. Making a statement such as "Jenny is now preparing a sandwich with only two verbal prompts" or "Timothy now waves hello when he enters the classroom in the morning 4 out of 5 days each week" communicates clearer and more objective messages.

Testing and Training Data

Different levels of evaluation can occur for each objective identified on an IEP. Test conditions and training conditions provide two contexts for obtaining valuable data (Farlow & Snell, 1994). *Testing* means that a person's performance is checked under criterion conditions (i.e., conditions that as closely as possible use natural contexts, cues, and consequences). Thus, the teacher typically provides no prompting or teaching assistance, reinforcement for task success or improvement, or any corrections. The goal of testing is to learn about a student's current performance under criterion conditions (specified in the objective), not to teach the student. Thus, testing is "an evil necessity"; students do not learn when tested, but testing must be done as frequently as needed to get an accurate picture of their performance under criterion conditions.

During *training,* or teaching, conditions, data are recorded while a student is assisted as needed to "get responding going"; the student is provided instructional feedback, given corrections for errors, and provided with appropriate reinforcement. Learning is the goal of training, so conditions are planned to promote improvement in performance and to advance the learner through the various stages of learning.

Because of the absence of prompts and reinforcement during testing, a student's performance is typically less proficient than under training conditions. Test data thus represent conservative measures of learning but may more accurately represent a student's performance in natural, unaided situations. Test data taken on a skill before a teaching program is initiated are called baseline data; data taken on a skill under testing conditions once a teaching program has been initiated are called probe data.

When Christine was first learning how to use her communication board to greet the cashier in the grocery store, her teacher initially "tested" her at the grocery store (i.e., she did a baseline test). Test data showed that Christine was unable to activate the correct greeting symbol. Instruction was implemented to teach her this skill during daily sessions at school in which her teacher recorded training data. When Christine went to the grocery store, her teacher again recorded test data (probe data) to determine how she was performing the skill in the natural context. When Christine performed some but not all of the steps, her teacher noted this and then immediately began teaching to prevent any more difficulty.

Measurement Strategies

In this section, we review several ways to measure student performance. The strategy selected should suit the behavior to be measured and the situation. Some of the strategies are easy to use and require little time away from the usual routine; other strategies, however, take more planning and time. These more challenging strategies may be used when a challenging situation in the class warrants additional investigation. Table 5–2 summarizes these measurement strategies: (a) permanent products, (b) frequency recording, (c) percentage, (d) rate, (e) duration, (f) task-analytic measurement, and (g) interval recording and time sampling.

TABLE 5–2
Measurement Procedures Appropriate for Classrooms

Description of Measurement	Advantages	Disadvantages	Examples of Behaviors Measured
Permanent products Direct measurement of lasting and concrete results of a target behavior	• Does not require continuous observation • Permits analysis of products for error patterns	• Behavior must have a tangible result • No immediate feedback	• Appropriate behaviors: the number of newsletters folded and stapled • Inappropriate behaviors: the number of buttons ripped from clothing
Frequency recording The number of times a behavior occurs within a specified period of time	• Is useful with a wide variety of discrete behaviors • Can be easily accomplished in the classroom • May be converted to a rate	• Necessitates continuous attention during the observation period • Yields less accurate results with high rate behaviors or behaviors of varying duration • Inappropriate for behaviors of long duration	• Appropriate behaviors: spontaneous requests for materials needed; initiation of greetings • Inappropriate behaviors: talkouts, hits, incorrect color sorting
Percentage The number correct compared with the number of opportunities (or intervals)	• Useful when the number of opportunities varies across sessions • Can be used to report task analytic measurements, duration, interval, and time sampling data	• Cannot distinguish the number of opportunities from the score • Cannot be used if there is no ceiling on the number of opportunities	• Appropriate behavior: Independent eating, correct signing • Inappropriate behavior: hits, self-injury, cursing, etc, if measured through interval recording or time sampling
Rate The frequency of a behavior and its relation to time expressed as a ratio	• Useful when the number of opportunities varies across sessions • Reflects proficiency	• Cannot distinguish the total time of the observation period	• Appropriate behavior: vocational tasks completed per minute, social interactions per hour • Inappropriate behavior: call outs per class period
Duration The total amount of time in which a targeted behavior occurs in a specified observation	• Yields a precise record of the length of the occurrence of a behavior • May be used to record the duration of each incident of behavior	• Necessitates continuous attention during the observation period • Requires a stopwatch for best accuracy • Inappropriate for frequent behaviors of short duration	• Appropriate behavior: attending to lesson, completion of hygiene routine • Inappropriate behavior: tantrums, stereotyped behavior

TABLE 5–2 (Continued)
Measurement Procedures Appropriate for Classrooms

Description of Measurement	Advantages	Disadvantages	Examples of Behaviors Measured
Task analytic measurement A record of the performance of each step in a sequence of behaviors comprising a task	• Useful in most skills in domestic, vocational, leisure and community domains • May be used to guide instruction • Enables a measurement of each behavior that comprises a skill • Can be summarized as a meaningful percentage or number of steps	• Requires a good task analysis of the skill being measured • Not suitable for measuring inappropriate behaviors • May focus too much on motor skills, neglecting qualitative aspects of the task	• Appropriate behaviors: bedmaking, playing a CD, assembly tasks, preparing a snack
Interval recording A record of the occurrence of behavior within each segment of time (intervals) within a single observation	• Requires less effort than continuous frequency or duration methods • Does not require as precise a definition of a unit of behavior • Applicable to a wide range of behaviors	• Provides an estimate only • The size of the interval must be appropriate for the behavior frequency • Accuracy is facilitated by timers or taperecorded countings of intervals	• Appropriate and inappropriate behaviors: any of the behaviors listed for frequency or duration
Whole interval Records whether behavior occurred continuously throughout the interval	• Useful when it is important to know that the behavior is not interrupted	• Underestimates the magnitude of the target behavior	• Appropriate behaviors: on-task behavior, engagement in play
Partial interval Records whether behavior occurred at any time within the interval	• Useful for behaviors that may occur in fleeting moments	• Overestimates the magnitude of the target behavior	• Appropriate behaviors: social interactions • Inappropriate behaviors: hitting, hand biting, tantrum
Momentary time sampling Records whether behavior occurred at the moment the interval ends	• Useful for behaviors that tend to persist for a while • Does not require continuous observation • Can be used with more than one student at a time	• Must sample at frequent and relatively short intervals	• Appropriate behaviors: on-task behavior, engagement in play • Inappropriate behaviors: tantrums, off-task behavior

Permanent Products

Many behaviors have a concrete result, or product, that lasts. Unlike behaviors that must be directly observed as they occur, behaviors that result in a product or physical outcome can be evaluated after the individual has performed the behavior. For example, Timothy's parents need not sit by his bed all night long to observe toileting accidents. Rather, evidence of accidents can be observed by looking at or touching the child's sheet in the morning. Jenny's teacher can simply look over her journal to check for the number and length of sentences written. Permanent product measures provide opportunities to detect error and quality patterns (e.g., particular words or sounds that may be problematic for Jenny). Because measurement of permanent products does not require continuous observation, it is convenient for classroom use.

Frequency Recording

Some behaviors are transitory and must be measured as they occur. Frequency recording measures the number of times a behavior (appropriate or inappropriate) occurs within a specified period of time (e.g., the number of times that a student throws his or her work materials onto the floor during a 30-minute work session, the number of times that the student greets people appropriately throughout the school day). Frequency has been used to measure many types of behaviors. Souza and Kennedy (2003) measured the frequency of social interactions (lasting longer than 15 minutes) that a 20-year-old student had with people without disabilities during a bus ride and at a food mall. Cooper and Browder (1998) counted the frequency of independent choices three adults with severe disabilities made in a variety of fast-food restaurants.

In order to have meaningful frequency data, it is necessary to specify the length of the particular time period and to compare data from the same length of time only. For example, a teacher may report that her student bit her hand 15 times on Monday but only five times on Tuesday. This certainly sounds like excellent progress. However, if the teacher observed the student for 3 hours on Monday but for only 1 hour on Tuesday, it is not possible to conclude whether there was any progress.

Behaviors measured in this way should be readily divided into discrete units, with a clear beginning and end, and be easily visible and countable. For example, stereotyped behavior, such as hand waving, may occur at such a high rate that it is impossible to count accurately. Attempting a frequency count of vocalizations may also be difficult if each vocalization does not have a clear beginning and a clear end. For these two examples, another measurement method (such as duration or interval) should be selected in place of frequency.

Finally, behaviors measured in this way should be relatively uniform in length and not occur for long periods of time. For example, a parent may report that her child sucked his thumb only two times. This is not helpful information if each occurrence of thumb sucking lasts 45 minutes! The frequency, in this case, does not reflect the amount of behavior. Other measures, such as duration, would be more appropriate for such behaviors. Frequency recordings would accurately measure Jenny's correct coin and value identification and the number of times Timothy waved to his teacher and peers.

Percentage

A percentage score can be used when a behavior can occur a fixed number of times in an observation session rather than an undetermined number of times. Percentage is calculated by dividing the number of behaviors observed by the number of opportunities to perform that behavior. This type of measure is used frequently in the general education system to evaluate mastery of academic concepts (e.g., percentage of words correctly spelled, percentage of math problems correctly completed). Timothy's teacher used a percentage to measure social interactions when she counted how many times he passed the materials to his neighbor when it was his turn; on one day she recorded correct responses for two of the five opportunities occurring during the morning song, or 40% of the opportunities. Percentages can also be used to measure the number of intervals in which a behavior occurred.

Many educators use percentages to measure performance on task-analyzed activities. For example, Taber et al., (2003) used a least-to-most prompting strategy to teach six secondary-age students with moderate cognitive disabilities the safety skill of using a cell phone when lost in the community. Students participated in a 10-step task analyses (i.e., either "answering the cell phone and providing information to gain assistance" or "identifying when lost and using speed dial on the cell phone"). Student performance on each of the steps was measured, and a percentage of steps correctly completed was calculated. These researchers found that all students learned 100% of their steps and were considered independent in the use of cell phones according to their task analyses.

Percentage measures are not appropriate when the number of opportunities to perform a behavior is not fixed or controlled. For example, it is inappropriate to write an objective that states that Christine will "greet her peers 80% of the time" if her teacher cannot determine the number of opportunities Christine has to greet her peers.

Rate

Rate can be used to determine the frequency of a behavior and its relation to time. A rate is expressed by the ratio of the number of behaviors divided by the unit of time (e.g., Jessie threw her materials on the floor 15 times in a 30-minute session, or 0.5 times per minute). In vocational training situations, for example, a goal may be to increase the number of cleaning tasks completed in a certain amount of time (e.g., from washing 5 windows in 30 minutes, or .17 per minute, to 10 windows in 30 minutes, or .33 per minute). Using communication books to remind students of possible conversation topics, Hughes et al. (2000) measured the rate of initiating interactions with familiar and unfamiliar general education conversational partners of five high school students. These researchers measured how frequently the participant initiated social interactions within a set period of time and then converted the frequency to a rate per minute.

Rate is also a helpful measure when the observation time of a session varies (e.g., to measure the number of spoonfuls of food Christine eats per minute with her self-feeder when the length of lunch time varies). An advantage of using rate to measure performance is that rate reflects both accuracy and speed, or fluency of performance, rather than just accuracy (Billingsley & Liberty, 1982).

Duration

A duration recording is used if the focus is the amount of time an individual is engaged in a specific behavior or activity. Sometimes it is desirable for a person to increase the amount of time engaged in an activity (e.g., brushing teeth, exercising, studying), and sometimes it is desirable for an individual to decrease the amount of time spent in an activity (e.g., watching television, displaying self-injurious behavior). Duration measures the total amount of time in which a targeted behavior occurs within a specified time period.

Harvey, Baker, Horner, and Blackford (2003) used duration of sleep to explore the presence of sleep problems in individuals with intellectual impairments living in community settings. They found that while the duration of sleeping of individuals in their sample was similar to those without disabilities, the quality of sleep was different (e.g., waking up in the middle of the night) as a function of the interaction between level of disability and the use of medications. Duration has also been used to record the number of minutes spent working when using a self-operated auditory prompting system (Grossi, 1998), to record the time that students were engaged in social interaction (Gaylord-Ross, Haring, Breen, & Pitts-Conway, 1984), and to identify reinforcer preferences by comparing duration of time spent operating various battery-controlled devices (Wacker, Berg, Wiggins, Muldoon, & Cavanaugh, 1985).

Duration can be recorded in three ways: (a) a total duration, (b) a percentage of time, and (c) by measuring each occurrence. In the total duration method, the teacher records the total amount of time the individual spent engaged in the behavior in the observation period. For example, Timothy's teacher may be interested in measuring the amount of time he spends engaged in independent play. Before starting the duration measure, the teacher must operationally define appropriate and independent play for Timothy, making sure that it is possible to clearly determine the onset and termination of the behavior. The teacher can then monitor the behavior using a stopwatch that is unobtrusively carried in her dress pocket. All the teacher has to do is to start the stopwatch when Timothy starts playing. As soon as he stops playing (e.g., participates instead in self-stimulatory behavior), the teacher stops the stopwatch. The teacher starts and stops the stopwatch accordingly for the course of the playtime. The amount of time accumulated on the stopwatch at the end of the playtime reflects a total duration.

A percentage of time can be derived by simply dividing the total time engaged in the activity by the length of the playtime. For example, Timothy may have played for a total of 5 minutes in a 15-minute playtime. The following equation represents the process for determining the percentage of time:

$$\frac{\text{Total duration of behavior}}{\text{Length of observation period}} = \frac{5 \text{ minutes}}{15 \text{ minutes}} = 33\%$$

Although the duration measure is simple and accurate (if the behavior is clearly defined), another piece of information makes the duration measure even more informative: the frequency of each occurrence. For example, we know that Timothy participated in playing for 5 minutes (or 33% of playtime); however, we do not know whether he played for 5 minutes in a row or if he played for only 30 seconds at a time but kept returning to the play area. Such information may be valuable in determining the type of intervention to use with Timothy to increase his play skills. The method of *measuring each occurrence* provides this information, although it is more time consuming than the previous two methods. To measure the occurrences, the teacher would start the stopwatch when Timothy started to play, turn the stopwatch off when he stopped playing, and then record the duration on a data sheet. The teacher would then return the stopwatch to 0. When Timothy started to play again, the teacher would start the stopwatch and have it continue until he stopped playing. When Timothy stopped again, the teacher would record this duration, and so on. At the end of the observation period (e.g., 15 minutes), the teacher would have a record of total duration (e.g., 5 minutes) as well as a count of the number of times Timothy started and stopped playing (e.g., eight times). In this case, the goal would be to increase the duration of time Timothy spent playing and to decrease the number of times that he got distracted from playing.

Task-Analytic Measurement

Task-analytic measurement focuses on a student's performance on a sequence, or chain, of behaviors during teaching or during testing. This type of measurement is the most frequently used method of instruction and evaluation of student performance of routines or complex activities. To implement task-analytic measurement, a teacher conducts a task analysis (see chapter 4), designs a data sheet to record student performance, and then records the student's performance on each of the steps delineated in the task analysis (or some portion of the steps if using backward or forward chaining).

During teaching, there are a variety of ways in which the teacher may evaluate the student: by recording a plus (+) or minus (−), by recording the prompt level (e.g., verbal or physical prompt) required for the student to complete the step, or by using another type of measure (e.g., the amount of time to complete a step). If the teacher is using a total task-chaining strategy (see chapter 4), then all the steps in the task analysis are scored. If the teacher is using a partial participation strategy or using forward chaining or backward chaining, then only the steps that the student is working on are scored. Table 5–3 shows a task analysis for the skill of making a peanut butter sandwich. Because Jenny can participate extensively in this type of activity, her teacher chose to use a total task-chaining strategy and a least-to-most prompting procedure. But, as Jenny's behavior has clearly indicated that she prefers not to be guided and touched in this way, her team decided to teach Jenny using just the verbal and model prompts. It was agreed that if Jenny did not complete a

step of the task analysis independently after a verbal prompt or a model, which was typically sufficient, the teacher would simply complete that step for her and allow her the opportunity to perform the next step of the sequence.

In general, Jenny's data reflect that she is slowly moving toward criterion; at the beginning of the week she achieved 60%, and at the end of the week she achieved 72%. Keeping track of individual steps of her task analysis, however, allows more detailed analysis that can contribute to constructive program modifications. Looking at individual steps on her data sheet reveals a few steps that seem to be problematic for her. Jenny is unable to open the peanut butter jar (step 12) and consistently requires *models* to complete step 5 (getting bread from bread box) and step 8 (getting plate). This information will allow her team to consider some modifications or adaptations for these steps. For example, should Jenny be provided with a rubber gripper that might make opening the jar easier? Should she be taught instead to ask someone for assistance to open up the jar? Could the bread box and the plates be moved closer to her to make accessing them easier? Or might pictures be helpful as a prompt to remind her of where the items that are needed are kept?

Table 5–4 shows another task analysis for the same activity. Christine, however, is expected to participate partially in the activity. Christine is scored on eight steps of the task, and her teacher (or peer for step 2) completes the steps that are marked with an X. Extension and enrichment skills (e.g., initiation, social skills, monitoring skills) form the steps in which Christine can likely achieve independence. These components allow for meaningful participation and control of the activity even though she cannot perform most of the motor components of the task (see chapter 3 and 4). The prompt procedure for Christine includes physical assistance.

During testing, task-analytic measurement can be carried out by using the *single-opportunity* or the *multiple-opportunity* method. The easiest, although less informative, method is the single-opportunity method. This approach is carried out as follows:

1. Conditions (including materials) are arranged as planned in the instructional program.
2. The instructional cue (if any) is given when the student is attending.
3. The student's response to each step in the task analysis is recorded until an error occurs.

TABLE 5–3
Jenny's Task Analysis for Making a Peanut Butter Sandwich

Name: Jenny   Teacher: Ms. Alpern

Activity: Making a peanut butter sandwich

Materials: Peanut butter sandwich supplies

Record number that indicates amount of assistance: 0, teacher completes; 1, model; 2, verbal; 3, independent

Routine steps	9/6/04	9/13/04	9/27/04	10/4/04
1. Initiate snack by going to home economics class	3	3	3	3
2. Go to refrigerator	2	2	2	2
3. Get out peanut butter	2	2	2	2
4. Put peanut butter on counter	2	2	3	3
5. Get bread from bread box	1	1	1	1
6. Put bread on counter	2	2	2	3
7. Get butter knife	1	1	1	2
8. Get plate	1	1	1	1
9. Put knife and plate on counter	3	3	2	3
10. Open bread bag	1	1	1	2
11. Remove two slices onto plate	3	3	3	3
12. Open peanut butter jar	0	0	0	0
13. Scoop out peanut butter with knife	1	1	2	1
14. Spread peanut butter on one slice	3	3	3	3
15. Repeat until preferred thickness	3	3	3	3
16. Put other slice on top	1	2	1	2
17. Put knife in sink	1	1	1	2
18. Put peanut butter away	2	2	2	2
19. Get napkin	1	2	2	2
20. Bring sandwich and napkin to table	3	3	3	3
Total	36/60 (60%)	38/60 (63%)	38/60 (63%)	43/60 (72%)

Dates

TABLE 5–4
Christine's Task Analysis for Making a Peanut Butter Sandwich

Name: Christine
Teacher: Ms. Washington

Activity: Making a peanut butter sandwich

Materials: Peanut butter sandwich supplies; meal preparation overlay for communication board

Record number that indicates amount of assistance: X, teacher or peer completes; 1, full physical; 2, partial physical; 3, model; 4, verbal; 5, independent

Routine steps	Dates				
	10/7/04	10/8/04	10/9/04	10/10/04	10/11/04
1. Initiate snack by activating communication device					
2. Peer assists into home economics class	X	X	X	X	X
3. Press switch when "peanut butter" is scanned on communication device					
4. Press switch when "bread" is scanned on communication device					
5. Teacher gets items, puts on counter	X	X	X	X	X
6. Press switch when "knife" is scanned on communication device					
7. Press switch when "plate" is scanned on communication device					
8. Press switch when "napkin" is scanned on communication device					
9. Teacher gets items, puts on counter	X	X	X	X	X
10. Teacher makes sandwich	X	X	X	X	X
11. Teacher gives her a sample of sandwich and asks if sandwich is OK	X	X	X	X	X
12. Press switch when "yes/no" is scanned on communication device					
13. Teacher fixes sandwich as necessary	X	X	X	X	X
14. Press switch when "thank you" is scanned on communication device					
Total					

4. The following rules can be used to handle errors, periods of no response, and inappropriate behavior:
   • Testing is stopped after the first error, and all remaining steps are scored as errors.
   • After a specified latency period of no response (e.g., 3 seconds), testing is stopped, and all remaining steps are scored as errors.
   • After a specified period of inappropriate behavior (e.g., 10 seconds of stereotypic behavior) or after a single inappropriate response (e.g., throwing

the soap or the towel), testing is stopped, and all remaining steps are scored as errors.

For many tasks, the steps performed are scored as correct if they correspond to the task description, regardless of the order in which they are carried out, as long as the result is satisfactory. For example, it is not important whether Timothy pulls his right or left arm out of his coat first. However, for many other tasks (e.g., certain assembly tasks), performing each step in order is crucial to the successful completion of the activity. In tasks where order is important, the first step out of sequence is scored as an error. In addition, when the rate of performance is important (as specified in the criteria or standards), the maximum length of time allowed is specified.

> *Once each week, Ms. Alpern probed Jenny's performance on packing her book bag. Using the single-opportunity method, Ms. Alpern observed Jenny following two instructional cues. First, she gave the entire class the instruction that they need to get their things together to go to music. Second, she told Jenny, as she always does before activity changes, to check her picture schedule to see what the next class is and what she needs to take with her. Following the natural cue of the other students in the class, she began to gather some things together. Ms. Alpern scored a "+" on her data sheet for the first three steps: taking out her book bag, unzipping it, and putting in her pencils. After these first three steps of the task analysis, Jenny stood up to join her friends in the front of the room. Ms. Alpern scored a "−" on her data sheet to indicate that she did not independently perform the fourth step of putting her music book in her bag. According to the single-opportunity testing method, all remaining steps were scored "−." Ms. Alpern then proceeded to implement teaching.*

The single-opportunity method generally is completed quickly. It provides a conservative estimate of the student's skills. Less instructional time is wasted because teaching can begin immediately after the first error. Further, learning is less likely to occur during testing; therefore, the single-opportunity method provides a more accurate estimate of the effect of instruction. However, a disadvantage of the method is that performance on task-analytic steps that occur after the first error are not measured because testing is terminated at this point. Thus, probes (testing done once intervention has started) do not initially reflect learning on later steps, and performance is underestimated. If a teacher is using backward chaining (i.e., teaching the last step first), the single-opportunity probe does not reflect any progress until training advances to the earlier steps in the chain. Therefore, in these cases, the multiple-opportunity probe produces more information.

The multiple-opportunity method used the following steps:

1. Conditions are arranged as planned in the instructional program.

2. The instructional cue (if any) is given when the student is attending.
3. The student's responses to each step in the task analysis are recorded as correct or incorrect (i.e., performed correctly or not performed at all).
4. Whenever an error occurs after a specified period of no response or inappropriate behavior, the step is completed by the teacher rather than by prompting the student to perform the step. Basically, the student is positioned for each step that follows an error, so performance on every step can be assessed.

In both assessment approaches, feedback is not provided to the student on the performance of the targeted skill. Withholding feedback differentiates between conditions of testing (which represent the most difficult conditions specified in the objective) and the conditions of teaching (when prompts and reinforcement are available). For some students, noncontingent reinforcement may be made available (i.e., reinforcement for something other than performance of the task or generic praise, like "Keep up the hard work!") to hold their interest during assessment.

Interval Recording

To use interval recording, the observer divides an observation session into short, equal intervals, and the occurrence of behavior within each interval is recorded. Interval recording is useful for those behaviors that do not have discrete start or stop times and that vary in length (Schloss & Smith, 1998), that are continuous (i.e., of longer duration), or that are high frequency (Alberto & Troutman, 2003). Interval recording has been used to measure both appropriate behaviors (e.g., peer social initiations and interactions in inclusive settings) and inappropriate behaviors (e.g., stereotypic, aggressive) in schools and other community settings (Frea, 1997; Hunt, Alwell, Farron-Davis, & Goetz, 1996; Koegel, Stiebel, & Koegel, 1998; Lee & Odom, 1996; Umbreit, Lane, & Dejud, 2004).

There are two types of interval recording strategies: whole interval and partial interval. In whole-interval strategies, the observer notes if behavior occurred continuously throughout the interval.

> *Christine's drama teacher thought that she was losing interest in the play. Lately, rehearsals were quite tedious, often focusing on just one or two students, with the other students sitting and reading or doing*

homework from other classes. In order to assess this, her teacher asked Christine's teaching assistant to conduct a whole-interval recording for 5 minutes, once at the beginning of the class, once in the middle of the class session, and once toward the end of the class session. Each of the 5-minute periods were divided into 30 brief intervals of 10 seconds. The teaching assistant noted whether Christine was engaged throughout each 10-second interval in either watching the play or interacting with others. Christine's teacher found that Christine was mostly inattentive to the play and had few interactions with her peers during these times. The first observation at the beginning of class revealed that she was engaged for 10 of 30 intervals (or 33%). In the middle of class, she was engaged for 5 of 30 intervals (or about 17%), and at the end of class it was only 2 of 30 intervals (or 6%). Christine's engagement decreased as the class period progressed. Christine's teacher, teaching assistant, and two of her friends decided that they needed to make sure that Christine had something to do during these downtimes.

In partial interval recording, the observer notes if the behavior occurs at all during the interval rather than if it occurs continuously throughout the interval. Once a behavior is observed and noted on the data sheet, further observation is not required for the remainder of that interval. Exactly how many times the behavior occurs during each interval is not recorded. Thus, interval recording provides an estimate of the occurrence of behavior. Because of this, interval size must be carefully chosen, only limited conclusions can be drawn from the data, and the data must be interpreted cautiously (Alberto & Troutman, 2003).

Timothy seems to be by himself more and more during free play, not interacting with other children. Mr. Grayson decides that they will use a partial interval recording to get a better idea of how much time Timothy is spending alone. Mr. Grayson selects a 10-minute period of time in the middle of the 9:30 a.m. free play and a 10-minute period of time during the 11:30 a.m. free play. Then he divides each of these observation sessions into 10 equal 1-minute intervals. Mr. Grayson records a plus (+) in the box if Timothy has any type of interaction with another student during the interval and a minus (−) if there is no interaction. Figure 5-1 shows that Timothy had interactions with other children in 2 of the 10 intervals during early morning free play (or 20%). The

data do not tell us, however, if Timothy had two very brief interactions with other children or spent a full 2 minutes interacting with them. Timothy had interactions with other children in 6 of the 10 intervals (60%) during the 11:30 free play.

If Mr. Grayson repeated this observation for a week, following implementation of an instructional strategy to increase interactions, he may still find no change in the data. However, it is possible that Timothy is having a significantly greater number of interactions with his peers, but because the interactions were clustered within two or three of the intervals, the progress cannot be seen. In this case, the results of the interval recording may be misleading.

Data from the 11:30 a.m. free play interval show a higher percentage of peer interaction (60% of the intervals). Continued recording will reveal either that this is an unusual day or if it is typical for Timothy to interact more with his peers in the later free play time. If Timothy interacts more in the later play session, then Mr. Grayson can analyze that play time to determine what variables might be contributing to the increased level of peer interaction. Comments on the data sheet suggest the possibility that when other students are loud, it may inhibit Timothy from interacting with them and that musical toys may contribute to increased interactions. Mr. Grayson can now investigate these variables further.

Selection of the appropriate interval method should be guided by the characteristics of the behavior and the goals of intervention. If the behavior is brief and the goal is to have the behavior occur on a consistent but not necessarily continuous basis (such as Timothy's interactions), the partial interval method must be used, or the behavior will not be detected. Other behaviors, such as attention to a task, appropriately occur in a more continuous fashion (such as Christine's attending example). Such behaviors are best measured by the whole-interval strategy.

When measuring behaviors targeted for reduction, it is best to use the method that provides the most rigorous information. For example, if the whole-interval method is used to record the extent of self-injurious behavior, the interval is checked only if the self-injury occurs for the entire length of the interval. It is possible for the data to reflect no occurrences when in fact the student engaged in extensive self-injury but not *continuous* self-injury. Thus, the partial interval method would be more appropriate.

FIGURE 5–1
Partial Interval Recording Form for Timothy's Peer Interactions

Name:	Timothy	Teacher:	Mr. Grayson
Date:	November 2, 2004	Behavior:	Peer interaction
Code:	(+) peer interaction; (–) no peer interaction		

9:30 Free Play

10 minutes

Minutes	1	2	3	4	5	6	7	8	9	10
	–	+	–	–	–	+	–	–	–	–

Total: 20%

11:30 Free Play

10 minutes

Minutes	1	2	3	4	5	6	7	8	9	10
	–	+	+	+	–	+	+	–	+	–

Total: 60%

Comments: *Seemed to initiate and sustain interactions when musical toys are involved. When other children got loud, Timothy seemed to move away.*

The length of the interval depends on both the behavior being observed (its average length and frequency) and the observer's ability to record the behavior, but interval length usually is measured in seconds (e.g., 5, 10, 30 seconds). The more frequent the behavior, the smaller the interval for observation should be so that the data yield a more accurate representation of behavior.

If large intervals (e.g., 15 minutes) were used with partial interval recording to measure Jenny's frequent behavior of smiling, for example, 100% would be the typical result. In other words, it is almost certain that Jenny would smile at least once within each 15-minute interval. This is not informative, for it does not provide knowledge of the density of the behavior, that is, if Jenny smiled 5 times or 150 times.

For behaviors that occur infrequently, the partial interval method can have longer intervals. For example, because Timothy infrequently initiates interactions

with his peers, observing for 30-second intervals makes no sense. It is not likely that Timothy will display the behavior within 30 seconds. However, if the interval is made too large, any instance of the behavior can artificially inflate the percentage of intervals. Thus, if Timothy interacts only two times in an hour but the intervals are 30 minutes long, statistically Timothy interacted for 100% of the intervals! This certainly does not reflect the quality of Timothy's behavior. Five-minute intervals might be more appropriate.

Interval recording cannot be done casually, as a teacher's total attention must be directed toward the student during the entire observation time. In addition, the teacher must know when to move from one interval to the next. It can be challenging to teach and collect interval data at the same time (Alberto & Troutman, 2003). A watch or clock with a second hand can be used to time the intervals, but checking the time interrupts the observer's concentration; a portable tape recorder with a tape of prerecorded intervals and earplugs may eliminate this problem, though it is somewhat obvious. Some observers build in a brief time period (e.g., 5 seconds) for recording between observation intervals (Alberto & Troutman, 2003). For longer intervals (e.g., 3 to 5 minutes), inexpensive egg timers and kitchen timers have been used. Still, teachers must be sensitive to the environment and should be as unobtrusive as possible. For example, it would be distracting to have a beep sound every 10 seconds when observing Christine's attention in her drama class.

Time Sampling

Time sampling is a type of interval measure that can be used more practically in teaching settings. As in the whole- or partial interval recording strategy, a specified observation period (e.g., 30 minutes) is divided into small units (e.g., 5-minute intervals). However, unlike interval recording, where a teacher observes the behavior throughout the entire interval, the teacher observes the student only at the *end* of the interval. Time sampling usually uses longer intervals (minutes) than does interval recording (seconds) (Maag, 1999). The teacher records on the data sheet whether the student was or was not engaging in the target behavior at the end of each interval. For example, Reinhartsen, Garfinkle, and Wolery (2002) investigated the effect of child choice of toys versus teacher choice of toys on the engaged and problem behaviors of three 2-year-old boys with autism in an inclusive preschool classroom. Using a time-sampling strategy, these researchers divided the play period into small intervals of time (30 seconds) and observed the children's behaviors at the end of every 5 seconds. The researchers found that when children chose the toys to play with, there was an increase in engaged time and fewer problem behaviors for two of the three boys.

Implementation of time sampling can be done flexibly. Instead of continuously observing and recording at the end of each interval, the teacher can set up random intervals within an observation period. For example, the teacher may decide on an observation period of 1 hour and select six random times to observe (rather than exactly every 10 minutes).

It is also possible to use time sampling across the day and randomly identify observation times. For example, Mr. Grayson could choose to use time sampling (instead of interval recording) to record Timothy's interactions with peers across the 3-hour day at school (e.g., centers, snack, lunch, circle time). This strategy is relevant if the goal is for Timothy to increase interaction with his peers across many activities, not just during playtime.

Because time sampling does not require continuous observation, teaching and data collection can occur simultaneously (Alberto & Troutman, 2003; Maag, 1999). In addition, because the observation is so quick (was the behavior occurring or not occurring at that moment?), teachers can use the strategy with more than one student at a time (Schloss & Smith, 1998). For example, a teacher could record the on-task behavior of a group of students at the end of every 2-minute interval during independent seat work. Every 2 minutes, the teacher would look up and see which of the students were or were not engaged in their independent work (previously defined by the teacher). She would record a "+" for those who were engaged and a "−" for those not engaged.

Like interval recording, however, time sampling provides only an estimate of the behavior. In fact, for low-frequency and short-duration behaviors, time sampling is even less accurate than interval recording. The less frequent or briefer a behavior, the shorter the interval must be. (Because a teacher is checking at the end of the interval only, he may miss the behavior if it does not occur frequently or if it is of short duration.) Thus, time sampling is most appropriate for measuring behaviors that occur frequently and are of long duration.

Data Sheets

Data sheets must allow teachers to systematically record data from their observations (e.g., frequency data, task-analytic data, interval data). It is important to record in a format that will allow subsequent data analysis. For example, some student performance data can provide the information for error analyses (e.g., which steps of the task analysis are consistently missed, such as in Table 5–3), and most data can be converted into graphs for easier visual analysis.

The basic elements of a data sheet are (a) the student's name; (b) the observer's name; (c) the date, time, and location of the observation; (d) the length of the observation; (e) the behavior(s) observed and, if necessary, a brief observable description of each; (f) adequate space for data recording (e.g., room for a 15-step task analysis or 10 2-minute intervals); (g) a scoring code; (h) a data summary; and (i) comments (see Figure 5–1 and Tables 5–3 and 5–4). In addition to providing the range of information necessary to make effective instructional decisions, a data sheet can also assist in functional behavioral assessment (Brown, 1991) (see chapter 6 for a discussion of functional behavioral assessment). For example, in the time-sampling procedure to measure Timothy's interactions with his peers across the day, his teacher could specify the time of day and the activity in which the data were measured. With this type of information, it is possible to analyze the events or variables (e.g., activities, time of day, different peers, materials) contributing to the presence or absence of peer interactions. Adding an extra column on the data sheet for recording the incidence of an inappropriate behavior may enable the teacher to see a trend in the relationship between an inappropriate behavior and the time of day or type of activity.

Measures of Accuracy

Because important decisions are made on the basis of data, team members must have confidence in the data they collect. Consider the following example where the relationship between accurate data collection and effective program evaluation is obvious.

Data recorded by Jenny's teaching assistant indicate that she can prepare her snack with only two verbal prompts. However, when her teacher assists Jenny in this activity, she finds that Jenny needs not only significant verbal prompts but also gestural cues. The discrepancy in these data may be because Jenny is not accustomed to preparing her snack with her teacher. If this is the case, then certain programmatic changes can help Jenny generalize her snack preparation skills in the presence of others. However, it is also possible that someone is not recording Jenny's data accurately. If this is the case, changes focusing on generalization would not be appropriate. Efforts should instead focus on increasing the accuracy, or reliability, of the data collection.

Interobserver (or Interrater) Reliability

Interobserver reliability is assessed to determine whether the target behavior is being recorded accurately (Miltenberger, 1997). One way to ensure that data are accurate, or reliable, is to have two independent observers record the behavior of a student at the same time, compare the two observations, and mathematically determine the extent of agreement of the data. The percentage of interobserver reliability can be calculated by dividing the number of agreements between the two observers by the number of agreements plus disagreements and multiplying by 100. The result of this calculation is a *percentage of agreement:*

$$\frac{\text{Agreements}}{\text{Agreements} + \text{Disagreements}} = \frac{\text{Percentage of}}{\text{Agreement}}$$

For example, two teachers use a partial interval recording to observe the presence of a specified behavior. A 5-minute observation period is divided into 10 30-second intervals. Each time they observe the target behavior, they record an X in the correct cell. The results of the observation are as follows:

30-second intervals	1	2	3	4	5	6	7	8	9	10
Teacher 1	X	X		X		X			X	X
Teacher 2	X	X	X	X		X			X	X

According to this formula, the reliability between the two teachers is as follows:

$$\frac{9 \text{ agreements}}{9 \text{ agreements} + 1 \text{ disagreement}} = \frac{9}{10} = 90\% \text{ agreement}$$

Generally, a reliability coefficient of .80, or 80%, is considered acceptable. Poor interrater reliability should prompt the team to improve their agreement in ways such as clarifying the behavioral definition of the behavior being observed, further training for staff collecting the data, or simplifying the observational system (Schloss & Smith, 1998).

Procedural Reliability

Procedural reliability (also referred to as treatment integrity) is the degree to which program procedures are implemented accurately. Procedural reliability asks the question, Did the teacher follow the instructional plan? If we do not assess the accuracy of the implementation of a program and a student is not having success, then we could not determine if it was actually the intervention that was ineffective (Lane & Beebe-Frankenberger, 2004). In an extensive discussion of procedural reliability, Billingsley, White, and Munson (1980) point out that all relevant variables of a program must be evaluated. Program components such as delivery of reinforcers, use of prompts, program setup, antecedent events, and consequent events should be examined (Billingsley et al., 1980). A behavioral checklist of each intervention procedure can be designed, and the teacher can "check off" each component used (Kerr & Nelson, 1998). Lane and Beebe-Frankenberger (2004) suggest designing checklists of the specific instructional components expected to be implemented by the educator. This checklist would then be used to assess whether the procedure was followed. Following are some specific questions to consider when assessing procedural reliability:

- Is the instructional plan implemented as frequently as planned?
- Does the instructor use the correct sequence and timing of instructional prompts?
- Does the instructor deliver the appropriate consequences?
- Are instructional cues delivered in the manner designated in the program plan?
- Were all the necessary instructional materials available?
- Was the program implemented in the correct environment?

Procedural reliability can be calculated in much the same way as interobserver reliability. Billingsley et al. (1980) offer the following formula:

$$\text{Procedural reliability (\%)} = \frac{(\text{TA} \times 100)}{\text{TT}}$$

In this formula, TA is the number of teacher behaviors in accordance with the program plan, and TT is the total number of teacher behaviors that could have been performed in accordance with the program plan. As an example, Christine was supposed to participate in the library with her nondisabled peers eight times each month (twice each week) but participated only six times last month. Applying this formula to intervention frequency, the procedural reliability is

$$\text{Procedural reliability (\%)} = \frac{6 \times 100}{8} = 75\%$$

Graphs

Although analysis of information on a data sheet may provide important details about performance during an instructional session (e.g., specific steps performed correctly or missed on a task analysis, number of interactions at the beginning versus the end of free time), there are significant limitations to leaving data in this form. For example, it is difficult to interpret or analyze

behavioral data from a data sheet alone, especially when weeks of data are considered. Behavioral data can be most effectively interpreted and analyzed when they are graphed. Graphs allow teachers to more easily detect trends of progress and thus to make more effective program decisions. When trends are positive, many teachers also find graphs reinforcing, as they are a continual source of feedback.

Although some teachers initially feel apprehensive or intimidated by graphs, most soon discover that graphs are actually simple to design and read. A graph is made up of two axes (Figure 5–2). The abscissa, or the x-axis, is the horizontal line. The abscissa usually represents the time frame of a measurement (e.g., each data point reflects the data from a day, week, or month). The ordinate, or the y-axis, is the vertical line. It is labeled with the target behavior being measured (e.g., peer interaction, number of words read) and the measurement that was used (e.g., duration, frequency, percentage of intervals). For example, on a graph of Timothy's interval data on interactions with peers, his teacher might label the abscissa as "school dates" and the ordinate as "the percentage of 1-minute intervals of interaction with peers."

Converting Data

Before any points can be plotted on the graph, data must be converted into a single numeric form for each data point. Frequency data can be tallied and presented as the total number in a given time period (e.g., number of times Timothy correctly looked at named peers during morning group). Total duration data may be presented as the total number of minutes or

FIGURE 5–2
Basic Components of a Graph

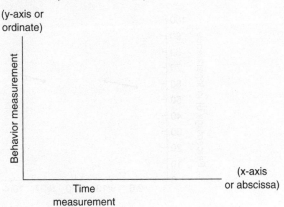

seconds during which a behavior occurred within a given time period (e.g., number of minutes spent in a 15-minute leisure activity). Duration data that are collected using the method of measuring each occurrence can be presented as duration (number of minutes spent interacting with peers during morning free play) or as a frequency (number of peer interactions during morning free play). Interval or time-sampling data can be converted into the number or percentage of intervals in which the behavior occurred. Converting task-analytic data, which involves multiple steps and may have a range of scoring codes, is a little more complex. Take the example of Jenny's 20-step task analysis of making a peanut butter sandwich (Table 5–3). As described previously, Jenny did not need physical prompts within an activity. Because of this, her teacher uses a four-component prompt hierarchy (0, teacher completes; 1, model; 2, verbal; 3, independent). The steps to convert Jenny's task-analytic data into a single numeric form for graphic presentation are the following:

1. *Figure out the most points that Jenny can earn in each session*: The teacher multiplies the number of steps in the task analysis (20) by the number of points possible in each step (3) for a total of 60 possible points that can be earned.
2. *Add the number of points earned in the session*: Jenny scored a total of 36 points (out of a possible 60) on September 6.

3. *Calculate the percentage*: Divide the number of points earned (36) by the total number of points possible (60) to calculate the performance percentage (60%).
4. *Plot the data*: Plot the performance percentages on the graph.

Setting Up a Graph
Once raw data have been converted into a single number to graph, it is easy to plot the data point. First, make sure to label the ordinate or vertical line (y-axis) with the behavior being measured and the type of measurement being used (e.g., % independence of vacuuming, number of verbalizations during lunch). Next, divide the ordinate into equal intervals that cover the possible range of data (e.g., 0% to 100%, 0 to 50). If there are no definite upper and lower limits, the range should extend from the baseline level to the target level, with some extra space added at both ends to allow for variability.

Data points within each phase of a program (e.g., baseline, intervention, reinforcer change) are connected by straight lines, but they should not be connected across vertical lines that indicate a phase change (e.g., the change from baseline to intervention). Each program phase is separated by a broken vertical line and should be labeled at the top of the graph to indicate the intervention used (e.g., baseline, picture prompting, peer model). To enhance the effectiveness of a graph for data analysis, date the graph along the abscissa (x-axis) using the same time intervals as the data

FIGURE 5–3
Four Days of Graphed Data for Jenny Making a Peanut Butter Sandwich

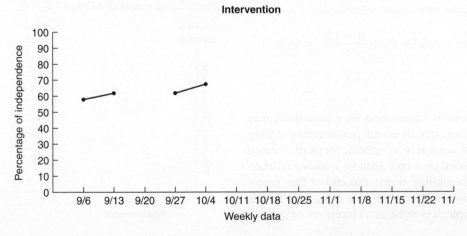

(e.g., daily, weekly, monthly). Figure 5-3 lists every week for 3 months because teaching data will be recorded on making a peanut butter sandwich on a weekly basis. It is important to delineate the dates before recording to allow automatic skipping of spaces for missing sessions. Because missed sessions can have a detrimental effect on a student's performance, it is important to be able to see these gaps in time. Notice that no data are recorded for September 20 in Figure 5-3. Jenny's teacher should investigate the reason for the absence of data collection and the effect of this absence on her performance.

Plotting Data Points

Figure 5-3 shows 4 days of data taken from Jenny's data sheet. To plot data, place each data point (i.e., the total for the session) at the intersection of the session date (on the abscissa) and the level of performance (on the ordinate). Notice the space between the dates of September 13 and September 27; it is best to skip the space to indicate the missed session. However, all consecutive sessions (according to the scheduled plan of intervention) are connected.

Many teachers find it useful to distinguish between graphs that reflect behavior targeted for acceleration versus graphs that reflect behavior targeted for deceleration. To distinguish, some use a dot to represent acceleration data and an X for deceleration data. This strategy makes successful and unsuccessful trends even more obvious during data analysis. It also allows

two related data paths to be plotted on the same graph. Figure 5-4 shows a graph for Timothy, using dots for acceleration data (percentage of intervals with appropriate peer interactions during free play) and Xs for deceleration data (number of times toys grabbed from peers). Note that Figure 5-4 uses two ordinates to identify the two target behaviors (i.e., peer interactions and frequency of grabbing) with two different measurement strategies (i.e., percentage and frequency). Figure 5-4 reflects a successful program. That is, the appropriate behavior (peer interactions) shows an increasing trend, and the inappropriate behavior (grabbing) shows a decelerative trend.

Using Self-Graphing Data Sheets

Some teachers find it efficient to combine the data recording sheet and the graph. This has been done to measure prompting levels (Alberto & Schofield, 1979), task sequences (Holvoet, Guess, Mulligan, & Brown, 1980), and task analysis (Bellamy, Horner, & Inman, 1979). Plotting data from a task analysis in this fashion has been referred to as an upside-down or self-graphing format (Test & Spooner, 1996). Figure 5-5 is a self-graphing data sheet to record progress on hair brushing.

A self-graphing data sheet can be used to record data by making a slash (/) through the step number if the student responds independently and an X through the step number if the student needs assistance to complete the step. At the end of the session, add the number of slashes and then circle the number correct

FIGURE 5–4
Use of Graph to Show Timothy's Progress and Program Changes During Free Play

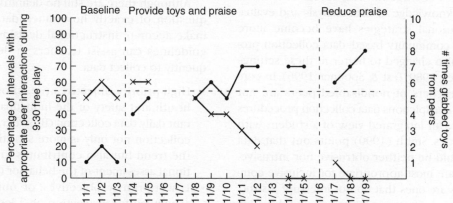

FIGURE 5–5

Self-Graphing Data Sheet for Hair Brushing

Program: Brush hair   Student: Jenny   Teacher: Ms. Dailey

Task analysis

Task analysis													
11. Puts brush away	X	X	X	X	11	11	11	11	11	11	11	11	11	11
10. Check hair for neatness	X	X	X	X	10	10	10	10	10	10	10	10	10	10
9. Brush left back of head	X	X	X	X	9	9	9	9	9	9	9	9	9	9
8. Brush left side of head	X	X	(8)	(8)	8	8	8	8	8	8	8	8	8	8
7. Brush front	X	(7)	X	X	7	7	7	7	7	7	7	7	7	7
6. Brush right side of head	X	X	X	X	6	6	6	6	6	6	6	6	6	6
5. Brush right back of head	X	X	X	X	5	5	5	5	5	5	5	5	5	5
4. Pick up brush	X	X	X	X	4	4	4	4	4	4	4	4	4	4
3. Selects desired materials	X	X	X	X	3	3	3	3	3	3	3	3	3	3
2. Locates brushing materials	X	X	X	X	2	2	2	2	2	2	2	2	2	2
1. Initiates brushing	X	X	X	X	1	1	1	1	1	1	1	1	1	1
	9/2	9/9	9/16	9/23										

Key: / = independent
       X = needs assistance

for the day. A graph is formed by connecting the circles across days.

Frequency of Data Collection

Early in the development of current data-based teaching models, it was fairly common to hear the advice to collect data each time an instructional activity was implemented. In fact, data collection practices recommended for teachers were similar to those used by researchers (Meyer & Janney, 1989). Although this may now sound excessive, it was an important phase, as it afforded educators additional understanding of the learning process of students with severe disabilities and increased knowledge of data analysis and evaluation. As educational strategies have become more integrated and community based, data collection procedures have also changed to better fit these settings (Meyer & Janney, 1989; Test & Spooner, 1996). In contexts where teachers of nondisabled peers are not recording data, conspicuous data collection procedures do not enhance an integrated view of a student with severe disabilities. Smith (1990) points out that data collection should be neither obtrusive nor intrusive. Measures that are most appropriate for inclusive community settings are ones that do not interrupt instruction, take minimal time to complete, are unobtrusive

and do not stigmatize the individual, and provide both objective and subjective observations.

Just how often a teacher should take data is a subject of great debate. Holvoet et al. (1983) point out the irony in this debate—the arguments about data collection do not appear to be data based. A teacher may find a wide variety of suggestions when reading the literature (e.g., collect data once each day, every time the skill is practiced, or once a week). Most discussions of frequency of data collection, however, suggest that once a skill is in the maintenance, fluency, or generalization stage of learning, data collection could be reduced (Farlow & Snell, 1994).

Although there are still no definitive answers to the question of exactly how much data are needed to make accurate instructional decisions, the following guidelines can assist teachers in deciding how frequently to collect data:

• High-priority objectives (i.e., those related to the health and safety of the individual or others) warrant daily data collection (Browder, 1991). Daily data collection not only is more sensitive to changes in the trend but also contributes to important functional assessment of the behavior (Brown, 1991).

• Lower-priority objectives, or objectives that are scheduled for instruction on a less-than-daily basis (e.g., grocery shopping), may be evaluated less frequently, for example, once every 1 or 2 weeks (Browder, 1991).

- Implementation of a new program requires frequent data collection. For the first 2 weeks of the instructional program, data could be collected daily or at every teaching session if the lessons are not held at least once a day. When the student has shown steady progress (e.g., 2 weeks of data), data collection could be reduced to weekly (Farlow & Snell, 1994).

- Skills being taught to replace problem behaviors can be measured in the same way as any other new program (e.g., data initially collected daily, then following progress reduced to weekly); however, these probes should be carried out in the context of relevant situations, persons, and environments (Meyer & Janney, 1989).

- Data that show progress as planned, with a clear accelerating trend, may be evaluated less frequently (Snell & Lloyd, 1991), such as on a weekly basis (Farlow & Snell, 1994).

- Data that do not show progress as planned or that are variable warrant evaluation on a more continual basis (Snell & Lloyd, 1991), minimally twice a week and ideally on a daily basis (Farlow & Snell, 1994).

- Anecdotal records or logs can be used once or twice weekly to record general information concerning a student's overall daily performance and to systematically assess responses to program efforts and any conditions that might affect a student's learning (e.g., tasks or activities that the student enjoys, tasks or activities that the student does not enjoy) (Farlow & Snell, 1994; Meyer & Janney, 1989). Such logs may be useful supplements to more precise, quantified data.

Analysis

Teams must feel confident that instruction is having the desired effect on student performance. It is also helpful to know that an intervention is responsible for the change in the student's performance, not just the passage of time or some other event. Sometimes simple single-subject designs (e.g., reversal, changing criterion) can help teachers feel more confident about the effect of their instruction or the impact of various changes in the educational environment.

Timothy's parents informed Mr. Grayson that Timothy was going to be placed on a new medication for a few weeks and that he should be observant to see if he noticed any changes in Timothy's on-task behavior. Mr. Grayson decided to draw in a vertical change line on his "on-task" graph to mark the beginning of the medication. At the end of 3 weeks, Mr. Grayson was informed that they would be discontinuing the medication; he then drew in another vertical line to indicate the discontinuation of the medication. At this point, Mr. Grayson was able to inform the team that during the time of the medication Timothy's on-task behavior improved and that when it was discontinued the behavior returned to premedication levels. The physician represcribed the medication, and Mr. Grayson drew in another change line and within a week saw the on-task behavior once again increasing.

Mr. Grayson used what is called an ABAB, or reversal design, to monitor the decisions of Timothy's family and doctor. After seeing an increase in the behavior following the medication, Mr. Grayson was not confident that it was actually the medication that was responsible for the change in behavior. After all, at around the same time, he added more picture cues to his instruction; perhaps it was the picture cues that helped Timothy stay on task. However, that the behavior decreased *each time* the medication was withdrawn and increased *each time* it was prescribed made Mr. Grayson and the team more confident that the medication was, at least in part, responsible for the change in Timothy's on-task behavior.

Although an in-depth discussion of single-subject experimental designs (e.g., reversal, multiple baseline, changing criterion) is not possible in this text, we recommend further reading in this area. There are a number of texts that provide excellent reviews of single-subject designs (e.g., Alberto & Troutman, 2003; Kerr & Nelson, 1998; Maag, 1999; Miltenberger, 1997; Schloss & Smith, 1998; Zirpoli & Melloy, 2001). We will limit our later discussion to the simplest classroom design that is nonexperimental in nature (i.e., baseline-intervention, or AB, design).

Merely collecting data is not sufficient; data must be used. Teams will carefully examine, analyze, and interpret data to contribute to the instructional process. The remainder of this chapter discusses the analysis of classroom data and ways in which this information can most effectively help teachers make instructional decisions.

To understand the variety of data analysis strategies available for classroom use, teachers first must understand two important terms: dependent variable and independent variable. The behavior to be changed and measured is the *dependent variable*. Examples of dependent variables include Timothy's peer interactions, Jenny's use of coins to make school purchases, and Christine's performance on the job at Wal-Mart. The instructional strategy that is manipulated by the teacher is the *independent variable*. Examples of independent variables include reinforcement, self-monitoring, reinforcement, and many other procedures that teachers use to try to change a target behavior. The purpose of a single-subject design (such as the reversal design described previously) is to demonstrate a functional relationship between the dependent and the independent variables, that is, to determine whether application of the independent variable (the teaching procedure) results in changes in the dependent variable (the target behavior). A simple way to remember the distinction between the dependent and the independent variable is to keep in mind that changes in the dependent variable "depend" on changes in the independent variable (Alberto & Troutman, 2003).

Types of Data

To understand whether students are benefiting from instructional programs, teachers should examine students' performance data during teaching as well as data from several other sources. Typically, the data are of several types:

- Anecdotal records (e.g., staff notes on unusual behavior or performance, comments sent by the teacher to the home or from the family to school)
- Ungraphed teaching data reflecting performance under training conditions on target skills (e.g., individual steps of a task analysis)
- Ungraphed test data reflecting performance on target skills under criterion conditions (e.g., what individual components of the shopping routine the student could perform in the grocery store without instructional prompts)
- Graphed teaching data on target skills
- Graphed test data on target skills

Because students do not learn during testing, teams should limit the amount of "test to teaching" data. The

"1 to 5 or less" rule of thumb can be used to keep testing infrequent (gather test data once every 5 days or every 2 weeks when teaching occurs daily). By contrast, teaching data can be recorded whenever the student is taught or less often.

Ungraphed Data

When raw, or ungraphed, data of performance on a multiple-stepped task are summarized and graphed, a certain amount of information is lost. For example, teachers looking at a graph on the accuracy of Jenny's sandwich making would know about her overall progress on the task across sessions, but they would not know the specific information available on her data sheet, such as which steps she missed or did correctly on a given day or if these missed or correct steps were consistent across days.

Teachers should preserve ungraphed data since response-by-response information may help them make decisions about program implementation when progress is poor (Farlow & Snell, 1994; Snell & Lloyd, 1991). Even with non–task-analytic, or discrete, data (e.g., the number of correct greetings made by Timothy at preschool), graphed summaries lose some of the information that can be preserved on the data collection sheets. For example, Timothy's teacher analyzed the ungraphed data to determine if his performance is better in the early part of the morning or in the later part of his school day or if he greeted certain peers or adults more than others.

Obtaining a Baseline

The first step in implementing systematic classroom instruction is to conduct a baseline measure. Baseline is the measure of a behavior (the dependent variable) before intervention (the independent variable). In other words, the baseline phase of measurement describes a student's performance under the naturally occurring conditions in his or her environment without instructional manipulations.

Mr. Grayson uses interval recording to measure Timothy's interactions with his classmates during two free play sessions for 3 days (Figure 5-1 shows recording on 1 day). Because Mr. Grayson observes Timothy in his naturally occurring environment, without intervening in any way, these 3 days are

considered baseline. After implementation of an intervention program to increase Timothy's interactions with his classmates, Mr. Grayson compares the baseline data with the intervention data to see whether there was an increase in peer interactions. Mr. Grayson was particularly interested in the effect of the intervention on Timothy's behavior during the 9:30 a.m. free play time.

A teacher should be cautious about how long a baseline condition is in effect. Generally, the rule is to continue baseline measures until there is a stable trend in the data. It is considered unethical, however, to continue a baseline in certain situations. First, if a behavior is dangerous, it is unacceptable to wait for a stable trend before beginning treatment. Many times, a teacher can find other forms of data to use as a baseline (e.g., incident reports, daily logs). Second, many students have little or no behavior related to the target objective (e.g., sign language for a student who has never used sign language). Again, it is considered unethical to delay instruction for an extended period of time when a student clearly cannot perform the behavior. Teachers must remember that baseline does not refer to absence of a program or to downtime; it refers to the time before a given program is implemented or the time when a particular program is withdrawn or stopped.

Third, if the direction of the baseline trend is opposite to the direction of the desired trend (e.g., the number of peer interactions are decreasing, aggression is increasing), collection of baseline data should be discontinued and intervention initiated. When this type of trend occurs, something in the baseline condition is either extinguishing the behavior (e.g., absence of intermittent teacher praise for playing with others was once reinforced and was withdrawn during baseline) or reinforcing the behavior (e.g., lack of teacher consequence for aggressive behavior allows the student to get attention from the other students).

Baseline-Intervention Design

Comparing a baseline condition (A) with an intervention condition (B) is called an AB, or baseline-intervention, design. This design is referred to as a nonexperimental design because no conclusive demonstration of a cause–effect, or functional, relationship between the intervention and the observed changes in behavior is

possible. Since there is no withdrawal of the intervention or replication of treatment effects, rival hypotheses based on factors not controlled by the teacher may have caused the changes in the behavior (e.g., maturation of the student across time, a new student in the class, a parent working on the skill at home).

Timothy's teacher decides to implement an intervention to increase his interactions during the 11:30 free play. Intervention consists of seating Timothy in proximity to two of his outgoing and friendly classmates, Floyd and Mario, and praising the students for all interactions. Timothy's interactions with his peers increased. Mr. Grayson wondered if it was his new intervention (i.e., praise and environmental manipulation) that increased the peer interaction or if, perhaps, it might be the new Power Ranger figures that Floyd was bringing to school.

Given the lack of experimental control, the AB design rarely is used by researchers, but it is appropriate for monitoring student performance within teaching settings, particularly when proven teaching strategies are used. Sometimes, however, it is possible for teams to use a reversal design (ABAB) as described earlier when Timothy's teacher had the opportunity to assess his behavior under medication and nonmedication phases.

When teams are familiar with a student's typical learning patterns and are aware of various events that affect performance, they can usually judge treatment effects with a considerable degree of certainty. Since student performance is monitored before teaching occurs (during baseline) and during different phases of teaching (independent variables), the AB design provides an objective (although not scientifically conclusive) description of a student's behavior before, during, and after training.

If a student's performance during the baseline progresses in the same direction expected during the intervention, teachers have difficulty interpreting the intervention data. That is, unless the intervention has a large effect, it is difficult to judge whether the change in the data (from the baseline to the intervention) is the result of the intervention or simply a continuation of the trend seen during the baseline. Because of this difficulty, teachers typically wait until baseline performance is relatively stable before starting intervention; however, in some instances discussed previously (e.g., dangerous behavior), teachers may not wait for a stable baseline or may not take a baseline at all before beginning intervention.

An AB design is shown in Figure 5-6. This example shows an increase in Christine's engagement during drama club after intervention. Intervention consisted of having her sit closer to peers, having the teaching assistant move to the back of the room to do paperwork, teaching her peers how to communicate with

FIGURE 5-6
An AB Design for Evaluating the Effects of Intervention on Christine's Engagement During Drama Club (with and without a mean line)

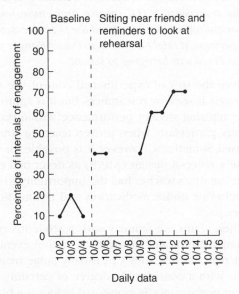

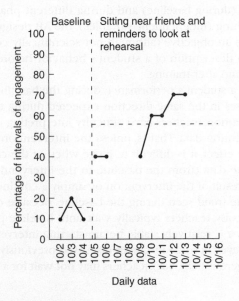

her, and programming her communication device with vocabulary suited to the class.

Graphing Conventions

As described earlier, the main purpose of converting raw data to graphs is to provide a summarizing picture of the student's performance and progress. These interpretations guide program modification. The ability to accurately interpret graphs is enhanced by the use of certain graphing conventions. Three major graphing conventions are recommended (Figure 5-4):

- *Broken vertical lines*, or phase changes, represent changes in the instructional program. These can include planned programmatic changes (e.g., changing from baseline to intervention (Figure 5-6), modification of the task analysis or materials, change in the time or setting of the instruction, or change in the reinforcement or prompt. Broken vertical lines can also be used to indicate situations or events that might indirectly or incidentally affect the student's performance. These events include, for example, changes in medications, staff changes, or a new student in the class.
- *Broken horizontal lines* (a criterion line) can be used to indicate the criterion for the program. This criterion should match the criterion stated in the behavioral objective of the program. Seeing this line on the graph gives the team a quick visual reminder of what the goal of the program is and where the student is in relation to the goal.
- *Connect data points* only for consecutive days within a phase. Data points should not be connected across phase change lines or across missed data days (e.g., student absent or session missed). This allows a clear picture of the effect of the program change but also allows the team to note the gaps in instructional opportunities and its effect on performance.
- *Show the expected trend.* Teams can quickly note if a graph represents a successful or unsuccessful program effort by using an X to represent behavior that is to be decelerated and dots to represent skill building. This graphing convention also allows multiple data paths on one graph (e.g., increasing toy play and decreasing self-stimulatory behavior during free play).

Timothy's teacher graphed his progress on increasing peer interactions in his 9:30 a.m. free play time.

Mr. Grayson decided that it would be helpful not just to note his progress on this social interaction skill but also to analyze the impact of the intervention on Timothy's behavior of grabbing toys from his peers. He drew a criterion line across the graph at 70% because the objective was to have Timothy engage in appropriate peer interactions in 70% of the intervals of the free play session (a percentage based on his observations of other children in the class playing together). When Timothy reached criterion on peer interactions and there was also a significant decrease in grabbing toys, Mr. Grayson decided that he should reduce the amount of praise he was giving to Timothy and his peers so that it was more typical of the frequency of praise he provided other children in the class. He was happy to note that the appropriate peer interactions remained high and that the grabbing remained at zero (see Figure 5-4).

Visual Analysis

Visual inspection of a graph is most frequently used to evaluate the effects of classroom data (Alberto & Troutman, 2003). That is, certain characteristics and comparisons of the data paths (e.g., data from the baseline compared to data from the first phase of instruction) are examined to judge the effectiveness of the instructional strategy. Sometimes, the effects of a program are so strong that the impact is obvious by just looking at ("eyeballing") the graph. In these situations, the graph itself will let you know all you need to know. For example, the top panel of Figure 5–6 shows a very distinct difference between baseline and intervention. It is easy to see on this graph a positive change in the trend (an accelerating data path) and the level of change (performance of 10% and 20% during baseline, which then jumped to 40% and higher during intervention).

However, teachers and researchers often find that their efforts in analyzing the trends on a graph are aided by several simple visual aids—the mean line, the aim line, and the trend line.

Mean Lines

An easy visual addition to a graph to help analyze intervention effects is looking at the mean (i.e., average) of each phase and comparing these lines. This can be done by calculating the mean of the data points in each phase and drawing a horizontal broken line corresponding to that value on the ordinate scale (Alberto &

Troutman, 2003). For example, we could calculate the average of baseline for Figure 5-6 in the following way:

1. Add baseline data point values:

$$10\% + 20\% + 10\% = 40\%$$

2. Divide total by number of days:

$$\frac{40\%}{3} = 13.3\%$$

3. Draw a horizontal broken line across baseline phase at 13%

The same would be done for intervention:

1. Add intervention data point values:

$$40\% + 40\% + 40\% + 60\% + 60\% + 70\% + 70\% = 380$$

2. Divide total by number of days:

$$\frac{380\%}{7} = 54.28\%$$

3. Draw a horizontal broken line across intervention phase at 54%

The bottom panel of Figure 5-6 shows the difference in the two horizontal lines and is an additional visual representation of the success of the intervention.

Aim Lines

The aim line is a more sophisticated version of the criterion line, calculated from a student's data collected during baseline or after several training days. Usually, the aim line starts at the initial performance level of the student when you begin instruction and extends over the instructional period to the criterion level and date you have set in the instructional objective (Farlow & Snell, 1994). This progress-monitoring visual aid is drawn onto a graph early in a program and allows the team to compare actual progress to their expectations for progress. Although they might look quite complicated, aim lines are simple to draw and easy to interpret. Aim lines result from connecting two points made by (a) the intersection of the middate and the midperformance of the first 3 training days (or last three baseline days) and (b) the intersection of the criterion performance with the goal date of accomplishment (aim date).

Jenny's team decided to graph the target skill of making purchases at school with combinations of coins. The first objective in the program was to teach

FIGURE 5–7

Jenny's Performance During a Month of Instruction on the Objective of Making Purchases at School Using Pennies (Assistance on these graphs is credited to Marci Kinas Jerome and Corey Jerome)

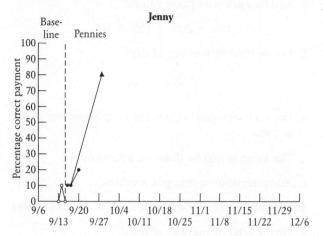

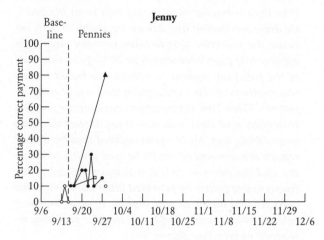

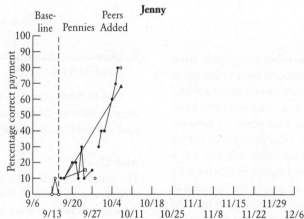

"penny." They started the program on 9/13 with an aim date of 9/28/04.

The graph at the top left of Figure 5-7 shows that she scored 10%, 10%, and 20% during the first 3 days of teaching pennies. They set the first endpoint for the aim line at the intersection of the second day of the program, or middate (September 17), and her mid-performance, which was 10% (i.e., the middle value of the three percentages). The aim line endpoint was set at the intersection of the criterion performance expected of Jenny (i.e., 80%) and the goal date for pennies (September 28). Jenny's teacher then drew a straight line between these two endpoints.

Selection of an aim date is influenced by several factors, including the school's typical evaluation periods (e.g., every 9 weeks), the urgency (or time line) for learning the skill, the difference between current per-

formance and the criterion, and the speed of learning on similar tasks in the recent past. Aim dates should not be excessively distant from implementation dates and may be set to correspond to more frequent marking periods used in general education (e.g., 9 to 12 weeks).

Trend Lines

The trend line is a line that roughly averages the direction and slope of a student's performance when the performance is uneven, variable, or difficult to interpret by just looking at the graph. Trend refers to the direction of graphed data as well as the slope, or steepness, of a data path. A trend can be of three general types:

1. *Ascending trends* have an upward slope on a graph and indicate improvement (or learning) when the behavior graphed is a skill or adaptive behavior. (If the goal of the program is to reduce a behavior, the

ascending trend would be interpreted as regression, or deterioration.)

2. *Flat trends* have either no slope or a very slight upward or downward slope. When the behavior graphed is a skill or an adaptive behavior, flat trends indicate no learning or improvement.

3. *Descending trends* have a downward slope and indicate regression, or deterioration, when the behavior graphed is a skill or adaptive behavior. (If the goal of the program is to reduce a behavior, the downward slope would be interpreted as indicating improvement.)

When the trend of graphed teaching data is not obvious or uniform, trend lines help teachers summarize and interpret the fluctuating, or variable, nature of performance (Tawney & Gast, 1984). Some researchers have defined an ascending slope as 30° or more in the positive direction and a descending slope as 30° or more in the negative direction (DeProspero & Cohen, 1979).

When the trend is obvious, there is no need to draw a trend line, but when a student's progress is below the aim line for three out of five consecutive data points and the trend is not obvious, a teacher should pencil in a trend line to define the trend. If the line indicates that the trend on a target skill is flat or descending (for skill-building programs), then the team should further analyze the data and other relevant information to decide whether specific program modifications are needed.

When Jenny's performance continued to be up and down and below the aim line after a week of

teaching, they decided to pencil in a trend line (graph on the top right of Figure 5-7).

There are several ways to draw trend lines, including the "quickie split-middle trend line" (White & Haring, 1980), which can be drawn simply and clarifies the general direction of change in the data as well as the relative rate of change (reflected in the slope). Although teachers may collect test (probe) data intermittently and add them to the same graph using differently coded lines or points, teaching or training data constitute the primary information used to make judgments about day-to-day progress (Browder, 1991; Farlow & Snell, 1994; Haring, Liberty, & White, 1980). Teachers should draw a trend line using the following four steps (Figure 5-8):

1. Take the last 6 to 10 days of teaching data collected and draw a vertical line to divide the data in half.

2. Look at the first half of the data (the first three, four, or five data points) and locate the middle date. Draw a small vertical line through this data point.
   - If an odd set of data points is considered (e.g., three or five), draw the line through the middle date.
   - If an even set of data points is considered (e.g., four), just sketch a pencil line between the dates for the second and third data points.

3. Look at the middle performance level and draw a short horizontal line through this data point. The middle performance level is not the average of the

FIGURE 5–8
Drawing a Split-Middle Trend Line

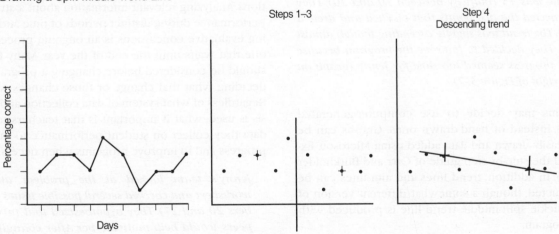

Steps 1–3

Step 4
Descending trend

performances for the data points in the set of three to five data points. It is simply the middle performance value.

- For an odd number of data points, select the middle value (e.g., for 10%, 15%, and 12%, the middle performance value is 12%).
- For an even number of data points, select a value halfway between the two middle data points (e.g., for 15%, 10%, 15%, and 11%, the middle value between 11 and 15 is 13%).

4. Extend the two lines until they intersect.
5. Repeat this process for the other half of the data.
6. Then draw a line connecting the two points of intersection from both halves of the data.

Once the trend line is drawn, visually judge whether the trend is ascending, flat, or descending. If the trend is flat or descending, teachers should hypothesize or determine why and make program modifications based on the hypotheses or explanations. If the trend is ascending but not fast enough, teachers may (a) make changes in the program (e.g., modify the materials or prompts, change the reinforcer) to try to speed progress or (b) adjust the aim line by lowering the criterion or moving the date further into the future. Alternately, teachers may do nothing to the program and look for other explanations for the student's reduced progress.

Jenny's team drew a trend line using the first 7 days of training. They divided it into two groups: the first three data points and the last four. For the first 3 days, the middle date was 9/17, and middle value was 10%; for the next 4 days, the middle date was halfway between 9/23 and 9/24, and the middle value was 15 (halfway between 10 and 20). They connected the two points that resulted and drew a line. The trend was slightly ascending though almost flat. They decided to improve the program because this progress seemed too slow for Jenny (graph on top right of Figure 5–7).

Teams may decide to use computer-generated graphs instead of hand-drawn ones. Graphs can be fairly easily drawn and data added using Microsoft Excel and the step-by-step guide of Carr and Burkholder (1998). In addition, trend lines and aim lines can be constructed, though a somewhat different version of the quickie split-middle trend line is produced with this program.

Evaluation

When a student's progress has been below aim for approximately three out of five sessions or if the trend is flat or descending (or ascending for deceleration programs), teachers should attempt to determine why and to make program improvements based on their analysis of the data (Farlow & Snell, 1994; Haring et al., 1980). Using a variety of information about the student and the program, along with the data collected on skill performance, team members can systematically develop hypotheses, or possible explanations, for a student's lack of progress. Changes should be implemented that correspond to the probable explanations, or the team may decide not to change the program but to wait and see if there is improvement. It is inappropriate, however, to wait too long before changing an ineffective program; if the team decides to wait beyond 2 weeks, the delay should be justified.

A number of educators and researchers have developed approaches for analyzing student performance data and making program changes (e.g., Browder, 1991; Farlow & Snell, 1994; Ford et al., 1989; Haring, Liberty, & White, 1981; Haring et al., 1980; Neel & Billingsley, 1989; Snell, 1988). Some approaches are simple, while others are complex; several approaches rest directly on research, while several do not. A team may use guidelines or checklists to help analyze potential problems with a given instructional program. The Program Analysis Worksheet (Figure 5–9) guides a team to think systematically about why a student is not progressing as planned (Farlow & Snell, 1994).

The process of data analysis is an important one if students are to benefit fully from the systematic data collected by their teachers and from informal observations. Analyzing relevant information about a student's performance during distinct periods of time and drawing evaluative conclusions is an ongoing process, not one that waits until the end of the year. Many factors should be considered before changing a program and deciding what that change or those changes will be. Regardless of what system of data collection and analysis is used, what is important is that teachers use the data they collect on student performance to monitor progress and to improve programs when necessary.

Jenny's team looked at the problem analysis worksheet and checked several possible issues (numbers 20 and 27). They hypothesized that involving peers would help motivate her. After changing the

FIGURE 5–9

Problem Analysis Worksheet

Problem Analysis Worksheet

Student: _____ Time Period: _____

Program: _____

Team Members present at meeting: _____

Directions: Put a check (√) by the statement that you feel describes the data collected during the latest review period. If you suspect the statement describes the data, but you need more data to address the issue, check the second column. (Check only one column.)

			Seems to be true	Need more data
1. The trend of the data is:	Ascending	1.	—	NMD
	Flat			
	Descending			
2. The data are:	Not variable	2.	—	NMD
	Variable			
3. The level of the data is:	Low	3.	—	NMD
	Moderate			
	High			
4. Student performance is related to medication		4.	—	NMD
5. Student has experienced a temporary environmental change/problem/stress		5.	—	NMD
6. The data may not be reliable		6.	—	NMD
7. The staff are not implementing the program reliably		7.	—	NMD
8. The trend or level of variability has changed since the last review		8.	—	NMD
9. The student used to perform the skill at higher levels		9.	—	NMD
10. The data pattern indicates that variability is random		10.	—	NMD
11. The data pattern indicates that variability is cyclical		11.	—	NMD
12. Test data conflict with the instructional data		12.	—	NMD
13. Test scores tend to be greater than instructional scores		13.	—	NMD
14. Errors typically occur on the same step(s) of the task analysis		14.	—	NMD
15. Student is not progressing through prompt levels		15.	—	NMD
16. Errors typically occur on the first trials of the day/session		16.	—	NMD
17. Errors typically occur on the latter trials of the day or session		17.	—	NMD
18. Errors occur more in some settings or with specific staff		18.	—	NMD
19. Student does not attempt the task		19.	—	NMD
20. Student is reluctant to participate in the task		20.	—	NMD
21. Student responds negatively to certain levels of prompts		21.	—	NMD
22. Student does not attend to the cues		22.	—	NMD
23. Student is receiving reinforcement for incorrect performance		23.	—	NMD
24. Student exhibits similar problems in other programs		24.	—	NMD
25. Interfering behaviors are present		25.	—	NMD
26. Problem behaviors are staying the same or increasing		26.	—	NMD
27. The program excludes student interaction with peers		27.	—	NMD
28. Other:		28.	—	NMD

State team's hypothesis about the instructional problems based on the above information:

Source: From *Making the Most of Student Performance Data,* by L. J. Farlow and Martha E. Snell, 1994, Innovations: Research to Practice Series, Washington, D.C.: American Association on Mental Retardation. Copyright 1994 by American Association of Mental Retardation. Adapted with permission.

aim date to 10/11 and including two classmates in the sessions, her progress improved (lower part of Figure 5-7).

Special Considerations in General Education Settings

This final section of the chapter discusses the importance of being unobtrusive in data collection, storage, and use. First, evaluation information is confidential. It should be available only to the student, family members, and professionals directly involved in the student's program. Just as a typical student's report card is never publicly displayed, neither should a student's progress graphs or data records be displayed for others to see. Graphs and data sheets should be organized and stored in record files accessible to teaching staff.

Unobtrusive collection of data is another challenge for teachers. It is easy to envision a data-collecting teacher or school psychologist armed with a clipboard, stopwatch, and portable video camera to record students' performance. When teaching staff are so obtrusive in their data collection efforts, they call unnecessary attention to their students and may inadvertently stigmatize them (Test & Spooner, 1996).

Behavior measurement must be relatively accurate and must provide relevant information. However, accuracy and relevance of data need not depend on obvious or bulky recording equipment, excessive adult observers, or measurement procedures that interfere with teaching or learning within the community or school setting. Typically, teaching staff (and sometimes peer tutors) collect data as they teach or record data after an instructional session, basing the data on the permanent products left as a result of a student's performance (e.g., counting the number of clean cafeteria tables). Additional observers usually are not needed or available.

The methods selected for directly measuring behavior in teaching settings should be as simple and time saving as possible (e.g., frequency or event counts for carefully selected and distinct periods of time or count of permanent products). Typically, teachers avoid methods requiring extensive observation time (e.g., frequency counts taken across an entire day) and avoid measurement equipment that interferes with teaching (e.g., a portable tape recorder and headset for an interval measurement). Teachers must make some compromises to obtain the maximum amount of information with the least effort and time commitment.

Minimizing the obtrusiveness of data collection typically can be accomplished with a little imagination and brainstorming. In some cases, typical measurement methods are used but the equipment is simplified. For example, a teacher who knows a task analysis fairly well can make notes on index cards or on small sticky notes. Some teachers may want to keep 3-inch by 5-inch cards in their pockets for reference, noting the specific step number (correct or prompted) on the card as the student performs the task. Sticky notes can be stuck to purses or watches, and hash marks can record the frequency of a target behavior. Wrist-worn or key-chain counters, calculators, or quiet counters also can be used to keep frequency counts unobtrusively and to time the duration of target behaviors. Some teachers have made simple bead counter bracelets using leather shoestrings and 19 plastic beads arranged in two differently colored groups of 9 and 10; the bead arrangement enables counting by 1s in the first group and by 10s in the second group for a possible total count of 109 before resetting the beads. In those instances when behaviors require the use of interval observations, teachers or psychologists may use headsets and precounted interval tapes on portable cassette recorders fairly unobtrusively, but this works only if the activity does not require the observer to instruct or interact with the student.

In other cases, teachers reduce the obviousness of their evaluation procedures by using less traditional measures. Meyer and Janney (1989) suggest a wide range of measurement tools that they call "user friendly." For example, once Timothy can enter his classroom reliably and safely in his "arrival program," the teacher may simply measure two products that result from Timothy's performance of the entire arrival chain: (a) whether his coat or sweater is hung on his hook and (b) whether Timothy is playing at the activity that he placed by his photo on the activity choice chart. This measure would be taken 10 minutes after his arrival. Other examples include using measurement of weight gains and ratings of spillage to evaluate the success of a feeding program or weight gain to evaluate the effectiveness of a program to reduce rumination and vomiting. Communication logs between home and school may be examined to ascertain a family's perception of student improvement and satisfaction with an instructional program. The list of examples for user-friendly measures depends on the imagination of teachers and family members about alternate ways to evaluate learning.

Summary

Teachers must evaluate each student's progress in his or her school program. Frequent and meaningful data collection that is individualized allows teachers to effectively design, evaluate, and modify their instructional strategies. This chapter discusses quantitative measurement strategies as well as outcome measures that focus on an individual's quality of life. For measurement to be useful and meaningful, it must be reliable (accurate), and it must measure behaviors and skills considered by the individual and significant others as socially valid; that is, the behaviors and skills measured must have a positive impact on the quality of the student's life. Measurement and evaluation strategies must be designed and implemented in ways that respect each student's privacy and participation in integrated and community-based environments.

Suggested Activities

1. Select one student in your class and examine the current measurement strategies used for each IEP objective.
   a. For each objective that includes a measurement strategy, consider whether that strategy is the most appropriate one to use. Would a different one be more meaningful?
   b. For each objective that does not include a measurement strategy, describe an appropriate and manageable one that could be used.
2. For this same student, design a graph for each instructional objective not currently displayed in graphic format.

References

Agran, M., Snow, K., & Swaner, J. (1999). Teacher perceptions of self-determination: Benefits, characteristics, strategies. *Education and Training in Mental Retardation and Developmental Disabilities, 34,* 291-301.

Alberto, P. A., & Schofield, P. (1979). An instructional interaction pattern for the severely handicapped. *Teaching Exceptional Children, 12,* 16-19.

Alberto, P. A., & Troutman, A. C. (2003). *Applied behavior analysis for teachers* (6th ed.). Upper Saddle River, NJ: Merrill/Prentice Hall.

Baer, D. M., Wolf, M. M., & Risley, T. R. (1968). Some current dimensions of applied behavior analysis. *Journal of Applied Behavior Analysis, 1,* 91-97.

Baer, D. M., Wolf, M. M., & Risley, T. R. (1987). Some still-current dimensions of applied behavior analysis. *Journal of Applied Behavior Analysis, 20,* 313-327.

Bambara, L. M., & Koger, F. (1996). *Opportunities for daily choice-making* (AAMR Research to Practice Series: Innovations). Washington, DC: American Association on Mental Retardation.

Bannerman, D. J., Sheldon, J. B., Sherman, J. A., & Harchik, A. E. (1990). Balancing the right to habilitation with the right to personal liberties: The rights of people with developmental disabilities to eat too many doughnuts and take a nap. *Journal of Applied Behavior Analysis, 23,* 79-89.

Bellamy, G., Horner, R., & Inman, D. (1979). *Vocational habilitation of severely retarded adults: A direct service technology*. Baltimore: University Park Press.

Billingsley, F. F., Gallucci, C., Peck, C. A., Schwartz, I. S., & Staub, D. (1996). "But those kids can't even do math": An alternative conceptualization of outcomes for inclusive education. *Special Education Leadership Review, 3,* 43-55.

Billingsley, F. F., & Liberty, K. A. (1982). The use of time-based data in instructional programs for the severely handicapped. *Journal of the Association for the Severely Handicapped, 7,* 47-55.

Billingsley, F. F., White, O. R., & Munson, R. (1980). Procedural reliability: A rationale and an example. *Behavioral Assessment, 2,* 229-241.

Browder, D. M. (1991). *Assessment of individuals with severe disabilities: An applied behavior approach to life skills assessment* (2nd ed.). Baltimore: Paul H. Brookes.

Brown, F. (1991). Creative daily scheduling: A nonintrusive approach to challenging behaviors in community residences. *Journal of the Association for Persons with Severe Handicaps, 16,* 75-84.

Brown, F., Gothelf, C. R., Guess, D., & Lehr, D. (1998). Self-determination for individuals with the most severe disabilities: Moving beyond chimera. *Journal of the Association for Persons with Severe Handicaps, 23,* 17-26.

Brown, F., & Lehr, D. (1993). Meaningful activities meaningful for students with severe multiple disabilities. *Teaching Exceptional Children, 25,* 12-16.

Carr, J. E., & Burkholder, E. O. (1998). Creating single-subject design graphs with Microsoft Excel. *Journal of Applied Behavior Analysis, 31,* 245-251.

Cooper, K. J., & Browder, D. M. (1998). Enhancing choice and participation for adults with severe disabilities in community-based instruction. *Journal of the Association for Persons with Severe Handicaps, 23,* 252-260.

DeProspero, A., & Cohen, S. (1979). Inconsistent visual analyses of intrasubject data. *Journal of Applied Behavior Analysis, 12,* 574-579.

Farlow, L. J., & Snell, M. E. (1989). Teacher use of student performance data to make instructional decisions: Practices in programs for students with moderate to profound disabilities. *Journal of the Association for Persons with Severe Handicaps, 14,* 13-22.

Farlow, L. J., & Snell, M. E. (1994). *Making the most of student performance data* (AAMR Research to Practice Series: Innovations). Washington, DC: American Association on Mental Retardation.

Fisher, M., & Lindsey-Walters, S. (1987, October). *A survey report of various types of data collection procedures used by teachers and their strengths and weaknesses*. Paper presented at the annual conference of the Association for Persons with Severe Handicaps, Chicago.

Ford, A., Schnorr, R., Meyer, L., Davern, L., Black, J., & Dempsey, P. (1989). *The Syracuse community-referenced curriculum guide.* Baltimore: Paul H. Brookes.

Frea, W. (1997). Reducing stereotypic behavior by teaching orienting responses to environmental stimuli. *Journal of the Association for Persons with Severe Handicaps, 22,* 28-35.

Fuchs, L. S., & Fuchs, D. (1986). Effects of systematic formative evaluation: A meta-analysis. *Exceptional Children, 53,* 199-208.

Gaylord-Ross, R. J., Haring, T. G., Breen, C., & Pitts-Conway, V. (1984). The training and generalization of social interaction skills with autistic youth. *Journal of Applied Behavior Analysis, 17,* 229-247.

Gothelf, C. R., & Brown, F. (1998). Participation in the education process: Students with severe disabilities. In M. L. Wehmeyer & D. J. Sands (Eds.), *Making it happen: Student involvement in education planning, decision making, and instruction* (pp. 99-121). Baltimore: Paul H. Brookes.

Grossi, T. A. (1998). Using a self-operated auditory prompting system to improve the work performance e of two employees with severe disabilities. *Journal of the Association for Persons with Severe Handicaps, 23,* 149-154.

Haring, N. G., Liberty, K. A., & White, O. R. (1980). Rules for data-based strategy decisions in instructional programs: Current research and instructional implications. In W. Sailor, B. Wilcox, & L. Brown (Eds.), *Methods of instruction for severely handicapped children* (pp. 159-192). Baltimore: Paul H. Brookes.

Haring, N., Liberty, K., & White, O. R. (1981). *An investigation of phases of learning and facilitating instructional events for the severely/profoundly handicapped learners.* Final project report. Seattle: University of Washington, School of Education.

Haring, T. G., & Breen C. (1989). Units of analysis of social interaction outcomes in supported education. *Journal of the Association for Persons with Severe Handicaps, 14,* 255-262.

Harvey, M. T., Baker, D. J., Horner, R. H., & Blackford, J. U. (2003). A brief report on the prevalence of sleep problems in individuals with mental retardation living in the community. *Journal of Positive Behavior Interventions, 5,* 195-200.

Holburn, S. (2002). How science can evaluate and enhance person-centered planning. *Research and Practice for Persons with Severe Disabilities, 27,* 250-260.

Holvoet, J., Guess, D., Mulligan, M., & Brown, F. (1980). The individualized curriculum sequencing model (II): A teaching strategy for severely handicapped students. *Journal of the Association for the Severely Handicapped, 5,* 337-351.

Holvoet, J., O'Neil, C., Chazdon, L., Carr, D., & Warner, J. (1983). Hey, do we really have to take data? *Journal of the Association for the Severely Handicapped, 8,* 56-70.

Hughes, C., Rung, L. L., Wehmeyer, M. L., Agran, M., Copeland, S. R., & Hwang, B. (2000). Self-prompted communication book use to increase social interaction among high school students. *Journal of the Association for Persons with Severe Handicaps, 25,* 153-166.

Hunt, P., Alwell, M., Farron-Davis, F., & Goetz, L. (1996). Creating socially supportive environments for fully included students who experience multiple disabilities. *Journal of the Association for Persons with Severe Handicaps, 21,* 53-71.

Kazdin, A. E. (1976). Statistical analysis for single-case experimental designs. In M. Hersen & D. Barlow (Eds.), *Single-case experimental designs: Strategies for studying behavior change* (pp. 265-316). New York: Pergamon.

Kazdin, A. E. (1977). Assessing the clinical or applied importance of behavior change through social validation. *Behavior Modification, 1,* 427-452.

Kazdin, A. E. (1980). *Behavior modification in applied settings.* Homewood, IL: Dorsey Press.

Kerr, M. M., & Nelson, C. M. (1998). *Strategies for managing behavior problems in the classroom* (3rd ed.). Upper Saddle River, NJ: Merrill/Prentice Hall.

Koegel, L. K., Stiebel, D., & Koegel, R. L. (1998). Reducing aggression in children with autism toward infant or toddler siblings. *Journal of the Association for Persons with Severe Handicaps, 23,* 111-118.

Lane, K. L., & Beebe-Frankenberger, M. (2004). *School-based interventions: The tools you need to succeed.* Boston: Pearson/Allyn & Bacon.

Lee, S., & Odom, S. L. (1996). The relationship between stereotypic behavior and peer social interaction for children with severe disabilities. *Journal of the Association for Persons with Severe Handicaps, 21,* 88-95.

Maag, J. W. (1999). *Behavior management: From theoretical implications to practical applications.* San Diego: Singular.

McGlashing-Johnson, J., Agran, M., Sitlington, P., Cavin, M., & Wehmeyer, J. (2003). Enhancing the job performance of youth with moderate to severe cognitive disabilities using the self-determined learning model of instruction. *Research and Practice for Persons with Severe Disabilities, 28,* 194-204.

McGrath, A. M., Bosch, S., Sullivan, C. L., & Fuqua, R. W. (2003). Reciprocal social interactions between preschoolers and a child with autism. *Journal of Positive Behavior Interventions, 5,* 47-54.

Meyer, L. H., & Evans, I. M. (1989). *Non-aversive intervention for behavior problems: A manual for home and community.* Baltimore: Paul H. Brookes.

Meyer, L. H., & Evans, I. M. (1993). Meaningful outcomes in behavioral intervention: Evaluating positive approaches to the remediation of challenging behaviors. In J. Reichle & D. P. Wacker (Eds.), *Communicative alternatives to challenging behavior: Integrating functional assessment and intervention strategies* (pp. 407-428). Baltimore: Paul H. Brookes.

Meyer, L. H., & Janney, R. (1989). User-friendly measures of meaningful outcomes: Evaluating behavior interventions. *Journal of the Association for Persons with Severe Handicaps, 14,* 263-270.

Miltenberger, R. (1997). *Behavior modification: Principles and procedures.* Pacific Grove, CA: Brooks/Cole.

Neel, R. S., & Billingsley, F. F. (1989). *IMPACT: A functional curriculum handbook for students with moderate to severe disabilities.* Baltimore: Paul H. Brookes.

Reinhartsen, D. B., Garfinkle, A. N., & Wolery, M. (2002). Engagement with toys in two-year-old children with autism: Teacher selection versus child choice. *Research and Practice for Persons with Severe Disabilities, 27,* 175-187.

Risley, T. R. (1970). Behavior modification: An experimental-therapeutic endeavor. In L. A. Hamerlynck, P. O. Davidson, & L. E. Acker (Eds.), *Behavior modification and ideal health services* (pp. 103-127). Calgary, Alberta, Canada: University of Calgary Press.

Ryndak, D. L., Clark, D., Conroy, M., & Stuart, C. H. (2001). Preparing teachers to meet the needs of students with severe disabilities: Program configuration and expertise. *Journal of the Association for Persons with Severe Handicaps, 26,* 96–105.

Schloss, P. J., & Smith, M. A. (1998). *Applied behavior analysis in the classroom* (2nd ed.). Boston: Allyn & Bacon.

Smith, M. D. (1990). *Autism and life in the community: Successful interventions for behavioral challenges.* Baltimore: Paul H. Brookes.

Snell, M. E. (1988). *Final report for the effective use of student performance data by teachers of students with severe handicaps* (Final Project Report for Grant #G008530150). Washington, DC: U.S. Department of Education, Office of Special Education and Rehabilitation Services.

Snell, M. E. (2003). Applying research to practice: The more pervasive problem? *Research and Practice for Persons with Severe Disabilities, 28,* 143–147.

Snell, M. E., & Lloyd, B. H. (1991). A study of the effects of trend variability, frequency, and form of data on teachers' judgments about progress and their decisions about program change. *Research in Developmental Disabilities, 12,* 41–61.

Souza, G., & Kennedy, C. H. (2003). Facilitating social interactions in the community for a transition-age student with severe disabilities. *Journal of Positive Behavior Interventions, 5,* 179–182.

Storey, K. (1997). Quality of life issues in social skills assessment of persons with disabilities. *Education and Training in Mental Retardation and Developmental Disabilities, 32,* 197–200.

Taber, T. A., Alberto, P. A., Seltzer, A., & Hughes, M. (2003). Obtaining assistance when lost in the community using cell phones. *Research and Practice for Persons with Severe Disabilities, 3,* 105–116.

Tawney, J., & Gast, D. (1984). *Single subject research in special education.* New York: Merrill/Macmillan.

Test, D. W., & Spooner, F. (1996). *Community-based instructional support* (AAMR Research to Practice Series: Innovations). Washington, DC: American Association on Mental Retardation.

Umbreit, J., Lane, K. L., & Dejud, C. (2004). Improving classroom behavior by modifying task difficulty: Effects of increasing the difficulty of too-easy tasks. *Journal of Positive Behavior Interventions, 6,* 13–20.

Utley, B. L., Zigmond, N., & Strain, P. S. (1987). How various forms of data affect teacher analysis of teacher performance. *Exceptional Children, 53,* 411–422.

Voeltz, L. H., & Evans, I. M. (1983). Educational validity: Procedures to evaluate outcomes in programs for severely handicapped learners. *Journal of the Association for the Severely Handicapped, 8,* 3–15.

Wacker, D. P. (1989). Why measure anything? *Journal of the Association for Persons with Severe Handicaps, 14,* 254.

Wacker, D., Berg, W., Wiggins, B., Muldoon, M., & Cavanaugh, J. (1985). Evaluation of reinforcer preferences for profoundly handicapped students *Journal of Applied Behavior Analysis, 18,* 173–178.

Walther-Thomas, C., Korinek, L., McLaughlin, V. L., & Williams, F. T. (2000). *Collaboration for inclusive education: Developing successful programs.* Boston: Allyn & Bacon.

Wehmeyer, M. L., & Schwartz, M. (1997). Self-determination and positive adult outcomes: A follow-up study of youth with mental retardation or learning disabilities. *Exceptional Children, 63,* 245–255.

White, O. R. (1986). Precision teaching—precision learning. *Exceptional Children, 53,* 522–534.

White, O. R., & Haring, N. G. (1980). *Exceptional teaching* (2nd ed.). New York: Merrill/Macmillan.

Wolf, M. M. (1978). Social validity: The case for subjective measurement or how applied behavior analysis is finding its heart. *Journal of Applied Behavior Analysis, 11,* 203–214.

Zirpoli, T. J., & Melloy, K. J. (2001). *Behavior management applications for teachers* (3rd ed.). Upper Saddle River, NJ: Merrill/Prentice Hall.

6

Positive Behavior Support
for Individuals with
Severe Disabilities

Robert H. Horner,
Richard W. Albin,
Anne W. Todd,
Jeffrey Sprague
University of Oregon

In this chapter, we provide an introduction to positive behavior support, a description of the core procedures that make positive behavior support effective, and examples of how this approach is applied with individuals who have severe disabilities. Throughout the chapter, we refer to two students, Maya and Isha, and to the activities that their support teams conducted to

illustrate the various features and procedures that constitute individualized student behavior support. Some terms used and procedures described in these examples may be unfamiliar and new to some readers. Bear with us; by the end of the chapter, all these terms and procedures will be explained and described. To start, meet Maya.

 Maya

Maya is 12 years old, lives at home with her family, and has Down syndrome and moderate to severe intellectual disabilities. Maya lives with her two high school–age brothers and both birth parents and recently entered sixth grade at her neighborhood middle school. She enjoys fish, has a fish aquarium, and hopes to work at a fish or pet

store in the future. Maya takes care of most of her dressing and personal care needs and enjoys cooking and listening to music with peers. She reads at a first-grade level; follows step-by-step directions by reading words, icons, and photos; adds and subtracts single-digit numbers; identifies numbers 1 to 10; and copies two- to three-word

---

Development of this chapter was supported by a grant from the Office of Special Education Programs, with additional funding from the Safe and Drug Free Schools Program, U.S. Department of Education (H326S030002). Opinions expressed herein are those of the authors and do not necessarily reflect the position of the U.S. Department of Education, and such endorsements should not be inferred. For additional information regarding the contents of this chapter, contact the first author (robh@uoregon.edu)

phrases. Maya also engages in problem behaviors that are becoming increasingly intense and currently threaten her continued participation in regular school settings. The major concern is that in situations where Maya is not receiving social attention from peers, she will yell at her peers and then sometimes hit them. Maya's behavior can escalate to dangerous levels. She also has a history of sticking her tongue out, spitting, and throwing objects when she has had very little peer attention.

Twenty-five years ago, Maya most likely would have been placed in a segregated school with a minimalist curriculum and behavior support that included the delivery of aversive events (e.g., physical punishment, restraint, and isolation). Today, the Individuals with Disabilities Education Act (U.S. Department of Education, 1997) and current U.S. Department of Education standards (Shavelson & Towne, 2002) require research-validated strategies that provide Maya with access to the least restrictive environment and help her meet her individual education plan (IEP) goals.

Positive behavior support (PBS) is about the redesign of environments to produce both decreases in problem behavior and increases in basic lifestyle goals such as improved learning, access to social networks, employment, and involvement in the full range of community activities. PBS builds directly from a powerful science of human behavior (Bijou & Baer, 1961; Bijou, Peterson, & Ault, 1968; Catania, 1992), advances in biomedical support (Reiss & Aman, 1998), and the strong values base provided by advocates of normalization (Nirje, 1969; Wolfensberger, 1983), self-determination (Wehmeyer & Schwartz, 1997), and person-centered support (Kincaid, 1996; O'Brien, O'Brien, & Mount, 1997).

At its core, PBS is the values-driven application of applied behavior analysis, biomedical supports, systems change, and education (Carr et al., 1999; Carr et al., 2002; Fox & Dunlap, 2002; Horner et al., 1990; Koegel, Koegel, & Dunlap, 1996; Sugai et al., 2000). The values of the focus individual and his or her family and advocates shape the outcomes that define successful intervention and the array of intervention options that are acceptable.

The science of human behavior defines the array of intervention options that are likely to result in desired effects. The organizational and social systems establish the foundation for sustainable effects. This blending of values, science, and organizational systems gives PBS strong promise as a viable approach for addressing the real and difficult challenges posed by problem behaviors such as defiance, self-injury, aggression, property destruction, noncompliance, and withdrawal.

The goal of PBS is to invest in understanding the vision and strengths of each individual and to use this information to craft an environment that promotes socially adaptive behaviors while simultaneously making problem behaviors irrelevant, inefficient, and ineffective. This represents a significant shift in perspective from a vision of behavior support as a process that "changes the person," or emphasizes delivering consequences that will guide a person toward adapting to an established setting (e.g., classroom, residential setting). Within the PBS approach, consequences (both positive and negative consequences) remain important, but a major focus is placed on the redesign of the setting to *prevent* problem behaviors (Carr et al.,1994; Durand, 1990). This focus on prevention is seen in the emphasis given to removing stimuli that promote or evoke problem behavior (e.g., changing activity schedules, tasks, and social contexts associated with problem behavior) and to investing in teaching new skills, such as communication and social skills, that can replace problem behavior (Dunlap, Foster-Johnson, Clarke, Kern, & Childs, 1995; Dunlap, Kern-Dunlap, Clarke, & Robbins, 1991).

Carr (1994, 2000) offered an important insight into PBS when he encouraged those who design support to focus as much or more on what happens *between* bouts of problem behavior (e.g., when the person is doing well) as they do on what is happening during a bout of problem behavior. Using information about situations where the person is successful can provide valuable guidance for identifying how to organize support in more difficult situations. To illustrate the implications of this idea, meet our second student, Isha, described next.

Isha

Isha is a 15-year-old young woman with autism and severe intellectual disabilities who was at risk of being excluded from her school because she would scream, pull at her own hair, and scratch at staff when she was asked to shift from one activity to another. Isha has some speech but primarily uses a symbol communication system for much of her "formal" communication. Isha does not like

change or new situations. She also is allergic to grass and tree pollens, which contributes to her challenges during parts of the year. Earlier efforts to "address her autism" and provide clear positive and negative consequences (e.g., token economies, dense schedules of reinforcement) had been ineffective. Isha's team decided to try a PBS approach. Her teachers looked carefully at the situations where she behaved well and considered the differences between situations where she was successful and those that were difficult for her. In Isha's case, a process of functional behavioral assessment (described in detail later in this chapter), a central feature of PBS, made it clear that when her day followed highly predictable routines, she did well. When she was asked to shift from her routine (even to preferred activities), she found the process highly aversive and engaged in dangerous behaviors. Her problem behaviors maintained over time because periodically Isha was successful in getting her predictable routine reinstated. Isha's behavior support plan emerged as a combination of schedule redesign to prevent problem situations, teaching her new ways to request predictability, systematic consequences to prevent problem behaviors from being rewarded, and

clear rewards for moving through her daily events. To provide predictability without succumbing to the trap of continually repeating a narrow daily routine, the staff taught Isha to use a picture communication system to review current activities and label what activity would come next (Flannery & Horner, 1994). New activities could be introduced as long as they had a picture, were reviewed in advance, and were to be followed by a preferred activity. The staff also learned to give Isha precorrection prompts (Colvin, Sugai, & Patching, 1993) 1 to 3 minutes before an activity change. Finally, staff made sure that Isha received her allergy medication during the spring and early summer pollen season. Together these efforts resulted in an 85% reduction in her problem behavior, the opportunity to remain in her neighborhood school, and the ability to sustain important social relationships with peers.

Cascading Model of PBS

In many ways, the process of PBS is a cascade of steps, each step building from its predecessor. Figure 6–1 offers an overview of this process and provides the

organizing structure for describing the specific practices and organizational systems for each step. We begin with a review of the whole process and then provide more detailed implementation recommendations and supporting research for each step.

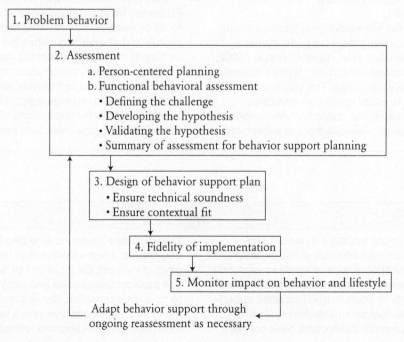

FIGURE 6–1
Cascading Structure of Behavior Support

1. Problem behavior

2. Assessment
   a. Person-centered planning
   b. Functional behavioral assessment
   • Defining the challenge
   • Developing the hypothesis
   • Validating the hypothesis
   • Summary of assessment for behavior support planning

3. Design of behavior support plan
   • Ensure technical soundness
   • Ensure contextual fit

4. Fidelity of implementation

5. Monitor impact on behavior and lifestyle

Adapt behavior support through ongoing reassessment as necessary

Step 1: Problem behavior. The cascade of activities begins when a problem behavior (or set of problem behaviors) is identified. If the problem behavior is of sufficient severity to require a formal plan of support, then an assessment is conducted. Note that from the beginning, problem behavior is (a) defined as problematic because it serves as a barrier to important lifestyle goals, including health, safety, and inclusion; (b) clustered into classes of behavior maintained by the same consequence (e.g., obtain attention, allow escape from an aversive activity); and (c) organized according to daily routines when it is most likely to occur (e.g., transitions, meal time, toileting, reading period), so the challenge shifts from simply reducing problem behavior to providing the support needed so the person is successful within daily routines. PBS focuses not just on reducing problem behavior but also on building the skills that result in success within routines that are difficult for the individual.

Step 2: Assessment. The assessment needed to guide PBS includes a *person-centered plan* that defines the personal goals and preferences of the individual and his or her family and a *functional behavioral assessment* that provides a clear statement defining (a) exactly what the problem behavior(s) looks like, (b) when it is most and least likely to occur, and (c) why the problem behavior keeps occurring. This information is obtained from review of the student's history; from active interviews with advocates, the student, and those who support the student; from direct observation; and, on occasion, from formal functional analysis.

Step 3: Design of support plan. The assessment information is used to construct a plan of support. In fact, a major feature of PBS is that the unique knowledge gleaned from the assessment process should directly guide the content of the support plan. A process known as "competing behavior analysis" (described later in this chapter) has been useful in moving from assessment results to a formal plan. PBS plans resulting from this process are characterized by (a) clear, operational definitions of the problem behavior(s); (b) a formal summary of the assessment outcomes; (c) specific strategies for altering the environment to prevent problem behaviors; (d) teaching objectives to build the desired skills that replace problem behaviors; (e) strategies for ensuring that desired behaviors are rewarded;

(f) strategies for minimizing the rewards associated with problem behaviors; (g) negative consequences for problem behaviors (if necessary); (h) strategies for minimizing the danger caused by severe problem behaviors (if necessary); and (i) formal procedures for assessing and adapting the plan over time.

Step 4: Fidelity of implementation. To increase the likelihood that behavior support plans are implemented as written, emphasis is placed on (a) clear description of the implementation process (who will do what, when) and (b) consideration of contextual fit, that is, the extent to which those individuals who are expected to provide support have the skills, resources, and support to be successful (Albin, Lucyshyn, Horner, & Flannery, 1996).

Step 5: Monitor and adapt support to achieve problem behavior reduction and lifestyle impact. For PBS to have substantive impact on not just problem behavior but also the options available for a desirable lifestyle, attention is needed for ongoing adaptation and sustainability. The vision of PBS is not that a brief intervention will "fix" or "correct" a person but that *ongoing* support may well be needed. Effective plans of support incorporate procedures for monitoring and adapting support strategies over time.

In the following sections, we will follow Maya through the cascade of PBS steps, with more detailed descriptions of the specific procedures that result in effective support. This example helps highlight the relevance of each step in the cascade of PBS steps.

Problem Behavior

The individualized student PBS process begins when a student is identified as having problem behavior(s) that requires more attention and support than is provided for the vast majority of students within the broader contexts of schoolwide and classroom behavior support systems (Sugai, Horner, & Gresham, 2002). In particular, PBS is used for students whose behavior raises concerns regarding the health and safety of the student, peers, school staff, or others; whose behavior interferes significantly with the student's educational program or the education of others; or whose behavior places the student at risk for loss of an inclusive educational placement and placement into a more restrictive or segregated setting. Consider Maya, who

was entering a regular middle school but whose problem behavior put her at risk for exclusion from that
school because of concerns about Maya's and other
students' safety.

> *Maya had a history of engaging in problem behav-
> ior that the middle school staff knew from her his-
> tory and files and from the transition process that
> was implemented to facilitate Maya's move from ele-
> mentary to middle school. Middle school staff was
> concerned about Maya's serious problem behaviors,
> which included hitting other students, spitting, and
> yelling, in addition to the annoying behavior of
> sticking her tongue out at other students. There also
> was concern that Maya's behaviors were becoming
> increasingly intense and that sometimes her behav-
> ior escalated out of control. From the very beginning
> of the school year, staff were alerted to Maya's behav-
> ior, and behavioral incidents in the hallways did oc-
> cur and were noted. If Maya was to be supported suc-
> cessfully in her new middle school, it was clear to
> Maya's teachers that an individualized behavior
> support plan (BSP) would be needed. A behavior sup-
> port team was created for Maya, and the process of
> designing and implementing a BSP was initiated.*

Assessment for Behavior Support Planning

Before a BSP can be developed for a student who is experiencing problem behavior, an assessment process is
initiated. In supporting students with disabilities, it is
advisable that two types of assessment be completed:
person-centered planning and functional behavioral
assessment.

Person-Centered Planning

In recent years, there has been growing recognition
that the outcomes of behavior support should include
not just the elimination or reduction of problem behavior but also an improvement in adaptive behavior
and overall quality of life (e.g., Koegel et al., 1996;
Meyer & Evans, 1989; Newton & Horner, 2004;
Schalock & Alonso, 2002). To be successful, the outcomes of behavior support must be referenced to the
personal values of the student receiving support and
his or her family.

This focus on quality of life, personal values, and
outcomes has resulted in people with disabilities, their

families, and teachers and other professionals working
to create processes for defining a person's values and
desired lifestyle and for rallying the support required
to achieve that vision. For example, the many varieties
of person-centered planning (see Holburn & Vietze,
2002; Kincaid, 1996; Mount, 1994) are designed to ensure that the person and those closest to the person
both (a) define a high-quality lifestyle from their personal perspectives and (b) discuss and develop broad
strategies for creating the conditions that will enable
that lifestyle. Person-centered planning assists support
teams to identify a "vision" for the focus student and to
place behavior support into the broader contexts of
the student's life and personal goals.

> *The design of behavior support for Maya began with
> her support team conducting a Personal Futures
> Plan meeting (Kincaid, 1996; Mount, 1994). The
> team that participated in the Personal Futures Plan
> was led to the greatest degree possible by Maya and
> included Maya's family, three middle school staff,
> Maya's fifth-grade teacher, the middle school behav-
> ior specialist, two friends, Maya's aunt, and Maya's
> longtime home care provider. This group of people
> met and then developed the following goals for
> Maya: (a) high school graduation; (b) living in an
> apartment with a friend; (c) employment in a fish or
> pet store; (d) skill development in cooking, clothing
> care, basic household chores, money management,
> personal care, and time management; (e) joining a
> community group; and (f) maintenance of good
> physical health through diet and exercise. These goals
> provided Maya's support team with a common vi-
> sion for Maya and for what they wanted and needed
> to accomplish with a BSP.*

Teachers and others providing support to students
with disabilities will want to be mindful that the development and implementation of any BSP should occur
within the context of broader lifestyle considerations
that have emerged from previously completed person-
centered planning processes. It is recommended that
person-centered planning occur on a regular basis,
given that students' aspirations may change across
time, particularly as the onset of their postschool lives
approaches. When students have the kinds of lives
they want and deserve, their problem behaviors may
decrease, and PBS can be initiated to address "residual"
problem behaviors. In dealing with such problem
behaviors and in supporting a student in the quest to

obtain a more desired life, the initiation of functional behavioral assessment will be vital (Holburn, Jacobson, Vietze, Schwartz, & Sersen, 2000).

Functional Behavioral Assessment

Functional behavioral assessment (FBA) is a central feature of PBS. FBA is a process for gathering information about problem behavior and the environmental conditions that predict and maintain it (Crone & Horner, 2003; O'Neill et al., 1997). The goal of FBA is to improve the effectiveness and efficiency of the BSP. The process of FBA involves gathering information about the problem behavior, the situations where problem behavior is most and least likely to occur, and the consequences that reward and maintain the problem behavior. This information is typically gathered through multiple methods, including interviews, rating scales, checklists, reviews of records and files, direct observations in natural settings, and the process of functional analysis. Not all methods are necessarily used within a single FBA. A major outcome of FBA is a hypothesis statement that identifies the function(s) (i.e., purpose) that the problem behavior serves for the person. FBA helps us understand why problem behavior occurs (i.e., variables that are associated with the problem behavior). Details on FBA procedures and outcomes are described in the following sections of this chapter.

An FBA of Maya's behavior was conducted through file reviews, interviews, and direct observations led by the behavior specialist on Maya's team. Situations were categorized where Maya was most likely and least likely to engage in hitting, spitting, yelling, and sticking her tongue out. Through functional assessment interviews with Maya's former and current teachers and her family and through systematic observations of her behavior during the school day, Maya's team identified two routines where her problem behaviors were most likely to occur: (a) hallway transition periods and (b) activities with minimal structure (i.e., lunch, recess, group activities). In both situations, Maya's team identified that Maya's problem behaviors were preceded by low levels of peer attention and were followed by and seemingly rewarded by immediate access to peer attention.

FBA is neither a process for producing a diagnosis nor a process for determining if a behavior problem is a manifestation of a disability (Carr et al., 1994; Durand, 1990; Sugai, Lewis-Palmer, & Hagan-Burke,

1999–2000). The focus of FBA is on understanding the relationship between environmental events and problem behavior, on how to change the environment, not the student. A medical approach would likely focus on identifying deficits in the *child*, but an approach based on FBA focuses on identifying deficits in the *environment* (i.e., the conditions that establish and maintain problem behavior). FBA and PBS emphasize the engineering of effective environments as the key to producing desired behavior change.

FBA is less concerned with the fundamental etiology of problem behavior (i.e., how it originated) and more concerned with the environmental conditions (i.e., consequences) that *currently* maintain the behavior. The conditions under which a problem behavior initially develops may be very different from the conditions that currently maintain it. For example, Guess and Carr (1991) have suggested that some forms of severe self-injury may have begun as simple forms of self-stimulation (or responses to short-term illness), only later to develop into complex and destructive behaviors maintained by their social consequences. O'Reilly (1997) found that a 26–month-old girl's self-injurious behavior was correlated with the presence of recurrent otitis media (an ear infection that produces ear pain, ear fullness, or hearing loss). Naturally, such behavior would draw the attention of any caring parent. Thus, although the behavior began as a reaction to ear pain, it was ultimately emitted in the absence of ear pain due to a parent's contingent attention. FBA and PBS (a) use a behavioral approach rather than a medical approach to focus on (b) environmental conditions that set up, trigger, and maintain problem behaviors rather than on diagnostic labels in order to (c) remediate deficient environments rather than "fix" or "cure" students with problem behaviors.

Why Conduct an FBA?

The 1997 amendments to the Individuals with Disabilities Education Act (IDEA) included the requirements that schools use FBA and PBS. Although many school personnel may have already considered the use of FBA and PBS to be "best practices" and begun to use them, the 1997 IDEA amendments provided a legal mandate. This mandate has triggered thoughtful reviews and questions about (a) the extent to which school personnel have the technical capability to implement effective FBA and PBS (e.g., Ervin et al., 2001); (b) the degree to which FBA and PBS demonstrate external validity across the full range of settings, students, and behaviors that constitute a school-based application (e.g., Nelson, Roberts, Mathur, & Rutherford, 1999); (c) the social validity of FBA (e.g., Reid & Nelson, 2002); and (d) the extent to which interventions based on FBA can be demonstrated to be more effective than interventions not derived from an FBA (e.g., Gresham et al., 2004). These are important questions that should trigger further research determining whether the federal confidence in FBA and PBS is warranted. Such research is beginning to emerge.

For example, two meta-analyses of behavior intervention and PBS research have found that the presence of pretreatment FBA was associated with increased effectiveness of an intervention (Didden, Duker, & Korzilius, 1997; Marquis et al., 2000). Marquis and colleagues found strong differences in the percentage of behavior reduction resulting from PBS interventions when FBA was conducted and used in planning the intervention. They concluded, "These results indicate that doing an assessment and using it to plan the PBS intervention probably results in a better outcome" (p. 161).

Further support for the beneficial effect of using FBA to plan interventions was provided in two recent studies involving students with problem behaviors in general education settings (Ingram, Lewis-Palmer, & Sugai, in press; Newcomer & Lewis, in press). These two studies compared interventions that were logically derived from a preceding FBA (i.e., were "FBA indicated") to interventions that were either "contraindicated" by FBA or not tied to a FBA hypothesis. In both studies, the interventions that were logically linked to an FBA produced substantial reductions in problem behavior in comparison to commonly used interventions that were not linked to FBA.

Finally, relevant to the question of whether FBA is doable by typical school personnel is a recent study by Bergstrom, Horner, and Crone (2004). This study found that, following training and limited technical assistance, school-based teams (a) independently developed FBA hypotheses that were later confirmed to be accurate by a researcher who independently conducted a functional analysis, (b) independently developed and implemented behavior support plans—based on the preceding FBA—that significantly reduced students' disruptive behavior and increased their on-task behavior, and (c) completed the FBA processes in a relatively short period of time, accurately implemented the interventions, and rated the interventions as being high in "acceptability."

In addition to informing decisions regarding the selection of effective behavior support procedures, FBA provides the conceptual logic needed to make multicomponent support plans work as intended. Many problem behaviors necessitate multicomponent support plans (e.g., modifying the curriculum, teaching new skills, reinforcing alternative behavior, and extinguishing problem behavior). However, the complexity of multicomponent interventions can increase the difficulty of implementation. Without the conceptual logic provided by an FBA, there is a danger that an individual intervention procedure that appears sound when examined in isolation may be revealed as illogical when considered as a component of an integrated intervention package. FBA helps ensure that the multiple elements of an intervention work together rather than at cross-purpose.

Recall Isha, who was at risk of being excluded from her school because she would scream, pull her hair, and scratch at staff when she was asked to shift from one activity to another. When Isha was requested to alter her typical routine in an unpredictable manner, she found the process highly aversive and engaged in these dangerous behaviors that often resulted in her predictable routine being reinstated. Based on this knowledge, her staff could have chosen to "extinguish" the problem behavior by disallowing her predictable routine to be reinstated, hoping to reduce the problem behavior by withholding the reinforcer. Although this might have worked and would have made some programmatic sense as an isolated support strategy, the staff instead chose to use a package of integrated procedures that combined (a) redesigning Isha's schedule to prevent problem situations, (b) teaching her new ways to request predictability, (c) introducing systematic consequences to prevent problem behaviors from being rewarded, and (d) providing clear rewards to Isha as she moved through her events.

The conceptual logic underlying FBA, as well as emerging research results demonstrating the effectiveness and utility of FBA, argues for continued research and application. Basing interventions on the function of problem behavior rather than attempting to overpower problem behavior through the application of interventions involving arbitrary contingencies of reinforcement appears to be a fruitful approach to helping students overcome problem behavior.

The Outcomes of FBA

Broadly considered, FBA produces information that results in six outcomes: (a) description of the student's problem behavior and daily routines; (b) identification of consequent conditions that maintain the problem behavior; (c) identification of antecedent conditions that set the occasion for (or "trigger") the problem behavior, as well as antecedent conditions that *do not* trigger the problem behavior; (d) identification of setting events that make the problem behavior more sensitive (or less sensitive) to the maintaining consequences and their associated antecedents; (e) production of a written hypothesis that synthesizes the foregoing information into a testable statement about the problem behavior; and (f) direct observations of the student during typical daily routines for the purpose of tentatively confirming (or disconfirming) the hypothesis (O'Neill et al., 1997).

Who Is Involved in FBA?

Depending on the school or district and its policies, the person (or persons) with the responsibility for conducting or leading an FBA may be a school psychologist, behavior specialist, counselor, special educator, teacher, or some other member of a behavior support team; however, FBA involves a team process with many team members sharing responsibilities. Typically, the process for achieving the six FBA outcomes begins with interviews of school personnel and others who are most knowledgeable about the student's problem behavior (e.g., people who have actually witnessed the student's problem behavior). The informants may include teachers, a bus driver, a school nurse, parents, and, if possible, the student him- or herself. A review of existing records and data also may be undertaken.

Various manuals and accompanying forms and questionnaires have been developed to aid in conducting interviews that identify problem behaviors, daily routines, and the problem behaviors triggering and maintaining consequences (e.g., O'Neill et al., 1997; see Dunlap & Kincaid, 2001, for a review of FBA manuals). As we note in a following section, there are also several instruments that can be used to facilitate direct observation of the student during his or her daily routines. However, even as we present such instruments in the following pages, we believe it is more important to understand the concepts that underlie the use of the instruments than to understand how to complete a specific questionnaire or form.

Regardless of the instruments used, it is useful to think of FBA as proceeding in three phases: defining the challenge, developing the hypothesis, and validating the hypothesis. Completing these phases is a necessary precursor to developing an effective and efficient BSP.

Defining the Challenge

This phase of FBA is concerned with achieving the first FBA outcome: a description of the student's problem behavior and daily routines. A successful behavior support effort cannot be initiated until those involved reach agreement about the nature of the problem behavior. This is best accomplished by first defining the problem behavior in operational terms. An operational definition specifically describes what the student is doing when he or she is said to be engaging in "problem behavior." A problem behavior that is described as "anger" or "frustration" lacks the clarity of a description such as "hitting," "refusing to follow the teacher's instructions," or "throwing textbooks." Operational definitions help ensure that those who are called on to implement the BSP are operating with a common understanding of the behavioral challenge. There are many tools that assist teams in identifying and defining problem behavior, identifying daily routines, and organizing problem behavior by daily routines. Two examples of tools we have used are the Teacher Assistance Team Request for Assistance form (presented in Figure 6-2) and the Functional Assessment Checklist for Teachers & Staff (FACTS—Part A) (presented in Figure 6-3). Maya's team used both of these tools in defining the challenge.

A sample Request for Assistance form was completed by Maya's homeroom teacher in collaboration with the school behavior specialist, Trudy Schwartz, on 09/18/03, to initiate a referral for assistance with Maya's problem behaviors. This request for assistance was the impetus to formalize convening a behavior support team in hopes that they could ultimately develop a BSP that would help Maya learn different ways to communicate rather than communicating by using problem behaviors. On the Request for Assistance form, Maya's problem behaviors initially were identified by her homeroom teacher as aggressiveness, poor attention, poor work completion, and disruptiveness.

Later, on 10/01/03, Trudy used "Part A" of a tool called the Functional Assessment Checklist for

FIGURE 6–2
Request for Assistance Form

Date _____**9/18/03**_____

Student Name _____**Maya**_____

Teacher/Team _____**Trudy**_____

IEP: (Yes) No (Circle)

Grade ___**6th**___

Situations	Problem Behaviors	Most Common Result
Various situations including lunch, hallways, recess, and classrooms	Shows aggression, is disruptive and inattentive; is not completing academic work.	Peers respond to her–laugh or confront her

1. What have you tried/used? How has it worked?
Talked with parents, teacher, and planned positive reinforcer

What have you tried to date to change the situations in which the problem behavior(s) occur?

___ Modified assignments to match the student's skills	___ Changed seating assignments	___ Changed schedule of activities	Other?
✓ Arranged tutoring to improve the student's academic skills	___ Changed curriculum	___ Provided extra assistance	

What have you tried to date to teach expected behaviors?

✓ Reminders about expected behavior when problem behavior is likely	___ Clarified rules and expected behavior for the whole class	___ Practiced the expected behaviors in class	Other?
✓ Reward program for expected behavior	___ Oral agreement with the student	___ Self-management program	
✓ Systematic feedback about behavior	___ Individual written contract with the student	___ Contract with student/with parents	

What consequences have you tried to date for the problem behavior?

___ Loss of privileges	___ Note or phone call to the student's parents	___ Office referral	Other?
___ Time-out	___ Detention	___ Reprimand	
___ Referral to school counselor	✓ Meeting with the student's parents	___ Individual meeting with the students	

Source: Todd, A. W., Horner, R. H., Sugai, G., & Colvin, G. (1999). Individualizing school-wide discipline for students with chronic problem behaviors: A team approach. *Effective School Practices, 17*(4), 72–82.

FIGURE 6–3
Functional Assessment Checklist for Teachers and Staff (FACTS—Part A)

Step 1   Student/Grade: __**Maya, Grade 6**__   Date: __**10/01/03**__
           Interviewer: __**Trudy**__   Respondent(s): __**Homeroom and Study Hall Teachers**__

Step 2   **Student Profile:** Please identify at least three strengths or contributions the student brings to school.
           __**Likes being around people, loves fish and aquariums, likes music**__

Step 3   **Problem Behavior(s): Identify problem behaviors**

✓ Tardy	✓ Fight/Physical Aggression	✓ Disruptive	__ Theft
__ Unresponsive	__ Inappropriate Language	__ Insubordination	__ Vandalism
__ Withdrawn	__ Verbal Harassment	__ Work not done	__ Other _____
	✓ Verbally Inappropriate	__ Self-injury	

Describe problem behavior: **hits peers, yells, spits, throws objects, sticks tongue out**

Step 4   **Identifying Routines: Where, when, and with whom problem behaviors are most likely**

Schedule (Times)	Activity	Likelihood of Problem Behavior	Specific Problem Behavior
9:00	Bus to class	Low 1 2 3 4 5 High (6)	Tongue out, yell, spit
9:15	Language Arts	1 (2) 3 4 5 6	
10:15	Break	1 2 3 4 5 (6)	Tongue out, yell, hit, spit
10:30	Math	1 (2) 3 4 5 6	
11:30	Homeroom	1 2 3 (4) 5 6	Tongue out
12:00	Lunch	1 2 3 4 5 (6)	Yell, spit, hit
12:30	Teen Health	1 2 (3) 4 5 6	Tongue out
1:30	Current Events	1 (2) 3 4 5 6	
2:30	Choir	1 2 3 (4) 5 6	Tongue out, yell
3:30	Class to Bus	1 2 3 4 5 (6)	Tongue out, yell, hit, spit
All day	Hallway transitions	1 2 3 4 5 (6)	Tongue out, yell, hit, spit

Step 5   **Select one to three routines for further assessment. Select routines based on (a) similarity of activities (conditions) with ratings of 4, 5 or 6 and (b) similarity of problem behavior(s). Complete the FACTS–Part B for each routine identified.**

Hallway transitions—arrival and dismissal, lunch

Teachers and Staff (FACTS) to begin an FBA interview with Maya's homeroom and study hall teachers. During these interviews, Maya's problem behaviors were more specifically defined as hitting peers, sticking out her tongue, spitting, yelling, and throwing objects.

In addition to identifying and operationally defining problem behavior(s), defining the challenge also involves identifying the student's typical daily routines and determining the occurrence of problem behavior(s) in those routines. Routines are sequences of behavior that are a usual part of daily life that result in socially important outcomes. For example, eating breakfast, traveling to school, participating in morning circle, engaging in recess activities, and transitioning from one school activity to the next are common routines for students. A routine involves a predictable sequence of events that results in predictable outcomes. A challenge of PBS is to ensure that a student is not excluded from typical routines because of problem behavior but rather is provided with behavioral support that results in the problem behavior being rendered irrelevant, ineffective, or inefficient during those routines.

We strongly recommend that an FBA describe the student's full daily routines and identify those routines where the student's problem behavior is most likely—and least likely—to occur. For students, a daily routine can be described in terms of the daily schedule of school activities. The FACTS—Part A (see Figure 6-3) incorporates this as step 4, providing a section to record the daily routines, to rate the likelihood of problem behavior within each routine, and to identify the specific problem behavior(s) that occurs within each routine.

During the course of leading the FBA interview for Maya, Trudy recorded Maya's school routines/schedule directly on Part A of the FACTS (see Figure 6-3). Organizing Maya's problem behaviors within the contexts of daily routines helped Maya's team understand that her problem behaviors were most likely to occur during (a) hallway transition periods (including transitions to and from the school bus area) and (b) activities with minimal structure (i.e., lunch, break, less structured group activities such as homeroom and choir). The specific problem behaviors identified were sticking out tongue, yelling, hitting, and spitting.

Developing the Hypothesis

Once the student's problem behavior has been operationally defined and organized within the contexts of his or her typical daily routines, we focus on gathering information that will lead to developing a hypothesis about when and why the problem behavior occurs. To gather the information required to arrive at a hypothesis, the person responsible for conducting the FBA will continue interviewing the school personnel and others who are most knowledgeable about the student's problem behavior. Depending on the time available, this may involve simply continuing with the same interview that produced the operational definition of the student's problem behavior and a description of his or her daily routine. Typically, it is useful to talk with at least two people who have daily contact with the student and have witnessed the problem behavior. As noted, it may also be appropriate to interview the student if he or she can participate in an interview effectively.

Interviews, Checklists, and Rating Scales Several interview instruments, checklists, and rating scales are available for gathering the information required to complete this phase of the FBA. Structured interviews (Crone & Horner, 2003; O'Neill et al., 1997; Willis, LaVigna, & Donnellan, 1987); checklists, such as the FACTS (Crone & Horner, 2003; March et al., 2000) and the Functional Analysis Checklist (Van Houten & Rolider, 1991); and rating scales, such as the Motivation Assessment Scale (MAS) (Durand, 1988), organize information about problem behaviors, antecedent stimuli (including setting events), and consequences to help determine behavioral function. Comprehensive interview forms (e.g., O'Neill et al., 1997; Willis et al., 1987) also solicit information about the student's repertoire of adaptive behavior, particularly behavior that may serve to replace the problem behavior, his or her communication skills, the quality of the support environment, and the success (or failure) of previous support plans. Interviews have the advantage of (a) being relatively low in cost, (b) allowing for the inclusion of multiple people who have important information about the student, and (c) providing a rich array of information that can be used to structure more detailed analyses of problem behavior.

An FBA interview concerning a complex, challenging pattern of behavior may take anywhere from 45 minutes to 2 hours. In our experience, the time required to complete an interview can vary considerably, depending not only on the complexity of the problem but also on the number of people participating in the interview and their knowledge of the student, talkativeness, and level of agreement. Using a structured interview or a checklist helps keep the process focused. Consistent with the outcomes of this phase of FBA, the interview should produce—at a minimum—the following: (a) identification of consequent conditions that maintain the problem behavior; (b) identification of antecedent conditions that set the occasion for (or "trigger") the problem behavior, as well as antecedent conditions that *do not* trigger the problem behavior; and (c) identification of setting events that make the problem behavior more sensitive (or less sensitive) to the maintaining consequences and their associated antecedents.

Identification of Consequent Conditions That Maintain the Problem Behavior An important aspect of behavior-environment relationships is the consequence(s) produced by a person's behavior, including problem behavior. Behavior is useful in that it serves a

function for the person. We assume that any behavior that occurs repeatedly is serving some useful function (i.e., is producing an outcome that is reinforcing).

Behavior may serve two major functions (i.e., produce two major outcomes): (a) *obtaining* something desirable or (b) *avoiding or escaping* something undesirable. In more technical terms, obtaining desirable things is referred to as *positive reinforcement*, while escaping or avoiding undesirable things is referred to as *negative reinforcement* (if such consequences result in continued occurrences of the behaviors). Figure 6-4 provides a framework for organizing the possible functions of problem behaviors into six categories (three under "Obtain" and three others under "Escape/Avoid"). Events that may be obtained or escaped/avoided may require interactions that involve other persons or things (i.e., are socially mediated events) or may be internal to the person with problem behavior and not require the presence of others. Some problem behaviors may serve multiple functions (Day, Horner, & O'Neill, 1994).

FIGURE 6–4
Functions of Behaviors

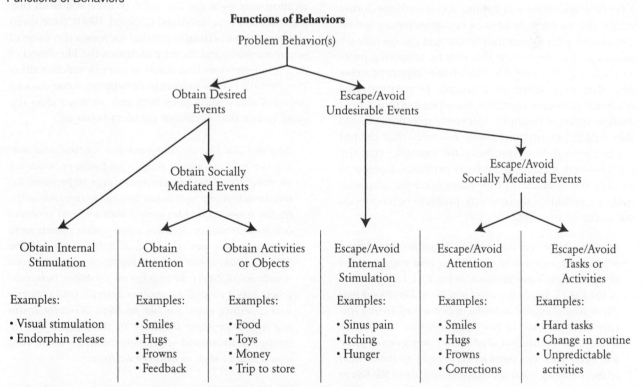

Source: From O'Neill, R. E., Horner, R. H., Albin, R. W., Sprague, J. R., Storey, K., & Newton, J. S. (1997). *Functional assessment for problem behavior: A practical handbook (2nd ed.).* Pacific Grove, CA: Brooks/Cole.

Developing a hypothesis about the function of problem behavior(s) based on the information collected in an interview(s) is a critical outcome of the FBA process and is essential for developing an effective and efficient BSP. Some FBA interview forms, such as the Functional Assessment Interview from O'Neill et al. (1997) and the FACTS—Part B (presented in Figure 6-5), provide a place on the form to record a hypothesis that identifies the function of problem behavior.

Using Part B of the FACTS Checklist, Trudy and Maya's team found that during the "hallway transitions" portions of Maya's routine (e.g., traveling from the school bus to her first class, during the break between her language arts and math classes), her problem behaviors were maintained by getting peer attention. This is noted in the Summary of Behavior section, step 6 on the form. (Note that Part B of the FACTS would be completed for each different type of routine associated with a high likelihood of problem behaviors.)

Identification of Antecedent Conditions That Do and Do Not Trigger the Problem Behavior
Interview questions will inquire about routines during which the problem behaviors occur, including *when*, *where*, and with *whom* they occur and the *specific activities* within the routine that may be triggering problem behavior. It is useful to identify any aspect of a routine that may serve as a trigger (e.g., particular academic demands, free time, transitioning to the next routine, types of prompts). Interview questions should also solicit information about routines that do not evoke problem behavior. Note, for example, that the FACTS—Part A (see Figure 6-3) provides a place to identify the likelihood of problem behavior across all routines, including those where problem behaviors do not occur or are unlikely.

The FBA interview concerning Maya produced findings about antecedent conditions that trigger—and do not trigger—her problem behaviors. Using Part A of the FACTS, Trudy inquired about the likelihood that Maya would engage in problem behaviors during specific time periods of her daily routine. The FACTS shows that the likelihood of Maya's engaging in problem behaviors was rated as very "high" in the context of the following routines: transitioning from the bus to class, break, lunch, transitioning from class to the bus, and throughout the day during hallway transitions.

Each of these routines involved a hallway transition for Maya (e.g., traveling from the school bus to her first class, going to lunch, going to break). In contrast, the likelihood of Maya's engaging in problem behavior was rated as relatively low during the following routines: language arts, math, and current events. These routines involved classroom activities that were highly structured. Step 4 of Part B of the FACTS indicates that during hallway transitions, relevant predictors (antecedent triggers) for Maya's problem behavior appear to be that she is (a) socially isolated, although (b) with peers, during (c) an unstructured time (transitions in the hallway).

Identification of Setting Events
Recognition of the role that setting events play in problem behavior is relatively new (Carr, Reeve, & Magito-McLaughlin, 1996; Horner, Day, & Day, 1997; Horner, Vaughn, Day, & Ard, 1996). Setting events are conditions that temporarily alter the value of reinforcers that maintain problem behaviors. For example, sleep deprivation is a setting event that may make some tasks more aversive than usual and decrease the value of the social praise obtained by doing these tasks. The result is that sleep deprivation may increase the value of escaping from boring tasks (e.g., via tantrums) (Durand, 1990). Time spent alone may be a setting event that increases the value of social attention and thereby increases the likelihood of problem behaviors that result in peer or teacher attention. Setting events help explain why on some days an instructional session goes well and on other days the same instruction occasions problem behavior.

Isha did not like shifting from her routine, and asking her to do so was a trigger for problem behavior. However, Isha did not always engage in problem behavior when she was asked to shift to another activity. On some days, Isha would shift without problem behavior. However, on days when pollen counts were very high and her allergy was acting up (and she had not taken her allergy medication), Isha was much more likely to engage in problem behavior when asked to shift to another activity. Isha's allergy was a setting event for her problem behavior. It did not trigger problem behavior by itself, but it did increase the likelihood of problem behavior when Isha was asked to shift to another activity.

The design of behavior support is improved when information about powerful setting events is available

FIGURE 6–5

Functional Assessment Checklist for Teachers and Staff (FACTS—Part B)

Step 1   Student/Grade: **Maya, Grade 6**   Date: **10/01/03**
         Interviewer: **Trudy**   Respondent(s): **Homeroom and Study Hall Teachers**

Step 2   **Routine/Activities/Context:** Which routine (only one) from the Facts–Part A is assessed?

Routine/Activities/Context	Problem Behavior(s)
Hallway Transitions	Sticking out tongue, yelling, spitting, hitting peers

Step 3   **Provide more detail about the problem behavior(s):**

What does the problem behavior(s) look like? **Tongue out, yelling, spitting, hitting peers during transitions**

How often does the problem behavior(s) occur? **Moderate to high frequency (lower in other routines)**

How long does the problem behavior(s) last when it does occur? **Until peer gives attention or teacher interrupts**

What is the intensity/level or danger of the problem behavior(s)?

Step 4   **What are the events that predict when the problem behavior(s) will occur? (Predictors)**

Related Issues (setting events)		Environmental Features	
___ illness	Other:	___ reprimand/correction	___ structured activity
___ drug use	**long breaks from school**	___ physical demands	✓ unstructured time
✓ negative social	**social isolation**	✓ socially isolated	___ tasks too boring
___ conflict at home	**before school**	✓ with peers	___ activity too long
___ academic failure		___ Other	___ tasks too difficult

Step 5   **What consequences appear most likely to maintain the problem behavior(s)?**

Things That Are Obtained		Things Avoided or Escaped from	
___ adult attention	Other:	___ hard tasks	Other: _____
✓ peer attention		___ reprimands	_____
___ preferred activity		___ peer negatives	_____
___ money/things		___ physical effort	_____
		___ adult attention	_____

SUMMARY OF BEHAVIOR

Step 6   **Identify the summary that will be used to build a plan of behavior support.**

Setting Events and Predictors	Problem Behavior(s)	Maintaining Consequence(s)
"Mondays" and low peer attention Hallway transitions	Sticking tongue out, yelling, spitting, and hitting	Peer attention

Step 7   **How confident are you that the Summary of Behavior is accurate?**

Strategies for Preventing Problem Behavior	Consequences for Problem Behavior
Not very confident	Very Confident

1	2	3	4	⑤	6

Step 8   **What current efforts have been used to control the problem behavior?**

Strategies for Preventing Problem Behavior		Strategies for Responding to Problem Behavior	
___ schedule change	Other: **peer mentor,**	___ reprimand	Other: **call home**
___ seating change	**precorrect behavior**	___ office referral	**teach to use conversation**
___ curriculum change	**before transitions**	___ detention	**book**

and is used to design support procedures that address relevant setting events and their effects. Because setting events may be distant in time (i.e., they may have occurred earlier in the day or the night before) and may not have clearly visible effects or indicators, asking interview questions about potential setting events may be the best way to learn about them. Thus, using the FBA interview to gather information about general medical status, social interaction patterns, daily activities, and other possible setting events that may increase (or decrease) the person's sensitivity to the previously identified maintaining consequences and their associated triggering antecedent conditions is an important aspect of the FBA interview.

Maya's team identified that possible setting events for Maya's problem behaviors are long breaks from school (a weekend, a holiday) and social isolation before school. These have been recorded on Part B of the FACTS in step 4.

Other Information of Interest Depending on the time available for the interview, gathering additional information can ultimately prove useful when the time comes to develop the BSP. For example, it will be useful to inquire about appropriate behavior that is already part of the student's repertoire, particularly behavior with which the student may be able to secure the maintaining consequence currently gained via problem behavior. For example, a student may have demonstrated that she can ask for help or ask for a break from an activity by signing or signaling. If the student appears to be engaging in tantrums to escape difficult academic tasks, the BSP could include a prompt for the student to use the sign or signal to ask for a break (and then provide the break) as an alternative to escaping from the task via a tantrum. If the student does not already have a usable signal, the BSP could include a teaching component designed to help the student acquire this important skill.

In thinking about appropriate alternative behaviors, communication is the single most important skill to be considered for students with severe problem behaviors. Different theories have been proposed to explain why this is so, but the consistent conclusion is that effective support requires understanding the ways in which a person communicates important information to others in the environment. PBS plans often include teaching or enhancing communication skills. Therefore, it is essential to inquire about the communication

skills a person currently uses (Donnellan, Mirenda, Mesaros, & Fassbender, 1984).

Isha had experience using a symbol system to communicate simple requests. Her support team recognized that this type of communication response could be used as an alternative behavior to replace Isha's problem behavior. Their hypothesis was that Isha's problem behavior was maintained by getting to stay in activities she was doing and getting activities reinstated when she was asked to shift to another activity. What Isha needed was a better way, an acceptable way, to communicate that she wanted to stay with her current activity. The team determined that they could teach Isha to request more time by pointing to a symbol in a communication book.

It may also prove wise to use the interview as an occasion to identify reinforcers that will be effective with the student (e.g., objects, events, activities). Prior to developing the BSP, one may want to assess the student's preferences with regard to reinforcing objects, activities, and events. Such assessments typically involve exposing the student to a variety of potential reinforcers, including edibles, toys/objects, entertainment (e.g., music, TV, movies), games, outings, domestic and personal care activities, and various forms of social attention and sensory stimulation (Green, Reid, Canipe, & Gardner, 1991; Pace, Ivancic, Edwards, Iwata, & Page, 1985).

Interviews with Maya's teachers and parents indicated that Maya thrived on peer attention and that many of her inappropriate behaviors are maintained by peer attention. Maya's desire to gain peer attention was incorporated into her support plan by arranging for Maya to have a peer mentor to be with during nonstructured routines on the bus and at school. Having a peer mentor during routines that were difficult for Maya meant that she had regular access to peer attention and did not need to engage in problem behavior to get peer attention (i.e., problem behavior was made irrelevant).

Finally, one may also want to ask about the history of the student's problem behavior (e.g., how long it has persisted), the various programs and interventions that have been used to manage the behaviors, and the degree of success achieved by implementing those programs. Learning about the types of supports that have been attempted and their effects can provide clues about the things that influence problem behaviors. For example, if a time-out program was tried in the past and had the effect of *increasing* the frequency of a behavior, this might indicate that the behavior is motivated by escaping or avoiding situations or demands. In many cases, it may be hard to obtain clear and reliable information about what has been tried and how well it worked or did not work; however, it is usually worthwhile to make the attempt.

Produce a Written Hypothesis as a Testable Statement At this point, one should be in a position to synthesize the previously gathered information into a testable hypothesis statement about the problem behavior. The hypothesis statement describes the relationship between setting events, triggering antecedents, the behaviors of concern, and maintaining consequences.

> *Trudy's hypothesis statement (Summary of Behavior) regarding Maya's problem behavior is recorded in step 6 on Part B of the FACTS. She has noted that Maya is likely to stick her tongue out at peers, yell, spit at them, or hit them during hallway transitions (particularly on Mondays after a weekend break from school) with the maintaining consequence (function) being to gain their attention. Trudy and her colleagues have indicated that they have a high degree of confidence in this hypothesis statement by giving it a rating of 5 on a 6-point scale in step 7.*

Table 6–1 provides samples of other hypothesis statements derived from hypothetical FBA interviews.

These statements are broken down into setting events, immediate antecedents, problem behaviors, and maintaining consequences.

Validating the Hypothesis

Once a testable hypothesis statement has been produced, the final stage of the FBA can occur: validating the hypothesis. Because the hypothesis statements will ultimately guide the development of a BSP and because it is often difficult to define hypothesis statements with a high degree of confidence, it is necessary to validate (test) the accuracy of the hypothesis. Two major strategies for validating hypothesis statements are (a) direct observation of the student in the context of the relevant routines and (b) formal functional analysis manipulations, where mini-experiments are conducted to demonstrate a functional relationship between the problem behavior and environmental events. Conducting a functional analysis requires a relatively great degree of skill. For this reason, we begin by discussing the direct observation option for verifying the hypothesis.

Direct Observation Direct observation of behavior has long been a cornerstone of applied behavior analysis (e.g., Baer, Wolf, & Risley, 1968). The antecedent, behavior, consequence (ABC) chart (Bijou et al., 1968) was an early method to supplement interview data with direct observation. ABC charting involves watching the focus person and recording, in narrative style, information about the problem behavior and its

TABLE 6–1
Sample Hypothesis Statements from Hypothetical FBA Interviews

1. When Sarah is getting little attention in morning circle, she is likely to shout profanities and throw things to get attention from her peers. The longer she has gone without direct attention, the more likely she is to engage in shouting profanities.
2. When Monica is asked to do independent seat work, she is likely to tear up materials and hit her teacher to escape from the task demands. This process is even more likely if she has had a negative interaction with the teacher earlier in the day.
3. When Jolene is prompted to stop using the computer, she is likely to fall to the floor and scream. The problem behaviors are maintained by keeping access to the computer, and the likelihood is greatest when Jolene has had limited time on the computer earlier in the day.
4. In situations with low levels of activity or attention at home, Dan will rock and begin to chew his fingers. These behaviors appear to be maintained by self-stimulation.
5. When Bishara is asked to dress himself or do other nonpreferred self-care routines, he will begin to slap his head. Head slaps appear to be maintained by escape from the self-care routines and are even more likely if he has been asked to stop a preferred activity to engage in the self-care routine.
6. When Anya begins to have difficulty with a reading or math assignment, she will put her head down, refuse to respond, and/or close her books. Anya's refusal is maintained by avoiding the assignment and is far more likely to occur if she has had less than 5 hours of sleep the previous night.

antecedent and consequent events. The narrative approach used in ABC charting is limited in that its narrative style does not lend itself to gathering measures of observational reliability. ABC charting can also be difficult to use when observing high-frequency behaviors. Finally, ABC charting may tell us little about conditions that are associated with the *absence* of problem behavior since ABC charting is event driven and occurs only when a problem behavior occurs.

An extension of the ABC chart, called scatter plot analysis, was developed by Touchette, MacDonald, and Langer (1985) and elaborated by Doss and Reichle (1991). The scatter plot is a grid that allows one to record the occurrence of problem behavior (via a shorthand behavior code) within designated time intervals (e.g., hour or half-hour periods) across multiple days. The scatter plot has the advantage of documenting both when problem behaviors occur and when they do not occur. Touchette et al. documented that by focusing on the features of those periods where problem behavior was observed, interventions that altered those periods resulted in reductions of problem behavior.

A more recent adaptation of the scatter plot observation form that also incorporates elements of ABC charting is the Functional Assessment Observation form (O'Neill et al., 1997). This system for conducting direct observations allows for the identification of events that reliably occur just prior to problem behaviors and events that occur just after problem behaviors. By identifying these relationships, one can infer antecedent events that trigger problem behaviors and consequence events that maintain the problem behaviors. When the contents of the form are structured in accordance with information previously gained via interviews (e.g., identified problem behavior, antecedents, consequences, routines), the form can be a useful tool. However, it should be noted that direct observation systems seldom focus on distant setting events.

While direct observation methods are more objective and precise than interviews, their results must also be viewed with caution. Given that simple direct observation does not involve manipulation or control of targeted variables, the data demonstrate correlations, not causal relationships, between environmental events and behavior. An example will illustrate the potential risk of relying solely on direct observation data to design a behavior support plan. Consider the case of a student who engages in severe head hitting.

A record of direct observations showed that when the student hit her head, the teacher usually went to her side, provided a reprimand, and attempted to redirect her to play with a toy. Multiple direct observations of this series of events suggested that the student's head hitting was maintained by the teacher's attention. However, a later, more extensive analysis indicated that the student had chronic sinus infections and that head hitting lessened the pain from the infections. In this case, attempts to replace head hitting with requests for attention would have been ineffective. However, medication to relieve the sinus pain was effective. Multiple factors can affect problem behavior, and care is needed when developing and confirming FBA hypotheses.

Some studies have documented that carefully conducted direct observations can be used as the basis for designing effective BSPs (Lewis-Palmer, 1998; Mace & Lalli, 1991; March & Horner, 1998; Repp, Felce, & Barton, 1988, Sasso et al., 1992), while others have demonstrated that less accurate findings also may work (Lerman & Iwata, 1993). The full range of appropriate applications of direct observation methods have not been documented across settings, subjects, and qualifications of personnel. Future investigations should delineate appropriate applications of direct observation versus experimental analysis methods (e.g., functional analysis).

At this time, it appears that interviews followed by direct observations designed to confirm (or disconfirm) hypotheses can lead to useful conclusions about the antecedents and consequent events controlling problem behavior. The relatively low cost, effort, and skill required to conduct interviews and direct observations offer a practical alternative to functional analysis for many practitioners.

It is important that direct observation procedures be structured to provide clear and useful information while not overburdening those responsible for collecting the data. The results of an FBA interview should be used to guide the direct observations. Observations and an observation data form should focus on the behaviors and environmental conditions identified during the interview process (O'Neill et al., 1997). Maya's team used the Functional Assessment Observation form (O'Neill et al., 1997) to collect data (see Figure 6–6).

On 10/06/03, 5 days after completing the FACTS, Trudy collected direct observation data to validate

FIGURE 6–6
Functional Assessment Observation Form

Functional Assessment Observation Form

Name: **Maya**

Starting Date: 10/06/04   Ending Date: 10/06/04   Perceived Functions

Time	Tongue out	Yell	Hit peer	Spit	Throw objects	Demand/request	Difficult task	Transitions	Interruption	Alone (no attention)	Hall	Classroom	Lunchroom	Attention	Desired item/Activity	Self-Stimulation	Demand/request	Activity (transitions)	Person	Other/don't know	Sit alone	Comments: (if nothing happened in period, write initials)
9:00 Hall	2	1,3	1,3	2				1,2,3			1,2,3			1,2,3						3		
9:15 Language Arts			4						4			4		4								
10:15 Hall/break	6	5,7	5,7	6				5,6,7			5,6,7			5,6,7						5,7		
10:30 Math																						E.G.
12:00 Lunch	8,10	9,10	9,10	8					8,9,10				8,9,10	8,9,10						10		
12:30 Teen Health																						S.P.
1:30 Current Events/ Choir																						C.J.
3:30 Hall		11	11						11					11						11		
Totals																						

Events: ~~1~~ ~~2~~ ~~3~~ ~~4~~ ~~5~~ ~~6~~ ~~7~~ ~~8~~ ~~9~~ ~~10~~ ~~11~~ 12 13 14 15 16 17 18 19 20 21 22 23 24 25

Date: 10/06/04

Source: O'Neill, R., Horner, R. H., Albin, R. W., Sprague, J. R., Storey, K., & Newton, J. S. (1997). *Functional assessment for problem behavior: A practical handbook* (2nd ed.). Pacific Grove, CA: Brooks/Cole.

(or disconfirm) the team's hypothesis that Maya is likely to stick her tongue out at peers, yell, spit at them, and/or hit them during hallway transitions (particularly on Mondays after a weekend break from school) for the function of gaining their attention. To collect the data, Trudy used the Functional Assessment Observation form. Data were collected for the entire school day across all of Maya's routines.

A quick orientation to other aspects of the structure of the Functional Assessment Observation form may be helpful. The first group of columns on the form lists the problem behaviors.

For Maya, these are sticking out her tongue, yelling, hitting peers, spitting, and throwing objects.

The second group of columns lists the hypothesized predictors (antecedent triggers) for the problem behaviors.

In Maya's case, generic predictors, such as "Demand/ Request" and "Alone," have been supplemented with more specific predictors: hall, classroom, and lunchroom.

The next set of columns lists the perceived functions of the problem behavior, organized into two subgroups: (a) get/obtain and (b) escape/avoid. Within each of these subgroups are listed generic functions of problem behavior (e.g., get attention, desired activity/item, self-stimulation, and escape/avoid a demand/request, activity, or person). Finally, the last set of columns provides a place to record actual consequences of a problem behavior (i.e., specific consequent events that occurred when problem behavior occurred).

In Maya's case, being made to sit alone is an actual consequence that she experienced when she hit another student.

On the Functional Assessment Observation form, problem behaviors are recorded as events rather than frequency counts. A single event includes all instances of a problem behavior of a given type (e.g., spitting) that are separated by no more than a 3-minute time gap. Counting behavior events is easier than trying to count every instance of a behavior, particularly with problem behaviors that have hard-to-determine beginnings and endings. Each time a problem behavior event occurs, the data collector records the sequence number of the event (e.g., 1 for the first event that occurred, 2 for the second event that occurred) in each of the relevant columns of the form.

Maya's first problem behavior event (i.e., event 1) occurred between 9:00 a.m. and 9:15 a.m. while she was making a hallway transition and included her yelling at and then hitting a peer (note the 1 in each of those columns). The data collector has also recorded that the predictors for event 1 were transitions and hall (note the 1 in each of those columns) and that the perceived function of the event was

attention (note the 1 in that column). There was no consequence delivered for event 1. During this same time period, two other distinct problem behavior events occurred (i.e., events 2 and 3). Event 3 involved Maya's yelling and hitting a peer again, and the data collector has recorded the predictors as transitions and hall, the perceived function as attention, and the actual consequence as Maya's being made to sit alone.

Note also that when no problem behavior events occur during an observed portion of a student's routine, the observer simply writes his or her initials in the final column of the form. This makes it clear that although an observation did occur, no problem behavior occurred.

The data on Maya's direct observation form show that she experienced no problem behaviors during her math, teen health, or current events classes.

In all, Maya engaged in 11 problem behavior events on 10/06/03, the last of which occurred around 3:30 p.m., when she was making a hallway transition. At the bottom of the form, the data collector has drawn a slash mark through events 1 through 11, drawn a vertical line after the number 11, and written the date as 10/06/03. Thus, a quick check reveals that 11 behavioral events occurred on 10/06/03. If the same form were to be used to collect data on the following day, 10/07/03, the first behavioral event of that date would be recorded as event 12.

Validation (or disconfirming) of the hypothesis can be undertaken once sufficient data have been collected.

There is confirmation that the FBA interview correctly identified Maya's problem behaviors in that no problem behaviors other than those that were revealed in the interview have been recorded. Maya engaged in four behavioral events that included sticking her tongue out (events 2, 6, 8, and 10), seven events that included yelling (events 1, 3, 5, 7, 9, 10, and 11), seven events that included hitting a peer (events 1, 3, 5, 7, 9, 10, and 11), and so on. Except for event 4, all behavior events included multiple problem behaviors, which may be an indication that the cluster of behaviors serves the same function.

The FBA hypothesis was that Maya was more likely to engage in problem behaviors during hallway transitions (particularly on Mondays after a weekend break from school) than at other times in order to gain their attention. A review of the data for 10/06/03 (a Monday) indicates that of the 11 behavioral events, seven (64%) occurred during hallway transitions (i.e., events 1, 2, 3, 5, 6, 7, and 11). This provides support for the hypothesis, although the data also reveal that three other behavioral events occurred during lunch (i.e., events 8, 9, and 10). For all 11 events, the form shows that the perceived function was attention, thus providing confirmation for that portion of the original hypothesis.

In summary, Maya's direct observation data provide a confirmation of the original hypothesis, although her BSP may need to address not only the problem behaviors that occur during hallway transitions but also those that occur during lunch. In developing such a plan, it will be important to consider the prevailing environmental conditions during Maya's math, teen health, and current events classes, when the probability of her problem behaviors appears to be low.

There are many forms for collecting direct observation data. The key issue is that direct observation systems can be used to validate FBA hypotheses developed through interview procedures. In cases where the hypothesis is at least tentatively confirmed, development of a related BSP can be initiated. In cases where the hypothesis is at least temporarily disconfirmed, the direct observations will either provide enough information to revise the hypothesis statement accordingly or launch another round of focused information gathering from additional informants, followed by another round of direct observations. Ideally, successive rounds of information gathering will be sharpened until a final round of direct observations succeeds in at least tentatively confirming the final hypothesis statement.

Where problem behaviors and environmental conditions are so complex that a series of direct observations fail to result in a tentatively confirmed hypothesis or where behavior support plans that have been implemented with fidelity nevertheless fail to produce reductions in problem behavior, it may be necessary to conduct a functional analysis. Technically, functional analysis is a process that is separate and distinct from FBA. Functional analysis should not be undertaken lightly; it requires time and a high level of behavioral skills. However, some problem behavior may be so complex that its solution requires a functional analysis.

Functional Analysis Within applied behavior analysis, functional analysis refers to the explicit manipulation of variables in order to demonstrate a functional relationship between an environmental event and a behavior. As such, a functional analysis is a mini-experiment. The conceptual foundation for functional analysis has been described by Bijou et al. (1968), Carr (1977), and Skinner (1953), among others.

In a highly influential study, Iwata, Dorsey, Slifer, Bauman, and Richman (1982) demonstrated what has become the classic methodology for conducting a functional analysis: *the manipulation of consequent variables.* They examined—in an analog setting—the relationship between self-injury and various consequent events (i.e., contingent attention, contingent escape from academic demands, alone, and unstructured play/control). This study conclusively demonstrated the wisdom of deriving interventions based on the function (or purpose) of a problem behavior rather than merely imposing arbitrary contingencies of reinforcement or punishment on problem behavior in a "trial-and-error" approach designed to overpower the problem behavior regardless of its function. The functional analysis conducted by Iwata et al. revealed that some participants engaged in high rates of self-injury only when self-injury resulted in escape from difficult tasks; other participants engaged in self-injury only when the behavior resulted in adult attention, and still others engaged in self-injury in all conditions.

Despite the success and widespread use of functional analysis by researchers, its "ecological validity" has sometimes been questioned (Hanley & Iwata, 2003). Functional analysis is usually conducted under well-controlled conditions in settings that may not entirely duplicate the settings in which the problem behavior occurs (e.g., a functional analysis might be conducted in the corner of a classroom rather than in the midst of the typical classroom activities). Nevertheless, functional analysis is not limited to such analog settings. Variations of the basic analog protocol have been demonstrated in schools and communities (Durand & Carr, 1991; Lalli, Browder, Mace, & Brown, 1993; Northup et al., 1995; Sasso et al., 1992; Sprague & Horner, 1992; Umbreit, 1995), clinical outpatient settings (Wacker, Steege, Northup, Reimers, et al., 1990), and homes (Arndorfer, Miltenberger, Woster, Rortvedt, & Gaffaney, 1994; Lucyshyn, Albin, & Nixon, 1997).

Regardless of the setting in which functional analysis is conducted, it is a complex procedure that is currently much more likely to be conducted by a trained behavior analyst than by a teacher. A particularly cautionary aspect of functional analysis is that, by its very nature, it evokes problem behavior. That is, in manipulating successive consequent variables, the behavior analyst is searching for the reinforcer for the problem behavior and the antecedent condition that reliably triggers the problem behavior by setting the occasion for delivery of the reinforcer (e.g., a difficult academic task that reliably evokes problem behavior because of a history of the problem behavior resulting in escape from the task). A functional analysis that targets, for example, aggression or self-injury is not to be undertaken lightly because the analysis will "cause" those problem behaviors to occur. Despite these cautions about functional analysis, there has been at least one demonstration of a methodology that effectively taught teachers to use functional analysis in actual elementary-level classroom settings (Moore et al., 2002) in which the target problem behavior was students' yelling out during class.

There are some variations in how functional analysis is conducted that could perhaps be adapted to increase the likelihood of its use by typical intervention agents, such as teachers. For example, Wacker and his colleagues (Northup et al., 1991; Wacker, Steege, Northup, Reimers, et al., 1990; Wacker, Steege, Northup, Sasso, et al., 1990) have developed a *"brief" functional analysis protocol* that involves an analog assessment phase followed by a "contingency reversal" phase. During the analogue assessment phase, functional analysis conditions (e.g., attention, escape) are alternated in rapid sessions (5 to 10 minutes per session, two or three consecutive sessions per condition) to identify the maintaining consequences (i.e., the function) of problem behavior. In the subsequent contingency reversal phase, the participant is taught an appropriate response that produces the maintaining consequence identified in the analog assessment phase (e.g., how to say "Come here, please" to gain attention). The effect on problem behavior of reinforcing or not reinforcing this new appropriate response is then tested in a series of contingency reversals. This brief functional analysis procedure can result in identification of maintaining consequences (functions) for problem behavior during the course of a 90-minute evaluation.

As an example of the brief functional analysis methodology, consider Figure 6–7. During the analog assessment phase, the hypothetical student's rate of aggression is high during the attention condition sessions (when the student is provided with attention contingent on engaging in aggression but otherwise ignored), and his rate of requesting attention or assistance is low. During the escape condition sessions (when the student is prompted/assisted through a difficult academic task and allowed to escape the task contingent on engaging in aggression), his rates of both problem behavior and requesting attention or assistance are low. The analog assessment phase suggests that aggression is maintained by getting attention. This hypothesis is further tested during the contingency reversal phase conditions. The first condition of the contingency reversal phase replicates the analog assessment condition that tested attention as the maintaining consequence. However, prior to the onset of this condition, the student is taught to sign "Come here, please," and attention is delivered to the student contingent on his signing. During this condition, the student's rate of aggression is low, and his rate of signing is high. This condition is then reversed to replicate the analog condition in which only aggression produces attention and then reversed one final time to assess the rate of aggression when attention is again delivered contingent on the participant's appropriate signing.

Another possibility for increasing the likelihood that functional analysis could be conducted in schools is the option of focusing on the *manipulation of antecedent variables* rather than consequent variables. This is sometimes referred to as a *structural analysis* (Axelrod, 1987). Structural analysis involves a focus on discovering a relationship between an antecedent condition and a behavior. This typically is done using a single-subject withdrawal (ABAB) design approach. Manipulating antecedent conditions while holding consequent conditions constant may be much easier—and even natural—for teachers (e.g., Vollmer & Van Camp, 1998; Wacker, Berg, Asmus, Harding, & Cooper, 1998). Many curricular, instructional, and other antecedent variables (e.g., type of task, task difficulty, level of attention, choice) can be, and have been, manipulated in school settings to identify relationships between antecedents and problem behavior (Carr & Durand, 1985a; Dunlap et al., 1991; Munk & Repp, 1994).

Although functional analysis is considered the "gold standard" for defining the maintaining function of problem behaviors, we recommend that functional analysis should be attempted (a) only with the support

FIGURE 6–7
Brief Functional Analysis

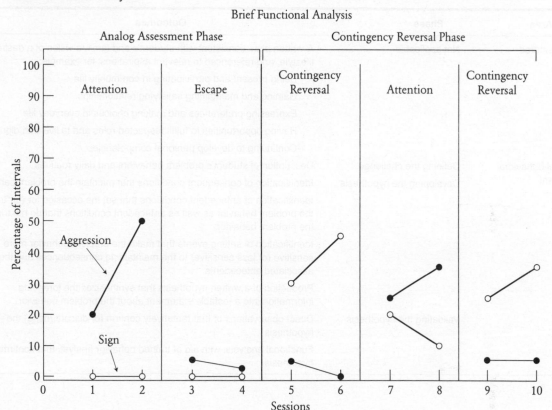

of a trained behavior analyst and (b) only when other sources of FBA do not provide a clear set of validated hypothesis statements.

Summary of Assessment for Behavior Support Planning

In completing the assessment processes that precede development of a BSP, you will have engaged in person-centered planning and will have conducted an FBA. The FBA will have produced six outcomes: (a) description of the student's problem behavior and daily routines, (b) identification of consequent conditions that maintain the problem behavior, (c) identification of antecedent conditions that set the occasion for (or "trigger") the problem behavior as well as antecedent conditions that *do not* trigger the problem behavior,

(d) identification of setting events that make the problem behavior more sensitive (or less sensitive) to the maintaining consequences and their associated antecedents, (e) production of a written hypothesis that synthesizes the foregoing information into a testable statement about the problem behavior, and (f) direct observations of the student during typical daily routines for the purpose of tentatively confirming (or disconfirming) the hypothesis (O'Neill et al., 1997). If necessary, you may also have requested the help of a trained behavior analyst in conducting a functional analysis.

The areas of assessment and their phases and outcomes are summarized in Table 6-2. After addressing the outcomes, you will be prepared to develop a BSP.

TABLE 6–2
Areas, Phases, and Outcomes of the Assessment Process

Area	Phase	Outcomes
Person-centered planning	Not applicable	A written plan, consistent with student's and family's vision of a desired lifestyle, and referenced to relevant aspirations; for example:
		Being present and participating in community life
		Gaining and maintaining satisfying relationships
		Expressing preferences and making choices in everyday life
		Having opportunities to fulfill respected roles and to live with dignity
		Continuing to develop personal competencies
Functional behavioral assessment	Defining the challenge	Description of student's problem behaviors and daily routines
	Developing the hypothesis	Identification of consequent conditions that maintain the problem behavior
		Identification of antecedent conditions that set the occasion for (or "trigger") the problem behavior as well as antecedent conditions that do not trigger the problem behavior
		Identification of setting events that make the problem behavior more sensitive (or less sensitive) to the maintaining consequences and their associated antecedents
		Production of a written hypothesis that synthesizes the foregoing information into a testable statement about the problem behavior
	Validating the hypothesis	Direct observations of that tentatively confirm (or disconfirming) the hypothesis
		Functional analysis, with aid of trained behavior analyst, that confirms the hypothesis

Using Assessment Information to Guide Behavior Support Plan Content

Once the assessment phase of the PBS process is completed, the next step is developing, implementing, and evaluating a comprehensive, positive behavior support plan (BSP). At this point in the support process, the six outcomes for a functional assessment should be completed, and a person-centered vision of broader lifestyle goals for the focus student should be agreed on by the support team. The information gathered in the functional assessment and person-centered planning processes provide the foundation for the BSP. However, as the development and implementation of the BSP progresses, it is important to remember that the functional assessment and person-centered planning processes are ongoing. Both assessment processes should be done on a recurring basis as the student's BSP impacts both appropriate and problem behaviors and as changes in lifestyle, routines, and living settings occur.

A BSP provides a guide for the behavior of those people providing support (e.g., teachers, parents, classroom assistants, specialists). We often think of a BSP as the plan for changing the behavior of a student with problem behaviors. In fact, although "designed" for a focus student, a BSP actually describes changes and behaviors that we as teachers, administrators, family members, friends, and peers will make happen and perform. A comprehensive BSP is a blueprint for designing and maintaining effective environments that render problem behaviors irrelevant, inefficient, and ineffective. The changes we make in the physical setting, the daily schedule, what we teach, the way we teach, and the way we respond to appropriate and problem behaviors are what will produce changes in the behaviors of the student. It is through changes in our behavior that we effect changes in the behavior of students with problem behaviors. As such, written BSPs should be clear in describing the exact changes expected in the behavior of those who will implement the plan and in the settings in which the plan will be implemented. In the following sections, we describe important features of a positive BSP.

A Positive BSP Should be Technically Sound

In designing comprehensive positive behavior support, it is essential that a BSP be *technically sound* (Crone & Horner, 2003; Horner, 1999; O'Neill et al., 1997). Technically sound means that the procedures in the support plan are logically linked to functional assessment hypotheses and also are grounded in the basic principles of human behavior and biomedical sciences (Alberto & Troutman, 2003; Carr et al., 2002). Interventions that are technically sound are also evidence based. Research or clinical application data should exist supporting the effectiveness and logic behind each procedure used in a plan (e.g., Carr & Carlson, 1993).

A Positive BSP Should be Contextually Appropriate

In addition to being technically sound, a BSP should be *contextually appropriate* (Albin et al., 1996; Horner, 1999; Lucyshyn, Kayser, Irvin, & Blumberg, 2002). Contextually appropriate refers to how well support plan procedures "fit" their implementers and settings. The term "contextual fit" (or "goodness of fit") has been used to describe the compatibility between a BSP and the values, skills, and resources of BSP implementers both at home and school (Albin et al., 1996). Contextual fit influences the selection of procedures within a BSP as well as whether the plan procedures are put into place at all, are implemented with fidelity, and are implemented for extended periods of time (Horner, Albin, Borgmeier, & Salantine, 2003; Moes & Frea, 2000; Sandler, 2001). To be effective, PBS plans must be implemented with fidelity by typical support providers, in natural school, home, and community settings, often for extended time periods. The contextual fit of the BSP is as important to its effectiveness as is the technical soundness of the plan.

A Positive BSP Should be a Collaborative Endeavor

We strongly recommend that a collaborative team process be used in the design, implementation, evaluation, and modification of the plan. The team should include all the key stakeholders involved in supporting a student with problem behaviors, including teachers and school staff who will implement the plan, family and friends, the student with problem behaviors (when appropriate), school and other administrators who must support the BSP implementation process, and any others (e.g., behavior or related-services specialists, respite providers) involved in supporting the student (Anderson, Albin, Mesaros, Dunlap, & Morelli-Robbins, 1993; Crone & Horner, 2003; Todd, Horner, Sugai, & Colvin, 1999). Collaboration among all stakeholders is likely to promote good contextual fit. A collaborative team process also provides the framework for a support approach that is dynamic and capable of responding to changing support needs. Behavior support needs of persons with severe problem behaviors are likely to be long term in nature. Support should be designed with longevity in mind and with the expectation that the nature of the support will change as the person's skills, needs, and preferences change. Sustained plan implementation, ongoing monitoring of effects, and timely adaptation and modification of plan procedures and features are essential elements of effective comprehensive behavior support. A collaborative team process involving all key stakeholders facilitates high-quality performance of these elements.

Todd et al. (1999) have described a team-based approach to PBS (i.e., "discipline") in schools that utilizes a two-tiered model. The first tier is a school-based "core behavior support team," consisting of a school administrator, someone with behavioral expertise, and a representative sample of school staff (i.e., teachers and others). The core team has responsibility for coordinating and managing all aspects of behavior support within a school, including both schoolwide and individual student systems of support. The core team serves as a resource for the school and staff in the area of behavior support. The second tier involves "action teams" that conduct the individualized behavior support process. Each student requiring a BSP would have his or her own action team. Each action team would consist of a member (or members) of the school's core team (e.g., a school behavior specialist), the student's teacher(s), the student's parents/family, and any other school or community members who are involved in the student's life or are interested in participating (e.g., a counselor, social worker, speech/language therapist, physical therapist, school bus driver, probation officer, respite care provider). In this two-tiered model, the core team is responsible for receiving and managing staff requests for assistance with students' behavioral problems, forming and supporting action teams, and assisting as needed in the design, implementation, and evaluation of BSPs. The action team is responsible for conducting person-centered planning and the FBA, developing and implementing a comprehensive positive BSP, supporting the student and teachers in support plan implementation, and collecting data to evaluate support plan effectiveness (Crone & Horner, 2003).

> *Maya's school had instituted a schoolwide PBS system that identified three expectations for all students: be respectful, be responsible, and be safe. School staff had translated these expectations into specific student behaviors that were expected in the various settings (e.g., hallways, cafeteria, classrooms, bus loading zone, playground) and activities (e.g., entering school, assemblies, fire drills, after-school functions) that make up a "school day." Importantly, staff had taught these expected behaviors to all students, so that students at Maya's school knew what behaviors were expected of them. In addition, Maya's school had strategies for monitoring students and rewarding them for doing expected behaviors (e.g., the school held a weekly raffle on Fridays and students received raffle tickets to acknowledge appropriate behaviors).*
>
> *Although Maya participated in the schoolwide system, by itself, the schoolwide system was not sufficient to meet Maya's behavioral support needs. Maya required more individualized support. That is why Trudy Schwartz, the behavior specialist, initiated the individual student behavior support system in Maya's school by completing a Request for Assistance form. With this Request for Assistance, an action team was set up for Maya that included Trudy, Maya's homeroom teacher and another regular education teacher who had her in class for part of the day, Maya's educational assistant, and Maya's mother. This action team set about the task of further assessing Maya's behavior and designing, implementing, and monitoring a BSP.*

A Positive BSP Should be Comprehensive

The goal of PBS is to have a broad positive impact on the life of a person with disabilities and challenging problem behaviors (Carr et al., 2002; Horner, 1999). Successful behavior support should translate into real differences in a person's life across all contexts in which behavior support needs are present (e.g., home, school, respite care, community). The following three features characterize a comprehensive BSP:

1. *All problem behaviors performed by the focus person are addressed*: The need for behavior support often is prompted by the occurrence of a few intense problem behaviors. Teachers and families have noted, however, that high-frequency occurrences of low-intensity behaviors (e.g., whining, refusal) may be as disruptive, problematic, and damaging to the student and those around him or her as higher-intensity aggression, self-injury, and property destruction (Horner, Diemer, & Brazeau, 1992; Turnbull & Ruef, 1996). Research also indicates the value of organizing support around all the problem behaviors that are maintained by the same function (e.g., all behaviors that produce attention, all behaviors that are maintained by escape from tasks) (Sprague & Horner, 1992, 1999). Both our current understanding of behavioral theory and the goal of producing change that is of broad impact argue for focusing behavior support on the full range of problem behaviors a person performs rather than on just one or two high-intensity behaviors.

2. *A comprehensive support plan is implemented across all relevant settings and times of day*: Just as addressing all problem behaviors is important, so too is implementation of behavior support procedures across the relevant scope of a person's entire day. In the past, it was not unusual for individual behavioral interventions to be implemented for limited periods of time, across limited settings or situations. The research literature shows clearly that single intervention procedures can have a dramatic effect in reducing severe problem behavior across brief periods in specific contexts. However, to achieve true lifestyle impact, behavior support must produce broad and lasting effects across the relevant range of contexts, conditions, activities, and routines that a person with severe problem behaviors experiences in the course of the day. A challenge for PBS is to develop comprehensive support strategies that can be implemented and sustained across the entire day and the full range of conditions encountered (Horner, 1999).

3. *A comprehensive support plan blends multiple procedures*: It would be unusual for a single intervention procedure to address the full spectrum of problem behaviors performed by an individual with severe problem behaviors and to cover the full range of settings where problems occur. Comprehensive support

will more likely involve the creative blending of multiple procedures. For example, strategies for curricular revision and schedule modification may be used to minimize contact with highly aversive events, instructional procedures will build new skills, and consequences throughout the day will be modified to increase the rewards associated with communication and learning and decrease the rewards that follow problem behaviors. Collectively, these multiple changes result in an environment that minimizes and redirects access to problem events, builds new skills, and provides constructive feedback that both promotes appropriate behavior and minimizes the rewards for problem behavior.

A Positive BSP Should be Sustainable

PBS has moved the delivery of behavioral intervention for persons with severe problem behaviors from specialized and restrictive settings into regular, integrated community settings. A challenge facing families, schools, and community support providers today is to deliver effective behavior support in typical homes, schools, and community settings for as long as such support is needed. PBS plans, in most instances, will be implemented by the "typical people" (e.g., family members, friends, teachers, and classroom assistants, paid caregivers) who live and work in those settings. To be effective over the long term, BSP implementation must be sustainable (i.e., capable of being implemented with reasonable fidelity by typical people for extended periods of time). We have two recommendations to facilitate sustained implementation of a BSP across all relevant settings and contexts in a student's life for extended periods. First, the BSP must continue to have good contextual fit over time. As the BSP changes over time, team members should continue to monitor for contextual fit. Second, it is important that the BSP procedures can be relatively easily embedded and implemented within the typical routines and activities that make up the student's daily life at school, at home, and in the community. If BSP procedures require teachers, families, or other support providers to make substantial changes in their daily or other regular routines and activities as part of plan implementation, then plan procedures are much less likely to be implemented across all contexts and times of day, and implementation is much less likely to be sustained over time.

Competing Behavior Analysis

Competing behavior analysis (CBA) provides a conceptual bridge for moving from functional assessment information to the design of a comprehensive BSP (Crone & Horner, 2003; Horner & Billingsley, 1988; O'Neill et al., 1997). Conducting a CBA provides a framework to logically link the multiple intervention procedures and support strategies of a comprehensive BSP to information collected in the FBA. Thus, CBA is a strategy for producing a BSP that is technically sound. A separate CBA should be completed for each response class of problem behaviors identified in a FBA. If a student performs one set of problem behaviors (throws and destroys materials) to escape difficult tasks and another set (calls out, pounds desk) to get attention, then two CBAs will be completed, one for each set of behaviors (i.e., each response class). If one set of behaviors serves multiple functions (Day et al., 1994), then separate CBA should be completed for each function.

The process for conducting a CBA involves four basic steps: (a) summarize the FBA information to construct a hypothesis statement for each response class of problem behaviors; (b) identify appropriate desired and alternative replacement behaviors and the contingencies associated with them; (c) identify potential intervention procedures, across four support strategy categories, that promote the occurrence of appropriate behaviors and make problem behaviors irrelevant, ineffective, and inefficient; and (d) select the set of strategies from the options proposed that are technically sound and likely to result in behavior change and are a good contextual fit (Crone & Horner, 2003; O'Neill et al., 1997).

The process of summarizing FBA information to construct a summary statement for a response class involves listing, from left to right, the setting event(s), immediate antecedents (predictors), problem behavior(s) in the response class, and maintaining consequence(s) that have been identified in the FBA. The maintaining consequence(s) for problem behavior indicates (or suggests) the function of the problem behavior (refer back to Figure 6–4 for a listing of potential functions). For example, the functional assessment summary statement for Isha (described at the beginning of the chapter) indicates that she screams, pulls her own hair, and scratches at staff (problem behavior) when she is asked to shift (transition) from one activity to another (antecedent). Isha's problem behaviors, at least sometimes, lead to a consequence of her getting to stay in her current activity (i.e., getting her predictable routine reinstated) (maintaining consequence). Screaming, pulling her hair, and scratching staff become more likely when Isha is in new or unpredictable situations or when she suffers from her pollen allergy (setting event). The consequence that occurs for Isha's problem behavior suggests that the function of her problem behaviors is escape from transitions, which are aversive to Isha. This information would be diagrammed as follows:

Setting Event	Antecedent	Problem Behavior	Consequence	Function
• New or unpredictable situations • Pollen allergy	Asked to shift to another activity	• Screams • Pulls own hair • Scratches	Gets to stay in current activity	Escapes aversive transition

The second step in completing a CBA is to identify a desired alternative behavior that will compete with the problem behavior. Two questions can be asked: (a) Given that the setting event(s) and predictor(s) have occurred, what is an appropriate behavior that would be the *desired behavior* for the person to perform in that situation? and (b) Given that the setting event(s) and predictor(s) have occurred, what would be an *alternative replacement* behavior that could produce exactly the same consequence as the problem behavior(s) (i.e., a functionally equivalent behavior) (O'Neill et al., 1997)?

For Isha, the desired behavior would be that she transition from activity to activity without incident when asked. The current (actual) maintaining consequence for shifting without incident for Isha is teacher praise and acknowledgment for "acting like an adult." A functionally equivalent alternative for Isha would be requesting predictability by asking to stay in the current activity using an appropriate communication response (e.g., a symbol requesting "more time"). Her team reasons that requesting to stay in the current activity is an appropriate functionally equivalent response (i.e., produces the same maintaining consequence as the problem behavior) that can compete as a replacement for Isha's problem behaviors (Carr, 1988). When she asks appropriately to stay in the current activity, Isha will receive additional time in the activity (e.g., 1 more minute). This is not what staff want Isha to do, but it is preferable to her problem behavior and is an acceptable option as staff work on other strategies in Isha's plan to address her problem behavior and transitions.

An important aspect of alternative replacement behaviors is that they may serve as short-term solutions while a support team also implements other strategies within a comprehensive support plan aimed at increasing desired behaviors and eliminating the need for alternative replacement behaviors. This CBA would be diagrammed as in Figure 6-8.

This depiction of the CBA provides support team members with a literal picture of the current contingencies for Isha in the context of transitions from activity to activity and sets the occasion for the team to define what to change in the context (e.g., contingencies, antecedents, skills, consequences) to make the problem behaviors irrelevant, ineffective, and inefficient.

The third step in the CBA process is to build a list of possible behavior support procedures. The goal here is not simply to look for a single intervention that would eliminate the problem behavior(s) but to identify a range of strategies and procedures that would reduce the likelihood of problem behavior(s) and increase the likelihood that either or both of the competing behaviors (i.e., desired or replacement) would occur. Such a multicomponent support plan might address setting events (e.g., for Isha, designing a schedule to reduce unpredictability of activities), the immediate antecedents (e.g., asking Isha to shift activities only after first presenting a preinstruction or reminder that a transition was coming), behaviors (e.g., teaching Isha to ask for more time on an activity), and consequences (e.g., increase reinforcers for the desired behavior of shifting to new activities throughout the day, ensure that problem behavior does not result in escaping the transition but that requesting more time does). A comprehensive BSP will have multiple components addressing the full range of variables that influence which behaviors occur from among the alternatives available. This third step often involves a brainstorming

FIGURE 6–8
Competing Behavior Analysis for Isha

Student Name: Isha

Beavior Support Plan: Competing Behavior Analysis

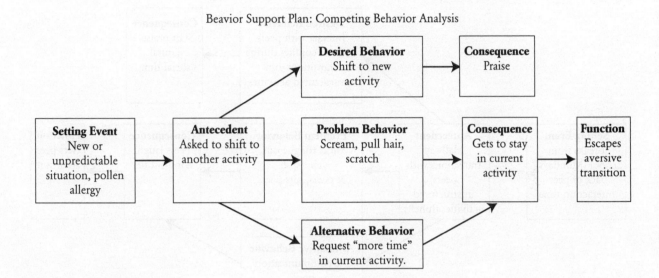

process to first create a menu of potential strategies from which support team members can then select the best options and strategies for their situation. In this way, the resulting plan is more likely to be both technically sound (i.e., based on the functional assessment) and have good contextual fit (i.e., strategies are identified that work best for the team members and context) (Albin et al., 1996; Crone & Horner, 2003; O'Neill et al., 1997).

The fourth step in building a plan of behavior support involves review of the proposed list of strategies and selection of specific procedures that the team identifies as effective, doable, and an appropriate fit with their skills, values, schedules, resources, and administrative support system. This fourth step is extremely important. The people who will be implementing the plan procedures (and, in many cases, the student with problem behaviors) decide on and define the final features (procedures) of the BSP. The first three steps have ensured that technically sound information is being considered. The features of effective behavior support are defined. The final step adds form to those features and addresses the issue of the plan being contextually appropriate and a good fit for the

student, plan implementers, and the context (settings) where the plan will be implemented. This fourth step is of particular importance when a behavioral consultant from "outside" the school is involved in the design of support. The behavioral consultant can be of tremendous assistance in the process of functional assessment and coordination of the competing behavior model. The final selection of the specific strategies that make up a behavior plan, however, must be done with very active participation of people who know the student best and who will be implementing the final plan. Support team consensus that a plan's procedures are doable, consistent with the team members' values and skills, in the best interest of the student, and likely to be effective is a key element in moving forward to implementation of the plan. Figure 6–9 presents a completed CBA for Maya illustrating the completion of these four steps.

The functional assessment hypothesis statement for Maya could be stated as follows: "During lunch, hallway transitions, and less structured activities, Maya engages in sticking her tongue out, yelling, hitting, and spitting at peers, with these behaviors maintained by

FIGURE 6–9
Competing Behavior Analysis for Maya

Student name: Maya

Behavior Support Plan: Competing Behavior Analysis

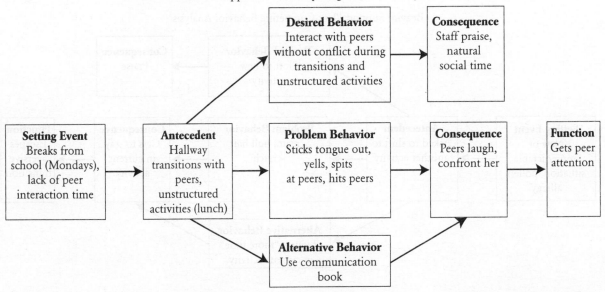

(Make problem behavior irrelevant)   *(Make problem behavior inefficient)*   *(Make problem behavior ineffective)*

Setting Event Strategies	Antecedent Strategies	Behavior Teaching Strategies	Consequence Strategies
• Call peer on phone on Sunday night • Provide peer mentor during unstructured times	• Provide pictorial schedule and review for social times • Staff and peers prompt use of communication book • Precorrect before all transitions • Increase hall monitoring by staff	• Teach how to use pictorial schedule as a communication book • Teach peers about communication book	• Ask peers to ignore inappropriate behavior • Peers ask Maya to use communication book (low-level problem) or notify staff (high-level problem) • Remove from setting if hitting occurs • Increase social times throughout day

Maya receiving attention from her peers, in the forms of laughter, yelling back, and confrontations when she does the behaviors. Maya's problem behaviors are even more likely when two setting events are present: breaks

from school ('Mondays') and lack of peer interaction time."

This hypothesis statement is diagrammed as follows:

Setting events	Antecedents	Problem behaviors	Consequences	Function
• "Mondays" • Lack of peer interaction time	• Hallway transitions • Unstructured activities (lunch, break)	• Yelling • Sticking out her tongue • Hitting peers • Spitting at peers	Peers laugh Peers yell back Peers confront	Obtains peer attention

The desired behavior for Maya in the problematic routines identified (hallway, lunch, unstructured activities) is that she talks and interacts with peers appropriately and without conflict. In assessing what consequences were currently present to maintain this desired behavior, Maya's team concluded that talking appropriately with peers would produce natural social time that would be reinforcing for Maya. They also tried to praise her for appropriate behavior.

A benefit of CBA is that it focuses attention on the existing consequences available to maintain desired behavior. Often, teams may find that the existing reinforcers for desired behavior are unimpressive and inadequate, particularly relative to the maintaining consequence for problem behavior.

The alternative replacement behavior identified by Maya's team was teaching Maya to use a communication book to initiate and conduct a conversation with peers. This behavior would produce the peer attention that Maya desired. Maya's peers also would be taught about the conversation book and how it worked with Maya.

The third step in the CBA for Maya had the support team identifying several potential intervention procedures and support strategies that could be used to make Maya's problem behavior irrelevant, inefficient, or ineffective. These procedures and strategies are organized as setting event, antecedent, teaching, and consequence manipulations.

After brainstorming a variety of potential support plan components, Maya's team carefully reviewed and discussed the procedures and identified which ones they would include in Maya's plan. In determining which procedures to actually implement, Maya's team considered how effective they thought each procedure would be with Maya; whether they had the skills, resources, and capacity to implement the procedure; how comfortable they were with implementing the procedure; and whether the procedure was reasonably doable within Maya's academic program and school routines. The strategies with an asterisk (*) next to them were selected by Maya's team for inclusion in her comprehensive BSP.

Contents of a Written BSP

Elements of Effective Behavior Support

Horner, Sugai, Todd, and Lewis-Palmer (1999–2000) presented a checklist for assessing the quality of behavior support that delineates 10 features of BSPs and the planning process that produces them. An adapted version of this checklist is presented in Figure 6–10. The 10 features include elements related to the completion of an FBA, the support planning process, the development and features of a written support plan, and the evaluation and assessment of the plan and its effects. In this section, we use the checklist as a guide in describing key elements of a written BSP as well as elements to address in the support planning process even if they do not need to be included in the written BSP.

The elements of a written positive BSP are organized around the goal of creating an effective environment that promotes and supports appropriate behavior and makes problem behavior irrelevant, inefficient, and ineffective. Accomplishing this goal typically necessitates development and implementation of a multi-component support plan that focuses on proactive strategies for prevention and teaching as well as on reactive strategies for responding to both appropriate and problem behaviors. The actual format, length, and style of a written BSP may vary. Rather than focusing on a particular form or format to use, we shall focus on the information presented in a written plan and on the processes described. Following are recommendations for the elements of behavior support planning and a written BSP (for more information, see Crone & Horner, 2003; Horner, Albin, Sprague, & Todd, 2000; Horner et al., 1999–2000; O'Neill et al., 1997).

1. *Define academic and lifestyle context for behavior support*: Person-centered planning is a key element of the assessment process in PBS. A written BSP should begin with a brief summary of the person-centered goals and vision that guide the BSP and the support team's planning efforts and decisions. This summary may also describe the connection between the BSP and desired or projected personal outcomes for the student. Whenever a BSP is proposed and developed, there should be a rationale for the plan and objectives for the plan's components that are directly related to the health, safety, and lifestyle of the focus student (Carr et al., 2002; Horner et al., 1990; Meyer & Evans, 1989). This summary places the BSP within the broader context of the student's life.

FIGURE 6-10

Checklist for Assessing the Quality of Behavior Support Planning:
Does the Plan (or Planning Process) Have These Features?

1. _____ Define academic and lifestyle *context* for behavior support

2. _____ Operational description of problem behaviors

3. _____ Problem *routines* identified

4. _____ Functional assessment hypotheses stated

5. Intervention/*Foundations* (issues that cut across routines)
   a) _____ health and physiology
   b) _____ communication
   c) _____ mobility
   d) _____ predictability
   e) _____ control/choice
   f) _____ social relationships
   g) _____ activity patterns

6. Intervention/*Prevention Strategies* (make problem behavior irrelevant)
   a) _____ schedule
   b) _____ curriculum
   c) _____ instructional procedures

7. Intervention/*Teaching Strategies* (make problem behavior inefficient)
   a) _____ replacement skills
   b) _____ new adaptive skills

8. Intervention/*Consequence Strategies*

   Extinction (make problem behavior ineffective)
   a) _____ minimize positive reinforcement
   b) _____ minimize negative reinforcement

   Reinforcement (make appropriate behavior more effective)
   _____ maximize positive reinforcement

   Negative Consequences (if needed)
   _____ negative consequences contingent on problem behavior

   Safety/Emergency Intervention Plan (if needed)
   _____ clear plan for what to do if/when crisis behaviors occur

9. Evaluation and Assessment
   a) _____ define the information to be collected
   b) _____ define the measurement process
   c) _____ define decision-making process

10. Ensure Contextual Fit
    a) _____ values
    b) _____ skills
    c) _____ resources
    d) _____ administrative system
    e) _____ perceptions that program is in best interest of student

2. *Operational description of problem behaviors*: Clear definitions of problem behaviors, stated in observable and measurable terms, are an important initial step in designing a BSP. Clear definitions assist a support team to reach agreement on the nature and severity of the problems faced. Definitions or descriptions of problem behaviors should focus both on individual behaviors (e.g., screaming, hitting, talking out, throwing objects) and on response classes (i.e., groups of behaviors maintained by the same consequences). It is rare that a student engages in only one problem behavior. More likely, a student engages in several behaviors that "work together" and are members of a response class. In some cases, behaviors in a response class may occur in very predictable patterns, such as an escalating sequence (Albin, O'Brien, & Horner, 1995), that can and should be identified as part of operationally describing the problem behaviors.

3. *Problem routines are identified*: An important consideration in describing problem behaviors is to define the behaviors within the routines and contexts in which they occur (Lucyshyn et al., 2002; O'Neill et al., 1997). Too often, problem behaviors are described or defined as if they were characteristics or traits of the person (e.g., he's aggressive, he's a biter, she's noncompliant). Defining problem behaviors within the routines in which they occur (e.g., Maya's problem behaviors occur during transitions and activities with minimal structure but do not occur in predictable and highly structured activities) emphasizes that a student's behavior must be understood in relation to the context in which it occurs (i.e., antecedent stimuli, setting events, and consequences). Defining problem behavior within routines assists the support team in understanding the function of the behavior, the environmental variables affecting and controlling the behavior, and the scope of behavior problems (e.g., whether behavior problems are limited to a single routine or a small number of routines or are present across a large number and broad range of routines) as well as in identifying patterns of problem behavior (e.g., finding similar problem behaviors or the absence of problem behaviors across routines with similar features).

4. *Functional assessment hypotheses are stated*: For each response class of problem behaviors identified in the FBA, a hypothesis statement should be presented that identifies setting events, antecedents/predictors, the behaviors in the response class, and the maintaining consequences. The hypothesis statement(s) provides the basis for a CBA and the subsequent generation of potential intervention procedures. For response classes that have multiple functions, a separate summary statement must be produced for each function, identifying the different setting events and predictors for each different maintaining consequence (i.e., function). Having the functional assessment hypothesis statements presented at the beginning of a written BSP serves as a reminder for plan developers and implementers of the underlying basis for the plan's procedures and goals. Hypothesis statements may be written in the BSP in sentence format or in a table format that presents the components of a hypothesis statement (setting events, antecedents, problem behaviors, consequences, and function). Examples of each format were presented for Maya in the CBA section earlier in this chapter.

5. *Intervention/Foundations (issues that cut across routines)*: One of the roots of PBS is the recognition that problem behaviors may result from and communicate, intentionally or unintentionally, the absence of or failure of living environments to provide basic foundational features in a person's life. These features cut across specific routines, activities, and settings. They include a person's health and physiological status, ability to communicate, mobility, predictability of environments, control and choice exercised by the person, social relationships, and activity patterns. These features must be addressed in the behavior support planning process. Some of them (e.g., mobility) may not be equally important or reflected within a written BSP for all people. However, for each of the features that are relevant for a focus person, the written BSP should describe the importance of the feature and the strategies and procedures of the plan that address the feature.

For Isha, predictability of the environment is a major factor in her problem behavior, and ensuring predictability is a guiding objective for her BSP.

For Maya, the ability to communicate effectively and appropriately is a major issue and a guiding factor in her support plan.

This should be communicated within the written plan.

6. *Intervention/Prevention strategies*: Prevention strategies help make problem behavior irrelevant. The guiding question in planning for prevention is, "How can we redesign environments (e.g., classroom, school,

home) proactively to eliminate or minimize as much as possible the occurrence of problem behaviors?" The overall goals of prevention strategies are making the environment as predictable as possible and providing opportunities for choices accommodating individual preferences. Three specific environmental manipulations include (a) *restructuring schedules* to modify or avoid antecedent stimuli that evoke problem behavior, to remove setting events that increase the likelihood of problem behaviors or to minimize their effects with neutralizing routines when they do occur (Horner et al., 1996, 1997), and to make positive reinforcers readily available for appropriate behavior so that positives far outweigh negatives (e.g., at least a 4:1 to 6:1 ratio of positives to negatives); (b) making sure *curricular content* is at an appropriate level for the learners and is relevant (e.g., age and context appropriate), useful (e.g., functional), interesting, and stimulating (Ferro, Foster-Johnson, & Dunlap, 1996); and (c) making sure *instruction* is appropriately designed, paced, and adapted for individual learners (Munk & Repp, 1994).

7. *Intervention/teaching strategies*: Teaching strategies help make problem behaviors inefficient by teaching students (a) appropriate replacement skills that are functionally equivalent to problem behaviors as identified within the CBA and (b) new adaptive skills that we want or expect them to perform as identified within the CBA. Academic and social skill deficits often are associated with increased levels of problem behavior or, at the least, put students at risk for problem behavior (Gresham, 2002). Adaptive skills to teach may include academic, social, community and independent living, leisure, recreational, self-management, and coping skills. Adaptive skills are often (or should be) the focus of long-term objectives on an IEP.

Appropriate replacement skills constitute an intermediary step toward performance of adaptive skills. A replacement skill within the CBA framework is an appropriate behavior that will produce the same maintaining consequence as problem behavior and thereby act as a replacement skill. The term "functional equivalence" is used in describing replacement skills because they produce the same maintaining consequence as problem behavior (Carr, 1988). Frequently, the alternative skill identified for teaching in a BSP is an appropriate communication response.

Isha engaged in problem behavior to avoid transitions to another activity. The alternative behavior identified for Isha in her CBA was an appropriate communication response: using a symbol to request more time in the current activity and thus avoiding the transition momentarily.

Teaching an alternative communication response is an intervention termed functional communication training (FCT) (Carr & Durand, 1985a; Carr et al., 1994; Durand, 1990). FCT is a well-researched and empirically documented procedure that builds on the idea that problem behavior frequently serves a communicative purpose, particularly for people with disabilities who may have limited communication skills and repertoires (Carr & Durand, 1985b, 1987; Donnellan et al., 1984). Teaching appropriate communication skills through FCT can have a rapid and long-lasting effect in reducing problem behavior to zero or near-zero levels (Berotti & Durand, 1999; Carr & Durand, 1985a; Durand & Carr, 1991, 1992). The basic steps for applying FCT include the following (see Carr et al., 1994, for a more complete description of FCT procedures):

1. Identify the function of the problem behavior through FBA. To use FCT, it is essential to know whether the function of problem behavior is to obtain desired reinforcers (e.g., attention, tangible materials or items, preferred activities, comfort) or to escape or avoid activities, items, or situations that the student finds aversive (e.g., things that are difficult, boring, painful, effortful, disliked).

2. Identify a request response to teach the student. This should be an appropriate response that will serve as a replacement behavior for problem behavior. The request response may be a verbal response; a manual sign; a gesture; the use of a card with a printed symbol, word, or picture; the use of an AAC device; or any other response that allows the student to communicate a message to others. The request response should be easy for the student to learn (perhaps a response already in his or her repertoire) and easy for others to perceive and interpret (or learn to interpret). The request response should match the function of problem behavior (e.g., getting attention: "I want to play"; getting more time on an activity: "More time please"; escaping a difficult task: "I want a break" or "Help me please").

3. Engage the student in an activity or context related to problem behavior and teach the student to use the alternative communication response. Do this by prompting the student to use the communication response before a problem behavior occurs and then immediately honoring the request. Fulfilling

the request immediately is very important, particularly in the beginning of teaching, so that the student learns that the appropriate response works to fulfill the request even more efficiently than problem behavior.

In addition to communication responses, functionally equivalent replacement skills may include self-management skills (e.g., self-scheduling to produce "predictability" or self-recruited feedback to produce teacher attention), self-control or coping responses (e.g., relaxation training to reduce stressful arousal), social skills (e.g., a social initiation response that produces peer attention), and appropriate responses to produce stimulation similar to that produced by problematic "self-stimulation" behavior.

8. *Intervention/consequence strategies*: Consequence strategies help make problem behavior ineffective. They also are used to promote the performance of desired behaviors. Consequence strategies are reactive, with consequences delivered after a response (behavior) has occurred. Traditionally, consequence strategies have served as the mainstay for applied behavior analysis and behavior management. While PBS emphasizes proactive and teaching strategies in providing behavior support, consequence strategies still play an important role and are likely to be included in a comprehensive BSP. This is particularly true with students, as schools have a long history of relying on consequence strategies to change behavior. Many school discipline policies spell out specific consequences (usually negative consequences, such as punishment) for infractions of school rules. Students requiring a BSP are likely to have consequence procedures incorporated into their BSPs.

The principles of human behavior identify three consequence procedures that are applied in the process of behavior support: extinction, reinforcement, and negative consequences (punishment). There has been much discussion and debate regarding whether any punishment procedure is acceptable within PBS (Horner et al., 1990; Repp & Singh, 1990). A goal of PBS is to minimize, if not eliminate, use of negative consequences to control people and their behavior. The use of severe punishers and heavy reliance on punishment procedures are not acceptable in providing behavior support. Procedures that cause or rely on pain, tissue damage, and humiliation should never be used, and those that seclude, restrict, or restrain students may also be unacceptable and require substantial

review and consideration. It is our experience and belief, however, that some negative consequences, including procedures that fit the technical definition of punishment, are a natural part of learning and life and, therefore, may be an appropriate part of a comprehensive positive BSP (Horner et al., 1990; Janney & Snell, 2000). The procedures that we believe are acceptable mirror procedures that would be typical of what is found in public schools and considered acceptable for nondisabled children. Such procedures should be age appropriate. Examples of punishment procedures that may be included in a BSP are mild reprimands and negative feedback (e.g., being told "no" or "that behavior is unacceptable"), redirection involving no or minimal physical contact, reasonable response cost or loss of activity (e.g., the blocks are put away when you throw them at classmates, computer time is lost when you push classmates to get to the computer first), and some mild forms of time-out (e.g., you have to sit on the bench for a minute because you were rough-housing in recess).

School-based support teams need to carefully consider, plan, and regularly review the use of appropriate consequences, both positive and negative, in a BSP. Many state and local education agencies have policies that guide and that may prohibit or restrict the use of different punishment procedures as well as the use of sweets and snacks as positive reinforcers. Teams should be aware of state and district policies, and BSP procedures should be in compliance with those policies.

Extinction Extinction is the withholding of reinforcement for a behavior that has been reinforced in the past. Extinction is used in a BSP to make problem behaviors ineffective. One objective for a BSP is to minimize the extent to which problem behaviors continue to "work" (i.e., produce desired reinforcers) for a student. Putting problem behavior "on extinction" is a procedure that will reduce the occurrence of problem behavior. However, implementers of extinction should anticipate the possibility of an increase in problem behavior—an extinction burst—when the procedure is first implemented. An extinction burst raises particular concerns if the problem behavior placed on extinction is dangerous. It is important to keep in mind that problem behavior may be maintained by either positive reinforcement (e.g., getting adult or peer attention, obtaining desired activities or objects) or negative reinforcement (e.g., escape or avoidance of aversive tasks or demands, having teachers or peers stay away or leave you alone). This will be identified in the FBA process, and an appropriate extinction procedure can be designed and implemented.

Extinction is a challenging intervention to implement logistically and can be problematic when implemented alone (Shukla & Albin, 1996). In a comprehensive BSP, an extinction contingency for problem behavior is typically used in combination with prompts and reinforcers for an alternative replacement behavior such as a functional communication response. The idea is to prompt and teach a replacement behavior that is effective and reinforced while making problem behavior ineffective by eliminating or reducing the reinforcement it receives.

Isha escapes transitions, which she finds aversive, by engaging in screaming, pulling her hair, and scratching at staff. These behaviors are negatively reinforced by Isha's avoiding transitions (i.e., staff let her stay with the activity she is doing). The team realizes that simply placing Isha's problem behavior on extinction would require staff to not allow her to avoid the transition. This strategy would probably be too difficult to carry out because staff would have to prompt and assist Isha through the transition, which could lead to dangerous situations (e.g., she might become highly agitated).

A better procedure is to combine extinction of problem behavior with prompting and teaching an alternative replacement behavior, a communication response.

Isha's team decided to teach her to ask for more time. When the problem behavior is placed on extinction, Isha also will be prompted and taught to ask for more time. When she asks appropriately, the communication response will be honored and reinforced with additional time on the current activity. The team reasoned that engaging in problem behavior should not lead to Isha's getting to stay in an activity longer but that asking appropriately for more time can be reinforced.

Reinforcement Procedures Positive reinforcement for desired and appropriate replacement behaviors is included in a BSP to help make those behaviors more effective and efficient, which also makes problem behavior relatively more inefficient. As noted in the CBA section of this chapter, the presumed maintaining consequences for desired behaviors are too often inadequate to compete successfully with the maintaining

consequences for problem behavior. The CBA helps show support teams when existing reinforcers are not strong enough and do not provide sufficient incentive to support performance of desired behaviors. An essential component in a BSP is the regular delivery of strong positive reinforcement in terms of both the quality and the schedule of reinforcers, contingent on the occurrence of desired appropriate behaviors. Reinforcers for desired behavior must be strong enough and delivered with sufficient frequency to compete successfully with the consequences that maintain problem behaviors. For some students, it may be necessary to identify effective reinforcers through systematic reinforcer or preference assessments (Durand, Crimmins, Caulfield, & Taylor, 1989; Green et al., 1991; Roane, Vollmer, Ringdahl, & Marcus, 1998).

A commonly heard comment regarding the frequency of positive reinforcement is that a student needs or demands too much positive reinforcement. The issue is often that teachers and other support providers have difficulty delivering reinforcers frequently enough to meet students' needs. Self-management strategies offer one solution for this problem. Students may be taught to self-monitor their behavior and then to self-recruit reinforcement or feedback from staff (Mank & Horner, 1987; Smith & Sugai, 2000; Todd, Horner, & Sugai, 1999). A self-management approach to delivering positive reinforcement reduces the demand on staff to constantly monitor student performance and remember to deliver frequent reinforcers while at the same time increasing the independence and self-determination of the student. The student self-monitors and then cues staff that a reinforcer or feedback of some type should now be delivered.

Punishment Procedures As noted previously, punishment procedures may be included in a BSP when they are useful in making a support plan effective and beneficial for a student with problem behavior, appropriate to the contexts in which they are used, and implemented ethically and reasonably. In some cases, school or district policies may delineate some punishment procedures that will be included and implemented for all students in a school regardless of whether they have an individual BSP or IEP. Mild punishment procedures may sometimes be used in a manner similar to extinction, that is, as a procedure that helps make problem behavior ineffective or inefficient. In these cases, mild punishment of problem behavior is used in combination with prompting and reinforcing or teaching an appropriate alternative behavior, such as a functional communication response.

If punishment procedures are included in a BSP, clear guidelines for the use of punishers must be included in the written BSP. Behavior(s) that result in delivery of punishment should be clearly defined. Students and staff should be informed regarding school disciplinary policies and how, when, and what punishments will be used. A significant problem with the use of punishment procedures in schools is inconsistent and confusing implementation (Mayer & Sulzer-Azaroff, 2002). Support teams should use the least intrusive punishment that they expect to be effective and should carefully monitor the implementation and effects, including side effects, of the punishment procedure. The level of intrusiveness of punishment should be logically balanced by the value of the anticipated behavior change for the student with problem behaviors (Horner et al., 1990).

Safety or Emergency Intervention Plan An emergency/crisis plan should be included in the comprehensive BSP for any student with severe problem behaviors who engages in (or has some likelihood of engaging in) high-intensity self-injurious, aggressive, or destructive behaviors that threaten his or her safety and health or the safety and health of others. The purpose of an emergency/crisis plan is to protect people from harm, not to teach or change behavior. An emergency/crisis plan should (a) precisely define what constitutes an emergency/crisis; (b) describe in detail the specific intervention procedures to be implemented, including procedures designed to defuse and deescalate crisis behavior as well as procedures to deal with crisis behaviors directly once they occur; (c) define specific criteria for ending implementation of any intrusive or restrictive emergency procedures (e.g., criteria for ending an emergency restraint procedure); (d) describe in detail specific procedures for data collection related to the emergency/crisis; (e) detail reporting procedures to be followed and identify who should be informed; (f) describe training and caregiver support procedures designed to maintain capacity to respond effectively to emergency/crisis behaviors; and (g) describe debriefing, feedback, and other follow-up procedures to be implemented after implementation of emergency/crisis intervention. Readers interested in learning more about behavioral crisis prevention and management are referred to Carr et al. (1994) and Colvin et al. (1993).

9. *Evaluation and assessment:* The written BSP should include descriptions of data collection procedures, including forms and directions for using them, and procedures for ongoing monitoring and evaluation of plan effects. The evaluation plan will specify the behaviors to be tracked, the form(s) to be used, procedures for summarizing and sharing the information collected, and the person(s) responsible for each of the evaluation activities. A process for regular review and analysis of evaluation information should be identified so that timely decisions can be made regarding ongoing implementation and modification of plan procedures. An effective strategy is to set a regular meeting schedule for the support team to review plan effects and any issues arising related to plan implementation.

10. *Ensure contextual fit:* A BSP will be effective only if it is implemented with consistency and fidelity. Ensuring contextual fit is an element of the support planning process that may not show up in the written BSP but is important to ensuring fidelity and sustainability of implementation of the plan (Albin et al., 1996). Factors to consider in assessing the contextual fit of a BSP are the values of the implementers, skills of the implementers, resources available for BSP implementation, and administrative support provided for BSP implementation. In addition, the extent to which the BSP is perceived by implementers as being in the best interests of the focus student and its perceived effectiveness are considerations for contextual fit and the fidelity and sustainability of BSP implementation.

BSP Implementation Plan

Another feature of effective behavior support planning and BSP implementation that promotes effective implementation of support plans, although it is not included on the Horner et al. (1999–2000) checklist, is a written implementation plan. An implementation plan that provides a guide for getting the procedures and features of a comprehensive BSP into place and operational is an often-overlooked element of effective behavior support. Unfortunately, we have experienced many cases in which excellent behavior support plans have been developed but never fully implemented. Developing an implementation plan as part of the overall process of providing comprehensive support facilitates both initial and sustained implementation of planned procedures. The implementation plan identifies responsibilities and time lines for activities required to make plan procedures happen. For example, it would identify who will obtain or develop needed materials and forms and when. The implementation plan also might describe procedures for implementing each of the various plan components, identify the sequence in which plan procedures will be implemented, and set target dates and time lines for implementation. The implementation plan can be used to identify any resources needed for plan implementation, training needs of those who will implement plan procedures, and strategies for meeting those training needs. Just as the comprehensive support plan itself is the product of a collaborative team

FIGURE 6–11
Sample Written Behavior Support Plan for Maya

Student: Maya Reimeriz   Adoption Date: 10/20/03
DOB: 06/14/91
Contacts: Mrs. J. Reimeriz (555-6789)—mother
Action team: Ms. Craig (homeroom teacher), Ms. Schwartz (behavior specialist), Mr. Martinez (teacher), Ms. Durham (educational assistant), Mrs. Reimeriz (mother)

Vision and Rationale for Support

Maya is 12 years old and lives at home with her parents and two older brothers. She has Down syndrome and moderate to severe intellectual disabilities (see student file for test scores). Her parents are very committed to Maya's inclusion in regular education classes and school settings. Maya enjoys fish, has a fish aquarium, and hopes to work at a fish or pet store in the future. A personal futures plan for Maya was done in September and produced the following goals: (a) high school graduation; (b) apartment living with a friend; (c) employment in a fish or pet store; (d) skill development in cooking, clothing care, basic household chores, money management, personal care, and time management; (e) joining a community group; and (f) maintenance of good physical health through diet and exercise. Currently, Maya reads at a first-grade level; follows step-by-step directions by reading words, icons, and photos; adds and subtracts single-digit numbers; identifies numbers 1 to 10; and copies two- to three-word phrases. She takes care of most of her dressing and personal care needs. Maya enjoys talking and listening to music with peers. Her mother notes that she likes to cook at home.

Maya engages in problem behaviors that are becoming increasingly intense. Her behaviors currently threaten her continued participation in regular school settings. The major concern is that in situations where Maya is not receiving social attention from peers, she will yell at the peers and then sometimes hit them. The hitting is becoming more frequent, and conflicts with peers are becoming more intense. She also sticks her tongue out at people and spits at people (although she rarely hits them with spit). She also has a history of throwing objects. Maya's parents and school staff are concerned for her future. Her team agrees that her life at school and home will be greatly improved by learning new social and communication skills to replace her problem behaviors.

Team Agreements

     ✓ Maya will receive her education in the neighborhood middle school.
     ✓ Maya's behavior support plan will be based on functional assessment outcomes.
     ✓ Maya's support plan will be implemented and evaluated on a consistent and regular basis for a specified period of time (i.e., the school year).
     ✓ Behavior support for Maya is a high priority since, with age, aggressive and inappropriate behaviors may become more frequent, disruptive, and problematic and may put her and those around her at even more risk.

FIGURE 6–11 (*Continued*)
Sample Written Behavior Support Plan for Maya

Description of Problem Behaviors

1. *Sticking tongue out*: Maya sticks her tongue out of her mouth as she orients her face to peers. Tongue protrudes clearly as she faces peer. Licking her lips and having her mouth relax open (no visibility of tongue) are not examples of sticking tongue out.

1. *Yelling*: Maya screams words (e.g., hey, hi-hi-hi, student names) or vocalizes (e.g., ahh) in a very loud tone. Intensity is clearly above hallway (or ambient) noise level. Speaking to peers and saying hi in a normal voice intensity are not examples of yelling.

3. *Spitting*: Maya spits in the direction of her peers. Spitting includes actual fluid being spit out or the imitation and intent to look as if fluid will be spit out. Spit does not need to hit someone to count as spitting.

4. *Hitting peers*: Hitting peers is defined as Maya striking (i.e., making contact with any degree of force) or attempting to strike (i.e., swinging at or punching at someone with no contact) peers with an open hand or fist. Accidentally bumping someone or tapping someone's shoulder to get their attention are not examples of hitting peers.

      Maya's behaviors often happen in a sequence. When she sticks her tongue out, her peers usually laugh and imitate her. When peers walk away from Maya or don't respond to her sticking out her tongue, she often yells or spits at the closest peer(s). If peers challenge her or yell back at her, she may hit them. If Maya is particularly agitated about peer attention, she may yell and hit from the very beginning.

Summary of FBA and Hypothesis Statement

The functional behavioral assessment included the completion of a Request for Student Support Team Assistance; the FACTS, Parts A and B; and a full day of direct observation on a Monday using the Functional Assessment Observation form (O'Neill et al., 1997). From this process, the team identified two routines where Maya's problem behaviors were most likely to occur: (a) hallway transition periods and (b) activities with minimal structure (e.g., lunch, recess, large-group activities). In each case, Maya's team identified that Maya's problem behaviors were preceded by low levels of peer interaction and attention and rewarded by immediate access to peer attention (peers laugh, make comments, and yell back at her). The team agrees that Maya's problem behaviors are maintained primarily by getting peer attention. A diagram of the summary hypothesis statement for Maya is included on her competing behavior analysis form (see attached form). [Note that this form, which is included as Figure 6-9 in this chapter, would be attached as part of the written behavior support plan.]

General Intervention Plan for Maya

Overview: The main goals of Maya's behavior support plan will be to (a) reduce the unpredictability of when Maya will have opportunities to have access to and interactions with peers by providing her with a picture schedule, (b) teach Maya to use her picture schedule as a conversation book so that she can approach peers and initiate a conversation in an appropriate and respectful manner, and (c) provide Maya with a peer mentor during less structured activities so that she will get peer attention naturally and not have to engage in her problem behavior routine to get it. To help make the conversation book work for Maya, the team has agreed to spend 15 to 20 minutes explaining it to the other students and explaining how they should respond when she approaches them with it.

FIGURE 6–11 (*Continued*)

Sample Written Behavior Support Plan for Maya

    Because hitting is not acceptable for any student, if Maya hits other students, the team and her parents have agreed to follow the school discipline policy on fighting. Maya will be removed from the situation to the vice principal's office, and her parents will be contacted.

Specific Procedures for Maya

Specific elements of Maya's behavior support plan are identified with an asterisk on the attached competing behavior analysis form.

Behavior Support Plan: Action Plan

Tasks	Person responsible	By when	Review date	Evaluation decision • Monitor • Modify discontinue
Prevention: Make problem behavior irrelevant (environmental redesign)				
Identify and schedule peer mentors	Ms. Craig	10/20	10/24	
Teaching: Make problem behavior inefficient (teach new skills)				
Teach use of picture schedule	Ms. Durham	10/30	10/31	
Teach use of communication book	Ms. Schwartz	10/30	10/31	
Extinction: Make problem behavior ineffective (minimize reward for problem behavior)				
Explain Maya's communication book and how to respond to it to students	Ms. Schwartz	10/30	10/31	
Reinforcement: Make desired behavior more rewarding.				
Ensure that Maya has opportunities for social interaction with peers	Ms. Craig and Ms. Durham	10/30	10/31	
Safety: Ensure safety of all (what to do in dangerous situations) (if needed)				
Use school discipline policy for hitting–give office discipline referral and send to vice principal	Ms. Craig informs staff	10/24	10/31	

FIGURE 6–11 (*Continued*)
Sample Written Behavior Support Plan for Maya

Behavior Support Plan: Evaluation Plan for Maya

Behavioral goal (use specific, observable, measurable descriptions of goal)

What is the short-term behavioral goal?

Teach Maya to use the communication book to approach peers in the hallway. Maya will approach peers in the hallway with her communication book at least once per transition for 5 consecutive days.

Expected date: 10/30/03

What is the long-term behavioral goal?

Maya will interact appropriately with her peers in all school settings (classrooms, hallways, and so on) for 4 weeks with no incidences of yelling, spitting or hitting.

Expected date: 05/31/04

Evaluation Procedures

Data to be collected	Procedures for data collection	Person responsible	Time line
Is plan being implemented?			
Peer mentor	Check in with teachers	Rachel	Daily for 2 weeks
Use of the communication book	Observations in the hallway	Trudy and Latisha	Daily for 2 weeks
Use of the picture schedule	Observations at bus and in classrooms	Latisha and teachers	Daily for 2 weeks
Is plan making a difference?			
Number of conversations with peers	Observations in hallway	Trudy and Latisha	Daily for 2 weeks
Number of incidents	Reports from staff	Trudy compiles	Weekly for first month
Office discipline referrals for hitting	SWIS™ system	Trudy checks	Check weekly to start

Plan review date: weekly review for first month

Note: If emergency behavior management procedures are necessary, attach safety plan as separate sheet.

process, an implementation plan also should reflect consensus from the support team.

The implementation plan can also provide aids (e.g., checklists, one-page summaries) to promote implementation fidelity and long-term maintenance (Lucyshyn & Albin, 1993). Team and caregiver support strategies and procedures for sustaining long-term implementation of a support plan can be incorporated into the implementation plan. Procedures for sustaining a collaborative team process over time and for maintaining the team's focus on their vision and goals for a focus person's lifestyle are essential for the long-term delivery of effective comprehensive behavior support.

Examples of a written behavior support plan and an implementation plan for Maya are presented in Figure 6–11.

Summary

PBS is among the most exciting developments in the support technology available to children and adults with severe disabilities. Problem behaviors have long been a major obstacle to important living, educational, and employment opportunities. For too long we have assumed that to be part of typical environments, a person first needed to acquire appropriate behaviors. We now have learned that appropriate behaviors are best learned when appropriate supports are delivered *in* typical contexts. The procedures associated with PBS provide the means for assessing and designing support that will both reduce problem behaviors and develop the constellation of skills needed to have a real impact on how a person lives.

This chapter provides (a) a structure for understanding problem behaviors; (b) a set of procedures for conducting assessments that can transform chaotic, painful, confusing situations into understandable, logical patterns that can be addressed; and (c) a process for building support plans that will be both effective and doable.

The science of behavior analysis has defined an important set of mechanisms that describe how human beings learn from their environment. This science has been transformed into teaching and support procedures that have the potential to produce important changes in the behavior of children and adults with disabilities. PBS is the marriage of this science with fundamental values about the way people with disabilities should be part of our society. The challenge is to use

the science with precision and the values with distinction. Those implementing PBS need the self-discipline to learn the science before they venture to change someone else's behavior, the wisdom to learn the values so they apply the technology with discretion, and the humility to work collaboratively and to continually assess the impact of interventions on the lives of those who receive support.

References

Alberto, P.A., & Troutman, A. C. (2003). *Applied behavior analysis for teachers* (6th ed.). Englewood Cliffs, NJ: Merrill/Prentice Hall.

Albin, R. W., Lucyshyn, J. M., Horner, R. H., & Flannery, K. B. (1996). Contextual fit for behavior support plans: A model for "goodness-of-fit." In L. K. Koegel, R. L. Koegel, & G. Dunlap (Eds.), *Positive behavioral support: Including people with difficult behavior in the community* (pp. 81–98). Baltimore: Paul H. Brookes.

Albin, R. W., O'Brien, M., & Horner, R. H. (1995). Analysis of an escalating sequence of problem behaviors: A case study. *Research in Developmental Disabilities, 16*, 133–147.

Anderson, J. L., Albin, R. W., Mesaros, R. A., Dunlap, G., & Morelli-Robbins, M. (1993). Issues in providing training to achieve comprehensive behavioral support. In J. Reichle & D. P. Wacker (Eds.), *Communicative alternatives to challenging behavior: Integrating functional assessment and intervention strategies* (pp. 363–406). Baltimore: Paul H. Brookes.

Arndorfer, R. E., Miltenberger, R. G., Woster, S. H., Rortvedt, A. K., & Gaffaney, T. (1994). Home-based descriptive and experimental analysis of problem behaviors in children. *Topics in Early Childhood Special Education, 14*(1), 64–87.

Axelrod, S. (1987). Functional and structural analysis of behavior: Approaches leading to reduced use of punishment procedures. *Research in Developmental Disabilities, 8*, 165–178.

Baer, D. M., Wolf, M. M., & Risley, T. G. (1968). Some current dimensions of applied behavior analysis. *Journal of Applied Behavior Analysis, 1*, 91–97.

Bergstrom, M. K., Horner, R. H., & Crone, D. A. (2004). *School-based team members conducting functional behavioral assessments in the general education environment. Manuscript under review.*

Berotti, D., & Durand, V. M. (1999). Communication-based interventions for students with sensory impairments and challenging behavior. In J. R. Scotti & L. H. Meyer (Eds.), *Behavioral intervention: Principles, models, and practices* (pp. 237–250). Baltimore: Paul H. Brookes.

Bijou, S., & Baer, D. M. (1961). *Child development: Vol. 1. A systematic and empirical theory.* New York: Appleton-Century-Crofts.

Bijou, S. W., Peterson, R. F., & Ault, M. H. (1968). A method to integrate descriptive and experimental field studies at the level of data and empirical concepts. *Journal of Applied Behavior Analysis, 1*, 175–191.

Carr, E. G. (1977). The motivation of self-injurious behavior: A review of some hypotheses. *Psychological Bulletin, 84*, 800–816.

Carr, E. G. (1988). Functional equivalence as a mechanism of response generalization. In R. H. Horner, R. L. Koegel, & G. Dunlap (Eds.), *Generalization and maintenance: Lifestyle changes in applied settings* (pp. 194–219). Baltimore: Paul H. Brookes.

Carr, E. G. (1994). Emerging themes in the functional analysis of problem behavior. *Journal of Applied Behavior Analysis, 27*, 393–399.

Carr, E. G. (2000). Reconceptualizing functional assessment failures: Comments on Kennedy. *Journal of Positive Behavior Interventions, 4*, 205–207.

Carr, E. G., & Carlson, J. I. (1993). Reduction of severe behavior problems in the community using a multicomponent treatment approach. *Journal of Applied Behavior Analysis, 26*, 157–172.

Carr, E. G., Dunlap, G., Horner, R. H., Koegel, R. L., Turnbull, A. P., Sailor, W., et al. (2002). Positive behavior support: Evolution of an applied science. *Journal of Positive Behavior Interventions, 4*, 4–16, 20.

Carr, E. G., & Durand, V. M. (1985a). Reducing behavior problems through functional communication training. *Journal of Applied Behavior Analysis, 18*, 111–126.

Carr, E. G., & Durand, V. M. (1985b). The social-communicative basis of severe behavior problems in children. In S. Reiss & R. Bootzin (Eds.), *Theoretical issues in behavior therapy* (pp. 219–254). New York: Academic Press.

Carr, E. G., & Durand, V. M. (1987, November). See me, help me. *Psychology Today*, 62–64.

Carr, E. G., Horner, R. H., Turnbull, A. P., Marquis, J. G., McLaughlin, D. M., McAtee, M. L., et al. (1999). *Positive behavior support for people with developmental disabilities: A research synthesis*. Washington, DC: American Association on Mental Retardation.

Carr, E. G., Levin, L., McConnachie, G., Carlson, J. I., Kemp, D. C., & Smith, C. E. (1994). *Communication-based intervention for problem behavior: A user's guide for producing positive change*. Baltimore: Paul H. Brookes.

Carr, E. G., Reeve, C. E., & Magito-McLaughlin, D. (1996). Contextual influences on problem behavior in people with developmental disabilities. In L. K. Koegel, R. L. Koegel, & G. Dunlap (Eds.), *Positive behavior support: Including people with difficult behavior in the community* (pp. 403–423). Baltimore: Paul H. Brookes.

Catania, A. (1992). B.F. Skinner, organism. *American Psychologist 47*(11), 1521–1530.

Colvin, G. (1993). *Managing acting-out behavior*. Eugene, OR: Behavior Associates.

Colvin, G., Sugai, G., & Patching, B. (1993). Precorrection: An instructional approach for managing predictable problem behaviors. *Intervention in School and Clinic, 28*, 143–150.

Crone, D. A., & Horner, R. H. (2003). *Building positive behavior support in schools: Functional behavioral assessment*. New York: Guilford.

Day, H. M., Horner, R. H., & O'Neill, R. E. (1994). Multiple functions of problem behaviors: Assessment and intervention. *Journal of Applied Behavior Analysis, 27*, 279–289.

Didden, R., Duker, P. C., & Korzilius, H. (1997). Meta-analytic study on treatment effectiveness for problem behaviors with individuals who have mental retardation. *American Journal on Mental Retardation, 101*, 387–399.

Donnellan, A. M., Mirenda, P. L., Mesaros, R. A., & Fassbender, L. L. (1984). Analyzing the communicative functions of aberrant behavior. *Journal of the Association for Persons with Severe Handicaps, 3*, 201–212.

Doss, S., & Reichle, J. (1991). Replacing excess behavior with an initial communicative repertoire. In J. Reichle, J. York, & J. Sigafoos (Eds.), *Implementing augmentative and alternative communication* (pp. 215–237). Baltimore: Paul H. Brookes.

Dunlap, G., Foster-Johnson, L., Clarke, S., Kern, L., & Childs, K. E. (1995). Modifying activities to produce functional outcomes: Effects on the disruptive behaviors of students with disabilities. *Journal of the Association for Persons with Severe Handicaps, 20*, 248–258.

Dunlap, G., Kern-Dunlap, L., Clarke, S., & Robbins, F. R. (1991). Functional assessment, curriculum revision, and severe behavior problems. *Journal of Applied Behavior Analysis, 24*, 387–397.

Dunlap, G., & Kincaid, D. (2001). The widening world of functional assessment: Comments on four manuals and beyond. *Journal of Applied Behavior Analysis, 34*, 365–377.

Durand, V. M. (1988). The Motivation Assessment Scale. In M. Hersen & A. Bellack (Eds.), *Dictionary of behavioral assessment techniques* (pp. 309–310). Elmsford, NY: Pergamon.

Durand, V. M. (1990). *Severe behavior problems: A functional communication approach*. New York: Guilford.

Durand, V. M., & Carr, E. G. (1991). Functional communication training to reduce challenging behavior: Maintenance and application in new settings. *Journal of Applied Behavior Analysis, 24*, 251–264.

Durand, V. M., & Carr, E. G. (1992). An analysis of maintenance following functional communication training. *Journal of Applied Behavior Analysis, 25*, 777–794.

Durand, V. M., Crimmins, D. B., Caulfield, M., & Taylor, J. (1989). Reinforcer assessment I: Using problem behavior to select reinforcers. *Journal of the Association for Persons with Severe Handicaps, 14*, 113–126.

Ervin, R. A., Radford, P. M., Bertsch, K., Piper, A. L., Ehrhardt, K. E., & Poling, A. (2001). A descriptive analysis and critique of the empirical literature on school-based functional assessment. *School Psychology Review, 30*, 193–209.

Ferro, J., Foster-Johnson, L., & Dunlap, G. (1996). The relationship between curricular activities and the problem behavior of students with mental retardation. *American Journal on Mental Retardation, 101*, 184–194.

Flannery, K. B., & Horner, R. H. (1994). The relationship between predictability and problem behavior for students with severe disabilities. *Journal of Behavioral Education, 4*, 157–176.

Fox, L., & Dunlap, G. (Winter 2002). Family-centered practices in behavior support. *Beyond Behavior 11*, 24–27.

Green, C. W., Reid, D. H., Canipe, V. S., & Gardner, S. M. (1991). A comprehensive evaluation of reinforcer identification processes for persons with profound multiple handicaps. *Journal of Applied Behavior Analysis, 24*, 537–552.

Gresham, F. M. (2002). Teaching social skills to high-risk children and youth: Preventive and remedial strategies. In M. A. Shinn, H. M. Walker, & G. Stoner (Eds.), *Interventions for academic and behavior problems II: Preventive and remedial approaches* (pp. 403–432). Bethesda, MD: National Association of School Psychologists.

Gresham, F. M., McIntyre, L. L., Olson-Tinker, H., Dolstra, L., McLaughlin, V., & Van, M. (2004). Relevance of functional behavioral assessment research for school-based interventions and positive behavioral support. *Research in Developmental Disabilities, 25*, 19–37.

Guess, D., & Carr, E. G. (1991). Emergence and maintenance of stereotypy and self-injury. *American Journal on Mental Retardation, 96*, 299–319.

Hanley, G. P., & Iwata, B. A. (2003). Functional analysis of problem behavior: A review. *Journal of Applied Behavior Analysis, 36*, 147–185.

Holburn, S., Jacobson, J. W., Vietze, P. M., Schwartz, A. A., & Sersen, E. (2000). Quantifying the process and outcomes of person-centered planning. *American Journal on Mental Retardation, 105*, 402–416.

Holburn, S., & Vietze, P. M. (2002). *Person-centered planning: Research, practice, and future directions.* Baltimore: Paul H. Brookes.

Horner, R. H. (1999). Positive behavior supports. In M. L. Wehmeyer & J. R. Patton, (Eds.), *Mental Retardation in the 21st Century* (pp. 181–196). Austin, TX: PRO-ED.

Horner, R. H., Albin, R. W., Borgmeier, C., & Salantine, S. P. (2003, May). *Moving from functional assessment to the design of behavior support.* Symposium presented at the Association for Behavior Analysis Annual Convention, San Francisco.

Horner, R. H., Albin, R. W., Sprague, J. R., & Todd, A. W. (2000). Positive behavior support. In M. E. Snell & F. Brown (Eds.), *Instruction of students with severe disabilities* (5th ed., pp. 207–243). Upper Saddle River, NJ: Merrill/Prentice Hall.

Horner, R. H., & Billingsley, F. F. (1988). The effect of competing behavior on the generalization and maintenance of adaptive behavior in applied settings. In. R. H. Horner, G. Dunlap, & R. L. Koegel (Eds.), *Generalization and maintenance: Lifestyle changes in applied settings* (pp. 197–220). Baltimore: Paul H. Brookes.

Horner, R. H., Day, H. M., & Day, J. (1997). Using neutralizing routines to reduce problem behaviors. *Journal of Applied Behavior Analysis, 39*, 601–614.

Horner, R. H., Diemer, S. M., & Brazeau, K. C. (1992). Educational support for students with severe problem behaviors in Oregon: A descriptive analysis from the 1987–1988 school year. *Journal of the Association for Persons with Severe Handicaps, 17*, 154–169.

Horner, R. H., Dunlap, G., Koegel, R. L., Carr, E. G., Sailor, W., Anderson, J., et al. (1990). Toward a technology of "nonaversive" behavioral support. *Journal of the Association for Persons with Severe Handicaps, 15*, 125–132.

Horner, R. H., Sugai, G., Todd, A. W., & Lewis-Palmer, T. (1999–2000). Elements of behavior support plans: A technical brief. *Exceptionality, 8*, 205–216.

Horner, R. H., Vaughn, B., Day, H. M., & Ard, B. (1996). The relationship between setting events and problem behavior. In L. K. Koegel, R. L. Koegel, & G. Dunlap (Eds.), *Positive behavioral support: Including people with difficult behavior in the community* (pp. 381–402). Baltimore: Paul H. Brookes.

Individuals with Disabilities Education Act, Amendments of 1997. (1997). H.R. 5, 105th Congress, 1st Sess.

Ingram, K., Lewis-Palmer, T., & Sugai, G. (in press). Function-based intervention planning: Comparing the effectiveness of FBA indicated and contra-indicated interventions plans. *Journal of Positive Behavior Interventions.*

Iwata, B. A., Dorsey, M. F., Slifer, K. J., Bauman, K. E., & Richman, G. S. (1982). Toward a functional analysis of self-injury. *Analysis and Intervention in Developmental Disabilities, 2*, 3–20.

Janney, R., & Snell, M. (2000). *Behavioral support.* Baltimore: Paul H. Brookes.

Kincaid, D. (1996). Person-centered planning. In L. K. Koegel, R. L. Koegel, & G. Dunlap (Eds.), *Positive behavior support: Including people with difficult behavior in the community* (pp. 439–465). Baltimore: Paul H. Brookes.

Koegel, L. K., Koegel, R. L., & Dunlap, G. (1996). *Positive behavioral support: Including people with difficult behavior in the community.* Baltimore: Paul H. Brookes.

Lalli, J. S., Browder, D. M., Mace, F. C., & Brown, D. K. (1993). Teacher use of descriptive analysis data to implement interventions to decrease students' problem behavior. *Journal of Applied Behavior Analysis, 26*, 227–238.

Lerman, D. C., & Iwata, B. A. (1993). Descriptive and experimental analysis of variables maintaining self-injurious behavior. *Journal of Applied Behavior Analysis, 26*, 293–319.

Lewis-Palmer, T. (1998). *Using functional assessment strategies in regular school classroom settings with students at-risk for school failure.* Unpublished doctoral dissertation, University of Oregon, Eugene.

Lucyshyn, J., & Albin, R. W. (1993). Comprehensive support to families of children with disabilities and behavior problems: Keeping it "friendly." In G. H. S. Singer & L. E. Powers (Eds.), *Families, disability, and empowerment* (pp. 365–407). Baltimore: Paul H. Brookes.

Lucyshyn, J. M., Albin, R. W., & Nixon, C. D. (1997). Embedding comprehensive behavioral support in family ecology: An experimental, single-case analysis. *Journal of Consulting and Clinical Psychology, 65*, 241–251.

Lucyshyn, J. M., Kayser, A. T., Irvin, L. K., & Blumberg, E. R. (2002). Functional assessment and positive behavior support at home with families: Designing effective and contextually appropriate behavior support plans. In J. M. Lucyshyn, G. Dunlap, & R. W. Albin (Eds.), *Families and positive behavior support: Addressing problem behavior in family contexts* (pp. 97–132). Baltimore: Paul H. Brookes.

Mace, F. C., & Lalli, J. S. (1991). Linking descriptive and experimental analysis in the treatment of bizarre speech. *Journal of Applied Behavior Analysis, 24*, 553–562.

Mank, D. M., & Horner, R. H. (1987). Self-recruited feedback: A cost-effective procedure for maintaining behavior. *Research in Developmental Disabilities, 8*, 91–112.

March, R., & Horner, R. (1998, May). *School-wide behavioral support: Extending the impact of ABA by expanding the unit of analysis.* Presentation at the Association for Behavior Analysis Annual Convention, Orlando, FL.

March, R., Horner, R. H., Lewis-Palmer, T., Brown, D., Crone, D., Todd, A. W., et al. (2000). *Functional Assessment Checklist for Teachers and Staff (FACTS).* Eugene: University of Oregon, Department of Educational and Community Supports.

Marquis, J. G., Horner, R. H., Carr, E. G., Turnbull, A. P., Thompson, M., Behrens, G. A., et al. (2000). A meta-analysis of positive behavior support. In R. M. Gerston & E. P. Schiller (Eds.), *Contemporary special education research: Syntheses of the knowledge base on critical instructional issues* (pp. 137-178). Mahwah, NJ: Lawrence Erlbaum Associates.

Mayer, G. R., & Sulzer-Azaroff, B. (2002). Interventions for vandalism and aggression. In M. R. Shinn, H. M. Walker, & G. Stoner (Eds.), *Interventions for academic and behavior problems II: Preventive and remedial approaches*. Silver Spring, MD: National Association of School Psychologists.

Meyer, L. H., & Evans, I. M. (1989). *Nonaversive interventions for behavior problems: A manual for home and community*. Baltimore: Paul H. Brookes.

Moes, D. R., & Frea, W. D. (2000). Using family context to inform intervention planning for the treatment of a child with autism. *Journal of Positive Behavior Interventions, 2,* 40-46.

Moore, J. W., Edwards, R. P., Sterling-Turner, H. E., Riley, J., DuBard, M., & McGeorge, A. (2002). Teacher acquisition of functional analysis methodology. *Journal of Applied Behavior Analysis, 35,* 73-77.

Mount, B. (1994). Benefits and limitations or personal futures planning. In V. J. Bradley, J. W. Ashbaugh, & B. C. Blaney (Eds.), *Creating individual supports for people with developmental disabilities* (pp. 97-108). Baltimore: Paul H. Brookes.

Munk, D. D., & Repp, A. C. (1994). The relationship between instructional variables and problem behavior: A review. *Exceptional Children, 60,* 390-401.

Nelson, J. R., Roberts, M. L., Mathur, S. R., & Rutherford, R. B., Jr. (1999). Has public policy exceeded our knowledge base? A review of the functional behavioral assessment literature. *Behavioral Disorders, 24,* 169-179.

New York State ARC v. Carey, 393 F. Supp. 715, 718-19 (E.D.N.Y. 1975) and *New York State ARC v. Carey,* No. 72-C356/357 (E.D.N.Y., 1975).

Newcomer, L. L., & Lewis, T. J. (in press). Functional behavioral assessment: An investigation of assessment reliability and effectiveness of function-based interventions. *Journal of Emotional and Behavioral Disorders.*

Newton, J. S., & Horner, R. H. (2004). Emerging trends in methods for research and evaluation of behavioral interventions. Pp. 495-515. In E. Emerson, T. Thompson, T. Parmenter, & C. Hatton (Eds.), *International handbook of methods for research and evaluation in intellectual disabilities*. New York: Wiley.

Nirje, B. (1969). The normalization principle and its human management implications. In R. Kugel & W. Wolfensberger (Eds.), *Changing patterns in residential services for the mentally retarded* (pp. 179-195). Washington, DC: President's Committee on Mental Retardation.

Northup, J., Broussard, C., Jones, K., George, T., Vollmer, T. R., & Herring, M. (1995). The differential effects of teacher and peer attention on the disruptive classroom behavior of three children with a diagnosis of attention deficit hyperactivity disorder. *Journal of Applied Behavior Analysis, 28,* 227-228.

Northup, J., Wacker, D., Sasso, G., Steege, M., Cigrand, K., Cook, J., et al. (1991). A brief functional analysis of aggressive and alternative behavior in an outclinic setting. *Journal of Applied Behavior Analysis, 24,* 509-522.

O'Brien, C. J., O'Brien, J., & Mount, B. (1997). Person-centered planning has arrived or has it? *Mental Retardation, 35,* 480-484.

O'Neill, R. E., Horner, R. H., Albin, R. W., Sprague, J. R., Storey, K., & Newton, J. S. (1997). *Functional assessment for problem behavior: A practical handbook* (2nd ed.). Pacific Grove, CA: Brooks/Cole.

O'Reilly, M. (1997). Functional analysis of episodic self-injury correlated with recurrent otitis media. *Journal of Applied Behavior Analysis, 30,* 165-167.

Pace, G. M., Ivancic, M. R., Edwards, G. L., Iwata, B. A., & Page, T. J. (1985). Assessment of stimulus preference and reinforcer values with profoundly retarded individuals. *Journal of Applied Behavior, 18,* 249-256.

Reid, R., & Nelson, J. R. (2002). The utility, acceptability, and practicality of functional behavioral assessment for students with high-incidence problem behaviors. *Remedial Special Education, 23,* 15-23.

Reiss, S., & Aman, M. (Eds.). (1998). *Psychotropic medication and developmental disabilities: The international consensus handbook*. Columbus: Ohio State University, Nisanger Center.

Repp, A. C., Felce, D., & Barton, L. E. (1988). Basing the treatment of stereotypic and self-injurious behaviors on hypotheses of their causes. *Journal of Applied Behavior Analysis, 21,* 281-289.

Repp, A. C., & Singh, N. N. (1990). *Perspectives on the use of nonaversive and aversive interventions for persons with developmental disabilities*. Pacific Grove, CA: Brooks/Cole.

Roane, H. S., Vollmer, T. R., Ringdahl, J. E., & Marcus, B. A. (1998). Evaluation of a brief stimulus preference assessment. *Journal of Applied Behavior Analysis, 31,* 605-620.

Sandler, L. (2001). *Goodness-of-fit and the viability of behavioral support plans: A survey of direct care adult residential staff*. Unpublished doctoral dissertation, University of Oregon, Eugene.

Sasso, G. M., Reimers, R. M., Cooper, L. J., Wacker, D., Berg, W., Steege, M., et al. (1992). Use of descriptive and experimental analyses to identify the functional properties of aberrant behavior in school settings. *Journal of Applied Behavior Analysis, 25,* 809-821.

Schalock, R., & Alonso, M. A. V. (2002). *Handbook on quality of life for human service practitioners*. Washington, DC: American Association on Mental Retardation.

Shavelson, R. J., & Towne, L. (Eds.). (2002). *Scientific research in education*. Washington, DC: National Academy Press.

Shukla, S., & Albin, R. W. (1996). Effects of extinction alone and extinction plus functional communication training on covariation of problem behaviors. *Journal of Applied Behavior Analysis, 29,* 565-568.

Skinner, B. F. (1953). *Science and human behavior*. New York: Macmillan.

Smith, B. W., & Sugai, G. (2000). A self-management functional assessment-based behavior support plan for a middle school student with EBD. *Journal of Positive Behavior Interventions, 2,* 208-217.

Sprague, J. R., & Horner, R. H. (1992). Covariation within functional response classes: Implications for treatment of severe problem behavior. *Journal of Applied Behavior Analysis, 25,* 735-745.

Sprague, J. R., & Horner, R. H. (1999). Low frequency, high intensity problem behavior: Toward an applied technology of functional analysis and intervention. In A. C. Repp & R. H. Horner (Eds.), *Functional analysis of problem behavior: From effective assessment to effective support* (pp. 98-116). Belmont, CA: Wadsworth.

Sugai, G., Horner, R. H., Dunlap, G., Hieneman, M., Lewis, T. J., Nelson, C. M., et al. (2000). Applying positive behavior support and functional behavioral assessment in schools. *Journal of Positive Behavior Interventions, 2*, 131-143.

Sugai, G., Horner, R. H., & Gresham, F. (2002). Behaviorally effective school environments. In M. R. Shinn, G. Stoner, & H. M. Walker (Eds.), *Interventions for academic and behavior problems: Preventive and remedial approaches* (pp. 315-350). Silver Spring, MD: National Association for School Psychologists.

Sugai, G., Lewis-Palmer, T., & Hagan-Burke, S. (1999-2000). Overview of the functional behavioral assessment process. *Exceptionality, 8*, 149-160.

Todd, A. W., Horner, R. H., & Sugai, G. (1999). Self-monitoring and self-recruited praise: Effects on problem behavior, academic engagement, and work completion in a typical classroom. *Journal of Positive Behavior Interventions, 1*, 66-76, 122.

Todd, A. W., Horner, R. H., Sugai, G., & Colvin, G. (1999). Individualizing school-wide discipline for students with chronic problem behaviors: A team approach. *Effective School Practices, 17*, 72-82.

Touchette, P. E., MacDonald, R. F., & Langer, S. N. (1985). A scatter plot for identifying stimulus control of problem behavior. *Journal of Applied Behavior Analysis, 18*, 343-351.

Turnbull, A. P., & Ruef, M. (1996). Family perspectives on problem behavior. *Mental Retardation, 34*, 280-293.

Umbreit, J. (1995). Functional analysis of disruptive behavior in an inclusive classroom. *Journal of Early Interventions, 20*, 18-29.

U.S. Department of Education. (1997). *To assume the free and appropriate education of all children with disabilities: Nineteenth annual report to congress on the implementation of the Individuals with Disabilities Education Act.* Washington, DC: Author.

Van Houten, R., & Rolider, A. (1991). Applied behavior analysis. In J. L. Matson & J. A. Mulick (Eds.), *Handbook of mental retardation* (pp. 569-585). New York: Pergamon.

Vollmer, T. R., & Van Camp, C. M. (1998). Experimental designs to evaluate antecedent control. In J. K. Luiselli & M. J. Cameron (Eds.), *Antecedent control: Innovation approaches to behavioral support* (pp. 87-111). Baltimore: Paul H. Brookes.

Wacker, D. P., Berg, W. K., Asmus, J. M., Harding, J. W., & Cooper, L. J. (1998). Experimental analysis of antecedent influences on challenging behavior. In J. K. Luiselli & M. J. Cameron (Eds.), *Antecedent control: Innovation approaches to behavioral support* (pp. 67-86). Baltimore: Paul H. Brookes.

Wacker, D. P., Steege, M., Northup, J., Reimers, T., Berg, W., & Sasso, G. (1990). Use of functional analysis and acceptability measures to assess and treat severe behavior problems: An outpatient clinic model. In A. C. Repp & N. Singh (Eds.), *Perspectives on the use of aversive and nonaversive interventions for persons with developmental disabilities* (pp. 349-359). Pacific Grove, CA: Brooks/Cole.

Wacker, D. P., Steege, M. W., Northup, J., Sasso, G., Berg, W., Reimers, T., et al. (1990). A component analysis of functional communication training across three topographies of severe behavior problems. *Journal of Applied Behavior Analysis, 23*, 417-429.

Wehmeyer, M., & Schwartz, M. (1997). Self-determination and positive adult outcomes: A follow-up study of youth with mental retardation and learning disabilities. *Exceptional Children, 63*, 256.

Willis, T. J., LaVigna, G. W., & Donnellan, A. M. (1987). *Behavior assessment guide.* Los Angeles: Institute for Applied Behavior Analysis.

Wolfensberger, W. (1983). Social role valorization: A proposed new term for the principle of normalization. *Mental Retardation, 21*, 234-239.

7

Special Health Care Procedures

Jane P. Rues
J. Carolyn Graff
Marilyn Mulligan Ault
Jennifer Holvoet

Students with special health care needs are similar to all other students in terms of their right to an appropriate education in the least restrictive environment, with full family participation. The presence of special health care needs, estimated at 3.8% to 32% depending on definition

and method of determination (Beers, Kemeny, Sherrit, & Palfrey, 2003), requires additional accommodations in the educational setting. This is best accomplished by training educational staff in the knowledge and skills needed to manage these procedures at school.

 Liz

Mark Vontz was not surprised when he learned that a student enrolling in his class next year would have special health care needs. He had become accustomed to "looking out" for a variety of his students' needs over his 8 years of teaching fifth- and sixth-grade math and science. In the past, he had encountered several medical situations, even emergencies, that had taken him to the emergency room with some students. The episodes that most clearly taught him the necessity of proper training and support resulted from the near death of two students during his fourth and fifth year of teaching. During a spring field trip to gather water quality samples, a student was stung by a bee. While Mr. Vontz was removing the

stinger, the student moved rapidly through the stages of anaphylactic shock. He was able to call an emergency medical technician (EMT) on his cell phone and arrange to meet an ambulance on the way to the hospital.

The second emergency didn't even occur off campus. During the hot days at the beginning of school, a student returned to his class from soccer practice. It soon became evident that the athlete was in respiratory crisis. Mr. Vontz was able to retrieve the student's inhaler from his gym bag and call for EMT assistance. It became very clear to him that the outcomes of these situations would not have been so positive had he not been knowledgeable about first aid, known about the medical status of his students, and had a good relationship with the EMT at the local hospital. More typical issues surrounding health care occurred throughout the years, including medication administration, burns and wounds, and allergies. Mr. Vontz felt quite confident that he was prepared to handle any health-related condition.

During the past 3 years of teaching, Mr. Vontz's school had actively moved toward the practice of full inclusion for all children. Children with a range of disabilities had been enrolled in his classroom, and he enjoyed the challenge of including them in science and math activities with their more typical peers. He felt he was a contributing part of a team trying to determine how the math and science content could be taught in a way that would be meaningful for their lives. With the support from the consultant teacher, he felt positive about his efforts and their results. Now he was presented with the challenge of

including a student with severe cognitive disabilities who also used a wheelchair to navigate around the building and his classroom. He had dealt with children having both these conditions before but not any children who had multiple needs. He knew he had to be prepared. This child, Liz, also used a gastrostomy tube for eating and nutritional needs. Mr. Vontz knew that the aide would assist the child with tube feedings. He would, however, have a significant role on the team planning for her full inclusion. He and all her other teachers had to understand her nonverbal communication not only about how she expressed herself in academic and social situations but also about the very critical basics, such as how she indicates hunger and thirst, knowledge of her oral and nonoral nutritional needs and how to respond, and how to integrate the needs of the health care procedure into her educational activities.

Throughout their careers, teachers encounter students who need a variety of special health care procedures to promote and maintain health (Ault, Guess, Struth, & Thompson, 1989; Batshaw, 2002; Graff, Ault, Guess, Taylor, & Thompson, 1990). This chapter focuses on special health care procedures that are common across a number of health conditions and diagnoses. It is organized to reflect a continuum of classroom use. Quality health care in the educational setting is also discussed with suggestions for integrating health care needs into the educational program and the role of prevention. The first section identifies a general body of knowledge and group of skills as "health and safety procedures." These procedures include infection control, cardiopulmonary resuscitation, and first aid. The second section includes a group of routine procedures that are identified as "routine prevention procedures" and include teeth and gum care, skin care, and bowel care. The third group of procedures, present less frequently, are identified as "specialized health care procedures." These include seizure monitoring, medication administration, growth monitoring, nutrition supplementation, and management of food intake. The final section addresses procedures that occur infrequently and that teachers may or may not be expected to participate in their implementation. These procedures, referred to as "low-incidence health care procedures," include nonoral feeding, atypical elimination, respiratory management, glucose monitoring, and shunt care. Each section addresses what is involved in the implementation of the procedure, why this particular knowledge and skills are necessary, and where to go for further information and training.

The Internet is one of the most valuable options available to educators and parents to quickly access current information on most health conditions or procedures. Box 7–1 provides advice about the Internet that should serve as a general guide and encouragement to use the links listed in this chapter.

Quality Health Care and Teaching

The process of establishing quality health care in the educational setting means a commitment to (a) integrating special health care needs into the student's ongoing educational program and (b) actively preventing the development of health-related problems or conditions. This commitment must be made by the educational staff as well as the administrative personnel. Teachers, additional staff members, and related service personnel must be willing to attend to special health care procedures throughout the educational day. The team (e.g., building principal, school nurse, general and special education teachers, director of special education, other administrative staff members, and parents) must be willing to support this commitment through the provision of necessary training, accessible location of the classroom or instructional setting within the school building, and availability of backup support personnel. Collaboration among each of these key groups is essential to the provision of health care that is safe and consistent and that involves the student to the greatest degree possible in implementation of the plan. This respect and collaboration is often

Box 7–1 Using the Internet for Further Information or Training

The Internet offers many sources of information about (a) specific disabilities and the typical characteristics associated with these disabilities, (b) typical (and alternative) medical treatments used to treat certain aspects of specific disabilities, and (c) opportunities to learn from and confer with other individuals who have a specific disability, are family members of children with that disability, or are teaching others with the disability.

Information About Disabilities

Accurate and current information about specific disabilities (even very rare syndromes) and health care conditions can be used to understand the disability, its natural history, and conditions associated with it that may also require educational support. Such information can generally be regarded as accurate if published on the Internet by medical practitioners or parent support groups. The information found in this chapter or through Internet sites will allow you to ask relevant and informed questions of parents of students with disabilities newly enrolled in your class. This information can also be helpful in ascertaining when certain behaviors may be part of a disability. For example, a student receiving a certain medication may experience dryness of the mouth or lethargy. Knowing this and using the tips that parents and educators have provided to address this problem can certainly make the education of a child more effective. Often these tips are found in discussion groups or chat rooms on Internet sites.

Most of the disability information on the Internet is written from a medical perspective, and a good medical dictionary or talking with the parents may help clarify many of these terms. Learning the terms is a worthwhile investment for an educator. It allows clearer and more professional communication with many support staff, such as occupational and physical therapists, and also allows better communication when you wish to ask questions of parents or experts either personally or via e-mail.

Some examples of this type of material are the following:

1. Awesome Library (has links to different types of disabilities and health-related needs):
   http://www.neat-schoolhouse.org/special~ed.html
2. Prader-Willi Association (click on the Basic Information link): **http://www.pwsausa.org**
3. Cerebral palsy: **http://www.ucpa.org**
4. Kids with Cancer: **http://www.kidswithcancer.com**
5. Asthma and Allergy Foundation: **http://www.aafa.org**
6. Alternative medicine: **http://www.alternative-medicine-info.com**

Medical Treatments

An educator may be interested in what medical treatments are associated with different disabilities. For example, knowing what types of medications are typically prescribed and the intended effect and possible side effects of the medication may help the educator be a more informed observer in the classroom. This would allow the educator to provide useful information to the parents and the physician as they attempt to manage the child's medications. If surgeries are scheduled for a student, knowing more about those surgeries and what type of care the student may need when he or she returns to school may make the experience less traumatic for both. The parent and hospital discharge plan will provide specific information about your student, but educators can also access general information online at **http://www.ccmckids.org/Patient__Education/hip.htm** and other similar sites.

In addition, an educator can search for specific information by using a search engine and typing in the name of the treatment (e.g., spica cast) or medication (e.g., phenytoin [Dilantin]). As a general rule, look for sites such as glossaries or patient information rather than sites that are clearly geared to physicians (e.g., *The Use of Dilantin in Febrile Seizure Management*) or that are clearly personal (*Patty's Dilantin Page*) to find general information. Hospitals or pharmacies often sponsor such sites. Some good sites to start your investigation are the following:

1. The Virtual Hospital: **http://www.vh.org/pediatric/index.html**
2. Connecticut Children's Center Patient Education Guides:
   http://www.ccmckids.org/patient_education/hip.htm
3. MedWeb: **http://gen.emory.edu/MEDWEB/keyword/patient_education/neoplasms.html**
4. Implant Dentistry: **http://implantdentistry.com**
5. Drug information: **http://www.rxlist.com**, **http://nlm.nih.gov/medlineplus/druginformation**, or
   http://www.smartbasic.com
6. Internet Public Library (medical text for health professionals): **http://www.mentalhealth.com/p30.html**

There are also many Internet sites focusing on disabilities that are developed and operated by parents. Often these sites have information about alternative treatments for various conditions. These treatments, however, often are not endorsed by the medical community and generally are promulgated by word of mouth, not research. When looking at alternative treatment literature, be sure to read both the pros and the cons so that you are an informed reader. You should not make recommendations about alternative treatments, but you could provide information from both sides of the controversy to a family or team searching for ideas, which, of course, should be reviewed by appropriate health care professionals.

Opportunities to Confer with Others

One of the most useful options available on the Internet is the ability to easily correspond with experts about specific problems or areas where more information is needed. Most pages related to a health condition and those that are sponsored by departments of education or special education also provide links to the Website manager. By clicking on that link, filling in the e-mail form that results, and clicking on Send, you can be put in touch with people who are in a position to help you maximize the positive effect of your interactions with a student who has special health needs or disabilities. The team can also confer with local experts around the complex health problems of a student. Often the regional children's hospital will provide Web pages that address a range of services (e.g., clinics serving children with cerebral palsy, interdisciplinary clinics serving children who have problems eating). These sites provide the educator with access either personally via a phone call or accompanying the student and family to a clinic visit or through e-mail with these local experts.

exemplified in a transdisciplinary team in which the unifying philosophy is a commitment to sharing information and skills among the various disciplines represented on the team. The richness of these interactions across time encourages team communication based on a shared understanding of terminology and procedures that contributes to achievement of students' educational goals. This team model can be effective, efficient, accountable, and proactive because each team member is responsible for implementing the goals throughout the school day using incidental and embedded teaching and partial participation.

Integrating Health Care Needs

The first commitment, addressing both the educational and the health requirements of students in the educational setting, confirms the unwillingness of teachers to divide students' needs into separate parts and instead to accept the responsibility to address the educational needs of the total student. The fact that a student has a gastrostomy tube (i.e., has a tube inserted through the wall of the abdomen in order to receive food and fluids), a tracheostomy (i.e., has an opening at the base of the throat in order to facilitate breathing), or is catheterized (i.e., has a tube inserted into the bladder to drain urine) can add to rather than subtract from situations that may provide the content or occasion for instruction. Take, for example, Liz's friend Gina, who is catheterized.

Gina, a 6-year-old student with spina bifida, attends a full-day kindergarten class at Liz's school. Gina's teacher, parents, and therapists collaborated on a program to improve Gina's fine motor skills. With stronger and more refined grasp patterns in her hands, Gina could be a more active participant in her intermittent catheterization program.

At least three instructional strategies facilitate the incorporation of health-related procedures into the educational day. These include incidental teaching, embedded skill teaching (see chapter 4), and partial participation (see chapters 4 and 9). Briefly, incidental teaching is a procedure during which a teacher follows a student's initiation in identifying an interest or a need. Once the teacher has responded to the signal or initiation presented by the student, the teacher offers an opportunity to practice specific skills. Incidental teaching, usually described in the context of language instruction, can also be applied when responding to a student's need for special health care procedures. Based on an initiation from a student (e.g., facial expression and an increase in body movement, pointing via eye gaze, or upper-extremity movement to a picture of the desired item), the teacher can provide, for example, humidified oxygen or a tube feeding or empty a colostomy bag.

Embedded teaching suggests that multiple skills, addressing many different goals, can be taught simultaneously. Critical skills such as language, reach and grasp, relaxation, and head control can be practiced in conjunction with daily health care procedures. For example, prior to the administration of medication, the student assumes an erect sitting posture, reaches and touches the glass of water to indicate readiness, and visually tracks the pill as it is poured from the bottle. With assistance from the teacher, the student brings the spoon (with pill and applesauce) to her mouth. She then chooses to wash it down with more applesauce or water.

With partial participation, the third instructional strategy, teachers support the student's involvement in a health-related activity as an educational objective. With this approach, the student is not required to independently perform a health care procedure but may practice and participate in many important component skills that are part of a special health care procedure; these can contribute to greater independence, control, and self-determination. Participating in components of a procedure, such as grasping a toothbrush and spitting after teeth and gum care, visually fixating and swallowing during medication administration, communicating the need for position changes, or grasping the syringe and visual tracking during tube feedings, all represent meaningful participation and contribution to health care procedures.

> *Mr. Vontz planned to implement a sequence in his math class that would allow Liz to keep an inventory of her medical supplies. This included sorting and counting the tubes, formula bottles, and bags. As part of a group activity with her peers related to sets, fractions, and projections, she would also keep a weekly total of intake and project her formula needs for the next week for the school nurse. Mr. Vontz would also make sure that he and her teammates in the class understood her sign for the need to have a drink. Once she signaled her need, a peer would call the health care aide.*

Preventing Additional Health Care Problems

In addition to being committed to meeting the present needs of students, teachers must participate in efforts designed to prevent the development of further health-related problems. Problems may result from complications from an already identified condition (e.g., contractures resulting from cerebral palsy) or from conditions not related to any currently identified

problem (e.g., food refusal due to gastroesophageal reflux). The instructional day must routinely include activities and procedures designed to promote the overall health of all students, including those with special health care needs. Implementation of special health care procedures must be a high priority in order to maintain student health as well as to contribute to the ability of students to optimally interact with the environment. Health-related activities and procedures that may prevent future problems include adequate nutrition and hydration, cardiovascular exercise and physical fitness, frequent movement, frequent positioning or repositioning in the upright position, changes in instructional environments and materials, and access to the outdoors and sunshine.

What Does a School Nurse Know?

Since the inception of school nursing, management of students with chronic health problems has been an expanding role (American Nurses Association, 2001). Originally, the major function of a school nurse was to protect the entire student population from the spread of common disease. This involved screening for contagious diseases, immunizing students, and implementing basic health instruction in the schools (Walker & Jacobs, 1984). The role of screening for hearing and vision problems was added later. The health services provided by school nurses today include monitoring immunization status, screening for hearing and vision, administering or supervising administration of medication, and preventing the spread of infections, along with numerous other services (Brener et al., 2001).

The number of students with special health care needs in the education setting is increasing because of scientific advances and increased access to public education. The role of school nurses has expanded via their contribution to the school team's plan for students with health care needs. An important component of the overall plan is the individualized health care plan (IHP), developed by the school nurse to meet the needs of students whose health needs affect their daily functioning. The use of current health care standards in the development of the IHP helps assure administrators, parents, and staff that the student is properly cared for. The IHP can be incorporated into the individualized education plan (IEP) when the health care issues are related to the educational needs of the student. The IHP serves as legal protection by showing that proper plans and safeguards, such as an emergency care plan, are in place for any student with a condition that has the potential for developing into a medical emergency.

A teacher should not assume, however, that the school nurse necessarily has the knowledge or skill to address all the special health care procedures that may be required in the schools. A school nurse may not have specific knowledge or skill in the implementation of certain procedures such as catheterization, tracheostomy suctioning, or gastrostomy tube feedings. But given his or her background and training, the school nurse is the most qualified member of the team to take a major role in identifying resources, training, and monitoring special health care procedures for individual students. (Students with Chronic Illnesses, 2003).

Health and Safety Procedures

These procedures contribute significantly to the overall health and safety of any student in any classroom but particularly to young children and youth with severe or profound disabilities. These procedures, *appropriate for all students*, include infection control, cardiopulmonary resuscitation, and first aid. The procedures (a) have a broad range of application across many different settings and (b) require that all staff members having direct contact with students be skilled in their application.

Infection Control

The purpose of infection control is to prevent the transmission of disease to children and youth and, secondarily, to prevent the infection of school personnel. Infections occur when organisms enter the body and find an environment that allows them to grow and spread. Some infections, such as the common cold, are an expected part of childhood. Other infections, such as AIDS or tuberculosis, which occur in the general public, present minimal risk in the schools if proper control procedures are followed. Infections can be caused by bacteria, viruses, fungi, protozoa, and helminthes (parasitic worms). Once an infection is established, there is always a potential for transmission to others.

What Is Involved

Infection control refers primarily to the efforts of public health and school officials to prevent the initial occurrence of infection. Secondarily, it refers to efforts to prevent the spread of an already established infection. Proper immunization, before school enrollment, is the major method of infection control. Children should have begun their immunizations before entry into schools (kindergarten or preschool) and should have received the following: HepB (hepatitis B vaccine), DTaP (diphtheria, tetanus, acellular (yes) pertussis vaccine), IPV (inactivated polio vaccine), MMR (measles, mumps, and rubella), Hib (haemophilus influenza type b conjugate vaccine), PCV (pneumococcal vaccine), and varicella (chickenpox). The schedules for these immunizations have been established by the Centers for Disease Control (**http://www.cdc.gov**). Hepatitis A vaccine is recommended for children and adolescents in selected states and regions and for certain high-risk groups; your local public health authority will advise you regarding the risk for your students. Influenza vaccine is recommended for children 6 months and older who have certain risk factors (including asthma, cardiac disease, sickle cell disease, human immunodeficiency virus [HIV], and diabetes). Despite many recent advances in vaccine delivery, in 2001 only 77% of U.S. toddlers 19 to 35 months of age had received their basic immunizations series (American Academy of Pediatrics, 2003b).

Infection control also involves using proper procedures to prevent the spread of infection to other children and youth as well as educators. When a student is identified as having an infection, consultation with the school nurse and the primary health care provider is necessary to determine whether the child should remain in or return to the classroom. If the student remains, then specific procedures designed to prevent the spread of infection without unnecessarily stigmatizing the student must be followed. Because certain students are more susceptible to infections than others, efforts must be made to maintain or promote the health of the student with the infection as well as those students potentially exposed. Frequent hand washing, particularly as the teacher moves from physical contact with one student to another, is an effective intervention for infection control in the classroom.

There are some viruses that may be present for varying lengths of time with no symptoms. These include but are not limited to cytomegalovirus (CMV), herpes virus, hepatitis A and B viruses, and HIV. Preventing the spread of these infections, therefore, requires a clear understanding of how infections are transmitted. For example, a child may have acquired CMV infection early in life. The virus will leave the body through saliva or urine only at certain times, with no sign that this is occurring. School policy may require, therefore, that disposable gloves be used whenever feeding or changing the child's diaper if such a level of support is required. Because there is a risk to pregnant women, many health authorities also recommend that pregnant staff persons not work directly with a child who has CMV infection. Procedures required to prevent the spread of HIV infection and hepatitis should be followed when individuals are exposed to blood, certain other body fluids (i.e., amniotic fluid, pericardial fluid, peritoneal fluid, pleural fluid, spinal fluid, cerebrospinal fluid, semen, and vaginal secretions), or any body fluid visibly contaminated with blood. Since HIV and hepatitis B virus (HBV) transmission have not been documented from exposure to other body fluids, such as feces, nasal secretions, sputum, sweat, tears, urine, and vomitus, extraordinary precautions do not apply. Extreme care procedures should be applied in dental or oral care settings in which saliva might be contaminated with blood (**http://www.cdc.gov/hiv/ pubs/facts/transmission.htm**).

Use in the Classroom

The best way to prevent the spread of infection in the classroom is for all students and staff to use clean procedures. The simple and most effective procedure is to engage in proper hand washing, which includes lathering hands with running water and soap. Proper hand washing should always occur after contact with an ill child, after feeding a child (or supporting a child to eat), and after contact with diapers. This is critical following toileting activities and before handling any food or liquid. Figure 7-1 presents one description of proper hand-washing techniques. Clean procedures also involve the proper washing of school items, such as toys and teaching materials, with disinfectants before the items are shared. This is particularly true if items are mouthed, if saliva is present outside the mouth (e.g., on the hands or clothing), or if sneezing or coughing onto materials is common. For the most effective implementation of clean procedures, classrooms should be equipped with or have access to toileting and hand-washing areas that are separate and distinct from food preparation areas. The teacher is responsible for promoting and maintaining a clean

FIGURE 7–1
Description of Proper Hand-Washing Techniques

How to Wash Your Hands
- Remove jewelry
- Rub foaming soap all over hands especially around and underneath nails and between fingers
- Rub hands under running water and rinse
- Use paper towel to dry, to turn off faucet (if necessary), and to open door to exit (if necessary)

Source: Adapted from Centers for Disease Control. (1985) *What you can do to stop disease in child day care centers.* Atlanta: Department of Health and Human Services. Obtain through your local or state department of health or write to: Public Health Advisor, Center for Professional Health and Training, Centers for Disease Control, 1600 Clifton Road, Atlanta, GA 30333.

classroom environment; activities can be delegated or shared with an aide, but the teacher must provide both the rationale and a protocol to support routine use of clean procedures.

Where to Go for Further Information or Training

Local health departments and local hospitals with departments or designated individuals responsible for infection control can be contacted for additional information. Many local hospitals are establishing Web pages for reference to immunization schedules and infection control procedures. The Centers for Disease Control and Prevention (**http://www.cdc.gov/ mmwr/preview/ mmwrhtml/rr5116a1.htm**) and the American Academy of Pediatrics (**htpp://www. aap.org**) provide information and guidelines about infectious diseases, symptoms, methods of transmission, and strategies for prevention.

Cardiopulmonary Resuscitation

Cardiopulmonary resuscitation (CPR) is an emergency procedure used when breathing or breathing and pulse have ceased. CPR is not considered a routine procedure for classroom implementation; rather, it is an emergency response. A presentation of CPR is included within the context of this chapter only to provide general information about the procedures. All teachers should receive CPR certification every 2 years and should not attempt intervention without current endorsement. CPR, while potentially life sustaining, may easily result in serious injury and death if not performed correctly (American Academy of Pediatrics, 1993; ParasolEMT, 1998; Sommers, 1992).

What Is Involved
The three basic rescue skills of CPR include opening the airway, restoring breathing, and restoring circulation. CPR applied immediately on discovery of a casualty and sustained until more advanced life support arrives is the key to saving lives. Teachers should be trained in all CPR procedures associated with the ages of the students they teach. Separate procedures have been developed for infants (birth to 1 year of age), children (1 to 8 years of age), and adults (8 years of age to adult). Disposable masks can be used by the rescuer and be obtained at the time CPR training is completed.

CPR guidelines implemented in 2001 recommend the use of automated external defibrillator (AED) as a part of treating cardiorespiratory arrest in adults and children older than 8 years (American Heart Association, 2000). The AED is a device used to restore a normal heartbeat in a student whose heart has suddenly stopped beating. The AED provides an electrical shock to the heart to help restore a normal rhythm.

If the student appears to be choking, identify if the airway is completely obstructed by determining if the student can speak or cough. If the student can do either, do not interfere with the student's attempts to force out the object blocking the airway. If the student is unable to speak or cough, the Heimlich maneuver is performed.

Use in the Classroom
Difficulty breathing is the most frequent medical emergency for children (Wong & Hockenberry, 2003; Young & Seidel, 1999). The need for resuscitation may result from injuries; suffocation caused by toys, foods, or plastic covers; smoke inhalation; sudden infant death syndrome; and infections, especially of the respiratory tract, among other conditions (Statistical Resources Branch, 1981). The majority of situations resulting in the need for CPR for children are preventable; therefore, instructional settings and routines must be established to ensure environments that are safe and foster independence.

Although any individual may need CPR, students with severe disabilities tend to have characteristics that increase the likelihood. Heart defects, seizure disorders, aspiration of fluids and/or food, tracheostomies, or excess fluids in the mouth are examples of these characteristics.

Eating characteristics that may result in the need for an emergency response are inadequate chewing and/or swallowing that can result in students aspirating portions of their meals. Children, when compared with older students, are at a higher risk for choking because their airways are smaller and their coughs are weaker (Harris, Baker, Smith, & Harris, 1984).

All teachers and staff at Mr. Vontz's school routinely update their CPR and first aid certification. Students who use wheelchairs require a slightly more involved response from staff should resuscitation be needed. Mr. Vontz's principal made sure that the local hospital provided one-on-one training in a response protocol for a student in a wheelchair, particularly for resuscitation and CPR. Most first aid situations did not require a different response for students who were or were not using a wheelchair.

Teachers and other professionals who interact on a regular and close basis with students having disabilities should be routinely certified in CPR. If a person who is trained in CPR does injure the victim, the state's Good Samaritan laws usually protect that person. The Good Samaritan doctrine is a legal principle that prevents a rescuer who has voluntarily helped a victim in distress from being successfully sued for "wrongdoing."

Where to Go for Further Information or Training
The American Heart Association (**http://www.americanheart.org**), local hospitals, the Red Cross (**http://www.redcross.org**), school districts, and other local agencies routinely conduct CPR and management of airway obstruction classes. A course, Heartsaver CPR in Schools, is offered through the American Heart Association to train students and teachers on the chain of survival and the warning signs of heart attack, cardiac arrest, stroke, and choking. There are also a number of Websites that deal with the implementation of CPR (e.g., **http://www.yahoo.com/health**). Many of these sites, however, do not outline the specific procedures because hands-on training is needed for certification.

First Aid

First aid refers to emergency care given before regular medical aid can be obtained. The "first aid" procedures administered in most schools are not lifesaving situations, yet unmanaged or improperly managed, these situations can become life threatening with serious consequences. Although a great deal of effort is expended to ensure a safe school environment, accidents and injuries will occur. The most frequent reasons for school-based emergency medical services are falls, other trauma (fracture or dislocation), and medical illness (e.g., breathing difficulty, seizures, and other illnesses) (Knight, Vernon, Fines, & Dean, 1999). These events require first aid procedures that can be carried out in the school by the first person on the scene and that can be supported by the school nurse or qualified school staff. Because these events often occur when the teacher is the first available source of assistance, first aid training should be required of all school staff and should be taught by competent and certified health care professionals.

It is often the teacher who first recognizes, interprets, and acts on a student's signs and cues that indicate a need for aid. Any child may need first aid at some point in their school career, such as for an episode of asthma, an allergic reaction to food, or a reaction to medication. Students with special health care needs may present additional challenges to school staff because their symptoms may be subtle and difficult to recognize or they may have difficulty communicating. For example, a student may experience a headache, nausea, or fever but be unable to describe these symptoms to others. Collaborative consultation with parents can provide for parental input on body language, facial expressions, and changes in appetite, which may be indicators of an illness in their child. An aware teacher can recognize these signs in all of his or her students.

What Is Involved

Planning Since situations requiring first aid generally arise unexpectedly, it is critical to have properly trained staff and emergency procedures in place. Careful planning for and anticipation of situations requiring first aid and identification of methods for prevention are essential in all schools. An emergency plan and procedures for school staff to follow should include not only the school setting and available resources in that setting but also settings away from the school campus (e.g., traveling to and from school by bus or a field trip). Plans and procedures for a school should be consistent with the policies established by the school district and with state laws and regulations for school staff. Procedures could include, for example, assignment of persons responsible for telephoning emergency assistance to transport the student to a source of emergency care

when needed; for calling the student's parents; for accompanying the student to the emergency room, physician's office, or other location to receive emergency care; and for attending to the needs of the other students who witnessed the event requiring first aid.

School staff should have telephone numbers for contacting the student's parents during the school day along with the names and telephone numbers of persons to contact when parents are not available. Additionally, the name and telephone number of the student's health professional should be easily available for school staff responsible for using this information. Telephone numbers for the school nurse, school administrator, ambulance, police department, fire department, paramedics, poison control center, and hospital emergency room should be posted at each telephone in the school.

The amount of responsibility individual school staff members have in administering first aid varies in each school district based on district policy. The number of health care professionals available in school districts also varies. In one school district, a school nurse may be assigned to an individual school and provide services to several hundred students in that school, while in another district, there may be only one nurse for the entire school district. In that instance, a school staff member who is properly trained in first aid or the school administrator may be the person who is contacted in emergency situations. A clearly outlined procedure of the steps to be followed in an emergency should be posted near all telephones.

Students who are at risk for health-related emergencies should be identified, with student and parental permission, and specific plans about what to do in the event of an emergency should be developed and in place (Porter, Haynie, Bierle, Caldwell, & Palfrey, 1997). At a minimum, the emergency plan should include the parents' names and telephone numbers, telephone numbers of alternate persons to contact in the event of difficulty reaching the student's parents, and the names and telephone numbers of the student's physician or health care professionals (e.g., nurse practitioner, clinical nurse specialist, or physician assistant). In addition to specific information about the steps to be followed for a specific procedure, written parental permission and medical authorization to carry out the interventions at school must be included. Information such as the student's allergies, status of immunizations, major medical problems, medications a student is receiving, and other pertinent information in the

FIGURE 7–2
Sample Individualized Health Care Plan for Liz

In Emergency, Notify:

Name: Kathy Clark   Phone: 235-5483   Relationship: aunt

Name: Mike Harmon   Phone 864-4954   Relationship: father

Jane Roaland   2003–2005   School Year
School Health Care Coordinator

Mike Slvoski
Education Coordinator

Individualized Health Care Plan

Student Information:

Liz Harmon	2-14-1994
Name	Birthdate
Mike and Beth Harmon	3316 SW 80 Street Terrace
Parent/Guardian	Address
Mother/Guardian: 295-2434	271-1800
Home Phone	Work Phone
Father/Guardian: 295-2434	864-4954
Home Phone	Work Phone
Primary Care Physician: N. Crouch	Phone: 545-2726

Specialty Physicians/Health Care Workers:

Wagner, speech/language	Phone 235-8476
Hoag, wheelchair care	Phone 235-8555
Martinez, R.N., skin care	Phone 675-7983
Berle, M.D., internist	Phone 295-3434

school records should be available to school staff responsible for using this information. An emergency care plan should also be a part of the student's IHP and IEP. Porter et al., (1997) present a collection of very useful documents for use when developing and implementing a plan for the inclusion of children and youth requiring specialized health care procedures in an educational setting. Figure 7–2 represents a portion of these documents adapted for Liz. The IHP could serve as part of the transition plan for children who are hospitalized for either elective or emergency care.

Borgioli and Kennedy (2003) note that students with multiple disabilities usually have higher rates of illness and hospitalization than do other children. Results of their survey indicated that only 1 in 46 students had a transition plan to deliver educational services while students were absent from school; this does little to address possible educational losses that might be associated with school absences.

An emergency identification bracelet or necklace should be worn or an emergency information card carried to identify any serious condition or allergies

FIGURE 7–2 (*Continued*)
Sample Individualized Health Care Plan for Liz

Student-Specific Staff Training:

Subject	Date	By	Attending
Colostomy bag changing at school	8/25/03	Hospital staff	Fifth grade staff
		Burgess	Secretary
Seizure monitoring at school	8/25/03	Hospital staff	Fifth grade staff
		Nelson	Secretary

General Staff Training:

Subject	Date	By	Attending
CPR	8/28-29/03	Red Cross	All staff

Peer Awareness Training:

Subject	Date	By	Attending
Wheelchairs on the playground	9/25/03	Smith	Fifth grade 3rd hr playground
Nonsymbolic communication	11/6/03	Wagner	Turgeon's math class

Source: Adapted from Porter, S., Haynie, M., Bierle, T., Caldwell, T.H., & Paltrey, J.S. (1997). *Children and youth assisted by medical technology in educational settings: Guidelines for care*. Baltimore: Paul H. Brookes.

the student has. Such conditions may include diabetes, epilepsy, hemophilia, and potentially serious allergic reactions to medications or insect stings. Along with the condition or allergy, the student's name and blood type should be included. Use of personal emergency identification is especially important as students become older, more independent, and less supervised by persons aware of their potential need for immediate intervention.

Certain supplies are necessary when administering first aid and are usually available in the office of the school nurse. Disposable gloves should be used when staff may have contact with body secretions. These secretions may include urine, blood, mucus drainage, or saliva. The special health care needs of an individual student may dictate additional items (e.g., blood sugar testing apparatus) that can be kept in a designated location for the student or with the student at all times. Supplies should be checked periodically and replaced as needed.

Although medications are frequently part of a first aid supply, it must be remembered that medication cannot be given without permission from the student's physician. Written parental and medical permission is required for school staff to administer medication. The exact procedure depends on the policies of the local school district and state laws and regulations. Exceptions to this are life-threatening emergencies in which EMT paramedics administer medications as recommended by a physician from the emergency room or hospital where a student is being transported. In this instance, administration of medications may take place on the school campus by staff from the emergency medical service.

Deciding if Emergency Attention Is Needed School staff should not call paramedics for minor injuries such as minor cuts, bumps, or sprains. Guidelines on when to contact medical professionals may be in place for an individual student, but unexpected emergencies can occur and must be handled immediately. During an emergency situation, such as severe bleeding, shock, or sudden unconsciousness, the paramedics or an ambulance service should be called to take the student to a hospital. When contacting emergency room staff or paramedics for assistance in determining the seriousness of the student's condition, school staff should minimally provide the following information: (a) student's specific complaints or symptoms; (b) when symptoms began; (c) what makes the pain or condition better or worse; (d) what the student was doing when the injury or illness occurred; (e) what changes have occurred since the onset of the injury or illness; (f) what, if anything, the student has swallowed; and (g) what medication(s) the student has been taking. When a student is known to have a health problem that can potentially result in a life-threatening situation, inform the emergency room staff and paramedics as allowed by the student's parents. Permission forms previously signed by the student's parents and filed in the student's school record allow this pertinent information to be shared.

First Aid in the Classroom

First aid procedures must be conducted with due regard for the danger of cross infection. Adherence to hand washing, as described previously, has been shown to reduce overall infection risks (Pittel, 2001). Before providing the aid, wash hands with soap and water or use an alcohol-based hand rub. For bleeding injuries that result from a burn, laceration, or puncture wound, many school districts recommend that school staff wear gloves when in contact with blood or body secretions that may contain blood. Concerns about

transmission of HIV, HBV, and other organisms that may be present in the blood have resulted in changes in policies in school districts. Authorities have emphasized that any transmission of HIV or HBV most likely involves exposure of skin lesions or mucous membranes to blood and possibly to other body fluids of an infected person (Education and Foster Care ..., 1985). During treatment, avoid coughing, breathing, speaking over the wound, and contact with body fluids and use only clean bandages and dressings. After treatment, wash your hands with soap and water.

Where to Go for Help

Emergency care resources in the community may include the local hospital and emergency room staff, health department, and trained EMT paramedics. In some communities, ambulance service, fire department, or police department staff may be properly trained to provide first aid in an emergency. Websites are also available with general information regarding first aid training (**http://www.redcross.org** and **http://www.americanheart.org**) or procedures (ParasolEMT, 1998). In the event that the student is stung by a bee or ingests a poisonous substance, the nearest poison control center is an excellent resource for the school nurse in determining what steps should be taken. A poison control center can be located at 1-800-222-1222 or **http://www.aapcc.org/findyour.htm**.

Routine Prevention Procedures

Teeth and Gum Care

The major components of teeth and gum care include oral hygiene, preventive dental care, and good nutrition and eating habits. Some of these components may be addressed instructionally during the school day, and some require collaboration between the school and home. The purpose of including teeth and gum care in the curriculum is that oral health is integral to general health of the student. Additionally, routine, effective oral hygiene will decrease the possibility of aspiration due to food particles remaining undetected in the mouth.

Oral Hygiene and Preventive Dental Care

Regular visits to the dentist may begin as early as 6 months of age. Many factors, such as an improperly formed jaw or teeth, prolonged dependence on the bottle, lack of stimulation from chewing, inadequate cleaning of the teeth and gums, infrequent dental care, and the side effects of medications, can result in unhealthy and malformed teeth and gums. For the child with a disability, it is recommended that dental care begin early, during the first year of life, to establish a preventive program with the parents. Establishing a schedule of routine dental care provides parents with guidance on toothbrushing and flossing, dental development, fluoride, oral habits, proper diet, and other issues unique to the child.

Infant Dental Care
Routine oral hygiene should begin as early as possible. Starting at birth, clean the baby's gums with a clean damp cloth and progress to toothbrushing as teeth appear. Regular attention to oral hygiene at an early age will establish a routine associated with eating for the child, establish the feeling of having a clean mouth, and desensitize the oral-motor area for the child with increased sensitivity to touch in and around the mouth. (See the recommended oral hygiene procedures by the American Dental Hygienists' Association, **http://www.adha.org**.)

Toothbrushing
Toothbrushing with a small, soft-bristled toothbrush can begin when the baby's first teeth begin to erupt. The American Dental Hygienists' Association recommends specific procedures for toothbrushing (**http://www.adha.org**).

Flossing
Although flossing can begin at age 2 to 3, most children will not have the dexterity to do it alone until age 7 or 8. The American Dental Hygienists' Association provides helpful recommendations for flossing student's teeth (**http://www.adha.org**).

Nutrition
Nutrition is integral to oral health (American Dietetic Association, 2003). Two primary oral infectious diseases are directly influenced by diet and nutrition: dental caries and periodontal disease. In addition to careful brushing and flossing, a healthy, balanced diet is necessary for teeth to develop properly and for healthy gum tissue to form around the teeth. A healthy diet includes the following major food groups each day: bread, cereal, rice, and pasta; vegetables; fruit; milk, yogurt, and cheese; and meat, poultry, fish, dry beans, eggs, and nuts. A diet high in certain types of carbohydrates, such as sugar and starches, may place a child at risk for tooth decay.

"Baby bottle" tooth decay can occur when an infant or toddler is given a bottle filled with milk, formula, fruit juice, or sugared liquids at bedtime, at naptime, or for long periods during the day. Excessive exposure to sugar in these liquids can cause teeth to discolor and decay. Dental caries (tooth decay) is the single most common chronic childhood disease—five times more common than asthma and seven times more common than hay fever (U.S. Department of Health and Human Services, 2000). In a 1-year study of nontraumatic dental emergencies from a pediatric emergency department, 73% of visits were the result of dental caries, and 185 resulted from baby bottle tooth decay (Wilson, Smith, Preisch, & Casamassimo, 1997). Children with oral motor problems are at increased risk for this problem because the bottle is often the primary source of nutrition long beyond 12 to 18 months of life. Rigorous attention to oral hygiene is required to maintain healthy teeth and gums.

Classroom Adaptations
Current data on child health suggest that few children receive early periodic screening, diagnosis, or preventive dental treatment. Anticipatory guidance provided through the school can facilitate an interchange on the provision of developmentally appropriate, preventive oral health information and care (Perlman, 1997). The development of a routine of oral hygiene, independent or assisted, that is ongoing and consistent between home and school will help (a) prevent periodontal (or gum) disease by maintaining healthy teeth and gums, (b) promote a healthy diet and good eating habits, and (c) promote correct speech habits and a positive body image (Mott, Fazekas, & James, 1985).

The time required to complete teeth and gum care must be included when planning for the student's individual program. Toothbrushing is performed after meals and snacks; flossing is performed at least once a day. The location (home or school) where flossing is conducted can be designated during the IEP process. Gloves should be used when completing any oral hygiene procedure. Initially, the student with a disability may require complete assistance with toothbrushing and flossing. The goal of instruction is for the student to be able to brush his or her teeth independently or with minimal assistance from staff and meaningfully participate in the process.

As the strength in Gina's hands increased, she was able to grasp a toothbrush with a built-up handle.

Gina's teacher, mother, and occupational therapist collaborated on the adaptation and resulting tooth-brushing program. An IEP goal was established to develop toothbrushing skills and was conducted at school and home. The aide carried out the program following lunch.

To promote adequate oral hygiene, the student must be positioned to facilitate toothbrushing and flossing. For the student who sits in a wheelchair, the adult can stand or sit behind the student and reach around with one hand supporting the student's chin and opening the student's mouth. The teeth can then be brushed using the other hand. The student can sit on the floor while the adult sits behind him or her on a chair, with the student's head straddled by the adult's thighs. The adult can reach around with one hand supporting the student's chin and brush the teeth with the other hand. If unable to sit up, the student can be turned onto the side with the face along the edge of a pillow and a towel and basin placed under the chin.

Occasionally, a child with a severe physical disability and poor oral motor skills has a bite reflex. This involuntary reflex or response often occurs when a spoon, toothbrush, or other object is placed in the child's mouth. If this is a problem when cleaning the teeth, a padded tongue blade or a new, clean rubber doorstop can be placed between the biting surfaces of the upper and lower jaw (Woelk, 1986). This will protect the child's teeth and the individual who is assisting the child with oral hygiene. Toothbrushing can then be carried out with this device holding the mouth slightly open. Alternately, students with this bite reflex have learned to partially participate in toothbrushing by learning some of the steps involved, including holding open the mouth for 5 seconds while one quadrant of teeth is brushed (Snell, Lewis, & Houghton, 1989). Brushing should be accomplished in the bathroom in front of a sink with both the student and the teacher looking in the mirror.

Additional Resources

The American Dental Association provides information on care of teeth and gums. Information can be obtained from local dentists, the local health department, or the following:

American Academy of Pediatric Dentistry
211 East Chicago Avenue, Suite 700
Chicago, IL 60611-2616
http://aapd.org

Academy of Dentistry for Persons with Disabilities
http://www.scdonline.org/ADPD_Index.htm

Mental Retardation: A Review for Dental Professionals
http://www.saiddent.org/modules.asap

Developmental Disabilities Digest
http://www.ddhealthinfo.org

Skin Care

The most appropriate skin care treatment in the schools focuses on the prevention of skin breakdown and the development of pressure sores. Because some students spend the majority of their day in a wheelchair, braces, or splints and are dependent on others for changing their position, it is critical that skin care and skin monitoring be systematically addressed in the classroom. Four objectives must be considered when promoting healthy skin: (a) keeping the skin clean and dry, (b) maintaining proper nutrition, (c) maintaining adequate activity, and (d) reducing periods of continuous pressure on parts of the body across the day.

Clean, dry skin is a necessary requirement for healthy skin. This is particularly important for skin that comes in contact with feces or urine. A primary skin care program should include efforts to reduce or eliminate incontinence, establish a regular toileting schedule, establish catheterization, or establish frequent routines of checking and changing diapers and cleansing the skin to reduce prolonged exposure of the skin to feces or urine. Moisture, stool, and frequent and excessive washings cause a decrease in the skin's tolerance to friction, leaving it more vulnerable to chafing by diapers and clothing (Jeter & Lutz, 1996). This exposure can also result in the softening or maceration of the skin. Softened skin is at an increased risk for the development of sores. Moisture, from any source, accumulated in folds of the skin around the genitals, thighs, or any place where the skin can rub together will result in redness, irritation, and the eventual development of sores (Jeter & Lutz, 1996). Maceration of skin by urine and feces adds to the excoriating (skin cutting) effects of the decomposing substances in the urine and the infective organisms present in the feces to already damaged tissue, increasing the likelihood that sores will develop.

Sacco (1995) recommends the maintenance of adequate nutrition and hydration as an important strategy in the prevention of pressure sores. Adequate nutrition and hydration allows the body to develop healthy skin and more resistance to bacteria and to pressure sores. Proper nutrition is also critical to support healing when a sore has developed.

Optimal levels of activity also must be encouraged as part of a proactive skin care program. Inactivity can result in increased opportunities for the student to experience pressure on the skin surfaces. Pressure occurs when the skin and subcutaneous tissue is squeezed between an underlying bony prominence and a hard surface, such as a bed or a chair. Unrelieved pressure on the skin squeezes tiny blood vessels that supply the skin with nutrients and oxygen. Sliding down in a chair or bed (friction or shear force) can stretch or bend blood vessels. When skin is starved of nutrients and oxygen for too long, the tissue dies and a pressure ulcer forms (Bryant & Doughty, 2000). Certain parts of the body sustain more weight when sitting and lying and are considered pressure-sensitive areas (e.g., the heels, bony prominences along the spinal column, or the buttocks). A change in position should occur *about every 1 to 2 hours* for those students with severe physical disabilities to relieve continuous pressure as well as to increase blood circulation (Sacco, 1995).

The student, whether active or inactive, may also experience pressure from braces, shoes, or sitting in a wheelchair. The same concern about pressure resulting from inactivity applies to pressure resulting from ill-fitting equipment. The skin underneath braces and splints or wheelchair seats should be checked daily to identify persistent red spots. If the spots do not fade within 20 minutes after the pressure is relieved, the health care worker should be notified of (a) ill-fitting equipment and (b) the potential for the development of a pressure sore.

When providing care to unhealthy skin, the focus is on treating the skin to promote a return to a healthy condition. The actual care of the unhealthy skin is prescribed by the student's physician or other health care provider or endorsed by the health care worker in the school.

Classroom Adaptation
The student's skin should be examined daily by the teacher or designate, emphasizing areas of the body susceptible to the development of pressure sores. The school health care worker or the primary care physician should write a general health plan for the student

at risk for skin problems. The plan should address the need for routine position changes, cleansing, maintenance of nutrition, and use of lotions or oils on the skin.

It is important that the student has some way to communicate the presence of discomfort. This is an opportunity for the parents and school team to collaborate in the identification of signals that the student uses to indicate that a position change is necessary. If a signal is difficult to identify or not readily recognizable, a communication objective for teaching such a response should be developed.

Because Gina has reduced sensation and spends the majority of her time sitting in a wheelchair, her skin care program includes diet and fluid monitoring and twice-daily skin checks. These checks are implemented by the school health professional in the late morning and in the afternoon before she goes home. Gina's team has also worked to develop a signal for position change while strengthening her elbow extensors so that she can raise herself out of the chair to relieve pressure on her bony prominences (buttocks). Gina does this routinely between classes, providing a minimum of six hourly position changes across the day.

Additional Resources
The student's family and physician or health care provider working with the physician can provide valuable assistance and direction to the educational staff on prevention or treatment of skin problems. The enterostomal therapist from a local hospital can provide assistance in care of the student's skin and the physical, and occupational therapist in the school system can help identify positions that will be suitable for the student during certain activities yet prevent prolonged pressure on a few skin areas. (See also **http://www.1uphealth.com/health** or **http:// www.healthfinder. gov**, a general health information locator provided by the U.S. government.)

Bowel Care

The purpose of bowel care is to increase awareness of factors that may affect the elimination schedule and to promote the overall health of a student. Constipation occurs in 5% to 10% of all children (Leung, Chang, & Cho, 1996) but occurs in 70% to 90% of children with cerebral palsy and other significant developmental disorders (Bohmer, Taminiau, Klinkenberg-Knol, &

Meuwissen, 2001; Del Giudice et al., 1999; Kozma & Mason, 2003). Increased or decreased muscle tone affects coordination of the anal muscles or muscles of the pelvic floor, making it more difficult for the student to have regular bowel movements. These muscle tone differences are often compounded by insufficient fiber and water consumption, disorders of gastrointestinal motility (Del Giudice et al., 1999), and immobility and may be a side effect of certain medications. Symptoms of constipation can include unexplained fussiness, apparent abdominal pain, decreased appetite, and a swollen abdomen (Hirsch, 1997).

Factors that contribute to optimal bowel functioning include a diet high in fiber, adequate fluid intake, a regular daily schedule for elimination, an established plan for toilet training (if applicable), an environment conducive to elimination, proper positioning for elimination, and daily physical activity or exercise (Hirsch, 1997; Leung et al., 1996).

Fiber and Fluid Intake
Diet, particularly fluid and fiber content, is often the first line of intervention to manage the toileting process (Sullivan-Bolyai, Swanson, & Shurtleff, 1984). Fiber is found in raw fruits and vegetables, whole-grain breads, and cereals. When the student has difficulty chewing and swallowing, an increase in fiber content may be difficult to achieve. Shaddix (1986) has recommended that the student progress from blended, pureed, or baby foods as rapidly as possible. Unfortunately, commercial baby foods contain very little fiber. To supplement the low fiber content, table foods can be placed in a baby food grinder or food processor to obtain the best texture for the student with oral-motor impairment. Shaddix (1986) also recommends serving bran cereal for breakfast or mixing unprocessed bran in food each day to supply additional fiber.

A dietitian is the best person to make changes in the fiber content of the student's diet. Studies have demonstrated that even when families are instructed on how to increase fiber intake, follow-up reveals that their children still consume less than the recommended fiber intake (McClung, Boyne, & Heitlinger, 1995). Dietary management requires intensive and ongoing counseling to be effective. The student's physician or other health care professional may recommend a dietitian for this purpose. Most children need between 1 and 2 quarts of fluid a day. Shaddix (1986) recommends using unsweetened juice and water. Prune juice has a natural laxative effect and can be combined with

another fruit juice to be more readily accepted by the student if he or she dislikes the taste. Thickening liquids with items such as infant cereals, blended fruit, or unflavored gelatin may change the consistency of the fluid to be more easily accepted by the student with oral-motor problems. Frequent opportunities to drink small amounts of fluid are often scheduled throughout the day to better meet the fluid needs of the student with difficulty swallowing.

Use in the Classroom
Normal bowel functioning means that the student has a normal schedule of elimination. This developing or existing pattern may be incorporated into an ongoing or new toilet training program. Stimuli or activities that aid in or detract from the process of defecation should be identified through discussion and collaboration with the family and school personnel. These include (a) promoting a normal schedule of elimination by placing the student on the toilet for approximately 10 minutes after meals and snacks to take advantage of the gastrocolic reflex that usually occurs 15 to 30 minutes after meals, (b) proper positioning of the student to increase the student's overall muscle tone (e.g., a squatting position), (c) using adapted equipment (e.g., toilet chairs), and (d) promoting physical activity and exercise to help the fecal material move through the large intestine toward the rectum.

Where to Go for Further Information or Training
Each individual has unique patterns of bowel functioning, and the student with a disability brings additional complications to the issue of bowel control. These complications can include oral-motor impairment, resulting in inadequate intake of fiber and fluids; medications that alter the consistency, color, and frequency of bowel movements; decreased levels of activity resulting in improper emptying of the intestines; inadequate innervation of the rectal sphincters; and inability to recognize the urge to defecate.

These problems, if not addressed, affect the student's participation in the curriculum because of either discomfort from chronic constipation or increased frequency of bowel movements. Both of these conditions will limit participation and interfere with bowel-training programs. The physical therapist or occupational therapist can provide a plan for positioning the student during meals and elimination. The dietitian is an important source of information on incorporating fiber in the meals and should work with the occupational therapist on developing an eating plan that addresses both dietary needs and the oral-motor skills of the student.

The student's physician can be helpful in solving problems with diarrhea, constipation, and skin irritation. When diet and adequate fluids are not enough, the physician may recommend supplemental fiber, laxatives, medications, or occasional suppositories and enemas. The communication between school and home regarding the student's status with the bowel management program is critical for success. A typical bowel elimination procedures (ileostomy and colostomy) are discussed later in this chapter.

When Gina started preschool, she did not have reliable bowel control. This created problems socially and limited participation in activities on a daily basis. When Gina was enrolled in kindergarten, a bowel-training program was developed by her physician, nutritionist, parents, and school nurse and incorporated into her IHP and IEP. The collaboration that occurred resulted in a comprehensive, consistent approach to bowel training that resulted in more dependable schedule for elimination while decreasing accidents.

Specialized Health Care Procedures

There are a number of specialized health care procedures that are often required for students with severe or profound disabilities (Ault et al., 1989). These procedures are those that require monitoring during the school day. Teachers or designated staff members may be required to record occurrences of an event and monitor the student; no other intervention is required. These procedures include seizure monitoring, medication administration, and nutrition monitoring and supplementation.

Seizure Monitoring

Seizure monitoring provides a record of the frequency of seizures during the school day and assists the parents and health care professionals to evaluate the effectiveness of the seizure medications. Monitoring, using a form as shown in Figure 7–3, allows us to carefully observe and summarize information about a student's seizures. Systematic observations over time help us distinguish behaviors that are and are not related to the seizure and communicate these observations to the

parents and physician (Neville, 1997; Williams et al., 1996). Careful observation of the child's seizures helps us physically protect the child during a seizure.

A seizure is sudden, abnormal bursts of electrical activity in the brain, resulting in a temporary change in behavior. This change in electrical activity may be limited to one area of the brain or may begin in one area and spread to other areas of the brain. If the electrical disturbance is limited to only part of the brain, then the result is a partial seizure. For example, the child may experience stiffening or jerking of one arm or leg. If the electrical disturbance affects the entire brain, the result is a generalized seizure, also referred to as grand mal or tonic-clonic seizure.

Epileptic seizures, including febrile seizures, occur in .5% to 1% of children; of the 125,000 new cases that develop each year, up to 30% occur in children and adolescents (**http://www.epilepsyfoundation.org**; Boss, 2002). Children with cerebral palsy and other health and developmental problems are less likely to "grow out of their seizures" and less likely to achieve optimal control with anticonvulsants (Carlsson, Hagberg, & Olsson, 2003; Singhi, Jagirdar, Khandelwal, & Malhi, 2003). Thus, the monitoring of students' seizures has been identified as one of the major health-related procedures performed by the classroom teacher (Ault et al., 1989; Batshaw, 2002) (see Box 7–2 and 7–3).

Normally, a seizure lasts from 30 seconds to 3 minutes; recording the duration of a student's seizure provides a record of the "typical" length of the seizure. A series of consecutive seizures with no recovery of consciousness lasting longer than 30 minutes is called status epilepticus; this condition is life threatening and requires immediate medical care (Boss, 2002).

Classroom Application

Timely and comprehensive seizure monitoring requires the teacher to be prepared with a systematic approach to collecting behavioral data. Adequate preparation for meeting the needs of students with epilepsy requires that the educational staff work closely with the family to gain all the necessary information, such as the types of seizures to be prepared for, as well as typical behaviors seen before, during, and after a seizure.

Collaboration among school, family, and health care providers will increase the usefulness of seizure monitoring; for example, school staff aware of medication changes can provide feedback to the family and physician on changes in frequency and intensity of seizures. This information is critical, particularly if the physician

FIGURE 7–3
Sample Documentation Recording Form

Seizure Monitoring Form

Name of Student: _____   Date: _____

Seizure medication: _____   Time of last
                                                                               administration: _____

Careful observation and documentation will allow you to describe three possible components of the seizure: 1) antecedent events: activities preceding the seizure; 2) seizure activity: motor behavior during the seizure; and 3) postictal state: behavior after the seizure. For each of the following descriptors, note the occurrence or nonoccurrence and indicate by numbering if there was a sequence evident.

Antecedent Events

Classroom activity preceding seizure: _____

Change in student's behavior: _____

Time of onset: _____

Seizure Activity

Areas and sequence of body involved:

      face _____ R arm _____ L arm _____

      trunk _____ R leg _____ L leg _____

Muscle tone: limp _____, rigid _____, alternating limb movements _____

Position of eyes: rolled back _____, turned to R _____, turned L _____

Breathing: beginning of seizure: normal _____, interrupted _____

              middle of seizure: normal _____, interrupted _____

              end of seizure: normal _____, interrupted _____

Skin color: pale _____; blue _____; red _____; other _____

Incontinence: bladder _____; bowel _____

Postictal Activity

Time seizure ended: _____

Duration of seizure: _____

Behavior immediately following seizure:

awake, inactive _____   awake, active _____

crying, agitated _____   drowsy, asleep _____

_____

Person observing seizure/completing form: _____

---

is in the process of evaluating the student's prescription and dosage. An increase in the number of seizures per day or per week may indicate that the student is not receiving medication as prescribed or that the student is in need of a change in medication as a result of a change in the student's metabolism or altered utilization of the

medication (Low, 1982). Careful, accurate reporting of seizure activity to parents and health care providers should result in improved seizure management.

Liz has a seizure disorder that is controlled with medication. At Mr. Vontz's request, the parents shared

Box 7–2 What to Do During a Seizure

1. Remain calm. Remember that no one can stop a seizure once it has started.
2. Stay with the student to monitor the student's activity during the seizure.
3. Mentally sequence the events that occurred before the seizure so you can record them later on an appropriate form (see Figure 7–3).
    a. Did the student recognize or signal the onset of the seizure? If so, how was this done?
        i. Did the student cry out or yell?
        ii. What was the student's activity immediately before the seizure?
        iii. Who noticed a change in the student's behavior?
4. Loosen tight clothing, especially around the neck.
5. Ease the student to the floor (to avoid a fall) if the student is standing or sitting when the seizure begins. This should be done even if the student is secured in adaptive equipment (i.e., wheelchair, standing frame, prone board).
6. Place a cushion or blanket under the student's head to prevent injury to the head.
7. If possible, position the student on his or her side so that the tongue does not block the airway and the student does not choke on secretions.
8. *Do not place anything* (e.g., fingers, objects) in the student's mouth. This could injure the student or result in vomiting.
9. Do not give the student medications or anything to drink during the seizure. (Some students may receive rectal medication such as Diastat to diminish the seizure.)
10. Mentally sequence the student's activity during the seizure so that behaviors related to the seizure can be recorded later on an appropriate form (see Figure 7–3).
    a. What time did the seizure begin?
    b. Where on the body did the seizure begin, and did it move to another body part?
    c. What were the movements of the head, face, eyes, arms, and legs?
    d. Was the student's body limp or rigid?
    e. Were the student's eyes rolled back, to the right, or to the left? Did they appear glassy?
    f. Did the student stop breathing?
    g. Did the student bite or chew the tongue?
    h. Was the student's skin pale, blue, or reddened?
    i. What time did the seizure end?

  ## Box 7–3 What to Do After a Seizure

1. Monitor the student's breathing. If breathing is absent, the emergency medical system must be notified immediately and resuscitation efforts begun.
2. Roll the student onto the left side and clear secretions from the mouth with a suction machine, bulb syringe, or gloved hand wrapped in a handkerchief.
3. Talk or interact with the student to determine level of awareness (i.e., alert, drowsy, confused, unable to respond) and record this information.
4. Determine whether the student is able to move his or her arms and legs or if there is any change in the student's ability to move.
5. Check for loss of control of urine and stool (this can be embarrassing for the student) and determine if the student sustained any injuries (e.g., bleeding from the mouth).
6. Make the student comfortable and quiet, allowing an opportunity to sleep if necessary (a student may sleep for several hours after a seizure).
7. Record the length of the seizure (in seconds or minutes) and what happened before and during the seizure as described previously.

with the team characteristics of Liz's seizures at an IEP meeting. This allowed Mr. Vontz to be prepared when Liz had a seizure at school. Liz stiffened in her chair as the students were getting ready to go out to the playground. Mr. Vontz quickly released the seat belt and placed Liz on the floor with her coat underneath her head. He moved the desks out of the way and sent another student to get assistance. Although he had forgotten to time it, Liz's tonic-clonic seizure was brief. Mr. Vontz had a change of clothing for Liz, which he gave to the school nurse. Liz normally slept for several hours after a seizure in the school nurse's office.

Understanding the behaviors that occur before, during, and after a seizure will help the staff prepare the school areas accordingly. For example, a student may become somewhat drowsy approximately 2 hours after administration of a seizure medication, which is generally around 9:30 a.m. In this instance, the teacher needs to plan for activities requiring less interaction and participation from the student at this time of day. A student who produces large amounts of secretions during a seizure will need a suction machine or bulb syringe available in the classroom to remove secretions from the mouth.

The potential for injury to the student during a seizure is a concern for all school staff. Students whose seizures are not well controlled can experience a head injury as a result of a seizure-related fall. Often, these students wear a lightweight helmet to protect the head. Efforts should be made to make this protective device as age appropriate and unstigmatizing as possible. The student must *never* be restrained during a seizure because of the possibility of physical harm (to the child or the school staff) while the student is held or restrained.

Additionally, the school environment must be as safe as possible for students with seizures. Objects (e.g., furniture, equipment, or toys) that could cause an injury should be portable and easy to remove during a student's seizure. Pathways and instructional environments should be wide and free of unnecessary objects (i.e., unused wheelchairs or storage boxes) to minimize the chance of injury during a fall.

Additional Resources
The Epilepsy Foundation sponsors a wide variety of programs and activities for persons with epilepsy as well as workshops and training for staff and educa-

tional materials developed for school personnel working with students with epilepsy. Local affiliates can be located in local telephone directories or searching for locally based Epilepsy Foundation at **http://www.epilepsyfoundation.org**. Information from the national organization is available from the following:

Epilepsy Foundation
4351 Garden City Drive
Landover, MD 20785
Phone: 1-800-332-1000
http://www.efa.org

Medication Administration and Monitoring

The general purpose of administration of medication is to relieve symptoms, to treat an existing disease, or to promote health and prevent disease. Since most medications require administration across the day, many students would be unable to attend school unless medication administration were provided.

Preparation for Administering Medication
Before administering any medication, the policies of the school district related to approval or consent for medication administration must be reviewed. The American Academy of Pediatrics (2003a) has issued a policy statement to guide prescribing physicians as well as school administrators and health staff on the administration of medications to children at school. In addition to prescribed medications, the statement also addresses over-the-counter products, herbal medications, experimental drugs that are administered as part of a clinical trial, emergency medications, and principles of student safety. Administration of any prescribed medication requires a written statement from the parent and the physician that provides the name of the drug, the dose, the approximate time it is to be taken, and the reason the medication is needed. In the absence of trained medical staff, the school principal or designee (e.g., teacher) will be trained to administer medication to students. Secure storage for the medication (Gadow & Kane, 1983; Sheets & Blum, 1998) is also a requirement. A physician's written approval may also apply for over-the-counter medications. Any administration of a medication should be recorded, using a log similar to that presented in Figure 7–4.

FIGURE 7–4
Medication Information Form

Medication Information Form

Name _____   Age _____

Route _____

Administration Analysis:

Date	Medication	Dosage Indicated	Time Received	Full dosage Received at Time Prescribed		Initials
_____	_____/_____	_____	_____	Y	N	_____
_____	_____/_____	_____	_____	Y	N	_____
_____	_____/_____	_____	_____	Y	N	_____
_____	_____/_____	_____	_____	Y	N	_____
_____	_____/_____	_____	_____	Y	N	_____
_____	_____/_____	_____	_____	Y	N	_____
_____	_____/_____	_____	_____	Y	N	_____
_____	_____/_____	_____	_____	Y	N	_____
_____	_____/_____	_____	_____	Y	N	_____
_____	_____/_____	_____	_____	Y	N	_____

Maintenance/Episodic Meds and Side Effects

M/E 1. _____

M/E 2. _____

M/E 3. _____

M/E 4. _____

M/E 5. _____

M/E 6. _____

Possible Interactions of Medications

1. _____ & _____ = _____

2. _____ & _____ = _____

3. _____ & _____ = _____

4. _____ & _____ = _____

5. _____ & _____ = _____

6. _____ & _____ = _____

Administering Medications

The method of administration depends on the developmental age of the student and the student's ability to chew and swallow. For students who are not yet sitting independently or for those who have difficulty retaining food or fluid in the mouth, the student is usually supported in a sitting position. The smaller student may be held; the larger student may remain in a wheelchair or chair (Wong & Hess, 2000). When holding or supporting a student, maintain a relaxed position to decrease the chances of choking. This may be achieved by ensuring that the student's neck is flexed, the shoulders are rounded, and the student is in a slightly forward position.

The medication is carefully measured and placed in the student's mouth from a spoon, plastic dropper, or plastic syringe (of course, a syringe without a needle). The dropper or syringe is placed along the side of the student's tongue. The medication is given slowly to ease swallowing and avoid choking. For the student with tongue thrust, it may be necessary to rescue medications from the student's lips or chin and readminister it. If the student uses a suck to take in liquid, the medication can also be slowly pushed into a nipple while the student is sucking (Wong & Hess, 2000).

If the student is able to swallow a tablet, the medication may be placed on the middle of the tongue. The student can then swallow it with juice or water (Potter & Perry, 2001). Because of the possibility of aspiration (pulling the tablet or secretions into the lungs), a whole tablet should not be given until the student is about 5 years old or demonstrates the necessary oral-motor control to safely swallow the tablet.

Use in the Classroom

Medication given during the school day must be made available at the school. The medication container must be labeled with the student's name, dosage, frequency of administration, and the prescribing physician's name. A system for recording and documenting when the medication was administered to a student must be established. Finally, the school district's policy should be reviewed to determine who can administer the medication in the school setting. Although medications are often administered in the school nurses office, there may be some unique administration scheduling requirements (e.g., medications must be given with food) that could result in the medications being given in the lunch room. Regardless of the location, the nurse or designate must identify the best location to promote student participation while ensuring privacy. "Five rights" of medication administration have been identified regardless of who administers them: the person administering the medication makes certain that the *right dose* of the *right medication* is given to the *right student* at the *right time* by the *right route* (Potter & Perry, 2001). These guidelines are used every time a medication is given. A few minutes of double-checking a medication or writing down the routine procedure can prevent a serious error that may result in unfortunate experiences for the school staff, the student, and the family.

Where to Go for Further Information or Training

School staff can find more information on administration of medication in the references listed at the end of this section (Potter & Perry, 2001; Wong & Hess, 2000; Wong & Hockenberry, 2003). Nurses in the school, the physician's office, public health department, or local hospital can provide assistance on methods of administration, side effects and toxic effects of medica-

tions, and setting up a medication log for the student. The occupational and physical therapists can provide guidance on proper positioning for medication administration and suggestions on oral or motor problems hindering medication administration. A pharmacist and the student's physician can provide information about the student's medication (i.e., side effects, toxic effects, and interaction among medications).

An interactive training source, "Assisting Children with Medications at School: A Guide for School Personnel," can be obtained from Learner Managed Designs, Inc., P.O. Box 747, Lawrence, KS 66044; phone: 1-800-467-1644; fax: 316-773-7488; **http://www.lmdusa. com/cdschoolage.html**.

Growth Monitoring, Nutrition Supplementation, and Management of Food Intake

Eating is one of the primary experiences in life. It is a universal event for children of all ages, from all cultures, from all socioeconomic classes, and regardless of the child's disabilities and abilities. The well-nourished child grows at an expected rate, is resistant to illness, and has the energy to take advantage of social and educational opportunities. Adequate nutrition is critical to achieving potential for brain and physical development. A review of the research in this area shows that 30% to 90% of individuals with major motor and/or cognitive disabilities have difficulties eating, and evidence of malnutrition has been reported in up to 90% of children with cerebral palsy who are nonambulatory (Rempel, Colwell, & Nelson, 1988). To initiate appropriate intervention, the school team must be aware of students at risk for nutrition problems and the simple screening methods used to identify these children.

Growth Monitoring Procedures

Growth is a sensitive measure of health, nutritional status, and development. We can monitor the nutritional status of a student by measuring his or her growth. Trends revealed through repeated height and weight measurements can be used to detect growth abnormalities, monitor nutritional status, or evaluate the effects of nutritional or medical interventions (see Figure 7–5). Growth measurements must be made accurately and recorded correctly at least three times a year.

FIGURE 7–5
Growth Monitoring Form

Growth Monitoring Form

Name _____ Age _____

Special Considerations _____

I. AT RISK FOR GROWTH PROBLEMS
Refer if weight for height is <5% or >95% **OR** if there is no weight gain over 9 month period

FALL _____ WINTER _____ SPRING _____
          (date)   (date)   (date)

Height: Height: Height:

Weight: Weight: Weight:

Ht/Wt%:   Ht/Wt%:   Ht/Wt%

(Plot growth on chart)

II. AT RISK DUE TO MEALTIME CHARACTERISTICS
Refer if 2 or more of these characteristics apply.

_____ Meal lasts longer than 40 minutes.

_____ Student displays discomfort during or after meal, such as

_____ excessive crying, whining, or signs of discomfort or

_____ frequent gagging, coughing, choking.

_____ Meal consistently contains items from only two of the four food groups (meat, dairy, vegetables, fruits) or contains less than suggested amounts of food for height.

_____ Drinks less than 4-6 glasses of fluid per day.

III. CHECK MEDICATION INFORMATION FORM FOR MEDICATION THAT COMPROMISES NUTRIENTS AND/OR SUPPRESSES APPETITE

In order to obtain an accurate weight, a beam scale with nondetachable weights is recommended. This type of scale is commonly found in physician's offices and in the school health office. The student is weighed in light clothing with shoes removed, wearing as little clothing as possible with consideration given to privacy needs. If the child is unable to bear weight in standing, an adult may hold the student and obtain a combined weight. The adult then subtracts his or her weight obtained on the same scale at that time from the combined weight. A measure of weight does not provide maximum information without corresponding measures of height. Both are needed for an accurate analysis of growth.

In measuring height, a metallic tape or yardstick attached to a flat wall should be used. Any measuring rods attached to a platform or scale or plastic or cloth tapes are considered inaccurate and should not be used. Ideally, the student must be able to cooperate and stand upright. If not, measures of length may be taken with the student lying down.

If a student is less than 2 years of age or is unable to stand unassisted and straight, then he or she may be measured lying down on a measuring board. One person (possibly a parent) holds the student's head so the eyes are looking vertically upward with the crown of the head firmly against the fixed headboard. The second person holds the student's feet with knees and hips extended and toes pointed directly upward. A movable foot board is brought firmly against the student's heels. Individualized methods of assessing length are necessary when a student is unable to lie with shoulders, hips, and heels aligned. This type of measuring device may be available in the primary health care provider's clinic or in a public health clinic, or the school nurse should be able to locate a measuring board.

In addition to weight and height measurements, body mass index (BMI) is calculated to provide information about a student's growth. The BMI expresses the relationship between height and weight. It is of particular importance in monitoring many students with profound disabilities because these students frequently do not grow at the same rate as other individuals of the same age.

Monitoring Nutritional Supplementation and Food Intake

Many children with multiple or profound disabilities experience difficulty in eating. This may be the result of chronic health problems, early negative oral experience (e.g., tube feedings, intubation, suctioning), neurological problems, fatigue during meals, or a combination of these factors. The special education teacher, trained as an observer of behavior, can play an important role in monitoring the child's eating abilities and behaviors, food intake, and preferences.

Because the process of mealtime or eating extends well beyond the school day, it is critical that the school and family work together and exchange information about changes in eating behavior or volumes of food consumed. Specific behaviors to monitor include (a) whether a meal lasts less than 10 minutes or longer than 40 minutes; (b) student's behaviors, such as excessive whining, crying, or signs of discomfort, including frequent gagging, coughing, or choking; and (c) whether the meal consistently contains items from only two of the five food groups or contains less than suggested amounts for height and weight.

Recording the foods eaten at each meal and the student's responses to the various textures, tastes, and consistencies can provide the family and school with important information about preferences and differential oral-motor responses to the various foods. Some students with multiple or profound disabilities are tube fed or receive a combination of tube and oral meals. For these youngsters, it is important to monitor over time the amount and types of food ingested both orally and through the tube.

The effect of body position, particularly the head and trunk, on the student's ability to eat are additional observations. These monitoring functions can provide information important to the identification of simple positional interventions or lead to appropriate referrals.

Increasing Caloric Intake It is a myth that "failure to thrive" is a necessary part of having a disability. The reason for a student's BMI being less than desired is often because the child does not get enough calories. Simply increasing the amount of food to increase weight gain is often unsatisfactory because of impaired oral-motor function or effects of fatigue. Frequent illness or infection may also decrease a child's appetite, as do certain medications.

There are several techniques to increase the number of calories a student ingests when not enough food is consumed to maintain an appropriate rate of growth. The addition of fats (a particularly concentrated source of calories), evaporated milk, wheat germ, or eggs in the preparation of foods increases the caloric and nutrient intake without requiring the students to eat more food. A regular meal pattern with two or three high-calorie snacks per day is also recommended to promote weight gain.

Increasing Fluid Intake Adequate fluid intake is essential for maintaining health. Children with oral or motor problems often have difficulty with consuming sufficient liquids. This may be caused by an inability to communicate thirst, problems with hand-to-mouth coordination, or problems with sucking, swallowing, and/or heavy drooling. Many students with oral-motor difficulties are able to consume thickened liquids more successfully than thin liquids. Products commonly used to thicken thin liquids include pureed fruit, baby cereal, yogurt, dehydrated fruits and vegetables, mashed potato flakes, gelatin (added to warm liquids), or commercially available products designed specifically for thickening foods. Fruits and vegetables such as canned fruit, watermelon, cucumbers, and squash are also excellent sources of water.

Classroom Adaptations and Applications

Growth is a sensitive measure of health and development. Recording and plotting a child's height and weight, using forms such as Figure 7–5 at the beginning, middle, and end of the school year, will help monitor the student's growth. Trends revealed through repeated height and weight measurements can be used to detect growth abnormalities, monitor nutritional status, or evaluate the effects of nutritional or medical interventions. A variety of growth charts are available for assessing the growth of children. The growth charts revised in 2000 by the National Center for Health Statistics (**http://www.cdc.gov/growthcharts**) can be used to assess the growth of most children and should be a permanent part of a child's record. Recognizing that children with disabilities may have different growth expectations than children without disabilities has prompted the development of separate growth charts for children with Down syndrome, Prader-Willi syndrome, Turner syndrome, and achondroplasia. Generally, these data are recorded and plotted by the school nurse or dietitian, but any member of the team can be trained to measure and record a child's growth.

A referral to a nutritionist should be made when the following occur:

1. Weight for age is at or below the 5th percentile or at or above the 95th percentile.
2. Length for age is at or below the 5th percentile.
3. BMI is at or below the 5th percentile or at or above the 85th percentile.
4. No weight gain in 1 month (for infants from birth to 12 months of age).
5. No weight gain in 3 months (for children from 1 to 2 years of age).

Additional Resources

A registered dietitian can be contacted through a local medical center, hospital clinic, county or state extension service, or state or local chapter of the American Dietetic Association at **http://webdietitians.org/Public/index.cfm**. The request should be for dietitians who work with children who have special health care needs or profound disabilities. In addition, the state's services for children with special health care needs and university centers of excellence in developmental disabilities can offer consultation and technical assistance for the development of nutrition services in schools. These agencies may also provide an interdisciplinary feeding clinic or assist you in locating a clinic for evaluation and follow-up of children with complex, chronic feeding disorders.

An additional resource is the University of Iowa Virtual Children's Hospital at **http://www.vh.org/pediatric/index.htm**. Look further in the site to find Patient Information by Department: Pediatric Nutrition at **http://www.vh.org/navigation/vch/topics/pediatric_patient_nutrtion.html**.

Low-Incidence Health Care Procedures

Procedures occurring with low frequency, in less than 25% of students with disabilities, are identified in this chapter as "low-incidence health care procedures." These procedures require additional equipment and specialized training. This section describes the low-incidence procedures of various nonoral methods for providing nutrients, atypical methods of elimination of feces and urine, respiratory management procedures, and shunt care.

Nonoral Feeding Procedures

Gastrostomy and nasogastric tube feedings are two methods of providing nourishment other than by mouth. Either of these may be necessary if the student cannot eat enough food orally to get needed nutrients and fluid. A *gastrostomy tube* (G-tube) is a tube extending through the abdomen into the stomach. The purpose of this tube is to allow liquid nutrients to move into the stomach when a student is unable to eat by mouth or is unable to eat adequate amounts of food by mouth. Gastrostomy tubes are used for long periods of time or even on a permanent basis. Some students may have a G-tube and not require feedings through the tube during school hours. Their tubes may be used to supplement oral intake or used when the student is ill or oral intake is not adequate. A *jejunostomy tube* (J-tube) extends through the abdomen into the jejunum, or the second part of the small intestine. Students with a G-tube or J-tube whose oral motor skills allow and who are not at risk for aspiration may be able to eat and drink by mouth. This allows students to continue activities that will promote oral-motor skills during mealtimes with their peers. Some students may receive their tube feeding after eating food by mouth in the cafeteria. The G-tube or J-tube is usually covered by the student's clothing. Students' participation in activities such as physical education and sports depends on their individual skills, not on the presence of a G-tube or J-tube.

A *nasogastric tube* (N-G tube) extends through the nose, down the throat and esophagus (or food pipe), and into the stomach. Some students have N-G tubes placed for each feeding, while others have tubes in for several weeks at a time. An N-G tube is typically a short-term solution to assist a student temporarily unable to meet his or her nutritional needs by mouth. Since this may be related to an illness or hospitalization, school staff are less likely to have contact with students having N-G tubes and therefore may avoid the issue of accidental placement of a N-G tube into the respiratory tract or lungs (Orr, 1997).

What Is Involved

Liquid nutrients can be given as formula or regular food carefully blended to be administered through the tube. Feedings are either continuous (liquid nutrients slowly drip through the feeding tube over the entire day or night) or intermittent (larger amounts of liquid nutrients are given during five to eight feedings in a day). The amount of liquid nutrients given through the tube varies for each student and must be determined by the student's health care professional. In addition to formula or blended food, the student's health care professional will recommend a specific amount of water to be given each day.

Students may be fed by *gravity drip, pump, or syringe*. A student fed by gravity drip has a container of formula hanging from 8 to 24 inches above the level of the stomach. A clamp is used to regulate the flow of the formula. Students may receive nutrients by gravity drip continuously or intermittently. However, most students receive the formula by a pump that automatically regulates the flow of liquid nutrients into the gastrostomy tube. The pump may be electric or battery operated. The student may receive the nutrients by syringe, a third method. A large syringe is attached to the end of the feeding tube, and liquid nutrients are poured into the syringe. When the remaining liquid nutrients have flowed into the bottom of the syringe tip, the appropriate amount of water is poured into the syringe and flows into the feeding tube to clear the tube of any remaining formula. Liquid is never forced through the tube.

Instead of a G-tube that extends out of the student's stomach through the abdomen and is secured beneath the clothing, the student may have a *button gastrostomy*. This is a short tube that fits against the skin on the abdomen and has a small plug that can be removed for feeding. The button G-tube fits snugly against the student's skin and is not as noticeable to others or to the student. Tubing connected to the pump can be placed into the button opening, allowing liquid nutrients to flow into the stomach or jejunum (i.e., the first 10 inches of small intestine). When the student has received the proper volume of formula, the tubing is disconnected, and the opening is closed by the small plug attached to the button gastrostomy tube.

Use in the Classroom

Regardless of the method of ingestion, food intake should occur during the mealtime or snack time of peers. Students should participate in their meals in as typical a manner as possible to promote the development of mealtime skills and to have the opportunity to engage in all the social interactions that should be occurring around mealtime.

Students' position is important while the formula is flowing through the tube. Generally, students are in a sitting or upright position and remain sitting or upright for 1 hour after all the formula has entered the stomach. Oral stimulation activities can be carried out as the student receives formula through the tube, particularly if a student cannot eat food or drink by mouth. Oral hygiene procedures or mouth care should be provided, especially if the student does not eat or drink by mouth. If eating by mouth becomes a possibility, it will be important to introduce the food that can be eaten orally before the formula is given through the tube so that hunger works as a stimulus for eating.

If a child's N-G tube or G-tube comes out during the school day, a clean gauze pad or clean cloth is placed over the opening. The school nurse, as well as the student's parents, may be trained to replace the tube, so an extra tube is kept at school. It is important to replace a G-tube within 2 hours or before the next feeding (Cusson, 1994). If a J-tube comes out, the student's physician must replace it. The student's peers should understand the purpose of the tube and any equipment such as the pump and connecting tubing to help avoid accidental pulling on the tube.

Where to Go for Further Information or Training

Nurses in the local hospital, pediatrician's office, public health office, or home health agency can provide information on intake of nutrients by tube. Dietitians in the local hospital or health department can provide information about many formulas given by tube. Medical supply companies may provide information and training in use of the equipment (e.g., G-tube, connecting tubing, and pump).

"Gastrostomy Feedings" can be accessed through **http://wellness.ucdavis.edu.**

Videotapes include the following:

"Home Gastrostomy Care for Infants and Young Children"
Learner Managed Designs, Inc.
P.O. Box 747
Lawrence, KS 66044
Phone: 785-842-9088
Fax: 785-842-6881

"Making That Important Decision: Parents' Perspectives on a G-Tube"
"Life After Your Child's G-Tube Placement"
Monroe-Meyer Institution
Media Resource Center
985450 Nebraska Medical Center
Omaha, NE 68198-5450
Phone: 402-559-7467 or 1-800-656-3937 ext. 7467
Fax: 402-559-5737

Atypical Elimination Procedures: Bowel or Intestinal Ostomy Care

Atypical elimination procedures address methods of eliminating feces and urine that require some type of assistive device or special procedure. While the goal is independent performance of these procedures, students with severe and multiple disabilities generally require assistance. In these situations, partial participation goals are appropriate for the student.

What Is Involved

An *ostomy* is a surgically created opening in the body for the discharge of body wastes; there are two main types: a *colostomy* and *ileostomy*. When the opening is created from the bowel or intestine and leads to the abdominal surface, a student is able to eliminate feces from the bowel without using the rectum. *Colostomy* refers to an opening created when a portion of the colon or large intestine is removed and the remaining colon is brought to the surface of the abdomen. An *ileostomy* refers to an opening of some portion of the ileum (lower part of the small intestine) onto the abdomen. Feces are eliminated through this opening and collected in a small pouch or bag. The pouch is tightly adhered to the skin around this opening on the abdomen, called a stoma. Since there is no control over when feces move into the pouch, feces collect in the pouch during the school day. This is especially true when a student has an ileostomy. The fecal material passing through the stoma is liquid or a pasty consistency

and contains digestive enzymes that can be irritating to the skin. Ostomy care involves procedures to collect feces in an odor-free manner and to keep the skin and stoma healthy and free of irritation.

Ostomy care should be conducted in an area that is private and allows a student to be in the best position for emptying or replacing the pouch. This may be a sitting or reclining position. Extra supplies for changing the pouch should remain at school at all times, along with an extra change of clothes (Haynie, Porter, & Palfrey, 1989). A procedure for ostomy care should be developed by the student's parents, school nurse, teacher, and other school staff that respects the student's right to privacy but includes the student's participation in the procedure to the greatest degree possible. Efforts are made to prevent skin irritation around the ostomy and beneath the pouch, eliminate odors due to gas accumulation in the pouch, and prevent loosening of and leakage from the pouch. Careful attention must be given to hand washing before and after the ostomy pouch is drained or changed. School staff must wear gloves during these two activities.

Use in the Classroom

A colostomy or ileostomy pouch is usually changed at home. A student, however, may require a change at school for a variety of reasons. A bag may become loose or leak as a result of activity or unintentional pulling on the pouch. A student may also develop diarrhea or excessive gas. Changing of the pouch is recommended between meals, not right before meals, because the signs and smells of the ostomy may reduce the student's appetite.

Ostomy care may be done by the student, school nurse, or other school staff person who is properly trained. Some students may require distraction during ostomy care to keep their hands from exploring the pouch and stoma. However, other students may be able to participate in the ostomy care by holding supplies and helping clean the stoma area, or they may carry out the procedures themselves (Wong & Hockenberry, 2003). Students need to be aware and responsible for the pouch to avoid negative responses from peers. Parents can offer school staff suggestions about ways a student can participate in ostomy care. IEP objectives that address communication and fine motor skills related to ostomy care will increase the student's participation in this long-term need.

School staff who have regular contact with the student should receive specific training about the colostomy or ileostomy and potential problems. Understanding how to manage problems can allow students to continue classroom activities with little interruption. The goal is to promote as much independence and participation as possible.

Where to Go for Further Information or Training

Information and literature on colostomy or ileostomy care can be obtained from the following:

The United Ostomy Association
19772 MacArthur Boulevard, Suite 200
Irvine, CA 92612-2405
Phone: 1-800-826-0826

The International Association for Enterostomal Therapy
27241 LaPaz Road, Suite 121
Laguan Nigel, CA 92656
Phone: 714-476-0268

The American Cancer Society at
http://www. cancer.org

The United Ostomy Association Inc. at
http://www. uoa.org

Atypical Elimination Procedures: Clean Intermittent Catheterization

Students having defects of the spinal cord, such as spina bifida or myelomeningocele, may also have neurological impairment of the bladder (*neurogenic bladder*) resulting in little or no control over bladder emptying. Typically, the bladder stretches as it fills with urine until full, when nerve signals cause the bladder to contract and empty. Usually, a person can delay bladder emptying and control the occurrences of urination. A neurogenic bladder may overstretch or contract frequently or irregularly, resulting in constant dribbling or incomplete evacuation. *Clean intermittent catheterization* is a procedure to empty the bladder and is most frequently used in students with neurogenic bladder (Vigneux & Hunsberger, 1994).

Clean intermittent catheterization involves the insertion of a catheter through the urethra (passageway between the bladder and the opening to the outside of the body) into the bladder. This usually is done every 2 to 4 hours during the day (McLone & Ito, 1998), taking into consideration other activities in the student's day, such as meals and snacks. The area chosen to carry out the procedure should provide privacy and have a sink to allow proper cleansing before and after the procedure.

During the catheterization, a student may sit on the toilet, stand, or lie down. The urine, if not emptied directly into the toilet, should be collected in a container. After thorough hand washing, the area around the opening to the urethra is cleansed with a towelette or with soap and water. Nonlatex gloves are worn, unless the student completes this procedure independently (Haynie et al., 1989).

Use in the Classroom

Clean intermittent catheterization is a health or related service (Individuals with Disabilities Education Act, 1997) that must be provided to students requiring this procedure during the school day. In an important decision issued by the Supreme Court (*Irving Independent School District v. Tatro*, 1984), clean intermittent catheterization was identified as a related service that should be provided during school hours and included in the child's education program when needed (Glucksman, 1984; Vitello, 1986).

A student with a neurogenic bladder has little or no control over the process of emptying the bladder and needs assistance in controlling the release of urine during the school day. The teacher involved in this process should encourage the student to participate in his or her own urinary catheterization as much as possible. The extent of participation in catheterization will depend on the student's fine motor control to manipulate the catheter and clothing and, of course, the student's motivation. Students should be encouraged to participate as much as possible by washing their hands, holding equipment, or participating in whatever activities are appropriate (Taylor, 1990). Collaboration with the family will support consistency of procedures and generalization.

> *Gina actively participates in her clean intermittent catheterization. Her teacher and family collaborated on a task analysis of Gina's participation in the catheterization. She hands the equipment to the health care professional in the requested order and signals verbally when done. Gina's assistant talks with her during the activity to increase her level of participation and understanding of the process. She also incorporates questions about family activities from a list the parents provide weekly.*

When students are unable to control the bladder, they may not achieve complete dryness, so protective clothing may be used. Students may also experience leakage when laughing, coughing, or sneezing. An extra set of clothing may be kept at school in case of an accident.

Where to Go for Further Information or Training

Nurse specialists in clinics, urological specialists, and hospitals serving children with myelomeningocele can provide information and assistance in this area. Videotapes on catheterizations, such as "Clean Intermittent Catheterization," can be useful in training others to perform this procedure (available from Learner Managed Designs, Inc., P.O. Box 747, Lawrence, KS 66044; phone: 1-800-467-1644; fax: 316-773-7488). Guidelines for "CIC—Clean Intermittent Catheterization" can be accessed at **http//:www.medicine.uiowa.edu/uhs/ cicprint.cfm**.

Respiratory Management: Tracheostomy Care

Respiratory management involves procedures to maintain an adequate oxygen level in the bloodstream; it is the process of helping students maintain respiration or breathing. Typically, respiratory management procedures in school involve tracheostomy care, suctioning, oxygen supplementation, and assisted ventilation.

What Is Involved

A *tracheostomy* is a surgically created opening into the trachea. It is created when there is an obstruction in the respiratory tract to prevent movement of oxygen through the trachea and allows for long-term assisted ventilation and a way to remove aspirated oral secretions by suctioning (Hunsberger & Feenan, 1994). A hollow plastic or Silastic tube, called a *tracheostomy tube*, is placed in this opening and secured by cotton ties or other ties around the neck. The student can then breathe through the trachea rather than through the mouth or nose.

Care of the tracheostomy so that air can move freely includes removal of secretions from the student's trachea, cleaning the tracheostomy tube, care of the skin around the tube, changing the tracheostomy ties, and changing the tracheostomy tube. Changing a tracheostomy tube and cleaning the old tube should be done at home. The skin around the tube is cleaned at least once daily and more often as needed. The student may wear a bib or dressing around the tube to collect secretions coming out of the tube. When the bib is soiled, it is changed during the school day. School staff should carefully examine the skin around the tube for any signs of redness or irritation. Staff should wear gloves and wash their hands carefully before and after tracheostomy care at a sink that is not used for food preparation. Proper hand washing (Figure 7–1) following procedures involving body secretions is an effective method of minimizing the risk of infections to students and staff in the classroom.

Use in the Classroom

Although the overall number of tracheostomies being performed for children is decreasing, the length of time tracheostomies remain in place is increasing (Carter & Benjamin, 1983; Line, Hawkins, Kahlstrom, MacLaughlin, & Ensley, 1986; Wetmore, Handler, & Postic, 1982). Parents are routinely trained to care for a child with a tracheostomy at home. When school staff know that a student will have a tracheostomy tube placed, one or more of the school staff should also be trained with the parents before the student's discharge from the hospital. Even though a teacher may not be designated as the person routinely responsible for changing the tube, all classroom personnel should be able to respond in the event of an emergency. This preparation can help alleviate concern on the part of parents and the school staff and minimize potentially negative responses from the student and the student's peers. Supplies should always be available at school. In addition to learning tracheostomy care, school staff should be trained in cardiopulmonary resuscitation of a student with a tracheostomy.

Students may use a speaking valve that allows the student to speak as a result of a positive pressure closure valve that opens only when the student breathes in to allow air to enter the tracheostomy tube. After the student has breathed in, the positive closure mechanism shuts, forcing air out through the vocal cords, nose, and mouth, thus creating speech (Passy, 1986). The Passy-Muir speaking valve is being used with infants and children to promote speech and language development (Engleman & Turnage-Carrier, 1997).

Other students in the classroom may be curious about the tracheostomy. They should be informed about the purpose of the tracheostomy tube and its importance to the child. They may need reminders not to touch, pull on, or put objects into the tube. When the student is exposed to cold or windy weather, the tracheostomy tube should be covered. The student may wear light clothing to cover the tube or a small pouch known as an "artificial nose" over the opening of the tracheostomy tube. As the student breathes in and out through the "artificial nose," the air is warmed and humidified. This nose can prevent tracheal spasm caused by cold air or irritation of the trachea by dust particles (Wong & Hockenberrry, 2003). Although the student may play outdoors, play near water, such as a swimming pool or stream, is restricted to avoid accidentally getting water in the opening of the tracheostomy tube. Care should also be taken to avoid any talc product, such as baby powder, and fumes, such as paint, varnish, or hair spray (Wong & Hess, 2000).

Where to Go for Further Information or Training

Qualified persons, such as nurses and respiratory therapists who have taught the student's parents, can teach tracheostomy care. Cardiopulmonary resuscitation for a person with a tracheostomy requires specialized devices and training.

Resources include the following:

"Home Tracheostomy Care for Infants and Young Children"
Available from "Learner Managed Designs, Inc.
P.O. Box 747
Lawrence, KS 66044
Phone: 1-800-467-1044
Fax: 316-773-7488
http://www.lmdusa.com

"Suctioning" from Children's Health, University of California, Davis
http://www.wellness.ucdavis.edu/general_health/family_practice/tracheostomy

Respiratory Management: Suctioning

Suctioning is the removal of secretions from the respiratory tract to allow for breathing. Suctioning may be done through the nose (nasopharyngeal), mouth (oropharyngeal), or trachea. Suctioning in the school setting is most likely to be done through the mouth by the school nurse or designated staff trained in this procedure. A suction catheter (attached to a suction machine by connecting tubing), a bulb syringe, or a DeLee suction catheter may be used to remove secretions from the mouth. These machines produce a suctioning sound when in operation. Because of the unusual char-

acteristic of this sound, it is important to introduce both the machine and its operation to the student's peer group.

What Is Involved

Suctioning is carried out when a student is unable to remove secretions effectively and requires assistance in moving the secretions from a certain area of the body. Signs that a student may need suctioning include audible secretions, symptoms of obstruction, and signs of oxygen deficiency. Large amounts of secretion in the mouth may be visible or partially visible and can be removed by suctioning. Positioning the student on one side allows secretions to move out of the mouth to be suctioned more easily.

Secretions removed with a bulb syringe should be expelled onto a disposal tissue before a second attempt is made to remove additional secretions. Gloves should be worn, and care must be taken to avoid skin contact with the secretions removed from the student's mouth or nose. Thorough hand washing before and after suctioning is essential.

Where to Go for Further Information or Training

Home health nurses, nurses in local hospitals, and respiratory therapists can provide information about and assistance with suctioning. Also look for assistance in your area through the American Lung Association at **http://www.lungusa.org**.

Respiratory Management: Oxygen Supplementation

Oxygen supplementation is necessary if the current level of oxygen in the body is inadequate because of respiratory or cardiac conditions. Oxygen is given through a nasal catheter (a small catheter is placed into one nostril), nasal prongs or cannula (two small plastic prongs fit into the student's nostrils), a face mask (a plastic mask fits over the student's mouth and nose), or a trachea mask (a plastic mask fits loosely over the student's tracheostomy tube). Nasal prongs are the most frequently used method of administering oxygen to children in the home, school, and the community.

What Is Involved

Oxygen should not be given over a prolonged period of time without humidification since it can dry up secretions and mucous membranes. The flow rate of oxygen is not changed unless ordered by the student's primary care provider. Occasionally, a student needs to have more oxygen during mealtime or certain activities. The student's primary care provider must prescribe this change in flow rate. Indications that the student has an inadequate supply of oxygen include difficult breathing, irritability, increase in respirations, fatigue, pale color, cyanosis (i.e., bluish lips and nail beds), or increase in the heart rate.

Use in the Classroom

Most likely, a student will receive oxygen from a portable oxygen tank that is attached to a wheeled device or wheelchair and is carried by or with the student. Because oxygen is highly combustible, caution should be taken to avoid using highly flammable substances while oxygen is administered. Open flames from cigarettes or candles, Bunsen burners in chemistry class, electrical equipment that can produce sparks, and items that can produce static electricity must be avoided. Areas where oxygen is being used should be marked with large, easily read warning signs. Administration of oxygen may be a necessary part of a student's health care plan. Oxygen supplementation may be required at all times or may be given at certain times, such as during meals, snacks, naps, or other activities.

Liz's oral-motor skills improved throughout the school year, so she began accepting small amounts of pureed food before formula was given through her gastrostomy tube. However, her respiratory status became a problem after an episode of pneumonia. Liz continued accepting small amounts of pureed food but needed oxygen during and after she ate by mouth. She also experienced breathing problems when she became excited or stressed. Her classmates learned to recognize her distress and need for oxygen and call the teacher's attention to Liz.

Where to Go for Further Information or Training

Respiratory therapists and pediatric nurses in a local hospital and home health care staff members may provide information about administration of oxygen to children. Medical equipment supply companies can provide useful information about the oxygen tank, humidifier, and the tubing used to administer oxygen. The student's physician is a resource for school staff members when questions arise about the student's responses to oxygen supplementation.

The videotape "Home Oxygen for Infants and Young Children" is available from Leaner Managed Designs, Inc., P.O. Box 747, Lawrence, KS 66044; phone: 1-800-467-1044; fax: 316-773-7488. "Home Oxygen Therapy" can be found at **http://www.aarc.org/patient_education/tips/homeox.html**.

Respiratory Management: Mechanical Ventilation

Mechanical ventilation is required when the student is unable to breathe in or breathe out adequately; oxygen supplementation is accomplished using the student's current breathing pattern. Students may be dependent on a ventilator as a result of conditions such as neurological damage, muscle weakness, or severe pulmonary disease (Haynie et al., 1989). Respiratory management in the schools involves monitoring the necessary equipment to allow breathing and to intervene in emergency situations.

What Is Involved

Although there are many different types of ventilators, the most common is a *positive pressure ventilator*. This ventilator breathes for the student by forcing air into the lungs, usually through a tracheostomy tube. A *negative pressure ventilator* creates a negative pressure that pulls the student's chest wall out and air moves into the lungs as a result of this negative pressure. An example of a negative pressure ventilator is the iron lung. These ventilators are used less often than the positive pressure ventilators and do not require a tracheostomy tube. Noninvasive positive pressure ventilation (NPPV) has been used for children. This uses a nasal or oral mask attached to the ventilator. Three types of NPVV are (a) continuous positive airway pressure, (b) intermittent positive-pressure breathing, and (c) bilevel positive airway pressure (O'Neill, 1998). A student may require ventilation only during sleep and can attend school with oxygen supplementation. Another student may require ongoing ventilation and attends school with the constant attention of a home health nurse or other health care professional.

Use in the Classroom

Students require assisted ventilation for a variety of reasons: fatigue from the increased work of breathing, periods when breathing does not occur spontaneously, or periods when conditions restrict or prevent adequate ventilation. Students who require ventilatory assistance, as well as their parents, are often anxious when others become responsible for managing this aspect of their daily routine. Anxiety can increase the student's respiration and possibly lead to hyperventilation. Training school staff about the ventilator and what to do in case of an emergency can increase the student's and parents' confidence in the staff and decrease the student's and parents' anxiety about the school experience.

Carefully planned training sessions with the school staff members who will carry out procedures with the student are crucial. Staff members must feel confident and secure in the procedures they are using, have a clear understanding of all aspects of the procedures, and have plans to follow if problems arise. A nurse or respiratory therapist who has received specialized training to manage mechanical ventilation should perform care. A trained caregiver should be available to the student in the classroom and in transit to and from the school. In addition to knowing how to care for the student and ventilator, these trained persons must know how to provide CPR for the student with a tracheostomy. Backup electrical power should be available for mechanical ventilator at all times. A resuscitation bag, spare tracheostomy tube, and suction supplies should always be with the student.

Where to Go for Further Information or Training

Respiratory therapists, home health care staff members, nurse specialists working with the student in the hospital setting, and the student's physician can provide information to develop and implement an overall plan for a student's respiratory management.

See also **http://www.healthfinder.gov**, a general health information locator provided by the U.S. government. Also available is "Allergies and Asthma Network Mothers of Asthmatics" at **http://www.aanma. org**, a nonprofit membership organization founded in 1985 to help families in their quest to overcome and maintain control of asthma, allergies, and related conditions. Several children's hospitals also provide Web-based information: University of Minnesota Department of Pediatrics (**http://www.peds.umn. edu**) and Gillette Children's Hospital (**http://www. gillettechildrens.org**). A videotape, "Breathing Easy: Children on Ventilators at School," is available from Learner Managed Systems, Inc.

Glucose Monitoring

Glucose monitoring is a procedure used to identify the amount of glucose (sugar) present in the blood. This is often carried out by the school nurse for students who have diabetes, a disorder in which carbohydrates are unable to be used because of inadequate production or use of insulin. Excessive amounts of glucose are then found in the student's blood and urine.

Type 1 diabetes occurs when insulin is not produced, resulting in problems getting glucose into the cells of the body. Five percent to 10% of Americans with diabetes have type 1 diabetes. Type 2 diabetes results from the body's failure to use insulin properly, along with a deficiency of insulin in the body. Around 90% to 95% of Americans with diabetes have type 2 diabetes. Type 1 diabetes occurs more frequently in children, but an increasing number of children are developing type 2 diabetes because of obesity and lack of exercise; previously, type 2 diabetes occurred more often in adults. The four aspects of therapy for type 1 diabetes are (a) blood glucose monitoring, (b) exercise, (c) diet, and (d) medication (Maffeo, 1997). Persons with type 1 diabetes usually require testing of blood glucose levels three or four times per day; this will likely affect the classroom routine. The number of times a student's blood glucose level is checked will depend on whether the student is taking insulin or other diabetic medication, is having a hard time controlling blood glucose levels, has severe low blood glucose levels or ketones from high blood glucose levels, or has low blood sugar levels without warning signs (**http://www.diabetes.org**). Another test used to measure blood glucose levels is glycosylated hemoglobin. The result of this test reveals the overall glucose control over several months and can serve as a "report card" (Bayne, 1997) on dietary and insulin management.

What Is Involved

Glucose monitoring is taught to students and their parents as a method of achieving optimal control of blood glucose levels and can be carried out relatively easily during the school day. The student's fingertip is pricked with a lancet or spring-activated lancet by the student, school nurse, or designate. When a drop of blood forms, the blood is allowed to drop from the student's finger onto a special reagent strip. The strip is placed into a special meter. A reading of the student's glucose level appears on the meter's screen. If this device is not used, the color of the reagent strip can be compared with the color blocks on the reagent container; this method results in a probable range of glucose levels (Graff et al., 1990). It is important to follow the directions that come with the child's device.

Use in the Classroom

A team approach to therapy or management includes informing teachers, school staff, the student's peer group, bus drivers, and others who interact with the student about diabetes. The student may wear a Medic Alert bracelet or necklace to provide identification that could be lifesaving. The teacher and peer group can play a role in helping the student manage his or her disease by providing sugar-free treats or other appropriate foods during holiday and birthday celebrations. Careful monitoring provides accurate, current information on the student's glucose level and allows treatment of levels that are too high or too low. Foods can be given to provide extra glucose, foods can be limited, or insulin can be given. Glucose levels that are too high or too low can affect a student's ability to perform in the classroom. In a position statement on medical care for persons with diabetes, the American Diabetes Association (1997) noted that it is desirable to test blood glucose levels at school before lunch and when signs or symptoms of abnormal levels are present.

When glucose levels are too high, insulin may need to be given. Since students with disabilities may not communicate symptoms of low or high glucose levels, parents can be extremely helpful in identifying behaviors that indicate glucose levels are not within the desired range. The school nurse or person designated by the school nurse monitors the student's glucose levels. When possible, the student should have some responsibility to assist with monitoring. The student's IEP and IHP will most likely reflect the efforts of the school nurse and teacher to monitor the student's glucose levels yet minimize the interruptions related to glucose testing during the student's school day.

Where to Go for Further Information or Training

Information about diabetes can be obtained through diabetes educators, nurses working with children who have diabetes, and dietitians in local hospitals. The American Diabetes Association may have local affiliates that can be contacted for more information:

American Diabetes Association
1701 North Beauregard Street
Alexandria, VA 22311
Phone: 1-800-342-2383
http://www.diabetes.org

Juvenile Diabetes Research Foundation
International
120 Wall Street
New York, NY 10005-4001
Phone: 1-800-533-2873
http://www.jdf.org
E-mail: infor@jdrf.org

Medic Alert Foundation International
2323 Colorado Avenue
Turlock, CA 95382
Phone: 1-888-633-4298
http://www.medicallert.org

Internet resources linking to diabetes-related resources include the following: **http://www.childrenwithdiabetes.com** and **http://www. clevelandclinic.org/socialwork/ diabetes.resource_guide.htm**.

Shunt Care

Hydrocephalus is a condition in which the accumulation of excess amounts of fluid in the cerebral ventricles results in enlargement of the ventricles. This enlargement may eventually lead to enlargement of the head and subsequent brain damage. Some causes of hydrocephalus are Arnold-Chiari malformations, brain tumors, Dandy-Walker syndrome, and meningitis (Wong & Hockenberry, 2003). A student with hydrocephalus may have a shunt that drains excess fluid from the ventricles of the brain into another part of the body. This fluid is called cerebrospinal fluid and is formed primarily in the ventricles. Shunt care almost exclusively involves procedures to identify when the shunt has malfunctioned.

What Is Involved

Surgical placement of a shunt is the treatment for hydrocephalus and allows fluid to leave the cerebral ventricles and to move to one of several possible locations for elimination by the body: (a) the peritoneal cavity (ventriculoperitoneal, or V-P, shunt) and (b) the right upper chamber (atrium) of the heart (ventriculoatrial, or V-A, shunt). If a shunt becomes obstructed or malfunctions, fluid begins to build up, creating increased pressure in the brain. Signs of shunt malfunction in students include headache, vomiting or change in appetite, lethargy or irritability, swelling along the shunt tract, seizures, deterioration in school performance, neck pain, or personality change (McLone & Ito, 1998). Double vision or blurred vision may also occur.

Use in the Classroom

To ensure proper functioning of the shunt, there must be careful observations and reporting of complications to parents or the student's physician. School staff must be aware of the student's usual behavior, level of activities, and responses (Graff et al., 1990). This knowledge will help the school team note changes in level of activity, behavior, and response to and awareness of the environment, which may indicate that the shunt is not working. Lethargy, nausea, and vomiting are common signs of shunt malfunction, but idiosyncratic behaviors are best identified through discussion with the student's parents. There are generally no restrictions on a student's activities, with the exception of exclusion from contact sports when there is a high risk of head injury (Jackson, 1980). Carpeted floors in the classroom can help protect a student who falls in school.

Where to Go for Further Information or Training

Health care professionals working with the student, such as the student's physician (pediatrician or family physician, neurologist, neurosurgeon) and a nurse specialist working with children who have neurological disorders, can provide additional information. The student's parents can be exceptional resources by providing information about the student's usual behaviors and behaviors that can be expected when the shunt is not functioning properly.

The Hydrocephalus Association, National Hydrocephalus Foundation, and the Spina Bifida Association of America provide families and professionals with resources on hydrocephalus and its management. The Hydrocephalus Association offers support, education, and advocacy to families and individuals (Tatter, Owen, & Kenyon, 1998):

Hydrocephalus Association
870 Market Street, Suite 705
San Francisco, CA 94102
Phone: 415/732-7040 or 1-888-598-3789
http://www.hydroassoc.org

National Hydrocephalus Foundation
12413 Centialia Road
Lakewood, CA 90715-1623
Phone: 526-402-3523
http://www.nhfonline.org

The Spina Bifida Association of America
4590 MacArthur Boulevard, NW, Suite 250
Washington, DC 20007-4226
Phone: 202-944-3285 or 1-800-621-3141
Fax: 202-944-3295
E-mail: sbaa@sbaa.org

Issues in Providing Special Health Care

Participation in Integrated Settings

In the past, the rationale for placement of students requiring complex special health care procedures in restricted, segregated settings was that the resources (personnel and equipment) were more efficiently, economically, and reliably provided if all students requiring special health care procedures at school were in close proximity. Separation from peers, however, is in opposition to current efforts toward attending one's neighborhood school (Meyer, Peck, & Brown, 1991). Proponents of inclusion of children with special health care needs support the position that if a student has been discharged from a hospital to the home and nonnursing personnel can accomplish the necessary special health care procedures in the home, it is also possible to provide these same procedures in the school setting (Porter et al., 1997). Medically, there does not appear to be a reason for school segregation.

When Liz was born and the degree of her disabilities became increasingly clear, her parents were very much afraid that Liz would not have the same educational and social opportunities and experiences growing up that her sisters had. The family liked their neighborhood, their school, and their community. They felt Liz should be a part of all this, just as her sisters were. Since her birth, Liz had been receiving services through the school district, with home visits from infant and early childhood teachers. When Liz turned 6, she started in a segregated school, but soon the district moved her to an inclusive placement in Liz's neighborhood school. Though often a challenge, the process of including Liz with her peers was and is being accomplished. Her parents, again, were faced with the familiar fears and concerns when Liz had the G-tube placed. The school personnel, though initially hesitant, were willing to "give it a try." Liz's mom and dad worked closely with the district's health care coordinator to develop a plan for her health management at school. Together they developed a strategy to address the technical skills that are needed by school personnel as well as any emotional or philosophical supports that might be provided to the school as they begin to participate in this new health care procedure. Aside from a few days missed because of colds and one case of diarrhea, Liz's attendance has been very good.

Inclusion is a major objective of legislation such as the Individuals with Disabilities Education Act (IDEA) and the Americans with Disabilities Act. All students, including students with disabilities and health care needs, have rights to participate in a regular classroom with appropriate supports during the school day. The responsibility of school districts to provide necessary health services to students with disabilities has been upheld in court cases such as the *Tatro* case (Vitello, 1986) and *Cedar Rapids Community School District v. Garrett F.* (Katsiyannis & Yell, 1999). In the *Tatro* case, a "three-part test" (**http://www.ideapractices. org/law/regulations/searchregs/300subpartA/As ec300.24.php**) was adopted by the Supreme Court in which services affecting the educational and health needs of a student must be provided under IDEA if (a) the student's disability requires special education services, (b) the service is necessary to assist the student in benefiting from special education, and (c) a nurse or other qualified person who is not a physician can provide the service.

Children in Pain

Pain is a sensation in which an individual experiences discomfort, distress, or suffering resulting from irritation or stimulation of sensory nerves (Thomas, 1985). The interpretation of pain usually leads that individual to communicate, either verbally or nonverbally, the onset, intensity, and occurrence of pain. Therefore, subjective information and an interpretation of another's communication (see chapter 11 for a discussion of nonsymbolic communication) is often the basis for treatment or management of pain.

Pain in children has been challenging to assess, particularly when children are preverbal or nonverbal (Foster, Hunsberger, & Anderson, 1989). The presence of language and cognitive disabilities makes it difficult to rely on reports of pain, and teachers must be very aware of each student's strategy for communicating discomfort or pain (see chapter 11 for more information). The student's behaviors, expressions, fears, and sources of comfort provide objective information about the student's experience of pain. The different ways a child or youth may express pain are very individual. If possible, a student may gesture toward or favor specific areas of the body if the pain is localized. For example, if experiencing a fracture, a student may guard an arm or try not to bear weight on a leg. The student may hold his or her head or stomach, a common response for all persons with stomachaches or headaches, or wince when swallowing or breathing. Often, however, the pain is not localized, or the child is not able to localize the pain or protect an area of the body. In these instances, the only indication that the student is in pain is the student's different behavior. Is the child, for example, more quiet, more irritable, or more lethargic than usual?

It may be the case that some students overreact to episodes of pain. Others, however, may not be aware of pain as an indicator that an injury has occurred. Students with spina bifida have decreased sensation in the lower extremities and may not feel pain, even with a severe injury, such as a burn or fracture (Holvoet & Helmstetter, 1989). Assessment instruments have been developed to assess behavior changes associated with pain, but no useful instruments exist for assessing pain in students with disabilities, who often express themselves nonverbally (Foster et al., 1989). School staff must rely on their own observations and knowledge about the student along with the information provided by the student's family to make an objective interpretation about a student's experiences with pain.

Children Who Are Dying

When a student's health begins to deteriorate because of an underlying health condition or illness, plans for the student's educational program may need to be adjusted to the physical changes that are occurring. The course of the decline as communicated by the parents and physician may allow school staff members to adjust the school program. It is important to plan strategies to assist the student, his or her peers, and school staff for the deterioration of the child's abilities. Everyone involved with the child should work toward being emotionally prepared.

When a student's condition is expected to worsen or when death is expected within months or years, four options are available. These include (a) focusing on skill training that will maintain the child's present skills as long as possible; (b) teaching skills that are needed in order to compensate for lost ability; (c) aiding the student, family, school, and other students in dealing with increasing deterioration; and (d) lessening the likelihood of secondary complications, such as pain or additional impairment. These options are based on the assumptions that it is important for the student's life to be as normal as possible and that part of a child's normal life includes school (Holvoet & Helmstetter, 1989). Some or all of these options may be selected, depending on the student's condition. It is especially important that families, school staff, and health professionals work closely during this time.

School staff can gain understanding of the degenerative illness and feel more comfortable with the student by meeting with the parents and medical staff to (a) learn about the student's condition, (b) learn what the student can and cannot do, and (c) clarify how to recognize and respond to emergencies (Holvoet & Helmstetter, 1989). When a student dies, school staff members are dealing not only with their own feelings but also with the feelings of classmates, families, and other staff members. It is important to discuss a student's death openly and allow others to express their feelings.

Withholding Treatment

Box 7–4 discusses the special case of withholding CPR and was written by a physician with a long history of educating health care providers in the process of ethical decision making, particularly at the end of life. These are issues that we are facing with increasing frequency; thoughtful discussion will assist us in understanding and evaluating the values involved, our respective roles and responsibilities, and the process through which decisions are made or changed. The intent of this feature is not to tell you "what to think" but rather "how to think" about these difficult issues.

  ### Box 7–4 Withholding CPR

William G. Bartholome, M.D., M.T.S.

The possible withholding of a specific health care intervention-such as cardiopulmonary resuscitation, or CPR-is an example of the challenges facing teachers and schools when a student may have a life-limiting or even terminal illness. The notion of training teachers and other appropriate school personnel to provide CPR is based on the underlying assumption that any student who would suddenly stop breathing or whose heart would suddenly stop beating would be provided this emergency medical intervention in an effort to rescue them, to resuscitate them.

For some children, parents and health care providers may decide that CPR is either (a) "futile" in the sense that it is unlikely to be effective or (b) inappropriate given the nature of the child's medical condition and prospects for living (Landwirth, 1993). Studies of patient outcomes after CPR have demonstrated that it is often the case that CPR is a brutal and fruitless procedure (Blackhall, 1987). It is now known that, in certain populations of seriously ill children, CPR is so rarely successful in saving lives that decisions to withhold it are not only reasonable but ethically required in order to protect the child from the burdens of this highly invasive and often futile procedure (Nelson & Nelson, 1992). In most cases, the decision to withhold CPR will be made initially during the course of the child's hospitalization. Since cardiopulmonary resuscitation is a "routine" procedure in most hospital settings, the decision to withhold CPR is implemented through the mechanism of a "do not resuscitate," or DNR, order. When a patient with a DNR order experiences a "respiratory or cardiac arrest" (the patient stops breathing or the patient's heart stops beating), attempts to restore breathing or heart function (CPR) are not undertaken, and the patient is allowed to die.

While it is clearly the case that health care professionals and the facilities in which they work have become increasingly comfortable with decisions to limit certain kinds of life-sustaining treatments (Bartholome, 1991), this is often not the case when these same patients leave the hospital to go back out into the community or back to school. In the past few years, health care professionals, institutions, organizations, and families have worked diligently with emergency medical services (EMS) and agencies to develop methods of implementing the decision to limit treatment, especially decisions to withhold CPR from patients after discharge from hospital (Sachs, Miles, & Levin, 1991). Some communities have developed computer registries of DNR patients; some use special out-of-hospital DNR forms, or even special DNR medical alert bracelets. While these procedures may well result in protecting people from inappropriate CPR in their homes, it is unclear how these developments would serve these same individuals outside of the home, in the school.

When children with DNR orders are discharged to home or to another facility, such as a long-term care facility, steps are taken to ensure that the order is honored after the child has been discharged. The result is that teachers and school districts are now being asked to develop procedures for including children with DNR orders in the classroom. If teachers and school personnel are to be provided training that would allow them to provide CPR in a school setting, is it also the case that they should be provided training in how to respond to children with DNR orders? If school officials are willing to develop procedures to respond to the special needs of children who may experience a respiratory or cardiac arrest while at school, should they also be willing to develop policies and procedures for honoring DNR orders while these special students are at school? If hospitals and other health care facilities are willing to develop policies and procedures for protecting their patients from inappropriate resuscitative efforts, should no schools, which have adopted policies of always attempting CPR, be willing to do the same to protect students from inappropriate CPR?

Should Schools Honor DNR Orders?

Some have argued that it is one thing for health care professionals or even family members to accept the responsibility of honoring DNR orders but another to expect this kind of responsibility to be undertaken by teachers or school personnel. Younger (1992) argues that since school personnel "have neither first-hand knowledge of the patient's clinical status nor the training necessary to make clinical judgments," they should *not be expected to honor DNR orders* in the classroom. Younger also points out that school personnel, unlike families, have not been provided with training in dealing with and responding to a child who is experiencing a sudden cardiac or respiratory arrest. It may well be the case that a child from whom CPR is withheld may experience seizures or gasping respirations or another kind of "terminal crisis" before death. Is it reasonable to expect that a teacher in a classroom with other students would be capable of providing effective "comfort" to the dying student? Younger proposes that individual schools work out agreements with local EMS agencies to respond to the 911 call for help but to provide only comfort to the child. This proposal implies that school districts would "honor DNR orders" by transferring this responsibility on a case-by-case basis to local EMS agencies. Although I feel that there is considerable merit in Younger's proposal, it may not be the case that such arrangements can be made in advance for all children.

Many children who are appropriate candidates for DNR orders have conditions for which a wide range of other life-sustaining treatments (e.g., antibiotics, treatment for status epilepticus) are appropriate and utilized. A DNR order is nothing more than a decision to withhold a specific, burdensome, and often unsuccessful intervention, namely, CPR (Council on Ethical and Judicial Affairs, 1990). It has also been argued that a parent's request that a school district honor a student's DNR order might be a very reasonable request but that it conflicts with the school's obligation to protect other students from the harm that might come from having to witness the child's death in the classroom. No one who has ever witnessed a full-blown CPR attempt, particularly a prolonged and unsuccessful one, would ever make this claim. It could clearly be argued that witnessing the brutality to the child involved in an attempt at CPR is likely to be much more difficult for the child's fellow students than witnessing the loving and caring response of school personnel to a classmate while she or he experiences something that the class had been previously told might happen and had been prepared to deal with if it did.

Summary

To establish quality health care in the educational setting, teachers must (a) incorporate special health care procedures into the educational day and (b) actively prevent the development of related health problems and conditions. This chapter offers guidelines for establishing programs responsive to all the needs of students. These guidelines address assessing needs, scheduling, gathering student information, monitoring routine procedures, and including special health care procedures as part of the instructional day.

Procedures that should be a part of training for all classroom personnel include infection control, first aid, and CPR. Teachers also should have readily available information concerning the special health care needs of students. This information should minimally include (a) seizure information, with the type, frequency, and response; (b) medication information, with the type, purpose, schedule of administration (even at times other than school hours), and possible side effects or interactions; (c) emergency numbers for family members, the medical facility of choice, and the primary care provider; and (d) specific protocols, or descriptions, of the implementation of special health care procedures for individual students, the person primarily responsible for implementing the procedures, designated backups, and the dates of training of school staff members for the implementation of the procedures.

Teachers should consider the nutrition and hydration needs of their students. BMI, calculated regularly over time, provides information on the overall growth and nutritional status of students. Following meals and snacks, some students may need teeth and gum care. Routine monitoring also may include the color of the skin under a brace or at the hips and tailbone. The risk status for pressure sores provides information for considering routine positioning, repositioning a minimum of every 20 minutes, and frequent rotations into the upright position. The frequency of bowel movements and the frequency and qualities of urination are other considerations.

The student's health care needs are best addressed through collaboration between the school, family, and health professionals. When it is clear to everyone, including the student, why a particular procedure is required, the student's health and ability to participate in the educational process is enhanced through inclusion of procedures in the IHP and/or IEP. Creativity and consistency in implementation and monitoring can be an outcome. It is hoped that this chapter will provide team members with the information and resources to serve students with a variety of health care conditions comfortably and safely.

Suggested Activities

1. Complete training for CPR with an emphasis on children and a basic Red Cross first aid course.
2. Monitor the BMI of a student for whom you feel normal growth is at risk. Plot growth over several months and determine if the student's weight for height places the student below the fifth percentile. Determine whether growth is occurring at an acceptable rate. Discuss your findings with the school nurse or nutritionist and the parents.

3. Spend approximately 2 hours participating in a specialty medical clinic focusing on pediatrics, such as a cerebral palsy clinic, a feeding clinic, or a home health nurse clinic. Learn to implement a special health care procedure for a student with whom you are familiar. Develop at least two or three instructional skills that are appropriate for the student to practice during the implementation of the special health care procedure. If possible, implement a plan for the student to practice the skills during the procedure.
4. Find a Website that addresses issues of right to treatment and disability. Make sure the site is produced by a medical center, pediatric hospital, state or federal agency, or university.

References

American Academy of Pediatrics. (1993). Basic life support training in school. *Pediatrics, 91*(1), 158-159.

American Academy of Pediatrics. (2003a). Guidelines for the administration of medication in school. *Pediatrics, 112*(3), 697-699.

American Academy of Pediatrics. (2003b). Increasing immunization coverage. *Pediatrics, 112*(4), 993-996.

American Diabetes Association. (1997). Standards of medical care for patients with diabetes mellitus. *Diabetes Care, 20*(1), S5-S13.

American Dietetic Association. (1997). Nutrition in comprehensive program planning for persons with developmental disabilities—Position of the ADA. *Journal of the American Dietetic Association, 97*, 189-193.

American Dietetic Association. (2003). Position of the American Dietetic Association: Oral health and nutrition. *Journal of the American Dietetic Association, 103*, 615-625.

American Heart Association. (2000). Part 9: Pediatric Basic life support. *Resuscitation, 46*, 301-341.

American Nurses Association. (2001). *Scope and standards of professional school nursing practice.* Washington, DC: Author.

Ault, M. M., Guess, D., Struth, L., & Thompson, B. (1989). The implementation of health related procedures in classrooms for students with severe multiple impairments. *Journal of the Association of Persons with Severe Disabilities, 13*, 100-109.

Bartholome, W. G. (1991). Withholding/withdrawing life-sustaining treatment. In B. Woodrow & M. D. Burgess (Eds.), *Contemporary issues in pediatric ethics* (pp. 17-40). Waterloo, Ontario: Edwin Mellen Press.

Batshaw, M. L. (2002). *Children with disabilities* (5th ed.). Baltimore: Paul H. Brookes.

Bayne, C. G. (1997). How sweet it is: Glucose monitoring equipment and interpretation. *Nursing Management, 28*(9), 52, 54.

Beers, N. S., Kemeny, A., Sherrit, L., & Palfrey, J. S. (2003). Variations in state-level definitions: Children with special health care needs. *Public Health Reports, 118*(5), 434-447.

Blackhall, L. J. (1987). Must we always use CPR? *New England Journal of Medicine, 317,* 1281-1285.

Bohmer, C. J., Taminiau, J. A., Klinkenberg-Knol, E. C., & Meuwissen, S. G. (2001). The prevalence of constipation in institutionalized people with intellectual disability. *Journal of Intellectual Disability Research. 45 (Pt 3), 212-218*

Borgioli, J. A., & Kennedy, C. H. (2003). Transitions between school and hospital for students with Multiple disabilities: A survey of causes, educational continuity, and parental perceptions. *Research and Practice for Persons with Severe Disabilities, 28,* 1.

Boss, B. (2002). Concepts of neurologic dysfunction. In K. L. McCanse & S. E. Huether (Eds.), *Pathophysiology* (pp. 438-549). St. Louis, MO: Mosby.

Brener, N. D., Burstein, G. R., Dushaw, M. L., Vernon, M. E., Wheeler, L., & Robinson, J. (2001). Health services: Results from the School Health Policies and Programs Study 2000. *Journal of School Health, 71*(7), (yes) 294-304.

Bryant, R. A., & Doughty, D. (Eds.). (2000). *Acute and chronic wounds: Nursing management* (2nd ed.). St. Louis, MO: Mosby.

Carlsson, M., Hagberg, G., & Olsson, I. (2003). Clinical and aetological aspects of epilepsy in children with cerebral palsy. *Developmental Medicine and Child Neurology, 45*(6), 371-377.

Carter, P., & Benjamin, B. (1983). Ten-year review of pediatric tracheotomy. *Annals of Otology, Rhinology, and Laryngology, 92,* 398-400.

Council on Ethical and Judicial Affairs, American Medical Association. (1990). Guidelines for the appropriate use of do-not-resuscitate orders. *Journal of the American Medical Association, 265,* 1868-1871.

Cusson, R. M. (1994). Altered digestive function. In C.L. Betz, M.M. Hunsberger, & S. Wright (Eds.) *Family-centered nursing care of children (2nd ed.) (pp. 1413-1505).* Philidelphia: W. B. Saunders.

Del Giudice, E., Staiano, A., Capano, G., Romana, A., Florimonte, L., Miele, E., et al. (1999). Gastrointestinal manifestations in children with cerebral palsy. *Brain and Development, 21*(5), 307-311.

Diabetes statistics for youth. (n.d.). Retrieved January 30, 2004, from http://www.diabetes.org/diabetes-statistics/children.jsp

Education and foster care of children infected with human T-lymphotropic virus type lymphadenopathy-associated virus. (1985). *Morbidity and Mortality Weekly Report, 34,* 517-520.

Engleman, S. G., & Turnage-Carrier, C. (1997). Tolerance of the Passy-Muir speaking valve in infants and children less than 2 years of age. *Pediatric Nursing, 23*(6), 571-573.

Foster, R. L. R., Hunsberger, M. M., & Anderson, R. D. (1989). *Family-centered nursing care of children.* Philadelphia: W. B. Saunders.

Gadow, K. D., & Kane, K. M. (1983). Administration of medication by school personnel. *Journal of School Health, 53,* 178-183.

Glucksman, J. (1984, November). Clean intermittent catheterization— The law. *Spina Bifida Spotlight,* 1-2.

Graff, J. C., Ault, M. M., Guess, D., Taylor, M., & Thompson, B. (1990). *Health care for students with disabilities: An illustrated medical guide for the classroom.* Baltimore: Paul H. Brookes.

Harris, C. S., Baker, S. P., Smith, G. A., & Harris, R. M. (1984). Childhood asphyxiation by food. *Journal of the American Medical Association, 251*(17), 2231-2235.

Haynie, M., Porter, S. M., & Palfrey, J. S. (1989). *Children assisted by medical technology in educational settings: Guidelines for care.* Boston: Project School Care, The Children's Hospital.

Hirsch, D. (1997). Constipation. *Exceptional Parent, 27*(8), 60-63.

Holvoet, J. F., & Helmstetter, E. (1989). *Medical problems of students with special needs: A guide for educators.* Boston: College-Hill.

Hunsberger, M., & Feenan, L. (1994). Altered respiratory function. In C. L. Betz, M. M. Hunsberger, & S. Wright (Eds.), *Family-centered nursing care of children* (2nd ed., pp. 1167-1275). Philadelphia: W. B. Saunders.

Individuals with Disabilities Education Act Amendments of 1997, Public Law 105-17, 20 U.S.C. 1400 et seq.

Jackson, P. L. (1980). Ventriculo-peritoneal shunts. *American Journal of Nursing, 80,* 1104-1109.

Jeter, K. F., & Lutz, J. B. (1996). Skin care in elderly, dependent, incontinent patients. *Advances in Wound Care, 9*(1), 29-34.

Katsiyannis, A., & Yell, M. (1999). Education and the law: School health services: *Cedar Rapids Community School District v. Garrett F. Preventing School Failure, 44*(1), 37-38.

Knight, S., Vernon, D. D., Fines, R. J., & Dean, N. P. (1999). Prehospital emergency care for children at school and nonschool-based locations. *Pediatrics, 103*(6), e81 (yes).

Kozma, C., & Mason, S. (2003). Survey of nursing and medical profile prior to deinstitutionalization of population with profound mental retardation. *Clinical Nursing Research, 12*(1), 8-22.

Landwirth, J. (1993). Ethical issues in pediatric and neonatal resuscitation. *Annals of Emergency Medicine, 22*(2, Pt. 2), 502-507.

Leung, A., Chang, D., & Cho, H. (1996). Constipation in children. *American Family Physician, 54*(2), 611-620.

Line, W. S., Hawkins, D. B., Kahlstrom, E. J., MacLaughlin, E.F., & Ensley, J. L. (1986). Raceotomy in infants and young children: The changing perspective 1970-1985. *Laryngoscope, 96,* 510-515.

Low, N. L., (1982). Seizure disorders in children. In J.A. Downey & N.L. Low (Eds.) *The child with disabling illness: Principles of rehabilitation (pp. 121-144). New York: Raven Press*

Maffeo, R. (1997). Helping families cope. *American Journal of Nursing, 97*(6), 36-39.

McClung, H. J., Boyne, L., & Heitlinger, L. (1995). Constipation and dietary fiber intake in children. *Pediatrics, 96,* 997-1000.

McLone, D. G., & Ito, J. (1998). *An introduction to spina bifida.* Chicago: Children's Memorial Hospital Spina Bifida Team.

Meyer, L. H., Peck, C.A., & Brown, L. (1991). *Critical issues in the lives of people with severe disabilities.* Baltimore: Paul H. Brookes.

Mott, S. R., Fazekas, N. F., & James, S. R. (1985). *Nursing care of children and families.* Menlo Park, CA: Addison-Wesley.

Nelson, L. J., & Nelson, R. M. (1992). Ethics and the provision of futile, harmful, or burdensome treatment to children. *Critical Care Medicine, 20,* 427-433.

Neville, B. G. R. (1997). Epilepsy in children. *British Medical Journal, 315,* 924-931.

O'Neill, N. (1998). Improving ventilation in children using bilevel positive airway pressure. *Pediatric Nursing, 24*(4), 377-381.

Orr, M. E. (1997). Nutrition. In P. A. Potter & A. G. Perry (Eds.), *Fundamentals of nursing: Concepts, process, and practice* (pp. 1089-1127). St. Louis, MO: Mosby.

ParasolEMT. (1998). http://www.parasolemt.com.au.

Passy, V. (1986). Passy-Muir tracheosotmy speaking valve. *Otolaryngology and Head and Neck Surgery, 95,* 247-248.

Perlman, S. P. (1997). Putting teeth into oral health care: Good care of oral hygiene begins at home. *Exceptional Parent, 27*(8), 32-35.

Pittel, D. (2001). Improving adherence to hand hygiene: A multidisciplinary approach. *Emerging Infectious Diseases, 7*(2), 234-240.

Porter, S., Haynie, M., Bierle, T., Caldwell, T. H., & Palfrey, J. S. (1997). *Children and youth assisted by medical technology in educational settings: Guidelines for care.* Baltimore: Paul H. Brookes.

Potter, P. A., & Perry, A. G. (2001). *Fundamentals of nursing* (5th ed.). St. Louis, MO: Mosby.

Rempel, G. R., Colwell, S. O., & Nelson, R. P. (1988). Growth in children with cerebral palsy fed via gastrostomy. *Pediatrics, 82,* 857-862.

Sacco, M. (1995). Four-step multidisciplinary approach to wound management pays off. *The Brown University Long-Term Quality Letter, 7*(5), 1-2.

Sachs, G. A., Miles, S. H., & Levin, R. A. (1991). Limiting resuscitation: Emerging policy in the emergency medical system. *Annals of Internal Medicine, 114,* 151-154.

Sheets, A. H., & Blum, M. S. (1998). Medication administration in schools: The Massachusetts experience. *Journal of School Health, 68*(3), 94-98.

Shaddix, T. (1986). *Meal planning for the childhood years: Nutritional care for the child with developmental disabilities.* Birmingham, NY: United Cerebral Palsy of Greater Birmingham.

Singhi, P., Jagirdar, S., Khandelwal, N., & Malhi, P. (2003). Epilepsy in children with cerebral palsy. *Journal of Child Neurology, 18*(3), 174-179.

Snell, M. E., Lewis, A. P., & Houghton, A. (1989). Acquisition and maintenance of toothbrushing skills by students with cerebral palsy and mental retardation. *Journal of the Association for Persons with Severe Handicaps, 14*(3), 216-226.

Sommers, M. S. (1992). The shattering consequences of CPR: How to assess and prevent complications. *Nursing, 22*(7), 34-41.

Statistical Resources Branch, Division of Vital Statistics. (1981). *Final mortality statistics.* Hyattsville, MD: Author.

Students with chronic illnesses: Guidance for families, schools, and students. (2003). *Journal of School Health, 73*(4), 131-132. Available at: http://www.nhlbl.nih.gov/health/public/lung/asthma/guidfam.pdf.

Sullivan-Bolyai, S., Swanson, M., & Shurtleff, D. B. (1984). Toilet training the child with neurogenic impairment of bowel and bladder function. *Issues in Comprehensive Pediatric Nursing, 7*(1), 33-43.

Tatter, S.B., Owen, C., & Kenyon, L. (1998, June 2). Hydrocephalus Associaiton Homepage. (online). Available: http://neurosurgery.mgh.harvard.edu

Taylor, M. (1990). Clean intermittent catheterization. In J. C. Graff, M. M. Ault, D. Guess, M. Taylor, & B. Thompson (Eds.), *Health care for students with disabilities: An illustrated medical guide for the classroom* (pp. 241-252). Baltimore: Paul H. Brookes.

Thomas, C. L. (1985). *Taber's encyclopedic medical dictionary.* Philadelphia: F.A. Davis.

U.S. Department of Health and Human Services. (2000). *Oral health in America: A report of the surgeon general.* Washington, DC: Author.

Vigneux, A., & Hunsberger, M. (1994). Altered genitourinary/renal function. In C. L. Betz, M. M. Hunsberger, & S. Wright (Eds.), *Family-centered nursing care of children* (2nd ed., pp. 1516-1517). Philadelphia: W. B. Saunders.

Vitello, S. J. (1986). The Tatro case: Who gets what and why. *Exceptional Children, 52*(4), 353-356.

Walker, D. K. & Jacobs, F. H. (1984, Winter). Chronically ill children in school. *Peabody Journal of Education 61*(2), 28-76.

Wetmore, R. F., Handler, S. D., & Postic, W. P. (1982). Pedidatric tracheosotmy: Experience during the past decade. *Annals of Otology, Rhinology, and Laryngology, 96,* 628-632.

Williams, J., Grant, M., Jackson, M., Shema, S., Sharp, G., Griebel, M., et al. (1996). Behavior descriptors that differentiate between seizure and nonseizure events in a pediatric population. *Clinical Pediatrics, 35*(5), 243-250.

Wilson, S., Smith, G., Preisch, J., & Casamassimo, P. (1997). Nontraumatic dental emergencies in a pediatric emergency department. *Clinical Pediatrics, 36*(6), 333-338.

Woelk, C. G. (1986). The mentally retarded child and his family. In G. M. Scipien, M. U. Barnard, M. A. Chard, & P. J. Phillips (Eds.), *Comprehensive pediatric nursing* (pp. 639-666). New York: McGraw-Hill.

Wong, D. L., & Hess, C. S. (2000). *Wound and Whaley's clinical manual of pediatric nursing.* St. Louis, MO: Mosby.

Wong, D. L., & Hockenberry, M. J. (2003). *Nursing care of infants and children.* St. Louis, MO: Mosby.

Young, K. D., & Seidel, J. S. (1999). Pediatric cardiopulmonary resuscitation: A collective review. *Annals of Emergency Medicine, 33,* 195-204.

Younger, S. J. (1992). A physician/ethicist responds: A student's rights are not so simple. (Case presentation and three commentaries in response to the question: Should a school honor a student's DNR order?) *Kennedy Institute of Ethics Journal, 2*(1), 13-19.

8

Addressing Motor Disabilities

Philippa H. Campbell

Quality programs for individuals with motor disabilities include both instructional programs and physical management routines. Instructional programs work to develop specific movements for use in performing functional outcomes in communication, mobility, socialization, work, and learning. For example, teaching an individual to stand and move with assistance from a chair to a toilet, a sofa, or the floor requires an instructional program. However, individuals with motor disabilities also require conscientious management of their physical needs while in their home, school, work, and community environments. Lifting, carrying, positioning, feeding, toileting, dressing, and other similar routines must be managed when a person is not able to do the routine independently or may not be independent in all settings. Physical management routines allow adults (or peers) to use therapeutic procedures for the muscles, bones, and joints and compensate for overall motor limitations that may be present. Lifting a child from an adaptive chair can be done in ways that promote relaxation or in ways that make a child stiff,

uncomfortable, or fearful. A child may sit comfortably in an adaptive chair or may sit uncomfortably with poor positioning in an ill-fitting chair. Occupational therapists and physical therapists, together with family members, teachers, and others, can ensure that the easiest and most efficient ways are used to manage physical care needs in all settings. How students' needs are addressed depend on their age and size, the degree and type of motor disability, the setting, and the person who will be carrying out the routine. In addition to the team, there are many useful Internet resources, such as the Website for the National Academy of Cerebral Palsy and Developmental Disabilities (**http://www.aacpdm.org**) or United Cerebral Palsy Associations (**http://www.ucpa.org**). An Internet search through Google.com yielded over 1 million sites providing information about children with motor disabilities.

This chapter provides an overview of the guidelines used to accommodate the physical care needs of individuals with motor disabilities so that they will be able to participate as fully as possible in activities in

291

everyday settings. Two children, Susan, a 4-year-old preschooler, and Mackenzie, a high school freshman, are described here and used as examples to illustrate the ways in which general handling and care routines are individualized for specific children and circumstances.

 Susan

At age 6, Susan, who has been diagnosed as having cerebral palsy with spastic quadriplegia, remains dependent on caregivers for all her care. Susan likes a lot of activities that other kindergartners enjoy, such as being read stories, making art projects, and playing with toys. Susan might like to be as independent as other children, but severe stiffness in her arms and legs prevents such independence. Susan needs extensive assistance while eating, dressing, and bathing as well as when she is lifted and carried from place to place. Susan attends kindergarten and, when her mother is working, is cared for in a community day care center. At school and the child care center, Susan receives special education and therapy services through her local school district. These specialists help the educational and child care program staff and Susan's family manage her care and maximize her participation.

Much of the assistance provided to small children by adults in physical management routines will be necessary for Susan throughout her life. However, over time and with the help of her family and team members, Susan will learn to take part in daily care routines and to perform other routines independently. For example, Susan participates in dressing and bathing, and her mother, teacher, and the child care workers are helping Susan learn to eat without assistance. The team's goal is to use resources and methods to manage Susan's physical care routines, help her participate fully in activities and routines, and promote her ability to become as independent as possible.

 Mackenzie

Mackenzie has been receiving special education and a variety of related services for the past 14 years. "Mac" was diagnosed with cerebral palsy at 6 months and began receiving early intervention services shortly thereafter. Now 15 years old, she is a veteran of numerous orthopedic surgeries, and just last year, a selective dorsal rhizotomy surgery was done to help lower the muscle tone in her legs. The surgery improved the ease with which Mac's care needs can be addressed and allowed her to stand with considerable support and assistance.

Mac attends her local high school, where she is enrolled in many classes with her peers. She also participates in other classes to learn community skills, such as riding public transportation and ordering food in a restaurant. Her high school peers have grown up with Mac, who has attended regular schools since kindergarten, and many of them are sensitive to her needs. One of her friends assists her during lunchtime each day in the cafeteria. Another spends time with her during swimming. A paraeducator has been assigned to work with Mac and other students with special needs. The paraeducator assists "Mac" in the bathroom and in moving her from one piece of equipment to another. The paraeducator follows team recommendations and helps by making special adaptations and modifying materials so that Mac can do her schoolwork with her peers. Mac is able to get around the school independently using a power chair. She communicates her wants and needs with a communication device and uses a computer with a switch to participate in her classes. Mac receives occupational, physical, and speech language therapy. Her team, which includes her teacher, parents, therapists, and lots of friends, recognizes her many strengths and has established individualized educational program (IEP) goals that will enable her to be as independent as possible on graduation.

Key Concepts in Understanding Motor Disability

Most types of pediatric physical disability are identified during infancy or early childhood years. Children with the most severe physical disabilities are likely to be diagnosed at or shortly after birth, while those with mild physical disabilities or those with some forms of genetically based physical limitations may not be identified until their toddler or preschool years or sometimes later in school. Physical disability also may be the result of accident or injury that may occur at any time during childhood; it may be the only disability the child has or may be accompanied by other disorders, such as vision or hearing impairment, intellectual disability, or other types of learning disorders (see Batshaw, 2002). As a result of the physical or combined disability, children may have difficulties with physical development, learning, or performance.

Susan has a physical disability that is influencing her participation during many kindergarten activities (art, motor, snack time, and transitions) as well as her performance of self-care routines and communication.

Movement Abilities, Adaptation, and Participation

Motor disability may range from severe to mild and may involve the whole body (i.e., arms, legs, head, trunk) or only parts of the body (e.g., one side or both legs). When the motor disability is severe, the whole body is more likely to be involved than when the disability is mild or moderate (Palisano et al., 1997). When motor disability is mild to moderate, there is a greater chance that children will learn to perform the same motor skills that typically developing children master during their early years. Children with mild to moderate disability will learn basic gross motor skills, such as sitting, crawling, and walking, although they may look different or be less coordinated than children without motor disability or may achieve skills at a later time than typical children. Children with severe motor disability may never be able to perform these basic skills because the degree of motor impairment may prevent them from doing so. Severe motor disability may not just affect gross motor skills like mobility but may also influence whether a child is able to learn to eat independently, play with toys, hold a pencil, manage clothing, or use the bathroom independently. Severe motor disability impacts performance in many different areas (Dormans & Pellegrino, 1998).

Throughout the childhood years, whether at home, in school, or in community settings, participation in typical activities and routines must be promoted no matter how severe the motor disability. *Activities* include all the academic, leisure, and social events that occur for students of a particular age and grade level during and after school; *routines* are more basic events often associated with completing basic self-care tasks and include the assistance of others that is needed to manage a routine (e.g., lifting, helping the student to use the bathroom, helping someone eat). When a motor disability limits performance of skills, participation in typical settings is ensured through accommodations, adaptations, assistive technology, or other strategies. The terms *accommodation* and *adaptation* are often used interchangeably, but both terms relate to physical accessibility, or program modifications made to promote access and participation. *Accessibility* results from environmental adaptations (or modifications) that allow an individual with a disability to enter into and use a particular setting. Designing a bathroom with wider doors, grab bars, a higher toilet, special water spigots, or other modifications makes it possible for people with physical disabilities to go into and use the bathroom facilities. Program adaptations allow an individual with a disability to participate in the activities and routines of a particular environment or setting by changing the ways in which information is presented. A museum that provides exhibit information in Braille has made program modifications to allow people with visual disabilities to enjoy exhibits. A teacher who tapes a paper to the desk of a student with a physical disability so that the student may still write, draw, or paint on the paper has adapted the activity for the student. Simple adaptations such as a picture board that a student may use communicate by pointing to pictures or placing a nonslip mat under a plate so it won't move during eating are considered within the definition of assistive technology or may simply be seen as adaptations. *Assistive technology* includes a variety of items, ranging from items that are readily available and used by people with or without disabilities to those that have been developed specifically for use by individuals with disabilities. Simple adaptations of readily available items are often classified as "low tech," while those that are specific to individuals with disabilities are defined as "high tech" (Best, Bigge, & Heller, 2004; Campbell & Wilcox, 2004; Mistrett, 2001). Assistive technology can help individuals perform specific skills in a different way than is typically done. Communication devices, referred to as Alternative and Augmentative Communication devices (AAC), enable students who cannot speak to communicate using another means. The device may be as simple as pictures or symbols pasted onto cardboard (an example of a low-tech assistive device) or as complicated as a computerized device that both speaks and writes (an example of a high-tech device). Accommodations, adaptations, and assistive technology all enable children with disabilities to fully participate in typical home, school, and community activities. For example, a child with a physical disability who is unable to run may still be able to participate in a community baseball program (such as Little League) by using an adaptation to hit the ball or by "running" bases by moving a wheelchair.

> *Mac is improving her skills in using her power wheelchair during times when ninth graders change classes. She and another student leave class a little bit earlier than the others so that Mac has more time to get to the next class. Her student helper walks along with her and provides assistance when she has difficulty negotiating through doorways or steering around obstacles in the halls.*

When motor disability is severe and limits performance of self-care skills, the basic needs of an individual must be managed in the environments or settings where the person spends time (Campbell, 1995). For a child to participate in baseball, strategies for managing eating, toileting, and other care needs during the baseball game and in the settings where baseball takes place must be identified. Often such care falls on parents, other family members, or hired personal care assistants; a child may be permitted to participate only with family members or a personal care assistant present. There are many reasons why children may be required to participate only if adults are present, and these include perceived safety, liability and risk management, and views that the child needs more assistance than may actually be the case. A better alternative involves good planning and instruction of people who spend time with an individual in a particular setting. For example, the places where baseball takes place may be assessed to determine the accommodations and adaptations necessary for an individual's eating, drinking, and toileting needs to be met. People who are at the community games, such as the coaches or perhaps an older high school student who wishes to volunteer or, depending on age and the situation, the friends and peers of the child, may be taught the best ways of addressing individual needs during baseball games and practice. Assisting in determining strategies for managing care needs is generally the role of the occupational therapist (or sometimes the physical therapist), but family members and others who are familiar with the child may also be knowledgeable about easy and effective strategies.

Movement Form and Function

Most motor disabilities start with an impairment in the brain or in the nerves, muscles, or joints of the body. When these impairments are present before or in the early period immediately after a child's birth, they may affect the development of the motor (or other) skills that occur so naturally during most children's early years and lead to lifelong motor disabilities.

> *Susan's motor disability affects not just her acquisition of motor skills, such as walking, but also speaking, eating, and toileting. Her limited skill performance, in turn, influences the ways that she participates in activities and routines at home, at school, and in the community.*

Most motor disabilities are not static; that is, they do not remain the same throughout an individual's lifetime. Some children may acquire motor skills later than would be expected for most children. A child, for example, may learn to walk at age 5 rather than at age 1, which would be more typical. By the time that student has reached adulthood, walking may no longer be possible or preferred. The individual may have learned other more efficient and less taxing ways of getting around, such as using a power chair.

Every motor skill has both a form (the pattern and coordination of the movement, the way a person moves) and a function (the purpose of the movement). The purpose (function) of walking is to enable a person to get around in the environment, to go from place to place. The form of walking differs based on individual circumstances. People may walk with their legs held far apart or close together, on their toes, with their knees held together, or using many other patterns. Children with motor disabilities may learn a motor skill but may use a different form or pattern to accomplish the same purpose or function. For example, the function of walking may be achieved by propelling a wheelchair or by using a power chair. Children with motor disabilities may move from place to place on their hands and knees or by using a walker. They may use a walker in their homes or classrooms but may use a wheelchair at the shopping center or when outside on the playground. The more severe the motor disability, the more likely a child will use different rather than typical ways of accomplishing motor functions. These different ways of accomplishing motor functions are likely to depend on adaptations including assistive technology devices. If a child's hands are fisted and difficult to open for grasp and release, an adapted holder may help the child to hold objects in order to write, paint, or draw. However, creative expression, a function of writing, drawing, and painting, may be accomplished using a computer with a mouse and appropriate software. Children do not necessarily use assistive technology devices naturally or without instruction. Most often, the adaptations and assistive technology devices that help children accomplish basic motor functions, such as mobility, communication, or self-care skills, must be collaboratively taught by occupational and physical therapists, speech and language pathologists, teachers, family members, and others who are involved with the child. Look at Figures 8–1 and 8–2 and read the vignette about Susan that follows.

Susan's therapists worked with her family to purchase a gait trainer that allows her to help her dad wash the family car. When Susan was an infant, she learned how to put weight on her legs by using a stander while watching videotapes with her brother and sister.

Opportunities for people with motor disabilities to participate in activities and routines may be limited when the people in those settings do not *expect* participation. Susan's father expected her to help wash the car and "created" opportunities for her to help. When adults, children's siblings, or peers do not "create" opportunities, the child with a disability may learn that nothing is expected, that it is better to be "helpless" (Seligman, 1975). On the other hand, when expectations and circumstances provide insurmountable challenges, the person may not be able to be successful and may have low self-esteem or an attitude of never being able to be "right" (Kunc, 1996). By using adaptations and assistive technology devices, a "bridge" is created between a child's abilities and the challenges of the environment that may result in the "just right" challenge where children can be successful. The goal is for the student to use movement as functionally as possible even if the form is different from that used by typical peers. Adaptations and assistive technology are types of intervention that can facilitate successful participation.

FIGURE 8–1
When positioned in a gait trainer, Susan is able to help her dad wash the car.

FIGURE 8–2

When Susan was an infant, she learned how to bear weight on her legs by being positioned in a stander.

The Importance of Weight Shifting to Movement Abilities

Posture describes the position of the body—sitting, standing, on hands and knees, lying down. *Alignment* describes the position of the body in relationship to physical planes of space. For example, a person who is sitting in a chair and leaning backward against the back of the chair is in a sitting posture but is out of alignment. An aligned sitting posture in a chair occurs when the person sits straight, with the feet on the floor and the hips and knees bent at right (or 90°) angles. It is important to observe alignment when motor disability is present because the way in which the body is out of alignment is defined by the muscle tone differences, the acquired secondary motor disabilities, and the compensations that are being used to remain upright against gravity or comfortable in a position. Movement results when (a) the body is moved within the same posture, such as when a person reaches down to the floor but remains in sitting or leans forward in sitting to reach an object that is past arm's length, or (b) when the body is moved through space,

such as in rolling, crawling, walking, running, ice skating, or climbing steps.

All gross motor movements are made up of combinations of weight shifts of the body in different planes of space. Weight-bearing surfaces cannot move. To lean forward in sitting, the weight of the body must be shifted forward. To walk, body weight must be shifted from side to side and frontward. When weight is shifted, the weight of the body comes off of one part, resulting in an unweighting that allows movement of an extremity or body part that is not weight bearing. When a person is standing, for example, the weight of the body is on both feet. The weight has to be shifted off of one leg to allow the unweighted leg to move. The unweighted leg moves forward in front of the body, and then the weight has to be shifted forward onto that leg so that the back leg may be unweighted and move forward, resulting in walking.

Motor skills, such as walking, reaching, or getting into and out of positions, are made up of weight shifts. Particular weight shifts may be difficult for individuals with motor disabilities. A student with spasticity in the legs may have her pelvis and hips pulled backward by the spasticity and tightness in the hip or leg muscles and, therefore, may have difficulty shifting weight forward over the legs, a weight shift that is needed to stand up or be easily assisted into standing.

Spasticity in the hip and leg muscles was one of the problems that Mac had before her surgery, and spasticity is also an emerging issue with Susan, even though she is still young. Susan's therapists work to prevent the development of secondary disabilities in Susan's hips and promote opportunities for her to practice shifting her weight forward.

Weight shifts that are important for a child to learn and use should be incorporated into all routines and activities, including physical management routines.

For Susan, the desired motor skill of an anterior-to-posterior weight shift (i.e., moving the body forward and backward at the hips, such as in leaning forward or backward when sitting) was incorporated into as many physical management routines as possible so that, for example, when Susan was being moved from a chair, the person lifting her created an opportunity for her to practice the anterior-to-posterior weight shift by encouraging her to lean forward before lifting her. Susan needs to be lifted to be positioned in different types of equipment during kindergarten. When she comes to school in the morning in her wheelchair, her kindergarten teacher makes sure that Susan helps by leaning forward before she lifts her out the chair to position her on the floor for morning circle.

Barriers to Skilled Movement

The severity of the motor disability is dependent not just on the neurological or neuromuscular impairment but also on the interaction between the limitations of the impairment and environmental challenges, circumstances, and expectations across the life span of the individual (Campbell, 1997). The degree of muscle tone and secondary motor disabilities are two barriers to performing skilled movement patterns (Stamer, 2000), while limited opportunity for learning and practice is another barrier (Larin, 2000).

Muscle Tone

Many individuals have motor disabilities that are related to atypical muscle tone. *Muscle tone* is a measure of the tension in individual muscles (or muscle groups). The term *postural tone* is also used to describe the degree of tension in muscles throughout the body. Normal postural tone provides sufficient tension in the muscles to hold the body up against gravity and to support coordinated movements into and away from gravity. Sufficient postural tone allows a variety of movements, such as reaching, which requires that the arm be held up against the influences of gravity, or rolling from the side onto the back, which requires controlled movement into gravity. Many functional movements are combinations of antigravity (away from gravity) and with-gravity (or into gravity) movement. Standing up from a chair requires movement into gravity to lean forward and away from gravity to put weight on the feet and stand up.

Some individuals with motor disabilities have *hypotonia*, or too little postural tone. This means that they may have difficulty with antigravity postures, such as sitting, or with antigravity movements, such as are required to get from sitting to standing. Other motor disabilities involve too much tone, either in particular muscle groups (such as those in the legs) or throughout the body. The terms *hypertonia* and *spasticity* are used to describe the stiffness that results when the muscles have too much tension. Often, the body or an extremity (e.g., the arms, legs, or head) are pulled by the spasticity into the opposite direction of where the movement should occur. A student who is sitting and who has significant spasticity in the arms may have the arms pulled backward behind the trunk by the spasticity rather than having the arms forward in front of the trunk, a position from which it would be possible to reach. Combinations of atypical muscle tone are also possible. For example, muscle tone may be low in the head and trunk (hypotonic) and high in the arms and legs (hypertonic or spastic).

Muscle tone, particularly hypertonia, is influenced not just by the original brain impairment but also by environmental conditions, which may change tone to sudden stiffness throughout the body or in one or more extremities. An unexpected loud noise, for example, may cause a student to become even more spastic. Picking a student up from the floor without warning, for example, or using inappropriate techniques may activate spasticity (and make the motor disability even more difficult to manage). By contrast, appropriate physical management routines may maintain the student's muscle tone within more appropriate ranges, making the student more able to assist in the process and making the procedures safer and easier for the people supporting the student.

Secondary Motor Disabilities

A cycle illustrating the ways in which posture and movement may become more abnormal over time is illustrated in Figure 8-3. The cycle shows the process that occurs when infants are born with abnormal tone or when atypical muscle tone is acquired through brain damage from accident or injury. Muscle tone, particularly in the head and trunk, is hypotonic for a majority of infants who are born very prematurely. Other infants with motor conditions may also have low tone in the head and trunk during their early development. Over time, many of these infants develop increased tone in the extremities and, to a lesser extent, in the head and trunk so that by school age they may demonstrate muscle tone that is described as hypertonic or spastic.

Various types of secondary motor disabilities, disabilities with which an infant was not born, can occur as a child gets older. The cycle of abnormal movement illustrates how children with abnormal muscle tone develop these secondary motor disabilities over time. First, reliance on body adjustments or on the arms to support antigravity postures may promote use of compensatory movement patterns, which in turn lead to practice of poorly coordinated movement patterns, which in turn may create secondary physical changes in the muscles and joint structures, which in turn may result in orthopedic deformities, which induce further development of compensatory patterns, secondary physical changes, and perhaps more orthopedic deformities. By the time many children with motor disabilities reach school age, secondary motor disabilities and orthopedic deformities have been added to the original motor disability that was present during their infant and early childhood years.

Secondary Physical Changes *Secondary disabilities* include physical limitations in range of movement in the joints so that, for example, a child may not be able to fully straighten the arms. Limited range of movement may be related to another secondary disability that is present with spasticity, namely, muscle tightness. Tight muscles are those that do not easily stretch out to their full length, thereby maintaining a joint in limited range of motion. For example, a student who acquires tightness and shortening in the muscles

FIGURE 8–3
Cycle of the Development of Abnormal Movement. This diagram illustrates the ways in which posture and movement develop abnormally over time. Deviations in postural tone result in postural adjustments that compensate for the inability of tone to hold the body upright against gravity. These adjustments, in turn, influence the kinds of movements that are possible.

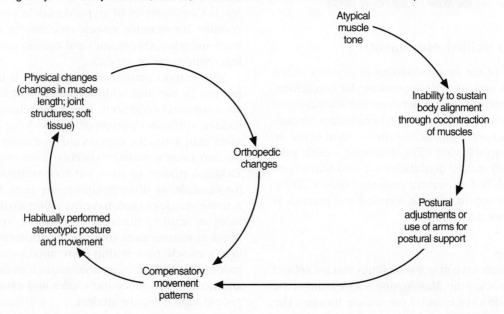

of the hips and knees so that they are in a bent position most of the time (as happens when children are positioned too often in sitting) may be unable, as an adolescent or adult, to straighten the hips and knees to stand, making it necessary for two people to move the student from a chair to the toilet, onto a school bus, into a car, or into any other position. Some children have muscle tightness in the muscles on the inside of their legs that keeps their legs tightly together or sometimes even with one leg crossing over the other. It may be difficult for them or another person to move their legs widely apart or to turn their legs outward. Severe muscle tightness and limited range of motion may result in orthopedic changes. For example, children's leg bones may become dislocated from the pelvic bone when muscle shortening and tightness in the legs is severe. Muscles may also become overlengthened or overstretched. A child whose upper back is rounded may have muscle tightness in the shoulder muscles that pull the shoulders forward, thereby overlengthening the upper back muscles. Muscle weakness is another type of secondary disability that may develop from limited use of certain muscle groups. Muscle weakness may be associated both with spasticity or with low muscle tone. Children with spasticity and underlying muscle weakness may still be unable to move well even after spasticity is reduced.

Compensatory Movement Most infants and young children are intrinsically motivated to move; therefore, children with disabilities move in whatever ways are possible for them. Some of these ways of moving compensate for basic physical limitations. A common example among children with tightness in the leg muscles is that their knees are bent when sitting on the floor (rather than sitting with the legs straight out), or, if children have arm movement, they may support their bodies with their arms (Figure 8–4a) or pull forward at the shoulders, as is illustrated in Figure 8–4b. Either of these floor sitting positions compensates for shortness or tightness in the leg muscles (in particular, hamstring muscles). Another way of compensating is to use the arms to accomplish what the body muscles are unable to do. For example, young children may sit on the floor only when supporting themselves with their arms to compensate for the inability of the trunk muscles to maintain the body upright without arm support (Figure 8–4c).

While each of the children in Figure 8–4 is achieving some degree of independent floor sitting, they are doing so at high physical cost. The long-term negative outcomes of each child achieving sitting may be forgotten when an immediate focus is on gross motor development or skill performance. The fact that a child has accomplished something independently should not outweigh concern about the ways in which this independence has been achieved. The child in Figure 8–4a shows increased tone (or spasticity) in the head and arms. This high tone is stiffening the top of the body so that the child is able to stay upright against gravity with the support of the adult. The child is not in alignment (or truly upright) against gravity but is tilted forward because of lack of sufficient extensor tone in the trunk. This extensor tone would straighten the trunk so that she was sitting on her hips (rather than forward of her hips, as is the case in the illustration). The preschooler in Figure 8–4b is able to floor sit without adult assistance but does so with the upper back rounded forward, the head turtled or sunk into the shoulders, and the arms pulled forward to his chest.

The child in Figure 8–4c compensates with arms that are held out and away from the body for balance and stability. The sitting patterns of each of these children, while different from each other, all rely on adjustments of the body as well as use of the arms to compensate for low tone in the head and trunk. None of the children are upright and in alignment against gravity, although all of them are sitting. While these compensations make sitting possible, they also are associated with (a) increased muscle tone, so that the children are using spasticity to attain sitting; (b) posture that is not aligned against gravity; and (c) reliance on use of the arms to hold the body upright (making the arms unavailable for functional activity, such as playing with toys or doing other things that would typically be done in a sitting position). Most children do not sit as an end in itself. Rather, they sit so that they can play with objects, watch what is going on around them, or move from sitting into another position, such as crawling, standing, or walking. These children with motor disabilities are able to sit but are not able to sit functionally.

Preventing Secondary Motor Disabilities A goal of therapeutic intervention is to prevent or limit the development of spasticity and secondary disabilities. From infancy, therapists work to maintain range of motion and muscle strength while teaching children to move without using spasticity. This is accomplished through proper positioning, therapeutic techniques such as active and passive range of motion, resistive

FIGURE 8–4
Patterns of Muscle Tone and Biomechanical Adjustments of Body Parts

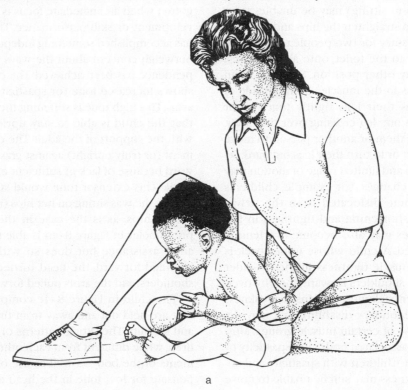

a

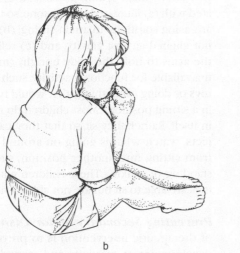

b

c

exercise, or movement facilitation and motor learning–based approaches (Bly, 2000; Stamer, 2000). Even with the best attempts, secondary disabilities may be difficult to prevent. Thus, older children are likely to have movement that is limited by the primary disability as well as by the secondary disabilities that have developed over time.

Even though Mac has received services since infancy, secondary disabilities were acquired. The amount of spasticity in her legs prevented her from being transferred easily from one position to another, so a recent surgical procedure has decreased the spasticity in her legs and allows her the possibility of learning to stand supported for a few seconds — long enough to be moved from one position to another. Even though the surgery has reduced the spasticity, Mac needs to practice using her legs for supported standing so that she can develop muscle strength and learn to stand as a part of moving from one position to another.

Limited Opportunity for Learning and Practice

Sufficient opportunity to perform motor skills within the situations in which they are functionally used is necessary so that children have opportunities to learn and practice movement. This means that a particular motor skill must be practiced often enough to become firmly established as "automatic." When a child is first learning to go up and down steps, for example, the required movements are thought out and made carefully and slowly. As the child goes up and down steps again and again, greater skill and precision result from the practice of repeating these movements. After much practice, going up and down steps becomes automatic: a motor skill that is performed without even thinking. Many functional motor skills become automatic or are performed without conscious thought: walking, drinking from a glass, feeding oneself, riding a bike, playing volleyball, reaching for objects, washing dishes, or communicating with signs.

Individuals with motor disabilities can best learn new skills through practice. Opportunities for practice are provided by creating situations throughout the day where a child performs a specific motor skill. These practice opportunities may be incorporated into both physical management routines and participation in typical classroom activities. A child may be required, for example, to lift the arms up toward the adult before being picked up from the floor, before the tray on the wheelchair is put on or taken off, or before being moved out of a chair. By incorporating movement of the arms into many physical routines, an individual not only partially participates in the care routine but also uses the same motor skill (in this case, lifting the arms up) across routines, thereby practicing this movement numerous times throughout the day.

Susan's kindergarten teacher has created many additional practice opportunities. For example, she has all the children lift their arms up many times during morning circle song, has incorporated this movement into the actions that children perform when listening to stories, and requires Susan to lift her arms up before putting on or taking off the smock she wears during art and snack. These natural opportunities for Susan to use her arms allow her to learn and practice functional arm use across a variety of situations. Because Susan's caregivers, teachers, and therapists all incorporate this arm movement into everything they do with Susan, more than 100 opportunities a day to practice lifting her arms are provided! This approach means she will learn to lift her arms up more quickly than if she practiced only during therapy sessions, and she is less likely to develop muscle tightness and secondary disabilities in her arms and shoulders.

Getting Help from Therapists and Other Specialists: Working as a Team

There are people from many different disciplines who have specialized knowledge that may be helpful in planning how physical management routines will be implemented or in thinking of ways to promote participation in home, school, and community activities and routines. Helpful ideas may come from occupational and physical therapists, speech and language pathologists, assistive device specialists, and professionals from other disciplines, such as rehabilitation engineers, nurses, or respiratory therapists.

Susan's older brother Steven plays soccer in a community league. Susan has attended these games since she was an infant and may want to participate when she is old enough for the league. Though Susan will never run or kick a ball, there may be ways that she can participate in sports through the community league. Another sport may be easier to adapt for Susan's physical participation. For example, in baseball, she may be able to attempt hitting the baseball by using a T-ball support. Or she may be able to be on the swim team, where adaptations will allow her to stay afloat and move her arms and legs. At the least, if sufficient adaptations cannot be made to support her physical participation, she might be the scorekeeper, equipment manager, or timekeeper or participate on the team in some way other than by playing the actual sport. Promoting her participation in a sports activity can occur when specialists team with families and coaches to promote participation in whatever ways are possible.

The activities that a particular person participates in are linked directly to settings in neighborhoods and communities where the individual spends time. When children are young, those activities are influenced by

decisions and preferences of their families as well as by opportunity. Children who attend typical child care, preschool, or general education programs or adults who work in typical work settings have more opportunities for a wider range of experiences and social contacts than do children whose education is based in special settings or individuals who are employed in sheltered workshops. Promoting participation in activities that take place in everyday settings results from collaboration among the individual, the family, specialists, and the people associated with the particular activity or setting.

Susan wants to swim in the swimming program with her brother and sister in her neighborhood recreation center. For this to happen easily, collaboration must occur among the swimming instructor, Susan's family, and the specialists. The outcome of the collaboration is not to increase Susan's motor skills, necessarily, but to allow her to benefit (including social

---

  ### Box 8–1 Integrated Therapy

Until recently, most therapy services have been provided to students *directly*; that is, therapists work one on one with students in their classrooms, homes, or in other environments. In many instances, therapists establish their own goals (e.g., physical therapy goals) that may or may not be related to those established by a student's teacher or another therapist and then work with students individually or in small groups to provide the types of interventions that will assist the student to achieve therapy goals. More recently, therapists have begun to provide services to students by consulting or collaborating with individuals who spend the most time with a child. Therapists consult and collaborate with teachers, family members, child care providers, and others to (a) promote a student's participation in home, school, and community settings and (b) show others how to work on a child's or student's goals within these natural contexts.

Integrated therapy is a term that has gained increasing popularity as a way of describing an approach to providing therapy services for infants, toddlers, and students of all ages. Integrated therapy does not describe a particular model for providing therapy services but is a general term used to describe a variety of approaches, most of which share the following features:

- One set of functional goals are outlined on the IFSP or IEP, and various services or disciplines contribute their unique expertise and perspective to teaching and learning.
- Services are provided within the context of activities and routines that occur in various home, school, or community settings; that is, students are not removed from typical activities to receive therapy services.
- All the professionals in disciplines associated with a child's or student's needs collaborate together and with the family to determine priorities, plan and implement interventions, and monitor progress.

Other terms besides integrated therapy may be used to describe approaches with similar components, including *transdisciplinary, consultative,* or *collaborative teaming* (Orelove, Sobsey, & Silberman, 2004). Another term that is sometimes used is *coaching*, which emphasizes a therapist's role in helping other individuals, such as families or teachers, work effectively with students. Students who receive therapy services in an integrated manner appear to make greater gains in skill learning and have better skill generalization than do students whose therapy is provided totally through more traditional direct, one-on-one therapy in which services are provided outside of natural contexts (Giangreco, 1986). The important point is not what an approach is labeled but rather that people collaborate and solve problems together so that individuals with motor disabilities may participate fully in life.

benefits) from being in the swimming program. Susan's participation will be facilitated through management routines for dressing, undressing, toileting, lifting, carrying, and positioning and potentially may require modifying the swimming setting or the typical swimming activities (see Box 8–1).

A Framework for Team Decision Making

Teams need a framework to guide decision making about children's participation and learning within the context of typical everyday activities and routines. Home, school, and community settings provide a context for specifically designed interventions. There are two general categories of intervention approaches that may be used with children with disabilities. One intervention approach relies on *accommodations and adaptations*, including assistive technology devices, for the purpose of making it possible for a student to participate in the activities and routines of home, school, and community settings as successfully and fully as possible. The second intervention approach is designed *to teach new skills and abilities* by embedding specially designed special education and therapy intervention strategies (or techniques) into existing activities and routines. Both of these intervention approaches are likely to be most successful when a "fit" is created between the intervention and the requirements of the setting. Traditional therapy methods, for example, were designed for use within clinical or specialized educational settings where one therapist is working with one child at a time. These methods do not necessarily adapt easily or well to typical contexts where adult-to-child ratios may be larger and where the focus in on the activity as a whole rather than on individual student goals.

A first goal for all specialists is to ensure that a child is fully included in the activities and routines that characterize typical settings (Udvari-Solner, Causton-Theoharis, & York-Barr, 2004). This goal is generally best achieved through the use of accommodation and adaptation interventions that may not result directly in a student's acquiring specific skills but that will allow successful participation in a particular activity or routine.

Susan's family enjoys and values sports. Each member of the family is involved in some sort of community sports activity, so it is logical that Susan's family would want to create opportunities for her to participate in

sporting activities. Susan is interested in sports because she has attended sporting activities with other family members, and she likes to go swimming. However, it is not necessarily a goal for Susan to learn to swim or to be able to participate in swimming in ways that other children her age do. However, knowing of the family's priority and Susan's interest in swimming, specialists can develop the adaptation interventions that will let Susan to participate in the community swim program with her family. Susan's therapists wanted her to learn to put her coat on independently, so they suggested that the kindergarten teacher use therapeutic techniques to help Susan put her arms into her coat sleeves before going out for recess and when leaving school. This approach did not work well within the kindergarten routine. Susan's teacher really did not have the time to focus only on Susan when so many children also needed help with their coats. Instead, Susan's mother purchased a poncho that could be put on easily by putting her head through the neck hole of the poncho. Having Susan wear a poncho rather than a coat was an adaptation that allowed her to participate successfully in a routine of getting ready to go outside.

A second goal is to use successful activities and routines of home, school, and community settings as contexts for individualized learning and practice. Routines or activities that are going well can provide a context into which specialized teaching or therapeutic strategies can be embedded.

One of Susan's goals was to reach forward. Opportunities for practice as well as therapeutic interventions were embedded into as many kindergarten activities and child care routines as possible. For example in her coat-on routine, once Susan was able to easily put her head through the hole of the poncho, her therapists showed her teacher how to use facilitation techniques to help Susan reach up and grasp the poncho and guide it over her head independently.

Specialists, families, and community program personnel can use the decision making framework in Figure 8–5 to aid in making decisions about the best ways to meaningfully include students with a disability into their school and community as well as to determine opportunities for addressing the individual's special learning and therapeutic needs. The process starts by identifying outcomes, which can be done by the student, family members, child care providers, peers and

FIGURE 8–5

This diagram provides a framework for making decisions about whether and when to embed motor learning into activities and routines. A first step is to find out about activities and routines that may not be going well so that the routine or activity itself can be improved through adaptations or other means. Routines and activities that are going well provide opportunities for learning and a context in which to embed motor learning strategies.

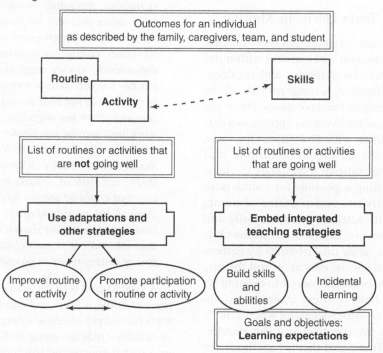

friends, teachers, or other people who spend time with the person. Person-centered planning processes such as the McGill Action Planning System, commonly known as MAPS (Vandercook, York, & Forest, 1989), or discussion with students and their family members also can help identify desired outcomes (refer to chapter 3 for more on MAPS). Outcomes are not necessarily written as goals but often represent a broader context or framework for specific goals. For example, when parents and children identify desired outcomes, they are likely to use the context of their family's values, roles, priorities, and concerns as a framework. Outcomes may be expressions of things they would like to change (e.g., "I wish I understood better what John is trying to tell me" or "I'd like be able to bathe Shawn more easily") or things they would like to do (e.g., "We go skiing a lot, and we want Stacey to be able to do this with us"). Outcomes generally fall into three categories. They may

relate to participation in activities (e.g., go skiing), to better management of routines (e.g., bathe more easily), or to learning particular skills (e.g., communicate more clearly). When professionals identify goals for students, they too use their experiences with children as a contextual framework. This perspective typically emphasizes skills that come from developmental tests or other types of evaluations they have used as a basis for understanding a child's needs. Professionals are more likely to identify outcomes and goals that are descriptive of skill learning (e.g., walk without support, eat with a spoon, communicate with peers), and if they use developmentally referenced tests as a primary way of identifying those goals, the skills may not necessarily be functional or necessary for a given student.

Mac was unable to hold a pencil or any writing instrument when she was younger and, therefore, was unable to independently do seat work required in kindergarten. Her therapists identified holding a pencil as a goal but then quickly revised this goal into a broader functional goal, namely, that Mac would access a computer using a switch device so that she could do written work independently. Like other children, Mac did not learn to use the computer just because she was given a computer and a switch device. The "best" switch had to be identified, and Mac needed to learn to activate the switch and use different types of software and to be given practice opportunities. As she got older, different types of software were needed, and, like others, she has needed instruction to use these new programs.

When Susan's family identified an outcome of participating in community swimming with family members, the school team working with Susan started by using the framework outlined in Figure 8-5 to solve problems regarding Susan's participation in swimming and to identify opportunities within swimming for her to learn and practice goals and objectives included on her IEP. They viewed the swimming program as a setting with various routines and activities. The first step in their problem-solving analysis was to talk with the swim program personnel to identify any activities and routines that were not going well. The second step was to use adaptation interventions (Figure 8-6) so that Susan could participate as fully as possible in all the swim program activities and routines. The third step was to identify activities and routines that were going well so that these could provide a context for Susan to learn specific skills. The fourth step was to decide which intervention techniques could be successfully embedded into these activities and routines so that Susan would have opportunities to learn and practice skills.

In Susan's swim program, the routine of getting the children undressed, in their suits, into the pool area, and into the pool was somewhat chaotic for everyone. The specialists who were working with Susan talked to the swim teacher and asked her to identify what was going well and not so well. The teacher thought that the swimming activities were going well but that the routine of getting into the pool was not going well. Susan's team then used the framework in Figure 8-6 to identify adaptation interventions to improve this routine and to promote Susan's participation.

FIGURE 8–6
Accommodation and Adaptation Framework. Accommodations and adaptations, including assistive technology devices, may be used to improve activities or routines that are not going well in classroom, school, home and community settings with the goals of (a) improving the overall activity or routine for all children who are participating and (b) promoting participation in the activity or routine of the person with a motor disability.

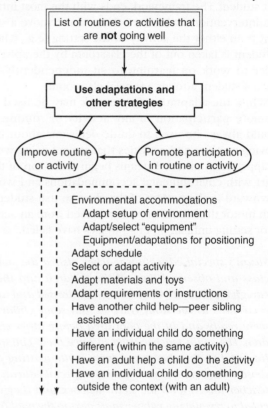

Adaptation Interventions to Promote Participation

The adaptation framework outlined in Figure 8-6 lists the types of accommodations and adaptations, including assistive technology, that can be designed to promote children's participation in any activity or routine (Campbell, 2004.) The framework begins with the least intrusive and generally easiest and least expensive interventions. These involve modifying the environment or setting where an activity takes place. For example, a student can be taught to negotiate around desks and other equipment in a classroom, or the classroom desks can be rearranged so that the student is able to

negotiate independently. Other adaptations involve selecting or modifying materials used in the activity or altering the activity requirements or its schedule. When
a student is provided with extra time to complete a
math project, for example, the schedule of the activity
has been modified. When a teacher provides a preschooler with easy-to-grasp crayon knobs, the materials necessary for art have been specially selected for
that student. The framework ends with the most intrusive interventions, which are those that remove a student from either the activity or the setting (e.g., when
a student is taken out of the classroom by therapist in
order to work on learning to sit independently or
when a student attends a special classroom).

While the adaptation framework may be used to
promote participation in any activity or routine, it
should always be used to guide decisions about improving routines and activities that are not going well.
To apply the framework, teams begin at the top of the
chart with environmental accommodations and work
downward to the bottom of the chart so that students
with motor disabilities are not removed from an activity or setting until all other strategies have failed.

*Susan's special education teacher visited the swim
class and observed that all the children and their
caregivers did not necessarily get undressed and into
their suits at the same time so that some children
were ready and in the pool area before other children. The swim teacher tried to have these children
line up but they became fidgety while waiting for
those who were not yet ready. The special education
teacher talked with the swim teacher, and they decided to try placing rubber mats next to the pool (environmental modification) so that each child would
have his or her own mat and would sit down next to
the pool when they were ready. In this way, children
were not milling around, they were using a familiar
routine (e.g., sit on a mat), and they could still splash
their feet in the water while waiting. The teachers
also decided to have Susan come early to allow
enough time for her to get into her swimsuit so that
she was ready at the same time as the other children
(adapting the schedule).*

Individuals with motor disabilities may be prevented from participating in a variety of community
programs when physical management needs are not
easily met. For example, any difficulty in getting Susan
undressed or dressed, managing her toileting needs, or

lifting, carrying, and positioning her in the pool area or
in the water may become obstacles to her participation in the swimming activity.

*Susan's mother or babysitter dresses and undresses
her in the locker room for the pool. The adult strad-
dles the bench and sits Susan on the end of the bench
between the adult's legs. By leaning forward, the
adult is able to control the position of Susan's hips
and pelvis, keeping them forward to prevent her legs
from stiffening. (If her legs became too spastic, she
would be difficult to control and might slip off the
bench.) In this position, the adult's hands are free to
move Susan's arms and legs, using facilitation techniques taught by the physical therapist and making
the activity of dressing or undressing one in which
specific therapeutic intervention methods are used to
promote practice of specific skills (e.g., reach forward, forward and backward weight shifts). After
Susan's clothes have been removed and she is in her
swimming suit, the adult places her arm under Susan's thighs and stands up, lifting Susan at the same
time and positioning her so she can be carried to the
swimming pool. Susan's undressing is going so well
that the therapist has suggested that Susan may be
able to move her own arms out of the shirt sleeves
when taking her shirt off or learn to stand up, assisted, from sitting on the bench so that she can walk
a few steps assisted before being carried the rest of
the way into the pool.*

Only when routines are going well for a student can instruction or therapy techniques be embedded in that
routine. For example, it would be very difficult to use
the undressing routine as an opportunity for new skill
learning if getting ready for swimming were not going
well, not just for Susan but for all the children in the
swimming class.

The same process of identifying activities and routines within a particular setting (Figure 8–5) and of systematically designing adaptations (Figure 8–6) was applied to resolve Mac's physical management needs
during a Girl Scout troop outing.

*When Mac was in fifth grade, her Girl Scout troop
was going to visit a farm house, a hands-on museum
about living on a farm. The two-story farmhouse had
been built in the early 1900s, presenting innumer-
able architectural barriers to her participation.
Many routines, such as positioning, lifting, and toileting, were going to be difficult in this situation. The*

obvious "solutions" were (a) having Mac miss the trip or (b) having her mother go along so that someone would be available to lift, carry, and give assistance. Instead, Mac's mom and the scout leader used the process outlined in Figure 8-6 to identify adaptation interventions for promoting Mac's participation. First, they considered adapting the environment. While it was not possible to modify the farmhouse setting, it was possible to position Mac in her regular wheelchair, one that was lighter and smaller, instead of her power chair so that she could remain seated and be moved easily around the first floor of the museum by another member of her troop (equipment/adaptations for positioning). The troop leader called ahead to tell the museum about Mac's abilities and ask about the activities that would take place at the museum so that materials and modifications could be brainstormed ahead of the visit. The troop made cookies in the farmhouse kitchen. Mac was able to slip her hand through the large handles of the old-fashioned cookie cutters and cut out cookies using a large breadboard that was placed across her knees (adapt materials). A partner used a spatula to move the cookies onto the cookie sheet. Fortunately, the farmhouse had a large bathroom on the first floor. Mac could be pushed into the bathroom and lifted onto the toilet. While she was not wonderfully positioned, the troop leader supported Mac from the front and then lifted her back into her chair (adult assistance). Mac is usually transported in her power chair in her family's van, which is equipped with a lift. For the farmhouse trip, she used a special adult-size support car seat borrowed from a local equipment exchange program that her therapist knew about, and she rode in a regular car (equipment/adaptations for positioning).

For this field trip, Mac's needs were managed without her mother being required to attend and without total adult assistance. More lifting and carrying than normal were needed because all the special equipment and adaptations that Mac uses were not available or possible at the farmhouse. Mac's therapist spent time one afternoon after school with the Girl Scout troop and showed the troop leaders how to lift and carry Mac easily and how to make sure that she was positioned well in her regular chair. This information was helpful to her troop leaders, who previously had not needed to lift or carry her because Mac attended the troop meetings in her power chair.

Specialists have information about ways to adapt environments or settings as well as ideas about the positions that may work best for an individual with motor disabilities in a particular circumstance. They know also how to adapt materials or change the sequence of steps in a routine or alter its requirements. Teachers, family members, and other adults who interact with students with motor disabilities can see specialists as sources of information and ideas that may help another adult manage physical needs easily and with limited effort. However, managing care routines easily and efficiently requires both adaptations and skillful use of techniques. Knowing how to lift a student, for example, is only one part of the process; the second part is carrying it out correctly. Many therapists have so many years of experience in using these techniques that they are able to do them automatically and with greater ease than a person who is a first learner. When techniques seem difficult to implement, practice can help make them easier to use. Practice of any motor skill is important because it leads to competence, making the skill easier to use over time.

Many therapists are only now learning how to change their roles and to function as consultants (not just direct providers of one-on-one interventions) to others. As consultants, therapists are collaborating with teachers and family members to make sure that students' physical needs are managed easily and efficiently. When specialists do not ask how routines are working or what activities are going well or not so well, teachers and parents must communicate this information and ask for assistance. In the absence of assistance, many families alter their activities because they can't figure out how to do them and include their child with a disability. When routines and activities are not going well, teachers and other professionals may view the situation as "unworkable" or "not possible," essentially excluding a child from participation. Another commonly used strategy is to ask for adult assistance in the form of a personal assistant for the student. In essence, adults have a natural tendency to start at the bottom of Figure 8-6 and work upward rather than starting at the top and working down. Teams of educators, family members, and specialists working with a particular student can focus on ways of making participation in typical environments possible. By sharing information and resources, collaborating, and using a problem-solving focus, the physical management routines of students with even the most severe motor disabilities may be managed easily and efficiently in practically all settings and environments.

When specialists help families figure out how their children can participate on the playground or in the local park, suggest ways to go camping or what to do so a child can ride in an amusement park, or determine how a young adult can work for pay in an office setting or manage more independently in a restaurant, students' social and environmental experiences are broadened, as are their opportunities for learning. Similarly, when general education teachers share with specialists what is difficult within the context of their classrooms, specialists may contribute strategies that will make the situation successful rather than stressful. Problem solving by individuals with various backgrounds and expertise is important. Many of the issues that teams need to address do not have "known" solutions. Rather, the team may have to generate what seems to be an optimal solution (Rainforth & York-Barr, 1997).

Coordination of Services and Supports

Professionals of many different disciplines may be involved in working with and assisting individuals with physical disabilities. Physical and occupational therapists, speech language pathologists, assistive technology specialists, vision or hearing specialists or teachers, adaptive physical educators, or recreation therapists are some of the specialists who may be involved with children with disabilities in addition to regular or special education teachers, paraeducators, child care providers, or other paid caregivers. One of the primary issues for families and people with disabilities is coordination of these services and supports, especially since the constellation of services and supports needed by individuals with motor disabilities of all ages is often provided by a variety of separate agencies, including schools, child care programs, or human service and home health agencies. Various team structures have served as a traditional way for coordinating services (Campbell, 1987; Downing, 2002; Giangreco, 1994; Rainforth & York-Barr, 1997), particularly in school settings. Service coordination is required in publicly funded statewide systems of early intervention but not for students in school settings. Service coordinators help families locate and use a variety of services and supports and coordinate these services so that they are provided in ways that help promote the development of infants and toddlers with delayed development. In education, the teacher, special educator, a school social worker, or the child's family may

coordinate services. Plans such as the individual family service plan (IFSP), used in early intervention; the IEP, required in education; or other plans, such as the individualized habilitation (or service) plan, which is for individuals beyond school age or those residing in various types of out-of-home living arrangements, help specify the ways in which services contribute to attainment of desired outcomes, goals, and objectives.

At times, conflicts arise because each professional discipline may view children's disabilities and development from a different perspective; sometimes these underlying perspectives result in different priorities or goals for children. For example, an occupational therapist who is approaching a child from a particular perspective, such as sensory integration (a focus on ways in which the child is processing sensory information), may identify and view a child's skill limitations in terms of processing of sensory information. The therapist in such a situation would likely establish goals to improve the integration of sensory stimuli as a means of enhancing a child's motor abilities. However, this same child's teacher may have a priority of teaching the child to write and may be more interested in adaptations, such as computer word processing programs that allow a child to write in spite of deficient motor abilities. The occupational therapist in this example is focused on improving performance, but the teacher is interested in improving participation in academic skills and access to the general education curriculum. Both professionals recognize the limitation in fine motor skills and the effect of this limitation on a performance area such as writing, but the occupational therapist is using a remedial approach to prepare the child to learn to write using a pencil, and the teacher is addressing the issue from the standpoint of compensation for the fine motor and writing limitation.

As Mac entered high school, the limitations that she had in writing became pronounced. Her writing was not easily intelligible and was very laborious, making it difficult for her to write as clearly and as quickly as was needed in her high school program. The occupational therapist wished to have her use a computer for writing but also wanted to spend individual therapy time working on fine motor coordination so that Mac's writing would ultimately be improved. Her teacher wanted everything to be adapted so that Mac would not need to write at all and could participate in the academic curriculum via assistive technology. Each of these team members viewed the challenges with Mac's writing from a different underlying perspective.

Sometimes different perspectives and approaches can coexist if professionals and families are working together. A physical therapist can work on unassisted walking as long as adaptations are in place that allow the individual to get around as independently as possible while acquiring the skills for walking.

Susan's family, teacher, and child caregivers needed her to be able to get from place to place without a great deal of assistance. Susan's physical therapist identified walking unassisted for short distances as a goal that Susan could attain and was reluctant to have too many adaptations used for fear these would negatively influence her ability to walk. The physical therapist wanted Susan to be helped to walk without too much assistance, for example, when her parents were going between the house to their car or when Susan needed to move from one activity to another in kindergarten and child care. By talking with the family and Susan's teachers, the physical therapist learned about the importance of Susan's independence in mobility. She suggested using a gait trainer so that Susan could be independent in mobility at home and in school and also negotiated with Susan's parents to move the furniture in their family room closer together so that Susan could practice unassisted walking by moving from one piece of furniture to another.

The different viewpoints that may result from multiple perspectives need to be coordinated and integrated if students are to be maximally successful. Participation in typical activities and routines is critical, but participation is not enough to ensure improvements in current motor skills and abilities or the acquisition of new motor abilities. Motor competence provides a base for future development, learning, and participation and prevents the development of other disabilities that are secondary to the original disability and that occur as a child ages (Campbell, 1997).

While Susan may never learn to walk without any assistance at all or to use walking as her primary form of mobility, opportunities to practice walking are important so that she learns how to bear weight on her feet and move her legs to move forward even short distances. When she is older, being able to walk with minimal assistance will be important as a way

of moving her from one situation to another (e.g., moving her into an unmodified bathroom into which her wheelchair won't fit or into a stall in a bathroom or from one location in a room to another).

Many of the professionals who come into contact with individuals with motor disabilities do so for only short periods of time in that individual's life. One set of therapists and teachers may shift to a new set when a student moves from early intervention to preschool. Professionals may shift again each time a student moves within the educational system from elementary to middle to high school and then to postschool education or work. Families are the constant in their children's lives and are often the "historians" of what has occurred earlier in their child's life (Salisbury & Dunst, 1997). Families usually know what has worked or not worked, what has been tried with what result, and what may be easiest for their children. Professionals who develop positive and respectful relationships with parents and family members can learn a great deal about what has happened with the student before that professional entered the student's and family's life. Making sure that parents see themselves as "experts" about their children is an important role for all professionals to play. Most motor disabilities are lifelong: they do not go away or decrease with age or programming. In many instances, motor disabilities become more limiting because of secondary changes that result from poor physical management, insufficient use of adaptive equipment or assistive devices, or overemphasis on independent performance of gross motor skills.

Proper Physical Management

The first goal of proper management is maintaining normal body alignment. Atypical muscle tone may allow the body to fall out of alignment with less-than-normal tone (hypotonia) or may pull the body out of alignment with greater-than-normal tone (hypertonus). The child previously illustrated in Figure 8–4b is being pulled out of alignment by spasticity in the shoulders and arms as well as by spasticity in the hips. The hips have been pulled backward, causing the shoulders and arms to pull forward to allow the child to remain upright. The result is that his back is rounded and not straight (or aligned) over his hips. In contrast, the child in Figure 8–4c is out of alignment because she is falling into gravity. Holding her arms out to the side provides balance and stability so that she does not fall all the way forward. The result is that her spine is not in alignment over her hips, and her back is rounded rather than straight (or upright) against gravity. Postural alignment can be achieved with proper positioning and with handling that minimizes the effects of atypical muscle tone and maintains body alignment.

A second goal of proper management is to encourage as much participation as possible by the individual and to prevent the development of secondary muscular and structural disabilities. Individuals who are being moved, fed, dressed, lifted, or positioned may become passive during physical management routines. Opportunities for an individual to physically participate in the physical management routine may become lost when full assistance in routines become automatic. Sometimes a major part of a routine may be difficult for an individual to perform and may take too long given the setting or situation in which the routine is being used. For example, a student may be able to walk to the bathroom with supervision, but it may require 30 minutes for the student to get to the bathroom. Students may participate within routines through communication, such as vocalizing that they are ready to be moved or using eye movement to look at the plate or glass to indicate what they might want next, or through small motor movements, such as opening their hands to have the spoon put in their hands before a hand-over-hand feeding routine or opening their mouths for the spoon or cup. There are many creative ways in which some participation can be incorporated into every physical management routine for every student (see chapters 4, 9, and 11 for further discussion of participation in activities and routines). Many individuals remain dependent on others to physically move them because of the degree of their physical impairment. However, all individuals can learn the motor movement necessary to participate partially and meaningfully in one or more steps of a physical management routine.

The third goal of proper physical management is to move and position individuals in ways that allow desired motor skills to be used in as many situations as possible. Often there are one or more motor skills that are important for an individual to practice. These skills may be incorporated into several physical management routines so that many opportunities to practice are provided throughout the day. Incorporating motor

skills into many routines is especially important for individuals with severe motor disabilities and for younger children who are just beginning to learn and practice these abilities. Students with severe disabilities are at great risk for developing secondary motor disabilities such as muscle tightness, limitations in range of motion, or orthopedic disabilities. Motor abilities such as range of motion can be maintained when children are expected to perform the movement numerous times throughout the day. For example, if a student has difficulty extending her arms the full length for reaching, if adults or peers hold or place objects away from the student, opportunities are created for the student to reach with her arm fully extended. For younger children who may be just learning a particular motor ability, opportunities for practice enable children to fully integrate the skill across various routines.

Physical Management Routines

Most adults lift, carry, or feed infants and young children without thinking how they are doing these things. When individuals have severe physical disabilities, however, caregivers must use specific procedures to promote participation, provide opportunities for practice, and prevent development of secondary motor disabilities. Thus, simple care activities become consistent physical management routines that, ideally, are used by all people involved in caregiving, including parents, teachers, paraprofessionals, therapists, sitters, nurses, siblings, friends, and peers.

Physical management routines should reflect both the environments in which the routines will be used and the physical needs of the individual. In developing these routines, the team of parents, friends, and professionals who are involved with the individual should also consider the efficiency with which the routines can be carried out (Campbell, 1995). In classroom or group settings, individual caregiving routines should not prevent students from participating in group activities or isolate students from their peers. Eating routines provide a good example. When a student's eating routine takes 1 hour at school and, therefore, the student eats in a classroom rather than a cafeteria, the social interactions that normally occur in conjunction with eating are lost, and the physical management routine isolates the student from his or her classmates. When even 15 minutes are required to reposition a child in adaptive equipment to allow participation in a kindergarten group activity, such as art or reading, the other children are likely to be completing the activity just as the student who has been repositioned is ready to join.

Ecological assessment strategies (chapter 3) can help teams establish the steps of a routine and the natural opportunities for participation (Baumgart et al., 1982; Campbell, 1997; Rainforth & York-Barr, 1997). Management routines are not isolated activities. They have beginning and ending points that link them with events occurring before and after.

Susan's team completed an ecological inventory (Table 8-1) to help determine the ways in which Susan could participate in the eating routines in kindergarten and in her child care setting. The assessment process helped the team determine how Susan,

who had been viewed as "needing to be fed," might be able to participate as fully as possible during lunch and snack.

Physical management routines should be individualized according to a child's needs, but they also should include a series of steps that are incorporated into all routines (Stremel et al., 1990). These steps include the following:

1. Making contact with the individual
2. Communicating what is going to happen in a way the individual can understand
3. Preparing the individual physically for the routine
4. Performing the steps of the routine in ways that require the individual to participate as much as possible

TABLE 8–1
Ecological Inventory of Snack Time

Name: <u>Susan</u>		Environment: <u>4-year-old classroom</u>		Activity: <u>Snack time</u>	
Plan					**Observation**
Preschooler inventory	Inventory of Susan	Skills Susan may acquire	Skills Susan may *not* acquire	Adaptation possibilities	Assessment and plan
Children are at various learning centers and are cleaning up to prepare for snack; children move to snack table and seat themselves. (time = 8 minutes).	Susan is standing in stander at art easel being cleaned up by TA, who removes Susan from stander, carries her to snack table, and positions her in snack chair (time = 10 minutes).	Use a motorized chair to go to the snack table.	Transfer form stander to chair or walking device; walking; moving chair with her arms	Motorized chair	Equipment dealer has been contacted to obtain loaner chair to try; Susan will be placed in a regular wheelchair and will vocalize to indicate that she would like to be pushed or moved and will point with arm movement to show where she wants to go. TA will push Susan when she indicates and to where she points. Motorized chairs will be tried when available from dealer.
Children wait while designated helper children pass out juice boxes, snack food, and napkins.	Susan is not yet to the snack table; her food is placed in front of the spot where she will sit.	Susan can get to the snack table on time if started out from the preceding activity earlier than other children; she is already able to sit and wait.		Adapted chair is needed (and is already available); chair sits on wheeled platform.	TA will start transition from learning centers to snack earlier so that time is available for clean up, transfer, and movement to the snack table and Susan is with other kids.

TABLE 8–1 (Continued)
Ecological Inventory of Snack Time

Name: Susan	Environment: 4-year-old classroom			Activity: Snack time	
Plan					**Observation**
Preschooler inventory	Inventory of Susan	Skills Susan may acquire	Skills Susan may *not* acquire	Adaptation possibilities	Assessment and plan
Children insert straws in juice boxes, drink independently, and eat snack foods independently, requesting more if they would like additional liquid or food.	Susan is unable to insert juice straw, drink from straw, or eat finger foods.	Eating spoon foods; drinking from cup with long straw(?) or if held for sipping; can vocalize to request more and can use large arm movement to indicate choice	Finger feeding, especially small foods; drinking from juice box straw	Try different cups; may be able to use Rubbermaid juice box, which has large straw; needs shallow spoon with built up handle: Big Mac switch for requesting more	Embed strategies to teach spoon feeding within snack; work with teacher to have spoon-fed snacks rather than finger foods. Susan will use Big Mac switch to request more and large arm movement to indicate choice.
Children clean up after snack by throwing juice boxes and napkins away; one helper child passes the basket.	Susan throws away her napkin (once she is able to grasp it) and can make large arm movements to wipe table				
Children who need to use the restroom do so after snack; others begin next activity.	Susan's diapers are changed but she is transferred to the potty for toilet training after snack; this makes her miss the next activity.	She may become toilet trained; learn to transfer from chair to toilet independently; communicate her bathroom needs.		Toilet chair	Wheel (or carry) to the potty chair and place on the chair; do Susan's clothes for her; sit her on potty for a maximum of 10 minutes, making sure that her tone is relaxed. Encourage Susan to participate as much as possible. Reward for successes! Take Susan to next activity.

Note: TA - teaching assistant.

Making contact is important because many individuals with severe disabilities have disorders in vision, hearing, posture, and movement. Contact to prepare for a physical management routine may include touching, speaking, gesturing, signing, attracting the individual's attention visually, or a combination of these approaches. When individuals use specific communication systems, such as object cuing, an object may be used in conjunction with speaking to prepare the individual for the caregiving activity (Rowland & Stremel-Campbell, 1987). It is equally important to communicate

what is going to happen next (e.g., "It's time to get on the bus and go home, so let's move to your wheelchair") in ways that the individual can understand. This may mean using speech and gestures, simple language, object cuing, or nonverbal systems, such as tactile or regular signing. A speech and language pathologist or others who know the best ways for a student to receive and understand language can help design optimal communication strategies.

Basic guidelines for each type of caregiving routine (e.g., lifting, carrying) that apply to all individuals with

TABLE 8–2
A Routine for Lifting and Carrying

Name: <u>Susan</u>		**Date**: <u>5/11/99</u>

Lifting and Carrying Routine
Follow these steps each time you pick Susan up from the floor or move her from one piece of equipment to another or move her in the classroom from one location to another.

Step	Activity	Desired response
Contacting	Touch Susan on her arm or shoulder and tell her you are going to move her from _____ to_____	Wait for Susan to relax.
Communicating	Tell Susan where you are going and show her a picture or object that represents where she is going. For example, show her coat and say, "We are going outside now to play."	Wait for Susan to respond with facial expressions and vocalizations. (Try not to get her so hyped that she becomes more spastic.)
Preparing	Make sure Susan's muscle tone is not stiff before you move her. Use deep pressure touch with a flat hand on her chest area to help relax her.	Wait to make sure that Susan's body is relaxed and in alignment (as much as possible).
Lifting	Place Susan in a sitting position and lift her from sitting unless she is in the stander, where she will need to be lifted from standing. Tell her that you are going to lift her. Put your arms around Susan's back and under her knees and bend her knees to her chest so that you maintain her in a flexed position.	Wait for Susan to reach her arms forward toward you and facilitate at her shoulders if she does not initiate reach within 10 seconds.
Carrying	Turn Susan away from you so that she is facing away and can see where you are moving. Lean her back against your body to provide support and hold her with one arm under her hips with her legs in front. If her legs become stiff, use your other arm to hold her legs apart by coming under one leg and between the two legs to hold them gently apart.	Susan will be able to see where she is going and can use her arms to indicate location (grossly).
Repositioning	Put Susan in the next position she is to use for the activity. Tell her what is happening; "Music is next, and you are going to sit on the floor so you can play the instruments with Jilly and Tommy."	Susan is ready to participate in the next activity.

physical disabilities are discussed next. These guidelines must be individualized to suit a student's age, size, motor abilities, and ways of communicating, and the environments in which the routines are used. Table 8–2 is an example of a lifting and carrying routine written for Susan. This routine is implemented during kindergarten and at Susan's child care center in the afternoons each time she is lifted and carried to another location. What works best for Susan's parents at home may not be as easily implemented by her teacher or the caregivers in her child care center (and vice versa because of the unique requirements of environments and people). Physical and occupational therapists are resources for individualized caregiving routines. Together with teachers and family members, written or picture instructions can be developed for how each individualized caregiving routine is to be implemented each time the routine is needed.

Mac's needs are addressed by a number of people, including her family and friends, people with whom she spends time in community activities, the paraeducator, and a number of teachers with whom she interacts during a typical high school day. Mac carries her generic instruction plan (Table 8–3) with her in the backpack attached to her wheelchair.

Methods of Changing Position
Many different times during a day, individuals who are unable to move themselves independently may need to be lifted and moved from one position to another. Every attempt should be made to design routines that allow participation in whatever ways possible, however limited. A student who is unable to stand independently may still be able to stand briefly when being moved from a chair by using the feet as a point for pivoting the body from a wheelchair to a classroom chair

TABLE 8–3
Generic Instruction Plan for Mackenzie

When Mackenzie's peers are participating in:	Mackenzie can:
Lessons at their desks	Be called on to participate Have a peer assist her in writing Use her computer Be involved in community-based instruction
Lunch	Eat with her peers in the lunchroom Be assisted by a peer to go through the lunch line (Mac needs help with reaching and grasping food items.) Balance her cafeteria tray on her lap Use her eyes (eye-pointing skills) or vocalization to answer "yes" or "no" so that she can make choices Be assisted in eating and drinking by her friends Carol or Shawn
Changing classes	Use her motorized chair to get through the halls, especially if she leaves class a few minutes early Be accompanied by another classmate so that someone is available if she needs assistance
Using the bathroom	Use the bathroom on the first floor that has been specially adapted for her Be taken to the bathroom by a female student (Joanie and Susan are often available) Be taken to the bathroom by an aide Help when being transferred from her chair to the toilet (She needs a lot of physical assistance from an adult or another high school student.) Use the toilet independently Assist in managing her clothing Wash her hands independently

Source: Plan modified from Rainforth & York-Barr (1997), *Collaborative teams for students with severe disabilities: Integrating therapy and educational services* (2nd ed.). Baltimore: Paul H. Brookes.

or onto the toilet. A child who is unable to get to a sitting position by herself may be able to bend her neck and head forward to make it easier for the adult to move her into sitting and then pick her up from the floor.

Lifting Several standard procedures are incorporated into any method of lifting to make the task physically easier for caregivers. All individually designed lifting programs, even those for infants and small children, should incorporate these procedures. In general, the rule is for adults to lift with the legs rather than with the back by squatting down next to a person who is on the floor, holding the person, and then standing up. Lifting improperly may result in physical problems for parents, teachers, or other adults who perform this activity frequently. Back pain and more serious complications are frequent results of using incorrect lifting methods. Younger children are lifted easily by one person. Older children or adults who are severely dependent may require two people to lift them safely.

A number of factors must be considered when determining methods for moving a student. These include the following:

1. The specific movements that the student is able to perform either independently or with assistance
2. The degree of discrepancy in postural tone (i.e., higher- or lower-than-normal tone)
3. The positions (postures) to be used for instructional activities and to which the student will be moved
4. The adaptive equipment being used to position the student
5. The number, size, and strength of the adults (or peers) who will be moving the student
6. The size and weight of the student

Individuals with severe discrepancies in postural tone (either very low tone or very stiff/hypertonic) are lifted more easily from the floor if they are placed in a sitting position before being lifted. Many children and adults are able to participate partially in a transition from stomach or back lying to a sitting position and may be able to hold on to the caregiver, maintain head position, or assist in other ways during lifting.

Many children are lifted from adaptive equipment, such as wheelchairs or specialized classroom chairs. Figure 8-7 illustrates the routine used to lift a preschooler with stiffness (hypertonus) throughout the body. The adult in this picture is kneeling beside the child, who is being lifted out of her adaptive chair. By kneeling next to the child, the adult does not need to bend over and place stress on the back. Instead, the adult will be able to easily pick the child up out of her chair and then stand up from the kneeling position. Physical and occupational therapists can work with teachers and parents to design individualized procedures for specific children.

Transfers Many individuals with motor disabilities may not need to be lifted or may not require lifting in all situations. Standard methods are typically used to

teach children and adults to move independently from one situation into another (e.g., from a chair to the floor, from a chair to the toilet, from one chair to another). The specific methods used to move (or transfer) depend on two factors: (a) the situation (the points between which the individual will be moving) and (b) the parts (or steps) of the routine that an individual can perform independently (Jaeger, 1989). For example, transfer is different from a bed to a chair than from a chair to the floor, and the ways used to accomplish this transfer would depend, for example, on whether the individual can use the arms to partially participate in the transfer.

Physical or occupational therapists should analyze home, school, and typical community environments to determine the most appropriate procedures for each environment and to help individuals achieve transfer as independently as possible. To be motorically efficient, transfer routines for each environment should achieve biomechanical advantage for both the person with a disability and the person helping, if help is needed. Two frequently used basic approaches are standing transfers and sliding transfers, both of which may be accomplished either independently or assisted by another person, depending on the extent of the motor disability. Standing transfers require a minimum of assisted weight bearing on the legs. Sliding transfers require use of the arms for balance and support.

FIGURE 8–7
Proper Lifting of a Small Child. Lifting a small child from a chair is easier when the adult kneels down next to the child so that the adult can pick up the child and then stand up using her legs rather than her back.

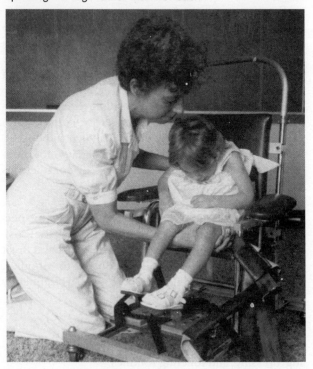

Carrying Many younger children must be carried regardless of where they are. Infants are likely to be carried by parents and teachers more often than are school-age children or adults. Children with severe dysfunction in posture and movement can be difficult to carry for long distances, even when small in size. Instructional programs that focus on independent mobility are important to reduce the need for carrying as children get older and bigger in size. Backpacks or "frontpacks" can be used to carry infants, while strollers can be selected or specifically designed for infants, toddlers, and preschoolers. Wheelchairs and other types of adaptive seating can be designed for children who are older or extensively dependent.

There are several important guidelines for carrying:

1. The distance any individual is carried should be as short as possible.
2. Routines should be designed to allow maximum individual participation, provide therapeutic management, and capitalize on biomechanical efficiency.

3. Children should be carried in ways that control muscle tone, achieve body alignment, and allow independent performance of selected movements.

4. Methods should be used that are appropriate for the size and strength of the adult as well as for the situation(s) in which carrying is being used.

5. Carrying routines that require adults to use both arms for carrying do not work as well as those requiring one arm or use of the second arm intermittently because caregivers often need the second arm to open car doors or house doors, carry items (such as a diaper bag), or hold on to another child.

Carrying routines are best designed for the individuals who will use them and the settings where they will be used. Occupational and physical therapists can design strategies that will work for the caregivers, teachers, and other personnel who will be carrying an infant or child. Illustrated examples of carrying routines can be found in reference texts (Finnie, 1975; Jaeger, 1989; Rainforth & York-Barr, 1997; Stamer, 2000). For example, a younger child with hypertonus (increased tone, spasticity) in the legs may be carried over one of the caregiver's hips to spread the legs and allow the legs to relax or become less stiff. A student with low tone and difficulty with head control may be easier to carry facing frontward, with the legs held together and supported underneath by the caregiver's arm. When muscle tone is not controlled in some way, carrying children, especially for long distances, requires a great deal of strength and endurance on the part of the caregiver. Ideally, carrying routines capitalize on each child's individual abilities to distribute his or her weight evenly and make carrying easier and more efficient.

Proper Positioning and Adaptive Equipment

The use of adaptive positioning equipment for proper positioning is an essential intervention for most individuals with severe motor disabilities. Well-aligned posture results from muscle contractions that maintain the body in positions against varying influences of gravity. Increased muscle tone frequently occurs in response to gravitational effects on the body. An individual who is able to lie on the floor with reasonable postural tone may become hypertonic when placed in a sitting position or may slump. Such changes occur when the motor system is unable to coordinate tone

and muscle contractions against the influences of gravity.

Proper positioning can help maintain body alignment and reasonable levels of postural tone by accounting for gravitational influences. Many individuals can be positioned to receive adequate postural support and alignment without the use of extensive adaptive equipment. However, most individuals with severe physical disabilities require at least some adaptive equipment to provide postural support (Breath, DeMauro, & Snyder, 1997; Rainforth & York-Barr, 1997; Trefler, Hobson, Taylor, Monaham, & Shaw, 1996). It is critical to take several precautions when using adaptive equipment:

1. Well-selected and well-fitted equipment can only maintain postural tone levels and body alignment, not produce normalized tone or proper body alignment.

2. Adaptive equipment maintains body alignment only when it is well fitted and when the individual has been placed properly in the equipment.

3. Adaptive equipment may not produce the specific results desired for each individual, so teachers, parents, and therapists must carefully observe the individual using the equipment over time and in a variety of situations to determine whether the desired function is achieved.

4. Because many individuals with motor disabilities may lack the postural tone necessary to remain in static positions for long periods, the length of time the individual is placed in equipment varies on an individual basis.

5. Restricting people to one position (even in equipment that fits well and is otherwise comfortable) can produce secondary problems, such as poor circulation or skin ulcerations, or secondary motor disabilities, such as muscle tightness or contractures that lead to deformity.

Teachers and parents should ask therapists to specify the length of time each individual can be positioned in equipment. Some individuals can stand or sit comfortably for long periods of time (2 to 3 hours). Other individuals should be repositioned as frequently as every 20 to 30 minutes.

Positioning for Self-Care Routines

Positioning affects a child's ability to participate in eating, dressing, and toileting routines.

Eating Well-coordinated contractions of the oral motor muscles result in appropriate use of the lips, teeth, tongue, and jaw for eating and drinking (Klein & Morris, 1999; Lowman & Murphy, 1999). Since the muscles in the oral-motor area are not able to contract in coordinated ways if posture is misaligned severely, particularly in the head and shoulders, alignment through good positioning is the first step for implementing appropriate eating and drinking. Most individuals are fed in a seated position; therefore, alignment should start with the position of the pelvis and hips, which are the primary weight-bearing surfaces in sitting. The spine should align from the supporting base of the pelvis and hips to allow alignment of the head on an erect spine. Good alignment is achieved through proper positioning using specialized adaptive equipment where necessary. Only after a student is seated with good alignment will techniques specific to the oral-motor area be maximally effective (Lowman, 2004).

Toileting Proper positioning is an essential component in effective toileting. Of particular importance are muscle tone, alignment, and postural control in the muscles of the pelvis, hips, and trunk. Reasonably normal degrees of tone must be attained for elimination. For example, individuals with hypertonus, particularly in the pelvis, hips, and legs, may have even greater increases of tone during toileting, thereby preventing elimination. An individual with low tone may lack the muscle contractions necessary for effective bowel and bladder elimination. Proper positioning can promote alignment while providing postural support. Therefore, as with other self-care routines, a first step is to make sure that the individual is properly positioned for the routine.

Adaptive equipment can assist a student to sit appropriately for toileting. Many types of toileting equipment are commercially available (see Figure 8–8 for one example). Additional modifications (e.g., towel roll supports or pads) may be necessary to ensure proper support and alignment when using commercial equipment. Most toileting areas of community buildings have been modified for use by people in wheelchairs by installing grab bars and high toilets to make independent transfer from a wheelchair easier (or, in some cases, possible). These bathroom facilities, however, may not be easily used with children with severe motor disabilities who may need supports for sitting in addition to assistance in moving from their wheelchair to the toilet.

FIGURE 8–8
Adapted Toilet Chairs Position Comfortably for Toileting.

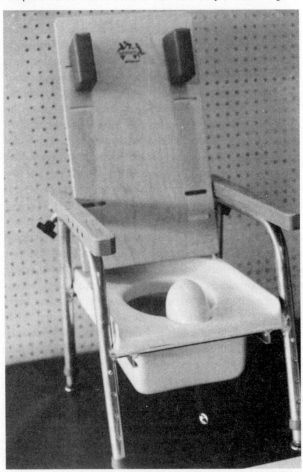

Mackenzie is learning assisted transfer from her power chair (and her regular wheelchair) at school. One bathroom in her high school has been equipped with grab bars and with the special toilet adaptation that Mac needs in order to sit. Although she is able to lean forward and grasp the grab bars, she needs assistance to get out of the chair, turn, manage her clothing, and seat herself on the adapted toilet insert. Mackenzie will probably never be fully independent in toileting because many of the places where she will need to use the bathroom will not have the special adaptations and equipment that are required for her to become independent. However, as Mac learns to assist with the transfer, managing her toileting routine is easier for the caregiver. When

Mackenzie was much younger, her mother and her preschool teachers worked to teach her to communicate when she needed to use the bathroom. They used a Big Mac switch, programming it to say "I need to pee" and making it available to Mackenzie throughout the day. They also made sure that she drank a lot of liquid and that they knew approximately what times during the day she was likely to need to use the toilet. Then they asked her if she needed to go to the bathroom and prompted her arm movement onto the switch. As soon as Mac activated the switch, the adults lifted her from wherever she was positioned and carried her to a special potty chair. They left her on the chair for a few minutes, using rewards and attention when she was successful.

Dressing Typically, children above the chronological age of 12 to 18 months should be dressed and undressed in a sitting position. Sitting is a chronologically age-appropriate position from which to learn necessary arm movements in a less passive position than back lying. Supported sitting, achieved either with equipment or with adult support, is necessary for individuals who are unable to sit independently or balance in a sitting position using the trunk muscles. Individuals who need to use their arms to hold themselves upright in sitting are unable to use their arms for movements in and out of clothing and should be supported by equipment or caregivers to allow arm movements.

A variety of types of adaptive equipment may be used to support students who are able to balance in a sitting position and move their arms and legs. Individuals who lack sitting balance or who require considerable guidance of arm and leg movements can be provided with postural support when positioned in sitting (floor, bed) with the adult positioned behind them. For example, by positioning the child in a sitting position on the adult's legs, the adult is able to provide postural support and maintain this child's muscle tone so that she does not increase her muscle stiffening during dressing. Alternate positions that can be used for dressing and undressing can be designed by physical and occupational therapists, or examples are available in reference texts such as Best et al., (2004) and Finnie (1975).

Some activities, such as changing diapers and dressing or undressing infants, cannot be accomplished well with an individual in a sitting position. Changing diapers when infants or young children are lying on their backs is easiest. However, some children with spasticity may become stiffer when placed on their backs. Placing a small pillow under the head or applying pressure with the hands on the chest while bending the individual's hips and legs toward the chest may help reduce stiffness in the legs and make managing the diaper easier. Many children will be easier to lift and carry after diaper changing if moved first from a back lying to a sitting position and then lifted and carried.

Selecting Adaptive Equipment

Equipment is available from a wide variety of commercial sources. Each piece of equipment varies in purpose, cost, and durability. Some individuals require equipment that is durable enough to last for several years. Others need positioning equipment only temporarily until their size changes or their skills change. Because infants and young children are growing, their needs may be met most appropriately by equipment that is highly adjustable or low enough in cost to be replaced when they outgrow it. For example, an insert may be fabricated from triwall (e.g., appliance carton weight cardboard) to help position an infant in alignment in a high chair. When this baby becomes a preschooler, a more substantial insert may be needed for the child to sit at the table for snack time at Sunday school.

When Susan was a toddler, she was easily able to be positioned in a wagon for transportation using two paper towel rolls to support her trunk (Figure 8–9). Now that she is in kindergarten, proper positioning is more difficult to attain. In Figure 8–10, Susan is sitting inside a laundry basket inside the wagon. Her position is so flexed that she is unable to use her arms well in this position.

Equipment must also be appropriate to the environment. A normalized appearance of equipment enhances the social integration of an individual. Figure 8–11 shows a preschooler with severe disabilities who is learning how to use a motorized car to move around independently in outside environments and in his preschool program. Another consideration is the extent to which a particular piece of equipment may result in isolation of the infant or child from peers. Much of the currently available equipment for infants and young children has been designed for ease of use by adults or for use in classrooms or programs that are attended only by students or adults with motor disabilities. For example, wheelchairs such as Tumbleform Carrie Chairs, Snug

FIGURE 8–9
As an infant, Susan and her brother were transported in a wagon. Because Susan was not able to sit up independently, her mother positioned her in a laundry basket with paper towel rolls in order to keep her upright.

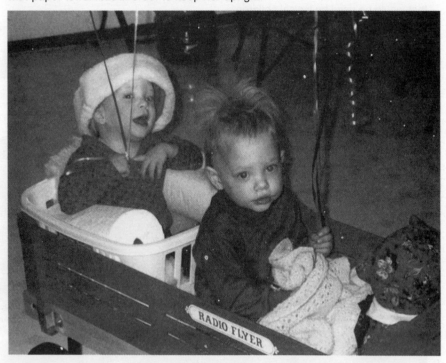

FIGURE 8–10
Now that Susan is older, she still sometimes rides in the wagon, but since she is bigger, she is able to fit in the laundry basket only in a position where her whole body is flexed (or bent). While she enjoys riding in the wagon, the amount of flexion in her body results in increased spasticity in her arms so that they pull in toward her chest for support instead of being available for her to hold on in order to support herself.

FIGURE 8–11
Young children who cannot walk can learn to use modified off-the-shelf cars to get around outside, on playgrounds, or in other open spaces. Michael's car was modified in order to allow him to operate it with a switch instead of the foot pedals that would be used by typical children.

Seats, and travel chairs position young children so that the adults pushing them do not have to bend over. When such wheelchairs are used for activities other than just transporting, young children with physical disabilities become positioned higher than their peers and are physically isolated. Young children should be at the same level as their peers so that they can play and be together with children who do not have physical disabilities in child care, preschool, or community settings. Being familiar with major equipment vendors or with equipment available through catalogs can help keep teachers and therapists current on the features of various types of equipment that may be used easily in the community and in school.

Most individuals with severe motor disabilities receive equipment through a number of sources. Some physical and occupational therapists who work with the students in school settings suggest particular pieces of equipment and are responsible for securing and fitting equipment. Alternately, if an individual has been referred by a physician or therapist, seating clinics that are operated by hospitals and agencies in various states can prescribe equipment (all equipment or only seating devices). In other instances, equipment is purchased by families, therapists, or teachers who reviewed product literature and catalogs. Equipment that is paid for through insurance, medical health care plans, or federal medical programs (such as Medicaid) requires a physician's prescription. Some manufacturers and distributors help families and professionals secure the right prescription and complete the necessary paperwork correctly. Seldom are individuals with severe physical disabilities able to use commercially available equipment without some adaptation.

Parents may experiment with adaptations or may return to clinics or distributors to fit and adjust equipment. Physical and occupational therapists also may fit and adjust equipment. It is important to contact professionals when equipment does not position an individual adequately or when the body seems to be misaligned.

Use of poorly fitting adaptive equipment may result in secondary motor disabilities, such as changes in muscle length or development of orthopedic deformities. When equipment is too big or too small, for example, the person being positioned is likely to be out of alignment. Being out of alignment may be uncomfortable and make it more difficult for the person to function, but misalignment also changes the length of the muscles or the position of the joints, resulting in the development of additional motor disabilities that were not present during infancy or early years. The most common secondary deformities are those involving the spine. Improper positioning may contribute to scoliosis (i.e., a "C" curve in the spine), kyphosis (i.e., a rounding of the shoulders), or lordosis (i.e., positioning of the pelvis in a tipped forward position with a "swayback").

Purposes of Adaptive Equipment

Adaptive equipment has three major purposes:

1. Prevention of secondary motor disabilities, including deformities
2. Increasing use of functional motor skills
3. Promotion of participation in activities and routines in home, school, and community settings

Sometimes, these purposes may conflict. For example, many individuals with severe motor disabilities are able to perform functional arm and hand skills best when positioned in sitting, resulting in their being positioned in sitting most of the time. Sitting, also, may be the easiest position in which to manage a person with motor disabilities across many different environments, another factor that may contribute to sitting being selected as a preferred position. When Susan was beginning preschool, a special adapted chair was obtained so that she would be functional in her school setting (Figure 8–12). Even though sitting may appear to be the ideal position, when an individual spends most of the time in only one position, secondary disabilities may develop (even when equipment is well fitted and used appropriately). Changes in the length of muscles

FIGURE 8–12

Wheelchairs are helpful for transporting children from one location to another but often do not work well for classroom positioning. Other chairs, like the one Susan is sitting in, that are adapted for good positioning and that fit under tables or desks may be needed.

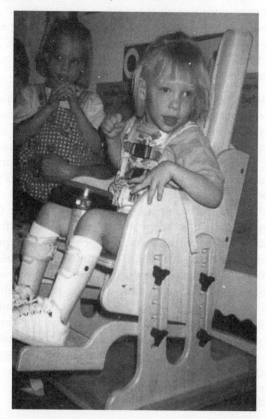

in the hips and legs occur frequently when an individual is positioned in sitting for a majority of the day. Tightness (or contractures) of the flexor muscles may result, causing the hips and knees to remain in a flexed (or bent) position and preventing them from straightening (or extending) in order to stand or lie with the legs straight. When any one position such as sitting is used in a particular setting such as school for a majority of the day, other positions and types of equipment are necessary to place an individual in alternate positions to compensate and prevent secondary disabilities. Alternate positions for sitting are those that place the body muscles in an opposite pattern. Standing or side lying straightens the hips and knees and puts the muscles in the opposite position (extension) from sitting where the hips and knees are flexed. Alternate positions may require additional types of adaptive equipment. The functional appropriateness of a position in relation to the setting and activity in which it will be used is of primary importance.

Positioning Mac, a high school student, in a side-lying position during art class is not socially appropriate, even though the position may work well for her and the equipment is available. Side lying is a good position to use for watching TV at home, for sleeping, or for just relaxing. Standing is the best alternative to sitting in a majority of settings.

Most children with severe motor disabilities require several types of positioning equipment at home and as they begin child care or school. For example, they may need positioning for floor sitting, chair sitting, standing, mobility, and toileting. Many types of adaptive equipment are available for positioning; new types are produced every year (see Figures 8–8 and 8–13).

Physical and occupational therapists who are employed in clinic or hospital settings may not be fully aware of the environments in which adaptive equipment will be used. When equipment is acquired through a clinic or vendor, parents, teachers, and school-based therapists must describe these settings and the activities involved. Several pieces of equipment may appropriately position an individual; however, only one piece may be suited to a school environment,

FIGURE 8–13
Types of Adaptive Equipment Available to Position Students with Motor Disabilities
(a)

(b)

(c)

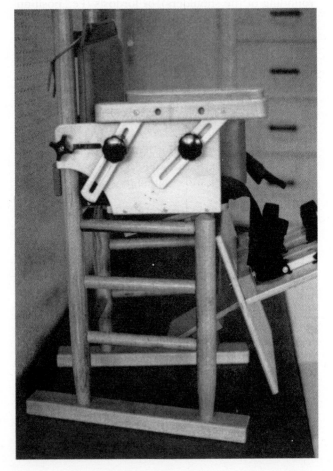

(d)

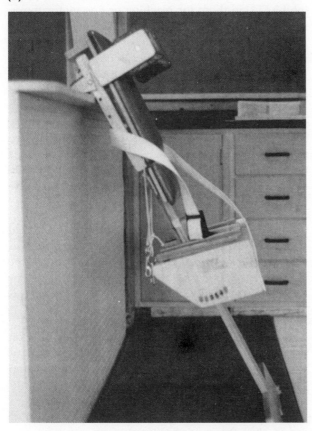

be transportable in the family's car or van, or work best in the home or settings where a family spends time with their children. To find out after a piece of equipment has been purchased that it won't fit in the bathroom of the school or in the family car is unfortunate. Most pieces of equipment are quite costly, and seldom is their purchase fully covered by insurance or other health care programs; therefore, environmental factors must be considered before equipment is ordered, purchased, or fitted.

Increasing Use of Functional Motor Skills

Teachers, therapists, and parents must select and use equipment that places individuals with motor disabilities in positions where they can easily perform functional movements. When motor disabilities are severe, functional skills such as mobility, communication, eating, or class participation are likely to be limited by motor disabilities. Most individuals with severe motor

disabilities will learn to perform these and other functional skills through the use of assistive technology devices. In many instances, arm and hand, head, or leg movements will be used to operate an assistive device.

Mac operates her power chair by using a switch interface device that is placed in her headrest. Her head movement activates and directs the movement of the chair.

Other types of switch interface devices, computers, communication aids, writing devices, adapted feeding equipment, or environmental control units are used by people with disabilities. Functional assistive devices enable a person to participate in the task or activity in spite of significant motor disabilities. There are many types of assistive technology devices that have been designed to provide an alternate way of performing a functional skill. Power wheelchairs, augmentative and alternative communication devices, environmental control units, or computers are examples of specially designed devices that use high technology to enable people with motor disabilities to be functional in many different settings. Usually, high-technology devices are not easily used without training, instruction, or practice in their use. In other words, a child does not just begin "talking" because he or she has been given an alternative communication device that uses voice output when activated. Low-technology devices (or adaptations) are as important as complex high-tech devices specially designed for use by people with disabilities, and they may be easier for a student to use, less expensive, and more useful across settings and activities. A power wheelchair, for example, is useful in many settings but will not fit onto an airplane or in many cars. Because of the limitations of high-technology devices, most individuals need a combination of high- and low-technology devices in order to perform functional skills across a wide variety of settings and activities.

Mac uses a communication device to express wants and needs and a computer, both of which are high-tech devices, but she removes printed paper from her printer by using a block of wood that she is able to grasp that has a substance to which the paper adheres. Mac is unable to pick up and grasp the paper with her hand but does so independently using this low-tech device. With her communication device, she is able to ask the paraeducator or the teacher to help her in the bathroom, and when she is positioned in her power chair, she can get to the bathroom inde-pendently, change classes by herself, and get to the cafeteria, the bus, and her after-school clubs and ac-tivities. Mac is not able to transfer to the toilet with-out assistance or manage her clothing, but manag-ing her toileting routine is far easier because of the independence provided through her positioning equipment and other devices.

Susan uses a variety of communication aids, such as pictures and a single switch interface, when on a kindergarten class trip to the zoo (Figure 8–14B). She also uses a simple device that holds her cup and al-lows her to move the cup toward her for drinking and out of the way when she is finished. She falls for-ward a lot in sitting, so when she is doing a painting activity, her teacher makes sure that she has an easel in front of her. Sometimes Susan stands to paint at the easels in the classroom, and sometimes her teacher uses a cardboard tabletop easel that she has made by taping cardboard into a triangular shape.

Without sufficient trunk control to maintain an up-right posture in sitting or standing equipment, many students may automatically use their arms to help hold the trunk upright. Using the arms for postural support inhibits using them for reaching or fine motor move-ment. A student may be unable to eat independently, manipulate learning materials, or even activate an as-sistive technology device when the arms are used to maintain an upright position (rather than for func-tional skills). Adaptive positioning equipment enables students to more easily perform functional skills, with or without the use of assistive technology devices, by supporting the trunk so that the head and arms are free for movement. Effective positioning (a) provides body alignment to prevent secondary motor disabili-ties, (b) allows for functional movement, and (c) pro-motes participation in an activity or routine.

When Susan wanted to paint at an easel or help to feed the fish in the kindergarten's aquarium, she was able to do so more easily in a standing position. The therapists and teachers decided that a gait trainer or supine stander would be most appropriate for this activity.

Standing equipment would probably *not* be best on the playground or when playing a game like baseball or when working with other children in a group tabletop

FIGURE 8–14
Susan relies on different pieces of equipment and adaptations, including both low- and high-technology devices. When positioned in a walker, Susan can be close to the activity (photo A). In photo B, she communicates both by pointing to pictures pasted on her wheelchair tray and by accessing a high-technology communication device with voice output. She also uses a cup holder device so that she can drink from a cup when she is thirsty.   **(a)**

activity. Easel or mural painting, board work, or washing dishes may be more easily facilitated in standing than with sitting equipment, while independent mobility (moving from place to place) will be easier using adapted seating. A motorized or power chair enables a student to get from place to place but may not provide the best seating position when the student is doing class work with a computer; another type of adapted chair may promote better seating. Seating that transports a student safely to and from school may be inappropriate for classroom use because the student's movement, while restricted sufficiently to ensure safety when on the bus, may be too restricted to function in the classroom. Most individuals require a variety of positions and adaptive equipment not only to prevent secondary disabilities and deformities and maintain alignment but also to promote function within the context of specific activities.

Promoting Participation

Many young children and school-age students receive services in schools and programs that are attended by peers and participate with their families and friends in all sorts of community activities. They may visit the firehouse with a Cub Scout troop, attend a birthday party at the home of a friend, swim at the Y or a

community recreation program, attend church or religious classes, go shopping, visit amusement parks, go to day or overnight camps, see plays or movies, or participate in any number of other settings. In an ideal world, all environments and settings would be usable by individuals with motor disabilities. In reality, the necessary adaptations or devices may not always be available in all settings.

> Mac can get to any bathroom independently in her power chair but often is unable to get through a standard doorway, which is likely to be too narrow to accommodate her chair. Sometimes when visiting a museum or another community building, she is unable to get in the building unassisted because of steps or ramps that are too narrow for her chair.

Because all settings are not fully accessible or don't accommodate all types of adaptive equipment, therapists and others need to design secondary strategies for overcoming these architectural barriers. Lifting and carrying routines may be needed in some settings even when individuals are independent in others. Partial or full independence in self-care routines such as toileting, eating, bathing, or other care activities may be possible only through environmental accommodations, adaptive equipment for positioning (e.g., wheelchairs, toilet chairs, bathing chairs), assistive devices (e.g., grab bars around the toilet, adapted handles on the sink faucets, special plates and utensils, bars around a person's bed, a washcloth mitt), or other such aids. Students may be more dependent in a routine when environments have not been designed or fully modified for individuals with physical disabilities or when needed equipment and devices are not available. When circumstances or settings are less than ideal, teams should problem solve solutions.

When Mac needs to use a restroom in the community, her toileting routine is more difficult than when she is at home or at school. She still can communicate her needs with her communication device and, if in her power chair, get to the bathroom independently. Since her rhizotomy surgery, she can bear weight momentarily on her legs and feet, so it is possible to transfer her to a toilet using an assisted standing transfer, which can be managed by one adult. Before the surgery, her legs were so stiff and bent that Mac could not physically help in the transfer, and two people were needed to lift her onto or off a toilet. Once on the toilet, someone has to hold her in place, which is not necessary at home or in school, where an adapted toilet chair is used.

Summary

Managing the physical care needs of individuals with severe motor disabilities requires teamwork, creativity, planning, and skill. Physical management routines include lifting, transferring, carrying, positioning, eating and drinking, toileting, and dressing. When these care routines accommodate the needs of each individual, they provide opportunities for participation and may also help prevent the development of secondary motor disabilities. Allowing individuals to participate in their own caregiving to the greatest extent possible may prevent learned helplessness as well as make them less dependent on assistance from others.

Physical management routines need not yield full independence in a particular care activity; many individuals with severe motor disabilities require assistance in these activities throughout their lives. The purposes of these routines are to address care needs with dignity and in ways that promote participation, to manage routines efficiently, and to reduce the likelihood of secondary physical limitations and deformities.

Suggested Activities

1. At the beginning of each school year, work with therapists to assess whether each student's adaptive equipment is suitable for the student and is used properly. Answer the following questions:
   a. Does the equipment fit the student?
   b. Do the staff members place the student properly in the equipment?
   c. Does the equipment produce the desired function over time and across activities?
   d. How long should the student remain in the piece of equipment before being repositioned?
   e. Is the equipment suited to the student's chronological age, and does it allow for a normalized appearance?
   f. Does the equipment isolate the student from an activity because of its size, height, or purpose?
2. Observe the typical routines that your students follow during their school day (e.g., arrival and departure on a bus, movement to and from scheduled school locations, use of the restroom, change of diapers, change of clothing for physical education class, or use of the library). For students who are not independent in their movements or ability to communicate, check to see if the following four activities occur during these routines:
   a. The adult or peer makes physical contact with the student.
   b. The adult or peer communicates what is going to happen in a manner that the student can understand.
   c. The adult or peer prepares the student physically for the routine.
   d. The adult or peer performs the steps of the routine in ways that allow the student to have choices and require as much participation as possible.

References

Batshaw, M. L. (2002). *Children with disabilities* (5th ed.). Baltimore: Paul H. Brookes.

Baumgart, D., Brown, L., Pumpian, I., Nisbet, J., Ford, A., Sweet, M., et al. (1982). Principle of partial participation and individualized adaptations in educational programs for severely handicapped students. *Journal of the Association for the Severely Handicapped, 7*(2), 17–27.

Best, S., Bigge, J. L., & Heller, K. W. (2004). *Teaching individuals with physical or multiple disabilities* (5th ed.). New York: Pearson/Prentice Hall.

Bly, L. (2000). *Baby treatment based on NDT principles.* Tucson, AZ: Therapy Skill Builders.

Breath, D., DeMauro, G., & Snyder, P. (1997). Adaptive sitting for young children. *Young Exceptional Children, 1*(1), 10–16.

Campbell, P. H. (1987). The integrated programming team: An approach for coordinating professionals of various disciplines for students with severe and multiple handicaps. *Journal of the Association for Persons with Severe Handicaps, 12*(2), 107–116.

Campbell, P. H. (1995). Supporting the medical and physical needs of students in inclusive settings. In N. Haring & L. Romer (Eds.), *Welcoming students who are deaf-blind into typical classrooms* (pp. 277–305). Baltimore: Paul H. Brookes.

Campbell, P. H. (2004). Participation-based services: Promoting children's participation in natural settings. *Young Exceptional Children, 8*(1), 20–29.

Campbell, P. H., & Wilcox, M. J. (2004, February). Tots-n-tech research institute on assistive technology for infants and toddlers: Briefing book. Available at **http://tnt.asu.edu**

Campbell, S. K. (1997). Therapy programs for children that last a lifetime. *Physical and Occupational Therapy in Pediatrics, 17*(1), 1–15.

Dormans, J. P., & Pellegrino, L. (1998). *Caring for children with cerebral palsy: A team approach.* Baltimore: Paul H. Brookes.

Downing, J. (2002). Working cooperatively: The role of team members. In J. Downing (Ed.), *Including students with severe and multiple disabilities in typical classrooms: Practical strategies for teachers* (2nd ed., pp. 147–162). Baltimore: Paul H. Brookes.

Finnie, N. (Ed.). (1975). *Handling your young cerebral palsied child at home.* New York: E. P. Dutton.

French, C., Gonzalez, R. T., & Tronson-Simpson, J. (1991). *Caring for people with multiple disabilities: An interdisciplinary guide for caregivers.* Tucson, AZ: Therapy Skill Builders.

Giangreco, M. F. (1986). Effects of integrated therapy: A pilot study. *Journal of the Association for Persons with Severe Handicaps, 11*, 205–208.

Giangreco, M. F. (1994). Effects of a consensus-building process on team decision-making: Preliminary data. *Physical Disabilities: Education and Related Services, 13*(1), 41–56.

Jaeger, D. L. (1989). *Transferring and lifting children and adolescents: Home instruction sheets.* Tucson, AZ: Therapy Skill Builders.

Klein, M., & Morris, S. (1999) *Mealtime participation guide.* Tucson, AZ: Therapy Skill Builders.

Kunc, N. (1996, April/May). The right to be disabled. *Pennsylvania Early Intervention, 7*(7), 1, 4.

Larin, H. (2000). Motor learning: Theories and strategies for the practitioner. In S. K. Campbell, D. W. Vander Linden, & R. J. Palisano (Eds.), *Physical therapy for children* (pp. 170–197). Philadelphia: W. B. Saunders.

Lowman, D. K. (2004). Mealtime skills. In F. Orelove, D. Sobsey, & R. Silberman (Eds.), *Educating children with multiple disabilities: A collaborative approach* (4th ed., pp. 563–607). Baltimore: Paul H. Brookes.

Lowman, D. K., & Murphy, S. M. (1999). *The educator's guide to feeding children with disabilities.* Baltimore: Paul H. Brookes.

Mistrett, S. (2001). Synthesis on the use of assistive technology with infants and toddlers (birth through age two). Final Report to OSERS, Contract No. HS97017002.

Orelove, F., Sobsey, D., & Silberman, R. K. (2004). *Educating children with multiple disabilities: A collaborative approach* (4th ed.). Baltimore: Paul H. Brookes.

Palisano, R., Rosenbaum, P., Walter, S., Russell, D., Wood, E., & Galuppi, B. (1997). Development and reliability of a system to classify gross motor function in children with cerebral palsy. *Developmental Medicine and Child Neurology, 39*, 214–223.

Rainforth, B., & York-Barr, J. (1997). *Collaborative teams for students with severe disabilities: Integrating therapy and educational services* (2nd ed.). Baltimore: Paul H. Brookes.

Rowland, C., & Stremel-Campbell, K. (1987). Share and share alike: Conventional gestures to emergent language for learners with sensory impairments. In L. Goetz, D. Guess, & K. Stremel-Campbell (Eds.), *Innovative program design for individuals with dual sensory impairments* (pp. 49–75). Baltimore: Paul H. Brookes.

Salisbury, C. L., & Dunst, C. J. (1997). Home, school, and community partnerships: Building inclusive teams. In B. Rainforth & J. York-Barr, *Collaborative teams for students with severe disabilities: Integrating therapy and educational services* (2nd ed., pp. 57–87). Baltimore: Paul H. Brookes.

Seligman, M. (1975). *Helplessness: On death, depression, and development.* San Francisco: W. H. Freeman.

Stamer, M. (2000). *Posture and movement of the child with cerebral palsy.* Tucson, AZ: Therapy Skill Builders.

Stremel, K., Molden, V., Leister, C., Matthews, J., Wilson, R., Goodall, D. V., et al. (1990). *Communication systems and routines: A decision making process.* Washington, DC: U.S. Office of Special Education.

Trefler, E., Hobson, D., Taylor, S., Monaham, L., & Shaw, C. (1996). *Seating and mobility for persons with physical disabilities.* San Antonio, TX: Psychological Corporation/Therapy Skill Builders.

Udvari-Solner, A., Causton-Theoharis, J., & York-Barr, J. (2004). Developing adaptations to promote participation in inclusive environments. In F. Orelove, D. Sobsey, & R. Silberman (Eds.), *Educating children with multiple disabilities: A collaborative approach* (4th ed., pp. 151–192). Baltimore: Paul H. Brookes.

Vandercook, T., York, J., & Forest, M. (1989). The McGill Action Planning System (MAPS): A strategy for building the vision. *Journal of the Association for Persons with Severe Handicaps, 14*(3), 205–215.

Teaching Self-Care Skills

Leslie J. Farlow
Martha E. Snell

The development of the ability to care for oneself represents the beginning of independence from one's parents. The first time children complete self-care routines, like using the toilet or getting dressed "all by themselves," is considered a major event in most families to be celebrated and recorded. We define the self-care domain to include the basic and routine tasks of maintaining personal hygiene: toileting, eating, dressing, and grooming. For children and young adults with severe disabilities, the ability to manage personal care is of paramount significance even if there continues to be some reliance on others. A range of obstacles (e.g., intellectual, physical, or behavioral disabilities, along with lowered environmental expectations or poor

instruction) may slow, limit, or indefinitely postpone development of such basic adaptive skills. This chapter describes proven and socially acceptable methods for assessing and teaching these skills.

Before we begin, we'd like to introduce three students: John, a kindergarten student; Jamal, a teenager in middle school; and Alycin, a young woman well into her transition to adulthood. Within the chapter sections on toileting, mealtime, and dressing and grooming, we share the related issues faced by these three students and their educational teams. Their instructional programs should help you apply chapter information to your own practices with students.

John

This is John's first year in an inclusive kindergarten classroom. He is very social and appears to like everything about school, especially music and reading. He has a great sense of humor and enjoys "tricking" his teachers into believing that

he can't do something. John is identified as having multiple disabilities: cerebral palsy and severe mental retardation. There are 20 students in his class. Ms. Johnson, the kindergarten teacher, has the supports of a part-time teaching assistant and a consulting special education teacher, Ms. Perez. Ms. Perez typically spends about a half hour daily in the kindergarten class teaching small groups of children or working one on one with John. John's mother participates actively on his team along with an occupational therapist (OT), a physical therapist (PT), and a speech and language pathologist (SLP), all of whom provide services to him several times a week in the context of kindergarten activities.

John uses a wheelchair to travel distances of more than a few feet, but he can walk 3 feet using two canes and up to 10 feet when an adult holds him from behind and facilitates hip rotation. John is not toilet trained and still wears diapers. He eats finger foods and uses a spoon, but he is messy and does not appear to chew his food thoroughly. John participates in most grooming skills with verbal and physical assistance.

 Jamal

Jamal is an eighth grader with autism. At age 13, he is fairly social with staff and peers and well liked. Jamal is part of a Lunch Bunch Club, which means he interacts daily with many other eighth graders, even though he spends about half his school time learning apart from peers (e.g., in the special education room and in many community locations). Jamal uses signing, conventional gestures, and a pocket communication book of symbols and printed words to communicate. Instead of showing his dislike of activities jumping up and down, tearing around the room, and yelling, he is learning to communicate his dissatisfaction with head shakes and asking to choose another activity. Jamal likes being around peers but dislikes excessive noise and often reacts by covering his ears.

Unlike many of his peers, Jamal is somewhat oblivious to his appearance, though, at his mother's insistence, he always looks neat and fashionable. His grooming goals include generalization of independent tooth-brushing, initiation of hand washing before handling food, and checking his face in the mirror after eating and brushing his teeth. In the dressing area, Jamal is aiming for independence in the school bathroom (i.e., unfastening and fastening his pants, exiting the bathroom with clothes properly arranged and underpants not showing), handling all fasteners on clothing and jackets, and tying his shoes. At lunchtime, Jamal's focus is on asking for what he needs and fluently cleaning his own place after lunch.

 Alycin

Alycin, who is 17, will complete her high school program next year and start a post–high school program located in the community. Because of her extensive cerebral palsy, she uses a wheelchair and a computerized communication device with voice output and regularly uses other pieces of adaptive equipment (toileting and shower chairs, adapted desk and chair, and wedges for positioning). Alycin's vision is limited, which means her parents, teachers, and peers rely a lot on telling her

where things are and "talking her through" what is happening around her. For her transition years, Alycin and her team have identified skill targets that emphasize less dependence on others and have problem solved common challenges to her self-care routines. Her self-care skills include indicating when she needs to use the bathroom, partial participation in toileting and grooming tasks, and active participation in eating, including the use of a mechanized self-feeder for some meals.

A Rationale for Attaining Proficiency in Self-Care Routines

Increasingly, students with severe disabilities are being educated with nondisabled peers in neighborhood schools. While proficiency in self-care skills is needed for health, self-determination, and access to some environments, some educators might question how appro-

priate it is to teach students such skills in school settings. Self-care routines are part of all individuals' daily activities, and they have strong, lifelong influences on health and positive self-image. Activities of daily living are a priority for many parents. If not performed by the student, these routines must be completed by someone else or medically managed if the person is to remain healthy.

The attainment of basic self-care skills contributes to individual self-determination. Initiation, persistence, choice making, self-regulation, and self-efficacy are components of self-determination (Brown & Cohen, 1996). Think about it:

- People have many natural opportunities to initiate and persist while completing necessary self-care routines.
- Eating, grooming, and dressing require many choices.
- Independent performance of self-care tasks is a milestone in the development of self-regulation for typically developing young children.

Progress in self-care skills provides a sense of self-control and accomplishment for students with disabilities. The attainment of proficiency in basic self-care skills (even with some necessary accommodation) allows students to be more independent and meet their own personal needs.

Regardless of whether or not it should be, independence in self-care skills increases students' access to some environments and social acceptability with others. Starting in the adolescent years, appropriate dressing and grooming skills are often necessary for acceptance in a peer group. The accommodations that are allowed and available during the school years often change when students leave school. Young adults who lack a high degree of independence in their daily hygiene may be excluded from many community, work, and living environments as a result.

With instruction, students with disabilities make progress in self-care skills and learn to demonstrate some level of independence from parents and other support providers.

Problems with Current Research

Even though self-care skills contribute to health, reduce dependence, and add to quality of life, the research basis for instruction of these skills is surprisingly limited and exhibits one or more difficulties: (a) it was conducted in segregated settings, (b) it included aversive procedures as part of the intervention, and (c) it is dated. Today, segregated placements and aversive procedures are not acceptable practices for students with disabilities because (a) we know the power that ordinary peers and life experiences can have for students with disabilities (Meyer, Park, Grenot-Scheyer,

Schwartz, & Harry, 1998) and (b) we have seen that more problems than solutions result from the use of aversive methods (Carr et al., 1999).

Despite the need for more research in inclusive educational settings, research in the functional skill domains, including self-care, appears to be declining (Nietupski, Hamre-Nietupski, Curtain, & Shrikanth, 1997). The most recent studies continue to be conducted in restricted settings (cf. Ahearn, 2003; Cicero & Pfadt, 2002; Tarbell & Allaire, 2002), segregated preschool settings (cf. Bainbridge & Myles, 1999) or the home (cf. Denny et al. 2000; Najdowski, Wallace, Doney, & Ghezzi, 2003). Furthermore, with a reduction in self-care research in general, the areas of dressing and grooming instruction have been significantly less studied than have toileting and eating instruction (Snell, 1997).

General Principles for Developing Self-Care Instruction

Our eight general principles for developing self-care instruction are listed in Table 9–1 and discussed in greater detail next. Teachers, in collaboration with family members, related service personnel, general educators, and the student, choose which skills to target but pay close attention to social, cultural, and age characteristics of teaching procedures and the perspective of peers. Selection is based on an inventory of the environment to determine which self-care routines and skills are the most important for the student to master and what the best schedule and settings are for instruction. When appropriate and with careful monitoring, the team may choose a goal of *partial participation* on some tasks (Baumgart et al., 1982) rather than total participation in an ordinary manner. Partial participation refers to the process of empowering the student to do as much of a task as he or she can independently while getting support for some steps through adapted materials, automated devices, changed sequences, or personal assistance. Uncomplicated and effective teaching methods should be chosen on the basis of the student's learning characteristics, stage of learning, and the teaching setting. Finally, the team should identify any related skills (e.g., social, communicative) to teach. These eight principles are repeatedly applied by teams as the decision cycle to select skills, evaluate progress, and adjust teaching strategies.

TABLE 9–1

Principles for Developing and Implementing Self-Care Teaching Programs

- Collaborate with all team members
- Conduct meaningful assessment and use the results
- Use procedures that are socially valid as well as age and culture appropriate
- Involve peers in the process
- Use partial participation carefully
- Select appropriate and respectful environments for instruction
- Select uncomplicated and effective instructional methods
- Consider related skills for instruction

Collaborate with Team Members

The collaborative team is an ongoing process in which many decisions are made about what to teach, how to teach, and how to improve teaching (Snell & Janney, 2005). If teams are to be student centered, the student must be a team member. When students are present at their own individualized educational plan (IEP) meetings and team members seek to understand their feelings, ideas, and choices about self-care skills, team decisions are more likely to reflect the student's wishes. We know of several teams who routinely put the student's picture on the meeting table when he or she cannot be present.

Family Members

Family members and support providers can provide the team with perspectives that no professional members have, especially in the self-care domain. Involvement of the family in instructional plans can facilitate skill generalization from the school to the home environment. If teachers are limited to the traditional school day and settings for instruction and observation, then family members or other support providers must encourage students' use of the self-care routines where they are especially needed—in the home and the community. Parents have been taught to use functional analysis and behavior management strategies to teach their children to eat (Denny et al., 2000; Najdowski et al., 2003; Tarbell & Allaire, 2002), to use the toilet (Bainbridge & Miles, 1999), and to complete self-care routines (Reamer, Brady, & Hawkins, 1998).

Self-modeling or video modeling was applied to teach parents the use of task analysis, prompting, and reinforcement (Reamer et al., 1998). Parents were videotaped interacting with their children during routines including dressing and brushing teeth. These videos were then edited to include three positive examples (correct use of prompts and task analysis) and one negative example. While parents viewed the tape with the parent educator, they described their actions and received feedback on the positive examples; then they practiced a step in the task analysis that had not been performed correctly. The program was effective as measured by an increase in the steps completed independently by children and a decrease in parental assistance provided. Their children demonstrated progress in skills, and parents generalized their skills to teaching other behaviors.

Tarbell and Allaire (2002) were able to teach parents to improve their children's food consumption and eating through a program that included education in typical child development, behavior management, and the progression of eating skills. At an inpatient clinic, parents observed members of an interdisciplinary team instructing their children and were coached in their child's individualized eating program for 2 to 3 weeks. Children's performance improved at the clinic and the home, indicating that parents continued to implement the programs.

Teachers

Typically, special educators take the lead contacting parents on self-care priorities and progress, writing task analyses, measuring and keeping records of student progress on IEP objectives, and providing training and oversight to paraprofessionals who help implement self-care instruction. General education teachers must be involved as core members, too, because (a) their classroom activities and teaching schedule are the context for assessment and instruction and (b) classmates may be included as informal models for self-care.

Related Support Providers

When self-care skills are a priority, related services staff make essential contributions for many students. Occupational therapists have expertise in the activities of daily living and the fine motor development required. For example, Reese and Snell (1991) consulted with an OT to determine the most appropriate steps for putting on and removing coats and jackets. Physical therapists are sources of knowledge on adaptive equipment and positioning considerations, which both influence skill performance. Speech and language therapists have expertise in oral musculature that may be useful in the evaluation of eating and oral hygiene activities. For example, Snell, Lewis, and Houghton (1989) consulted with an SLP to determine the most appropriate steps for brushing teeth. School nurses may directly assess nutrition, bowel and bladder characteristics, and health concerns (e.g., seizure disorders, urinary tract infections, vision and hearing limitations) or consult with the student's physician. Sometimes paraprofessional staff, adaptive physical educators, and vision specialists are included because they fill important team roles.

Related support services may be best provided in an integrated model. When services are integrated, decision-making and teaching roles are shared rather than having some team members make recommendations as experts. Scott, McWilliam, and Mayhew (1999) reported that the integrated therapy model (a) has been shown effective for student learning, (b) may facilitate better skill generalization, and (c) is preferred by teachers and related service personnel. Students who receive therapy in natural and integrated contexts make progress similar to students receiving therapy in pullout settings.

Paraprofessionals

Paraprofessionals, also referred to as teaching aides or assistants, are critical members of the student's educational team. Their role as instructors has continued to increase. Students who are not independent in self-care routines may require assistance during the day that may be provided by paraprofessionals. While paraprofessionals with instructional experience can contribute to student progress, problems can also result from relying too much on paraprofessionals for instruction. Giangreco and his colleagues used interview and observation to identify several problems: (a) the separation of students with disabilities from peers resulting in decreased interactions; (b) the development of dependence on the paraprofessional rather than an increase in independent performance; (c) the reduction of choice and personal control when paraprofessionals make decisions for the student; (d) the loss of gender identity, commonly observed when children are taken into the restroom appropriate for the paraprofessional's gender rather than the student's; and (e) limitations on delivery of competent instruction when the paraprofessional is left to develop instruction, select goals, and adapt instruction (Giangreco, Edelman, Luiselli, & MacFarland, 1997).

Considering the findings of Giangreco et al. (1997) and the advice of Freschi (1999) and Doyle (2002), we make the following recommendations:

1. Specify the role of the paraprofessional staff (and/or other instructional staff) when developing instructional plans. Plan to fade instructional personnel in the same way that other instructional components are faded.
2. Provide education to the entire instructional team regarding the student's instructional program and the possible negative effects of adult proximity. When all team members are familiar with instructional strategies for a student, there is less likelihood that instructional decisions will be left solely to the paraprofessional.
3. Teach paraprofessionals to implement individualized programs systematically and fade their assistance.
4. Provide regular supervision to paraprofessionals and give them feedback on their teaching.
5. While accountability for instruction resides with professional staff, encourage paraprofessionals to contribute their knowledge to the planning process.
6. Maintain the role of the teacher as the instructional leader for all students in the classroom, determining which topics of instruction are implemented when. Discourage any competition with this role.
7. When hiring paraprofessionals and developing job descriptions, consider the needs of all students in the classroom. The paraprofessional should "belong" to the classroom rather than a single student: do not hire a paraprofessional for one student. Clarify responsibilities and schedule activities with other students.
8. Paraprofessionals need training to be effective instructors, in such areas as general instructional principles, how to teach and support specific students, how to work on the team, and confidentiality (Doyle, 2002).

Conduct Meaningful Assessment and Use the Results

Assessment is necessary to determine the following:

- What skills the student is able to perform
- What skills the student does not perform or does not perform completely
- What unlearned skills are a priority now or in the future

- Whether known skills are performed fluently
- Whether known skills are performed across settings
- Whether the student is making progress in instruction
- Whether changes are needed in instruction

Typically, self-care assessments include the use of interviews and adaptive behavior checklists with family members, environmental assessments, and direct observation (see chapters 3 and 5 for more on assessment). Assessment should reflect the settings that students use or will use. For example, if a student eats meals in the school cafeteria, then the related skills of cafeteria use may be a priority, such as getting in line, selecting food, and carrying a tray. As a student becomes older and receives more instruction in the community, then the associated skills of packing a lunch and eating at work or restaurant use are appropriate teaching targets. Family-style dining may become a priority if it is preferred by the family or if the student's future placement indicates the need.

Interview or Self-Report

Information may be collected from team members through interview using a checklist of self-care skills. Interviews may begin with general questions, such as "Describe Jamal's typical morning routine getting ready for school," and move to more detailed aspects about skills that appear to be priorities (Brown, Evans, Weed, & Owen, 1987), such as the following:

- Can Jamal brush his teeth? What kinds of assistance does he need (e.g., complete, more than half, less than half, little, or none)?
- In the toothbrushing routine, does Jamal initiate the task, resolve problems that arise, monitor his quality or speed, or terminate the task when done?
- Does he seem to like or dislike the task or parts of the task? Which parts?
- In the toothbrushing routine, does Jamal make choices, use his communication, or have interfering behavior?

Sometimes individuals or agencies outside the team are also asked about what self-care skills are required in settings that the student uses or may use in the near future.

As John's teachers prepared for him to enter an inclusive kindergarten, they learned that children went to the restroom in groups. They also knew that

John could probably learn to wash his hands after toileting by watching his peers. Thus, a preschool objective was to teach John to attend to several peers.

Alycin's team called six potential postschool adult agencies to see what kinds of self-care skills were required to participate. Unfortunately, only two provided assistance in toileting transfers and at mealtime; all others required independence or attendant services. This news made the team place more emphasis on improving Alycin's ease with assisted transfers and fluency in feeding herself (finger foods or the self-feeder).

Direct Observation

Some self-care skills, such as taking a bite, taking a drink, or eliminating in the toilet, can be separated from the chain (or routine) for instructional purposes, but these behaviors usually are taught as part of a routine. For example, the target skill of bladder elimination may be taught in the context of the toileting routine, which is task analyzed into its component behaviors: walking to the toilet, unfastening clothing, pulling down pants, and so on. For some students, extension and enrichment skills, such as initiating by asking permission to go to the bathroom, or problem solving by requesting assistance are taught concurrently or added after progress is made on the core steps.

Published task analyses such as those by Baker and Brightman (1997) can be used to guide assessment observations and instruction, but teachers often conclude that it is more practical to develop their own task analyses (chapter 4). Task analyses may be developed by performing the task, observing capable peers perform the task, observing focus students performing the task, and getting team input. Task analyses should be socially valid in that they reflect the ways others around the student do the task (family members or peers at school) and include materials used at home or school or other relevant environments. For many students and self-care targets, consultation with family members and related services staff (the OT, PT, or SLP) greatly improves the task analysis (see Box 9–1).

Use Socially Valid Procedures, Appropriate for Age and Culture

Social validity refers to the acceptability of procedures and outcomes according to social norms. For example, what are priorities and concerns that families

Box 9–1 An Example of Meaningful Self-Care Assessment

Ms. Perez, John's special education teacher, and Mr. Lee, the occupational therapist, visited John's family at home about a month before his IEP meeting was scheduled. Ms. Perez chose to use the Vineland Scale of Adaptive Behavior to interview John's mother on his adaptive behaviors, in addition to an informal interview and environmental assessment. She took advantage of being in John's home to assess the environments where John completed self-care tasks: his bedroom, the bathroom, the kitchen, and the dining room. Ms. Perez discussed the family's routine in the morning getting ready for school, in the evening getting ready for bed, and mealtimes at home and in the community. What follows are the assessment findings:

John's scores range from 1 year to 3 years on the Vineland. While not toilet trained and still using diapers, his physician says John is physiologically capable of toileting independence. John does eat finger foods without assistance and uses a spoon, but he is messy and does not appear to chew his food thoroughly. John participates in most grooming skills but still requires some verbal and physical assistance. He can dress independently in clothing with no fasteners, such as elastic-waist pants and T-shirts, but he needs full physical assistance with zippers, buttons, and snaps.

Based on these findings, the team decided a number of things: (a) John's priorities for self-care instruction are toileting independently, chewing food, using a fork, and washing his hands and face; (b) John will receive instruction in mealtime behaviors and fastening clothing only as natural opportunities present themselves; (c) task analyses will be used to guide teaching and to measure John's progress; and (d) the members of the team will keep a time chart to record toileting successes and accidents and a frequency count of correct and incorrect bites for chewing.

or support providers have for students? What standards do the student's peers have for performing self-care skills? What community norms are relevant to a task being performed in an acceptable way? Social validity is important when teams select a skill to teach, plan how the student will be taught to perform the skill (including prompting and consequence procedures), decide how the skill will be performed (materials, location), select criteria for acceptable performance, and plan how to evaluate learning.

The acceptability of teaching strategies cannot be ignored. For example, overcorrection, or the repeated performance of the correct behavior after an error, has been demonstrated as an effective component in some toilet-training programs. In the Azrin and Foxx (1971) program, a student who has had a toilet accident was required to pull down pants, sit on toilet, stand, and pull up pants five times after each accident. While this procedure may indeed have been effective in reducing toileting accidents, there are many alternative strategies that are both positive and effective ways to improve toileting skills. Most team members view overcorrection as punishing, demeaning, stigmatizing, and intrusive and thus unacceptable.

Teams should compare their teaching methods to methods used to teach students without disabilities in similar settings and judge the appropriateness of the techniques. Family members should also evaluate the

fitness of the technique for their son or daughter. Because of the personal and private nature of many self-care skills, it is even more critical that team members evaluate their comfort level with teaching plans. In one study addressing how menstrual care might be taught, nondisabled women in the community were surveyed to determine if instruction should be conducted using a doll rather than directly with the students themselves (Epps, Stern, & Horner, 1990). Women in the community indicated a preference for instruction using a doll, citing the intrusiveness of instruction on the student and the potential to negatively react to such an approach.

Self-care routines targeted for instruction, as well as the procedures for instruction and monitoring progress, should be age and culture appropriate. Skills are *chronologically age appropriate* for a student if performed by others of the same age. The specific ways skills are accomplished, as well as the materials and setting used, can be influenced by a student's age. Whether a skill becomes a priority may also be determined by a student's chronological age. For example, completely independent toileting is not an appropriate goal for a preschool or primary school–aged child since typical children of this age receive assistance from parents or siblings in public toilets, with soap and towel dispensers, and even with getting on and off the toilet and manipulating doors because of the height, size, and novelty of the equipment. When students in elementary and middle school are still dependent on others for toileting, eating, and grooming assistance, however, their differences may isolate them from their peers. Age appropriateness may also affect the selection of criteria. For example, Young, West, Howard, and Whitney (1986) recorded the dressing rate of skilled peers with and without disabilities to calculate an average of these rates, which became the goal rate for instruction.

Like some of his peers, Jamal wears button-fly designer jeans, but the buttons are very difficult for him to fasten and unfasten. Many peers also wear snap-and-zip jeans, which would be easier for him to handle.

At 17, Alycin has her legs and armpits shaved by her mom; in the summer, because Alycin likes to swim, she also has a bikini shave! Alycin likes to pick out the shaving cream.

Culturally-appropriate criteria, or practices that family members value that relate to heritage, religious practices, and beliefs, may influence the performance of some self-care skills, particularly dressing and diet. Not enough attention has been given to the impact of family values and culture on teaching content. Listening to families as valued team members gives others on the team opportunities to learn about cultural preferences the family may have.

Involve Peers

The ways in which peers perform tasks are important in selecting skills for instruction and determining how they will be performed. Research shows that the attitudes of typical peers toward students with disabilities are better when students who have disabilities are viewed by their peers as being similar to them (Bak & Siperstein, 1987). For example, in the grooming area, this can mean several things: (a) looking similar to their peers in dress, hairstyle, and grooming habits and (b) performing grooming skills at the same time and place. Especially in dressing and grooming, peers may be better models than professional teachers.

Now that Alycin spends more time in community-based instruction, she and her team, including her friends, feel she must "dress the part." This means no skirts because they ride up in the wheelchair and none of the other girls wear skirts and no shorts because they are not suitable for a job; instead, she wears long, lightweight pants that she and several high school friends picked out.

Nondisabled peers can be involved as task companions, partners, models, or assistants with students who have severe disabilities, though caution must be applied so that one-way helping is not the only outcome. Mike's peers in Figure 9–1 assist him by handing him a milk carton and providing assistance with his lunch when he needs it. Those who have used this approach often comment on how students' motivation for learning is high when peers replace adults as learning partners.

John likes to trick adults by pretending that he cannot do things, but he is very responsive to praise and encouragement by his peers and being liked by his classmates. Ms. Perez and Ms. Johnson acknowledge John's accomplishments and encourage classmates to praise John when he is successful in a task "all by himself."

FIGURE 9–1
Mike's Lunch Routine
Mike's routine illustrates partial participation, interaction with peers, and embedded skills: (a) Mike cannot reach into the cafeteria line refrigerator where milk is kept, so a classmate lends a hand; (b) Mike has learned to grasp his lunch money and reach and extend it to the cashier to pay and (c) get his lunch; (d) Mike can eat independently with an adapted spoon and bowl; (e) when Mike needs assistance, he gets it from classmates.

(a)

(b)

(c)

(d)

(e)

Staub, Spaulding, Peck, Gallucci, and Schwartz (1996) taught adolescents in junior high to be student aides, which involved ability awareness training, adult modeling, and an accountability system for participation in the student aide program. They scheduled student aides to lend a range of support to students with disabilities in general education classes. Support was given in social, academic, communication, and daily living skills and for appropriate behavior and resulted in many positive outcomes. Here are a few quotes from those who supported during self-care routines:

Peer: "Another change is that he can tie his shoes by himself. I taught him how to do that" (p. 201).

Physical education teacher: "Kelly initially relied on her aide to help her with the locker routine. But now she's doing a great job at it and she's even helping another student in the class with disabilities with her locker routine" (p. 201).

Use Partial Participation Carefully

Completion of most self-care routines tends to be necessary, and when not performed by a student must be performed by someone else for the student. Still, there are many physical and sensory disabilities that interfere with attaining independence. The team may want to consider using partial participation (Baumgart et al., 1982) and adaptations that allow students to take part to some degree in activities, to attain dignity, and to profit from good grooming rather than remaining totally dependent on others. Modifications for partial participation include the following:

1. Modified or adapted materials (e.g., toothbrushes, combs, forks, and cups that are designed for easier gripping; Velcro fasteners in place of buttons, hooks, or snaps)
2. Adaptive switches or automated appliances (e.g., hair dryers activated by a pressure switch, battery-powered toothbrushes that provide scrubbing action automatically)
3. Changed sequences within an activity (e.g., allowing a student to put her bathing suit on under her clothes before going to a public pool, sitting on the toilet for balance and then scooting underwear down)
4. Personal assistance (e.g., fastening pants for a child in the bathroom, guiding a student's hand to scoop food)

Teachers should not eliminate skills for instruction merely on the basis of perceived difficulty or student characteristics. When the team decides to use partial participation, any adaptations should be designed to be age appropriate, nonstigmatizing, and practical (Ferguson & Baumgart, 1991). When developing partial participation activities, the team should take care that student participation is active, is meaningful to the function of the activity, and is not scheduled at the same time as other valuable classroom instruction. As with all instructional strategies, ongoing evaluation of partial participation is needed to determine when assistance can be faded or eliminated to ensure that modifications result in satisfactory outcomes and empowered students. Partial participation should enable respectful inclusion of students in more activities and interactions with peers.

At home, Myra (Alycin's mom) and Alycin have a long history of using partial participation strategies in self-care tasks. For example, Alycin can grasp a wet washcloth and has the wiping motion, but because of her cerebral palsy, she does not apply enough pressure to get her mouth or arms clean. Still, when showering, Myra gives Alycin a soap mitt and lets her spread the soap on her body, while Myra does any scrubbing that is needed. During the morning routine, Alycin helps by holding up her arms as her mom applies deodorant. When it is time to brush teeth, Myra asks Alycin which of several flavors she wants and gives her a "filled" electric brush, and Alycin does the lateral motion up front; then Myra gets the back teeth as Alycin holds her mouth open. Myra adds, "I do the floss, she holds her mouth open, and the job is done!"

Select Appropriate and Respectful Environments for Instruction

Once priority skills are selected, teams must determine the time and places for instruction. Teaching in the places and at the times when the activity is routinely used is a characteristic of quality programs for students with severe disabilities because this practice uses normalized routines, allows peer modeling, and promotes skill generalization (Losardo & Bricker, 1994; Sewell, Collins, Hemmeter, & Schuster, 1998). The ultimate goal of instruction is to enable students to use self-care skills appropriately with as much independence as possible alongside others or in private at home, at friends' homes, at school, and in the community. Given this goal and the fact that students with severe disabilities have difficulty generalizing learned skills from one setting to another, there is clear support for instruction in natural settings.

When students are segregated from their peers for instruction, the social interaction opportunities are reduced, the probability of skill generalization is lessened, and the use of staff time may be inefficient. There are functional settings for teaching self-care skills at school, such as the restrooms for toileting and grooming skills and locker rooms for dressing and showering. Much younger students will have opportunities to dress up and put on art smocks. These are activities that school-age peers complete alongside each other, and peers make the best models for age-appropriate dress and grooming styles.

For some skills, *privacy* will be a critical consideration for when and where to teach. The team may decide to conduct instruction in a natural setting at a time when peers are not present (e.g., teaching grooming during class instead of between classes) or in a location not used by peers for the activity (e.g. a bathroom by the nurse's office or eating in a classroom instead of the cafeteria). Many self-care tasks are conducted in private, especially toileting, bathing, and dressing. When peers see that a student beyond the preschool years requires instruction in toileting or basic grooming skills, it could be stigmatizing for the student with disabilities and uncomfortable for peers. Peers may perceive the student as less able in all areas of functioning. Students may learn to think that it is acceptable to be exposed in public restrooms or that they should be compliant with any adults in any situations, which may make a student vulnerable to exploitation. These factors argue for teaching some skills in isolated settings. Other reasons given in the literature for privacy during instruction include use of specialized equipment and the establishment of a calm environment to facilitate muscle tone in students with physical disabilities (Vogtle & Snell, 2004).

The decision to teach a student in private away from peers must be made cautiously. We recommend that the team follow these guidelines when making this decision.

- If the self-care activity is one that other class members perform openly at school (e.g., hand washing, using a utensil at lunch, taking outer garments off on arrival and putting them on for recess), then activity-based, nonisolated teaching may be appropriate. For example, most students do not brush their teeth at school, so if toothbrushing is a priority and school time is devoted to its teaching, then isolated teaching may be best.
- If privacy is natural and appropriate to the task (e.g., toileting, menstrual hygiene, changing clothes for swimming), then any instruction should take place in private although during expected times so that task completion leads to natural outcomes (e.g., swimming follows changing into a swimsuit).

For reasons of safety, the student should be taught some skills in addition to basic self-care. When teaching skills that are typically conducted privately, the student should know the following:

- When it is appropriate to perform tasks
- With whom it is appropriate to perform tasks
- Who may give directions for these tasks
- When exceptions would be made to privacy standards

These questions have not been answered by research but are ones that the team should evaluate together. It is critical to consult with the family and the student to determine the best choices for time and location of instruction.

Select Uncomplicated and Effective Instructional Methods

The commonsense guideline for designing teaching programs is that programs be easy to use and practical but that they work! This same message has been designated as the *principle of parsimony* by Etzel and LeBlanc (1979): when several approaches work, select the simplest. We have found that the most "doable" program that works with an individual student is team developed: it reflects input from all team members, is built on consideration of assessment results and the student's stage of learning, involves peers when appropriate, respects student preferences, is sensitive to the student's age and culture, and uses proven procedures. Stages of learning (e.g., acquisition, fluency, maintenance, and generalization), which were described in chapter 4, influence the selection of teaching strategies. The next section provides suggestions from current research to help teams design programs to teach self-care skills.

Acquisition Stage Strategies

During the acquisition stage of learning, the student does not know how to perform the task without assistance. The goal of instruction during this stage is to provide maximal information to the student about how to perform the core steps and related behavior in the routine. Students in acquisition perform between 0% and 60% of the task correctly on assessment probes. Students who have demonstrated performance above 60% are probably in the fluency, maintenance, or generalization stages, and acquisition strategies will not be effective. Most self-care studies have addressed skills in the acquisition stage of learning and thus have used some sort of physical prompting across steps in a task analysis. Table 9–2 describes instructional strategies and cites supportive research studies for each (also see chapter 4; Duker, Didden, & Sigafoos, 2004; Steere & Pancsofar, 1995).

Task Analyses and Chaining Approaches for Instruction Most self-care instruction will require a task analysis during the acquisition stage. To teach the sequence of steps in a task, teams choose one of three chaining approaches: total task, forward chaining, and backward chaining.

The *total task approach* involves teaching a student each task step in order during every instructional opportunity. This approach has several advantages: the

TABLE 9–2
Effective Strategies for Teaching Self-Care Skills

Strategy	Research on self-care skills	Considerations: Beneficial features and *Cautions*
Generic strategy: Provide opportunities and reinforce appropriate behavior Identify natural occasions during the schedule or create opportunities for students to use the target skills. Embed teaching in these activities, thereby distributing teaching trials and teaching in natural contexts. Emphasize or give natural reinforcers (praise neat eating after checking table and floor for spillage, go outside after putting on jacket); encourage self-monitoring of performance (check appearance in mirror).	**Toileting** (Hobbs & Peck, 1985) **Eating** (Nelson, Cone, & Hanson, 1975; Riordan et al., 1980, 1984; Smith, Piersel, Filbeck, & Gross, 1983)	• Simple strategy, appropriate in most settings • Embedding instruction appears to increase generalization both by its association with natural stimuli and response variations and distributed rather than massed trials • Embedding involves distributed learning trials and natural stimuli, both of which seem to improve student motivation • *Many students need more information via prompts or other instruction to perform the behavior; having an opportunity is not enough*
Generic Strategy: Shaping Reinforce successful approximations of the desired behavior, expecting better and better performance with less assistance over time. Follow reinforcement guidelines.[1] Generally, shaping is a part of all successful teaching procedures.	**Eating** (Luiselli, 1991; O'Brien, Bugle, & Azrin, 1972) **Toileting and related skills** (Levine & Elliot, 1970; Luiselli, 1996; Marshall, 1966; Richmond, 1983)	• Allows student to experience success by reinforcing any improvements in performance • *May require extra materials or time to allow for gradually increased task demands (e.g., using a variety of clothing sizes so student is exposed to first to over-sized clothing and later to natural-sized clothing)*
Chaining: Backward Chaining Providing instruction on the final step(s) of a task until mastery on final step(s) is achieved, then providing instruction on the next step(s) from the end until mastery and so on. Follow reinforcement guidelines.[1]	**Eating** (Hagopian et al., 1996, Luieselli, 1991)	• Task is broken into small teachable units for students who learn better with shorter sequences rather than receiving instruction through the entire task • Begins instruction with completing the task, which can be naturally reinforcing • *Students may be prompted through steps that they may be able to perform independently*
Chaining: Forward Chaining Teach the first step(s) of a task until mastery is achieved, while guiding student through rest of task on each trial. Then expect student to complete first learned step and shift instruction to the next step(s) until mastery (and guide through rest of task) and so on. Follow reinforcement guidelines.[1]	**Toileting and related skills** (Bettison, 1982) **Dressing** (Alberto, Jobes, Sizemore, & Doran, 1980) **Menstrual care** (Epps et al., 1990; Richman et al., 1984)	• Breaks tasks into small teachable units for students who are frustrated by being prompted through the entire task • *May be more difficult for student to understand function or outcome of performance, which may affect student's motivation*
Chaining: Total Task Teach all steps of a task at the same time in a forward order. Use a prompting system on each step. Follow reinforcement guidelines.[1] As student masters a given step, expect student to perform that step without assistance.	**Eating** (Denny et al., 2000) **Dressing** (Reese & Snell, 1991) **Other daily living skills** (Matson et al., 1990)	• May be the most natural chaining approach, as all steps treated as learning opportunities • Works best if chain *not too long*; can subdivide into shorter task clusters and use total task on each cluster • *Learning may be faster when used after student has reached end of acquisition phase (has learned one*

339

TABLE 9–2 (*Continued*)
Effective Strategies for Teaching Self-Care Skills

Strategy	Research on self-care skills	Considerations: Beneficial features and *Cautions*
		third to half the task); thus might start with backward or forward chaining and then switch to total task when one third or so of the steps have been learned
Prompting: Graduated Guidance and Decreasing Assistance Provide physical assistance to the student to complete the task, gradually decreasing the amount as the student begins to perform the task either (a) by reducing pressure or (b) by moving your hand from the student's hand to the wrist, to the elbow, to the shoulder, and away. Reduction of assistance can be based on probe performance or the independent movement cues of the student. Follow reinforcement guidelines.[1]	**Eating** (Albin, 1977; Azrin & Armstrong, 1973; Denny et al., 2000; Miller, Patton, & Henton, 1978; Simbert, Minor, & McCoy, 1977) **Dressing** (Reese & Snell, 1991; Sisson et al., 1988) **Other daily living skills** (Matson et al., 1990)	• Provides maximal information about how to perform the task, especially for students new to the task, for students with physical disabilities or visual impairments, and for other students who respond positively to physical assistance • Eliminates time going through prompt levels that the student does not respond to • *May limit opportunity for students to perform some steps independently or with less assistance; some risk for providing "too much help"; need a plan for fading assistance* • *Not for students who find physical assistance aversive*
Prompting: Modeling or Observational Learning Arrange students so they can watch other classmates being taught and then be provided direct instruction to complete the task. Students are taught in groups of two or three. Each student is prompted to watch the whole task while the others are instructed. Follow reinforcement guidelines.[1]	**Dressing** (Biederman et al., 1998; Wolery et al., 1980) **Other daily living skills** (Wolery, Ault, Gast, Doyle, & Griffen, 1991) **Handwashing** (Biederman et al., 1998)	• May assist students in learning to "learn by watching others," a useful self-instruction approach • Allows for efficient instruction by grouping students • *Does not provide for privacy* • *Requires focused visual attention, memory, and ability to imitate* • *Not appropriate for instructor to perform some self-care tasks for observation (e. g., toileting, complete undressing)*
Prompting: Simultaneous Prompting Cue the student to look at task materials, give a task request, and immediately prompt student through each step of the task without a latency. Continue prompting until probe trials indicate student has reached mastery on a step.	**Dressing** (Sewell, et al., 1998)	• Provides maximal information about how to perform the task, especially for students new to the task, ensuring success • *May limit opportunity for students to perform some steps independently or with less assistance; some risk for providing "too much help"*
Prompting: System of Least Prompts Select a hierarchy of two to four prompts of increasing assistance (e. g., verbal, model, physical), give the cue to the student, and pause a fixed latency for student response (e.g., 3 seconds). If student is incorrect or does not respond,	**Eating** (Benerdt & Bricker, 1978) **Brushing teeth** (Horner & Keilitz, 1975) **Dressing skills** (Young et al., 1986)	• Provides opportunities for the student to perform each step independently or with the least amount of assistance required. • Strategy is easily implemented with multiple-step tasks

• May work better once student has learned about a third or more of the task steps; start with a most-to-least system and then switch

• May be time inefficient for students who require most prompts at the most intrusive end of the hierarchy to perform the task correctly

• Provides maximal assistance for student success
• Prompts are easily matched to individual students characteristics
• Delay is individualized and allows student opportunity to perform independently before receiving assistance
• *Not for students who have difficulty waiting for assistance (progressive time delay may be more effective than constant time delay with these students)*

present the next least intrusive prompt and again pause. Repeat the procedure until the student is successful with least intrusive prompt. Follow reinforcement guidelines.[1]

Prompting: Time Delay

Initially, position student for task and give a single effective prompt with no latency for each step with praise for performance and reinforcement at the end. Over successive trials, insert small amounts of time between natural cues (or earlier step in chain) and instructional prompts to allow for student to initiate step. May follow 0-second delay sessions with either a constant amount of delay (such as 4 seconds) or a progressive but gradually increasing amount of delay (e.g., 1, 2, 3, 4 seconds) over successive session. Decrease delay following errors. Follow reinforcement guidelines.[1]

Eating (Collins et al., 1991)

Brushing teeth (Snell et al., 1989)

Other daily living skills (Wolery et al., 1991)

[1]**Reinforcement guidelines:** When using shaping or any of the prompting or chaining procedures, reinforcement follows a similar pattern: Give quick reinforcement for independent steps and for cooperating or performing teaching step (e. g., praise, smile, pat) with more reinforcement or natural reinforcement at the end of the task. Reinforcement must be individualized.

task gets done, and students have the opportunity to see the functional outcome of the task, which may not be apparent if only one step is taught at a time. The disadvantage is that lengthy tasks may make early learning too complex, and it may be too time consuming to proceed through the whole task. Thus, for some students who can do less than a third of the task on their own, backward chaining, forward chaining, repeated practice on problem steps, or instruction in smaller skill clusters (e.g., core steps only) is more appropriate. After students begin to master around half the task, teachers shift the teaching focus to performing fluently, completing entire routines (total task approach), and transferring the skill to a range of natural environments.

While there are no rigid rules for deciding which instructional procedure is most effective at a given stage, there are "rules of thumb." For students who are completely new to a skill (in the acquisition stage), more intrusive prompts, such as *physical prompts* or *physical guidance*, may be best. This might mean using graduated guidance, time delay with physical prompts, or a decreasing assistance prompt hierarchy. During the acquisition stage, many students cannot respond to minimal verbal or gesture cues. Teaching time can be lost moving through two or more prompt levels in an increasing prompt hierarchy, such as a least prompts system, especially when the least intrusive prompts may not yet be meaningful. For example, during initial instruction for combing hair, the verbal prompt to "make a part" may not be understood by some students, while others may not be able to imitate a model prompt to make a part. Students with motor disabilities also may need physical guidance initially to learn the movements necessary to perform skills. The exception is students who are less able to tolerate physical prompts.

A second chaining approach used during acquisition is called *backward chaining*. To implement backward chaining, the teacher guides the student through all but the last step in the task and then teaches the last step. When the last step is mastered, the student is assisted through all steps up to the next-to-the-last step, and instruction is given, after which the student is expected to perform the last step. When this second-to-the-last step is mastered, instruction shifts backward to the third-to-the-last step, after which the student performs the last two steps without instruction. Additional steps are added until the student performs the entire task independently. Hagopian, Farrell, and Amari (1996) used backward chaining to teach cup usage to a 12-year-old boy who refused liquids and food. The

student was first taught to swallow and then was expected to accept liquids and to swallow to be reinforced. The final step taught was to bring the cup to his mouth, accept the liquid, and swallow.

Prompting Procedures Several prompting approaches have been used successfully in early learning: graduated guidance, time delay, simultaneous prompting, and system of least prompts. While graduated guidance is one of the most intrusive and intensive approaches we describe, it has been used to teach self-care skills more often than any other method reported. Prompts are intensive initially and then faded (e.g., Denny et al., 2000). Reese and Snell (1991) used graduated guidance to teach three children with severe disabilities, including motor and sensory impairments, to put on and take off jackets and coats. Instruction began with oversize clothes and involved individualized task analyses. They used three levels of prompts, which progressively faded guidance from full to none:

- Full assist (teacher assists by placing a hand over the student's hand)
- Partial assist (teacher uses only an index finger and thumb to assist)
- Touch assist (teacher assists with only one finger)

Full assistance was provided initially and was continued on each task step until the student indicated that less help was needed. This was communicated by (a) pressure cues from the student, (b) correct responses made during the latency period, or (c) evidence from instructional data that the student had been successful with less help in the previous teaching trials.

Graduated guidance also may be faded by *hand-to-shoulder* fading (Azrin & Armstrong, 1973; Simbert, Minor, & McCoy, 1977). In this approach, guidance is faded from hand-over-hand assistance first to a gentle touch on the hand, then to the forearm, to the elbow, to the upper arm, and finally to the shoulder and upper back. A third way to fade guidance is through *backward chaining*, in which guidance is provided from the beginning of the task though all but the last step, when guidance is reduced or delayed. Guidance is gradually faded by reducing assistance on more and more steps from the end to the beginning of the task.

Another strategy for fading graduated guidance is to use performance on probes, referred to as *decreasing assistance*. Matson, Taras, Sevin, Love, and Fridley (1990) used probe performance to decide when to withdraw assistance in teaching brushing teeth, combing hair, dressing, and eating skills to three students with autism and mental retardation. The teacher modeled the entire task, physically guided the student through the task, and had the student perform the task under probe conditions. On the next instructional session, guidance was not provided for those steps that the student had performed correctly under the probe condition.

In addition to the use of probes and pressure cues from the student, the level of guidance is sometimes reduced after a set numbers of trials. For students with multiple disabilities who were learning to dress, Sisson, Kilwein, and Van Hasselt (1988) reduced the level of assistance after every 10 teaching trials.

Time delay is another effective teaching method. Constant time delay, which involves initial 0-second latencies followed by 4-second latencies, has been successfully applied to teach basic eating skills (Collins, Gast, Wolery, Halcombe, & Leatherby, 1991). Table 9–3 shows the task analyses Collins et al. used to teach a group of young students to eat with a spoon, drink from a cup, and use a napkin at meals. Teachers may either increase the delay period gradually in small increments of 1 to 2 seconds (progressive delay) or increase delay quickly by moving from no-delay trials to trials

delayed by 4 seconds (constant delay). Applying the principle of parsimony (Etzel & LeBlanc, 1979), we recommend using constant delay, which is easier to use than progressive time delay and is effective.

Simultaneous prompting is a more recent approach that involves ongoing use of a single effective prompt on every step of a task with no response latency. Teachers know to completely fade the prompt on task steps as soon as a probe indicates that the student can complete that step independently. One study applied this prompting approach with preschoolers and the self-care task of dressing (Sewell et al., 1998), and another used this approach to teach hand-washing skills (Parrott, Schuster, Collins, & Gassaway, 2000).

The *system of least prompts* has been applied to teach dressing skills (Young et al., 1986). During acquisition, the students were prompted first with verbal and gestural prompts when they did not respond or when they made an error. If the verbal or gestural prompt did not result in correct performance, graduated physical guidance was given. Students were given intermittent praise for success during teaching and praise, hugs, pats, and stickers at the end of the task whenever performance was improved over the

TABLE 9–3
Task Analyses for Teaching Mealtime Skills with Constant Time Delay

Behavior	Discriminative Stimuli	Response
Spoon	"Eat"	Grasp spoon
	Spoon in hand	Scoop food
	Food in spoon	Raise spoon to lips
	Spoon touching lips	Open mouth
	Mouth open	Put spoon in mouth
	Food in mouth	Remove spoon
	Spoon out of mouth	Lower spoon
	Spoon on table	Release grasp
Cup	"Drink"	Grasp cup
	Cup in hand	Raise cup to lips
	Cup touches lips	Tilt cup to mouth
	Liquid in mouth	Close mouth and drink
	Liquid swallowed	Lower cup to table
	Cup on table	Release grasp
Napkin	"Wipe"	Grasp napkin
	Napkin in hand	Raise hand to face
	Napkin touching face	Wipe face
	Face wiped	Lower napkin
	Napkin on table	Release grasp

Reprinted from "Using Constant Time Delay to Teach Self-Feeding to Young Students With Severe/Profound Handicaps: Evidence of Limited Effectiveness" by B. C. Collins, D. L. Gast, M. Wolery, A. Halcombe, and J. Letherby, 1991. *Journal of Developmental and Physical Difficulties, 3*, p. 163, Copyright © 1991 by Plenum Publishing. Reprinted by permission.

previous session. Once the student could perform a task correctly in a consistent manner without prompts, the training procedure was changed to improve the students' fluency or rate of responding. Difficult steps, which were characterized by hesitation, more frequent errors, or self-correcting, were identified and given repeated practice. Thus, if a student usually hesitated and sometimes erred only when pulling a shirt off his head, he was given 10 consecutive trials on this step alone.

Fluency Stage Strategies

During fluency learning, students understand the task requirements but need more practice to perform the skill consistently and at an appropriate pace. Students need to be motivated to improve fluency. When students are near mastery of acquisition learning (more than 60% of steps correct), it is often time to revise a program, reduce prompts, and address motivation (e.g., shift from antecedent prompting tactics to consequences, making reinforcement contingent on faster or more perfect performance). Targeting more fluent performance in self-care routines often means emphasizing timed performance: teachers or students might time their performance or students may learn to "beat the clock" to be ready for a preferred activity that follows the routine. Other strategies to increase student motivation for practicing and perfecting skill routines include providing choices, recruiting peer support, and introducing more challenging or extended steps.

Sometimes the task steps need to be looked at and improved. When difficult steps are simplified or eliminated or students are given extra practice on them, errors can be reduced and fluency enhanced. Fluency training in self-care routines may be necessary if adults are to let students use their skills. For example, in a busy family, parents may dress a child who takes too much time to dress by herself.

When Jamal finds something intolerable, he jumps up and down, screams, and runs. Intolerable events may be unfamiliar situations, changes in familiar routines, or a task he finds too difficult. One example of a difficult task for Jamal was buttoning his button-fly jeans. In the toileting routine, Jamal was independent except for this step. This meant he would leave the bathroom with his pants open, which constituted a social disaster at school! His teacher described one of two things that would happen at these times: (a) he'd wait until someone buttoned his

pants or gave him hand-over-hand prompting, which he hated, or (b) his teacher would "back off" and give minimal cues but repeat her requests to hurry him, and he'd get very upset. After meeting to solve the problem, the team changed the program. His mom agreed to replace button-fly jeans with zipper jeans as he outgrew them, which would simplify the task. The occupational therapist cut the buttonholes a little bigger, making them easier to button and unbutton (simplify task). Staff let him pick a preferred activity photo that he traded in right after buttoning his pants (motivation). He worked by himself but could request "help" by signing (communication in place of problem behavior). Staff helped out little by little and praised him for the buttons he had done alone. Currently, Jamal buttons three and sometimes four of the five buttons.

Maintenance Stage Strategies

When students begin to demonstrate some mastery of a task, teachers should select less intrusive strategies, provide more opportunities for students to perform independently, build skill performance into the schedule as a routine, fade artificial reinforcement that may have been used, and fade their presence altogether. Teachers can fade instruction and build routine performance in a number of ways, including the following:

- Stepping behind, then away from the student, and engaging in other tasks nearby
- Leaving the task area at gradually increasing but unpredictable times (Dunlap & Johnson, 1985)
- Introducing peers into the instructional area so that teacher time and attention are divided among students and less focused on the target student
- Eliminating intrusive prompts, such as physical guidance and modeling, and using simple pointing gestures or nonspecific verbal prompts (e.g., "What's next?")
- Using picture task schedules as "permanent prompts" for students to self-manage their daily self-care and chore routines and involving students in selecting and arranging task photos in a schedule book each morning (Bambara & Cole, 1997; Irvine, Erickson, Singer, & Stahlberg, 1992) (chapter 14 expands on ideas for self-prompting)

Teaching students to self-manage their dressing or grooming performances is a well-documented maintenance strategy. Several types of stimuli (e.g., pictures, picture checklists, tape-recorded messages, and video-tapes) can be used to teach students to prompt and monitor their own performance of a series of self-care tasks that they already know how to accomplish in part. For example, Garff and Storey (1998) taught young adults to use a checklist to self-manage hygiene during work, while Lasater and Brady (1995) used video self-modeling to teach shaving. Material prompts like these may or may not be faded, depending on the student, but such prompts are designed by the team to be nonstigmatizing, easily carried, and independently used. For example, students can select and arrange pictures of morning routine tasks in a pocket-size booklet to be used like a schedule. For other students, a booklet of task pictures (used initially during acquisition training) may be shortened to single-task photos and continue to remind students of task steps after teachers have faded their ongoing supervision (Figure 9–2). For students able to operate a small cassette tape recorder, the Pocket Coach (Attainment Company, Inc.) can facilitate self-management. Teachers let students or peers record ahead a series of up to 15 12-second self-prompting messages (e.g., brush teeth, shave, shower and shut curtain all the way; dress, comb hair, straighten bed, take medication, and eat; pack lunch and get bus money). When a person presses the play button, the message plays or repeats, but when the done button is pressed, the tape progresses to the next message. More information on assistive technology and links to vendors can be found at http://www.abledata.com, http://www.ataccess.org, and http:// www.vats.org.

Generalization Stage Strategies

During generalization and the other advanced stages of learning (fluency and maintenance), it is important to reduce prompting and to fade from artificial to natural consequences. To make school and community environments supportive of skills, teachers may involve peers and show them how to give more natural forms of reinforcement (e.g., high five, "All right!") and error correction (e.g., "Try it again," point to mistake). Environments should be arranged so that students can use their acquired skills regularly and obtain approval (or learn to give self-approval) for task completion at the end of a time period or after a cluster of related routines are completed (e.g., the three interrelated tasks of using the bathroom, washing hands, and returning independently to work). When students use self-scheduling photo books to plan their daily school schedule, self-reinforcement can be an added component of instruction.

Using multiple instructors (i.e., teachers, peers, therapists, parents) also enhances generalization because students learn (a) that "who's present" is less relevant than are task stimuli and (b) that they can complete the task despite differences between teachers. Generalization is facilitated when students are expected to use the target skill during all opportunities across multiple environments (e.g., eating in the school cafeteria, home economics room, and restaurants; using the toilet and washing hands in the classroom toilet, the school restroom, the restaurant restroom, and the locker room). Teaching across multiple settings requires the student to adjust performance to apply the skills across (a) differences in materials, (b) changing background stimuli (e.g., noise, commotion, temperature), and (c) varying problems that may arise. For example, differences from one bathroom to another include the door into the toilet, the presence or absence of a stall, the type of lock on a stall, the height of the toilet, the presence or absence of wall supports, the location of supports, the location and type of the toilet paper dispenser, the height of the sink and faucets, the type of soap dispenser, the type of paper towel dispenser, and the location of the trash container. Even in one bathroom, it is not unusual to have several different types of soap and towel dispensers! Teaching across multiple task opportunities facilitates generalization, although learning may be slow initially.

FIGURE 9–2
Task Step Photos for Teaching Jamal Hand Washing

Reinforcement

If reinforcement is to be effective, it must be individually planned. What is reinforcing varies from student to student. Some students may need more concrete reinforcers (e.g., associated object present, not a photo), while others may need more frequent reinforcement (e.g., praise during the task, preferred activity at the end). What to use, how much, and how to use it must be designed to suit a given student. The goal is to teach students to attend to natural reinforcers so their performance is not dependent on artificial reinforcers:

- John's independent toileting is reinforced by having dry pants, increased independence, and privacy and by being like his peers. Feeding himself without spilling is reinforced by reducing his hunger more quickly and being neat like others.
- Jamal's ability to fasten and unfasten his pants by himself means that he finishes faster, without frustration, and he can go alone to the boy's bathroom.
- If Alycin can learn to change her feminine pad by herself, she can enjoy the privacy that goes with performing a very personal task on her own.

Still, during early instruction, especially if students have limited experience with natural reinforcers, completion of self-care activities alone may not be very reinforcing. Teachers should be prepared to use and systematically fade artificial reinforcers during these later phases of instruction.

Consider Related Skills for Instruction

Self-care tasks and routines have several components:

- *Core steps:* The essential behaviors that are involved in task completion
- *Enrichment skills:* Task-related skills that are not critical to the independent performance of a routine but add to the quality of its performance (e.g., expressive communication, social behavior, and preference or choice)
- *Extension skills:* Task-related skills that expand meaningful participation but without extensive physical requirements (e.g., initiation, preparation, monitoring the quality, monitoring the tempo, problem solving, and termination) (Brown et al., 1987)

Understandably, many teachers focus on the core skills first since these behaviors are what "gets the job done." But self-care routines provide opportunities to teach beyond the core, extending the task to a more useful level of performance and enriching the routine in ways that integrate it with social and communication skills. For example, evening mealtimes for many of us signal a time to relax and connect with friends and family; thus, we socialize, talk to each other, and make choices (all enrichment skills). As shown in Figure 9–3 for Annie and Frank, students who have severe multiple disabilities may find extension and enrichment skills to be a more meaningful way to participate in the activity than completing all the core steps.

Jamal has learned that the lunch bell signals that his "lunch bunch" peers will arrive and they'll head to the cafeteria, get and pay for their lunches, and eat together, cleaning up when finished. When Jamal learned to respond to the lunch bell and his lunch partners' arrival, he learned to initiate on his own. Mastering the lunch line (waiting, getting each item, paying) allowed Jamal to carry out preparation steps on his own. Jamal learned to watch his peers' cues to monitor his eating tempo (eat until the group is done) and to monitor quality and solve problems by watching others as they cleared their places and recycled their trash into the right receptacles. Once done, he knew that lunch was over (termination) and headed back to his homeroom.

Reflect on the school-age self-care routines that lend themselves to socialization, communication, and choice: the extension skills. It is not unusual to see high school girls conversing while doing hair and putting on makeup between classes. Joyce's fingernail-painting routine (Figure 9–4) is one routine that embeds many social, choice-making, and communication skills. We recommend that teachers enhance task analyses by adding extension and enrichment components to the core task and that they plan to teach during natural opportunities for these routines to occur, particularly when peers are involved. Students can be taught to communicate the desire to begin and end grooming tasks. For example, a student without independent mobility skills could request to be taken to the school bathroom to brush her hair after recess and request to be taken to class before she is late. Choice and approval of finished products are also communication skills that can be embedded into self-care routines. For example, a student who does not have the motor skills to style her hair may be able to initiate a need for grooming, make choices about style and accessories, and approve the final style.

FIGURE 9–3

Middle School Students Extend and Enrich Lunch Time. (a) Annie has the opportunity to communicate with the cafeteria cashier and (b) interacts with a peer who helps her balance a cup for drinking. (c) Frank at a community-based eating activity where he communicates his need for assistance in getting more food by pointing to his picture board on his lap, and (d) Frank chooses what he wants, and his teacher gives physical guidance with serving.

(a)

(b)

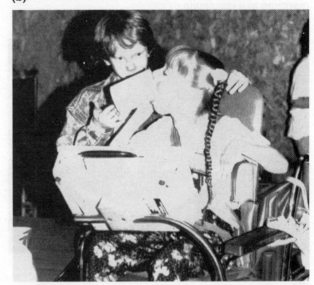

(c)

(d)

FIGURE 9–4
Painting Fingernails
Student partially participates in nail care actively by (a) requesting application of nail polish and giving directions on color preference with an eye gaze communication board, (b) holding still as nails are done, and (c) showing manicure to a classmate.

(a)

(b)

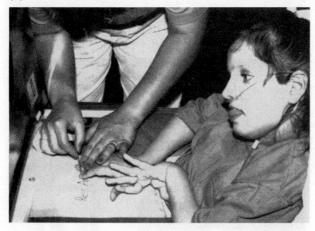

In the remainder of the chapter, we discuss toileting skills, feeding, and finally dressing and grooming skills.

Special Considerations for Toileting

Assessment and Instruction

Toileting behavior is one of the most difficult self-care skills to teach because it requires an awareness of internal stimuli (e.g., bladder fullness, bowel tension)

(c)

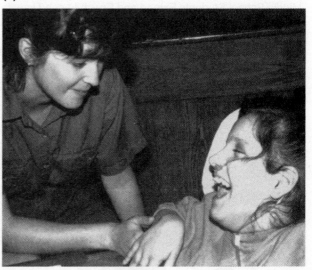

and a lengthy sequence of related skills that must be learned in part or full for the skills to be useful. In this section, we discuss the process for teaching toileting: (a) the prerequisites, (b) assessment, and (c) approaches for teaching. (See chapter 7 for bowel and bladder management for students who require atypical elimination procedures and chapter 8 for specific positioning considerations for students with motor disabilities; see also Barnes & Case-Smith, 2004; Orelove, Sobsey, & Silberman, 2004; Shephard, Procter, & Coley, 1996.)

Prerequisites for Toilet Training

Three characteristics are essential for toilet-training readiness. These characteristics are interdependent and relate to the maturity of the central nervous system and the muscle sphincters involved in elimination. Students must exhibit the following:

- Stability in the pattern of elimination
- Daily 1- to 2-hour periods of dryness
- A chronological age of 2 years or older

Generally, students who are ready for training have one bowel movement daily and three to five urinations, but many differ from this pattern. Bowel responses and some urination responses should occur within predictable daily time periods, not randomly. Being ready for instruction must be balanced with the teaching setting; ideally, students are taught these skills during the preschool years or at home. Toilet training gets more problematic when students move into elementary grades and beyond. Teams should emphasize toilet training at younger ages when schedules are more flexible and social stigma is less likely.

Assessment of Toileting Performance

Assessment of toileting performance should be used to determine the student's natural pattern of elimination as well as to measure progress in the toileting program. A toileting record may be kept on a grid of days by time intervals. We recommend the use of 15- or 30-minute intervals. While these shorter intervals demand more staff time, they provide a more accurate picture of the student's elimination pattern. Other considerations for assessment of toileting include whether data will be collected across environments (e.g., at home, in the community, all school environments), the length of the day (e.g., an interval of the school day, the whole school day, all waking hours), and who collects the data. The elimination record in Figure 9–5 was designed for John. The record illustrates 7 school days with 15-minute intervals.

To determine the natural pattern of elimination, check the student at the end of each time interval and record dryness, urination, or bowel movement. Also record if an elimination was correct (e.g., in the toilet) or an accident. At least during baseline (the period before a teaching program starts), it is important to change the student into dry clothing immediately after each accident, accompanied by neutral teacher–student interaction (neither punishing or reinforcing). This ensures that recent accidents are not confused with earlier accidents. To discover whether reliable toileting patterns exist and what these patterns are, most recommend that baseline charting continue for a minimum of at least 2 weeks, with a possible extension to 30 days if necessary (Baker & Brightman, 1997; Fredericks, Baldwin, Grove, & Moore, 1975; Giles & Wolf, 1966). The team may also want to record whether correct eliminations are self-initiated or prompted.

In the general education classroom, peers may become aware that a classmate is being toilet trained because of the frequency of removing the child to a nearby bathroom. As such issues arise, teachers should handle them with care and perhaps as part of peer

planning or support groups (Snell & Janney, 2000). The team must be sensitive to the student's right to privacy when selecting the location for baseline assessment and training. We suggest that records be easily accessible by team members who will be recording information but still secure and private—never taped to the bathroom wall.

For 1 week, Ms. Perez and her assistant, Ms. Anderson, collected baseline data somewhat sporadically on a 30-minute interval elimination record, but no steady pattern emerged. Because this was a priority skill for John, the team decided to take 2 more weeks of data but increase pants checks to 15-minute intervals, as illustrated in Figure 9–5, and to assign staff to time intervals to improve their record keeping. At each interval, the assigned adult removed John to a private area and checked his diapers. If he had urinated, a U was recorded in the pants column; if he was dry, a D was recorded in the same column. Whenever he used the toilet, his performance was recorded in the toilet column as student initiated (1) or adult initiated (2). John did not have a bowel movement at school during baseline, which is why BM was not recorded. Ms. Johnson offered her students an opportunity to go to the bathroom on arrival, on the way to and from physical education and lunch, and before leaving school. During these times, John was taken to the bathroom, and these opportunities are recorded in the toilet column. On only one adult-initiated opportunity did John eliminate on the toilet (day 7 at 1:05). On day 6, staff found they were not as regular in their checks as they wanted to be and decided to record the exact time John was checked or eliminated (if known).

Ms. Anderson reviewed all 10 days of baseline data (5 of which are shown in Figure 9–5) and selected teaching times 5 to 10 minutes before John's usual times for urination: 9:45—before the 9:45 to 10:00 time when John usually urinated; 11:30—before lunch; 12:45—after lunch (because John used the bathroom then to clean his face and hands) before the 1:00 time John usually urinated; and right before dismissal because John's mother reported he was often wet when he arrived home. Because John was usually wet on arrival at school, he was always changed at 8:15.

The team may want to teach skills in the toileting routine other than elimination, such as lowering pants

FIGURE 9–5

Data Recorded During the Last 7 Days of Baseline and the First 2 Days of Instruction from John's Toileting Program

Elimination Record

Student's Name: John   Recorder(s): Perez, McLean, Lee, Anderson

	Baseline Data: Week 2										Instruction			
	Day 1		Day 2		Day 3		Day 4		Day 5		Day 6		Day 7	
	Mon		Tues		Wed		Thurs		Fri		Mon		Tues	
Time	Pants	Toilet	Pants	Toilet	Pants	Toilet	Pants	Toilet	Pants	Toilet	Pants	Toilet	Pants	Toilet
8:30 arrival		D–		D–		D–		D–	U			D–		D–
8:45 ind	D				D		D		D					
9:00 group	D		D		D		D		D		D		D	
9:15 group	D		D		D		D		D					
9:30 center	D		U		D		D		D			U (9:30)	D	
9:45 center	D		D		U		D		D					U (9:47)
10:00 center	U		D		D		U		U			D–		D–
10:15 PE		D–		D–	U			D–		D–		D–		
10:30 PE														
10:45 language		D–	U			D–		D–		D–				
11:00 language	D		D		D		D		D			U (11:05)	D	
11:15 prep		D–		D–		D–		D–		D–		D–		D–
11:30 lunch	D		U		D		D		D			U (11:30)		U (11:35)
11:45 lunch														
12:00 story		D–		D–		D–		D–		D–		D–		D–
12:15 rest	D		D		D		D		D					
12:30 rest	D				D				D		D		D	
12:45 art	U		D		U		U		U (12:45)					U (12:50)
1:00 recess	D		U		D		D		D			D–		U– (1:05)
1:15 group	D		D		D		D		U			D–		
1:30 dismissal	D		D		D		D		D			D–	D	

Key: D = dry; U = urination; BM = bowel movement; toilet codes: + = student initiated, − = adult initiated; blank = unable to check; L = lunch.

Other: _____

Note: If it is possible to record the exact time of the elimination, use the second line for that time period.

or latching a stall door. While Table 9-4 sets forth 12 basic toileting components and lists potential teacher cues and student behaviors that relate to each component, the actual skills should be individualized to address student needs for instruction, the home and/or school setting, and the care providers or staff involved. Some components, such as pants down and up and hand washing, have multiple steps. The team should consider use of a task analysis that is generic enough to be used with the variety of toilets a particular student uses during the training period.

Other considerations include the order of steps in the task. For example, with younger children, a better method of teaching wiping requires the child to stand up and then wipe rather than to remain seated. In addition, if skirts or dresses are worn, the "pants up and down" sequence changes. Some students with physical disabilities may be more independent if they sit or lean on the toilet to remove their pants. The most "typical" urination position for boys is to stand and face the toilet, and for girls, it is to sit. However, initially, boys as well as girls are taught to use the toilet while sitting; later, boys who have adequate motor control will be taught to stand.

> *Whenever team members took John to the toilet, they taught John to use his canes to walk from his wheelchair to the toilet and provided related skills instruction. On the days when he wore clothing with fasteners, they taught fastening and unfastening, but he was taught to flush and wash his hands after toileting.*

For Alycin, partial participation is necessary for the task steps of pulling pants down and sitting on the toilet. Partial participatory steps are incorporated into her task analysis.

> *At home, Alycin's mom uses a one-person supported transfer, which involves Alycin being pulled to standing (Alycin can bear weight), pivoted in place, having her pants lowered (by mom), lowered onto the adapted toilet seat, and having the seat belt fastened. School staff will work with the OT, PT, and mom to modify their two-person transfer so it can be safely executed by one person, making toileting at job settings more feasible. The three will also problem solve ways for Alycin to be actively involved.*

As Alycin's case illustrates, the toileting components, teachers' teaching cues, and student behaviors listed in the task analysis must be individualized.

Approaches for Teaching Toileting

In this section, we describe several broad approaches to teaching toileting: traditional, improved traditional, and rapid. The primary difference between traditional and rapid methods is the toileting schedule:

- Traditional methods rely on toileting students when they are likely to experience bowel or bladder tension (when the bowel or bladder is naturally full).
- Rapid methods require students to consume extra fluids, creating more frequent bladder tension and thus additional opportunities for toileting.

Most children learn to control their bowel movement without accidents before they acquire bladder control, and they master daytime before nighttime control. This general pattern is also typically true for individuals with disabilities.

Traditional Toilet-Training Methods
Training Considerations Before beginning instruction, the team must consider clothing, toileting position, and task order. Clothing students in training pants or ordinary underwear rather than diapers is recommended, as it can facilitate detection of accidents during baseline and training (Dunlap, Koegel, & Koegel, 1986). This allows learners to experience the naturally unpleasant feedback from wet or soiled clothing that modern disposable diapers have virtually eliminated; these naturally occurring, uncomfortable consequences of accidents can contribute to faster learning. Wearing diapers may lead to substantially more urinary accidents and fewer successful voids even when taken to the toilet regularly (Tarbox, Williams, & Friman, 2004). However, without diapers, students' toileting accidents can be noticed by peers and be stigmatizing, especially beyond the preschool years. Teams (including family members) must decide the appropriateness of having students wear diapers and may make exceptions to this guideline with older students to avoid noticeable accidents. Training pants with plastic pants over them may allow the student both privacy and feedback. For some students, it may be best to remove diapers only with intensive or isolated instruction or if training occurs at home during summer vacation. Teams may decide that wearing diapers in school even when training is under way is the appropriate choice.

TABLE 9–4

Basic Behavior Components in Toilet Training with Teaching Cues and Initial Student Behaviors

Behavior component	Teacher's training cue (individualized to suit student)	Initial forms of student's behavior[3]
Recognizing the need	Do you have to go?[1]	Senses internal stimuli May show outward behavior (grabs genitals, grimaces)
Waiting	Do you have to go?[1]	Senses internal stimuli May show outward behavior (grabs genitals, grimaces)
Entering the restroom	Go to the toilet.	Walks directly to restroom
Pulling pants down	Pull your pants down.	(Unfastens belt, buttons, zippers) Hooks thumbs into tops of underpants Pushes underwear and outerwear to at least midthigh
Sitting on the toilet	Sit on the toilet.	Sits on the toilet seat
Eliminating	"Pee."[2]	Eliminates
Using toilet paper	Wipe yourself.	Stands Reaches and grasps toilet paper Pulls out and tears off an appropriate amount Bends and wipes self Drops paper into toilet
Pulling pants up	Pull up your pants.	Grasps top band of underpants. Pulls up and into place Grasps outer pants at waist Pulls up and into place (Fastens buttons and zippers)
Flushing	Flush the toilet.	Places hand on top of flusher Pushes down on flusher
Washing hands	Wash your hands.	Approaches sink Turns water on Wets hands Picks up soap and rubs hands Replaces soap Soaps hands Holds hands under water and rinses hands
Drying hands	Dry your hands.	Reaches for and grasps paper towel dispenser crank Turns crank several turns to release appropriate amount Grabs paper and tears off Holds paper between hands while turning hands Drops paper into trash
Exiting the restroom	Time for _____	Leaves restroom Goes to next activity

[1]The internal cue of bladder or bowel tension becomes the controlling stimulus after training is complete.

[2]Use language suited to the student's chronological age, the setting (school or home), and family practice.

[3]Behavior form may change in later learning (e.g., boys may stand to urinate); task steps will vary to suit conditions and student.

Stages of Toileting Training

Usually as students learn toileting, they move through stages, somewhat parallel to the stages of learning discussed earlier. Some students attain all three stages; others may attain only the first or the first and second stages.

Stage 1: Regulated Toileting The first stage of toileting is learning to become regulated to a toileting schedule (also called habit trained or conditioned). Students who acquire reliable patterns of bowel movements and urination can stay dry if someone else reminds or assists them to go to the toilet at scheduled times. School staff can observe the signals that elimination is imminent and then prompt students to use the toilet. Keeping a fairly stable eating and drinking pattern paired with reinforcement for correct toileting behavior helps students achieve toileting regulation.

John's data in Figure 9–5 indicate that he is at this stage of toilet training: regular periods of dryness and elimination but only rare eliminations on the toilet and no self-initiations.

Stage 2: Self-Initiated Toileting The second toileting stage toward independence involves learning to discriminate the natural cues of bladder fullness (for bladder control) and pressure in the lower bowel (for bowel control). During this stage, we want students to make a connection between these internal stimuli and the response of eliminating on the toilet. Noticing their signals that elimination is imminent and prompting them to the toilet as well as giving positive feedback immediately on elimination on the toilet helps them make this connection. Once a student is sitting on the toilet, teachers may make regular checks and (depending on its appropriateness) listen or look for urination or defecation so that they can provide reinforcing feedback with little delay. Whenever students tell someone, signal a need to use the bathroom, or simply initiate toileting on their own, staff must give enthusiastic praise and get them to a bathroom quickly with as little help as necessary.

Generally, Alycin initiates the need for toileting, and her pattern of elimination is very regular. But there are challenges in several areas: (a) Alycin being able to reliably signal others with her electronic communication board, (b) staff learning to attend to Alycin's requests and act on them, (c) staff more efficiently

providing assistance to get her to a toilet and make the transfers from wheelchair to toilet, and (d) Alycin learning to participate in the toileting components more quickly.

Stage 3: Toileting Independence The final stage in the toileting process is gaining independence. Independent students not only are aware of the need to toilet but also manage clothing and related cleanup skills (e.g., wiping, flushing, washing hands). At this stage, trainers fade themselves out of the bathroom during routine toileting, and the focus shifts to skill generalization, fluency and proficiency issues (e.g., speed, elimination of all accidents, social awareness), and routine performance.

Jamal is working on independence: he self-initiates, has not had an accident at school for over a year, and can perform most of the related skills. Once Jamal learns to unfasten and fasten his pants, he will have achieved independence.

Steps for Using a Traditional Approach

Traditional toilet training (referred to as habit training in stage 1) begins with taking a child to the toilet at regular intervals throughout the day or when the child demonstrates the need to toilet (e.g., grabbing their crotch, increased movement). Children are praised for elimination on the toilet and remaining clean and dry. While these simple steps are successful for most children when they are at the readiness stage, several authors recommend training steps and related practices that may make traditional bowel or bladder training more successful (Baker & Brightman, 1997; Fredericks et al., 1975; Linford, Hipsher, & Silikovitz, 1972; Schaefer & DiGeronimo, 1997):

1. Continue diapers when students are neither bladder nor bowel trained and focus on bowel training first because it is easier to learn. Any accidents are changed in the bathroom without a fuss. When bladder training, training pants are better than diapers, but the team needs to decide, depending on the circumstances.
2. Learn how the student signals the need to eliminate. Signals for a bowel movement are more obvious (e.g., gets quiet, squats, strains, red in face). Whenever these signals occur, take the student to the bathroom even if it is not a scheduled time and then record these times on the record.

3. Establish a toileting schedule and follow it consistently. Adjust times only if the program is unsuccessful; make adjustments based on an analysis of the student's elimination pattern.
4. Use the regular toilet, with adaptations added only as necessary: (a) to keep the student's feet flat on the floor or on a nonslip support and (b) to keep the student sitting securely (e.g., toilet seat inset). Sometimes needed (as in Alycin's case) are specialized toilet chairs, support bars (as in John's case), or perhaps even potty seats (if the child is younger than age 5 and very small). If students are unstable while sitting, they will have trouble relaxing the sphincters that control elimination. When needed, team members should pool their talents to generate appropriate adaptations that are nonstigmatizing and practical.
5. Keep the toileting time positive but not distracting. Any rewarding activities should take place after toileting and out of the bathroom. Unneeded conversation (e.g., social talk, singing, rhymes) is kept to a minimum, though talking about the toileting task in ways suited to the student is appropriate.
6. Take the student to the toilet according to schedule or when a need is signaled, approximately (a) 15 minutes before the scheduled time for bowel training and (b) 5 to 10 minutes before the scheduled time for bladder training. The specific length of time for sitting on the toilet should be determined on the basis of individual student characteristics. The

student should be placed on the toilet long enough to have the opportunity to eliminate but not for so long that toileting becomes aversive.
7. Reinforce the student when elimination occurs. If elimination does not occur, return the student to the classroom for a 5- to 10-minute interval and then back to the toilet. Continue the alternating intervals until elimination occurs. Record any extra toileting times and the outcomes.
8. Continue elimination records so the team can evaluate progress and adjust toileting times as needed.
9. Consider extending goals as the student is successful (e.g., add more times, add bladder training, shift to self-initiation and then independence).

Table 9–5 illustrates some of the basic rules of a traditional toilet-training approach (Hobbs & Peck, 1985).

Improved Traditional Methods
When traditional toilet training is insufficient, teachers may consider one or more of the following procedures: (a) regular toileting without diapers, (b) pants inspections, (c) consequences for accidents, (d) increased fluids, (e) the use of moisture-signaling devices, (f) transfer of stimulus control, or (g) priming.

Regular Toileting Without Diapers While there is limited testing for this approach of regular toileting without diapers, its simplicity and reported success with an older person make it worth describing. It is

TABLE 9–5
The Rules of Toilet Training

Do	Do not
• Reinforce students for using the toilet (e.g. praise, physical contact, tangibles, as appropriate for age, student, setting).	• Do not reinforce students when wet. Do not talk, scold, or give eye contact or unneeded touch.
• When there is an accident, clean the student without delay.	• Avoid letting students get social reinforcement while wet or soiled.
• Until students are clean, remove them from class activities, without reprimand.	• Do not let students get used to being wet or soiled.
• In private, clean students impersonally with damp towel after accidents (should be neutral, not reinforcing); dress in dry clothing.	• Do not give showers or baths to wet or soiled students.
• Give students regular opportunities to use the toilet (e.g., once every 2 hours or more often).	• Do not let students eat or continue eating when an accident occurs before or during a meal. Clean the student first.
• Stay with or nearby students while they are on the toilet, listen and watch for their elimination, and reinforce eliminations immediately.	• Do not skip or delay a scheduled toileting.
	• Do not leave students during toileting because you may miss an opportunity to reinforce eliminations. Do not delay reinforcement.

Source: Adapted from Hobbs, T., & Peck, C. A. (1986). Toilet training people with profound mental retardation: A cost effective procedure for large residential settings. *Behavioral Engineering, 9*, p. 53.

likely that regular toileting without diapers is more appropriate for older students who have learned the basic toileting routine but continue to have accidents and wear diapers as a matter of convenience. In a recent study, Tarbox et al. (2004) tested this simple method with a 29-year-old adult with developmental disabilities who routinely wore adult diapers (Depends®) to his work setting. Two conditions were compared within a withdrawal design. First, the man's diaper was removed on arrival at work, and he was asked to use the toilet every 30 minutes, which he did independently and received praise for successful voiding. After 6 days, the man was allowed to wear adult diapers while at work and was still asked to use the toilet every 30 minutes. These two treatments (no diaper and diaper) were alternated several times for 4 to 7 days each. Data were gathered on his daily occurrences of urinary accidents and his successful voids on the toilet. The findings showed that when the man did not wear a diaper, his urinary accidents decreased to an average of 0.1 instance per day, and his successful voids increased to 1.8 times per day, but when he wore a diaper, his accidents increased to an average of 1.5 per day, and successful voids decreased to an average of 0.5 per day. The findings suggest that wearing a diaper may set the occasion for having accidents and that negative reinforcement is involved: disposable diapers decrease the unpleasant sensation of wetness, others' awareness of accidents, and the need to use the toilet. Additionally, the extra social reinforcement for successful voiding may have helped increase his use of the toilet.

This approach is fairly straightforward, but it requires more supervision than simply having adults or students wear diapers. Additional replication of these findings will strengthen it as an option for reducing incontinence.

Pants Inspections and Reinforcement Pants checks consist of assessing whether a student is wet or dry and providing appropriate feedback (reinforcement for continence or signaling a need to change if wet). During the first two phases of toileting (regulation and self-initiation), pants checks serve to increase student awareness of being wet or dry. When learning to become independent, pants checks can help students maintain continence. These checks were introduced as a component of rapid training programs (Azrin & Foxx, 1971; Foxx & Azrin, 1973). We recommend asking the student if he or she is dry in a form of

communication that is neutral and that the student will understand. Also, teaching students to discriminate wet and dry first can improve their ability to answer accurately when asked. If the pants are dry, reinforce with praise for dryness and a reinforcer appropriate for the student ("Good, you have dry pants! Pick out a CD to listen to."). See the section that follows on consequences for accidents to select a response for wet or soiled pants. Some students may not be able to determine or communicate whether they are dry. These students may be taken to the bathroom and privately checked, giving feedback to the student about dryness.

Teams will want to individualize the specific length of intervals between pants checks, their timing, the feedback given for wetness and dryness, and the reinforcement for continence. Feedback should always be directed toward increasing student awareness of being dry and wet; when wet, pants should be changed. The pants check approach is less accurate with disposable diapers than with training pants.

John's first instructional program in preschool consisted of the traditional methods described previously, half-hourly pants inspections, and enthusiastic verbal praise for dry pants. When this was not successful, pants checks in the bathroom were increased to 15-minute intervals whenever sufficient staff were present in the room.

Consequences for Accidents When students are learning elimination control and are purposefully taken out of diapers, some accidents must be expected. Thus, a regular procedure for responding to accidents should be planned by the team. In most cases, extinction (planned ignoring) is an appropriate strategy; however, the team may consider several options:

1. *Extinction*. Following an accident, change the student's pants and clean the student in a neutral manner, with little socialization. Be careful not to provide any reinforcing activity too soon after an accident (Hobbs & Peck, 1985).
2. *Mild Disapproval*. As soon as an accident is discovered, approach the learner in a manner that respects his or her privacy, have the student feel and look at the pants, and express some age-appropriate form of disapproval in your words and facial expressions ("Oh, you wet your pants," "No music. You have wet pants."). Change the student as with the extinction procedure.

3. *Cleanup.* Require the student to participate in washing him- or herself with a damp cloth and changing clothes. Student cleanup should be implemented as a natural consequence with little socializing. Requiring the student to participate in an overcorrection procedure, that is, repeatedly practicing going to the toilet or doing more than required (e.g., mop the entire floor where the accident occurred instead of just cleaning the soiled area of the floor), is aversive and should not be used. Use the cleanup participation strategy cautiously, as students who require prompting to clean themselves may be reinforced by attention for the accident or may become upset emotionally. In addition, some who clean themselves independently may find it reinforcing to leave classroom demands.

The approaches for handling accidents must be carefully matched to a given student. Note that if extinction is selected, neither disapproval nor student cleaning up of accidents should be used. However, disapproval and cleanup consequences may be used together, or disapproval may be used alone. Cleanup typically involves mild disapproval. Most experts and practitioners agree that it is the positive aspects of teaching that lead to learning new skills, not the negative consequences.

Increasing or Regulating Fluids Increasing the fluids that a student consumes will increase the opportunities to urinate and thus to be taught and to obtain reinforcement. However, increasing fluids to boost the quantity of bladder-training sessions must be accompanied by certain precautions. When the intake of water or other liquids is forced or encouraged over an extended period, the balance of electrolytes in the body may be seriously endangered. Hyponatremia, or a low serum sodium level, while rare may result and is associated with nausea, vomiting, muscular twitching, grand mal seizures, and coma (Thompson & Hanson, 1983). This condition "constitutes a serious medical emergency requiring prompt sodium replacement therapy and other medical support" (p. 140). If the team decides to increase fluids, we recommend that fluids not be increased by more than three small servings during the school morning or day. This allows increased opportunities for instruction without putting the child's health at risk.

Loosely regulating fluids simply involves scheduling the times of day that a student has fluids (not necessarily an increased amount) to make the student's urination schedule more predictable. For example, if during baseline a teacher notes that a student tends to urinate approximately 2 hours after drinking, the teacher could schedule a fluid break 2 hours before a convenient time to implement toileting instruction in an appropriately private setting. We do not know of any research on this method of informally redistributing the fluids that would be drunk or offering an extra drink to coincide with scheduled toilet training, but it worked for John, the student in our example (see Box 9–2).

Moisture-Signaling Devices One possible reason students may not learn toileting is delayed feedback. Students who wear modern disposable diapers often feel little discomfort when they are wet, and teachers may be unable to identify if they are wet or exactly when elimination occurred. Learning to associate bowel or bladder tension with elimination (e.g., sphincter relaxation) is facilitated when students are quickly taken to the toilet during urination or bowel movement and receive approval. Moisture-signaling devices are used to signal the moment of elimination.

Two types of moisture-detection or urine-signaling devices have been used along with other teaching methods:

1. *Toilet alert.* A special potty chair or a small toilet bowl that fits under the regular toilet seat that catches eliminations and triggers an auditory signal through the detection of moisture (Foxx & Azrin, 1973; Herreshoff, 1973).
2. *Pants alert.* Training underpants that detect moisture when students eliminate in their clothing (Mahoney, Van Wagenen, & Meyerson, 1971; Smith, 1979; Van Wagenen & Murdock, 1966). These special underpants involve a circuit and switch plan somewhat similar to the toilet signal; the signaling device is attached to the pants, shirt, or vest pocket.

Both devices involve a low-voltage circuit being completed when moisture activates the switch for the auditory signal. The signal allows staff to provide students with appropriate feedback the moment elimination occurs. Moisture-detecting switches connected to a potty chair or toilet inset signal the moment for positive reinforcement; moisture-detecting underpants signal the moment an accident occurs. Thus, reinforcement and accident procedures can be implemented without delay (refer to Azrin, Bugle, and O'Brien, 1971;

Box 9–2 John's Toilet Training

When John's team looked at his Instructional data, they decided that his pattern of elimination was too variable to predict full bladder times accurately. They decided to attempt to stabilize the morning urination pattern by giving John a 6-ounce beverage of his choice as soon as he arrived at school, and again at lunch. With the fluid increase, John consistently urinated around 9:30 and 12:30, so his teachers selected 9:20 and 12:20 for toileting times. On John's first occurrence of urinating in the toilet (2 days after the program revision), Ms. Perez cheered for him. John praised himself, saying that he had gone to the bathroom "like big boys do." Within 2 weeks, John was no longer having accidents at school. His mother reported that John was still arriving home wet. When giving John an additional opportunity to use the toilet before leaving was unsuccessful, the team decided to eliminate the extra fluid at lunchtime. This solved the problem on the bus, but John continued to have toileting accidents at home.

The next phase of the program planning concerned the home: (a) the use of diapers was stopped, (b) John's mom took him to the toilet every 2 hours, and (c) John was praised for having dry pants. These procedures were successful in getting John to maintain dry pants for 1 month both at home and school.

Then John's team began self-initiation training at school. Instead of automatically taking John to the bathroom at designated times, they asked (as is typical to dc in Kindergarten), "Does anyone need to use the bathroom?" If John did not respond, they prompted him to raise his hand and took him to the bathroom. When he responded in the affirmative to the question without prompts for 1 week, they no longer prompted him to use the toilet. If he raised his hand, they took him to the toilet; if he did not, they allowed him to continue his classwork. John remained dry and spontaneously requested to go to the bathroom. At this point, the teacher withdrew the increased fluids.

John successfully maintained dry pants for 2 months with self-initiated requests only. Then his mother reported that he began having accidents at home and on the bus again. Within a few days, the accident began at school also. John's mother reported that his father had received a temporary transfer and was living in another town for 3 months. John's accidents seemed to occur only when his father was away, not when the father was home with the family. The team decided that John's mom and his two teachers would reinstitute verbal reminders for using the toilet. Every hour, John was taken to the bathroom if he needed to go. His response was honored; if he said yes, he'd go to the toilet, but if he said no, he continued his activity. Finally, his dad agreed to call daily and praise John for his successes at school and home in toileting and other areas. This procedure reduced accidents to one or two a month. When John's father returned home, the hourly prompts were faded, and John continued his success toileting.

Herreshoff, 1973). These devices are available through the Sears and the J. C. Penney catalogs and are carried by many local pharmacies; pediatricians also can direct parents or teachers to suppliers.

Despite the efficiency of signaling the moment of elimination, the disadvantages of moisture-signaling equipment in a toileting program are many. The equipment, which is noisy and fairly obvious (especially when it signals), can be quite stigmatizing to students who use it. If students spend time in regular education classes and activities in the school and community, this equipment is not appropriate. Other problems with the device include expense, breakdown, or failure (Mahoney, et al., 1971; Smith, 1979). Teams should view moisture-signaling devices as an option for use in unusual situations in which toileting progress has been minimal and toileting control is relatively important for the individual. However, for some students, moisture-signaling equipment may be appropriate during, for example, an at-home summer program.

Transfer of Stimulus Control When a behavior happens consistently in the presence of a particular stimulus, it is said to be under stimulus control. For example, if someone answers the phone whenever it rings, the behavior of picking up the receiver and saying "hello" is under the control of the telephone ring. For the child who regularly urinates in his or her diaper, urination may be under the control of the diaper. Luiselli (1996) reported a procedure for transferring stimulus control in toilet training. The student was placed in training briefs at the beginning of the school day. Four times a day, she was taken to the bathroom, put in a disposable diaper instead of the training briefs, and placed on the toilet. If she urinated in 3 minutes, she was rewarded with stickers and was read a book. If not, she was simply put back into training briefs and returned to the classroom. At the end of 2 weeks of training, the diaper was physically faded by cutting holes in it. On the third day, she got on the toilet and urinated on her own before being dressed in the diaper. The diaper was then eliminated, and she continued using the toilet success-fully after a 1-month follow-up. Because this strategy worked once with one student, it should be used cau-tiously with others. Nonetheless, it appears promising, is less intrusive than many of the other methods de-scribed, was demonstrated in an inclusive setting, and was not part of a package treatment.

Priming Bainbridge and Myles (1999) demonstrated the use of priming to toilet train a child with autism. The student watched a video that showed children go-ing to the bathroom at a birthday party. The student watched the film three times a day at home and was given the prompt "It's time to go potty." The student increased the number of self-initiations for toileting and the number of dry diapers during checks. Re-search is limited, but it appears to be a promising strat-egy for students who watch videos and respond to visual cues.

Rapid Training Programs
Current Views of "Rapid" Approaches "Rapid" toilet-training methods actually are rather complex training packages based primarily on the research of Azrin and Foxx (Azrin & Foxx, 1971; Foxx & Azrin, 1973, 1974) or of Van Wagenen, Mahoney, and col-leagues (Mahoney et al., 1971; Van Wagenen, Meyerson, Kerr, & Mahoney, 1969; Van Wagenen & Murdock, 1966). Some components of the packages (e.g., pants inspections, moisture-detection devices) have already been discussed. The packages are described as "rapid" because the program usually is delivered with high in-tensity, and rapid changes in student performance have been reported. However, some of the methods and the intensity of its delivery conflict with today's best prac-tices; in addition, the speedy results have not been con-sistently replicated by researchers.

Most applications of rapid approaches to toilet training have employed one or more of the following questionable practices: (a) fluid increases that may be dangerous, (b) removal of the student from all or most instruction other than toileting, (c) removal of the stu-dent from opportunities to participate in interactions with nondisabled peers, and (d) the likelihood of ex-cessive punishment (cf. Cicero & Pfadt, 2002, as a most recent example). Two rapid approaches (Mahoney et al., 1971; Richmond, 1983) are less intrusive and non-aversive in their application; we describe only Rich-mond's procedure because, unlike Mahoney's approach,

it does not require expensive, specialized signaling equipment.

Richmond's Rapid Procedure Four preschool chil-dren with profound retardation were successfully toi-let trained with increased opportunities to use the toi-let. Intervention consisted of four training phases (i.e., toileting every 15 minutes, every 30 minutes, every hour, every 2 hours), each lasting 1 week and followed by a posttraining or maintenance phase. Each toileting trip was preceded by a pants check. If no accident was detected, the child was praised for having dry and clean pants. The teacher then asked the child, "Do you need to use the toilet?" The child was prompted to re-spond and go to the restroom. In the restroom, the child was praised for engaging in the related toileting behaviors (e.g., pulling pants down and up). If neces-sary, graduated guidance was used to prompt these be-haviors. Social praise and liquids were given for suc-cessful toileting, and no comments were made when accidents occurred. Extra fluids served both as rein-forcers and to increase the frequency of urination. When an accident was detected, the teacher gave a brief reprimand and simple correction (i.e., the child was responsible for getting a clean set of clothes, re-moving the dirty clothes, washing soiled body areas, disposing of dirty clothes, and dressing). The morning preschool schedule continued even with the frequent toileting interruptions.

Richmond's results offer encouraging news to teachers of younger children: simple toileting methods applied in a consistent manner can be effective over a 9- to 15-week period without extreme techniques or schedule changes. Frequency of toileting, while impor-tant to learning bladder control, is problematic when students move into elementary grades and beyond. Teams should emphasize toilet training at younger ages when schedules are more flexible and social stigma is less likely.

Eliminating Toileting Accidents
There is less research that deals with the problems of partial toileting control during waking hours. Two some-what different approaches have been used to eliminate toileting accidents once bladder control is attained. The first approach is to ensure continuity of treatment across the settings a person uses daily. Dunlap, Koegel, and Koegel (1984) employed the combination of train-ing methods (i.e., pants checks, urine-sensitive pants,

reinforcement for success, and graduated guidance for related behaviors) on a schedule of once or twice per hour. They found that when similar approaches were employed at either the schools or the homes of three young students with autism, students made no clear progress toward mastery. Only when training methods were consistently and simultaneously implemented across these and the other community settings that the students visited daily were steady gains made in successful toileting. One adult per child was designated as the program coordinator, whose job it was to (a) initiate contact with a designated support provider in each setting, (b) ensure that this person understood the teaching and data collection methods, (c) ensure that the child carried written instructions to facilitate consistent use of procedures by staff, (d) ensure full-day coverage, (e) contact trainers immediately after the first day to check the procedure and answer questions, and (f) continue regular phone contacts with trainers to promote coordination and consistent implementation of treatment. For two of the four students, however, infrequent bowel accidents continued for several months after bladder control was attained, making the effects of the continuity-of-treatment approach on bowel accidents less clear.

In the second approach to reducing bladder accidents, Barmann, Katz, O'Brien, and Beauchamp (1981) combined hourly pants checks with a somewhat normalized version of positive practice or cleaning up after accidents. For example, when the three boys with moderate to severe mental retardation were dry, they were praised verbally, but when wet, they were required to (a) get a towel, (b) clean up all traces of urine or feces, (c) go to their bedroom and get clean pants, and (d) place the wet pants in a diaper pail. For all three students, the procedures led to substantial improvements over their baseline accident levels of three to four accidents daily. Once overcorrection was instituted in the home, there was an immediate decline in accidents there and at school, followed by no more accidents.

Encopresis, or partial bowel control, can take two forms: (a) retentive (extreme constipation) and (b) nonretentive (soiling). Treatment programs must match the type of encopresis and the actual and likely reasons for its presence. Boon and Singh (1991) and Doleys (1985) recommend individually designed teaching programs that emphasize reinforcement for appropriate bowel movements, periodic pants checks,

and possible use of laxatives or enemas in the early stages of training, but no punishment.

Special Considerations for Eating and Mealtime

Assessment and Instruction

Eating is perhaps the most functional and frequently used of all self-care skills. When developing individualized plans for teaching eating and mealtime behavior, teams focus on the general goals of healthy eating (e.g., meeting nutritional needs, eating without choking) and eating as independently as possible. This section addresses elements of assessing and teaching basic mealtime skills in learners whose objectives primarily concern aim for self-feeding. Two other chapters address issues that we do not cover but that are relevant for many students: nutrition monitoring and supplementation and nonoral feeding procedures (chapter 7) and specific considerations for students with motor disabilities (chapter 8). Other references supplement the coverage of these topics (Case-Smith & Humphry, 1996; Christaisen, 2004; Lowman & Murphy, 1999; Orelove et al., 2004).

Eating is unique in the self-care domain for several reasons. First, in addition to filling our primary needs for nutrition, mealtimes are often a time for socializing. Mealtimes mean conversation, getting together with friends and family, sharing, and enjoying food. This should be true for students with disabilities, too. Pleasant and gratifying mealtimes can enhance the use of eating skills and the social and communication skills embedded in eating routines. Teams should structure mealtime and eating instruction so that learning and enjoyment result.

Second, the priority for instruction must be weighed against students' nutritional needs. Individual student characteristics will influence the amount of teaching time. Ideally, some instruction can be provided throughout each entire meal and snack. However, some students (e.g., those with physical disabilities or exhibiting interfering behaviors) require unusually long mealtimes and may become fatigued and discontinue eating. If a student is not eating enough to maintain nutrition or the mealtime instruction is interfering with time to teach other priority goals, teachers may initially teach for the first one third to one half of the meal and more fully assist the student during the remainder.

The Sequence for Teaching Mealtime Skills

The core eating skills typically are taught in a general developmental sequence beginning with various aspects of dependent feeding (e.g., anticipates spoon, uses lips to remove food with utensils), eating finger foods, eating with a spoon, drinking from a cup, using a fork, spreading and cutting with a knife, serving food, using condiments, and displaying good table manners. In general, targets should be both realistic in relation to the current performance of students and immediately or subsequently relevant (prioritized by the family or teacher as being needed on a regular basis). Additionally, students must learn to eat a variety of foods since food refusal and food overselectivity can put students at risk nutritionally, for growth, and for other health problems.

Not all eating skills, however, should be taught in a developmental sequence. Incorporating into mealtime routines the related skills a student can do or can learn will facilitate improvements in independence later.

When Alycin was very young and highly dependent on others for feeding, parents and teachers taught her to initiate eating by making a modified sign for eat and vocalizing the "Eee" sound. Then they put her bib on her tray, and she learned to feel for and grasp it.

Likewise, teaching skills in a functional order, even if not the developmental order, may be the best option. For example, Mary, who is age 8, knows how to use a spoon without spilling but does not use a fork or cut with a knife. Developmentally, she "should" master these first, but her team has decided that using a napkin and going through the lunch line are more functional, even if she bypasses fork and knife use for now.

Prerequisites for Instruction in Eating Independently

For students to be successful in learning to eat independently, they need an active gag reflex and the skills of sucking, maintaining closed lips, swallowing, biting, and chewing. Mastery of these basic skills greatly reduces the risk of choking. Before beginning assessment or instruction, students should be in the proper position for eating, even when they do not have extensive or obvious motor disabilities or high or low tone in their muscles. Proper position has a big impact not only on learning and success with eating but also on the prevention of choking and the aspiration of food. The student's head must be stable, in midline, and with the chin and jaw as near to parallel with the floor as possible (chapter 8).

Monitoring Student Performance at Mealtimes

Monitoring at mealtimes can be challenging during phases when the student still requires physical assistance. Eating skills and related mealtime behaviors may be measured in several ways: (a) frequency or percentage of correct responses, (b) duration or rate of correct responses, (c) frequency or percentage of errors, (d) duration or rate of errors, and (e) task-analytic assessment. (Chapter 5 describes these measurement methods in more detail.) Team members can observe and assess throughout an entire meal routine, for part of a meal, or for several trials (e.g., eating with a spoon, drinking from a cup) or can observe the after-effects of eating by measuring "permanent products" (e.g., assess the mess on the table and floor). How the target eating behavior is defined will influence how it is measured. For example, if spoon use is defined as a discrete behavior—"Moving appropriate food from the container with the spoon held in one hand, by the handle, right side up and without spilling (except back into the container from which the food was taken)" (O'Brien & Azrin, 1972, p. 391)—then it is often counted but it could be timed if fluency is an issue. If the same skill is defined as a task made up of component steps—"Grasp spoon, scoop food, raise spoon to lips, open mouth, put spoon in mouth, remove spoon, lower spoon, release grasp" (Collins et al., 1991, p. 163)—then task-analytic assessment or percentage of correct responses would be used (see Table 9–3).

Related and embedded skills may also be a focus for monitoring instruction. Figure 9–6 shows how a teacher collected data on the component skills for eating lunch in a school cafeteria by using a task analysis while counting the number of correct fork use responses in the first 10 opportunities.

Mike has just gotten an electric wheelchair and needs to learn how to control it. In addition, he is beginning to use an augmentative communication device (i.e., a folder with pages for specific activities during the day). Mike has some verbal language, so his teacher is monitoring greeting skills, too. Skills in these three areas (i.e., mobility, communication, social) are embedded in the task of getting lunch in the cafeteria. The targeted eating skill for Mike is stabbing bites of food with his fork. The teacher collects data on the number of correct stabs (e.g., stabs a bite of food on

FIGURE 9–6

Data Sheet for Component Skills of Eating in School Cafeteria

Student: _Mike_   **Setting and Time:** _Lunchroom, 11:35_
Program Manager: _Carla_   **Peers:** Bill, Jane, Karen
Stimulus: _Teacher tells student that it is time for lunch_
Procedure: _System of least prompts (SLP) for all steps except wheelchair_
Graduate guidance (GG) for wheelchair steps

Date	10/5	10/6	10/7
1. Initiates driving wheelchair to area where one folder is kept (mobility)	H	H	H
2. Picks up folder and places on tray	P	P	G
3. Navigates hallway to get to cafeteria (mobility)	H	H	H
4. Enters line and positions chair in front of cooler (mobility)	H	H	H
5. Opens folder and points to picture indicating milk choice (communication) (Peer: Gets milk and puts on tray)	P	G	V
6. Moves to food area (mobility)	H	H	H
7. Greets cafeteria worker (social) (Cafeteria worker: Asks Mike what he wants to eat)	V	+	+
8. Points to picture indicating choice (communication) (Peer: Puts plate on wheelchair tray)	G	V	+
9. Moves to salad/dessert area (mobility)	H	H	H
10. Points to salad/dessert choices on communication folder (communication)	V	V	V
11. Moves chair to cashier (mobility)	H	H	L
12. Greets cashier (social)	V	V	+
13. Hands lunch money to cashier	G	G	G
14. Waits for change before saying "thank you." (social)	+	+	+
15. Goes to lunch table (mobility)	H	H	H
Percentage of steps correct (out of 15)	0%	13%	33%
• Correct fork use responses during first 10 opportunities	III	JHT	JHT
Embedded Skills			
• Communication (3)	0	0	2
• Mobility (7)	0	0	0
• Social (3)	1	2	3

Note: + = independent; SLP: verbal (V), gesture (G), shadow (S); GG: hand over hand (H), light touch (L), shadow (S).

the first attempt and moves the food into his mouth with no spilling). In the cafeteria line, peers help Mike reach for food items and put them on his tray and also provide guidance on operating the wheelchair. The steps that peers and cafeteria workers do for Mike are noted in parentheses in the task analysis.

For Mike's instructional program, data are summarized by percentage of steps correct in the total task, the frequency of bites with appropriate fork use (i.e., no assistance and no spills off the plate), and the frequency of embedded skills (e.g., communication, mobility, and social).

During the first 2 weeks of the program, the teacher monitors Mike's and his peer tutors' performance and models appropriate prompts for the peers to use; she collects data daily during this initial period. As peers begin to provide appropriate levels of assistance, the teacher withdraws and lets the peers provide assistance on their own, observing and collecting data less often, while Mike, the peer assistants, and the cafeteria workers informally report on Mike's progress.

Using peers as assistants requires careful supervision to avoid creating "little teachers" (see chapter 10 for suggestions), but the alternative options of using occupational therapists or health aides to teach basic eating skills can be very restrictive socially. The combination of embedding related priority skills into the lunch routine with using supervised peer models constitutes a powerful approach for building mealtime skills.

Team members should expect students to be messy while they are learning to eat. Spilling and other errors of untidiness go along with learning to eat with one's fingers and with utensils, using adapted utensils or eating equipment, and drinking from a glass. If spilling and messiness errors continue as students acquire the basic steps, teachers should conduct observations to determine where the errors occur in the response chain (e.g., locating food, grasping utensils, scooping) and why (e.g., poor lip closure around spoon, hurrying). Messiness is influenced both by the student's level of skill and by the student's muscle tone and control, the sitting position, the type and consistency of food, and the utensils, cups, or adapted equipment.

Alycin has been making progress using her electric eating device. Once set up and positioned, the device requires that someone monitor the food on *the rotating plate, but Alycin can operate the switch to activate the spoon that dips automatically into the food as the plate turns. Alycin's mom has learned a lot about the required food consistency that keeps spilling to a minimum. She makes lasagna 16 different ways and freezes it so the family can eat most meals together! A new device they hope to purchase will help Alycin eat soups, cereal, and ice cream.*

At an early planning meeting, the OT suggested adapted equipment to help John with his messiness. Thus, he now uses a bowl with a built-up side and utensils with built-up handles. Although John is neater with these materials, he complains about not having a cafeteria tray like others. So his team decides to eliminate the special bowl and utensils and reinforce neatness. At school, neatness is rewarded with preferred activities. At home, John's mother agrees to serve ice cream contingent on having a clean table and floor area after eating. This is effective on most days, but some foods, like spaghetti, prove particularly difficult to eat. For difficult foods, John is given the adapted materials. With these procedures in effect, John eats more neatly at school and at home.

Instructional Strategies for Eating and Mealtimes

A variety of methods have been successful in teaching mealtime skills (Table 9–2). Specifically, shaping and physical prompting procedures (including physical prompts on time delay and graduated guidance) have been shown to promote the acquisition of eating skills. Sometimes, these strategies have been combined with error correction, but positive procedures alone have proven adequate in other cases. Generally, graduated guidance and shaping are the recommended procedures for building basic eating and skills for independent eating during the acquisition stage.

Once students have learned the basic core eating skills (e.g., pick up spoon, scoop food), other teaching methods have been demonstrated as more effective during advanced stages. For example, skills can be maintained and made more fluent with simple reinforcement (e.g., praise and confirmation: "That's right!") and error correction. Procedures used to correct errors in these later stages may include teachers' or peers' verbal statements and models (observation learning; see Table 9–2).

Eating Finger Foods

The first sign of independence in eating is the predictably messy stage of consuming finger foods. If the team's initial observations emphasize needs in utensil use *and* coordinating grasp, lift, and placement of finger foods in the mouth, finger food instruction should have priority. At this early stage, students use pincer grasps and hand-to-mouth movements to pick up food in combination with the sucking, gumming, chewing, and swallowing of many soft foods, such as bananas and saliva-softened toast. Eating finger foods provides essential opportunities to improve the movements needed for later utensil use. Eating finger foods also allows opportunities for continued instruction in chewing. Teachers can use meal and snack times to introduce students to a variety of textures and tastes.

For Alycin, an adapted sandwich holder does not really work; it tends to smash her sandwich, and she cannot eat its end; instead, Alycin eats a lot of finger foods, which someone simply holds out for her to grasp. Her favorites are rolled up cheese and sandwich meat.

Drinking from a Cup or Glass

Initially, students help parents or teachers hold the cup or glass and lift it to their mouth. At this early stage and when individuals first drink from a cup independently, they use both hands. When students have the potential to master drinking from a cup without assistance, straw use also may be taught, but typically this is not taught until after drinking from a cup is learned. For students like Alycin, who cannot learn independence in cup drinking, drinking liquids from stabilized cups through straws is a good alternative means for becoming independent.

Alycin has been drinking from a cup on her own for years. She uses her DynaVox (or indicates by yes or no responses) to tell what beverage she wants, and, once poured into her sports cup (a covered cup with an extended straw), it is placed into a stabilized cup holder within reach on her tray or in a holder on her self-feeder tray.

Use of a straw also may be a functional skill for students in restaurants and cafeterias, where most people use them. As with eating with fingers, the learning process is messy.

The type of cup chosen for training may influence the initial success of students. Stainback and Healy

(1982) suggest that short, squat cups that do not turn over easily and can be held without difficulty are best to begin with. With preschool-age students, a weighted cup may be appropriate, although most cups of this style have a clear association with infants and are not age appropriate. Similariy, whereas double-handled cups are easier to hold, they also are not age appropriate in their design. However, plastic-handled coffee mugs (with or without the top) may be a good substitute. Durable plastic cups are obviously safer to use than are containers made of glass, brittle plastic, or paper. Spouted or nipple cups should never be used because they stimulate abnormal sucking and do not allow students to master the correct drinking response, but sports cups with built-in straws are easily available and often used by teens and adults. To reduce spilling, the amount of liquid in a cup should not be excessive but also should not be so insufficient that students need to tip their heads too much to drink, increasing the difficulty of the task. Adapted cups that are cut out on the upper side (for the nose) can allow students with physical disabilities to drink all the fluid without tilting their heads at all.

After students learn to drink holding handled cups or small glasses with both hands, teachers can begin to emphasize a reduction in spilling. Spilling can occur while drinking but may also happen as a cup or glass is grasped, lifted, or replaced on the table. As drinking from a glass improves, students should be reminded to lift glasses with only the dominant hand.

Using Utensils

Once students have the skills of grasping finger foods, moving food from a table to the mouth with their fingers, along with the basics (i.e., lip closure, chewing, and successful swallowing), teams can plan instruction on using utensils. At this time, observations should be made to assess the student's ability to pick up and eat with a spoon. Using utensils can be taught simultaneously with instruction on drinking from a cup.

Typically, utensil use is taught sequentially, from the easiest skill to the most difficult. Spoon use is the simplest, followed in order of difficulty by eating with a fork, transferring spreads with a knife, spreading with a knife, cutting finger-grasped bread with a knife, and cutting meat with a fork and knife. The typical sequence is (a) spoon, (b) fork for spearing, (c) knife for spreading, and (d) knife and fork for cutting. Children may be able to eat using utensils in a palm-down finger or fist position (Figure 9–7). Teachers may use this

FIGURE 9–7

Everyone Benefits When Students Learn to Eat Independently

grasp for initial instruction and teach the more mature, palm-up position after students have improved their eating independence.

At age 6, John needs to learn to cut bites of food with a fork. At a team meeting, the OT shares her concerns that John will not learn to cut with a fork until his fine motor abilities improve. The team still decides to teach fork use, but it is not a priority for John. Ms. Perez and an assistant teach cutting with a fork, using graduated guidance at the beginning of lunch whenever soft foods require cutting. The prompt levels that they use are full assistance on the hand, light assistance on the hand, assistance on the wrist, assistance at the elbow, assistance at the shoulder, and independence. Ms. Perez and the assistant fade the prompts as they notice improvement in his independent movements. Although John does not master cutting with a fork before the end of the year, he learns to cut soft foods like cooked vegetables by himself.

Addressing Problem Behaviors at Mealtimes

A large portion of research on eating has addressed related problem behaviors, such as eating too rapidly (Favell, McGimsey, & Jones, 1980; Knapczyk, 1983; Luiselli, 1988) and eating too slowly (Luiselli, 1988). In

this section, we describe teaching approaches found useful in shaping skills, promoting neatness, and reducing problem eating behavior (e.g., eating too fast or too slowly, food refusal, food selectivity). More serious eating problems, such as pica (i.e., eating nonedible substances), excessive weight gain, and extreme food refusal, are not addressed here. Teams facing these problems may need to broaden the team membership to include medical input and to use additional assessment tools (e.g., functional assessment to study the conditions that seem to be maintaining the behavior, medical assessments, and health monitoring). (Chapter 6 addresses functional assessment; chapter 7 discusses health monitoring.)

Rate of Eating Instruction aimed at pacing may be needed for some students in the fluency stage of learning, such as students who eat finger foods, use utensils, or drink from cups but do so too quickly or too slowly. Pacing prompts have been used to slow down or speed up a student's rate of eating and establish an appropriate eating speed. Excessively rapid eating can be a serious problem because of social acceptability and potential health problems (e.g., vomiting, aspiration, poor digestion). A survey of persons with severe and profound retardation living in institutions (Favell et al., 1980, p. 482) defined "normal" eating rates as about eight bites per minute with the total meal consumed in 15 to 20 minutes. "Rapid" eaters, however, "consumed food at rates sometimes exceeding 20 bites per minute, and finished their entire meal within 1 to 3 minutes" (p. 482).

Knapczyk (1983) used pacing prompts to reduce rapid and sloppy eating in a student with severe disabilities, cerebral palsy, and poor arm and hand coordination. The student used a spoon to eat pureed foods but did not pause between bites. During the first phase of instruction, the teacher placed one spoonful of food into an empty bowl and gave verbal instructions with manual guidance to eat the spoonful and lay down the spoon. This phase continued until the student followed the request without help. Then the amount of food was gradually increased until the student was able to consume his entire meal and still pause between bites. During follow-up, pureed food was changed to solid food without any disruption of pausing between bites.

Pacing prompts have also been used to increase the rate of eating. For example, Luiselli (1988) increased the rate of eating in a girl with dual sensory impairments who took approximately 1 hour to complete meals. The teacher provided pacing prompts to her after every 40-second pause, guiding the girl's hand to grasp the food and bring it to her mouth. The girl's eating rate increased, and her need for prompts decreased.

Food Selectivity and Refusal Food refusal refers to the behavior of refusing to eat a sufficient amount of food to maintain one's health. Food selectivity refers to eating a few foods and no others. Students who exhibit either behavior are at serious risk for malnutrition and the associated health problems. Several researchers have demonstrated the effectiveness of positive reinforcement for increasing the variety of foods that a student eats. Food selectivity has been successfully treated by simple reinforcement of new choices (Najdowski et al., 2003; Riordan, Iwata, Finney, Wohl, & Stanley, 1984; Riordan, Iwata, Wohl, & Finney, 1980). The researchers determined student food preferences by observing their responses when presented with a variety of foods. The foods that students accepted were identified as preferred foods, and the foods that were refused were identified as nonpreferred foods. Children in all the studies increased the variety and amount of food consumed when bites of nonpreferred foods were followed by bites of preferred foods. Several studies have shown the importance of making reinforcement contingent on swallowing rather than accepting food (Najdowski et al., 2003; Riordan et al., 1980). Riordan et al. (1984) compared different schedules of reinforcement and found that intermittent reinforcement (providing bites of preferred food throughout the meal) was more effective than providing preferred foods at the end of a meal of nonpreferred foods.

Ahearn (2003) illustrated the use of an antecedent strategy to address food selectivity in a child with autism in a multiple baseline design across different vegetables. Ahearn used a pretest procedure to determine the child's preferred foods, primarily condiments. Then the child was presented with vegetables with his favorite condiments on top; for example, the child ate broccoli when covered with ketchup, barbecue sauce, or Italian dressing but not without condiments. Using condiments paired with nonpreferred foods increased the variety and amount of vegetables that the child ate.

Tarbell and Allaire (2002) describe a comprehensive and holistic program to address food refusal in children placed on feeding tubes because they did not eat

sufficiently to maintain their health. The Encouragement Feeding Program was designed to teach children to be successful eaters so they could be weaned from feeding tubes and consisted of individualized mealtime therapy, occupational therapy, therapeutic recreation, and preschool. Individual barriers to eating were identified for each child. For example, children described as needing to establish *hunger/satiety* were those who never regulated their own appetite in terms of a lack of food or fullness; their program consisted of food exploration (introduced to pureed foods followed by a gradual increase in food variety) and parent education. *Inexperienced eaters* were children who had no experience with eating. These children were provided with intensive oral therapy and taught to bite and chew. As with the first group, these students were also introduced to pureed foods, and the variety of foods was gradually increased. The group of children described as having *psychosocial issues* had difficult parent interactions around eating. The focus for these students was on improving parent–child interactions through mealtime management and recreational therapy. Children with *sensory/anxiety* disorders demonstrated problems with transitions, extreme food phobias with "fight-or-flight behavior," and oral defensiveness. Their treatment focused on sensory play on a daily basis. The researchers reported that parents in all groups were able to maintain eating programs and that children continued to make gains after they returned home.

Eating problems have to be carefully observed and analyzed in order for teams to design an appropriate intervention.

Informal assessment revealed that John could chew his food, keep his mouth closed while chewing (although he didn't usually do so), and respond to verbal cues. The team decided that Ms. Perez and the assistant should use verbal prompts and reinforcement to teach John to consistently and thoroughly chew his food with his mouth closed. But once the program was under way, they noted that he sometimes responded to verbal prompts by opening his mouth wider, thrusting his tongue, shaking his head from side to side, and laughing. His peers often laughed in response. To counter these "silly" behaviors, the team discussed using a brief interruption-extinction consequence along with the prompting program—that is, if John opened his mouth while chewing, they would remove his tray briefly until he closed his mouth, completed chewing, and swallowed. But

Ms. Perez argued that peers' laughter seemed to be maintaining John's sloppy eating and wanted to try a more normalized approach of peer modeling. She talked to John's peers to problem solve how they might help reduce John's silliness. His classmates decided they would not laugh or smile when John engaged in silly behaviors but would try hard to notice his neat eating (with his mouth closed). Several classmates who were extra-good models sat near John. After 2 weeks, peer modeling proved to be an effective approach for John.

Special Considerations for Dressing and Grooming

Assessment and Instruction

Having some ability to participate, fully or partially, in grooming and dressing activities and the responsibility for doing so not only lightens the load on care providers but also creates opportunities for choice and control in one's life. Individuals who dress and groom themselves to suit peer and community standards make better impressions on others. In this section, we discuss the teaching of dressing and grooming skills and cover (a) the range of skills, (b) instructional considerations, (c) materials, (d) embedded behaviors, and (e) recent research. Our focus is primarily on learners who will become actively involved or independent in their daily routines of dressing and grooming. For more coverage of teaching tactics for students with motor disabilities, refer to chapter 8; see also Christiansen and Matuska (2004); Orelove et al. (2004); Shephard et al. (1996); and Vogtle and Snell (2004).

Range of Skills

The dressing and grooming curriculum for students with severe disabilities encompasses routines that almost everyone engages in daily from brushing teeth to evaluating one's appearance and making adjustments if necessary. The more difficult tasks in dressing and undressing include shoe tying and fastening and unfastening buttons, snaps, hooks, zippers, ties, and belts. Grooming routines performed less frequently include clipping, filing, or painting fingernails; menstrual hygiene; shaving face, underarms, or legs; and applying makeup. Routines such as shaving and makeup are specific to the student's gender, culture, and personal

preference. Other skills, such as bathing or showering, washing hands, brushing teeth, and menstrual care, are critical for maintaining good hygiene. Finally, skills that are nonessential, such as painting fingernails (see Figure 9-4), wearing makeup, or grooming a beard, can still be very important to certain individuals.

Schedule and Location of Instruction

One challenge in teaching grooming and dressing skills in school settings is that other students do not typically learn these skills at school. Nonetheless, dressing and grooming opportunities are available at school. Preschool and kindergarten children use dressing skills in dress-up situations (Sewell et al., 1998), while older students dress for physical education classes. High school students often complete grooming routines between classes. Use of these natural times and locations may be the most effective learning environments. Learning grooming tasks under natural conditions (e.g., time of day, location) is likely to increase the rate of learning (Freagon & Rotatori, 1982) and to promote skill transfer and retention (Reese & Snell, 1991; Snell et al., 1989). The practice of scheduling lots of opportunities to practice a task being taught facilitates learning (Lehr, 1985), while spacing the learning opportunities across the day is also more conducive to learning than is massing trials into a concentrated shorter period of time (Mulligan, Lacy, & Guess, 1982).

Teaching in natural settings and at natural times allows peers and siblings to serve as models. When students with disabilities have friends of the same age and gender who are able to perform the skills they are trying to master, learning by observing them and by getting their assistance offers a viable supplement to teacher-directed trials (see Table 9-2). Finally, making the teacher's presence and supervision less predictable to learners has been shown to result in increased attending and better performance in children with autism (Dunlap & Johnson, 1985). Taken together, these studies lend some support to the use of typical peers as models and informal task assistants during natural grooming opportunities at school.

When scheduling dressing and grooming instruction at school, teachers may find that some students require more intensive instruction than is possible during natural opportunities. In these cases, the instructional team must balance individual student needs for intensive instruction in these areas with other needs for instruction. Some students may need to have additional instruction scheduled at other times in alternate locations. For example, a student may practice brushing teeth after breakfast and lunch (a natural time but a task not done by peers at school) in the restroom off the nurse's office (a natural setting but not with peers present). Students also may get indirect practice on grooming skills, as illustrated by Jamal.

Jamal will need a lot of instruction before he can tie his shoes by himself, but his teacher is optimistic. She lets him get extra practice on tying simple knots by tying the plastic grocery bags when he gathers and packages things for recycling with other eighth graders. Since they have started recycling three times a week, Jamal has learned to make the half knot. Peers also are good models: they are willing to slow down their tying and verbalize the steps while he watches.

Dressing and Grooming Materials

When selecting materials for instruction, teachers should use real materials (e.g., clothing, toothbrushes, deodorant) as much as possible. However, the use of larger clothing for initial instruction, faded over time to appropriate clothing sizes, has been demonstrated as a potent strategy (Azrin, Schaeffer, & Wesolowski, 1976; Diorio & Konarski, 1984; Reese & Snell, 1991). Initial teaching of buttoning with larger buttons was also effective (Kramer & Whitehurst, 1981). Surprisingly, Kramer and Whitehurst (1981) also found it easier for students to button the top buttons that were out of view rather than to begin the task with lower buttons.

To promote generalization of dressing and grooming skills to new materials and settings, students must learn to use a variety of materials and settings. Teams should decide what materials and what settings are most appropriate (e.g., nonstigmatizing, preferred, privacy) and most feasible (e.g., nearby, fit daily schedule). Sometimes in grooming instruction, teachers cannot use real materials and may supplement with artificial or simulated materials. For example, menstrual hygiene instruction for women with severe disabilities takes longer than a single menstrual cycle. Epps et al. (1990) compared two instructional approaches, both of which involved simulation: (a) changing artificially stained underwear or a pad on oneself and (b) using a doll and materials to practice these same maneuvers. Women taught using the dolls did not demonstrate generalization of their skills to themselves, but once they were given instruction on

themselves, they were able to perform these same skills during their menses. When using task simulations to teach, match the simulation to the actual task as much as possible. The authors in this study agreed with this general practice. They noted that changing pads on dolls differs greatly from performing the same task on oneself. In addition, they found that when the simulated menstrual amount and stain was dissimilar from the woman's actual menses onset, generalization was worse than when the similarity was close. Their materials included examples of different colors and styles of underwear, underwear with stains in different locations, and underwear with no stains. As we mentioned earlier in this chapter, Epps and her colleagues also learned that ordinary women in the community expressed a preference for teaching initially on dolls rather than on the individual herself; thus, instructional methods need to be designed to promote efficient learning and generalization for individual learners while also being socially acceptable both to those who do the teaching and to who are taught.

Dressing and Grooming Routines

Dressing and grooming routines provide numerous opportunities to develop self-determination through enrichment skills, such as making choices, communicating preferences, and interacting socially. For some, dressing and grooming are opportunities to express creativity in choosing fashionable clothing and hairstyles. The extension skills of initiating tasks, persisting through completion, solving problems, and monitoring speed and quality are a big part of independence in the grooming and dressing domain. Extension skills can be fully or partially performed.

Instructional Strategies for Teaching Dressing and Grooming Skills

All the instructional strategies discussed earlier in this chapter (Table 9–2) have been used successfully to teach grooming and dressing skills. Next, observation learning, self-modeling, and forward chaining are discussed in more detail.

Observation Learning or Modeling
Several studies lend support to the practice of learning by watching others perform competently or by watching others being taught. This ordinary teaching approach has been called by different names: observation

learning (Shoen & Sivil, 1989; Wolery, Ault, & Doyle, 1992) and passive modeling (Biederman, Fairhall, Raven, & Davey, 1998). Biederman et al. (1998) demonstrated that for teaching hand-washing and dressing skills passive modeling was more effective than both interactive modeling (i.e., hand-over-hand instruction with ongoing verbal prompts and praise) and less rigorous verbal prompting.

Wolery et al. (1992) described an approach for using observation learning in small groups:

- Students addressing similar skills are taught in small groups of two or three.
- Students are asked or prompted to watch who is being taught as he or she performs the skill.
- Students in the group take turns performing the target skill while others observe.
- One student can be taught half the task while others watch; instruction then moves to another in the group for the other half. Typically, students will learn some or all of the task steps that they have only observed.

Video self-modeling differs from live observation learning as students observe videos of their own mastery performances, edited to omit errors and produce a recording of "advanced" skills. Dowrick and Raeburn (1995) made videos of self-modeling available to a group of students over a 2-week period. Tapes containing close-ups of key component behaviors were edited so that no errors or prompting was shown. The researchers included dressing as one of the skills that was taught. Consistently, children were judged to have made significantly more progress when tasks involved self-modeling, and those gains did not lapse but continued over time. These findings on the positive effects of video replay suggest the potential that self-observation may have as a teaching strategy for dressing, alone or in combination with other methods (see Box 9–3).

Simultaneous Prompting

Simultaneous prompting for self-care skills involves ongoing physical prompting, with fading determined by student performance on regularly conducted probe trials. During probe trials, students are asked to perform the entire task without assistance, errors are ignored, and these steps are completed for the student without comment. Training trials involve cuing the student to look at task materials, giving a task request, and prompting and praising the student on each step of the task, with a choice of activity reinforcer offered at the end.

Sewell et al. (1998) used simultaneous prompting during activity-based routines to teach two preschoolers

  Box 9–3 Grooming Application to John

John's team views dressing and grooming as priority areas. Because he is 6 years old and has many other needs and motor limitations, most objectives in the dressing and grooming areas reflected partial participation. The skills his team selects for instruction are those John uses most often; washing hands, washing face (needed after all meals), and unfastening and fastening clothing for toileting.

The team examined John's schedule and identified natural opportunities for teaching these skills. Washing hands and manipulating fasteners are taught whenever John goes to the bathroom. Washing his face is taught after lunch. At school, Ms. Perez or her assistant teach all skills in the boy's bathroom. At home, John's mother teaches in the family bathroom. Later in the school year, when a male teaching assistant, Mr. Mclean, is hired to work with the primary grades, the team decides to ask him to teach John when other boys are present in the bathroom. John has some experience with washing his face and hands, and he is able to complete some steps with minimal guidance. These skills are task analyzed and taught to John, using a system of least prompts.

Manipulating fasteners is a more difficult skill for John because of the fine motor requirements. The OT helps team members design a simple version of graduated guidance to teach the skills, so John will get the feel of the motions required. Prompting begins with full physical assistance but changes based on the pressure cause of John's improved performance of the skill steps; as he initiates successfully, guidance is reduced to shadowing.

At the end of the year, John sometimes demonstrates the ability to wash his face and hands independently, but he also requires verbal reminder at times. The team's plan is to fade verbal reminders by having Mr. McLean stand just outside the bathroom door to observe and praise successful efforts. He notes that John sometimes throws away a paper towel without washing his hands. Although John is not at 100% accuracy, he is correctly imitating the behaviors of his typical peers, who do not always wash their hands either. By the end of the school year, John needs only reminders to check how his face looks after washing but still requires some physical assistance with fasteners.

with developmental delays to take off shoes, socks, and pants and to put on shirts, shoes, and jacket. Skills were taught in the context of routine activities that required the skill (e.g., taking off socks before dress-up play, sensory play, ball-bin play, and rest time; putting shirt on for dress-up play, water play, and "messy" art activities). The teacher assessed student performance in a probe trial each morning and completed one-on-one instruction throughout various times of the day. The teacher first provided an attentional cue (e.g., "Look, [student's name]" or "Look at [article of clothing]") and then gave full physical assistance and verbal directions and explanations throughout the task. The student received continuous verbal reinforcement as long as she allowed physical assistance. The students also got to perform a preferred task after the dressing skill was performed. The teacher used a variety of clothing to encourage generalization. Once students correctly performed a skill without assistance for 3 consecutive days, the teacher shifted to maintenance, withholding prompts and thinning continuous praise to praise following successful completion.

Forward Chaining

Another method used with grooming skills is forward chaining, which involves teaching in a forward direction through task steps and "building" a student's performance as each additional step is learned (Figure 9–8). Forward chaining has been used to teach menstrual care (Epps et al., 1990; Richman, Reiss, Bauman, & Bailey, 1984). Epps et al. (1990) faded prompts by requiring students to return to the beginning of the

FIGURE 9–8
Physical Therapist Uses a Forward Chaining Total Task Approach to Teach Natalie to Wash Her Hands

task after errors until they performed without a prompt. Thus, whenever students made an error, they practiced the appropriate response with the prompt until performed correctly. Then the student was taught to begin the task again, and no prompt was given. Richman et al. (1984) used an alternate forward chaining approach to teach feminine hygiene. On the first trial, the women were prompted through the entire task. Then they were allowed to perform independently on the task until their first error. Errors were followed by having the women practice the missed step with verbal assistance until they could complete the step independently. Next, they were asked to begin the task again from the beginning. These chaining strategies can be applied to a variety of grooming skills.

Team members have many proven teaching strategies to select from when addressing grooming and dressing IEP objectives. When planning how to teach, teams again must select methods that meet the principle of parsimony (Etzel & LeBlanc, 1979): procedures that are both relatively easy to use and have been demonstrated to be effective with students who have severe disabilities.

Summary

The self-care domain consists of basic tasks for maintaining personal hygiene: toileting, eating, dressing, and grooming. Independence or even active participation in one's own self-care contributes to personal and emotional well-being and self-determination. Assessment, program development and implementation, and evaluation require close team collaboration.

Effective strategies in the self-care domain include contingent reinforcement, shaping, chaining approaches, and prompting strategies. Special considerations in toileting include examination of students' physiological readiness and assessment of natural toileting patterns. Instruction in toileting may be successful using traditional methods or improved traditional methods, including reinforcement for dry pants, consequences for accidents, regulating toileting times, or moisture-signaling devices. Some students may require rapid training programs.

Eating and mealtime instruction also requires the assessment of physiological readiness. Additionally, consideration of appropriate foods and materials for instruction is required. Eating finger foods is typically the first self-feeding skill to be learned, followed by drinking from a cup and using utensils. Additional instructional strategies demonstrated to improve eating skills include pacing prompts.

Individual preference and having control of the activity is a critical consideration in many grooming and dressing skills. Careful communication with the student, family, and peers is necessary to determine appropriate choices in this area. There are fewer natural opportunities for dressing and grooming during school than for the other self-care areas of eating and toileting, forcing the educational team to sometimes consider the use of artificial times and places for instruction if dressing is a priority for the student. Recent research in this area has shown that various forms of observational learning (i.e., modeling, passive modeling, and video self-modeling), as well as simultaneous prompting, are successful in teaching grooming and dressing.

Suggested Activities

1. Are your instructional programs in self-care consistent with current best practices? Find out by completing the following program evaluation and improvement checklist for each self-care objective for a particular student you know well.

The Skill or Routine

- Is it functional for this student (i.e., needed now and in the future, essential to health or social acceptability, valued by family and peers)?
- Is it appropriate for the student's age and setting?
- Do the conditions and criteria reflect peer standards for performance in similar environments?
- Does the routine include extension skills beyond the core task steps and opportunities for enriching the task with student communication, choice, and socialization?

Teaching Methods

- Do methods emphasize natural cues and task materials?
- Is a range of routine times and locations used to teach?
- Can natural incentives be used to promote motivation?
- Are methods that have worked before with this student being used again?
- Are methods socially and culturally valid?

- If adaptations are needed, are they nonstigmatizing and used only as necessary?
- Are the teaching strategies team generated?
- Are all staff well informed on all program components?

Evaluation

- Were the starting points for teaching determined from baseline assessments?
- Has the team developed simple but effective methods to monitor student performance and learning across settings?
- Are performance data used to make program improvements?

2. Are you using partial participation with students to complete self-care routines? If so, answer the following questions to check the appropriateness of your application.
   - Did planning include input from therapists, the student, and family members?
   - If adaptations are used to simplify the cognitive aspects of a task, does the student know how to use the adaptations, or will instruction address this learning?
   - Does the student have some control in the task or routine?
   - Will you monitor the student's performance regularly so that participation can be increased or made more natural?
   - Is the form of partial participation used suited to the student's age and personal preferences?
   - If prostheses or adaptive equipment are used, are they durable and suited for use in all or most environments where the skill is needed?
   - Does partial participation appear to improve the student's enjoyment of the task, inclusion with peers, and the ease with which the student completes the task?
   - Does partial participation result in good outcomes in this routine (e.g., clean teeth)?
   - Is the partial participation approach practical for the student and for care providers or peers who might assist?

References

Ahearn, W. H. (2003). Using simultaneous presentation to increase vegetable consumption in a mildly selective child with autism. *Journal of Applied Behavior Analysis, 36*(3), 361–365.

Alberto, P., Jobes, N., Sizemore, A., & Doran, D. (1980). A comparison of individual and group instruction across response tasks. *Journal of the Association for Persons with Severe Handicaps, 5*, 285-293.

Albin, J. B. (1977). Some variables influencing the maintenance of acquired self-feeding behavior in profoundly retarded children. *Mental Retardation, 15*(5), 49-52.

Azrin, N. H., & Armstrong, P. M. (1973). The "mini-meal": A method for teaching eating skills to the profoundly retarded. *Mental Retardation, 11*(1), 9-11.

Azrin, N. H., Bugle, C., & O'Brien, F. (1971). Behavioral engineering: Two apparatuses for toilet training retarded children. *Journal of Applied Behavioral Analysis, 4*, 249-253.

Azrin, N. H., & Foxx, R. M. (1971). A rapid method of toilet training the institutionalized retarded. *Journal of Applied Behavior Analysis, 4*, 89-99.

Azrin, N. H., Schaeffer, R. M., & Wesolowski, M. D. (1976). A rapid method of teaching profoundly retarded persons to dress by a reinforcement-guidance method. *Mental Retardation, 14*(6), 29-33.

Bainbridge, N., & Myles, B. S. (1999). The use of priming to introduce toilet training to a child with autism. *Focus on Autism and Other Developmental Disabilities, 14*(2), 106-109.

Bak, J. J., & Siperstein, G. N. (1987). Similarity as a factor effecting change in children's attitudes toward mentally retarded peers. *American Journal of Mental Deficiency, 91*, 524-531.

Baker, B. L., & Brightman, A. J. (1997). *Steps to independence: Teaching everyday skills to children with special needs* (3rd ed.). Baltimore: Paul H. Brookes.

Bambara, L., & Cole, C. L. (1997). Permanent antecedent prompts. In M. Agran (Ed.), *Self-directed learning: Teaching self-determination skills* (pp. 111-143). Pacific Grove, CA: Brookes/Cole.

Banerdt, B., & Bricker, D. (1978). A training program for selected self-feeding skills for the motorically impaired. *AAESPH Review, 3*, 222-229.

Barmann, B. C., Katz, R. C., O'Brien, F., & Beauchamp, K. L. (1981). Treating irregular enuresis in developmentally disabled persons. *Behavior Modification, 5*, 336-346.

Barnes, K. J., & Case-Smith, J. (2004). Adaptive strategies for children with developmental disabilities. In C. Christiansen & K. M. Matuska (Eds.), *Ways of living: Self care strategies for special needs* (3rd ed., pp. 109-147). Rockville, MD: American Occupational Therapy Association.

Baumgart, D., Brown, L., Pumpian, I., Nisbet, J., Ford, A., Sweet, M., et al. (1982). Principle of participation and individualized adaptations in educational programs for severely handicapped students. *Journal of the Association for Persons with Severe Handicaps, 7*, 17-27.

Bettison, S. (1982). *Toilet training to independence for the handicapped: A manual for trainers.* Springfield, IL: Charles C Thomas.

Biederman, G. B., Fairhall, J. L., Raven, K. A., & Davey, V. A. (1998). Verbal prompting, hand-over-hand instruction, and passive observation in teaching children with developmental disabilities. *Exceptional Children, 64*, 503-511.

Boon, F. F. I., & Singh, N. (1991). A model for the treatment of encopresis. *Behavior Modification, 15*, 335-371.

Brown, F., & Cohen, S. (1996). Self-determination and young children. *Journal of the Association for Persons with Severe Handicaps, 21*, 22-30.

Brown, F., Evans, I., Weed, K., & Owen, V. (1987). Delineating functional competencies: A component model. *Journal of the Association for Persons with Severe Handicaps, 12*, 117-124.

Carr, E. G., Horner, R. H., Turnbull, A. P., Marquis, J. G., McLaughlin, D. M., McAtee, M. L., et al. (1999). *Positive behavior support for people with developmental disabilities: A research synthesis.* Washington, DC: American Association on Mental Retardation.

Case-Smith, J., & Humphry, R. (1996). Feeding and oral motor skills. In J. Case-Smith, A. S. Allen, & P. N. Pratt (Eds.), *Occupational therapy for children* (3rd ed., pp. 430-460). St. Louis, MO: Mosby.

Christiansen, C. H., & Matuska, K. M. (Eds, 2004). *Ways of living: Adaptive strategies for special needs* (3rd ed.). Bethesda, MD: American Occupational Therapy Association.

Cicero, F. R., & Pfadt, A. (2002). Investigation of a reinforcement-based toilet training procedure for children with autism, *Research in Developmental Disabilities, 23*, 319-331.

Collins, B. C., Gast, D. L., Wolery, M., Halcombe, A., & Leatherby, J. G. (1991). Using constant time delay to teach self-feeding to young students with severe/profound handicaps: Evidence of limited effectiveness. *Journal of Developmental and Physical Disabilities, 3*, 157-179.

Denny, M., Marchand-Martella, N., Martella, R., Reilly, J. R., Reilly, J. F., & Cleanthous, C. C. (2000). Using parent-delivered graduated guidance to teach functional living skills to a child with cri du chat syndrome. *Education and Treatment of Children, 23*, 441-454.

Diorio, M. A., & Konarski, E. A., Jr. (1984). Evaluation of a method for teaching dressing skills to profoundly mentally retarded persons. *American Journal of Mental Deficiency, 89*, 307-309.

Doleys, D. M. (1985). Enuresis and encopresis. In P. H. Bornstein & A. E. Kazdin (Eds.), *Handbook of clinical behavior therapy with children* (pp. 412-440). Homewood, IL: Dorsey Press.

Dowrick, P. W., & Raeburn, J. M. (1995). Self-modeling: Rapid skill training for children with physical disabilities. *Journal of Developmental and Physical Disabilities, 7*, 25-37.

Doyle, M. B. (2002). *The paraprofessional's guide to the inclusive classroom: Working as a team* (2nd ed.). Baltimore: Paul H. Brookes.

Duker, P., Didden, R., & Sigafoos, J. (2004). *One-to-one training: Instructional procedures for learners with developmental disabilities.* Austin, TX: PRO-ED.

Dunlap, G., & Johnson, G. (1985). Increasing the independent responding of autistic children with unpredictable supervision. *Journal of Applied Behavior Analysis, 18*, 227-236.

Dunlap, G., Koegel, R. L., & Koegel, R. K. (1984). Continuity of treatment: Toilet training in multiple community settings. *Journal of the Association for Persons with Severe Handicaps, 9*, 134-141.

Dunlap, G., Koegel, R. L., & Koegel, L. K. (1986). *Toilet training for children with severe handicaps: A field manual for coordinating procedures across multiple community settings*. Huntington, WV: Marshall University, Autism Training Center.

Epps, S., Stern, R. J., & Horner, R. H. (1990). Comparison of simulation training on self and using a doll for teaching generalized menstrual care to women with severe mental retardation . *Research in Developmental Disabilities, 11*, 37-66.

Etzel, B. C., & LeBlanc, J. M. (1979). The simplest treatment alternative: The law of parsimony applied to choosing appropriate instructional control and errorless learning procedures for the difficult-to-teach child. *Journal of Autism and Developmental Disorders, 9*, 361-382.

Favell, J. E., McGimsey, J. F., & Jones, M. J. (1980). Rapid eating in the retarded: Reduction by nonaversive procedures. *Behavior Modification, 4*, 481-492.

Ferguson, D. L., & Baumgart, D. (1991). Partial participation revisited. *Journal of the Association for Persons with Severe Handicaps, 16*, 218-227.

Foxx, R. M., & Azrin, N. H. (1973). *Toilet training the retarded: A rapid program for day and nighttime independent toileting.* Champaign, IL: Research Press.

Foxx, R. M., & Azrin, N. H. (1974). *Toilet training in less than a day.* New York: Simon & Schuster.

Freagon, S., & Rotatori, A. F. (1982). Comparing natural and artificial environments in training self-care skills to group home residents. *Journal of the Association for Persons with Severe Handicaps, 7*(3), 73-86.

Fredericks, H. D. B., Baldwin, V. L., Grove, D. N., & Moore, W. G. (1975). *Toilet training the handicapped child.* Monmouth, OR: Instructional Development Corporation.

Freschi, D. F. (1999). Guidelines for working with one-to-one aides. *Teaching Exceptional Children, 23*(4), 42-45.

Garff, J. T., & Storey, K. (1998). The use of self-management strategies for increasing the appropriate hygiene of persons with disabilities in supported employment settings. *Education and Training in Mental Retardation and Developmental Disabilities, 33*, 179-188.

Giangreco, M. F., Edelman, S. W., Luiselli, T. E., & MacFarland, S. Z. C. (1997). Helping or hovering? Effects of instructional assistant proximity on students with disabilities. *Exceptional Children, 64*, 7-18.

Giles, D. K., & Wolf, M. M. (1966). Toilet training institutionalized severe retardates: An application of operant behavior modification techniques. *American Journal of Mental Deficiency, 70*, 766-780.

Hagopian, L. P., Farrell, D. A., & Amari, A. (1996). Treating total liquid refusal with backward chaining and fading. *Journal of Applied Behavior Analysis, 29*, 573-575.

Herreshoff, J. K. (1973). Two electronic devices for toilet training. *Mental Retardation, 11*(6), 54-55.

Hobbs, T., & Peck, C. A. (1985). Toilet training people with profound mental retardation: A cost effective procedure for large residential settings. *Behavioral Engineering, 9*, 50-57.

Horner, R. D., & Keilitz, I. (1975). Training mentally retarded adolescents to brush their teeth. *Journal of Applied Behavior Analysis, 8*, 301-309.

Irvine, A. B., Erickson, A. M., Singer, G. H., & Stahlberg, D. (1992). A coordinated program to transfer self-management skills from school to home. *Education and Training in Mental Retardation, 27*, 241-254.

Knapczyk, D. R. (1983). Use of teacher-paced instruction in developing and maintaining independent self-feeding. *Journal of the Association for Persons with Severe Handicaps, 8*(3), 10-16.

Kramer, L., & Whitehurst, C. (1981). Effects of button features on self-dressing in young retarded children. *Education and Training of the Mentally Retarded, 16*, 277-283.

Lasater, M. W., & Brady, M. P. (1995). Effects of video self-modeling and feedback on task fluency: A home-based intervention. *Education and Treatment of Children, 18*, 389-407.

Lehr, D. (1985). Effects of opportunities to practice on learning among students with severe handicaps. *Education and Training of the Mentally Retarded, 20*, 268-274.

Linford, M. D., Hipsher, L. W., & Silikovitz, R. G. (1972). *Systematic instruction for retarded children: The illness program. Part 3. Self-help instruction.* Danville, IL: Interstate.

Losardo, A., & Bricker, D. (1994). Activity-based intervention and direct instruction: A comparison study. *American Journal on Mental Retardation, 98*, 744-765.

Lowman, D. K., & Murphy, S. M. (1999). *The educator's guide to feeding children with disabilities.* Baltimore: Paul H. Brookes.

Luiselli, J. K. (1988). Improvement of feeding skills in multihandicapped students through paced-prompting interventions. *Journal of the Multi-Handicapped Person, 1*, 17-30.

Luiselli, J. K. (1996). A case study evaluation of a transfer-of-stimulus control toilet training procedure for a child with a pervasive developmental disorder. *Focus on Autism and Developmental Disabilities, 11*, 158-162.

Mahoney, K., Van Wagenen, R. K., & Meyerson, L. (1971). Toilet training of normal and retarded children. *Journal of Applied Behavior Analysis, 4*, 173-181.

Marshall, G. R. (1966). Toilet training of an autistic eight-year-old through conditioning therapy: A case report. *Behaviour Research and Therapy, 4*, 242-245.

Matson, J. L., Taras, M. E., Sevin, J. A., Love, S. R., & Fridley, D. (1990). Teaching self-help skills to autistic and mentally retarded children. *Research in Developmental Disabilities, 11*, 361-378.

Meyer, L. H., Park, H., Grenot-Scheyer, M., Schwartz, I. S., & Harry, B. (1998). *Making friends .* Baltimore: Paul H. Brookes.

Mulligan, M., Lacy, L., & Guess, D. (1982). Effects of massed, distributed, and spaced trial sequencing on severely handicapped student's performance. *Journal of the Association for the Severely Handicapped, 7*(2), 48-61.

Najdowski, A. C., Wallace, M. D., Doney, J. K., & Ghezzi, P. M. (2003). Parental assessment and treatment of food selectivity in natural settings. *Journal of Applied Behavior Analysis, 36*, 383-386.

Nietupski, J., Hamre-Nietupski, S., Curtain, S., & Shrikanth, K. (1997). A review of curricular research in severe disabilities from 1976 to 1995 in six selected journals . *Journal of Special Education, 31*, 36-55.

O'Brien, F., & Azrin, N. H. (1972). Developing proper mealtime behaviors of the institutionalized retarded. *Journal of Applied Behavior Analysis, 5*, 389-399.

O'Brien, F., Bugle, C., & Azrin, N. H. (1972). Training and maintaining a retarded child's proper eating. *Journal of Applied Behavior Analysis, 5*, 67-73.

Orelove, F. P., Sobsey, D., & Silberman, R. K. (2004). *Educating children with multiple disabilities: A collaborative approach* (4th ed.). Baltimore: Paul H. Brookes.

Parrott, K. A., Schuster, J. W., Collins, B. C., & Gassaway, L. J. (2000). Simultaneous prompting and instructive feedback when teaching chained tasks. *Journal of Behavioral Education, 10*, 3-19.

Reamer, R. B., Brady, M.P., & Hawkins (1998). The effects of video self-modeling on parents interactions with children with developmental disabilities. *Education and Training in Mental Retardation and Developmental Disabilities, 33*(2), 131-143.

Reese, G. M., & Snell, M. E. (1991). Putting on and removing coats and jackets: The acquisition and maintenance of skills by children with severe multiple disabilities. *Education and Training in Mental Retardation, 26*, 398-410.

Richman, G. S., Reiss, M. L., Bauman, K. E., & Bailey, J. S. (1984). Teaching menstrual care to mentally retarded women: Acquisition, generalization, and maintenance. *Journal of Applied Behavior Analysis, 17*, 441-451.

Richmond, G. (1983). Shaping bladder and bowel continence in developmentally retarded preschool children. *Journal of Autism and Developmental Disorders, 13*, 197-205.

Riordan, M. M., Iwata, B. A., Finney, J. W., Wohl, M. D., & Stanley, A. E. (1984). Behavioral assessment and treatment of chronic food refusal in handicapped children. *Journal of Applied Behavior Analysis, 17*, 327-341.

Riordan, M. M., Iwata, B. A., Wohl, M. K., & Finney, J. W. (1980). Behavioral treatment of food refusal and selectivity in developmentally disabled children. *Applied Research in Mental Retardation, 1*, 95-112.

Schaefer, C. E., & DiGeronimo, T. F. (1997). *Toilet training without tears* (Rev. ed.). New York: Signet Books.

Scott, S. M., McWilliam, R. A., & Mayhew, L. (1999). Integrating therapists into the classroom: *Young Exceptional Children, 2*(3), 15-24.

Sewell, T. J., Collins, B. C., Hemmeter, M. L., & Schuster, J. W. (1998). Using simultaneous prompting within an activity-based format to teach dressing skills to preschoolers with developmental delays. *Journal of Early Intervention, 21*, 132-142.

Shephard, J., Procter, S. A., & Coley, I. L. (1996). Self-care and adaptations for independent living. In J. Case-Smith, A. S. Allen, & P. N. Pratt (Eds.), *Occupational therapy for children* (3rd ed., pp. 526-580). St. Louis, MO: Mosby.

Shoen, S. F., & Sivil, E. O. (1989). A comparison of procedures in teaching self-help skills: Increasing assistance, time delay, and observational learning. *Journal of Autism and Developmental Disorders, 19*, 57-72.

Simbert, V. F., Minor, J. W., & McCoy, J. F. (1977). Intensive feeding training with retarded children. *Behavior Modification, 1*, 512-529.

Sisson, L. A., Kilwein, M. L., & Van Hasselt, V. B. (1988). A graduated guidance procedure for teaching self-dressing skills to multi-handicapped children. *Research in Developmental Disabilities, 9*, 419-432.

Smith, A. L., Jr., Piersel, W. C., Filbeck, R. W., & Gross, E. J. (1983). The elimination of mealtime food stealing and scavenging behavior in an institutionalized severely mentally retarded adult. *Mental Retardation, 21*, 255-259.

Smith, P. S. (1979). A comparison of different methods of toilet training the mentally handicapped. *Behaviour Research and Therapy, 17*, 33-34.

Snell, M. E. (1997). Teaching children and young adults with mental retardation in school programs: Current research. *Behaviour Change, 12*, 73-105.

Snell, M. E., & Janney, R. E. (2000). *Practices for inclusive schools: Social relationships and peer support.* Baltimore: Paul H. Brookes.

Snell, M. E., & Janney, R. E. (2005). *Practices for inclusive schools: Collaborative teaming* (2nd ed.). Baltimore: Paul H. Brookes.

Snell, M. E., Lewis, A. P., & Houghton, A. (1989). Acquisition and maintenance of toothbrushing skills by students with cerebral palsy and mental retardation. *Journal of the Association for Persons with Severe Handicaps, 14*, 216-226.

Stainback, S. S., & Healy, H. A. (1982). *Teaching eating skills: A handbook for teachers .* Springfield, IL: Charles C Thomas.

Staub, D., Spaulding, M., Peck, C. A., Gallucci, C., & Schwartz, I. S. (1996). Using nondisabled peers to support the inclusion of students with disabilities at the junior high school level. *Journal of the Association for Persons with Severe Handicaps, 21*, 194-205.

Steere, D. L., & Pancsofar, E. L. (1995). Cues, prompts, and correction strategies. In W. W. Woolcock & J. W. Domaracki (Eds.), *Instructional strategies in the community: Instruction for persons with disabilities* (pp. 35-53). Austin, TX: PRO-ED.

Tarbell, M. C., & Allaire, J. H. (2002). Children with feeding tube dependency: Treating the whole child. *Infants and Young Children, 15*(1), 29-41.

Tarbox, R. S. F., Williams, W. L., & Friman, P. C. (2004). Extended diaper wearing: Effects on continence in and out of the diaper. *Journal of Applied Behavior Analysis, 37*, 97-100.

Thompson, T., & Hanson, R. (1983). Overhydration: Precautions when treating urinary incontinence. *Mental Retardation, 21*, 139-143.

Van Wagenen, R. K., Meyerson, L., Kerr, N. J., & Mahoney, K. (1969). Rapid toilet training: Learning principles and prosthesis. *Proceedings of the 77th Annual Convention of the American Psychological Association, 4*, 781-782.

Van Wagenen, R. K., & Murdock, E. E. (1966). A transistorized signal-package for toilet training of infants. *Journal of Experimental Child Psychology, 3*, 312-314.

Vogtle, L., & Snell, M. E. (2004). Methods for promoting basic and instrumental activities of daily living. In C. H. Christiansen & K. M. Matuska (Eds.), *Ways of living: Adaptive strategies for special needs* (3rd ed., pp. 85-108). Rockville, MD: American Occupational Therapy Association.

Wolery, M., Ault, M. J., & Doyle, P. M. (1992). *Teaching students with moderate to severe disabilities*. White Plains, NY: Longman.

Wolery, M., Ault, M. J., Gast, D., Doyle, P. M., & Griffen, A. K. (1991). Teaching chained tasks in dyads: Acquisition of target and observational behaviors. *Journal of Special Education, 25*, 198–220.

Young, K. R., West, R. P., Howard, V. F., & Whitney, R. (1986). Acquisition, fluency training, generalization, and maintenance of dressing skills of two developmentally disabled children. *Education and Treatment of Children, 9*, 16–29.

10

Peer Relationships

Ilene S. Schwartz
Debbie Staub
Charles A. Peck
Chrysan Gallucci

- Waving hello to your teacher when you enter the classroom
- Sharing materials with your classmates during an art project
- Arguing with a friend about who gets to use the swing first
- Helping a classmate clean up materials at the end of a science project

These are all examples of social behaviors that students with and without disabilities could practice at school. The development of these simple, as well as more complex, social behaviors are among the most important developmental outcomes of childhood (Shonkoff & Phillips, 2000). Human beings are the most profoundly social of all creatures. Our development, well-being, and happiness are utterly dependent on the quality of our relationships with others. From the earliest establishment of regularity and predictability of social exchanges between infants and caregivers (Kaye, 1982) to our uniquely human construction of "webs of significance" and meaning as adults (Geertz,

1973), the social relationships of our lives form the crucible within which we come to know the world, each other, and ourselves (Bruner, 1990). With this viewpoint in mind, we attempt in this chapter to highlight the role that social relationships play in the development of children and youth with disabilities and to describe some of the strategies teachers and other caregivers can use to support this process.

The study of social behavior has always been intricately woven into the study of educating people with disabilities. Although some early work in this area put the emphasis on skills (while ignoring the context in which the skills needed to be performed), current work in developmental psychology, special education, and applied behavior analysis emphasizes relationships and the context of those relationships. For example, Vygotsky (1978) and other social-cultural theorists place issues of relationships at the fulcrum of their claims about how children become competent members of human communities (e.g., Bruner, 1996;

Cole, 1996; Lave & Wenger, 1991). Behavior analysts emphasize the need to look at behavior in context, encouraging educators, families, and researchers to attend to the social and ecological validity of their interventions (Baer, Wolf, & Risley, 1987; Schwartz & Baer, 1991; Wolf, 1977). The purpose of this chapter is to focus the discussion of the social lives of children with disabilities on relationships rather than skills. We want readers to consider the context and function of social behavior and think about how the presence or absence of meaningful social relationships can impact the quality of life of students with severe disabilities.

To help bring these concepts to life, we want to introduce you to three students with severe disabilities. All these students attend inclusive schools and have friends. We could not have made that statement when we first met these students. They made friends as a result of participating in inclusive educational placements that valued social relationships, developed and maintained the contexts to support peer relationships, and provided systematic instruction for students, with and without disabilities, focused on facilitating those relationships. These students have different diagnoses, strengths, interests, and challenges, but all have been enriched by social relationships with their typically developing peers.

 ## Three Case Examples

Sean

Sean is a first grader with autism. We first met Sean when he was attending an inclusive preschool. He was referred to the preschool after "being expelled" from three different child care programs. All the child care providers described Sean as a "sweet little boy, as long as you let him do his own thing." When Sean was asked by teachers or other children to participate in activities, he refused. Sometimes these refusals included screaming, hitting children, or throwing objects. Sean's parents were surprised when they observed him at the various child care programs and noticed that he was almost always "shunned" by the other children. But it was different in the inclusive preschool— Sean flourished. He learned to be more flexible, interact successfully with other children, and even manage his anger and disappointment. He also developed a love of baseball (shared by his parents) and learned how to trade baseball cards. In kindergarten, he learned to read, and by the beginning of first grade, he would often arrive at school after he had read the sports page for the latest update on his favorite teams.

Carrie

Carrie, who has Down syndrome, is in fourth grade and has attended inclusive classrooms since she was in second grade. Her teachers and peers characterize her as a playful, occasionally stubborn or shy, and always interesting child. Carrie has always been small for her age, and her carrot-top hair, perhaps a symbol of her fiery personality, hangs close to her shoulders. She loves to draw and is quite verbal but is often difficult to understand. She works with a communication specialist on her articulation and voice volume regularly. She is learning how to use pictures, symbols, and nonverbal communication to make herself better understood. Interestingly, often her peers

understand her communicative attempts better than adults. Her reading level is close to that of a typical first grader's. Carrie takes great pride in being a member of her school. In the past couple of years, she has shown significant growth in her ability to do things independently.

Cole

Cole is a 17-year-old young man with severe disabilities who attends high school as a junior. Cole started attending an inclusive school in third grade. His parents were active advocates for inclusion and believe that the presence of typically developing peers improved the quality of Cole's education and his life. Cole contracted spinal meningitis at age 1, resulting in early paralysis and severe seizures. Cole's serious health problems and challenging behaviors (e.g., tantrums, aggression toward adults and objects) have often been frustrating for both his family and teachers.

Described by his neurologist as having one of the most severe cases of seizure disorders in the state, Cole's "good" days and "bad" days are often determined by his rate of seizure activity and the effects of the medication he takes to control them. Cole uses an augmentative system as his primary mode for communication and is quite fluent with it. He has strong social initiation skills, and his expressive vocabulary has increased greatly in the past few years. With close friends and family, he is easily understood. Because of an increase in violent behaviors the summer of his seventh-grade year, Cole's parents enrolled him in a behavioral treatment group home for 18 months, where he lived full time as a resident. During that time, Cole was able to continue his education at the junior high school he had been attending. Currently, Cole lives with a foster family in close proximity to his parents, whom he sees regularly.

Peer Relationships and Developmental Outcomes

Social relationships are important both as developmental outcomes and as the context for learning. Researchers, educators, and parents all agree that developing friendships and positive relationships with peers is one of the important tasks of childhood (e.g., Hart & Risley, 1996; Hartup, 1983; Wolfberg, 1999). There is also increasing evidence that the lack of positive peer relationships (i.e., children who are ignored or rejected by their peers) is a risk factor for a number of troubling developmental outcomes, such as mental health problems and poor adjustment. Schools provide multiple opportunities for social interaction, and many classrooms actually require students to work together to achieve classroom and curricular goals. For example, in early childhood classrooms, using activity-based or embedded learning opportunities is considered a best practice (Sandall, Hemmeter, Smith, & McLean, 2004). In elementary schools, much of the curriculum is based on cooperative or experiential learning (Greenwood, Maheady, & Delquadri, 2002). Throughout school, the informal social curriculum is taught and learned on playgrounds, in clubs, and in the school hallways.

In addition to the personal satisfaction and support that people gain from personal relationships, students have the opportunity to learn important social, communicative, academic, and cognitive skills in the context of peer relationships. For example, during group activities in classrooms, students are participating in a social context in which they may learn to attend to group instructions, to observe what the group is doing as a cue for what is expected ("mass modeling"), and to make choices and regulate behavior without direct adult intervention. During free choice activities, students learn how to make choices, negotiate sharing materials with others, and are often highly motivated to learn the communicative, motor, or cognitive skills necessary to complete their preferred activities. All these may be recognized as critical skills for competent participation in a tremendous variety of highly valued activities, roles, and settings within our culture.

In the following section, we describe a conceptual framework we and our colleagues have developed that helps make sense of the complex connections between social experiences, skill acquisition, and participation in valued roles, activities, and settings (Billingsley,

FIGURE 10–1
Lunchtime is often hurried but filled with social exchanges between peers.

Gallucci, Peck, Schwartz, & Staub, 1996; Peck et al., 1994; Schwartz 2000). We then offer a set of recommendations for interventions based on this framework. We conclude our chapter with some suggestions regarding assessment and evaluation strategies that we believe are useful in documenting outcomes related to peer relationships and with comments related to the effect of experiences with the inclusion of students with severe disabilities on the lives of children and adolescents who are typically developing.

In this chapter and elsewhere (Billingsley et al., 1996; Peck et al., 1994; Schwartz, 2000), we make the claim that *participation in socially valued roles, activities, and settings is both the most fundamental outcome of the developmental process and the primary means by which development is achieved.* This view is at odds with views of development as acquisition of skills, which has dominated the field of special education, including special education for individuals with severe disabilities, for many years. We do not consider skills to be unimportant. Rather, we broaden our analysis of how students with severe disabilities come to be more competent members of human communities to include more detailed consideration of the relationships between skill acquisition and a variety of social context factors.

Our changing views of development have emerged in part from talking to the parents of children with severe disabilities who participated in inclusive educational placements and hearing their stories about the profound effects these placements had on all aspects of their children's development. Cole's mother shares a typical story.

> Her son attended a segregated preschool and early elementary program. Although she was pleased with some of the academic skills he was learning, he was not making friends, he was not connected to the school or community, and as his parent she felt it was difficult to be connected to the school since the location of his program changed almost every year. After attending an inclusive school for 1 year, Cole had friends, had been invited to a birthday party, and was recognized by classmates in the supermarket who came over to say hello. Cole's mother became a member of the Parent–Teacher Association at the school.

Although being invited to a birthday party is not a developmental outcome measured by any state test of educational achievement, it is an important indicator of belonging, friendships, and membership. After hearing many stories from parents about the changes inclusive education made in the quality of life for their children with severe disabilities, we designed a research project to help us describe the effects of inclusive education on the academic and social development of students with severe disabilities. We implemented a 4-year program of research in which we followed 43 children with moderate or severe disabilities who have been enrolled full time in regular classrooms (Consortium for Research on Social Relationships, Cooperative Agreement #H086A20003, awarded to Syracuse University from the U.S. Department of Education). We collected and analyzed data from multiple sources, including classroom observations; interviews with teachers, parents, nondisabled peers, and paraeducators; video recordings and documents such as individualized education programs (IEPs); and examples of children's work, in an effort to describe outcomes that occur for students in inclusive school programs.

An important feature of this work has been our efforts to construct an understanding of outcomes for students with disabilities in active dialogue with parents, teachers, and students. In these conversations and in the more "objective" data we collected, we were confronted again and again by compelling evidence of change in children's lives that was not adequately described in terms of the simple acquisition of skills. Analyzing hundreds of excerpts from our observational and interview data, we developed a conceptual framework that describes the types of outcomes we observed for students with severe disabilities in inclusive school settings. Because the framework was developed out of our observations of fairly typical school settings, including regular classrooms, playgrounds, cafeterias, and other activity contexts, it offers considerable guidance for teachers and specialists who wish to use these settings as a context for supporting the development of learners with severe disabilities.

The Outcome Framework

The outcome patterns that have emerged in our project are conceptualized in terms of three broad domains. First, our findings suggest that many of the children we studied in inclusive classrooms were in fact learning many of the same types of *skills* that have been the traditional focus of special education outcome assessment. These include social and communication skills, academics, and functional skills. A second domain of outcomes we observed was the extent to which children with severe disabilities achieve *membership* or a sense of belonging in the formal and informal groups that make up the social fabric of the classroom and school (Schnorr, 1990). Finally, we observed that children in inclusive classrooms may develop a wide variety of personal *relationships* with other children. Each of these broad outcome domains (i.e., skills, membership, and relationships) has strong effects on each other. Moreover, each of the domains may be viewed in terms of its relationship with a higher-order outcome, which we conceptualized as increased participation in valued roles, activities, and settings of the community and culture (Bronfenbrenner, 1979; Lave & Wenger, 1991). Figure 10–2 depicts the relationship between each of the three outcome domains and the higher-order goal of increased participation.

Ultimately, peer relationships are both an end in themselves (and an important one) and an important means of support that enable a child to participate in a variety of valued roles, activities, and settings. Relationships between children with severe disabilities and their nondisabled peers are strongly related to other types of outcomes, including the child's individual skills (e.g., social and communication skills) and status as a "member" of the class or social group. We describe each of these outcome domains in more detail.

FIGURE 10–2
Inclusive Education Research Group Outcome Framework

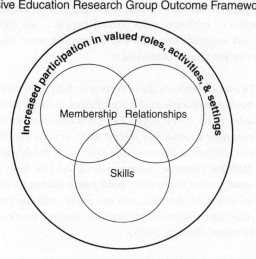

Membership

We use the term "membership" to refer to the phenomenological sense of belonging to a social group, such as a classroom, cooperative work group, or friendship clique. Membership is not something we can observe directly. However, we can make inferences about the extent to which a child is treated as a member of a group by observing things such as accommodations group members make to include a child, shared symbols used by the group (e.g., special T-shirts, team names, uniforms), and rituals that occur in the group context (e.g., special greetings, activities or roles performed only by group members).

Membership is an important outcome in and of itself in the lives of children, including those with severe disabilities (Ferguson, 1994). In fact, membership outcomes have received very high "importance" ratings from parents and teachers in social validation studies of the outcome framework (Peck et al., 1994). The extent to which students with severe disabilities are viewed as "members" of the classroom affects the kinds of opportunities they are likely to have for participating in social relationships and other classroom activities (Schnorr, 1990). Examples of membership include children with severe disabilities being included on the job chart alongside their nondisabled peers, providing a nonspeaking role (or a role using a voice output augmentative communication device) for a student with severe disabilities in a school play, and making sure that the names of the children with disabilities

are included on the monthly birthday list that is read by the principal at the school assembly (Copeland, Hughes, Agran, Wehmeyer & Fowler, 2002; Williams & Downing, 1998).

Relationships

This domain of outcomes refers to the characteristics and extent of personal (dyadic) relationships between children with disabilities and their peers. We characterized relationships between students with disabilities and other individuals (both with and without disabilities) on the basis of consistencies in their social interactions over time, interviews with teachers and parents, and (when possible) informal interviews with children themselves. As in most relationships, the qualitative features of the social relationships we observed between individual children are not static but often vary in specific contexts (Fiske, 1992).

Clearly, a high-priority outcome for children with severe disabilities, as for any child, is the development of friendships. Friendships have been the focus of most analyses of social relationships in the professional literature to date (Downing, Spencer, & Cavallaro, 2004; Fisher, 2001; Haring, 1991; Meyer, Park, Grenot-Scheyer, Schwartz, & Harry, 1998). However, other types of relationships also play an important role as sources of learning and support for students with severe disabilities. Our observations of the variety of relationships that emerge between children with disabilities and their nondisabled peers led us to identify four "types" of relationships—play/companion, helper (giver), helpee (receiver), and conflictual—each of which offers important learning opportunities for children. It is this range of relationships that adds richness and depth to the human interactions that factor into our quality of life. Examples of these relationships include the companionship of the person sitting next to you on the school bus, the helper who points out what page to turn to in the reading book, helping other students by handing out journals, and the conflict you may have with a peer when both of you want to use the last swing on the playground.

Skills

The third domain of outcomes we observed in inclusive classrooms is comprised of the academic and behavioral competencies children develop over time; these have been the predominant focus of traditional outcomes assessment in special education. Skills, particularly social and communicative skills, strongly affect (but do not exclusively determine) the extent to which students with severe disabilities are able to participate in a variety of social roles, activities, and settings. Our analysis of what children learn in inclusive settings and how they learn suggests that many critical skills are acquired in the contexts of social activities in which personal relationships and membership play an important part.

> *During one of our observations, Carrie and her classmates were going for a nature walk in the fields surrounding their school. Students were instructed to get their science notebooks so that they could write down the types of plants they identified during the walk. As the students gathered their notebooks and pencils, Carrie watched her peers, then went to her desk, picked up her science spiral notebook and her pencil, and got in line behind her friend Sophie. She watched as many children slipped their pencils down the spiral of their notebooks, and then after a little struggle and persistence she was able to store her pencil in the same manner.*

Carrie's imitation of peers, independent task management, and use of fine motor skills occurred without direct adult intervention (Apolloni & Cooke, 1975; Garfinkle & Schwartz, 2002).

We have observed children learning new skills in the context of signing in every morning as they entered the classroom, counting out materials for distribution to classmates, checking off the names of children for a lunch count, listening to a book on tape and then participating in literature group, and many other social activities. The essence of this domain is to acknowledge all the teaching (often by peers) and learning that takes place outside of explicit, teacher-led instruction. We do not discount the importance of explicit instruction, which is the cornerstone of specialized instruction; rather, we are urging the consideration of strategies to make the informal instruction that takes place even more effective.

Linkages Among Outcome Domains

The relationships among the outcomes described previously are transactional (Bronfenbrenner, 1979; Sameroff & Chandler, 1975). The quality of a child's social relationships with peers is affected by (and affects) the child's status as a member of the group and is also affected by (and affects) the skills the child develops. All these factors contribute to the student's access and participation in valued roles, activities, and settings in the school and community. The richest examples of inclusive educational practice we have observed suggest that multiple outcomes were likely to accrue for students involved.

> *In one classroom, we observed a child with severe behavior problems and a significant reading disability who read every night for 30 minutes into a tape recorder so that his friend with severe disabilities could listen to the story the next night for homework. Multiple positive outcomes resulted. The boys developed a nice friendship, both participated more fully in literature groups, and the child with the reading disability improved his reading fluency and comprehension (Pernat, 1995).*

The intersection of membership, relationships, and skill development yielded instructional practices that benefited all students.

The framework we have described has some important implications for understanding issues of curriculum and instruction for learners with severe disabilities and others. First, the framework rejects the separation of social and academic outcomes that has been so prevalent in the field of special education. In fact, our observations suggest that the social aspects of a child's life in school (which we have defined in terms of membership and relationships) constitute the motivational contexts in which many fundamental life skills are learned. The false dichotomization of social and academic skill outcomes may in fact lead teachers away from creating functional and meaningful instructional contexts for learners with severe disabilities.

Recognizing the important linkages among membership, relationships, and the development of critical skills suggests that removing students from rich social contexts to emphasize one type of outcome (e.g., pulling a student out of the regular classroom for one-to-one skill instruction) is likely to affect the student's opportunities related to other outcome domains (Schnorr, 1990). Our model suggests many ways in which interventions can be designed that take advantage of the natural learning processes that are embedded in typical classroom life and other rich social contexts.

In the following section, we illustrate how the outcome framework can be used to describe and evaluate the peer relationships in the lives of Sean, Carrie, and Cole, the three children introduced earlier in this chapter. In particular, we draw the reader's attention to the critical functions that each child's social relationships play in providing opportunities to learn new skills, to achieve a sense of membership or "belonging" to valued social groups, and to support participation in valued roles, activities, and settings.

Three Case Illustrations

Sean

Membership

Since Sean entered the inclusive kindergarten, there has been a major shift in his membership. At first he was aloof, he ignored his peers, and after a little while they began to ignore him. In teacher-directed small groups, his teacher had to directly facilitate interactions between Sean and his peers. For example, she taught Sean how to trade baseball cards, an activity that the boys in the kindergarten class enjoy very much. After a few months, it was clear that Sean was becoming a member of the class. He was easily included in friendship groups and in schoolwide and classwide activities. One of the nicest changes has been his membership in outside-of-school activities, such as his T-ball team and church youth group. His mother reported that the last time she took him to buy shoes, he and the salesperson talked about the local baseball team the entire time. She said, "Sean seemed to actually enjoy talking to the salesman—I could have gone out for coffee."

Relationships

> Sean and I are friends because we liked most of the things that the other one liked to do—like, I like to kick a ball, and he likes to kick a ball. I like to be with him, and he likes to be with me. I like to see him, and he likes to see me. He likes baseball, and so do I. He likes computer games, and I like computer games. He likes to look at pictures, and I like to look at pictures. He likes Harry Potter, and I like Harry Potter. (Typically developing classmate of Sean's)

Sean seems to have relationships across three of the four subdomains: play/companionship, helper, and helpee. We have never observed him engage in a conflictual interaction, and most often if conflict seems imminent, Sean leaves the area. In terms of play, he has found friends who share similar interests. He is an excellent reader and is often asked by other children to either read them stories during free choice or help them with their assignments during independent work. He has trouble with math and often asks other for help during this time and is also hesitant in crowded situations (e.g., lunch) and receives assistance from his peers to negotiate those situations.

Skills

Sean demonstrates close-to-grade-level academic work but still has severe deficits in social and communication skills. He works with a speech-language pathologist and a peer during choice time on storytelling and conversational skills. He receives social skills instruction during recess on the playground, and teachers have been taught how to use discrete-trial teaching techniques during ongoing classroom activities to help Sean receive instruction where and when he needs it (McBride & Schwartz, 2003). He attends a school that has implemented a schoolwide positive behavior support plan (Sugai, Horner, & Gresham, 2002) and benefits from the emphasis on social codes that pervade the curriculum as well as from small-group instruction that is available to all students who need it.

Carrie

Membership

> Yeah, she's a member of our class, I mean she does everything that everyone else does. She helps in the class garden, even though she might not do it as well as other kids can. I mean it's fine. It turns out in the end. She can say that she helped in the garden and she helped do stuff in our class because she does a lot of things. (Carrie's classmate)

The extent to which Carrie was viewed as a full member of her class varied over the course of the 4 years we followed her. Several factors contributed to this variation, but most notable was the type of classroom context in which Carrie participated. For example, the first year we observed Carrie, she was in class with a general education teacher who strongly supported cooperative learning. Carrie was included in all the class activities and assignments. However, with a more traditional general education teacher the next year, Carrie spent a considerable amount of her school day being pulled out of her classroom for specialized instruction. During her fourth-grade year, she was perceived by both the general education teacher and her peers as an important, contributing member of the class. She participated in small academic groups who were studying literature, social studies, and math. She was assigned roles in these groups, and accommodations were made so she could actively participate and contribute in a meaningful way.

Relationships

> I think one of the things I see right now is Carrie's ability to have true friends. I'm talking about kids who call her on the phone and invite her to their house. That has happened more and more this year. (Carrie's teacher)

For Carrie, interactions with her typically developing classmates have been her greatest source of support and joy. Her peers helped her with academic work, made accommodations to include her in activities, and gave her feedback about her social behaviors. Carrie developed several lasting friendships over the 4 years of our research. In fourth grade, she was a peer tutor ("helper") for a first-grade class and helped another child with disabilities at the school on an informal basis.

Conflictual interactions with peers have been an ongoing issue for Carrie (e.g., grabbing at others, trashing others' personal property), but in this area Carrie made perhaps her greatest improvement. After conducting a functional behavior assessment (FBA) to better understand what was motivating and maintaining this challenging behavior (see chapter 6 for a complete discussion of FBA and positive behavior support), we provided systematic instruction to Carrie to teach her how to gain attention from her peers in a more appropriate manner. In addition, her peers learned to communicate with her about their feelings regarding these behaviors, and Carrie, who very much wants to be liked by her peers, has responded to their feedback.

Skills

> I think that so much of her actual academic and functional development is because she has had lots of peers to model from, lots of peers to support her, to reinforce her. She sees meaning for what she is doing rather than being in some isolated situation. (Carrie's mother)

Carrie showed growth and improvement in all skill outcome areas. In fourth grade, Carrie's teacher reported that she exhibited more appropriate social skills with her peers and that she was making verbal requests to adults more frequently. Every year, Carrie showed academic improvement in math, reading, writing, and computer use. Carrie became more responsible and independent, both at home and at school. Carrie's mother and teacher also reported that Carrie made remarkable growth in her communication skills. Her articulation was greatly improved, and she was talking louder and more frequently to peers and adults. She also became more fluent in using symbols and gestures as repair strategies to help herself be more easily understood by peers and adults.

Cole

Membership

> Cole sat down between Paul and another of his classmates and started eating his lunch. He talked to Paul and sat listening to peers as they talked. He occasionally repeated things they said, and they all laughed. (Observation notes, sixth grade)

As a sixth grader, Cole was very much a member of his class. He attended sixth-grade graduation as well as an overnight camping trip with the entire sixth grade at his elementary school. During his first year at junior high, Cole followed a class schedule similar to that of his typically developing classmates. However, during the last 2 years, Cole began to spend more time helping with school jobs and engaging in schoolwide recreation activities. A favorite activity during his sophomore year was to attend the varsity football games.

Relationships

> Cole saw Chris (one of his student aides) walk in the room. As Chris walked toward Cole, Cole got very excited and said in a real distinct voice, "There's Chris! Look, he's back!" Chris smiled and said, "Hi, Cole." Cole said, "He's back, he's back!" (Observation notes during Cole's ninth-grade year)

Many of the interactions that Cole had with his peers in sixth grade were typical of "helpee" relationships. His peers helped Cole behave appropriately in class, and they found ways to ensure his participation. Outside of class, other boys often met him at the bus and invited him to play basketball during recess. His teacher commented, "You just get so much more out of Cole when he's with his peers." When Cole moved on to junior high, he was observed engaging in many friendly interactions with peers. He became particularly fond of older, typically developing male students at the junior high school and was often found "hanging out" with them. He continued to receive help from several student aides who accompanied him to his classes throughout the school day. While Cole's friendships with typically developing peers have not extended beyond the school campus, his peers seem very genuine in their affection for him.

Skills

> Cole used to be real shy. He'd duck his head and not say a word and close his eyes if someone came close. Now he can talk about anything! (Typically developing friend in eighth grade)

Cole's most significant growth has been in social communication. For example, he learned how to interact much more appropriately with his peers, how to share, and how to wait for his turn patiently. He also displayed better receptive communication skills, which were reflected in his increased ability to follow directions. We observed Cole initiating many more social interactions with his typically developing peers, and we noticed an increased use of complete sentences to express his feelings or describe his day. He has learned a limited number of traditional academic skills, such as number and word recognition and counting, as well as independently moving through functional routines in his school and community, such as packing his lunch, taking the bus, and moving between classes at the junior high.

Relationships and Learning

These vignettes about Sean, Carrie, and Cole show how central the social relationships of each of these students' lives are to their learning. Their opportunity to interact with their classmates is one of the strongest motivations to participate in classroom activities. Teachers for each of these students comment on how other children understand their communicative attempts, make accommodations to enable their participation in activities, and give them helpful prompts and feedback about their behavior. One day, we observed an interaction between Cole and two of his friends that brings many of these issues into focus.

> *Cole, Chris, and Justin are sitting together as one of several small groups in the class. Cole whispers to Chris and laughs. Chris laughs and then asks Cole to pay attention to the teacher. Cole watches the teacher for a few minutes then turns to Justin and burps. Justin laughs. Chris tells Cole to knock it off. Chris then scratches the top of Cole's head. Cole does the same thing back to Chris. When their group is called up to perform their report, Chris tells Cole, "Just watch me and do what I do."*

While some might see this interaction as a bit unruly and perhaps interfering with the lesson, we see it as a rich example of how typical classroom life is planted with opportunities for learning for students like Cole. It is clear that Cole is highly motivated to interact with his buddies. His communication attempts are, in fact, richly rewarded with their attention and laughter. In addition, one student takes an active role in teaching Cole to pay attention to what the teacher is saying and to what is happening in the group activity. Chris's final admonition to Cole, "Just watch me and do what I do," is perhaps one of the most important social skills Cole must learn if he is to get along without the direct assistance of others in complex social settings: observing the behavior of people around him as a source of guidance about how to "fit in" to a social situation.

In the following section, we use our conceptual framework to suggest a variety of curriculum goals related to social relationships as well as intervention strategies for addressing them. In making these recommendations, we promote a holistic view of student learning and development in which outcomes are conceptualized in terms of increased student participation in valued roles, activities, and settings. This approach recalls early insights about the value of "partial participation" proposed by Baumgart and her colleagues (Baumgart et al., 1982; Ferguson & Baumgart, 1991). That is, students should be encouraged to participate independently as much as possible and supported to complete the activity with assistance. Partial participation can also be facilitated by modifying or accommodating the activity (Sandall & Schwartz, 2002). For example, during a class meeting, students who are nonverbal can have the appropriate symbols in their communication book to participate in all activities of the meeting. We further develop the notion of participation here by placing it in the context of contemporary theories of *situated learning* (e.g., Lave & Wenger, 1991) as well as our own observations of student development in the context of inclusive schools. Situated learning means that instruction is provided in the context of meaningful and motivating activities and routines. Our assumption, supported by the theories of situated learning, is that students acquire specific skills (including important cognitive, communicative, and academic skills) in the context of engaging in meaningful activities in which their participation is supported by other children, teachers, and other adults.

Strategies for Intervention

Our suggestions for intervention strategies related to social relationships are based on three sources. First, recommendations are based on our own research and practice in working with students with severe disabilities in inclusive classrooms over the past years (Grenot-Scheyer, Staub, & Fisher, 2001; Meyer et al., 1998; Peck et al., 1992). Second, our observations are based on sociocultural theories of human development that we found of enormous value in making sense of what we observed (Cole, 1996; Lave & Wenger, 1991; Vygotsky, 1978). These views place the process of joint activity, or participation, at the center of the developmental process. Development is thus seen as a process of mutual change and adaptation rather than as a process that takes place exclusively within the learner (Lave & Wenger, 1991). The third source of influence consists of feedback from teachers, special educators, and parents about what is really workable in the context of typical practice (Meyer et al., 1998; Staub, 1998).

Designing "Usable" Interventions

The concept of *social validity* has been a key concept in behavioral interventions for over 25 years (Schwartz & Baer, 1991; Wolf, 1977). Socially valid interventions are those that are both effective and judged to be acceptable by consumers. Usable interventions are ultimately socially valid interventions. In an attempt to develop guidelines to help describe usable interventions, Meyer et al. (1998) held series of meetings with constituent groups, school-based teacher teams, and groups of adolescents attending inclusive schools. They suggest that usable interventions designed to affect the social lives of children with disabilities should be characterized as follows:

1. *Doable in context:* Interventions must be based on an understanding of the "average" classroom and what are practical and reasonable expectations.
2. *Feasible with available resources:* A careful analysis of long-term available resources should precede the implementation of an intervention.
3. *Sustainable over time:* Interventions are effective only if they are implemented correctly and consistently. For interventions to be usable, teachers and educational teams must be able to implement them for the long run, whether that is the school year or the entire time the student is in school. Time for sharing ideas and expertise is essential for sustaining the life and quality of an intervention.
4. *Constituency owned and operated:* Interventions that are created, facilitated, and supported by the ones carrying them make a large difference in how and for how long they are carried out.
5. *Culturally inclusive:* Interventions must be consistent with and respectful of the values, behaviors, and beliefs of the ones implementing and receiving them.
6. *Intuitively appealing:* Does the intervention make good, common sense? Is it appealing to the recipients and the ones carrying it out?

In the context of our research, we have had the opportunity to observe and record a variety of classroom practices that were associated with positive outcomes for children with and without disabilities. Although we organize our observations about classroom practice here in terms of specific domains and subdomains within our conceptual framework, many of the most promising things we have observed teachers doing are likely to have an effect on all three of the outcome domains (social relationships, membership, and skills).

Recognizing and Supporting Membership

Outcomes related to the domain we have termed "membership" are essentially phenomenological in nature, referring to the sense of "belonging," which students with disabilities may experience in a variety of formal and informal group contexts in inclusive schools. An important issue to consider in planning supports for students with disabilities in the membership domain is that the perceptions of adults regarding who is and is not a member of the group may not be consistent with those of students (Schnorr, 1990). In this context, teachers should listen carefully to what students have to say about their social experiences in the classroom and school (Grenot-Scheyer, Staub, Peck, & Schwartz, 1998).

We observed five contexts in which teachers, parents, and students viewed membership as an important outcome for students with disabilities. These include (a) small groups that were developed by teachers or peers, (b) the class, (c) the school, (d) friendship cliques, and (e) outside groups.

Small-Group Membership (Teacher Developed)

Carrie participates in a discussion with four typically developing classmates about the "Faithful Elephants," an award-winning short story. Carrie looks at sketches Anna has made from the story and points out different things she sees. Anna asks her, "Carrie, who do you think the person with the stick is?" Carrie smiles and says, "He feeds the elephant." Children around the group smile with appreciation at her response. Sharon, another group member, shares her "sketch to stretch" with the other students, and they respond to what they see in her sketch.

Description In our observations, we found that students with disabilities were often members of small groups at stations or centers, of reading or literature groups, in theme-related project groups, in art project groups, or in teacher-led games. We also found that the students with disabilities took a variety of roles in these groups, including listening, reading, sharing turn taking, and contributing to group work.

Strategies for Supporting Membership in Small Groups Perhaps the most critical strategy for supporting the membership of students with severe disabilities in small groups has to do with the general quality of the group work itself. There is a well-developed literature describing design and implementation of group work within regular classrooms that include a diverse array of student backgrounds and abilities (Cohen, 1986; Putnam, 1993). An important feature of cooperative learning methods within these small-group contexts is provision for each student to make a substantial contribution to the group without having to make the same contribution (Cohen, 1986).

Carrie's teacher often used reader's theater (Routman, 1994) as a means of demonstrating student's knowledge and comprehension at the completion of a novel or chapter of a book. As each reading group finished a novel, they wrote a script that represented the novel. All group members were expected to participate in the skit about the book, including Carrie, who was a beginning reader. However, the lines of the script that Carrie was expected to read, while they gave her a meaningful and sometimes central role in the skit, were tailored to her reading abilities. Carrie's general education teacher wrote about these experiences: "The students with disabilities have shined during these skits. They take pride in their performance and become totally engaged in the learning experience. At times they need prompts or reminders, but their group members take ownership and help each other as needed."

In order for some students with disabilities to participate as members of small groups, teachers may need to make accommodations in the activities. The special education consulting teacher can assist the classroom teacher to plan roles and accommodations for individual student participation in groups. However, we have observed some of the best accommodations to be those invented by other students. Theresa found various ways to communicate with her classmate Cathy, who is nonverbal. Based on her experiences, Theresa played an active role in developing a communication book for Cathy and showing others how to use it. Nondisabled students are able to invent these and other accommodations for peers with disabilities only when they are in classrooms in which teachers respect their ideas and actively solicit their input.

Small-Group Membership (Peer Developed)

Description This outcome theme refers to formal and informal groups organized by students themselves, such as teams for basketball at recess or groups of children playing a game during free time in the classroom. Cole, a student with severe developmental delays, participated in a daily basketball game at recess.

Cole is waiting his turn to shoot the ball during the basketball game. He takes two steps forward and shoots underhand, his preferred method of shooting. He misses the first shot but makes the second. (You're allowed only one shot, but nobody says anything about him making a second shot.) After he makes it, he looks around, and all four of the kids in line say, "Good job," or "All right Cole!" (Observation notes from Cole's sixth-grade year)

Many of the same qualities of the small groups that are developed by teachers were evident in small groups that are peer developed. For instance, students with disabilities in these small groups were given a role, specific accommodations were made by typically developing students to support their participation, and rituals (such as "high fives" and exclamations of "nice shot") were performed by group members.

Strategies for Supporting Small-Group Membership (Peer Developed) Teachers can support membership in small groups developed by students by creating unstructured situations for play and exploration (e.g., setting up free choice centers, not excluding students with disabilities from important "breaks" such as recess, providing games and other interactive materials for use during free time). Teachers can also plan ahead for peer support by conducting ability awareness training, setting up buddy systems, and having class discussions about ways in which peers with disabilities can be included in peer-directed activities (Gallucci, Staub, Peck, Schwartz, & Billingsley, 1996).

Class Membership

Description This outcome theme refers to the student's belonging to the class as a social group. We observed many examples of students with disabilities receiving the same roles, symbols, and rituals of the class as their typically developing peers, suggesting that they were "members" of these communities.

Ninth-grade band: Cole walks to the band room with his "student aide" for that period. About 30 kids are hanging out in front of the classroom. Cole is greeted by several students as they wait for the teacher. "Are you going to the game this afternoon?" one student asks. Cole nods. The teacher arrives, and the kids file into the room and start to take their instruments out and practice. The band teacher hands Cole a couple of percussion sticks and reminds him what to do. Cole hits his sticks together in time with the rest of the band members. (Observation notes, Cole's ninth-grade year)

The examples of class membership we found included students having roles in special events such as class plays, assembly presentations, parades, games, or celebrations. Students with disabilities were also often assigned roles within the class, such as taking attendance or passing out materials. Symbols of class membership we observed included certificates, portfolios, class hats worn for special occasions, being the "kid of the week," or being included on a classroom reading chart. Students with disabilities followed class schedules similar to those of their classmates and were included in the activities of their classes with adult and peer support.

Strategies for Supporting Class Membership

The overall social climate and sense of community that prevails in a classroom has a great impact on the likelihood that students with disabilities will be included as full members. One of the processes through we which we observed classroom teachers develop a stronger sense of community is the class meeting (Nelson, Lott, & Glenn, 1993). Class meetings are conducted in the general tradition of the "town meeting"; they may take a variety of forms but have as a common goal the creation of opportunities for children to have a voice in decisions about how the class is conducted and in setting norms and expectations for behavior in the classroom community. Schneider (1996) suggests that the first meeting begin with the inquiry, "What kind of classroom community do we want to have?" The meetings, once established, become a regular event.

In one fifth-sixth, multigrade class we observed, the topic of class membership came up during a class meeting. The group of students were concerned that one of their classmates, a student with autism, was being excluded from literature groups to work individually with a special education assistant. The group of students felt this was an important time for their classmate to be included "in the work we do." The students talked about the issues and agreed that everyone should participate in literature groups in whatever way they could. Adjustments were made in the schedule of the

student with disabilities, and accommodations were made to the curriculum. The student with autism soon became an active and valued member of a literature group. Equally important, all the students in this class experienced themselves as having some influence over how their class was run. Indeed, it actually became more of "their" class through this process of figuring out how to include their classmate with autism.

School Membership

Description Membership outcomes at the school level were indicated by (a) the student's participation in school rituals and activities, (b) by accommodations made by adults and other students to support such participation, (c) by the display of symbols of membership (such as school sweatshirts, logos, or other artifacts), and (d) by their presence in special settings, such as schoolwide assemblies and sporting events. Many times, the participation of students with disabilities in these events took on a personal and social significance that reflected the importance of membership to the student and others.

> *It is Friday morning assembly time. The principal of Austen Elementary School reads a list of names of all the students who have completed school service projects. The principal calls out Carrie's name. Carrie stands up with the rest of the students whose names the principal has called. She has a big smile on her face. Everyone clearly knows her, and the students clap for her and others as she beams with pride.*

Strategies for Supporting School Membership

Opportunities for students to participate in school events that both reflect and contribute to a sense of membership are plentiful in most schools. In many schools we have observed, however, the importance of these opportunities is not recognized for children with disabilities. Teachers, administrators, and parents who appreciate the value of children's experience of belonging at school can include students with disabilities in active roles at school, such as taking turns announcing the daily bulletin over the school public address systems or taking tickets at a school basketball game. In addition, membership can be promoted by planning necessary supports and accommodations to ensure that students participate in schoolwide rituals and celebrations, including, of course, graduation. We found symbols of membership more evident at the upper elementary and middle school years, when these issues become more salient for *all* students. For example, symbols of membership at the middle school level included students having a class schedule, receiving a report card, carrying a school bag, or wearing a school sweatshirt. While many of these symbols of membership are taken for granted by many students, the absence of such symbols for students with severe disabilities may serve as subtle indicators to other students and adults of the marginalized social position of students with disabilities.

Friendship Groups/Cliques

Description Membership within a friendship group/clique refers to a student belonging to a group of mutual friends whether or not there is a close relationship with any individual in the group. Carrie played each day with the same group of girls from her fourth-grade class during recess for more than 2 months.

> *Carrie leaves the cafeteria with Lindsay, Chelsea, and Jackie, heading to the playground, all holding hands. They run to the tire swing. Carrie, Lindsay, and Chelsea climb on the tire, and Jackie pushes them. Chelsea climbs off and sits on a log watching. Carrie and Lindsay swing for a while. Both are laughing really hard and trying to make the swing go faster.*

Strategies for Supporting Membership in Friendship Cliques As any parent knows, a child's membership in a friendship clique is one of the most valued experiences in a child's life, and if it doesn't occur naturally, it is one of the most difficult outcomes for adults to create. In our observations, this outcome was a relatively rare occurrence. The heart of friendship is voluntary association. Adults can create environments in which it is relatively safe for children to befriend vulnerable peers (Haring & Breen, 1992; Staub, 1998), and they can create social contexts in which it is attractive for nondisabled students to "hang out" (Gaylord-Ross, Haring, Breen, & Pitts-Conway, 1984; Gibbs, 1995; Snell & Janney, 2000), but friendship is ultimately a matter of choice among peers. The few examples we found of this included children playing with the same group of peers every day at recess or walking home regularly with the same group of friends.

While it may be difficult for teachers to "program" membership in friendship cliques for their students with severe disabilities, there are things that can be done that might facilitate the development of groups

from which these cliques may spring. For example, in several schools, we worked with teachers to create a regular meeting time for peers to discuss issues of inclusion, which resulted in the continued development of support systems for peers with disabilities. We did not include the students with disabilities in these discussions because the typically developing students expressed that they would be uncomfortable talking about their classmates in their presence. One of the effects of these groups was that some typically developing students began to feel more skillful at including students with disabilities in a variety of regular peer activities, some of which extended beyond school contexts (Gallucci et al., 1996).

Outside Groups

Description This final membership theme reflected a student's membership in community-based groups such as church choir, soccer team, Cub Scout troop, and an after-school folk dancing club. These groups may not be formally affiliated with the school but nevertheless may be composed of children who meet each other at school or who develop relationships that extend across both settings. In our research, parents reported a variety of these kinds of experiences. Karly was a member of her Brownie troop, which met once a week for an hour. Jonathan, a nonverbal student with autism, participated in his Sunday school classes at his community church. Carrie received her first communion with her typically developing peers from school.

Strategies to Support Inclusion in Outside Groups Interventions to support a student's membership in groups outside of school need not be highly technical. Parents need to identify groups that they would like their children to join. These may be sports, dance, scout or religious groups. Parents and teachers may advocate for the student's participation in these groups and provide an array of peer supports and accommodations in much the same way as in classroom settings. Intervention begins, of course, with recognition of the value of membership in these groups as both an experience in itself and a context for the development of skills and the enhancement of personal relationships. Often interventions to facilitate participation in these groups are quite simple, such as helping group leaders prepare visual supports and schedules for the student or brainstorming with group members about how a student can participate in the activity.

Recognizing and Supporting a Range of Relationships

Social relationships between students with severe disabilities and their peers take a wide variety of forms. We identified four major types of peer relationships that were evident in the lives of the students we studied: (a) play/companionship, (b) helpee, (c) helper, and (d) conflictual. Each of these types of relationships offers somewhat different developmental opportunities; participation in such a "range of relationships" is an important advantage to students (Gaylord-Ross & Peck, 1985). In the next section, we present examples of each of these types of relationships and describe some strategies we have observed teachers use to support students' learning in each.

Play/Companion Relationships

The play/companionship theme refers to relationships that revolve around the mutual enjoyment of an activity or interaction. The importance of play/companionship relationships and friendship as a dimension of a satisfying human life is widely acknowledged (Haring; 1991; Strully & Strully, 1985). We also believe that these kinds of relationships are extremely important for children as contexts for the development of social and communication skills and as avenues for achieving membership in larger social groups. When children repeatedly choose to spend time playing together or "hanging out," showing a preference for each other's company, they begin to achieve some of the richer outcomes of "friendship" (Copeland et al., 2002; Staub, 1998). The following excerpt from our observations illustrates the kind of play/companion relationship we often saw in inclusive classrooms.

> It is free time. Marcy, a second-grade student with Down syndrome and moderate developmental delays, goes to the house area in the loft. Mellanie, a typically developing classmate, is there. Marcy smiles happily on seeing Mellanie, and the girls begin to chase each other up and down the loft. Both girls are laughing and smiling. Mellanie stays in the loft, and Marcy runs up the loft. Mellanie then chases Marcy to the stairs. Marcy runs back up the stairs. They do this over and over—maybe 20 times—before the teacher calls an end to free time.

In spite of the instructional technology that has been made available to educators today, teachers cannot "program" their student's friendships. But they can build connections that may help foster and support friendships between and among their students. Teachers can use practices that encourage student participation, they can provide situations like the free-time activity described previously that encourage playful interactions to occur, and they can model caring, respectful, and interested attitudes toward each of their students. The following are some strategies for supporting play/companion relationships.

Time and Opportunity Students with moderate and severe disabilities and their classmates need varied, frequent, and regular opportunities to interact with each other. No matter how supportive the classroom may be for building and sustaining friendly relationships, if the student with disabilities is seldom present, it will be difficult for them to develop relationships in that setting (Schnorr, 1990; Snell & Janney, 2000; Staub, 1998). Furthermore, students with disabilities who do spend the majority of their school day in their general education classroom need to be engaged in activities that encourage frequent peer interaction and general social skills development. Our observations suggest that classrooms in which positive social relationships are more likely to develop are those in which children are given lots of opportunities to work together in a variety of small and large groups, to talk with each other about the work in which they are engaged, and to assist one another with academic and other classroom activities (Salisbury, Gallucci, Palombaro, & Peck, 1995; Salisbury & Palombaro, 1998). The richness of Carrie's relationships with her peers during her sixth-grade year was directly related to her teacher's design of a classroom environment with these very characteristics. In contrast, classrooms that are dominated by teacher talk, individual seat work, and activities in which helping one another is viewed negatively (and sometimes even defined as "cheating") are less suited for peer interactions of any kind, much less those we advocate here.

Classroom Climate The impact of the general emotional tone or climate of a classroom on children's feelings and performance has been well documented (Janney & Snell, 1996, 1997). While many benefits for children with and without disabilities derive from establishment of a warm and caring classroom environment (Hedeen, Ayres, & Tate, 2001), the emergence of play/companion relationships between children with severe disabilities and their typically developing class-mates is likely to be particularly affected. In a climate in which children feel themselves vulnerable to judg-ment, rejection, and exclusion, they are not likely to take social risks inherent in affiliating themselves with peers who are obviously "different" in ways that are de-valued in our culture. In order to make the classroom a place where typically developing children could de-velop positive personal relationships with their most vulnerable peers, it must be made a safe place for all kinds of differences to be acknowledged and ac-cepted. The establishment of such a climate may not be an easy task in schools and communities in which some students experience judgment and exclusion related to race, social class, gender, or ethnicity. Thus, the task of making the climate of classrooms and other social settings safe and supportive for children with disabilities is fundamentally and inextricably linked with making these settings safe and supportive for all children (Meyer et al., 1998).

Paradoxically, the obvious vulnerability of students with severe disabilities may function as an opportunity for teachers to create a more caring and accepting classroom climate by demonstrating that even its most vulnerable members are respected and included (Peck, Gallucci, Staub, & Schwartz, 1998). For example, in Sean's kindergarten class, the "talking stick" activity honored a different student each day for their unique contributions to the class.

> *The "talking stick," a short totem pole such as a piece of wood, is passed around the circle of students. Each day the talking stick is given to a selected "honored student," and the other classmates go around the cir-cle and make compliments to him or her. (Observer comment about the "talking stick" activity)*

Sean was never shortchanged on compliments by his classmates on the day he was the "honored" student for the talking stick activity. Sean's classmates were able to identify his unique strengths and thus celebrate his dif-ferences. Moreover, the participation of Sean and oth-ers we observed in regular classrooms served as a con-text for students to clarify and affirm important values and practices related to individual rights, inclusion, and participation in the classroom.

Cooperative Goal Structures Bryant (1998), Putnam (1993), Sapon-Shevin (1992), and others have noted that classrooms using cooperative goal structures may help generate friendships and foster the development of a variety of social and communicative skills that are important for all students. However, setting up cooper-ative group activities does not in itself ensure that pos-itive interactions, relationships, and academic out-comes will occur (Ohtake, 2003). The success of such arrangements is dependent on thoughtful planning, guidance, and support from the teacher (Cohen, 1986). In cooperative activities that include students with severe disabilities, considerable creativity is often required to ensure their meaningful participation. While teachers must be careful not to delegate too much responsibility to their typically developing stu-dents for creating accommodations for students with disabilities, peers can be a valuable source of creative ideas (Salisbury et al., 1995), as the following excerpt reveals.

> *A group of students are planning a skit as part of their Winter Holiday pageant. One member of the group is Cathy, a student with moderate develop-mental disabilities and limited verbal skills. Her classmates are anxious that she not be left out of the dialogue of the skit and decide to record her parts on a tape player, which she activates when cued. (Observation notes)*

The planning and preparation of Cathy's role in the skit turned out to be one of the highlights of the work the students did on the skit and one of the most mean-ingful aspects of the pageant.

Classroom Structures: Physical Considerations
The physical arrangements of a classroom may set the occasion for student interactions and the development of social relationships. Flexibility of seating arrange-ments, the amount of space available to carry out ac-tivities, and the placement of the teacher's desk are all factors that influence interactions in the classroom set-ting (Epstein & Karweit, 1983).

> *In Carrie's classroom, her teacher had salvaged an old couch that he covered with an attractive blanket and placed by the only window in the classroom. This spot has become an important setting for Carrie to engage in many playful interactions with her nondisabled classmates. (Observer comment)*

Teachers as Models Studies suggest that children are more likely to acquire positive attitudes and behav-iors when they experience warm and affectionate relationships with their teachers (Grenot-Scheyer, Fisher, & Staub, 2001; Lipsky & Gartner, 1998; McGregor & Vogelsberg, 1998). Many of the teachers we observed successfully serving children with disabilities in their regular classrooms were also notable for the respect, warmth, and compassion they demonstrated for every one of their students. They designed their classroom environments to promote student interaction, but they also showed students the kinds of behavior they expected by taking time to listen to students, by treating their feelings with respect, and by avoiding critical and judgmental behavior toward students. We believe that nondisabled students are extremely sensitive to the ways in which the classroom teacher and other adults respond to children with disabilities. The extent to which they see acceptance and caring modeled by the teacher impacts their own interpretation of being "different" in the classroom not only for their peer with disabilities but also for themselves.

Helpee Relationships

We observed numerous social relationships in which the student with disabilities was the recipient of assistance or support from another child. We termed these "helpee" relationships. Clearly, these kinds of relationships evolve naturally in the context of many social settings in which students often need special support for participation.

> In eighth-grade home economics class, the teacher asks the students to go to their cooking stations and complete the steps of making lasagna. Jackie, a "student aide" for Gina, a 13-year-old girl with cerebral palsy who uses a wheelchair, pushes Gina to an adapted kitchen counter. The teacher hands Gina an egg. Jackie physically guides Gina, cracking open the egg and putting it in a bowl. While Jackie guides Gina through this process, she quietly encourages her and tells Gina, "You're doing a good job."

We found many examples of students with moderate and severe disabilities being helped by their typically developing peers in a variety of ways. There were many instances of typically developing students naturally helping out by picking up dropped items, cuing a student with disabilities to participate, or showing them where they should be. We observed peers helping classmates with disabilities with their school work, making transitions, and prompting appropriate behavior.

In these instances, it was often seat mates, buddies, or small-group members who offered the most help. While we observed help being provided in natural ways, we also found many examples of help being provided that was purposefully planned by teachers. At Gina's junior high school, for example, typically developing students were taught to be student aides to provide assistance to students with disabilities in each of their inclusive general education classes. We also noticed adults requesting help or support from nondisabled peers in the context of recess buddies, transition partners, or academic tutors.

There is a large body of literature on typically developing peers providing support to students with disabilities. Increases in social skills (e.g., Copeland et al., 2002; Hughes et al., 1999; Staub & Hunt, 1993), conversational turn taking (Hunt, Alwell, & Goetz, 1988), and improvements in academic skill development (Grenot-Scheyer et al., 1998) for students with moderate and severe disabilities at the elementary and secondary levels have all been associated with peer support programs.

Helping and Friendship Many researchers have noted the potential for relationships in which students were predominantly receiving help from others (what we have termed "helpee" relationships) to have adverse affects on the emergence of other kinds of peer relationships, including friendships (Copeland et al. 2002; Hughes et al., 1999; Meyer et al., 1998, Staub, Spaulding, Peck, Gallucci, & Schwartz, 1996; Voeltz, 1982). In our own research, Theresa and Cathy's story provides an illustration of how too much "help" may sometimes interfere with friendship.

> Theresa and Cathy's friendship began in the third grade when they first made a connection on the school playground. Theresa, a very shy typically developing child, saw that Cathy, who has severe disabilities, was in need of a friend. Perhaps identifying with this need, Theresa initiated an interaction with Cathy that led to a 2-year friendship between the girls. However, by the time the two girls were attending their inclusive fifth-grade class together, Theresa's friendship with Cathy had changed, and its primary function had become helping. Theresa's ability to understand Cathy's communication attempts may have been one important reason as to why their relationship had shifted, as teachers began to routinely assign Theresa to help Cathy in a variety of

classroom activities. Before the end of their fifth-grade year, Theresa had become Cathy's designated caretaker. Their classroom teacher and the special education assistant, challenged by supporting a classroom of 30 students, two of whom had moderate or severe developmental delays, began to rely on students who were most "connected" to the child with disabilities as a primary source of support. Sadly, Theresa became more and more overwhelmed as this responsibility grew, finally expressing relief when she and Cathy were not assigned to the same classroom the following year. What had begun as a true expression of interest, caring, and support had become an overwhelming responsibility for this fifth-grade girl, leading her to withdraw from the relationship. (Staub, Schwartz, Gallucci, & Peck, 1994)

Cathy and Theresa's relationship raises some important issues for consideration when assigning typically developing students to help classmates or peers with disabilities. First, if typically developing students are asked to take on the role of tutor or caretaker for a classmate with disabilities, are they given the opportunity to communicate their dissatisfaction, discomfort, or unpreparedness for this role? Second, how does the role of helper affect the relationships among teacher, students without disabilities, and the student with disabilities? Third, considering respect and value for individual diversity and ability levels, how much "help" should adults be expecting typically developing students to provide their peers with disabilities, and how should this help be structured so that there is a balance between giving and taking (Staub et al., 1994)? Finally, how can students with severe disabilities be provided with the opportunity to "choose" the student they would like to receive help from (Janney & Snell, 1996)?

Strategies for Supporting Helpee Relationships

Relationships in which students with severe disabilities receive help from peers are perhaps the most frequent and naturally occurring of those we observed. However, we have noted a tremendous difference between classrooms in which these relationships are planfully supported by adults and those in which students are left to themselves to figure out when and how to help. We have also noted several limitations of these types of relationships, especially when they become the predominant mode of relationship. Following are some

strategies for structuring and supporting helpee relationships:

1. *Classwide helping procedures.* Teachers can support *all* students to have a voice in how the classroom is conducted, addressing issues of providing "help" to each other in ways that do not take over the activity. Teachers can also discuss with their students the kinds of help peers with disabilities may require. If these discussions take place within the context of all students helping each other, more naturalized systems of support may develop. We observed several classrooms where students and teachers had incorporated "helping" rules (Janney & Snell, 1996). For example, in Karly's and Deanne's multigrade, K–2 classroom, the "ask three before me" rule required students to ask at least three other classmates before they went to the teacher for assistance. The "elbow partner" rule was used when students were in need of help. For this rule, they were to first ask a classmate to their right elbow for help and, if that didn't work, ask a classmate to their left elbow for help.

2. *Peer tutoring programs.* Teachers can also set up structured systems, such as peer tutoring or peer buddy programs. We have described one such program, operated at the junior high school level, in some detail (Staub et al., 1996). Several components of the program were believed to contribute to its success. First, the open and frank ability awareness discussions that took place during the first week of the school year gave students an opportunity to learn about differences among people, and in the discussions they could express any fears and misconceptions they may have regarding disability issues. Second, the student aide role at Kennedy Junior High was highly valued by teachers, staff, and fellow classmates. Students who participated in the program received a good deal of recognition for their work. Finally, the special education teacher who carried out the student aide program was planful about balancing "helping" with opportunities for friendly interactions to occur. The student aides and the students with moderate and severe disabilities went on outings in the community, played games during "downtime," and occasionally attended plays or sporting events after school hours.

Unhelpful Help Giangreco and his colleagues (Giangreco, Edelman, Luiselli, & MacFarland, 1997) have described some of the problems that may develop when adult aides are in one-to-one tutoring roles with students with disabilities in inclusive classrooms. We have noticed similar problems in some peer-helping relationships. Peers are sometimes unaware of the needs of students with disabilities to do things for themselves and may rush in to help in ways that interfere with learning. Students who are in helping relationships with peers who have disabilities should receive direct guidance and support from teachers in making judgments about when help is needed and when it is not. Furthermore, students need to learn to ask students with disabilities if they want or need help before assuming they do and providing the help anyway (Janney & Snell, 1996).

Helper Relationships

This outcome theme refers to relationships and interactions in which the student with disabilities provides support or assistance to another child. This type of relationship is relatively unusual for children with disabilities—an observation we find distressing. Examples we observed of children with disabilities participating in relationships as helpers rather than as "helpees" were rich with opportunities for learning and self-concept enhancement. These relationships may also serve an important function in educating others about the many ways in which individuals with disabilities can make meaningful contributions to the welfare of others.

> The students in Mr. Hathaway's sixth-grade class are working on their journals. Jonathan, a student with autism, is typing his journal onto the computer. As he slowly types the words into the computer, he is interrupted as Amy sits down beside him, her notebook in hand: "Hey, Jon, how do you spell 'conscience'?" asks Amy. A few minutes later, as Jonathan returns to his seat, another student stops him as he walks by, "Jon, how do you spell 'mechanical'?" (Jonathan is acknowledged to be the best speller in Mr. Hathaway's class.)

In another situation we observed, Carrie served as a "peer tutor" for a first-grade class during the year she was in fourth grade.

> Once a week, Carrie would visit the first-grade class to listen to the typically developing students read. This relationship gave Carrie a chance to experience herself in a role in which she was giving rather than receiving help, and she consistently responded with

some of her most independent and mature behavior. Likewise, she was providing an "ear" to the first graders who were in need of practicing their reading skills. The effects of such an experience on Carrie's self-esteem were certainly important. The first graders benefited from having an eager listener attend to their reading, and, perhaps more important, they had the opportunity to see an older child with Down syndrome as a competent and mature role model.

Strategies for Supporting Helper Relationships

Teachers and other adults must plan opportunities for students with disabilities to help others. These opportunities may be focused on helping individuals, such as Carrie's work with first graders, or they may be group focused, such as having a student regularly pass out materials to their classmates. When students have special skills, such as Jon's, teachers may create a role for the student in which those skills can be used to assist others.

With support from teachers, many older students with moderate or severe disabilities may be able to develop meaningful helper relationships with younger children. In schools with preschool programs, child care programs for younger children, and (in high schools) teen parent programs, there may be many useful contexts in which students with disabilities can develop relationships in which they are the "helper." In our experience, the possibility and value of such relationships is seldom recognized by adults.

Conflictual Relationships

Students with severe disabilities, like other students, have occasional conflict with peers (Lieber, 1994). In a few instances, we observed relationships in which there was repeated verbal or physical conflict between the same two students. We termed such relationships conflictual or adversarial. The following vignette is an example of two students, one with a disability and one without, who experienced conflict with one another for almost an entire school year over the attention of a girl in their fifth-grade class.

> Jake, a child with moderate developmental delays, walks over to Connor, a typically developing student, who is standing alone watching the other kids play at recess. Jake starts pushing Connor against the wall. He does this for several minutes. Connor walks away from Jake, but Jake follows him, still pushing at him. In between pushes, Jake gets right in Connor's face

and looks at him with an angry expression. (Observer comment: Earlier in the day, Connor pushed Jake out of the way so he could stand next to Erika in line [the girl they both like].)

Other instances of conflict we observed included students who were fighting, teasing, or arguing with each other. In younger children, we found conflict over toys or games, especially within unstructured situations such as free time or recess. In the intermediate grades, we sometimes observed instances of students with disabilities exhibiting aggressive or inappropriate behaviors toward other students, particularly on the playground. Although most conflictual or adversarial interactions we observed were fleeting and episodic, if these behaviors occur frequently or are chronic in nature, a functional behavior assessment should be conducted to help the educational team understand what is motivating and maintaining the challenging behavior and interfering with the development of more appropriate peer relationships (see chapter 6).

Strategies for Supporting Learning in Conflictual Relationships Conflictual relationships, although unpleasant, can serve as important learning opportunities. Teachers can be planful in problem-solving and conflict resolution skills in the hope that students will learn from their conflicts with their peers. In some cases, students may learn to use structured strategies, such as the "conflict wheel" (Jones & Jones, 2000), to solve problems with each other. In other cases, group discussion and collective brainstorming and planning in class meetings may be used to address problems with individuals, small groups, or the entire classroom community (Nelson et al., 1993).

A particularly problematic issue we have observed has to do with the reluctance of many typically developing students to provide direct and honest feedback to peers with disabilities about undesirable or inappropriate behavior.

Carrie is sitting with her friends Terry and Yolanda at lunch. The girls are chatting and eating. Carrie has gotten some mayonnaise from her sandwich on her hands. Suddenly she leans over and wipes her hand on Terry's sleeve. "Oh … gross," exclaims Yolanda quietly to Terry. Neither of the girls say anything directly to Carrie. They move down the table so Carrie cannot reach them. (Observation notes, Carrie's fourth-grade year)

This vignette illustrates the problem of "double standards," which both children and adults often use in responding to the behavior of students with moderate or severe disabilities. While there are many situations in which tolerance, understanding, and accommodation are called for in supporting students with disabilities, there are also many in which tolerance may be viewed as disabling. In this situation, Carrie needed clear and direct feedback from her peers about her inappropriate behavior. Equally important, her peers needed to know how to set boundaries for what they would tolerate in ways that allowed them to remain comfortable in their relationship with Carrie. Simply moving away from Carrie was not a productive solution to this conflict for any of the students involved. Teachers have an important role to play in teaching nondisabled children how to be honest and direct with their peers with disabilities. In many cases, this involves helping nondisabled students appreciate the importance of their feedback to the learning of their peers with severe disabilities.

The intervention strategies that have been presented here, although focused on supporting outcomes in membership and relationships, do not preclude the importance of traditional skill development for individuals with severe disabilities. Indeed, the very skills educators work so hard on "teaching" students with severe disabilities (e.g., social communication skills, functional routines) were often acquired as an embedded outcome, along with the outcomes of membership and relationships. The reader is referred to other chapters in this text for more information on skill development in specific areas for students with severe disabilities. Although our emphasis is on supporting membership and relationships, we must acknowledge the important of effective use of evidence-based instructional strategies with students with severe disabilities. We know that instruction works. When you refer to the diagram of our conceptual framework (Figure 10–2), it is the point at the center, when skill development, membership, and relationships all intersect, that the best outcomes for all children are achieved.

Recognizing and Supporting Skill and Knowledge

This domain is where most of the effort of traditional special education has focused. When special educators discuss specially designed instruction and identify objects for children's IEPs, they mostly identify discrete, objective, and measurable behaviors. It is important that special education not lose its focus on discrete skills. One purpose of the outcome framework is to help educators consider how and when the skills being taught are being used. By considering how skills facilitate group membership and individual relationships, educational teams can better identify target skills that will yield true meaningful outcomes for students.

Strategies

There are a number of highly effective strategies for teaching discrete social skills to students with severe disabilities (for interesting reviews, see Joseph & Strain, 2003; McConnell, Missall, Silberglitt, & McEvoy, 2002; and Rogers, 2000). The skill areas of communication, motor, and academics are covered elsewhere in this volume, so our discussion will focus on discrete social skills. Brown and his colleagues (Brown, Odom, & Conroy, 2001) present a model for social skills interventions that include interventions that range in intensity and focus. That is, the model begins with interventions that address all the children in a classroom and are less intensive and increases in intensity to interventions that are developed for a specific child. The less intensive interventions, such as environmental design and affective interventions to influence attitudes, help establish the classroom climate and set the stage for social interaction. These interventions are directed to *all* the children in the classroom. The next level of intervention targets children who may be at risk for social problems and increases the intensity of the intervention. This level of intervention includes strategies such as incidental teaching of social skills and group instruction. These interventions require more planning and intervention on the part of the teacher and include fewer children directly. Finally, the most intensive interventions are developed in response to the needs of individual students and are presented to single students or small groups of students.

All levels of intervention as proposed by Brown and his colleagues can help facilitate the skills that result in improved peer relationships. When Sean was in kindergarten, his teacher used many strategies to create an environment where he was actively participating, was assigned valued roles and responsibilities, and where he was supported to contribute to the conversations that occurred in the classroom.

In Sean's kindergarten class, they had "Buddy Day" once a week. Although peer interaction was encouraged at all times, once a week special attention was given to children working in dyads. Children were dismissed to recess in pairs, worked in pairs on art projects, and ate lunch with their buddies.

These simple interventions helped set the stage for increasing relationships and membership and provided valuable opportunities for Sean to work on social-communicative skills.

Sean's teachers also used incidental teaching to address social skill development in the classroom. Incidental teaching involves identifying a child's initiation as a teachable moment and requiring the child to expand or elaborate his response. (See chapter 12 for more information.)

Sean often watched children play T-ball on the playground during recess. His motor skills had improved to the point that he was quite adept at hitting the ball off the tee, but he was hesitant about joining the other children playing. His teacher observed Sean watching the children play and saw him point to the ball as a child hit it. The teacher took advantage of this teachable moment to help Sean pick up the ball and join the game.

Sean also benefited greatly from explicit social skills instruction. This instruction was sometimes teacher directed and sometimes peer mediated (Odom et al., 1999). For example, after discovering Sean's love of baseball, the teachers decided to use explicit instructional techniques to teach him how to trade baseball cards. This skill was an extension of his turn-taking and conversation programs and was a wonderful vehicle for developing meaningful social relationships. The field of special education has a rich history of using evidence-based instructional strategies to teach many functional skills. It is important for educators to apply these strategies to teach social skills and to conduct those interventions in inclusive contexts.

Assessment and Evaluation of Peer Relationships

Although assessment and evaluation have always been cornerstones of special education, the systematic assessment of social behavior of individuals with disabilities has lagged behind measurement in other developmental domains. One reason for this may be the nondiscrete and complex nature of social behavior, while another may be that while the most authentic assessment of social behavior should probably occur within the classroom, those who have traditionally conducted such assessments are not comfortable or familiar with doing so in the classroom setting.

Since the publication of Strain, Cooke, and Apolloni's (1976) seminal book on the measurement and analysis of social behavior of students with developmental, learning, and behavioral disabilities, assessment approaches have relied primarily on the methodological strategies of applied behavior analysis. These approaches to measurement have been extremely valuable in identifying functional relationships between a variety of instructional variables and student social behavior. Recently, behavior-analytic methods have been extended conceptually and methodologically to the analysis of contextual factors affecting the quality and quantity of social relationships between students with disabilities and their peers (Breen & Haring, 1991; Haring, 1992; Meyer et al., 1998). In addition, Kennedy and his colleagues (e.g., Kennedy, Horner, & Newton, 1989; Kennedy & Itkonen, 1994) have demonstrated the value of methods drawn from social and community psychology in analyzing the networks of social relationships in which individuals with disabilities participate. These measurement approaches share a common focus on dimensions of social behavior that may be reliably quantified, such as the number of interactions a student with disabilities has with his or her peers or the duration of engaged time spent participating in an activity. With adaptation, such techniques can be highly useful to classroom teachers. However, our own work has been inspired in good part by our experience that social relationships between children with disabilities and their nondisabled peers, as well as other outcomes of their participation in regular class settings, are often not described adequately by quantitative measures.

There are several issues that constrain the effectiveness of quantitative measures as a means of documenting and evaluating change in social relationships, particularly when they are used in isolation. These include (a) the relative inflexibility of such measures in capturing unanticipated dimensions of change, (b) their relative insensitivity to issues of meaning embedded in social situations, and (c) the fact that teachers often

find these data of limited value in their daily work (Ferguson, 1987; Grigg, Snell, & Lloyd, 1989; Meyer & Evans, 1993). We do not suggest that quantitative measures be abandoned; in fact, they may be the most appropriate type of measure for most data collection in schools. However, in our own efforts to document outcomes for students with severe disabilities that their parents and teachers affirm as meaningful and important, we have found narrative data to be extremely valuable (for an elaboration on these arguments, see Schwartz, Staub, Gallucci, & Peck, 1995) and an effective complement to more quantitative measures. We have used a variety of simple data collection techniques drawn from the qualitative research tradition to enrich our description, analysis, and understanding of what is happening in students' social lives at school and elsewhere. Next, we briefly describe some of these techniques, including narrative observational records and interviews, and how we have used them. More complete accounts of how qualitative research strategies may be used to describe and evaluate change in educational settings are offered by Bogdan and Biklen (1992), Hubbard and Powers (1991), and others. Then we describe some more traditional strategies for collecting data and suggest how they may blended to meet the unique measurement needs that social behaviors present (Schwartz & Olswang, 1996).

Narrative Observational Records

Observational data recorded as narrative offer a highly flexible means of documenting the rich and dynamic flow of classroom events. Rich narrative descriptions of behavior in situational contexts may be a valuable source of insight about what is going on in a social setting. These descriptions are time consuming, and if not completed carefully, they may not provide the type of information necessary to evaluate a student's current level on goals and objectives or provide information that is useful in program planning. Figure 10–3 presents a form that can be used to gather short notes about social behaviors that can turn the outcome framework presented previously into a planning tool for writing an IEP. For example, narrative descriptions of interactions might help identify issues related to the quality of "helping" relationships emerging for children across the school year. Five examples of issues that we have observed to be of concern in some classrooms

FIGURE 10–3
IEP Planning Form

Membership

Membership Subdomain	Present Level of Performance/Participation	Supports and Instructional Needs, Possible Goals
School membership		
Class membership		
Teacher-created small groups		
Student-created small groups ("friendship cliques")		
Outside-of-school groups		

Relationships

Relationships Subdomain	Present Level of Performance	Supports and Instructional Needs, Possible Goals
Play/companionship		
Helper		
Helpee		
Conflict (Note: It is important to conduct a functional behavior assessment if these relationships are problematic or result in challenging behaviors.)		

Skills

Skills Subdomain	Present Level of Performance	Supports and Instructional Needs, Possible Goals
Communication		
Academic		
Motor		
Independence		

and that might be evaluated using narrative data include the following:

1. To what extent is assistance from peers and adults really helpful (or unneeded, intrusive, stigmatizing)?
2. Are nondisabled children becoming de facto aides to children with disabilities?
3. What are the attitudes, interpretations, and responses of nondisabled children who are not directly involved

in inclusive classrooms (e.g., children on the playground or in the cafeteria)?
4. How do nondisabled peers respond to "inappropriate" behaviors of peers with disabilities? (e.g., Are they direct in giving feedback to the child? Do they respond pejoratively?)
5. In what ways are issues of inclusiveness part of regular class meetings and discussions, and to what extent are these issues considered to be about all

children in the classroom and not just those with identified disabilities?

Interviews

Interviews are another source of data teachers may find useful in evaluating social relationships among students. In fact, interviews provide a source of insight about how students perceive their relationships, which may be uniquely valuable to teachers and other adults, who often have only partial understanding of the students' point of view. Some disadvantages of interviews include the time-consuming nature of conducting and analyzing the interviews and the difficulty in using these data to document student progress.

If you choose to use interview, the type of questions you ask will affect the usefulness of the information you receive. We have found that interview protocols that begin with an open-ended question asking for description rather than evaluation of "what's going on" in relation to the student with disabilities or others in the classroom are the most effective. We also attempt to establish trust with the interviewee by assuring them that they do not have to answer every question and that they can stop whenever they want. Using an open-ended interview strategy allows the adult or student being interviewed an opportunity to bring up issues of concern that the interviewer may not know to ask about. This information may be of great value to teachers and others who are trying to develop a richer understanding of the social experiences and relationships of students with severe disabilities for the purpose of designing interventions as well as monitoring and evaluating change.

Analyzing and Evaluating Narrative Data

The value of narrative (qualitative) data as a source of information about what is going on in the social lives of students with disabilities is enhanced to the extent that these data are read and analyzed regularly. Simply jotting down observational notes or excerpts from conversations with children and others will not in itself necessarily lead to greater understanding of what is going on in the classroom. But the reflection involved in regular and systematic analysis of the data does. This analytic process need not be highly formal, but it should be ongoing. Furthermore, it should involve all the members of the team, including the special educator, general educator, parent(s), and any

other individuals providing services to the student (e.g., paraeducator, physical therapist). The use of a reflective journal may add considerably to the depth of this process of "re-searching" the data for patterns of behavior, context events, or other factors affecting social relationships. Hubbard and Powers (1991) describe a variety of specific techniques teachers have used for analysis of narrative data, such as looking for common themes across journal entries or identifying information that doesn't seem to fit to bring up possible issues *of concern*.

Blending Traditional and Alternative Data Collection Strategies

When discussing assessment and data collection, it is helpful to go back to the basics. The basic idea of assessment is to collect information that will help you answer a question. In special education, one can think of IEP objectives as the questions and data on child performance as the information we collect to attempt to answer those questions. Therefore, it is important that the type of data you collect is informed by the question you are asking (Schwartz & Olswang, 1996). In terms of child behavior, we can ask questions about how frequently behavior happened, how long it lasted, who was around when it happened, whether the child needed help, and even whether the child appeared to be happy when they were demonstrating the behavior. All this information could be important to answer questions about a child's social competence; however, the most important characteristic of the data we collect must be that it answers the question we are asking. For example, if I am interested in the fluency of a specific behavior, then knowing how long it lasted may help me answer my question. If I am interested in generalization, knowing that a child can name pictures at a rate of 35 a minute is not helpful.

The challenge of data collection, whether it is using quantitative or qualitative methods, is to match data collected to the question being asked. Figure 10–4 presents a matrix that can be used to help plan instruction and data collection. This sample matrix displays targeted behaviors by social domain across the activities of a typical school day for Sean. Although much instruction is embedded across the day and teachers are always encouraged to take advantage of teachable moments, this matrix indicates when teachers will include specially designed instruction and data collection. Teachers can also use the matrix to help

FIGURE 10–4
Planning and Data Collection Matrix

Student's Name: Sean		Week of: February 22, 2004	
Daily Schedule	**Membership**	**Relationships**	**Skills**
Arrival/transitions	Sign in and check job chart (frequency)	Greet peers by name (frequency) Respond to greetings (frequency)	Manage materials independently (count number of teacher prompts)
Journal writing	Share journal with his small group (count number of teacher prompts) Participate at his assigned seat (1–5 rating scale)	Hand out journal to group members (count number of teacher prompts) Ask peers for assistance (frequency)	Writing short sentences Drawing picture to match stories (work sample)
Reading	Participate in teacher-led and student-led groups (1-5 rating scale)	Assist other students with reading (duration of engagement) Work with peer on completing a book (duration of engagement)	Improve reading fluency (weekly probes) Improve comprehension (weekly probes)
Class meeting	Follow teacher-directed activity (count number of teacher prompts) Participate in group discussions and problem solving (frequency of turns)	Work collaboratively with peers (duration of engagement)	Conversation skills (number of turns) Question-answering skills (frequency) Problem solving (decrease in challenging behavior)
Math	Work on problems in teacher-assigned groups (count number of teacher prompts) Select partner for small-group work (count number of teacher prompts)	Receive or provide assistance to partners (frequency)	Understanding of basic arithmetic facts Basic concepts (weekly probes)
Lunch	Eat lunch with student-selected group (narrative)	"Hang out" with peers (narrative)	Manage materials independently (count number of teacher prompts)
Social studies	Participate in teacher-selected group (narrative)	Work with partner (narrative)	Basic concepts Language comprehension(weekly probes)
Independent work			Fluency of previously acquired skills (work samples) Self-regulation (decrease in challenging behaviors)
Choice	Participate in student-selected group (duration of engagement)	Participate in appropriate leisure skills with partner (duration of engagement)	Conversation skills (number of turns)
Recess	Participate in student-selected group (duration of engagement)	Participate in appropriate leisure skills with partner (duration of engagement)	Conversation skills (number of turns plus narrative to comment on content)

them keep track of what data have and have not been collected. This type of tool can also be extremely helpful in lesson planning and developing class activities.

Nondisabled Students and Severely Disabled Peers: All True Benefits Are Mutual

Facilitating the social relationships of people with severe disabilities has become a greater priority in recent years. Why, when general education is seemingly obsessed with high-stakes testing on traditional academic subjects, have professionals working with students with severe disabilities worked even harder on social relationships? One reason may be that family members, educators, and researchers value the role that satisfying social relationships play in the quality of life for people with disabilities and their families. It follows, then, that other people will also benefit from the improved social skills and social relationships of people with severe disabilities. Research and development work related to social relationships between children with severe disabilities and their nondisabled peers has been focused almost exclusively on the functions of these relationships in the lives of children with disabilities (Haring, 1991; Meyer et al., 1998; Strully & Strully, 1985). One of the most robust phenomena we have observed in our inclusive schools research is the positive value many nondisabled students place on their relationships with peers who have severe disabilities. Indeed, the relatively few studies that have been carried out to evaluate the impact of these relationships on nondisabled students are quite consistent in their findings (Staub & Peck, 1994–1995). Specifically, it is clear that nondisabled students are perceived by themselves, their parents, and their teachers as benefiting in a variety of ways from their relationships with peers who have severe disabilities. These include the following:

1. Increased understanding of how other people feel
2. Increased acceptance of differences in appearance and behavior
3. Increased sense of self-worth in contributing to the lives of others
4. Increased sense of commitment to personal principles of social justice (Biklen, Corrigan, & Quick, 1989; Helmstetter, Peck, & Giangreco, 1994; Murray-Seegert, 1989; Peck, Carlson, & Helmstetter, 1992;

Peck, Donaldson, & Pezzoli, 1990; Staub, 1998; Staub et al., 1994)

In addition, the academic progress of nondisabled students is not harmed by the inclusion of students with severe disabilities in regular classes (Hollowood, Salisbury, Rainforth, & Palombaro, 1995; Peck et al., 1992; Sharpe, York, & Knight, 1994).

Perhaps most exciting is the reciprocity of outcomes between students with and without moderate and severe disabilities that emerged from many of the relationships we observed over the course of our follow-along research. Three outcomes that we perceived to be mutually beneficial included (a) warm and caring companionships, (b) increased growth in social cognition and self-concept, and (c) the development of personal principles and an increased sense of belonging (Staub, 1998).

Companionship

One of the most important functions of relationships is to enable us to feel safe, loved, and cared for. When Karly and Deanne first became acquainted in their K–2, multiage class, each needed a friend. Both were shy, hesitant, and often intimidated by the activity that surrounded them. By becoming companions, they found comfort in each other's presence in an overwhelming situation.

> *Deanne is truly a friend for Karly. They hang out, they comfort each other, and they are always hugging and holding hands. Karly and Deanne truly have a "bud" friendship. You don't want to be friends with everyone in the classroom necessarily, but everyone has a need for at least one buddy. That's what they provide to each other. (Karly's and Deanne's teacher)*

Growth in Social Cognition and Self-Concept

We found that several of the nondisabled children who participated in our research identified as "connected" to their peers with disabilities became more aware of the needs of their disabled peers. These children became skilled at understanding and reacting to the behaviors of their classmates with disabilities. Stacey, a nondisabled peer of Carrie's who attended class with Carrie for many years, was perceived to have benefited from her long-standing relationship with Carrie.

I think Stacey is at a point where she looks at Carrie as a friend, and I think inclusion, overall, has benefited Stacey in the sense that Stacey will never judge someone by their mental ability, whether they have Down syndrome or are developmentally delayed. I think she's come to a point where later on in life, if she has a chance to hire someone that could do the job with a disability, she would be the first one to say "yeah." (Carrie's and Stacey's teacher)

Likewise, having a relationship with Stacey was very important to Carrie's own sense of self-worth. Stacey not only provided Carrie with a model for how to socialize appropriately but also helped Carrie feel better about herself.

Stacey has had an enormous impact on Carrie's behavior. Carrie wants to do the "right thing" in front of Stacey, and you can really tell that she feels reinforced when Stacey compliments her on her behavior or actions. (Carrie's mother)

Development of Personal Principles

Children are extremely vigilant about the way vulnerable peers are treated by other children and by adults (Bukowski, Newcomb, & Hartup, 1996). While the risks of vulnerability, including social rejection and exclusion, are commonly recognized for children with disabilities, the meanings that nondisabled students may construct about the experiences they observe in relation to their peers with disabilities have received little empirical attention from researchers and little practical attention from educators. We believe that there may be considerable risks for nondisabled students that are constituted by their belief that it is not safe to be weaker than others in our society. Significantly, the likelihood of children drawing this conclusion appears to be compounded, not reduced, when vulnerable peers are sent away (to other classes or to other schools).

Viewed from this perspective, the inclusion of children with severe disabilities in regular classes creates both risk and opportunity for all children. The creation of classroom and school communities in which developmental differences are accepted and in which vulnerability is not observed to produce exclusion may represent one of our most powerful opportunities to make schools psychologically safer and more humane places for all children. The social relationships that develop between children with disabilities and their nondisabled peers thus constitute a wonderful oppor-

tunity for all educators. For the benefits of these relationships to be realized, it is essential that educators, parents, and other adults concerned with the well-being and development of children recognize the deep ways in which our relationships with people with disabilities offer us possibilities to see and to redefine who we are.

Brittany [Sean's nondisabled classmate] definitely keeps us on our toes. One day last week, Sean was really having a hard time—lots of screaming and fussing. I asked his teaching assistant to take him for a walk. I was stressed that the kids were getting stressed. Brittany came up to me and said, "I think we should ignore Sean's screaming and find something that he wants to do in class. Think how bad he feels being sent out of the room." Well, how do you respond to that? What it did was force me to push for a better communication system on his part, and the special education staff have really responded positively. But really, it caused me to look at Sean differently, not as a child with disabilities but as a classmate, a peer. (Sean's teacher)

Summary

This chapter highlights the importance of social relationships in the lives of all children. The level of importance and value that teachers place on supporting and facilitating their students' relationships will influence greatly their successful development. It is our hope that this chapter has provided ideas and tools for teachers to use in this important capacity.

Suggested Activities

1. Plan to spend at least 40 minutes in an inclusive classroom to observe a target student's interactions with his or her peers. Write down your observations in an objective fashion (e.g., provide a running account of what you observe without comment or judgment). After your observation, read over your notes and write your responses to the following:

   a. What looked "right" about the interactions I observed? (For example, nondisabled students were treating student with severe disabilities respectfully, student with severe disabilities was included in conversations.)

b. What looked "uncomfortable" about the interactions I observed? (For example, nondisabled students were not treating the student with severe disabilities as a member of their class.)

c. What was working well in the classroom environment for promoting peer interactions? (For example, the arrangement of desks allowed for easy conversation among students, the teacher used cooperative learning activities to promote interactions.)

d. What barriers were evident in the classroom environment that interfered with students' interactions? (For example, a class rule was that students were not to talk with one another during activities.)

2. Looking back over your responses to the items in question 1, develop an action plan that specifies how the classroom environment could be arranged to facilitate more appropriate peer interactions. What are things the teacher(s) could do? What environmental changes would you recommend? What types of activities would facilitate more peer interactions?

References

Apolloni, T., & Cooke, T. P. (1975). Peer behavior conceptualized as a variable influencing infant and toddler development. *American Journal of Orthopsychiatry, 45*, 4-17.

Baer, D. M., Wolf, M. M., & Risley, T. R. (1987). Some still-current dimensions of applied behavior analysis. *Journal of Applied Behavior Analysis, 20*, 313-327.

Baumgart, D., Brown, L., Pumpian, I., Nisbet, J., Ford, A., Sweet, M., et al. (1982). The principle of partial participation and individualized adaptations in educational programs for severely handicapped students. *Journal of the Association for Persons with Severe Handicaps, 1*, 17-27.

Biklen, D., Corrigan, C., & Quick, D. (1989). Beyond obligation: Student's relations with each other in integrated classes. In D. Lipsky & A. Garnter (Eds.), *Beyond separate education: Quality education for all* (pp. 207-222). Baltimore: Paul H. Brookes.

Billingsley, F., Gallucci, C., Peck, C., Schwartz, I., & Staub, D. (1996). "But those kids can't even do math": An alternative conceptualization of outcomes for inclusive education. *Special Education Leadership Review, 3*, 43-56.

Bogdan, R., & Biklen, S. (1992). *Qualitative research for education: An introduction to theory and methods.* Boston: Allyn & Bacon.

Breen, C., & Haring, T. G. (1991). Effects of contextual competence on social initiations. *Journal of Applied Behavioral Analysis, 24*, 337-347.

Bronfenbrenner, U. (1979). *The ecology of human development.* Cambridge, MA: Harvard University Press.

Brown, W. H., Odom, S. L., & Conroy, M. A. (2001). An intervention hierarchy for promoting young children's peer interactions in natural environments. *Topics in Early Childhood Special Education, 21*(3), 162-175.

Bruner, J. (1990). *Acts of meaning.* Cambridge, MA: Harvard University Press.

Bruner, J. (1996). *The culture of education.* Cambridge, MA: Harvard University Press.

Bryant, B. K. (1998). Children's coping at school: The relevance of failure and cooperative learning for enduring peer and academic success. In L. H. Meyer, H. S. Park, M. Grenot-Scheyer, I. S. Schwartz, & B. Harry (Eds.), *Making friends: The influences of culture and development* (pp. 353-368). Baltimore: Paul H. Brookes.

Bukowski, W. M., Newcomb, A. F., & Hartup, W. W. (1996). *The company they keep: Friendship in childhood and adolescence.* New York: Cambridge University Press.

Cohen, E. (1986). *Designing groupwork: Strategies for the use of heterogeneous classrooms.* New York: Teachers College Press.

Cole, M. (1996). *Cultural psychology: The once and future discipline.* Cambridge, MA: Harvard University Press.

Copeland, S. R., Hughes, C., Agran, M., Wehmeyer, M. L., Fowler, S. E. (2000). An intervention package to support high school students with mental retardation in general education classrooms. *American Journal on Mental Retardation, 107*, 32-45.

Epstein, J. L., & Karweit, N. (1983). *Friends in school: Patterns of selection and influence in secondary schools.* New York: Academic Press.

Ferguson, D. L. (1987). *Curriculum decision making for students with severe handicaps: Policy and practice.* New York: Teachers College Press.

Ferguson, D. L. (1994). Is communication really the point? Some thoughts on interventions and membership. *Mental Retardation, 32*, 7-18.

Ferguson, D. L., & Baumgart, D. (1991). Partial participation revisited. *Journal for the Association for Persons with Severe Handicaps, 16*, 218-227.

Fisher, M. (2001). Andre's story: Frames of friendship. In M. Grenot-Scheyer, M. Fisher, & D. Staub (eds.), *At the end of the day: Lessons learned in inclusive education.* Baltimore: Paul H. Brookes.

Fiske, A. P. (1992). The four elementary forms of sociality: Framework for a unified theory of social relations. *Psychological Review, 99*, 689-723.

Gallucci, C., Staub, D., Peck, C., Schwartz, I. & Billingsley, F. (1996). *But we wouldn't have a good class without him: Effects of a peer-mediated approach on membership outcomes for students with moderate and severe disabilities.* Unpublished manuscript. Seattle: University of Washington.

Garfinkle, A. N., & Schwartz, I. S. (2002). Peer imitation: Increasing social interactions in children with autism and other developmental disabilities in inclusive preschool classrooms. *Topics in Early Childhood Special Education, 22*, 26-38.

Gaylord-Ross, R., Haring, T., Breen, C., & Pitts-Conway, V. (1984). Training and generalization of social integration skills with autistic youth. *Journal of Applied Behavior Analysis, 17*, 229-247.

Gaylord-Ross, R., & Peck, C. A. (1985). Integration efforts for students with severe mental retardation. In D. Bricker & J. Filler (Eds.),

Serving students with severe mental retardation: From research to practice (pp. 185-207). Reston, VA: Council for Exceptional Children.

Geertz, C. (1973). *Interpretation of cultures.* New York: Basic Books.

Giangreco, M., Edelman, S., Luiselli, T., & MacFarland, S. (1997). Helping or hovering? Effects of instructional proximity on students with disabilities. *Exceptional Children, 64,* 7-18.

Gibbs, J. (2000). *A new way of learning and being together.* Windsor, CA: Center Source Systems.

Greenwood, C. R., Maheady, L., & Delquadri, J. (2002). Classwide peer tutoring programs. In M. R. Shinn, H. M. Walker, & G. Stoner (Eds.), *Interventions for academic and behavior problems II: Preventive and remedial approaches* (pp. 611-650). Bethesda, MD: National Association of School Psychologists.

Grenot-Scheyer, M., Fisher, M., & Staub, D. (2001). *At the end of the day: Lessons kearned in inclusive education.* Baltimore: Paul H. Brookes.

Grenot-Scheyer, M., Staub, D., Peck, C. A., & Schwartz, I. S. (1998). Reciprocity and friendships: Listening to the voices of children and youth with and without disabilities. In L. H. Meyer, H. S. Park, M. Grenot-Scheyer, I. S. Schwartz, & B. Harry (Eds.), *Making friends: The influences of culture and development* (pp. 149-168). Baltimore: Paul H. Brookes.

Grigg, N. C., Snell, M., & Lloyd, B. (1989). Visual analysis of student evaluation data: A qualitative analysis of teacher decision making. *Journal of the Association for Persons with Severe Handicaps, 14,* 23-32.

Haring, T. G. (1991). Social relationships. In L. Meyer, C. Peck, & L. Brown (Eds.), *Critical issues in the lives of people with severe handicaps* (pp. 195-217). Baltimore: Paul H. Brookes.

Haring, T. G. (1992). The context of social competence: Relations, relationships and generalization. In S. Odom, S. McConnel, & M. McEvoy, (Eds.), *Social competence of young children with disabilities: Issues and strategies for intervention* (pp. 307-320). Baltimore: Paul H. Brookes.

Haring, T. G., & Breen, C. G. (1992). A peer-mediated social network intervention to enhance the social integration of persons with moderate and severe disabilities. *Journal of the Association for Persons with Severe Handicaps, 13,* 20-27.

Hart, B. M., & Risley, T. R. (1996). *Meaningful differences in the everyday experiences of young American children.* Baltimore: Paul H. Brookes.

Hartup, W. W. (1983). Peer relations. In E. M. Hetherington (Ed.), *Handbook of psychology: Vol. IV. Socialization, personality, and social development* (pp. 103-196). New York: Wiley.

Hedeen, D., Ayres, B., & Tate, A. (2001). Charlotte's story: Getting better, happy day, problems again! In M. Grenot-Scheyer, M. Fisher, & D. Staub (eds.), *At the end of the day: Lessons learned in inclusive education.* Baltimore: Paul H. Brookes

Helmstetter, E., Peck, C. A., & Giangreco, M. F. (1994). Outcomes of interactions with peers with moderate or severe disabilities: A statewide survey of high school students. *Journal of the Association for Persons with Severe Handicaps, 19,* 263-276.

Hollowood, T. M., Salisbury, C. L., Rainforth, B., & Palombaro, M. M. (1995). Use of instructional time in classrooms serving students with and without severe disabilities. *Exceptional Children, 61,* 242-253.

Hubbard, R., & Powers, B. (1991). *The art of classroom inquiry.* Portsmouth, NH: Heineman.

Hughes, C., Rodi, M. S., Lorden, S. W., Pitkin, S. E., Derer, K. R., Hwang, B., & Cai, X. (1999). Social interactions of high school students with mental retardation and their general education peers. *American Journal on Mental Retardation, 104,* 533-544.

Hunt, P., Alwell, M., & Goetz, L. (1988). Acquisition of conversation skills and the reduction of inappropriate social interaction behaviors. *Journal of the Association for Persons with Severe Handicaps, 13,* 20-27.

Janney, R., & Snell, M. (1996). How teachers use peer interactions to include students with moderate and severe disabilities in elementary general education classes. *Journal of the Association for Persons with Severe Handicaps, 21,* 72-80.

Janney, R. E., & Snell, M. E. (1997). How teachers include students with moderate and severe disabilities in elementary classes: The means and meaning of inclusion. *Journal of the Association for Persons with Severe Handicaps, 22,* 159-69.

Jones, V., & Jones, L. (2000). *Comprehensive classroom management.* Boston: Allyn & Bacon.

Joseph, G. E., & Strain, P. S. (2003). Comprehensive evidence-based social-emotional curricula for young children: An analysis of efficacious adoption potential. *Topics in Early Childhood Special Education, 23,* 65-76.

Kaye, K. (1982). *The mental and social life of babies: How parents create persons.* Chicago: University of Chicago Press.

Kennedy, C. H., Horner, R., & Newton, S. (1989). Social contacts of adults with severe disabilities living in the community: A descriptive analysis of relationship patterns. *Journal of the Association for Persons with Severe Handicaps, 14,* 190-196.

Kennedy, C. H., & Itkonen, T. (1994). Some effects of regular class participation on the social contacts and social networks of high school students with severe disabilities. *Journal of the Association for Persons with Severe Handicaps, 19,* 1-10.

Lave, J., & Wenger, E. (1991). *Situated learning: Legitimate peripheral participation.* New York: Cambridge University Press.

Lieber, J. (1994). Conflict and its resolution in preschoolers with and without disabilities. *Early Education and Development, 5,* 5-17.

Lipsky, D. K., & Gartner, A. (1998). Taking inclusion into the future. *Educational Leadership, 56,* 78-81.

McBride, B. J., & Schwartz, I. S. (2003). Effects of teaching early interventionists to use discrete trials during ongoing classroom activities. *Topics in Early Childhood Special Education, 23,* 5-18.

McConnell, S. R., Missall, K. N., Silberglitt, B., & McEvoy, M. A. (2002). Promoting social development in preschool classrooms. In M. R. Shinn, H. M. Walker, & G. Stoner (Eds.), *Interventions for academic and behavior problems II: Preventive and remedial approaches* (pp. 501-536). Bethesda, MD: National Association of School Psychologists.

McGregor, G., & Vogelsberg, T (1998) Inclusive schooling practices: Pedagogical and research foundations. A synthesis of the literature that informs best practices about inclusive schooling. Allegheny Univ. of the Health Sciences, Pittsburgh, PA.

Meyer, L., & Evans, I. (1993). Science and practice in behavioral intervention: Meaningful outcomes, research validity and usable knowledge. *Journal of the Association for Persons with Severe Handicaps, 18,* 224-234.

Meyer, L. H., Park, H. S., Grenot-Scheyer, M., Schwartz, I. S., & Harry, B. (1998). Participatory research approaches for the study of the social relationships of children and youth. In L. H. Meyer, H. S. Park, M. Grenot-Scheyer, I. S. Schwartz, & B. Harry (Eds.), *Making friends: The influences of culture and development* (pp. 3–30). Baltimore: Paul H. Brookes.

Murray-Seegert, C. (1989). *Nasty girls, thugs, and humans like us: Social relations between severely disabled and nondisabled students in high school.* Baltimore: Paul H. Brookes.

Nelson, J., Lott, L., & Glenn, H. (1993). *Positive discipline in the classroom.* Rocklin, CA: Prima.

Odom, S. L., McConnell, S. R., McEvoy, M. A., Peterson, C., Ostrosky, M., Chandler, L., et al. (1999). Relative effects of interventions supporting social competence of young children with disabilities. *Topics in Early Childhood Special Education, 19*, 75–91.

Ohtake, Y. (2003). Increasing class membership of students with severe disabilities through contribution to classmates' learning. *Research and Practice for Persons with Severe Disabilities, 28*, 228–231.

Peck, C. A., Carlson, D., & Helmstetter, E. (1992). Parent and teacher perceptions of outcomes for typically developing children enrolled in integrated early childhood programs: A statewide survey. *Journal of Early Intervention, 16*, 53–63.

Peck, C. A., Donaldson, J., & Pezzoli, M. (1990). Some benefits nonhandicapped adolescents perceive for themselves from their social relationships with peers who have severe handicaps. *Journal of the Association for Persons with Severe Handicaps, 15*, 241–249.

Peck, C., Gallucci, C., Staub, D., & Schwartz, I. (1998, April). *The function of vulnerability in the creation of inclusive classroom communities: Risk and opportunity.* Paper presented at the annual meeting of the American Educational Research Association, San Diego.

Peck, C. A., Schwartz, I., Staub, D., Gallucci, C., White, O., & Billingsley, F. (1994, December). *Analysis of outcomes of inclusive education: A follow-along study.* Paper presented at the annual meeting of the Association for Persons with Severe Handicaps, Atlanta.

Pernat, D. (1995). Inclusive education and literacy: Engaging a student with disabilities into language arts activities in a sixth grade classroom. *Network, 4*(4), 12–19.

Putnam, J. (Ed.). (1993). *Cooperative learning and strategies for inclusion.* Baltimore: Paul H. Brookes.

Rogers, S. J. (2000). Interventions that facilitate socialization in children with autism. *Journal of Autism and Developmental Disorders, 30*, 399–410.

Routman, R. (1994). *Invitations: Changing as teachers and learners in K–12.* Portsmouth, NH: Heineman.

Salisbury, C., Gallucci, C., Palombaro, M., & Peck, C. (1995). Strategies that promote social relationships among elementary students with and without severe disabilities in inclusive schools. *Exceptional Children, 62*, 125–137.

Salisbury, C., & Palombaro, M. M. (1998). Friends and acquaintances: Evolving relationships in an inclusive elementary school. In L. H. Meyer, H. S. Park, M. Grenot-Scheyer, I. S. Schwartz, & B. Harry (Eds.), *Making friends: The influences of culture and development* (pp. 81–104). Baltimore: Paul H. Brookes.

Sameroff, A., & Chandler, M. (1975). Reproductive risk and the continuum of caretaking casuality. In F. Horowitz, M. Hetherington, S. Scarr-Scalapatek, & G. Siegel (Eds.), *Review of research in child development* (Vol. 4, pp. 197–243). Chicago: University of Chicago Press.

Sandall, S. R., Hemmeter, , Smith, B. J., & M. E. McLean (Eds.). (2004). *DEC recommended practices in early intervention/early childhood special education.* Longmont, CO: Sopris West.

Sandall, S. R., & Schwartz, I.S. (2002). *Building blocks: A comprehensive approach for supporting young children in inclusive placements.* Baltimore: Paul H. Brookes.

Sapon-Shevin, M. (1992). Student support through cooperative learning. In W. Stainback & S. Stainback (Eds.), *Support networks for inclusive schooling* (pp. 65–80). Baltimore: Paul H. Brookes.

Schneider, E. (1996, September). Giving students a voice in the classroom. *Educational Leadership,* pp. 22–26.

Schnorr, R. (1990). Peter? He comes and he goes . . . First graders' perspectives on a part-time mainstreamed student. *Journal of the Association for Persons with Severe Handicaps, 15*, 231–240.

Schwartz, I. S. (2000). Standing on the shoulders of giants: Looking ahead to facilitate membership and relationships for children with disabilities. *Topics in Early Childhood Special Education, 20*, 123–128.

Schwartz, I. S., & Baer, D. M. (1991) Social validity assessments: Is current practice state of the art? *Journal of Applied Behavior Analysis, 24*, 189–204.

Schwartz, I. S., & Olswang, L. B. (1996). Evaluating child behavior change in natural settings: Exploring alternative strategies for data collection. *Topics in Early Childhood Special Education, 16*, 82–101.

Schwartz, I. S., Staub, D., Gallucci, C., & Peck, C. A. (1995). Blending qualitative and behavior analytic research methods to evaluate outcomes in inclusive schools. *Journal of Behavioral Education, 5*, 93–106.

Sharpe, M. N., York, J. L., & Knight, J. (1994). Effects of inclusion on the academic performance of classmates without disabilities. *Remedial and Special Education, 15*, 281–287.

Shonkfoff, J. P., & Phillips, D. A. (Eds.). (2000). *From neurons to neighborhoods: The science of early childhood development.* Washington, DC: National Academy Press.

Snell, M.E., & Janney, R. E. (2000). Teachers' problem-solving about children with moderate and severe disabilities in elementary classrooms. *Exceptional Children, 66*, 472–90.

Staub, D. (1998). *Delicate threads: Friendships between children with and without special needs in inclusive settings.* Bethesda, MD: Woodbine House.

Staub, D., & Hunt, P. (1993). The effects of a social interaction training on high school peer tutors of schoolmates with severe disabilities. *Exceptional Children, 60*, 41–57.

Staub, D., & Peck, C. A. (1994–1995). What are the outcomes for nondisabled kids? *Educational Leadership, 52*, 36–40.

Staub, D., Schwartz, I. S., Gallucci, C., & Peck, C.A. (1994). Four portraits of friendship at an inclusive school. *Journal of the Association for Persons with Severe Handicaps, 19*, 314–325.

Staub, D., Spaulding, M., Peck, C.A., Gallucci, C., & Schwartz, I.S. (1996). Using nondisabled peers to support the inclusion of students with disabilities at the junior high school level. *Journal of the Association for Persons with Severe Handicaps, 21*, 194–205.

Strain, P., Cooke, T., & Apolloni, T. (1976). *Teaching exceptional children: Assessing and modifying social behavior*. New York: Academic Press.

Strully, J., & Strully, C. (1985). Friendship and our children. *Journal of the Association for Persons with Severe Handicaps, 10*, 224-227.

Sugai, G., Horner, R. H., & Gresham, F. M. (2002). Behaviorally effective school environments. In M. R. Shinn, H. M. Walker, & G. Stoner (Eds.), *Interventions for academic and behavior problems II: Preventive and remedial approaches* (pp. 315-350). Bethesda, MD: National Association of School Psychologists.

Voeltz, L. M. (1982). Effects of structured interactions with severely handicapped peers on children's attitudes. *American Journal of Mental Deficiency, 86*, 380-390.

Vygotsky, L. (1978). *Mind in society*. Cambridge, MA: Harvard University Press.

Williams, L. J., & Downing, J. E. (1998). Membership and belonging in inclusive classrooms: What do middle school students have to say? *Journal of the Association for Persons with Severe Handicaps. 23*, 98-110.

Wolf, M. M. (1977). Social validity: The case for subjective measurement or how applied behavior analysis is finding its heart. *Journal of Applied Behavior Analysis, 11*, 203-214.

Wolfberg, P. J. (1999). *Play and imagination in children with autism*. New York: Teachers College Press.

11

Nonsymbolic Communication

Ellin Siegel
Amy Wetherby

Although people communicate with each other in many ways, talking is the most common way. Spoken words are a symbolic mode of communication because they rely on forms that represent, or stand for, something else. For example, the spoken word "shoe" is a symbol that refers to things that you put on your feet. Similarly, the sign for shoe and a picture of a shoe are also symbols because they represent or refer to the class of objects that we know as shoes. Language is a system for combining symbols with shared meaning using formal rules of grammar and conversation. A child who says "shoe off" is using symbolic communication to ask for his or her shoe to be taken off. While most children immersed in a language-rich environment learn to talk without being formally taught,

children with disabilities may face significant challenges learning to talk, which may affect their ability to understand what others say or their ability to express themselves with words. Many individuals with severe disabilities have limited ways of expressing themselves or understanding those around them; they may communicate symbolically or nonsymbolically. Using the shoe example, a child can use nonsymbolic communication to request help in tying by moving her untied shoe toward another person, rubbing the shoe and moaning, or just crying. While symbolic communication may be much more explicit than nonsymbolic communication, there are many different ways to communicate without symbols, and nonsymbolic communication can be very powerful.

Marina

Marina is 3 years old and began attending an early intervention center last year. At age 1, she was not walking or talking but laughed frequently and always wanted to be near the "action" of her two older siblings and her parents. Marina's parents became very skilled at noticing and interpreting her subtle movements and facial expressions.

405

FIGURE 11–1
Marina enjoys interactions with her mother. They have learned how to read each other's expressions, and their enjoyment in this familiar peek-a-boo game is obvious

She smiled often as her head bobbed up and down. Her parents helped her learn to make choices by directing her gaze toward desired items. Her family learned to understand when Marina's body movements meant that she wanted a favorite game or event to occur (see Figure 11–1). For example, Marina would rock back and forth in a wagon to get her brother to pull it and reach up and climb on her mother's back to get a ride.

By age 2, Marina began having seizures, and her parents sought further medical testing, which led to the diagnosis of Angelman syndrome. This syndrome was first identified by Dr. Harry Angelman in 1965. Major clinical characteristics include microbrachycephaly (small head with a flattened occiput), abnormal results on electroencephalogram (EEG), an awkward gait, severe language impairment (usually without speech), excessive laughter, a protruding tongue, the mouthing of objects, and intense curiosity (Clayton-Smith & Pembrey, 1992; Dooley, Berg, Pakula, & MacGregor, 1981; Williams & Frais, 1982; see

http://www.angelman.org for information about Angelman syndrome).

A great deal of familiarity with Marina and her subtle ways of communicating was needed before the intervention staff could readily interpret her behaviors. The onset of her seizures led Marina to regress. Now, medication controls her seizures but makes her fatigue easily and her abilities fluctuate. The staff members are trying not only to interpret Marina's behaviors but also to encourage her to use the behaviors that she was using before the Angelman syndrome progressed. They want to solidify Marina's communication by developing her awareness of the effects that her communicative behaviors have on other people. In addition, the staff and her family are trying to get Marina to use more conventional gestures (giving an object, raising her arms to be picked up, holding an object up to show it, and reaching) and to expand her use of eye gaze so she will be more understandable and readable to people who are less familiar with her.

 Ryan

When Ryan sees you approach him, he usually smiles, reaches toward you to shake hands, and vocalizes. He is a 16-year-old teenager who has limited peripheral vision and a mild hearing loss. He enjoys attention and expresses his interest by smiling at familiar people, extending his fisted hands toward objects or people, and making eye contact. Because of severe motor impairments, Ryan relies on others to move him. He has a variety of

supported positions: sitting in different adapted chairs, side lying, and sitting in a motorized wheelchair. It is difficult for Ryan to maintain his head erect for very long when seated and needs adaptations. He must be moved to new positions every hour.

Ryan attends the local high school in his community, where he rotates through many different subjects and spends part of the day in the community. He has developed some friendships with his peers, especially since he began assisting the football team. Paired with other assistants assigned to the football team, Ryan takes care of the team towels (i.e., laundering, folding, handing them). He also helps with getting drinks to the players.

Ryan tends to wait for others to interact with him but will indicate his interest in maintaining interactions by increasing his vocalizations or body movements. He turns his head away or is quiet when he wants to terminate or deter an interaction.

Nonsymbolic Skills

This chapter focuses on individuals who do not use or understand symbols and the rules of language. To communicate, these individuals rely on their own bodies and information from their current contexts or activities. Their communication may include facial expressions, body movements, gazing, gesturing, and touching. This communication has been referred to by many different terms, such as prelinguistic, prelanguage, and nonverbal. The authors of this chapter prefer the word "nonsymbolic" in order to focus on what individuals are doing. *Nonsymbolic behavior* is viewed as a legitimate form of communication, not just a transition to another stage. Because some individuals with severe disabilities rely primarily on nonsymbolic skills, it is crucial to recognize each individual's current communication repertoire and to expand it. Intervention that meets best practices treats the person with dignity and focuses on building on what the person can do. The basic right to affect others via communication is central to life (National

Joint Committee for the Communication Needs of Persons with Severe Disabilities, 1992) (see Box 11-1).

The Impact of the Disability

No single disability or combination of impairments distinguishes which individuals communicate primarily in a nonsymbolic manner. An individual who communicates in this way may have dual sensory impairments, a severe motor impairment, autism spectrum disorder, profound mental retardation, or a cognitive disability combined with a health impairment. Individuals who use nonsymbolic communication form a heterogeneous group. All young children communicate without symbols during the first year of life, and for some this mode continues for many years. Communication partners (school staff members such as teachers and speech-language therapists) must recognize nonsymbolic communication skills and have strategies to enhance these skills for young and older students who use this communication mode (see Box 11-2).

  Box 11–1 National Joint Committee

The National Joint Committee for the Communication Needs of Persons with Severe Disabilities (NJC) focuses on providing information on best practices. In 1992, the NJC established a communication *Bill of Rights* to relay the basic rights every individual has to affect interactions through communication. Everyone has the right to:

- Request what they want
- Refuse what they don't want
- Express preferences and feelings
- Be offered choices and refuse choices
- Request and get another's attention and interaction
- Request and get information about changes in routine or setting
- Get intervention to improve communication
- Get a response to their requests, even if not fulfilled
- Be able to get services and have communication aides at all times
- Be in settings with peers who don't have disabilities
- Be spoken and listened to with respect and courtesy
- Be spoken to directly, not talked about while present
- Have communication that is clear, meaningful, and culturally and linguistically appropriate

Website: **http://professional.asha.org/njc**

Table 11–1 displays nonsymbolic and symbolic behaviors and examples.

The Trifocus of Intervention

Most school staff and other communication partners expect to observe and respond to verbal or symbolic language. Educators and speech-language pathologists (SLPs) also need to understand the importance of nonsymbolic communication and to broaden the focus of their interventions and improve their responsiveness to nonsymbolic learners. Others' responsivity to child communication is viewed as a central influence on later child communication and language development (Harwood, Warren, & Yoder, 2002). Because most people typically use spoken language to communicate, it may be difficult for school staff as well as other partners to adjust their expressive messages to individuals with severe disabilities. Yet all of us use nonsymbolic expressions. When Mary asks you where Sam has gone, you tip your head in the direction Sam went. When a waitress is at the table next to you, you lift your coffee cup in the air, hoping that she will give you a refill. You may not be fully aware, however, of the many forms of nonsymbolic communication and may not use nonsymbolic communication to enhance your communication skills (Beukelman & Mirenda, 1998; Siegel & Cress, 2002; Stillman & Siegel-Causey, 1989).

Individuals who communicate nonsymbolically can have successful interactions with others. When a child cries, a staff member recognizes this as communication and tries to relieve discomfort. A reach toward the juice conveys the message for more. Nonsymbolic communication plays a key role in most interactions, especially with those who do not use symbols or have limited understanding of symbols (Stillman & Siegel-Causey, 1989).

The trifocus framework (Siegel & Cress, 2002; Siegel-Causey & Bashinski, 1997) incorporates concepts from various fields into three primary components: the learner, the partner, and the environmental context (Figure 11–2). The trifocus framework recognizes that communication partners and learners experience communication interactions mutually and that both parties are reciprocally affected. Because communication is a dynamic process involving at least two people, the willingness of individuals without disabilities to interact may be influenced by the limited behavioral repertoires

TABLE 11–1
Nonsymbolic and Symbolic Forms of Communication

Nonsymbolic	Symbolic
Vocal—Using sounds and utterances produced by voice	Verbal—Using words
Affect—Displaying a feeling or emotion	Sign language—Using system of hand and arm gestures
Tactual—Using touch (stimulation of passive skin receptors and active manipulation and exploration)	Photographs and pictures—Using visual representation or image
Body movement—General motion of body such as leaning, pulling away, or swaying	Representational objects—Using miniature objects to depict real objects or activity; using portions of a real object to depict a real object or activity.
Gestural—Using movement of the limbs or parts of body	Graphic system—Using a method of symbols (Blissymbolics, Rhebus pictures)
Physiological—Displaying functions of body such as alertness or muscle tone	
Visual—Using sense of sight	

Source: Adapted from "Introduction to Nonsymbolic Communication" by R. Stillman and E. Siegel-Causey. In *Enhancing Nonsymbolic Communication Interactions Among Learners with Severe Handicaps* (p. 4) by E. Siegel-Causey and D. Guess (Eds.), 1989, Baltimore: Paul H. Brookes. Reprinted by permission of Paul H. Brookes Publishing Company, P.O. Box 10624, Baltimore, MD 21285-0624.

FIGURE 11–2
The Trifocus Framework

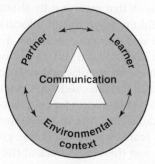

Copyright 1996 by E. Siegel-Causey and S. Bashinski. Reprinted with permission.

of individuals with severe disabilities. Therefore, one focus of intervention is on enhancing the communication skills of learners with nonsymbolic abilities by expanding their repertoire. A second focus of intervention is on enhancing the skills of communication partners. When interacting with individuals who are nonsymbolic communicators, the partner needs to take a more active role than when interacting with someone who talks. The partner needs to present information in a clear way without relying on symbols and be very responsive to nonsymbolic signals.

This framework recognizes the influence of the environmental context on communication interactions and in particular on the learner. Context encompasses all physical and social aspects of the setting. In order to enhance a student's nonsymbolic communication and responsiveness, partners will pay attention to the physical and social aspects of the environment. Physical refers both to the broad settings (e.g., home, school, and community) and the specific contexts that an intervention occurs within (snack, physical education, or break) as well as to the physical attributes of a setting (lighting, noise level, and materials) (Ault, Guy, Guess, Bashinski, & Roberts, 1995). Social environment includes aspects such as the peers and adults within close proximity of the learner, overall activity level of the setting, and the amount and type of social interaction or contact being provided to the learner by partners (Ault et al., 1995).

Figure 11–3 provides an overview of the trifocus framework. The multiple focus on learner, partner, and environment has considerations that should help the partner more effectively plan assessment and intervention. We organized this chapter using these three

FIGURE 11–3
Overview of Trifocus Framework

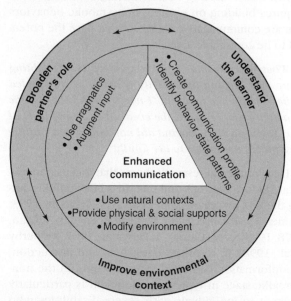

Copyright 1998 by E. Sigel-Causey. Reprinted with permission.

components: understand the learner (assessment), broaden the partner's role (use nonsymbolic input and be responsive to learner's nonsymbolic communication as part of intervention), and improve environmental contexts (modify the environment, use physical and social supports as part of intervention). The next section provides information related to early communication development, including the emergence and the parameters of nonsymbolic communication acquisition.

Early Communication Development

It is sometimes difficult to interpret messages of individuals who use nonsymbolic expressions, especially since most of us function in a world of symbols. Individuals with severe disabilities need to be systematically taught to interact, are likely to learn to communicate first about their own wants and needs, and are most likely to communicate in their familiar environments (Downing, 1999, Siegel & Cress, 2002).

Critical Aspects of Communication

Communication is a developmental process involving reciprocal interactions between individuals (Bates, O'Connell, & Shore, 1987; Duchan, 1995; Dunst, Lowe,

& Bartholomew, 1990; Wetherby, Reichle, & Pierce, 1998). Understanding and enhancing communication requires building on existing nonsymbolic behaviors that are communicative signals or that have the potential to be communicative.

When Marina smiled, her parents reacted by lighting up and keeping the activity going. They interpreted her smile as a signal of "I want" within the specific activity and repeated the event. At this early level of communication, Marina did not realize that smiling signaled a message to her family.

Developmental research shows that infants communicate before they talk and that this ability unfolds during the first few years of life (Bates, 1979; Bloom, 1993; Bruner, 1981; Dore, 1986; McLean & Snyder-McLean, 1978, 1999; Siegel-Causey & Downing, 1987; Wetherby et al., 1998). In terms of assessment and instruction, the information compiled from research on the nonsymbolic stage in typical development is particularly relevant to individuals with severe disabilities who communicate in a similar manner. Extensive reviews of the developmental research on nonsymbolic communication and the communicative abilities of children with severe disabilities include Siegel-Causey, Ernst, and Guess (1987, 1989), Siegel-Causey and Guess (1989), Wetherby and Prizant (1992), and Wetherby, Warren, and Reichle (1998).

A Three-Stage Communication Progression

The emergence of communication is a developmental process involving reciprocal interactions between a caregiver and child. Bates and associates (Bates, 1979; Bates, Camaioni, & Volterra, 1975) have provided a theoretical framework to describe the emergence of communication and language. Borrowing terminology from the speech act theory of Austin (1962), they identified three stages in the development of communication. From birth, the infant is in the "perlocutionary stage." The "perlocution" is the effect of the message on the communication partner who must interpret messages. The infant's behavior systematically affects the caregiver and thus serves a communicative function, although the infant is not yet producing signals with the intention of accomplishing specific goals. For example, when an infant cries, this may signal hunger to the caregiver, and the caregiver responds to the crying by holding the child and offering a bottle. The child's crying serves the function of requesting the caregiver's help although the child may not have deliberately tried to seek that outcome. By about 9 months of age, most children move to the "illocutionary stage" and begin to use preverbal gestures and sounds to communicate intentionally. The "illocution" is the purpose of the message as planned or intended by the speaker. At this stage, the child deliberately uses particular signals to communicate for preplanned effects on others. An example of intentional communication is when a child reaches toward a bottle, grunts, looks at the caregiver, and then looks back at the bottle to signal that he or she wants the bottle. At about 13 months of age, the child progresses to the "locutionary stage" and begins to construct propositions to communicate intentionally with referential words. The "locution" is the referential meaning of the message. At this stage, a child can request his or her bottle by reaching and using a word approximation, such as "baba," to refer to the bottle. Thus, communication and language development can be conceptualized as a three-stage process, involving movement from perlocutionary (preintentional, partner interpreted) communication to illocutionary (intentional nonverbal) communication to locutionary messages (verbal language) used intentionally to communicate. This model has been adapted for application to the emergence of communication in individuals with severe disabilities (e.g., Beukelman & Mirenda, 1998; McLean & Snyder-McLean, 1988; Musselwhite & St. Louis, 1988; Rowland & Stremel-Campbell, 1987). The speech act theory and its relationship to nonsymbolic behavior are described with examples in Table 11–2.

An important assumption of this three-stage progression is that all individuals communicate in some way. In applying this model to individuals with severe disabilities, communicative partners play a critical role in interpreting behaviors that are communicative. The model also highlights the broad range of communicative abilities spanning the perlocutionary and illocutionary stages. Understanding the developmental progression from perlocutionary to illocutionary communication can help partners detect and enhance progress in subtle but critical aspects of communicative development.

When Ryan was a preschooler, he did not intentionally communicate (perlocutionary stage). During this period, Ryan often interacted with nondisabled peers at preschool. On one such occasion, Tom, a peer,

TABLE 11–2
Speech Act Theory and Nonsymbolic Behaviors

Definition	Nonsymbolic messages	Interpretation or meaning	Speech act messages	Interpretation or meaning
Perlocution (Partner interpreted communication): the effect or function of the message on the listener; interpretation of behaviors as if they were intentional	Ryan's first moves toward his book bag.	His friend interprets this to mean that Ryan wants the book bag and says, "Hey, you want some help buddy?"	Says "mm" after he swallows a bite of his sandwich.	His teacher assumes that he wants another bite and says, "Here's your sandwich."
Illocution (Intentional communication): the meaning of the message as planned by the speaker; using behaviors and conventional gestures with the intent of affecting the behavior of others	Ryan looks at his friends when the bell rings before gym class.	Ryan wants his friend to push him to gym class.	Andy says "nn" and turns his head away when the teacher puts the sandwich toward his mouth.	Andy is full.
Locution (Intentional symbolic communication): using words with the intent of affecting the behaviors of others			Andy smiles and says "yes" when his teacher extends his cup of juice toward him.	Andy uses words to convey wanting a drink.

Source: Based on *How to Do Things with Words* by J. Austin, 1962, Cambridge, MA: Harvard University Press, and *The Emergence of Symbols: Cognition and Communication in Infancy* by E. Bates, 1979, New York: Academic Press.

and Ryan were seated across from each other at a table. On the table was a large switch connected to a toy that had sound and movement linked to many small, colorful toy birds. Ryan squealed in delight each time Tom used the switch to make the toy movements occur. Ryan's vocal expressions became a humming sound when the toy's noises and movements stopped. Tom, with help from staff, learned to react to the humming as if Ryan expressed "I want more." Later Ryan was taught to hum and look at Tom to signal "more," and he also was taught to use the switch.

It is important for communication partners to understand how communication emerges because nonsymbolic communication may be the primary or only means used by individuals with severe disabilities. Communicative interactions are rooted in early social and emotional development in infants. Gaze, the expression of emotion, body movement, and orientation are signals (or forms) that guide infants' responses and

regulate social interactions. The caregiver's ability to interpret and respond contingently to the preintentional communicative signals of infants plays an important role in the child's development of intentional communication (Dore, 1986; Dunst et al., 1990; Harwood et al., 2002; Yoder, Warren, McCathren, & Leew, 1998). Early social interactions involving shared experiences lead to awareness of the effects that their behaviors have on others (Bruner, 1981; Corsaro, 1981). Thus, the responsiveness of communicative partners to learners' preintentional communicative behaviors plays a major role in developing communication skill.

Intentional Behavior

Behavior is intentional if an individual has an awareness of or a mental plan for a desired goal as well as the means to obtain the goal (Piaget, 1952). For example, if a child wants a toy on a shelf out of reach, the child may pull a chair over to the shelf, climb on the chair, and get the toy. This example demonstrates cognitive intentional behavior. Parallels in the development of cognitive intentionality are seen in the social domain. For instance, the child may pull on the caregiver's pant leg, point to the toy, and vocalize until the caregiver gets the toy.

The constructs of intention and function are significant to a discussion of nonsymbolic communication. Since communication involves a dyadic interaction between a sender and a receiver, communicative intent must be considered in relation to the function of communication. *Intention* refers to the plan of the message sender, and *function* refers to the purpose of the act as interpreted by the message receiver. Look at Figure 11–4 and read about the following nonsymbolic communication act.

Marina looks at and reaches toward her ball, looks at her mother, looks back at the ball, and looks up at her mother. As a result, her mother tips the basket so that Marina can reach the ball. Marina's plan was to get the ball and play with Mom. The function of Marina's signal was to request an action, and her mother interpreted the signal as intended by Marina. The success of a communicative act depends on whether the sender's intention is appropriately interpreted by the receiver of the message. Marina's interaction with her mother was successful.

Wetherby and Prizant (1989) suggested that intentional communication develops along a continuum beginning with automatic, reflexive reactions. Children then develop awareness of goals but do not have plans to achieve the goals. As children gain more experience,

they learn to coordinate their behaviors to pursue their goals. Further development in intentionality is evident in the use of *repair strategies* (i.e., strategies used to clarify one's intentions when communicative attempts are unsuccessful). Rudimentary efforts to repair involve repeating a signal to persist in achieving a goal. For example, if a child reaches to request a bottle and the caregiver does not respond, the child may reach again. More sophisticated efforts involve modifying the form of the signal. Using the same example of reaching to request a bottle, a child may repair by reaching again and adding a vocalization and eye gaze. A child's ability to use simple plans, coordinated plans, and alternative plans to achieve goals develops from 9 to 18 months of age, during Piaget's sensorimotor stages V and VI (Bates et al., 1975; Harding, 1984; Wetherby, Alexander, & Prizant, 1998). The ability to repair is evidence of intentionality and would indicate illocutionary communication.

Ryan has developed repair strategies. For example, his friend Matt is helping him get to their next class, art. As they enter the room, his teacher points to Matt's project and says, "Ryan, where is your project?" Ryan looks at her and vocalizes, "Ehh." "Don't worry, Matt can take you back to your locker." The teacher did not understand his message, so Ryan has to add to it using a repair strategy. Ryan's repair strategy is to look at the art teacher, vocalize louder, and pull his head to the right side of his wheelchair. "Oh, is it in your backpack?" she says as she points to his backpack. Ryan smiles.

FIGURE 11–4
In the photo at left, Marina reaches toward the toy basket to request her ball (intention). In the photo (right), Marina's mother interprets the action to mean that Marina wants a toy (function) and tips the basket so that Marina can reach inside.

Communication Roles

Communication involves taking turns between being a sender of a message (expressive role) and being a receiver (receptive role). Communicative partners interacting with nonsymbolic learners must be aware of these dual roles. Individuals with disabilities also must function as senders and receivers of messages. Figure 11–5 shows Marina and her mother in these dual communication roles.

While nonsymbolic communicators are individuals who use primarily nonsymbolic communication as senders, their receptive abilities may be comparable to or better than their expressive abilities. Before children comprehend the meaning of words, they use a variety of contextual cues to figure out how to respond, and therefore they may appear as if they comprehend specific words (Chapman, 1978; McLean & Snyder-McLean, 1978; Miller & Paul, 1995). For example, when

FIGURE 11–5
Marina and her mother both act as senders and receivers of messages. Marina is the sender first and reaches toward the jar (top left), and her mother is the receiver and responds to her request by giving her the jar. Marina then gives the jar to her mother to request her to open it (top right), and her mother responds by opening the jar. Her mother is then the sender and shows Marina what is inside the jar, and Marina responds by looking in the jar (bottom left). Marina's mother then blows bubbles and tells Marina to pop them, and Marina responds by popping the bubbles (bottom right).

a child is standing in front of a sink and an adult points to the faucet while saying "wash hands," the child can figure out how to respond from the situation without comprehending the word "wash" or "hands." As children move to the illocutionary stage of communication expression, they begin to comprehend nonverbal cues provided by their caregivers, including gestures, facial expression, and directed eye gaze (e.g., an adult pointing to or looking at an object "means" the child should give or attend to that object). Children may also respond to intonation cues (i.e., the melody or tone of speech) to determine how to respond (e.g., mom's loud, deep voice "means" angry). At this stage, children also may respond to situational cues by using the immediate environment and knowledge of what to do with objects to respond (e.g., observe what others do in the situation, knowing that you drink from a cup, knowing to put objects in a container). As children progress to the locutionary stage of expression, they begin to comprehend the meanings of familiar words but continue to be guided by the context. It is easy to overestimate a child's comprehension of language if one is not aware of the nonverbal, intonation, or situational cues that the child may be using to determine how to respond. The development of response strategies serves as a bridge to the comprehension of word meanings: contextual cues give children strategies for responding and guidance to the meanings of words.

Recognizing Nonsymbolic Communication

Nonsymbolic communication is a reciprocal interaction involving understanding or reception and signaling others or expression (Figure 11–6). The overlapping circles depict the communication partner's abilities to use both nonsymbolic and symbolic behavior.

For nonsymbolic learners, it is necessary to identify the observable behaviors that may serve a communicative function. The first parameter to identify is *how* the learner communicates, or what *forms* of communication are used. Nonsymbolic communication may be conventional in form if the meaning of the behavior is shared by many partners and is generally recognizable. Examples of conventional gestures are giving, showing, reaching, pointing, and open-palm requesting. However, nonsymbolic communication may be unconventional or idiosyncratic and understood only by someone who is very familiar with the individual and the context. Table 11–3 presents examples of forms that nonsymbolic communication may take, including unconventional yet effective forms, such as standing by a sink to request a drink or scratching oneself to protest an action.

A second parameter to identify is the function, or purpose, served by the communicative behavior. Children use presymbolic gestures and vocalizations to communicate for a variety of purposes before they use words (Bates, 1979; Coggins & Carpenter, 1981; Harding & Golinkoff, 1979; Wetherby, Cain, Yonclas, & Walker,

FIGURE 11–6
Reciprocal Nature of Communication Interactions

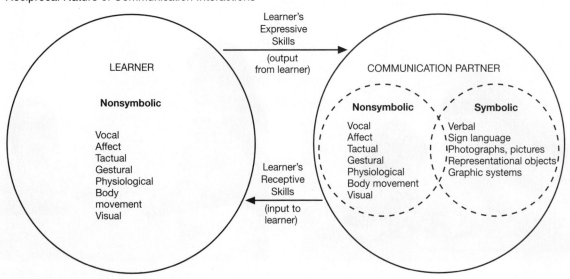

TABLE 11–3
Forms of Learner Nonsymbolic Communication

Generalized movements and changes in muscle tone
- Excitement in response to stimulation or in anticipation of an event
- Squirms and resists physical contact
- Changes in muscle tone in response to soothing touch or voice, in reaction to sudden stimuli, or in preparation to act

Vocalizations
- Calls to attract or direct another's attention
- Laughs or coos in response to pleasurable stimulation
- Cries in reaction to discomfort

Facial expressions
- Smiles in response to familiar person, object, or event
- Grimaces in reaction to unpleasant or unexpected sensation

Orientation
- Looks toward or points to person or object to seek or direct attention
- Looks away from person or object to indicate disinterest or refusal
- Looks toward a suddenly appearing familiar or novel person, object, or event

Pause
- Ceases moving in anticipation of coming event
- Pauses to await service provider's instruction or to allow service provider to take turn

Touching, manipulating, or moving with another person
- Holds or grabs another for comfort
- Takes or directs another's hand to something
- Manipulates service provider into position to start an activity or interactive "game"
- Touches or pulls service provider to gain attention
- Pushes away or lets go to terminate an interaction
- Moves with or follows the movements of another person

Acting on objects and using objects to interact with others
- Reaches toward, leans toward, touches, gets, picks up, activates, drops, or pushes away object to indicate interest or disinterest
- Extends, touches, or places object to show to another or to request another's action
- Holds out hands to prepare to receive object

Assuming positions and going to places
- Holds up arms to be picked up, holds out hands to initiate "game," leans back on swing to be pushed
- Stands by sink to request drink, goes to cabinet to request material stored there

Conventional gestures
- Waves to greet
- Nods to indicate assent or refusal

Depictive actions
- Mimes throwing to indicate "throw ball"
- Sniffs to indicate smelling flowers
- Makes sounds similar to those made by animals and objects to make reference to them
- Draws picture to describe or request activity

Withdrawal
- Pulls away or moves away to avoid interaction or activity
- Curls up, lies on floor to avoid interaction or activity

Aggressive and self-injurious behavior
- Hits, scratches, bites, spits at service provider to protest action or in response to frustration
- Throws or destroys objects to protest action or in response to frustration
- Hits, bites, or otherwise harms self or threatens to harm self to protest action, in response to frustration, or in reaction to pain or discomfort

Source: From "Introduction to Nonsymbolic Communication" by R. Stillman and E. Siegel-Causey. In *Enhancing Nonsymbolic Communication Interactions Among Learners with Severe Handicaps* (p. 7) by E. Siegel-Causey and D. Guess (Eds.), 1989, Baltimore: Paul H. Brookes. Reprinted by permission of Paul H. Brookes Publishing Company.

1988; Wetherby & Prizant, 1993). Bruner (1981) suggests that children use communication to serve three functions during the first year of life (Table 11-4):

- *Behavior regulation:* Communicating to get others to do something or to stop doing something (e.g., request an object or action or protest an object or action)
- *Social interaction:* Communicating to get others to look at or notice oneself (e.g., request a social game, greet, call, showoff)
- *Joint attention:* Communicating to get others to look at an object or event (e.g., comment, request information)

Studies of the communicative functions of individuals with severe disabilities also demonstrate a pattern of relatively strong use of behavior regulation functions and limited use of social interaction and joint attention

functions (Cirrin & Rowland, 1985; Ogletree, Wetherby, & Westling, 1992; Wetherby, Yonclas, & Bryan, 1989; Wetherby, Prizant, & Hutchinson, 1998).

The forms of communication used by individuals with severe to profound mental retardation has been analyzed on the basis of contact gestures versus distal gestures (McLean, McLean, Brady, & Etter, 1991). At about 9 months of age, children first use contact gestures, in which their hands come in contact with an object or person (e.g., giving or showing objects, pushing an adult's hand). By about 11 months, children use distal gestures, in which their hands do not touch a person or object (e.g., open-hand reaching, distant pointing, waving) (Bates et al., 1987). McLean et al. (1991) found that the adolescent and adult participants who used only contact gestures used communication for behavior regulation functions only, while the participants who used distal gestures used communication for

TABLE 11–4
Examples of Nonsymbolic Communicative Functions

Communicative function	Communication form (nonsymbolic examples)
Behavior regulation: to get others to do something or stop doing something	
Request object or action	• Learner *looks* at or *reaches* toward an object that is out of reach • Learner in need of assistance *gives* an object to open or activate it • Learner *holds* up an empty cup to get a refill
Protest object or action	• Learner *pushes* other's hand away to stop being tickled • Learner *cries* in response to a toy's being put away • Learner *throws* undesired object
Social interaction: to draw attention to oneself	
Request social routine	• Learner *taps* other's hand to request continuation of tickling • Learner *looks* at other and laughs to keep a peek-a-boo game going
Request comfort	• When distressed, learner *reaches* toward caregiver to get comforted • Learner *raises* arms to get picked up and comforted • Learner *wiggles* in chair to get other to adjust his or her position
Greet	• Learner *waves* hi or bye • Learner *extends* arm in anticipation of other's shaking to say good-bye
Call	• Learner *tugs* on other's pant leg to get other to notice him or her • Learner *vocalizes* to get other to come to him or her
Show off	• Learner *vocalizes* a raspberry sound, *looks* at other, and *laughs* to get a reaction
Request permission	• Learner *holds* up a cookie to seek permission to eat it
Joint attention: to draw attention to an object or event	
Comment on object or action	• Learner *shows* a toy to get other to look at it • Learner *points* to a picture on the wall to get other to look at it
Request information	• Learner *holds* up a box and *shakes* it with a questioning expression to ask what's inside • Learner *points* to a picture in a book and *vocalizes* with rising intonation to ask what it is

FIGURE 11–7
Marina is using contact gestures successfully with her mother.

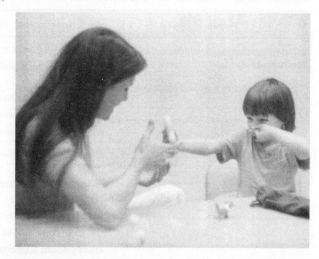

behavior regulation and joint attention functions. That is, the adolescents or adults who used contact gestures communicated by leading others' hands to request actions, while those who used distal gestures drew the attention of others to an object by pointing. Additionally, those using distal gestures attempted to clarify their messages when there was a communication breakdown and communicated at a higher rate than did those using contact gestures. Figure 11-7 shows Marina using contact gestures.

The Capacity for Symbols

Piaget (1952) suggested that sensorimotor cognitive knowledge (i.e., knowledge about how things in the world work) provides the basis for the emergence of using symbols. The ability to use language reflects a child's cognitive capacity to use symbols. There is accumulating evidence of parallels between cognition and the emergence of preverbal communication and first words (Bates & Snyder, 1987; Rice, 1983; Wetherby et al., 1998). In a cross-sectional study of 25 typically developing children, Bates (1979) found that the following sensorimotor skills were correlated with the emergence of language: imitation, tool use, communicative intent, and object use. Thus, the potential for movement toward a symbolic communication system in learners with severe disabilities may be better understood by considering skills that enhance the capacity for symbol use and understanding the developmental progression from nonsymbolic to symbolic skills.

Assessment

This section presents a structure for assessing the nonsymbolic communication of individuals with severe disabilities. Because the learner is interrelated with partners and environments, assessment should address each of these three aspects. Table 11-5 displays the tri-focus on learner, partner, and environment with assessment considerations (second column) and an overview of the interventions that are linked to each focus (third column).

Good communication assessment procedures measure typical and spontaneous behaviors, are conducted

TABLE 11–5

Considerations for Assessment and Intervention Focus Using the Trifocus Framework

Focus	Assessment considerations	Intervention focus
1: Understanding the learner who has severe disabilities	*What is the learner's communication profile?*	View challenging behavior as communication
	Consider the progression of communicative development	Relate learner's expressions to partners' actions
	Attend to behavior state patterns	Facilitate alert, responsive state behavior
	Identify learner's level of intentionality	
	Identify learner's level of symbolization	

2: Broadening the communication partner's role	*How can I help the learner communicate better?*	Use pragmatics:
		  Enhance sensitivity
		  Increase opportunities
		  Sequence experiences

	How can I communicate better with the learner?	Use a continuum of choice formats

	Consider the pragmatic perspective	Augment vocal input:
		  Enhance meaning
		  Facilitate retention

	Consider opportunities for communication	
	Identify social supports	
	Consider partner interaction style	
	Attend to elements of choice making	
	Consider augmented input	
3: Improving the environmental context	*What combination of influences can improve the context of the interaction?*	Provide both physical and social natural supports
	Attend to natural contexts	Use relevant, natural contexts

	Consider external influences on state behavior	Modify environment:
		  Adjust sensory qualities
		  Alter movement and orientation of the learner's body
		  Change learning atmosphere

		Modify combinations of environmental influences

Source: Adapted from Siegel-Causey, E., & Bashinski, S. M. (1997). Enhancing initial communication and responsiveness of learners with multiple disabilities: A tri-focus framework for partners. *Focus on Autism and Other Developmental Disabilities*, 12(2), 105–120.

by familiar persons, employ real-life materials and naturalistic activities, use a variety of assessment strategies, and translate information into relevant functional skills. It is important to assess both current and future needs for communication. Assessment strategies include commercially available instruments, communication and language samples, functional behavioral assessment, and oral-motor assessment. Further details about assessment are discussed by Snell (2002) and in chapters 3, 5, and 6.

In the next section, we address assessment from the trifocus framework. We discuss in order (a) the learner's profile of communication abilities, (b) the broadening the communication partner's role by assessing their patterns and style, and (c) improving the communication environment.

Assessment: Understanding the Nonsymbolic Communicator

The Learner's Profile

Assessment of nonsymbolic communication should identify not only what individuals cannot do but also what they can do. Assessment should build a profile of student limitations and abilities across cognitive, social, communicative, and motor domains.

Communication partners or team members (educator, SLP) should begin assessment with two assumptions: (a) everyone communicates, and (b) learners with nonsymbolic skills *are* communicating. The purpose of assessment is to identify *how* and *why* an individual uses communication. The profile of the learner's communication in Box 11–3 should guide the

Box 11-3 Learner Communicative Profile

1. Communicative forms
   a. Vocalizations, gestures, and so on
   b. Behavior state patterns
   c. High levels of challenging behavior
2. Communicative functions
3. Intentionality
4. Readability of signals
5. Repair strategies
6. Capacity for symbols

assessment of skills and developmental capacities that are important for intervention planning.

Communicative Forms

The first assessment task is to identify the kinds of forms the learner uses. A person's communication forms give information that will influence how he or she should be taught.

Vocalizations and Gestures The categories of nonsymbolic forms in Table 11-3 can guide the assessment process. Team members should be cognizant of both conventional forms and idiosyncratic forms that the learner may use. For gestural communication, contact gestures should be differentiated from distal gestures. Sometimes it can be difficult to distinguish communicative forms from more generalized behaviors in individuals with severe disabilities. Communicative forms need to be linked to specific situations and how the individual uses them to convey messages.

> *Using the categories from Table 11-3, Marina's communicative forms include generalized movements (e.g., increased hand shaking, moving torso), vocalizations (e.g., undifferentiated vowels, laughs, cries), facial expressions (e.g., smiles, grimaces), orientation with her head and eyes to objects or actions of interest, pauses and acting on objects (reaches toward desired objects, body movement to request action), and withdrawal to avoid activity.*

However, many of Marina's forms may not be exhibited by learners with more severe motor impairments than she has.

> *For Ryan and others with severe motor impairments, partners must be attuned to more subtle movements and a smaller range of movements as*

the communicative forms (e.g., increased tone, stop or start of a vocalization, change of expression).

One way to keep track of the learner's current repertoire of communicative forms is by using a gestural dictionary (Beukelman & Mirenda, 1998; Siegel & Cress, 2002) or, as we refer to it, a communication dictionary. This approach, illustrated in part for Ryan in Table 11-6, provides a way to document what the learner communicates, what the family and staff are interpreting each form of communication to mean, and how a partner should react when the form is expressed by the learner. Two considerations need to be addressed in setting up a communication dictionary: (a) how it is organized and (b) how it is displayed. The dictionary should be available for partners to access easily and can be organized in several ways, such as listing each form categorized by body parts starting with head (e.g., head: shaking, movement to side; face: wide open mouth, neutral) or in alphabetical order (e.g., "aah" sound, arching of back, body movement forward). The selected format should be easy for school staff/communication partners to use. Team members (educators, SLPs) have found it helpful to have the dictionary displayed in more than one way (poster board in classroom, listed on cards in a wallet-photo holder the learner carries, or in a notebook) so that all partners have access to the dictionary during their interaction with the learner. Collecting and revising the communication dictionary is part of assessing the learner's communication and building a communication profile. Periodically updating the communication dictionary documents the changes in forms used by the learner across the school year as more forms are developed or as forms become more conventional.

Behavior state is a physiologic condition that reflects the maturity and organization of an individual's

TABLE 11–6
Communication Dictionary

Student:	Ryan	Date:	October 1998

Settings: classes, one-to-one intervention

What the learner does (form)	What it means (function)	How we react (consequence)
Turns head away from activity or person	I don't want to do this or I am done	Respond as if expressed "no" and stop the activity. Tell Ryan what you responded to ("I see that your head turned.")
Increases vocalizations	I like this	Continue activity. Tell him what made you continue. ("I can hear that you like this.")
Eye gaze*	This is the item or person I want	Respond as if he selected what he gazed at. Tell him what made you respond. ("You are looking at Tom. Do you want to go with him?")

* Emerging

central nervous system. The term "behavior state" is also used to refer to an individual's ability to internally and externally mediate interactions with the environment (Rainforth, 1982). Behavior state observations generally include assessment of sleep, drowsiness, awake behavior (e.g., orienting, interacting), agitation (e.g., crying, aggression, self-abuse), and stereotypic behavior. Research suggests that state behavior has a significant influence on alertness and responsiveness of learners who have multiple disabilities and, indirectly, on their learning, development, and overall quality of life ((Guess, Roberts, Siegel-Causey, & Rues, 1995; Guess, Roberts, et al., 1993; Guess, Siegel-Causey, et al., 1993; Guess et al., 1990, 1991; Guy, Guess, & Ault, 1993; Richards & Sternberg, 1992, 1993). These learners' state profiles frequently reveal high occurrences of behaviors that impede progress in educational programs and particularly affect communication intervention (e.g., drowsiness, sleep, stereotypy). Low occurrences of overt responses or little action may be another characteristic of state organizational patterns in learners with

severe disabilities and may further result in an extremely limited response repertoire with reduced fluency in the complex environments of school and community. Learners who display low rates of overt responses, have externally limited response repertoires, and spend significantly less time in alert states than others will need considerable ongoing support to develop effective communication skills.

It is important assess a learner's typical levels of alertness in educational environments. Several authors have extended the research in behavior state and studied assessment strategies for use by educational personnel: (a) the ABLE (Analyzing Behavior State and Learning Environments) model (Ault et al., 1995) and (b) classroom observation methods (Richards & Richards, 1997). For example, both assessment approaches describe ways for team members to observe a student's level of alertness across the school day for its regularity. If irregular patterns are documented (e.g., excessive sleepiness or drowsiness, high rates of self-stimulation), they can be linked to interventions aimed at increasing or decreasing alertness levels. (Intervention is addressed later in regard to environmental considerations.)

High Levels of Alertness and Challenging Behavior An additional consideration is whether any communication forms may be socially inappropriate (e.g., self-injury, aggression). Behavior state research (e.g., Guess, Siegel-Causey et al., 1993) has identified patterns of stereotypy, agitation, aggression, or self-injurious behavior that appear to represent high levels of alertness. These same behaviors have been labeled as "challenging," or "problem," behaviors. If a behavioral state assessment (Siegel-Causey & Bashinski, 1997) was conducted as part of the communication profile, it should be reviewed to see if high level of arousal states were present (e.g., agitation, self-injury, stereotypy). When challenging behavior or high levels of arousal are found, they would be assessed further in terms of their communicative functions.

Whether the behaviors are judged to be part of the behavioral state schema or challenging behaviors, we believe they should be viewed as a form of communication and need to be understood in relation to an individual's entire repertoire of communicative forms. The first step in assessing these forms is to review the communication dictionary and note if any of these behaviors might indicate challenging behaviors (Table 11-6). The checklist in Figure 11-8 includes challeng-

FIGURE 11–8

Checklist of Communicative Functions and Nonsymbolic Forms

	Nonsymbolic Forms											Challenging Behaviors				
Communicative Functions	Acting on/Using Objects	Assuming Positions or Moving to Specified Places	Conventional Gestures	Depicting Actions	Facial Expressions	Generalized Movements or Tone Changes	Orientating or Eye Gaze	Touching or Manipulating Objects	Vocalizing	Withdrawing	Other:	Agitation	Aggression	Self-Injury	Self-Stimulation	Other:
Behavior Regulation																
Request Activity or Help																
Protest Object																
Request Access to Tangibles																
Escape Activity or Person																
Social Interaction																
Request Social Routine																
Request Comfort																
Greet																
Call																
Showing Off																
Request Permission																
Request Attention																
Joint Attention																
Comment on Object/Action																
Request Information																
Other Functions																
Sensory																

Student:_____

Date:_____ Setting:_____

Context:_____

_____

Observer:_____

*Italicized may be linked to challenging behavior © Siegel & Wetherby, 2004. Reprinted with permission.

ing behavior as forms of communication and can be used in the assessment process.

Communicative Functions

A second goal of assessment is to identify the *reasons* or *functions* that an individual uses communication. If an individual is at a nonintentional level (i.e., does not demonstrate any deliberate, goal-directed communication), assessment should identify any behaviors that serve a communicative function based on others' interpretation of these behaviors. For individuals demonstrating intentional communication, assessment should identify the range of communicative functions

expressed. A useful assessment framework described earlier is based on Bruner's (1981) categories of communicative functions that emerge in development prior to the onset of speech:

1. *Behavior regulation:* Acts used to regulate another's behavior to obtain or restrict environmental goals (e.g., request or demand access to actions, assistance, or activities or protest actions)
2. *Social interaction:* Acts used to draw another's attention to oneself for the purpose of making a social connection (e.g., request social game, attention greet, call, show off)

3. *Joint attention:* Acts used to direct another's attention to an object or event in order to sharing the focus of attention (e.g., comment on object, action, request information)

These categories of communicative functions vary in sociability, with behavior regulation having the least social demands and joint attention having the most. Children with severe disabilities and children with autism spectrum disorders in the early stages of communication have been found to express limited ranges of communicative functions, particularly the more social functions of social interaction and joint attention (Ogletree et al., 1992; Wetherby et al., 1998). Partners should determine whether an individual uses these major functions to convey messages.

> *Marina displays the communicative functions of regulating behavior (e.g., requesting and protesting objects or actions) and engaging in social interaction (e.g., requesting social games, calling) but does not yet communicate for joint attention.*

The Checklist of Communicative Functions and Nonsymbolic Forms Figure 11-8 can help the educational partner link the learner's forms and functions. A first step would be to circle the nonsymbolic forms across the top of the checklist that are known to be in the learner's repertoire; the partner may want to add in the specific types of behaviors the learner uses (e.g., gesture or reaching) or other forms unique to the learner that are not shown. The educator or SLP would then conduct observations in a natural context when the learner is participating in activities with partner(s). As the observation unfolds, the observer identifies (or hypothesizes) the possible function for each nonsymbolic form observed. The observer checks the specific function within each category: behavior regulation, social interaction, joint attention, or other functions. Videotaping oneself interacting with the learner and then completing the checklist is also beneficial in getting a full understanding of forms and functions. The checklist should be completed across a variety of activities and repeated periodically over the school year.

Challenging behaviors can take on functions of behavioral regulation (e.g., requesting item, escaping an action or person) and social interaction (e.g., requesting attention) and also may serve other purposes for the student within these three broad categories of function. The same challenging behavior may serve one or more communicative functions.

> *Ten-year-old Michael often flaps his hands. The assessor observes him during a cooking project. After the cookies are placed in the oven to cook, Michael begins flapping his hands. The paraeducator tells the small group to clean up. Michael's hand flapping continues. Gesturing to the oven, his friend Pete asks, "What's wrong, Michael? We get to eat a cookie when the timer goes off." Michael's hand flapping decreases in intensity. The observer marks "Self-Stimulation" under "Challenging Behaviors" and "Request Access to Tangibles" under "Behavior Regulation." A note is made that Michael may be using hand flapping as a display of agitation and/or as a request for tangibles and that staff should verify this by assessing across activities.*

A number of researchers (e.g., Horner, O'Neill, & Albin, 1991; O'Neill, Vaughn, & Dunlap, 1998; O'Neil et al., 1997; Reichle & Wacker, 1993; Wacker et al., 1990) have considered the impact of challenging behavior in terms of its communicative functions. They agree that much of the challenging behavior exhibited by those with severe disabilities may be a form communicative that serves a specific function or functions (Carr & Durand, 1985; Carr et al., 1994). Using a communicative approach guides the assessor to identify whether a particular communicative form functions to regulate another person's behavior (e.g., as a means to request a desired tangible or escape or avoid a situation) or to request social interaction (to draw attention to self; Brady & Halle, 1997; Carr et al., 1994; Durand & Crimmins, 1992; O'Neill et al., 1997). Thus, assessment with the checklist in Figure 11-8 may indicate a need for functional assessment to verify the function of challenging behavior and provide intervention strategies (also see chapters 6).

The information from the checklist provides a measure of the current repertoire of communicative forms and functions and an overview of the possible intervention: (a) altering or expanding number of forms used, (b) expanding frequency of use, (c) expanding number of functions used, (d) expanding frequency of use of functions, and (e) changing forms that are challenging behaviors.

Intentionality

A third goal of assessment is to identify the degree of intentionality for each communicative function. Recall that communication may range on a continuum from preintentional to intentional. Intentionality cannot be measured directly; it must be inferred from observable behaviors displayed during interactions. A nonsymbolic learner's degree of intentionality can be determined based on behavioral evidence (Bates, 1979; Bruner, 1978; Harding & Golinkoff, 1979), including the following:

1. Alternating gaze between the goal and the listener
2. Persisting in the signal until the goal is accomplished or failure is indicated
3. Changing the signal quality until the goal has been met
4. Ritualizing or conventionalizing the form of the signal over time within specific communicative contexts
5. Awaiting a response from the listener
6. Terminating the signal when the goal is met
7. Displaying satisfaction when the goal is attained or dissatisfaction when it is not

An individual may not display all these behaviors, but the more behaviors displayed, the more likely the behavior is intentional communication. Chris's photo in Figure 11–9 and the following explanation are good examples.

Chris is beginning to show evidence of intentionality in some play situations when he gazes directly at his friend Samantha (the listener). His team is teaching him to alternate this gaze between the listener and the object or event he desires. They know that he will display more intentionality if this skill is present. He does know to wait for Samantha's response of interest in the toy cow.

Learners should be assessed across a variety of activities to determine whether any of the seven intentional behavior indicators are present. The more behaviors present, the more intentional the communicator.

It is important to view intentionality as a developmental process and to evaluate the degree of intentionality in reference to changes in behaviors that indicate anticipation and expectation. Increases in intentionality are evidence of progress for nonsymbolic communicators.

Marina is showing intentionality by alternating her gaze and persisting until a goal is met. She recently began ritualizing communicative forms (e.g., using a brief back-and-forth body movement rather than an exaggerated bouncing movement to request a

FIGURE 11–9
Chris is positioned in the side-lyer next to his peer, Samantha, who holds the toy cow. As an educator assists him in finding the switch, Chris looks toward Samantha (function = engage in social interaction). Samantha smiles to indicate she wants Chris to activate the toy (function = behavior regulation).

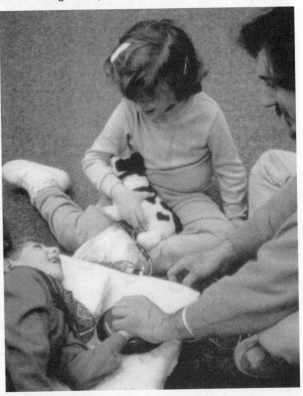

wagon being pulled) and terminating the signal when the goal is met (e.g., ceased the back-and-forth movement once the wagon movement is continued).

Readability of Signals

A fourth goal of assessment is determining how readable nonsymbolic communicative behaviors are. *Readability* refers to the clarity of a communicative signal and ease with which the signal can be interpreted. Readability is influenced by the degree of familiarity of the communication partner with the learner as well as the conventionality of the signal. Ability to use facial expression enhances readability by clarifying the learner's emotional state (Prizant & Wetherby, 1990; Kublin, Wetherby, Crais, & Prizant, 1998). Motor ability greatly influences the use of facial expressions and the clarity of gestural and vocal communication.

Marina's family members find Marina's subtle body movements and facial expressions to be very readable, but less familiar people find Marina's behaviors difficult to interpret.

Repair Strategies

A fifth goal of assessment is identifying repair strategies. Communication breakdowns are frequent when there is limited readability of signals. Thus, it is important for nonsymbolic learners to repair communicative breakdowns (Kublin et al., 1998; Prizant & Wetherby, 1990). An opportunity for repair occurs when a learner initiates a communicative behavior and the partner fails to respond or responds in a manner that violates the learner's intention.

Marina wiggles in her stroller to request out; when her mother fails to respond, this is an opportunity for Marina to repair in order to clarify what she wants. Marina starts vocalizing to communicate that she does not want to stay in the stroller.

In addition to natural opportunities to repair, "holding out" before responding to the learner's communicative intent in order to evaluate the ability to repair can also systematically provide opportunities. It should be determined whether the learner persists by repeating the same signal or by modifying the signal, such as changing the behavior or adding something to the behavior (e.g., adding a gaze or vocalization to a gesture). When learners abandon a communicative goal if it is not immediately achieved, they are lacking in repair strategies. The ability to modify a signal to repair communicative breakdowns allows greater reciprocity and promotes more successful social exchanges.

While Marina occasionally abandons a goal if it is not met immediately, she more often repeats her signals for behavior regulation and is beginning to modify her signals if her goals are not met. For example, if she requests to be pulled by bouncing her body back and forth and her mother does not respond right away, she looks at her mother and vocalizes.

The form provided in Table 11–7 can be used to assess in common situations when learners typically (a) express repairs and (b) do not express repairs but become agitated or withdraw. Those who do not use repair strategies should be taught to do so.

TABLE 11–7
Repair Strategy Assessment

Partner: _____   Activity: _____   Date: _____

Directions: Use this form to assess the learner's repair strategies across a variety of familiar activities. Whenever there is a breakdown in communication, complete columns 1 and 2. If the learner repaired the breakdown, complete column 3. If the learner did not repair the breakdown, complete column 4. Use column 5 to suggest repair strategies the learner could be taught.

1. Learner communicative behavior	2. Partner response	3. Did the learner repair? How?	4. Did the learner withdraw or become agitated? Describe.	5. List possible repair strategies to teach.

Brady, McLean, McLean, and Johnston (1995) studied repairs of 28 individuals with severe to profound mental retardation who resided in an institution. Each participant was provided with five opportunities to repair when adults did not respond to or misunderstood their requests for help or their requests for attention to an object or event. They found that 25 of the 28 participants initiated at least one repair. Significantly more participants repaired when requests for help were misunderstood. The participants who did repair tended to either repeat the same signal or change to a different signal. However, they rarely added information to their signals, suggesting that these repairs are harder to learn. Others have suggested that those who use serious challenging behavior as a form of communication may be using their problem behavior as a repair strategy in instances when their more conventional forms are unsuccessful. Furthermore, the ability to repair with appropriate behavior may lead to reductions in problem behavior (Wetherby, Alexander, et al., 1998).

Capacity for Symbols

A sixth goal of assessment is the learner's capacity for symbol use across activities. By definition, learners who communicate nonsymbolically do not use symbols expressively. However, there may be great variation in terms of their understanding (reception) of symbolic input: speech or graphics (e.g., such as line drawings, photos). Thus, the learner's assessment profile should include information on comprehension.

Knowledge of skill level on cognitive tasks that are correlates of language (i.e., tool use, causality, imitation, object use) can help partners understand the capacity of learners for communication skills. In other words, learners' communicative strategies should be considered in reference to their problem-solving and learning strategies. It is particularly important to consider how learners use objects to obtain a goal, understand the source of actions, observe and attempt to imitate the behaviors of others, and explore the functional uses of objects. For example, a child who attempts to obtain a cracker that is out of reach by scooting to the low cupboard that the cracker box sits on, reaching for the box, pushing it off the shelf, and vocalizing so someone will help open it is demonstrating mental representation skills in tool use.

An understanding of the cognitive skills of learners can provide information about strengths and interests that can be used to develop communication abilities. The transition from nonsymbolic to symbolic activities is a critical milestone that is evident in the use of objects and play. As children are able to symbolize, they show increasing capacity to use objects for specific functions, to engage in pretend actions toward others, and for adding actions during play (Lifter & Bloom, 1998). There is a strong relationship between object knowledge or use in play and the emergence of words. Wetherby and Prutting (1984) describe specific procedures adapted from developmental literature for setting up assessment probes for tool use, causality, imitation, and object use. For individuals with limited motor abilities, microswitches or other adaptive devices are needed to assess cognitive knowledge.

Strategies for Assessing Nonsymbolic Communication

Three strategies help assess nonsymbolic communicative behaviors:

1. Interviewing familiar people
2. Observing in natural contexts
3. Gathering communication samples

Interviews

The first strategy in assessing nonsymbolic communication is to interview people who are very familiar with the learner to document their forms and functions (teachers, care providers). Several guides exist for planning the interview. Peck and Schuler (1987) describe an interview format to identify forms, functions, and repair strategies. The Functional Assessment Interview (FAI) (O'Neill et al., 1997) explained in chapter 6 can be used to collect information about events that influence challenging behavior. Snell (2002) presents another example of an interview format and observation that incorporates the trifocus nonsymbolic framework and may be helpful for the educational team's assessment activities. Communication interviews provide a great deal of information about the learner in a relatively short period of time and may be used to plan further assessment.

Observations in Natural Contexts

A second strategy for assessment is to observe communicative behaviors of learners and partners that occur in natural contexts (Wetherby & Prizant, 1997). Observational checklists, such as Figure 11–8, can help organize recordings from naturalistic observations. Checklists are used most typically while observing children and while observing videotaped naturalistic communicative interactions in several environments.

Communication Sampling

The purpose of the third assessment strategy is to gather a representative sample of communicative behaviors in a relatively short period of time. Although sampling may be done while a school staff person observes, videotaping a communication sample is optimal. Videotapes offer the most objective and the richest data collection procedure for analyzing communicative behaviors. Videotapes also allow repeated observations of behaviors, providing opportunities to note subtle and fleeting behaviors that may be missed during ongoing dyadic interactions.

In contrast to the use of checklists, communication sampling involves designing situations to entice learners to initiate and participate in communicative interactions. Free play within joint-action routines may be used (Snyder-McLean, Solomonson, McLean, & Sack, 1984), but learners must have ample opportunities to initiate a variety of communicative acts. If a learner does not initiate readily, communicative temptations are useful (Wetherby & Prizant, 1989, 1993; Wetherby & Prutting, 1984).

Communicative temptations involve opportunities that entice specific attempts at communication. One example is activating a windup toy, letting it deactivate, and then waiting and looking expectantly at the learner. This gives the learner a chance to request assistance at getting the toy to activate, to protest about the ceasing of action, or to respond in other ways. Another example is giving the learner a block to put away in a box, repeating this several times so that the learner expects a block, and then giving a different object, such as a toy animal or a book. The novel object may tempt the learner to communicate about the unexpected object or to protest over the change in objects. In Figure 11–5, it appears that the bubbles that Marina's mother has deliberately placed out of reach tempt Marina.

Because temptations may be presented nonverbally, they circumvent the problem of a learner's limited comprehension of language. Although each temptation should be designed with at least one particular function in mind, any one temptation may potentially elicit a variety of communicative functions (Wetherby & Rodriguez, 1992). Communicative temptations should not be the only interactive technique used to sample but may be useful as warm-ups or supplements to unstructured interactions.

An accurate assessment of nonsymbolic communication depends on observation of a learner over a period of time in a variety of communicative situations with different partners. Assessment should be viewed as an ongoing process rather than episodic. Furthermore, since communication is a process between at least two people (speaker and partner), assessment must consider the learner's communicative behavior in relation to the interaction styles of communicative partners (Kublin et al., 1998; Mirenda & Donnellan, 1986; Peck & Schuler, 1987) and the characteristics of the environment (Siegel-Causey & Bashinski, 1997). This assessment focus was addressed previously in Table 11–5 (#1).

Assessment: Understanding the Social Environment

Assessment information gained from the "learner communicative profile" is only part of the picture. The team will also assess the communication qualities of the social environment to create the "partner communicative profile." These social qualities might include the following:

1. Opportunities to initiate and respond to communication
2. Social supports present
   a. What is there to communicate about?
   b. Who is available to interact with?
3. Interaction styles of communication partners

These qualities and the structure in Table 11–5 (#2) help us consider ways to assess the broad social aspects of the communication partners' roles.

Opportunities

Educational settings and activities vary a great deal in regard to the quality and quantity of opportunities for communication. School staff partners must ask whether situations and persons give enough opportunities for the learner to initiate and respond using all three major communicative functions. That is, do learners have opportunities to use communication in order to get others to do things (behavior regulation), to draw attention to themselves (social interaction), and to direct others' attention to objects or events (joint attention)?

Opportunities to use communication for behavior regulation generally involve instances when an individual needs to request assistance or objects that are out of reach, to make choices about desired objects or activities (e.g., food items, toys, or play partners), and to indicate undesired objects or activities. Opportunities to regulate behavior should occur throughout activities, not just when materials are first presented or activities are first initiated. An evaluation of behavior regulation opportunities tells team members whether there needs to be more (Peck, 1989).

Opportunities to use communication for social interaction and joint attention are more likely to occur within repetitive, turn-taking interactions. Bruner (1978, 1981) suggests that joint-action routines provide the best chance for communication development and learning to exchange roles in conversation. A joint-action routine is a repetitive turn-taking game or activity in which there are shared attention and participation by both the learner and the caregiver, exchangeable roles, and predictable sequences (Snyder-McLean et al., 1984). A classic example of a joint-action routine for infants and toddlers is the game of peek-a-boo (Bruner & Sherwood, 1976), which caregivers may play hundreds or thousands of times during the first year of a child's life. But joint-action routines exist across all ages. A joint-action routine may include activities involving preparation of a specific product (e.g., painting, food), organization around a central plot (e.g., pretending), or cooperative turn-taking games (e.g., smiling in response to one's name during a song) (Snyder-McLean et al., 1984).

In Ryan's role with helping the football team, there are many repetitive preparations that give structured opportunities for him to communicate. One joint-action routine begins as he and his friend Andy approach the clothes dryer and Andy assists setting up an adaptation that helps Ryan remove the clothes. The adaptation is a slanted board that clips on Ryan's tray and extends into the dryer. There is a large button that is attached to a switch. Each time Ryan hits the switch, it rotates a belt that circulates to draw the clothes to Ryan's tray. Ryan then pushes the clothing item/towel into a basket positioned to his right on the floor. They interact back and forth when Ryan smiles, and then Andy sets the jig each time by placing a clothing item on it to allow Ryan to pull the towels onto his tray and then to push them into the basket to the side of his wheelchair. The routine continues until each dryer is emptied.

In assessment, it is important to consider how the structure of activities influences communication. Snyder-McLean et al. (1984) delineate eight critical elements of successful joint-action routines for the assessment of the communicative environments (Table 11–8). These elements of quality as well as the quantity of joint-action routines should be evaluated. Activities that learners and partners routinely engage in at home, in the classroom, or in the community are potential joint-action routines that should be evaluated for these eight elements.

It is imperative to link these eight critical elements of joint-action routines with the learner's chronological age when selecting materials, settings, and people for the routines. Possible activities at home include eating meals, dressing, bathing, and playing; at school include eating snacks and meals, domestic activities (e.g., doing laundry and preparing meals), and art and leisure activities; and in the community include riding the bus, going shopping, and eating in a restaurant. The elements give joint routines a familiar, predictable structure that allows nonsymbolic learners to anticipate the activity's nature and sequence, participate maximally, and enhance their communication (Duchan, 1995; Kublin et al., 1998; Snyder-McLean et al., 1984).

The following joint-action routine uses these elements:

1. *Obvious unifying theme:* Preparing for football practice.
2. *Requirement for joint focus and interaction:* Both are assigned to get the locker room set up before practice begins.
3. *Limited number of clearly defined roles:* Andy assists with some of Ryan's setup. Ryan completes some tasks alone and some with assistance from Andy. Andy does some tasks on his own.
4. *Exchangeable roles:* For some jobs, it doesn't matter who does what task (shutting the dryer and washer doors).
5. *Logical, nonarbitrary sequence:* The young men proceed logically to wash, dry, fold, and store the locker room towels.
6. *Turn-taking structure:* Ryan's and Andy's turns are dependent on each other, so there is a balance of turns (e.g., Andy sets up the jig and Ryan pulls each item out of the dryer).
7. *Planned repetition:* There is built-in repetition with multiple items that need to be washed, dried, folded, and stored.

TABLE 11–8
Critical Elements of Effective Joint-Action Routines

1. *An obvious unifying theme or purpose* to relate the actions of different individuals engaged in the routine and provide a theme that is meaningful and recognizable to all participants. There are three general types of routines:
   - Preparation or fabrication of a specific product (e.g., food preparation, product assembly)
   - Routines organized around a plot or theme (e.g., daily living routines, pretend play scenarios)
   - Cooperative turn-taking games or routines (e.g., songs with spaces to fill in, peekaboo)
2. *A requirement for joint focus and interaction* to establish need for interaction and negotiation.
3. *A limited number of clearly delineated roles*, but at least two different roles that are definable and predictable (e.g., speaker and listener, giver and receiver).
4. *Exchangeable roles* so that the individual is assigned to more than one role in the same routine.
5. *A logical, nonarbitrary sequence* that is determined by the nature of the activity and can be predicted by the outcome or product.
6. *A structure for turn taking in a predictable sequence* that allows the individual to anticipate when to wait and when to initiate a turn.
7. *Planned repetition* over time to establish role expectancy and sequence predictability, used within a daily time block to offer several turns to each individual.
8. *A plan for controlled variation* that introduces novel elements against a background of familiarity and expectancy to evoke spontaneous comments in the following ways:
   - Interrupt the routine or violate expectations
   - Omit necessary materials
   - Initiate a routine and "play possum"
   - Initiate old routines with new contents
   - Introduce new routines with old contents

Source: Adapted from "Structuring Joint-Action Routines for Facilitating Communication and Language Development in the Classroom" by L.K. Snyder-McLean, B. Solomonson, J. E. McLean, and S. Sack, 1984, *Seminars in Speech and Language 5*(3), 216–218.

8. *A plan for controlled variation:* Natural interruptions or violations occur in their routine, such as finding personal clothes items with the towels or running out of soap. These events allow them to communicate with each other and, of course, goof around, such as when Ryan used his jig to fling a pair of underwear into Andy's pile of towels.

Social Supports
Learners' communication interactions are influenced by the social demands and supports provided in the environment. A nurturing atmosphere fosters warmth and security. Learners need to have responsive interactions with partners over time so that trust and sharing develops between them. Communication interventions should facilitate interactions and relationships with others, particularly with family members, school staff, and peers without disabilities. Assessment should help educators understand from the learner's perspective whether the social environment is positive and conducive to interactions: "What is there to communicate about?" and "Who is available to interact with?" Answering these questions may help staff assess social supports.

For individuals in the perlocutionary stage, social supports mean that structured opportunities are created within familiar activities to attract the learner's interest and give ways to participate and take turns. Partners need to be responsive to the communicative function of subtle behaviors.

When Marina first entered the preschool, staff and peers provided many opportunities for her to express whether she wanted an activity to continue and to choose what would happen next. A staff member watched her reaction, responded to what she seemed to be communicating, and made a record.

If some routines do not met these criteria (repetitive, familiar, and interesting), the assessment process is modified and expanded to examine the opportunities for communication.

As Marina's friend pushed her in the swing, he stopped the swing periodically and asked questions, pausing after each question to watch her response: "Fun, Marina?" "Do you want to swing more?" "Do you want to go on the merry-go-round?"

As individuals move toward the illocutionary stage, they should have social supports that allow them to initiate interactions, maintain interactions, and terminate interactions while realizing that their behaviors affect others.

As Marina learned that staff members and peers understood her expressions, she signaled her needs more readily. As she was swinging, she smiled and vocalized to her friend. When she wanted to stop, she put her head down and stopped vocalizing.

Interaction Style

Communicative behavior is influenced not only by the opportunities for communication but also by the interaction styles partners use in relation to the social supports available. Does a partner foster or inhibit communication? The caregivers' ability to respond contingently to a child's behavior has a major influence on the child's developing communicative competence (Dunst et al., 1990; Yoder, et al., 1998).

School staff partners should think about the unique ways that they talk, gesture, and share "who they are" as they interact with others.

Sam, Ryan's SLP, tends to speak quietly, look directly at his communication partners, and use touch only to emphasize important points. He always wears blue jeans and short-sleeve T-shirts, uses musk cologne, and has glasses. Martha, Ryan's teacher, speaks loudly, uses her tone of voice to convey emotion, and is affectionate and demonstrative with touch and gestures. She usually wears long dresses, wears her hair in a braid, and does not use perfume. Sam and Martha's interaction styles and personal behaviors influence the same learner in different ways.

The learner's ability to understand may be influenced by how communication partners express themselves. A student may receive the most salient information through nonsymbolic means.

Carol, a student who uses nonsymbolic communication, attends to Sam, the SLP, when he touches her or is close enough for her to smell his cologne, although for most of their interactions, she tends not to notice Sam until he redirects her attention by raising his voice and being more animated. She becomes very attentive and animated the moment she hears her teacher Martha's voice and strives to encourage

Martha to interact with her. Ryan, however, prefers Sam's quiet voice and limited touch and tries to avoid Martha's demonstrative nature and loud voice.

Developmental literature provides guidelines for assessing interaction styles of caregivers (Girolametto, Greenberg, & Manolson, 1986; MacDonald, 1989; MacDonald & Carroll, 1992; Yoder et al., 1998). Based on developmental guidelines for children at nonsymbolic stages of communication, interaction styles should be evaluated to determine if the following features are present:

1. Waiting for the learner to communicate by pausing and looking expectantly.
2. Recognizing the learner's behavior (form) as communication by interpreting the communicative function that it serves.
3. Responding to the communicative message (function) of the learner.
4. Matching the communicative level of the learner by expressing oneself with symbolic language paired with nonsymbolic communication.

Table 11-9 provides a format to assess partner interaction styles. Collaboratively conducting assessment allows each team member (and peers) to discover ways to improve their interaction styles. For example, if a learner is requesting an object, does the communicative partner give the desired object immediately?

Marina and her friend Jody, a peer without disabilities, are serving a snack. Jody has the juice pitcher and Marina the cups. Jody looks at Marina as they approach Arturo's place at the table (waiting for communication). Marina smiles and places the cup in front of Arturo. Jody looks at Marina and then at the cup (recognizing and interpreting the communication function). "OK, I pour juice, huh?" and Jody pours the juice (responding contingently and matching the communicative level).

Some interactions do not promote communication:

Marina and Lois, the paraeducator, are serving a snack. Lois smiles and says, "Give Arturo a cup next." This request will help Marina know how to proceed and will speed up the serving process. However, it does not give Marina an opportunity to communicate or allow her to "direct" Lois to pour juice. Thus, Marina's partner did not wait for her to communicate.

TABLE 11–9
Assessing Partner Interaction Styles

Partner: _____   Activity: _____   Date: _____

Directions: Use this form to assess your own (videotape) or other partners' interactions with the learner. Share self- and partner assessments to ensure consistency of instruction.

Features	If present, what was observed?	If not, what alternatives might be used?	Unclear? What might we try next time?
1. Does the partner wait for communication?			
2. Does the partner recognize the learner's form of communication and interpret the function that it serves?			
3. Does the partner respond to the communication function expressed by the learner?			
4. Is the partner's response expressed with symbolic and non-symbolic behavior that matches the learner's ability?			

Partners must adjust their behaviors to match the communication level of each learner. MacDonald (1989) provides the analogy of being on a staircase with a child so that the partner has one foot on the child's step and the other foot on the next step. In the assessment of a communication partner's interaction style, it is important to consider the balance between the individual and the partner. That is, communicative partners should ask whether the interaction is reciprocal: Does each individual influence and respond meaningfully to the other individual and have a balance of turns?

Assessment: Understanding the Physical Environment

In addition to the social aspects of the environment, the second primary dimension to consider is the effect of physical variables on the communication contexts and interactions. The profile of the physical environment should be assessed in terms of the following:

1. Learner's position in terms of stability, proximity, and access to the interaction
2. Learner's interest in the activity

3. Learner's access to materials given sensory and motor skills
4. Activity level of the immediate environment near the learner's activity

During instruction and interactions, the physical environment influences how well communication is exchanged between the learner and partner (Table 11-5, #3). It has been suggested that changes in behavior state can be improved when environments are intentionally arranged in favorable ways (Ault et al., 1995; Guess et al., 1990). Five primary variables have been documented to influence a person's alert or sleepy states: (a) the attention a learner gives to social contact, (b) a learner's static body position, (c) the type of activity, (d) availability of materials, and (e) activity level in the immediate environment. In addition, behavior state research (Ault et al., 1995) suggests that changing environmental characteristics will directly influence behavior state. A well-engineered environment is associated with learners' display of alert, responsive state behavior. Conversely, this study also demonstrated that when educational staff did not systematically manage environmental characteristics, learners displayed more behavior states that were

TABLE 11–10
Assessing the Physical Environment

Partner: _____   Activity: _____   Materials: _____   Date: _____

Directions: Use this form to assess routines and activities via videotape or in real time. Share results within team to improve consistency of instruction.

Features	If present, what was observed?	If not, what alternatives might be used?	Unclear? What might we try next time?
1. Is the learner supported adequately: A. Stable? B. Can access the activity materials?			
2. Is the activity of interest?			
3. Are the materials matched to learner's sensory and motor skills?			
4. Is the activity and noise level near the learner conducive to attending and interacting?			

nonoptimal for learning (i.e., sleep, drowse, daze, agitation). Systematic instructional application of the environmental techniques yielded significant decreases in nonoptimal behavior states.

There are some simple ways to assess these variables while also assessing partners' interaction styles. Team members can use Table 11–10 to observe familiar routines and activities that take place across the person's school day and assess the presence or absence of facilitative communication strategies and the ways that the physical structure of activities influences the learner's communication.

Teaching

Methods to Promote Communication

Traditionally, intervention has focused on promoting speech and language development. Speaking and communicating have been viewed as synonymous (Calculator, 1988). Efforts were focused on remediation, including drilling in discrimination and teaching speech as a behavior within one-to-one isolated therapy sessions (Bedrosian, 1988; Musselwhite & St. Louis, 1988).

This focus on speech excluded many students with severe disabilities who were described as "not ready" for communication development or enhancement. Previously, the belief was held that before a child could benefit from augmentative and alternative communication interventions, a criterion level of cognitive ability was necessary (Rice & Kemper, 1984). Such beliefs are no longer supported (National Joint Committee for the Communication Needs for Persons with Severe Disabilities, 1992; Snell et al., 2003). The current trend is to teach communication in ways that match the learner's skills regardless of the mode of expression. Current research and theory suggest the following:

1. Focus teaching on interactions that are learner centered in natural home, school, and community environments
2. Use responsive and nondirective systematic instruction
3. Use intervention strategies that enhance early communication, such as naturalistic teaching procedures, including time delay (Halle, Marshall, & Spradlin, 1979), mand model (Warren, McQuarter & Rogers-Warren, 1984), and incidental teaching (Hart & Risley, 1975) (see chapters 12)

4. Use a communication dictionary so that partners respond to idiosyncratic gestures consistently (Beukelman & Mirenda, 1998; Mirenda, 1988; Siegel & Cress, 2002)
5. Use scripted routines (Beukelman & Mirenda, 1998)
6. Use joint-action routines (Snyder-McLean et al., 1984)
7. Provide choice-making opportunities (Brown, Belz, Corsi, & Wenig, 1993; Downing, 1999; Guess, Benson, & Siegel-Causey, 1985; Peck, 1989)
8. Use augmented input (Romski & Sevcik, 1993; Rowland, Schweigert, & Prickett, 1995; Wood, Lasker, Siegel-Causey, Beukelman, & Ball, 1998)
9. Use interrupted behavior chains (Allwell, Hunt, Goetz, & Sailor, 1989; Goetz, Gee, & Sailor, 1985; Hunt, Goetz, Alwell, & Sailor, 1986)

Next we describe intervention strategies that facilitate communication interaction between both learners and their partners and synthesize many intervention methods. An overview of the intervention methods is shown in Figure 11–10.

A Reciprocal Assessment Focus That Leads to Intervention

The assessment strategies described earlier in this chapter help educational partners recognize the effect of communication interactions on both the learner and his or her partner(s) and target areas that might be enhanced through instruction. Communication intervention is best viewed as a reciprocal process between a partner and a learner. The learner may be the responder

FIGURE 11–10
Intervention Guidelines in Relation to the Context of the Environment

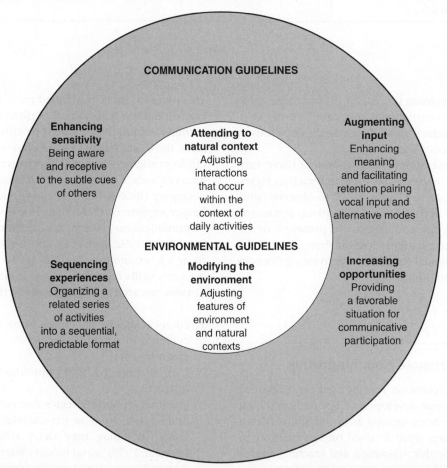

Source: Adapted from "Procedures for Enhancing Nonsymbolic Communication" by E. Siegel-Causey, C. Battle, and B. Ernst. In *Enhancing Nonsymbolic Communication Interactions Among Learners with Severe Handicaps* (p. 25) by E. Siegel-Causey and D. Guess (Eds.), 1989, Baltimore: Paul H. Brookes.

and thus influenced by how clearly he or she understands (responder-receptive understanding). In this case, intervention might focus on improving the partner's expressions. Alternately, the learner may be the initiator, in which case the partner's understanding is influenced by how clearly the learner expresses him- or herself (initiator-expressive competence). Intervention might focus on improving the learner's expressions and improving the partners' responsiveness and consistency. Interactions are influenced by what both the initiator and the responder do rather than assuming that either partner has deficits to remediate.

Using Functional, Systematic Methods in Natural Routines

As educational partners deliver communication instruction, they must incorporate systematic instructional methods regardless of the intervention approach. All communication instruction should occur within the routines of the day and natural environments (within the home, school, or community) so that learners not only communicate better or more but also recognize that communication always serves a purpose. This approach uses a collaborative model of service delivery, with all staff members working together to establish goals and facilitate cross-disciplinary training.

Potential Communication Content and Environmental Intervention Focus

In addition to being aware of the influence that partners' interactional styles have on receptive understanding, school staff partners should consider how the environment influences communication instruction. The center of Figure 11-10 displays the two environmental guidelines for teaching communication: (a) attend to natural contexts and (b) modify the environment to promote communication. To use these guidelines, the team will address several questions. What activities are conducive to joint-action or turn-taking segments? Are staff members and peers conducting activities that use these attributes? From the learner's perspective, what is there to communicate about in each familiar activity? Such questions may help partners discover potential communication content and interventions that focus on environmental arrangement(s).

Using an adaptation that facilitates handling and transferring, Ryan hands out towels to the team at the football games. This activity provides his team with many possible communication opportunities: Ryan *indicates to a peer that he is ready with a towel, that he recognizes individual friends and favorite players, that he wants to move his wheelchair or change his position, that he has finished the job, that he wants to start a conversation, and so on.*

By answering these questions, school partners will identify a wide range of teaching targets and may develop additional targets to generalize to other natural activities. Then the educational team can prioritize the targets that are most functional and will generalize across people, events, and settings.

Communication Intervention Guidelines

Four guidelines for improving communication intervention are shown in the outer circle of Figure 11-10: (a) enhance sensitivity, (b) sequence experiences, (c) augment input, and (d) increase opportunities. These guidelines evolved as part of an overall intervention for interacting with learners who have severe handicaps (see Siegel, in press; Siegel-Causey & Bashinski, 1997; Siegel-Causey & Guess, 1989). The guidelines are not arranged in a sequential manner; rather, educational partners should incorporate the relevant components of the guidelines during any individual communicative interaction.

The six guidelines in Figure 11-10 and their corresponding strategies form a philosophy of intervention based on two assumptions: (a) partners should expect learners to communicate and, (b) improving the partner's communication will positively influence interactions. Using this approach, partners should enhance the following (Figure 11-11):

1. Their use of nonsymbolic and symbolic expressions
2. Their understanding of the learner's nonsymbolic expressions
3. Their enhancement of communication contexts and attention to influences on the learner's state behavior

Jack, Ryan's friend, expects that Ryan will communicate as they take off their coats on entering the room. This allows Jack to be ready to respond to Ryan's initiations and expressions. Since Jack has had a variety of interactions with Ryan, he is familiar with Ryan's nonsymbolic ways of communicating, can predict what this activity will be like, and is alert to opportunities that occur naturally in their routine. (Jack uses the guideline of increasing opportunities and enhancing sensitivity.)

FIGURE 11–11
Intervention Guidelines and Corresponding Strategies

Enhancing the partners' nonsymbolic and symbolic expressions to the learner

Increase opportunities	Sequence experiences	Augment input
• Create need for requests	• Encourage participation	• Enhance meaning
• Facilitate alert, responsive state behavior	• Establish routines	• Facilitate retention
• Provide choices	• Provide turn-taking opportunities	
• Provide opportunities to interact		
• Use time delay		

Enhancing the partners' understanding of the learner's nonsymbolic communication

Enhance sensitivity
- Recognize individual's readiness for interaction
- Recognize nonsymbolic behaviors
- Respond contingently at the learner's level of communication
- Respond to expressions and challenging behavior as communicative behavior

Enhancing the learner's communication contexts and attending to external influences on the learner's state behavior

Attend to natural contexts	Modify environment
• Provide physical supports	• Adjust sensory qualities
• Provide social supports	• Alter movement and orientation of learner
	• Change learning atmosphere

Note: Based on Siegal-Causey, E., Battle, C., & Ernst, B. (1989). Procedures for enhancing nonsymbolic communication. In *Enhancing Nonsymbolic Communication Interactions Among Learners with Severe Handicaps* (p. 25) by E. Siegel-Causey and D. Guess (Eds.), Baltimore: Paul H. Brookes; and Siegel-Causey, E., & Bashinski, S.M. (1997). Enhancing initial communication and responsiveness of learners with multiple disabilities: A tri-focus framework for partners. *Focus on Autism and Other Developmental Disabilities,* 12(2), 105–120.

An initial focus of some communication interventions is to encourage learners to convey messages. Some learners are discouraged from communicating because of the great physical or cognitive effort required, while others have had infrequent opportunities to communicate (Downing, 1999; MacDonald, 1985; Musselwhite & St. Louis, 1988). Still others are at the perlocutionary stage and do not understand that their behaviors can affect others. Thus, a better focus may be to teach learners that they can affect people and events. We believe that all the guidelines and strategies in this section can help learners progress on a continuum of development from perlocutionary to locutionary to illocutionary expressions. In addition, the strategies allow learners to control interactions as they initiate, maintain, and terminate communication exchanges. When using the intervention guidelines, remember to do the following:

1. Use relevant and functional tasks and age-appropriate methods and materials and intervene within natural contexts and activities
2. Expect communication

Intervention Guidelines to Enhance Partners' Nonsymbolic and Symbolic Expressions

The first intervention guidelines we will review are listed in the top section of Figure 11-11: enhancing partners' expressions to the learner. The three strategies are to increase opportunities, sequence experiences, and augment input.

Increasing Opportunities

Creating situations that empower learners to communicate can promote their participation in interactions. The strategies to increase opportunities include (a) creating need for requests; (b) facilitating alert, responsive behavior; (c) providing choices; (d) providing opportunities to interact; and (e) using time delay (Halle, 1984; Siegel-Causey & Bashinski, 1997; Siegel-Causey & Guess, 1989).

Requests As learners move to a more illocutionary level, they can direct attention to an object or event (e.g., get peers' attention on the waves in a pool), seek to initiate social interaction, and attempt to create changes in actions or objects. If a need is created, these skills can be shaped into requests.

> *When Marina finishes her juice, her teacher acts "busy." Thus, if Marina wants more to drink, she will need to get the partner's attention so that he will pour the juice.*

Responsive State Behavior Intervention to facilitate state behavior at the perlocutionary level will focus on establishing the relationship between what the learner expresses and the actions of other people and environmental events. Perlocutionary nonsymbolic behaviors generally include relaxing or stiffening of the body; total body movement; arm, leg, or hand gestures or movements; and vocalizations (e.g., crying, cooing, noise making).

> *The peer stops the country music CD that he and Chris are listening to and starts to play another CD. Chris's legs stiffen, and he begins to vocalize. His peer looks over, attending to the change in Chris's expression. "Hey buddy, you want to hear it still?" He reactivates the music, and Chris relaxes and quiets down.*

When partners notice a learner's level of alertness and change an activity accordingly, they can facilitate responsive behavior.

Choices The right to choose is highly valued. Offering opportunities to choose has been shown to be a powerful intervention (e.g., Bambara & Koger, 1996; Bannerman, Sheldon, Sherman, & Harchik, 1990; Brown et al., 1993). Siegel-Causey and Bashinski (1997) suggested that choice making involves (a) displaying preferences and (b) making decisions. To display a preference, the learner recognizes that options exist, has a propensity (liking) toward something, and makes a communicative expression (choice) about that item or occurrence.

> *Ryan is given the opportunity to choose which peer he wants to work with during football practice tasks. To choose, he needs to recognize that there are peers present to choose from, to prefer being with one of them (propensity), and to convey this preference by gazing at the peer he prefers.*

For choice making to be effective, it is important to consider the learner's level of receptive understanding and symbolization, and it may be necessary to teach choice making. A simpler level of choice making applicable to learners who communicate nonsymbolically is the active or passive choice system with two options (Beukelman & Mirenda, 1998). The learner gets choice "X" when passive (for doing nothing) and choice "Y" when active (for doing something). A slightly more difficult option is two-item active choice making using real objects (Beukelman & Mirenda, 1998). The types of items in the two-choice array can be (a) two preferred options (Writer, 1987), (b) one preferred and one nonpreferred option, or (c) one preferred option and a "blank" or "distracter" option (Reichle et al., 1991; Rowland & Schweigert, 1990). Choice items should be used that will promote the learner's understanding that his or her behavior influenced the choice. Learning to make choices should be a positive experience; thus, starting with two preferred options is usually favored. Partners analyze each routine to identify the options for choice-making that exist during a scheduled class period or school day (for more information, refer to Brown et al., 1993).

Daily routines and activities in the school setting have many opportunities for choice making. Brown et al. (1993) presented a model of *choice diversity* that expands traditional choice-making options by analyzing opportunities for choices within specific routines. Seven categories of choice are available within the context of most daily routines. These categories include offering choices between activities and within activities, as well as giving students choices of refusing an activity, of terminating an activity, and when, where, and with whom an activity is performed.

> *During a leisure activity routine, Marina can be given the opportunity to choose listening to music or to have a book read to her (a choice between two activities). If Marina chooses to listen to music, she can be given the opportunity within that activity to choose listening to either rock or country music (choice within activity). Marina can also be given the opportunity to choose where (either lying on the mat or sitting in a rocking chair) and with whom to listen to music (either with Paul or with her friend Jody). Marina could choose not to listen to music or be read a book (refusal) and choose to end the activity when she wants (terminate). The educational team decides which aspects of these options would be implemented in the leisure routine with Marina.*

Opportunities to Interact Providing opportunities for the learner to interact and communicate is a central strategy of intervention. The learner who is building intentional behavior will use nonsymbolic behavior to affect actions of people and the environment. Partners can provide opportunities for the learner to use their behaviors within natural routines or activities that occur. Nonsymbolic behaviors used purposefully in the early stages of intentionality generally include actions such as approaching or avoiding people, materials, or activities; contacting or pushing or pulling people, materials, or activities; smiling; and pointing. Partners will provide opportunities for the learner to use these behaviors.

The learner who communicates at a nonsymbolic level is limited to expressions focused on his or her current behavior state or on something that can be touched, looked at, or directly perceived. Opportunities are enhanced when the partner provides materials within interactions that can form concrete input to a learner and gives meaningful content to communicate about. The preintentional and intentional behaviors may appear very similar in form and may affect the partner similarly whether the expressions were reactions (perlocutionary, partner interpreted) or actions displayed intentionally by the learner to get desired effects from the partner (illocutionary, intentional).

Time Delay School staff partners can insert pauses (time delay) in interactions so that learners can initiate a change in the interchange, maintain the interchange, or terminate it. Giving learners clear opportunities (with a delay) for them to take "their turn" and emit an expression can be beneficial to learners at both the perlocutionary and the illocutionary stage.

At the perlocutionary stage, partners can help learners recognize that they have signals. Thus, partners convey information with the behaviors expressed by the individual.

> *At a snack table with Marina and other children, the juice pitcher is passed around the table. John (the SLP) used Marina's own behavior, fluttering his hands and saying, "Ahga," as the juice pitcher gets closer to him. To expand the communication opportunities, John increased his vocalizations and looked at Marina (pausing rather than pouring the juice). Marina then had an opportunity to jointly attend to the juice pitcher, request juice herself, or terminate the interaction.*

Sequencing Experiences

Learners at the perlocutionary level do not realize that they can control their own behaviors or that their behaviors affect a game or routine. However, sequencing experiences allows them to experience maintaining and terminating interactions. As learners develop more illocutionary skills, they anticipate steps in a sequence and initiate parts of a routine or game. The second guideline for enhancing the partner's nonsymbolic and symbolic expressions to the learner is to sequence experiences; three strategies are used: (a) encourage participation, (b) establish routines, and (c) provide turn-taking opportunities.

Participation Partners can analyze routines that are already familiar and provide a role for the learner in the sequential components. Partners may select dialogues, scripted routines, or routine components to help sequence the experiences for the learner and thus encourage more participation and communication.

Routines Routines such as self-care, leisure, and transition between activities and places provide redundancy and reoccurrence across the day. These recurring events across environments can be structured to encourage the learner to anticipate what may occur next. Planned "dialogues" (Siegel, in press; Siegel-Causey & Guess, 1989) can structure routines for the multiple partners so that communication is expected and consistent reciprocal roles between the learner and partners is promoted. (An example dialogue within a routine is provided later in this chapter [Table 11–11].) Similarly, "scripted routines" delineate the specific verbal and touch cues the partner should provide and the pauses and the precise actions of the partner within natural events (Beukelman & Mirenda, 1998).

Turn Taking Games and familiar routines often have a component of "your turn, my turn," which helps learners realize that they can express themselves.

> *Marina helps pour juice for the class with her friend Jody. Each time that Jody moves the pitcher forward, Marina moves a cup toward the pitcher. This interchange occurs repeatedly.*

Since many routines and games have built-in roles of receivers and senders of communication, *turn taking* can be enhanced and emphasized as well as combined with increased opportunities.

TABLE 11–11
Dialogue Before Snack in Marina's Classroom

This classroom has students with disabilities and typical peers who are 3 to 5 years of age. It is time for snack, and each student has a role. The teacher, Rachel, has paired Marina and Jody together for many classroom activities. Marina has missed school for the last month because of hospitalizations for extensive seizures. Jody is a typical peer, who is extremely quiet and reluctant to interact with other children. Rachel feels that Jody can benefit from helping Marina get back into the school routine and from having structured interactions to communication about.

Intervention guidelines and strategies	Interventionist	Learner and peer
Opportunity: Provide opportunities to interact	Rachel says to the group, "Class, it is time to prepare for snack. You will find a job and a partner on the snack picture board here." Rachel points to the bulletin board that displays photographs of student pairs and a photograph of the job each pair is to complete. "Who wants to find a job?" Rachel *pauses* and *looks* around the circle. A few students raise their hand, and Rachel calls them up to find their picture. "What job did Andy and Josh find?" Rachel extends the photo that Andy and Josh found under their pictures and shows it to the children. She pauses in front of Jody. "What job is in this picture?"	
		Jody whispers, "Tablecloth."
	"Great, Jody. That's right, it is a tablecloth. Pass the photo to Marina. Marina, get ready." Rachel knows that Jody will barely extend the photo to Marina. Thus, Marina will have to reach out to get it. Rachel wants Marina to practice reaching out for items so that she can learn that this is a good way to request things she wants.	
Sequencing: Encourage participation	"Where is the photo, Marina?" Rachel says as she *looks quizzically and extends her palms upwards.*	
		Marina looks at Rachel's hands and laughs.
Sensitivity: Respond to the individual's level of communication	"You're happy! Let's find the photo." Rachel *guides Jody to extend the photo toward Marina.*	
		Marina laughs again and reaches toward the photo that Jody has extended in front of her.
Sensitivity: Recognize nonsymbolic behavior	"*Marina, you want the photo!*" Rachel exclaims.	
		Marina takes the photo.
Augmenting: Enhance meaning	Rachel points out the tablecloth in the photo that Marina now holds and *gestures, as if laying it out* as she says, "Put out tablecloth?"	
		Marina touches the photo. Jody looks over at the snack area, where the tablecloths are stacked on a shelf.
Sensitivity: Recognize nonsymbolic behaviors	"*Yes, Jody, I see you looking at the snack area.* Andy and Josh are going to put the tablecloth out." Rachel continues to call students up to find their snack jobs on the photo board. Soon, it is Marina and Jody's turn.	
Sequencing: Encourage participation	"*Who wants a job?*"	
		Jody looks at the photos of her and Marina.
Sensitivity: Respond contingently	"*Right, Jody, your picture is still here,*" Rachel says as she points to the photos of Jody and Marina.	

TABLE 11–11 (*Continued*)

Intervention guidelines and strategies	Interventionist	Learner and peer
Sequencing: Encourage participation	"Who is in the picture with you?" Rachel *asks*.	
		Jody looks at Marina. *Marina laughs.*
Sequencing: Provide turn taking	Rachel *extends the photo* toward the girls.	
		Marina turns toward the photo.
Sensitivity: Recognize non-symbolic behaviors	*"Yes, Marina, this is your job,"* says Rachel.	
		Jody moves toward Rachel, and Marina crawls *to follow her. Jody takes the photo from Rachel.*
	Rachel encourages Jody to show the photo to Marina in the same manner as they did with the photo of the tablecloth.	
Sequencing: Encourage participation	Rachel asks, "*What job is in the picture?*"	
		Jody whispers, "Napkins."
Sensitivity: Respond to the individual's level of communication.	"Napkins!" Rachel *says* as she *gestures toward Jody and Marina and pretends to hand out napkins.*	
Augmenting: Enhance meaning		
		Jody watches. Marina laughs and touches *Rachel's hands.*
Opportunity: Provide opportunities to interact	"Marina, where are the napkins?" Rachel *asks as she shrugs her shoulders and looks around the room.*	
		Marina turns toward the shelves and begins to *crawl to them.*
Sensitivity: Respond contingently	*"Marina sees the napkins,"* Rachel says with a *loud and happy tone in her voice.* "Are you going to help with your job, Jody?" Jody slowly follows Marina to the shelf.	
		Marina giggles and watches Jody follow her.
	Rachel continues to guide the girls as needed to complete their job of putting out the napkins and encourages them to interact as opportunities arise.	

Augmenting Input

The last intervention guideline for enhancing the partners' nonsymbolic and symbolic expressions to the learner is to augment input by enhancing meaning and facilitating retention.

Enhance Meaning The use of verbal input paired or "augmented" with another mode of communication may improve the learner's understanding. This commonly used strategy may help learners receive information more clearly because verbal input is elaborated on with another mode (such as concrete gestures, touch cues, real objects, photographs, or pictures).

Facilitate Retention Learners have better recall of events and messages through objects, gestures, or photographs than simply another's words. Thus, object schedules or calendar boxes may facilitate a learner's recall and anticipation of familiar activities (Blaha, 2001; Downing, 1999; Rowland & Schweigert, 1990).

When it is time to go to physical education class (PE), the teacher says "line up at the door." Harris, a learner with autism, notices the movement of his classmates and picks up his pencil (the object that signals writing tasks he was working on). He walks over to his object schedule and puts the pencil in the "finished" box. The next object in his schedule boxes are two wristbands that signal PE class. Harris puts them on his wrists. These objects help Harris recall the next event in his day.

Intervention Guidelines to Enhance the Partner's Understanding of the Learner's Nonsymbolic Expression: Enhance Sensitivity

If partners don't know what learners are communicating, there is a breakdown. The key guideline for improving partners' understanding is for partners to become sensitive to the nonsymbolic expressions of learners. In the middle section of Figure 11-11, five strategies help partners concentrate on what learners do: (a) recognizing readiness for interaction, (b) recognizing nonsymbolic behaviors, (c) responding contingently, (d) responding to expressions and challenging behavior as communicative, and (e) responding to the individual's level of communication.

Recognize Readiness for Interaction The learner's assessment profile and gestural dictionary are not strategies per se but sets of information that equip partners with concrete ways to understand both what the learner expresses and the alert, responsive behaviors that can be responded to in a consistent manner. Recognizing these alert behavior states helps the partner notice the learner's *readiness* for interaction. Thus, sensitivity is enhanced by being familiar with the learner's range of communication forms and by assigning meaning to those expressions.

> *Paul, a school staff partner, waits for Chris to indicate interest in activating the switch (increasing opportunities to create a need for requests) (Figure 11-12). When Chris smiles and vocalizes at Paul (his signals that communicate behavior regulation and social interaction), Paul helps position Chris's arm so that he can more easily engage the switch (enhancing sensitivity by responding contingently).*

Recognize Nonsymbolic Behaviors At the perlocutionary stage, learners do not realize that their behaviors can affect others, so the intervention focus is on always noticing and responding to the learners' expressions. As learners express themselves in a more illocutionary manner (with intentionality), partners can note nonsymbolic behaviors that display a readiness for interaction and respond with expressions that

FIGURE 11-12
Paul is following the intervention guidelines and strategies to enhance Chris's communicative expressions.

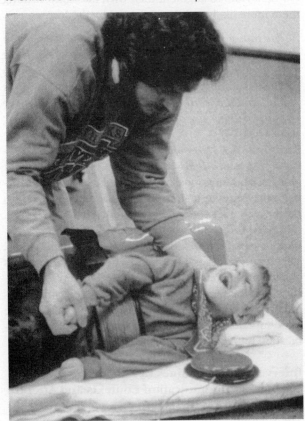

are at the same level. Regardless of the level of intentionality, partners can enhance their sensitivity to learner expressions and capitalize on opportunities for communication by thoroughly knowing the learner's current nonsymbolic behavior. Gestural dictionary (Beukelman & Mirenda, 1998) or communication dictionary (Siegel & Cress, 2002) is the best way to apply this strategy (Table 11-6 provides a format to report nonsymbolic and symbolic behavior).

Respond Contingently and at the Learner's Level of Communication Another aspect of being sensitive is for partners to *respond contingently* to nonsymbolic behaviors using a communicative level matched to the learner's understanding. Again, the dictionary is useful because it not only describes the learner's current forms of expression and their meanings but also gives suggestions for how to respond appropriately (what partners should consistently do). The dictionary also can guide partners to use the learners' behaviors to augment their own messages, making them more likely to be understood by the learner.

The music teacher, Anne, turns her head away from Ryan and says "no" to convey that she does not want to play the tambourine that is on the tray. Turning away is a nonsymbolic behavior Ryan uses to express "no," and the word "no" is a symbolic form that Anne pairs with her use of that nonsymbolic expression.

Respond to Expressions and Challenging Behavior as Communicative Behavior In the assessment of forms and functions, we described forms of challenging behavior (aggression, self-stimulation, self-abuse) as having potential communicative function (Table 11–8). As one considers intervention at the nonsymbolic level, partners should respond to all the learner's expressions. This includes assessing the function(s) of a learner's challenging behavior (escape, attention, tangible, sensory) and then responding to that communicative function by teaching an appropriate form that can serve the same function for the learner using functional communication training (chapter 6).

Intervention Guidelines to Enhance the Learner's Communication Contexts and Attend to Influences on the Learner's State Behavior

The final guideline in Figure 11–11 focuses on contexts and environment of the learner using the strategies of (a) attending to natural contexts and (b) modifying the environment.

Attend to Natural Contexts If interactions occur naturally or as part of daily activities and routines, then it is easier for partners to use the learner's communication interests and participation needs. At these times, partners embed their direct instruction, thereby highlighting for the learner the relationship of stimulus, response, and consequences (Noonan & Siegel, 2003). The milieu teaching techniques, described in chapters 12, embrace this approach by systematically teaching skills when they are needed and relevant.

Chris is relaxing on the floor after he has been taken out of his wheelchair for a short break. He notices the rest of his class putting away their materials. He vocalizes and moves his head toward the students' desks.

Paul sees Chris's communication and squats down near him on the floor. "I hear you Chris, what do you want?" and pauses, looking at Chris. Chris vocalizes again and scoots closer to his switch and puts his arm on it. Once activated, the Big-Mack switch relays "Help me." Paul responds to Chris's communication by saying, "OK, Chris, I'll give you a hand so you can be ready for story time," and initiates lifting him back into his wheelchair, which is positioned at the front of the room, where his peers are gathering to hear a story.

Physical Supports The partner may need to change the *physical supports* to increase the learner's performance. For example, physical supports that may enhance participation include adding interesting and manipulable materials, adapting the activity materials, or increasing personal assistance.

Social Supports Social supports may also enhance learner motivation and improve instruction. Examples include involving peers as facilitators, using group project activities, and teaching social communication strategies within the activity.

Modify the Environment Sometimes team members need to modify the environment so that the learner can interact with others in a functional manner while displaying more alert, responsive state behavior. Ault et al. (1995) validated techniques for improving alert, responsive behaviors and found three characteristics that most influenced responsive behaviors: (a) sensory qualities, (b) movement and orientation of the learner's body, and (c) learning atmosphere. These data suggest a direct relationship between changing environmental characteristics and influencing behavior state.

Adjust Sensory Qualities A range of sensory qualities can be modified: visual, auditory, tactile, gustatory, and olfactory stimuli. The partner determines whether certain features of sensory stimuli in the activity (or that could be added) would have an activating or soothing effect on the learner. For example, direct versus indirect light, materials highlighted with bright or neutral backgrounds, or a change from light to deep pressure may produce responsive behavior in the learner.

Alter Movement and Orientation Similarly, the partner can evaluate the effects of movement and orientation of the learner's body. Team members may consider tempo or movement of the learner's body parts or the learner's body tilt and position when on various adaptive equipment.

Change Learning Atmosphere The final consideration involves assessing the *learning atmosphere*. For example, what effects do secondary noise, location changes, and nearby activity level have on an individual learner? Making minor changes or manipulations in these environmental characteristics can easily be implemented within an activity in conjunction with partner strategies from this chapter (for more, refer to Ault et al., 1995).

Using the Intervention Guidelines: Examples

Intervention guidelines should be incorporated into natural routines, as displayed in the photo sequence in Figure 11–13.

> *Jona, a paraeducator, tells Chris that it is time for music. She waits for his vocal and hand movements that signal that he agrees, then she picks him up. Once he is face to face, she asks who he wants for a music buddy, says the name of two peers, and then repeats their names, pausing after each name for his response. He vocalizes to choose one peer, and she places him in his chair. She pauses before strapping his feet and looks at him; this is Chris's cue to move his foot into place; Jona thanks him.*

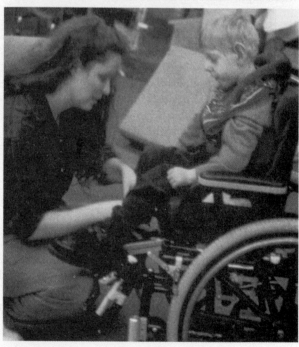

FIGURE 11–13
Jona, an interventionist, uses intervention strategies within the naturally occurring event of moving Chris to a new position.

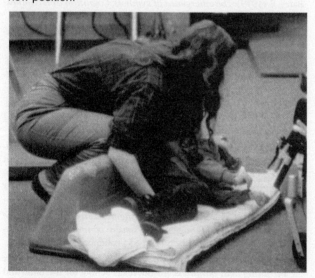

The dialogue in Table 11-11 illustrates ways to incorporate intervention into the daily context of interactions. The left-hand column of this table identifies partner behaviors and the intervention guideline or strategy being used. The italics in the middle column denote the partner's use of a specific intervention within the dialogue. Italics in the learner and peer column designate their communications.

Summary

The assessment and intervention methods in this chapter can help school staff members become effective communication partners with the learners who use nonsymbolic communication. Researchers and practitioners in the field of severe disabilities and speech-language pathology have only begun to recognize the broad spectrum of communication intervention needs of individuals who have disabilities. A new emphasis on and inclusion of instructional methods and procedures for enhancing the primary repertoire of communication forms a foundation for the development of symbolic and augmentative communication. The goal is to use methods that incorporate students' nonsymbolic skills and to build on their repertoires of communication skills so that they can understand and use more sophisticated symbolic skills.

Suggested Activities

1. Select a learner who uses primarily nonsymbolic communication. Write down the activities that occur with partners (peers or adults). Select one activity that you participate in and analyze the interaction using the following table:

Learner Behavior	What I Think it Means	How I Respond	Effectiveness of Interaction	Possible Changes

What intervention strategies will you apply based on your analysis?
2. Think about your personal style of interacting with learners who have severe disabilities.
   a. Pick one of these learners.
   b. Who are his or her favorite peers?

c. Who are his or her favorite adults?
d. What information can you gather that will help determine what interactional style this learner prefers?
e. What is your interaction style, and how does it match the learner's preferences?
3. Select a learner and an activity that you engage in with that learner. Analyze the activity in terms of the naturally occurring opportunities for the learner to communicate. Which opportunities do you respond to? Are there any opportunities that you inadvertently preempt? Write a dialogue to enhance the activity.

References

Alwell, M., Hunt, P., Goetz, L., & Sailor, W. (1989). Teaching generalized communicative behaviors within interrupted behavior chain contexts. *Journal of the Association for Persons with Severe Handicaps, 14,* 91-100.

Ault, M. M., Guy, B., Guess, D., Bashinski, S., & Roberts, S. (1995). Analyzing behavior state and learning environments: Application in instructional settings. *Mental Retardation, 33,* 304-316.

Austin, J. (1962). *How to do things with words.* Cambridge, MA: Harvard University Press.

Bambara, L. M., & Koger, F. (1996). *Opportunities for daily choice making.* Washington, DC: American Association on Mental Retardation.

Bannerman, D. J., Sheldon, J. B., Sherman, J. A., & Harchik, A. E. (1990). Balancing the right to habilitation with the right to personal liberties: The rights of people with developmental disabilities to eat too many doughnuts and take a nap. *Journal of Applied Behavior Analysis, 23,* 78-89.

Bates, E. (1979). *The emergence of symbols: Cognition and communication in infancy.* New York: Academic Press.

Bates, E., Camaioni, L., & Volterra, V. (1975). The acquisition of performatives prior to speech. *Merrill-Palmer Quarterly, 21,* 205-226.

Bates, E., O'Connell, B., & Shore, C. (1987). Language and communication in infancy. In J. Osofsky (Ed.), *Handbook of infant development* (pp. 149-203). New York: Wiley.

Bates, E., & Snyder, L. (1987). The cognitive hypothesis in language development. In I. Uzgiris & J. Hunt (Eds.), *Infant performance and experience* (pp. 168-204). Chicago: University of Illinois Press.

Bedrosian, J. L. (1988). Adults with mildly to moderately severe mental retardation: Communicative performance, assessment and intervention. In S. N. Calculator & J. L. Bedrosian (Eds.), *Communication assessment and intervention strategies* (pp. 265-307). Boston: College-Hill.

Beukelman, D. R., & Mirenda, P. (1998). *Augmentative and alternative communication: Management of severe communication disorders in children and adults* (2nd ed.) Baltimore: Paul H. Brookes.

Blaha, R. (2001). *Calendars for students with multiple impairments including deaf blindness.* Austin: Texas School for the Blind and Visually Impaired.

Bloom, L. (1993). *The transition from infancy to language.* New York: Cambridge University Press.

Brady, N. C., & Halle, J. W. (1997). Functional analysis of communicative behaviors. *Focus on Autism and Other Developmental Disabilities, 12*(2), 95-104.

Brady, N. C., McLean, J. E., McLean, L. K., & Johnston, S. (1995). Initiation and repair of intentional communication acts by adults with severe to profound cognitive disabilities. *Journal of Speech and Hearing Research, 38,* 1334-1348.

Brown, F., Belz, P., Corsi, L., & Wenig, B. (1993). Choice diversity for people with severe disabilities. *Education and Training in Mental Retardation, 28,* 318-326.

Bruner, J. (1978). From communication to language: A psychological perspective. In I. Markova (Ed.), *The social context of language* (pp. 17-48). New York: Wiley.

Bruner, J. (1981). The social context of language acquisition. *Language and Communication, 1,* 155-178.

Bruner, J., & Sherwood, V. (1976). Early rule structure: The case of peekaboo. In J. Bruner, A. Jolly, & K. Sylva (Eds.), *Play: Its role in evolution and development* (pp. 277-285). London: Penguin.

Calculator, S. N. (1988). Exploring the language of adults with mental retardation. In S. N. Calculator & J. L. Bedrosian (Eds.), *Communication assessment and intervention strategies* (pp. 523-547). Baltimore: University Park Press.

Carr, E. G., & Durand, V. M. (1985). Reducing behavior problems through functional communication training. *Journal of Applied Behavior Analysis, 18,* 111-126.

Carr, E. G., Levin, L., McConnachie, G., Carlson, J., Kemp, D., & Smith, C. (1994). *Communication-based intervention for problem behavior: A user's guide for producing positive change.* Baltimore: Paul H. Brookes.

Chapman, R. (1978). Comprehension strategies in children. In J. Kavanagh & W. Stragne (Eds.), *Speech and language in the laboratory, school and clinic* (pp. 308-330). Cambridge, MA: MIT Press.

Cirrin, F., & Rowland, C. (1985). Communicative assessment of nonverbal youths with severe/profound mental retardation. *Mental Retardation, 23,* 52-62.

Clayton-Smith, J., & Pembrey, M. E. (1992). Angelman syndrome. *Journal of Medical Genetics, 29,* 412-415.

Coggins, T., & Carpenter, R. (1981). The communicative intention inventory: A system for observing and coding children's early intentional communication. *Applied Psycholinguistics, 2,* 235-251.

Corsaro, W. (1981). The development of social cognition in preschool children: Implications for language learning. *Topics in Language Disorders, 2,* 77-95.

Dooley, J., Berg, J., Pakula, Z., & MacGregor, D. (1981). The puppet-like syndrome of Angelman. *American Journal of Disordered Children, 135,* 621-624.

Dore, J. (1986). The development of conversation competence. In R. Scheifelbusch (Ed.), *Language competence: Assessment and intervention* (pp. 3-60). San Diego: College-Hill.

Downing, J. E. (1999). *Teaching communication skills to students with severe disabilities.* Baltimore: Paul H. Brookes.

Duchan, J. (1995). *Supporting language learning in everyday life.* San Diego: Singular.

Dunst, C., Lowe, L. W., & Bartholomew, P. C. (1990). Contingent social responsiveness, family ecology, and infant communicative competence. *National Student Speech Language Hearing Association Journal, 17,* 39-49.

Durand, V. M., & Crimmins, D. B. (1992). *The motivation assessment scale (MAS) administration guide.* Topeka, KS: Monaco.

Girolametto, L. E., Greenberg, J., & Manolson, H. A. (1986). Developing dialogue skills: The Hanen early language parent program. *Seminars in Speech and Language, 7,* 367-382.

Goetz, L., Gee, K., & Sailor, W. (1985). Using a behavior chain interruption strategy to teach communication skills to students with severe disabilities. *Journal of the Association for Persons with Severe Handicaps, 10,* 21-30.

Guess, D., Benson, H. A., & Siegel-Causey, E. (1985). Concepts and issues related to choice making and autonomy among persons with severe disabilities. *Journal of the Association for Persons with Severe Handicaps, 10,* 79-86.

Guess, D., Roberts, S., Siegel-Causey, E., Ault, M. M., Guy, B., Thompson, B., et al. (1991). Investigations into the state behaviors of students with severe and profound handicapping conditions (Monograph No. 1). Lawrence, KS: University of Kansas Department of Special Education.

Guess, D., Roberts, S., Siegel-Causey, E., Ault, M. M., Guy, B., Thompson, B., et al. (1993). An analysis of behavior state conditions and associated environmental variables among students with profound handicaps. *American Journal on Mental Retardation, 97,* 634-653.

Guess, D., Roberts, S., Siegel-Causey, E., & Rues, J. (1995). Replication and extended analysis of behavior state, environmental events, and related variables in profound disabilities. *American Journal on Mental Retardation, 100,* 36-51.

Guess, D., Siegel-Causey, E., Roberts, S., Guy, B., Ault, M. M., & Rues, J. (1993). Analysis of state organizational patterns among students with profound disabilities. *Journal of the Association for Persons with Severe Handicaps, 18,* 93-108.

Guess, D., Siegel-Causey, E., Roberts, S., Rues, J., Thompson, B., & Siegel-Causey, D. (1990). Assessment and analysis of behavior state and related variables among students with profoundly handicapping conditions. *Journal of the Association for Persons with Severe Handicaps, 15,* 211-230.

Guy, B., Guess, D., & Ault, M. M. (1993). Classroom procedures for the measurement of behavior state among students with profound disabilities. *Journal of the Association for Persons with Severe Handicaps, 18,* 52-60.

Halle, J. (1984). Arranging the natural environment to occasion language: Giving severely language-delayed children reason to communicate. *Seminars in Speech and Language, 5*(3), 185-197.

Halle, J. W., Marshall, A. M., & Spradlin, J. E. (1979). Time delay: A technique to increase language use and facilitate generalization in retarded children. *Journal of Applied Behavior Analysis, 12,* 431-439.

Harding, C. (1984). Acting with intention: A framework for examining the development of the intention to communicate. In L. Feagans, C. Garvey, & R. Golinkoff (Eds.), *The origins and growth of communication* (pp. 123-135). Norwood, NJ: Ablex.

Harding, C., & Golinkoff, R. (1979). The origins of intentional vocalizations in prelinguistic infants. *Child Development, 50,* 33-40.

Hart, B., & Risley, T. R. (1975). Incidental teaching of language in the preschool. *Journal of Applied Behavioral Analysis, 8,* 411–420.

Harwood, J., Warren, S. F., & Yoder, P. (2002). The importance of responsivity in developing contingent exchanges with beginning communicators. In J. Reichle, D. R. Beukelman, & J. Light (Eds.), *Exemplary practices for beginning communicators* (pp. 59–95). Baltimore: Paul H. Brookes.

Horner, R. H., O'Neill, R. E., & Albin, R. W. (1991). *Supporting students with high intensity problem behavior.* Unpublished manuscript, University of Oregon, Eugene.

Hunt, P., Goetz, L., Alwell, M., & Sailor, W. (1986). Using an interrupted behavior chain strategy to teach generalized communication responses. *Journal of the Association for Persons with Severe Handicaps, 11,* 196–204.

Kublin, K. S., Wetherby, A. M., Crais, E. R., & Prizant, B. M. (1998). Using dynamic assessment within collaborative contexts: The transition from intentional to symbolic communication. In A. Wetherby, S. Warren, & J. Reichle (Eds.), *Transitions in prelinguistic communication* (pp. 285–312). Baltimore: Paul H. Brookes.

Lifter, K., & Bloom, L. (1998). Intentionality and the role of play in the transition to language. In A. Wetherby, S. Warren, & J. Reichle (Eds.), *Transitions in prelinguistic communication* (pp. 161–195). Baltimore: Paul H. Brookes.

MacDonald, J. D. (1985). Language through conversation. In S. Warren & A. Rogers-Warren (Eds.), *Teaching functional language* (pp. 89–122). Baltimore: University Park Press.

MacDonald, J. D. (1989). *Becoming partners with children: From play to conversations.* Chicago: Riverside.

MacDonald, J., & Carroll, J. (1992). Communicating with young children: An ecological model for clinicians, parents, and collaborative professionals. *American Journal of Speech-Language Pathology, 1,* 39–48.

McLean, J., McLean, L., Brady, N., & Etter, R. (1991). Communication profiles of two types of gesture using nonverbal persons with severe to profound mental retardation. *Journal of Speech and Hearing Research, 34,* 294–308.

McLean, J., & Snyder-McLean, L. (1978). *A transactional approach to early language training.* New York: Merrill/Macmillan.

McLean, J., & Snyder-McLean, L. (1988). Applications of pragmatics to severely mentally retarded children and youth. In R. L. Schiefelbusch & L. L. Lloyd (Eds.), *Language perspectives: Acquisition, retardation and intervention* (pp. 255–288). Austin, TX: PRO-ED.

McLean, J., & Snyder-McLean, L. (1999). *How children learn language.* San Diego: Singular.

Miller, J., & Paul, R. (1995). *The clinical assessment of language comprehension.* Baltimore: Paul H. Brookes.

Mirenda, P. (1988, August). *Instructional techniques for communication.* Paper presented at the Annual Augmentative and Alternative Communication for Students with Severe Disabilities Special Education Innovative Institute, Fremont, CA.

Mirenda, P. L., & Donnellan, A. M. (1986). Effects of adult interaction style on conversational behavior in students with severe communication problems. *Language, Speech and Hearing Services in the Schools, 17,* 126–141.

Musselwhite, C. R., & St. Louis, K. W. (1988). *Communication programming for persons with severe handicaps: Vocal and augmentative strategies* (2nd ed.). San Diego: College-Hill.

National Joint Committee for Communication of Persons with Severe Disabilities. (1992). Bill of rights. Retrieved January 5, 2004, from **http://www.asha.org/njc/bill_of_rights.htm**

Noonan, M. J., & Siegel, E. (2003). Special needs of young children with severe handicaps. In L. McCormick, D. Loeb, & R. Schiefelbusch (Eds.), *Supporting children with communication difficulties in inclusive settings: School-based language intervention* (2nd ed., pp. 405–432). Boston: Allyn & Bacon.

Ogletree, B., Wetherby, A., & Westling, D. (1992). A profile of the prelinguistic intentional communicative behaviors of children with profound mental retardation. *American Journal on Mental Retardation, 97,* 186–196.

O'Neill, R. E., Horner, R. H., Albin, R. W., Sprague, J. R., Storey, K., & Newton, J. S. (1997). *Functional assessment and program development for problem behavior: A practical handbook.* Pacific Grove, CA: Brookes/Cole.

O'Neill, R., Vaughn, B., & Dunlap, G. (1998). Comprehensive behavioral support: Assessment issues and strategies. In A. Wetherby, S. Warren, & J. Reichle (Eds.), *Transitions in prelinguistic communication* (pp. 313–341). Baltimore: Paul H. Brookes.

Peck, C. A. (1989). Assessment of social communicative competence: Evaluating environments. *Seminars in Speech and Language, 10,* 1–15.

Peck, C. A., & Schuler, A. L. (1987). Assessment of social/communicative behavior for students with autism and severe handicaps: The importance of asking the right question. In T. L. Layton (Ed.), *Language and treatment of autistic and developmentally disordered children* (pp. 35–62). Springfield, IL: Charles C Thomas.

Piaget, J. (1952). *The origins of intelligence in children.* New York: Basic Books.

Prizant, B., & Wetherby, A. (1990). Assessing the communication of infants and toddlers: Integrating a socioemotional perspective. *Zero to Three, 11,* 1–12.

Rainforth, B. (1982). Biobehavioral state and orienting: Implications for educating profoundly retarded students. *Journal of the Association for the Severely Handicapped, 6,* 33–37.

Reichle, J., & Wacker, D. (Eds.). (1993). *Communication and language intervention series: Vol. 3. Communicative alternatives to challenging behavior: Integrating functional assessment and intervention strategies.* Baltimore: Paul H. Brookes.

Rice, M. (1983). Contemporary account of the cognition/language relationship: Implications for speech-language clinicians. *Journal of Speech and Hearing Disorders, 48,* 347–359.

Rice, M. L., & Kemper, S. (1984). *Child language and cognition: Contemporary issues.* Baltimore: University Park Press.

Richards, S., & Richards, R. (1997). Implications for assessing biobehavioral states in individuals with profound disabilities. *Focus on Autism and Other Developmental Disabilities, 12*(2), 79–86.

Richards, S. B., & Sternberg, L. (1992). A preliminary analysis of environmental variables affecting the observed biobehavioral states of individuals with profound handicaps. *Journal of Intellectual Disability Research, 36,* 403–414.

Richards, S. B., & Sternberg, L. (1993). Corroborating previous findings: Laying stepping stones in the analysis of biobehavioral states in students with profound disabilities. *Education and Training in Mental Retardation, 28,* 262–268.

Romski, M.A., & Sevcik, R.A. (1993). Language learning through augmented means: The process and its products. In A. Kaiser & D. Gray (Eds.), *Enhancing children's communication: Research foundations for intervention* (pp. 85–104). Baltimore: Paul H. Brookes.

Rowland, C., & Schweigert, P. (1990). *Tangible symbol systems: Symbolic communication for individuals with multisensory impairments.* Tucson, AZ: Communication Skill Builders.

Rowland, C., Schweigert, P. D., & Prickett, J. G. (1995). Communication systems, devices, and modes. In K. M. Huebner, J. G. Prichett, T. R. Welsch, & E. Joffee (Eds.), *Hand in hand: Essentials of communication and orientation and mobility for your students who are deaf-blind* (pp. 219–259). New York: American Foundation for the Blind.

Rowland, C., & Stremel-Campbell, K. (1987). Share and share alike: Conventional gestures to emergent language for learners with sensory impairments. In L. Goetz, D. Guess, & K. Stremel-Campbell (Eds.), *Innovative program design for individuals with dual sensory impairments* (pp. 49–75). Baltimore: Paul H. Brookes.

Siegel, E. (in press). *Enhancing nonsymbolic communication for learners with severe disabilities and autism.* Baltimore: Paul H. Brookes.

Siegel, E., & Cress, C. (2002). Overview of the emergence of early AAC behaviors: Progression from communicative to symbolic skills. In J. Reichle, D. R. Beukelman, & J. Light (Eds.), *Exemplary practices for beginning communicators* (pp. 25–57). Baltimore: Paul H. Brookes.

Siegel-Causey, E., & Bashinski, S. (1997). Enhancing initial communication and responsiveness of learners with multiple disabilities: A tri-focus framework for partners. *Focus on Autism and Other Developmental Disabilities, 12*(2), 105–120.

Siegel-Causey, E., & Downing, J. (1987). Nonsymbolic communication development: Theoretical concepts and educational strategies. In L. Goetz, D. Guess, & K. Stremel-Campbell (Eds.), *Innovative program design for individuals with dual sensory impairments* (pp. 15–48). Baltimore: Paul H. Brookes.

Siegel-Causey, E., Ernst, B., & Guess, D. (1987). Elements of nonsymbolic communication and early interactional processes. In M. Bullis (Ed.), *Communication development in young children with deaf-blindness: Literature review III* (pp. 57–102). Monmouth, OR: Communication Skills Center for Young Children with Deaf-Blindness.

Siegel-Causey, E., Ernst, B., & Guess, D. (1989). Nonsymbolic communication in early interactional processes. In M. Bullis (Ed.), *Communication development in young children with deaf-blindness: Literature review IV* (pp. 69–122). Monmouth, OR: Communication Skills Center for Young Children with Deaf-Blindness.

Siegel-Causey, E., & Guess, D. (Eds.). (1989). *Enhancing nonsymbolic communication interactions among learners with severe handicaps.* Baltimore: Paul H. Brookes.

Snell, M. E. (2002). Using dynamic assessment with learners who communicate nonsymbolically. *Alternative and Augmentative Communication, 18,* 163–176.

Snell, M. E., Caves, K., McLean, L., Mineo Mollica, B., Mirenda, P., Paul-Brown, D., et al. (2003). Concerns regarding the application of restrictive "eligibility" policies to individuals who need communication services and supports. *Research and Practice for Persons with Severe Disabilities, 28,* 70–78.

Snyder-McLean, L. K., Solomonson, B., McLean, J. E., & Sack S. (1984). Structuring joint-action routines for facilitating communication and language development in the classroom. *Seminars in Speech and Language, 5*(3), 213–228.

Stillman, R., & Siegel-Causey, E. (1989). Introduction to nonsymbolic communication. In E. Siegel-Causey & D. Guess (Eds.), *Enhancing nonsymbolic communication interaction among learners with severe disabilities* (pp. 1–13). Baltimore: Paul H. Brookes.

Stremel-Campbell, K., & Rowland, C. (1987). Prelinguistic communication intervention: Birth-to-2. *Topics in Early Childhood Special Education, 7*(2), 49–58.

Wacker, D. P., Steege, M.W., Northup, J., Sasso, G., Berg, W., Reimers, T., et al. (1990). A component analysis of functional communication training across three topographies of severe behavior problems. *Journal of Applied Behavior Analysis, 23,* 417–429.

Warren, S. F., McQuarter, R. J., & Rogers-Warren, A. K. (1984). The effects of mands and models on the speech of unresponsive socially isolated children. *Journal of Speech and Hearing Disorders, 47,* 42–52.

Wetherby, A., Alexander, D., & Prizant, B. (1998). The ontogeny and role of repair strategies. In A. Wetherby, S. Warren, & J. Reichle (Eds.), *Transitions in prelinguistic communication* (pp. 135–160). Baltimore: Paul H. Brookes.

Wetherby, A., Cain, D., Yonclas, D., & Walker, V. (1988). Analysis of intentional communication of normal children from the prelinguistic to the multi-word stage. *Journal of Speech and Hearing Research, 31,* 240–252.

Wetherby, A., & Prizant, B. (1989). The expression of communicative intent: Assessment issues. *Seminars in Speech and Language, 10,* 77–91.

Wetherby, A., & Prizant, B. (1992). Profiling young children's communicative competence. In S. Warren & J. Reichle (Eds.), *Causes and effects in language assessment and intervention* (pp. 217–253). Baltimore: Paul H. Brookes.

Wetherby, A., & Prizant, B. (1993). *Communication and symbolic behavior scales—Normed edition.* Chicago: Applied Symbolix.

Wetherby, A., & Prizant, B. (1997). Communication, language, and speech disorders in young children. In S. Greenspan, J. Osofsky, & S. Wieder (Eds.), *Handbook of child and adolescent psychiatry* (pp. 473–491). New York: Wiley.

Wetherby, A., Prizant, B., & Hutchinson, T. (1998). Communicative, social-affective, and symbolic profiles of young children with autism and pervasive developmental disorder. *American Journal of Speech-Language Pathology, 7,* 79–91.

Wetherby, A., & Prutting, C. (1984). Profiles of communicative and cognitive-social abilities in autistic children. *Journal of Speech and Hearing Research, 27,* 364–377.

Wetherby, A., Reichle, J., & Pierce, P. (1998). The transition to symbolic communication. In A. M. Wetherby, S. F. Warren, & J. Reichle (Eds.), *Transitions in Prelinguistic Communication* (pp. 197–230). Baltimore: Paul H. Brookes.

Wetherby, A., & Rodriguez, G. (1992). Measurement of communicative intentions during structured and unstructured contexts. *Journal of Speech and Hearing Research, 35,* 130–138.

Wetherby, A., Warren, S., & Reichle, J. (Eds.). (1998). *Communication and language intervention series: Vol. 7. Transitions in prelinguistic communication.* Baltimore: Paul H. Brookes.

Wetherby, A., Yonclas, D., & Bryan, A. (1989). Communicative profiles of handicapped preschool children: Implications for early identification. *Journal of Speech and Hearing Disorders, 54,* 148-158.

Williams, C., & Frais, J. (1982). The Angelman ("happy puppet") syndrome. *American Journal of Medical Genetics, 11,* 453-460.

Wood, L., Lasker, J., Siegel-Causey, E., Beukelman, D., & Ball, L. (1998). Input framework for augmentative and alternative communication. *Augmentative and Alternative Communication, 14,* 261-267.

Writer, J. (1987). A movement-based approach to the education of students who are sensory impaired/multihandicapped. In L. Goetz, D. Guess, & K. Stremel-Campbell (Eds.), *Innovative program design for individuals with dual sensory impairments* (pp. 191-223). Baltimore: Paul H. Brookes.

Yoder, P., Warren, S., McCathren, R., & Leew, S. (1998). Does adult responsivity to child behavior facilitate communication development? In A. M. Wetherby, S. F. Warren, & J. Reichle (Eds.), *Transitions in prelinguistic communication* (pp. 39-58). Baltimore: Paul H. Brookes.

12

Teaching Functional Communication Skills

Ann P. Kaiser
Joan C. Grim

Communication skills are essential for everyday social and learning interactions. Most students with severe disabilities need systematic instruction to learn communication forms and strategies that are easily understood by others. Efficiently teaching functional skills so that students can participate in everyday interactions is the primary goal for systematic instruction in communication. Functional communication skills are dependable, consistent forms used in a manner that informs listeners of students' needs, wants, interests, and feelings. Such skills may take many different forms, including words, phrases and sentences, signs, gestures, and the use of augmentative devices. Functional communication skills allow students to participate in social interactions by giving them a means to express their intentions and to respond to others. For the majority of learners with severe disabilities, functional communication skills are acquired most easily when they are taught in everyday interactions and routines to achieve specific social goals with familiar conversational partners.

Naturalistic Approaches to Teaching Communication

During the past three decades, naturalistic strategies for teaching functional communication have been demonstrated to be effective for increasing everyday communication by students with severe disabilities across school, home, and work settings. Naturalistic teaching strategies begin with the student's intention to communicate and systematically provide models of appropriate communication forms and meaningful social consequences for communication attempts. These strategies are designed to teach new forms of language while simultaneously promoting social communication in everyday conversational contexts. By embedding instruction in ongoing interactions and everyday activities, students may immediately use the forms being taught to express their needs and wants and experience the functional consequences of their communication (see Table 12-1).

447

TABLE 12–1
Key Terms

Key terms	Definition	Examples
Functional communication	Communication acts that have the intended effect on the listener; that is, acts that achieve the goals of the speaker by gaining the desired response from others. Any communicative act, in any mode, can be functional, depending on the response of the communication partner.	• Student verbally requests assistance • Student points to picture for "help" • Student signs "help" and adult responds with indicated assistance
Form	The mode of communication and, within modes, the topography and systematic organization of symbol or sign use.	• Words • Signs • Grammar • Computer vocal output • Pictures
Function	The social purpose of a communication event and, especially, the actual effect of the individual's communicative act. Function is established by the consequences experienced by the communicator. Functional communication has the intended effect on the listener.	• Greeting • Protest • Comment • Agree
Naturalistic communication intervention strategies	Techniques for teaching communication in the context of ongoing daily activities, using the social and physical context, the need for communication, and natural consequences as an integral part of the teaching episode. Teaching is incidental, dispersed across the day, and embedded in activities rather than occurring in massed practice trials for specifically teaching a skill.	• Responsive interaction • Milieu teaching • Enhanced milieu teaching • Prelinguistic milieu teaching • Incidental teaching
Social communication	Exchange of information, including expression and understanding of expressed needs, wants, and feelings, between two persons.	• Verbal conversations • Hugging • Mutual gaze • Gesturing that is understood by partner
Augmentative and alternative communication (AAC)	Use of an integrated system of components (symbols, aids, strategies, and techniques) to support communication by persons with severe impairments in verbal communication. The system may include visual, auditory, or tactile representations of concepts and includes gestural communication; multimodal communication is most common.	• Gestures • Signs • Pictures • Printed words • Computer-based technologies • Using any of the above with speech

Naturalistic teaching is grounded in social communication. That is, teaching occurs when two persons have a shared goal of exchanging information within a social interaction. One person (e.g., the teacher) supports social communication or the construction of a shared meaning by conversational partners in a communicative interaction by modeling, prompting, or cuing communication for the less skilled partner. Typically, social communication is verbal and linguistic (i.e., uses words and sentences), but communication can also be nonverbal, symbolic, or gestural. Naturalistic teaching supports effective social communication by responding to and expanding the students' current form and mode of communication. Thus, students' use of words, signs, natural gestures, or simple or complex augmented communication modes will be responded to with meaningful communication, and models of more complex forms will be provided. The goal of naturalistic teaching is to make the student's current form of communication functional in the ongoing interaction and also to provide models of more complex forms. Sharing information and sustaining meaningful interaction between partners co-occur with instruction about communication form. Thus, naturalistic teaching emphasizes both function and form while using everyday communicative context for teaching.

Naturalistic approaches to teaching communication skills build on principles of behavioral teaching technology that have been used to teach specific skills to individuals with limited language for more than 30 years. Teaching functional communication skills to students with severe disabilities requires an approach to

intervention that emphasizes useful communication and promotes generalization and maintenance of newly learned skills. Limited generalization is a major barrier to acquisition of a functional communication repertoire (Kaiser, Hester, & McDuffie, 2001). Both longitudinal analysis (Warren & Rogers-Warren, 1983) and specific experimental analyses (Anderson & Spradlin, 1980) have demonstrated that limited generalization of newly learned language skills by individuals with severe disabilities is a typical training outcome when training occurs outside the settings where the newly learned skills are required.

 Case Studies

Lizabeth

Lizabeth is a 4-year-old with autism. At this time, she has no spoken words but is learning to use the Picture Exchange Communication System (PECS) to signal her requests to her teachers. She has learned to use pictures to request her favorite stuffed toy, food, or activity; to ask for help; to indicate she needs to use the bathroom; and to say no. She will soon be learning to use more pictures for other preferred items and activities. Lizabeth has attended a preschool sponsored by her family's church since age 3. She is the only child with a disability in a class of 12 children. An itinerant special education teacher visits the classroom 4 days a week, and a speech-language pathologist (SLP) visits 2 days a week. Both work with Lizabeth in the classroom. The special education teacher consults with the SLP and the two classroom teachers. The two most challenging issues for her teachers are understanding Lizabeth's needs and wants and engaging her in the activities of the classroom.

Kristi

Kristi is a bright-eyed 9-year-old with a charming smile and lots of energy. She is a full participant in the third-grade classroom she attends in her neighborhood school. Along with 20 other children, she receives academic instruction that is designed to fit her developmental needs in the context of cooperative learning groups, individualized tutoring, and classroom activities. Kristi's special education teacher collaborates with her classroom teacher in planning and implementing instruction. In addition, Kristi works with an SLP and a physical therapist 3 days each week. Kristi has multiple disabilities: a vision impairment corrected with glasses, a moderate level of motor control that limits her mobility, and cognitive delays. Although she is socially engaging and frequently smiles and gestures at adults and peers, her formal communication skills are limited. Only when prompted does Kristi currently

use the four pictures on her StepTalk™ (Voice Output Communication Aide, VOCA) that she learned in one-to-one training with her speech therapist. Kristi does not yet use the device with peers or initiate communication. Her parents are interested in learning ways to facilitate her use of the VOCA at home, and her teachers want to enhance her participation.

Carter

Carter is a 10-year-old boy with autism. His spoken language is limited to one- and two-word utterances, but he understands longer sentences if the topic is concrete. Carter's favorite activities include visiting his grandparents and looking at family picture albums. He is a fan of all kinds of sports, and he likes to throw a football with his older brother. Carter is sometimes echoic (e.g., repeats the last word or two) of phrases directed to him. His mother, Catherine, has been taught to use responsive interaction and milieu teaching during interactions with him at home. She is careful to respond to Carter's verbal and nonverbal initiations, expand his utterances into short sentences, and prompt him to verbalize choices when appropriate.

Michael

Michael is a 15-year-old student with mental retardation and a moderate hearing loss. He uses a wheelchair. His communication skills include single words and two-word phrases. He struggles to articulate sounds clearly because of his hearing loss. It is important to maintain face-to-face visual contact with Michael when speaking to him so that he can see as well as hear what is being said. Michael uses a DynaMyte™ (an electronic VOCA with three levels) and his voice, especially with peers who have difficulty understanding him. Michael is socially responsive to peers and enjoys participating in a variety of activities.

Michael is enrolled in a multiability, prevocational high school program where much of the instruction takes place in community settings. Michael has several different teachers across a typical school day. His teachers and SLP work together to individualize his vocational and academic instruction to fit his communication abilities.

For students like Kristi and Lizabeth, emphasizing functional communication skills translates into (a) selecting an alternative mode of communication (e.g., a VOCA or the PECS book) (Frost & Bondy, 1994, 1996) that is easier for them to acquire than the verbal mode, (b) teaching responses that have an immediate use in indicating needs and wants, and (c) providing specific training to promote generalized use of new skills in everyday conversational contexts. To ensure that skills are functional and generalized, training occurs in several different settings where communication is needed. Dinner at home, recess on the playground with peers, lunch in the cafeteria, and bus rides to school are settings for training in addition to the regular education classroom and the speech therapy room. Teaching[1] communication is a collaborative process, involving regular and special educators, SLPs, other professionals, family members, and peers and friends who are conversational partners. Before teaching new skills, the team must assess the student's needs for communication and the demands for communication across settings.

Overview of Enhanced Milieu Teaching

This chapter discusses one method of naturalistic teaching, enhanced milieu teaching (EMT) (Kaiser, 1993). EMT is the third generation of naturalistic teaching strategies. It builds on the principles of incidental teaching (Hart & Risley, 1968) and milieu teaching (Hart & Rogers-Warren, 1978) and adds systematic principles for responsive conversational style. EMT is a naturalistic approach to teaching communication skills

in everyday communication contexts based on (a) responding to the meaning of students' communication while providing models of elaborated communication, (b) embedding supportive prompts for elaborated communication within ongoing social interactions, and (c) providing functional consequences for students' communicative attempts. Figure 12–1 provides a schematic overview of the components of milieu teaching procedures.

Three Naturalistic Strategies

EMT was designed for use in everyday communication environments by teachers, SLPs, other educational team members, and parents and adult family members. EMT shares an emphasis on social interaction with at least two other prominent naturalistic teaching

FIGURE 12–1
EMT Overview

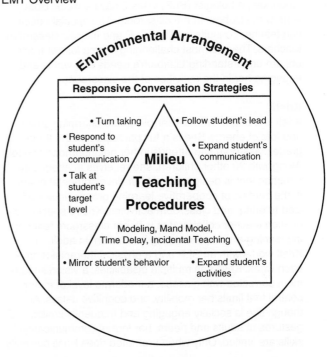

---

[1]Throughout this chapter, the term "teachers" is used to include any adult who teaches new communication skills—special education teachers, regular education teachers, classroom assistants, speech and language therapists, other therapists, parents, friends, assistants, and other adults who interact with students to promote their communication development. Peers can also facilitate and support the use of new communication skills; however, their role will most often be as conversational partners or as a collaborator with an adult rather than as an instructor.

strategies: PECS (Frost & Bondy, 1994, 1996) and Pivotal Response Training (PRT) (Humphries, 2003; Koegel, Koegel, Harrower, & Carter, 1999). These three naturalistic teaching procedures are designed for use in homes and classrooms, with a range of communication partners providing systematic language support, and use behavioral teaching strategies (prompts, shaping responses, facing cues, reinforcement, environmental arrangement). EMT and PECS specifically teach new skills in response to students' immediate interests and intentions in classroom, community, and home settings. PRT teaches a repertoire of behaviors that help students express their needs and wants and increases their responsiveness to environmental cues for communication. Some portion of PRT training may occur in a clinic-type setting, but the goal is sustained support for communication in everyday settings by persons who typically interact with the student. All three intervention approaches have the goal of spontaneous, initiated social communication (see Table 12–2).

TABLE 12–2
Naturalistic Teaching Procedures Compared

Naturalistic strategies	Training focus	Communicative partners during training	Where training procedures are delivered
Enhanced milieu teaching (EMT)	• Adults arrange the environment to engage child's interests. • Child is taught how to respond during natural communicative exchanges. • Child learns to attend to and respond to socio-communicative cues. • Turn taking is taught through both motor exchanges and verbal exchanges to reinforce reciprocity in social interactions. • Child play behaviors are verbally modeled by teacher. • Reinforcers are directly related to activity. • All attempts by the child to communicate are reinforced.	• Teachers • Parents • Peers	• Clinic and classroom • Training is embedded in daily routines and activities
Pivotal response training (PRT)	• Teaches a repertoire of pivotal behaviors, such as persistence, play, and social exchanges. • Child makes choices during preferred activities. • Tasks are varied to maintain interest. • Mastered tasks are interspersed with new tasks to ensure that child will attempt task again. • Teacher models appropriate social interchanges. • Teacher uses natural reinforcers directly related to the task. • All attempts by the child to respond are reinforced.	• Teachers • Parents • Peers	• Clinic (for initial parent training) • Training is embedded in daily routines and activities
Picture Exchange Communication System (PECS)	• Teaches child how to make requests. • Teaches child to gain the attention of the communicative partner by initiating the request. • Child requests highly desirable items by exchanging a picture for the item. • Child preferences are pretested and ranked throughout the training. • All correct exchanges are reinforced by giving child the requested item, paired with a verbal model.	• Teachers • Parents • Peers	• Clinic and classroom • Training is embedded in daily routines and activities

Considerations for AAC

The principles outlined in this chapter can be applied to teaching communication using alternative and augmented modes of communication as well as verbal communication. An alternative and augmentative communication (AAC) system is "an integrated group of components, including symbols, aids, strategies, and techniques used by individuals to enhance communication" (American Speech-Language-Hearing Association, 1991, p. 10). Multimodal teaching approaches are needed to teach communication through an AAC mode. Thus, when using EMT, teachers will model and respond with both spoken language and the student's AAC mode (e.g., by pointing to a picture in the PECS book or by demonstrating the use of a VOCA).

1. The selection of communication mode should be based on current student and environmental assessments (Beukelman & Mirenda, 1998; Romski & Sevcik, 1992; Wacker & Reichle, 1993) and requires knowledge of the student's physical, cognitive, and intentional communication abilities as well as knowledge of the opportunities for and barriers to communication for the student.

   Kristi is capable of waving and identifying pictures. Therefore, her gestures, combined with pictures on her VOCA (StepTalk™), become functional forms of communication training across her day. She is taught to wave "hi" to her classmates when she enters her classroom at morning arrival time, and her classmates wave or say "hi" in response. While the wave gesture alone works for Kristi in the classroom, when she enters the crowded cafeteria, she is taught to combine her wave gesture with a picture selection to solicit a response from a partner. She may need to wave and point to the picture of her friend Julie to gain her teacher's attention and indicate that she wants to sit with her friend Julie.

   Expert assistance should be sought to evaluate students for their use of AAC modes. The large quantity of AAC devices available ranges from very low technical options, such as picture books, to complex multilayered computer based systems, such as the Freestyle/Speaking Dynamically Pro™. Students may begin with a relatively simple system and move to more complex systems as their communication skills develop.
2. In some cases, students may need exposure to or practice using a new mode of communication in addition to naturalistic teaching. For example, students may require initial practice in operating a computer-based communication system or in learning sufficient motor imitation skills to allow efficient imitation of a simple sign. These practice opportunities can occur concurrent with naturalistic teaching; there is no advantage to waiting until the student is "ready" for teaching in functional contexts.

   Kristi's teacher will need to be sure that Kristi can match the photos of her friends to the actual individuals. She may want to teach photo matching in a more structured classroom activity before she teaches Kristi to use them in the cafeteria.

3. In order for a communication system to be functional, the student's communication partners must have enough knowledge of the system to respond to the student's communicative attempts. Communication partners who are teaching new forms (signs, pictures) need a repertoire of those forms so that they can model and expand in natural contexts.

   Kristi's peers are included in the natural communicative exchanges. They point to pictures on her communication device as they respond to her. Peers are natural sources of content topics for the device. They provide generation-appropriate phrases that can be used on Kristi's communication device.

4. There is no evidence to suggest that using an alternative communication mode reduces a student's chances of learning to speak; in contrast, pairing nonverbal and verbal communicative forms may facilitate learning both forms (Goldstein, 2002; Romski & Sevcik, 1992). Thus, introducing an AAC system as soon as the student demonstrates the minimal cognitive and intentional communication abilities to support the use of the system is highly recommended. Spoken language can always be modeled concurrently to provide opportunities to learn both verbal and alternative forms of communication.

With these caveats in mind, examples of applications with learners who use AAC systems have been included throughout the chapter (see also chapter 11). Table 12–3 illustrates a range of ACC devices suited to naturalistic teaching procedures.

TABLE 12–3

List of AAC Devices

No tech/low tech	Medium-tech devices	High-tech devices
Pictures/photographs/line drawings	6-Level Communicator™	DynaMyte™
Gesture/sign language	Tech Talk™	Freedom 2000/2000Lite™
Written language	Tech Speak™	Head Mouse
PECS	Macaw™	Vanguard™
Simple voice output (VOCA):	Alpha Talker™	Freestyle/Speaking Dynamically Pro™
Big Mac Switch™	Superhawk™	Intellikeys™
Step-by-Step Communicator™	Message mate 8/20/40™	Optimist™
Cheap Talk 4/8™	Hand-Held Voice™	
Twin Talk™	Digivox™	
Chat Box™		
Voice-in-a Box™		
Listen to Me™		
Stepper™		

Low tech: Nonelectronic devices, usually pictures, photographs, or objects representing vocabulary; requires little or no training of teachers or families to use and maintain.

Medium tech: Electric or nonelectric devices, usually battery operated; typically has electronic voice output; accommodates several pictures or words for vocabulary; does not require specialized programming skills but requires some assistance to set up, use, and maintain the device.

High tech: Electronic devices: uses specialized computerized programs to display vocabulary; one symbol represents classes of words embedded in the device; has electronic voice output and some have word prediction capabilities; requires specialized training to program, use, and maintain.

Companies who sell AAC devices:

Mayer-Johnson, Inc.—http://www.mayer-johnson.com

Don Johnston—http://www.donjohnston.com

Enabling Devices—http://www.enablingdevices.com

Naturalistic Teaching Procedures and Students with Autism

Difficulty in acquiring social communication skills is a core characteristic of students with autism (National Research Council, 2001). Intensive intervention to teach functional communication skills that generalize and maintain is essential for these students. There has been much controversy about the timing, amount, and types of intervention that are likely to produce optimal outcomes for students with autism. Although there have been no large clinical studies comparing communication approaches or investigating the parameters of intensity, duration, and timing on the outcomes of milieu teaching approaches with students with autism, there are studies demonstrating the effectiveness of milieu teaching with children who have autism (Goldstein, 2002; Hancock & Kaiser, 2002; Kaiser, Hancock, & Nietfeld, 2000; McGee, Almeida, Sulzer-Azaroff, & Feldman, 1992; McGee, Morrier, & Daly, 1999;

Miranda-Linne & Melin, 1992). Naturalistic teaching approaches, particularly EMT, are appropriate for use with students who have autism for several reasons. First, EMT focuses on teaching functional communication in social contexts; thus, it addresses both the key skill deficit and the problem of use within social interaction that are most difficult for students in autism. Second, EMT embeds the types of behavioral teaching procedures that have been shown to be consistently effective in teaching new skills to students with autism. Third, by teaching functional communication skills across settings and by involving several responsive communication partners, it is possible that EMT promotes generalization across stimuli, settings, and persons that is most difficult for children with autism.

EMT can be used to teach a range of skills, from single words to sequential responses in conversation; thus, it is a technique that may be appropriate for students with widely different skills and for students over a fairly long period of development. Finally, EMT emphasizes the acquisition of spontaneous communication skills that express student needs and communicative intentions. For many students with autism, the transition into spontaneous, initiated communication is very difficult. EMT procedures that systematically reduce the level of prompts and supports may provide a framework for moving from imitation (modeling) to choice making (manding) to spontaneous production (time delay and incidental teaching). As we illustrate in the case examples for Kristi and Michael, EMT can be combined with other strategies to teach communication skills. The choice to use EMT as the primary intervention or as a strategy to promote generalization should be based on students' needs and available teaching resources and teaching contexts.

The Goals of Language Intervention

The overriding goal of language intervention is to increase students' functional communication. As obvious as this goal is, functional communication can be forgotten in classrooms where several students have significant communication needs and teaching new skills requires many trials before a new response is learned. Faced with the many needs and modest skill repertoires of individuals with severe disabilities, it is easy to lose sight of the primary task of language intervention, which is increasing students' abilities to share information, feelings, and intentions with communication partners.

Communication as a Short-Term Target

Functional communication is both a short-term training objective and a long-term goal. Target forms (words, signs, gestures, picture exchanges) should be usable immediately. Although some potential targets may be logical in terms of existing skills, they may not be functional in terms of immediate usefulness. For example, naming colors, an early skill acquired by typical children, may not be immediately functional for students with severe disabilities and limited communication repertoires.

The specific form does not render a target dysfunctional. Instead, the usefulness of the form in the student's everyday communicative environment determines its function. For example, emerging phonemes such as /ba/ and /ma/ are highly functional communication forms for very young children who are developing normally. Caregivers for such young children

attend to new phonetic forms as if those forms had communicative intent. Contrast this with Kristi's team's view.

> *Kristi's team feels that teaching her to articulate early phonemes such as /ba/ and /ma/ will do little to increase her current functional communication skills unless persons in the environment respond to them in functional and systematic ways. Instead, they will use signs, picture selection, or communication using a simple electronic board, as these are forms that Kristi can use immediately to indicate desired objects or activities.*

Making Training Functional

Three steps can be taken to increase the functionality of short-term training targets: (a) select forms known to be functional in a particular setting frequented by the student, (b) teach the student to use new forms in practical ways, and (c) prepare conversational partners to respond to new forms in ways that make these forms useful. Functional forms for training can be determined by observing the settings where students spend time and noting their interactions and the communication needed to participate in those interactions.

> *Kristi's team reflects on her interactions throughout her day and compiles a list of communication opportunities. They decide that Kristi needs greeting skills as she gets on the bus and as she enters the classroom. She needs simple requests to obtain classroom materials and to ask for assistance. She needs to be able to indicate her food preferences at lunch. It would be enjoyable for her to be able to indicate to a peer that she would like to play and to comment on her favorite activities.*

From the list of opportunities, a set of potential target forms can take into account Kristi's preferences. It makes sense to teach generic forms (such as "help"); however, specific forms that allow her to get what she prefers (i.e., a hug, a favorite book, access to a computer game) also should be taught.

Forms become functional only when the environment responds to their use in particular ways. Teaching a form in its functional communicative context gives meaning to an otherwise arbitrary sign or word. Meaning derives from the consequences of attempted communication.

At the lunch table, Kristi combines a waving gesture and selects a picture of Julie on her VOCA that says, "Julie come." Her friend understands Kristi's meaning and joins her at the lunch table.

Ensuring functional use may require intervention to help partners become responsive to the emerging communication skills of students. This is particularly true when students are using an alternative communication mode, have unclear articulation, or have a history of limited language use. Often the greatest barrier that students must overcome is the effectiveness of less desirable strategies, such as hitting others or grabbing materials. If conversational partners respond more quickly and consistently to these behaviors than to emerging forms of "standard" communication, it will be difficult to learn new forms.

Functional Communication

Communication shares feelings, needs, or information. Functional communication (a) begins with a connection between people, (b) does not depend on the specific form of communication, but (c) does depend on shared understanding or meaning.

In Kristi's case, signaling her request for a friend to come is not functional unless her friend responds to the request. Her friend may need support from a teacher (such as a prompt to respond to Kristi's gesture and VOCA) to understand and respond to Kristi's attempt to communicate.

Training parents, classroom aides, community members (i.e., bus driver), and peers to pay attention and respond to communication attempts is often critical for functional language intervention.

Effective social communication interventions, such as EMT, require increasing the interaction skills of the target students and their conversational partners (Hunt, Alwell, & Goetz, 1988; Kaiser, Hancock, McLean, & Stanton-Chapman, 2001; Ostrosky, Kaiser, & Odom, 1993). Coaching peers to initiate communication and to respond to students' communication attempts may be nearly as important as teaching new forms. Similarly, supporting conversational interaction by providing a common topic (e.g., a photo album containing pictures of a student's family and favorite activities [Hunt et al., 1988]) or providing toys or activities enjoyed both by students with disabilities and by their peers (Ostrosky et al., 1993) may be a necessary modification.

Lizabeth's 4-year-old classmates easily learned words for the pictures in her PECS communication book when their teacher used a large-group time to talk about ways to communicate. The teacher first asked the children to name some ways they let people know what they want. They talked about using words and about pointing, nodding heads, and taking things they wanted. The teacher showed them Lizabeth's book and asked them to name each picture. Some pictures were easy to name (i.e., potty, toy); others were a little harder (i.e., more, no, help). They practiced pointing to and naming the pictures. The teacher told them that Lizabeth was just learning to use these pictures to communicate. She suggested that they watch very carefully when Lizabeth attempted to give them a picture and that they say the name of the picture so Lizabeth could hear the word. Every day for 2 weeks after the initial large-group activity, the teacher asked the children to name a time when they had helped Lizabeth use her book. During play and snack, the teacher set up opportunities for Lizabeth to communicate with peers and used the EMT strategies to prompt peer-directed communication.

EMT Strategies

EMT refers to language and communication training procedures that are (a) brief and positive in nature, (b) carried out in the natural environment as opportunities for teaching functional communication occur, and (c) occasioned by student interest in the topic. EMT provides specific instruction about the form, the function, and the social use of language. Instruction takes place using a responsive conversational style, and the environment is arranged to support student communication. Naturalistic modeling of what, how, and when to communicate is combined with systematic prompts and consequences for communication. Teaching opportunities that are embedded in the context of meaningful social interaction between partners with shared interests are most likely to result in learning new, functional communication forms.

Guidelines for Using EMT

- Teach when the student is interested
- Teach what is functional for the student at the moment

• Stop while both the student and the teacher are still enjoying the interaction

There are important differences between traditional direct instruction to teach language and EMT. In traditional direct instruction, the basic structure of the teaching interchange is predetermined by the adult's agenda for training. Specific discrete trials are constructed to provide massed practice with particular linguistic forms, and standard consequences are selected to reinforce or correct the responses of students. Discrete-trial training focuses on teaching the student to respond to specific cues or stimuli in exact ways. For example, students may be taught to label objects ("chair") or to respond precisely to pictures with short descriptive phrases ("boy sits chair"). Trials are grouped together to give students intensive practice with consistent feedback for their performance. Teaching occurs in one-to-one or small-group settings in order to help students focus their attention and to limit interference from ongoing activities or other students. Potentially, discrete-trial training can be used effectively to establish an initial repertoire of sounds or acquisition of motor responses needed for operating an electronic communication device. The controlled and systematic sequencing of stimuli, responses, and consequences in discrete-trial training promotes rapid acquisition of relatively narrow responses but does not readily facilitate generalized use of new forms for social communication. See Table 12–4 for comparison of teaching principles and procedures of four intervention language procedures.

For example, during a 20-minute session, a student might be presented with 30 opportunities to name common objects. Each time, the teacher holds up the object and says, "What is this?" When the student responds, the teacher praises her; if the student gives an incorrect answer or does not answer at all, the teacher models the correct response. Although EMT shares some of these features, it differs in important ways. EMT occurs in the natural environment in response to the interests of students and incorporates functional consequences. Successful EMT more closely resembles a conversation than a rote instructional episode. During EMT, teachers or peers and the student communicate in a meaningful, responsive way.

Effective use of EMT requires that teachers do the following:

1. Arrange the environment as a context for conversation

2. Communicate with students using a responsive, interactive style and model language at the student's target level
3. Be able to fluently use the four core EMT techniques (i.e., model, mand model, time delay, and incidental teaching)
4. Be skilled in assessment and planning for EMT
5. Be sufficiently skilled in classroom management to ensure classroom time, space, and opportunities for communication
6. Collaborate with other communication team members

Why EMT Is Effective for Learners with Severe Disabilities

EMT procedures are well suited for teaching functional language skills to students with severe disabilities.

Michael is a 15-year-old student with mental retardation and a moderate hearing loss. When teaching Michael new language skills, his teachers match his intentions (e.g., greeting, answering, requesting, commenting) and the complexity of his language (e.g., single words with some simple two-word requests). They model appropriate new vocabulary and two- and three-word phrases when his attention is focused on something of interest to him (e.g., a favorite material, an activity, a peer), when he has a specific need or desire, or when he can make a choice. Because Michael's speech is difficult to understand, he uses both verbalizations and his DynaMyte to communicate; teachers model using language and his DynaMyte.

Teachers try to match their requests for language and their models to Michael's emerging skills. They teach forms that are just slightly more advanced than his current spontaneous language. Since Michael uses a few two-word utterances, such as "want" plus a noun (e.g., "want Coke") to make requests, the teachers work to expand his requesting repertoire by modeling a variety of new nouns in combination with the verb "want" and by adding a pronoun (e.g., "I want chips"). Modeling a new form occurs as Michael attends to the specific aspect of the environment that the new form describes. Teachers encourage increasingly complex skills, increased vocabulary, and Michael's use of the DynaMyte by pointing to the pictures representing new labels while verbally modeling the complete utterance.

Successful EMT occurs when a student's communication works to control the immediate environment.

TABLE 12-4
Comparison of Language Teaching Procedures

	Core principles	How taught	Where technique occurs	Who teaches
Enhanced milieu teaching	• Naturalistic approach to teaching communication • Focus is on child's interest. • Increase student's functional communication. • Pragmatic outcomes for child and communicative partner.	• Environmental arrangement • Responsive style • Model, mands, and time delay • Incidental teaching	• Everyday contexts • Natural routines • Preplanned playtimes	• Everyone who comes into contact with the child • Support provided for each component of the procedure
Picture Exchange Communication System	• Focus of communication is on the exchange with the communicative partner, not the referent. • Children learn to use reliable methods to request. • Spontaneous, nonprompted communication is the goal. • Children learn to persist in establishing communication with a partner.	• Environmental arrangement • Errorless learning and correction strategies • Time delay • Prompt fading • Correspondence checks • Interrupted chains	• Everyday contexts • Natural routines • Preplanned training environments	• Any persons trained to implement the PECS system • Training completed after multiday didactic instruction
Pivotal response training	• Teaches children pivotal behaviors that spread across all areas of their behavioral repertoire. • Focus on improving children's motivation, responsivity to cues in the environment, and self-management. • Emphasis on generalization of treatment. • Designed to address specific behavioral characteristics of autism spectrum disorder.	• Target behaviors taught • Direct and natural reinforcement • Interspersed easy and difficult tasks • Child responds to multiple cues • Systematic fading of reinforcement and adult supervision	• Clinic for initial parent training • Home • Preplanned training environments	• Parents and peers after 15 hours of training
Discrete-trial teaching	• Goal of communication is on responding to teacher-chosen referents. • Focus on child's verbal response followed by adult-delivered consequences. • Therapist holds up stimulus item; item not functional within interaction.	• Numerous discrete skills taught by repeated trials • Verbal prompts • Direct reinforcement • Prompt fading	• Clinic • Isolated room in home • Designated classroom areas	• Any person trained to implement the program with intense (usually weekly) training • Child receives daily (20 to 40 hours per week) directing teaching

457

First, teaching new requesting forms is most effective when a student has indicated the desire for a specific object or a specific activity. Initiations and requests signal when a student has specific communicative intentions and has already made discriminations among many aspects of the communication context (e.g., what he wants, presence of a cooperative partner, that language is needed to communicate). Prompting or modeling language that matches the student's intentions help her learn how language functions to control the environment. Furthermore, requiring elaborated language also teaches the student that specific forms work more effectively than general or incomplete ones.

Modeling a New Form in a Functional Context

MICHAEL: (Reaching for a CD that has fallen on the floor)

TEACHER: Want CD. [verbal model plus activates the pictures for "want" and "CD" on his DynaMyte]

MICHAEL: Want (activates "want" on VOCA). [incomplete response]

TEACHER: Say "Want CD." [corrective model plus activates "want" and "CD" on Dynamyte]

MICHAEL: Want CD (activates "want" and "CD"). [complete response]

TEACHER: Oh, you want the CD. (Activates the pictures) Let me get it for you. (Picks up CD from the floor and hands it to him)

EMT also may help students develop strategies that increase their naturally occurring language learning. Michael is being taught to attend to both the presence of a conversational partner and his own needs as opportunities to talk. When he initiates, his verbal behavior results in specific consequences. Thus, EMT is likely to increase Michael's initiations and positive interactions with adults.

EMT promotes establishment of groups of related responses composed of functionally equivalent communication forms (response classes). In EMT episodes, Michael hears at least two utterances that serve the same purpose: the original form he produces and the elaborated form that is modeled by the teacher. He also has the forms modeled in speech and on his DynaMyte.

When Michael requests more milk at lunch by saying "milk" and/or selecting the picture of milk on his DynaMyte, his teacher models a slightly more elaborate request, "milk, please." Michael has an opportunity to equate his existing single-word request with a more polite form of requesting. When teachers and his parents provide Michael with another container of milk accompanied by additional descriptive talk (e.g., "it's chocolate milk" or "yes, you can have more milk"), several forms are paired with the same function in a brief interaction.

Finally, teaching in communicative contexts facilitates generalization to other conversational interactions. Teaching incorporates a variety of stimuli that occur in naturalistic contexts. Thus, students are not likely to become "stimulus bound" to the same extent observed after traditional one-to-one training. Teaching in response to Michael's attention to a specific object or event increases the likelihood that Michael will learn new labels and simple request forms without the use of massed trials and intensive practice or teacher-selected reinforcers that may mitigate against generalization.

Core Milieu Teaching Procedures

This section describes four core milieu teaching procedures: (a) modeling, (b) mand model, (c) time delay, and (d) incidental teaching. Table 12-5 summarizes these teaching techniques.

Modeling Procedure

Modeling is used during the initial stages of teaching a new form (e.g., a new sign, word, or picture) when a student has not acquired independent use of the form. Modeling may be considered the most fundamental milieu teaching process. The four primary goals of child-directed modeling are (a) building turn-taking skills, (b) training generalized imitation skills, (c) establishing a basic vocabulary, and (d) participating in conversations that occur outside the training context. Modeling can be used in environments that are arranged to facilitate communication by students. The teacher first establishes joint attention, meaning that the teacher will focus attention on the student *and* on what the student is interested in. Next, the teacher presents a verbal or gestural model that is related to the student's immediate interest. If the student imitates the model correctly, immediate positive feedback (which includes an expansion of the student's response) and the material of interest are offered to the student. Then the teacher expands the student's response to present a more complex communication form.

TABLE 12–5
Core EMT Teaching Techniques

Modeling procedure	Mand-model procedure
• Use the modeling procedure to teach new forms. • Note student interest. • Establish joint attention. • Present a verbal model related to the student's interest. • A correct student response receives immediate praise, verbal expansion, and (when material is being withheld) access to material. • An incorrect or absent student response is followed by a corrective model. • A correct student response receives immediate praise, verbal expansion, and access to material. • An incorrect or absent response to the corrective model is followed by corrective feedback plus access to material.*	• Use the mand-model procedure to prompt functional use of emerging forms. • Note student interest. • Establish joint attention. • Present a verbal mand related to student interest. • A correct student response receives immediate praise, verbal expansion, and (when material is being withheld) access to material. • An incorrect or absent student response is followed by a second mand (when student attention is high and when the student is likely to know the answer) or a model (when student interest is waning and the student is unlikely to know the answer). • A correct response to a mand or model is followed by immediate praise, verbal expansion, and access to material. • An incorrect student response to the corrective mand or model should be followed with the steps of the model procedure IF the child remains interested*.
Time delay procedure	**Incidental teaching procedure**

• Use time delay to teach more spontaneous use of emerging forms.
• Identify occasions when a student is likely to need materials or assistance.
• Establish joint attention.
• Introduce time delay.
• A correct student response (i.e., student communicates what he or she needs) receives immediate praise, verbal expansion, and materials or assistance.
• An incorrect or absent student response is followed by application of the mand-model procedure (if student interest is high and the student is likely to know the answer) or application of the model procedure (if student interest is waning and the student is unlikely to know the answer).*
	• Use incidental teaching whenever the student requests.
	• Identify occasions when a student is verbally or nonverbally requesting materials or assistance.
	• Establish joint attention.
	• Use the occasion to teach more intelligible, complex, or elaborated language/communication skills by applying steps of the following:
	  a. Model procedure (use to train new or difficult forms or structures or to improve intelligibility)
	  b. Mand-model procedure (use to train complexity and conversational skills)
	  c. Time delay procedure (use to train a student to initiate verbal or nonverbal communicative behavior about environmental stimuli)

* If the child loses interest (reaches for another toy, starts playing with something else) before any prompting procedure is "completed," discontinue that episode (set the requested material aside in case the child becomes interested again—do not give it to them!) and follow the child's lead, watching for other opportunities. Child interest is paramount to functional and meaningful milieu teaching.

If the student does not respond to the initial model or responds with an unintelligible, partial, incorrect, or unrelated response, the teacher establishes joint attention again and presents the model a second time (a corrective model).

A correct student response results in immediate positive feedback, expansion of the student's utterance, and access to the material. If an incorrect response follows the corrective model, the teacher provides corrective feedback by stating the desired response and then gives the topic material to the student. All milieu procedures have a modeling component that includes the

steps described here. Figure 12–2 contains a flowchart showing the steps of the modeling procedure.

Modeling Language That Matches the Student's Intention

MICHAEL: (Touching the front of his jacket and looking at the teacher)

TEACHER: Say, "New jacket." [verbal model plus activates pictures on Dynamyte] (Model is followed by a teacher pause to give the student time to respond)

MICHAEL: . . . jacket (activates "jacket" picture).

FIGURE 12–2

The Modeling Procedure Flowchart

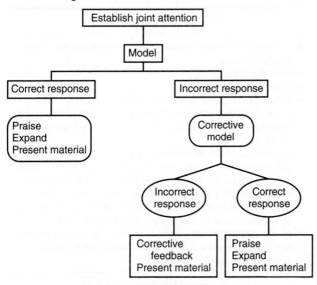

TEACHER: *New* jacket. [verbal model plus activates pictures].

MICHAEL: New jacket (activates "new" and "jacket"). [complete response].

TEACHER: Oh, I like your new jacket! Let me see the back.

Modeling may be used to increase the complexity of Michael's requesting.

Michael and two peers are taking CDs from the shelf to play music for the class. Michael looks at his friend, who is holding a favorite CD, and gestures to request the friend to give the CD to him.

TEACHER: Tell Jamie, "Play CD." [verbal model plus activates pictures]

MICHAEL: Play (activates "play" picture). [partial student response]

TEACHER: Play *CD.* [corrective verbal model plus activates pictures]

MICHAEL: Play CD (activates "play" and "CD"). [correct student response]

TEACHER: Right, you want Jamie to play the CD for you. Let's help him put it in. [acknowledgment+ expansion+natural consequence]

Mand-Model Procedure

The mand-model procedure was developed by Rogers-Warren and Warren (1980) to actively program for the generalization of language skills from one-to-one

sessions to the classroom. Generalization was facilitated by training classroom teachers to increase the number of opportunities for students to display newly learned language in the classroom. During the mand-model procedure, a variety of interesting materials are provided. When a student approaches a material (a basket containing several toy cars and trucks), the teacher mands (verbally instructs) the student to request what he or she wants (e.g., "Tell me what you want"). If the student gives an appropriate response (e.g., want truck), the teacher responds positively and descriptively (e.g., "Okay, you want the red truck") and provides the requested material. If the student does not respond or gives an incorrect response (e.g., "Points to truck, no verbalization"), the teacher provides a model for the student to imitate. By presenting choices among interesting materials, the teacher allows the student to make language immediately functional in indicating his or her choice.

Use of the mand-model procedure is arranged and initiated by teachers. Teachers are responsive to what students are interested in and present mands only when there is a meaningful opportunity for the student to control the environment through communication. The particular goals toward which the mand-model process is directed are (a) establishing joint attention (topic selection) as a cue for verbalization, (b) teaching turn-taking skills, (c) teaching students to provide information on verbal request or instruction, and (d) teaching students to respond to a variety of adult verbal cues. The mand-model procedure differs from the model procedure by including a nonimitative verbal prompt in the form of a question (e.g., "What do you need?"), a choice (e.g., "We have crayons or paints; which one would you like?") or a request (e.g., "Tell Jamie what you want") rather than providing an initial model. The presentation of corrective models of appropriate responses when a student responds incorrectly or fails to respond to the mand (i.e., question, choice, or request) is identical to the sequence in the model procedure (see flowchart in Figure 12–3).

Choice-making mands are particularly effective variants of the mand-model procedure. Choice-making mands begin with a statement to students about the available choices (e.g., "There are cheese sandwiches and peanut butter sandwiches"). They are followed by asking students to indicate a preference (e.g., "What would you like?"). The subsequent steps are identical to those just described. Asking students to indicate a preference using a familiar question or request form

FIGURE 12–3
The Mand-Model Procedure Flowchart

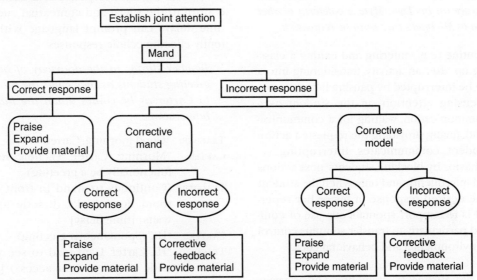

promotes generalization in similar but nonteaching choice situations.

Real questions or real choices form the basis of the mand-model procedure. Real questions and choices allow the student to truly communicate preferences and gain control over the environment. In contrast, questions that test the student's knowledge or seek only to get the student to perform a response are not truly functional communication exchanges because the adult already knows the answer. Use of the mand-model procedure should support both (a) students in becoming more independent and (b) teachers in learning to ask for and respond to student preferences.

Time Delay Procedure

Conversation should involve not only responding to another person's models and mands for verbalization but also initiating communication about various aspects of the environment. The time delay procedure was developed to establish environmental stimuli instead of simply presenting models and mands as cues for verbalization. The effects of the time delay procedure alone were experimentally demonstrated by Halle and his colleagues (Halle, Baer, & Spradlin, 1981; Halle, Marshall, & Spradlin, 1979). Adults in these studies (e.g., caregiving staff members and teachers) were instructed to attend to individual students by introducing a time delay in situations where the students were likely to need assistance or materials. Time delay has also been used in

combination with interrupting a chain of behaviors (Gee, Graham, Goetz, Oshima, & Yoshioka, 1991) and with a systematic reduction in prompting (Gee, Graham, Sailor, & Goetz, 1995). For example, when a student is assembling a pizza box as part of his vocational training, he learns sequential steps: (a) place cardboard, (b) fold along lines, (c) tuck end tabs, (d) secure with tape, and (e) fold down top. A time delay just before step d might be used to prompt the student to request help from his job coach to "hold please."

Steps of the time delay procedure include the following:

1. The teacher is in proximity to and looking at the student.
2. The teacher pauses when student attends to the material (e.g., looks at job coach and then at box) or nonverbally signals his communicative intent (e.g., points to the object).
3. The teacher waits for the student to verbalize.
4. If the student does not respond to the time delay within 5 seconds, the teacher models an appropriate verbal request ("hold please").
5. Positive feedback and immediately offering the desired material or assistance follow student verbalizations.

Michael's teachers decide to use a time delay procedure to prompt his language interactions with persons at school and in the community. His social studies teacher casually will block the door while talking to another student until Michael verbalizes and selects a picture on his DynaMyte. A cafeteria worker may hold on to Michael's tray until he requests it.

Any regular routine (e.g., entering and exiting a classroom, cleaning up after an activity, transitioning into a new task) may be interrupted by pausing between routine steps, focusing attention on the student as a prompt for communication, waiting for a communicative request, and, finally, providing the requested action when the student communicates. Interrupting sequences of behavior by blocking students' next actions should be used infrequently and only when the student already has the desired response in his or her repertoire. The goal is to support spontaneous use of communication and particularly to transfer stimulus control to nonverbal environmental and behavioral cues.

At his work site, Michael is assembling a bicycle gear by taking parts from each of six containers and fitting them together. The second container, which holds washers, is empty.

TEACHER: (Looks at Michael and waits for him to initiate communication) [delay or pause 2 to 5 seconds]

MICHAEL: Washer (activates "washer"). [partial student response]

TEACHER: Say, "Need washers." [corrective verbal model plus activates picture on VOCA]

MICHAEL: Need washers (activates "need" and "washers"). [correct student response]

TEACHER: Yes, Michael, you need more washers. Help yourself. (Giving him a large box of washers to fill his container) [acknowledgment+expansion+natural consequence]

Time delay alone or in combination with other fading and chaining procedures may be especially useful with students who are echolalic (e.g., frequently imitate or repeat the exact words spoken to them). Students with autistic characteristics may repeat the last words of a prompt. These echoic repetitions can be functional; that is, the student may be communicating a specific intention such as greeting the listener or indicating his or her agreement. By observing the context in which the student uses an echoic utterance, it may be possible to use the occasion to prompt a more standard, spontaneous utterance that serves the same

function. Nonverbal prompting helps avoid the automatic echoing of a response and transfers stimulus control to the social and contextual cues. For Carter, time delays can prompt language without inadvertently eliciting echoic responses.

Teacher stands in the doorway of her homeroom greeting students as they enter the room. She speaks to Carter as he comes down the hall toward his homeroom.

TEACHER: "Good morning, Carter."

CARTER: "Morning, Carter." (Echoic response; may functionally be a greeting)

TEACHER: (Continues to stand in front of the home room door, looks directly at Carter and waits) [time delay]

CARTER: "Hi." (Spontaneous greeting)

TEACHER: "Hi, Carter. I am glad to see you!" (Moves aside to give Carter access) [acknowledgment+natural consequence]

Incidental Teaching Procedure

A fourth strategy has been developed for teaching more elaborate language and improving conversational skills about particular topics. Incidental teaching is used when the student makes a request. The first step in the incidental teaching procedure is to arrange the environment in ways that encourage the student to request materials and assistance. This can be done by displaying potential reinforcers attractively within the student's view but out of reach. A student who verbally or nonverbally requests materials or assistance is identifying what is reinforcing at that moment. The teacher responds by modeling, manding, or delaying for a more elaborated response or for additional information. When the student responds appropriately, the teacher gives the item of interest while affirming and repeating the answer in an expanded fashion (see Figure 12-4).

FIGURE 12-4
The Incidental Teaching Procedure Flowchart

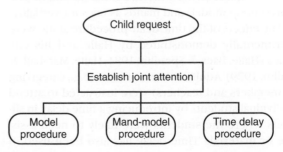

If the student does not respond appropriately to the mand or time delay prompts, the teacher moves to a simpler prompt and instructs the student to imitate a model. The adult then confirms the accuracy of the student's imitation, repeats and expands what the student said, and gives the student whatever he or she requested. Only if the student loses interest does instruction stop.

Because teaching to a reinforcer is possible only as long as the item or event is really of interest to the student, episodes are brief and positive in nature. Ability to request verbally or nonverbally and ability to imitate target forms are the only prerequisite student skills for incidental teaching.

> *Carter and a peer have been taken to a variety store to purchase a birthday present for a classmate. They are looking at a rack of baseball caps.*

CARTER: (Pointing to a blue cap) Cap. [initiation]

TEACHER: Tell me which one you like. [mand]

CARTER: (Continuing to point)

TEACHER: Say, "Blue cap." [corrective model]

CARTER: Blue cap. [correct student response]

TEACHER: Here you go. You like the blue cap. Do you think Jimmy will like this one? [natural consequence + acknowledgment + expansion]

CARTER: (Nodding his head yes)

There is real joy in teaching functional communication forms to a student who is interested and motivated to use the form at the moment. Teaching only when students are highly motivated to respond may reduce the number of teaching episodes, but it ensures that teaching and learning are exciting positive events for both teachers and the students.

When to Use Each of the Four Procedures

Two general guidelines apply when selecting one of the four milieu procedures. First, select the procedure that is the most natural to the ongoing interaction. For example, asking a question (using the mand-model procedure) is natural when a student's intentions or desires are not clear or when asking for specification would be usual (e.g., "Would you like milk or iced tea?"). The modeling procedure is used whenever the student does not know the appropriate response. For example, if the student does not know the name of an object, it is natural to model the label for the student (e.g., "These are Lego blocks").

Second, use the procedure that provides the level of support the student needs to make an appropriate communicative response. Modeling provides maximum support for a student's response. The mand-model procedure provides a middle level of support and can be tailored to fit a student's skills by either asking a question only or providing two named choices followed by a question (e.g., "I have cheese sandwiches and peanut butter sandwiches. What do you want?"). Time delay provides no initial verbal support.

Incidental teaching differs from the other three procedures because it always follows a student request. Thus, incidental teaching should be used only when the student has made a request. Requests can be verbal, vocal, or gestural. How the teacher responds to the student's request in order to prompt elaborated language depends on the level of support the student requires to respond appropriately. In all uses of the milieu procedures, incomplete or incorrect student responses are followed by support for a correct response (i.e., if a student cannot respond to a mand, a model of the correct response is offered). Every episode includes a positive consequence, continuing communication, and modeling of an expanded form of the prompted response. The goals in all the procedures are to ensure that the interaction is as communicative, natural, and positive as possible and that interactions end with the students' gaining the specified reinforcers.

Learning to notice individual students' varied forms of requesting is a challenging task for teachers who want to use incidental teaching. Echoes, rote utterances, repeated gestures, problem behavior, and other behaviors (e.g., banging a hand on the table) and vocalizations with and without gestures may be requests. Systematic observation can help determine if these behaviors are intended to be requests. For students with limited physical mobility, eye gaze and head turns may function as requests. Students with autism and limited verbal skills may have very few obvious requests, but systematic observation can help in identifying their unique forms and reinforcers. *Every student communicates and almost every student requests.* The challenge for teachers is recognizing and responding to these requests as opportunities to teach (see also chapter 11).

Environmental Arrangement Strategies

Using the environment to prompt language involves (a) a focus on making language part of students' routines, (b) including interesting materials and activities in the environment, (c) having adults and peers who encourage students to use language and who respond to their attempts to communicate, and (d) establishing a contingent relationship between language use and access to materials or assistance during some routines and activities. Research suggests that environmental arrangement is an important strategy for teachers who want to promote communication in classrooms (Alpert, Kaiser, Hemmeter, & Ostrosky, 1987; Haring, Neetz, Lovinger, Peck, & Semmel, 1987; Kaiser, Ostrosky, & Alpert, 1993; McCathren, 2000). To encourage the use of language, classrooms and other communication settings require interesting materials and activities. Teachers should intervene by presenting desired materials and activities in response to students' requests and other uses of language (Hart & Rogers-Warren, 1978). Contingent provision of desired materials acts to reinforce language use.

Six strategies have been shown to increase the likelihood that students will show interest in the environment and make communicative attempts and that teachers will prompt language about things of interest to the students (see Table 12–6). The goal of these strategies is to provide clear and obvious prompts, while attractive materials and activities function as both discriminative stimuli and reinforcers for language use.

Interesting Materials

When materials and activities that students enjoy are available, students are most likely to initiate communication about the things that interest them. Thus, increasing interest in the environment increases the likelihood of language use as well as opportunities for language teaching. It may be helpful to assess students' preferences and to arrange settings so that preferred materials and activities are included. Students' preferences

---

TABLE 12–6
Arranging the Environment to Encourage Communication

1. **Interesting materials.** Students are likely to communicate when things or activities in the environment interest them.

Example: James lay quietly on the rug, with his head resting on his arms. Ms. Davis sat at one end of the rug and rolled a big yellow ball right past James. James lifted his head and looked around for the ball.

2. **Out of reach.** Students are likely to communicate when they want something that they cannot reach.

Example: Mr. Norris lifted a drum off the shelf and placed it on the floor between Judy and Annette, who were both in wheelchairs. Mr. Norris hit the drum three times and then waited, looking at his two students. Judy watched and clapped her hands together. Then she reached for the drum with both arms outstretched.

3. **Inadequate portions.** Students are likely to communicate when they do not have the necessary materials to carry out an instruction.

Example: Mr. Robinson gave every student except Mary a ticket to get into the auditorium for the high school play. He told his students to give their tickets to the attendant. Mr. Robinson walked beside Mary toward the entrance. When Mary reached the attendant, Mr. Robinson paused and looked at Mary. She pointed to the tickets in his hand and signed, "Give me." Mr. Robinson gave her a ticket, and she handed it to the attendant, who said, "Thank you. Enjoy the play."

4. **Choice making.** Students are likely to communicate when they are given a choice.

Example: Peggy's favorite pastime is listening to tapes on her tape recorder. On Saturday morning, Peggy's father said to her, "We could listen to your tapes" (pointing to the picture of the tape recorder on Peggy's communication board) "or we could go for a ride in the car" (pointing to the picture of the car). "What would you like to do?" Peggy pointed to the picture of the tape recorder. "OK, let's listen to this new tape you like," her father said as he put the tape in and turned on the machine.

5. **Assistance.** Students are likely to communicate when they need assistance in operating or manipulating materials.

Example: Tammy's mother always places three clear plastic containers with snacks (cookies, crackers, popcorn) on the kitchen table before Tammy returns from school. When Tammy arrives home and is ready for a snack, she goes to the table and chooses what she wants by handing the container with her chosen snack to her mother. Her mother responds to this nonverbal request by modeling a request form that specifies Tammy's choice (e.g., "Open popcorn").

6. **Unexpected situations.** Students are likely to communicate when something happens that they do not expect.

Example: Ms. Esser was helping Kathy put on her socks and shoes after rest time. After assisting with the socks, Ms. Esser put one of the shoes on her own foot. Kathy stared at the shoe for a moment and then looked up at her teacher, who was smiling. "No," laughed Kathy, "my shoe."

along with age and context appropriateness should be considered.

Out of Reach

Placing some desirable materials within view but out of the students' reach prompts students to make requests to gain access to the materials. Materials may be placed on shelves, in clear plastic bins, or simply across a table during a group activity. Students' requests create opportunities for language teaching. When students request a specific material, he or she is specifying their reinforcer at that moment (Hart & Rogers-Warren, 1978). Thus, a teacher who prompts language and provides the requested material after a communicative response effectively reinforces that response. For students who have limited motor skills, materials should be within their visual field, slightly out of reach, and far enough apart from other materials to allow a teacher or peer to interpret the nonverbal or verbal requests.

> At home, Carter's mother keeps three of his favorite objects (a pack of baseball cards, a small trophy from his softball team, and a yo-yo) on the windowsill above the sink. At supper time, Carter likes to be in the kitchen while she cooks dinner and later cleans up. Carter cannot reach over the sink to the window. He initiates by pointing and naming the object he wants. Carter's mother uses this opportunity to prompt a short sentence (e.g., "I want yo-yo") in an incidental teaching episode. Responding to Carter's initiations also reminds his mom to take a few minutes to talk to Carter during this busy time of day. Her attention to his initiations supports his positive behavior at a time of day when he may be challenging.

Inadequate Portions

Providing small or inadequate portions of preferred materials (e.g., blocks, crackers, or turns on a computer game) is another way to arrange the environment to promote communication. During an activity that students enjoy, the teacher can control the materials so that students have only a limited amount. When they have used up the materials, they are likely to request more. When they initiate with requests for more, the adult has the opportunity to model and prompt more elaborate language as well as to provide functional consequences for the communicative attempts.

Teachers may also set up the environment so that students request materials from each other.

Choice Making

On many occasions, two or more options of activities or materials can be presented so that students can make a choice. To encourage students to initiate language, the choice may be presented nonverbally (e.g., by holding up two tools for opening a carton in either hand or by presenting three snack options on a tray). Students may be most encouraged to make a choice when one of the items is much more preferred and the other is much less preferred or disliked.

> Lizabeth's teacher sets up a tray with two options at snack time: apples and crackers with peanut butter. She offers each child in the class a choice of snacks. Lizabeth prefers apples and does not like peanut butter. When the teacher holds out the tray with choices and Lizabeth reaches for the apples, the teacher prompts Lizabeth to give her the picture of apples from the communication book and says, "Oh Lizzie, you want apples. Good choice!" After the snack routine is established, the teacher prompts Lizabeth to indicate to a peer what she wants using her book (e.g., the peer will say, "Lizzie, what do you want?," as she waits for Lizabeth to hand her a picture).

Assistance

Creating a situation where students are likely to need assistance increases the likelihood of communication about that need. Attractive materials that require assistance may encourage students to request help. For example, a difficult-to-open container of a preferred food (e.g., chocolate milk) may provide an excellent opportunity to prompt "open" or "help."

Unexpected Situations

The final environmental strategy is to create a need for communication by setting up situations that go against the expectations of students. Children learn routines and expect that things will happen in a particular order. When something unexpected happens, they may be prompted to communicate. Of course, use of this strategy must be tailored to the student's skills and to their familiar routines. At times, students need help recognizing that something is funny or unusual.

Ideally, use of the environmental strategies results in stimulating students' interest and communication.

Teachers should either reinforce acceptable responses that result or use a milieu teaching procedure to (a) prompt a contextually relevant and appropriate response, (b) correct a response, or (c) evoke a more complex response. Nonverbal cues accompanying the environmental arrangement strategies should be faded out over time so that students are responding more to things of interest in the environment and less to arranged cues (Halle et al., 1979). For example, it may be necessary at first for teachers to shrug their shoulders, raise their eyebrows, and tilt their head while extending their hands containing two different materials in order to direct students' attention to the materials and to the opportunity for choice making. As students begin initiating requests, teachers will prompt less often and less overtly.

Environmental strategies must be tailored to each student's cognitive level and responsiveness to the environment. For example, if a student does not notice an unexpected situation created for communication, there is no opportunity to practice a communicative response. Environmental strategies are most effective when they cue communicative responses that are emergent in students' repertoires. Environmental arrangements provide nonverbal cues for communication that may facilitate students' progress toward spontaneous use of their new skills.

Inadequate portions of Kristi's favorite food at lunch serves as a cue to give her PECS card for "more."

When a peer who is handing out passes for the Friday night football game gives Michael only one pass (a planned implementation of inadequate portions), Michael indicates, "I want two" using his DynaMyte.

How teachers and others respond to students' communication attempts when these attempts are elicited by environmental arrangement is extremely important. Immediate attention, feedback, and access to the desired material or requested assistance, as well as a positive response, are essential for reinforcing communication attempts. As in all applications of EMT, episodes that begin with environmental arrangement should be brief, positive, successful for students, and reinforcing for the use of language and social engagement with adults.

The best uses of environmental arrangement are natural opportunities. The strategy of giving choices can be used naturally in many contexts. Other strategies, such as inadequate portions and out of reach, should not be overused because they can be disliked by students. Environmental arrangement strategies also support peer communication, as peers can provide materials and activities a student requests. It is important to help peers understand the basic principles of EMT if they are going to be prompting specific forms of communication (e.g., teach to the students' interests, be positive, keep episodes short, and always follow through with natural consequences), but increasing responding to student communication may require only brief instructions and feedback to peers.

Using Environmental Arrangements to Promote Peer Interactions

Peer interaction is promoted when the interaction setting is organized so that peers (rather than adults) give assistance or materials contingent on the student's communication. At these times, peers can also present choice-making opportunities and interact more easily with the student in the context of interesting materials (Farmer-Dougan, 1994; McGee et al., 1992). Teachers can mediate interactions with peers by directing the student to communicate with the peer (i.e., provide prompts to the student to address the peer: "Tell Janie, I want another turn shooting the basket"). In addition, peers can be taught simplified milieu strategies to use directly with the student (Hancock & Kaiser, 1996). In Figure 12–5, Elise uses her Dynavox to plan a party with her friend Sarah.

Elise and Sarah are in Elise's backyard—a natural location for the two to play together after school. They are trying to decide who to invite to Elise's birthday party. Elise's mother has given Sarah paper and pencil to write down Elise's ideas for the party. Sarah asks Elise to tell her who to invite and what she wants to eat, and she writes down what Elise tells her.

Responsive Conversational Style

One of the important evolutions in naturalistic communication intervention during the past few years is the greater emphasis on responsive conversational style (Kaiser, Hancock, & Hester, 1998). EMT embeds the milieu teaching procedures into conversational

FIGURE 12–5
Elise using her Dynavox to plan a party with her friend Sarah

interactions by taking advantage of both the turn balance of good conversations and ongoing opportunities for modeling (without requiring a response) the forms and functions of communication (Kaiser, 1993; Kaiser & Hancock, 2000).

Responsive conversational style is a general interaction approach that supports students' communication and greatly enhances the naturalistic qualities of milieu teaching. Responsive conversational style sets a social context for language in the same way that environmental arrangement sets a physical context. Together, responsive conversational style and environmental arrangement create a supportive interactional context for conversation-based teaching. When a responsive interaction is established between teachers and students, communication is ongoing and offers many opportunities for specific but highly natural teaching. Responsive conversational style has four components:

1. Establishment of joint and mutual attention
2. Turn taking
3. Contingent responsiveness
4. Positive affect

As previously defined, *joint attention* occurs when teachers and students are focused on the same activity or material. For example, when a teacher watches closely while a student moves a toy truck back and forth on the floor, the teacher and student are jointly attending to the student's activity. *Mutual attention* occurs when students and teachers look at each other as they talk. In an ideal conversation, there is both joint attention to the student's ongoing activity and mutual attention between the student and the teacher. Joint attention allows teachers to focus their comments and requests for language on the objects and activities that are of immediate interest to the students. Mutual attention helps maintain communicative engagement between the conversational partners and increases the likelihood that students' requests and comments will be understood and responded to appropriately.

Turn taking refers to the exchange of communication turns by students and teachers in a conversation. Ideally, conversational turns are balanced so that each communicator's turns are of similar length and complexity. Turns can be taken nonverbally or verbally. Because many students with severe disabilities initiate infrequently, developing a more even balance of turns may require teachers to talk less, take shorter turns, and attend carefully to the students' ways of taking turns and attempts to communicate. Pausing to allow time for students to respond is an easy way to increase opportunities for students to take their turns. Ending an adult turn with a question can also promote student turn taking, but the adult must ask a question the student understands and then wait for a response.

The following examples illustrate balanced and unbalanced turn taking.

Unbalanced Turn Taking

MR. G.: Hi there, Markus! What are you doing? Do you like that puzzle? It's a baseball player.

MARKUS: Me ball, too.

MR. G.: Oh, you like baseball? Do you watch baseball on TV? I never miss a game. I watched three games this weekend. Well, it's time to clean up. Do you need some help? OK, you do it.

Balanced Turn Taking

MR. G.: Hi there, Markus! (Pause)

MARKUS: Hi!

MR. G.: Hey, you've got the baseball player. (Pause)

MARKUS: Me ball, too.

MR. G.: You like baseball?

MARKUS: (Nods yes)

MR. G.: You like baseball. I bet you watch it on TV. (Pause)

MARKUS: Me. (Nods yes)

MR. G.: You watch baseball on TV.

Contingent responsiveness means that teachers respond to students' communication attempts quickly and meaningfully. Noticing and responding to student communication attempts are essential in establishing a conversation. Such responsiveness reinforces attempts to communicate and indicates to students that teachers are available as communication partners. Although some attempts will be missed in the context of a busy classroom, teachers should seek to be as responsive as possible to student communication attempts. When students communicate at low rates and there are relatively few potential communication partners in a setting, teacher responsiveness is especially important. Clearly, inclusive settings offer more opportunities for positive communicative interactions with a range of partners; however, teachers' modeling of responsive styles of interaction is often important for both students and other teachers.

To respond in a meaningful way, teachers must try to understand what it is that students intend to communicate and tailor their responses accordingly. The communicative attempts of students with severe language disabilities are not always easily understood. However, when teachers have established joint and mutual attention and have arranged the environment to promote communication, understanding students' messages is easier. The following examples contrast a conversation in which a teacher is contingently responsive with one in which she is not.

Contingently Responsive Conversation

Marci is emptying her backpack (a book, her glasses, a note from her mother, a package of tissues). Her teacher, Mrs. B., is standing by Marci's locker, waiting for Marci to finish.

MARCI: (Takes out her glasses and looks at them)

MRS. B.: Oh, Marci, there are your glasses. (Pause) Shall I help you put them on?

MARCI: (Hands Mrs. B. the glasses and looks at her)

MRS. B.: (Takes the glasses, looks back at Marci, smiles, and then helps Marci put the glasses on)

MARCI: (Takes out the note from her mother and plays with it)

MRS. B.: You brought a note from your mom. (Watches Marci and pauses) Marci, is that note for me?

MARCI: Note. Un-huh.

MRS. B.: (Looks at Marci, extends her hand, and waits)

MARCI: Here. (Gives note)

MRS. B.: Why, thank you, Marci. Let's see what your mom has to say. (Holds note where she and Marci can look at it while she reads it)

Noncontingent Conversation

MRS. B.: Good morning, Marci. Put your things away and come sit down.

MARCI: (Takes out her glasses)

MRS. B.: Hurry, Marci. We're running late.

MARCI: (Takes out a note from her mother)

MRS. B.: (Reaches for note and takes it) Thank you. I'll read this later.

MARCI: Note?

MRS. B.: Hurry. It's late.

Positive affect includes smiling, gentle touching, use of the student's name, a warm tone of voice, and an affirming style of interaction. Students who have limited verbal communication may be particularly sensitive to the nonverbal messages that communication partners send. Teachers who indicate their interest in a student by making themselves physically available and affirming students' attempts to communicate invite conversation. In contrast, adults or peers who speak loudly, do not match their pace and style to that of the students, and are not gentle in their physical contact with students discourage communication even if they do not intend to do so. Positive affect indicates interest, liking, respect, and availability for conversations with students. Positive affect should be an ongoing aspect of interactions with students who have severe disabilities as well as creating a social context for milieu teaching. Responsive, contingent conversation takes time because teachers must focus attention on students, wait for their responses, and pace subsequent comments and responses to match the students' style of communication. The time required is offset by the benefits of connecting and communicating with the student and by setting up opportunities to effectively teach functional communication skills (see also chapter 11).

Michael's job coach is careful to establish physical contact with him at the beginning of a work period. He greets Michael face to face and shakes his hand or touches his shoulder. He expresses his positive regard for Michael with smiles, nods, and gestures as well as words. Because Michael has a hearing loss, his job coach makes sure peers also communicate with Michael with their facial expressions, physical proximity, gentle touching, and gestures.

Peers may need special instructions about the importance of these aspects of communication for students with disabilities. Talking with a warm tone, conveying positive affect, and being relatively gentle in physical exchanges do not come naturally to most children and teens. Teacher modeling of a responsive conversational style with all students and some open discussion of ways in which students can communicate with each other, especially their peers with disabilities, can prompt modest improvements in interactional style.

Research on Milieu Teaching and EMT

Milieu teaching and EMT have a long history of research. More than 50 empirical studies have examined the effects of milieu teaching. Four variants of Hart and

Risley's (1968) original model of incidental teaching have been analyzed experimentally: (a) modeling (Alpert & Kaiser, 1992; Alpert & Rogers-Warren, 1985), (b) manding and modeling (Cavallero & Bambara, 1982; Hemmeter, Ault, Collins, & Meyers, 1996; Mobayed, Collins, Strangis, Schuster, & Hemmeter, 2000; Warren, Gazdag, Bambara, & Jones, 1994; Warren, McQuarter, & Rogers-Warren, 1984),), (c) time delay (Angelo & Goldstein, 1990; Charlop & Trasowech, 1991; Charlop & Walsh, 1986; Halle et al., 1979, 1981; Miller, Collins, & Hemmeter, 2002; Oliver & Halle, 1982; Schwartz, Anderson, & Halle, 1988), and (d) incidental teaching (Alpert & Kaiser, 1992; Farmer-Dougan, 1994; Hart & Risley, 1968, 1974, 1975, 1980; Hemmeter & Kaiser, 1994; Hemmeter et al., 1996; Lennox & Brune, 1993). In general, modeling, mand modeling, and time delay are variants of the original incidental teaching model. In these procedures, there is increased adult support for children who are low-frequency initiators and whose language skills are relatively limited. Incidental teaching is simply the use of models, mands, and time delays in response to student requests.

Milieu teaching involves the application of behavioral teaching procedures in naturalistic, conversational settings (Hart & Rogers-Warren, 1978). Research has demonstrated that milieu teaching is effective in teaching a range of productive language skills to individuals with mental retardation and other language-related disabilities (Kaiser, Yoder, & Keetz, 1992.) A range of language responses (e.g., single words, adjectives, simple utterances [one to four words], compound sentences, specific requests, general requests) in both verbal and nonvocal modes have been taught. Milieu teaching positively affects general language skills as measured by changes in complexity of utterances and vocabulary diversity (Hart & Risley, 1975, 1980; Kaiser, 2000; Kaiser & Hancock, 2000; Kaiser et al., 2000; Rogers-Warren & Warren, 1980; Warren et al., 1984). Generalization across settings has been reported for some subjects in each study in which it has been assessed (Alpert & Kaiser, 1992; Alpert & Rogers-Warren, 1985; Cavallero & Bambara, 1982; Halle et al., 1979, 1981; Hancock & Kaiser, 1996; Hart & Risley, 1974, 1975; Kaiser et al., 2000; McGee, Krantz, & McClannahan, 1985; Miranda-Linne & Melin, 1992; Warren et al., 1984). Finally, for children with initially low levels of responsiveness and initiations, milieu teaching has resulted in increased levels of these specific social communicative behaviors (Halle et al., 1981;

Hancock & Kaiser, 1996, 2002; Hart & Risley, 1980; Kaiser et al., 2000; Mobayed et al., 2000; Rodi & Hughes, 2000; Warren et al., 1984).

There is considerable evidence that children's initiations, responses, participation in conversation, and requesting using trained utterances can be systematically increased using milieu procedures (Charlop & Carpenter, 2000; Charlop & Walsh, 1986; Farmer-Dougan, 1994; Haring, Roger, Lee, Breen, & Gaylord-Ross, 1986; Haring et al., 1987; Hemmeter et al., 1996; Matson, Sevin, Box, Francis, & Sevin, 1993; Schwartz et al., 1988). Studies that have measured broader effects on language development (Alpert & Rogers-Warren, 1985; Hart & Risley, 1975, 1980; Hemmeter & Kaiser, 1994; Warren & Bambara, 1989; Yoder, Kaiser, & Alpert, 1991) report modest changes in more global measures of language development. In two studies (Kaiser, 2000; Kaiser & Hancock, 2000) comparing applications of milieu teaching by parents and therapists of preschool children with significant language disabilities, results indicated that children in both the parent- and the teacher-implemented conditions made and maintained significant gains in most measures of language development. These findings support the value of involving family members in the use of milieu teaching.

Children with autism increased their verbal communication during the milieu teaching interventions when implemented by either parents (Kaiser et al., 2000) or therapists (Hancock & Kaiser, 2002), and the results for children with autism did not differ from those of other children (Kaiser, Hancock, Nietfeld, & Delaney, 1996; Kaiser et al., 1998). These results, along with those of additional studies (Charlop & Carpenter, 2000; Hamilton & Snell, 1993; McGee et al., 1992, 1999), suggest that milieu teaching may be successful in improving the communication skills of students with autism. There has been much discussion on the outcomes of intensive didactic intervention on the functioning of children with autism (McEachin, Smith, & Lovaas, 1993); however, findings to date do not establish that didactic training is better than more naturalistic approaches to language intervention (Green, 2001; Gresham & MacMillan, 1997; Matson et al., 1993), and at least one study found that milieu teaching techniques resulted in equal retention, greater generalization and equal or greater spontaneous language use than didactic training (Miranda-Linne & Melin, 1992). To date, there is evidence that milieu teaching and EMT procedures can increase the language and communication skills of students with autism.

Implementing EMT

Implementing EMT requires more than skill in using each of its three components. Assessment of child skills, selection of targets, structuring the setting to promote naturalistic teaching, and evaluating both the implementation and the student's progress must be addressed to ensure that this instructional strategy is effective.

Data Collection and Evaluation

Effective milieu language teaching is data based. Many aspects of the process may be monitored. At a minimum, it is recommended that data be kept on the following dimensions:

1. *The number of milieu teaching episodes per day and the targets taught in these episodes:* A total of 20 to 25 episodes per day is a reasonable teaching base. Typically, students will have a small number of targets (two to five), and there should be at least five opportunities to teach each target. If students are not learning quickly with this number of opportunities, it is important to determine if more concentrated practice is needed to acquire the targeted form of communication. Massed trial practice can be used to shape sign production, acquire skills for operating an electronic device, or practice discrimination skills that form the conceptual bases for word meanings but is not usually sufficient for establishing the functional use of the communication form.

2. *The number of student initiations across the day or during selected activities:* An increase in the number of student initiations is often one of the primary effects of EMT. Initiations typically are defined as directed intentional communication that occurs in the absence of an adult verbal stimulus (e.g., a request). Noting the content of student initiations helps to assess progress; select activities, materials, and consequences; and establish new targets.

3. *The responsiveness of the student to EMT procedures:* Responsiveness can be measured by counting the number of appropriate student responses to questions, mands, models, and delays. For example, a teacher could determine the number of times a student responded to 10 different questions across the day. Responsiveness to 65% to 70% of the EMT procedures should be considered adequate if each episode ends positively and contains appropriate models of the target behavior.

4. *Use of the target skills by students outside of teaching episodes:* This indicates a level of unprompted generalizations of the target skill across forms, people, and settings.

Each of these dimensions can be monitored using a simple tally sheet. Data sheets can be sticky notes or index cards attached to a lesson plan. An activity-specific data sheet cues the teacher when and how to prompt and provides space for data collection. Sticky notes on the student's communication book, wheelchair, or desk can be used for simple data collection. While daily monitoring is ideal, systematic sampling of different activities across several days yields a more balanced evaluation than does casual monitoring across an entire day. Non-data-based EMT is likely to be highly erratic and, like any such approach, may prolong the use of ineffective strategies, depriving students of critical learn-

ing time. Monitoring is especially important when several students are being targeted for EMT. Table 12–7 is a sample data sheet used to collect data for Kristi across three school settings.

How to Use EMT

EMT can be either used as a primary language intervention approach or combined with direct teaching one on one to facilitate generalization and promote further acquisition. When used as a primary intervention approach, EMT should be applied systematically in routine interactions with the student, in small groups, and at any other time a need for language use can be specified. Skilled teachers can use EMT within the context of classroom and daily living activities without disrupting them.

TABLE 12–7
Sample Data Sheet for a Student

Student: Kristi			
Setting	**Occurrences of target responses**	**Prompts used**	**Student response acknowledged**
Target 1: greet peers "hi"			
Arrival	///	MQ, MQ, MQ	
Breakfast	/	M	+
Target 2: request assistance "help"			
Arrival	/	S	+
Departure	/	S	+
Target 3: "more"			
Breakfast	//	TD, TD	+ +
Lunch	/	TD	+

Setting: Specify activity when response occurred.

Occurrences: Use slash (/) for each time child uses target response.

Prompts: (Record a symbol each time a prompt is used). M = model, MQ = mand or question, TD = time delay.

Acknowledge: + = target response was acknowledged by adult or peer + either with the corresponding prompt or S+ for adult/peer acknowledgment of spontaneous target response without a prompt.

TABLE 12–8
EMT Planning and Data Collection Form for Two Preschool Children in an Activity

Activity: PlayDoh	Materials of Interest	Basic Arrangement
Date: 8-1-03	1. 2 cans of PlayDoh 2. 4 cookie cutters 3. 2 rolling pins	1. Cookie cutters on tray 2. Lids on PlayDoh 3. Rolling pins on shelf

Child	Communication target	Environmental arrangement	Milieu procedure	Child response	Comments
Margaret	Sign "help"	1. Opening PlayDoh (assistance)	Model	Signed "help"	Only one model
	Point to preference	2. Present two cookie cutters (choice making)	Model with physical assistance	Initiated point	Did not need prompt
	Sign "want more"	3. Small portion of PlayDoh (small portions)	Model "want more"	Signed "want more"	Needed two models
	Sign shape of cookie cutter	4. Present two cookie cutters (choice making)	Time delay and model "want star"	Signed "more"	Time delay, two models, then physical guidance for "star"
Mary	Verbalize "help, please"	1. Opening PlayDoh (assistance)	Incidental teaching	"Help, please"	Mary is requesting
	Verbalize "want ____"	2. Present two colors of PlayDoh (choice making)	Incidental teaching	No response	Consistently nonverbal
	Verbalize "want pin"	3. Roll PlayDoh without pin (assistance)	Incidental teaching	"Want pin"	Models are effective, mands are not
	Verbally request PlayDoh	4. Small portion of PlayDoh (small portion)	Time delay	"PlayDoh"	Exaggerated time delay to elicit response
	Point to cookie cutter	5. Present three cookie cutters on tray (choice making)	Time delay	Points to cookie cutter	Exaggerated time delay to elicit response

Teaching procedures used: model, mand model, time delay, and incidental teaching.

Planning classroom activities and routines around EMT opportunities ensures that training will occur. Routines provide extra support to students who are learning language because the context is familiar and the expectations for communication are clear. Table 12-8 is a completed EMT planning sheet used to organize the classroom activities of two preschool students.

Activity-based instruction (Bricker & Cripe, 1989) is similar to EMT except that it includes a range of social, motor, communicative, and cognitive skills. In activity-based instruction, materials are selected and settings arranged to facilitate active child engagement, provide opportunities for learning language and other skills, and promote natural opportunities for incidental teaching. Another highly effective strategy is to embed EMT into instruction on academic, work, or independent living tasks. Communication integrated with teaching of other skills further ensures that the natural functions of communication are being learned.

Michael is learning to ride the bus from his home to his job training site. His job coach prompts him to use his Dynamyte to greet the driver, to respond when other passengers ask him questions (e.g., "How are you? Where are you going?"), and to thank the driver as he gets off the bus. These communication skills are functional and well integrated with other daily living skills: waiting for the bus, getting on, putting money in the coin receptacle, watching for his stop, and checking for his belongings before departing the bus.

Communication goals may be embedded in tasks that teach several skills simultaneously. For example, teaching signs during grooming helps Kelly acquire situation-specific language.

In the grooming sequence, Kelly practices washing her face after lunch. The teacher uses time delays to prompt Kelly to sign for soap, towel, finished, and, if needed, help from the teacher. Initially, the teacher modeled by pointing to the photos, providing the verbal label, and prompting Kelly to imitate, but now she focuses her attention on Kelly and waits for Kelly to request the needed objects.

Table 12–9 shows communication targets and EMT procedures for three students during lunch. These students routinely enter the lunch room, ask for specific foods, make a choice of drinks, move to a table, and ask to sit next to a peer. Each student has three communication targets, appropriate for aspects of their established routine. Note that for Kristi, who is just learning to use

her VOCA, pointing to communicate is taught along with the sign "eat" to specify her food choices because she does not have specific food labels yet. Similarly, Jamie, who uses a picture book to communicate, is encouraged to point, vocalize, and attempt "please." Data can be collected on the lesson plan sheet using the columns immediately adjacent to where the target is listed. Social goals, such as looking at peers, getting peers' attention before communicating, and using "please," are taught concurrently with the target communicative form.

Assessment

When EMT is proposed as an intervention strategy, assessment serves two general purposes:

1. To describe the student's existing communication skills
2. To gather a database for developing treatment goals and intervention strategies

Performing an Environmental Inventory

The purpose of an environmental inventory is to identify the settings in which students need communication skills. Since almost every setting requires such skills, the first step of the inventory is to list the settings where a student spends the majority of his or her time. First, settings are identified (e.g., home, school, church,

TABLE 12–9
EMT Prompts and Communication Targets for Three Students During Lunch

Students		Date: 10-25-04						Total correct
Lunch contexts		Order food		Order drinks		Ask to sit with peer		
Jamie	Prompt	Model		Mand-model		Model		
	Target	Point + "eat" (sign)	+	"Juice" or "milk" (sign)	−	"Sit" (sign) + look at peer	+	2/3
Martin	Prompt	Time delay		Time delay		Mand model		
	Target	"I want + _____" (three-word request)	+	"I want + _____" (three-word request)	+	"(Name), sit here."	−	2/3
Kristi	Prompt	Mand model		Mand model		Model		
	Target	Show picture	+	Show picture	+	Show picture + vocalize to get attention	+	3/3

+ = correct response; − = incorrect response; NR = no response.

TABLE 12–10
Environmental Inventory for Communication Opportunities: Taking the Bus to School

Activities	Communication demands/functions	Possible training site	Possible teacher	Comments	Target forms
Getting on bus	Greet driver	Yes	Mom or sibling	Mom willing; sibling may be	"Good morning"
Greeting driver	Ask social questions	No	No one, driver too busy	Check for generalization from other social talk training	
Greeting riders	Friends greet, ask social questions	Yes	Normal peer or sibling	Two classmates are willing and ride the same bus	"Hello" + (name) "I'm fine" "I'm _____"
Ride to school	Varied questions, can comment on environment	Yes	Normal peer or sibling	Two classmates	Three words context appropriate; also yes or no
Getting off bus	Say good-bye to driver and passengers, greet teacher or aide who meets the bus	Maybe	Aide who greets students at school	Could coordinate with Mom on greeting	"Good-bye" "Hello" + (name)

transportation vehicles); then specific activities (e.g., eating, helping with chores at home, ordering and paying in a restaurant) within each setting are listed and particular communication demands identified.

Table 12-10 is an environmental inventory that describes communication opportunities during a ride to school each morning. The setting (bus to school) is identified, and five discrete activities during the ride are indicated. For each activity, general communication opportunities are listed, and a potential teacher is identified. An intervention plan requires that specific forms and functions of language be delineated and potential teachers identified.

An environmental inventory should be based on direct observation of the student in the potential teaching settings plus informal interviews with significant others. Interviews are especially helpful in deciding where to teach and in clarifying whether information gained during direct observation actually represents the student and the environment. Table 12–11 summarizes a plan for intervening to teach a student to greet the driver and peers during the student's ride to school.

Assessing Student Skills

Two general classes of assessment information are related to student skills. The first is a comprehensive overview that describes cognitive functioning, social skills, motor skills, and communication abilities, a topic

that is beyond the scope of this chapter. The second type of assessment examines students' actual performance of communicative behaviors in the settings identified through environmental inventory. This section focuses on the second type of assessment information. (More information is available in chapter 3 and 11.)

Functional Communication Skill Assessment

Assessing functional communication skills involves observing students in the activities identified in their environmental inventory and answering the following five questions:

1. *What do the students find interesting in this setting?* To answer this question, observe the students and note the people, objects, and events to which they attend. Determine if and how the students initiate socially to the people in the setting and if they are responsive to particular people.

2. *What communication functions do the students exhibit in this setting?* Seven basic communication functions should be considered: greetings, protests, requests for objects, requests for attention, requests for assistance, commenting, and answering (Table 12–12). Settings in which adult-initiated interactions are infrequent may offer few opportunities for answering and commenting. Note both whether opportunities occur and how the students respond to those opportunities.

TABLE 12–11
Using EMT to Teach Greetings with Multiple Teachers on Bus to School

Student: Tommy			Trainer responsible: Teacher aide with sibling	
New training _____		Date: January 10–30, 2004	Generalization training: √	

Activity	Trainer	Language targets	Procedures	Data/monitoring
Greeting driver	Sibling	"Good morning" + eye contact, smile	Sibling *models*, verbal praise for success, one corrective model, driver responds positively	
Responding to driver	Sibling	"Fine" in response to "How are you?"	Sibling *models*, prompts if needed, acknowledges	Sibling records on note card for teacher aide who summarizes and gives sibling feedback
Greeting friends	Sibling	"Hello" + (name)	Sibling *models* (say "hello" to your friend), *models* if needed expands, and acknowledges	
Responding to friends	Sibling	Varies: Reply "hello" Answer "fine" Answer "yes" or "no"	Sibling *models* appropriate reply, uses delayed modeling, expands, and praises	
Getting off bus	Teacher's aide	"Good-bye" "See you"	Aide *models*, prompts if needed, acknowledges	

3. *What forms do the students use to express these functions?* Communication functions can be expressed verbally and nonverbally. As described in chapter 11, students with severe disabilities often have idiosyncratic ways of expressing functions. For example, a student may throw objects in protest rather than nod or say, "No." Kristi, who has a limited verbal repertoire, uses a single gesture to indicate requests for help, for objects, or to invite joint play. Understanding a student's idiosyncratic communication forms is sometimes difficult but always worth the time invested in observation and analysis because current communication forms are the beginning point for teaching more elaborated language.

4. *What communication skills in the student's repertoires can be the base for building new language skills?* General information about students' skills gleaned from the review of existing language assessments can help determine the beginning skills to be taught with milieu methods. For example, the test results on Kristi's picture identification or on Michael's one- and two-word vocabulary should be added to their respective assessments of communication performance in natural settings.

Kristi's teacher reviewed her records and prepared a list of pictures she had been taught in the past. Using this list, the teacher constructed a probe or test in which Kristi was given two opportunities to use each picture on her VOCA in response to planned presentations of objects or events. Any pictures that Kristi mastered in the probe or test setting were then assessed in everyday settings. Information collected in natural settings indicated whether Kristi spontaneously used her VOCA to request or initiate interactions or whether she used her VOCA in response to questions (e.g., "What do you want?") or mands (e.g., "Tell me what you want to do next.")

Discrepancies between tested performance and naturalistic performance are ideal beginning points for milieu teaching interventions to promote generalization. The milieu method teaches skills slightly in advance of the students' current functional repertoires. Often, this requires generalization training to transfer already learned forms into their functional contexts. Language goals may include enlarging the student's vocabulary, extending the number of different forms used to express an already mastered communicative function (e.g., greetings), and teaching new ways to use and combine existing skills. Language skills that already have been acquired receptively but are not yet in the productive repertoire are also potentially excellent targets.

Michael understands many more labels than he uses spontaneously; these labels would be good targets in

TABLE 12–12
Seven Basic Communication Functions

Functions	Possible forms
Greetings	Waves Eye contact "Hello" "Name"
Requests for assistance	Gesture to come Giving object for which assistance is needed Taking the adult's hand and directing the adult to the task Crying "Help" Use of the adult's name
Request for object	Pointing Attempting to grab the object Taking the adult's hand and directing it to the object Verbal request: "Give me," "Want that" Naming object
Requests for information	Echoic imitation "What?" Eye contact plus quizzical look Showing object (requesting name or function of object)
Protests	"No" Pushing the adult away Crying Turning away from the adult or peer Throwing objects
Comments	Echoic imitation Pointing to the object Showing the object to the adult

simple two-word phrases with already mastered verbs (e.g., go library, go gym, go homeroom).

5. *What social communication strategies are used by the students?* To answer this question, students must be observed interacting to identify when they are socially responsive and what basic interactional skills they already have. EMT procedures teach and strengthen interactional skills as well as communication skills.

Combining Environmental Information and Student Assessments

The final step in assessment is to combine information gathered about the environment and students' skills in order to design a teaching plan. The teaching plan should specify the following:

1. The mode(s) for student communicative responses (e.g., verbal, sign, symbol system, or a combination of these)
2. Specific communication targets described in terms of both linguistic form and communicative function
3. Where and when teaching will occur
4. How the teaching environment should be restructured to include EMT interactions
5. Who will do the teaching
6. What assistance the teacher may need to use EMT strategies
7. Whether supplemental instruction is needed in addition to EMT and when this instruction will be provided

The student communication mode(s) and specific training targets should be derived primarily from student assessments with the communication team's consensus, but targets and mode(s) should also be determined by the characteristics of the settings. For example, if no one in a student's most frequented settings has knowledge of signs and if the student's significant others are unwilling to learn a signing symbol system, a communication board with pictures may be a more useful mode of communication. Many students will use multiple modes of communication.

The first training setting should be one in which the target skills will be most functional, but it should also be one in which milieu intervention is relatively easy to apply. Identification of teachers who can apply the milieu techniques effectively is essential. Often, new instructors need support to begin intervention. Assistance in identifying interactions for teaching and training specific language targets and instruction in modeling, manding, time delay, and feedback should be part of the trainers' preparation. Continued feedback to teachers is also needed if the intervention is to be effective.

Some skills may need intensive practice in the communication setting. For example, when teaching a student an initial set of signs or to associate pictures with objects, places, and activities, massed trial practice may be useful for training the basic motor skills involved in producing the response. Intensive instruction and EMT can proceed concurrently. Trainers can determine if more intensive teaching is needed by monitoring student performance and noting the actual number of EMT trials that students are receiving and their progress toward criterion performance. If the number of trials is low or students are not acquiring a specific target form after a reasonable length of time (e.g., 3 weeks of 10 trials each day), then massed trial instruction may be added to facilitate acquisition while continuing milieu teaching to ensure generalization to functional use. Other considerations include the symbol system taught, the functionality of the specific student's targets, and the adequacy of implementation of the milieu procedures.

To meet the goal of functional language, the effectiveness of intervention must be assessed at frequent intervals in natural settings. If students' functional communication repertoires are not expanding during intervention, adjustments in teaching tactics and target skills should be made. A sort of bottom-line question should be posed at 3-month intervals: What does this student communicate effectively now that he or she was unable to communicate 3 months ago? Assuming regular teaching sessions, even students with severe disabilities should show progress toward more functional skills after 3 months of training.

Generalized Skills Teaching

One of the strengths of EMT is that it is designed to facilitate generalization. Multiple exemplars (e.g., several linguistically similar forms that serve the same function) in functional communication contexts and naturally occurring reinforcers make the generalization of newly trained forms likely. When students have several appropriate forms that communicate their needs and wants effectively, they are likely to use them. However, when planning a milieu intervention, it is still important to consider the generalization of language training.

Language generalization occurs at several levels. Using a specific communication function (e.g., requests) or form (e.g., adjective–noun combinations, such as "red ball") across individuals and settings is an important but relatively simple type of generalization. Formation of a generalized concept, such as "ball," "cup," or "go," without either overgeneralizing (i.e., child says "goed" for "went" or refers to all red, round things as "ball") or undergeneralizing (i.e., child uses "ball" only when she sees a red, round ball but not when she sees a football) the word representing the concept is a more difficult type of generalization. The most complex type of generalization is generative language use (i.e., spontaneously initiating novel, meaningful word combinations in varied situations).

Generalization is an aspect of the learning process. As described in chapter 4, learning may be characterized as consisting of four overlapping levels or stages. First is the acquisition level, where students learn the basic response or skill (e.g., the word "ball" is associated with a spherical object). Language teaching typically is concentrated on this level. Simple form–object and form–event relationships are taught, and new skills are introduced as soon as students evidence associative learning. At the second or maintenance level of learning, students learn to routinely use the skill. They practice the skill in one or two functional contexts until appropriate use of the skill is well established and dependable. Next is the generalization level, when students begin to use the new response under a variety of conditions. They may overgeneralize or undergeneralize use of the response as they explore its potential functions and discover its essential attributes and delimiters. This level of language learning frequently has been ignored in language teaching, although many students with severe disabilities need help "fine-tuning" their use of forms. Finally, the fourth level of learning is characterized by competence, or fluency, in using the learned response. At this level, students approximate adult competence in use of the response. Students know when to use and not use the response. The response is used generatively—it is integrated with other communicative responses in the students' repertoires. This level of language learning is the desired outcome of intervention but typically has been overlooked.

Carter is beginning to learn some three-word phrases (e.g., "give me some," "play new game"). He typically uses his newly learned phrases in one of two ways: he either undergeneralizes and uses the phrase only in the exact circumstance it was learned or overgeneralizes and uses the phrase across many settings and contexts, some of which are not appropriate. Carter may say "give me some" when requesting popcorn from his mother but not when requesting other foods or requesting comic books from his friends. EMT may be used to prompt Carter to apply his newly learned phrases to a variety of appropriate contexts.

Initial acquisition, maintenance, generalization, and fluency are influenced by a number of variables that relate to the nature of the training, environmental support for trained language, and the criteria for mastery of the trained responses. Variables that relate specifically to training outcomes include (a) what is taught; (b) who teaches; (c) how functional, reinforcing, and consistent the consequences for communication are; (d) where teaching occurs; (e) how the content is organized; (f) what criteria for learning are applied; and (g) how responsive students' environments are to new learning.

What Is Taught?
Both the forms of communication (e.g., words, sentences, signs, use of picture, responses using a communication device) and their functions (e.g., greetings, commenting, questioning, requesting) must be learned if new skills are to be used. Simply put, the content of training must be functional for students, and they must have experience using the content in a functional manner during training.

New forms should reflect communicative functions that students have already acquired. For example, since

Michael already requests objects (e.g., milk, his favorite CD), a new form of requesting (e.g., "give me"+noun label) can be taught easily. New forms for training should be only slightly more complex than the forms that students currently use to express a particular function. Conversely, when teaching a new function, such as requesting information, it is easiest to begin with an already known form, or to teach the function with a single, simple form.

Who Teaches?
The simple answer to this question is everyone. As many people as possible who come in contact with students regularly and are willing to be either spontaneous teachers or trained teachers should be involved. Responsive conversational style as well as use of the four milieu teaching techniques can enhance the natural abilities of teachers, therapists, and parents to promote communication in context. The milieu methods have been learned and effectively applied by teachers and other professional staff, paraprofessionals, and parents. EMT is a particularly feasible approach because training can be incorporated easily into routine activities throughout the day. Parents and significant others can be effective in facilitating generalization through their use of the components of EMT.

When family members are willing, they can also teach new skills appropriate to settings outside of schools (Kaiser et al., 2001). Family members are especially important for ensuring that students maintain newly learned skills. These people may use EMT across the range of daily interactions to prompt functional use of forms that students have already learned. EMT procedures implemented in a naturalistic and conversational style should promote the functional use of students' skills without changing conversations into formal teaching interactions. Research comparing parent-implemented and therapist-implemented EMT found that young children with disabilities, including children with autism, showed greater language growth over a 6-month period after intensive intervention when their parents implemented EMT than when it was implemented only by a therapist (Kaiser et al., 1998). Parent-implemented training may be especially important for students who require intensive intervention over long periods of time and practice in specific social contexts. (Table 12–13 shows adaptations of EMT procedures for teaching students with autism.)

TABLE 12–13
Adaptations of EMT for Students with Autism

Environmental arrangement

- Select and arrange materials and the setting to minimize interfering behaviors
- Select high-preference materials
- Change materials before student loses interest
- Develop specific procedures for managing the child's interfering behaviors

Responsive conversational style

- Define limits to following the child's lead and interest (do not follow inappropriate or stereotypic behaviors)
- Establish patterns of turn taking and shared engagement with materials before introducing prompts
- Repeat and expand student's communication attempts
- Use imitation of student's actions (mirroring) to maintain engagement
- Match affect, volume, and pacing with the student's
- Expand nonverbal behavior toward appropriate play and use of objects

Milieu teaching

- Abbreviate the sequence of milieu prompts in order to maintain the child's focus of attention
- Use choice mands with visual choices
- Model targets alone ("Ball") rather than "Say ball" to reduce inappropriate echoing of the prompt ("Say")
- Use time delay to promote verbal initiations

How Are Students Reinforced?

To be generalized, language must come under the control of a breadth and range of naturally occurring consequences. To the greatest extent possible, only student-selected, naturally occurring reinforcers should be used in training (e.g., preferred activities, toys, or materials). If this is not possible initially with some training targets, then systematic introduction of naturally occurring consequences must be a central part of the training process. Consequences should always include continued positive interaction with teachers, meaningful comments related to students' responses, and expansions of student's utterances. These types of consequences are the typical natural results of everyday language use.

Where Does Teaching Occur?

Language should be taught in settings where communication naturally occurs: at home, on the playground, in the lunchroom, in the community, during academic activities, in the hallway, on the bus, during family outings, and in all the daily routines in which language is functional. With normally developing children, parents and teachers rarely set aside a particular time for specifically teaching language or other skills. There are too

many other things to be done. Language is taught informally in the course of typical activities, such as eating, dressing, toileting, bathing, and transitions between activities. In general, the same model should apply for students who have severe disabilities. In the classroom and in community instruction, it is important to integrate language learning into the teaching of other skills within which the use of language normally occurs.

Responsive Environments Enable New Learning and Generalization

One way to program for generalization is to introduce a new skill into its natural community of reinforcement (Stokes & Baer, 1977), that is, to allow the student to experience the naturally occurring positive outcomes of communication. As students acquire new skills and their behaviors change, natural environments must respond in ways that support those changes. During normal development, adaptation naturally occurs in mother–child interactions. Mothers are aware of their children's improved skills because they are in close contact with the children and expect them to change (Newport, 1976). When students have severe disabilities, adults sometimes lose the expectation that the students will change. In busy classrooms, teachers may not have much time to notice a student's attempts to comment using newly learned signs, pictures, or words. Thus, potential conversational partners may fail to respond differentially when change and growth do occur. Peers, teachers, and parents can become more responsive when they have information about changes in the students' communication. When these people respond to new forms and provide consequences for their use, they help students generalize and maintain new skills. Again, providing opportunities for students to use new forms is an important step toward ensuring maintenance.

Michael's and Kristi's parents should be provided with regular updates on newly learned words and pictures. In classrooms, demonstrations of new skills can help peers and teaching staff members recognize new communication forms.

Kristi is given the opportunity to use the new pictures she has learned on her Stepper™ in a large-group activity. Michael is invited to show his friends pictures on his DynaMyte and to label these pictures with his newly learned words.

Each of the preceding variables (what to teach, who teaches, where teaching occurs) should be directly addressed in designing an individualized communication training program for a student. Generalization should

be assessed on a weekly basis. Parents should be asked to note the use of new forms, and their help in promoting generalization should be sought. A simple report form, such as the one shown in Table 12-14, can be used to both assess generalization and prompt adults to facilitate language use.

Table 12-15 is a generalization planning worksheet developed to monitor and plan for generalization. The basic strategy is to plan training to include multiple, functional exemplars; to probe for simple generalization across persons, settings, and objects; to monitor generalization observed in functional contexts; and to remediate any observed problems in generalization. The worksheet should be updated on a weekly basis and shared with everyone involved in the students' training. Sharing data and brainstorming innovative approaches to support generalization and maintenance should be a collaborative team activity.

Designing an Optimal Teaching Approach

In the following paragraphs, we apply EMT strategies to Jordon.

An Application of Milieu Teaching

Jordon is a 5 year old boy. When he was 4 months of age, Jordon contracted cerebrospinal meningitis and was hospitalized for a period of 5 weeks. As a result

TABLE 12–14
Report Form for Assessing Generalization

Student: Kristi		Date: March 3, 2005	
Person reporting: Sharon (Mom)		Mode: Sign	

Target	Status	When was target used? How often?	New context
1. Help	Kristi has this one really well at school	Opening jar, one time; trying to get toys from sibling, three times	Trying to get arm in coat
2. Candy	Kristi's favorite	Lots of times! She really likes to try this request	None
3. Potty	Maintaining use of this word as a request	About five times (always appropriate)	No, she uses it by herself appropriately
4. Hug	Just started training this word	Not seen	Build a routine with Mom and Dad
5. _____			

Comments and suggestions: I think "hug" will need prompting. Kristi doesn't know how to ask for hugs yet. I may be missing some things she signs because her signing is not precise and I sometimes don't recognize her gestures as specific signs.

TABLE 12–15
Generalization Planning Worksheet

Student: Michael				Trainer: Martha (teacher)		Date: 1/30/05	
Form	Initial training criterion met (date and %)	Generalization probed			Spontaneous use observed		Further training needed? (date, plan, person responsible)
		Setting (%)	Trainer (%)	Stimuli (%)	Prompted (no, and occasion)	Unprompted (no, and occasion)	
Photo + label (help, book, finished)	10/14/04 100	100	100	85	One time (book) in response to time delay by teacher	Three times (help): 1. When he couldn't reach his jacket 2. When he wanted teacher assistance with his backpack 3. When a peer took his paper	"Finished" will be trained at home beginning 2/12/05. Mom and Dad will build into mealtime routine in morning and evening.

of the meningitis, Jordon experienced significant brain damage, which resulted in hemiplegia of the left side and severe mental retardation. Jordon lives at home with his mother, his 12 year old sister, and his maternal grandmother. He attends a regular kindergarten class from 9:00 a.m. to 3:00 p.m., Monday through Friday. Jordon is seen by the school's speech and language clinician twice each week for small group language instruction. Both the speech clinician and the special education teacher consult with Jordon's kindergarten teacher. Late afternoons are spent at home with his grandmother and his sister, when she arrives home from school. Jordon's mother comes home from work around 6:00 p.m. Weekends are generally less structured. On Saturday mornings, Jordon usually attends a young children's story hour at the local library. Jordon also spends time on other activities, such as going to the grocery with his mother, going to the playground with his sister, and accompanying his grandmother as she does chores around the house.

Jordon has very little "language." He vocalizes and/or points to request; smiles and sometimes produces a string of syllables in response to adult attention; and dependably waves "hello" and "goodbye" with his right hand. He responds inconsistently to peer initiations and protests to peers, but does not initiate contact, vocalizations, or smiling to peers.

Jordon's special education teacher, his regular kindergarten teacher, his SLP, and his mother form a planning team that focuses on his communication needs. This team follows a series of steps in developing a functional language training program for Jordon that uses EMT strategies.

Gathering New Information

First, functional communication skills that will give Jordon more control over his physical and social environment are identified by conducting an environmental inventory in the settings in which Jordon spends the majority of his time. For these environments (his kindergarten class, playground, and home), the following information is determined:

1. The major activities that occur within each environment:
   - Kindergarten class—large group, small group, snack or lunch, and gym or recess
   - Playground—swings, riding push toys, and slide
   - Home—meals, bedtime or story time, trips in the car, and play with favorite toys
2. Basic communication skills that will help Jordon function more independently and that will facilitate increased participation in activities
3. The individuals in each environment or activity who would be logical milieu teachers and their current skills
4. Whether the materials available and the arrangement of the environment are optimal for promoting Jordon's initiations and choice making and facilitating the use of EMT procedures

Information needed to complete the environmental inventories for Jordon's classroom activities is readily available. His mother describes his home activities. Jordon's special education teacher and his SLP divide the responsibility of observing Jordon at school and at home after school. For each environment, they obtain information about strategies currently being used to teach language, the responsiveness of teachers to Jordon when he shows interest in something or attempts to communicate, and opportunities for Jordon to control his physical and social environment.

Second, interviews are conducted to get information from significant others as a basis for planning a functional communication program. Five questions are posed:

1. What does Jordon find interesting in this setting?
2. What communication functions does he exhibit in this setting?
3. What forms does he use to express these functions?
4. What existing communication skills can be the basis for building new skills?
5. What social communication strategies does Jordon use in this setting?

The special education teacher interviews the teacher and teaching assistant in the kindergarten class, the physical therapist, and the peer tutor who works with Jordon. Jordon's mother interviews his grandmother, his sister, and the story-time coordinator at the Saturday morning library program. The interviews are designed to obtain specific information about the existing environmental demands for Jordon to communicate, the social and communicative behaviors exhibited by Jordon in each setting, and the minimal skills that Jordon needs to improve his ability to interact and communicate with others in the environment. The planning team uses the interview data to verify, clarify, and augment their observational data and to gain insight into the ability of significant others to identify and foster Jordon's communicative behavior.

Third, in addition to taking into account environmental characteristics and demands, Jordon's planning team specifies child characteristics essential to consider in developing an individualized, functional communication training program. Test results (including the results of diagnostic testing) and informal observation provide relevant information about Jordon's receptive language and expressive communication skills, motor development, and sensory abilities. Reports from teachers and significant others provide information about his social interaction strategies, preferred activities, and engagement with the physical environment:

1. *What does Jordon find interesting?* Jordon's interests vary by setting. At home, he likes to look at books alone or with an adult or his sister, to be pushed in a swing, and to ride the merry-go-round on the nearby playground. He likes to ride in the car. He also likes to look at mechanical things, such as the vacuum cleaner, the coffeemaker, and the blender when they are operating. He enjoys meals and especially likes having a snack with his sister when she arrives home after school. He seems to enjoy story time at the library as long as he can see the pictures. At school, Jordon does not seem interested in many of the classroom activities (e.g., large group, going to most centers, working independently on preacademic tasks). He does like to look at books, watch and manipulate trucks and cars, and be pushed on the swing during outdoor time. The physical therapist reports that Jordon seems very interested in mechanical toys (e.g., a windup top, a toy truck with a turning cement mixer, race cars that move on a track).

2. *What communication functions does Jordon exhibit?* At home, he dependably greets his family and protests when he does not get his way or does not want to do something. He sometimes requests objects and assistance. At school, Jordon demonstrates these same functions (i.e., greetings, protests, requests) but seems less consistent. For example, he greets his physical therapists and SLP but does not always greet his classroom teacher and never greets peers. He does protest when peers take toys or interfere with his activities.

3. *What forms does Jordon use to express these functions?* In all settings, Jordon vocalizes to greet others (except peers). He reaches for objects, looks at adults, vocalizes to request, and vocalizes cries and sometimes tantrums to protest. Jordon spontaneously produces a variety of one-syllable sounds but does not yet use them to signal specific functions. His mother reports that he can wave good-bye with his right hand with minimal prompting. He waves good-bye at story time and with familiar adults if his mother prompts him.

4. *What existing skills can be the basis for building new skills?* Jordon can take turns nonverbally (e.g., alternating putting objects in a basket, pushing a car back and forth) and vocally (e.g., making sounds when an adult imitates him). He is able to do picture-to-object and object-to-picture matching, and he is working on a program that teaches him to point to an object after presentation of its verbal label. He can also imitate motor gestures with his right hand (e.g., wave "hi," touch his head). He responds to the word "no" by stopping whatever he is doing. Testing has shown that Jordon has good visual and auditory functioning. His motor development limits both his mobility and, to an extent, his engagement with objects, toys, and peers. He basically does not use the left side of his body; rather, his left hand is tightly clenched and his arm drawn upward. He can sit independently for long periods and can pivot around in a circle. He is able to roll from one place to another but typically relies on prompting to do so.

5. *What social communication strategies does Jordon use?* Jordon gets attention from his mother, his sister, his grandmother, his teachers, and his physical therapist by visually following the person until he can establish eye contact. On making eye contact, Jordon smiles and sometimes produces a string of sounds. He can also vocalize and reach for objects and coordinate his attention by looking at an adult, reaching for the object and vocalizing, then looking back at the adult. He smiles and turns toward adults when they speak to him. He responds to his name and to familiar words and simple phrases (e.g., his sister's name, car, eat, potty, time to go) with appropriate anticipatory responses (e.g., looking around for his sister, vocalizing and smiling when it is time to go in the car or eat). He will occasionally respond to peers by taking a toy they offer. He will protest to peers but does not initiate eye contact, vocalizations or smiling toward peers.

Planning the Functional Communication Program

Fourth, Jordon's team plans his functional communication program by considering the data on child performance and learning characteristics in light of the data obtained from the environmental inventories. They begin by determining target responses that are slightly above Jordon's current level of functioning and that are functional across environments and activities. Se-

lected training targets include "more," "help," and pointing to one of two pictures to choose one of the two represented objects (i.e., choice making). The team feels that many natural opportunities to teach each of these targets will occur across the primary activities and environments.

His team next considers the communication mode to be used in teaching each response. A review of Jordon's expressive modalities indicates that he spontaneously produces a variety of sounds but does not imitate sounds. He uses his right hand to point to things that he wants and also for picture–object and object–picture matching. He has virtually no use of his left hand, placing limitations on the repertoire of signs he can ultimately produce. Because he already shows some degree of skill using pictures, Jordon's teachers decide that his primary communication system should involve a picture communication board, but they will always include models of verbal responses.

In summary, three beginning goals are selected for Jordon:

1. Sign "help" (modified)
2. Sign "more" (modified)
3. Indicate choices by pointing on a communication board

The next step in planning Jordon's communication program is determining how and when to teach these goals. Appropriate vocal stimuli (words) will be paired with pictorial stimuli (pictures representing concepts). Vocal imitation training will be given at the same time he is taught to use signs and pictures. Initially, concrete pictoral stimuli should be used. This poses a problem for teaching the more abstract concepts of "help" and "more." The team decides to teach Jordon to express these responses by producing modified signs that will accommodate his physical disability. Verbal imitation training of "help" and "more" will accompany the respective sign training.

The third goal, indicating choice, uses the communication board. Initially, two pictures are presented. Beginning with two pictures is appropriate because Jordon already understands that pictures stand for objects and actions. As Jordon becomes more proficient in using the communication board, additional pictures will be added gradually. The pictures on the board vary and are functionally related to the activity at hand. Once Jordon indicates his choice, he is given access to that material.

In their fifth step, the planning team discusses the techniques they will use to train the target responses. Several EMT procedures are selected.

Modeling Procedure   Initially, modeling would be used to teach "help" and "more" at times when Jordon appears to need help or want more of something. The team agrees that they will attempt to give him the opportunity to express each function himself before modeling the appropriate (modified) sign. For example, when Jordon correctly imitates each sign 80% of the time, the teachers will interchange use of the mand-model and time delay procedures (rather than the model procedure) to elicit responses. (Attempts by Jordon to indicate "help" or "more" that are followed by the model, mand-model, or time delay procedure technically represent applications of the incidental teaching procedure, i.e., a child's request followed by the model, mand-model, or time delay procedure.) In addition to collecting performance data on sign production, the team collects data on vocal imitation training that accompanies each nonverbal training trial. The mand-model, time delay, and incidental teaching procedures are used to teach Jordon to make choices using the communication board. An example of how each of these techniques is applied for this purpose follows.

Mand-Model Procedure   The mand-model procedure is used when Jordon indicates a choice in response to his teacher's presenting two alternatives.

After Jordon has learned to respond by imitating his targets (help and more) during the model procedure, the mand-model procedure is introduced. When it is Jordon's turn during music group, the teacher shows him the bells and the tambourine. She then places in reach his communication board that shows a picture of each of these objects and asks, "Which musical instrument do you want?" If Jordon does not respond or if he makes an incomplete or unclear response, she prompts by presenting a model of the correct response (i.e., demonstrates a clear pointing response to the picture that Jordon appears to favor), or she physically prompts Jordon to make a clear response. The teacher then verbally expands his nonvocal response (e.g., "You want the bells") and provides a verbal model that is for the situation and his skill level (e.g., "bells"). Following the model procedure to train "bells," he is given the bells to shake.

Delay Procedure   The delay procedure is used to support Jordon in learning to initiate use of his communication. Delay will be introduced after Jordon has some success using targets in the model and mand-model procedures.

In free play, when Jordon visually expresses interest in a toy, the teacher presents his communication board displaying pictures of the toy of interest and another toy. The teacher looks at Jordon for about 5 seconds but says nothing (delay). If Jordon points to either picture, he receives the corresponding object. A point to the "wrong" picture (i.e., Jordon shows displeasure on receiving the object) or an incomplete or unclear response results in a mand (tell me what you want) or model prompt (teacher signs an option) with or without a physical prompt, as necessary. An appropriate verbal model is presented before delivering the chosen toy.

Incidental Teaching Procedure   The incidental teaching procedure is used on occasions when Jordon requests a material or activity. It can be introduced at any point in training because it embeds the model, mand-model, or time delay procedures as needed to support Jordon's use of his targets.

If Jordon points to the record player, the teacher presents his communication board, displaying pictures of the record player and something else. She then uses the mand-model (what do you want?) or delay procedure (waits 5 seconds while looking at Jordon but says nothing) to elicit a pointing response. Verbal and physical prompts are presented as needed. Before giving Jordon access to the record player, the model procedure is applied to elicit an appropriate vocal or pointing response.

As a sixth step, several additional tasks are completed in developing Jordon's communication training programs. The team writes task-analyzed instructional programs, including levels of prompts, vocal imitation training procedures, and criterion performance levels for each communication objective. Procedures for data collection and data sheets also are developed. The members of the team agree to do EMT whenever naturalistic opportunities occur and especially in the context of other kinds of skill training. Data are collected daily on a minimum of 10 trials for each objective. However, training occurs during other naturalistic teaching opportunities throughout the day. The teachers decide to use certain situations as training settings and other situations as generalization settings. In school, Jordon's communication goals are trained formally during small-group sessions in both his early intervention class and his kindergarten class, during snack, and at recess. Probes for generalization are conducted during large-group sessions, lunch, and gym. Jordon's environmental inventory indicates that his mother and grandmother are willing to use environmental arrangement strategies and the EMT procedures. Jordon's early intervention teacher, who has had previous EMT experience, plans to provide EMT training by visiting Jordon's home once each week for 2 months. Periodic posttraining visits will be made to Jordon's home to assess the family members' use of EMT and to provide feedback and additional training as necessary.

Seventh and finally, the team considers whether didactic communication training should be conducted in conjunction with the naturalistic communication training. The consensus is to implement only the naturalistic training procedures initially. Jordon's vocal imitation skills are monitored carefully, and if the anticipated rate of acquisition is not achieved within 4 months, the issue of concomitant didactic training on vocal imitation skills will again be considered.

Summary

Teaching functional language is a curriculum goal that requires support from a variety of persons in the larger ecosystem in which instruction occurs. EMT strategies are selected and purposefully embedded into the social interactions of activities and across settings. Training needs to be more frequent and dispersed than can easily be managed by speech clinicians who see individual children for two or three sessions each week. Thus, language teaching is a responsibility shared by school staff and family members and cannot be taught separately from other skills if it is to be functional. Assigning responsibility, providing necessary training, facilitating access to appropriate training settings, and sharing information are essential aspects of allocating resources for functional language training. The development of problem-solving strategies through team collaboration is necessary with functional communication teaching because problems undoubtedly arise when such broad-based instruction is undertaken.

Suggested Activities

1. Observe a student with disabilities for a period of 1 to 2 hours. Note the ways in which the child attempts to communicate and the ways in which the adults in the environments respond. From these observations and your notes, identify at least five opportunities to teach a functional language skill. Describe the context, the skill, and the procedure you would use to teach the skill.

2. One of the most important skills that a teacher must master is clear communication about communication. Review Michael's case study at the beginning of this chapter. Then role-play, explaining his skills, his needs, and the basics of milieu teaching to Michael's homeroom general education teacher. This exercise works best in teams of three: (a) one person explains, (b) one person plays the general education teacher, and (c) one person evaluates the interaction and gives feedback. Switch roles and use what you learn from one another. Summarize what you have learned after all three people have role-played.

3. Consider how to create a classroom that is a "context for conversation." Choose a type of classroom that reflects the age and most appropriate options for students of interest to you. Include the following: (a) how teachers will interact with students, (b) the classroom schedules, (c) the physical design of the classroom, and (d) training for teaching assistants and peers. List five simple things that you might do to promote communication in the classroom.

References

Alpert, C. L., & Kaiser, A. (1992). Training parents as milieu language teachers. *Journal of Early Intervention, 16*(1), 31–52.

Alpert, C. L., Kaiser, A., Hemmeter, M. L., & Ostrosky, M. (1987, November). *Training adults to use environmental arrangement strategies to prompt language.* Paper presented at the annual meeting of the Division of Early Childhood, Council on Exceptional Children, Denver.

Alpert, C. L., & Rogers-Warren, A. K. (1985). Communication of autistic persons, characteristics and intervention. In S. F. Warren & A. K. Rogers-Warren (Eds.), *Teaching functional language* (pp. 123–155). Baltimore: University Park Press.

American Speech-Language-Hearing Association (ASHA). (1991). Report: Augmentative and alternative communication. *Asha* 33 (supl. 5),10.

Anderson, S. R., & Spradlin, J. E. (1980). The generalized effects of productive labeling training involving comment object classes. *Journal of the Association for the Severely Handicapped, 5,* 143–157.

Angelo, D. H., & Goldstein, H. (1990). Effects of a pragmatic teaching strategy for requesting information by communication board users. *Journal of Speech and Hearing Disorders, 55*(2), 231-243.

Beukelman, D. R., & Mirenda, P. (1998). *Augmentative and alternative communication: Management of severe communication disorders in children and adults.* Baltimore: Paul H. Brookes.

Bricker, D., & Cripe, J. (1989). Activity-based intervention. In D. Bricker (Ed.), *Early intervention for at-risk and handicapped infants, toddlers and preschool children* (pp. 251-274). Palo Alto, CA: VORT Corp.

Cavallero, C. C., & Bambara, L. (1982). Two strategies for teaching language during free play. *Journal of the Association for the Severely Handicapped, 7*(2), 80-93.

Charlop, M. H., & Carpenter, M. H. (2000). Modified incidental teaching sessions: A procedure for parents to increase spontaneous speech in their children with autism. *Journal of Positive Behavior Interventions, 2*(2), 98-112.

Charlop, M. H., & Walsh, M. E. (1986). Increasing autistic children's spontaneous verbalizations of affection: An assessment of time delay and peer modeling procedures. *Journal of Applied Behavior Analysis, 19*, 307-314.

Charlop, M. H., & Trasowech, J. E. (1991). Increasing children's daily spontaneous speech. *Journal of Applied Behavioral Analysis, 24*, 747-761.

Farmer-Dougan, V. (1994). Increasing requests by adults with developmental disabilities using incidental teaching by peers. *Journal of Applied Behavior Analysis, 27*(3), 533-544.

Frost, L. A., & Bondy, A. S. (1994). *The picture exchange communication system training manual.* Cherry Hill, NJ: Pyramid Educational Consultants.

Frost, L. A., & Bondy, A. S. (1996). *The picture exchange communication system training manual.* Cherry Hill, NJ: Pyramid Educational Consultants.

Gee, K., Graham, N., Goetz, L., Oshima, G., & Yoshioka, K. (1991). Teaching students to request the continuation of routine activities by using time delay and decreasing physical assistance in the context of chain interruption. *Journal of the Association for Persons with Severe Handicaps, 16*, 154-167.

Gee, K., Graham, N., Sailor, W., & Goetz, L. (1995). Use of integrated general education and community settings as primary contexts for skill instruction for students with severe, multiple disabilities. *Behavior Modification, 19*, 33-58.

Goldstein, H. (2002). Communication intervention for children with autism: A review of treatment efficacy. *Journal of Autism and Developmental Disabilities, 32*(5), 373-396.

Green, G. (2001). Behavior analytic instruction for learners with autism: Advances in stimulus control technology. *Focus on Autism and Other Developmental Disabilities, 16*, 72-85.

Gresham, F. M., & MacMillan, D. L. (1997). Autistic recovery? An analysis and critique of the empirical evidence on the early intervention project. *Behavioral Disorders, 22*(4), 185-201.

Halle, J. W., Baer, D. M., & Spradlin, J. E. (1981). Teachers' generalized use of delay as a stimulus control procedure to increase language use in handicapped children. *Journal of Applied Behavior Analysis, 14*, 387-400.

Halle, J. W., Marshall, A. M., & Spradlin, J. E. (1979). Time delay: A technique to increase language use and facilitate generalization in retarded children. *Journal of Applied Behavior Analysis, 12*, 431-440.

Hamilton, B., & Snell, M. E. (1993). Using the milieu approach to increase spontaneous communication book use across environments by an adolescent with autism. *Augmentative and Alternative Communication, 9*, 259-272.

Hancock, T. B., & Kaiser, A. P. (1996). Siblings' use of milieu teaching at home. *Topics in Early Childhood Special Education, 16*(2), 168-190.

Hancock, T. B., & Kaiser, A. P. (2002). The effects of trainer-implemented enhanced milieu teaching on the social communication of children with autism. *Topics in Early Childhood Special Education, 22*(1), 39-54.

Haring, T. G., Neetz, J. A., Lovinger, L., Peck, C., & Semmel, M. I. (1987). Effects of four modified incidental teaching procedures to create opportunities for communication. *Journal of the Association for Persons with Severe Handicaps, 12*, 218-226.

Haring, T. G., Roger, B., Lee, M., Breen, C., & Gaylord-Ross, R. (1986). Teaching social language to moderately handicapped students. *Journal of Applied Behavior Analysis, 19*, 159-171.

Hart, B. M., & Risley, T. R. (1968). Establishing the use of descriptive adjectives in the spontaneous speech of disadvantaged preschool children. *Journal of Applied Behavior Analysis, 1*, 109-120.

Hart, B. M., & Risley, T. R. (1974). Using preschool materials to modify the language of disadvantaged children. *Journal of Applied Behavior Analysis, 7*, 243-256.

Hart, B. M., & Risley, T. R. (1975). Incidental teaching of language in the preschool. *Journal of Applied Behavior Analysis, 8*, 411-420.

Hart, B. M., & Risley, T. R. (1980). In vivo language intervention: Unanticipated general effects. *Journal of Applied Behavior Analysis, 12*, 407-432.

Hart, B. M., & Rogers-Warren, A. K. (1978). Milieu teaching approaches. In R. L. Schiefelbusch (Ed.), *Bases of language intervention* (Vol. 2, pp. 193-235). Baltimore: University Park Press.

Hemmeter, M. L., Ault, M. J., Collins, B. C., & Meyers, S. (1996). The effects of teacher-implemented feedback within free time activities. *Education and Training in Mental Retardation and Developmental Disabilities, 31*, 203-212.

Hemmeter, M. L., & Kaiser, A. P. (1994). Enhanced milieu teaching: Effects of parent-implemented language intervention. *Journal of Early Intervention, 18*, 269-289.

Humphries, T. L. (2003) Effectiveness of pivotal response training as a behavioral intervention for young children with autism spectrum disorder. *Bridges: Practice Based Research Synthesis, 2*(4), 1-10. Available at http://www.researchtopractice.info

Hunt, P., Alwell, M., & Goetz, L. (1988). Acquisition of conversation skills and the reduction of inappropriate social interaction behaviors. *Journal of the Association for Persons with Severe Handicaps, 13*, 20-27.

Kaiser, A. P. (1993). Functional language. In M. E. Snell (Ed.), *Instruction of students with severe disabilities* (4th ed. pp. 347-379). New York: Macmillan.

Kaiser, A. P. (2000, June). *Research on parent-implemented early language interventions.* Paper presented at the Symposium on Research in Child Language Disorders (SRCLD), Madison, WI.

Kaiser, A. P., & Hancock, T. B. (2000, April). *Supporting children's communication development through parent-implemented naturalistic interventions.* Paper presented at the 2nd Annual Conference on Research Innovations in Early Intervention (CRIEI), San Diego.

Kaiser, A. P., Hancock T. B., & Hester, P. P. (1998). Parents as co-interventionists: Research on applications of naturalistic language teaching procedures. *Infants and Young Children, 10*(4), 1-11.

Kaiser, A. P., Hancock, T. B., McLean, Z. Y., & Stanton-Chapman, T. L. (2001, October). *Building social communication skills during peer interaction: Kidtalk for Peers.* Paper presented at the Head Start University Grantees Meeting, Alexendria, VA.

Kaiser, A. P., Hancock, T. B., & Nietfeld, J. P. (2000). The effects of parent-implemented enhanced milieu teaching on the social communication of children who have autism [Special issue]. *Journal of Early Education and Development, 4,* 423-446.

Kaiser, A. P., Hancock, T. B., Nietfeld, J. P., & Delaney, E. (1996, December). *Adapting enhanced milieu teaching for children with autism.* Paper presented at the meeting of DEC International Early Childhood Conference on Children with Special Needs, Phoenix, AZ.

Kaiser, A. P., Hester, P. P., & McDuffie, A. S. (2001). Supporting communication in young children with developmental disabilities. In D. Felce & E. Emerson (Eds.), *MRDD Research Reviews* (Vol. 7 (2):, pp. 143-150).

Kaiser, A. P., Ostrosky, M. M., & Alpert, C. L. (1993). Training teachers to use environmental arrangement and milieu teaching with nonvocal preschool children. *Journal of the Association for Persons with Severe Handicaps, 18*(3), 188-199.

Kaiser, A. P., Yoder, P. J., & Keetz, A. (1992). Evaluating milieu teaching. In S. F. Warren & J. Reichle (Eds.), *Causes and effects in communication and language intervention* (pp. 9-47). Baltimore: Paul H. Brookes.

Koegel, L. K., Koegel, R. L., Harrower, J. K., & Carter, C. M. (1999). Pivotal response intervention. I: Overview of approach. *Journal of the Association for Persons with Severe Handicaps, 24*(3), 174-185.

Lennox, D. B., & Brune, P. (1993). Incidental teaching for training communication in individuals with traumatic brain injury. *Brain Injury, 7*(5), 449-454.

Matson, J. L., Sevin, J. A., Box, M. L., Francis, K. L., & Sevin, B. M. (1993). An evaluation of two methods for increasing self-initiated verbalizations in autistic children. *Journal of Applied Behavior Analysis, 26,* 389-398.

McCathren, R. B. (2000). Teacher-implemented prelinguistic communication intervention. *Focus on Autism and Other Developmental Disabilities, 15*(1), 21-29.

McEachin, J. J., Smith, T., & Lovaas, O. I. (1993). Long-term outcome for children with autism who received early intensive behavioral treatment. *American Journal on Mental Retardation, 97,* 359-372.

McGee, G. G., Almeida, M. C., Sulzer-Azaroff, B., & Feldman, R. S. (1992). Promoting reciprocal interactions via peer incidental teaching. *Journal of Applied Behavior Analysis, 25*(1), 117-126.

McGee, G. G., Krantz, P. J., & McClannahan, L. E. (1985). The facilitative effects of incidental teaching on preposition use by autistic children. *Journal of Applied Behavior Analysis, 18,* 17-31.

McGee, G. G., Morrier, M. J., & Daly, T. (1999). An incidental teaching approach to early intervention for toddlers with autism. *Journal of the Association for Persons with Severe Handicaps, 24,* 133-146.

Miller, C., Collins, B. C., & Hemmeter, M. L. (2002). Using a naturalistic time delay procedure to teach nonverbal adolescents with moderate-to-severe mental disabilities to initiate manual signs. *Journal of Developmental and Physical Disabilities, 14*(3), 247-261.

Miranda-Linne, F., & Melin, L. (1992). Acquisition, generalization, and spontaneous use of color objectives: A comparison of incidental teaching and traditional discrete-trial procedures for children with autism. *Research in Developmental Disabilities, 13*(3), 191-210.

Mobayed, K. L., Collins, B. C., Strangis, D. E., Schuster, J. W., & Hemmeter, M. L. (2000). Teaching parents to employ mand-model procedures to teach their children requesting. *Journal of Early Intervention, 23*(3), 165-179.

National Research Council. (2001). *Educating children with autism.* Washington, DC: National Academy Press.

Newport, E. L. (1976). Motherese: The speech of mothers to young children. In N. J. Castellan, D. B. Pisoni, & G. R. Potts (Eds.), *Cognitive theory* (Vol. 2, pp. 177-218). Hillsdale, NJ: Lawrence Erlbaum Associates.

Oliver, C. B., & Halle, J. W. (1982). Language training in the everyday environment: Teaching functional sign use to a retarded child. *Journal of the Association for the Severely Handicapped, 7*(3), 50-62.

Ostrosky, M. M., Kaiser, A. P., & Odom, S. L. (1993). Facilitating children's social communicative interactions through the use of peer-mediated interventions. In A. P. Kaiser & D. B. Gray (Eds.), *Enhancing children's communication: Research foundations for intervention* (Vol. 8, pp. 7-43). Baltimore: Paul H. Brookes.

Rodi, M. S., & Hughes, C. (2000). Teaching communication book use to a high school student using a milieu approach. *Journal of the Association for Persons with Severe Handicaps, 25,* 175-179.

Rogers-Warren, A. K., & Warren, S. F. (1980). Mand for verbalization: Facilitating the display of newly-taught language. *Behavior Modification, 4,* 361-382.

Romski, M. A., & Sevcik, R. A. (1992). Developing augmented language in children with severe mental retardation. In S. F. Warren & J. Reichle (Eds.), *Causes and effects in communication and language intervention* (pp. 113-130). Baltimore: Paul H. Brookes.

Schwartz, I. S., Anderson, S. R., & Halle, J. W. (1988). Training teachers to use naturalistic time delay: Effects on teacher behavior and on the language use of students. *Journal of the Association for Persons with Severe Handicaps, 14,* 48-57.

Stokes, T. F., & Baer, D. M. (1977). An implicit technology of generalization. *Journal of Applied Behavior Analysis, 10,* 349-367.

Wacker, D. P., & Reichle, J. (1993). Functional communication training as an intervention for problem behavior: An overview and introduction to our edited volume. In J. Reichle & D. P. Wacker (Eds.), *Communicative alternatives to challenging behavior: Integrating functional assessment and intervention strategies* (Vol. 3, pp. 1-8). Baltimore: Paul H. Brookes.

Warren, S. F., & Bambara, L. M. (1989). An experimental analysis of milieu language intervention: Teaching and action-object form. *Journal of Speech and Hearing Disorders, 54,* 448-461.

Warren, S. F., Gazdag, G. E., Bambara, L. M., & Jones, H. A. (1994). Changes in the generativity and use of semantic relationships concurrent with milieu language intervention. *Journal of Speech and Hearing Research, 37*(4), 924-934.

Warren, S. F., McQuarter, R. J., & Rogers-Warren, A. K. (1984). The effects of teacher mands and models on the speech of unresponsive language-delayed children. *Journal of Speech and Hearing Research, 51,* 43-52.

Warren, S. F., & Rogers-Warren, A. K. (1983). Setting variables affecting the display of trained noun referents by retarded children. In K. Kernan, M. Begab, & R. Edgerton (Eds.), *Environments and behavior: The adaptation of mentally retarded persons* (pp. 257-282). Baltimore: University Park Press.

Yoder, P. J., Kaiser, A. P., & Alpert, C. L. (1991). An exploratory study of the interaction between language teaching methods and child characteristics. *Journal of Speech and Hearing Research, 34,* 155-167.

General Curriculum Access

Diane M. Browder
Lynn Ahlgrim-Delzell
Ginevra Courtade-Little
Martha E. Snell

This chapter addresses how teachers can apply successful methods to teach academic skills to students with severe disabilities by accessing general education curriculum. The following case studies, based on real students, will be used to illustrate how to apply the concepts described.

 Brett

Brett, an 8-year-old boy with severe disabilities, communicates through eye gaze, touch/reach, and vocalizing. He laughs when happy but whines, cries, and pushes objects or people away when unhappy. He allows staff to utilize hand-over-hand assistance when using his Tech-Talk® (Advanced Multimedia Devices) but has shown little inter-

est in using it himself (see the appendix at the end of this chapter). Brett sits and walks short distances without help. He relies on staff assistance to eat and is on a toileting schedule. Brett does not yet use symbols for communication or academic learning.

 Amy

Amy is a fifth grader with a traumatic brain injury. She has a seizure disorder controlled with medication and shunts. She is nonambulatory and quadriplegic and is dependent on caregivers for all activities of daily living. She receives occupational, physical, and speech therapy. Her voluntary movements consist of slight head turns and eye movement.

Amy responds to auditory and tactile stimulation and communicates through the use of augmentative and alternative communication devices. She seems to enjoy music, sensory stimulation, and being read a story. Amy has some emerging use of symbols to communicate but has not yet learned to use them for academic tasks.

Ricky

Ricky is a 13-year-old boy with severe disabilities. He has a visual impairment and is transported to school in a wheelchair. Ricky demonstrates interest in school by becoming increasingly alert and responsive as the day's routine begins. He understands verbal requests and responds positively when spoken to in a soft, calm tone of voice. He acknowledges familiar people by saying "mama." Ricky uses objects to communicate. When given a choice between two objects, he will push away the object he does not want and take the object he does want. He uses a yellow triangle to express that he is ready to walk and work and a tape to express that he wants to listen to a book on tape. Ricky indicates "yes" by smiling and "no" by pushing away.

Dominique

Dominique is a 16-year-old girl with Down syndrome. She was born in Costa Rica, where she attended school sporadically for approximately 5 years. She has lived in the United States for 2 years. Dominique's primary language is Spanish, but she seems to understand some English. She is very shy and covers her face with her hands. She is in need of corneal transplants for both eyes and receives visual impairment services. Dominique can see enlarged text, reads some sight words, and is learning to write her name and other functional words. She expresses herself by giving thumbs up to questions like "Do you have to use the restroom" and points to what she wants to eat.

The Meaning of Having Access to the General Education Curriculum

Having access to the general curriculum means having the opportunity and instructional support to learn the core academic content typical of one's grade level. Inclusion in typical classes is an important way to enhance this access, but inclusion is not synonymous with having access to the general curriculum. Inclusion involves creating opportunities for students to attend their neighborhood schools and general education classes. With full membership and individualized supports, students can benefit socially and academically from being included in general education. Planning access to the general curriculum in these settings

Box 13–1 Having the Opportunity to Learn Academic Skills

All students should have the opportunity to learn academic skills like reading and math. Educators have not always agreed with this assumption. Students have sometimes been given labels to distinguish those who could learn academics ("educable") from those who could not ("trainable"). Not much is known about the academic potential of students with severe disabilities because educators have often made assumptions that academics were a lower priority than acquiring other basic life skills. In our own earlier work, we sometimes described how to make decisions about who should or should not learn academics (Browder & Snell, 2000). Our thinking has changed. We now propose including all students in academic instruction for several reasons. First, parents have shown us the flaw in our prior logic that students' life skills should take priority over and sometimes replace academic instruction. Students not classified as having disabilities are not required to demonstrate that they can tie their shoes or keep their rooms clean before learning to read. Second, students have taught us that they value academics. From adults who have asked to learn to read to children in general education classes, we have learned how much some individuals value learning the "real" school curriculum. As one adult with disabilities said in a recent focus group, "Why would you not give every child the chance to learn to read? How do you know someone can't learn to read if they are never taught?" Finally, recent legislation like the No Child Left Behind Act (2002) requires assessing progress in reading, math, and science for all students. These assessments will have little purpose if students have not also had the opportunity to learn these skills.

can be the most efficient approach because the curriculum is already in place. But simply placing a student in a typical class does not create access to the general curriculum. Students with severe disabilities in any setting need instruction in core academic content to prepare for the assessments required by the No Child Left Behind Act.

Inclusion involves developing strategies for students to receive instruction on their individualized education program (IEP) in these typical settings. But this instructional support may not create access to the general curriculum if the IEP is not "standards-based"—does not include goals that align with state academic content standards. Access to the general curriculum gives the opportunity to learn content like reading, math, science, and social studies and to have the instructional support to show academic gains. Access does not mean that a student with severe disabilities will master all of the same grade-level expectations, but it does mean mastering some priority skills at each grade level that promote literacy, numeracy, and other academic learning.

Legal Precedents for Access to General Curriculum

One reason it is important to understand how to create access to the general curriculum is that recent legislation has mandated that all students have this access. The 1997 Amendments of the Individuals with Disabilities Education Act (IDEA) included students with disabilities in the standards-based school reform movement by requiring their participation in state and district accountability systems. In the past, students with moderate or severe disabilities were often exempt from the large-scale assessments that were a key component of school reform. In the mid-1990s, the National Center for Education Outcomes drew attention to this practice, noting that students not included in accountability systems could easily be bypassed in efforts to measure educational progress (Erickson, Thurlow, & Thor, 1995). The concern was that if students with disabilities were left out of accountability systems, they also would be left out of policy decisions. The goal was to include students with disabilities in state and local accountability reform programs to promote access to the general education curriculum (Kleinert, Kearns, & Kennedy, 1997), set higher expectations for learning outcomes (Thompson, Quenemoen,

Thurlow, & Ysseldyke, 2001), and improve instruction (Browder, Spooner, et al., 2003; Kleinert & Kearns, 2001).

The 1997 Amendments to IDEA specifically required that information regarding a student's access to the general curriculum be documented in the IEP through (a) a list of the services, modifications, and supports to "ensure access of the child to the general curriculum, so that he or she can meet the educational standards within the jurisdiction of the public agency that apply to all children" (§300.26[b] [3]); (b) a statement of how the disability affects the involvement and progress in the general curriculum; and (c) a statement of the goals to enable involvement and progress in the general curriculum. IDEA 1997 also mandated inclusion of students with disabilities in state- and districtwide assessments. States were required to develop an alternate assessment to be conducted by July 1, 2000, for students unable to participate in typical assessments (§300.138[b]). When IDEA 1997 was passed, only one state, Kentucky, had developed an alternate assessment system (Thompson & Thurlow, 2000), while the other 49 states had to create new procedures quickly. States struggled with whether students with severe disabilities were in a separate functional curriculum or in the general curriculum with adaptations or both. Functional curriculum, first promoted by Brown et al. (1979), focuses on instruction related to students' current and future environments in the domains of home, community, recreation, and vocational skills. This curriculum has dominated instructional planning for students with severe disabilities for the past two decades (Browder, Spooner, et al., 2004). In contrast, general curriculum and content standards are organized by academic domains like language arts, math, science, and social studies. When states first developed their alternate assessments, many focused on documenting progress on functional life skills, but by 2001, most states were using state standards (typically academic) as the basis for alternate assessments (Thompson & Thurlow, 2001). In fact, reading and math were the most frequently used categories for the alternate assessment in 2001–2002 (Browder, Ahlgrim-Delzell, et al., in press).

This focus on academic assessment for all students was further promoted through No Child Left Behind Act (2002). The act required reporting outcomes on state standards in math, language arts, and science for all students, including those with severe disabilities. By the 2002–2003 school year, all states brought reading and math into their alternate assessments, although a few continued to include life domains like community and home skills. Subsequent rule making for the No Child Left Behind Act (U.S. Department of Education, 2003) allowed for alternate standards for no more than 1% of all students in the grades assessed; and alternate standards must be aligned with a state's academic content standards and reflect professional judgment of the highest learning standards possible for these students.

Increasing Expectations for Students with Severe Disabilities

In addition to these legal precedents, educators have developed increasing expectations for the educational outcomes for students with severe disabilities. At first, educators focused on students' rights to an inclusive education and its social benefits. Built on the philosophy of normalization, early proponents of inclusion viewed inclusive school programs as a civil right (*Board of Education Sacramento City Unified School District v. Holland*, 1992; *Brown v. Board of Education*, 1954; Lipsky & Gartner, 1989; Meyer, 1994). Early inclusion resources stressed social inclusion and its benefits for all children (e.g., Certo, Haring, & York, 1984; Downing, 1996; Haring & Romer, 1995), but the curricular content typically focused on teaching individualized, age-appropriate, functional curriculum. In some cases, inclusion itself became the curriculum, while membership in the classroom with opportunities for social and communication with peers was the goal (Dymond & Orelove, 2001). While these goals continue to be important for all students, educators now are also focusing on how to help all students make progress in the general curriculum.

This focus is increasingly reflected in the strong academic emphasis in states' alternate assessments. In a content analysis of six states' alternate assessment performance indicators, Browder, Spooner, et al. (2004) found that the predominant curricular philosophy reflected in the *specific skills targeted for assessment* were academic. In contrast, the most frequent type of *activities in which the skills were to be performed* were functional (i.e., real-life activities). This blending of academic tasks and functional contexts is interpreted to mean that while educators continue to value having students learn skills using real-life materials and activities, they prefer to assess academic skills within functional contexts.

Can Students with Severe Disabilities Master Academic Skills?

In response to the increased focus on the general curriculum for all students, many question whether students with severe disabilities can master academic skills.

Brett has never had IEP objectives with an academic focus. Because of his extensive life skills needs, his prior education has focused primarily on daily living skills along with his therapy needs. Brett also has not had the opportunity to participate in typical classes. His team wonders what access to the general curriculum will mean for Brett. They question if there is any research evidence to support teaching him academics.

There is little doubt at this point that inclusive schooling positively impacts the social skills of students with severe disabilities (Giangreco, Dennis, Cloninger, Edelman, & Schattman, 1993; Hanline, 1993; Hunt, Alwell, Farron-Davis, & Goetz, 1996). There is also evidence that students can master IEP skills in inclusive contexts. For example, Hunt, Staub, Alwell, and Goetz (1994) demonstrated how three second-grade students with severe cognitive and physical disabilities in a general education classroom increased their ability to identify picture symbols and respond to their names. The teaching strategies included cooperative learning techniques, informal facilitation strategies, and systematic instructional support from a special education consultant who worked cooperatively with the teacher. Although this study occurred in the context of a math class, math skill acquisition was not reported.

In contrast, only a few studies have focused on documenting academic growth in inclusive contexts. Giangreco et al. (1993) reported an increase in academic skills of students with severe disabilities in inclusive classrooms though a series of teacher interviews. A 7-year case study by Ryndak, Morrison, and Sommerstein (1999) followed a young woman with severe cognitive and physical disabilities throughout middle school, high school, and some college. After applying a variety of adaptations, modifications, and supports, including team decision making, peer tutoring, speech/language therapy, and limited resource room assistance, the student showed tremendous growth in her vocabulary, articulation, and handwriting legibility. The young woman surpassed team expectations by acquiring knowledge of material addressed in general classrooms not specifically identified as IEP goals.

McDonnell, Mathot-Buckner, Thorson, and Fister (2001) documented the achievements of three randomly selected middle school students with moderate to severe disabilities who had peer tutors in typical classrooms. The general and special education teachers developed individualized objectives for each student for skills connected to the general education curriculum and developed individualized accommodations such as use of a calculator, prompting, and verbal directions in place of written directions. Students made progress in math, history, and physical education; increased their rate of academic responding; and decreased their rate of competing behaviors.

Basil and Reyes (2003) reported academic progress for six students with severe disabilities using a computer program for 30 minutes twice a week for 3 months. These students, ages 8 to 16, had made minimal academic progress in a special education context using traditional reading instruction but with the use of the computer program learned to select words to form phrases that the program vocalized and animated. The students progressed from an average of three element phrases ("The *bee hides* the *carrot*") to seven elements ("The *singing fox runs over* the *bridge* and *hugs* the *cat*"). Three of the six students increased their ability to identify pictures from an average of three to eight pictures. These three students also developed the ability to segment words into syllables and transferred some of this knowledge to the elements of writing, as evidenced by scribbling in a line, scribbling longer as in word formations, writing individual letters, and spelling some words correctly.

This emerging research shows that students with severe disabilities can master academic skills. However, educators continue to have substantial work ahead to demonstrate effective practices for teaching them the wide range of academic skills typical of the general curriculum. A review of 785 articles addressing students with severe disabilities found that only 10% focused on cognitive/academic skills and that there had been a *decrease* in research in this area (Nietupski, Hamre-Nietupski, Curtin, & Shrikanth, 1997). Most studies of academic skills for this population have targeted teaching either functional sight words (Browder & Xin, 1998) or money skills (Browder & Grasso, 1999). While these skills are important, they relate to only a small portion of national and state standards.

For students like Brett and the others described in the case studies, educators are just beginning to discover how to access to the general curriculum.

This chapter will highlight the research on teaching academic skills to students with severe disabilities and offer practical ideas based on some of the innovations currently being tried by teaching teams. This chapter also provides examples of how to create a link between the students' IEP and a state's academic content standards.

Ways to Create Access to the General Curriculum

While there are many ways to promote inclusion, less is known about gaining access to typical grade-level curriculum. Four strategies for creating curricular access include (a) using principles of universal curriculum design for all students, (b) promoting self-directed learning within typical class activities, (c) using direct and systematic instruction of specific target skills, and (d) creating a standards-based IEP.

Use Universal Design of Curriculum for All Students

The beginning point for gaining entry to general curriculum is to consider all students' needs when creating standards and curricular resources. When the content, materials, and teaching strategies are developed to consider the needs of all students, including those with disabilities and other learning needs, educators are using what is known as "universal design" (CAST, 1998a). This term has also been applied to creating buildings that are responsive to the needs of all users (e.g., with accessible entries). These accommodations are considered "universal" because they allow access to everyone, not just those with disabilities. For example, a curb cut provides access not only to the individual in a wheelchair but also to the parent pushing an infant in a stroller. Universal design is achieved by providing flexible materials that accommodate individuals with wide variations in sensory, learning, and physical abilities. Universal design does not lower the standards but offers ways to access the standards.

There are three essential qualities of universal design for learning: (a) multiple means of representation, (b) multiple means of expression, and (c) multiple means of engagement (CAST, 1998b). Multiple means of representation utilizes digital materials that can be transformed in size, shape, or color or transferred into speech or pictures with captions. This includes using various computer programs and other forms of technology such as voice recorders, palm pilots, and digital camcorders. Multiple means of expression provides digital alternatives to pencil and paper such as scanning, enlarged keyboards, spell-checkers, multimedia presentation, and graphics. Digital technology provides multiple transformations that are immediate and easily accessible. Multiple means of engagement provide flexible supports and levels of challenge, personalized scaffolding, and options for repetition, familiarity, novelty, and variations in culture to keep students engaged. All three of these qualities are best achieved when developed *within the curricular materials from the onset.* For example, digital textbooks can contain multiple options for content (e.g., pictures to define words, size of letters, highlighting key phrases), response mode (e.g., composing written response or using switch to select picture), and options for engagement (e.g., fast-paced content or repetition). In a universal design, computer-based software applications become a key component for accessing the curriculum for students with severe disabilities (Wehmeyer, Sands, Knowlton, & Kozleski, 2002). The computer applications are not an "add-on" for this group of students but rather an option available for all students.

In the future, educators will probably have digitized texts and other software in which the publisher provides the universal design. The current reality is that most teams must adapt from the classroom teaching methods that do not contain these design features. A student may participate in an inclusive class in which the teacher relies primarily on hard-copy textbooks for content and students' written responses to check understanding. Even if the teacher uses alternative formats like cooperative learning strategies and computer software, these may not have been developed for use by students who have severe disabilities. To have universally designed curricula with classrooms responsive to the needs of students with severe disabilities, collaboration between general and special educators is needed to identify ways to create accessibility. Through collaboration, materials are selected and instructional activities planned for use with all students, thereby also accommodating the needs of students with severe disabilities. Thus, rather than a reactive approach in which the special educator must always adapt from existing lesson plans and materials, collaborative planning produces instruction that works for everyone in the class.

Onosko and Jorgensen (1998) describe ways for high school teachers to collaborate in developing instructional units and lessons that are responsive to all students by incorporating technology, modified materials, people supports, and individualized expectations to enable all students to reach the objectives of the instructional unit. For example, if everyone participates with a peer partner, the individual supports needs of the student with severe disabilities are built in. If all students use digital pictures combined with texts in preparing their reports, the student who does not yet read words can view peers' projects with increased understanding as well as preparing a report using primarily pictures.

Amy receives instruction in a typical fifth-grade class. Her special education teacher used to wait until the fifth-grade teacher developed her lesson plans for the week, and then she would determine ways for Amy to participate in each activity. Some activities were difficult to adapt, such as when the students worked independently on math problems in their book. Because Amy needed to be engaged to keep alert, it was difficult for her to spend large amounts of time without interaction. The special education teacher noticed that Amy was not the only one becoming drowsy during the seat-work time. Together the special and general education teachers applied universal design to develop new activities for the entire class in place of doing problems in the book. One activity was a collaborative task where each student, including Amy, had different clues for how to solve a math problem. They had to determine what they needed to do next and who had the clue to help them do it. Amy used a Touch Talker to give her clue.

Promote Self-Directed Learning

Besides working with general educators to make the curriculum universally designed for all students, another important strategy is to prepare students with disabilities to be self-directed (Wehmeyer, Palmer, Agran, Mithaug, & Martin, 2000). Being self-directed may mean learning to solve problems or regulating their own behavior in the context of general education classes (Agran, Blanchard, Hughes, & Wehmeyer, 2002; Wehmeyer, Yeager, Bolding, Agran, & Hughes, 2003) as well as learning to follow visual or auditory cues or verbal self-instructions to complete typical classroom tasks (Agran, King-Sears, Wehmeyer, & Copeland, 2003).

Because Ricky displays both a preference and skill for listening to books on tape, audiotaped instructions may be a useful way to support him when he participates in academic lessons. As typical students complete independent seat work that involves composing written answers to questions, Ricky may listen to a tape that helps him select objects to show understanding of the lesson. In science, the tape might say, "Reach into the box and find the rock. Turn off the tape." Once he has the rock, he restarts the tape and it says, "Feel the rock with your fingers to see if it has smooth edges or rough edges. Turn off the tape." Ricky explores the rock and then restarts the tape. Next the tape says, "This rock is rough. It is a crystal. Notice how crystal feels. Now find the second box and pick up that rock. Turn off the tape." Because Ricky is visually impaired, this self-directed seat-work opportunity gives him the opportunity to access different qualities of rock formation that other students may have learned from the pictures in their book. To check for understanding at the end of independent work time, the teacher can ask Ricky to select the crystal when given two rocks.

Apply Direct, Systematic Instruction to Teach Target Skills

In addition to universally designed curriculum and promoting self-directed learning, getting into the general curriculum also requires some direct, systematic instruction in typical settings. Schoen and Ogden (1995) demonstrated how a general education teacher might deliver this individualized instruction. In their study, the general education teacher used a constant time delay procedure (see chapter 4) with attentional prompts to instruct three students to read sight words. One of the students with moderate mental retardation and two who were at risk were taught 24 unknown vocabulary words. Eight of these words were taught through direct instruction, while 16 words were taught with observational learning: watching peers in the group read the words. Similarly, the special education teacher or a paraprofessional might instruct either the individual student or a small group that includes other students who need systematic drill and practice. For example, a teacher uses flash card drills to teach math facts or equations to several students, while the student with severe disabilities is taught to identify numbers.

Besides individual or small-group instruction, the general or special educator might use some whole-class instruction that embeds target material for the student with severe disabilities. Collins, Hall, Branson, and Holder (1999) found that students with moderate cognitive disabilities were able to learn factual statements that the general education teacher presented repeatedly throughout a group lecture. Some students might need the opportunity to respond after these facts are presented. For example, during a social studies unit on state government, the teacher might repeatedly note that "Our state is *North Carolina*." Each time the teacher says the state name, the student finds and marks the picture of the state's outline to parallel other students' note taking.

Typical peers can learn to provide this individualized instruction. Hunt et al. (1994) investigated the extent to which three students with severe disabilities who were full-time members of elementary classrooms could learn communication and motor objectives during academic activities in cooperative learning groups. The students with disabilities were assigned to cooperative groups with their nondisabled peers; peers were taught to give designated cues, prompts, and reinforcements for the students with disabilities in their groups. By the end of the study, each student with severe disabilities was independently producing his or her targeted communication or motor skill during the math activities.

Dominique participates in English as a second language in her high school. Although the class is taught in English, the teacher is fluent in Spanish and provides praise and encouragement to Dominique in her native language. She uses two strategies for Dominique to expand her English skills through systematic instruction. As she teaches English phrases, she repeats selected phrases throughout the lesson for Dominique ("What is your name?" and "Who is here today?"). Dominique's goal is to give an English reply. As needed, the teacher models the correct answer. When Dominique masters the answers, the teacher adds new phrases. The teacher also uses conversation partners to promote fluency in English. While all students in this class are allowed to use written phrase cards as discussion starters, Dominique uses her sight words.

Developing Standards-Based IEPs

While inclusive contexts provide ways for students to learn functional skills like learning to make choices or increasing range of motion, access to the general curriculum also means selecting specific target skills with direct links to the academic content. These target skills are both (a) the variety of responses that students will make to participate in the daily reading, math, or other academic lesson and (b) their priority IEP objectives in academic content areas. On an ongoing basis, the educational team plans ways for the student to participate in the full range of the grade-level curriculum. Annually, the team targets specific academic goals for the IEP that will be used for promoting progress in this curriculum. The states' alternate assessment serves as an additional indicator of whether the student is achieving state standards for reading, math, and science. For students to be able to achieve these state standards, they need instruction that is aligned to them.

A standards-based IEP is one that not only is responsive to the student's individual needs but also defines how this student will demonstrate performance of state standards from the general curriculum. In the past, educators have often based IEPs for students with severe disabilities on either a separate, functional curriculum or an undefined, vague curricular focus with little knowledge of the general curriculum (Browder, Spooner, et al., 2004; Thompson, Thurlow, Esler, & Whetstone, 2001). Sands, Adams, and Stout (1995) found that only 15% of special educators believed that outcomes related to the general education curriculum should be the primary focus of IEPs. Even when the IEPs contain academic goals, these goals may not link to state standards or guide instruction. Fisher and Frey (2001) followed three students with severe cognitive and physical disabilities who were being provided a fully included educational experience for 3 years. While these students' IEPs reflected academic outcomes, the authors reported that their teachers never referred to the IEP document. The IEP objectives were also not consistent with the general education classroom practices, nor were they based on state standards applicable to other students in the class. These findings imply that teachers need guidance in aligning instructional goals, the IEP, and state standards. Thompson, Thurlow, et al. (2001) suggest that part of the difficulty in focusing on state standards is the fact that many IEP forms created by states do not reference state standards, so they are overlooked.

Some team members may have concerns that a standards-based IEP takes the individualization out of the IEP process, but this does not have to be true if the educational team focuses on the individual's needs and the skills required to access the general curriculum.

Standards-based IEPs have several potential advantages (Hock, 2000): (a) they can promote inclusion by linking the IEP to goals that schools have said were important for all students, and (b) they help to establish priorities with a long-term focus and in a language common to general educators.

Thompson, Quenemoen, et al. (2001) describe the steps educators can take to create a standards-based IEP. In Table 13–1, we modified these steps by including strategies to identify skills that access the general curriculum and applied these steps to the case student Brett.

Become Familiar with State Standards and Grade-Level Curriculum and Review Students' Needs

In conducting a study on state curriculum standards and alternate assessment, Browder, Flowers, et al. (2004) found that some special education teachers who participated in a focus group reported a lack of familiarity with state standards and the general curriculum. Agran, Alper, and Wehmeyer (2002) also found that some teachers did not consider access to the general curriculum important for students with severe disabilities. Thus, an important starting point for the educational team is to be sure that all members have copies of the state standards and examples of grade-level curricula used to address these standards. Most states publish their standards and other special education teaching resources on their department of education Website (e.g., Colorado: **http://www.cde.state.co.us/cdesped/StuDis-Sub1.htm**; Massachusetts: **http://www.doe.mass.edu/mcas/alt**). Many states use standards developed by national associations in the different content areas as a basis for constructing state-specific standards. Excerpts of these national standards appear in subsequent sections of this chapter as we discuss each content area. Becoming familiar with state standards may involve participation in general education curriculum workshops. The general education member(s) of the planning team can be a resource for understanding the standards concepts.

Using curriculum-based assessments and prior experience, the team should clarify the students' priorities so their individual needs will not be lost when linking to state standards. A curriculum-based assessment is an evaluation that is directly related to the educational objectives and the academic curricula that the student will learn in the classroom.

TABLE 13–1

How to Build a Standards-Based IEP

Step	Actions	Application
Step 1: Learn about district and state standards	Familiarize yourself with state and district standards	Brett's IEP team reviews their state standards to familiarize themselves with the academic expectations for students on the third-grade level since Brett is 8 years old.
Step 2: Learn how students are included in district and state standards	Consult your state alternate assessment manual, general education standards, and other state department Websites	The team then reviews a state curriculum guide that gives examples of skills that link to the state standards.
Step 3: Determine present level of educational performance with standards in mind	Conduct a curriculum-based assessment	Because Brett does not yet have academic skills, his assessment focuses on what responses could be used to access general curriculum. His need for symbol use is a high priority, but his meaningful eye gaze is a good starting point to get him engaged in activities by focusing on materials.
Step 4: Develop annual goals based on present level of performance and progress toward standards	Determine the critical function of the standards and consider alternative ways the student might address them; focus on active participation, functional context, and students' level of symbol use and embed self-determination	To help determine the essence of the standard, Brett's IEP team relies on the expertise of the third-grade teacher to consider "Is this skill really language arts? (math, science, etc.). Is it the same type of skill intended by this standard?" They also consider functional applications (e.g., using numbers in daily living activities) and ways to promote self determination (e.g., making choices using word/symbol combinations).
Step 5: Examine previous IEP goals that do not seem to reflect progress toward standards	Determine if these skills can be modified so they address a standard through an academic response	Brett's team decides to modify his former IEP goal to use a Tech-Talk® with symbols in reading activities. They decide that his goal to learn to eat with a spoon continues to be important and does not need an academic link.
Step 6: Examine standards that are not addressed by IEP goals	Make sure each standard has an IEP goal connected to it	The team reviews Brett's final IEP to be sure they provide ways to access the range of reading and math skills in third-grade curriculum. They add an objective to answer "What" questions by eye gazing to one of two pictures or objects so that Brett can demonstrate his comprehension.
Step 7: Document goals and standards on IEP	Check with your school administrator to find out how to document the link between the IEP goals and the standards	Brett's team documents which state standards are addressed with each objective next to the goals because there is not an area specified on the state-developed IEP document.
Step 8: Figure out how student will take state/district assessments; document participation on IEP	Determine how the student will be included in state/district assessments	Brett's IEP team reviews the states' assessment guidelines and determine that he is a candidate for the alternate assessment.

Source: Adapted from Thompson, Quenemoen, Thurlow, and Ysseldyke (2001). Used with permission.

Ricky starts middle school with an IEP focusing solely on functional life skills. Ricky's special education teacher also has no experience or training in teaching the general curriculum. Her first step is to get a copy of her state's standards and to study the state's resources on preparing for the alternate assessment by teaching students skills linked to these standards. Because the middle school is organized by clusters of classes or "pods" at each grade level, the teacher finds it difficult to know how to promote inclusion and form partnerships with these teaching teams. She begins by planning with Ricky's IEP team for him to be included in the sixth-grade pod called the "Wonders." General education teachers share state standards and some sample sixth-grade lesson plans with all members of the team, including Ricky's parents, the therapists, and Ricky. The special education teacher describes Ricky's strengths, ways of communicating, educational needs, and preferences. The special education teacher attends the pod's planning meetings now that Ricky has joined these classes.

Consider the "Critical Function"

Once the educational team is familiar with the state's standards and grade-level curriculum, they can identify target skills for the individual student in the general curriculum. Kleinert and Thurlow (2001) describe how to use White's (1980) concept of "critical function" to align an IEP objective with learning standards from the general curriculum. This is done by looking beyond the *form* of an academic content standard to the *function* of the standard in enhancing the student's life. For example, a state standard may be "Students will develop and apply enabling strategies to read and write" (North Carolina Department of Public Instruction, 1985). This goal has numerous subobjectives at each grade level K–12. The critical function of this standard is the ability to communicate using printed materials. For many students, this is demonstrated by reading a passage and producing a written response. Alternative forms to demonstrate this learning standard include producing written products using computer software that translates speech into written words and comprehending written text by using picture clues and key words. Many states have developed curricular materials to help teachers define the critical function of state academic content standards that are available on their state education Websites in the guidelines for alternate assessment (e.g., Kentucky:

http://www.ihdi.uky.edu/kap; Massachusetts: http://www.doe.mass.edu/mcas/alt/; North Carolina: http://www.ncpublicschools.org/accountability/testing/alternate). States have used a number of terms to identify these functions such as "access skills," "essence of the standard," or "essential skills."

Brett is participating in the state's alternate assessment. In reviewing the third-grade objectives for the standard "The learner will develop enabling strategies and skills to read and write," the special education teacher notices the focus on becoming fluent in applying decoding skills. The third-grade teacher explains how at this age students need to be fluent in their decoding of words because the focus in reading is beginning to shift to passage comprehension. Together the two teachers consider what might be the critical function of this standard and how it can be accessible to Brett given that he does not yet have symbolic communication. They decide that the critical function of this first standard is to gain competence in identifying symbols and words and to become engaged with books and other forms of literature.

Promote Active Participation

Once the team is familiar with state standards and has reviewed any state guidelines on how to understand their critical function, they are ready to identify specific skills for the student. In choosing these skills, it is important to consider ways for the student to be an active learner. Billingsley (1993) has used the term "active education" to refer to having the student actively participating in classroom learning versus merely receiving social benefits. For general curriculum access, active participation occurs when the student acquires independent responses like choosing, matching, and answering that demonstrate understanding of the academic content standard. In contrast, a "passive" skill is one in which the student simply has to cooperate with or tolerate physical or other guidance. For some students with severe cognitive and physical disabilities, it may be difficult to target an independent response, but active participation is possible if the student has at least one voluntary movement.

For example, a student who has physical disabilities may not have the fine motor skills to fill in a bar graph to create a data display in math. A passive approach to this goal would be to use physical guidance to color in the graph. In this example, unfaded prompts mask active and independent responding and prevent the student from demonstrating ability or understanding of a concept. An *active* alternative would be to have the student use eye gaze (independent, voluntary response) to indicate which of several graphs best represent the number of items. Or the student might use computer software to generate the graph by clicking and selecting (independent, voluntary response) the best chart option. It will be important for the teacher to use a prompting and fading strategy so the student can learn these skills independently, for example, physically guiding the students' hand to hit the switch to select the chart option, then using time delay to fade the guidance (see chapter 4). Table 13-2 provides several examples of how to modify objectives to promote active academic learning.

For Brett, it is easy to inadvertently target passive participation for the state's standard on developing enabling strategies for reading and writing. For example, goals like "listen while a peer reads a story" and "hit the Touch Talker with hand-over-hand guidance" are passive goals, making it difficult for his teachers to determine if Brett has learned reading skills or simply is complying. Because Brett needs focused work on acquiring symbols, the team decides to teach him to select between two symbols to identify the named activity on his Touch Talker. To be sure the symbol has meaning, the teacher immediately

shows him an item associated with the named activity (a book for "reading"). He is then given a choice between two preferred books. He chooses either by eye gazing or by using a switch to select between two digital pictures of books on the computer.

Use Functional Activities to Address Academic Skills

Another consideration that can help the team identify target skills for general curriculum access is to consider how the standards can be addressed through functional activities. While participating in the general curriculum places more emphasis on academics than students with severe disabilities have had in the past, it is still necessary for these students to learn these skills in functional and meaningful contexts. Many state academic standards can be learned in the classroom and applied to real-life situations. The following examples, selected from several states' resources on alternate assessment, illustrate how academic skills can be embedded in typical daily routines:

- Creates a list of things to bring to school (writing)
- Locates a house by its house number (math)
- Uses a keypad on a microwave (math)
- Locates the weather page using newspaper index (reading)
- Follows a picture recipe (reading)

TABLE 13–2
Active Versus Passive Objectives for Academic Learning

Passive responses that do not indicate if student understands the concept	Active responses that simplify physical demands and focus on understanding
Dominique chooses a picture by touching one, but it is not clear if she is making an intentional choice or randomly touching a picture.	Dominique identifies pictures named by teacher or peer. After identifying pictures, she chooses ones to use in her science report.
A peer counts out five objects saying, "1, 2, 3, 4, 5." Brett makes no response except to "watch."	Peer counts "1, 2, 3, 4 . . . ," and Brett hits Tech-Talk® to finish counting with "5." Next, peer goes "1, 2 . . . ," Brett "3," and peer "4, 5."
The teacher guides Amy's hand to write her name on her paper. This "prompt" cannot be faded because Amy's disability makes it unlikely that she will gain use of her hands.	Amy eye gazes between a name stamp and pen to indicate whether she wants her name stamped or written for her.
The teacher reads a story and Ricky "listens," but it is unclear whether the story had any meaning to him.	As the teacher reads the story on auto racing, she asks students to anticipate what comes next. Ricky can choose between hitting a switch to say "I'm not sure" or using a model car to show what he thinks will occur next.

TABLE 13–3
Examples of How Brett's IEP Goals to Learn to Use an Adaptive Switch Can Address Multiple State Standards

To make a request	Reading: When given a switch in conjunction with pictures/word symbols, Brett will use a Tech-Talk® labeled with picture symbols to request leisure choices.
To print from a computer	Writing: Brett will activate a switch to print a note he has composed for a peer.
	Math: Brett will choose a graph, then activate a switch to print the graph that represents the daily work he has completed.
To operate a microwave	Math: Brett will hold a switch for a count of 10 to heat his snack or lunch in the microwave.
To indicate desire to walk or to operate a wheelchair	Math: Using a switch for "up," "down," "left," and "right," Brett will indicate the direction he would like to walk or wheel himself during physical therapy.

Although each state standard to be addressed by same-grade-level peers should be addressed within an IEP, it is not necessary that each IEP objective be connected to a standard. Some goals may remain purely functional, not connected to the standards because they are still important. It also is not necessary to have a different IEP objective for every state standard. A carefully constructed IEP goal can address more than one standard, and some standards may not be addressed. For example, an objective on using a personal schedule might address standards in reading and math. Table 13-3 shows the application of a communication goal (use of assistive technology) to multiple state standards.

Find Opportunities to Practice Self-Determination

When defining skills for students with severe disabilities that align to state standards, the principles of self-determination must not be overlooked. Lack of training in the components of self-determination has been speculated to be one reason students with disabilities continue to leave school inadequately prepared for adult life despite 15 years of special education (Wehmeyer, et al., 2002). Self-determination is the characteristic of "acting as the primary causal agent in one's life and making choices and decisions regarding one's quality of life free from undue external influence or interference" (Wehmeyer, 1996, p. 24). Several studies show that students with severe disabilities can learn to make preference selections consistently and to generalize them to other settings (Belfiore, Browder, & Mace, 1994; Browder, Cooper, & Lim, 1998; Cooper & Browder, 1998; Kennedy & Haring, 1993). While there is less research on the extent these students can learn other

components of self-determination, such as self advocacy (Algozzine, Browder, Karvonen, Test, & Wood, 2001), this may be due to a neglect of these components when planning instruction. For example, while a majority of teachers appear to agree that self-determination skills are an important curricular area, this belief does not translate into the development of IEP goals designed to teach these skills (Agran, Snow, & Swaner, 1999; Wehmeyer, Agran, & Hughes, 2000). Table 13-4 provides examples that can be taught concurrently with academic skills.

Apply Levels of Symbol Use to Guide Instruction

Another consideration in identifying target skills to access the general curriculum is the level of symbol use the student has mastered. Knowing some words and numbers opens up many more options for learning language arts and math. In contrast, students with no use of symbols can still acquire emerging literacy and numeracy skills (a) by considering ways to present tasks that introduce new symbols or (b) by performing tasks without knowledge of any symbols. Three levels to consider are presymbolic, early symbolic, and expanded symbolic.

Presymbolic Language Arts and Math
If a student has not yet acquired the skills to discriminate between pictures or other symbols, then an important focus of a curriculum should be those skills that will build language arts and math concepts. To demonstrate, consider a general education writing competency. Writing skills can be defined broadly as those responses that produce a permanent product to communicate with others. While the student may not

TABLE 13–4
Teaching Self-Determination Skills While Addressing Academic Standards

Skill	Academic applications
Choice making	Choose pictures for picture journal
	Choose whether to buy soda with dollar or quarters
Decision making	Decide whether to buy or pack lunch after reading school menu
	Decide which is the best after-school job after comparing hourly rates
Problem solving	Look at picture diagram for battery placement to solve why CD player will not play
	Determine how much more money must be earned for desired purchase after counting money
Goal setting	Use computer software to copy and paste goals from goal list
	Use number stamp to target the number of sight words to learn this week
Self-management	Use object graph to indicate how many jobs completed
	Select word that best describes how well a lesson was completed ("great," "okay," "not okay")
Self-awareness	Develop picture/word autobiography
	Develop and learn to read a list of "facts about me" or "likes/dislikes"

be able to write or type words, it may be realistic to learn how to develop a product that enhances communication. For example, the student might use eye gaze to select pictures for a picture journal entry about horseback riding. Symbols that are easier to learn at this stage are those that are highly familiar, regularly encountered, and associated with preferred activities. These early symbols include objects that represent a familiar activity (toothbrush, jacket, a pet's leash), commercial symbols (an illustration of a favorite toy or food name brand, the "golden arches"), and photographs of friends and family members in routine or favorite activities (Mirenda, MacGregor, & Kelly-Keough, 2002).

As part of social studies, Amy's fifth-grade class goes on a field trip to a working farm. Amy is alert and interested in the sound and sight of the horses they encounter during this trip. When the class returns from the trip, the teacher asks them to write a composition about what they had learned about the farm. Working with a peer, Amy uses her eye gaze to select digital pictures from choices displayed on the computer screen to develop the content for her report. The teacher is persuaded that her selections were purposeful, not random, because her report focuses more on horses than the other animals and farm activities.

Early Symbolic Language Arts and Math
Students at this second level use some symbols including objects, pictures, or a few sight words or numerals. For example, following an object schedule teaches

students "comprehension of objects as symbols," a typical language arts competency. Students who are learning the meaning of sight words, for example, by preparing a word/picture recipe are working on comprehending what they read. If the school schedule is consistent across days, students can learn the expected sequence of events associated with the objects, which is a competency area in math. A schedule can also incorporate time ("I do this first, this second, and after lunch I will do this"), another area of math competency.

Ricky is learning to indicate the upcoming activity in his daily schedule by using objects that have the printed word attached to them. A little book indicates reading, a stamp indicates writing, a spoon indicates lunch, and a tape indicates leisure time. When given his schedule and asked if it is time for reading or lunch, Ricky is learning to give his teacher the next object on his schedule.

Expanded Symbolic Language Arts and Math
Students at this third level have mastered some sight words and number use and may have some functional academic skills like using money to make a purchase or locating community signs like restrooms. These students can build their language arts and math skills. Students who can read some words might learn to use these words along with pictures to begin "writing" journal entries about their activities by typing or pasting words and pictures on a page. They may respond well to learning to answer questions about stories they helped compose or familiar stories. Others who can

use numbers across a variety of daily activities might learn to keep track of their work or count how many table places to set.

All students in Dominique's school are expected to maintain a daily agenda to help them keep up with their schedules and class work. The school provides them with a spiral-bound day planner for this purpose. Dominique uses the same planner but keeps track of her day using both pictures and words. Her teacher posts a picture symbol/word schedule on the board each morning. She tapes picture symbols into the agenda, then writes the corresponding word next to the picture. As she completes her classes, she puts an "X" through the picture symbols and words.

Language Arts Instruction

Language arts includes a broad range of skills: reading, writing, listening, speaking, viewing, and visually representing. Teachers will want to select skills that are needed by students and teach these skills in ways that emphasize their use in every day life. For example, in reading, students can be taught to read pictures or words in order to understand instructions, to select leisure options, to find locations, to identify products while shopping, to gain information, and to participate more fully in social settings. In addition, it is important to teach comprehension skills as part of reading instruction. When the student understands the meaning of the word or picture in context of daily routines, reading becomes functional.

Before considering how to create access to language arts instruction for students with severe disabilities, it is important to review how general educators have defined language arts. There are no nationally sanctioned standards in the English language arts, but the International Reading Association (IRA) and National Council of Teachers of English (NCTE) offer a set of recognized K–12 standards that most states have used to guide the development of their content standards (IRA/NCTE, 1996). Table 13-5 shows excerpts of these standards and examples of how to connect a student's level of symbol use to standards. The standards focus on the broad outcomes of students becoming knowledgeable, reflective, and critical participants in a literate society. This chapter focuses on the components of reading and writing.

The reading component includes (a) phonological awareness, letter–sound correspondence, and alphabetic principle; (b) word identification, decoding, and word study; (c) fluency; (d) vocabulary; and (e) comprehension (Bos & Vaugn, 2002). Phonological awareness is the knowledge that spoken language is broken down into smaller units (words, syllables, phonemes) that can be manipulated. Implicit in this knowledge is the alphabetic principle where sounds relate to letters. Phonological skills include discriminating between sounds, identifying syllables, rhyming, blending sounds together to form words, producing tongue twisters, and manipulating sounds to create different words. It is also important to have a sight word vocabulary and a decoding strategy to identify words not in that sight word vocabulary. (A sight word is a word that is recognized automatically rather than decoded.) A number of strategies are used to decode words: letter–sound correspondences (phonics), spelling patterns (onset rimes), knowledge of word structures such as suffixes and prefixes (structural analysis), syllable types (syllabication), and word order (syntax) and context (semantics). Fluency is the ability to read a text quickly and accurately. Fluency is most often measured by the number of words read correctly in 1 minute. Comprehension is the construction of meaning from text. Vocabulary is the stock of words available to a student in order to read, write, and speak.

Elements of written expression include the writing conventions, writing process, spelling, and handwriting (Bos & Vaugn, 2002). Writing conventions are skills such as punctuation, capitalization, and quotation marks. The writing process involves selecting topic to write on, composing the written work, revising and editing, and publishing. Elements of handwriting skills include legibility, fluency, posture, pencil grip, and position of the paper.

Creating Access to Language Arts for Students with Severe Disabilities

In planning access to language arts instruction for students with severe disabilities, it is important to address the full array of skills that promote literacy. Unfortunately, there is scant research on how to teach students with severe disabilities many of these skills. In this section, we offer guidelines based on existing research and practical procedures for teaching students at the three levels of symbol use.

TABLE 13–5

An Excerpt of IRA/NCTE (1996) Standards for the English Language Arts with Student Examples

Excerpt	Student examples (Key: P = presymbolic, ES = early symbolic, ExS = expanded symbolic)
1. Read print and nonprint texts to acquire new information, for personal fulfillment	P–Ricky activates a switch to listen to books on tape. ES–Brett points to his printed name when paired with other names of classmates. ExS–Dominique scans the newspaper to find key information (i.e., weather words to find out how to dress, reading a TV schedule to find her favorite show).
2. Use tactics to understand texts using prior experience and reading ability	P–Amy opens her eyes or looks away from the peer reader when asked, "Should I keep reading?" ES–Ricky uses objects with word labels to indicate what the upcoming activity is in his daily schedule. ExS–Dominique reads functional sight words to perform daily living tasks (e.g., cooking).
3. Students communicate with different audiences	P–Using a Step Talker, Brett takes turns sharing a story with his class or family. ES–Ricky uses IntelliKeys® (AbleNet) to create picture/word notes to share with people who understand his object system. ExS–Dominique follows sight word notes to lead her IEP meeting.
4. Students write to communicate with different audiences	P–Brett activates a switch to print a note he has composed with the help of a peer. ES–Ricky uses IntelliKeys® (AbleNet) to compose a picture/word message. ExS–Dominique composes a variety of messages using picture symbols/words (e.g., grocery lists, journal entries).
5. Apply knowledge of language to create, critique, and discuss texts	P–Amy eye gazes to indicate her choice of book she would like read to her. ES–Ricky indicates whether he likes a book on tape by using a digital picture program to add it to his "Favorites" files. ExS–Dominique uses a checklist to indicate what she liked about a picture symbol/word newsletter she has read (i.e., "I liked the article topic," "I did not like joke of the week").
6. Conduct research by using resources; gather, evaluate, and synthesize data to communicate their discoveries	P–After a community or special school experience, Amy reviews and selects digital pictures that she has seen, using eye gaze, to create a journal. ES–Ricky finds locations of books and magazines about sports (or other topics) in the media center and uses pictures of sports stars to poll peers about their favorites. ES–Dominique uses the Internet to view video clips and pictures from potential employers' Websites and makes a picture/word list of what she likes/dislikes in each job site.
7. Students develop an understanding of diversity in language use across cultures, ethnic groups, geographic regions, and social roles	P–Amy eye gazes to select from digital pictures to provide illustrations for her group's report on a cultural group. ES–Ricky participates in a class discussion (e.g., black history month) by pressing a Step by Step switch that communicates information about key facts. ExS–Dominique creates a picture/word report about a cultural group different from her own.
8. Use visual, spoken, and written language to accomplish their own purposes	P–Brett uses a Tech-Talk® with picture symbols to communicate with his peers. ES–Ricky uses an object/word board to select leisure choices to a variety of people. ExS–Dominique keeps a personal journal and writes notes to peers using pictures and words.

Presymbolic Language Arts Instruction

Research on presymbolic language arts skills for students with severe disabilities is limited. This is unfortunate because participating in the general education curriculum is complicated when students do not respond to words and picture symbols. However, there is a body of research on the acquisition of nonsymbolic communication (Downing & Siegel-Causey, 1998; Kaiser & Goetz, 1993) that gives direction in how to teach these students and how they can most meaningfully participate in the general education curriculum. There is also a growing body of literature on nonsymbolic communication as a means to determine student preferences (Lohrmann-O'Rourke, Browder, & Brown, 2000; Lohrmann-O'Rourke & Gomez, 2001). Building on this work, the starting point for literacy may be to explore students' preferences for different types of literature. Does a student like Amy show an interest in different types of poems, drama, humorous stories, or anecdotes about people she knows? The teacher can also consider ways to get the student independently engaged with books using assistive technology, such as a switch to activate a book or view a digitized book.

Teachers can promote "emergent literacy" with such reading experiences. Sulzby (1991) defines emergent literacy as "the reading and writing behaviors that precede and develop into conventional literacy" (p. 88). Written language experiences should not be withheld just because a student has not yet met some communication milestones (Erickson & Koppenhaver, 1997). Instead, literacy can be integrated into daily routines through books on tape, artwork and writing centers, use of their names, and opportunities to explore books.

Amy presents complex challenges for planning early literacy training because of her lack of symbol use and the team's lack of success in finding a communicative device that she can physically activate. Currently, the team relies primarily on her use of her eyes to communicate. Amy's teacher decides to see if she can increase Amy's participation in reading by having her classmates read to her. Her goal is for Amy to ask to have the peer continue reading by opening her eyes wide (a response she would sometimes make when showing interest in sounds or touch). Over time, Amy begins to open her eyes when the peer pauses and asks, "Should I keep reading?" Amy's teacher also wants her to begin to comprehend and use symbols. She makes book selection cards by taking digital pictures of the covers of some books Amy has read. She places these pictures on the four corners of a black poster board so Amy can direct her eyes toward her choice. She also wants to be sure Amy comprehends the book titles she is choosing, so she uses the computer to show a digital picture of one book cover at a time. She asks Amy to look at her when they find the book they read today. The teacher then types "Today I wanted to read (name of book)" and shows the printout to Amy. Amy determines whether to let her family know what she read answering the question "Do you want to let your family know what you read today?" by eye gazing between a symbol for "yes" (green smiling face) and "no" (red frowning face).

Early Symbolic Language Arts Instruction

Students who are at the early symbolic level of language arts are using some symbols, including pictures. Recent studies support both the feasibility and the benefits of teaching picture "reading" to students with severe disabilities. Cafiero (2001) found that the use of picture communication boards increased both communication and positive behaviors in a student with autism. Grunsell and Carter (2002) found that four

FIGURE 13-1

This student has chosen picture/word symbols to place on a choice board that represent activities he prefers throughout the day. The board and his headstick enable him to inform others of his choices. BoardMaker for Windows (Mayer-Johnson, Inc., 1998). Credits: The Picture Communication Symbols™ © 1981–2004, Meyer-Johnson, Inc. All Rights Reserved Worldwide.

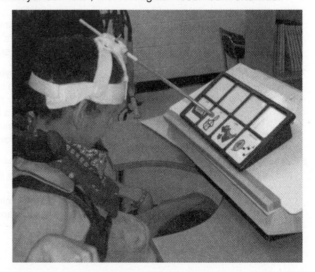

students with mental retardation and severe communication disorders learned to request using graphic symbols and generalized these skills to two untaught routines. Koppenhaver, Erickson, and Skotko (2001) found that access to communication symbols, assistive technologies, and parent training consistently enhanced children's frequency of labeling/commenting and appropriate symbolic communication.

Using BoardMaker for Windows (Mayer-Johnson, Inc., 1998) or Writing with Symbols 2000 (Mayer-Johnson, Inc., 1999), teachers can create class schedules and give students choices that they can read and use to control their environment (Figure 13–1).

Pairing picture symbols with simple books can give students at the early symbolic level the opportunity to read books independently (see Figure 13–2).

FIGURE 13–2

An adaptation of the book *The Magic School Bus Plays Ball: A Book About Forces* that Brett's teacher created using the software Writing with Symbols 2000. Credits: The Picture Communication Symbols™ © 1981–2004, Mayer-Johnson, Inc. All Rights Reserved Worldwide.

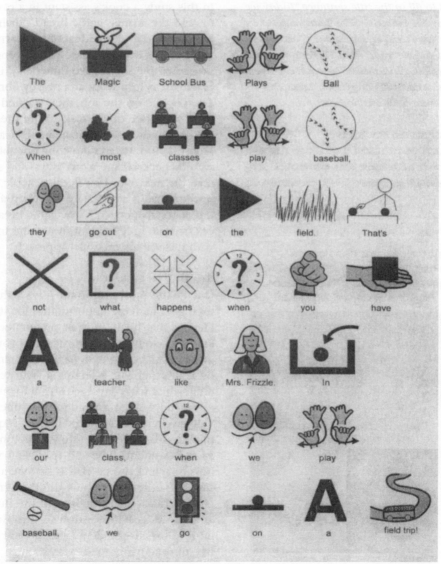

Although Brett is just learning to use symbols, his teacher wants to promote literacy by showing him stories that use word–symbol combinations. She adapted the book The Magic School Bus Plays Ball: A Book About Forces *using the software Writing with Symbols 2000. In her reading lesson, she first reads the book to the group (including Brett). To build comprehension, she gives Brett an individual summary of the story using symbols (Figure 13-2). As she reads the story summary slowly, she helps him find and mark the symbol for "bus" and "ball" using a Bingo marker (Bingo markers are easy to grasp and simply touching the picture creates a see-through dot). To build comprehension, the teacher has Brett find the symbols to fill in the title sentence "Today we read _____" using the computer. The teacher types in the symbols for "bus" and a distractor ("cat") and asks him, "What did we read about?" Brett needs a gesture and physical guidance to select the correct pictures for "bus" and "ball." They then print this report for Brett to share with his parents.*

Picture-Word Instruction Booklets

Picture-word instructions can help individuals manage or control their own activities; this promotes self-determination. As shown in Figure 13-3, picture-word

FIGURE 13–3
This student creates a daily agenda using picture symbols to help him transition throughout the day. Credits: The Picture Communication Symbols™ © 1981–2004, Mayer-Johnson, Inc. All Rights Reserved Worldwide.

booklets have been designed to guide students through daily tasks, teach cooking with recipes, multiple-step housekeeping chores, and other daily living skills (Browder, Hines, McCarthy, & Fees, 1984; Johnson & Cuvo, 1981) and to increase independence in vocational settings (Agran, Fodor-Davis, Moore, & Deer, 1989).

Teaching younger students the skills of following picture-word instruction booklets also can have long-term benefit for self-instruction on new skills. Some students may be able or may prefer to use books that only have words. For example, Browder and Minarovic (2000) taught three adults with moderate mental retardation to read sight words that helped them remember a sequence of job tasks in their paid community jobs. In this study, a cook's assistant in a restaurant learned to read the words "garlic bread," "dishwasher," "pots," and "trays." The individuals first learned to read the sight words during massed trial (repeated) practice prompted by progressive time delay; instruction took place just before work at a nearby library or at home. Then, while on the job, they learned to self-manage their sequence of job tasks using these words and a "did-next-now" self-management strategy (Agran & Moore, 1994). After completing one job, the employee would check off the word "trays" and say, "Did 'trays'"; read the next word on the list, "garlic," and say, "Next, 'garlic bread'"; and restate the word as she moved to the materials needed: "Now garlic bread." The employees became independent in moving from task to task with this self-instructional approach.

Reading to Make Choices

One of the most important ways sight words can be used is to increase opportunities for students to make choices that relate to their preferences. For example, knowing some sight words can provide students a means of selecting options from a menu, finding a favorite Internet site, selecting a favorite TV show, communicating what flavor ice cream to buy, or obtaining a preferred soda at a vending machine. Some choices will have "correct answers" that are required to participate appropriately or safely in community settings, such as students who can read sight words and symbols to select the correct restroom, avoid doors that say "Use other door," pick the theater in a multiplex cinema that corresponds with the purchased ticket, and so on. Teachers can also introduce "menus" of options that the student can read and choose, such as free time activities in the classroom.

In addition to his object schedule, Ricky has a leisure choice board. The board is labeled with objects that represent leisure activities he has shown interest in. For example, a tape represents a book on tape, a CD represents listening to music, and a small wheel represents his wheelchair being pushed for a walk. When it is leisure time, Ricky is given his choice board. He feels the choices and then removes one object to indicate his preference for that period. Because Ricky has mastered these symbols, the teacher decides to make them more symbolic by gluing them to cardboard so that he must finger scan them rather than holding the object (Ricky is visually impaired). She also glues the first letter sound in the word below it ("B" for book, "M" for music, "W" for wheelchair).

Reading for Orientation and Mobility

Sight words can enhance students' mobility in a variety of places, enabling them to find their way around school buildings, and in stores, libraries, restaurants, and medical office buildings. For example, aisle marker words from the grocery store may be taught to improve the ability to locate products (Karsh, Repp, & Lenz, 1990); signs of familiar landmarks like "barber," "KOA," and "Denny's" can be taught to help students identify community landmarks (Singleton, Schuster, & Ault, 1995). Familiar street signs and bus names are other options for this instruction.

Dominique is learning how to read grocery words using the Edmark Functional sight word program (PRO-ED, Inc., 2002). Using this program, she is learning to read words like "bread" and "dairy." She is now able to go into the grocery store and find the aisle that these items are in by reading the sight words on the aisle markers.

Container and Product Discrimination

Shopping for groceries, preparing food, doing laundry, and other daily living activities often require discrimination between different containers. Sometimes students benefit from learning to select their family's cereal or detergent brands; parents might send money and a short shopping list to school, thereby providing a meaningful task for the community-based training context. Other students will benefit from learning to discriminate edible products from nonedible products. Store coupons provide an easily accessible material

for teaching product reading, and they also contain the natural cues for product discrimination (e.g., the color of the box, product logo). Grocery shopping may also be taught using videotaped instruction of a grocery store's aisles and pictures of products to be located (Alcantara, 1994). Aeschleman and Schladenhauffen (1984) had students develop their own symbols for grocery item groups (e.g., a pretzel symbolized salty snacks) that students then used on their shopping lists.

Reading to Gain Information or to Participate in Social Settings

Even with limited reading skills, students can use their reading to gain information or to function in social settings. For example, students who recognize their own names can use this information to find their own belongings or assigned areas (e.g., names on desks or work lockers). Knowledge of a few weather sight words and symbols and practice with the newspaper will allow an individual to determine the upcoming weather from the paper's daily report.

Communication skills can sometimes be enhanced by teaching students to read and use symbols or words. For example, Osguthorpe and Chang (1988) taught students who had no reading or symbolic communication skills to use a computerized Rebus symbol processor to communicate. The students learned to associate a Rebus picture with spoken labels of things and events in their environment (e.g., ride, bus, want, good-bye). Because the computer printed out communication as Rebus word combinations, others could read their communication as well.

Even though most of Brett's instruction is focused on learning to recognize symbols, his teacher decides to also introduce one important sight word: his name. She writes his name and those of his classmates in large letters on separate poster boards. She uses practice drills in which she has him touch the poster with his name. In the beginning, she prompts him to select his name by modeling how to point to it and uses time delay to fade pointing. Throughout the day, she gives Brett reasons to find his name (e.g., his seat, locker, lunch bag).

Another category of sight words that provides information includes product warning labels. For example, in Collins and Stinson's (1995) work, students learned to read words like "precaution," "harmful," "induce vomiting," and "caution." The teacher used instructive feedback to teach students the definitions of these words. For example, when showing the word card for "harmful," the teacher would say "'harmful if swallowed' means 'don't drink it.'" Students were probed on their ability to read these words on actual product labels. Linking reading instruction to actual products and contexts is basic to their functional use. Teaching a word like "danger" or "caution" in isolation may not help a student avoid a dangerous situation. By contrast, teachers can teach students to read the safety word ("caution") and to verbalize its meaning ("don't walk there") and then purposefully expose students to the safety words during community-based instruction and query their meaning (e.g., the word "caution" on yellow warning tape at a construction site means an area closed to pedestrians).

Students Who Are Linguistically Diverse

Some students with severe disabilities are from linguistically diverse homes. For example, in Dominique's home, Spanish is the primary language, but English is the primary language at school. When teaching sight words to students like Dominique, it is important to conduct ecological inventories (see chapter 3) and determine if the words they will encounter at home are English, Spanish, or some other language. Teachers should not assume that the printed language encountered most often outside of school is English. For example, some neighborhoods may have most signs in Spanish (e.g., food words on grocery store, street signs), while other neighborhoods will be predominantly English. In a study evaluating bilingual instruction with students having moderate mental retardation who came from Spanish-speaking homes, Rohena-Diaz (1998) found that most community signs were in English in the favorite stores used by the families. Thus, English aisle marker words were taught, but the language of instruction was varied between English and Spanish. Using constant time delay and massed trial classroom instruction, Rohena-Diaz found comparable word acquisition and generalization to store settings with both English and Spanish instruction compared to a control condition of word exposure only. Results may also have been influenced by the teacher's skill in talking informally in Spanish with the students and their families when not conducting the reading lessons. Still, these findings demonstrate that linguistically diverse students with moderate mental retardation can learn English sight words with time delay instruction.

Expanding Symbolic Reading: Bridging to Literacy

Some students gain enough of a sight word vocabulary to be able to scan printed materials and glean the key information needed in a given activity.

Dominique is learning to scan a TV program listing, locate the name of a favorite show, and identify the time it begins. In the morning, she can scan the weather report in the newspaper, picking out key words to learn how to dress appropriately. At her after-school job, she can check the bulletin board for simple messages like "Friday—casual dress" or "Pick up paycheck by 4:00 p.m."

If students make good progress learning how to read functional words or if students are young, it may be valuable to introduce a vocabulary of often-used words found in most printed literature. For example, Fry's list of 300 "instant words" (Fry, 1957, 1972), the Dolch list of 200 words (Dolch, 1950), and the revised Dale list of 769 words (Stone, 1956) are lists of words that appear frequently in beginning reading programs. The school's reading specialist may be a good resource for these word lists. The Dolch word list can be found in many commercial beginning reading materials. Many of these high-frequency words do not have an immediate functional application as isolated words (e.g., "red," "in"), but they can be combined into functional phrases with the targeted activity-related words. For example, the teacher might use recipe phrases (e.g., "Put in" with picture of oven). These words may also help students participate in general education activities where high-frequency words often appear in class work directions, word experience stories, charts, class newspapers, and bulletin boards.

Another important category of functional words are the names of key people and labels in students' environments and daily routines. Many elementary general education classes repeatedly use words like "math" and "reading" to help students know their schedule and assignments. Similarly, the names of some staff and classmates might be taught to help students know who will be working with them.

Amy has many peer tutors and assistants who come in the classroom to work with her. Her teacher has paired pictures of the tutors and assistants with their names on flash cards to show Amy. Each morning, Amy is shown two of the cards and asked whom she would like to work with that day. Amy indicates her preference by eye gazing to a picture/name.

One limitation of whole-word methods of teaching reading is that students may not generalize their skills to new words; words are learned as separate units rather than teaching phonetic rules. Some research with individuals with moderate mental retardation has demonstrated that these students can learn several methods of word analysis (e.g., Entrikin, York, & Brown, 1977; Hoogeven, Smeets, & Lancioni, 1989):

1. Phonetic analysis, or sounding out words
2. Structural analysis, or recognizing meaning units such as parts of compound words, prefixes, suffixes, and contractions
3. Contextual analysis, or using the meaning of the sentence and preceding sentence to determine an unknown word

Many commercial materials exist that provide skill sequences for teaching phonics and other word analysis skills, such as *McGraw-Hill Education's Science Research Associates' Developmental 1 Reading Laboratory* (McGraw-Hill Education, 1998). The general education teacher or reading specialist often can recommend materials for students who will benefit from instruction in word analysis. Because word analysis training is difficult to apply to immediate functional use (e.g., identifying the short "a" sound), it should augment, not replace, sight word instruction. Learning sight words only without any word analysis goals may be the main focus for some students because of their age, rate of learning, or the need for application to daily routines.

Comprehension Skills

Comprehension is a critical focus for all reading instruction. The first step in reading is to identify a word or picture symbol that is named (e.g., "Find coffee"), by pointing to it in an array (receptive reading), or by saying it aloud when presented with a single flash card (expressive reading). However, comprehension requires making a second response to the sight word that shows that the student understands the meaning of the printed word or picture. Comprehension can be shown by asking the student (a) to pair a word with a picture, (b) to demonstrate the activity, (c) to pair the word or picture with an associated object or location,

FIGURE 13–4
This student has produced a mask in her art class that represents the Native American groups she has been learning about in class. One of the key vocabulary words for the unit was "mask" which she has learned to identify and spell through sign.

or (d) to make some other type of academic comprehension response (e.g., circle a word or a picture). Functionality is increased when comprehension involves using the word in the context of a daily routine (Figure 13–4).

Ricky's teacher is having him learn to use raised letters or objects attached to cards to indicate his choice of activities. To be sure his choices are meaningful, she sometimes pairs his favorite activities with a nonpreferred object (glove). She decides to continue to expand Ricky's comprehension by beginning to label familiar belongings. Before going outside, she has him find the raised letter "d" (door) that is posted near the door along with a distractor letter "z." Prior to lunch, he must find the "l" (lunch) paired with a napkin to symbolize eating on his schedule board. He then scans the edge of the storage shelves to find the entire word in raised letters "Ricky," which marks where his lunch is stored.

Some students with severe disabilities are excellent decoders and can read many words but do not understand their meanings. These students have generalized word analysis skills but lack word comprehension. A lack of reading comprehension usually indicates that the student is deficient in language comprehension. To help students begin making links between printed words and their meanings, the teacher can probe students' listening (auditory) comprehension. That is, the teacher says the word and notes whether a student understands its meaning (e.g., finds the gym bag when the teacher says "gym"). If not, the teacher will want to focus sight word instruction on using the word in context rather than in a tabletop drill. For example, the teacher might show a student word cards representing their key schedule classes (e.g., physical education, chorus, homeroom, math) and ask the student to read the word and locate the associated photo of the classroom and teacher. Even if students cannot read entire sentences, instruction would begin at the level of the student's listening comprehension (e.g., single sight words or short phrases).

Comprehension can be encouraged by using a language experience approach (LEA), which involves composing simple stories (Nessel & Jones, 1981). This approach has the advantages of using familiar vocabulary that relates to recent experiences. In the LEA process, the student dictates a story to a teacher or tutor who then records it, adding words if needed. Once written, reading instruction focuses on the dictated story or passages. Topics for the story can be school events, community-based instruction, activities with friends, family events, or other areas of interest to the student. To use this passage for reading instruction, the teacher or peer tutor may (a) put new words on flash cards for sight word instruction, (b) ask comprehension questions, (c) ask the student to select a picture or photograph for the story, or (d) have the student photocopy, type, or recopy the story for a permanent storybook. Word cards can be arranged to make new sentences. Some students like to have a storage box for their words, and, depending on their skills, word cards can be arranged behind alphabet cards, making them easier to find. This arrangement also allows additional learning opportunities that involve alphabetization and initial letter recognition whenever getting out or

replacing word cards. Figure 13–5 shows a student-dictated story whose underlined words were those supplied by the teacher.

Teaching Writing Skills

Typically, writing is thought of as a pencil-and-paper task. But we can expand on the concept of writing to include students with significant disabilities who physically may not be able to write. To illustrate, students can learn to use stamps to produce their names, to select photographs to journal their activities, to record information on adapted computers, and to develop sentences and lists using specialized software that produces picture symbols for words. Once the concept of writing is expanded, the writing opportunities become considerable.

Limited research has been published that involves writing skills for students with severe disabilities. However, if writing is a goal, a good starting point is the student's own name. Students who are only learning to read a few sight words may be able to learn to write their name for lifelong use as a signature. One method for teaching this skill is to task analyze the individual letters of the student's name. Using the curricular materials *Handwriting Without Tears* (Olsen, 2003), students can learn a sequence of letter formations. Students practice with miniature chalkboards and chalk, which may be easier for some students to manipulate in early instruction on writing. An alternative approach to teaching a student to write a signature is to encourage the student to make distinctive markings on a page. The teacher can then shape these marks toward a signature. For example, pointing to a straight mark, the teacher might note how it looks similar to the way someone would begin to write a "T" for "Tom."

Students physically unable to write may learn to use rubber stamp signatures; stamps can be made that have the student's full name on them. Students would be

FIGURE 13–5
Example of a Language Experience Story Composed by a Student and Used to Teach Passage Reading.

The underlined words were provided by Dominique's teacher after she dictated the story:
I went to McDonald's. I ate a Big Mac, fries, and a coke. I paid $5.00. Carlos came with me. He is my brother.

taught that the stamp produces their name, and when asked for a signature, they would use the stamp. These also need to learn the proper placement of the stamp on a line. When students are unable to grip a writing utensil, they may be able to hit a voice output device that states "Write my name for me" whenever a signature is needed. For some students, learning to type their name on the computer would be a more accessible format. Whatever approach is taught, students need frequent practice on name writing during the day (e.g., on papers, to sign up for an activity, to sign out).

Ricky cannot grasp a pencil or pen, but he is able to grasp a stamp with a large handle. Ricky's teachers purchased a stamp with his name on it and the letter "R" imprinted in the handle. Ricky is able to find the stamp by touch. His teachers are instructing him on the proper way to hold the stamp so that the stamped letters are printed right side up.

Handwriting is only one component of literacy. Another important competency is composition. The "critical function" or "essence" of composition is to produce a printed communication. The outcome is a permanent product that can be saved for personal use or shared with others. Although some students may be unable to develop handwriting skills, they still may learn to produce meaningful composition. Students at the presymbolic level may learn to use a computer and select digital pictures of familiar school routines to create a picture journal about their daily activities. Students might also develop self-expression through art activities like making a block-printed cover for their journals. Similarly, computer-generated reports for academic subjects can be developed with pictures selected through a similar "click to select" process.

Students who are at an early symbolic level may be able to use picture/word combinations to begin developing phrase, sentences, simple stories, or reports. The student might use sentence starters like "I like . . ." or "My grocery list . . ." and select pictures with word captions to complete the thought. A software program that types in picture symbol/word combinations that some students benefit from learning is Writing with Symbols 2000 (Mayer-Johnson, Inc., 1999). With this program, teachers produce a bank of picture symbols and a sentence starter or phrase. Then students are taught to click on the pictures in the bank and complete the sentence. Figure 13–6 shows how a student can use Writing with Symbols 2000 to produce a grocery list.

Students at the expanded symbolic level will benefit from learning to spell sight words to use in composing reports, stories, and other forms of writing. Incidental learning or spelling sight words as they are taught is one way to teach spelling. For example, Wolery, Ault, Gast, Doyle, and Mills (1990) spelled each sight word in a group lesson with students who had mild disabilities. Spelling the words helped focus the students' attention, and some students also learned to spell the words. Students who need extra assistance with spelling can use a computer program to create grammatically correct sentences. Programs such as Write: OutLoud (Don Johnston, Inc., 1996) and Co-Writer (Don Johnston, Inc., 2000) allow students to type in the first few letters of a word and then view options of correctly spelled words. Students then chose from those options to compose sentences. Teachers may assist students with compositions by writing down sentences the students have dictated and have the students copy them by writing or typing.

Math Instruction

A second key area of academic instruction is math. The National Council of Teachers of Mathematics (NCTM) produced a set of standards titled *Principles and Standards for School Mathematics* (NCTM, 2000) that provide a comprehensive foundation of mathematics knowledge and skills recommended for all students. They specify the understanding, knowledge, and skills that students should learn from prekindergarten through grade 12 in five content areas (Table 13–6). Grade-level expectations, sample activities, and video clips of the standards in action can be found on the NCTM Website (**http://standards.nctm.org/index.htm**). These standards, along with specific state standards, can be used to develop age- and grade-appropriate activities in line with grade-level expectations. For students with severe disabilities, math instruction, like reading, builds on a student's assessed level of symbol use: presymbolic, early symbolic, or expanded symbolic. Students at a presymbolic level can be taught to apply counting skills to daily routines, while those at an early symbolic level can learn to manage their time and money and to recognize numbers in everyday activities. Students at the expanded symbolic level can learn to generalize their math skills into many different contexts and can master practical aspects of computation, geometry, and data analysis.

FIGURE 13–6
The Writing with Symbols 2000 program (Mayer-Johnson, Inc., 1999) can be used
by students to produce grocery lists. Credits: The Picture Communication Symbols™
© 1981–2004, Mayer-Johnson, Inc. All Rights Reserved Worldwide.

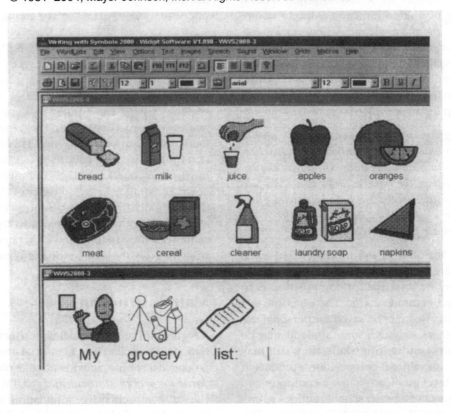

Presymbolic Math Instruction

There is very little research on teaching math skills to students at the presymbolic level. However, since the No Child Left Behind Act requires documenting progress in math, teachers are beginning to explore how to address the "critical function" of standards like those in Table 13-6. One way to address number and operations standards is to introduce counting and number use into students' daily routines. Students who do not count or recognize numbers may learn to pace a daily routine by counting.

> *While Ricky has learned some symbols for language arts, he does not recognize numbers. To start, Ricky's teacher decides to introduce the concept of numbers to him in the context of functional activities. She is teaching him to hit a switch to operate a blender on a set count. Ricky is learning not to hit the switch on "1" or "2" and not to wait for "4" but to hit on "3." The teacher uses other numbers for other activities (e.g., "Let's put your coat on in "5"). As Ricky comprehends different numbers, the teacher lets Ricky select the count by asking him, "Ricky, do you want to hit the switch on the count of '3' or '10'?" Ricky is also learning that "5" means a longer wait than "3."*

Students at the presymbolic level can learn beginning money and time concepts. Before learning to make purchases, a student learns to distinguish between money and nonmoney.

> *Ricky's teacher shows Ricky a dollar bill in his right hand and a pencil or other distractor in his left and asks him, "What do you need to buy more lemonade mix?" Ricky is also learning to manage his personal time by hitting a switch that requests a new activity whenever his watch beeps.*

TABLE 13–6
Excerpts of Mathematics Content Standards and Expectations (NCTM, 2000) and Student Examples

Content areas	Examples (Key: P = presymbolic, ES = early symbolic, ExS = expanded symbolic)
Number and operations	P–Ricky demonstrates the concept of numbers under 5 by hitting a switch to operate an appliance on a set count (i.e., start the blender on 3, 1 . . . 2 . . . 3). ExS–Dominique counts up to 10 objects (i.e., packages that are sold at the school store).
Algebra	P–Ricky selects the set count prior to performing different activities (start the blender on count of 3, put on jacket on count of 5). ES–Brett follows a variety of visuals to complete daily living activities (i.e., a place-setting model to set the table). ExS–Dominique fills in missing numbers in a copy of her social security number.
Geometry	P–When asked, "Where do you want to be?" and shown up and down arrows, Amy will eye gaze "up" or "down" to tell where she wants to be moved when positioned. ES–Brett matches geometric shapes as part of his work system (i.e., triangle to start, circle to stop). ExS–Dominique locates places on maps given simple relationships such as "near to" another area.
Measurement	P–Ricky selects money from nonmoney objects. ES–Dominique matches the clock on her personal time schedule to a wall clock and moves to the classes when the clocks match. ExS–Dominique keeps a simplified checkbook using computer software.
Data analysis and probability	P–Ricky tracks his correct answers in math by hitting his talking switch to ask a peer to add a square to his math bar graph that is displayed in his file on the computer in front of him. ES–Ricky self-evaluates after completing a snack preparation activity by using a graph with stickers. ExS–Dominique fills in a bar graph to track the number of items she has packaged for her school store.

Students at a presymbolic level might also focus on data analysis standards by learning to use object graphs to self-evaluate their work. For example, students might keep track of how many tasks they complete by using stickers on a chart, marbles in a jar, colored bar graphs, or rings on a dowel.

Ricky keeps track of his correct answers in math by hitting his talking switch to ask a peer to add squares to his math bar graph displayed on the computer in front of him.

Early Symbolic Math

Research on teaching students math skills at the early symbolic level address primarily money skills and time management. McDonnell (1987) found that students with severe cognitive disabilities could learn to purchase food items priced under $1.00 when prompted using constant time delay. In this early approach to money, students can learn to exchange some predetermined amount of money (e.g., dollar bill) to obtain an item and to spend money using predetermined money categories. For example, Gardill and Browder (1995) taught students to select a $5 bill for lunch, a $1 bill for

the school store, or quarters for the vending machine. Instruction focused on teaching students to match the correct money amount to a picture of the item placed alongside a sample of the money needed (e.g., picture of lunch next to a sample $5 bill). Over time, students learn to select the correct money amount without the picture and sample.

At the next level, students may learn to read and count out amounts of money up to 10, giving a functional context to apply number reading and counting skills. For example, McDonnell and Ferguson (1988), McDonnell, Horner, and Williams (1984), and Westling, Floyd, and Carr (1990) all found that the next-dollar strategy (i.e., giving the cashier one more dollar than the stated price) was an effective way to teach purchasing skills to students with severe cognitive disabilities. Test, Howell, Burkhart, and Beroth (1993) tested different approaches for teaching the next-dollar strategy (also known as the "one more than" strategy). For example, if the requested amount is "thirteen dollars and eight cents," the student, using $1 bills, counts out one more than the number of dollars named (counts out 14). Another strategy called the "One More Than Plus the Cents Pile Modification" is to have the student, using $1 bills, put $1 aside in the "cents pile," count out the requested dollar amount, then combine the two piles for a total of $14. Another approach called the "Say Back Method" is used when the student is asked for an amount in a shortened form, omitting the word "dollar" (e.g., "Two sixty"). The student is taught to say back the amount in terms of dollars and cents (i.e., "Two dollars and sixty cents") before counting out the correct number of dollar bills.

An alternative to the next-dollar strategy is to teach the use of a number line. Sandknop, Schuster, Wolery, and Cross (1992) found that students with severe cognitive disabilities could successfully use an adaptive number line to select lower-priced items. The students were taught using a task analysis in which they compared the first number, then the second, and so on until they could determine the lower price. Because number lines may be stigmatizing in public, this method may be more appropriate for early acquisition of the counting response.

Students at an early symbolic level may learn to manage their time and follow schedules. Because of the proliferation of digital watches and clocks and the comparative ease of digital displays over analog clocks, the most efficient format for teaching time telling will be digital numbers. A good beginning point is to teach students to read key times in their daily schedules and to identify when they appear on a watch. A skill sequence to teach digital time might shape students' discrimination across numbers. For example, the sequence of instruction for *digital clocks* might be as follows:

1. Recognize a number that comes just before time for the next activity (e.g., after the clock shows 7, student watches for the number 8 to turn on television show)
2. Recognize two numbers that tell the time of the next activity (e.g., student is cued beforehand and then checks her watch for the number 12 to go to the lunch room [12:00] or the number 10 in last two numbers to go home [3:10])
3. Recognize two or three numbers (numerals 1 to 59) to know the exact time (e.g., student learns to punch in at job training site at exactly 8:47)

One disadvantage of digital time telling is that it is more complex to determine how close a given time is to the target time (e.g., 2:27 is very close to 2:30, as is 1:57 to 2:00). *Analog clocks* allow one to watch the minute hand to see it getting closer to the target time. Thus, some will prefer to teach students a sequence of skills for telling time on analog clocks. First, the

student might learn to identify all the numbers on the clock (e.g., "point to 3"). Then the student learns to read the time on the hour using these numbers (e.g., "three o'clock"). For nonverbal students, the teacher might use three pictures of clocks showing different times and say, "Point to 3:00." Next, the teacher introduces time on the half hour (e.g., "Point to 8:30"). Once the student can identify clocks at both the hour and the half hour, the nearest quarter hour can be taught (e.g., "Quarter to 9; quarter after 9"). Finally, some students may learn to count by fives to do the nearest 5 minutes ("2:35").

For time management, students also need to follow schedules and use a calendar. Martin, Elias-Burger, and Mithaug (1987) taught students in a vocational training program to change work tasks based on a printed schedule of words or pictures paired with times. If students did not change work stations within 5 minutes of a scheduled time, they received a verbal prompt to do so and were prompted to look at the time and activity schedule. Younger students learn to use classroom clocks to self-initiate changes from one activity to the next according to schedules with times. Older students might use personal time schedule cards and their own watch to monitor when to change classes, attend therapy, or meet the bus for community-based instruction.

Dominique participates in a general education science and social studies class. She has learned what time she needs to leave her class to get to these classes on time. On Monday, Wednesday, and Friday, she uses a personal time schedule along with her agenda to move from class to class. She matches the clock on her personal time schedule to her watch or the wall clock and leaves when the clocks match.

Calendar time can help to plan daily, weekly, and monthly activities. This task might be taught using individual appointment books or small month-by-month calendars (week and daily planners are less functional, as they correspond less to the monthly calendars used in most places). Students learn to locate the current month and day to note any special events. Future events are recorded by finding the month and day.

Students at the early symbolic level can be taught to use numbers for specific purposes. For example, students can learn to pull numbered work tasks by locating the corresponding number on a materials shelf. Students learning personal information might be taught to point to their telephone number from a series of other telephone numbers. For example, a student whose phone number is 704-555-1234 would learn to look at the following series (in any order) and point to his or her phone number:

704-555-4321   704-555-9851   704-555-1234

Symbolic Math Instruction: Bridging to Numeracy
Some students with severe disabilities will learn a variety of money combinations and price reading, to tell time, and to compute small sums with or without a calculator (e.g., to balance a checkbook). Students who have generalized outcomes will be able to transfer these skills to novel contexts, such as reading prices on a variety of price tags or telling time from a mixture of clocks. Moving from this level of performance to greater competence will require that teachers address a broader range of math standards than those considered as functional math. Students will need to know more about numbers, computation, geometry, and data analysis. A research-based set of sequenced steps for

teaching counting, one-to-one correspondence, and using numerals (Resnick, Wang, & Kaplan, 1973) can be found in Table 13-7.

When using a math skill sequence, it is wise to use materials from daily classroom, school, and home routines and then find ways to apply each skill once learned (Figure 13-7). For example, Wacker et al. (1988) taught students with moderate mental retardation to enter numbers into computer files, checkbooks, and calculators. This data entry skill was enhanced by having students say the number aloud before entering it, using what they called a "say, then do" approach. Being able to read ("say") and enter ("do") numbers helps in planning purchases, performing simple data entry jobs, and using calculators.

Some students can learn to name numbers when taught by flash card drills with simple feedback or time delay procedures. Others may benefit from a task demonstration method involving stimulus shaping and general case instruction to teach generalized number naming (Repp, Karsh, & Lenz, 1990). In this method,

TABLE 13–7
Sequenced Objectives for Counting, One-to-One Correspondence, and Numerals

Units 1 and 2: Counting and one-to-one correspondence

1. The student counts by rote.
2. Given a set of movable objects, the student counts by moving them out of the set while counting (touch-move-counting).
3. Given a fixed ordered (unmovable) set of objects, the student counts the objects.
4. Given a fixed unordered set of objects, the student counts the objects.
5. Given a stated number and a set of objects, the student counts out a set of the stated size.
6. Given a stated number and several sets of fixed objects, the student identifies a set that matches the stated number.
7. Given two sets of objects, the student pairs objects and states whether the sets are the same in number.
8. Given two unequal sets of objects, the student pairs objects and states which set has more.
9. Given two unequal sets of objects, the student can pair objects and state which set has less.

Units 3 and 4: Numerals

1. Given two sets of numerals, the student matches the numerals.
2. Given a numeral stated and a set of printed numerals, the student selects the stated numeral.
3. Given a numeral (written), the student reads the numeral.
4. Given several sets of objects and several numerals, the student matches numerals with appropriate sets.
5. Given two numerals (written), the student states which shows more (or less).
6. Given a set of numerals, the student places them in order.
7. Given numerals stated, the student writes the numeral.

Note: Units 1 and 3 involve sets of up to five objects; units 2 and 4 involve sets of up to 10 objects.
Source: From "Task analysis in curriculum design: A hierarchically sequenced introductory mathematics curriculum," by L. B. Resnick, M. C. Wang, & J. Kaplan, 1973, *Journal of Applied Behavior Analysis, 6*, p. 699. Copyright 1973 by *Journal of Applied Behavior Analysis.* Adapted with permission.

FIGURE 13–7

This student counts the number of boys and girls present in his class each day. He finds the corresponding numbers, then adds them together to get a total of how many students are present that day.

numbers are introduced using a variety of sizes and colors so students learn to focus on the relevant stimulus (number configuration) versus irrelevant ones (e.g., color). Students learn to select the correct number (e.g., "7") first when given no distractors, then with highly dissimilar distractors (e.g., 7, 999, 04, M), and finally learn to select from among more similar distractors (7, L, Z, 1).

Dominique is learning to use numbers 1 to 12 in a variety of ways: naming numbers on flash cards, clock faces, and other materials. She also is learning to type numbers into a spread sheet in business class. Currently, she is given one number at a time on a flash card, finds the number on the keyboard, and types it into the first box on the spreadsheet. She is learning to use an analog watch to tell time to the quarter hour and keep track of her schedule.

Some students benefit from learning addition and subtraction skills, which also can be taught as a sequenced curriculum or through a commercial program. Some students may learn to add by using their counting skills. For example, Irvin (1991) taught children with

moderate mental retardation to rote count to 20 and to count up from any number (e.g., from 5 to 10). Using these skills, students learned to add by counting sets of dots. For example, to add 3 to 5, the student would be given sets of three dots and five dots. The student would count the three dots and then shift to the next set counting up from three (i.e., 4, 5, 6, 7, 8) to get the sum of eight.

Flash card drills of basic addition and subtraction facts can help build these skills fluent. Using flash card drills with constant time delay, Whalen, Schuster, and Hemmeter (1996) taught students in groups to add and subtract. Students learned both their own targeted math facts and those of their peers. Students also can learn to compute using calculators and to discriminate between whether to add or subtract (Lancioni, Smeets, & Oliva, 1987). Some students with disabilities may be able to keep pace with the general education math class assignments by using calculators (Horton, 1985). If such skills are taught, teachers are urged to find many ways for students to add and subtract in their daily routines with functional materials and realistic situations.

As Kerry improves in using data entry on a spreadsheet, she is learning to keep a simplified checkbook with money management software. She enters the dollar amount of her purchase after clicking on the word "withdrawal." For now, she skips the options to type in other information and just focuses on the amount left after the automatic subtraction. She demonstrates the skill using dollars for her teacher.

For some students, learning basic measurement of length (ruler), volume (cups and tablespoons measures), and weight (scale) will be important. Smeenge, Page, Iwata, and Ivancic (1980) developed a skill sequence to teach measurement to several individuals with multiple disabilities. They learned to compare lengths to determine if they were the same or different, then to determine if one was shorter or longer, and finally to use a ruler to measure feet and inches.

Some students with expanded math concepts may learn to count a variety of coins and bills. With older students, it may be more efficient to begin instruction with counting a variety of bills (Table 13–8) rather than focusing first on coins. Younger students may benefit from learning to count and combine coins as a functional application of their emerging counting skills. The Syracuse Community-Referenced Curriculum Guide (Ford, Davern, Schnorr, Black, & Kaiser, 1989) provides a skill sequence for counting and using a number line and calculator to plan and make

TABLE 13–8
A Dollar-First Sequence for Teaching Money Skills

1. One-Dollar Bill. Use of $1 for small purchases.
2. Ones to Tens. Use $1 bills needed for purchases up to $10 by using the "one-more-than" strategy (e.g., for $5.49, give five ones and "one more").
3. Ten-Dollar Bill. Use $10 bills for large purchases. Use a number line or "one-more-ten-than" strategy (e.g., for $36.59, give three tens and "one more ten").
4. Mixed Tens and Ones. Student learns to count up "one more than" using first tens, then ones (e.g., for $36.59, give three tens, six ones, and "one more" $1 bill).
5. Equivalence. Student learns to use equivalent bills (e.g., $5 bill = five ones).
6. Coins. Teach counting coins after use of bills is mastered.

TABLE 13–9
A Sequence to Teach Counting and Money Skills Simultaneously

1. Count pennies to 10 cents (count by ones to 10)
2. Equate 10 pennies to one dime (both are 10)
3. Count dimes to one dollar (count by tens)
4. Count quarters to one dollar (25, 50, 75, 1 dollar)
5. Equate two quarters plus dimes to one dollar (count by tens beginning with 50)
6. Count nickels to one dollar (count by fives)
7. Count quarters plus nickels (count by fives beginning with 25, 50, or 75)
8. Count dimes plus nickels (count by tens and then switch to counting by fives)
9. Count quarters plus dimes (count by fives beginning with 25 or 50)
10. Count quarters, dimes, and nickels (count 25 or 50, then by tens, and then by fives)
11. Count $1 bills to $10
12. Count $1 and $5 bills to $20
13. Count $10 and $1 bills to $20
14. Count $10, $5, and $1 bills to $20
15. Use a calculator to compute affordability of multiple purchases

purchases (Table 13–9). A critical feature of this program is that students use whatever level of money and number line skills they have to make purchases. Thus, students with skills to count pennies would count how many pennies they have (e.g., seven) and then consult the number line to see if this is enough to purchase five cents' worth of gum. Checking the amount also might be taught by matching the pennies to five circles on a picture of gum to see if there are enough pennies.

For older students, dollar bills may still be used for most purchases, but coin counting can be taught on vending machines (Trace, Cuvo, & Criswell, 1977). Lowe and Cuvo (1976) designed a skill sequence for teaching coins in which students learn to count all coins in varying units of fives (e.g., count two dimes by

tapping each twice and counting: "five-ten" then "fifteen-twenty"). Each coin was also associated with a finger(s) prompt. To count nickels, students used their index finger counting by five for each nickel. After mastering nickels to a dollar, students learned to count dimes. Dimes were counted by giving two taps per coin with the paired index and middle finger ("five-ten" . . . "fifteen-twenty" for two dimes). Next, students learned to count combinations of nickels and dimes, continuing to count by fives. After learning to count nickel and dime combinations, quarters were learned by tapping each coin five times with all fingers of the hand and counting by fives to 25. Pennies were learned last and require counting up by one (may be omitted). Additional research revealed that moving the coins a short distance from the group of uncounted coins while counting (a touch-move-count approach) facilitated learning (Borakove & Cuvo, 1976). In the Lowe and Cuvo coin counting sequence, students learned to arrange coins by decreasing value and then count the more valuable coins first, with pennies counted last.

Dominique is being taught to count a combination of five coins totaling 55 cents (one quarter, two dimes, and two nickels) by arranging them as follows: quarter, dime, dime, nickel, nickel. She learns to use the counting sequence and finger-tapping outlined as follows:

Coin	Finger prompt	Student taps coin and says
Quarter	5 fingers	"5, 10, 15, 20, 25
Dime	2 fingers	30, 35
Dime	2 fingers	40, 45
Nickel	Index finger	50
Nickel	Index finger	55 ... it's 55 cents."

One of the most complex money skills is change computation. This skill, if taught, probably should be taught last in a money sequence. Cuvo, Veitch, Trace, and Konke (1978) taught change computation to

students with moderate mental retardation who knew how to count coins. Students learned to count correct change given back after a purchase. Since most of us do not take the time to count their change, it seems reasonable that this complex skill may be one that is not taught unless there is specific reason to target it (e.g., training as a cashier).

Students who are expanding their math skills may be able to learn to use an analog clock. As stated previously, digital time telling has the disadvantage of not being able to visually see how close a given time is to the target time, while analog clocks allow one to watch the minute hand's movement toward the target time. An early resource on time telling (Thurlow & Turnure, 1977) suggested the following skill sequence: (a) discriminate the minute and hours hands, (b) telling time to the hour (o'clock), (c) telling time to the half hour, (d) telling time to the quarter hour, and (e) telling time to the minute.

Other Academic Areas

Teaching science and social studies to students with severe disabilities has a limited research base. Teachers can start by becoming familiar with the national

TABLE 13–10
Excerpts of the National Science Education Standards (NRC, 1996) and Student Examples

Category excerpts	Examples
Concepts and processes	Brett will identify how heat and cold affect liquids through food preparation activities. Dominique will identify chemical reactions by learning safe and unsafe uses for cleaning products.
Science as inquiry	Ricky will discover and classify substances by their smell. Dominique will learn to ask or write a question to be answered in a science activity.
Physical science	Brett will learn to indicate whether an electric circuit is on and to complete a circuit using a switch (e.g., to activate a CD player). Ricky will learn to identify what is magnetic and use magnets in a variety of daily activities (magnetic letter board, post notes).
Life science	Amy will eye gaze at picture symbols to indicate what is needed to care for a plant in helping to maintain a class garden. Kerry will identify which foods have protein and which have carbohydrates to plan a menu.
Earth and space science	Ricky (who is visually impaired) will classify rocks based on touch in developing a personal rock collection. Amy will identify a constellation through eye gazing at pictures or in a planetarium.
Science and technology	Brett will select pictures from a Website showing satellite pictures of space to identify stars. Kerry will learn to use a microscope.
Personal and social perspectives	Brett will recycle aluminum cans and newspapers. Kerry will identify pictures of different forms of energy.

science and social studies standards. Next they will identify useful skills that connect to the standards but that also balance with students' ages, skill levels, and functional priorities. This process, similar to that outlined for selecting target skills in language arts and math, reflects the steps outlined earlier in Table 13-1.

Science

Science can be taught alone or integrated with other academic areas (Polloway, Patton, & Serna, 2001). One study that provides an example of how to teach science-related skills focused on comprehension of newspaper weather reports. Browder and Shear (1996) taught weather words to students with moderate mental retardation and severe behavior disorders using an interspersal drill sequence. Interspersal involved presenting new weather words (e.g., sunny, cloudy, rain) "sandwiched" between flash cards of known words (e.g., the, cat, is) in a rapid drill sequence. Students also learned to read "story starters" that were teacher made beginning reading stories with the new words (e.g., "It is cloudy. It may rain. It is cloudy today."). Students mastered the weather sight words and made improvements in reading the daily weather report.

The National Research Council (NRC), the principal agency that provides services to the government, scientific community, and the public, developed the National Science Education Standards (NRC, 1996). These standards outline skills needed to achieve scientific literacy in eight categories (Table 13-10).

Social Studies

The National Council for the Social Studies (NCSS) has identified content standards for social studies teachers. While not recognized as national standards, they offer a starting point in determining what may be appropriate content to teach students with disabilities. As shown in Table 13-11, the Curriculum Standards for Social Studies (NCSS, 1994) developed 10 thematic strands and performance expectations for early grades, middle grades, and high school.

One resource for social studies materials for students with disabilities is the *News-2-You* (**http://www.news-2-you.com**) weekly newspaper written with BoardMaker picture symbols that addresses current events. This online publication provides "big picture" news to individuals who need "concise, visual concepts." The paper includes news, recipes, activity pages, and jokes that are all related to the weekly lead stories. Additional pages can be created by subscribers to include weather, sports, birthday news, movies reviews, and so on. *News-2-You* is written at various levels (regular edition, simplified edition, higher edition)

TABLE 13–11

Excerpts of Social Studies Curriculum (NCSS, 1994) and Student Examples

Excerpts	Examples
Cultural diversity	Kerry completes a report about her country of origin and shares it with the class using PowerPoint. Brett chooses between pictures of historical leaders as part of a group project on African American heritage.
People, places, and environments	Amy chooses between pictures to show contrasts in geographic regions (e.g., mountains vs. ocean, hot vs. cold). Kerry uses a globe to locate where different members of her extended family live.
Individual development and identity	Ricky learns to prepare foods that reflect his ethnic heritage. Brett develops a poster of pictures of his family tree.
Interactions among individuals and groups	Kerry fills in sentences with five key facts about U.S. policies on immigration. Amy identifies a picture of one or more key political leaders (e.g., president, governor).
Organization, production, distribution, and consumption of goods and services	Kerry makes a notebook of job options based on the production and distribution of goods in her community (e.g., grocery store jobs, warehouse jobs, farming jobs). Brett distinguishes between pictures of community helpers (police, fire, postman).
Democratic ideals, principles, and practices of citizenship	Kerry learns to self-advocate for a needed service by using an "I want . . ." statement. Ricky demonstrates a way to show the school's featured character trait for each month in interactions with peers (e.g., sharing).

FIGURE 13–8
An article from *News-2-You*, an online weekly newspaper written with BoardMaker picture symbols (Mayer-Johnson, Inc., 1998) that addresses current events.

Source: Used with permission, News-2-You, Inc. The Picture Communication Symbols™ © 1981–2004, Mayer-Johnson, Inc. All Rights Reserved Worldwide.

to include access for a wide variety of individuals (Figure 13–8).

Assistive Technology Information

Technology	Contact information
Step-by-Step®	AbleNet, Inc. (800-322-0956) **http://www.ablenetinc.com**
Tech-Talk®	Advanced Multimedia Devices, Inc. (1-888-353-AMDI) **http://www.amdi.net**
Pathfinder®	Prentke Romich Co. (800-262-1984) **http://www.prentrom.com**
Edmark Functional Word Series®	PRO-ED, Inc. (800-897-3202) **http://www.proedinc.com**
Write: OutLoud Co: Writer®	Don Johnson, Inc. (800-999-4660) **http://www.donjohnson.com**
IntelliKeys®	IntelliTools, Inc. (800-899-6687) **http://www.intellitools.com**
Boardmaker®	Mayer-Johnson, Inc. (800-588-4548) **http://www.mayer-johnson.com**
Writing with Symbols 2000®	Widgit Software, Ltd (01223) 425-558 **http://www.widgit.com**
Microsoft Money Software®	**http://www.microsoft.com**

Summary

In today's schools, academic instruction is part of the curriculum for all students. To identify the skills needed by students and specify functional outcomes, teachers must become familiar with their state standards and then apply several guidelines: (a) consider the "critical function" of the standard, (b) choose skills that promote active participation, (c) teach within functional activities to give the skill meaning, (d) apply a universal curriculum, and (e) incorporate self-determination and self-directed learning. The level of skill complexity will relate to students' ability to use symbols. Academic skills should both increase students' participation in general education and be relevant in their daily lives.

Suggested Activities

1. Outline a talk for parents that discusses the importance of providing access to the general curriculum for all students. Share ways to promote access and discuss different levels of symbol use (presymbolic, early symbolic, expanded symbolic) in language arts and math. Solicit their feedback on the academic outcomes they hope to see their children attain.
2. Develop an instructional plan to teach Brett to spell his name using an adapted keyboard and a switch. Incorporate direct, systematic instruction; small-group instruction using peer tutors; and whole-class instruction to embed Brett's name spelling into the lessons.
3. Obtain a copy of your school district's standard course of study for one grade level or subject area (language arts or math). Brainstorm how students at the presymbolic, early symbolic, and expanded symbolic levels could acquire the critical essence of these skills.

References

Aeschleman, S. R., & Schladenhauffen, J. (1984). Acquisition, generalization, and maintenance of grocery shopping skills by severely mentally retarded adolescents. *Applied Research in Mental Retardation, 5*, 245-258.

Agran, M., Blanchard, C., Hughes, C., & Wehmeyer, M. L. (2002). Increasing the problem-solving skills of students with developmental disabilities participating in general education. *Remedial and Special Education, 23*, 279-288.

Agran, M., Fodor-Davis, J., Moore, S., & Deer, M. (1989). The application of a self-management program on instruction-following skills. *Journal of the Association for Persons with Severe Handicaps, 14*, 147-154.

Agran, M., King-Sears, M. E., Wehmeyer, M. L., & Copeland, S. R. (2003). *Student-directed learning.* Baltimore: Paul H. Brookes.

Agran, M., & Moore, S. C. (1994). *Innovations: AAMR Research to Practice Series.* How to teach self instruction of job skills. *Innovations.* Washington, DC: American Association on Mental Retardation.

Agran, M., Alper, S., & Wehmeyer, M. (2002). Access to the general curriculum for students with significant disabilities: What it means to teachers. *Education and Training in Mental Retardation and Developmental Disabilities, 37*, 123-133.

Agran, M., Snow, K., & Swaner, J. (1999). Teacher perceptions of self-determination: Benefits, characteristics, strategies. *Education and Training in Mental Retardation and Developmental Disabilities, 34*, 293-301.

Alcantara, P. R. (1994). Effects of videotape instructional package on purchasing skills of children with autism. *Exceptional Children, 61*, 40-55.

Algozzine, B., Browder, D., Karvonen, M., Test, D. W., & Wood, W. M. (2001). Effects of interventions to promote self-determination for individuals with disabilities. *Review of Educational Research, 71*(2), 219-277.

Basil, C., & Reyes, S. (2003). Acquisition of literacy skills by children with severe disability. *Child Language Teaching and Therapy, 19*(1), 27-49.

Belfiore, P. J., Browder, D. M., & Mace, F. C. (1994). Assessing choice-making and preference in adults with profound mental retardation across community and center-based settings. *Journal of Behavioral Education, 4*, 217-225.

Billingsley, F. F. (1993). In my dreams: A response to some current trends in education. *Journal of the Association for Persons with Severe Handicaps, 18*(1), 61-63.

Board of Education Sacramento City Unified School District v. Holland, 786 F. Supp. 874 (E. D. Cal. 1992).

Borakove, L. S., & Cuvo, A. J. (1976). Facilitative effects of coin displacement on teaching coin summation to mentally retarded adolescents. *American Journal of Mental Deficiency, 81*, 350-356.

Bos, C. S., & Vaugn, S. (2002). *Strategies for teaching students with learning and behavior problems* (5th ed.). Boston: Allyn & Bacon.

Browder, D. M., Ahlgrim-Delzell, L., Flowers, C., Karvonen, M., Spooner, F. H., & Algozzine, B. (in press). How states implement alternate assessments for students with disabilities and recommendations for national policy. *Journal of Disability Policy Studies*.

Browder, D. M., Cooper, K. J., & Lim, L. (1998). Teaching adults with severe disabilities to express their choice of settings for leisure activities. *Education and Training in Mental Retardation and Developmental Disabilities, 33*(3), 228-238.

Browder, D. M., Flowers, C., Ahlgrim-Delzell, L., Karvonen, M., Spooner, F. H., & Algozzine, B. (2004). The alignment of alternate assessment content to academic and functional curricula. *Journal of Special Education, 37*(4), 211-223.

Browder, D. M., & Grasso, E. (1999). Teaching money skills to individuals with mental retardation: A research review with practical applications. *Remedial and Special Education, 20*, 297-308.

Browder, D., Hines, C., McCarthy, L. J., & Fees, J. (1984). Sight word instruction to facilitate acquisition and generalization of daily living skills for the moderately and severely retarded. *Education and Training in Mental Retardation, 19*, 191-200.

Browder, D. M., & Minarovic, T. (2000). Utilizing sight words in self-instruction training for employees with moderate mental retardation in competitive jobs. *Education and Training in Mental Retardation and Developmental Disabilities, 35*, 78-89.

Browder, D., & Shear, E. (1996). Interspersal of known items in a treatment package to teach sight words to students with behavior disorders. *Journal of Special Education, 29*, 400-413.

Browder, D. M., & Snell, M. (2000). Teaching functional academics. In M. Snell & F. Brown (Eds.), *Instruction of students with severe disabilities* (5th ed., pp. 493-542). Columbus, OH: Charles E. Merrill.

Browder, D. M., Spooner, F. H., Ahlgrim-Delzell, L., Flowers, C., Algozzine, B., & Karvonen, M. (2004). A content analysis of the curricular philosophies reflected in states' alternate assessment performance indicators. *Research and Practice for Persons with Severe Disabilities, 28*(4), 165-181.

Browder, D. M., Spooner, F. H., Algozzine, R., Ahlgrim-Delzell, L., Flowers, C., & Karvonen, M. (2003). What we know and need to know about alternate assessment. *Exceptional Children, 70*, 45-62.

Browder, D. M., & Xin, Y. P. (1998). A meta-analysis and review of sight word research and its implications for reaching functional reading to individuals with moderate and severe disabilities. *Journal of Special Education, 32*, 130-153.

Brown v. Board of Education, 347 U.S. 483 (1954).

Brown, L., Branston, M. B., Hamre-Nietupski, S., Pumpian, I., Certo, N., & Gruenwald, L. (1979). A strategy for developing age appropriate and functional curricular content for severely handicapped adolescents and young adults. *Journal of Special Education, 13*, 81-90.

Cafiero, J. (2001). The effect of an augmentative communication intervention on the communication, behavior, and academic program of an adolescent with autism. *Focus on Autism and Other Developmental Disabilities, 16*, 179-189.

CAST. (1998a). A curriculum every student can use: Design principles for student access. Retrieved February 27, 2003, from http://www.cec.sped.org/osep/ud-sec3.html

CAST. (1998b). Three essential qualities of universal design for learning. Retrieved February 27, 2003, from http://www.cec.sped.org/osep/appendix.html

Certo, N., Haring, N., & York, R. (1984). *Public school integration of severely handicapped students: Rational issues and progressive alternatives*. Baltimore: Paul H. Brookes.

Collins, B. C., Hall, M., Branson, T. A., & Holder, M. (1999). Acquisition of related and unrelated factual information delivered by a teacher in an inclusive setting. *Journal of Behavioral Education, 9*, 223-238.

Collins, B. C., & Stinson, D. M. (1995). Teaching generalized reading of product warning labels to adolescents with mental disabilities through the use of key words. *Exceptionality, 5*, 163-181.

Cooper, K. J., & Browder, D. M. (1998). Enhancing choice and participation for adults with severe disabilities in community-based instruction. *Journal for the Association for Persons with Severe Handicaps, 23*(3), 252-260.

Cuvo, A., Veitch, V., Trace, M., & Konke, J. (1978). Teaching change computation to the mentally retarded. *Behavior Modification, 2*, 531-548.

Dolch, E. W. (1950). *Teaching primary reading* (2nd ed.). Champaign, IL: Garrard Press.

Don Johnston, Inc. (1996). *Write: OutLoud*. Wauconda, IL: Author.

Don Johnston, Inc. (2000). *Co-Writer*. Volo, IL: Author.

Downing, J. E. (1996). *Including students with severe and multiple disabilities in typical classrooms*. Baltimore: Paul H. Brookes.

Downing, J., & Siegel-Causey, E. (1988). Enhancing the nonsymbolic communicative behavior of children with multiple impairments. *Language, Speech, and Hearing Services in Schools, 19*, 338-348.

Dymond, S. K., & Orelove, F. P. (2001). What constitutes effective curricula for students with severe disabilities? *Exceptionality, 9*(3), 109-122.

Entrikin, D., York, R., & Brown, L. (1977). Teaching trainable level multiply handicapped students to use picture cues, context cues, and initial consonant sounds to determine the labels of unknown words. *AAESPH Review, 2*, 169-190.

Erickson, K. A., & Koppenhaver, D. A. (1997). Integrated communication and literacy instruction for a child with multiple disabilities. *Focus on Autism and Other Developmental Disabilities, 12*(3), 142-151.

Erickson, R. N., Thurlow, M. L., & Thor, K. (1995). *State special education outcomes, 1994*. Minneapolis: University of Minnesota, National Center on Educational Outcomes. (ERIC Document Reproduction Service No. ED404 799)

Fisher, D., & Frey, N. (2001). Access to the core curriculum: Critical ingredients for student success. *Remedial and Special Education, 22*(3), 148-157.

Ford, A., Davern, J., Schnorr, R., Black, J., & Kaiser, K. (1989). Money handling. In A. Ford, R. Schnorr, L. Meyer, L. Davern, J. Black, and P. Dempsey (Eds.), *The Syracuse community-referenced curriculum guide for students with moderate and severe disabilities* (pp. 117-148). Baltimore: Paul H. Brookes.

Fry, E. (1957). Developing a word list for remedial reading. *Elementary English, 33*, 456-458.

Fry, E. (1972). *Reading instruction for classroom and clinic.* New York: McGraw-Hill.

Gardill, M. C., & Browder, D. M. (1995). Teaching stimulus classes to encourage independent purchasing by students with severe behavior disorders. *Education and Training in Mental Retardation and Developmental Disabilities, 30*, 254-264.

Giangreco, M. F., Dennis, R., Cloninger, C., Edelman, S., & Schattman, R. (1993). "I've counted Jon": Transformational experiences of teachers educating students with disabilities. *Exceptional Children, 59*(4), 359-373.

Grunsell, J., & Carter, M. (2002). The behavior chain interruption strategy: Generalization to out-of-routine contexts. *Education and Training in Mental Retardation and Developmental Disabilities, 37*, 378-390.

Hanline, M. F. (1993). Inclusion of preschoolers with profound disabilities: An analysis of children's interactions. *Journal of the Association for Persons with Severe Handicaps, 18*(1), 28-35.

Haring, N. G., & Romer, L. T. (1995). *Welcoming students who are deaf-blind into typical classrooms: Facilitating school participation, learning and friendships.* Baltimore: Paul H. Brookes.

Hock, M. L. (2000). Standards, assessments, and individualized educational programs: Planning for success. In R. A. Villa & J. S. Thousand (Eds.), *Restructuring for caring and effective education* (pp. 208-241). Baltimore: Paul H. Brookes.

Hoogeven, F. R., Smeets, P. M., & Lancioni, G. E. (1989). Teaching moderately mentally retarded children basic reading skills. *Research in Developmental Disabilities, 10*, 1-18.

Horton, S. (1985). Computational rates of educable mentally retarded adolescents with and without calculators in comparison to normals. *Education and Training of the Mentally Retarded, 20*, 14-24.

Hunt, P., Alwell, M., Farron-Davis, F., & Goetz, L. (1996). Creating socially supportive environments for fully included students who experience multiple disabilities. *Journal for the Association for Persons with Severe Handicaps, 21*, 53-71.

Hunt, P., Staub, D., Alwell, M., & Goetz, L. (1994). Achievement by all students within the context of cooperative learning groups. *Journal of the Association for Persons with Severe Handicaps, 19*, 290-301.

International Reading Association and National Council of Teachers of English. (1996). *Standards for the English language arts.* Newark, DE: Author.

Irvin, K. (1991). Teaching children with Down syndrome to add by counting-on. *Education and Treatment of Children, 14*, 128-141.

Johnson, B. F., & Cuvo, A. J. (1981). Teaching cooking skills to mentally retarded persons. *Behavior Modification, 5*, 187-202.

Kaiser, A., & Goetz, L. (1993). Enhancing communication with persons labeled severely disabled. *Journal of the Association for Persons with Severe Handicaps, 18*, 137-142.

Karsh, K. G., Repp, A. C., & Lenz, M. W. (1990). A comparison of the task demonstration model and the standard prompting hierarchy in teaching word identification to persons with moderate retardation. *Research in Developmental Disabilities, 11*, 395-410.

Kennedy, C. H., & Haring, T. G. (1993). Teaching choice making during social interactions to students with profound multiple disabilities. *Journal of Applied Behavior Analysis, 26*(1), 63-77.

Kleinert, H. L., & Kearns, J. F. (2001). *Alternate assessment measuring outcomes and supports for students with disabilities.* Baltimore: Paul H. Brookes.

Kleinert, H. L., Kearns, J. F., & Kennedy, S. (1997). Accountability for all students: Kentucky's alternate portfolio assessment for students with moderate and severe cognitive disabilities. *Journal of the Association for Persons with Severe Handicaps, 22*, 88-101.

Kleinert, H. L., & Thurlow, M. L. (2001). An introduction to alternate assessment. In H. L. Kleinert & J. F. Kearns (Eds.), *Measuring outcomes and supports for students with disabilities* (pp. 1-15). Baltimore: Paul H. Brookes.

Koppenhaver, D., Erickson, K., & Skotko, B. (2001). Supporting communication of girls with Rett syndrome and their mothers in storybook reading. *International Journal of Disability, Development and Education, 48*, 395-410.

Lancioni, G. E., Smeets, P. M., & Oliva, D. (1987). Introducing EMR children to arithmetical operations: A program involving pictorial problems and distinctive-feature prompts. *Research in Developmental Disabilities, 8*, 467-485.

Lipsky, D. K., & Gartner, A. (1989). *Beyond separate education: Quality education for all.* Baltimore: Paul H. Brookes.

Lohrmann-O'Rourke, S., Browder, D., & Brown, F. (2000). Guidelines for conducting socially valid systematic preference assessments. *Journal of the Association for Persons with Severe Handicaps, 25*, 42-53.

Lohrmann-O'Rourke, S., & Gomez, O. (2001). Integrating preference assessment within the transition process to create meaningful school-to-life outcomes. *Exceptionality, 9*, 157-174.

Lowe, M. L., & Cuvo, A. J. (1976). Teaching coin summation to the mentally retarded. *Journal of Applied Behavior Analysis, 9*, 483-489.

Martin, J. E., Elias-Burger, S., & Mithaug, D. E. (1987). Acquisition and maintenance of time-based task change sequence. *Education and Training in Mental Retardation, 22*, 105-119.

Mayer-Johnson, Inc. (1998). *BoardMaker for Windows.* Solana Beach, CA: Author.

Mayer-Johnson, Inc. (1999). *Writing with Symbols 2000.* Solana Beach, CA: Author.

McDonnell, J. (1987). The effects of time delay and increasing prompt hierarchy strategies on the acquisition of purchasing skills by students with severe handicaps. *Journal of the Association for Persons with Severe Handicaps, 12*, 227-236.

McDonnell, J., & Ferguson, B. (1988). A comparison of general case in vivo and general case simulation plus in vivo training. *Journal of the Association for Persons with Severe Handicaps, 13*, 116-124.

McDonnell, J. J., Horner, R. H., & Williams, J. A. (1984). Comparison of three strategies for teaching generalized grocery purchasing to high school students with severe handicaps. *Journal of the Association for Persons with Severe Handicaps, 9,* 123–133.

McDonnell, J., Mathot-Buckner, C., Thorson, N., & Fister, S. (2001). Supporting the inclusion of student with moderate and severe disabilities in junior high school general education classes: The effects of classwide peer tutoring, multi-element curriculum, and accommodations. *Education and Treatment of Children, 24*(2), 141–160.

McGraw-Hill Education. (1998). *Science Research Associates' (SRA) Developmental 1 Reading Laboratory.* Carlsbad, CA: Author.

Meyer, L. H. (1994). Editor's introduction: Understanding the impact of inclusion. *Journal of the Association for Persons with Severe Handicaps, 19,* 251–252.

Mirenda, P., MacGregor, T., & Kelly-Keough, S. (2002). Teaching communication skills for behavioral support in the context of family life. In J. M. Lucyshyn, G. Dunlap, & R. W. Albin (Eds.), *Families and positive behavior support: Addressing problem behaviors in family contexts* (pp. 185–207). Baltimore: Paul H. Brookes.

National Council for the Social Studies. (1994). Curriculum *standards for social studies.* Washington, DC: Author.

National Council of Teachers of Mathematics. (2000). *Principles and standards for school mathematics.* Retrieved September 12, 2003, from http://standards.nctm.org

National Research Council. (1996). *National Science Education Standards.* Washington, DC: National Academy Press.

Nessel, D. D., & Jones, M. B. (1981). *The language experience approach to reading.* New York: Teachers College Press.

Nietupski, J., Hamre-Nietupski, S., Curtin, S., & Shrikanth, K. (1997). A review of curricular research in severe disabilities from 1976 to 1995 in six selected journals. *Journal of Special Education, 31,* 36–55.

No Child Left Behind Act of 2001, Pub. L. No. 107–110, 115 Stat. 1425 (2002).

North Carolina Department of Public Instruction. (1985). *North Carolina Standard Course of Study.* Raleigh, NC: Author.

Olsen, J. (2003). *Writing without tears.* Cabin John, MD: Author. Available at http://www.hwtears.com

Onosko, J., & Jorgensen, C. (1998). Unit and lesson planning in the inclusive classroom. In C. Jorgensen (Ed.), *Restructuring high schools for all students: Taking inclusion to the next level* (pp. 71–105). Baltimore: Paul H. Brookes.

Osguthorpe, R. T., & Chang, L. L. (1988). The effects of computerized symbol processor instruction on the communication skills of nonspeaking students. *Augmentative and Alternative Communication, 4,* 23–34.

Polloway, E. A., Patton, J. R., & Serna, L. (2001). *Strategies for teaching learners with special needs* (7th ed.). Upper Saddle River, NJ: Merrill/Prentice Hall.

PRO-ED, Inc. (2002). *Edmark Functional Word Series.* Austin, TX: Author.

Repp, A. C., Karsh, K. G., & Lenz, M. W. (1990). Discrimination training for persons with developmental disabilities: A training for persons with developmental disabilities. A comparison of the task demonstration model and the standard prompting hierarchy. *Journal of Applied Behavior Analysis, 23,* 43–52.

Resnick, L. B., Wang, M. C., & Kaplan, J. (1973). Task analysis in curriculum design: A hierarchically sequenced introductory mathematics curriculum. *Journal of Applied Behavior Analysis, 6,* 697–710.

Rohena-Diaz, E. (1998). *A comparison of English and Spanish instruction in teaching sight words to students with moderate mental retardation who are linguistically diverse.* Unpublished doctoral dissertation, Lehigh University, Bethlehem, PA.

Ryndak, D. L., Morrison, A. P., & Sommerstein, L. (1999). Literacy before and after inclusion in general education settings: A case study. *Journal of the Association for Persons with Severe Handicaps, 24*(1), 5–22.

Sandknop, P. A., Schuster, J. W., Wolery, M., & Cross, D. P. (1992). The use of an adaptive device to teach students with moderate mental retardation to select lower priced grocery items. *Education and Training in Mental Retardation, 27,* 219–229.

Sands, D. J., Adams, L., & Stout, D. M. (1995). A statewide exploration of the nature and use of curriculum in special education. *Exceptional Children, 62,* 68–83.

Schoen, S., & Ogden, S. (1995). Impact of time delay, observational learning, and attentional cueing upon word recognition during integrated small group instruction. *Journal of Autism and Developmental Disorders, 25,* 503–519.

Singleton, K. C., Schuster, J. W., & Ault, M. J. (1995). Simultaneous prompting in a small group instruction arrangement. *Education and Training in Mental Retardation and Developmental Disabilities, 30,* 218–230.

Smeenge, M. E., Page, T. J., Iwata, B. A., & Ivancic, M. T. (1980). Teaching measurement skills to mentally retarded students: Training, generalization, and follow-up. *Education and Training in Mental Retardation, 15,* 224–229.

Stone, C. B. (1956). Measuring difficulty of primary reading material: A constructive criticism of Spache's measure. *Elementary School Journal, 6,* 36–41.

Sulzby, E. (1989). Assessment of emergent and children's language while writing. In L. Morrow & J. Smith (Eds.), *The role of assessment in early literacy instruction,* (pp. 83–109). Englewood Cliffs, NJ: Prentice-Hall.

Test, D. W., Howell, A., Burkhart, K., & Beroth, T. (1993). The one-more-than technique as a strategy for counting money for individuals with moderate mental retardation. *Education and Training in Mental Retardation, 28,* 232–241.

Thompson, S. J., Quenemoen, R. F., Thurlow, M. L., & Ysseldyke, J. E. (2001). *Alternate assessments for students with disabilities.* Thousand Oaks, CA: Corwin Press.

Thompson, S. J., & Thurlow, M. L. (2000). *State alternate assessments: Status as IDEA alternate assessment requirements take effect* (Synthesis Report No. 35). Minneapolis: University of Minnesota, National Center on Educational Outcomes. Retrieved January 24, 2003, from http://education.umn.edu/NCEO/OnlinePubs/Synthesis35.html

Thompson, S. J., & Thurlow, M. L. (2001). *2001 state special education outcomes: A report on state activities at the beginning of a new decade.* Minneapolis: University of Minnesota, National Center on Educational Outcomes.

Thompson, S. J., Thurlow, M., Esler, A., & Whetstone, P. J. (2001). Addressing standards and assessments on the IEP. *Assessment for Effective Intervention, 26*(2), 77–84.

Thurlow, M. L., & Turnure, J. E. (1977). Children's knowledge of time and money: Effective instruction for the mentally retarded. *Education and Training of the Mentally Retarded, 12,* 203–212.

Trace, M. W., Cuvo, A. J., & Criswell, J. L. (1977). Teaching coin equivalence to the mentally retarded. *Journal of Applied Behavior Analysis, 10*, 85-92.

U.S. Department of Education. (2003, December 9). *Federal Register*, Section 100.13 (c) (1).

Wacker, D. P., Berg, W. K., McMahon, C., Templeman, M., McKinnery, J., Swarts, V., et al. (1988). Evaluation of labeling-then-doing with moderately handicapped persons: Acquisition and generalization with complex tasks. *Journal of Applied Behavior Analysis, 21*, 369-380.

Wehmeyer, M. L. (1996). Self-determination as an educational outcome: Why is it important to children, youth, and adults with disabilities? In D. J. Sands & M. L. Wehmeyer (Eds.), *Self-determination across the life span: Independence and choice for people with disabilities* (pp. 17-36). Baltimore: Paul H. Brookes.

Wehmeyer, M. L., Agran, M., & Hughes, C. (2000). A national survey of teachers' promotion of self-determination and student-directed learning. *Journal of Special Education, 34*(2), 58-68.

Wehmeyer, M. L., Palmer, S. B., Agran, M., Mithaug, D. E., & Martin, J. E. (2000). Promoting causal agency: The self-determined learning model of instruction. *Exceptional Children, 66*, 430-453.

Wehmeyer, M. L., Sands, D. J., Knowlton, H. E., & Kozleski, E. B. (2002). Technology and students with mental retardation. In M. L. Wehmeyer, D. J. Sands, H. E. Knowlton, & E. B. Kozleski (Eds.), *Teaching students with mental retardation: Providing access to the general curriculum* (pp. 252-265). Baltimore: Paul H. Brookes.

Wehmeyer, M. L., Yeager, D., Bolding, N., Agran, M., & Hughes, C. (2003). The effects of self-regulation strategies on goal attainment for students with developmental disabilities in general education classrooms. *Journal of Developmental and Physical Disabilities, 15*, 79-91.

Westling, D. L., Floyd, J., & Carr, D. (1990). Effects of single setting versus multiple setting training on learning to shop in a department store. *American Journal on Mental Retardation, 94*, 616-624.

Whalen, C., Schuster, J. W., & Hemmeter, M. L. (1996). The use of unrelated instructive feedback when teaching in a small group instructional arrangement. *Education and Training in Mental Retardation and Developmental Disabilities, 31*, 188-202.

White, O. (1980). Adaptive performance objectives: Form versus function. In W. Sailor, B. Wilcox, & L. Brown (Eds.), *Methods of instruction for severely handicapped students* (pp. 47-69). Baltimore: Paul H. Brookes.

Wolery, M., Ault, M. J., Gast, D. L., Doyle, P. M., & Mills, B. M. (1990). Use of choral and individual attentional responses with constant time delay when teaching sight word reading. *Remedial and Special Education, 11*, 47-58.

14

Home and Community

Linda M. Bambara
Diane M. Browder
Freya Koger

Approaches to supporting individuals with severe disabilities within their homes and communities are undergoing important transformations as self-determination and full inclusion are more fully understood. Consider the focus of the past three decades. In the 1970s, many professionals believed that individuals with severe disabilities needed to earn the right to live in the community by learning skills that qualified them for deinstitutionalization. Rulings such as *Haldermann v. Pennhust State School and Hospital* (1979) established the legal right of community living. Individuals no longer needed a certain level of daily living skills for community access. In the 1980s, a large body of research emerged on teaching skills to individuals with severe disabilities for managing their homes and gaining access to their communities. Teachers focused on teaching skills in home and community settings, and students often spent large portions of their day away from the school building. In the 1990s, students with severe disabilities gained increased access to membership in general education. With the advent of inclusion and

the Individuals with Disabilities Education Act of 1997 (IDEA '97), special education teachers often struggled with the trade-off between offering life skills instruction in "real" nonschool environments and encouraging students with severe disabilities to have a typical school day in general education classes accessing the general education curriculum. Fortunately, at the beginning of the 21st century, curriculum access is broadly defined to include academic content in general education and "access to the content inherent within participation in *all the experiences that comprise general education life*" (Ryndak & Billingsley, 2004, p. 50, emphasis added). This definition applies to general education experiences in and outside of school contexts important for school and community life. With this new interpretation, life skill instruction fits within curriculum for learners with severe disabilities if blended with general education experiences.

This chapter adheres to several values in describing how teachers can encourage students to gain skills for

526

their homes and community. First, decisions on what and where to teach must be made in partnership with students and their families. Second, instruction needs to be planned to encourage the student's self-determination by teaching choice making, honoring preferences, and encouraging self-directed learning. Third, instructional strategies need to be blended with typical general education experiences while encouraging interaction with peers. Fourth, home and community skills gain

importance as students become older. While children rely mostly on their caregivers for daily living and community access, an important part of adolescents' transition to adulthood is their increased autonomy in their home (e.g., fixing their own breakfast) and community (e.g., meeting friends at a restaurant). We illustrate these four values with the lives of three students: Julia (age 14), Rico (age 9), and Aaron (age 20). We will begin with Julia.

                                Julia Romano

Julia, a petite 14-year-old with moderate cognitive disabilities, is an active, happy eighth grader in her middle school. Since Julia's earliest school days, her parents have insisted that she be included in general education classrooms and have full opportunity to participate in the school activities of her choice. Although Julia's eighth-grade schedule was difficult to design, she now attends an array of academic and nonacademic classes with her schoolmates. Julia is also a member of the middle school chorus and an after-school art club. As an active teen with tremendous school spirit, Julia loves to attend school games and dances with her friends.

Early in the school year, Julia's parents received an invitation to attend a transition planning meeting with the school's transition coordinator. This invitation took Julia's parents by surprise. Like many parents of young teens, they were more focused on Julia's current needs as a teenager than on her adult life. Julia had not thought much about her life as an adult either and her goals were uncertain. As they began to talk, both Julia and her parents expressed their dream for Julia to live in her own

home someday, work in a job she enjoys, and be active in her community as she has been at school. They recognized the importance of beginning to plan now.

Although the Romanos believed it would be beneficial for Julia to begin learning the daily living and community skills needed for postschool life, they had one unsetting concern. They worried that training for adult living would take Julia away from what she loved most—her school classes, activities, and classmates. Julia's parents had worked hard for Julia to be fully included. They were not willing to sacrifice Julia's current needs as a middle school student in planning for her future needs, at least not at age 14. They feared that during the transition planning meeting, they would have to make a choice.

Questions for Planning and Instruction

1. How can Julia's instructional needs in home and community skills be addressed without detracting from typical school experiences?

2. What skills should be addressed that could best address her current and future needs?

Planning Instruction to Enhance Skills for Home and the Community

Supporting individuals to have enhanced quality of life in their homes and communities involves much more than instruction. For some, the primary support need may be getting help to complete parts of a routine rather than learning to perform specific tasks within a routine. For example, assistance with budgeting may make it possible to buy prepared meals or to get help for housecleaning. Some daily routines can be managed by relying on a roommate or family member or

significant other who is especially adept in home management: one roommate may do all the cooking, and another does the laundry. In contrast, some people pursue home and community skills as a special interest or hobby. When activities such as home management and shopping are highly preferred, the individual may engage in extensive training in these areas. For example, a high school student may take 3 years of home economics classes or do an internship to learn more about banking. Planning instruction to enhance home and community skills reflect a person-centered perspective with self-determination as both a context and a goal of instruction.

Self-Determination: A New Era for Instruction

During the 1990s, we entered a new pedagogical era of self-determination, one that emphasizes the value of individuals with disabilities directing their own lives. Martin and Marshall (1995) describe self-determined individuals as people who "know what they want and how to get it" (p. 147). This simple definition provides the overall context or value base for determining what to teach and how to teach in a way that encourages student empowerment and self-directed learning.

With regard to determining what to teach, skills for home and community living should be directly related to the student's and family's preferences and visions for the future. More than being "functional" in the eyes of professionals, instructional goals are personalized according to the individual's unique interests and needs. Almost any daily living or community skill could potentially enhance learner control; however, those that facilitate self-determination are those that are useful from the learner's perspective (Bambara, Cole, & Koger, 1998). Such skills could be ones needed to participate in preferred activities (e.g., school chorus, Little League baseball) and necessary activities (e.g., taking medications, food shopping) to achieve long-range goals (e.g., using a bus to go to work).

Home and community skills for Julia will take into account her current interests as an active teen as well her and her parents' vision to live independently in her own home some day. Skills for Rico Hernandez, introduced later in this chapter, will differ not only because of differences in the two students' preferences and goals for the future but because of differences in their cultural heritage as well. Self-determination for most Anglo-Americans emphasizes independence and autonomy. In other cultures, including Hispanic ones, interdependence and shared autonomy with other family members is valued (Dennis & Giangreco, 1996). While skills for independent living will be stressed in Julia's program, skills for shared homemaking while living with his extended family will be the targets for Rico.

Broadly classified, skills for self-determination related to this chapter include (a) task-, activity-, or routine-specific skills, such as matching clothing, preparing dinner, or getting ready for work in the morning, and (b) generic empowerment skills that are applicable across tasks, activities, and routines. Generic empowerment skills, like choice making, decision making, and problem solving, enable learners to initiate, take action, and direct the course of their lives.

Self-determination influences how we teach by emphasizing student-directed learning and control. The learner is viewed as a partner in the instructional process so that instructors give them some control by offering multiple and diverse opportunities for choice making (Bambara & Koger, 1996; Brown, Belz, Corsi, & Wenig, 1993). For example, the instructor might offer the student a choice of when or where to participate in a lesson, a choice of materials, a choice of activity sequence or instructional formats, and the opportunity to change, take a break from, or terminate an activity if the student is experiencing difficulty. The instructor also follows the student's lead and interests, and this means honoring the student's spontaneous choices for instruction and modifying instruction according to the student's preferred learning style.

Self-determination can be enhanced during instruction via the principle of partial participation (Ferguson & Baumgart, 1991). Under this principle, students are never denied access to preferred or meaningful activities because they lack the skills for complete independent participation. Rather, teachers ask the following:

- What noninstructional supports are needed to make participation meaningful for the student?
- How much does the student wish to actively participate?
- How can instruction be used to enhance the student's independence, albeit partial independence?

Once these questions are answered, the instructor carefully blends instructional support with other forms of personal assistance and adaptive aids or permanent prompts to provide immediate access to daily routines and preferred activities.

Julia makes use of a personal assistant. After swimming lessons at her school, Julia turns the hair dryer on and off and blows the dampness from her hair, while her buddy Susan directs the tip of the dryer for final styling.

The main point is that whether acting independently or with the assistance of others or adaptive aids, students are able to set the direction and course in their lives.

Guidelines to Plan Instruction

At the beginning of this chapter, several values were stated to guide planning instruction for home and the community. These values are now translated into specific guidelines for instructional planning.

   Value One

Plan in Partnership with Students and Their Families

Guideline One: Use Person-Centered Planning Strategies

If instruction is viewed as a form of support, then the question is, What form of instruction is needed or wanted? To enhance self-determination, the focus and methods of instruction must fit within the context of the student's and family's preferences, priorities, and future goals. Person-centered planning is a collaborative process involving the student, family members, teachers, specialists, and, as needed, support personnel from nonschool services. Through problem solving and discussions among team members, person-centered planning aims to (a) describe a desirable future for the student, (b) delineate the activities and supports necessary to achieve the desired vision, and (c) mobilize existing resources to make the vision become a reality (Vandercook, York, & Forest, 1989). From an instructional perspective, person-centered planning can help coordinate teaching with other forms of support and unify the goals of instruction with a person's own goals. There are two approached to person-centered planning.

Structured Action Planning

A variety of structured person-centered planning processes have emerged over the past 20 years (Holburn & Vietze, 2002) that guide educational teams through information gathering and planning to address the student's wants and needs. Some of these include Personal Futures Planning (Mount, 2000); Life Style Planning (O'Brien, 1987); Making Action Plans, or MAPS (Forest & Pearpoint, 1992; O'Brien & Pearpoint, 2003); and Planning Alternative Tomorrows with Hope, or PATH (O'Brien & Pearpoint, 2003; Pearpoint, O'Brien, & Forest, 1992). Each differs somewhat in format and focus. For example, Life Style Planning focuses

on community participation for adults, while MAPS emphasizes the school inclusion for students. All the structured processes guide teams to consider at least five essential questions.

First, what is the student's history and current life situation? Here team members contribute information that will paint a life history for the student. Both positive and negative events in the student's past and current life are noted.

Second, what are the strengths and gifts of the student? The purpose of this question is to focus the team on building a vision based on the student's strengths and preferences rather than the student's deficits.

Third, what is the vision or dream for the student? Team members discuss what an ideal life might be for the student for the next several years of childhood or as an adult. Team members think about what they want for the student and what the student would want for himself or herself.

Fourth, what are the team's fears, obstacles, or challenges to building a better life for the student? This question guides teams to consider fears about change and obstacles that may thwart the student's dreams with the aim of eliminating them.

Fifth, what are the priorities and goals for the future, and what will it take to make the vision happen? Once a vision for the future has been established, team members focus on how to get there. They set priorities for achieving both short- and long-range goals, consider how to eliminate obstacles, and identify how to use supports to achieve desirable outcomes.

Because of their comprehensiveness, structured action planning approaches are useful when it is important to set new directions for the student, such as planning for transition to postschool life or greater inclusion in school.

Mr. and Mrs. Romano were concerned about the transition planning process for their daughter, Julia. They feared that planning would result in a heavy vocational emphasis and take her away from the current school activities that she loved. Julia's parents were later relieved to discover that the transition coordinator selected MAPS to help them clarify what was important to Julia and to begin to think about her future as an adult. The MAPS process let them set priorities for the next 3 years (Table 14-1). They decided that Julia will continue in general education classes, but her curriculum will be modified to reflect a stronger focus in home and community instruction.

TABLE 14–1
MAPS Outcomes for Julia

What is Julia's history?

Julia is a 14-year-old teen with Down syndrome.
Julia's parents have always felt strongly about inclusion.
Julia attended segregated preschool and school programs until age 8.
At her parents' insistence, Julia was fully included in a second-grade class.
Continued full inclusion through the eighth grade (current grade).
Julia has had a happy childhood, doing activities typical for her age.
Grade 6 was bad for Julia—first year at middle school. "New" kids from other elementary schools ridiculed her, called her "retard."
Problem solved after a schoolwide intervention emphasizing friendships for all.

Who is Julia?

Julia is a friendly, social girl who enjoys typical "teen" stuff.
She is very persistent.
She likes to be independent.
She likes to complete what she has started.
She is very methodical in her approach to things.
She laughs and giggles easily.
She's a "girl's girl": likes to primp, were new clothes, have her nails done, wear makeup.
She likes to stay busy and go places.
She loves to sing and draw.
She is somewhat gullible—easily led by peers she considers to be her friend.

What is your dream for Julia? What are your dreams for her as an adult?

In General:

For Julia to continue to be a part of her school.
For Julia to be happy, healthy, and safe.
To be able to pursue activities that she enjoys.
To have friends and people who care about her.

As an adult:

To live in an apartment with friends, family, or people who care about her.
To live close to family.
To have her independence but also the supports she needs to do what she wants.
To be involved in her community doing things she wants to do.
To have a competitive job that she likes.
To live in a community that will offer many opportunities and that will accept her for her gifts and talents.

What is your nightmare?

That Julia will be denied typical middle school and high school experiences.
That the focus on her "adult" needs will take her away from typical school activities.
That she will be lonely.
That she will be unhappy.
That once she graduates she will not be given the support she needs to achieve her goals.
That she will be put on a waiting list for adult services.
Once living on her own, she will be completely dependent on the "good" graces of others: lack independence.
Once she graduates, the good life that she has built so far will stop: no more friends, no more activities, waiting for a job.

What are Julia's strengths, gifts, and abilities?

Julia is very persistent and will work hard at the things she enjoys or wants.
Julia has wonderful social skills, people are drawn to her.
She's easygoing.
Julia loves to sing, draw, and swim.
Julia loves to be around people.

What are Julia's needs?

Julia enjoys and therefore needs to attend school with her same-age peers, doing typical school activities.
Julia needs to continue with the school activities that she enjoys: swimming, chorus, art.
Julia and her family need to begin exploring options for Julia's adult life.

TABLE 14–1 (*Continued*)

Julia needs to develop daily living and community living skills that will enhance her independence now and in the future. Some areas include:

- Basic cooking skills
- Community travel and safety skills
- Consumer skills (e.g., purchasing clothing, food shopping, ordering at restaurants)
- Use of communication tools (e.g., using the telephone, using newspapers and Internet to access information)

Julia needs to develop personal care skills appropriate for her age (to help Julia to feel good about herself). Some areas include:

- Skin care for a teen
- Teen grooming (e.g., styling hair, applying makeup and nail polish)
- Clothing selection and care
- Sex education

What would Julia's ideal day look like and what must be done to make it happen?

For at least the next 3 years:

Julia will maintain her current level of participation in regular education classes and after-school activities.
Daily living and community living skills will be integrated within her regularly scheduled classes. For community-based instruction, Julia will meet with a community training specialist one period a day, four times per week.
Julia's weekly schedule will reflect her interests as well as her academic, social, and daily and community living needs (e.g., school chorus, swimming/gym, home economics, social studies, science, art, computers, community-based instruction).

To prepare for the future:

Julia and family will explore adult services options.

Instructional targets will include skills that will be useful now and in the future and that can be taught within general education classes. Julia and her mother decided to meet periodically throughout the school year to target critical skills that Julia can learn at home (e.g., scheduling and self-initiating home chores). Julia will work with the community training specialist for one period, 4 days per week. Through the use of simulations in the school building and in actual community sites (e.g., the mall or music store), the community training specialist will teach Julia an array of skills appropriate for an active teen (e.g., how to use a cell phone, make purchases at fast-food restaurants, rent DVDs, shop for clothing) and, very

importantly, how to keep safe in the community. Julia's family explore options for home-living, community, and employment supports. The transition coordinator will help Julia and her family connect with adult services for this initial planning.

Collaborative Meetings

Not all person-centered planning requires a comprehensive, structured approach. Sometimes, teams need to come together to solve problems around specific issues, focusing on the goals and preferences of the student and family. This can be accomplished through informal, collaborative meetings, as in Rico's case.

 Rico Hernandez

Rico Hernandez, 9 years old, attends a third-grade class in his neighborhood school with the assistance of a full-time one-to-one paraprofessional. He has autism and is performing close to grade level academically in most subject areas, but he requires intensive wraparound support through mental health services because of severe behavioral challenges and life skill needs.

Mrs. Hernandez, Rico's mother, thought she would never see the day when her son would be in a general education classroom. She and her husband are extremely proud of their son's accomplishments, yet at the same time, they were becoming increasingly concerned about Rico's display of challenging behaviors at home and his lack of participation in household and family activities. They asked for a team meeting, consisting of Rico's teachers, support staff, and behavior specialists from the mental health services, to address their concerns.

After conducting a functional assessment and through many team discussions, it appeared that Rico's challenging behaviors, consisting of screaming, tantruming, and self-injury (face slapping), were most often associated with transitions or changes in routines or activities. The team speculated that from Rico's perspective almost any activity not anticipated by him (e.g., being asked to put his toys away while watching TV, going to a different grocery store, having an unexpected visitor in the home) constituted a change of activity. As Rico's tantrums increased in frequency and intensity as a result of his physical growth, Mrs. Hernandez placed less demands on him to participate in household activities. With the family's hectic schedule, it was often easier to complete Rico's chores for him.

Mrs. Hernandez also feared bringing Rico with her in the community. She worried not only about the potential for challenging behavior but also for Rico's safety. Rico would become preoccupied with other thoughts and frequently wander away from his mother. Mrs. Hernandez reported that one day, while grocery shopping, she turned her back for a minute, only to find Rico walking aimlessly in a busy parking lot. With the growing concerns about Rico's safety and behavior, he spent most of his free time at home doing little but watching television.

The team noted that Rico had had important success at school. With the assistance of the paraprofessional, he was completing adapted class assignments and participating in activities. In contrast, Rico rarely interacted with his peers. Mrs. Hernandez expressed her concern to the team that her son was socially isolated at school and had no friends. Rico often sat alone at recess while his classmates played kickball and volleyball. Mrs. Hernandez said she was worried that Rico was becoming increasingly dependent on the paraprofessional and could not function without her. She also wondered if the other children hesitated to play with Rico because he always had an adult nearby.

Questions for Planning and Instruction

1. How can Rico's participation in family routines and activities be enhanced while decreasing instances of challenging behaviors?
2. How can Rico be encouraged to have more involvement with his peers during leisure at school and home?
3. How can Rico's community access be encouraged? What supports will be needed for his behavior and safety?
4. In what ways can Rico's teachers and home support work together to meet Rico's needs at home?

In Rico's case, Mrs. Hernandez, Rico's teachers, the behavior specialist from mental health services, and the therapeutic support staff (TSS) met to address Rico's team's four questions. The team members discussed how to coordinate their support for Rico and his family. The teacher agreed to design instructional strategies to meet priority objectives, teach as many as were relevant in school, and teach the TSS how to teach these skills at home. Instructional targets selected were to teach Rico (a) to follow a picture schedule to enhance predictability of activities at home and increase independence at school, (b) to complete daily routines at home, (c) to learn community travel skills (e.g., following his parents or classmates when traveling independently around the school), and (d) to master the basics of organized ball games, such as kickball and soccer. Instructional targets were integrated with other forms of support, including behavioral support, respite care, enrolling Rico in Junior League sports, and getting him involved in school recess activities.

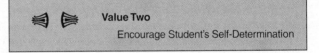
Value Two
Encourage Student's Self-Determination

Guideline Two: Enhance Choice-Making, Self-Cuing, and Self-Management Skills

Self-determination is an ongoing, developmental process. The more opportunities for self-determination, the greater its growth. More than just an outcome of instruction, self-determination should be viewed as a source of empowerment during instruction—students are more motivated when involved in their own learning through, for example, choice making, goal setting, and self-evaluation. Here we discuss three such approaches: (a) choice, (b) self-cuing, and (c) self-management.

Choice

When teachers select instructional goals that reflect preferences, they are honoring student choice. This is the first level of choice in instruction. The second level involves embedding multiple opportunities into for choice instruction so that students can self-direct their own learning.

Choice, or the act of selecting among presented alternatives, is an expression of preference. All people have preferences. The role of the instructor is to ensure that student preferences for learning are recognized and honored. This communicates respect for each student's individuality and enhances motivation for learning. Not surprisingly, many studies have shown that when preferences are incorporated during instruction, student participation is enhanced (e.g., Cole & Levinson, 2002; Cooper & Browder, 1998; Dunlap et al., 1994; Seybert, Dunlap, & Ferro, 1996). Furthermore, choice can lead to the reduction of problem behaviors, especially when student protests or disruptions during instruction are related to low opportunities for student control (e.g., Bambara, Koger, Katzer, & Davenport, 1995; Cole & Levinson, 2002; Dunlap et al., 1994; Peterson, Caniglia, & Royster, 2001; Seybert et al., 1996).

The choice diversity model (Brown et al., 1993) provides one strategy for embedding choice into the instruction of daily home and community routines. In this approach, teachers first analyze steps or component parts of a routine and then identify options that can be made available during each step. Teachers might first consider offering between-activities options to start an activity.

In a kitchen cleanup routine at home, Rico is offered the choice of clearing the table or stacking the dishes in the dishwasher. Then, once an activity is selected, Rico's mother give additional options within the activity: offers him a choice of materials (e.g., sponges, dish soap), choice of sequence (e.g., cups or plates first), choice of when to complete the activity (e.g., now or later), and choice of partners (e.g., with or without help from Mom).

Two additional options, the choice to not participate and to terminate an activity, are opportunities that must always be made available to students during instruction. If refusals are high, it may suggest that the activity is not meaningful or preferred by the student.

Instructors also should consider how to best present options to match the learner's comprehension and indication skills (Bambara & Koger, 1996). With regard to comprehension, some learners benefit when options are presented with actual objects, and some respond better to pictures than to words. In addition, consideration should be given to the type of choice-related questions or prompts. Closed questions that delineate alternatives (e.g., "Do you want to iron in the living room or in the kitchen?") are useful when the student is unfamiliar with potential choice. Teachers may prompt choice by using open-ended questions (e.g., "What do you want to do now?") after the student has become familiar with the available options. Students may express their choice by labeling, pointing, grimacing, or moving closer toward a preferred object. Table 14–2 illustrates how teachers might present between- and within-activity choices to learners with different comprehension and indication skills. To enhance self-initiation, instructors are encouraged to honor students' spontaneous choices whenever practical (e.g., "Thanks for telling me you want to wear your *blue sweater*!") and should expect that, as students learn the power of their choice making, spontaneous choices will increase.

Not all students know how to make choices. In such cases, choice making can be taught during home and community routines by (a) prompting the student to make a choice response (e.g., guiding the student to touch a preferred item) and (b) providing the selected item on each choice selection (Bambara & Koger, 1996). Through repeated opportunities across daily routines, the student will learn how to make true selections. In the meantime, instructors should attend to learners' subtle, nonverbal cues of preference (e.g., active participation, smiles) and rejection (e.g., facial grimace, pushing objects away) to ensure that the learners' preferences are being honored.

Self-Cuing

Teaching students to learn for themselves or from natural opportunities in their environment can also facilitate self-determination. Learners with severe disabilities can become overly dependent on instructor cues and fail to self-initiate home and community skills or self-correct when problems arise. Self-learning may be enhanced by teaching students to self-cue or to respond to natural cues or permanent prompts.

TABLE 14–2

Examples of Choice Options According to Skill Level

Task skill level	Cooking choices offered before cooking activity (between activities)	Choices offered within dessert activity
Beginner	Present bowls of ready-made Jell-O and pudding with the box for each displayed next to it. Teacher prompt: "Point to the one you want to make."	Options: • Two flavors of Jell-O (e.g., orange and cherry) • Two shapes to make Jell-O jigglers (e.g., star and circle)
Intermediate	Present student with three or four boxes of Jell-O and pudding that depict different flavors. Teacher prompt: "Would you like to make chocolate pudding, vanilla pudding, or cherry Jell-O?"	Options: • Three or four flavors of Jell-O • Mold or cookie cutters • Two or three different fruits to add
Advanced	Present student with picture recipe book that has several options for pudding or Jell-O. Teacher prompt: "Look through the recipe book. Which would you like to make?"	Options: • Two or three different Jell-O desserts • Array of molds, parfait glasses, cookie cutters • Array of items to add

Ford and Mirenda (1984) describe ways to build natural cues into instruction by pointing out salient features of natural cues (e.g., wrinkles in a bed) and using nonspecific prompts (e.g., "What's next?"). Sometimes natural cues are not salient enough and need to be enhanced through adaptations, such as by (a) color coding or labeling possessions with name tags; (b) using placement as a cue, such as hanging matching outfits together; (c) color coding temperature levels on stove or oven dials; (d) amplifying natural auditory cues, such as traffic sounds for pedestrian training; and (e) using unrelated, naturally occurring events to signal the onset of an activity (e.g., begin dinner when the television news starts or ends).

Even with adapted cues, students may make errors. In many cases, errors do not pose dangers, and teachers should encourage students to self-correct using the cues provided by the error. This means that teachers modify their teaching approach so that increased response prompts are withheld for a longer latency after a student error has been made or replaced by gestures or questions that emphasize error cues.

If Julia forgets to get all the items from the refrigerator to make a meal, the teacher may hesitate when Julia reaches the step requiring that item (mixing in the eggs) and let her discover the eggs are missing. If Julia somehow skips the step, the teacher might ask, "What did you forget?"

Such approaches probably work best once students have learned some of the task rather than in the early acquisition stage.

Some students may have difficulty knowing when to initiate activities or what comes next in a routine or activity even after they have been taught to respond to natural or adapted cues. In such cases, students may be taught to use permanent prompts to guide their learning. Permanent prompts are "extra" stimuli or cues, such as pictures, written words, or tape recordings, that students learn to use to enhance their independence. Permanent prompts act like memory aids, similar to recipe books, appointment books, and things-to-do lists.

Pictures can provide an excellent form of graphic assistance for students with severe disabilities because of their versatility with nonreaders. Typically, pictures representing an activity or a step in a routine or task are placed in a photo booklet or on a wall chart for easy accessibility. Students are then taught to "look and do," which means referring to the pictures as they complete each activity or step in a sequence. Again, as much as possible, these activities should incorporate student preference.

Pictures of Rico's after-school home routine (e.g., put backpack away, make a snack, take out the trash, watch TV, set the table for dinner) are placed on a wall chart in the kitchen. Rico is guided to look at the chart, initiate the first activity, and return to the chart for the next activity once the previous one was completed.

Students with disabilities have been taught to follow pictures as a guide to preparing meals (e.g., Martin, Rusch, James, Decker, & Trytol, 1982), to setting up and performing complex job tasks (e.g., Copeland & Hughes, 2000; Johnson & Miltenbeger, 1996; Mechling & Gast, 1997), to using a microcomputer (Frank, Wacker, Berg, & McMahon, 1985), and for managing daily or weekly schedules for leisure activities, work, housekeeping, or grooming (e.g., Anderson, Sherman, Sheldon, McAdam, 1997; Bambara & Ager, 1992; Bryan & Gast, 2000; Irvine, Erickson, Singer, & Stahlberg, 1992). Pictures also may be used to assist learners to shop for groceries (e.g., Matson, 1980) and order foods at restaurants.

In addition to promoting independence, picture prompts can help students generalize learned tasks or routines to new settings. Once a student learns how to "read" pictures in one situation, the pictures may then be used in different settings to guide student performance on the same or similar tasks (Irvine et al., 1992; Johnson & Miltenberger, 1996). In other words, the same picture cues used at school may be used at home to encourage student initiations in similar home activities with little or no additional instruction.

When pictures are not suitable to particular settings or learner needs, other forms of self-cuing can be tried. For example, Alberto, Sharpton, Briggs, and Stright (1986) taught four adolescents with moderate and severe disabilities to use self-operated audio prompts played through a Walkman-type cassette player to guide them through operating a washing machine, preparing a meal, and performing a vocational assembly task. Like pictures, audio prompts have enhanced learners' generalization to different settings (Post & Storey, 2002). Word checklists also can effectively cue students to complete home and work routines once sight words for specific tasks are taught (Browder & Minarovic, 2000). With personal handheld computers becoming increasingly prevalent in our society, individualized personal systems involving digital pictures of actual work tasks along with audio prompts offer tremendous promise for enhancing learner independence in the immediate future (Davies, Stock, & Wehmeyer, 2002, 2003).

Self-Management

Another way to promote self-direction in daily routines is to incorporate self-management in instruction. Self-management means a "personal and systematic application of behavior change strategies that result in the desired modification of one's own behavior" (Heward, 1997, p. 517).

A picture schedule was created for Rico that depicted each activity for his day and was placed in a binder on his desk. Each day Rico selected the order of classroom activities whenever it was possible (goal setting). He monitored the completion of activities by turning the page over (self-monitoring). At the end of the day, he reviewed how well he did on each completed activity (self-evaluation).

Technically speaking, choice making and use of permanent prompts are aspects of self-management; however, to truly self-manage behavior, a combination of multiple components is needed, such as goal setting (setting personal performance goals), self-monitoring (recording progress toward goals), self-evaluation (evaluating the acceptability of performance outcomes), and self-reinforcement (rewarding oneself for a job well done).

Two methods of self-management—self-instruction and self-scheduling—have direct applicability for home and community use. In self-instruction, students are taught to self-talk through the steps of a home, community, or leisure activity and self-evaluate their performance as they go along. Browder and Minarovic (2000) taught self-initiation of job tasks (i.e., cafeteria, grocery store, and garment factory) to four adults with mental retardation in their work settings. The employees were taught to verbalize a "did-next-now" strategy to complete and initiate the next job activity on their task work list (e.g., I did fill the bags, next I'm going to sweep the floor, now I'm sweeping the floor). Hughes (1992) taught four students with severe disabilities to use self-instruction to solve task-related problems at home by identifying the problem (e.g., "lamp not plugged in"), stating the correct response (e.g., "got to plug in"), evaluating the response (e.g., "fixed it"), and self-reinforcing (e.g., "good"). More recently, Bambara and Gomez (2001) used self-instruction to teach complex problem solving to adults with severe disabilities in their home. In this study, the adults were guided to consider more than one solution to a problem (e.g., "My toothbrush is missing. Look on the counter. Look in the cabinet. Ask for help.").

Self-scheduling can give people with severe disabilities a way to self-direct and control the multiple tasks needed for daily living. Learners are guided to select activities that are both enjoyable and necessary, plan when to do them that day or several days in advance, and use their schedule to initiate the planned activities (Anderson et al., 1997; Bambara & Ager, 1992; Bambara & Koger, 1996). Self-scheduling systems can be (a) teacher made by using materials such as pictures from magazines, photographs, or drawings or (b) supported through assistive technologies. For example, there are several computerized handheld scheduling systems developed specifically for people with disabilities (**http://www.abilityhub.com**, **http://www.ablelinktech.com**, **http://www.maxiaids.com**).

Self-determination skills are important for Aaron to learn as he prepares to move into his new apartment.

He is a young man in his last year of public school services and is working hard with his parents and the transition team to plan his next steps as an adult.

When Aaron and his team met, they discussed ways to enhance Aaron's skills to "be on his own." They compared living in an apartment to his current life at home. The team quickly realized that Aaron would have a lot more choices to make when he was on his own! For example, he would be deciding what to have for dinner, when to go to bed, what to wear, and whom to invite for a visit. He might decide to go out for the evening and would need skills to request support from his personal attendant. Aaron and his parents made a list of decisions that he could begin making right away in his family home, and his teacher helped him list decisions he could make at school. The team targeted self-scheduling as a way for Aaron to take more control of his day.

 Aaron Williams

Aaron is a young man with severe cognitive delays and physical disabilities. Because of a stroke at age 8, he is paralyzed from the waist down and has limited use of his right arm and hand. He moves about freely in his automated wheelchair and communicates with gestures, pictures, and a laptop computer.

At age 21, Aaron is in his last year of public school services. This last year is devoted to helping Aaron transition to his own apartment and find a job. Aaron has completed several years of person-centered planning with his transition team, and his goals are clear. He wants to live in his own apartment with a roommate who shares his interest in music and sports. He also wants a job that pays well, but gives him flexible or part-time hours because he tires easily. Because of his love of school and desire to improve his career options, Aaron has been taking classes at the community college since he was 18 with support from the public school transition coordinator. Aaron wants to continue taking courses and maybe explore a new college environment. Because of his physical challenges, Aaron will need 24-hour support from a personal care attendant to address his basic daily living, health, and safety needs. He also needs specialized transportation. Another challenge Aaron faces is that he has not had many experiences of being "on his own." Partially resulting from his physical challenges, Aaron has spent most of his

time at school or home. His family has worked hard to make their home accessible for Aaron but have found it difficult to find the resources (e.g., finances, physical assistance, transportation) to help Aaron spend time in the community. Aaron has had training in community activities through his school program.

Aaron's transition into a job and a home of his own will require the coordinated efforts of his planning team, which includes his parents, the transition coordinator, the county case manager from developmental disabilities services, and representatives from supported employment and supported living providers. The team has begun to brainstorm ways to help Aaron meet his goals. For example, the case manager will help the family explore affordable housing options, locate groups on campus related to music and sports that he can join, and adult residential services will assist Aaron in finding a roommate and creating a home based on his preferences.

Questions for Planning and Instruction

1. What skills does Aaron need and want that will enhance his competence and help him maintain control over the direction of his life?
2. How can instructional support be coordinated with the other forms of support that Aaron needs and wants?

Value Three

Choose Instruction That Blends with
General Education Contexts and
Encourages Peer Interaction

Guideline Three: Choose Appropriate Instructional Settings, Plan for Generalization, and Use Efficient Strategies

In order to maintain school inclusion and peer interaction, planning teams may need to give new thought to how skills for home and community settings can be taught. Questions that can be asked to guide this planning are the following:

- What setting will be used for instruction? Can the skills be embedded in typical school activities and routines? If not, will a simulated activity be feasible and effective, or is it best to schedule instruction in the settings where the skills are typically used?
- How can generalization be encouraged? How many different settings will be needed for this generalization to occur?
- How can instruction be made more effective and efficient? Can peers be involved?

Choosing the Instructional Setting

The challenge in teaching students skills for the home and community is that these settings differ greatly from typical school settings. Students may not generalize skills taught in school to community contexts (Snell & Browder, 1986). Students also need general educational experiences even though the skills taught there may not address those needed in the home and school. To meet this challenge, teachers can consider three options for instruction: (a) embedding home and community skills in typical school routines and settings, (b) using school-based simulations of home and community settings, and (c) conducting in vivo instruction. If one of the first two school-based options is selected, some instruction in community settings and interaction with families will help generalize skills to these settings.

The first setting option is *to embed skills in typical school routines*. In this option, the teacher considers how each priority skill can be incorporated in existing school or classroom activities. For example, Gardill and Browder (1995) taught purchasing skills using the school store, cafeteria, and vending machines as well as community settings. Similarly, food preparation might be incorporated with a general education unit in social studies when learning about other cultures or during a home economics class. Some housekeeping skills can be taught during cleanup time in the classroom where all students can share responsibilities with chores (e.g., emptying trash, cleaning a classroom sink after art projects). Most middle and high schools have home economics suites that offer a context for all students to learn many home skills during their school day. This instruction may be incorporated into general education classes in home economics through team planning, or students may receive private tutoring during periods when the room is free.

The second setting option is to *use school-based simulations of community and home activities*. Some skills cannot be blended into typical school activities because the skills are so discrepant from the general education curriculum that instruction requires activities or materials not usually provided in schools. In such cases, teachers can create simulations in school settings where home and community skills can be taught. For example, Sowers and Powers (1995) implemented a community training program that included simulation to teach fast-food purchase. First, they developed a task analysis for making a fast-food purchase and then observed the students' performance at a local fast-food restaurant. Each step of the activity was reviewed to determine if the student required an adaptation to complete the step. For example, some of the adaptations targeted for a participant named Paul were the following:

- Paul will always have his scooter so he can drive up to the clerk at the counter to place his order.
- Paul will use a fanny pack that is positioned in the front so he can carry his money and access it easily.
- Paul will use a drink cup holder secured on his scooter to place his drink when the clerk hands it to him.

To teach the adapted task analyses, the classroom teacher turned the school conference room into a simulated fast-food restaurant where the students could practice their skills in placing an order, paying for their purchase, and consuming it. The teacher had planned for instruction ahead of time by purchasing the desired food items for each student from the fast-food restaurant earlier in the day. The students then practiced placing an order with the teacher using role plays and received the actual food items after placing an order. Two practice trials were conducted by rewrapping the food after the first trial. The student could eat the food after the second practice. Once students had mastered the steps of the task analysis, the instructor invited the students' caregiver (e.g., parent or group home staff) to come to school to participate in the simulation. The caregiver watched the instructor give the student any needed assistance in the role play of purchasing the food and then provided assistance on the second trial. They were also given a list of suggestions for encouraging the student to perform the steps for him- or herself during home outings at the fast-food restaurant. Observations of the students demonstrated that they were able to generalize their skills from the simulated fast-food restaurant in the school conference room to community restaurants with both their teachers and caregivers.

As illustrated by Sowers and Powers (1995), simulations must be carefully planned if students are to generalize skills learned in simulations to home or community settings. To be effective, teachers must consider the following. First, the simulation should carefully replicate the stimuli and responses found in the community or home setting where the student is expected to perform the target skill under natural conditions (Horner, McDonnell, & Bellamy, 1986; Nietupski, Hamre-Nietupski, Clancy, & Veerhusen, 1986). This means using actual items from the criterion setting and/or creating replicas. Actual items that teachers might use in simulations include food and beverage containers, menus from area restaurants, city bus schedules, food cartons or wrappers of favorite snacks, and deposit slips and checks from the local bank. When actual items are impossible to bring to school settings, teacher-made replicas can be used. Browder, Snell, and Wildonger (1988) used photographs of actual vending machines when teaching vending machine use in the classroom. Each photograph was enlarged and glued to a stationary box to form a miniature machine. To make the simulation as real as possible, a "coin" slot was cut on the picture where students could hear a "clinking" sound as they dropped coins into the box. Additionally, the teacher pushed the food or drink out from under the box when the student

pushed one of the buttons on the picture. Similarly, Shafer, Inge, and Hill (1986) simulated an automatic teller (ATM) to teach banking skills. To create the simulation, the instructors located the ATM machine that was within walking distance of the students' homes and created a replica out of a cardboard box by modeling the features (e.g., button and slot positions, screen printouts) of the ATM the student would be using under natural conditions.

A second consideration when planning simulations is to use multiple exemplars and stimulus variation. Specifically, teachers should consider the types of possible variations a student may encounter in natural settings. For example, Neef, Lensbower, Hockersmith, DePalma, and Gray (1990) used multiple exemplars in simulated and in vivo instruction to teach laundry skills. In multiple exemplar training, the student either went to multiple laundromats or trained with multiple sets (several simulated box models) of washers and dryers. Interestingly, Neef et al. (1990) found that students generalized their laundry skills when introduced to multiple exemplars during classroom simulations. Variations in washing machines were achieved by using several different replicas of washing machines (i.e., exemplars) that the students might encounter in their community. Each was slightly different (e.g., position of button, doors) to expose students to as many variations as possible. Other examples of planned variations include using (a) a variety of hand soaps (e.g., bar, liquid, wipes) to teach hand washing, (b) a variety of responses (e.g., out of an item, too little money) during purchasing simulations, and (c) a variety of similar cooking ingredients (i.e., butter in tubs, sticks, and squeeze containers) while learning a new recipe. Instruction that embeds variation across teaching materials will give students opportunities to practice their new skills under as many as different conditions as possible, enhancing their ability to generalize from simulations to home or community settings.

The third consideration in using school-based simulations is to include some opportunities to apply skills in actual community or home settings. Research suggests that well-planned simulations can result in generalization to community contexts (e.g., Mechling, Gast, & Langone, 2002; Neef et al., 1990; Shafer et al., 1986); however, generalization is not guaranteed for all students (e.g., Alcantara, 1994; McDonnell, Horner, & Williams, 1984). To ensure that students use their skills in natural settings, teachers should plan some community-based instruction to supplement simulations. The advantage of using simulations is that community-based instruction may be scheduled much less frequently than would be needed if relying on community-based instruction alone. At the minimum, teachers should assess whether students do generalize from school simulations to community settings and teach in actual settings if they do not. For home skills, collaboration with caregivers can help determine if skills performed at school are being used at home. A parent conference similar to that in Sowers and Powers (1995) in which the caregiver sees and participates in the simulation may be especially beneficial in encouraging this generalization.

The third option for choosing instructional settings is to teach "in vivo." This means teaching directly in home or community settings through community-based instruction. When students are past typical school age but still receiving educational services (i.e., ages 19 to 21), the focus of instruction will probably shift from school to job training and community access. Students over the age of 18 are likely to receive instruction that is heavily if not entirely community based (Grigal, Neubert, & Moon, 2001), and school systems may move the "homeroom" base away from the high school to a community college or a nearby university campus. Inclusion takes place in the community where many of their same-age peers now hold jobs, attend postsecondary schools, and recreate. During the transition years (age 14 and older), students may also have direct community-based instruction for part of their school day, especially when (a) this is a student and parental priority, (b) this instruction can be scheduled as one or more periods of the student's class schedule and does not require the student to be removed in the middle of a general education class, and (c) other students leave school on a regular basis (e.g., to travel with school teams to sports events, to work at a half-day job program, to participate in honors activities, to attend a vocational-technical center). At the elementary level, direct community-based instruction is likely to be far less of a priority, as it is more disruptive to peer interaction and the classroom routine. Sometimes, direct community-based instruction may be a strong student and parent priority (e.g., to teach safe street crossing) and may be less disruptive (e.g., in elementary schools that use a lot of individualized pull-out programs for music, sports, the arts, and other special interests).

Maintaining inclusion in general education contexts is an important priority. Community-based instruction can compete with this goal unless careful consideration is given to student's age, individual priorities, and the school culture.

Plan for Generalization: General Case Instruction

When teaching skills for home and community, it is important to plan for generalization from school to home and community settings. Carefully planned simulations, coupled with some community-based instruction, can achieve this goal. However, generalization *across* home and community settings is also important. Teaching a student to purchase fast food at McDonald's does not necessarily mean that the student will know how to make purchases at Burger King, Wendy's, and Taco Bell. Each setting is slightly different, requiring a different set of responses or skills. General case instruction is one way to maximize generalization across different community settings (see Box 14–1). This approach has been effective in teaching students to generalize skills across various vending machines (Sprague & Horner, 1984), telephones (Horner, Williams, & Steveley, 1987), and restaurants (McDonnell & Ferguson, 1988) and to teach requesting help in different community contexts (Chadsey-Rusch, Drasgow, Reinoehl, Hallet, & Collet-Klingenberg, 1993).

Consider how Rico's teachers use general case instruction to teach Rico to use convenience stores with a companion:

First, an instructional universe is defined. Rico's teachers must answer several questions: Is the goal for Rico to be able to use all convenience stores in his neighborhood? In his region? In the United States? The teacher decides to focus on teaching Rico to use convenience stores in his region (the Lehigh Valley of Pennsylvania).

Table 14–3 shows the four convenience stores identified by the general case analysis.

Second, the teacher writes a generic task analysis for purchasing a snack at the store and then analyzes the stimulus and response variation in each store (Table 14–3). Third, the teacher selects which stores will be used for training. The teacher chooses a 7-Eleven, a Penn Supreme, and the school cafeteria

Box 14–1   General Case Instruction

General case instruction emphasizes selecting and teaching examples so that students learn to perform skills across the full range of settings and materials that they confront. The five steps to set up general case instruction are the following:

1. Define the instructional universe
2. Write a generic task analysis
3. Select teaching and testing examples that sample the range of stimulus and response variation
4. Teach
5. Test
6. Repeat steps 1 to 5.

TABLE 14–3

General Case Analysis

Generic responses: Task analysis (TA)	Instructional universe: Convenience stores in Lehigh Valley, Pennsylvania, assessment data: Sites to sample stimulus/response (S/R) variation (parentheses show S/R variation for that TA step in that site)				Assessment summary: Generalization
	Penn Supreme	**Nick's**	**7–Eleven**	**Kate's**	
1. Enter store	+ (electric door)	− (push)	− (pull)	− (push)	Push/pull door
2. Locate item	− (multiple aisles)	− (display case)	− (aisles)	+ (behind clerk)	Scan aisles and cases
3. Pick out item	+ (bottom shelf)	− (open case)	− (top shelf)	+ (clerk selects)	Shelf location and opening case
4. Take item to counter	+ (large counter)	− (small counter)	− (small counter)	N/A	Size/location of counter
5. Wait in line	+	+	+	N/A	Mastered
6. Pay cashier	− (clerk states price)	+ (clerk extends hand)	− (clerk states price)	− (clerk states price)	Verbal cue states
7. Take change/item	− (change with no bag)	− (no bag)	− (change and bag)	+ (bag)	Unbagged item Change cups
8. Leave store	+ (electric door)	− (pull)	− (push)	− (pull)	Push/pull door
Number correct/ Total Responses: Date of probe:	5/8 Nov. 3	2/8 Nov. 10	1/8 Nov. 12	3/6 Nov. 15	

Key: + = independent correct; − = incorrect or needed prompting, N/A = not applicable to that site.

Note: Reprinted from "Functional Assessment" by R. Gaylord-Ross and D. M. Browder, in *Critical Issues in the Lives of People with Severe Disabilities* (p. 58) by L. H. Meyer, C. A. Peck, and L. Brown (Eds.), 1991, Baltimore: Paul H. Brookes. Reprinted by permission.

snack line (which offers snack foods like ice cream) because these three stores sample the range of variation in Rico's region. The teacher will also test Rico at other stores, including Nick's Market and Kate's

One-Stop Shopping. Rico will get daily instruction in the school cafeteria and weekly instruction at a convenience store on Fridays. Every fourth Friday, the teacher will use a novel convenience store to check for generalization. This will continue until Rico demonstrates both mastery and generalization.

Efficient Teaching Strategies

Three ways teachers can maximize instruction and teach efficiently are to (a) use observational learning, (b) provide additional or "extra" information while teaching and (c) involve peers in instruction. In an example of observational learning, Griffen, Wolery, and Schuster (1992) used a small group to teach students with cognitive disabilities to make a milkshake, scrambled eggs, and pudding. To maximize instruction, one student received direct instruction using prompting for each step of the task analysis with constant time delay. At the same time, the instructor prompted and reinforced the other two students to observe and follow instructions by turning the pages of a picture recipe. Although each student received direct instruction on only one of the three recipes, they learned most of the steps of all three.

Observational learning also may be facilitated through teacher demonstration. Smith, Collins, Schuster, and Kleinert (1999) taught high school students to clean tables using a task analysis and a least prompts system. During each instructional session and after the students cleaned the tables, the instructor directed the students to watch him as he rinsed and put away the cleaning materials. Pre- and postassessments showed that through observational learning, the students were able to do most of the cleanup steps without direct instruction. Saving instructional time is a key advantage of observational learning. Critical steps not yet acquired by students can be taught directly, but teachers can still save time by not having to directly teach every step in a task analysis.

Instructional time may also be enhanced by providing additional or extra information during instruction of targeted skills. Taylor, Collins, Schuster, and Kleinert (2002) employed a system of least prompts to teach four high school students a routine for doing laundry. During instruction, they added extra information by inserting eight related functional sight words (e.g., detergent, normal, rinse, presoak, softener) printed on flash cards into the steps of the task analysis. Additional information was added as a consequent event. As the student performed a step, the teacher praised the student and then pointed to and said the word before the student continued with the next step. Students learned the laundry task

analysis and most of the words. Like observational learning, the sight words were acquired without direct instruction.

Involving peers as tutors can enhance efficiency by saving teacher time while also promoting interaction with classmates who have disabilities. For example, Collins, Branson, and Hall (1995) taught high school students from an advanced English class to teach recipe sight words to students with moderate cognitive disabilities. Students read each word and then found it in the recipe on the product's box or container. The advanced English students wrote about their teaching experiences as part of their English assignments. The students with disabilities learned to read the recipe words and could prepare the recipes when tested in the home economics room and at a nearby home.

Because many instructional procedures involving lengthy error correction strategies can interfere with typical peer interactions, teachers might consider using less intrusive instructional procedures with peer tutors. Tekin-Iftar (2003) used simultaneous prompting with peer tutors who taught middle school students with disabilities to read community signs. A key advantage of simultaneous prompting is that the peer tutor needs only to model the response (in this case, say the word) and then wait for the student to respond. If incorrect, the peer tutor simply goes on to the next word or instructional opportunity. Although not used by the researchers in this way, peers can easily incorporate simultaneous prompting during typical peer activities without appearing overly teacherlike. For example, community sight words can be taught as peers walk down the school hall together or participate on field trips (e.g., "This sign says 'women,'" "This sign says 'exit.'"). In the cafeteria, just before paying for lunch, peers could label the coins needed for purchasing. Teachers would assess student learning at another time.

Teachers can be effective and efficient by planning for generalization, using strategies that save teacher time, and collaborating with peers and families to teach new skills.

 Value Four
Home and Community Skills Gain
Importance as Students Become Older

Guideline Four: Use Transition Planning to Focus Community-Based Instruction

The seven most common transitions youth with disabilities face as they approach adulthood concern employment, living arrangements, getting around in the community, increased financial independence, making friends, sexuality and self-esteem, and having fun (Wehman, 1997). To help adolescents meet these challenges, work, community, and social skills gain increasing priority as students progress through their last years of school. Many of the skills described in this chapter are more suitably age appropriate for adolescents and young adults than children. Adolescents may open their first bank account, prepare meals, and start going to the movies without their parents, while children may do chores, pick up their laundry, and fix snacks but typically go to the movies alone.

Thus, teachers may focus more time on skills for the home and community during the transition years (age 14 and older).

Julia, who is 14, will probably have more objectives related to domestic and community skills than Rico, who is 9 years old. Aaron's greatest instructional needs at age 20 are using community resources, establishing his own home, and obtaining a job. Many of the objectives for his individualized education program (IEP) will be related to home, community, and employment skills.

The transition years is a time for increased community-based and home instruction (Figure 14–1). Still, as Julia's and Aaron's program show, individualization is important. Community-based instruction for Julia is carefully balanced with general education experiences in her high school. At age 14, maintaining relationships with high school buddies and being

FIGURE 14–1
Robert, at age 20, receives most of his educational support in community settings. One of the benefits of his part-time job in a martial arts center is free classes.

involved in a full range of high school activities (e.g., attending general education classes, pep rallies, school clubs) are important. By contrast, Aaron's program is entirely community based. At age 20, his peers have graduated from high school and are either attending college or working. Participating in high school activities is no longer age appropriate for Aaron.

For students between the ages of 18 and 21, commencement programs (Morningstar & Lattin, 2004) are an option offered by many school districts. Students attend graduation ceremonies with their peers but continue to receive services from their school district on transition-related IEP objectives until services are no longer needed or they turn 21. Commencement programs are fully community based. Program offices and some instructional space may be housed in postsecondary campuses (e.g., vocational or trade schools, community colleges, 4-year colleges) or at various community locations (e.g., storefront, office in an apartment complex or commercial building) (Grigal et al., 2001; Morningstar & Lattin, 2004).

Commencement programs are highly individualized, as they are guided by the student's transition and person-centered plans. Careful consideration is given to student preferences for what to learn and where to learn it. Students may receive instruction in any combination of settings, including community colleges, vocational schools, in the community, at the job, and in their home by teachers, job coaches, or paraprofessionals employed by the school district or other human service agencies. Although instruction for the home and the community is the focus, helping the student make connections with same-age peers is critical for full community inclusion and membership.

Aaron's program is housed at his local community college, where he attends two college art classes three times per week. At the college, he also receives private tutoring from a special education teacher on home and personal management where Aaron learns money and budgeting skills and learns how to schedule his weekly activities using a computerized handheld personal organizer. During lunch, he practices ordering and purchasing skills in the college cafeteria assisted by a friend from one of his art classes. Together, they hang out during lunch with mutual friends. Three times a week in the afternoon, Aaron meets up with his community/job coach. Because Aaron is unsure about what type of job he would like to have, his job coach arranges for him to

sample a variety of different employment settings. Additionally, his coach supports him to use an ATM machine to withdraw or deposit money; he practices the skills learned in personal management class in actual situations. At the end of the day, Aaron and his coach frequently go to a local coffee shop near his home where many young adults relax after work. His coach discreetly gives Aaron ideas about how to greet and meet new people. Once a week, Aaron gets instruction on menu planning and cooking meals in his family's home. When he transitions to his new apartment, which will be fully accessible for his wheelchair, home instruction will intensify. Several times per month, Aaron meets up with his Best Buddy, Jason, who attends the same community college, for evening fun. They go to college games, attend concerts, go to the movies, or just hang out with mutual friends.

Resources for Planning Instructional Support

Skills for the Home

To recap the discussion thus far, before teaching home and community skills, teachers need to consider what, where, and how to teach while also honoring student and family preferences and students' ages and selecting instructional strategies that are effective and efficient. Next, we describe specific ideas for teaching skills that are necessary in home settings. Many valuable commercially produced materials are available to help (e.g., **http://www.attainmentcompany.com**, **http://www.stanfield.com**).

Food Preparation

Students are often highly motivated to participate in food preparation instruction because they can consume the results! In contrast, food preparation can be difficult to plan and teach because of the specialized setting and equipment needed. In middle and high schools, home economic rooms are ideal locations, but supplies may be expensive. Schuster (1988) suggested several ways that a program may offset the expense, including (a) obtaining donations from civic organizations, (b) using lunch money (with the parents' permission) to prepare the student's lunch, (c) collecting lab fees from parents, (d) operating a school vending machine and using the profits to cover the costs of food, and (e) operating a schoolwide food service program on a cost basis (e.g., selling bagels or donuts in the morning). Students also may be able to reuse preparation materials several times before cooking the food for consumption. For example, Schleien, Ash, Kiernan, and Wehman (1981) had students practice boiling an egg, broiling a muffin, and baking a frozen dinner. The same egg was reboiled for practice, and the "frozen dinner" was an empty tray with foil. Although students need the natural consequences of consuming the food they prepare, they may be able to understand the importance of practicing before using the real materials.

Food preparation instruction has several components: planning, food preparation, safe food storage, and cleaning up. When teaching students to plan what foods to prepare, honor any dietary restrictions, respect both cultural and familial preferences (e.g., meatless or no pork), honor personal preferences, and encourage nutrition. Some students may benefit from learning recipe planning as described by Sarber and Cuvo (1983). In their study, adults with disabilities learned to plan meals using a board that had color cues for each food group. For example, peaches were cued for the fruits and vegetable group. Beef stew was cued as both meat and vegetables. After planning the menus, the adults learned to develop grocery lists to purchase necessary items. Arnold-Reid, Schloss, and Alper (1997) implemented the system of least prompts to teach participants to plan meals according to the four food groups: vegetables/fruit, meat, dairy, and bread/cereal. Because one participant had to limit sweets because of health concerns, these were listed in a column called the "Dreaded Other." Another student learned to have an item in the "Dreaded Other" column as an occasional treat. Since participants had difficulty filling out the chart, instruction was adapted by teaching either sight words or picture identification related to commonly eaten foods and enlarging the chart. After completing the chart, the participants planned a grocery list. Participants who do not have the academic skills to read or write food names in planning menus or self-monitoring their diet may benefit from a picture system. The Select-A-Meal Curriculum (Attainment Company, **http://www.attainment.com**) provides commercial materials that can be helpful for menu planning or restaurant use.

Besides teaching healthy menu planning, food preferences should be honored. Some students may be able to describe the foods they want to learn to prepare. For students with more severe disabilities, preference assessment can be applied to determine which foods to select (Lohrmann-O'Rourke, Browder, & Brown, 2000). To conduct this preference assessment, the teacher might show the student an array of pictures or packages of food and wait for the student to select one by touching it, gazing at it, or making some other response. Or the teacher may offer samples of foods and then have students choose from among the samples. The teacher would repeat the choices, rotating some different food options to see if a preference emerges.

Once the specific foods have been selected, consideration can be given to how to teach the recipe. One option is to use a special picture recipe book, such as the Home Cooking Curriculum (Attainment Company). Singh, Oswald, Ellis, and Singh (1995) taught individuals with profound mental retardation to prepare a dessert (pineapple mousse) using a picture cookbook with line drawings. First the instructor pretrained the recipe by demonstrating each step and having the participant practice it five times (guided rehearsal) per session. The instructor continued to this method for 5 instructional days. Then, to teach the student to cook by following the pictures, the instructor used a most to least intrusive prompting system beginning with gestural and verbal prompts and fading to verbal prompts and then no prompting.

Rather than using pictures, some students may be taught sight words to read directions on packages or to follow simple recipes. Although sight words may be taught while the student learns food preparation steps, some students may benefit from sight word instruction outside of cooking sessions.

Audiotaped recipes can be helpful to students who have difficulty using words or drawings. Trask-Tyler, Grossi, and Heward (1994) taught adolescents with developmental disabilities to prepare recipes using audiotaped directions. The participants carried a tape recorder in the pocket of a cooking apron. At the end of each step, the tape beeped, and students learned to turn it off and perform the step. The instructor used a system of least to most intrusive prompts to teach students to use the taped messages. Students mastered the recipes taught and generalized to similar recipes using the audiotape.

The advantage of employing picture, word, or audiotaped recipes is that they encourage self-directed learning. Often students will need teacher prompting to learn to use the materials for self-direction. While teachers have several alternatives for prompting, one alternative is the system of least intrusive prompting (Mechling & Gast, 1997; Trask-Tyler et al., 1994). For example, Mechling and Gast (1997) taught students to use a combination picture and audiotape recipe book that was made with a communication board with picture overlays and speech output. If students were unsure of the step, they re-pressed the button to hear the instructions over. The instructor gave progressive assistance, which is described in Table 14–4.

Time delay, another prompting alternative, can be used to teach participants to read sight words contained in recipe or instruction booklets (Browder, Hines, McCarthy, & Fees, 1984; Gast, Doyle, Wolery, Ault, & Farmer, 1991). Constant time delay is effective for teaching food preparation in a group format (Griffen et al., 1992; Hall, Schuster, Wolery, & Gast, 1992). The challenge of teaching food preparation to a group is having enough supplies. Rarely is it practical for each person in the group to perform all the steps of the cooking task. If four students in a group each prepare a box of instant pudding, there will be 16 servings to consume! Teachers can have each student prepare part of the recipe while the others watch.

Sometimes students are taught to prepare simple items for which no recipe is needed. Schuster and Griffen (1991) used constant time delay to teach students to prepare a drink mix (Kool-Aid). Students with moderate cognitive disabilities all learned to make this drink independently. However, when food preparation

is more complex, most of us rely on recipes. Teacher prompting can be crucial in assisting students with severe disabilities to learn to use picture, commercial, or audiotaped recipes. The goal of instruction is student-directed learning: students use recipe aides to guide themselves in food preparation without help. The teaching challenge is to design instruction so it is efficient and effective while also encouraging generalized use of self-prompting guides. Use the following guidelines to make instruction efficient while encouraging self-directed learning:

1. Where possible, teach food preparation in a small group of two or three, giving each person a chance to prepare part of the recipe while the others watch and follow the recipe using pictures, an audiotape, or the package

   In preparing a box cake mix, Sam adds the ingredients and prepares the pan using a picture recipe while Julia follows along using her own picture recipe. Then Julia uses the mixer and pours the mix into the pan and places it in the oven while Sam follows along on his picture recipe.

2. Use a prompt system like time delay or the system of least prompts to teach students to follow the recipe steps

   The teacher uses a verbal and gesture prompt: "Look at the next step and do it."

TABLE 14–4
Instructions for Audiovisual Self-Prompting System

Task: Making microwave popcorn
Self-prompting system: Digivox Communication Board with picture overlay and speech output

Sample step	Visual cue (picture)	Auditory cue
1. Put bag in, right side up	Bag inside, right side up	"Put bag in, like this"

Teacher's use of system of least prompts to encourage use of audiovisual system

1. Verbal:	"Touch the picture again." (Referring to picture overlay on device)
2. Verbal:	"Touch the picture again to hear how to put the bag in." (Referring to audio)
3. Gesture:	"Touch the picture like this." Touches picture and points to bag.
4. Model:	Repeats verbal prompt above and then models placing bag in microwave.
5. Physical:	Repeats verbal prompt above and guides hand to place bag in microwave.

Note: From L. C. Mechling & D. L. Gast, 1997. Combination audio/visual self-prompting system for teaching chained tasks to students with intellectual disabilities. *Education and Training in Mental Retardation and Developmental Disabilities, 32*, 138–153. Copyright (1997) by Division of Mental Retardation and Developmental Disabilities, Council for Exceptional Children. Used with permission.

3. Consider including additional information about nutrition or safety in the prompting or feedback

   The teacher consistently uses the same statement (e.g., "Use a hot mitt to keep from being burned").

4. Probe to assess learning

   Ask Julia to make a boxed cheesecake by following the picture recipe and record the steps she can do alone.

5. Probe for generalization

   Give Sam and Julia untrained recipes with pictures similar to the cheesecake and other learned recipes. Can they use the pictures to follow new recipes?

Housekeeping

To manage a home, individuals need strategies to keep pace with the ongoing demands of housecleaning and laundry (Figure 14–2). Even when outside help can be procured (e.g., a maid service or cook), ongoing chores still must be performed. As students make the transition from relying on their parents to clean and do their laundry to caring for their own clothes and living space, they need to learn two important sets of skills: (a) how to perform housekeeping and laundry tasks and (b) how to manage their time so they complete these tasks regularly.

Instructors typically use a task analysis of the skill and a prompting system (such as least intrusive prompts or time delay) to teach housekeeping tasks. Whether to teach the entire task (i.e., whole-task instruction) or some portion of it (i.e., chaining) will depend on the complexity of the task and the students' current skill level. For example, McWilliams, Nietupski, and Hamre-Nietupski (1990) taught students bed making using a system of least prompts and forward chaining in which steps of the task analysis were taught to mastery one at a time. In contrast, Snell (1982) used progressive time delay to teach the entire task of bed making, prompting students through the whole-task analysis during each teaching session.

Similarly, in teaching laundry skills, researchers have used the system of least prompts (Cuvo, Jacobi, & Sipko, 1981), time delay (Miller & Test, 1989) and most to least prompting (Miller & Test, 1989). For this task, McDonnell and McFarland (1988) found whole-task instruction to be more efficient than chaining, while Miller and Test (1989) found time delay to be slightly more efficient than most to least prompting. In applying these strategies to individual students, it is important to consider how the student learns best. One teacher might follow the research on efficiency and begin by teaching the entire task analysis using a time delay system. Another teacher might choose an approach after observing the student's prior performance with these methods.

Another alternative is to encourage student-directed learning by using a self-operated audio-prompting system (Post & Storey, 2002). Briggs et al. (1990) taught students with moderate and severe disabilities to operate a washing machine, clean a toilet, and clean mirrors using a taped script that they played while wearing a Walkman tape player. The script gave both verbal prompts and praise. The following sample from the Briggs et al. (1990) audiotape illustrates how the script contained prompting, self-checking of outcomes, seeking help as needed, and praise. When the bell sounded, the student turned off the tape and performed the step.

"Open the box and take out one set (two packets) of blue detergent. Put them in the washer." (bell)

"Can you see the blue packets on top of the clothes? If you can't see them, call the teacher for help." (bell)

"Good job! Now close the detergent box and put it back in the cabinet. Close the cabinet door." (bell)

Once students learn the basics of housekeeping, they need self-management skills to keep pace with the demands of these chores. Pierce and Schriebman (1994) taught children with autism used pictures to self-manage chores. Students were given a photo album with one step on each page and a picture for that step of the task analysis. To make album pages easier to turn, felt dots were glued to the bottom each page. Instructors taught in three phases. In the first, the instructor taught receptive labeling of all the photos. In the second, students learned to choose a reinforcer, turn a page in the book, perform the response, and self-reinforce. In the third phase, the instructor faded her presence by saying, "Good work. I'll be back in a minute," and leaving the area while the student worked alone. Students were able to use the picture books to set a table, make a bed, make a drink, get dressed, and do laundry without an adult nearby.

Once students know a skill on their own, they can learn to self-schedule these activities. Lovett and

FIGURE 14–2
This student is learning to use a community laundromat. Here he is learning the steps of a task analysis for folding clothes. He also has instructional plans for using the coin-operated washer and dryer.

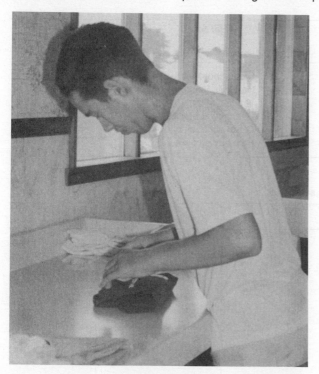

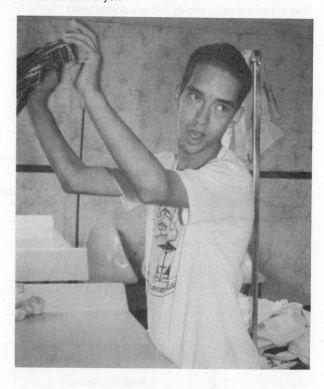

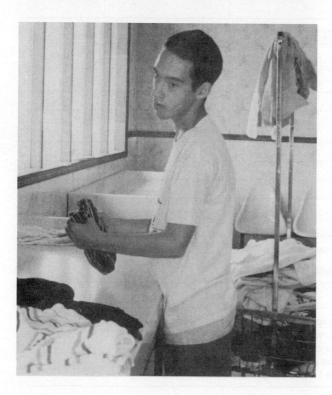

Haring (1989) taught adults with mild and moderate disabilities to self-manage their daily living skills using self-recording, self-evaluation, and self-reinforcement. Tasks were divided into daily, weekly, and occasional schedules. Participants used a planning form to self-select these tasks. Using instructions, modeling, and feedback, the teachers taught participants to use the same form to self-record when each task was completed. If participants did not achieve 100% accuracy for self-recording, they were taught to self-reinforce, (e.g., participate in a leisure activity) in order to improve their accuracy. After mastering self-recording, participants learned to graph their performance on a simple percentage chart and then determine whether they had made progress. Once successful in self-evaluation, all participants learned to self-reinforce when tasks were completed on time. An example of this self-management training is shown in Table 14–5.

The teacher helped Julia and her mother identify Julia's chores and determine flexible times for their completion. In a language arts class, the teacher and peers taught Julia to read the names of her chores

TABLE 14–5
Self-Management of Daily Living

Step 1: Identify daily, weekly, and occasional tasks

<u>Student</u>: Julia   **Age: 14**

Tasks	Daily	Weekly	Occasional
	Wash hair Blow-dry hair Wash face Select clothes Feed cat Help with dishes	Clean bedroom Help with laundry Vacuum den Change cat box Clean out book bag Help buy groceries	Budget allowance Shop for clothes

Step 2: Have student select when to perform these tasks

Julia's daily schedule

Time	Task	Yes	No	Notes
6:30 a.m. 7:00 a.m.	Wash hair, face			
After breakfast 7:15 a.m.	Select clothes			
After dressed 5:00 p.m.	Blow-dry hair			
Before dinner 6:00 p.m.	Feed the cat			
After dinner	Help with dishes			

Julia's weekly schedule

Day	Task	Yes	No	Notes
Sunday	Free!!			
Monday	Change cat box			
Tuesday	Help with laundry (wash towels)			
Wednesday	Free!! Pep club night			
Thursday	Help with groceries			
Friday	Clean out book bag			
Saturday	Vacuum den Clean bedroom			

Step 3. Teach student to self-record when task completed and to self-reinforce

Julia's "treats" for getting chores done

When I finish . . .	I will . . .
My hair and getting dressed	Treat myself to cherry lip gloss, nail polish, a hair clip, or other item from my treats drawer.
Feeding the cat	Hold the cat as she purrs.
Helping with dishes	Pick out snack cake or other treat.
"Extra" from my weekly list	Eat my snack cake and watch a TV show.
My Saturday chores	Call whichever relative I choose (e.g., Aunt Marie).

and the days of the week. The teacher also taught her how to make checks on the form by talking about what Julia had or had not done the night before at home. Once Julia could check the form accurately, the teacher met with Julia and her mother to review how Julia could "take charge" of her own chores using her charts and planned her list of "treats" for self-reinforcement. Julia then used her new self-management program at home with support from her mother as needed.

In doing housekeeping and laundry, students will encounter problems that prevent task completion unless they develop problem-solving skills. Hughes, Hugo, and Blatt (1996) taught students to use self-management strategies to solve several problems: (a) not having the right utensil to make toast, (b) trying to vacuum when the vacuum was unplugged, and (c) cleaning up when there were bread crumbs under the table or game pieces in the area to be vacuumed. The self-instruction strategy involved students learning to (a) state the problem, (b) state the response, (c) self-evaluate, and (d) self-reinforce. The instructor taught the strategy by modeling the problem-solving step, having the participant state what to do as the instructor performed it, and then having the participant do the step while saying the problem-solving strategy. For example, to cope with an unplugged vacuum, the participant would say the following:

1. "The vacuum won't run." (state the problem)
2. "Plug it in." (state the response)
3. "I plugged it in." (self-evaluate)
4. "Great job!" (self-reinforce)

Home Safety
Many skills constitute being safe at home (Collins, Wolery, & Gast, 1991), including recognizing and avoiding hazards (e.g., electric shock, hot burner), creating a safe home environment (e.g., locking doors, using matches appropriately), responding to emergencies (e.g., calling 911, evacuating a building), and using first aid (e.g., treating cuts and burns, responding to minor illnesses). Safety skills are taught like any other skill, but simulation and role play may be needed to create "dangers" not typically present in everyday settings. Haney and Jones (1982) taught four school-age children to escape from a simulated fire in a home setting. Props were designed to make the training more realistic. For example, hot and cold pads were used to change the touch temperatures of doors and a tape

recording of the home's fire alarm system was played. The instructor used a system of least prompts to teach the steps of the task analysis. Rae and Roll (1985) similarly employed a system of least prompts to teach evacuation. They also measured evacuation time to be sure students could leave the building in the time recommended by the fire department. Sometimes, for students like Rico, school fire drills can be upsetting and confusing (Box 14–2), and steps must be taken.

Students also may encounter emergencies that require knowing first aid skills. Spooner, Stem, and Test (1989) taught students to communicate an emergency, apply a bandage, take care of minor injuries, and respond to someone who was choking. The instructor used a group format followed by individual practice sessions with modeling and a probe. The task analyses used are shown in Table 14–6. These first aid skills can also be taught with constant time delay (Gast, Winterling, Wolery, & Farmer, 1992), by using puppet simulations (Marchand-Martella et al., 1992a), or by peers who role-play having wounds (Marchand-Martella, Martella, Christensen, Agran, & Young, 1992b).

In addition to using simulations, safety skills can be taught by embedding opportunities in daily routines or during instruction of other skills. Safety skills also can be taught by adding safety steps to task analyses or routines.

After preparing a meal, Aaron is prompted, as part of his food preparation task analysis, to check that all appliances (e.g., coffeemaker, burner, oven) are turned off before he leaves the kitchen. When he enters his home with his community teacher, Aaron is taught to lock the door behind him before he hangs up his coat.

In place of direct instruction, adding extra information is an ideal way of embedding safety skill information during instruction of home tasks or routines (Jones & Collins, 1997).

While teaching Aaron to use a microwave, his teacher tells him that if he sees smoke while cooking, he should quickly turn the microwave off. When Aaron reaches for his toast, his teacher says, "If the toast ever gets stuck, unplug the toaster, then use a rubber spatula to get the toast out."

For critical safety skills, teachers should consider setting up minisimulations to observe whether the student can apply the extra information when needed.

Box 14–2 How Rico Learned to Participate in Fire Drills

Whenever the school fire alarm sounded Rico would begin to scream and slap his face. Feeling pressured to evacuate the students safely, the third-grade teacher and paraprofessional would plead with him to leave. They had even tried carrying him out of the building, but Rico became aggressive. The special education teacher designed a fire evacuation simulation training program for Rico. Each day, at a different time each day the special education teacher or the paraprofessional asked Rico to choose two classmates from among those who had finished their work to practice a fire drill. In the first phase the teacher rang a small buzzer briefly (a second) and used least prompts to teach Rico to follow the two chosen classmates to the school yard. Rico received continuous praise by the teacher and peers as he followed them without screaming or self-injury. When he returned to the classroom he was given the choice of listening to a musical relaxation tape or looking at a book (activities which he liked and found calming). Over time the teacher made the buzzer longer and louder until it was more similar to the school fire alarm. When the next fire drill occurred, the peers went to Rico and calmly asked him to follow them. Rico went with them but wanted to hold their hands. He cried but was not screaming. At the end of the fire drill Rico returned and went directly to the relaxation tape just as he had done during simulations. The decision was made to continue the training program, but to fade to a weekly schedule.

TABLE 14–6
Task Analysis of First Aid

Communicating an emergency	Applying a plastic bandage
1. Locate phone	1. Look at injury
2. Pick up receiver	2. Find bandages needed
3. Dial 9	3. Select proper size
4. Dial 1	4. Find outside tabs of wrapper
5. Dial 1	5. Pull down tabs to expose bandage
6. Put receiver to ear	6. Find protective covering on bandage
7. Listen for operator	7. Pull off by tabs, exposing gauze portion
8. Give full name	8. Do not touch gauze portion
9. Give full address	9. Apply to clean, dry skin
10. Give phone number	
11. Explain emergency	
12. Hang up after operator does	

Taking care of minor injuries	First aid for choking
1. Let it bleed a little to wash out the dirt	1. Let the person cough and try to get object out of throat
2. Wash with soap and water	2. Stand behind victim
3. Dry with clean cloth	3. Wrap your arms around victim
4. Open plastic bandage	4. Make a fist with one hand, placing the thumb side of the clinched fist against the victim's abdomen—slightly above the navel and below the rib cage
5. Cover with bandage (hold by the edges)	
6. Call 911 if severe and no adult available	5. Press fist into abdomen with a quick, upward thrust
	6. Repeat step 5 as needed

Note: From "Teaching First Aid Skills to Adolescents Who Are Moderately Mentally Handicapped" by F. Spooner, B. Stem, and D. W. Test, 1989, *Education and Training in Mental Retardation, 24*, p. 343. Copyright 1989 by the Division on Mental Retardation and Developmental Disabilities, Council on Exceptional Children. Reprinted by permission.

Aaron's teacher deliberately inserted folded bread in the toaster to see whether Aaron would unplug the toaster before removing the stuck toast.

Telephone Use

Telephone use relates to many daily living skills, such as placing orders, calling friends, or coping with an emergency. Emergency telephoning has been successfully taught to students with disabilities (Risley & Cuvo, 1980; Spooner et al., 1989) using task analyses and pictures of emergency situations to begin each simulated emergency call.

Horner et al. (1987) applied general case instruction to teach generalized phone use to four high school students with moderate and severe disabilities. The instructional universe included frequently made and received calls. Training variations included the type of phone, its location, the person calling or being called, and the topic of conversation (e.g., to leave a message, place an order). Once instructed on these variations, students learned to make a wide range of phone calls.

Using general case instruction to teach Julia how to make phone calls is an ideal strategy for her. As an active teen, she will need to use the phone for a variety of purposes like calling home to ask permission to visit a friend after school, calling friends to chat, and making emergency calls when she needs help. Julia's need to use a variety of phones (cell, school, and home phones) can be addressed with a general case instruction approach.

Sometimes students lack the academic skills needed to dial the phone. Lalli, Mace, Browder, and Brown (1989) taught an adult with little number recognition to dial the phone by matching numbers to the numbers on the phone. Current technology makes it possible to bypass this step altogether by using speed dialing or voice activation on a home or cell phone. But number matching may still be important for using public phones.

Sexuality Education

Another relevant skill area for the home is sexuality education. Sexuality education is broader than just "sex ed." While sex typically refers to a sex act, sexuality refers to one's total being, including being male or female, feeling good about oneself, caring for others, and expressing oneself through intimacy. Fostering healthy sexual attitudes and behaviors are critical goals of sexuality education (Hingsburger & Tough, 2002). Unfortunately, sexuality education for learners with severe disabilities is typically overlooked or avoided. As a result, many adults with disabilities are uneducated about basic sex facts (e.g., names of body parts, knowledge of bodily functions, sexual acts) (McCabe & Cummins, 1996), are vulnerable to sexual abuse partially because of their lack of knowledge (Sobsey & Doe, 1991), and hold negative feelings about sexual issues (Garwood & McCabe, 2000). Some adults with disabilities may believe that it is never appropriate to enter into an intimate relationship with another because sex is "dirty" or "bad," or, if they do, they feel guilty about being bad (Lesseliers & Van Hove, 2002). Others, acting on their sexual urges without proper education, will act inappropriately (e.g., engage in public masturbation, make sexual advances toward the wrong person) (Hingsburger & Tough, 2002).

Feeling good about one's sexuality and having the opportunity to enter into intimate, loving relationships with others adds to personal happiness. To reverse the negative cycle of poor or no education, sexuality education should be viewed comprehensively and developmentally, focusing on (a) knowledge about basic sex facts, (b) skills (knowing how and when to act), (c) feelings (fostering positive attitudes), and (d) relationships (understanding and respecting others). Not everything can or should be taught at once. Some components will require the foundation of others, while all sexuality education must be age appropriate. Some guidelines about what to teach are offered by Schwier and Hingsburger (2000) in Table 14–7.

Commercial sexuality curricula are available to guide instruction (see Blanchett & Wolfe 2002), but most curricula are limited because they rely on lecture, discussion, and line drawings to explain concepts. Many learners with severe disabilities may not comprehend the information or know how to apply it. Commercial curricula can be useful for suggesting important sexuality topics, but teachers and parents need to teach so the content can be understood and used by students.

The best way to teach sexuality concepts is by infusing them into students' typical home or school routines and natural life experiences. For instance, body part names can be taught during dressing and bathing routines at home and, with parents' permission, at school when assisting the student to toilet or undress and dress for swimming. Learning anatomically correct names is critical for unambiguous communication (e.g., if abused, students can explain exactly where they were touched). Learning about public versus private areas of the home and school are important discriminations needed for acting sexually appropriate and for self-protection (Schwier & Hingsburger, 2000). During home routines, parents can label the bedroom and bathroom as private areas used for private activities such as dressing and masturbating. Private activities are not allowed in public areas of the home. Further, parents can teach their children that only certain people (friends, family members) may enter a private area of the house, but first they must ask permission (e.g., knock on the door). At school, teachers can encourage privacy by teaching students to close the bathroom door and to wrap a towel around themselves after showering.

Personal hygiene is an important component of sexuality education. Research examples provide some guidance on how to teach menstrual care. For example, Epps, Stern, and Horner (1990) taught girls to manage their periods by using simulations and general case instruction. A training video, "Janet's Got Her Period" (James Stanfield Publishing, **http://www.stanfield. com**), is a good resource to introduce the concept of menstrual care. The video shows a sister and mother teaching Janet to use sanitary products to manage her period. Personal hygiene should stress not only management of bodily functions but also looking good and feeling attractive. Wherever possible, teachers and parents can help students make the connection between their personal care routines and social activities. Getting ready for a party or a school dance, for example, can involve choosing nice clothes, styling hair in a special way, wearing special makeup, or choosing new perfume or cologne. Telling the student that he or she looks great, beautiful, or handsome can go a long way in bolstering the student's self-confidence and feelings of pride.

One area of sexuality education that can be especially appropriate to teach for school and the community is that of recognizing and respecting social boundaries. Students sometimes do not discriminate between who can be trusted with a hug and who cannot or lack understanding about their personal versus public body parts or activities. The "Circles" curriculum (Stanfield Company) provides videotapes and color coding to teach students to discriminate among different types of relationships. For example, the purple private circle is

TABLE 14–7
Sexuality Content Guidelines: What to Teach When

Age	Content
Early Years, 3–9	• Difference between boys and girls • Body names and functions • Public and private places • Modesty • How babies are born
Puberty, 9–15	• Hygiene (looking good, looking cool) • Physical changes • Menstruation • Wet dreams • Inappropriate touching and saying "no" • Social boundaries and social manners • Sexual feelings • How babies are made
Older Teens, 16 and up	• Dating preparation • Relationships (love vs. sex) • Handling sexual/emotional feelings • Laws/consequences for inappropriate touching • Sexual intercourse/other sex acts • Prevention of pregnancy • Prevention of STDs • Marriage/parenting

Adapted with permission from Schwier, K. M., & Hingsburger, D. (2000), *Sexuality: Your sons and daughters with intellectual disabilities* (p. 32). Baltimore: Paul H. Brookes which was adapted from: Maksym, D. (1990). *Shared feelings: A parent guide to sexuality education for children, adolescents and adults who have a mental handicap.* North York, Ontario, Canada: The Roeher Institute.

for the student alone. Some "circles" (relationships) welcome hugs, but some hugs should give the people space between bodies (friends versus lovers). People in the red zone (strangers) are not given physical or verbal contact. This program can be used to teach avoidance of sexual harassment and abuse and helps students know how to let relationships develop from acquaintances into friendships. By selecting photographs of people the student knows and color coding them, the discrimination can be made more concrete. Students may need to practice their ability to discriminate when encountering people in the community. For example, the teacher might say, "What zone is Mr. Jones? He's an acquaintance. What do we do? Just wave—no hugs." If a student makes inappropriate physical contact with a teacher or others, the teacher may use color coding on clothing to help the student know what "zones" are appropriate (e.g., a green patch on the arm to tap her for attention).

Teaching protection from abuse is also critical. Sadly, people with disabilities are highly vulnerable to sexual abuse, with most abuse incidents occurring with *familiar* people, not with strangers (Sobsey & Doe, 1991). Teachers can teach students abuse protection responses at school, but practice and reminders at home are important if students are to report actual abuse incidents wherever they occur. The "No-Go-Tell" is one effective strategy. Lumley and colleagues taught adult women with disabilities how to respond to unwanted sexual advances that potentially could be made by their support staff (Lumley, Miltenberger, Long, Rapp, & Roberts, 1998). By presenting scenarios (e.g., "What would you do if staff touched your breasts?") and participating in role play, the women learned a three-step sequence: No—verbally refuse the lure or action; Go—leave the situation; and Tell—report the incident to a trusted adult. Discriminating between what are appropriate and inappropriate sexual advances is an important prerequisite. Combining the circles curriculum with No-Go-Tell may help students learn these discriminations (e.g., "Kissing [long and on the mouth] is okay with a boyfriend or girlfriend when you both like it, but kissing [like that] is never okay with a stranger, your teacher, or a member of your family.").

Planning what sexuality skills to teach can be difficult. Collaboration between the teacher and parents is important to honor the family's values and determine what information is most relevant for an individual student. Because of the highly individualized and comprehensive nature of sexuality education, Lumley and Scotti (2001) recommend a person-centered planning approach during students' transition years so that sexuality education and related noninstructional supports can be tailored to the student's needs and vision for the future. Table 14-8 illustrates some relevant questions that can be incorporated in person-centered planning (Bambara, Koger, & Nonnemacher, 2002). Because of the highly sensitive nature of sexual issues, some questions are best discussed privately with the student and/or family rather than in the presence of an entire team. With the student's and parent permission, information may be brought back to the team for planning, as is shown for Aaron in Table 14-8.

After Aaron's last transition planning meeting, Mr. Delaney, the transition coordinator, privately asked the Williamses if they had considered Aaron's sexual needs and the possibility of sexual relationships. The Williamses admitted that they had never considered the questions given Aaron's paralysis but did say that one of their greatest fears about Aaron's transition to supported living was that someone would sexually abuse him. They shared that they did not know how to talk to Aaron about sex. When Mr. Delaney spoke with Aaron privately, Aaron clearly expressed an interest in girls but seemed resigned to the idea that having a girlfriend was not for him. After further talk, Mr. Delaney could not tell what Aaron knew or didn't know about sex. Once the Williamses thought about it, they were open to the idea that Aaron should have a normal life as possible, including girlfriends and maybe even marriage some day. Together with Mr. Delaney and Aaron, they developed a plan for Aaron's sexuality education. First, one of the school district's special education teachers would offer Aaron basic sexuality education and abuse protection education in a class format along with three other young men who needed similar training. Using slides, videotapes, discussions, and, where appropriate, role play, basic sexual facts (e.g., body changes, sexual acts), STD and pregnancy prevention, and sexual abuse protection will be presented. The teacher will also invite Aaron's college Best Buddy and young adults from Aaron's community college who did date-rape prevention training to talk about self-esteem and the body. Mr. and Mrs. Williams agreed to discuss their values about sex with their son at home. Second, the Williamses and Aaron will attend a program at Aaron's community college on "Sexuality and Disability." At this program, several couples with physical disabilities would

TABLE 14–8
Planning for Aaron's Sexuality Education: Person-Centered Questions and Outcomes

What are Aaron's dreams for the future and interests in social relationships?	• Aaron wants to live in his own apartment and hold a part-time job as he attends community college. • Aaron expresses interest in girls but doesn't believe having a girlfriend is appropriate for someone like him.
What does Aaron need to know about sexuality? What skills are needed? Any concerns?	• Aaron's family is concerned about the potential for sexual abuse. • It's unclear what Aaron knows about sex, sexual relationships, or sexual abuse protection. • Aaron needs a healthier view about the possibilities of having a girlfriend and about his self-image.
What types of sexuality education and supports are needed?	• Basic sex education • Knowledge and skills for abuse protection • Awareness of disability and intimate relationships • Specific sexuality information and training regarding physical disabilities • Support and encouragement to seek social opportunities and date

How will support be provided? Who will provide it?	• Basic sexual education and abuse protection training
	  • Mr. Burk, special education teacher
	  • Parent support at home
	• Disability awareness:
	  • Attend program at the community college
	• Specific sexuality information regarding physical disabilities:
	  • Sexuality therapist (as needed)
	  • Attend support group (maybe)
	• Support for social opportunities
	  • Community college coach
	  • Job coach
	  • Parents

share their stories about overcoming obstacles to dating, privacy, and marriage. One of the couples agreed to help Aaron make connections with a sexuality therapist with expertise in physical disabilities if he chooses to learn more specifically about sexual positions and adaptations. Third, Aaron's Best Buddy at the community college and his job coaches agreed to help Aaron make social connections at school and work. They will look for social opportunities at school clubs and parties where Aaron can meet girls, and encourage and support Aaron's social initiations (e.g., arrange for Aaron to meet a girl at the library, write phone numbers in his social book).

Skills for the Community

An important part of a student's transition to adult living is to acquire the skills needed for community settings: public safety, mobility in the community, and use of community resources like stores, banks, and restaurants. As described earlier in this chapter, teachers will

often use a combination of school and community instruction to address these skills for students who are in the middle and high school years. Students who are beyond high school age need age-appropriate alternatives to a high school building, such as a job, college classes, and an apartment with substantial community-based instruction. Younger students (elementary age) may focus more on school-based skills but also may receive some community-based instruction, depending on their individual needs and parental preferences.

Safety Skills
Community safety skills are critical. As students gain increased independence in the community, they are exposed to greater risks. Like home safety, community safety requires a wide variety of abilities, including recognizing and avoiding dangerous situations (e.g., walking away from strangers, avoiding certain streets), preventing hazards (e.g., safe street crossing), and knowing how to seek help when needed (e.g., going to a police offer, using the telephone). The same instructional

strategies used for home safety may be applied when teaching public safety. These include role play and simulations and embedding direct instruction or adding extra information about safety during other instruction of other community skills. An additional strategy involves embedding problem solving opportunities within community-based instruction. Based on procedures developed by Agran, Madison, and Brown (1995), Aaron was taught to travel to the bus stop after evening recreational activities at his community college.

As Aaron approached an unlit area of campus, he was taught to ask and respond to the following questions: (a) "What is dangerous?" ("Walking in very dark streets."), (b) "Why is it unsafe?" ("I can get mugged."), and (c) "What can I do to make it safe?" ("I can go another way.").

Some concepts of community danger and safety are abstract. Students may need to "experience" them before understanding how to respond. Using a "No-Go-Tell" strategy, Watson, Bain, and Houghton (1992) taught children with disabilities to refuse advances from a stranger, leave the area, and tell a trusted adult what happened. Once the children learned the sequence through role play, people unfamiliar to the children were employed by the researchers to approach the children in the community to determine if the children had mastered the skills. Parent permission for this approach is essential.

In another example of making abstract safety concepts real, Taber, Alberto, Hughes, and Seltzer (2002) developed a three-phase program to teach middle school students with disabilities how to use a cell phone when lost in the community. The first phase of instruction took place in the school building where the students defined being lost (i.e., not being able to find the person with whom you arrived at a community location) and then pretended to be. While pretending, the students were taught via a task analysis and system of least prompts how to use their cell phone to call for assistance. Two important steps in the task analysis were staying put and describing landmarks in the immediate surrounding so that the students' location could be identified by the person receiving the call. In the second phase, instruction took place in three community settings: grocery store, department store, and public library. In these locations, the students were required to use the calling sequence, as their instructor removed herself from the students' sight. If the student did not respond or make the call correctly within 5 minutes of being "lost," the instructor approached the student and reviewed the sequence. In

the third phase, during typical community-based instruction in the same settings, the instructor on occasion left the students' sight to assess whether they would call under more natural situations (i.e., being lost is not to be expected with each community trip). In both community phases, the students were always shadowed by another adult to ensure their safety.

In a replication study, Taber, Alberto, Seltzer, and Hughes (2003) modified emergency cell phone use for students who had difficulty dialing and/or trouble identifying when they are lost. The modifications included one-step speed dialing and answering a ringing cell phone when an adult discovered that the student was missing. When answering the phone, students were taught to provide relevant information about their immediate location (e.g., "What do you see?") so that they could be found.

Purchasing

Another important area of instruction is making purchases in the community (shopping). This may include making purchases for groceries, clothing, dining and snacking, household goods, and personal care and leisure items. Teachers need to consider four questions before teaching students to make purchases:

1. What stores does the student need to learn to use?
2. Is the goal to teach the student to make a specific purchase or a set of purchases (e.g., shop at several convenience stores)? That is, to what extent will generalization be taught?
3. To what extent will the student be taught to use money while purchasing versus using compensatory strategies (e.g., preselected money amount)?
4. How can the student gain autonomy in purchasing?

If the goal is for the student to learn to purchase a short list of items in the grocery store that is used consistently by the student's family, the teacher might focus on teaching list reading and item selection in a school simulation and then provide community-based instruction in that one store. In contrast, if the goal is for the student to be able to use a variety of stores to make a range of purchases (e.g., clothing, leisure materials, groceries), training should focus on this variation in both school- and community-based instruction.

Generalization in Purchasing General case instruction is one method of encouraging generalization across different community sites (Box 14–1 and Figure 14–3). When the goal is to teach generalized purchasing, general case planning can be used to infuse variation in simulations as well as in vivo instruction. McDonnell and Ferguson (1988) compared the relative effectiveness of general case in vivo instruction (variations that resulted by teaching in three different fast-food restaurants representing the range of stimuli) and general case simulations (variations were achieved by infusing a range of stimuli in school simulations). Because simulations should always include some community-based instruction, general case simulation was alternated each day with teaching in one community restaurant. After instruction, the students in both general case groups were assessed to see if they could generalize their purchasing skills to three new restaurants not used during instruction. Both general case in vivo and general case simulations were effective in teaching generalized purchasing skills. Students in both groups could apply their skills in novel restaurants without additional instruction.

The implication of this study is that when planning for generalized purchasing, teachers have some options. For older students whose instruction may be entirely community based, general case in vivo may make the most sense. For younger middle school- or high school–age students, teachers may select either option, with consideration given to student preferences for in-

structional settings, instructional costs, resources, and scheduling. For example, one advantage of choosing simulation is that it may be more practical for schools with limited transportation resources, and less travel time means more time in the school setting.

Computer-based video instruction is a type of simulation that may hold promise for teaching generalized purchasing (Mechling & Gast, 2003; Mechling et al., 2002). Mechling et al. (2002) videotaped three different grocery stores to teach four students with moderate intellectual disabilities to read aisle signs and locate items in a grocery store. The videotapes illustrated travel throughout the stores, the location of aisle signs, and items within the aisle. To teach aisle sign reading, when a still photograph of an aisle sign appeared on a computer screen, selecting the correct word on the screen caused the computer to show movement down the aisle for a certain item. Students were taught to shop for items by identifying the correct aisle. The results showed that the computer-based instruction taught students generalized reading of aisle signs (across different store examples) and the location of items in an actual store not used in the video instruction. With the assistance of a technology consultant, similar programs can be designed for schools so that

FIGURE 14–3

(a) Pete "preps" for his trip to the community with his teacher by making a picture shopping list and then gathering his money and ID. (b) Once at K-Mart, Pete and his teacher practice safe crossing of the street, (c) get a shopping cart, and begin searching for the items on their list. Pete searches the shelf (d) while using his picture shopping list and (e) compares the brand picture to the actual items in order to select an item that matches his list. Finally, (f) Pete finds a short line and pays for the items he has selected. Thanks to Vickie Block of Charlottesville High School and Deb Morris of Walker School and their students for sharing their work with us.

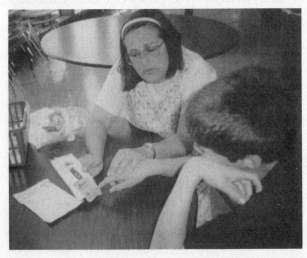

a

b

FIGURE 14–3 (*Continued*)

c

e

d

f

older students could learn grocery shopping skills while taking computer classes with peers.

Teaching Money Use A second aspect of teaching purchasing is to help students know how to use their money.

Recommendations for teaching money skills can be found in chapter 13, including supplying students with a preselected amount of money (McDonnell & Horner, 1985) or teaching a "one more than" money counting strategy (Test, Howell, Burkhart, & Beroth, 1993).

To gain autonomy in purchasing, students need to know how to use money, how to plan their purchases, and how to perform the steps of a purchasing routine (Figure 14–3). To teach students to plan purchases, Sandknop, Schuster, Wolery, and Cross (1992) taught students to select the lower-priced item from among grocery prices. Using constant time delay, students learned to look at two prices on a number line that was written vertically to determine which was "lower." Across training phases, students learned to compare not only the first digit of the price but then the second, third, and fourth. Frederick-Dugan, Test, and Varn (1991) developed a general case analysis of three types of purchases: food, clothing, and hygiene items. The instructor showed the student pictures of items from each category and a price up to $20. The students determined if they could buy the items by using a calculator. The instructor used progressive time delay to teach the students to compare the price to the money they had to determine if it could or could not be purchased.

Autonomy in Purchasing Autonomy can also be encouraged by teaching students to make a purchase with little to no teacher assistance. To be successful, the student may need social skills and the skills of making the purchase at the register. Westling, Floyd,

and Carr (1990) taught these social skills as part of a purchasing program. These social skills are shown in Table 14–9 in a program designed for Julia to purchase items at discount department stores. By learning skills such as asking for help and being polite, Julia is more likely to have positive experiences when shopping alone or with friends.

Sometimes when shopping, people need to ask for help. Chadsey-Rusch et al. (1993) developed a general case approach to teach students to request help in community settings. For example, students might ask for help to negotiate curbs in getting into the store. Or, like Julia's example in Table 14–9, students may learn to ask for help across a variety of situations encountered in the store (e.g., finding the store section, finding the item on the shelf). With these social and communication skills, students can learn to navigate community routines like purchasing with no more teacher assistance than they need or want.

Community Leisure
Besides dining out, another enjoyable community activity is participating in leisure activities. These activities may include going to concerts or movies, participating in fitness classes, walking in the park, participating in clubs, and going to special community events. The

TABLE 14–9
Task Analysis of Shopping Skills

Student: Julia	Skill: Purchasing at discount department stores (e.g., K-Mart, Wal-Mart)
Purchasing step	**Related social skill**
1. Enter door	Wait turn if needed
2. Go to correct store section	Ask help to find correct section Say "thank you" when given help
3. Find correct shelf	Ask help if can't find item on shelf Say "thank you" when given help
4. Select correct item(s)	
5. Go to register	Wait turn at checkout counter Keep cart from bumping others
6. Put item on counter	Greet cashier
7. Take out money	
8. Use "next dollar strategy"	
9. Give money to cashier	
10. Put change and receipt away	
11. Pick up purchased item	Say "good-bye" or "thanks"
12. Exit store	Wait turn at door to exit

Note: From D. L. Westling, J. Floyd., & D. Carr, 1990. Effects of single setting versus multiple setting training on learning to shop in a department store. *American Journal on Mental Retardation, 94,* 616–624. Copyright (1990) by American Association on Mental Retardation. Adapted with permission.

biggest challenge in leisure instruction is determining where and how to teach so that students learn skills without losing the chance to make friends and have fun. One opportunity to provide intensive leisure instruction in inclusive contexts for school-age students is a school- or community-sponsored summer program. Hamre-Nietupski et al. (1992) described an approach to extended school year programming that focused on inclusive leisure activities. An extended school year program is a public school service that is offered to students with severe disabilities beyond the typical 180-day school year in order to prevent skill regression. Not all students with severe disabilities qualify for these services, but those who do sometimes end up in segregated summer programs unless inclusive leisure options are considered. Hamre-Nietupski et al. (1992) selected local playground programs, the swimming pool, and weeklong camps. The special educators planned jointly with the recreational staff to adapt activities for increased participation. For example, T-ball was used during softball, and a large dowel was used for roasting hot dogs.

In addition to summer programming, school and community extracurricular activities provide opportunities for leisure instruction. For example, many schools have music groups, pep clubs, computer clubs, and intramural sports. Through collaboration with the sponsors of these activities and the student's caregivers, arrangements can be developed for students to have access to these opportunities. Important considerations in planning these activities include (a) assessing and honoring individual preferences for activities, (b) teaching individuals to self-initiate leisure activities, and (c) providing instruction or support to participate in inclusive settings.

Honoring Choice in Leisure Activities Most people pursue leisure activities for relaxation, fun, friendship, or fitness. An important aspect of leisure activities that makes them fun and relaxing is that they are optional. People choose what to do with their leisure time, including the choice to do nothing! Similarly, individuals with severe disabilities need the opportunity to choose how to spend leisure time. While some will be able to make these choices by telling others what they want to do or by initiating activities on their own, others need the opportunity to sample new leisure options to decide which to pursue. Sometimes these choices can then be expressed through selecting pictures of the activities or by using some other communication system (e.g., signing, communication board).

A challenge some teachers face is understanding the activity preferences of students who do not have a formal system of communication. Research on preference assessment with students who do not have symbolic communication has focused on selecting objects that can then be used or consumed (Lohrmann-O'Rourke et al., 2000). In contrast, selecting an activity requires using some type of symbolic representation of the options. Browder, Cooper, and Lim (1998) demonstrated how to teach using symbols to choose leisure activities. In a three-phase study, they first assessed participants' preferences for activities at community sites and in a day program by timing the duration of their participation in activities at each site. Once clear preferences emerged, they taught the participants to select an object to represent each activity. Using massed trials and a time delay prompting system, the instructor taught the participants to select a golf ball for golf, a library card to go to the library, a name tag for a club, or shoes for an aerobics class. This instruction occurred immediately before the leisure activity. Because the focus of the study was the choice of leisure settings (community versus day program), participants learned to associate different objects with the same activity in different settings. For example, an orange golf ball was chosen for the day program site and a white golf ball for the community golf course. Once the participants mastered associating the object with the activity, the third phase of the intervention was to give the participants a choice between settings (e.g., orange versus white golf ball). The participant was then given assistance (e.g., transportation and an instructor) to go to the chosen setting and engage in the activity. Interestingly, all participants consistently chose the community-based activities.

We recommend teaching objects associated with different leisure activities that are *all* community based. For example, an empty popcorn container or a ticket might be used for the movies, a baseball cap of a favorite team might be selected for attending a sports event, or a program might be used for the theater or a concert. Whatever object is chosen, the student may need direct instruction for several months to master the association between the object and the activity before using the object to make a meaningful choice. Actual visits to the leisure settings along with photos of the student participating in the activity can be used to help teach this association.

Teaching Self-Initiation of Leisure Activities The second consideration in planning instruction for leisure activities is to encourage the students' self-directed participation. The pictorial self-management that Pierce and Schriebman (1994) developed to teach children with autism to self-initiate daily living activities might be adapted for leisure activities. For example, students could be taught to use a photo book to select and begin an activity. Students who can use picture symbols may also be able to learn to self-schedule leisure activities. Bambara and Ager (1992) taught adults with developmental disabilities to use pictures to self-schedule leisure activities for the upcoming week. The participants also initiated contact with staff to request any necessary support (e.g., an escort or transportation). The pictures used were from the Attainment Company's "Plan Your Day Curriculum." Devine, Malley, Sheldon, Datillo, and Gast (1997) also evaluated an intervention to teach adults to initiate leisure activities. Similar to Bambara and Ager (1992), they taught participants to use a calendar and pictures for self-scheduling. They also compared (a) having the participants put a reminder on their wall calendar to (b) giving participants a morning phone call to prompt the selected activity. Both prompting methods increased participants' self-initiation of community leisure activities.

Instruction for Participation in Leisure Activities

Some students will benefit from direct instruction in the activity. For example, Zhang, Gast, Horvat, and Datillo (1995) taught adolescents with severe disabilities "lifetime sport skills," including bowling, overhand throwing, and short-distance putting. The instructor employed a physical prompt and constant time delay to fade teacher assistance. All participants mastered the sport skills. Similarly, Bolton, Belfiore, Lalli, and Skinner (1994) taught adults with severe disabilities to putt in golf. They used stimulus fading by introducing guide boards for the golf ball that were then faded in size until the participant could get the ball in the hole with no guide.

Leisure skills can also be taught using self-directed learning strategies. LeGrice and Blampied (1994) employed videotaped prompting to teach adolescents with moderate cognitive disabilities to operate a video recorder and personal computer. To teach the students to use the video to self-instruct, the instructor gave a nonspecific verbal prompt (e.g., "What's next?") and showed the videotaped step. If a student did not perform the step, the video was rewound, and the step was shown again until the student performed the step

using the video. Self-management strategies can be especially useful for fitness activities. Ellis, Cress, and Spellman (1990) taught individuals to increase their duration of walking in either hallways or on a treadmill with self-monitoring and self-reinforcement. During hall walking, the participant carried batons (like relay racers in the Olympics) and discarded one after each lap. When they had discarded all batons, they gave themselves a sticker in a notebook. Using a changing criterion design, the instructor helped the participants increase the number of batons carried (laps walked) across time. Similarly, in using the treadmill, the participants learned to set the timer for longer periods of time across weeks of training.

Since many leisure skills are performed with family members or at home, it may also be beneficial to get interested family members involved in instruction of leisure skills. For example, Wall and Gast (1997) taught caregivers (i.e., adult sibling, parent, houseparent) to teach leisure skills to adolescents. The caregivers learned to use task analyses and constant time delay to teach activities like horseshoes, checkers, croquet, board games, and turning the radio to a preferred station.

If developed well, leisure instruction need not impede the social benefits of participating in inclusive leisure settings. Vandercook (1991) taught adolescents two activities that were popular with youth in their school (bowling and pinball). After determining the least intrusive effective prompt for each student, the teacher instructed the students in the bowling and pinball skills at the community bowling alley. Once a week, students bowled with peers who were nondisabled. During this weekly bowling time with peers, the teacher did not interact with the dyad or prompt performance of bowling and pinball. As participants increased their bowling and pinball skills with the teacher, they generalized these skills to their weekly time with a peer. The peers also indicated a significant increase in their scores on attitude toward individuals with disabilities.

Breen and Haring (1991) evaluated how important it was for the peers with disabilities to have direct training in the leisure activity selected for peer inclusion. They selected eight computer games and provided intensive training in four of the games before setting opportunities for the adolescents with disabilities to play the games with their peers who were nondisabled. The instructor used a task analysis and least prompts system to teach the four trained games. Using an alternating treatment design, they found that social initiations, game satisfaction, and peer satisfaction were all higher when playing the trained games versus the untrained games. This study and the work of Vandercook (1991) illustrate the potential need to provide intensive teacher training as an adjunct to opportunities to engage in activities with peers.

While both of these studies trained and then simply observed peer interaction, some individuals with more severe disabilities may need ongoing, intensive support to participate in the leisure activity. When this occurs, the teacher may be able to transfer support to peers in the context of the activity. For example, Cooper and Browder (1997) trained adults with severe disabilities to participate in a water exercise class at the YMCA. Once each participant performed the exercise response with little prompting, the instructor encouraged nondisabled adult peers also taking the class to exercise beside the participant and offer occasional verbal prompting.

Another way to promote self-initiated leisure skills is to teach students an entire leisure routine, core task steps plus related extension and enrichment skills (Brown et al., 1993). Sometimes students do not self-initiate a leisure activity because they have learned only one component of the activity (e.g., the core steps of how to bowl) rather than the entire routine (including initiating and terminating) and related social and communication skills. Schleien, Certo, and Muccino (1984) illustrated how to teach an entire routine of using a bowling alley to a student with severe mental retardation. Instruction focused not only on how to bowl but also on how to purchase a drink and use the vending machine. The participant generalized these skills to three other bowling alleys without additional instruction. In another example, Taylor, McKelvey, and Sisson (1993) taught the entire routine for two skills (ordering a pizza and renting a video) to individuals with multiple disabilities (visual and physical impairments, mental retardation). For ordering the pizza, the skill cluster included using the phone, interacting with the delivery person, cutting and serving the pizza, and cleaning up. The students were also taught problem-solving skills. In renting a video, the students learned to ask the counter person to recommend a video if they could not find one that they liked or to help them find one on the shelf. Both skill clusters were taught in school simulations using a system of least prompts and "props" (e.g., pizza box, video boxes, phone) along with in vivo training in the community.

Banking

To participate in many community activities, students will need to acquire money management skills. While chapter 13 explains how to instruct money skills, this section describes approaches to teaching bill paying and banking. LaCampagne and Cipani (1987) tested a method for teaching adults with disabilities to pay their bills. Instructional materials included a checkbook, check recorder, several real bills with their payment envelope (e.g., electric company, credit card, telephone bill), and a calculator. The participants learned to perform the task-analyzed steps to write a check, record the amount in their checkbook, and put the payment in the payment envelope. Zencius, Davis, and Cuvo (1990) taught similar skills but used a personalized system of instruction in which students could proceed through learning the materials at their own pace.

Some students will benefit from knowing how to use the bank. McDonnell and Ferguson (1989) taught high school students with moderate disabilities both to use an automated teller and to cash checks in a bank while also comparing the use of a decreasing prompt hierarchy with constant time delay. All instruction was community based. Both methods of prompting were effective, but the decreasing prompts were slightly more efficient. Using an automatic teller also can be taught in school through simulated instruction. Shafer et al. (1986) made a simulated automatic teller from plywood. They found that the simulated instruction was more private and prevented the problem of the machine confiscating the card when too many mistakes were made. Bourbeau, Sowers, and Close (1986) developed a comparable simulation in a school workroom. The participants mastered using the simulated automated teller and generalized their skills to a real machine in the community. In contrast, Shafer et al. (1986) found that generalization to the community automated teller was incomplete until some community-based instruction was conducted.

Community Mobility

Community mobility involves pedestrian safety, being able to use public transportation, and finding locations in the community. The research on street crossing demonstrates the clear advantages that in vivo instruction has over classroom simulations (Marchetti, McCartney, Drain, Hooper, & Dix, 1983; Matson, 1980; Page, Iwata, & Neef, 1976). For some students, the most important street crossing skill to master is crossing streets with an escort (a partial participation goal). The task analysis would address walking or propelling a wheelchair near the escort, stopping at curbs, crossing when given a verbal or physical cue, and crossing without stopping in the street. For other students, the outcome is independent street crossing. When independence is the goal, it is important to take a general case approach to teach the variations of streets encountered in a particular community (Horner, Jones, & Williams, 1985). For example, the range of stimulus variation the student may encounter includes the speed of cars, the number of cars, changes in lights, the type of pedestrian signals (e.g., words, pictures), the number of lanes, traffic directions (e.g., one way or two way), the angle of crossing (e.g., straight, diagonal), and the type of street (e.g., stop sign, traffic light). Horner et al. (1985) trained on 10 different streets daily and probed with untrained streets until it was clear that participants could cross a variety of streets safely.

In Aaron's pedestrian program, he is taught to indicate when it is safe to cross; to choose to operate his motorized wheelchair alone or to request assistance, depending on the type of street and his own preference at the time; to steer his wheelchair safely near other pedestrians using the sidewalk; and to choose safe routes to travel.

Some individuals with severe disabilities need instruction to learn to walk from one location to another without stopping, wandering, or sitting down on the ground. For example, Spears, Rusch, York, and Lilly (1981) taught a boy to walk from his school bus to his classroom. They used pacing prompts (verbal reminders) to encourage the boy to keep walking without pausing. Teachers might consider having the student walk with peers to establish pacing. Another pedestrian skill is to find the way to a given location. Finding locations in some communities is complex and may require recognition of key landmarks. Singleton, Schuster, and Ault (1995) taught students to recognize community signs (e.g., "barber," "Denny's," "KOA") and their meaning. For example, students learned that a barber gives a haircut. Although not a focus of their instruction, recognition of community signs could be combined with teaching individuals a familiar route, such as walking to work or to the local community recreation center.

In some contexts, getting to these desired locations requires using public transportation, such as the bus or subway. Bus riding can be taught with some simulated practice. For example, slides taken in the local community can help students learn key landmarks to know when to get off the bus (Neef, Iwata, & Page, 1978; Robinson, Griffith, McComish, & Swasbrook, 1984). Such simulations do not always produce generalization

TABLE 14–10
Task Analysis for Teaching Bus Riding with Simulation

Students: Julia, Tom, Sarah	Skill: Bus riding
Step of task analysis	Video, slide, or picture simulation
1. Walk to bus stop	Pictures of nearby bus stops
2. Wait at bus stop	Show people waiting for bus
3. Identify correct bus	Pictures of buses that come to that stop
4. Signal bus to stop	Show person waving hand
5. Wait in line to enter bus	Show people in line
6. Enter front door of bus	Pictures of both bus doors
7. Give driver bus pass	Show driver and have real passes
8. Sit in empty seat or stand	Show seats that are empty and full
9. Identify destination	Pictures of landmarks
10. Pull cord for stop	Picture of cord
11. Exit rear door	Picture of inside bus doors
12. Move away from bus	Show person correct (moving away) and wrong (walking in front of bus)

to actual buses (Coon, Vogelsberg, & Williams, 1981); in contrast, individuals with severe disabilities can learn bus riding when all instruction is community based (Sowers, Rusch, & Hudson, 1979). Table 14–10 provides a response sequence for teaching bus riding that uses simulations as an adjunct to community-based instruction. To practice bus riding, the teacher shows slides (or video clips) for each response in the task analysis.

> *When teaching Julia and some classmates to take the city bus to the mall, the teacher showed a video clip or slides of bus stops near the school. When the correct bus stop was shown, students were encouraged to raise their hands. The teacher asked one student to verbalize what they do: "We get on the bus by Jack's Diner." She then showed video clips or slides of the various buses that stop at that destination. When the bus that says "West Mall" was shown, students again raised their hands, and someone stated the step. This procedure continued until all steps were rehearsed. Next, the students applied these skills in an actual trip to the mall.*

Summary

This chapter describes how daily living and community skills can be taught in ways that honor and encourage self-determination and general education inclusion. Based on the research literature to date, some community-based instruction or probes are needed to ensure that skills learned through school opportunities or simulations generalize to real settings. For students who are beyond the typical school age, most of this instruction will probably take place in the community. Evidence-based procedures were described to teach skills for home and the community that encourage student-directed learning, incorporate peer instruction and interaction when possible, and use powerful teaching strategies, such as constant time delay and least intrusive prompting.

Suggested Activities

1. Plan a school schedule for a student like Aaron, who was described in this chapter. Assume that because Aaron is 20 years old, he will receive instruction in community contexts. If Aaron has a part-time job

that lasts 3 hours per day, how and where will he spend the rest of his 6-hour school day? Who will give job and community instruction?
2. Given the person-centered planning for Julia shown in Table 14–1, brainstorm a list of leisure activities. Consider her preference for being with her middle school friends. How could some of the community and home skills she needs be taught in the context of these activities?
3. Identify two community activities for Rico. What method of prompting might be used in teaching these skills to Rico? How can you avoid stigmatizing Rico while teaching in the community? Also make a list of several ways that choice making can be added to community-based instruction of these activities with Rico. How will you encourage Rico to make choices while in community activities? What advantages might this choice making have for Rico?

References

Agran, M., Madison, D., & Brown, C. (1995). Teaching supported employees to prevent work injuries. *Journal of Vocational Rehabilitation, 5,* 33–42.

Alberto, P. A., Sharpton, W. R., Briggs, A., & Stright, M. H. (1986). Facilitating task acquisition through the use of a self-operated auditory prompting system. *Journal of the Association for Persons with Severe Handicaps, 11,* 85–91.

Alcantara, P. R. (1994). Effects of a videotape instructional package on the purchasing skills of children with autism. *Exceptional Children, 6,* 40–55.

Anderson, M. D., Sherman, J. A., Sheldon, J. B., & McAdam, D. (1997). Picture activity schedules and engagement of adults with mental retardation in a group home. *Research in Developmental Disabilities, 18,* 231–250.

Arnold-Reid, G. S., Schloss, P. J., & Alper, S. (1997). Teaching meal planning to youth with mental retardation in natural settings. *Remedial and Special Education, 18*(3), 166–173.

Bambara, L. M., & Ager, C. (1992). Use of self-scheduling to promote self-directed leisure activity in home and community settings. *Journal of the Association for Persons with Severe Handicaps, 17,* 67–76.

Bambara, L. M., Cole, C., & Koger, F. (1998). Translating self-determination concepts into support for adults with severe disabilities. *Journal of the Association for Persons with Severe Handicaps, 23,* 27–37.

Bambara, L. M., & Gomez, O. N. (2001). Using a self-instruction package to teach complex problem-solving skills to adults with moderate and severe disabilities. *Education and Training in Mental Retardation, 36,* 386–400.

Bambara, L. M., & Koger, F. (1996). *Innovations: AAMR Research to Practice Series—Opportunities for daily choice making.* Washington, DC: American Association on Mental Retardation.

Bambara, L. M., Koger, F., Katzer, T., & Davenport, T. (1995). Embedding choice in daily routines: An experimental case study. *Journal of the Association of Persons with Severe Handicaps, 20*, 185–195.

Bambara, L. L., Koger, F., & Nonnemacher, S. (2002, December). *Using a person-centered approach to support sexuality.* Paper presented at the 27th annual meeting of the TASH, Boston.

Blanchett, W. J., & Wolfe, P. S. (2002). A review of sexuality education curricula: Meeting the sexuality education needs of individuals with moderate and severe intellectual disabilities. *Research and Practice for Persons with Severe Disabilities, 27,* 43–57.

Bolton, J. L., Belfiore, P. J., Lalli, J. S., & Skinner, C. H. (1994). The effects of stimulus modification on putting accuracy for adults with severe or profound mental retardation. *Education and Training in Mental Retardation and Developmental Disabilities, 29,* 236–242.

Bourbeau, P. E., Sowers, J., & Close, D. W. (1986). An experimental analysis of generalization of banking skills from classroom to bank settings in the community. *Education and Training of the Mentally Retarded, 21,* 98–106.

Breen, C. G., & Haring, T. G. (1991). Effects of contextual competence on social initiations. *Journal of Applied Behavior Analysis, 24,* 337–348.

Briggs, A., Alberto, P., Sharpton, W., Berlin, K., McKinley, C., & Ritts, C. (1990). Generalized use of a self-operated audio prompt system. *Education and Training in Mental Retardation, 25,* 381–389.

Browder, D. M., Cooper, K. J., & Lim, L. (1998). Teaching adults with severe disabilities to express their choice of settings for leisure activities. *Education and Training in Mental Retardation and Developmental Disabilities, 33,* 228–238.

Browder, D. M., Hines, C., McCarthy, L. J., & Fees, J. (1984). A treatment package for increasing sight word recognition for use in daily living skills. *Education and Training of the Mentally Retarded, 19,* 191–200.

Browder, D. M., & Minarovic, T. J. (2000). Utilizing sight words in self-instruction training for employees with moderate mental retardation in competitive jobs. *Education and Training in Mental Retardation and Developmental Disabilities, 35,* 78–89.

Browder, D. M., Snell, M. E., & Wildonger, B. A. (1988). Simulation and community-based instruction of vending machines with time delay. *Education and Training in Mental Retardation, 23,* 175–185.

Brown, F., Belz, P., Corsi, L., & Wenig, B. (1993). Choice diversity for people with severe disabilities. *Education and Training in Mental Retardation, 28,* 318–326.

Bryan, L. C., & Gast, D. L. (2000). Teaching on-task and on-schedule behaviors to high functioning children with autism via picture activity schedules. *Journal of Autism and Developmental Disorders, 30,* 553–567.

Chadsey-Rusch, J., Drasgow, E., Reinoehl, B., Hallet, J., & Collet-Klingenberg, L. (1993). Using general-case instruction to teach spontaneous and generalized requests for assistance to learners with severe disabilities. *Journal of the Association for Persons with Severe Handicaps, 18,* 177–187.

Cole, C. M., & Levinson, T. R. (2002). Effects of within-activity choices on the challenging behavior of children with severe disabilities. *Journal of Positive Behavior Interventions, 4,* 29–37.

Collins, B. C., Branson, T. A., & Hall, M. (1995). Teaching generalized reading of cooking product labels to adolescents with mental disabilities through the use of key words taught by peer tutors. *Education and Training in Mental Retardation and Developmental Disabilities, 30,* 65–75.

Collins, B. C., Wolery, M., & Gast, D. L. (1991). A survey of safety concerns for students with special needs. *Education and Training in Mental Retardation, 26,* 305–318.

Coon, M. E., Vogelsberg, R. T., & Williams, W. (1981). Effects of classroom public transportation instruction on generalization to the natural environment. *Journal of the Association for the Severely Handicapped, 6,* 46–53.

Cooper, K. J., & Browder, D. M. (1997). The use of a personal trainer to enhance participation of older adults with severe disabilities in community water exercise classes. *Journal of Behavioral Education, 7,* 421–434.

Cooper, K. J., & Browder, D. M. (1998). Enhancing choice and participation for adults with severe disabilities in community-based instruction. *Journal of the Association for Persons with Severe Handicaps, 23,* 252–260.

Copeland, S. R., & Hughes, C. (2000). Acquisition of a picture prompt strategy to increase independent performance. *Education and Training in Mental Retardation, 35*(3), 294–305.

Cuvo, A. J., Jacobi, E., & Sipko, R. (1981). Teaching laundry skills to mentally retarded students. *Education and Training of the Mentally Retarded, 16,* 54–64.

Davies, D. K., Stock, S. E., & Wehmeyer, M. L. (2002). Enhancing independent task performance for individuals with mental retardation through use of handheld self-directed visual and audio prompting system. *Education and Training in Mental Retardation and Developmental Disabilities, 37,* 209–218.

Davies, D. K., Stock, S. E., & Wehmeyer, M. L. (2003). A palmtop computer-based intelligent aid for individuals with intellectual disabilities to increase independent decision making. *Research and Practice for Persons with Severe Disabilities, 28,* 182–193.

Dennis, R. E., & Giangreco, M. F. (1996). Creating conversations: Reflections on cultural sensitivity in family interviewing. *Exceptional Children, 63,* 103–116.

Devine, M. A., Malley, S., Sheldon, K., Datillo, J., & Gast, D. L. (1997). Promoting initiation of community leisure participation for adults with mental retardation. *Education and Training in Mental Retardation and Developmental Disabilities, 32,* 241–254.

Dunlap, G., dePerczel, C. S., Clarke, S., Wilson, D., Wright, S., White, R., & Gomez, A. (1994). Choice making to promote adaptive behavior for students with emotional and behavioral challenges. *Journal of Applied Behavior Analysis, 27,* 505–518.

Ellis, D. N., Cress, P. J., & Spellman, C. R. (1990). Using timers and lap counters to promote self-management of independent exercise in adolescents with mental retardation. *Education and Training in Mental Retardation, 27,* 51–59.

Epps, S., Stern, R. J., & Horner, R. H. (1990). Comparison of simulation training on self and using a doll for teaching generalized menstrual care to women with severe mental retardation. *Research in Developmental Disabilities, 11,* 37–66.

Ferguson, D. L., & Baumgart, D. (1991). Partial participation revisited. *Journal of the Association for Persons with Severe Handicaps, 16,* 218–227.

Ford, A., & Mirenda, P. (1984). Community instruction: A natural cues and correction model. *Journal of the Association for Persons with Severe Handicaps, 9,* 79–88.

Forest, M., & Pearpoint, J. C. (1992). Putting all kids on the MAP. *Educational Leadership,* 50, 26–31.

Frank, A. R., Wacker, D. P., Berg, W. K., & McMahon, C. M. (1985). Teaching selected microcomputer skills to retarded students via picture prompts. *Journal of Applied Behavior Analysis, 18,* 179–185.

Frederick-Dugan, A., Test, D. W., & Varn, L. (1991). Acquisition and generalization of purchasing skills using a calculator by students who are mentally retarded. *Education and Training in Mental Retardation, 26,* 381–387.

Gardill, M. C., & Browder, D. M. (1995). Teaching stimulus classes to encourage independent purchasing by students with severe behavior disorders. *Education and Training in Mental Retardation and Developmental Disabilities, 30,* 254–264.

Garwood, M., & McCabe, M. P. (2000). Impact of sex education programs on sexual knowledge and feelings of men with mild intellectual disability. *Education and Training in Mental Retardation and Developmental Disabilities, 35,* 269–283.

Gast, D. L., Doyle, P. M., Wolery, M., Ault, M. J., & Farmer, J. A. (1991). Assessing the acquisition of incidental information by secondary-age students with mental retardation: Comparison of response prompting strategies. *American Journal on Mental Retardation, 96,* 63–80.

Gast, D. L., Winterling, V., Wolery, M., & Farmer, J. A. (1992). Teaching first-aid skills to students with moderate handicaps in small group instruction. *Education and Treatment of Children, 15,* 101–124.

Griffen, A. K., Wolery, M., & Schuster, J. W. (1992). Triadic instruction of chained food preparation responses: Acquisition and observational learning. *Journal of Applied Behavior Analysis, 25,* 257–279.

Grigal, M., Neubert, D. A., Moon, M. S. (2001). Public school programs for students with significant disabilities in post-secondary settings. *Education and Training in Mental Retardation and Developmental Disabilities, 36,* 244–254.

Hall, M. G., Schuster, J. W., Wolery, M., & Gast, D. L. (1992). Teaching chained skills in a non-school setting using a divided half instructional format. *Journal of Behavioral Education, 2,* 257–279.

Hamre-Nietupski, S., Nietupski, J., Krajewski, L., Moravec, J., Riehle, R., McDongal, J., Sensor, K., & Cantine-Stull, P. (1992). Enhancing integration during the summer: Combined educational and community recreation options for students with severe disabilities. *Education and Training in Mental Retardation, 27,* 68–74.

Haney, J. L., & Jones, R. T. (1982). Programming maintenance as a major component of a community-centered preventive effort: Escape from fire. *Behavior Therapy, 13,* 47–62.

Heward, W. L. (1997). Self-management. In J. O. Cooper, T. E. Heron, & W. L. Heward (Eds.), *Applied behavior analysis* (pp. 515–549). Columbus, OH: Merrill.

Hingsburger, D., & Tough, S. (2002). Healthy sexuality: Attitudes, systems, and policies. *Research and Practice for Persons with Severe Disabilities, 27,* 8–17.

Holburn, S., & Vietze, P. M. (2002). *Person-centered planning: Research, practice, and future directions.* Baltimore: Paul H. Brookes.

Horner, R. H., Jones, D. N., & Williams, J. A. (1985). A functional approach to teaching generalized street crossing. *Journal of the Association for Persons with Severe Handicaps, 10,* 71–78.

Horner, R. H., McDonnell, J. J., & Bellamy, G. T. (1986). Teaching generalized skills: General case instruction in simulation and community settings. In R. H. Horner, L. H. Meyer, & H. D. Fredericks (Eds.), *Education of learners with severe handicaps: Exemplary service strategies* (pp. 289–314). Baltimore: Paul H. Brookes.

Horner, R. H., Williams, J. A., & Steveley, J. D. (1987). Acquisition of generalized telephone use by students with moderate and severe mental retardation. *Research in Developmental Disabilities, 8,* 229–248.

Hughes, C. (1992). Teaching self-instruction utilizing multiple exemplars to produce generalized problem-solving by individuals with severe mental retardation. *American Journal on Mental Retardation, 97,* 302–314.

Hughes, C., Hugo, K., & Blatt, J. (1996). Self-instructional intervention for teaching generalized problem-solving within a functional task sequence. *American Journal on Mental Retardation, 100,* 565–579.

Irvine, B. A., Erickson, A. M., Singer, G., & Stahlberg, D. (1992). A coordinated program to transfer self-management skills from school to home. *Education and Training in Mental Retardation, 27,* 241–254.

Johnson, R., & Miltenberger, R. G. (1996). The direct and generalized effects of self-instructions and picture prompts on vocational task performance. *Behavioral Interventions, 11,* 19–34.

Jones, G. Y., & Collins, B. C. (1997). Teaching microwave skills to adults with disabilities: Acquisition of nutrition and safety facts presented as non-targeted information. *Journal of Developmental and Physical Disabilities, 9,* 59–78.

LaCampagne, J., & Cipani, E. (1987). Training adults with mental retardation to pay bills. *Mental Retardation, 25,* 293–303.

Lalli, J. S., Mace, F. C., Browder, D. M., & Brown, D. K. (1989). Comparison of treatments to teach number matching skills to adults with moderate mental retardation. *Mental Retardation, 27,* 75–83.

LeGrice, B., & Blampied, N. M. (1994). Training pupils with intellectual disability to operate educational technology using video prompting. *Education and Training in Mental Retardation and Developmental Disabilities, 29,* 321–330.

Lesseliers, J., & Van Hove, G. (2002). Barriers to the development of intimate relationships and the expression of sexuality among people with developmental disabilities: Their perceptions. *Research and Practice for Persons with Severe Disabilities, 27,* 69–81.

Lohrmann-O'Rourke, S., Browder, D. M., & Brown, F. (2000). Guidelines for conducting socially valid systematic preference assessments. *Journal of the Association for Persons with Severe Handicaps, 25*(1), 42–53.

Lovett, D. L., & Haring, K. A. (1989). The effects of self-management training on the daily living of adults with mental retardation. *Education and Training in Mental Retardation, 24,* 306–323.

Lumley, V. A., Miltenberger, R. G., Long, E. S., Rapp, J. T., & Roberts, J. A. (1998). Evaluation of a sexual abuse prevention program for adults with mental retardation. *Journal of Applied Behavior Analysis, 31,* 91–101.

Lumley, V. A., & Scotti, J. R. (2001). Supporting the sexuality of adults with mental retardation: Current status and future directions. *Journal of Positive Behavior Interventions, 3,* 91-101.

Marchand-Martella, N. E., Martella, R. C., Agran, M., Salzberg, C. L., Young, K. R., & Morgan, D. (1992a). Generalized effects of a peer-delivered first aid program for students with moderate intellectual disabilities. *Journal of Applied Behavior Analysis, 25,* 841-851.

Marchand-Martella, N. E., Martella, R. C., Christensen, A. M., Agran, M., & Young, K. R. (1992b). Teaching a first aid skill to students with disabilities using two training programs. *Education and Treatment of Children, 15,* 15-31.

Marchetti, A. G., McCartney, J. R., Drain, S., Hooper, M., & Dix, J. (1983). Pedestrian skills training for mentally retarded adults: Comparison of training in two settings. *Mental Retardation, 21,* 107-110.

Martin, J. E., & Marshall, L. H. (1995). Choice Maker: A comprehensive self-determination transition program. *Intervention in School and Clinic, 30,* 147-156.

Martin, J. E., Rusch, F. R., James, V. L., Decker, P. J., & Trytol, K. A. (1982). The use of picture cues to establish self-control in the preparation of complex meals by mentally retarded adults. *Applied Research in Mental Retardation, 3,* 105-119.

Matson, J. L. (1980). A controlled group study of pedestrian-skill training for the mentally retarded. *Behavior Research and Therapy, 18,* 99-106.

McCabe, M. P., & Cummins, R. A. (1996). The sexual knowledge, experience, feelings, and needs of people with mild intellectual disability. *Education and Training in Mental Retardation and Developmental Disabilities, 31,* 13-21.

McDonnell, J. J., & Ferguson, B. (1988). A comparison of general case in vivo and general case simulation plus in vivo training. *Journal of the Association for Persons with Severe Handicaps, 13,* 116-124.

McDonnell, J. J., & Ferguson, B. (1989). A comparison of time delay and decreasing prompt hierarchy strategies in teaching banking skills to students with moderate handicaps. *Journal of Applied Behavior Analysis, 22,* 85-91.

McDonnell, J. J., & Horner, R. H. (1985). Effects of in vivo versus simulation-plus-in vivo training on the acquisition and generalization of grocery item selection by high school students with severe handicaps. *Analysis and Intervention in Developmental Disabilities, 5,* 85-91.

McDonnell, J. J., Horner, R. H., & Williams, J. A. (1984). Comparison of three strategies for teaching generalized grocery purchasing of high school students with severe handicaps. *Journal of the Association for Persons with Severe Handicaps, 12,* 123-133.

McDonnell, J. J., & McFarland, S. (1988). A comparison of forward and concurrent chaining strategies in teaching laundromat skills to students with severe handicaps. *Research and Intervention in Developmental Disabilities, 9,* 177-194.

McWilliams, R., Nietupski, J., & Hamre-Nietupski, S. (1990). Teaching complex activities to students with moderate handicaps through the forward chaining of shorter total cycle response sequences. *Education and Training in Mental Retardation, 25,* 292-298.

Mechling, L. C., & Gast, D. L. (1997). Combination audio/visual self-prompting system for teaching chained tasks to students with intellectual disabilities. *Education and Training in Mental Retardation and Developmental Disabilities, 32,* 138-153.

Mechling, L. C., & Gast, D. L. (2003). Multi-media instruction to teach grocery word associations and store locations: A study of generalization. *Education and Training in Developmental Disabilities, 38,* 62-76.

Mechling, L. C., Gast, D. L., & Langone, J. (2002). Computer-based video instruction to teach persons with moderate intellectual disabilities to read grocery aisle signs and locate items. *Journal of Special Education, 35,* 224-240.

Miller, U. C., & Test, D. W. (1989). A comparison of constant time delay and most-to-least prompts in teaching laundry skills to students with moderate retardation. *Education and Training of the Mentally Retarded, 24,* 363-370.

Morningstar, M. E., & Lattin, D. L. (2004). Transition to adulthood. In C. H. Kennedy & E. M. Horn (Eds.), *Including students with severe disabilities* (pp. 282-309). Boston: Allyn & Bacon.

Mount, B. (2000). *Person-centered planning.* New York: Graphic Futures.

Neef, N. A., Iwata, B. A., & Page, T. A. (1978). Public transportation training: In vivo versus classroom instruction. *Journal of Applied Behavior Analysis, 11,* 331-344.

Neef, N. A., Lensbower, S., Hockersmith, I., DePalma, V., & Gray, K. (1990). In vivo versus simulation training: An interactional analysis of range and type of training exemplars. *Journal of Applied Behavior Analysis, 23,* 447-458.

Nietupski, J., Hamre-Nietupski, S., Clancy, P. L., & Veerhusen, K. (1986). Guidelines for making simulation an effective adjunct to in-vivo community instruction. *Journal of the Association for Persons with Severe Handicaps, 11,* 12-18.

O'Brien, J. (1987). A guide to lifestyle planning: Using the Activities Catalog to integrate services and natural support systems. In B. Wilcox & G. T. Bellamy (Eds.), *A comprehensive guide to the Activities Catalog: An alternative curriculum for youth and adults with severe disabilities* (pp. 175-189). Baltimore: Paul H. Brookes.

O'Brien, J., & Pearpoint, J. (2003). *Person-centered planning with MAPS and PATH: A workbook for facilitators.* Toronto: Inclusion Press.

Page, T. H., Iwata, B. A., & Neef, N. A. (1976). Teaching pedestrian skills to retarded persons: Generalization from the classroom to the natural environment. *Journal of Applied Behavior Analysis, 9,* 433-444.

Pearpoint, J., O'Brien, J., & Forest, M. (1992). *PATH: Planning alternative tomorrows with hope.* Toronto: Inclusion Press.

Peterson, S. M. P., Caniglia, C., & Royster, A. J. (2001). Application of choice-making intervention for a student with multiply maintained problem behavior. *Focus on Autism and Other Developmental Disabilities, 16,* 240-246.

Pierce, K. L., & Schriebman, L. (1994). Teaching daily living skills to children with autism in unsupervised settings through pictorial self-management. *Journal of Applied Behavior Analysis, 27,* 471-481.

Post, M., & Storey, K. (2002). Review of using auditory prompting systems with persons who have moderate to severe disabilities. *Education and Training in Mental Retardation, 37,* 317-320.

Rae, R., & Roll, D. (1985). Fire safety training with adults who are profoundly mentally retarded. *Mental Retardation, 23,* 26-30.

Risley, R., & Cuvo, A. (1980). Training mentally retarded adults to make emergency telephone calls. *Behavior Modification, 4,* 513-525.

Robinson, D., Griffith, J., McComish, L., & Swasbrook, K. (1984). Bus training for developmentally disabled adults. *American Journal of Mental Deficiency, 89*, 37-43.

Ryndak, D. L., & Billingsley, F. (2004). Access to the general education curriculum. In C. H. Kennedy & E. M. Horn (Eds.), *Including students with severe disabilities* (pp. 33-53). Boston: Allyn & Bacon.

Sandknop, P.A., Schuster, J.W., Wolery, M., & Cross, D. P. (1992). The use of an adaptive device to teach students with moderate mental retardation to select lower priced grocery items. *Education and Training in Mental Retardation, 27*, 219-229.

Sarber, R. R., & Cuvo, A. J. (1983). Teaching nutritional meal planning to developmentally disabled clients. *Behavior Modification, 7*, 503-530.

Schleien, S. J., Ash, T., Kiernan, J., & Wehman, P. (1981). Developing independent cooking skills in a profoundly retarded woman. *Journal of the Association for the Severely Handicapped, 6*, 23-29.

Schleien, S. J., Certo, N. J., & Muccino, A. (1984). Acquisition of leisure skills by a severely handicapped adolescent: A data-based instructional program. *Education and Training of the Mentally Retarded, 19*, 297-305.

Schuster, J.W. (1988). Cooking instruction with persons labeled mentally retarded: A review of literature. *Education and Training in Mental Retardation, 23*, 43-50.

Schuster, J. W., & Griffen, A. K. (1991). Using constant time delay to teach recipe following skills. *Education and Training of the Mentally Retardation, 26*, 411-419.

Schwier, K. A., & Hingsburger, D. (2000). *Sexuality: Your sons and daughters with intellectual disabilities.* Boston: Paul H. Brookes.

Seybert, S., Dunlap, G., & Ferro, J. (1996). The effects of choice-making on the problem behaviors of high school students with intellectual disabilities. *Journal of Behavioral Education, 6*, 49-65.

Shafer, M. S., Inge, K. J., & Hill, J. (1986). Acquisition, generalization, and maintenance of automated banking skills. *Education and Training of the Mentally Retarded, 21*, 265-272.

Singh, N. N., Oswald, D. P., Ellis, C. R., & Singh, S. D. (1995). Community-based instruction for independent meal preparation by adults with profound mental retardation. *Journal of Behavioral Education, 5*, 77-92.

Singleton, K. C., Schuster, J., & Ault, M. J. (1995). Simultaneous prompting in a small group instructional arrangement. *Education and Training in Mental Retardation and Developmental Disabilities, 30*, 218-230.

Smith, R. L., Collins, B. C., Schuster, J.W., Kleinert, H. (1999). Teaching table cleaning skills to secondary students with moderate/severe disabilities: Facilitating observational learning during instructional downtime. *Education and Training in Mental Retardation and Developmental Disabilities, 34*, 342-353.

Snell, M. E. (1982). Teaching bed making skills to retarded adults through time delay. *Analysis and Intervention in Developmental Disabilities, 2*, 139-155.

Snell, M. E., & Browder, D. M. (1986). Community-referenced instruction: Research and issues. *Journal of the Association for Persons with Severe Handicaps, 11*, 1-11.

Sobsey, D., & Doe, T. (1991). Patterns of sexual abuse and assault. *Sexuality and Disability, 9*, 69-81.

Sowers, J., & Powers, L. (1995). Enhancing the participation and independence of students with severe physical and multiple disabilities in performing community activities. *Mental Retardation, 33*, 209-220.

Sowers, J., Rusch, F. R., & Hudson, C. (1979). Training a severely retarded young adult to ride the city bus to and from work. *AAESPH Review, 4*, 15-23.

Spears, D. L., Rusch, F. R., York, R., & Lilly, M. S. (1981). Training independent arrival behaviors to a severely mentally retarded child. *Journal of the Association for the Severely Handicapped, 6*, 40-45.

Spooner, F., Stem, B., & Test, D. W. (1989). Teaching first aid skills to adolescents who are moderately mentally handicapped. *Education and Training in Mental Retardation, 24*, 341-351.

Sprague, J. R., & Horner, R. H. (1984). The effects of single instance, multiple instance, and general case training on generalized vending machine use by moderately and severely handicapped students. *Journal of Applied Behavior Analysis, 17*, 273-278.

Taber, T.A., Alberto, P.A., Hughes, M., & Seltzer, A. (2002). A strategy for students with moderate disabilities when lost in the community. *Research and Practice for Persons with Severe Disabilities, 27*, 141-152.

Taber, T.A., Alberto, P.A., Seltzer, A., & Hughes, M. (2003). Obtaining assistance when lost in the community using cell phones. *Research and Practice for Persons with Severe Disabilities, 28*, 105-116.

Taylor, J. C., McKelvey, J. L., & Sisson, L. A. (1993). Community-referenced leisure skill clusters for adolescents with multiple disabilities. *Journal of Behavioral Education, 3*, 363-386.

Taylor, P., Collins, B. C., Schuster, J.W., & Kleinert, H. (2002). Teaching laundry skills to high school students with disabilities: Generalization of targeted skills and nontargeted information. *Education and Training in Mental Retardation and Developmental Disabilities, 37*, 172-183.

Tekin-Iftar, E. (2003). Effectiveness of peer delivered simultaneous prompting on teaching community signs to students with developmental disabilities. *Education and Training in Developmental Disabilities, 38*, 77-94.

Test, D.W., Howell, A., Burkhart, K., & Beroth, T. (1993). The one-more-than technique as a strategy for counting money for individuals with moderate mental retardation. *Education and Training in Mental Retardation, 28*, 232-241.

Trask-Tyler, S.A., Grossi, T.A., & Heward, W. L. (1994). Teaching young adults with developmental disabilities and visual impairments to use tape-recorded recipes: Acquisition, generalization, and maintenance of cooking skills. *Journal of Behavioral Education, 4*, 283-311.

Vandercook, T. (1991). Leisure instruction outcomes: Criterion performance, positive interactions, and acceptance by typical high school peers. *Journal of Special Education, 25*, 320-339.

Vandercook, T., York, J., & Forest, M. (1989). The McGill action planning system (MAPS): A strategy for building the vision. *Journal of the Association for Persons with Severe Handicaps, 14*, 205-215.

Wall, M. E., & Gast, D. L. (1997). Caregivers' use of constant time delay to teach leisure skills to adolescents or young adults with moderate or severe intellectual disabilities. *Education and Training in Mental Retardation and Developmental Disabilities, 32,* 340–356.

Watson, M., Bain, A., & Houghton, S. (1992). A preliminary study in teaching self-protective skills to children with moderate and severe mental retardation. *Journal of Special Education, 26,* 181–194.

Wehman, P. (1997). *Life beyond the classroom: Transition strategies for young people with disabilities* (3rd ed.). Baltimore: Paul H. Brookes.

Westling, D. L., Floyd, J., & Carr, D. (1990). Effects of single setting versus multiple setting training on learning to shop in a department store. *American Journal on Mental Retardation, 94,* 616–624.

Zencius, A. H., Davis, P. K., & Cuvo, A. J. (1990). A personalized system of instruction for teaching checking account skills to adults with mild disabilities. *Journal of Applied Behavior Analysis, 23,* 245–252.

Zhang, J., Gast, D., Horvat, M., & Datillo, J. (1995). The effectiveness of constant time delay procedure on teaching lifetime sport skills to adolescents with severe to profound intellectual disabilities. *Education and Training in Mental Retardation and Developmental Disabilities, 30,* 51–64.

15

Vocational Preparation and Transition

Katherine J. Inge
Virginia Commonwealth University

M. Sherril Moon
University of Maryland

This chapter provides a framework for preparing secondary students with severe disabilities for meaningful employment outcomes. We illustrate with the example of three students (Heather, Jane, and Robert) how to plan and implement transition activities. We also describe the essential characteristics of secondary vocational programs for students with severe disabilities. Throughout this chapter, we emphasize how vocational preparation must be coordinated along with many other facets of secondary programming as students make the transition from school to adulthood.

Heather

Heather is a 16-year-old sophomore who has Down syndrome and moderate to severe mental retardation. She has no major physical limitations, a functional vocabulary, and can read and understand most words and phrases considered essential for community mobility. She can use money to make purchases using a "next dollar" strategy. She is very social and has participated in many school, church, and community extracurricular activities, such as Scouts, church camp, Sunday school, pep club, YMCA programs, and Special Olympics Partners sports activities. Her 18-year-old sister has included her in many social activities with slightly older teenagers.

Two years ago, Heather entered her neighborhood middle school, where she participated in four inclusive class periods (i.e., language arts, physical education, social studies, and science), one resource room period, and 2 hours of community-based and functional academic training. She had several peer buddies and peer tutors and was a member of the science club and pep club. Part of her community-based instruction included career exploration. She indicated a preference for office and clerical work or work in retail clothing stores, though she performed well as a school office messenger in an in-school work internship. Currently, she is working in a 6-week unpaid internship at Kohl's department store as a stocker.

Heather is in her first year of a comprehensive high school where her sister is a senior. She is included in regular academic classes during the morning and two afternoons each week. On Mondays, Wednesdays, and Fridays, she receives vocational training and functional skills instruction in the community. Her next internship will be in the fast-food area to provide additional workplace experience to help Heather choose the type of job that she may be interested in pursuing. Specific preference data will be documented during this internship. Heather is slated to participate in the school's summer work program for students with disabilities, where she will be paid as an hourly employee. The goals of her vocational training program during the school year is to identify two job categories in which she shows a preference and to increase skill acquisition so that she can have a paid work experience in one of those areas during the summer.

 Jane

Jane is a 19-year-old student whose abilities are challenged by cerebral palsy and moderate mental retardation. She has limited use of her arms and hands as a result of spasticity, which is evident when she attempts to complete motor activities. Jane's hands usually are fisted, and she has a great deal of difficulty opening them to use functionally. Jane independently uses a power chair by using her head to push the control panel. She communicates verbally with family members and friends; however, unfamiliar persons usually do not understand Jane.

Jane can read on a first- or second-grade level and has a functional vocabulary. She can do simple addition and subtraction and uses a calculator to figure multiple purchases. She has just opened a joint savings and checking account at a local bank and is working on managing a monthly budget. Jane is friendly but very shy and does not have many friends, an area in which she has expressed concern. She is an only child who lives with her mother and her maternal grandmother.

For the first 3 years of high school, Jane has attended a self-contained class in a regular high school that is not her neighborhood school. For the past year, she has attended a community-based program for secondary students in her home school. Jane has individualized education program (IEP) goals related to mobility training, unpaid job training in at least three different job categories, finding the appropriate assistive technology, and making friends. Her teacher has helped her get involved with Best Buddies, and she spends time with a college student in a variety of after-school social activities.

Jane and her mother have expressed an interest in Jane's attending a new postsecondary program for students between the ages of 18 and 21 who are still receiving special education and are working toward an alternative diploma. This program, located at a local community college, would allow Jane to audit classes, get paid employment training, and participate in a variety of social activities with peers her age. Jane has a good chance of getting accepted into the postsecondary program if she can get to the community college without using school transportation, successfully identifies and completes job training in at least two jobs in which she is interested, and begins to use an alternative communication system that can be understood by unfamiliar persons.

 Robert

Robert is 19 years old with a grade 3 traumatic brain injury as a result of a car accident at the age of 12. His challenges related to the brain injury include right-side hemiplegia, severe ataxia, short-term memory impairment, and a slow speech pattern. Robert is able to walk with the assistance of a walker. He was very athletic prior to his accident and played soccer. He has not participated in any team sports since and reports that this frustrates him. His primary social activity is going to the local YMCA at least three times a week with his father and occasionally his brother. Robert has an outgoing personality for interacting with the public.

Since his accident, Robert has been included in regular education classes with one-to-one support from an aide. He did not graduate with his class the previous school year, and until this year, his school program has consisted of in-school academic course work. He reports that this has been too difficult for him, and he is not interested in going to college. Robert, his family, and transition team decided that a total program of academics was not meeting his needs and that he should have opportunities for career exploration. This year in school has been a balance between working on functional academics and community-based work experiences. His transition goal is to identify a career path and get a job for the summer that will contribute to building a work history.

Valued Employment Outcomes

Graduation from high school is a "right of passage" for most students. Some leave home for college and dream of future careers, while others leave to begin new jobs and start families. For most, it is an exciting time of transitioning from school to adulthood and independence. Unfortunately, the vast majority of students with severe disabilities do not leave high school to go on to college or to become part of the nation's workforce. Less than 1 out of 10 youth with disabilities transition from school and attain integrated employment outcomes, and many find themselves on long waiting lists to receive employment services (Wills Wills & Luecking, 2003; U.S. General Accounting Office, 2001).

Despite the Americans with Disabilities Act (ADA) and other federal initiatives, competitive employment still is not the first choice for the majority of individuals with disabilities (Wehman, Revell, & Brooke, 2003 is the correct date). Most are either unemployed or "underemployed" in stereotypical jobs that result in low wages, no benefits, and no opportunity for career advancement. Many people with severe disabilities and high support needs are placed in "Special Minimum Wage" programs under Section 14(c) of the Fair Labor Standard Act earning less than minimum wage. A U.S. General Accounting Office report (2001) estimated that 424,000 employees with disabilities are working under Section 14(c) with approximately 95% of this number in extended employment (formerly known as sheltered employment).

While segregated day services may be well intentioned, they are inconsistent with the core values of community inclusion and independence, which underlies recent disability legislation (Wehman, 2001). Designed as part of a service continuum, individuals with disabilities are supposed to move from segregated services as they gain skills to less restrictive settings and eventually community employment (Rogan, Held, & Rinne, 2001). However, few have moved through this "readiness" continuum to achieve integrated employment as an outcome.

Advocates of segregated employment endorse this as a postschool outcome based on individual choice indicating that some people with disabilities prefer to work in segregated facilities. However, many have never had the opportunity to participate in community work experiences in order to make informed choices. Smull (1998) suggests that preferences can be defined as something that people want. If students have never participated in community-based work experiences, then how will they know that community-integrated employment is their preferred transition outcome?

Another barrier to integrated employment has been low expectations for the postschool outcomes of students with severe disabilities. There is research and practice demonstrating that individuals who are viewed as "unemployable" can be successful in jobs earning minimum wage or above that include benefits and opportunities for career advancement. The number of people participating in supported employment in the United States has increased within a decade from less than 9,800 to over 140,000 (Wehman, Revell, & Kregel, 1998). Customized employment supports and strategies such as supported employment, supported entrepreneurship, coworker supports, job restructuring and negotiation, workplace accommodations, and federal legislation have facilitated the integrated employment outcomes for these individuals. In addition, policy shifts have expanded opportunities for integrated employment.

Unemployment and underemployment may be related more to services and supports that students do not receive when exiting the school system than a function of the students' disabilities (Getzel & Kregel, 1997). The use of supports is a way to expand a student's employment potential that focuses on identifying the needed supports for community inclusion rather than on a readiness approach that limits community access. Vocational preparation during the school years should include opportunities for training experiences in the community to determine job interests and preferences. Included in these opportunities should be the identification of the student's support needs for successful transition into paid employment. Educators, parents, and students with disabilities also must become familiar with the services and supports that are

TABLE 15–1
Employment Values

Values	Description
Presumption of ability	An individual with a disability, regardless of the severity of the disability, can achieve employment and other rehabilitation goals if the appropriate services and supports are made available.
Integrated employment	The goal is employment in an integrated community business making at least minimum wage.
Self-determination and choice	People with disabilities have the ability to guide their own careers and control the services and supports needed to facilitate integrated employment outcomes.
Commensurate wages and benefits	An individual should have the same opportunity to earn wages and benefits equal to that of coworkers without disabilities who are performing the same or similar jobs.
Capacity and abilities	A belief that all individuals are viewed in terms of their abilities, strengths, and gifts rather than on their disabilities.
Importance of relationships	A realization that community connections and supports, both at the workplace and in the community, are critical to maximize employment outcomes.
System change	A conviction that traditional systems must be challenged and changed to ensure that individuals have control and choice over their postschool employment outcomes.

available within their communities and facilitate collaboration between school, community agencies, and businesses. The anticipated vocational outcome should be integrated employment in regular community businesses. Table 15-1 lists the values associated with employment as a postschool outcome that should guide the transition process from school to work.

Defining Transition

Employment is only one area in which middle and secondary school–age students with disabilities must receive consistent transition planning and instruction. Other areas for which students must be prepared to live happily as adults include coordination of service and supports, independent living, community mobility, financial and medical security, friendship and sexuality needs, physical fitness and recreation access, and choice making and self-determination, or self-advocacy (Wehman 1996). To ensure that students receive transition service delivery in these areas as part of their special education programs, the Individuals with Disabilities Education Act (IDEA), P.L. 101-476, signed into law in October 1990, defined transition as the following:

[A] coordinated set of activities for a student, designed within an outcome-oriented process, which promotes movement from school to post-school activities, including post-secondary education, vocational training, integrated employment (including

supported employment), continuing and adult education, adult services, independent living, or community participation. The coordinated set of activities shall be based upon the individual student needs, taking into account the student's preferences and interests, and shall include instructions, community experiences, the development of employment and other post-school adult living objectives, and when appropriate, acquisition of daily living skills and functional vocational evaluation ... (D) A statement of the needed transition services for students beginning no later than age 16 and annually thereafter (and, when determined appropriate for the individual, beginning at age 14 or younger), including, when appropriate, a statement of the interagency responsibilities or linkages (or both) before the student leaves the school setting, and (F) In the case where a participating agency, other than the educational agency, fails to provide agreed upon services, the educational agency shall reconvene the IEP team to identify alternative strategies to meet the transition objectives. (National Association of the State Directors of Special Education, 1990, p. 2)

The 1997 IDEA Amendments, P.L. 105-17, broadened the focus of transition by lowering the age at which transition service needs are stated in the IEP; P.L. 105-17, Section 614, states that

beginning at age 14, and updated annually, a statement of the transition service needs of the child under the applicable components of the child's IEP that focuses on the child's courses of study (study as participation in advanced-placement courses or a vocational education program). (IDEA, 1997, p. 84)

The 1997 Amendments in Section 602 also state that

beginning at age 16 (or younger, if determined by the IEP team), a statement of needed transition services for the child, including, when appropriate, a statement of interagency responsibilities or any needed linkages. (IDEA, 1997, p. 46)

According to IDEA regulations, assessment, training, and support needs related to the transition outcomes of employment, independent living, or any area of adult functioning should be included in the IEP. A statement of needed services is required along with goals and related activities or objectives, time lines for meeting each goal, and persons or agencies responsible for implementing each goal. Goals must be based on student interests and preferences, which must be documented in the IEP. Education personnel responsible for initiating the transition planning process when or before a student turns 14 must invite the student, parents, and other advocate or agency representative outside the school who potentially would facilitate the accomplishment of any current or future transition goals.

When Heather's transition team began planning for her community-based vocational experiences, they first discussed her interests and preferences in an IEP meeting that included Heather and her parents. These interests were then used to develop specific goals for Heather's IEP. In this case, Heather had a goal to participate in a minimum of three community-based nonpaid work experiences during the school year to assist in identifying her vocational preferences.

Characteristics of Effective Vocational Preparation and Transition Programs

There is still limited empirical evidence indicating which transition practices lead to successful adult outcomes (Baer, McMahan, & Flexer, 2004), especially for students with the most severe disabilities. However, several common themes have been identified in the literature as promising (Greene & Kochar-Bryant, 2003; Hasazi, Furney, & DeStefano, 1999; Kohler & Field, 2003; Phelps & Hanley-Maxwell, 1997; Wehman, 1996).

Those practices targeted to students with severe disabilities most frequently cited by advocates, researchers, and policymakers include the following:

1. Student or person-centered planning resulting in an IEP that focuses on a student's preferences and needs and the unique school and community services that can be developed for that student
2. Interagency collaboration that strives to develop appropriate services and supports for each student even when the range of services and supports needed by students and their families don't exist
3. A secondary curricula including instruction in functional life skills, the opportunity to be involved in general education environments to age 18, access to paid work training opportunities while attending school, the teaching of self-determination strategies, and the planning for postsecondary opportunities regardless of degree of disabilities
4. Family involvement in the transition process that truly focuses on individual family's self-identified needs and concerns
5. Program structures or policies that allow for local interagency collaboration, written policy development, resource allocation specific to transition, program evaluation, and training for professionals and families

Supporting Families

As a student with disabilities reaches adolescence and then later reaches adulthood, the family faces two of the most difficult and stressful transitional periods (Turnbull & Turnbull, 1997). Educators must support families in a variety of areas, such as deciding what to include in the school curricula (e.g., sexuality education, self-determination skills, postsecondary access) and looking into future supported work and living options. Although parental participation is considered a key transition best practice (Kohler & Field, 2004) and research has shown that family involvement in the process improves postschool outcomes (Blackorby & Wagner, 1996), parental priorities are still undervalued in most IEP and transition planning processes (Salembier & Furney, 1997; Steineman, Morningstar, Bishop, & Turnbull, 1993). Turnbull and Turnbull (2001) wrote that insufficient progress has been made in achieving self-determination for people with severe disabilities and their families and that the cultural expectations of families are rarely considered in the self-determination planning process. The long list of concerns that families must deal with in order to improve the quality of life for their adult sons and daughters such as Medicaid waiver eligibility, behavioral supports across all environments, housing options based on preferences and needs, and the arranging of long-term financial needs are rarely addressed in secondary transition plans. Professionals must realize that families are usually the only consistent support for members with disabilities (Hanley-Maxwell, Pogoloff, & Whitney-Thomas, 1998); thus, their active participation in determining IEP transition goal priorities is crucial.

We must continually obtain information from parents by asking them questions and listening and by using written questionnaires and person-centered planning meetings (Flannery et al., 2000; Miner & Bates, 1997). Parents must assume more responsibility by signing off on the IEP as the responsible party on particular goals; exploring residential, employment, and leisure options; sharing specific paid job leads; promoting independence and self-determination in their sons

or daughters; and inviting particular agency and advocacy groups to become part of the transition process. For example, Hutchins and Renzaglia (1998) found that families could help in seeking and developing long-term job placements for students with severe disabilities through the use of a comprehensive vocational interview process. Benz, Johnson, Mikkelson, and Lindstrom (1995) found that transition efforts in general could be improved when parents were provided with more informational materials, had a single knowledgeable contact person, were given the opportunity to attend resource fairs, and could attend training sessions with both school and adult service providers present. Families and professionals should participate together in evaluating existing school and community programs and in the start-up of new or improved support or services systems. The questions for evaluating transition practices in Table 15–2 should help families, educators, and professionals work together in planning for a meaningful transition from school to adult life.

TABLE 15–2

Questions for Secondary School Programs to Evaluate Secondary Transition Practices for Students with Severe Disabilities

---

- Does the school system collect outcome data for former students including employment, independent living status, use of community services, and family/student satisfaction with the transition process and adult service provision?
- To what degree are students included in the regular education curriculum, and what is the participation rate in regular classes and extracurricular activities? Do parents and students want more inclusion than is facilitated?
- Is functional skills instruction individualized to meet the specific needs of students and their families? What is the extent to which individual students could participate in functional skills instruction within the context of a regular classroom environment?
- Do students receive community mobility skills training based on individualized assessment?
- Are students with the most severe disabilities receiving vocational education services?
- Are students given the opportunity to participate in a variety of vocational training experiences and ultimately paid employment opportunities?
- Do students' vocational training and paid employment opportunities reflect student and family preferences and interests?
- Do students receive formal transition planning beginning at the age of 14, and is this reflected in IEP goals?
- Are parents and students actively involved in transition planning through person-centered planning?
- Are family needs and preferences for residential services, behavior support, employment options, and financial supports considered when developing transition IEP goals?
- Do parents and other team members understand how to apply for Social Security benefits, Medicaid, Medicaid waivers, state developmental disabilities case management services, and vocational rehabilitation? Are representatives from these agencies participating in transition planning or IEP meetings?
- Do educators and parents know which adult services and supports are provided by certain local nonprofit or government agencies and which funding sources can be used to fund these services? Do they understand the eligibility and application requirements for adult service providers?
- Are the cultural values, preferences, and expectations of families considered in transition planning for individual students?
- Is estate-planning information provided for families as part of the transition process?
- Do parents and professionals set opportunities for training and information sharing related to the questions listed here?

Available Vocational Services and Supports in the Community

Successful transition depends on local collaboration among educational and community agencies, businesses, and families. The number of services that are available has rapidly evolved and expanded in recent years. Each community agency has a different set of eligibility requirements and rules that must be met in order for a student to access funding. This can be particularly confusing to both school personnel as well as family members when attempting to blend resources to obtain the supports and services needed for each student. Although schools must take the lead in coordinating the planning process and providing initial case management and skills training, the process cannot be completed until other community agencies or individuals assume the responsibility for follow-up services and continual case management. Meaningful transition cannot occur unless educators use ecological analysis and functional needs assessment to explore and update all possible local employment and volunteer work options while students are still in school (Neubert, 2003). Table 15-2 includes some of the critical questions that should be asked when evaluating the appropriateness and effectiveness of transition practices for students with significant disabilities.

Before a student reaches the age of 14, educators must determine what services exist, what services need improvement, and what services must be created and share this information with families for their consideration. Transition personnel who are working with students with severe disabilities and their families must help them understand where and with whom to apply for funding for services and also to apply for the actual service delivery. Many families do not understand that their son or daughter leaving public school must qualify for certain federal or state benefits such as Social Security, Medicaid waiver, and state developmental disabilities monies in a particular category (i.e., residential, vocational, respite, family services) or vocational rehabilitation services. These monies pay for the services provided by local nonprofit agencies. In other words, the dual process of qualifying for funding and then applying for the actual services is quite overwhelming and should be facilitated by secondary special educators or other team members. In fact, including the application for these services as IEP transition goals can be extremely helpful to families, as there is no single system to coordinate this process once a student exits the public school (Neubert & Moon, 1999).

Vocational Rehabilitation

Vocational rehabilitation is one of the primary facilitators and providers of employment supports for individuals with disabilities. Vocational rehabilitation counselors can provide their customers with such services as (a) vocational evaluations, (b) vocational counseling, (c) job placement, (d) vocational training (e.g., courses at a vocational center or rehabilitation facility), (e) college or university courses, (f) personal assistance services, (g) assistive technology services and devices, and (h) supported employment. The Rehabilitation Act funds vocational services and has been amended on numerous occasions since individuals with mental retardation were included in the 1943 provisions. In 1954, the amendments authorized the funding and building of rehabilitation facilities for extended employment (formerly sheltered employment) for individuals with severe disabilities. The next significant changes occurred in 1973 with the passage of the Vocational Rehabilitation Act (P.L. 93-112). This law denied federal funding to agencies that discriminate against individuals who are disabled under Section 504. Section 504 states that "no otherwise qualified individual [with a disability] shall by reason of his [disability] be excluded from the participation in, be denied the benefits of, or be subjected to discrimination in any program or activity receiving federal financial assistance" (29 U.S.C. 794).

Also in this legislation was the mandating of the Individualized Written Rehabilitation Program (IWRP). The IWRP must be developed by the vocational rehabilitation counselor and the individual with a disability to include long-range rehabilitation goals, intermediate objectives to reach the goals, a statement of the specific services to be provided, a date for the initiation and duration of services, and specified criteria with evaluation procedures. In 1998, the IWRP was renamed the Individual Plan for Employment (IPE) as part of the Workforce Investment Act with increased emphasis on the partnership between the individual with a disability and the vocational rehabilitation counselor in developing the IPE.

Robert's vocational rehabilitation counselor became a member of his transition team during his junior year of school. This meant that he had an open case that allowed the counselor to pay for support services during summer months between his junior and senior years when the school system was not providing services. In addition, money was available when he needed the assistance of a rehabilitation engineer to fabricate an accommodation at his paid work site.

The reauthorization of the Rehabilitation Act in 1986 included supported employment as a reasonable rehabilitation outcome for individuals with severe disabilities in Title IV, Part C (Revell, 1991). Supported employment is defined as competitive work in an integrated work setting with extended support services for individuals with severe disabilities for whom competitive employment has not traditionally occurred or has been interrupted or intermittent as a result of severe disabilities (*Federal Register,* August 14, 1987, p. 30551, 363.7).

The Rehabilitation Act was amended in 1992 as P.L. 102-569 and defined transition services for the first time. These regulations mandated a state plan requiring that the state rehabilitation agency address the development of policies that ensure coordination between the rehabilitation and state education agencies. The expected outcome is that students who need rehabilitation services will exit the public schools without a break in service (Button, 1992). Most important, the act included for the first time the concept of "presumption of ability" (Table 15-1). The assumption is that a person with a disability, regardless of the severity of the disability, can achieve employment and other rehabilitation goals if the appropriate services and supports are made available.

Prior to 1992, an individual with a disability was evaluated to determine his or her rehabilitation potential and the "feasibility" for employment. Often these evaluations concluded that the individual was not eligible for services. After 1992, eligibility determinations must focus on the use of existing data, particularly on information provided by the individual with a disability, his or her family, or advocates, and information provided by education agencies, Social Security agencies, the individual's personal physician, previous or current employers, and any organization or person referring the individual for services (Inge & Brooke, 1993).

One-Stop Career Center System

The most recent reauthorization of the Rehabilitation Act Amendments occurred in 1998 as part of the Workforce Investment Act (WIA). WIA authorized the development of a One-Stop Career Center system designed to meet the needs of all job seekers, including people with disabilities (Fesko, Hoff, Jordan, Fichera, & Thomas, 2000). Additional federal programs, including vocational rehabilitation, were identified as required partners in the One-Stop system with the "goal of giving all Americans access to comprehensive services, information and resources that can help them in achieving their career goals" (*Federal Register,* April 8, 2004, p. 18629). The intent was to provide access to a network of programs and services within a central location. WIA established state and local workforce investment boards for strategic planning, policy development, and oversight of the system.

With the passage of WIA, individuals with the most severe disabilities are now referred to as individuals with significant disabilities. There is increased emphasis on informed consumer choice to ensure that the person receiving services is a joint partner in rehabilitation planning. This includes providing information and support services to assist people with disabilities in exercising informed choice throughout the vocational rehabilitation process. Another key point is that individuals receiving Supplemental Security Income (SSI) or Social Security Disability Insurance (SSDI) benefits are automatically eligible for vocational rehabilitation services and do not need to go through eligibility reviews. In addition, state vocational rehabilitation agencies are encouraged to assist schools in identifying transition services and to participate in the cost of these services for any student with a disability who is determined eligible.

The One-Stop system is still in development. However, there are three levels of services that are to be available through a One-Stop (Fesko et al., 2000). These include core services, intensive services, and training services. An individual begins with core services as the first level and moves to intensive services if the core services are not sufficient to meet the person's needs. The third level, training services, is available if an individual meets the eligibility requirements and has not been successful in achieving employment with the core and intensive services. Table 15-3 provides a sample list of services that may be available through the One-Stop system.

WIA gives individuals with disabilities the ability to choose between receiving services from the traditional disability service system and the array of services and supports used by the nondisabled public when seeking jobs. Choice in what services are desired

TABLE 15–3
One-Stop Career Center Services

Sample core services	Sample intensive services	Sample training services
• Intake and orientation • Work skills exploration • Resource library, including access to computers, telephones, fax, and copy machines • Searches for jobs and training • Access to job banks or listings of available jobs • Internet access • Résumé development • Job search skills training • Networking skills workshops • Interview techniques workshops • Referral to an employer with current job openings • Customer satisfaction follow-up • Determination of eligibility for additional services	• Comprehensive assessments of skills and service needs • Development of an individual employment and career plan • Customized screening and assessment • Reference/background checks • Intensive career counseling • In-depth interviewing skills development • Computer workshops • One-to-one assistance with updating a résumé, cover letters, and thank-you letters • Case management	• Occupational skills training • On-the-job training • Up-to-date work skills • Job readiness training • Adult education and literacy • Customized training for an employer who commits to hiring

and delivered by providers specifically selected by the customer has historically been a barrier in the disability service delivery system (Racino, 1998). With the implementation of WIA, the potential for customer choice, inclusion, and self-determination have become a possibility for many individuals with disabilities who may no longer have to depend on a specialized service system to obtain employment (Bader, 2003).

When identifying vocational services and supports, the transition team should consider the services available through the One-Stop system. Currently, 14 states have implemented the Disability Program Navigator Initiative. These states are Arizona, California, Colorado, Delaware, Florida, Illinois, Iowa, Maryland, Massachusetts, New York, Oklahoma, South Carolina, Vermont, and Wisconsin (*Federal Register,* April 8, 2004, p. 18630). The program is a demonstration project jointly sponsored by the Department of Labor, Employment, and Training Administration and the Social Security Administration (SSA), which are jointly funding and training individuals as Navigators to address the needs of people with disabilities when seeking training and employment opportunities through the One-Stop system (SSA, 2004). The Navigator will provide information and serve as a resource to increase the self-sufficiency for individuals

with disabilities by linking them to employers and by facilitating access to supports and services within the system (*Federal Register,* April 8, 2004, p. 18647). Transition teams need to consider this resource and determine if their local One-Stop Career Center has a Navigator who could serve as a resource to the team and students with significant disabilities.

Eligibility

An important change in the vocational rehabilitation system occurred in 2001. The Rehabilitation Services Administration amended its regulations governing state vocational rehabilitation programs to redefine the term "employment outcome" to mean an integrated setting "typically found in the community in which applicants or eligible individuals interact with non-disabled individuals, other than non-disabled individuals who are providing services to those applicants or eligible individuals, to the same extent that non-disabled individuals in comparable positions interact with other persons."

(*Federal Register,* January 22, 2001 p.4387)

For decades, extended employment (formerly sheltered employment) was an acceptable outcome for individuals receiving vocational rehabilitation services. The new definition removes this type of employment as an approved outcome because extended/sheltered employment uses nonintegrated work settings.

The array of vocational rehabilitation supports that are available to students once they exit high school are significant. However, students are entering an adult service world driven by eligibility. Eligibility for vocational rehabilitation is based on (a) documentation of the presence of a disability that constitutes a substantial impediment to employment and (b) a reasonable expectation that vocational rehabilitation services will assist the individual with a disability achieve an employment outcome (*Federal Register,* January 17, 2001). Students must apply and have their vocational rehabilitation cases "open" prior to graduation in order to prevent a gap in service delivery.

"Presumption of ability" has already been mentioned, but some students still may be identified as unable to benefit from a rehabilitation program based on their disabilities. In other words, the student may be identified as not able to achieve an employment outcome and consequently denied services. However, the law stipulates that there must be clear and convincing evidence that a person cannot benefit before vocational rehabilitation services can be denied. One way to facilitate eligibility is to provide vocational rehabilitation with existing data to include reports from community-based vocational training experiences and paid work experiences prior to graduation. Students will then have résumés and references from previous and/or current employers to demonstrate the feasibility of employment outcomes.

If services are denied, the individual or his or her advocate can ask for a trial work experience to assist in demonstrating that the person can benefit. Trial work experiences are experiences "in which the individual is provided appropriate supports and training" to determine eligibility for services. WIA states,

> *In making the demonstration required under subparagraph (A), the designated State unit shall explore the individual's abilities, capabilities, and capacity to perform in work situations, through the use of trial work experiences with appropriate supports provided through the designated State unit, except under limited circumstances when an individual can not take advantage of such experiences. Such experiences shall be of sufficient variety and over a sufficient period of time to determine the eligibility of*

> *the individual or to determine the existence of clear and convincing evidence that the individual is incapable of benefiting in terms of an employment outcome from vocational rehabilitation services due to the severity of the disability of the individual.*

It is critical that the transition planning begins early in order to ensure that students with severe disabilities are able to access vocational rehabilitation services. Waiting until the last year of school to identify vocational supports and services may result in long waiting periods before the student achieves a meaningful employment outcome.

Medicaid Home and Community-Based Waiver

Home and community-based waivers (HCBS) were established by the U.S. Congress to address the rising cost of institutional care and to address the concern that people with disabilities could receive support such as personal care and training only in institutional settings (Endependence Center, 2003). Established in 1981, states were given the option of developing waiver programs as alternative services for people who were eligible for institutional placement. The recent U.S. Supreme Court decision in *Olmstead v. L.C.* gives legal weight to the use of HCBS (Smith et al., 2000). Through the waiver program, many individuals with mental retardation and related conditions have been able to avoid out-of-home or out-of-community placements (West et al., 2002). Now, families no longer have to place their sons and daughters in state-owned and -operated residential facilities if they do not have the resources to care for family members with disabilities. Instead, a family can use waiver funding to purchase supports such as personal assistance services to care for the individual at home.

Many states are using Medicaid waivers to design innovative and fiscally responsible long-term service programs. These programs enable people with intensive support needs to live in their communities and offer them more control over the services that they receive. For instance, Virginia's Consumer-Directed Personal Assistance Services MR and DD waivers facilitate choice and control by the individual with a disability:

> *Consumer-directed services are controlled directly by the person with a disability or their family if the person is a child or not capable of managing their staff.*

*You have the choice and control to determine what
activities assistance is needed with, who will provide
the service, when it will be provided, where it will be
provided and how it will be provided. You will have
the flexibility and responsibility to recruit, hire,
train, supervise, and fire your consumer-directed
staff . . . your staff will not work for an agency. They
will work directly for you. (Endependence Center,
2003, p. 12)*

States have flexibility in designing their waiver programs, allowing them to use funds to reimburse service providers for extended habilitation services such
as personal care assistance, assistive technology, in-
home residential support, day support, respite care,
and supported employment, to mention only a few
possible services. Some states have done particularly
well in providing employment supports to individuals
with severe disabilities through their HCBS waiver programs providing the ongoing support funding to maintain competitive employment in integrated settings.

West and his colleagues (2002) found that the majority of states (27, or 87.1%) showed a growth in their
supported employment participation through the
waiver with six states reporting that over one fourth of
their HCBS waiver participants were receiving these
services in 1999. The waiver provides an alternative avenue for providing services to those individuals with
severe disabilities who may be on waiting lists for
needed employment supports. Transition teams should
work within their states to determine the range and
types of waivers that are available that can support integrated community employment outcomes.

Social Security Benefit Issues Affecting Transition Age Youth

Social Security benefits offer cash payments and access to health insurance as well as work incentives that
are specifically designed to increase an individual's employment and earnings capacity. The SSA has two programs: SSI and SSDI. SSI is designed to provide income
to individuals with disabilities in financial need. SSI recipients in some states are automatically eligible for
Medicaid coverage with eligibility beginning the same
month as SSI eligibility. Other states require a separate
application for Medicaid, while still other states have
their own eligibility requirements (Newcomb, Payne,
& Waid, 2003). These state-specific application and

eligibility requirements for Medicaid should be determined during transition planning.

SSDI is a Social Security insurance program available to those who have worked and contributed to the
Social Security trust fund. A student with a disability
over the age of 18 who has not worked may receive
SSDI based on the work record of a parent with a disability who contributed to the Social Security trust
fund. After a 2-year wait period, individuals receiving
SSDI automatically begin to receive Medicare coverage. Beneficiaries of both the SSI and SSDI programs
are those who are determined as too disabled to work
(Brooke & O'Mara, 2001).

Many parents of school-age youth have expended a
great deal of time and energy to establish eligibility for
their sons and daughters. They may view paid employment as a significant risk to loss of benefits and Medicaid coverage (Miller & O'Mara, 2003). School personnel may face opposition to employment as a transition
outcome because of this fear, resulting in limited employment participation and earnings. However, Social
Security benefits can actually serve as a valuable resource to eligible students as they transition from
school to adult life. Individuals involved in transition
planning must become more knowledgeable of the issues affecting this group of beneficiaries in order to
provide accurate information regarding the impact of
employment on benefits.

While school personnel should become more knowl-
edgeable, they do not need to become experts in Social
Security disability benefits information. The Ticket to
Work and Work Incentive Improvement Act (Ticket to
Work Program) was enacted into law in December 1999
(P.L. 106-70). This legislation directed the SSA to establish
a community-based benefits planning and assistance
program to provide information on work incentives to
SSA beneficiaries with disabilities. The SSA has established a program of cooperative agreements across the
United States to provide benefits counseling and assis-
tance and conduct outreach efforts to inform beneficiaries of available work incentives.

This program, the Benefits Planning, Assistance, and
Outreach Program (BPAO), provides opportunities for
beneficiaries to receive the needed information and
services for them to become employed and more self-
sufficient (Kregel & Head, 2001). The BPAO has created
a national cadre of certified benefits specialists who
can serve as a valuable resource in the transition planning process. These services are free to individuals receiving SSDI or SSI benefits based on disability. Benefits

specialists may be located within a vocational rehabilitation agency, a community rehabilitation program, a protection and advocacy organization, a center for independent living, or a local Social Security office. This varies from state to state and from community to community, and therefore part of transition planning should be identifying where this key resource is located.

Eligibility

Parent-to-Child Deeming
SSI is a means-tested program; that is, eligibility for benefits is based on parental income and/or resources for children under 18 years of age (Hammis, 2002). In other words, some children cannot qualify for SSI benefits because the family income and resources are too high. This is referred to as "parent-to-child deeming" and will impact whether a child with a disability is found eligible to receive monthly cash SSI payments. This means that although a child may be eligible for SSI based on his or her own income and resources, he or she may still be determined as ineligible for SSI because of the income or resources from a parent or parents.

Once the SSA determines that a child under the age of 18 is eligible, the amount of the SSI check will be based on the current year's federal benefit rate. This is the maximum dollar amount that any single person can receive in a month and is established by Congress in January of each year. In 2004, the dollar amount was $564 a month for an eligible individual.

The exact dollar amount that a child receives each month is determined on a case-by-case basis. There are many deductions and exclusions that the SSA takes into consideration when determining how much of the parents' income and resources are considered in order to determine the monthly cash payment (e.g., the general income exclusion and the earned income exclusion), so parents should not assume that their sons or daughters would not be eligible for SSI benefits until they complete the application process. Nor should they consider an ineligibility decision "permanent" (Miller & O'Mara, 2003). Trained benefits specialists can assist parents in understanding the deeming rules for SSI and how the process works.

SSI Age 18 Redetermination
SSI eligibility must be redetermined when a child who has been receiving benefits reaches age 18 since the adult definition of disability for SSI is different than for

a child. This age-18 redetermination takes place sometime during the 12 months after the child turns 18, and parents will receive written notification from their local SSA field office (Miller & Brooke, 2003). If the age-18 redetermination process finds the student eligible for SSI, he or she will receive benefits under the adult SSI program. If the individual is found ineligible, benefits will terminate 2 months after the date of determination.

Once the student reaches age 18, parent-to-child deeming no longer applies when making SSI eligibility determinations or in calculating the amount of the SSI payment. Transition-age youth who were determined ineligible for SSI benefits under the age of 18 because of parent-to-child deeming should be encouraged to reapply after the 18th birthday. Although parent-to-child deeming no longer applies, other factors are considered in determining eligibility, known as "in-kind support and maintenance," which is considered unearned income provided in the form of food, clothing, or shelter by someone who pays for these supports, including parents or another individual who lives outside the household. This can cause the young adult to be found ineligible for SSI benefits or reduce the amount of paid benefits. The rules that the SSA applies to determining the value of in-kind support and maintenance are complex. Transition teams should encourage parents and students to consider seeking the assistance of a trained benefits specialist during the age-18 redetermination process.

Failure to reestablish SSI eligibility during the transition process means that the student will lose access to critical supports. School personnel and other involved professionals in the transition process can be of assistance in making sure the redetermination process is accurate and fair. Documentation from teachers and vocational rehabilitation professionals should be provided that indicates the level of support that is needed to perform work activities. In many instances, the lack of information on true work performance and support needs leads to an inaccurate assessment of the individual's future ability to earn income (Miller & Brooke, 2003). Participation in community-based work experiences can provide information that may assist the young adult in maintaining SSI eligibility.

If the student is found ineligible, those involved should encourage the young adult and parents to file an appeal to the SSA. Also important to note is that those students who are found ineligible at age 18 can continue to receive benefits if they began receiving vocational rehabilitation services prior to the 18th birthday (Miller & Brooke, 2003; Miller & O'Mara, 2003). This Social Security provision, referred to as Section 30, allows the young adult to maintain SSI benefits while participating in an approved vocational rehabilitation program. Clearly, those students who are in danger of losing eligibility need to be referred to vocational rehabilitation as part of the transition process in order to take advantage of this provision.

Ticket to Work Program

There are almost 1 million youth under the age of 18 receiving SSI benefits from the SSA (Maximus, 2003). One estimate is that approximately 70% of this number will access the Ticket to Work Program when they reach 18 years of age. The Ticket to Work Program provides financial support to employment networks (ENs) that in turn provide job acquisition and job retention services to SSA disability beneficiaries. The goal of this program is to assist individuals with disabilities to become employed and self-sufficient in order to leave the SSA's disability rolls (Berkowitz, 2003; Wehman & Revell, 2003).

The Ticket to Work Program is voluntary, and beneficiaries who receive tickets can contact one or more ENs or state vocational rehabilitation agencies to discuss services and going to work. The beneficiary can choose to assign or not to assign his or her ticket. In other words, the beneficiary can choose not to work. If the beneficiary chooses to work, he or she selects an EN and assigns the ticket to that EN in order to receive employment supports. Together the EN and the individual develop an individual work plan that outlines the services to be provided for reaching the beneficiary's employment goal.

The Ticket to Work Program can provide supplemental funding to schools for 18- to 21-year-old students who have been redetermined as eligible for disability benefits as adults. A school can apply to become an EN and provide services to those beneficiaries who are 18 years of age or older who have assigned their tickets to that school (Maximus, 2003). Or a school may collaborate with another community agency that is an EN to provide services and split the payments. Additional information on the Ticket to Work Program and how to become an EN can be found online at **http://www.yourtickettowork.com**.

Social Security Work Incentives

One of the SSA's highest priorities is to assist individuals with disabilities achieve independence through employment supports (SSA, 2004). These supports were designed to allow an individual to continue receiving a SSI check and/or Medicaid while working toward independence. Students who receive SSI and go to work can take advantage of a variety of employment supports, including the Earned Income Exclusion, Student Earned Income Exclusion, Impairment-Related Work Expense, Blind Work expense, Plan for Achieving Self-Support (PASS), and 1619 A and B, which protects Medicaid coverage (Ferrell, Brooke, Kregel, & Getzel, 2002). All these employment supports continue to be available to individuals with severe disabilities when they leave school except the Student Earned Income Exclusion as long as the individual is working and receiving SSI. However, if a student begins to earn wages, regardless of the amount, that money must be reported to the SSA. Failure to report relevant information to the SSA such as earnings can cause substantial overpayment of benefits that may take many years for the individual to pay back to Social Security (Ferrell et al., 2002).

Earned Income Exclusion

Social Security does not count all the income that an individual with a disability earns when determining the amount of the SSI payment (SSA, 2004). An individual will always have more money by working than by not working when receiving SSI (Ferrell et al., 2002). Clearly, this is important information for parents and transition-age youth to consider when planning for postschool employment outcomes. The SSA excludes the first $65 of an individual's wages in any month and $85 if the person does not have any other unearned income. Then, only half the remainder of the individual's wages is counted.

Student Earned Income Exclusion

This work incentive helps students retain more of their original SSI checks while working and remaining in school. If a student is under age 22, not married or the head of a household, and regularly attending school, he or she can take advantage of the Student Earned Income Exclusion. As an example, in 2004, Social Security would not count up to $1,370 of a student's earned income per month when calculating the monthly SSI payment amount. The maximum yearly exclusion was $5,520. The Student Earned Income Exclusion applies consecutively to months in which there is earned income until the exclusion is exhausted, or the student is over 22. For example, a student goes to work and earns $600 a month while in school. Since this amount is less than $1,370, there would be no reduction in the student's monthly Social Security check until wages earned in a calendar year totaled $5,520 based on the calculations for 2004.

Impairment-Related Work Expense

The Impairment-Related Work Expense (IRWE) allows individuals with disabilities to deduct the cost of work-related expenses from their earnings before calculations are made to determine their SSI cash benefit. An IRWE is not a written plan but rather a monthly report of expenditures used by the Social Security representative in calculating total countable income and determining continued eligibility or the amount of monthly cash payments. The SSA must have proof for every IRWE claimed by the individual with a disability, including (a) the name and address of the prescribing source (e.g., doctor, vocational rehabilitation counselor), (b) the impairment for which the IRWE is prescribed, and (c) receipts and canceled checks showing that the expense was paid for by the individual and not someone else. Some of the expenses that may be reimbursed using an IRWE include attendant care services, job coach services, assistive technology, drugs and medical services, special door-to-door transportation costs, and guide dogs.

Plan for Achieving Self-Support

SSI recipients who need additional financial resources to help them get or maintain employment may submit a Plan for Achieving Self-Support (PASS). A PASS can help an individual establish or maintain SSI eligibility and can increase the SSI monthly payment amount (SSA, 2004). Specifically, the SSA can exclude wages when calculating the monthly SSI check if the person sets aside an approved amount in a special savings account to save and pay for services toward achieving employment goals. In addition, a person could also use a PASS to save unearned resources such as an allowance, child support, savings bonds, or gifts toward the individual's career goals.

A PASS may be used in combination with the Student Earned Income Exclusion while a student is still in school to save for needed postschool supports and services toward a specific career goal (Miller & O'Mara, 2003). While using the Student Earned Income Exclusion and PASS in combination, the student would keep most if not all of the SSI payment intact while saving for a career goal. Other sources of funding are available to fund education and career development that can be used in combination with a PASS. As previously mentioned, a student may access training services through the One-Stop Career Centers if determined eligible through an Individualized Training Account. These funds are not counted as income or resources for SSI purposes and could be set aside in a PASS. A PASS that includes multiple funding streams is often more likely to be approved by the SSA (Miller & O'Mara, 2003).

1619 A and B

Once a person goes to work, a general rule of thumb is that the SSI check will be reduced $1 for every $2 in wages (Ferrell et al., 2002). However, 1619 A and B protect a person's Medicaid coverage while working and receiving SSI. Under 1619A, as long as the person maintains even 1 cent in the SSI check, he or she will continue to be eligible for Medicaid. Once the person is working and the check is reduced to 0, he or she is protected by 1619 B. This allows the SSA to keep the individual's file open while stopping the SSI check. If the person's wages decrease or the individual loses the job, he or she can notify the SSA. The individual would not need to reapply, and SSI checks would begin again.

Under 1619 A and B, an individual still would not be able to have more than $2,000 in resources to meet the eligibility requirements. For 1619 B, there is a "threshold" amount for wages in all states or a maximum amount that a person can earn and still maintain Medicaid coverage. The exact amount of wages that a person can earn per year and still keep Medicaid can be determined by reviewing the current year's threshold amounts at **http://www.ssa.gov**.

This section has provided information on Social Security benefits and SSI issues related to the needs of transition-age youth. The chapter only touches on the wealth of information that is available, and other rules apply for students who are receiving SSDI. Please refer to the resources listed in this chapter or contact the benefits specialist in your community who can provide support to transition teams of students receiving these benefits. Transition teams need to consider creative ways of blending funding sources, including Social Security, vocational rehabilitation, the One-Stop

Career Center system, Medicaid waivers, and other state-specific funding sources, with school resources to fund the needed supports for students to transition successfully to postschool integrated employment outcomes.

Determining Student Preferences and Interests

Fortunately, student or adult choice now is recognized as the focus of service delivery. Many agree that students with disabilities who practice self-determination have better adult outcomes (Wehmeyer & Kelchner, 1995). Self-determination emerges across the life span as individuals learn skills and develop attitudes that enable them to be "causal agents" in their own lives (Wehmeyer, Palmer, Agran, Mithaug, & Martin, 2000). The implication is that students must participate in a wide variety of employment situations so that they can develop true preferences or dislikes and so that they can accurately express employment choices over time (Winking, O'Reilly, & Moon, 1993). Realistic, community-based assessment procedures must also be used so that students are not unfairly deemed ineligible for vocational education and vocational rehabilitation programs, as historically has been the case. A variety of ecological assessment procedures (Neubert, 2004) and entire curricula (Martin, Mithaug, Oliphint, Husch, & Frazier, 2002; Wehmeyer, Agran, & Hughes, 1998) now exist that promote student choice and self-determination in the secondary schools and transition process. Legal mandates in IDEA and Rehabilitation Act Amendments also require the documentation of student preferences for transition goals in the IEP and individual choice in the development of IPE goals.

One of the best ways to ensure active student involvement in the transition process is to use a student or person-centered planning process to establish transition goals (Miner & Bates, 1997) (corrected in the reference list). The approach, which focuses on the desires and needs of the student and his or her family in helping the student achieve his or her dreams, has three characteristics (Mount, 1994): (a) focusing on everyday activities as a basis of planning for the future, (b) emphasizing family and community connections rather than particular services, and (c) not relying on a single person or agency to do everything. A variety of person-centered planning approaches exist and have

been referred to as personal futures planning, essential lifestyle planning, circles of friends, McGill Action Planning System (MAPS), and Planning Alternative Tomorrows with Hope (PATH) (Falvey, Forest, Pearpoint, & Rosenberg, 1993). More on person-centered planning can be found in chapter 3 and later in this chapter.

Balancing Vocational Preparation with Inclusion and Other Integrated Opportunities

Most secondary programs for students with severe disabilities have emphasized job training and community functioning in natural settings and, in so doing, have also limited the amount of time these older students spend in integrated academic or social settings in their neighborhood schools with peers of the same age (Fisher & Sax, 1999). Billingsley and Albertson (1999) proposed that special educators should be able to work with regular educators to implement functional skill activities within regular education classes and extracurricular activities. When functional skills are an instructional focus for students with severe disabilities in high school, it should be scheduled "during periods that do not interfere with general education classes that would address other educational needs of higher priority" (p. 300).

When students participate in employment related activities before the age of 18, they could do so in the same manner as their same-age peers, such as working or volunteering after school and during the summer. The rationale for providing different services for these students after age 18 is based on the need for age-appropriate experiences in postsecondary courses (e.g., adult and continuing education and community colleges) and in employment sites in the community. These experiences would be based on a person-centered planning process that takes into account the wishes, needs, and interests of the student, his or her family, and significant friends or professionals who support the student (Baird & Everson, 1999).

With the success of inclusive education now well documented, the lack of access to inclusive school-based activities and classes for secondary students with severe disabilities raises many concerns (Tashie & Schuh, 1993). This is particularly true when students lack opportunities to learn social and communication skills by interacting frequently with same-age, nondisabled peers

(McDonnell, Mathot-Buckner, & Ferguson, 1996). Inclusion in school-based programs promotes social skills development, the most critical skill in job retention, and it helps students without disabilities develop positive attitudes toward their peers with disabilities (Wehman, 1996). Considering this, one must ask whether work or community-based programs are always more appropriate than an academic setting for teaching these related skills.

Some experts have advocated that secondary students with severe disabilities spend the entire school day in school-based inclusive programs while receiving job and community-based training on weekends, during summer vacation, or after school hours. Unfortunately, in most states there are no programs or individuals other than public school personnel who can do this kind of training for school-age individuals, and it is unrealistic to expect educators to work these extra hours when most are already overworked and underpaid. Therefore, secondary programs must seek a balance for each student during regular school hours. The amount of job training should depend on a number of factors, including age, student preference, availability and quality of social interaction in each setting, and level of social, work-related, and specific vocational skill development. As Agran, Snow, and Swaner (1999) noted, there is no empirical evidence supporting which curricular emphasis is most critical, but many secondary teachers support a combination of both inclusion and functional skill training.

As students with severe disabilities reach the age of 18 or 19, a time when most students are graduating from high school, it is age appropriate for them to spend more time in employment or other postsecondary situations where they can take classes, work, and interact socially with other young adults. Many school systems are now starting postsecondary programs for students with severe disabilities who are ages 18 to 21 that are located on local college campuses (Grigal, Neubert, & Moon, 2001; Neubert, Moon, & Grigal, 2004). These postsecondary programs have been implemented in a number of states, including California, Louisiana, Kentucky, Maryland, and Oregon (Grigal, Neubert, & Moon, 2001; Hall, Kleinert, & Kearns, 2000; National Transition Alliance, 2000). These programs have been developed on college campuses and in the community to serve high school students with severe disabilities who are 18 years or older in their final years of public school. The students who attend these programs typically have been in high school for 4 or more years and may receive an alternative exit document (e.g., certificate of attendance, IEP diploma) as they exit public school. These programs are located not on high school campuses but in various postsecondary locations, such as universities, community colleges, community businesses, or adult service agencies.

Postsecondary programs located on college campuses or in the community typically serve between 8 and 21 students a year and are staffed by a special educator or transition specialist and instructional assistants who are funded by the school system (Grigal et al., 2001). Students' activities and schedules differ depending on their goals and needs; however, most programs offer some classroom-based instruction (e.g., functional academics) along with opportunities to enroll in college classes, to work on campus or in the community, and to participate in social and recreational activities with college-age peers. Programs located in postsecondary sites often include best practices in transition such as functional academics, paid job training and follow-along, assessment activities including person-centered planning, self-determination skills instruction, social and recreational skill development, community mobility training, and collaborating with families and postsecondary providers to ensure future access to adult services and supports.

One of the key features of postsecondary programs is that services are coordinated outside the high school from a designated location in the community. Choosing a site for the program requires collaboration of members from the school system and the community. A planning committee, which includes representatives from the various key organizations including school personnel, the program host (college or business), employers, local adult service providers, rehabilitation personnel, and, of course, parents and students should be the starting point. The planning committee should conduct a needs assessment to determine what kinds of postsecondary services are needed and where and how to provide them (Neubert, Moon, & Grigal, 2002). Neubert et al. (2004) found in a survey of Maryland postsecondary programs that paid employment training and interagency collaboration was a strength for these programs but that attendance in college classes and extracurricular activities was still limited in some cases.

Another framework some school systems have used to provide students with severe disabilities services outside high school after age 18 is based on the provision of individual supports (Hart, Zafft, & Zimbrich, 2001; Neubert et al., 2002; Weir, 2001). Using individual supports, students receive educational and community supports outside high school without attending a site-based program. A critical feature of individual supports is that they are provided and coordinated for one student at a time. The student receives services in a number of locations (e.g., college, employment site, and community environment) that are determined by their personal needs and goals instead of attending a program at a specific site. Using this approach, a student is not limited to existing programs or sites. The student and a support team create and implement an individualized schedule of work, college classes, or age-appropriate social activities. Those providing individual supports often use a person-centered planning process to (a) determine the student's interests, needs and goals, (b) identify the environments where these goals can be met, (c) determine the financial and human supports needed to access the environments and obtain the goals, and (d) monitor the coordination of support and progress toward goals. Supports can be provided by a number of individuals from the school system, the college, or agencies such as vocational rehabilitation. Coordination of services and supports usually remains the responsibility of someone in the school system until the student exits at age 21.

Proponents of this approach maintain that each student requires a unique support system that is based on individual choice. In addition, students with severe disabilities are seen as college students or employees, not as people with disabilities from a "program." This approach clearly enhances opportunities for inclusion with age-appropriate peers in community settings.

Providing individual supports to students after the age of 18 requires school personnel, students and their families, and college personnel to rethink how services and supports are delivered on college campuses and in the community (Neubert et al., 2002). Typically students with disabilities receive their instruction and supports from personnel paid by the school system until the age of 21 or 22. Using the individual supports approach, support is coordinated through various means, including the local school system, a college disability support office, or state agencies such as vocational rehabilitation (Hart et al., 2001). This approach requires continuing dialogue of "who pays for what" and ongoing collaborative efforts on the part of school systems, colleges, and adult service providers to find creative solutions.

Hart et al. (2001) summarized how the roles and responsibilities for teachers must be designed when using individualized supports. These include a move from teaching to service coordination or case management; training and supervising of instructional assistants and job coaches; working a variable, 12-month schedule; and assisting students develop self-determination skills in preferred environments. While many of these responsibilities are similar to what a transition specialist might provide in public schools (Asselin, Todd-Allen, & deFur, 1998; Council for Exceptional Children, 2000), this approach requires staff and administrators to truly reconsider how case management roles can be undertaken by teachers and specialists who support older students. Teacher and instructional assistants must be allowed to spend their time outside the confines of the high school; work flexible, nontraditional schedules; and determine how natural supports can be used in postsecondary settings. School administrators must understand the need for these changing roles and support teachers appropriately in terms of their caseload, the time needed for planning and collaborative efforts, and the resources allocated to the students and staff. Finally, community agency personnel must be involved in supporting students before they exit school. This too will require a shift in fiscal resources and staff responsibilities for some personnel. Individuals interested in planning, evaluating, and implementing postsecondary services for students with significant disabilities should visit the On Campus Outreach Website at **http://www.education.umd.edu/oco**.

Collaborating with a Team for Successful Transition

Effective transition planning depends on formal, functional agency linkages at the national, state, and local levels. Planning also must occur at the individual levels among the student, family, educators, human services agencies, local service providers, advocates, and businesses. Recent research has shown that collaborative structures at the state and, most important, at the local levels are crucial in successful service delivery (Furney, Hasazi, & DeStefano, 1997). The efforts of several states to formalize transition practices across agencies has been thoroughly documented (Bates, Bronkema, Ames, & Hess, 1992). Everson (1993) wrote that states must develop formal *cooperative agreements* between state-level agencies (such as education, vocational rehabilitation, and developmental disabilities) in order to shape legislation, to provide a framework for local planning, and to advocate for appropriate budgets. Cooperative agreements can specify functions such as establishing agendas for in-service training, defining responsibilities of various team members, and providing some standard procedures for local teams (Wehman, 1996). Fortunately, IDEA provides some guidelines for implementing IDEA transition requirements.

Local teams, comprised of representatives from agencies or individuals typically on an IEP team, collaborate for the purpose of assessing, changing, and monitoring local transition efforts, and a team functions according to the needs of transition-age students and the quality of secondary and adult service programs. Local teams must also provide avenues for information exchange and training among families, agencies, and businesses. Ultimately, a local team must examine IEPs to make sure that they are functional, promote self-determination, and lead to effective adult outcomes and that they will transfer over into goals on adult service plans, such as IPEs and individual habilitation plans.

Individual Transition Planning and the IEP

The individual transition planning team consists of the student and significant others to the student; educators; adult service providers at the local level; appropriate human service agencies who provide case management, funding to local providers, or direct services; advocates; and local employers. Team members must collaborate to develop and implement transition goals and activities on a student's IEP. These goals must be based on the student's preferences and interests, ideally determined by multiple experiences and a long-running personal futures planning process. IDEA further facilitates the monitoring of transition goals by stating that any agency or individual on the planning team, either from within or outside the school system, can sign off as the responsible party for seeing that a particular goal is met. To establish priority goals for any student with severe disabilities, an individual transition team should consider developing goals and related activities from the following areas: vocational training, paid employment, postsecondary education,

independent living, financial supports, health insurance or medical supports, daily living needs, recreation, medical needs, transportation, advocacy or self-advocacy needs, and social and sexual needs.

The number and type of transition goals depends on the needs of each student within and across all areas.

Heather needs several goals related to vocational training because, at age 16, her skill level and preferences are not yet established. In addition, she is already included in regular education classes and many extracurricular activities in which other skills can be developed. Jane, aged 19, on the other hand, has paid employment, but she needs skill development and support in other areas, particularly social and friendship development, assistive technology, and community transition supports. Therefore, her vocational goals may not be priority until after she is accepted into the postsecondary program. Robert has determined that he does not want to explore postsecondary programs. His transition goals focus on career exploration activities and establishing a work history.

A sample IEP transition goal for Heather, related to vocational training and employment, is shown in Figure 15-1.

School-Based Vocational Preparation

Vocational preparation at the middle and high school levels should lead to meaningful work in the community, as workplace supports and developing technology has made paid work possible for citizens with the most severe disabilities (Inge, 2001; Wehman, 2001). One of the most important research findings shows that paid or unpaid work experiences for students with disabilities facilitate the acquisition of higher-paying jobs postgraduation (Blackorby & Wagner, 1996; Colley & Jamison, 1998; Luecking & Fabian, 2000). Effective vocational training actually starts during the elementary years, during which learning to take responsibility, paying attention to natural cues, using a schedule, acquiring social skills, appropriate communication skills, self-monitoring and choice-making skills,

FIGURE 15–1

Heather's Sample IEP Vocational Training Goal

Goal #1

Heather will participate in unpaid work training in three job types to include stocking, food industry, and hotel positions so that she can express more accurately her preferences for paid employment positions by the end of the school year.

Level of current performance

Heather participated last year in an in-school work internship for 6 weeks as a school office messenger. She has expressed the desire to do this type of work in the future. To date, she has no other training experiences.

Activities needed to accomplish goal

1. Heather will work in all training sites on Mondays, Wednesdays, and Fridays for 2 hours per day, for 8 to 12 weeks in each site. Time of day will vary to include a workday of 7:30 a.m. to 9:30 a.m. at site #1, 9:30 a.m. to 11:30 a.m. at site #2, and 12:30 p.m. to 2:30 p.m. at site #3.

2. At 1-week intervals on each site, Heather will verbally answer questions concerning her desire to do future work in this area.

3. Job supervisors will evaluate Heather's performance at midterm and at the end of each training cycle.

4. Heather will review a videotape of her work at the end of each training period and discuss her work performance and preferences for future work of this type.

5. Heather will develop a résumé at the end of the school year listing her work experiences and strengths in each position.

Date of completion

6/1/04

Individuals(s) responsible for implementation

Heather, transition specialist, job trainer (teaching assistant)

---

and understanding the meaning of jobs or careers are emphasized.

As the student becomes older, inclusion in school programs and activities shifts to community programs in which job-related tasks, community mobility, and functional academic skills are taught in the settings in which they will be used (McDonnell et al., 1996). Actual training in real jobs should begin at the secondary level, where this instruction must be balanced with teaching work-related academic skills, social skills, and age-appropriate curriculum content areas in school settings alongside same-age peers who are not disabled (Putnam, 1994; Stainback & Stainback, 1992). The final years of school for students with severe disabilities between the ages of 19 and 22 should involve paid work and opportunities to continue learning and socializing with young adults. This implies that education moves out of the high school and into community, work, and postsecondary academic settings for the entire school day. Regardless of the age of the student, vocational training must focus on common outcomes and incorporate critical elements. These elements or

outcomes are listed in Table 15–4 and described further in the following sections.

Longitudinal Instruction of Work-Related Skills Across Grades and Settings

Vocational training must be coordinated with all other areas of a student's life, especially for those with the most severe disabilities, for whom life skills in domestic and community environments and appropriate social and communication skills may ultimately be more critical (Wehman, 1996). Therefore, instruction of generalized work behaviors that are also crucial to survival in other environments should comprise much of the vocational curriculum until the student is in the last 3 or 4 years of school (usually ages 18 to 22). This kind of approach allows for some job sampling in real job sites and even some part-time paid employment while still permitting inclusion in age-appropriate content areas and instruction in nonvocational community skills, such as transportation and community leisure participation.

TABLE 15–4
Critical Elements and Outcomes of School-Based Vocational Preparation

- Longitudinal instruction of work-related skills occurs across grades and settings, including inclusive school-based activities and classes, work sites, and community environments.
- Continual assessment of work preferences and interests begins in middle school and is documented in the IEP starting at age 14 so that a career path is identified.
- Community-referenced employment training is based on the local economy.
- Job training occurs across a variety of real jobs in real employment settings.
- Training sites are established in community businesses.
- Community-based training sites meet labor law requirements.
- Systematic instruction and workplace supports, including coworker supports, are used to teach vocational skills.
- Assistive technology is used when needed to facilitate student independence.
- Paid work is sought for students exiting school along with appropriate support services, such as vocational rehabilitation, Medicaid waivers, Social Security benefits, work incentives, and so forth.

Heather spends a good portion of her school week in regular school programs but still has unpaid job experiences in real employment sites where her preferences are assessed and specific work behaviors are taught. She also spends some time in other community environments learning mobility skills, functional academic, and communication techniques and sampling leisure and social alternatives. Paid work opportunities are part of her summer school program, an age-appropriate option for a 16-year-old. Most of Heather's functional academic, social, and communication needs are taught both in school settings through the modification of curriculum content areas and in the context of community and job site training programs.

Many work-related behaviors can be taught early on, usually beginning in the elementary grades. These work-related behaviors include caring for personal hygiene needs; using various transportation modes; taking short breaks; appropriately asking for assistance; getting to tasks or areas on time and within a certain time frame; learning to delay reinforcement; paying attention to natural cues and directions; getting along socially with individuals and groups of people; sharing items; adjusting to changes in a schedule; following a schedule in some format; understanding basic access, safety, and danger symbols used in the community; eating a meal or snack in a public area or fast-food environment; using a communication system with strangers or coworkers; making purchases such as vending items; responding to correction or criticism; understanding the concept of pay for work; and budgeting from a paycheck.

Continual Assessment of Work Preferences and Interests

Critical to developing vocational goals and activities for transition is the concept of identifying the career path that a student wishes to pursue. Using person-centered planning strategies (Parent, Unger, & Inge, 1997; Wehman, Everson, & Reid, 1996) can lay the foundation for this career path. With support, the student identifies a group of people or "circle of support" to assist in exploring what his or her future would be like. The central concept to a person-centered approach is encouraging students and their families to "dream" about their futures and possible careers. Existing services and programs should never limit a student's dreams about work. For instance, professionals who do not believe that a student with severe disabilities can be competitively employed may discourage many students with the most severe disabilities. They may be directed to existing vocational training experiences that have been established for other students rather than the more challenging task of identifying training sites specific to a student's interests. In some cases, students may even be directed toward more restrictive choices, such as segregated day activity programs or extended employment (formally sheltered workshops) because the transition team lacks the vision to push the service delivery system. The transition years must be used to fully explore options and visions for all students.

A student with a disability who dreams of being a movie star, for instance, is no different from students without disabilities who have the same dream. Instead of telling the student with a disability that her dream is unrealistic, she should be directed to work experiences in environments that reflect her interests. She may pursue part-time jobs such as the ticket taker or concession stand operator at the local movie theater. There also may be opportunities in a video store, a costume store, or some other similar environment in which the student is exposed to a component of the dream. Once these environments are identified, the student should have vocational training experiences across several options to see if any of these will meet her interests or preferences.

MAPS as a Planning Tool

MAPS is one person-centered tool that has been used to assist students in planning their futures (Falvey et al., 1993). This is an adult- or peer-facilitated process in which a facilitator and sometimes a recorder work with a student and a student-selected support team to identify the student's gifts and strengths as well as to plan for the future. The student selects people to assist in the planning process. There are eight key questions that should be addressed during a MAPS meeting: (a) What is a MAP? (b) What is the person's history or story? (c) What are your dreams? (d) What are your nightmares? (e) Who is the person? (f) What are the person's strengths, gifts, and talents? (g) What does the person need? and (h) What is the plan of action?

The key to the successful completion of a MAPS plan is to have a positive approach to the process. The student's gifts and talents should be highlighted, and he or she should never be described in terms of a disability label or problem. If a specific issue challenges the student, the team needs to state the issue in terms of support needs. For example, Jane dreams of becoming a secretary or teacher. This became clear to her parents when they initiated a MAPS meeting to plan for their daughter's future. Instead of making judgments about this being an unrealistic goal, her circle of support has begun to make plans to determine a career path in one of these areas.

PATH as Planning Tool

PATH is another process that can be used to identify a student's dreams and goals for employment. PATH evolved from the MAPS process and was designed to put into place a plan of action for the focus person (Pearpoint, O'Brien, & Forest, 1993). Literally, the process can identify an employment "path" for the student to pursue.

Similar to MAPS, the PATH process consists of a series of steps or questions that constitute the meeting, which is led by a group facilitator. The facilitator is preferably neutral and not a member of the student's transition team. The facilitator's responsibility is to assist the group in addressing each of the eight steps of PATH. These steps include (a) the dream; (b) sensing the goal, positive and possible; (c) grounding in the now; (d) who is enrolled; (e) recognizing ways to build strength; (f) charting actions for the next 3 months; (g) planning the next month's work; and (h) committing to the next steps.

The discussion of the PATH steps can direct the student's transition activities for the coming year. The team must be committed to following through with the plan; otherwise, the process yields a creative graphic with no outcomes.

MAPS, PATH, and Collaborative IEPs

MAPS and PATH do not take the place of transition plans or IEPS (Malatchi & Inge, 1997). They are companion tools that can enhance transition planning. They can give direction to the legal documents and provide a starting point in identifying the student's goals for the future. There are no rules related to whether a team uses a MAPS or PATH approach, and both seem to be excellent tools when beginning a transition planning process. Some teams may choose to use MAPS initially and then use PATH in later years when vocational interests become clearer. These person-centered tools facilitate positive input from all participants, create positive pictures of a student, and actively involve the student in his or her transition plan.

Community-Referenced Employment Training Based on the Local Economy

In some instances, students may be able to identify a specific career path in their person-centered plans. Others have such limited exposure to the workplace that they need to have a variety of experiences that reflect the local labor market. These training experiences assist in the identification of the student's preferences, abilities, and support needs. Therefore, each school system's vocational curriculum should be specific to the community as well as based on the expressed interests of the students. This requires ongoing assessment of the local labor market to determine the major employers in the community, the types of employment most commonly available, and the type of employment that has been obtained by individuals with disabilities (Brooke, Inge, Armstrong, & Wehman, 1997).

This may be accomplished by surveying the local Chamber of Commerce, contacting the One-Stop Career Center, reading the newspaper want ads, looking in the telephone yellow pages, completing follow-up contacts with school graduates, and contacting adult service agencies and employment programs. The school system should identify who will conduct the analysis of the local economy and who will make the contacts. A school system may consider appointing a task force to complete these activities when first beginning a community-based training program.

A labor market analysis in some communities, such as a small rural community, may reveal limited employment options for students with severe disabilities. Self-employment may be a viable option for students in these communities as well as any other community as a postschool vocational outcome. Self-employment as a relatively new concept but shows great promise for individuals with severe disabilities (Griffin & Hammis, 2003; Rucker & Brooks-Lane, 2003). Self-employment provides an opportunity for individuals to create an employment situation specifically tailored to meet their personal interests and abilities and support needs. The process is not unlike the start-up of a business for anyone without a disability including business planning and testing the feasibility of the proposed business.

Many may think that business ownership is beyond the capabilities of a person with severe disabilities. In thinking about this concept, the reader is encouraged to consider the general contractor as an analogy (R. Shelly, personal communication, April 19, 2004). The general contractor does not have all the skills to complete a job but hires others to support the project. The student with a severe disability may need a key support person as well as a business development team to include the transition specialist, vocational rehabilitation counselor, case manager, and family member and other community supports to assist the individual in realizing the goal of self-employment. The team assists the individual by using a person-centered business planning process (Griffin & Hammis, 2003). Funding sources for the business can include vocational rehabilitation, individual training accounts from the One-Stop Career system, the SSA's PASS, and other innovative strategies (described earlier) that are state specific.

Self-employment also includes resource ownership or owning a "business within a business" (Rucker & Brooks-Lane; 2003). Consider the following examples described by Rucker and Brooks-Lane (2003):

Kay is a young woman who loves children. She also has an interest in computers. Her business within a business was negotiated at a day care center that did not have the means to expand into providing computer experiences for the preschoolers. Kay purchased a computer, software, computer table, and chair and set up her business within the day care center to work with the preschool children.

Pam is a young woman who always keeps her fingernails polished and styled. In working with Pam, it was determined that this is very important to her. She was assisted in purchasing products that are related to nail care, and these are displayed in a cabinet for her to sell. Pam's business of selling beauty products is located within a local hair salon.

John has a love of pets and animals and wanted to work in a veterinarian clinic. Using the resource ownership model, John purchased a hydraulic table that can be used for grooming. His pet grooming business is located within the local veterinarian clinic.

The transition team that assists a student toward self-employment as a vocational goal must consider how the business may impact the student's Social Security benefits. A benefits specialist would be an important transition team resource in this instance.

The transition team is encouraged to view students from a capacity perspective believing that a student's dreams of business ownership are possible. Many resources are available to assist with supporting a person to set up a business (e.g., Griffin, 1999; Griffin & Hammis, 2003; Griffin et al., 2001; Shelly et al., 2002).

Job Training Across a Variety of Real Jobs in Real Employment Settings

Options for vocational training can include simulated work in the classroom, school building, and grounds; "real" work in the classroom obtained from community organizations; school-based vocational activities alongside actual school employees; community-based training sites; volunteer work; and supported employment positions in the community. Regardless of the setting, job-training experiences should be based on a student's preferences, interests, and IEP goals and not on convenience of the location. When designing vocational training experiences, school personnel must consider the difficulty of simulating the demands of a real work environment within the school setting, such as interactions with coworkers and customers, productivity issues, and other characteristics of the workplace (e.g., noise, orienting in a large space) (Inge, 1997). Another caution is related to volunteer experiences. If a student volunteers in the community, the work tasks should not be part of a job that others would receive payment for completing.

There are many benefits to providing a student job training in real employment settings. First, the student's interests related to employment in real jobs (not simulated) that exist in the community can be explored for a potential career. Second, ideal job characteristics can be pinpointed that match the student's abilities and interests. Third, training experiences within work settings can assist the student in identifying interests, preferences, and support needs that could be realized through self-employment or a "business within a business." Fourth, community-based experiences provide an opportunity to identify a student's work challenges within a real environment in order to determine how workplace supports and training can eliminate these challenges. Therefore, each student's schedule should reflect a portion of his or her vocational activities in the community as well as within the school building. Following are some considerations when designing a vocational program using a school- or community-based training approach.

Identifying Real Jobs Using a Community Labor Analysis

A community labor analysis should be completed to guide the selection of vocational objectives that reflect real jobs in the student's community regardless of the training location. Do not fall into the trap of obtaining work from the school office or a community agency to complete in the classroom if it does not reflect future job possibilities or the interests of the student. Simulated work that is not reflective of the local labor market does not give the students experiences that can help with identifying future job preferences.

School Versus Real Work Sites

School-based programs should be reserved for younger students (under age 14) when vocational training in a real work site is not an option because of the labor law

requirements. When using the school as a setting, students should be trained alongside school employees if possible, remembering to take into consideration the preferences of the students for these positions. Requiring a student to work in the school cafeteria, if he or she is not interested in this job, does not reflect best practices for vocational training. Teachers need to be sensitive when using the school as a work setting and consider the impact that this may have on peer relationships. In addition, if the school hires external agencies such as a business from the community to do work that the student is doing, all labor law guidelines must be met as if this were a nonpaid work experience in the community (Inge, Simon, Halloran, & Moon, 1993).

Transitions in School Programs

As students move from elementary school to high school, they should have the opportunity to complete a variety of jobs in a number of different settings to assist in developing a work history, determining job preferences, identifying future training needs, and determining skill characteristics for job matching. This information can be shared, as the student moves through the school years, with teachers and adult service agencies to facilitate the transition process from school to work. As previously stated in this chapter, students who have documentation that they are able to achieve an employment outcome have a solid foundation for entering the vocational rehabilitation system.

Figure 15–2 provides a vocational community-based training summary for Heather at the end of the semester or three 6-week grading periods in which she experienced three different training sites. Since she was uncertain of her job preferences, her transition team determined that she would have the opportunity to experience three different sites during the school year. Her documentation includes work task and environmental preferences, training needs, and recommendations for matching her abilities to a paid work experience.

Establish Community-Based Training Sites

The steps in developing community-based training sites include (a) identifying appropriate businesses, (b) contacting the personnel director of employer, (c) identifying and analyzing appropriate jobs, and (d) scheduling community-based instruction.

FIGURE 15-2

Report of Vocational Training Experiences: Community-Based Training Report

---

Student: Heather

Date of Report: June 1

During the past 4½ months (one semester), Heather has received community-based training at Hechinger, Howard Johnson's, and Shoney's. She worked at each job site for 2 hours, 4 days a week, over a 6-week period. Each of the training sites involved different job duties and work environments.

Training Site #1

At Hechinger's, Heather had several work stations where she put up stock and "fronted" the shelves. This required her to reposition merchandise from the back of a shelf to the front, organizing the items in neat rows. Heather was required to orient to large areas in the store and had frequent contact with customers. By the end of the training session, she was able to independently match stock in boxes to the correct location on the shelves, lift stock weighing up to 20 pounds, recognize and set aside damaged items and opened packages, maneuver a loaded stock cart throughout the store, and respond appropriately to customer questions; Heather was taught to say "please ask at the service desk" when customers approached her for information.

Training Site #2

At Howard Johnson's, Heather's job was to clean the restroom (e.g., sinks, toilets, sweeping, mopping) and vacuum the motel lobby. The position involved moving between two different work stations in the front of the motel. Heather reached skill acquisition on the bathroom tasks within 4 weeks of training; however, she could not perform the skill to production standards, and therefore the remainder of her placement focused on increasing her speed. During the last 2 weeks, her time to complete the task decreased from 90 minutes after a reinforcement program was implemented. Heather did not reach skill acquisition on the vacuuming task.

Training Site #3

Heather's position at Shoney's focused on busing tables and rolling silverware. Rolling silverware was a seated job duty that occurred in a secluded section of the dining room; busing tables required orienting to the entire restaurant, continuous standing, and frequent interactions with customers and coworkers. Heather reached independence on both tasks by the end of the training period. She was meticulous and took great care in performing her work. At times, this hampered her ability to achieve the production speed of her coworkers.

Summary

Heather performed well in both large and small work environments and was able to remain on task in environments where there were unfamiliar people. She seemed to prefer working in public environments with Shoney's being the work site of choice. Heather consistently displayed a positive attitude, arriving at work each day motivated and eager to work. Her interactions with customers and coworkers were both appropriate and pleasant. She was able to respond to yes or no questions accurately, initiate "hello" and "good-bye," and carry on short conversations with coworkers. Training sessions were scheduled between 7:30 a.m. and 3:00 p.m., and she maintained the same enthusiasm and speed across all training times. The system of least intrusive prompts was the most effective instructional strategy used with Heather. She consistently worked at a slow, steady pace for up to an hour and half before needing to take a break. Heather's physical strength is good, and she was able to carry a 30- to 40-pound bus pan full of dishes from the dining room to the dish room.

Points to Consider When Seeking Employment

1. The best instructional strategy for Heather is the system of least prompts.
2. Heather likes to self-monitor her work using a picture card and check system. She learned to do this independently during the Shoney's placement.
3. Heather is able to orient in large and small work environments.
4. She prefers to work in settings where she has frequent contact with coworkers and customers. She appeared especially motivated in the food service setting.
5. Heather has a positive attitude. She is motivated by work and is receptive to instruction from a job trainer.
6. Heather's endurance remained consistent for 1½ hours between 7:30 a.m. and 3:00 p.m.
7. Physical strength is good, and Heather can carry a 40-pound bucket for short distances (about 15 feet).

FIGURE 15–2 (*Continued*)

Future Training Recommendations

1. Increase opportunities for Heather to purchase items in the community using a "money card." She is currently unable to perform tasks such as using a vending machine independently.

2. Provide opportunities for Heather to perform tasks while standing to increase her endurance. She also has a tendency to stand and rock from foot to foot rather than maintaining a firm base of support.

3. Establish jobs and errands for Heather to complete that require her to verbally interact with adults. Focus on maintaining eye contact when performing these duties.

4. Provide opportunities for Heather to work toward increasing her speed and production rate on a task.

5. Refer to supported employment placement during next year of school before graduation.

Identifying Appropriate Businesses

Inge, Dymond, and Wehman (1996) state that it is helpful to identify businesses that offer several different job types. For instance, a local mall may have several businesses that could provide training sites while dispersing students and trainers within a reasonable distance of each other. Other options could include the local hospital, an industrial park or business complex (assuming the businesses targeted are considered nonhazardous), or a community college or university. The businesses should represent jobs that reflect student choice as well as ones that are available and within a reasonable distance from the school and student's homes. It may not be appropriate to select a job at a local business complex that would translate into a 45-minute ride to and from the school building or student's homes.

Contacting the Personnel Director or Employer

The school may identify a task force or business advisory board to identify businesses to contact for community-based instruction. This task force may serve as a network in the business community, which can provide invaluable employer contacts and resources (Brooke et al., 1997). In addition, the network can include school system contacts as well as contacts provided by parents, family members, friends, and the business community.

One individual, often the transition coordinator, should be identified to approach employers regarding use of their business for community-based training sites. If it is not possible for a single person to make all initial contacts, the school should maintain a list of businesses that have been approached as community-based training sites to prevent duplication of effort. This transition coordinator or teacher would be responsible for contacting the personnel director or company manager by phone or letter to set up an appointment to discuss the school's program in detail.

During the initial site visit, the teacher should discuss the responsibilities of the school trainer, student, employer, and coworkers. In addition, the employer should understand the labor law requirements that need to be met regarding unpaid work experiences. The contact person also should be prepared to discuss insurance coverage by the school system and liability issues as well as the development of a training agreement with the business. If the employer agrees to establish a training site, the teacher should schedule a time to meet with the department supervisors where the students will be working in order to develop task analyses and job duty schedules. A thank-you note is always appropriate regardless of the outcome of the initial contact.

Analyzing the Work Culture and Identifying Potential Duties

During this step, the teacher or community-based trainer needs to determine if there are any special requirements that the students must follow while on the work site. For instance, does the employer or supervisor want the student(s) to wear a uniform or specific clothing? Is there a particular entrance to the facility that should be used on arrival? Should the student report to the supervisor on arrival? Do employees have assigned lockers, and can one be available to the student(s)? Is there an identified break area and employee bathroom? Are there any restricted areas or activities in the facility? All this information should be recorded and placed in a file that can be accessed by all school personnel. This would be particularly important during teacher absence when another school employee must supervise the site.

Initial information to identify potential jobs within a business can be obtained from the personnel director or employer. Often this individual will be able to provide written job descriptions that can be used to identify job types; however, observation at the work sites usually is more beneficial for job identification (Brooke et al., 1997).

Scheduling Community-Based Instruction

Creative use of school personnel to schedule, transport, and train students for community-based instruction clearly is the greatest challenge for administrators and teachers. Staffing solutions may include team teaching; use of volunteers, paraprofessionals, peer tutors, graduate students, and student teachers; heterogeneous grouping of students; staggered student training schedules; and hiring staff to serve as "job coaches" within the community business. Transportation issues have been resolved using volunteers' or parent's cars with mileage reimbursement, coordination of training schedules with regular school bus schedules, use of public transportation, use of school district vehicles, and walking to sites within short distances. Each school system must select procedures that are effective for their specific needs. A rule of thumb for scheduling and training purposes is to have no more than three students per training site per instructor; however, one to one would be most effective for skill development.

Community-Based Training Sites Meet Labor Law Requirements

Understanding a number of key concepts and issues is critical to successfully implementing the guidelines that were released by the Departments of Education and Labor. First, the primary intent of the Fair Labor Standards Act is to ensure that individuals are not exploited in the workplace (Halloran & Johnson, 1992). One way to make certain that students with disabilities are not exploited in nonpaid vocational training is to ascertain that a "nonemployment relationship" exists

between the students and the employer. In other words, the relationship exists for training purposes only, and activities completed by students do not result in an immediate advantage to the business.

A number of factors are considered when determining whether a business is benefiting from having students in community-based instruction. First, the student(s) and teacher (or other school representative) cannot complete an employee's job duties while the employee is reassigned to other work tasks that are not usually his or her responsibility. For example, a student and the teacher should not deliver mail in a business while the administrative assistant who typically does this job is assigned additional word processing responsibilities. The employee must continue to do his or her work while the student is trained on those tasks as well. This has been referred to as "shadowing" the regular employee (Inge et al., 1993). In addition, students cannot perform services that, although not ordinarily performed by employees, clearly benefit the business. As an example, it would be unacceptable for students to clean an office as an unpaid work experience once a week if a business only hires a work crew to clean the office once a month.

Before placing a student in a community business for instruction, the transition team must identify the goals and objectives that are to be taught and include them in the student's IEP (see Figure 15-1). In addition, the teacher must make sure that the employer, student, and parent understand that the placement (a) is intended for training purposes and (b) is a nonpaid experiences and that (c) the student is not guaranteed a job after the training is complete. It is important to develop an agreement between all parties concerned that specifically states the intent of community-based vocational instruction including the Department of Labor and Department of Education guidelines. This agreement will be signed and dated by parents and student, school representative, and business representatives. The following situations, related to Heather and Robert, show how some training or unpaid work experiences can conflict with labor law guidelines.

 Heather's Case

Heather's transition team, consisting of her teacher, the transition coordinator, her parents, and Heather, decides that she should participate in a minimum of three vocational training placements during the school year. Heather has not yet expressed a specific career preference, so

she will have three different training opportunities that reflect job opportunities in her local labor market, including retail sales and food service. The transition team identifies two retail experiences—a hardware store and a clothing store environment. All work tasks are specified in

Heather's IEP, data will be collected, and a summary of each training experience will be written up for her school records. Heather, her parents, and each employer will sign an agreement before training, stating that these are nonpaid work experiences to benefit Heather and not the companies. A teacher or aide will be with Heather at all times to provide supervision, instruction, and data collection. Each experience will provide 120 hours of training experience within a real work environment.

Response to Heather's Case

One problem area is that the community-based training experiences at the hardware store and clothing store represent the same job type (e.g., Heather will be stocking merchandise). Some teachers may interpret the guidelines to mean that Heather could have 120 hours at

the clothing store and 120 hours at the hardware store during the school year since they are two different work sites. This is not the case because the tasks performed at both locations are not clearly different job classifications. In Heather's example, the teacher should monitor the training experiences to ensure the Heather receives only 120 hours of vocational training in stocking regardless of the number of sites in any one school year. A second problem exists with the agreement with the various employers; it also should specify that Heather and her teacher are not displacing company employees, filling vacant positions, or otherwise benefiting the business during community-based instruction. For instance, Heather and her teacher would need to "shadow," or work alongside, regular employees while completing the work tasks at the job sites.

 Robert's Case

Mrs. Jones is the school's transition coordinator and is attempting to find all her students "volunteer" positions within the community for at least 2 hours per week to help them gain work experiences. Mrs. Jones's neighbor, Mr. Andrews, works at a university as the Webmaster for the athletic department. Mr. Andrews tells Mrs. Jones that he is willing to have one student work for him every Friday afternoon from 3:30 p.m. to 5:30 p.m. checking the links on the department's Website. This job would be considered a "volunteer position." Mrs. Jones thinks that this might be a great opportunity for Robert since he is so interested in sports and he will have an opportunity to be around college students his own age. Mrs. Jones doesn't plan on listing these activities as part of Robert's IEP since he is volunteering his time during nonschool hours.

Response to Robert's Case

Students who have disabilities can volunteer their time in the same way as their peers without disabilities (Inge et al., 1993). For instance, Mrs. Jones might try to identify typical volunteer positions with the YWCA, church, or other local charity organization for Robert that reflect his interests in sports. In this situation as described, it is unlikely that a 19-year-old student would volunteer for 2 to 4 hours of nonpaid office work. Robert should be paid at

least minimum wage if this is not a training experience. Or Mrs. Jones could work with the athletic department to set up a nonpaid training experience for Robert. If it is a training experience, it must be in the IEP and meet all labor law guidelines already outlined in Figure 15–2.

Another option to volunteering might be to determine if Robert is able to meet the production levels for this particular job. If Robert did not meet the production standard, Mrs. Jones could assist the employer in filing for a 14(c) Special Wage Certificate. This certificate can be used when production levels for a particular job fall below the norm. The employer is generally responsible for obtaining a certificate of this type; however, a rehabilitation counselor or school representative can submit a group application for all students and employers participating in a school's work experience program. The important thing to note is that the certificate must be in effect before employment. Regional Department of Labor offices, Wage and Hour Divisions, have the directions and forms. Robert may quality for subminimum wage if he cannot work at the established company rate of production, but if he is meeting the standard set by the company, he should be paid minimum wage for his work. When approaching employers, school personnel should not just assume that businesses would not pay for a student's work experiences.

Selecting Systematic Behavioral Procedures to Teach Vocational Skills

Once the sites have been identified and a schedule for student placement has been determined, the educator who is assigned to work with the students on-site must

design instructional programs outlining how each student will be taught job skills and other related activities, such as social skills. This analysis includes identifying the areas in which various job tasks are performed, establishing a work routine, identifying natural/

coworker supports and natural cues in the workplace, and designing appropriate training and support strategies. The trainer should be able to complete these activities in one work shift prior to introducing the students to the site. Remember that each skill that a student is learning on a job site must have an objective in the student's IEP. Each vocational skill is written as a behavioral objective and should include the observable behaviors that will be taught, the conditions under which they will occur, and the criteria that will be used to evaluate the student's performance. Ensuring that objectives are written for each student will also decrease the chance that community-based instruction turns into field trips.

The following sections will provide an overview of systematic instructional strategies related to the development of task analyses, systematic prompting procedures, and data collection as they apply to the workplace (see chapters 4 and 5 for more information on specific instructional and measurement strategies). Specifically, strategies that use natural supports, natural cues, and compensatory strategies will be discussed.

Identifying Natural Supports

The first step in training is to identify the natural supports that may be available to students in the workplace and assist the student in accessing those supports. The use of the word *natural* implies that the supports are ones that are typically available to all workers in the workplace, not artificially contrived by the trainer. As such, natural supports can be referred to as the workplace supports that are provided to any employee in the workplace. Workplace supports may include but are not limited to such things as a coworker mentor who assists a student in learning the job; a supervisor who monitors work performance; a coworker who assists the student in developing social relationships, orientation training, or other company-sponsored training events; and an employee assistance program.

The role of the trainer is to assist the student in identifying and reviewing the variety of supports available and in selecting the ones that facilitate inclusion in the workplace. Companies vary in the number of workplace supports available. For instance, one company may have an intensive orientation and training program, while another has none. In addition, the support must be analyzed to determine if it meets the needs of the student. A one-time, 2-hour lecture on

company policies may be of little benefit to the student, while a coworker who explains the "unwritten rules" of the workplace to all new employees may be an extremely valuable resource.

The trainer should not expect that employers and coworkers would automatically know how to provide supports to a student with severe disabilities. Some individuals initially may feel uncomfortable providing instruction and supervision to a worker with a disability. The trainer should model appropriate social interactions and training techniques that will assist coworkers and supervisors to become proficient and comfortable in assisting the student. This can be as subtle as encouraging coworkers to direct questions and conversation to the student rather than to the trainer from the first day of the community-based training experience. Another example may be the teacher who assists the student in learning the names of coworkers as quickly as possible. Trainer support must be analyzed carefully. Something as simple as where the teacher stands during instruction can place a barrier between the student and coworkers. Inge and Tilson (1997) suggest that four questions be considered when choosing the best supports for the student in the workplace:

1. What are the possible workplace support resources?
2. What strategies match the learning style or needs of the student?
3. What are the student's, employer's, and coworkers' choices?
4. Which support option results in or promotes student independence?

Initially, identifying and discussing the various support options with the student, employers, and coworkers is the teacher's role during community-based training. In most instances, a combination of strategies will be selected to promote skill acquisition. This combination of supports may include natural supports from coworkers, natural cues, compensatory strategies, and instruction from the teacher or coworkers. In other words, all supports needed may not be natural! Determining which combination promotes learning is the key to gradually increasing the student's independence in the workplace. Table 15–5 provides a summary of a range of supports that may assist a student in becoming independent in the workplace.

TABLE 15–5
Examples of Workplace Supports

Strategy	Example
Self-monitoring	Student has difficulty completing work within a specified time period. Student uses a timer and a chart to monitor how long it takes to complete a specific job duty. Feedback from the chart assists the worker in meeting the job expectations.
Picture cue	Student has difficulty discriminating between work supplies. Tape a picture of the work task on each container.
Color cue	Student has difficulty selecting her time card to punch in. Put a colored dot on the time card to assist the student in selecting her card.
Pretaped instructions	Student has difficulty reading copy requests to determine work assignments. Tape-record instructions for copy requests.
Visual cue	Student has difficulty remembering when to restock the condiment bar. Place a piece of masking tape on the inside of the condiment bar as a visual reminder.
Auditory cue	Student has difficulty taking breaks on time. Student uses a preprogrammed wristwatch.
Coworker support	Student has difficulty orienting in more than one to two work areas. Coworkers bring copy requests to the copy room rather than ask the student to collect the work across multiple offices.
Reinforcement	Student has difficulty meeting production standard. Provide feedback hourly and ask student to assist with greeting restaurant patrons if a pre-agreed-on amount of work has been completed.

Source: Adapted from Inge, K. J., & Tilson, G. (1997). Ensuring support systems that work: Getting beyond the natural supports vs. job coach controversy. *Journal of Vocational Rehabilitation*, 9, 133–142.

Natural Cues

A natural cue represents some feature of the work environment, job tasks, or activities that signal to a student what to do next. Typically, a natural cue is one that the student can see, hear, touch or feel, or smell and has not been changed or added to the work site. Examples include the color of a cleaning supply, an on/off indicator light, a buzzer on the service door, the telephone ringing, announcements over a loudspeaker, the "body language" of a coworker, and the placement or location of work materials (e.g., mail in an in-box, dirty dishes on an unoccupied table).

One goal of instruction is to have the student respond correctly (e.g., participate in the work task) to natural cues in the environment without additional cues from the teacher or coworkers. When a natural cue is present or occurs during the student's work routine, however, he or she may not yet have learned to attend to the cue and respond correctly but instead may not attend to the cue at all or may respond incorrectly. For instance, a student may respond to the buzzer on the service door by opening it for the delivery person (the correct action), he or

she may ignore the buzzer and continue pricing merchandise (no response), or he or she may go ask another worker to open the door (incorrect response). Obviously, if the student attends to and responds to a natural cue, instruction is not required. However, some students must learn to recognize and attend to these cues. The teacher should work with the student, the employer, and coworkers to identify the natural cues in the workplace that can assist the student in completing his or her tasks successfully. Often, the coworkers and supervisor can be the most valuable source for this information.

One way to call attention to an identified natural cue may be to initially add an extra or artificial cue to the natural one. This extra cue can enhance the relevant features of the naturally occurring one.

Heather, who is filling a condiment bar on an "as needed" basis at her Shoney's vocational training placement, did not respond to the naturally occurring cue of the empty bins. A piece of tape was placed on the inside of the bins to signal her that a bin needed filling. The tape highlighted the relevant feature of the work task, the empty bin, to which Heather was not responding.

Whenever extra cues are added to the work environment or work tasks, the teacher needs to consider fading them as the student begins to notice and correctly respond to the naturally occurring ones.

Compensatory Strategies

Adding compensatory strategies to an instructional program can enhance a student's ability to learn and perform work tasks correctly. A compensatory strategy is any material or additional instruction, such as audiotaped directions or a jig for counting items, that compensates for the inability to independently perform certain aspects of a job (Inge, 1997). In some instances, using a compensatory strategy can eliminate instructions and allow the student to participate in activities that he or she otherwise could not. For instance, a student may use a "money card" to purchase a soda from the break room vending machine. A money card can be a piece of paper with the picture of the coins needed to purchase a soda from the soda machine. Use of the card eliminates the need for the student to learn the differences among coins or the actual amount that is required to use the machine.

If compensatory strategies are targeted, they must be designed with input from the student, employer, and coworkers. In addition, care should be given to the design and construction of materials to ensure that they do not stigmatize the student. Materials, when possible, should be those that any adult could access within a work environment and would be accepted by the work culture where they are used. For instance, if a picture book is selected to assist a student in remembering his or her work schedule, the employment specialist and student should work together in the design of the booklet. Some of the things to consider in their planning include identification of pictures that are useful, concise and eliminate unnecessary information, the number of pictures in the booklet to be used (e.g., too many may distract or confuse the student rather than assist in task completion), and the optimal size of the booklet (e.g., could it be made small enough to fit in a pocket?).

The same questions applied to designing a schedule reminder can be applied to almost any compensatory strategy used on a job site. Compensatory strategies should be simple to use and concise, and the least intrusive strategy should be selected that will assist the student in performing his or her job duties. A list of common compensatory strategies used in vocational training programs can be found in Table 15–6.

TABLE 15–6
Compensatory Strategies

Challenge	Possible solutions
The student can't remember his or her sequence of job duties.	Written list Audiocassette Picture book Assignment board Flowchart
The student has difficulty reading copy request to determine work assignments.	In-/out-boxes for each coworker, requesting work with name or picture of coworker on box Special form highlighting relevant features of the task, such as thickly outlined box where number of copies is written Audiocassette requests for copy work
The student can't count to package work materials.	Strips of tape on table that correspond to number of items in package Picture of number of items in the package Box with the number of dividers that corresponds to the number of items in package Sample of package for matching work
The student can't distinguish money to purchase a snack in the snack bar.	A money card to match amount for standard purchases Correct change in a coin purse Next-dollar-amount strategy

Self-Management Strategies

Self-management has included such terms as self-monitoring, self-observation, self-evaluation, self-reinforcement, self-instruction, and self-assessment. The following strategies may be applied either before or after the targeted job duty or skill to assist the student in performing a task successfully and independently:

- The student may use a preset alarm on a watch to determine when it is time to take a break.
- A student may use a compensatory strategy to assist him- or herself to self-monitor, such as a picture book to check off work tasks as they are completed during the day.
- A student may evaluate his or her work performance in order to self-reinforce, such as marking checks on a card for a specific amount of work, which is later exchanged for a reinforcer.

Self-management usually entails instructing the student to independently self-monitor by using natural cues, adding external cues and prompts, compensatory strategies, or assistive technology devices. A teacher, friends, a family member, a coworker, or the supervisor can be identified to assist the student in learning how to use the strategy. For instance, a family member may assist the student in checking off days on a calendar to determine when he or she goes to the community-based training site. A coworker may instruct the same student to use a timer to monitor production, while the teacher assists the student in using a picture book to sequence job tasks. Clearly, combining the use of compensatory strategies, natural cues, natural supports, and systematic instruction is the key to successful skill acquisition for students with significant disabilities in the workplace.

Special Considerations for Students with Physical Disabilities

Assistive Technology

A student with physical challenges has specialized support needs that should be identified before graduation that are related to independent living as well as employment (Inge & Shepherd, 1995; Shepherd & Inge, 1999). These challenges can often be met with assistive technology devices and services. The 1994 reauthorization of the Technology-Related Assistance for Individuals Act defined assistive technology devices and services:

The term assistive technology device means any item, piece of equipment, or product system, whether acquired commercially off the shelf, modified, or customized, that is used to increase, maintain, or improve functional capabilities of individuals with disabilities. (20 U.S.C. § 140[25])

The term assistive technology service means any service that directly assists an individual with a disability in the selection, acquisition, or use of an assistive technology device. (20 U.S.C. § 140[26])

There is a continuum of complexity in technology related to the device as well as the type of materials or manufacturing techniques used to produce the device (Inge & Shepherd, 1995). Low technology usually includes devices that are simple, with few or no movable parts. These are devices that students use on job sites that may include (a) a dycem, which is a nonskid mat that can stabilize work materials for the student; (b) key guards; (c) book stands; (d) reachers; (e) a lap tray; or (f) built-up or enlarged handles on utensils or work tools.

Low-tech devices can be purchased almost anywhere, from hardware stores to catalogs, or can be made from materials that are found in a home workshop. Usually, these devices are low cost and can be obtained quickly. High-tech devices are defined by the use of electronics and specialized manufacturing techniques and materials. High technology is most often associated with computers, robotics, environmental control units, and so forth. High technology could include augmentative communication devices, power wheelchairs, specialized software (e.g., Dragon Dictate™, TextHelp™), specialized input devices (trackball, eye gaze, touch screens), and other computer equipment. High-tech devices are typically available through vendors from companies specializing in this merchandise.

Possible sources for funding assistive technology include IDEA, Section 504 of the Rehabilitation Act, Medicaid, Social Security work incentive programs, and private insurance (Wallace, 1995). School district obligations to provide assistive technology services and devices are defined by federal and state laws requiring school districts to provide special education and related services to students with disabilities and federal and state laws prohibiting discrimination against persons with disabilities. In addition, policy letters have been issued by the Office of Special Education Programs (OSEP) that have clarified the school districts' responsibilities in providing assistive technology (Inge & Shepherd, 1995). In August 1990, OSEP stated that assistive technology is a part of establishing the student's IEP (RESNA, 1992). This policy letter made it clear that school districts cannot deny assistive technology to a student with a disability if the technology has been deemed necessary for the child to receive a free and appropriate public education.

Selecting the Device

Technology support needs should be identified after the student has selected a career path or potential job. This is very different from identifying devices and services and then trying to fit them into a job site. Once vocational training opportunities or a paid work experience are identified, options for supporting the student using technology should be explored. Some ways to address these needs include (a) renting equipment, (b) borrowing a device from another individual who is using the technology that is being considered, (c) contacting the state assistive technology project (many programs have lending libraries), and (d) using equipment that is owned by the school system. Often, low-tech solutions can be purchased or made at minimal cost that can be absorbed by the school system.

Typically, team members who may assist in the identification and purchase of technology for use on the job include occupational, physical, and speech therapists; teachers; parents; a rehabilitation engineer; and the student (Inge & Shepherd, 1995). These individuals should be involved as well as the employer, coworkers, and school staff (e.g., the on-the-job CBI (community-based instruction) trainer) who provide support to the student within the workplace. Devices can be purchased both "off the shelf" and can be custom made. Low-cost solutions such as going to the local hardware store rather than a technology vendor may save time and money. For example, a lapboard constructed by the school's vocational tech program will cost significantly less than one fabricated by a rehabilitation engineer. The team must become familiar with the assistive technology resources available in the community as well as how to access the most cost-effective support solution.

All options for assisting the student in completing the job task should be considered. High-tech devices are not always the best solution. Alternatives may include adapting the skill sequence, eliminating difficult steps from the task analysis, or asking a coworker to provide assistance. As with all solutions, the least intrusive and most natural one should be identified. A student may be able to use a high-tech device, but a quicker and more natural solution may be to seek personal assistance. In addition, the physical characteristics of the device must be acceptable to the student; otherwise, he or she will simply not use the assistive technology. A list of considerations when using assistive technology to facilitate community employment is provided in Table 15–7.

TABLE 15–7
Assistive Technology Considerations

- Do assistive technology assessments occur within "real work" environments?
- Have the student's dreams for employment guided the selection of technology for community-based vocational training sites?
- Has the student been able to test or use the technology in real work settings (not simulated or clinical settings)?
- Can the technology be rented or borrowed before purchase for trial purposes to determine reliability, usefulness, and ease of use?
- Does the student already use technology that can be applied in a workplace?
- Have low-tech options been considered before high-tech options?
- Is the appearance and design of the technology acceptable to the student?
- Does the technology fit within the physical, social, and cultural environment?
- Does the technology facilitate interaction with coworkers?
- Is the technology expandable to other work sites and/or student needs?
- Who will assist the student in learning how to use the technology in the workplace?
- Who will be available in the workplace to assist the student in troubleshooting assistive technology problems (e.g., a coworker or supervisor)?
- Have all aspects of workplace/assistive technology support needs been considered (e.g., personal care, social skills, communication, mobility in the workplace)?

After Jane's person-centered planning meeting, Jane and her teacher went to the local community college to review the new postsecondary program for students with severe disabilities. During the visit, they realized that she would have a great deal of difficulty getting around the campus in her current power chair, which was more than 8 years old and did not navigate the gravel and dirt paths. Jane's transition team referred her for an evaluation by the school's physical therapist. The therapist visited the campus, evaluated Jane's chair, and made recommendations to her physician. This included a head-activated switch rather than joystick since the physical therapist felt that the use of her arm increased Jane's spasticity and difficulty in moving. The physician also felt that a new chair was necessary, and he wrote a prescription for the device. Since this was considered durable medical equipment, the funding source of choice was Medicaid. By using this option, the power chair purchased belonged to Jane and would transition with her to future environments.

Jane was accepted to the postsecondary program in the fall of the following school year as planned by her transition team. The community college had a part-time position located with the registrar's office that matched Jane's interests in secretarial or office work. Jane and her transition team decided that this would be a job that could assist her in making some decisions about future employment. The supervisor in the office agreed to hire Jane for 10 hours a week to assist the office manager in maintaining a database on current and past students. The task identified for her was to assist the office manager in entering student data. At first, this task seemed too difficult since Jane was unable to use her hands to manipulate papers. The task was analyzed by the school system's occupational therapist, and a number of simple solutions were identified. Jane's technology solutions can be found in Figure 15–3.

In addition, the teacher provided input into systematic instruction procedures that would assist Jane in learning the task. Time delay with a verbal prompt (see chapter 4) was used to teach her the data entry program. Thus, a combination of assistive technology, coworker supports, and teacher training facilitated Jane's independence in this workplace. A table of how these supports combined to facilitate community employment for Jane can be found in Figure 15–4.

Finally, Jane's teacher knew that she must consider the instruction of related issues that are critical to employment success for students with severe and multiple disabilities. These may include using the bathroom, eating and drinking, communication, and mobility. These tasks, as well as the actual work duties, must be taught in the natural environment using systematic instruction procedures and may require modification from the manner in which they are typically performed at home or school. Jane chose to wear an adult protection garment rather than ask a coworker to assist her in the restroom. However, a student coworker volunteered to assist Jane with filling her sport bottle and eating a snack during break. This provided for important socialization time between Jane and her coworker and ultimately developed into a nonwork relationship. It is important to note that some students may not want to ask coworkers to assist with personal care, and a personal care attendant may be needed during portions of the workday.

Paid Employment

Providing students with a variety of work experiences using the strategies described in this chapter increases the chances of paid employment for many students with disabilities. Whether the work is part time or full time will depend on the needs and preferences of each student and his or her family. It will also depend on the capacity of businesses, family and friend networks, and community systems to provide continual support to the student. Most experts agree that paid employment experiences before graduation should be the ultimate vocational goal for most students with severe disabilities. Research has shown that students with paid jobs before graduation are more likely to be employed as adults (Blackorby & Wagner, 1996). Of course, a transition team must consider a variety of factors before paid jobs are pursued. For example, younger students between the ages of 16 and 19 may benefit more from inclusion in school-based classes where social and communication skills and work-related academic skills through participation in short-term training placements may be more crucial. Older students may benefit from inclusion in regular vocational education programs as long as the content is directly related to the local labor market.

FIGURE 15–3

Jane's Assistive Technology Solutions

Jane's job: Entering names and addresses into a mailing list

Jane's Strengths
- Types simple letters to friends and family members using a head pointer on a manual typewriter.
- Can copy whatever is written on paper with accuracy even if she can't read the words.
- Is very social and expresses an interest in learning to use a computer for data entry.
- Uses a power chair for mobility.
- Can lift her right arm to shoulder height.
- Is extremely motivated to work.

Jane's Work Challenges
- Cannot use her fingers to grasp objects.
- Is not able to manipulate paper for data entry.
- Must rely on others for daily care activities.
- Does not have any computer training or previous work experiences.

Issue/challenge	Solution
Issue #1: Jane's head pointer slips when striking the keys.	An eraser was put on the end of her head pointer.
Issue #2: Jane cannot access uppercase keys or press more than one key at a time.	A DOS-based program called "Sticky Keys" was put on Jane's computer.
Issue #3: The computer is placed at a low level; accessing it is awkward.	A stand was made to position the computer keyboard at an angle that was easy for Jane to access.
Issue #4: Jane has difficulty keeping her place on the paper that lists the data to enter.	A stand, which was available at an office supply store, was adapted with a motorized paper guide. Jane used a switch to move the guide down the page. This assisted her in keeping her place for data entry.
Issue #5: Jane cannot manipulate paper for data entry. Requests arrive on telephone message pads, business cards, and scrap pieces of paper.	Jane's supervisor suggested taping requests to standard-size paper. She offered to do this for her.
Issue #6: Jane has difficulty reading small print.	Type was enlarged on the copy machine.
Issue #7: How will Jane turn the sheets of paper?	Jane pushes the pages off the typing stand using her head pointer.
Issue #8: Jane couldn't stack finished work.	A box that caught the finished pages was attached to her stand.
Issue #9: Jane can't use the telephone to call her supervisor for assistance.	The phone receiver was placed on a gooseneck holder. Jane uses her head pointer to access the touch-tone buttons. She was also given an emergency alarm button. The supervisor keeps the receiver unit. Whenever she needs immediate assistance, Jane can push her alarm button.

Robert's Case

Once Robert and his transition team determined that he wanted to pursue paid employment, his parents, teacher, support staff, and Robert participated in a PATH meeting to identify his career goals and dreams. During his PATH, Robert expressed an interest in becoming a physical therapist or working at a gym. This information assisted Robert, his family members, and professionals in selecting community-based training experiences to assist him in further clarifying his career goals. The one-to-one aide who had been providing support during his academic school program was identified as the support staff person who would assist in training Robert during community-based

FIGURE 15–4

Jane's Supports for Data Entry Job at the Community College

Jane's job: Enter data into community college mailing list

Challenges:
- Learning how to use the data entry program
- Physically manipulating the work materials
- Meeting production goals

Task 1: Student needs to enter addresses using a computer.

1. Accommodations (low-tech devices)	Teacher works with supervisor and student to modify the workspace. Teacher finds a worktable that is accessible for student. Work site pays for table. Teacher gets blocks to raise the table to adequate work height. Student brings head pointer to work to use for data entry. Stand is made to tilt computer keyboard for easy access. "Sticky Keys" is loaded onto the computer.
2. Instruction (time delay)	Teacher and coworker develop task analysis for data entry. Student, supervisors, and teacher decide that the teacher will assist the student in learning the data entry program using a time delay strategy with a verbal prompt. Teacher carefully fades assistance, using the time delay strategy.
3. Color cue	Student and teacher discuss mistakes in data entry. Student is having difficulty distinguishing among the number "one", the letter "el" (l), and the letter "eye." The teacher uses a pink and green highlighter pen to add a color cue. This cue is faded as the student begins to distinguish the letters.

Task 2: Student needs to use the telephone to buzz supervisor for assistance.

1. Accommodations (low-tech device)	Teacher brainstorms with the supervisor and employee how the student will contact the supervisor when assistance is needed. Teacher identifies a device to hold the telephone receiver. Supervisor provides money to pay for device. Student uses head pointer to punch buttons on the phone.
2. Coworker assistance	Coworker offers to check to make sure phone is in the device at the beginning of the workday.

Task 3: Student needs a way to manipulate the paper with names for data entry.

1. Specialized accommodation	The therapist designs a work stand and paper holding device with a paper guide that the student moves down the page by pushing a switch.
2. Coworker assistance	Coworker offers to place pages on device at the beginning of the workday. She also offers to type on the pages on the copy machine so that it is easier for student to read.
3. Instruction	Student, teacher, and supervisor discuss training on device. Student decides that the teacher will develop a task analysis and train her to use the device.

Task 4: Student needs to increase data entry speed.

1. Self-monitoring	Supervisor, student, and teacher discuss the need for increased production. Teacher obtains a timer and records student's data entry speed. He presets the timer for a faster time. Student uses the timer to monitor data entry speed.
2. Reinforcement	Coworker offers to check on the student and praise when she notices that student is meeting the time requirement.

Source: Adapted from Inge, K. J., & Tilson, G. (1997). Ensuring support systems that work: Getting beyond the natural supports vs. teacher controversy. *Journal of Vocational Rehabilitation, 9*(2), 133–142. Reprinted with permission.

instruction. Specific goals and objectives were developed for Robert's IEP, which stated that he would participate in nonpaid community-based vocational training experiences during the school year: one at a medical center and one at a health club facility. Both were for 3 days a week, 2 hours per day, for a total of 6 hours of training.

Medical Center

Robert's first experience was at a medical center. This work experience allowed him to see many different aspects of the medical profession while capitalizing on his people skills. His responsibilities included delivering reports to the nurses' stations and participating in patient transport to physical therapy. Robert reported to the volunteer room each day that he went to the medical center. As requests came into the room, he was assigned to the specific activities. The trainer assisted him in finding his way around the hospital.

Robert quickly reported that he did not like working at the hospital and was "uncomfortable" around critically ill patients. He complained that he did not like to walk around the hospital, and the mobility requirements of this type of position proved to be challenging. After completing 1 month of training, Robert decided that he was not interested in pursuing a career in a hospital setting.

YMCA

The second placement was as a front-desk attendant at the YMCA. The responsibilities of this position included scanning customer cards, greeting guests, answering phones, and responding to customer inquiries about programs. Robert's abilities did not match some of these job duties. Therefore, he was assigned the scanning and greeting tasks, which he completed alongside the coworker who was responsible for this job. The aide provided one-to-one training to Robert on the job duties assigned at this site.

Although Robert did not become independent at the YMCA, his attitude at this job site was significantly different than his attitude at the hospital. He was stationed at a specific location and did not have to walk around the gym. In addition, Robert reported that he preferred the staff at this position, interacting with customers, and the personal trainers and that he liked the general work environment. After the completion of these two training experiences, Robert's work preferences had become clearer, and he decided that he would like to have a paid job during the summer at a health club.

Paid Employment

After his community-based experiences, Robert's transition team assisted him in applying to the Department of Vocational Rehabilitation. The team recognized the importance of having his "case opened" with vocational rehabilitation since they knew that he would require this agency's support once he graduated. Robert subsequently was able to access the services of the department's rehabilitation engineer when he became competitively employed.

A position was negotiated for Robert at a private gym. He was hired for 2 days a week, 3 hours each day, or a total of 6 hours per week during the summer months. He was paid minimum wage, from the first day of employment, plus free gym privileges. Robert's negotiated duties included greeting customers, scanning cards, handing out locker keys and towels, and doing some light cleaning of the equipment. He also worked with another staff member during his shifts who answers the telephone, responds to guest inquiries, and completes new membership and program applications.

Simple task modifications were made to remove some of the physical demands of the tasks. In order to increase his work pace, for example, items that Robert uses regularly are placed closer to his work station. In addition, individual stacks of the different-size towels are placed directly under the key rack so that Robert is able to collect a customer's keys and towels without extraneous movement.

The assistive technology that was introduced to Robert's job site was predominantly low technology and simple in design. First, an office chair with arms was purchased in order to provide a stable working surface. Without the arms for support, Robert had a difficult time controlling his movements because of ataxia and therefore could not effectively manipulate items and distribute the towels and keys. In addition, the chair swiveled so that he could turn to reach items rather than move his body. Since Robert was unable to use both hands, the rehabilitation engineer attached a mount for his card scanner to the arm of the chair. The scanner was positioned at the end of the armrest, which allowed Robert to use the arm as a stable base while scanning cards. This low-tech accommodation reduced the effects of his ataxia when he was attempting this task. Finally, a small Plexiglas container was obtained to store the keys. The board where these keys were typically stored was not within Robert's reach. All the low-tech devices introduced to this job site served to increase Robert's skills and efficiency. He was able to work independently after the accommodations were put into place and with 50 hours of job site training.

Response to Robert's Case

When Robert returned to school in the fall, his transition team realized that he had other transition issues once he was successful in his first paid job. Since his accident at age 12, he had relied on others to meet many of his needs.

However, once he began to participate in community-based training experiences and was subsequently employed, his transition team's expectations for him increased. For instance, members of Robert's transition team have begun to focus on extending his independence beyond the job site. Recently, Robert began instruction with a life skills trainer at home to improve his ability to function in that environment. He and his trainer focus on doing laundry, using the microwave, shopping, caring for his personal belongings, and menu planning.

In order to achieve independence in his transportation needs, Robert is now learning to use the public bus system in his community. This will allow him to go where he needs to go without depending on his family for transportation. In addition, after his paid summer work experience, the school system has begun to teach Robert to write independently through the use of technology. After experimenting with different modes of computer access, he has chosen to use "intellikeys™," which is an alternative keyboard, with a word prediction program. This focus on all of Robert's transition needs during his school program may also impact his future career options. For instance, use of "intellikeys™" may expand his job choices by allowing Robert to increase job responsibilities at the current site as well as open up future job tasks in other environments. Certainly, traveling independently will expand his choice of future employment settings. His transition team is also considering with Robert how he might develop a business within a business or resource ownership to expand his postschool vocational options.

Employment Support After Graduation

The transition team responsible for providing on-the-job training during a student's final paid job placement before graduation must address a number of issues, including job-specific skill training, changes in Social Security benefits, family satisfaction, transportation details, social and communication skill development, and, most important, who will assume responsibility for the student's job performance after he or she graduates. This final issue is probably the most pressing one facing families and individuals with disabilities today because no particular agency is mandated to serve individuals with disabilities in any capacity once they leave special education.

Despite the lack of appropriate community services available to young workers with severe disabilities, agencies are slowly changing, and newer, more innovative employment supports are springing up across the country. In addition, creative solutions to the problems are being developed as special and vocational educators forge agreements and work cooperatively with businesses, government, and community agencies. One of the most exciting developments is the use of workplace supports (Inge & Tilson, 1997), as described earlier in this chapter, that allow school or community service agencies to more quickly fade financial and personnel support from workers.

When workers with disabilities need continuing supported employment services, a variety of funding and program options should be sought (Brooke et al., 1997). Specifics have been provided within this chapter. In most localities, employment support services for adults with disabilities are provided by not-for-profit agencies that receive funding on a per customer basis from a variety of sources including vocational rehabilitation, state developmental disabilities agencies, Medicaid, Social Security work incentives, and special state-legislated allocations. It is imperative that a transition team specifically inquires about how training and support are provided before a student moves into one of these agency programs. In most states, dollars can be shifted from segregated service delivery modes to integrated employment through creative and collaborative agreements at the local, state, and federal levels.

By using the questions in Table 15–2, a transition team can assess the ability of an adult agency to provide appropriate employment support to a young adult leaving school. Regardless of the quality of services provided by any agency, it can accept or reject a potential student of its services based on eligibility requirements despite the needs or desires of that student. Most adult services have long waiting lists, and entry into any program is typically competitive. The individual who receives support from a community agency is the one whose team worked very early on to understand exactly how to qualify for each particular program. Ultimately, the best way for a school vocational program to ensure that a student gets and keeps paid employment is to help the student get a job and develop long-term supports that are not agency specific and that are firmly in place before graduation.

Summary

IDEA (P.L. 105-17), according to the 1997 Amendments, broadened the focus of transition and lowered the age at which these services begin to age 14. This law mandates that the assessment, training, and supports related to employment, independent living, or any area of adult functioning be included in a student's IEP. Providing transition services is a longitudinal process involving collaboration among a student, his or her family, school professionals, community support services, and the business community. Although special education is ultimately given the responsibility of implementing transition goals and activities, transition planning affects all curriculum areas. Decisions continually have to be made regarding which instructional areas are most important and when and where training and support should be provided. Student preferences must be assessed throughout the years, and this must be matched to the availability of employment, residential options, and social or leisure programs in the community.

Although the availability and quality of community support services for adults with disabilities are improving, there still are long waiting lists for all programs. Therefore, transitions teams must still work to find the critical supports or teach the most important skills related to adult functioning before the young adult reaches age 21 and must leave the school system. They must also work together to understand the strengths and needs to current school and community programs so that families, at an early stage, can begin to untangle the array of laws, agencies, and programs that will affect their sons or daughters with a significant disability through the life span.

Suggested Activities

1. Design a transition planning process appropriate to your community. Identify the agencies, organizations, and individuals representing those groups that should meet to establish the transition procedures for students with disabilities.
2. Identify employment opportunities in your community based on the following:
   a. Conversations with a Chamber of Commerce representative
   b. Meetings with the local One-Stop Career Center
   c. Conversations with the labor department
   d. Conversations with the vocational rehabilitation agency
   e. Meetings with the Small Business Administration or similar agency in your community
   f. Follow-up surveys of graduates who are employed in the community

References

Agran, M., Snow, K., & Swaner, J. (1999). A survey of secondary level teacher's opinions on community-based instruction and inclusive education. *Journal of the Association for Persons with Severe Disabilities, 24,* 58–62.

Asselin, S. B., Todd-Allen, M., & deFur, S. (1998). Transition coordinators: Define yourselves. *Teaching Exceptional Children, 30*(3), 11-15.

Bader, B. A. (2003). *Identification of best practices in One Stop Career Centers that facilitate use by people with disabilities seeking employment.* Unpublished doctoral dissertation, Virginia Commonwealth University.

Baer, R. M., McMahan, R. K., & Flexer, R. W. (2004). Transition models and promising practices. In R. W. Flyer, T. J. Simmons, P. Luft, & R. M. Baer (Eds.), *Transition planning for secondary students with disabilities* (2nd ed., pp. 53–82). Upper Saddle River, NJ: Merrill/Prentice Hall.

Baird, P. A., & Everson, J. M. (1999). *Person-centered planning: A guide for facilitators and participants.* New Orleans: Human Development Center, Louisiana State University Health Sciences Center.

Bates, P., Bronkema, J., Ames, T., & Hess, C. (1992). State-level interagency planning models. In F. Rusch, L. DeStefano, J. Chadsey-Rusch, L. Phelps, & E. Szymanski (Eds.), *Transition from school to adult life: Models, linkages, and policy* (pp. 115–129). Sycamore, IL: Sycamore Publishing.

Benz, M. R., Johnson, D. K., Mikkelson, K. S., & Lindstrom, L. E. (1995). Improving collaboration between school and vocational rehabilitation. Stakeholder-identified barriers and strategies. *Career Development for Exceptional Individuals, 18,* 133–144.

Berkowitz, M. (2003). The Ticket to Work program: The complicated evolution of a simple idea. In K. Rupp & S. H. Bell (Eds.), *Paying for results in vocational rehabilitation: Will provider incentives work for Ticket to Work?* (pp. 13–29). Washington, DC: Urban Institute.

Billingsley, F. F., & Albertson, L. R. (1999). Finding a future for functional skills. *Journal of the Association for Persons with Severe Disabilities, 24,* 298–302.

Blackorby, J., & Wagner, M. (1996). Longitudinal postschool outcomes for youth with disabilities: Findings from the National Longitudinal Transition Study. *Exceptional Children, 62*(5), 399–419.

Brooke, V., Inge, K. J., Armstrong, A., & Wehman, P. (Eds.). (1997). *Supported employment handbook: A customer-driven approach for person with significant disabilities.* Richmond, VA: Virginia Commonwealth University, Rehabilitation Research and Training Center on Workplace Supports.

Brooke, V., & O'Mara, S. (2001). Social Security work incentives: Issues in implementation. In P. Wehman (Ed.), *Supported employment in business: Expanding the capacity of workers with disabilities* (pp. 227-238). St. Augustine, FL: Training Resource Network.

Button, C. (1992, October/November). P.L. 102-569: A new season for the rehabilitation act. In *Word from Washington* Washington, DC: United Cerebral Palsy Association. (I no longer have the original source.)

Colley, D.A., & Jamison, D. (1998). Post school results for youth with disabilities: Key indicators and policy implications. *Career Development for Exceptional Individuals, 21,* 145-160.

Council for Exceptional Children. (2000). *What every special educator must know* (4th ed.). Alexandria, VA: Author.

Endependence Center. (2003). *Home and community-based services for people with disabilities: There's no place like home.* Richmond: Virginia Board for People with Disabilities.

Everson, J. (1993). *Youth with disabilities: Strategies for interagency transition programs.* Boston: Andover Medical Publishers.

Falvey, M. A., Forest, M., Pearpoint, J., Rosenberg, R. L. (1993). *All my life's a circle: Using the tools of circles, MAPS and PATH.* Toronto: Inclusion Press.

Ferrell, C., Brooke, V., Kregel, J., & Getzel, E. (2002). *Get a job! How employment affects your Supplemental Security Income and Medicaid benefits.* Richmond: Virginia Commonwealth University, Rehabilitation Research and Training Center on Workplace Supports, and the Social Security Administration.

Fesko, S., Hoff, D., Jordan, M., Fichera, K., & Thomas, C. (2000). *One-stop centers: A guide for job seekers with disabilities.* Retrieved April 26, 2004, from **http://www.communityinclusion. org/publications/text/onestop.html**

Fisher, D., & Sax, C. (1999). Noticing differences between secondary and postsecondary education: Extending Agran, Snow, and Swaner's discussion. *Journal of the Association for Persons with Severe Disabilities, 24,* 303-305.

Flannery, K. B., Newton, S., Horner, R., Slovic, R., Blumberg, R., & Ard, W. (2000). The impact of person centered planning on the content and organization individual supports. *Career Development for Exceptional Individuals, 23,* 123-137.

Furney, K., Hasazi, S., & DeStefano, L. (1997). Transition policies, practices, and promises: Lessons from three states. *Exceptional Children, 63,* 343-355.

Getzel, E. E., & Kregel, J. (1997). Transitioning from the academic to the employment setting: The employment connection program. In P. Wehman, J. Kregel, & M. West (Eds.), *Supported employment research: Expanding competitive employment opportunities for persons with significant disabilities* (pp. 167-183). Richmond: Virginia Commonwealth University, Rehabilitation Research and Training Center on Supported Employment.

Greene, G., & Kochar-Bryant, C. A. (2003). *Pathways to successful transition for youth with disabilities.* Upper Saddle River, NJ: Merrill/Prentice Hall.

Griffin, C. C. (1999). Rural routes: Promising supported employment practices in America's frontier. In G. Revell, K. J. Inge, D. Mank, & P. Wehman (Eds.), *The impact of supported employment for people with significant disabilities: Preliminary findings from the National Supported Employment Consortium* (pp. 161-178).

Richmond: Virginia Commonwealth University, Rehabilitation Research and Training Center on Workplace Supports.

Griffin, C. C., Flaherty, M., Hammis, D., Katz, M., Maxson, N., & Shelley, R. (2001). *People who won themselves: Emerging trends in rural rehabilitation.* Missoula, MT: University of Montana, Rural Institute.

Griffin, C. C., & Hammis, D. (2003). *Making self-employment work for people with disabilities.* Baltimore: Paul H. Brookes.

Grigal, M., Neubert, D. A., & Moon, M. S. (2001). Public school programs for students with significant disabilities in post-secondary settings. *Education and Training in Mental Retardation and Developmental Disabilities, 36,* 244-254.

Grigal, M., Neubert, D. A., & Moon, M. S. (2002). Postsecondary options for students with significant disabilities. *Teaching Exceptional Children, 35*(2), 68-73.

Hall, M., Kleinert, H. L., & Kearns, F. J. (2000). Going to college! Postsecondary programs for students with moderate and severe disabilities. *Teaching Exceptional Children, 32*(3), 58-65.

Halloran, W. D., & Johnson, W. (1992). Education-industry collaboration: Guidelines for complying with the Fair labor Standards Act. *American Rehabilitation, 18*(4), 21-23.

Hammis, D. (2002). Parent to child deeming. Retrieved January 10, 2005, from http://www.vcu-barc.org/news.html

Hanley-Maxwell, C., Pogoloff, S.M. & Whitney-Thomas, J. (1998). Families: The heart of transition. In F. R. Rusch and J. Chadsey-Rusch (Eds.) Beyond high school: Transition from school to work (pp. 234-264) Belmont, CA: Wadsworth Publishing.

Hart, D., Zafft, C., & Zimbrich, K. (2001). Creating access to college for all students. *Journal for Vocational Special Needs Education, 23,* 19-31.

Hasazi, S. B., Furney, K. S., & DeStefano, L. (1999). Implementing the IDEA transition mandates. *Exceptional Children, 65*(4), 555-566.

Hutchins, M. P., & Renzaglia, A. (1998). Interviewing families for effective transition to employment. *Teaching Exceptional Children, 30*(4), 72-78.

Individuals with Disabilities Education Act, 20 U.S.C. 1400 (1997).

Inge, K. (2001). Supported employment for individuals with physical disabilities. In P. Wehman (Ed.), *Supported employment in business: Expanding the capacity of workers with disabilities* (pp. 153-180). St. Augustine, FL: Training Resource Network.

Inge, K. J. (1997). Job site training. In V. Brooke, K. J. Inge, A. J. Armstrong, & P. Wehman (Eds.), *Supported employment handbook: A customer driven approach for persons with significant disabilities* (pp. 159-200). Richmond: Virginia Commonwealth University, Rehabilitation Research and Training Center on Supported Employment.

Inge, K. J., & Brooke, V. (Eds.). (1993, Winter). *Rehabilitation Act Amendments of 1992 Newsletter.* Richmond: Virginia Commonwealth University, Rehabilitation Research and Training Center on Supported Employment.

Inge, K. J., Dymond, S., & Wehman, P. (1996). Community-based vocational training. In P. J. McLaughlin & P. Wehman (Eds.), *Characteristics of mental retardation and developmental disabilities* (2nd ed., pp. 297-316). Austin, TX: PRO-ED.

Inge, K. J., & Shepherd, J. (1995). Assistive technology applications and strategies for school system personnel. In K. F. Flippo, K. J. Inge, & J. M. Barcus (Eds.), *Assistive technology: A resource for school, work, and community* (pp. 133-166). Baltimore: Paul H. Brookes.

Inge, K. J., Simon, M., Halloran, W., & Moon, M. S. (1993). Community-based vocational instruction and the labor laws: A 1993 update. In K. J. Inge & P. Wehman (Eds.), *Designing community-based vocational programs for students with severe disabilities* (pp. 52-71). Richmond: Virginia Commonwealth University, Rehabilitation Research and Training Center on Supported Employment.

Inge, K. J., & Tilson, G. (1997). Ensuring support systems that work: Getting beyond the natural supports versus job coach controversy. *Journal of Vocational Rehabilitation, 9,* 133-142.

Kohler, P. D., & Field, S. (2003). Transition-focused education: Foundation for the future. *Journal of Special Education, 37*(3), 174-183.

Kregel, J., & Head, C. (2001). *Promoting employment for SSA beneficiaries: 2001 annual report of the Benefits Planning, Assistance and Outreach Program.* Richmond: Virginia Commonwealth University Benefits Assistance Resource Center.

Luecking, R., & Fabian, E. S. (2000). Paid internships and employment success for youth in transition. *Career Development for Exceptional Individuals, 23*(2), 205-221.

Malatchi, A., & Inge, K. J. (1997). *Whose life is it anyway? A look at person-centered planning and transition.* Richmond: Virginia Commonwealth University, Rehabilitation Research and Training Center on Workplace Supports.

Martin, J. E., Mithaug, D. E., Oliphint, J. H., Husch, J. V., & Frazier, E. S. (2002). *Self-directed employment: A handbook for transition teachers and employment specialists.* Baltimore: Paul H. Brookes.

Maximus. (2003). *Youth in transition: The Ticket to Work Program and youth in transition.* Retrieved March 8, 2004, from **http://www.yourtickettowork.com/youth**

McDonnell, J., Mathot-Buckner, C., & Ferguson, B. (Eds.). (1996). *Transition programs for students with moderate/severe disabilities.* Pacific Grove, CA: Brooks/Cole.

Miller, L. A., & Brooke, V. (2003). *Supplemental Security Income and age 18 redetermination.* Retrieved March 8, 2004, from **http://www.vcu-barc.org/keyfacts.html**

Miller, L. A., & O'Mara, S. (2003). *Social Security disability benefit issues affecting transition aged youth.* Retrieved March 8, 2004, from **http://www.vcu-barc.org/news.html**

Miner, C. A., & Bates, P. E. (1997). The effect of person-centered planning activities on the IEP/transition planning process. *Education and Training in Mental Retardation and Developmental Disabilities, 32*(2), 105-112.

Mount, B. (1994). Benefits and limitations of Persons Futures Planning. In V. J. Bradley, J. W. Ashbaugh, & B. C. Blaney (Eds.), *Creating individual supports for people with developmental disabilities: A mandate for change at many levels* (pp. 97-108). Baltimore: Paul H. Brookes.

National Association of the State Directors of Special Education. (1990). Education of the handicapped act amendment of 1990 (P.L. 101-476): Summary of major changes in parts A through H of the act. Washington, DC: Author.

National Transition Alliance. (2000, June). 1999 Selected model programs/promising practices. *Alliance Newsletter, 4,* 3-15.

Neubert, D. A. (2003). The role of assessment in the transition to adult life process for students with disabilities. *Exceptionality, 11*(2), 63-75.

Neubert, D. A., & Moon, M. S. (1999). Working together to facilitate the transition from school to work. In S. Graham & K. R. Harris (Eds.), *Teachers working together: Enhancing the performance of students with special needs* (pp. 186-213). Cambridge, MA: Brookline Books.

Neubert, D. A., Moon, M. S., & Grigal, M. (2002). Post-secondary education and transition services for students ages 18-21 with significant disabilities. *Focus on Exceptional Children, 34,* 1-11.

Neubert, D. A., Moon, M. S., & Grigal, M. (2004). Activities of students with significant disabilities receiving services in postsecondary settings. *Education and Training in Developmental Disabilities, 39*(1), 16-25.

Newcomb, C., Payne, S., & Waid, M. D. (2003). What do we know about disability beneficiaries' work and use of work incentives prior to Ticket? In K. Rupp & S. H. Bell (Eds.), *Paying for results in vocational rehabilitation: Will provider incentives work for Ticket to Work?* (pp. 31-69). Washington, DC: Urban Institute.

Parent, W., Unger, D., & Inge, K. J. (1997). Customer profile. In V. Brooke, K. J. Inge, A. Armstrong, & P. Wehman (Eds.), *Supported employment handbook: A customer-driven approach for persons with significant disabilities* (pp. 46-97). Richmond: Virginia Commonwealth University, Rehabilitation Research and Training Center.

Pearpoint, J., O'Brien, J., & Forest, M. (1993). *PATH: A workbook for planning positive possible futures: Planning alternative tomorrows with hope for schools, organizations, businesses, and families.* Toronto: Inclusion Press.

Phelps, L. A., & Hanley-Maxwell, C. (1997). School-to-work transitions for youth with disabilities: A review of outcomes and practices. *Review of Educational Research, 67*(2), 197-226.

Putnam, J. W. (1994). *Cooperative learning and strategies for inclusion: Celebrating diversity in the classroom.* Baltimore: Paul H. Brookes.

Racino, J. A. (1998). The promise of self-advocacy and community employment. In P. Wehman & J. Kregel (Eds.), *More than a job: Securing satisfying careers for people with disabilities* (pp. 47-69). Baltimore: Paul H. Brookes.

Revell, G. (1991). Current regulations and guidelines. In S. L. Griffin & G. Revell (Eds.), *Rehabilitation counselor desk top guide to supported employment* (pp. 25-35). Richmond: Virginia Commonwealth University, Rehabilitation Research and Training Center on Supported Employment.

RESNA Technical Assistance Project (1992). *Assistive technology and the individualized education program.* Washington, DC: RESNA Press.

Rogan, P., Held, M., & Rinne, S. (2001). Organizational change from sheltered to integrated employment for adults with disabilities. In P. Wehman (Ed.), *Supported employment in business: Expanding the capacity of workers with disabilities* (pp. 195-214). St. Augustine, FL: Training Resource Network.

Rucker, R., & Brooks-Lane, N. (2003). *Systems change: Providing quality service delivery for persons with disabilities.* Retrieved April 29, 2004, from **http://www.t-tap.org/training/onlinecourses/oc.html**

Salembier, G., & Furney, K. S. (1997). Facilitating participation: Parents' perceptions of their involvement in the IEP/transition planning process. *Career Development for Exceptional Children, 20,* 29–42.

Shelley, R., Snizek, B., Westfall, M., Newman, L., Griffin, C., & Fogerty, L. (2002). No lone wolves: *Partnering for self-employment success.* Missoula: University of Montana, Rural Institute.

Shepherd, J., & Inge, K. J. (1999). Occupational and physical therapy. In S. deFur & J. Patton (Eds.), *Transition and school-based services: Interdisciplinary perspectives for enhancing the transition process* (pp. 117–165). Austin, TX: PRO-ED.

Smith, G., O'Keeffe, J., Carpenter, L., Doty, P., Kennedy, G., Burwell, B., et al. (2000). *Understanding Medicaid home and community services: A primer.* Retrieved April 21, 2004, from **http://www.aspe.hhs.gov/daltcp/reports/primer.htm#Intro**

Smull, M. (1998). Revisiting choice. In J. O'Brien & C. L. O'Brien (Eds.), *A little book about person centered planning* (pp. 37–49). Toronto: Inclusion Press.

Social Security Administration. (2004). *Redbook.* Retrieved April 19, 2004, from **http://www.socialsecurity.gov/work/ResourcesToolkit/redbook_page.html**

Stainback, S., & Stainback, W. (1992). *Curriculum considerations in inclusive classrooms: Facilitating learning for all students.* Baltimore: Paul H. Brookes.

Steineman, R. M., Morningstar, M. E., Bishop, B., & Turnbull, H. R. (1993). Role of families in transition planning for young adults with disabilities. *Journal of Vocational Rehabilitation, 3*(2), 52–61.

Tashie, C., & Schuh, M. (1993, Spring). Why not community-based instruction? High school students belong with their peers. *Equity and Excellence,* pp. 15–17.

Turnbull, A., & Turnbull, H. R. (1997). *Families, professionals, and exceptionality.* Upper Saddle River, NJ: Prentice Hall.

Turnbull, A., & Turnbull, H. R. (2001). Self-determination for individuals with significant cognitive disabilities and their families. *Journal of the Association for Persons with Severe Handicaps, 26,* 56–62.

U.S. General Accounting Office. (2001, September 4). *Special minimum wage program: Centers offer employment and support services to workers with disabilities, but labor should improve oversight* (GAO-01-886). Washington, DC: Author.

Wallace, J. K. (1995). Creative financing of assistive technology. In K. F. Flippo, K. J. Inge, & J. M. Barcus (Eds.), *Assistive technology: A resource for school, work, and community* (pp. 245–268). Baltimore: Paul H. Brookes.

Wehman, P. (Ed.). (1996). *Life beyond the classroom: Transition strategies for young people with disabilities* (2nd ed.). Baltimore: Paul H. Brookes.

Wehman, P. (Ed.). (2001). *Supported employment in business: Expanding the capacity of workers with disabilities.* St. Augustine, FL: Training Resource Network.

Wehman, P., Everson, J., & Reid, D. H. (1996). Beyond programs and placements: Using person-centered practices to individualize the transition process. In P. Wehman (Ed.), *Life beyond the classroom: Transition strategies for young people with disabilities* (2nd ed., pp. 91–126). Baltimore: Paul H. Brookes.

Wehman, P., & Revell, W. G. (2003). Lessons learned from the provision and funding of employment services for the MR/DD population: Implications for assessing the adequacy of the SSA Ticket to Work. In K. Rupp & S. H. Bell (Eds.), *Paying for results in vocational rehabilitation: Will provider incentives work for Ticket to Work?* (pp. 355–393). Washington, DC: Urban Institute.

Wehman, P., Revell, W. G., & Brooke, V. (2003). Competitive employment: Has it become the first choice yet? *Journal of Disability Policy Studies, 14*(3), 163–173.

Wehman, P., Revell, W. G., & Kregel, J. (1998). Supported employment: A decade of rapid growth and impact. *American Rehabilitation, 24*(1), 31–43.

Wehmeyer, M. L., Agran, M., & Hughes, C. (1998). *Teaching self-determination to students with disabilities: Basic skills for successful transition.* Baltimore: Paul H. Brookes.

Wehmeyer, M., & Kelchner, K. (1995). *Whose future is it anyway? A student directed transition planning process.* Arlington, TX: ARC National Headquarters.

Wehmeyer, M. L., Palmer, S. B., Agran, M., Mithaug, D., & Martin, J. (2000). Promoting causal agency: The self-determined learning model of instruction. *Exceptional Children, 66,* 439–453.

West, M., Hill, J. W., Revell, G., Smith, G., Kregel, J., & Campbell, L. (2002). Medicaid HCBS waivers and supported employment pre- and post-balanced Budget Act of 1997. *Mental Retardation, 40*(2), 142–147.

Weir, C. (2001, May). *Individual supports for college success* (On-Campus Outreach, Fact Sheet 7). Retrieved October 12, 2001, from **http://www.education.umd.edu/oco**

Wills, J., & Luecking, R. (2003). *Making the connections: Growing and supporting new organizations: Intermediaries.* Washington, DC: Office of Disability Employment Policy, National Collaborative on Workforce and Disability for Youth.

Winking, D., O'Reilly, B., & Moon, M. S. (1993). Preference: The missing link in the job match process for individuals without functional communication skills. *Journal of Vocational Rehabilitation, 3*(3), 27–42.

≈16≈

The Promise of Adulthood

Philip M. Ferguson
Dianne L. Ferguson

In his last year of high school, Ian Ferguson learned to fly. This was quite an accomplishment for someone labeled severely mentally retarded and physically disabled. As Ian's parents, we marveled at his achievement and worried about the law of gravity. Let us explain.

As part of Ian's final year as a student, he enrolled in "Beginning Drama." Following his carefully designed transition plan, Ian spent most of the rest of his day out in the community: working at various job sites, shopping at various stores, eating at various restaurants. But he began each day in drama class with a roomful of other would-be thespians. The logic behind Ian's participation in the class at the time was that it might lead somehow to his adult participation in some aspect or other of community theater. You see, while Ian's vision is poor, his hearing is great. In fact, he finds odd or unexpected sounds (human or otherwise) to be endlessly amusing. During high school, one of our more insightful friends bought Ian a set of sound effects tapes of the type used by theater groups (e.g., "Sound A-24, woman

screaming, 27 seconds" [screaming ensues]; Sound A-25, man sneezing, 15 seconds ...") as called for by various productions. Surely, we reasoned, Ian could learn to control his laughter long enough to help in such offstage activities as the making of sound effects. Furthermore, the drama teacher at Ian's high school just happened to be quite active in community theater in our town. Our objective, then, was really to see if we could figure out how Ian might participate in community theater productions as an adult leisure activity, possibly "networking" with the drama teacher to gain an entrée into that group.

To our pleasure, Ian benefited in many more unexpected ways from his introduction to the dramatic arts: memorization, articulation, expressiveness, and social interaction. He also learned to "fly." A major part of the first few weeks of class involved Ian's participation in "trust" exercises. Some students fell off ladders, trusting their classmates to catch them. Others dived off a runway with the same belief that their friends would break their fall. The exercise that Joe Zeller, the teacher, picked to challenge Ian was called "flying."

Seven or eight of Ian's classmates were to take him out of his wheelchair and raise him up and down in the air, tossing him just a little above their heads.

Now, the first time they tried this everyone was very tense. Both Mr. Zeller and Leah Howard (Ian's support teacher) were nervous; it was an adventure for them as well. The students released Ian's feet from their heel straps, unbuckled his seat belt, and, leaning over en masse, lifted him out of his chair. Joe and Leah positioned themselves at the most crucial locations on either side of Ian and slowly—together with the students—began to raise Ian's supine body with their hands. Now it was Ian's turn to be nervous. Ian's spasticity makes it impossible for him to break a fall by throwing out his arms. Several painful crashes have left him with a strong fear of falling at the first sensation of being off balance or awkwardly positioned. Like many folks who experience his kind of physical disability, Ian has a hard time trusting strangers to move the body that he has so little control over. As the students lifted him, he clutched nervously at the only wrist within reach of the one hand he can use, trying to find something to hold on to. His voice anxiously wavered "Leah, Leah," seeking reassurance that this was, in fact, a wise course of action. It was pretty scary for Ian and pretty risky for everyone else. But the exercise went well. Months later, when the drama class repeated some of the same trust exercises, Ian greeted the suggestion that he "fly" with an eager response of "Out of chair! Out of chair!" That is how Ian learned to "fly" in his last year of school. The secret was learning to control the fear of falling, and it's a lesson that has served us well in the ensuing years.

We tell this story about "flying" in drama class because it also captures the simultaneous sensations of excitement and anxiety that we experienced as Ian finished high school and launched into adulthood. We were fairly certain that Ian had some mixed feelings as his old routines and familiar settings vanished and new activities and settings took their place. The people in Ian's social network of formal and informal supports and friendship also recognized the responsibility that enough hands be there to "catch" Ian if he started to fall. As Ian left the relative stability of public school, grounded as it is in legal mandates and cultural familiarity, we worried about the thin air of adulthood where formal support systems seemed to promise little and accomplish even less.

Ian is 34 now. He lives in his own home, works at a job that he has enjoyed for nearly 12 years, and actively participates in a full schedule of household tasks, social engagements, parties, chores, weekends away, and occasional vacations. He did participate as a member of the cast in a local production of *Oklahoma!* directed by his high school drama teacher as we had hoped. He is supported in his adult life by a network of paid and unpaid people, a personal support agent who also provides direct support, and our ongoing involvement to ensure that his life is more okay than not okay from his point of view most of the time.

Our journey through these years has been difficult, often confusing and frustrating, but also filled with many exciting achievements. We have all learned a good deal about how one young man can negotiate an adult life and the kinds of supports that requires. Still, we continue to struggle with a variety of thorny issues. How do we make sure that Ian's life is really *his* life and not one that merely reflects the regulations, individual support plan procedures, agency practices, and other formal service trappings? How do we ensure that Ian's life is not a program? How do we assure ourselves that Ian is somehow contributing to all the choices that get made about what constitutes a good adult life for him? We have created new options for Ian and others as we have struggled to answer these questions. We have also increased our understanding of what it means for someone who has a variety of severe disabilities to be adult.

Exploring the Promise of Adulthood

In this chapter, we want to explore this status of adulthood and how it applies to people with severe disabilities. Our point is not that people with severe disabilities who are over the age of 18 or 21 are somehow not adults; of course they are adults. The problem is that our field has not spent enough time thinking through exactly what that means in our culture and era. Adulthood is more than simply a chronological marker that indicates someone is above a certain age. As important as having a meaningful job is or living as independently as possible, adulthood seems to involve more than this. As one social commentator has framed this distinction, "In many ways, children may always be children and adults may always be adults, but conceptions of 'childhood' and 'adulthood' are infinitely variable" (Meyrowitz, 1984, p. 25). If it is our responsibility as teachers and parents of students with severe disabilities to "launch" them as successfully as possible into adulthood, then it should be worthwhile to reflect on what promises such a role should hold. What is the promise of adulthood for people with severe disabilities?

We are not so bold as to think we can fully answer that question in this chapter. Our effort here will be to begin a discussion of the issue that we think needs to continue within the field of severe disabilities in general. We will organize our effort into three main sections: (a) understanding adulthood, (b) denying adulthood, and (c) achieving adulthood. Finally, throughout our discussion, our perspective will be unavoidably personal as well as professional. We will not pretend to be some anonymous and "objective" scholars writing dispassionately about the abstraction of adulthood for people with severe disabilities. Our son, Ian, is one of those people, and he is far from an abstraction to us. We will mention him throughout this chapter to illustrate some points we make and to explain our perspective better. However, we will also not write only as Ian's parents. We will draw on our own research and that of other professionals and scholars in disability studies to bolster our discussion as well. Such a mixture of the personal and professional perspective does not only affect us as the writers; it should also affect you as a reader. You should read and respond to this chapter as a discussion of the concept of adulthood in general but also as it fits (or does not fit) with your own personal experiences of people with severe disabilities.

Understanding Adulthood

The concept of adulthood is a fluid one that changes from era to era and from culture to culture (Ingstad & Whyte, 1995). For most European cultures, adulthood has a strong individualistic (or "egocentric" in anthropological terms) emphasis on personal independence and achievement. For many non-Western cultures, however, adulthood has a stronger emphasis on social affiliations and connectedness (or "sociocentric"). Even within our own American culture, the interpretation of adulthood has always undergone gradual historical shifts, influenced by all the factors that go into our social profile: demographic trends, economic developments, educational patterns, cultural diversity, even technology (think of how the availability of the automobile—both front and backseat—has changed the experience of adolescence). A quick historical review may help.

The Changing Status of Adulthood

The status of adulthood in our society is simple and complex, obvious and obscure. At one level, it is a straightforward matter of age. Anyone who is over the age of 18 (or certainly 21) is an adult, pure and simple. The process is automatic: one "gains" adulthood through simple endurance. If you live long enough, you cease being a child and become an adult. In legal terms, one could even be judged incompetent to manage one's affairs but still remain an adult in this chronological sense.

At an equally basic level, adulthood can mean simply a state of biological maturity. In such terms, an adult is someone who has passed through the pubertal stage and is physiologically fully developed. As with the chronological meaning, this biological interpretation also is still common and largely accurate as far as it goes: to be an adult is, at least in a physical sense, to be grown up, mature, fully developed.

However, it seems clear to us that the matter has always been more complicated than either chronology (Kett, 1977; Meyrowitz, 1984) or biology (Bouwsma, 1976; Dannefer, 1984). These factors convey a sense of precision and permanence about the concept that simply ignores the process of social construction by which every culture imbues such terms with meaning (Ingstad & Whyte, 1995; Kalyanpur & Harry, 1999).

For example, historically we know that the beginning age for adulthood has been a surprisingly flexible concept even within the confines of Western culture (Modell, Furstenberg, & Hershberg, 1978). Philippe Aries (1962) has even argued that childhood itself, as a social distinction, was not "discovered" in Europe until the 16th century. Before then, he argues, children were treated as little more than the "miniature adults"—much like they were portrayed in medieval art (Aries, 1962). Adolescence, for example, was reported in a 16th-century French compilation of "informed opinion" as being the third stage of life, lasting until 28 or even 35 years of age (Aries, 1962). On the other hand, in colonial New England, legal responsibility for one's personal behavior began at "the age of discretion," which usually meant 14 to 16 years old (Beales, 1985), and many children left home for their vocational apprenticeships as early as age 10 or 12 (Beales, 1985; Kett, 1977).

At the end of the 19th century in Europe and America and continuing today, a period of postadolescent "youth" emerged, where children of the upper and middle classes (mainly males at first but now including females) could choose to postpone their adulthood by extending their professional training into their late 20s. As defines this role, the key distinction in this delayed adulthood was the extended status of economic dependency for these college students (e.g., Wohl, 1979). Taylor (1988) is even more specific: "Physically and psychologically adults, these individuals have not yet committed to those institutions which society defines as adult—namely, work, marriage and family" (p. 649). In many areas of the country, both urban and rural, this extended economic dependency continues to shape the cultural expectations of a "successful" transition to adulthood (Furstenberg, Cook, Eccles, Elder, & Sameroff, 1999; Magnussen, 1997). Most social historians seem to agree that, after a period of compression and inflexibility in the decades following World War II, the "acceptable" time span for transition from childhood to adulthood has become a mosaic of cultural and class variations (Elder & Rand, 1995; Kalyanpur & Harry, 1999; Modell et al., 1978).

What remains is a curious interaction of fixed periods of institutional transition (graduation, voting, legal status) with fluid patterns of family and cultural change (economic separation, living apart from parents, sexual activity, postsecondary education) (Mallory, 1995). As America grows more diverse, it seems likely that the traditional cultural markers of adulthood will only become more problematic and situational. Kalyanpur and Harry (1999), for example, point out that for many non-Anglo families, "it is assumed that the son will continue to live in the parents' home, regardless of economic or marital status, and that the daughter will leave after marriage only to move in with her husband's family" (p. 106). Turnbull and Turnbull (1996) report in their research that many Latino families stressed the values of unity and permanence in family relationships over "mainstream" values of independence and separation (pp. 200–201) when it came to goals for their children. At the same time, many children from poor families feel early pressures to contribute to the economic survival of the family and their own material well-being. In many aspects of social life, teenagers engage in "adult" behavior at earlier and earlier ages (Furstenberg et al., 1999, p. 8).

Given this cultural and historical variability, how might we elaborate an understanding of adulthood that goes beyond age? How can we describe the social construction of adulthood? Finally, how do these social and cultural dimensions of adulthood affect the experiences and opportunities of people with severe disabilities? We will address these questions by examining some of the dimensions of adulthood and their symbolic significance.

The Dimensions of Adulthood

As Ian's parents, we naturally thought it was important that Ian graduate from high school. More to the point, however, we felt it was extremely important that he participate as fully as possible in his high school's commencement exercises. The graduation ritual itself seemed crucial to us. It took planning, coordination, cooperation, and compromise by a number of people to make that participation happen, but happen it did, as the picture of Ian in his cap and gown shows (Figure 16–1). Now, while Ian certainly enjoyed his graduation (especially the part where people applauded as he crossed the stage), we don't know if he fully appreciated all the cultural symbolism attached to such events for many of the other participants. Missing the graduation ceremony

FIGURE 16–1
Ian at his High School Graduation Ceremony

would not have lessened the skills Ian had learned in high school, threatened the friendships he had forged, or worsened his prospects for a smooth transition from school to work. In other words, the importance of Ian's participation in commencement was largely symbolic. It symbolized for us many of the same things that a son or daughter's graduation from high school symbolizes for most parents.

Few events are as loaded with symbolism as a graduation ceremony. It is perhaps the closest our particular society comes to a formal rite of passage from childhood to adulthood. Of course, other societies and traditions might have other symbols equally powerful and not include anything related to ceremonies about finishing schooling. Much of what we are trying to capture in an understanding of adulthood occurs at this symbolic level of meaning. There are three important dimensions to this symbolic understanding (Table 16-1).

The Dimension of Autonomy

Perhaps the most familiar and common symbols of adulthood in our society are those that convey a sense of personal autonomy. This dimension emphasizes the status of adulthood as an outcome, a completion. It is the *achieving* of adulthood that is the main focus;

what happens throughout the adult years in terms of learning and growth or the physical changes that accompany aging are less the point. More specific features of autonomy can be seen in several aspects of life commonly associated with adulthood.

Self-Sufficiency One of the most often cited features of adulthood is an expectation of self-sufficiency. At the most fundamental level, this usually means economic self-sufficiency. Whether by employment, inherited wealth, or social subsidy, adulthood entails the belief that one has the resources to take care of oneself. This sense of self-sufficiency entails a transition from a primary existence of economic consumption and dependency to one of rough balance between consumption and production. Theoretically, even our welfare system works to preserve and enhance the self-sufficiency of individuals by providing temporary support and training.

However, self-sufficiency goes beyond this economic sense to also include elements of emotional adequacy. Adulthood usually has the sense of having the emotional as well as economic resources to "make it on one's own." People who are thought to whine about trivial complaints are often told to "grow up" or "quit acting like a baby." Moreover, there are important

TABLE 16-1
Dimensions of Adulthood

Autonomy:	Being your own person, expressed through symbols of:	
	Self-sufficiency:	Especially economic self-sufficiency, or having the resources to take care of oneself. Includes emotional self-sufficiency, or the ability to "make it" on one's own. Marks a shift from economic consumption to consumption and production.
	Self-determination:	Assertion of individuality and independence. The ability to assure others that one possesses the rational maturity and personal freedom to make specific choices about how to live one's life.
	Completeness:	A sense of having "arrived." A shift from future to present tense. No more waiting.
Membership:	Community connectedness, collaboration, and sacrifice expressed through symbols of:	
	Citizenship:	Activities of collective governance from voting and participation in town meetings to volunteering for political candidates; expressing your position on issues with money, time, or bumper stickers; or recycling to protect the shared environment.
	Affiliation:	Activities of voluntary association, fellowship, celebration and support from greeting the new family in the neighborhood with a plate of cookies to being an active member of the church, a participant in the local service or garden club, or a member of the local art museum.
Change:	Adulthood as an ongoing capacity for growth rather than the static outcome of childhood. Change occurs for adults as they change jobs, move to new apartments or houses, relocate to new communities, or go back to school to learn new jobs or hobbies. Change also occurs as old friends and family members move away and new friendships are formed.	

gender differences in how our culture portrays emotional maturity. Still, in some sense or other, emotional competence in the face of life's adversities is presented as an expectation for adults.

> *Last year, Ian earned about $3,200 in his job at the university. This annual income has varied over time from a high of $4,500 to a low of $3,000 as his responsibilities changed, as supervisors changed, and as other parts of his life took precedence. While this job and these earnings are important to his life as an adult, they do not begin to cover his living, to say nothing of his recreational, expenses. Even with the social service support dollars made available to him, the life he is creating for himself exceeds his available economic resources too much of the time. However, Ian has a job and social service dollars to support his efforts. Many people with severe disabilities have none, or what they do have are woefully inadequate. Poverty and disability have a long history, and self-sufficiency and poverty are incompatible.*

Self-Determination   Self-determination and self-sufficiency are often treated as synonymous features of adulthood. However, while recognizing that the terms are closely related, we want to use the term "self-determination" to refer to a more active assertion of individuality and independence. An autonomous adult in this sense is someone who has the rational maturity and personal freedom to make specific choices about how to live his or her life. Autonomous adults make decisions and live with the consequences.

Certainly, from the perspective of childhood, this dimension of autonomy is probably the most anticipated. Self-determination involves all the freedoms and control that seem so oppressively and unreasonably denied as we suffer through the indignities of adolescence. We can live where we want, change jobs if we want, make our own judgments about what debts to incur and what risks to take, and make our own decisions when faced with moral dilemmas. We can even stay up late if we want or go shopping at 10:00 in the morning. However, these new privileges are quickly coupled with new responsibilities.

For persons with severe disabilities, the concept of self-determination is challenging and promising and has become a new focus of discussion and research (D. L. Ferguson, 1998; Priestley, 2001; Wehman, 2001; Wehmeyer, Agran, & Hughes, 1998). As a concept, self-determination could change not just what happens in the lives of people with severe disabilities but, more fundamentally, how we think about such things as services, supports, interventions, and outcomes.

One example of the role of self-determination and the challenges in understanding and interpreting it for people with severe disabilities first came to us wrapped in a Christmas Eve invitation.

> *Ian invited us to his house for Christmas Eve for the first time about 4 years ago. Previously we had always celebrated holidays in our home, even after Ian moved into his own house. Of course, most families eventually face such a time when the location for holidays and other family rituals shifts from the parents' home to the children's. What is hard for us to unravel in our relationship with Ian, however, is just how this particular transitional invitation occurred. Did Ian somehow arrive at the determination that it was time to shift our holiday celebrations to his own home? Did his housemates, Robin and Lyn, who had been helping him can fruits and vegetables, make jam and breads, and decorate and arrange baskets for weeks, "support his choice" to invite us over or shape his choice on his behalf? Did they somehow teach him how and why he might wish to request our presence at this holiday celebration? Since this first invitation, we have had many more—sometimes for holidays, sometimes just for an ordinary Wednesday or Friday. Whatever Ian's exact role in the decision to invite, it is clear that he enjoys having us in his house in a quite different way than he seems to enjoy visiting ours.*

For individuals whose communication skills are limited and for whom our understanding of their preferences and point of view can be incomplete, it is sometimes difficult to figure out when they are making choices—determining things for themselves—and when it is the interpretations of others that shape the outcomes. At the same time, it seems better to try to guess at another's perspective and preferences than to ignore them altogether. At still other times, it may well be that no choice is made despite the opportunity.

> *"Do you want eggs, pancakes, or bagels for breakfast tomorrow?" we asked Ian recently during an overnight visit. "Bagels," was his prompt reply. "Do you want bagels, pancakes, or eggs?" Phil tried again, wondering if Ian was really listening and choosing. "Eggs," Ian just as promptly replied.*

Over the years, we have tried various little tests like this to check whether Ian's answers are choices or just his effort to support the conversational exchange by repeating the last thing he heard. Of course, questioning his apparent choices could seem unsupportive of his efforts to determine things for himself. Perhaps the admission that we question his response is as important as whether he is really choosing. These are the essential questions and dilemmas of self-determination for Ian and others with similar disabilities.

Completeness Perhaps the common element in all the features of adulthood as autonomy is a sense of completeness. What one gains with self-determination and self-sufficiency is clearly more than the imagined pleasures of doing totally as one pleases. Adulthood brings no guarantees of living happily ever after. Rather than the rewards of choosing well and wisely, adulthood seems only to finally offer the opportunity to make those choices, from silly to serious, on one's own. Rather than working at learning all one needs to be an adult, one now finally *is* an adult, presumably putting to use all that learning and preparation. Adulthood has to do with the feeling of knowing how to act and what to do, such as what to order and how much to tip in any restaurant. Most of us have felt the pain of youthful uncertainty in "grown up" situations. We struggle to manage our youthful discomfort in the belief that each event will eventually bring the longed-for knowledge and confidence to cover all situations. In reality, of course, the completeness really comes with the ability to be comfortable with one's uncertainties.

Adulthood brings a sense of completeness—of preparation achieved—that is never there during childhood. The fact that many of us continue to feel uncertain in some situations well past middle age merely attests to the power of the notion of completeness to our understandings of adulthood. Even though as adults we continue to learn and grow, that learning is not in *preparation* for adulthood the way most of our learning was before achieving adult status. Even if we are unsure in some situations, it is not so much because we aren't prepared to handle it but rather because our knowledge and experience make the choice of action more ambiguous.

A continuing struggle for us is to make sure that Ian's adulthood is complete in this way. Even though he has continued to learn many things since high school graduation, we have tried to make sure that his learning

of new skills or information is not a requirement placed on Ian by his supporters for achievement of adulthood. He is an adult even if he never learns another skill. It is a difficult balance to achieve. Ian (and all other adults) needs to be afforded opportunities to continue to learn and grow but without the trappings of preparatory training or schooling. If we think of life as a type of language, then adulthood as autonomy would seem to be a move from the future to the present tense.

The Dimension of Membership

Sometimes it seems that we allow the dimension and symbols of autonomy to exhaust our understanding of adulthood. Adulthood in this view is essentially a matter of independence. This can create problems when we ask society to respond to all people with severe disabilities as "fully adult" since many are limited by their disability from demonstrating such independence in ways that are similar to how others without disabilities demonstrate them. Indeed, for many people, this limited independence is precisely what the label of "disability" means in the first place. However, we would argue that limiting our understanding of adulthood as "being able to do it by yourself" is problematic for all adults whether or not they have a disability. There is an equally important dimension in understanding adulthood that serves as a crucial counterbalance to the individualistic emphasis on autonomy. This dimension includes all those facets of adulthood that involve citizenship and affiliation and that must be supported by the collaboration and sacrifice of others. We collectively refer to these facets as the dimension of membership. If adulthood as autonomy is a move to life in the present tense, then adulthood as membership recognizes that life is plural rather than singular, communal as well as individual.

Citizenship Anthropologists have probably contributed most to our understanding of the communal aspects of adulthood in most cultures, including our own. They have described in detail the rituals and responsibilities that societies attach to adult status. In a very real sense, it is only with these rites of passage into adulthood that we become full members of our communities. In part, this involves an element of responsibility for others and the community in general. Voting and other acts of collective governance are the most obvious signs of this theme and perhaps seem the most daunting for some adults with severe disabilities.

We have not pursued voting as a way for Ian to explore this aspect of membership, mostly because we fear that providing the assistance he would need might really just result in one of us having the advantage of two votes. However, there are other ways Ian can exercise community responsibility. Stuffing envelopes, for example, passing out campaign information, or expressing an opinion through yard signs are ways Ian can and does contribute to the political life of his community. Actively recycling by using his backpack instead of bags when shopping and expressing his political opinions on issues of accessibility with the "Attitudes Are the Real Disability" bumper sticker affixed to the back of his wheelchair are examples of ways in which Ian participates as a citizen of our community.

Affiliation The communal dimension of adulthood is not only about a grudging performance of civic duties or even a cheerful altruism of civic sacrifice. An important aspect of communal adulthood lies in the various examples of voluntary association, fellowship, celebration, and support that adults typically discover and create. One of the most common signs of adulthood, for example, is the intentional formation of new families and the extension of old ones. Through formal and informal affiliations, adults locate themselves socially as well as geographically (Figure 16–2). You might live on the east side of town, belong to the square-dance club, attend the Catholic church, and have a spouse and two

FIGURE 16–2
Ian Often Meets Friends at One of the Local Pubs

kids. We might live in a downtown condo, belong to the library patrons' society, participate in community theater, and volunteer at the local rape crisis center. The particular array of affiliations can differ dramatically. However, in the aggregate, those affiliations help define a community just as the community, in turn, helps define each of us as adults. Through their affiliations, adults support and define each other.

The definitional power of our affiliations seems to us very true for Ian and other adults who require similar supports. Ian's life tends to reflect the people in his life. Right now, his two primary support people like to camp, give big parties, and garden. So Ian does, too. Moreover, Ian's community of Eugene, Oregon, is one that prizes such outdoor activities, and so there are many groups and opportunities that encourage these hobbies. When Ian was in his early 20s, dancing and pool were favorite pursuits of his supporters, and Ian obligingly enjoyed these activities just as much. At the same time, Ian has his own long-standing hobbies (e.g., casino gambling), and any long-term friends will probably need to enjoy the bells and whistles of Las Vegas, Reno, or a local casino as well (Figure 16–3).

The Dimension of Change
We said earlier that adulthood as autonomy could be described as a move from the future to the present tense. The dimension of adulthood as membership shows that the description requires a plural rather than a singular construction. Let us follow the logic in this final dimension of adulthood and argue that a dynamic approach to life demands that adulthood must finally be understood as a verb, not a noun. In the biological sense, adulthood may indeed represent a developmental maturity; in a social and psychological sense, it can also represent phases of continued growth.

Of course, this aspect of adulthood has been the focus of increased attention in developmental psychology since the seminal work of Erik Erikson (1950) on the eight "crises" or stages of the life cycle, four of which occur in adulthood. Subsequent psychologists have variously refined and revised this work (Erikson & Martin, 1984; Levinson, 1978; Vaillant, 1977). Sociologists and historians have added an important sociocultural perspective to these stages within the life span (Dannefer, 1984; Elder, 1987; Hareven, 1978). In general, however, these developmentalist writers help us understand that adulthood has its own stages of growth, change, and learning. It is a period of both realization and continued transition.

FIGURE 16–3
A Favorite Activity is Hitting the Slot Machines at a Nearby Casino

As with most scholarly "discoveries," the understanding of adulthood as full of change and development is neither new nor scholarly. As a theme, it runs through some of our richest traditions. One theologian (Bouwsma, 1976) has identified the Judeo-Christian tradition as one in which adulthood "implies a process rather than the possession of a particular status or specific faculty" (p. 77). He goes on to describe the key element for adulthood in this tradition not as the completion of growth but as the "capacity for growth" (p. 81). However, it is perhaps the Confucian tradition that best captures this understanding of adulthood with its depiction of life as a journey in which one is always "on the way."

> *Ian is now 34. He seems to have transitioned, along with his housemates, into the very beginnings of the ever-changing span of time we call "middle age." He is a different person than he was at 21. His tastes in music are still eclectic, but he seems to enjoy visiting his parents and singing along to old Paul Simon,*

Beatles, or Simon and Garfunkel CDs more than he did 7 or 8 years ago. He's gained some weight, and we've been told he has a few early gray hairs (we haven't spotted them yet). He's getting a little arthritis in his knees. More than changes in his appearance, however, he approaches his middle 30s with a different demeanor. He can be serious or consoling when the occasion demands, although he might not describe the emotion in those terms. He has experienced the death of grandparents, lost friends and support workers, and learned how to be alone in ways that are different than when he lived with us.

His parents have moved to work in a new state. Although Dianne is still working in Eugene part time and is around part of every month, Phil visits only a few times a year and talks to Ian a couple of times a week by phone. These changes mark a new phase in all our lives. We all miss living close to each other as Ian expresses clearly each time he meets one of us at the airport with smiles, enthusiasm, and sometimes flowers. We worry about the distances, but for now Ian's adulthood is secure enough, even with all the continuing challenges, to make this kind of change possible for all of us.

For many people with disabilities, these three dimensions of adulthood occur only partially, often as approximations of the symbols the rest of us use to identify others and ourselves as adults. Table 16–2 illustrates some examples of these symbols that are present in many adult lives, though not in as many adult lives of people with disabilities. If we only assess the symbols we each can claim, however, we may make the mistake of denying the status of adulthood to people with disabilities. Symbols are important, but they are not the whole story. One way we evaluate our success at supporting Ian's adulthood is to examine periodically just how each of these dimensions is visible in his life. How does the daily round of Ian's life reflect ways of becoming a unique member of our community? Are his activities, affiliations, and ways of participating varied? Do they change over time? Do they reflect a changing understanding among his circle of family, friends, and supporters of Ian's own preferences and choices? We'll return to these questions later with examples that might help you see how these dimensions of adulthood can apply in the life of a person with severe disabilities. First, however, let us examine more completely why these notions have been so difficult to apply to this group of people.

TABLE 16–2
Symbols of Adulthood: Some Examples

Symbols of autonomy
- Having a source of income, a job or wealth.
- Making your own choices, both the big important ones and the little trivial ones.
- No more waiting for the privilege of doing what you want, how you want, when and with whom you want to do it.

Symbols of membership
- A voter registration card.
- Membership cards for organizations and clubs.
- An appointment calendar and address book.
- Season tickets, bumper stickers, charitable contributions of time and money.

Symbols of change
- Marriage
- Acquiring new hobbies
- Children
- New jobs and homes
- Learning new skills
- Old friends

Denying Adulthood

If the meaning of adulthood involves the dimensions of autonomy, membership, and change, then how have those dimensions affected our understanding of adults with severe disabilities? There are undeniable improvements over the past decade in the movement of people with intellectual disabilities into community-based jobs and residences (Blanck, 1998; Prouty, Smith, & Lakin, 2002). However, the evidence of continuing problems in the quality of life for many of these individuals is apparent even to the casual observer. Most states continue to have long waiting lists for residential and employment opportunities. According to one poll (Louis Harris and Associates, 2000), between 65% and 70% of people with disabilities are unemployed (Wehman, 2001). As of 2002, almost 60,000 individuals were estimated to be waiting for residential services outside their family homes (Prouty et al., 2002). Although the number of people with developmental disabilities residing in large private or public institutions has dramatically declined over the past two decades, the federal government still spends some $5.6 billion (for fiscal year 2000) to keep people in large congregate care facilities (Braddock, Hemp, Rizzolo, Parish, & Pomeranz, 2002). In other words, although

only 10% to 15% of people with developmental disabilities receiving residential services (not including individuals sharing a home with a relative) lived in large, public institutions, almost half (45%) of the federal MR/DD Medicaid spending went to support those individuals (Braddock et al., 2002; Lakin, Prouty, Polister, & Coucouvanis, 2003). For over 15 years, evidence has mounted for the economic and social benefits of supported employment for adults with developmental disabilities. Yet unemployment and segregated workshops and day programs still dominate the vocational services offered (Blanck, 1998; DeLio, Rogan, & Geary, 2000; Wehman, 2001). For individuals with severe disabilities, in particular, this empirical evidence of a poor quality of life must also be understood in a historical context.

If you examine the history of adulthood for people with severe disabilities, you find a story not only of symbolic deprivation but also of economic deprivation. Indeed, at the heart of our discussion is the belief that the two are inextricably related. Symbols of adulthood accompany the practice of being an adult. Or, to reverse the logic, the denial of adulthood to people with severe disabilities has been symbolic as well as concrete. Recent movements to recognize the full range of rights and responsibilities of adults with

TABLE 16–3
Symbols of Denial of Adulthood: Some Examples

Unending childhood

- Childish, diminutive names like Bobby and Susie.
- Enforced dependency that permits others to make all important choices.
- Few life changes.

Unfinished transition

- No more school but no job, home, or affiliations in the community.
- Rituals for ending but not for beginning.
- Acquisition of visible but empty symbols like beards and pipes but no jobs, homes, or community affiliations.

Unhelpful services

- Clienthood: A focus on remediation and readiness determined through the mechanisms of professional preciousness.
- Anonymity: Service standards and procedures that overwhelm individuality and uniqueness.
- Chronocity: The professional decision to deny lifelong change because the client is insusceptible to further development.

severe disabilities can best be understood in light of this history of denial. Table 16-3 summarizes some of the symbols of denial of adulthood across the dimensions discussed next.

Unending Childhood

Wolfensberger (1972) not only helped popularize the principle of normalization as a basic orientation for human services but also deserves credit for raising our awareness of the symbolic dimensions of discrimination and stigma in the lives of people with severe disabilities. In particular, he helped highlight how society referred to people with mental retardation in terms and images that suggested a status of "eternal childhood." Nearly 30 years later, it is still frustratingly common to hear adults with severe disabilities described by the construct of "mental age": "Johnny Smith is 34 years old but has the mind of a 3-year-old." In an interview we did some years ago (P. M. Ferguson, Ferguson, & Jones, 1988), an elderly parent of a 40-year-old son with Down syndrome described him as a sort of disabled Peter Pan: one of the "ever-ever children." "This thing about normalizing will not happen . . . they'll always be childlike" (p. 109).

Fortunately, the myth of eternal childhood as the "inevitable" fate for people with severe disabilities is much less powerful than it was 10 or 20 years ago. We like to think that today's generation of young parents is less likely than our generation to learn from professionals that their sons and daughters are "ever-ever children." Increasingly, it seems that both professionals

and the general public are aware of the stigmatizing assumptions built into childish terms of reference. Appearance and activities are more and more likely to avoid the most obviously childish examples (e.g., adults playing with simple puzzles or toys, carrying school lunch boxes to work). We are gradually moving away from our infantilizing images of the past.

Of course, if symbols are the only thing to be changed, then the true movement to adulthood will still be stalled. We remember working at a large state institution for people with severe disabilities some 25 years ago. This institution closed in June 1998, but at the time, a number of people who worked there had apparently gotten only part of the message about treating people as adults. As a result, over a period of months, all the adult men on one ward grew beards and smoked pipes. Nothing else changed in their lives to encourage their personal autonomy, much less their membership in the community. The beards and pipes were simply empty symbols of adulthood that had no grounding in the daily lives of indignity and isolation that the men continued to lead. Alternatively, allowing someone the choice to risk his or her health by not wearing a seat belt in the car or by eating three large pizzas for dinner in the name of autonomy and adult independence also misses the point, resulting instead in a limitation of adulthood, perhaps quite literally if that person's health is threatened by such risky choices.

Even at 34, Ian might choose to watch cartoons and always choose to drink chocolate milk or any number of other choices that might be more typical of a young child. Once in a while, these choices are fine. But as a steady diet, such choices do not communicate the full range of options most adults enjoy. Part of truly supporting Ian's adulthood is making sure he has enough experience of lots of different options to make adult decisions. He still does choose chocolate milk, but probably more often now, he chooses Dr. Pepper or a beer. And his taste in beer has grown more sophisticated in the past half dozen years. The point is not so much to deny revisiting the preferences of childhood but to create the many more varied choices of adulthood as just as frequent options.

Unfinished Transition

An important part of the move away from the unending childhood view of severe disability has occurred in the increased programmatic attention paid to the transition period from school to adult life (Jorgensen, 1998; Wehman, 2001; Wehmeyer, 2001; Wehmeyer, et al., 1998). This focus on transition has certainly clarified the right of people with severe disabilities not to remain forever imprisoned by images of childhood. It has led to a heightened awareness on the part of the special education community that *what happens after a student leaves school is perhaps the most crucial test of how effective that schooling was.* In terms of program evaluation, the emphasis on transition planning in the schools has clearly identified adulthood as the ultimate outcome measure for the process of special education.

However, as a cultural generalization, an escape from unending childhood has not yet meant an entrance into full-fledged adulthood for many people with severe disabilities. Instead of eternal childhood, we see their current status as one of stalled or unfinished transition: a "neither-nor" ambiguity in which young people with severe disabilities are no longer seen as children or yet as adults. As with adulthood itself, however, transition too can be viewed symbolically. It is in this symbolic sense that people with severe disabilities can become embedded in a permanent process of incomplete transition.

Several scholars have suggested the anthropological concept of liminality as most descriptive of this situation (Murphy, Scheer, Murphy, & Mack, 1988; Mwaria, 1990). Liminality refers to a state of being when a person is suspended between the demands and opportunities of childhood and adulthood. Many societies use various rituals of initiation, purification, or other transitions to both accomplish and commemorate a significant change in status. In many cultures where these rituals retain their original intensity, the actual event can last for days or months. During such rituals, the person undergoing the process is said to occupy a liminal (or "threshold") state. According to one author,

> *People in a liminal condition are without clear status, for their old position has been expunged and they have not yet been given a new one. They are "betwixt and between," neither fish nor fowl; they are suspended in social space without firm identity or role definition….In a very real sense, they are nonpersons, making all interactions with them unpredictable and problematic. (Murphy et al., 1988, p. 237)*

For too many adults with severe disabilities, one could say the transition to adulthood is a ritual that once never began and now begins but seldom ends. Instead, they remain on the threshold of adulthood in a kind of permanent liminality—"suspended in social space."

We see this liminality in the kinds of social responses to adults with severe disabilities that perpetuate social isolation in the name of autonomy. Professionals who tell parents they need to "back off" from involvement in their newly adult son's or daughter's life so that they can begin to build their own separate life apart from the ties of family and home sometimes end up isolating the new adult by removing the most effective advocates for an expanded membership in the community. Parents and professionals who conspire (usually with purely benevolent intentions) to create a facade of independence for adults with severe disabilities by allowing them trivial, secondary, or coerced choices instead of true self-determination (Knowlton, Turnbull, Backus, & Turnbull, 1988) trap adults in the isolation of liminality in another way.

In still other instances, adults are given a plentiful supply of token affiliations and social activities with no attention to the symbols of self-sufficiency represented by a real job with real income, making the illusion incomplete in yet another way. Such an ambiguous social status will continue to frustrate individuals in their efforts to define themselves as adult. Society in general will continue to feel uncomfortable in the presence of such people, not knowing how to respond.

Ian's own transition seemed at risk of an extended liminal status for the first few months after graduation. He continued to live in our home, and his only "job" was a volunteer job that he had begun when in high school. His personal agent and personal support staff created a schedule of personal and recreational activities to fill his days. While Ian certainly enjoyed this round of activity, it felt to us, and we think to him as well, like a kind of holding pattern. He was waiting for his chance to enter the routines and responsibilities of adulthood. The "meantime schedule" of activity was a substitute and one that, in the end, did not last long. We'll have more to say about Ian's adult life later and how his daily and weekly routines simply are his life and substitute or wait for nothing.

Unhelpful Services

Although the special education system must share part of the blame for unfinished transition, much of the responsibility must fall on an "adult" service system historically plagued with problems of poor policy, inadequate funding, and ineffective programs (P. M. Ferguson & Ferguson, 2001; P. M. Ferguson, Hibbard, Leinen, & Schaff, 1990; Smull & Bellamy, 1991). There are significant exceptions to this generalization across the domains of residential programs (Howe, Horner, & Newton, 1998; Taylor, Bogdan, & Racino, 1991), employment support (Mank, Cioffi, & Yovanoff, 1997), and leisure and recreation (Anderson, Schleien, & Seligmann, 1997; Dattilo & Schleien, 1994; Germ & Schleien, 1997), but for far too many, the promise of adulthood remains an unfilled promise.

Many analysts of the social service system continue to point to fundamental inadequacies in adult services (Bérubé, 2003; Drake, 2001; Ferguson, 2003; Fleischer & Zames; 2001; McKnight, 1995). Although each of these analyses has its own list of problems, they all include some basic complaints. We will briefly mention three of these issues that correspond to the three dimensions of adulthood we have already set forth. These three issues are (a) clienthood, (b) anonymity, and (c) chronicity.

Clienthood

The traditional service system promotes "clienthood" rather than adulthood. Dependency unavoidably fosters the role of clienthood either explicitly or implicitly, and dependency is the status of many individuals "served" by the traditional service system. The role has many versions, but perhaps the most familiar is that which imposes a model of medical or behavioral

deficit as the dominant rationale for service decisions. In this version, the essential orientation for service delivery is that the individual with the disability has something that needs to be cured or remediated. Just as patients are expected to follow the doctor's orders and take the prescribed medicine, so are people with disabilities expected to follow their "individual habilitation (or support) plans," work hard to improve themselves (Bickenbach, 2001; Drake, 2001; McKnight, 1995; Phillips, 1985), and abide by the suggestions of their designated professionals (e.g., case managers, job coaches, residential providers).

This dependency is perhaps most familiar in those aspects of the welfare system (e.g., Supplemental Security Income, Social Security Disability Income, Medicaid) that can unintentionally create economic disincentives to vocational independence. But it is equally powerful at the more personal level through a tendency that Sarason (1972) has called "professional preciousness." Professional preciousness refers to the tendency of professionals to define problems in ways that require traditionally trained professionals (like themselves) for the solution. Thus, case managers sometimes define a client's needs according to what the system happens to provide (Drake, 2001; Taylor, 2001). Opportunities for meaningful employment are overlooked or unsought unless they have been developed through the proper channels of certified rehabilitation professionals rather than untrained but willing coworkers (Nisbet & Hagner, 1988). Those who find the penalties too high for participation in such a system can "drop out" but only at the risk of losing all benefits (especially health care) and without official standing as "disabled" at all (P. M. Ferguson et al., 1990). By limiting the avenues for achieving jobs, homes, and active social lives to the "disability-approved" services offered through the formal service system, clienthood undermines autonomy (P. M. Ferguson & Ferguson, 2001; Williams, 2001).

We realize we have drawn a pretty bleak picture. Our point is not that that all public policy is somehow bad or that it does not sometimes contribute in very real ways to realizing adulthood for many with disabilities. We are saying that people with severe disabilities will more often than not suffer less rather than more at the hands of the formal system. We and many other families have struggled to "tweak" and bend the demands of the formal system to allow it to better meet the needs of our sons and daughters. Our successes, when they occur, best serve to make our point that we need a system that doesn't require extraordinary effort to resist the clienthood, anonymity, and chronicity that too often describe our current system of service.

We have strived to create options for Ian that use the social service system but reject this status of clienthood, at least from Ian's point of view and, perhaps more important, from the point of view of his direct supporters. Although Ian's living situation is possible because of the official funding category of "supported living" and his job support dollars are provided through the category of "supported employment," we have redirected these dollars from the familiar residential or vocational programs to a process that allows Ian, his family, and supporters to directly decide how to use these dollars. Along with a small number of friends and colleagues, we operate a nonprofit organization that does not decide for Ian or the three others we are currently also supporting but rather manages the paperwork, rules, reports, and budgets that permit Ian and those most directly involved in his life to direct how the support dollars are best used to support his adulthood. Our collective efforts to support Ian's definition of his own life have allowed us to meet the necessary rules and regulations but protect Ian and his supporters from having to attend to them constantly. It has become the responsibility of Ian's personal support agent to make sure that the penalties of participation in the service system are minimized so that Ian may develop his own adult identity apart from that of social service system client.

Anonymity

The traditional system not only promotes dependency for many but also creates a kind of bureaucratic isolation in which procedures replace people and standardization overwhelms context. Certainly this is partly and simply a function of the size of the programs and the numbers of people involved. However, it goes beyond this to a style of centralization and control that pursues efficiency above all else. This style often leads to situations of sterility and isolation in programs that are ostensibly intended to increase a person's social integration. The need for efficient purchasing and supply can lead to so much similarity in the possessions and activities of clients that the individual becomes swallowed up in a collective that diminishes each member's uniqueness. It seems unlikely that the individuals in a dozen group homes and apartments operated by the same supported living agency all like the same brand of ice cream, prefer the same laundry detergent, and choose the same color paper napkins, for example.

An even more powerful example involves the types of relationships many people with severe disabilities experience. One thing that seems important to the social relationships and friendships that most of us enjoy is "knowing each others' stories." The very process of a developing friendship usually involves learning about each other through the stories of experiences and history shared in conversation.

When people enter Ian's life, we support the developing relationship by sharing much of Ian's story for him. If he lived in a community residential program, however, the constant turnover of staff and the demands for confidentiality might so limit what others know about his life that he is rendered virtually anonymous except for what can be readily observed and directly experienced.

Chronicity

The final barrier that seems an unavoidable facet of the traditional support system is something we term "chronicity." Chronicity is the officially delivered, systematic denial of lifelong change and growth. Chronicity is created by professional pronouncements that someone or some group is unsusceptible to further development. Again, this barrier results from the dominance of what might be called a "therapeutic model" in the overall design of services. For those who "respond to treatment" in this model, there is a future of more treatment, more programs, and more clienthood. However, for those whose disability is judged so severe as to be beyond help (e.g., "incorrigible," "incurable," "hopeless," "ineducable"), there is a professionally ordained abandonment (P. M. Ferguson, 2002). The person becomes "caught in the continuum" (S. Taylor, 1988), whereby expansion of adult opportunities is denied as premature while commitment to functional improvement is abandoned as unrealistic. For example, even service reforms such as supported employment that were initially developed specifically for people with severe disabilities have been denied to people with the most severe disabilities, who are judged to be "incapable of benefiting" from vocationally oriented training (D. L. Ferguson & Ferguson, 1986; P. M. Ferguson, 2002). In this orientation, the system presents full adulthood for people with severe disabilities as something that must be "earned," a reward handed out by professionals to people judged capable of continuing to progress. Failure to progress in the past justifies compressed opportunities in the future.

The Dilemma of Adulthood

All this leaves those of us who wish to see the promise of adulthood fulfilled for people with severe disabilities with a frustrating dilemma: How can we help people with severe disabilities gain access to the cultural benefits of community membership and personal autonomy associated with adulthood without neglecting the continued needs for adequate support and protection that did not end with childhood? How can we achieve this in the context of the current service system that can be more unhelpful than helpful? Let us offer a fairly minor example of this dilemma.

> *If someone asked Ian if he wanted to watch a Beavis & Butthead video or* 60 Minutes, *he would almost certainly choose the Beavis & Butthead. It's lively, has lots of odd (sometimes rude) noises, and has plenty of music. An Ed Bradley interview just does not match up.*

Concerned as we are with Ian's adult status, should we honor his choice as an autonomous adult and turn on the video even though we know it is an activity commonly associated with younger folks? Or should we override his choice in the belief that in this case the outcome (i.e., watching more adult entertainment) is more important than the process (i.e., allowing him to independently choose what he watches)? Perhaps we should not offer him the choice in the first place, confident that we will select a much more age-appropriate program. In the long run, we might argue, this will enhance Ian's image and expand his opportunities for affiliation and membership in a community of adults. Or is it okay to watch the Beavis & Butthead video once for every two or three times he watches Mike Wallace? Finally, we might look at this example of his viewing habits as an area of learning for Ian and emphasize the dimensions of change for him. In so doing, we might honor Ian's choice for now while simultaneously exposing him to more options that might be equally appealing but less childish (perhaps MTV as a compromise between Mike Wallace and Beavis).

Excessive emphasis on symbols of autonomy might actually diminish a person's access to membership symbols. Having only a volunteer job is not the same as volunteering your free time after work at a paid job. Making sure a young adult lives apart from previous family and friends in the pursuit of an image of self-sufficiency, for example, may restrict the adult's involvement in activities and groups that those very family and friends might help to access.

Similarly, excessive emphasis on change might perpetuate the liminal position of being permanently stuck on the threshold of full adulthood, spending one's days in endless preparation for life instead of actually living it. This is perhaps most common for those young adults who leave the preparatory experience of schools only to find themselves in a day program or residential service that continues a readiness training focus. Many young adults with severe disabilities still leave high school for the continued preparation of work training programs and sheltered workshops where many will labor for 30 to 40 years in a parody of productivity. We wonder how many adults "retire" from such programs when they reach their 60s without ever "graduating" to real jobs.

Indirectly, such one-dimensional service offerings can deemphasize the importance of social reform to accommodate a broader range of acceptable adult behavior. Instead, we believe that a full understanding of the multidimensional aspects of adulthood in our tradition and culture allows a more productive and flexible approach to the dilemma of balancing self-sufficiency with support and social accommodation with personal development.

> *Ron works at the same university we have for many years. He lived in a large institution for people with mental retardation until he was in his 40s. Now he works delivering mail from the dean's office to other parts of the college. Ron doesn't talk and has a history of lashing out at himself and others when he is confused or unclear about what is happening to him. When you encounter him in the mail room and say "hello," he will often respond by withdrawing, avoiding eye contact, and making his own unique sounds. To many people, these responses seem like he is retreating and uncomfortable with these interactions. Over time, however, those who persistently greet and interact with Ron realize that these responses are an acknowledgment and, perhaps, recognition of a familiar face.*

For us as parents, it seems that the professionals have done a good job of convincing society to recognize the importance of a transition from childhood but have not fully discovered what that process should be a transition to. We are, as it were, still in mid-journey on the trail toward adulthood for people with severe disabilities. As professionals, it seems to us that our field has not adequately understood the complexity of the journey or the character of its destination. Without such an understanding, the processes of achieving adulthood—symbolically or otherwise—for people with severe disabilities will never reach a conclusion.

Having said that and having explored the dilemma of adulthood for people with severe disabilities, we must now turn to the good news. Answers are emerging. Perhaps we have moved past the midpoint of our journey, at least for some adults with severe disabilities. Our last section will explore some of these developments after a brief summary review.

Achieving Adulthood

To summarize, the promise of adulthood in our society should be more than a job, a place to live, and being on one's own. A full understanding of the meaning of adulthood must look at the structure of symbols and imagery that surround this culturally defined role. In looking, we found that we could organize that symbolic structure around the three dimensions of autonomy, membership, and change. We elaborated the dimension of autonomy into three elements (self-sufficiency, self-determination, and completeness) and membership into two elements (citizenship and affiliation). Then we discussed the ways in which our current service options often tend to deny full participation in these dimensions. Even though some of the symbols of autonomy, membership, and change might be attempted, too often the result for persons with severe disabilities is really an experience of unfinished transition or unhelpful services.

Despite recent and helpful moves within the field of special education and disability services to focus on the importance of the transition process from school to adult life, we argued that most adults with severe disabilities remain on the threshold of adulthood in the fullest sense of substantive participation in both the symbols and the substance of multidimensional adulthood. An unhelpful service system helps perpetuate this unfinished transition by encouraging dependency, social isolation, and personal chronicity. This leaves us with a dilemma of how to surround people such as Ian with resources that recognize their needs without denying their adulthood. The good news is that it really is possible. The bad news is that it is present for only a few so far. There is still much to do.

We believe that the solution to the dilemmas we have raised about adulthood lies in the merger of a reformed support system with a multidimensional understanding of adulthood. In this section, we first outline some of the key themes of this new paradigm for support services that respond to the barriers to adulthood that the current system continues to create and maintain despite these new efforts. Next we will look at how these themes are starting to emerge in terms of the three dimensions of full adulthood that we have discussed. We think that, taken together, these expanded versions of support and adulthood provide an inclusive approach to achieving a high quality of adult life for all people, even those with the most severe disabilities or intensive support needs. Finally, we freely admit that probably nowhere in our country could one find all the elements of this new approach in place, fully functioning. However, we also believe that each of the elements does exist somewhere for some people right now, and for some, we are beginning to achieve several elements. There is increasing reason for optimism that systemic change is starting to occur. The challenge we face is "simply" to fill in the gaps.

The Concept of Support

The significant reforms of the past 25 years in developmental disabilities have occurred mainly under the banners of deinstitutionalization and normalization. We need to recall the massive shift of people from large, segregated settings to more community-based arrangements that has occurred in less than 3 decades (Braddock et al., 2002; Lakin et al., 2003; Prouty et al., 2002). In the past few years, even some of the money to support these people has made a similar shift from institution to community (Braddock et al., 2002). However, while only partially achieved, normalization and deinstitutionalization now need to be joined (or perhaps even replaced) by a new banner if we are to revitalize the move toward continued restructuring of policy and practice (P. M. Ferguson, Ferguson, & Blumberg, 1997; Linton, 1998; McKnight, 1995; Nerney, 2000; O'Brien & Murray, 1997). It is increasingly possible to see the outline of an effort to move beyond the perceived limitations of deinstitutionalization and normalization as policy guidelines to an emphasis on support and self-determination.

The central feature of this new, and admittedly sporadic, effort to radically reorient adult services is an expanded understanding of the concept of "support" and its relationship to self-determination. One way of summarizing the conceptual model that seems to govern this effort is "supported adulthood." The supported adulthood approach is the result of an inductive process. Its unifying vision has emerged out of disparate reform initiatives from across several service domains, including supported employment, supported living, supported education, supported recreation, and supported families.

What Is New About Supported Adulthood?

Supported adulthood is more than a simple commitment of the field to redress past institutional wrongs by eliminating segregated options. It is also more than an attempt to make people "appear" normal. The central theme is in the expanded interpretation of what is and is not supportive of a full adult life in the community. The common purpose is in the effort to recognize a dual sense of independence and belonging as the most basic benefits of social support programs. This enriched notion of "support" has indicated a way out of the conceptual dilemma whereby people with disabilities had to either earn their presence in the community with total independence and self-sufficiency or be inserted there with the type of bureaucratic arrogance so common to social welfare programs. In either case, the result was all-too-clustered isolation associated with the overlapping problems of perpetual clienthood and excessive individualism already described. The image of the 10-bed group home comes to mind, with residents separated from their neighbors simply by the size and regimentation of their house. It became a place of work for direct care staff rather than a home where people lived. To adopt the terminology of the New Testament, adults with severe disabilities were "in" the community but not "of" it.

What is new in the notion of supported adulthood is a guiding commitment to participation and affiliation rather than control and remediation. "Support" becomes an adjective, modifying and enriching an adult's capacity for participation in and contribution to his or her community. Support cannot be a predefined service available to any who meets eligibility criteria. The real message of initiatives such as supported employment and supported living is—or should be—that all people do not have to be totally independent in terms of skills or fully competitive (or even close) in terms of productivity to be active, growing, valued adult members of their communities.

Components of Supported Adulthood

There are at least five features of this expanded approach to support for adults with severe disabilities and their families: (a) natural contexts, (b) informal supports, (c) user definitions, (d) local character, and (e) universal eligibility.

Natural Contexts

The traditional welfare approach to services for people with severe disabilities has been the creation of special settings, with special staff, and separate bureaucracies (e.g., institutions, self-contained schools, and sheltered workshops). Part of the economic irrationality of many of the current approaches is that funding tracks continue to direct financial resources into these settings even as the field increasingly recognizes their inadequacies (e.g., the continuing institutional bias of federal Medicaid programs; see Braddock et al., 2002). Certainly, the situation is improving, as states have finally tipped the balance in financial support toward community programs. The growing use of Medicaid waivers for community support (Braddock et al., 2002) has allowed the federal government to work more closely with states in removing policy barriers that previously kept Medicaid dollars from flowing into progressive community settings. All these trends show a growing appreciation for the value of the natural context as the location of choice for people with disabilities regardless of the domain of life being discussed.

Supported adulthood requires a reliance on natural contexts in the design and location of its supports. Support must become an adjective or adverb that "modifies" an existing, natural setting rather than meaning the creation of a separate one. This shift directly challenges the traditional belief that the more intensive the support needs, the more segregated the setting had to be (S. J. Taylor, 1988, 2001). Instead, the focus on natural settings allows the intensity of support to be truly individualized from context to context instead of programmatically standardized along an arbitrary service continuum (American Association on Mental Retardation, 2002).

The supported adulthood approach brings progressively intensive support to those individuals who need it without abandoning the community setting. The assumption driving the design of services within this approach is that vocational "programs" for people with severe disabilities should occur in those settings within the community where work naturally occurs, not in specially created sites or segregated settings (Mank, 1996). Homes should be in neighborhoods where other people live (P. M. Ferguson et al., 1997; Walker, 1999). A preference exists for the generic service instead of the specialized one whenever possible. The appeal of natural contexts, then, is twofold: it returns to a reliance on the community setting, thereby combating the isolating tendencies of "specialized" programs, and it encourages independence by placing people outside the "protected" environment of segregated programs.

A shift to natural contexts first began for Ian during his last years of high school. One of the community jobs he explored—doing laundry at the local YMCA for the next day's fitness enthusiasts—continued as a volunteer job that earned Ian a free membership for a couple of years after he finished school. Now all his life and supports occur in natural contexts. He lives in a home in a typical neighborhood much like his parents (see Figure 16-4). His job for the past 12 years is with the university food service part of the student union and involves him traveling all over campus

(Figure 16-5). But even beyond these major components of his life, being part of the natural context over the years—for living, work, and recreation—has resulted in the emergence of natural supports, such as patrons who are used to Ian and his paid support person coming to the pub on High Street and who lend a hand with his chair when he occasionally needs to use the bathroom that is up a couple of steps or the concertgoers who are familiar with Ian's attendance at such events and let him break into the intermission refreshment line to join them and say hello.

Informal and Formal Support Resources

A second, related element is the recognition that support should be informal as well as formal. This element directly challenges the problems identified with the traditional client-based role for individuals with severe disabilities and their families. In practical terms, informal—or natural—support is what people who are not paid for the "services" provide (e.g., emotional support, practical assistance, moral guidance) like the community members in the previous example. As we mentioned earlier, as long as a professional client model governs the provision of adult developmental disability services, then support, by definition, will be organized and controlled by the formal service system.

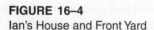

FIGURE 16–4
Ian's House and Front Yard

FIGURE 16–5
Ian at Work with Cart

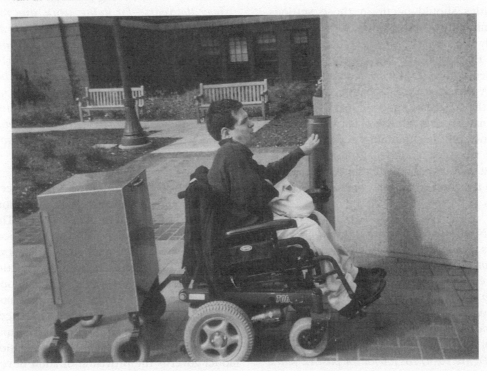

Efforts that most closely adhere to a supported adulthood approach are always bureaucratically "thin" and not necessarily oriented toward direct service provision. Such efforts recognize that the best support is that which is most natural and most embedded within the social relationships of the individual with disabilities. As with the element of natural contexts, this has the added benefit of economic prudence.

Of course, natural support can take time to develop. Many members of the community have grown up not knowing much about disability and, because of the tradition of segregated services, sometimes not encountering people with disabilities. Even when they try to interact or be supportive, sometimes their efforts can fall short or simply be inappropriate because they have so little experience with people with disabilities. Some individuals with disabilities can be difficult to get to know or talk to, furthering the challenge for those who might provide natural supports. While natural support can take time to develop and nurture, the presence of people with disabilities in natural settings as described is an important precursor to the development of these supports. Over time, with

more community participation and visibility of people with all manner of disabilities, more and more community members will feel comfortable and able to lend a hand when it is needed (see Figure 16-6).

The critical outcome measure is no longer whether someone receives "services" but rather whether someone's quality of life improves. The emphasis is that the individual finds the support needed regardless of where that support originates. The neighbor who decides at the last minute to invite Ian to accompany him to a ball game or over for dinner is just as supportive— if not more so—of leisure activity as the official recreational therapist with a scheduled swim time each week, and should be recognized as such. The point—at least from our perspective—is not that all formal support services should be withdrawn or avoided but that they should be seen as only one source of the support that all of us need at one time or another.

User Defined

An emphasis on informal supports and natural contexts leads logically to a third feature of the supported adulthood approach. The individual receiving the

FIGURE 16–6
Ian with Coworker

support is the only one who can define what is or is not supportive. Again, this directly challenges the controls of the bureaucratic structures to establish what "services" shall be available to an adult with a severe disability. Instead, the approach endorsed by all the examples of supported adulthood is to empower the individual to make such determinations. For example, a young man with aggressive behavior might use his behavioral repertoire to indicate a clear preference for spending his residential support dollars to maintain him in a duplex with one other roommate rather than the eight-person group home originally offered him. In some situations, the "user" might be a whole family rather than any one individual. So, for example, parents might need to help define what type of service would be most supportive for a son or daughter or what balance of informal and formal supports would best match their own contributions to his or her lifestyle.

Local Character

A fourth common feature in examples of supported adulthood is recognition that support should be community referenced. The emphasis here is not only that individuals should define what is and is not supportive but also that, once defined, that support should then take on the shape and texture of the local culture's traditions, values, and opportunities. The most obvious level of community referencing is at the basic effort to "fit in." For example, using a group home model as the exclusive type of residential service arrangement may foreclose the opportunities provided in many urban communities of apartment settings. Recreational opportunities should support and (if needed) provide training in locally valued activities (e.g., making a good ski run in Colorado, making a good pastrami on rye in New York City) instead of rigidly adhering to some standardized agenda that seems to imply, "All people with severe disabilities should learn to bowl." Community referencing should draw on the traditions and values within a local culture. A tradition of resistance can also be supportive when identified as a valuable and important part of a local culture. What we are advocating by "local character" is not just nostalgia for some imagined era of the small-town simple life; tradition can include recognition of difference, even tension, that support for people with severe disabilities should not ignore in the pursuit of peaceful conformity.

Ian lives in Oregon in a city with an active tradition of strong minority voices and social activism. Environmental issues alone offer any number of opportunities for citizenship and affiliation, depending on the side you choose to support. Ian already contributes his voice to at least some environmental debates in his use of canvas bags or his backpack when shopping. During a public employees' strike a few years ago at the University of Oregon, Ian joined in support of his coworkers on picket lines. Ian may not have understood all the issues involved in the strike, but he was aware that the routines were different and that people he worked alongside were not at their posts. Joining the community expression of resistance, regardless of what he understood about the issues, not only allowed Ian to support his coworkers but also increased their willingness to contribute to his support in other ways.

There is also a strong disability rights organization in our community. Although individuals with cognitive disabilities have not been well represented in the disability rights movement and while Ian is not yet a member of the local group, he is assisted to contribute his support for disability issues. In the course of his job, Ian serves the university as a semiofficial "accessibility tester." During one period, he began to consistently run into trouble with one of the automatic doors at the same campus building. The building was first on his morning route to deliver food supplies to cafés around campus. When he pressed the access panel to operate the door, nothing happened. Repeated calls by Ian's coworker to the physical plant resulted in frustration on all sides for a while. Whenever the repair team tested the panel, it worked, but the very next morning it would not work for Ian. Eventually, careful sleuthing by his coworker and others resulted in the discovery that during routine maintenance at night, the emergency switch was being turned off. After this incident, Ian was occasionally asked to try out a new door or entry or ramp to test its effectiveness for someone with Ian's type of wheelchair and skills. Our point is that supported adulthood requires attention not just to local traditions of peace, harmony, and patriotism but also to the minority voices and social activism that might afford rich and preferred opportunities for community participation and contribution.

Universal Eligibility

Finally, a fifth feature of most of the emerging examples of supported adulthood—and perhaps the most controversial—is the principle of universal eligibility. Everyone who requires support to experience the full promise of adulthood should receive it. Unfortunately, since there are simply not enough formal resources for all who genuinely require them, only those who meet a more stringent test of poverty or extremity of need, whether temporary or chronic, receive services. In Moroney's now classic analysis (1986), approaches that focus on a subgroup who are somehow "in most need" are described as reactive or residual. That is, such limited approaches perpetuate the problems of the welfare state programs that we summarized earlier. They tend to be stigmatizing, lack cost-effectiveness (because not preventative), and are destructive of personal independence and community membership (because of competition for services).

The customary rationale for this limited eligibility is inevitably tied to the professional client orientation to support services. If we break away from that constraint, however, then the universalizing of disability policy

seems much more feasible (Bickenbach, 2001; McKnight, 1995; O'Brien & Murray, 1997). For example, if formal support services are the only officially recognized, legitimate responses to an identified social need, then competition for scarce resources seems inevitable. If informal supports are included and existing natural contexts are preferred, then the available resources for support are dramatically multiplied. The addition of informal support to the equation automatically increases the total of recognized resources. Equally important, formal support dollars become more cost effective when used to encourage this informal sector rather than to pay the salaries of bureaucrats.

There is danger here as well, of course. The emphasis on informal supports can provide "cover" for those politicians and administrators who simply want to avoid the expense and challenge of meeting their responsibilities. The legal protections embedded in such landmark legislation as the Individuals with Disabilities Education Act and the Americans with Disabilities Act remain necessary for neglect of responsibility. Recognizing the value of informal supports should never become an excuse for not providing a social safety net for those who need it most.

Dimensions of Adulthood Revisited

Given the elements of the reform of supported adulthood that seeks to reconceptualize services, we now want to return our attention to the three key dimensions of adulthood that we have discussed throughout this chapter. How might the elements of supported adulthood reveal themselves across the three dimensions of autonomy, membership, and change? We again use Ian's experiences to personalize our discussion.

Supported Autonomy

The years since graduation have been exciting and productive for Ian. He now enjoys many symbols of autonomy. Still, Ian will never be completely self-sufficient in many of the most important aspects of life. He will probably never be able to make independent and reliable decisions about some of the more fundamental areas of life: religious beliefs and abstract principles of moral behavior, long-term financial planning, or even when it is safe to cross a busy street corner. However, with appropriate support, he can attend church if he wants to (assuming it is accessible), reciprocate the kindness of friends and strangers, help manage a small bank account, and even negotiate some intersections. Self-sufficiency certainly entails a number of discrete skills and resources that Ian will never be able to develop or discover on his own. However, self-sufficiency also conveys a pattern of life that goes beyond individual tasks or skills. In this expanded sense, Ian's autonomy is enhanced by appropriate types and levels of ongoing support.

Work life is perhaps the single area that is most commonly associated with personal autonomy. For Ian, the promises of supported employment have been exciting and rewarding. He has a great job—and one that is uniquely suited to his skills and personality. Ian is a very outgoing kind of guy who likes to be out and about, driving his wheelchair and meeting people. The food services located in the university's student union decentralized by putting small cafés in a number of the classroom buildings around campus. However, space is at a premium, and the cafés can store only a small number of supplies. Ian's wheelchair offered a legal vehicle that could convey supplies within the center of campus. With the assistance of vocational rehabilitation, a carrier was designed that fits on the back of his wheelchair for carrying these supplies, and he enjoys a regular route that takes him all over campus, meeting and greeting lots of different people. His job has changed over the years: adding tasks like collecting the receipts or breaking down cartons that once held supplies, adding new stops on the route, and increasing responsibilities for stocking at the main union.

Getting and maintaining this job has not always been easy. Some of the coworkers hired to support Ian have not been as successful as others. As supervisors and student employees change, Ian's personal support agent—a person hired by Ian and his family as an advocate and intermediary with family, officials, and support providers (P. M. Ferguson et al., 1997)—has sometimes needed to help the new coworkers understand supported employment and its role in Ian's life. Despite these continuing challenges, however, Ian enjoys his job and misses working when the university is on term break. We have seen his language and communication skills continue to grow and expand in the years since graduation and suspect that his daily encounters with new people have contributed. Ian illustrates just how

important it is for the developmental disability service system to ensure appropriate levels and types of ongoing support to maintain him in his job. It is a commitment that should be more universally made and kept (Bellamy, Rhodes, Mank, & Albin, 1988; Kiernan & Schalock, 1989; Mank, 1996; Wehman & Kregel, 1995).

Ian also illustrates the contribution that effective high school transition services can make to successful adult experiences after school. Ian did not learn to deliver food in high school. However, what he did learn was what it meant to "have a job." He did learn about making decisions. He did learn how much he enjoyed "going to work." That is, the dimension of autonomy gained important concrete application for Ian as he sampled a variety of possible employment opportunities in high school and participated in other opportunities for making choices that mattered.

In March 1997, Ian moved into his own home. Several years later, he moved into a somewhat larger house in a different part of town, enjoying the new space, larger yard, and excitement of moving that this event offered. His housemates have changed as well in this time, but the couple who live with him now are about to celebrate their seventh year with him. With this stability has also come a regular routine. Weekdays always involve a morning at work (unless the university is on break) with the remainder of the day punctuated by haircuts, a massage every few weeks, swimming to maintain range of motion and combat the gradual weight gain that seems endemic to middle age, and Wednesday nights with an old friend from high school. Weekends are the time for dinner parties with us (we get invited over often!) or other friends, short weekend camping trips to the coast or the hot springs, working on a large variety of art and craft projects—some of which become wonderful gifts for friends and family—as well as movies, a beer or coffee somewhere in town, or just as visit to the park to feed the ducks.

The year is punctuated with a round of parties and special events. The Easter egg hunt and Halloween haunted house draw larger and larger crowds from the neighborhood. The food is always good, the music and games are fun, and the atmosphere is celebratory. September brings some kind of theme party in honor of Ian's, his father's, and several other friends' birthdays—a Hawaiian luau has been one popular theme. Late summer usually involves a holiday—sometimes we all save up for something special like a trip to Reno or Las Vegas—but other times camping on the coast or the San Juan Islands of Seattle offers the needed respite from routine. Ian and his supporters are systematically exploring the accessibility of campgrounds in Oregon and Washington (Figure 16-7). But then there's always gardening to be done, canning and freezing of vegetables, painting the living room, fixing up the craft room, cleaning the wheelchair, making bread, picking up Dianne or Phil at the airport when they come back from trips—all the comfortable routine chores and tasks that have become a regular part of Ian's daily, weekly, monthly, and yearly life.

Ian is benefiting from the increasing availability of "supported living" options within the service system. Simply put, supported living means that, despite Ian's limits, he should be able to live where he wants (in his own home), with whom he wants, for as long as he wants, with the ongoing support needed to make that happen (Howe et al., 1998; Taylor, Biklen, & Knoll, 1987; Taylor et al., 1991). For Ian, this support comes from Robin, his personal support agent, and Lyn, both his live-in companions; Charly, Shane, and Andy, who support him during some parts of his week; and Susan, the manager of the supported living program that manages his income from the service system along with other critical bureaucratic tasks. Ian receives several sources of income: the support dollars that come through mental health that pay his supporters, his

earnings from his job along with Supplemental Security Income and Social Security Disability Insurance that pay for many of his personal needs and weekly expenses (food, some rent, spending money, haircuts, personal stuff, massages, swimming, gas for his van), and contributions from his parents that help cover his mortgage and utilities as well as contributing to his vacations.

Supported Membership

For us, as Ian's parents, it seems that the community is the safest place for him to be. The more hands that are there to catch him when he falls, the better. We firmly believe that the more deeply embedded Ian is in the life of his neighborhood, workplace, and the city in general, the more people there will be who will notice if he is not there and who will work to keep him there as a member of his community. Part of this involves some effort to allow Ian to fulfill his duties of citizenship. Ian has volunteered for several agencies or causes that he supports and enjoys. In addition to volunteering at the YMCA that we mentioned earlier, Ian has also delivered mail at a nearby long-term-care facility and helped a couple of times to put up posters around town advertising upcoming concerts for a local musical festival. It is important for Ian's membership in his community that he be given the support he needs so that he can, in turn, support his friends and neighbors.

Affiliations for pure fun and recreation are also important. The obvious term to capture the spirit of such activities is "supported recreation." Instead of separate, specialized, professionally defined recreational opportunities, the emphasis within progressive programs is now on the use of generic programs in the local community. Instead of Ian going to a special bowling night for all the people labeled mentally retarded in the whole county, the effort might be to let him choose what he wants to do for fun in the community and then arrange the supports and small groups necessary to allow those choices to be honored (Dattilo & Schleien, 1994; Germ & Schleien, 1997).

Supported Change

Perhaps the central aspect here is to make sure Ian has the information and opportunity to expand the choices he has surrounding his autonomy and membership. Supported change should not involve a lifetime of programs, interventions, training, and habilitation plans.

FIGURE 16–7
Ian and Lyn Enjoy Camping Trips to a Nearby Lake

However, it should encourage a lifelong growth and development that will allow Ian to change his preferences as he learns new things. It should allow his relationships with people to evolve and develop without the frenzied impermanence of various paid staff who are here one month and gone the next. Ian should be supported in activities that will create new levels of independence but even more in activities that will create new breadth of experience. Finally, Ian should be helped to learn how to make his choices known in effective yet appropriate ways. Supported change should help Ian alter or minimize those behaviors that reduce his personal attractiveness to other members of his community (D. L. Ferguson, 1998).

Many of these natural changes are occurring for Ian. His volunteer jobs have changed, as have his duties at his paid job. His first housemate, Faith, moved on to another phase of her own life, making it possible for Robin, who had worked for Ian some years previously, to come back into his life. New support people—Lyn, Alina, Kareem, Jennifer, Shane, and Charly—each of whom has spent several years in Ian's life, have introduced him to new experiences and opportunities. Ian continues to learn. He is certainly talking more and about more things. Under Robin's tutelage, his "cook's helper" skills have greatly expanded, and we hear that he is actually beginning to enjoy sleeping outside during camping trips!

Through all these changes, we learn more about how to engage Ian as an author in the adult life that is emerging. As we have watched Ian gradually separate his life from ours, our goal has not so much been one of self-determination in the particularly individual sense in which it is often applied to people with severe disabilities (Brown, Gothelf, Guess, & Lehr, 1998; P. M. Ferguson & Ferguson, 2001; Wehmeyer et al., 1998). Instead, we have sought with Ian a good life. We can support Ian's autonomy, membership, and change. We can also support a growing self-sufficiency and completeness, but supporting self-determination has forced us to shift our thinking from Ian's individual agency to our collective negotiations.

Philosophers have long talked about the importance of "agency" to our understanding of what it means to be an individual. What they mean by that term is our personal ability to act on the world around us, to be our own agents of change. The challenge of Ian and others with even more significant cognitive

(and physical, and sensory, and medical) disabilities is how close they seem to come to the absence of agency in key parts of their lives. We do not really know what Ian realizes about himself, though we would dearly love to know. Perhaps we should not assume that Ian finds meaning similar to our own experiences of the characteristics of self-regulation, empowerment, and autonomy so often cited as central to self-determination. Certainly we are all interdependent, but the truth of the matter is that the balance of interdependence in Ian's relationships is disproportionate in most matters as compared with our own. He is more dependent. He requires more care. He determines fewer things in the course of a day, week, or year than each of us do. Yet he does contribute in some very important ways to what occurs in his life. Does he choose? Sometimes and increasingly more so. But more often, he more indirectly influences people and events to end up being more okay than not okay from his point of view even when we do not know and perhaps cannot imagine what his point of view is at the time. We want Ian to have a life that is more okay than not okay from his point of view most of the time.

One way we have found helpful to think of these issues is to borrow a couple of literary metaphors. Literary critics try to discover what a particular text means. Part of discovering the meaning of a text, or the "social text" of any person's life, is finding out what the authors of that text intended it to mean—to gather and take into account all the possible meanings. That is never enough, however. The meaning of any text, including the social text of a life, belongs as well to the text itself and gets determined by each of us who "read" or participate in it. What even casual observers think about Ian's life contributes to his story and influences the next chapters.

Like many conventional texts, social texts often have multiple authors. Ian and others with limited communication skills can contribute as coauthors to the text. Even if they do not noticeably interpret any particular experience for themselves, in any strong sense of human agency, by shaping the collective story in whatever way others can comprehend, the social text is enriched with their contribution for others to interpret and elaborate (P. M. Ferguson & Ferguson, 2001).

This past Christmas, Ian made us bulletin boards— decorated around the edge with buttons and charms and pieces of old clocks. He gets help to pick the colors and textures, and he helps with most of the gluing. In past years, he also made raspberry jam, marinated mushrooms, canned pears, and applesauce. He has also made refrigerator magnets, tree ornaments, and hand-painted mugs and plates. Over the years, he has gone shopping for socks, tea, coffee, really good chocolates, jewelry, winter scarves, and decorative candles. The results of his holiday efforts are certainly shaped by those that support his participation in the season. This is a part of the complexity of Ian's adulthood that we have come to understand. His taste and choices always reflect the people in his life. Our Christmas gifts come as much from them as from Ian. For our part, we have come to love the variety and choice that go into the content of Ian's gifts. Of course, we also cherish the self-satisfied smile that he always has when he hands us the present as something that is uniquely Ian's.

Christmas is beginning to have a comfortable annual routine. The first holiday we went to Ian's house seemed odd, much like it must for all parents and their adult sons and daughters. Ian comes to our house now for Christmas Eve, Christmas morning, and sometimes Christmas dinner. Then we go to his house for dessert and more gift opening and good company with Robin and Lyn and some of their family and friends. The routine varies somewhat, but it is a routine that we all enjoy and anticipate—and it is one we have all created together.

Multidimensional Adulthood

For us the final key to understanding the full meaning of supported adulthood—indeed, of adulthood itself—is to recognize that it has no one single meaning. Autonomy is a very important dimension of adulthood, but there are others. Unfortunately, most attempts to describe the promise of adulthood for people with severe disabilities have tried to accomplish it by making careful discriminations in the meaning of autonomy and independence so as to account for the genuine limits in self-sufficiency that severe disability might actually impose (this seems especially true of severe cognitive disability).

We believe that a multidimensional approach to adulthood allows a clearer way of interpreting the situation. Instead of trying to subsume everything that we want to include under the single rubric of independence, a multidimensional approach allows us to thicken our description of adulthood with the

additional—but coequal—strands of membership and change that lead to the more accurate notion of adult "interdependence."

As we have described earlier, Ian's cognitive limitations and multiple disabilities are significant enough that the strand of autonomy in his version of adulthood may not be as strongly visible as his strand of membership. The strand of personal change and growth may allow the balance between the other two strands to change over his lifetime. It seems to us that a full understanding of adulthood in our society would allow us to avoid dilemmas of linear, one-dimensional thinking where degrees of "adultness" occur on a single line of autonomy and independence. Adding other dimensions is not an excuse for limiting Ian's independence; it is an interpretation that expands his adulthood. Ian's adulthood is an expression of the relationships he has with his parents, his paid supporters, his friends, and his neighbors that contribute to defining what happens to him day to day. To truly support his adulthood, we are striving for relationships that nourish rather than smother, relationships that flourish rather than atrophy, and relationships that author rich stories of lives lived rather than reports of outcomes achieved.

Some Dangers Ahead

A Cautionary Conclusion About Unkept Promises

Supported adulthood seems to provide an important summary of how social services might accomplish a practical merger of personal independence and community support. However, claims of relevance and value for such ideas should always be chastened by the history of social reform efforts in our country. Too often our reform optimism has been followed by decades of unintended consequences that seem all too predictable in retrospect.

There is a definite danger that arguments in favor of the supported adulthood approach could overemphasize the cost-effectiveness of such elements as the use of natural contexts and the encouragement of informal supports. Some economic savings may, indeed, be available through natural contexts and natural supports. However, as experience with the deinstitutionalization movement has shown, effective community support can suffer if justified primarily on the basis of financial savings. The arguments for adopting supported adulthood logic must be careful not to imply any enthusiasm for underfunded social programs. The economic justification for the approach is that it rationalizes spending by tying it directly to valued outcomes, not that it saves money.

A second danger with supported adulthood is to justify unintentionally an even greater reliance on a charity model of social support. One of the risks in calling for procedures such as increased reliance on community-based responses that encourage informal supports is the creation of a one-sided, libertarian abandonment of legitimate government responsibility to ensure the health and welfare of its citizens with disabilities. Of course, this move to the privatization of welfare gained popularity during the Reagan administration and seems to be enjoying continuing appeal. The problem is that the charity model almost unavoidably accepts the systemic inequities that occasion the need for charity in the first place. An effective disability policy must challenge inequity and discrimination in our society with distributive and protective systems within the formal structure of social agencies. Supported adulthood should illuminate a comprehensive, egalitarian approach to a national disability policy, not just look for volunteers to step up in an age of social divisions resulting from our class structure and continuing racial, gender, cultural, and religious discrimination.

A final danger in the approach is closely related to the potential overemphasis on charity. Just as the rediscovery of informal supports and natural contexts can be exaggerated into a privatized social policy of volunteers and cheerful givers, so can the concomitant deemphasis on traditional versions of formal supports lead to an overblown antiprofessionalism. Certainly, those within the field of disability services must recognize the value of properly focused expertise and technology in improving the quality of some people's lives. The contention that excessive professionalism has often encouraged a dependency role for disabled people should not entail the abandonment of all the wonderful advances made in the behavioral and life sciences.

Despite these very real dangers of misapplication or distortion, the value of moving rapidly toward a vision of supported adulthood is worth the risk. To us it seems to represent the only hope that Ian's "flight" into full adulthood will be a smooth one. There are thousands of Ians "taking off" every year in our society. There are thousands more making their way as adulthood moves from "young" adulthood to middle age and beyond. We have made implicit promises to all of them for as full and rewarding a lifetime as they can achieve.

The true risk is the human cost of not doing everything we can to fulfill those promises.

Suggested Activities

Think about and discuss with your colleagues the ways in which you do and do not operate as an "adult" in terms of (a) self-sufficiency and (b) autonomy.

1. Think about and discuss with your colleagues all the things, events, and supports you obtain from your own parents or other family members.
2. Inventory services available for an individual with severe disabilities in your community. Try to identify the following things about each agency or group providing services:
   a. Mission and philosophy of those providing the service
   b. Role of the family in program design, monitoring, and improvement
   c. Role of the adult in program design, monitoring, and improvement
3. Visit a residential or vocational program in your community that provides services for individuals with severe intellectual disabilities. Try to listen and notice things that reveal the ways in which the people served and supported by the program or service think of themselves as adults and are thought of by others as adults.
4. Talk with someone who works directly with individuals with severe disabilities (e.g., in a vocational support agency or a residential program). Find out how he or she views adulthood for the people they try to support.
5. Talk with a parent or a sibling of an adult with severe disabilities about his or her perspectives on how best to support the family member with the disability.

References

American Association on Mental Retardation. (2002). *Mental retardation: Definition, classification, and systems of supports* (10th ed.). Washington, DC: Author.

Anderson, L., Schleien, S. J., & Seligmann, D. (1997). Creating positive change through an integrated outdoor adventure program. *Therapeutic Recreation Journal, 31,* 214–229.

Aries, P. (1962). *Centuries of childhood: A social history of family life* (R. Baldick, Trans.). New York: Vintage Books. (Original work published in 1960.)

Beales, R. W., Jr. (1985). In search of the historical child: Miniature adulthood and youth in Colonial New England. In N. R. Hiner & J. M. Hawes (Eds.), *Growing up in America: Children in historical perspective* (pp. 7-24). Chicago: University of Illinois Press.

Bellamy, G. T., Rhodes, L. E., Mank, D. M., & Albin, J. M. (1988). *Supported employment: An implementation guide.* Baltimore: Paul H. Brookes.

Bérubé, M. (2003). Citizenship and disability. *Dissent, 50*(2), 52-58.

Bickenbach, J. E. (2001). Disability human rights, law, and policy. In G. L. Albrecht, K. D. Seelman, & M. Bury (Eds.), *Handbook of disability studies* (pp. 565-584). Thousand Oaks, CA: Sage.

Blanck, P. D. (1998). *The Americans with Disabilities Act and the emerging workforce: Employment of people with mental retardation.* Washington, DC: American Association on Mental Retardation.

Bouwsma, W. J. (1976). Christian adulthood. *Daedalus: Journal of the American Academy of Arts and Sciences, 105*(2), 77-92.

Braddock, D., Hemp, R., Rizzolo, M. C., Parish, S., & Pomeranz, A. (2002). The state of the states in developmental disabilities: Summary of the study. In D. Braddock (Ed.), *Disability at the dawn of the 21st century and the state of the states* (pp. 83-140). Washington, DC: American Association on Mental Retardation.

Brown, F., Gothelf, C. R., Guess, D., & Lehr, D. (1998). Self-determination for individuals with the most severe disabilities: Moving beyond chimera. *Journal of the Association for Persons with Severe Handicaps, 23*, 17-26.

Dannefer, D. (1984). Adult development and social theory: A paradigmatic reappraisal. *American Sociological Review, 49*, 100-116.

Dattilo, J., & Schleien, S. J. (1994). Understanding leisure services for individuals with mental retardation. *Mental Retardation, 32*, 53-59.

DeLio, D., Rogan, P., & Geary, T. (2000). APSE's position statement on segregated services: A background paper for advocates. *Advance, 10*(4), 1-2.

Drake, R. F. (2001). Welfare states and disabled people. In G. L. Albrecht, K. D. Seelman, & M. Bury (Eds.), *Handbook of disability studies* (pp. 412-429). Thousand Oaks, CA: Sage.

Elder, G. H., Jr. (1987). Families and lives: Some developments in life-course studies. *Journal of Family History, 12*, 179-199.

Elder, G. H., Jr., & O'Rand, A. M. (1995). Adult lives in a changing society. In K. S. Cook, G. A. Fine, & J. S. House (Eds.), Sociological Perspectives on Social Psychology (pp. 452-475). Boston: Allyn and Bacon.

Erikson, E. H. (1950). *Childhood and society.* New York: W. W. Norton.

Erikson, V. L., & Martin, J. (1984). The changing adult: An integrated approach. *Social Casework: The Journal of Contemporary Social Work, 65*, 162-171.

Ferguson, D. L. (1998). Relating to self-determination: One parent's thoughts. *Journal of the Association for Persons with Severe Handicaps, 23*, 44-46.

Ferguson, D. L., & Ferguson, P. M. (1986). The new victors: A progressive policy analysis of work reform for people with very severe handicaps. *Mental Retardation, 24*, 331-338.

Ferguson, P. M. (2002). Notes toward a history of hopelessness: Disability and the places of therapeutic failure. *Disability, Culture, and Education, 1*(1), 27-40.

Ferguson, P. M. (2003). Winks, blinks, squints and twitches: Looking for disability and culture through my son's left eye. In P. Devlieger, F. Rusch, & D. Pfeiffer (Eds.), *Rethinking disability: The emergence of new definitions, concepts and communities* (pp. 131-147). Philadelphia: Garant/Coronet Books.

Ferguson, P. M., & Ferguson, D. L. (2001). Winks, blinks, squints and twitches: Looking for disability, culture and self-determination through our son's left eye. *Scandinavian Journal of Disability Research, 3*(2), 71-90.

Ferguson, P. M., Ferguson, D. L., & Blumberg, E. R., with Ferguson, I. (1997). Negotiating adulthood: Kitchen table conversations about supported living. In P. O'Brien & R. Murray (Eds.), *Human services: Toward partnership and support* (pp. 189-200). Palmerston North, New Zealand: Dunmore Press.

Ferguson, P. M., Ferguson, D. L., & Jones, D. (1988). Generations of hope: Parental perspectives on the transitions of their children with severe retardation from school to adult life. *Journal of the Association for Persons with Severe Handicaps, 13*, 177-187.

Ferguson, P. M., Hibbard, M., Leinen, J., & Schaff, S. (1990). Supported community life: Disability policy and the renewal of mediating structures. *Journal of Disability Policy Studies, 1*, 9-35.

Fleischer, D. Z., & Zames, F. (2001). *The disability rights movement: From charity to confrontation.* Philadelphia: Temple University Press.

Furstenberg, F. F., Jr., Cook, T. D., Eccles, J., Elder, G. H., Jr., & Sameroff, A. (1999). *Managing to make it: Urban families and adolescent success.* Chicago: University of Chicago Press.

Germ, P. A., & Schleien, S. J. (1997). Inclusive community leisure services: Responsibilities of key players. *Therapeutic Recreation Journal, 31*, 22-37.

Hareven, T. (Ed.). (1978). *Transitions: The family and the life course in historical perspective.* New York: Academic Press.

Howe, J., Horner, R. H., & Newton, J. S. (1998). Comparison of supported living and traditional residential services in the state of Oregon. *Mental Retardation, 36*, 1-11.

Ingstad, B., & Whyte, S. R. (1995). Disability and culture: An overview. In B. Ingstad & S. R. Whyte (Eds.), *Disability and culture* (pp. 3-32). Berkeley: University of California Press.

Jorgensen, C. M. (1998). *Restructuring high schools for all students: Taking inclusion to the next level.* Baltimore: Paul H. Brookes.

Kalyanpur, M., & Harry, B. (1999). *Culture in special education: Building reciprocal family-professional relationships.* Baltimore: Paul H. Brookes.

Kett, J. F. (1977). *Rites of passage: Adolescence in America, 1790 to the present.* New York: Basic Books.

Kiernan, R. W., & Schalock, R. L. (Eds.). (1989). *Economics, industry, and disability: A look ahead.* Baltimore: Paul H. Brookes.

Knowlton, H. E., Turnbull, A. P., Backus, L., & Turnbull, H. R., III. (1988). Letting go: Consent and the "Yes, but . . ." problem in transition. In B. L. Ludlow, A. P. Turnbull, & R. Luckasson (Eds.), *Transitions to adult life for people with mental retardation: Principles and practices* (pp. 45-66). Baltimore: Paul H. Brookes.

Lakin, K. C., Prouty, R., Polister, B., & Coucouvanis, K. (2003). Selected changes in residential service systems over a quarter century, 1977-2002. *Mental Retardation, 41*, 303-306.

Levinson, D. (1978). *Seasons of a man's life.* New York: Knopf.

Linton, S. (1998). *Claiming disability: Knowledge and identity.* New York: New York University Press.

Louis Harris and Associates. (2002). *The N.O.D./Harris survey program on participation and attitudes: Survey of Americans with disabilities.* New York: Author.

Magnussen, T. (1997). Marginalised young men and successful young women? In J. Wheelock & A. Mariussen (Eds.), *Households, work, and economic change: A comparative institutional perspective* (pp. 187-194). Boston: Kluwer Academic.

Mallory, B. L. (1995). The role of social policy in life-cycle transitions. *Exceptional Children, 62,* 213-224.

Mank, D. (1996). Natural support in employment for people with disabilities: What do we know and when did we know it? *Journal of the Association for Persons with Severe Handicaps, 21,* 174-177.

Mank, D., Cioffi, A., & Yovanoff, P. (1997). Analysis of the typicalness of supported employment jobs, natural supports, and wage and integration outcomes. *Mental Retardation, 35,* 185-197.

McKnight, J. L. (1995). *The careless society: Community and its counterfeits.* New York: Basic Books.

Meyrowitz, J. (1984). The adultlike child and the childlike adult: Socialization in an electronic age. *Daedalus: Journal of the American Academy of Arts and Sciences, 113*(3), 19-48.

Modell, J., Furstenberg, F. F., Jr., & Hershberg, T. (1978). Social change and transitions to adulthood in historical perspective. In M. Gordon (Ed.), *The American family in social-historical perspective* (pp. 192-219). New York: St. Martin's Press.

Moroney, R. M. (1986). *Shared responsibility: Families and social policy.* Chicago: Aldine.

Murphy, R. F., Scheer, J., Murphy, Y., & Mack, R. (1988). Physical disability and social liminality: A study in the rituals of adversity. *Social Science and Medicine, 26,* 235-242.

Mwaria, C. B. (1990). The concept of self in the context of crisis: A study of families of the severely brain-injured. *Social Science and Medicine, 30,* 889-893.

Nerney, T. (2000). *Challenging incompetence: The meaning of self-determination.* Retrieved [January 5, 2005] at **http://www.self-determination.com/publications/incompetence3print.htm**

Nisbet, J., & Hagner, D. (1988). Natural supports in the workplace: A re-examination of supported employment. *Journal of the Association for Persons with Severe Handicaps, 13,* 260-267.

O'Brien, P., & Murray, R. (Eds.). (1997). *Human services: Towards partnership and support.* Palmerston North, New Zealand: Dunmore Press.

Phillips, M. J. (1985). "Try harder": The experience of disability and the dilemma of normalization. *Social Science Journal, 22*(4), 45-57.

Priestley, M. (Ed.) (2001). *Disability and the life course: Global perspectives.* New York: Cambridge University Press.

Prouty, R. W., Smith, G., & Lakin, K. C. (Eds.). (2002). *Residential services for persons with developmental disabilities: Status and trends through 2002.* Minneapolis: University of Minnesota,

Research and Training Center on Community Living, Institute on Community Integration.

Sarason, S. B. (1972). *The creation of settings and the future societies.* San Francisco: Jossey-Bass.

Smull, M. W., & Bellamy, G. T. (1991). Community services for adults with disabilities: Policy challenges in the emerging support paradigm. In L. H. Meyer, C. A. Peck, & L. Brown (Eds.), *Critical issues in the lives of people with severe disabilities* (pp. 527-536). Baltimore: Paul H. Brookes.

Taylor, S. J. (1988). Caught in the continuum: A critical analysis of the principle of the least restrictive environment. *Journal of the Association for Persons with Severe Handicaps, 13,* 45-53.

Taylor, S. J. (2001). The continuum and current controversies in the USA. *Journal of Intellectual and Developmental Disability, 26*(1), 15-33.

Taylor, S. J., Biklen, D., & Knoll, J. (Eds.). (1987). *Community integration for people with severe disabilities.* New York: Teachers College Press.

Taylor, S. J., Bogdan, R., & Racino, J. (Eds.). (1991). *Life in the community: Case studies of organizations supporting people with disabilities.* Baltimore: Paul H. Brookes.

Taylor, T. (1988). The transition to adulthood in comparative perspective: Professional males in Germany and the United States at the turn of the century. *Journal of Social History, 21,* 635-658.

Turnbull, A. P., & Turnbull, H. R., III (1996). Self-determination within a culturally responsive family systems perspective: Balancing the family mobile. In L. E. Powers, G. H. S. Singer, & J. Sowers (Eds.), *On the road to autonomy: Promoting self-competence in children and youth with disabilities* (pp. 195-220). Baltimore: Paul H. Brookes.

Vaillant, G. E. (1977). *Adaptation to life.* Boston: Little, Brown.

Walker, P. (1999). From community presence to sense of place: Community experiences of adults with developmental disabilities. *Journal of the Association for Persons with Severe Handicaps, 24,* 23-32.

Wehman, P. (2001). *Life beyond the classroom: Transition strategies for young people with disabilities.* Baltimore: Paul H. Brookes.

Wehman, P., & Kregel, J. (1995). At the crossroads: Supported employment a decade later. *Journal of the Association for Persons with Severe Handicaps, 20,* 286-299.

Wehmeyer, M. L. (2001). Self-determination and transition. In P. Wehman, *Life beyond the classroom: Transition strategies for young people with disabilities* (3rd ed., pp. 35-60). Baltimore: Paul H. Brookes.

Wehmeyer, M. L., Agran, M., & Hughes, C. (1998). *Teaching self-determination to youth with disabilities: Basic skills for successful transition.* Baltimore: Paul H. Brookes.

Williams, G. H. (2001). Theorizing disability. In G. L. Albrecht, K. D. Seelman, & M. Bury (Eds.), *Handbook of disability studies* (pp. 123-144). Thousand Oaks, CA: Sage.

Wohl, R. (1979). *The generation of 1914.* Cambridge, MA: Harvard University Press.

Wolfensberger, W. (1972). *The principle of normalization in human services.* Toronto: National Institute on Mental Retardation.

❧ Name Index ❧

⚜ Subject Index ⚜